A Companion to
Biological Anthropology

The *Wiley Blackwell Companions to Anthropology* offers a series of comprehensive syntheses of the traditional subdisciplines, primary subjects, and geographic areas of inquiry for the field. Taken together, the series represents both a contemporary survey of anthropology and a cutting edge guide to the emerging research and intellectual trends in the field as a whole.

Forthcoming

A Companion to Biological Anthropology

Edited by
Clark Spencer Larsen

Second Edition

WILEY Blackwell

Dedicated to biological anthropologists and
Companion to Biological Anthropology authors and friends

Phillip L. Walker (1947–2009)
Robert W. Sussman (1941–2016)
Gary D. James (1954–2020)

Contents

Notes on Contributors

C. Eduardo Guerra Amorim is Assistant Professor of Biology at California State University Northridge. His research uses genetic data from ancient and present-day humans to study local adaptation and resistance against pathogens. Recent research projects include the study of the peopling of the Andes and host-pathogen coevolution using ancient DNA.

Cynthia M. Beall is Distinguished University Professor and the S. Idell Pyle Professor of Anthropology at Case Western Reserve University. Her scientific focus is to understand human biological variation, past and present. Her research deals with the processes resulting in the different patterns of adaptation to high-altitude hypoxia on the three major plateaus. She serves as the Editor-in-Chief of *Evolution, Medicine, and Public Health*. She is a Fellow of the American Association for the Advancement of Science and Member of the National Academy of Sciences, the American Academy of Arts and Sciences, and the American Philosophical Society.

David R. Begun is a Professor in the Department of Anthropology at the University of Toronto. His main interests are the functional anatomy, phylogeny, and paleobiogeography of Miocene apes and the emergence of Pliocene hominins. He served as the co-editor of the *Journal of Human Evolution*. He is the author of *The Real Planet of the Apes* (2015) and the editor or co-editor of *Function, Phylogeny and Fossils: Miocene Hominoid Origins and Adaptations* (1997), *Geology and Vertebrate Paleontology of the Miocene Hominoid Locality of Çandır* (2003), *The Evolution of Thought: Evolutionary Origins of Great Ape Intelligence* (2004), and *A Companion to Paleoanthropology* (2013).

Barry Bogin is a Professor Emeritus of Biological Anthropology of the School of Sport, Exercise & Health Sciences at Loughborough University, the William E Stirton Professor Emeritus of Anthropology of the University of Michigan-Dearborn, and an active member of The Center for Academic Research and Training in Anthropogeny. Bogin has expertise in human physical growth and development, nutritional ecology, evolutionary biology, Maya people, and human adaptation. The focus of his research is to explain how Social-Economic-Political-Emotional (SEPE) forces influence human physical development.

Among his publications are the books *Patterns of Human Growth*, 3rd edition (2021), *Human Biology: An Evolutionary and Biocultural Approach*, 2nd edition (2012), *The Growth of Humanity* (2001), and *Human Variability and Plasticity* (2005).

Jesper L. Boldsen is Professor of Forensic and Biological Anthropology and a faculty member in the Department of Forensic Medicine at the University of Southern Denmark. His research interests are in the history of human health and human skeletal biology with a particular focus on age estimation, paleodemography, and paleoepidemiology. He is the founder and present head of the skeletal collection (ADBOU) at the University of Southern Denmark. He actively promotes trans-Atlantic scientific collaboration and has hosted many senior researchers and graduate students from North America and Europe. He is a former Vice President of the European Anthropological Association.

Anne V. Buchanan served a Research Associate in the Department of Anthropology at the Pennsylvania State University. She has a long-standing interest in complex traits, including disease, and has worked on many projects in genetic epidemiology and developmental genetics.

Jane E. Buikstra is Regents' Professor of Bioarchaeology and Founding Director of the Center for Bioarchaeological Research at Arizona State University. Her research focuses on the changing human condition over time, as documented through human remains recovered from archaeological contexts. She is a former president of the American Association of Physical Anthropologists[1] and the American Anthropological Association and is a Fellow of the American Association of the Advancement of Science and Member of the National Academy of Sciences and the American Academy of Arts and Sciences. She is the co-author of *The Bioarchaeology of Tuberculosis: A Global View on a Reemerging Disease* (2003) and editor of *Bioarchaeologists Speak Out* (2019) and *Ortner's Identification of Pathological Conditions in Human Skeletal Remains* (2019).

Luis L. Cabo is the Director of the Forensic and Bioarchaeology Laboratory and serves as the Graduate Research Director at the Department of Applied Forensic Sciences at Mercyhurst University. With a background in zoology and systems biology, his interests span forensic anthropology, bioarchaeology, zooarchaeology, and human paleontology, with a focus on quantitative applications in taphonomy, evolutionary anatomy, and biological profile estimation methods.

Rachel Caspari is Professor of Anthropology at Central Michigan University. She has worked on fossil human remains from Europe, Africa, and Asia. Her research focusses on the role of changes in population structure and life history in the Middle/Upper Paleolithic transition and the origin of modern *Homo sapiens*. She has a long-standing interest in the relationship between race and epistemology in paleoanthropology and is the co-author of *Race and Human Evolution*.

Mary E. Cole is a biological anthropologist and skeletal biologist in the Skeletal Biology Research Laboratory, Injury Biomechanics Research Center at Ohio State University's College of Medicine. Her research interests pertain to the microstructural determinants of bone quality and strength. Her methodological focus is the development of new microscopic visualization techniques for bone tissue microstructure, especially bone loss. She has published in *Interdisciplinary Reviews Forensic Science* and *The Anatomical Record*.

Fabian Crespo is Associate Professor of Anthropology at the University of Louisville. He received his PhD in Biology from University of Buenos Aires and conducted his postdoctoral research in human immunology at the School of Medicine, University of Louisville. His research addresses the role of infectious diseases in shaping inflammatory responses and immune competence in humans. His reconstructions of past epidemics and pandemics in the context of complex biosocial landscapes combines experimental immunology, bioarchaeology, and history. His publications have appeared in the *American Journal of Biological Anthropology*[2], *International Journal of Paleopathology*, and *Centaurus: International Journal of the History of Science and Its Cultural Aspects*.

Douglas E. Crews is Professor of Anthropology and Public Health at The Ohio State University. He is a biomedical anthropologist specializing in human adaptability, aging, senescence, stressor responses, and allostatic load and frailty among elders in Japan, Kuwait, American Samoa, and Poland. Recent publications have appeared in *PLoS One*, *American Journal of Physical Anthropology*, *General and Comparative Endocrinology*, and *Stress*. He co-edited *Biological Anthropology and Aging: Perspectives on Human Variation over the Life Span* (1994), co-authored *Introduction to Biological Anthropology Laboratory Manual* (2021), and authored *Human Senescence: Evolutionary and Biocultural Perspectives* (2003).

Dennis C. Dirkmaat is Professor in the Department of Applied Forensic Sciences, Mercyhurst University. He is a Diplomate in the American Board of Forensic Anthropology. In 2020, he received the first-awarded *Outstanding Mentor Award* from the Anthropology Section of the American Academy of Forensic Science. In 2021, he was awarded the section's *T. Dale Stewart Award for Lifetime Achievement* in Forensic Anthropology. He serves as the national forensic anthropologist for the National Center for Missing and Exploited Children (NCMEC) and as the forensic anthropologist for Singapore and Puerto Rico. Since 1986, Dirkmaat has conducted 1,000 forensic anthropology cases throughout the United States. He is the editor of *A Companion to Forensic Anthropology* (2012) and co-author of the chapter on forensic archaeological practices in the United States in *Forensic Archaeology: A Global Perspective* (2015).

Darna L. Dufour is Professor Emeritus of Anthropology at the University of Colorado Boulder. Her research interests focus on biocultural aspects of nutrition in contemporary human populations. She has completed long-term field projects in Latin America in both the Amazon region and urban environments. She is a co-author of *Disasters in the Field: Preparing for and Coping with Unexpected Events* and co-editor of *Nutritional Anthropology: Biocultural Perspectives on Food and Nutrition*.

James H. Gosman is Adjunct Professor of Anthropology at The Ohio State University. His research interests encompass skeletal biology and bioarchaeology. His publications and presentations focus on human trabecular bone growth and development related to locomotion. In a parallel career path, he serves as a consulting physician, being supported by an MD and Board Certification in Orthopedic Surgery. He currently serves as the co-director of the global health research arm of the nonprofit foundation, ConnectMed International.

Michael C. Granatosky is Assistant Professor of Anatomy at the New York Institute of Technology. His research interests pertain to functional morphology and evolutionary biomechanics with a focus on the origins and evolution of quadrupedal locomotion in primates and other animal taxa.

Debbie Guatelli-Steinberg is Professor of Anthropology at The Ohio State University. Her research area is dental anthropology, with a focus on developmental, morphological, and functional aspects of nonhuman primate and hominin teeth. Currently, she is engaged in projects on growth rhythms in enamel, functional aspects of dental form in monkeys, and patterns of enamel growth disruption in nonhuman primates and hominins. She is a Fellow of the American Association for the Advancement of Science and the author of *What Teeth Reveal About Human Evolution* (2016).

Kristen Hawkes is Distinguished Professor of Anthropology at the University of Utah. Her research uses comparisons among people (especially hunter–gatherers) and other primates with evolutionary modeling to develop and test hypotheses about the evolution of human life history and social behavior. She is a member of the Scientific Executive Committee of the Leakey Foundation, the National Academy of Sciences, the American Academy of Arts and Sciences, and the American Philosophical Society.

Leslea J. Hlusko is an Investigator at the National Center for Research on Human Evolution (CENIEH) in Spain and holds a full professorship at the University of California Berkeley. Her research uses quantitative genetics to identify how genes influence skeletal variation. She applies this knowledge to the fossil and bioarchaeological records to gain new insights to human evolution and adaptation. Her paleontological fieldwork has primarily focused on sites in eastern Africa. She is a Fellow of the American Association for the Advancement of Science, and former Vice President (2020–2022) and current President (2022–) of the American Association of Biological Anthropologists.

Whitney M. Karriger is a faculty member at the Auburn campus of the Edward Via College of Osteopathic Medicine where she taught anatomy and has now joined the Department of Biomedical Sciences at the College. She earned her PhD in Anthropology from Tulane University and has conducted research on Neandertal dental microwear and on craniofacial ontogeny in Neandertals and modern humans.

Lyle W. Konigsberg is Professor of Anthropology and a faculty member in the Carle Illinois College of Medicine at the University of Illinois at Urbana-Champaign. His research interests are in human skeletal biology with a focus on age estimation in forensic anthropology and paleodemography. He is a co-author with James H. Mielke and John H. Relethford of *Human Biological Variation*, 2nd edn. (2011), a former Vice President and former Secretary/Treasurer of the American Association of Physical Anthropologists, and the Editor-in-Chief of the *Yearbook of Biological Anthropology* (2019–2023).[1]

Christopher W. Kuzawa is a biological anthropologist with interests in developmental biology, human evolution, and health. He is Professor of Anthropology and Faculty Fellow with the Institute for Policy Research at Northwestern University, and Member of the US National Academy of Sciences and the American Academy of Arts and Sciences. He received his PhD in Anthropology and MSPH in Epidemiology from Emory University. His research explores developmental influences on adult biology and health, the psychobiology of human fatherhood, non-genetic forms of biological inheritance, and the energetics and evolution of the human brain.

Clark Spencer Larsen is Distinguished University Professor at The Ohio State University. His research focusses on bioarchaeology, examining adaptive transitions in a range of global settings. He co-directs the Global History of Health Project, a study of worldwide trends in health over the last 10,000 years of human evolution. He is the author of *Bioarchaeology: Interpreting Behavior from the Human Skeleton*, 2nd Edition (2015) and *Our Origins: Discovering Biological Anthropology*, 5th Edition (2020). Larsen is a Fellow of the American Association for the Advancement of Science and Member of the National Academy of Sciences and the American Academy of Arts and Sciences. He served as the Vice President and President of the American Association of Physical Anthropologists and as Editor of the *American Journal of Physical Anthropology*.[1]

Michael A. Little is Distinguished Professor Emeritus at Binghamton University, State University of New York. He is a human biologist who has conducted research in the Peruvian Andes on cold and hypoxic adaptation in Quechua-speaking Native Americans, and then in the northwestern Kenyan savanna on the ecology of Turkana pastoral nomads. Within recent decades, he has pursued historical and biographical research in biological anthropology. He has edited *Man in the Andes* (Baker and Little, 1973), *Turkana Herders of the Dry Savanna* (Little and Leslie, 1999), and *Histories of American Physical Anthropology in the Twentieth Century* (Little and Kennedy, 2010).

Sergi López-Torres is Assistant Professor of Evolutionary Biology at the University of Warsaw, Poland. His work focuses on understanding the evolutionary relationships among early members of Euarchontoglires, including the study of the earliest stages in the evolution of Primates and Glires. His research interests also encompass functional anatomy of primitive euarchontogliran groups, as well as reconstructing their dietary behavior and brain evolution.

Melissa B. Manus is a postdoctoral fellow at the Children's Hospital Research Institute at the University of Manitoba. Her research uses ecological and evolutionary perspectives to investigate connections between early life environments, the microbiome, and health. She received an MSc in Global Health from Duke University and a PhD in Biological Anthropology from Northwestern University, where her dissertation explored the influence of the social environment on the development of the infant microbiome. Her broader interests include applying microbiome science to address social and health inequities.

W. Scott McGraw is a Professor of Anthropology and Chair of the Department of Anthropology at The Ohio State University. He is co-director of the Taï Forest Monkey Project in the Ivory Coast where he has worked since 1992. He has also carried out fieldwork in the Democratic Republic of Congo and Ghana. His research combines aspects of behavior, anatomy, and evolution and he has published on a variety of topics including primate positional behavior, feeding and foraging, locomotor morphology, cranio-dental anatomy, and predator–prey dynamics. As a member of the Primate Specialist Group in the International Union for the Conservation of Nature, he is actively involved in African primate conservation, including contributing to the recently published *Red colobus (Piliocolobus) Conservation Action Plan 2021–2026* (IUCN 2021).

Rachel A. Menegaz is Assistant Professor of Anatomical Sciences at the University of North Texas Health Science Center at Fort Worth. Her research program is focused on the biomechanics, growth, and function of the mammalian feeding apparatus. She uses experimental approaches to better understand the relationship between diet and morphology during mammalian evolution.

Elaine N. Miller is a doctoral candidate at the Center for the Advanced Study of Human Paleobiology at The George Washington University in Washington, DC. She is broadly interested in human brain evolution and the neuroanatomical substrates that give rise to human sociality. Her dissertation work is an examination of how social adversity experienced in early life can impact neural development in chimpanzees and rhesus macaques. She is a National Science Foundation Graduate Research Fellow.

George R. Milner is a Distinguished Professor of Anthropology at The Pennsylvania State University. His research combines archaeology and biological anthropology, with an emphasis on the population structure and disease experience of past societies. His work with human skeletal remains also has forensic significance, especially regarding age and sex estimation. He has conducted archaeological excavations in North America, Europe, Africa, and Oceania. He is a Fellow of the American Association for the Advancement of Science and Member of the National Academy of Sciences.

James F. O'Connell is Distinguished Professor (Emeritus) of Anthropology, University of Utah, Salt Lake City. He has extensive ethnographic and archaeological field experience in western North America, central Australia, and East Africa. His research deals with variation in hunter–gatherer foraging and food sharing practices, the relationship between hunter–gatherer behavior and its archaeological consequences, and the implications of both for ideas about human ecology and evolution in the Pleistocene. He is a Member of the National Academy of Sciences, Fellow of the American Association for the Advancement of Science, Honorary Fellow of the Australian Academy of the Humanities, and Foreign Associate of the Australian Institute of Aboriginal and Torres Strait Islander Studies.

Carolyn Orbann is Associate Teaching Professor of Health Sciences at the University of Missouri-Columbia. Her current research interests include infectious disease in historic human populations and the impact of culture on disease spread. She uses historic data, including primary and secondary sources, to understand epidemics in the past, primarily 1918 influenza and diseases of colonization in eighteenth-century California. She uses computer simulation models to test ideas about the impact of human culture on infectious disease dynamics.

Dennis H. O'Rourke is Foundation Distinguished Professor of Anthropology at the University of Kansas. He is an anthropological geneticist whose research focuses on the use of ancient DNA to reconstruct regional population histories and early human dispersal in the Americas, especially the North American Arctic, and on the use of sedimentary ancient DNA in paleoenvironmental reconstruction. He is a Fellow of the American Association for the Advancement of Science and Past-President and Vice-President of the American Association of Physical Anthropologists and of the American Association of Anthropological Geneticists.

Barbara A. Piperata is Professor of Anthropology at The Ohio State University. Her research program focuses on nutritional anthropology and how resource insecurities affect maternal mental health and child growth and development. Her field research in the Brazilian Amazon explored how cultural beliefs and practices in the postpartum affect maternal reproductive energetics, as well as the role of poverty alleviation programs in driving the nutrition transition in rural communities. Ongoing research in Brazil and Nicaragua explored how food and water insecurity influence children's gut and oral microbiomes during critical windows of development.

Briana Pobiner is a research scientist and museum educator in the Human Origins Program at the Smithsonian Institution's National Museum of Natural History. Her zooarchaeological and taphonomic research centers on the role of meat-eating in the evolution of Stone Age human diets with a focus on the use of bone surface modifications including human butchery marks and predator tooth marks on modern and fossil bones. She also leads the Human Origins Program's education and outreach efforts, including managing public programs, website content, social media, and exhibition volunteer training.

Laurie J. Reitsema is Associate Professor of Anthropology at the University of Georgia. Her research pertains to the links between biology, culture, and environment, focusing on stable isotope analysis and the study of human stress, disease, and nutrition. Her bioarchaeological work is informed by ties to human biology and primatology.

John H. Relethford is SUNY Distinguished Teaching Professor Emeritus at the Department of Anthropology, State University of New York College at Oneonta. His research and teaching interests are human evolution, human biological variation, and human population genetics. Much of his research has focused on global patterns of craniometric variation, modern human origins, and the population history of Ireland. He is a former Vice President and President of the American Association of Physical Anthropologists and has received the Gabriel W. Lasker Distinguished Service Award from that organization. He is a Fellow of the American Association for the Advancement of Science. His books include *50 Great Myths of Human Evolution* and *Reflections of Our Past*, Second Edition, co-authored with Deborah Bolnick. He retired from teaching in 2020.

G. Philip Rightmire is Research Associate in the Department of Human Evolutionary Biology at Harvard University and Distinguished Professor of Anthropology (Emeritus) at Binghamton University (SUNY). His interests encompass the evolution of earliest *Homo*, first dispersals from Africa, species origins, and systematics. He has studied human fossils and participated in field excavations in southern and eastern Africa, western Asia, Europe, and the Far East. For all the support and opportunities that have come his way, he thanks his lucky stars!

Lisa Sattenspiel is Professor of Anthropology at the University of Missouri-Columbia. Her research focuses on understanding the impact of social and demographic factors on patterns of interaction of people from various walks of life and has involved work on hepatitis A, HIV, measles, the 1918 influenza pandemic, and COVID-19. Her two most recent projects are a comparison of the 1918 influenza and 2020 COVID-19 pandemics in rural vs. urban counties in the US state of Missouri and a study of the 1918 influenza pandemic among indigenous peoples in Alaska, USA and Labrador, Canada. She is a Fellow of the American Association for the Advancement of Science and is the author of *The Geographic Spread of Infectious Diseases: Models and Applications* (2009).

Christopher W. Schmidt is Professor of Anthropology and Chair of the Department of Anthropology at the University of Indianapolis. His research focuses on human diet and subsistence and includes dental microwear texture analysis (DMTA). One of his primary initiatives is the DENTALWEAR project, which has generated DMTA data from over 1,000 predominantly Holocene humans from around the globe. His recent books include *Long "on" the Tooth: Dental Evidence of Diet* and *Dental Wear in Evolutionary and Biocultural Contexts* (co-edited with James T. Watson).

Margaret J. Schoeninger is Professor Emeritus of Anthropology and Co-Director of the Center for Academic Research and Training in Anthropogeny (human origins) at the University of California at San Diego. Her research centers on subsistence strategies of humans and nonhuman primates to address the social, behavioral, and ecological aspects of human uniqueness. She has participated in archaeological, paleontological, and ethnographic fieldwork projects in North America, Mesoamerica, Peru, Pakistan, India, Kenya, and Tanzania. Her laboratory analyzes carbon, nitrogen, and oxygen stable isotope ratios in various biological materials including hair, bone collagen, and bone carbonate. She is a Fellow of the American Association for the Advancement of Science.

Chet C. Sherwood is Professor of Anthropology at the George Washington University. His research investigates how brains differ among primate species and how this variation is correlated with behavior, shaped by the rules of developmental biology, impacted by experience, and encoded in the genome. He co-directs the National Chimpanzee Brain Resource and the Great Ape Neuroscience Project. He received a James S. McDonnell Foundation Scholar Award in Understanding Human Cognition. He is a member of the National Academy of Sciences.

Mary T. Silcox is Professor of Anthropology at the University of Toronto, Canada. Her research program focusses on characterizing and interpreting the earliest phases of primate evolution from both a phylogenetic and an adaptive perspective. In addition to doing fieldwork in the western North America, her research program involves the use of high-resolution X-ray computed tomography to uncover previously unavailable aspects of anatomy. She is particularly interested in methods of quantifying dental anatomy to study diet through time and in refining our study of the evolution of the brain using endocasts.

Scott W. Simpson is a Professor of Anatomy in the Case Western Reserve University School of Medicine. His current research involves study of the biology and context of late Miocene to Pleistocene hominins including paleoanthropological field research experience with the Middle Awash and Gona Research Projects and currently he is the Principal Investigator of the Galili Paleobiology Project in the Afar region of Ethiopia. He is a member of the African Rift Valley Research Consortium and co-edited the volume *Methods in Paleoecology* (2018) with D. A. Croft and D. F. Su.

Fred H. Smith is a paleoanthropologist whose research focusses on Neandertals and the origin of modern people. He is University Distinguished Professor of Anthropology and Biological Sciences Emeritus at Illinois State University and an adjunct professor at the University of Colorado, Boulder. He is the author of numerous scholarly publications, including his book co-authored with Matt Cartmill, *The Human Lineage*, Second Edition (Wiley-Blackwell, 2022). Smith has received awards for his work from institutions in the United States, Ireland, Germany, and Croatia.

Anne Stone is an anthropological geneticist whose research and teaching focuses on the evolutionary history of humans and our pathogens. She is a Regents' Professor in the School of Human Evolution and Social Change at Arizona State University and a member of the Center for Bioarchaeological Research, the Center for Evolution and Medicine, and the Institute of Human Origins. Stone was elected Fellow of the American Association for the Advancement of Science in 2011 and to the National Academy of Sciences, USA in

2016. She currently serves on the scientific executive committee of The Leakey Foundation, the advisory board for the Center of Excellence for Australian Biodiversity and Heritage, and as Associate Editor for *Philosophical Transactions of the Royal Society*.

Samuel D. Stout is Professor Emeritus in the Department of Anthropology at The Ohio State University. His research interests are in skeletal biology, focusing upon the microscopic (histomorphological) level of structural organization of bone, and its applications in bioarchaeology, paleopathology, and forensic anthropology. He is a Fellow of the American Association for the Advancement of Science and the American Academy of Forensic Sciences. He is co-editor (with Christian Crowder) of *Bone Histology: An Anthropological Perspective* (2015, CRC Press).

Karen B. Strier is the Vilas Research Professor and Irven DeVore Professor of Anthropology at the University of Wisconsin-Madison. Her main research interests are to understand the behavioral ecology of primates from a comparative perspective and to contribute to conservation efforts on their behalf. She leads a long-term field study on the critically endangered muriqui monkey in the Brazilian Atlantic Forest. She is a Fellow of the American Association for the Advancement of Science and Member of the National Academy of Sciences and American Academy of Arts and Sciences. She is the author of *Primate Behavioral Ecology, 6th edition* (2021).

Douglas H. Ubelaker received his PhD from the University of Kansas in 1973. He serves as Curator and Senior Scientist in the Department of Anthropology of the National Museum of Natural History, Smithsonian Institution, Washington DC. He has reported on over 980 forensic cases, primarily at the request of the Federal Bureau of Investigation, USA. He has published extensively on topics related to forensic anthropology and bioarcheology. He served as the 2011–2012 President of the American Academy of Forensic Sciences and has received numerous awards.

Alexis Uluutku is a PhD candidate at The George Washington University studying at the Center for the Advanced Study of Human Paleobiology under Bernard Wood. She is interested in the effects of competition between early *Homo* and *Paranthropus* in eastern Africa during the Pleistocene. She uses geometric morphometrics to test for sympatry and morphological change through time as they relate to ecological incumbency and character displacement.

Peter S. Ungar is Distinguished Professor of Anthropology and Director of Environmental Dynamics at the University of Arkansas. His main research interests focus on the evolution of diet in and impacts of environmental change on humans and other mammals. Much of this work involves the study of microscopic use-wear of teeth for traces of past diet, as well as dental topography for evidence of adaptations for specific sorts of foods. He is a Fellow of the American Association for the Advancement of Science and a member of the American Academy of Arts and Sciences, and the author of *Evolution's Bite* (2017), *Teeth: A Very Short Introduction* (2014), and *Mammal Teeth* (2010).

Qian Wang is Professor of Anatomy at the Texas A&M University School of Dentistry. His research concerns adaptation, function, disease, and evolution. He is involved in studies examining craniofacial bone elastic properties and the biology and biomechanics of craniofacial sutures using a variety of research methods, including an ultrasonic technique and finite element analysis. He is the editor of *Bones, Genetics, and Behavior of Rhesus Macaques: Macaca mulatta of Cayo Santiago and Beyond* (2012). His current research focuses on paleopathology of recent human populations in the context of environmental and socioeconomic factors.

Kenneth M. Weiss is Evan Pugh Professor Emeritus at Pennsylvania State University. His research is on evolution as a process, and specifically on how it generates the genetic basis of complex morphological traits such as the teeth and the skull. He has written widely on how simple biological principles, which go beyond basic Darwinian ones, produce complexity on both the developmental and evolutionary timescales. He is a Fellow of the American Association for the Advancement of Science and the author of *Genetic Variation and Human Disease: Principles and Evolutionary Approaches* (1995).

Bernard Wood is University Professor of Human Origins at George Washington University. He is the author or co-author of 20 books ranging from a 1991 door-stopping monograph on the hominid cranial remains from Koobi Fora to the nontechnical *Human Evolution, A Very Short Introduction* (2019), the author of over 240 scientific articles and book chapters, and a slew of commentaries in *Nature* and other journals. His research interests are taxonomy, phylogeny reconstruction, and comparative morphology. He is an Honorary Fellow of the Royal College of Surgeons of England. In his spare time, he looks after a 1799 house in rural Virginia where he curates his collection of English salt-glaze stoneware.

Jesse W. Young is an organismal biologist with broad interests in understanding the developmental and evolutionary biomechanics of the mammalian locomotor system. Specific research foci include: (1) the functional, and adaptive, links between somatic growth and locomotor development in mammals and (2) the evolutionary biomechanics of primate arboreal locomotion. He is the author of *Skeletal Anatomy of the Newborn Primate* (2020).

Andrea M. Zurek-Ost is a PhD candidate at the University of North Carolina at Chapel Hill. Her research in the Basque Country focuses on the intersection of transience and skeletal health in the past through stable isotope methods. Her past research has explored the efficacy of morphological traits of the pelvis in age-at-death estimations, the application of taphonomic principles to crime scene reconstructions, and the role of the forensic anthropologist at fatal fire scenes. She has assisted with forensic casework across the northeastern United States and Puerto Rico and is a team member with Kenyon International Emergency Services. She has also overseen the curation of donated human and zooarchaeological skeletal collections at Mercyhurst University.

Acknowledgments

My thanks and my gratitude go to all the authors for their contributions to the second edition of *Companion to Biological Anthropology*. Their individual chapters provide comprehensive overviews of the past and recent advances in the science of biological anthropology, from the study of evolution and variation from the appearance of the first primate-like animals living 65 million years ago to the origins of human-like ancestors beginning some six to seven million years ago. The individual and collective leadership, knowledge, and commitment over the course of the development of the book made this an especially enjoyable project for me personally. The authors' wide span and depth of expertise and skills in key areas of research and investigation in biological anthropology ensured a flawless process in the preparation, production, and publication of the book. Thanks go to all authors for their superb contributions and steadfast commitment to the book project.

The book chapter drafts were evaluated by reviewers representing all areas of biological anthropology. I thank the following biological anthropologists and authorities from allied disciplines for their reading and recommendations for revisions of manuscripts: Leslie Aiello, Eduardo Amorim, Katherine Baloia, Daniel Benyshek, Tracy Betsinger, Michelle Bezanson, Claudio Bravi, Daniel Brown, Noel Cameron, David Cooper, Douglas Crews, Deborah Cunningham, Eric Delson, Darna Dufour, Arthur Durband, Heather Edgar, Leslie Eisenberg, Mohammed Elsalanty, John Fleagle, Laura Fulginiti, Teresa Gildner, Anne Grauer, Drew Halley, Ashley Hammond, Kristin Hedges, Michael Hermanussen, Nick Herrmann, David Himmelgreen, Daryl Holman, Daniel Hruschka, Keith Hunley, Richard Kay, Annie Katzenberg, Kristen Krueger, Susan Larson, Pierre Lemelin, Lee Lyman, Jonathan Marks, Thomas McDade, Stephanie Melillo, George Milner, Monique Borgerhoff Mulder, Rob O'Malley, John Relethford, Neil Roach, Dennis O'Rourke, Michael Plavcan, James Rilling, Alex Robling, Eric Seiffert, Katerina Semendeferi, Lynette Sievert, David Strait, Daniel Temple, Adam Van Arsdale, Bruce Winterhalder, Todd Yokley, and Sonia Zakrzewski. It was very nice to be able to interact with this group of biological anthropologists. We covered quite a lot of territory in our various discussions.

I give a special acknowledgement to the staff at Wiley-Blackwell for their continuous and unwavering support at all stages of the book's development. I thank Rachel Greenberg who extended the invitation to me to develop and edit a second edition of *Companion to Biological Anthropology* and for her support in preparing the proposal for the book project.

Thanks go to Charlie Hamlyn and Clelia Petracca for their guidance and advice and leading me through the myriad of details and all matters relating to areas ranging from invitations to prospective authors, the questions prospective authors had for me, and the preparation of the content and plethora of inquiries that I had for authors over the course of the last several years. I thank Verity Stuart who advised me on selection of images for figures for the book's cover. The development of the book had challenges for everyone involved on both sides of the Atlantic, made especially demanding owing to the unprecedented circumstances of the pandemic.

One of the first things I learned when I started taking anthropology courses in my freshman year at my undergraduate *alma mater*, Kansas State University, and reinforced ever since, is the remarkable biocultural and behavioral resiliency of humans, their ability to address challenges, to develop solutions to these challenges, and to adapt. For me, working on this book with all the authors reinforced that sense of resiliency. Everyone involved in the book made it possible to meet the challenges of the past several years. I cannot imagine a more collaborative and committed group than all who I have worked with from the beginning to the end of the book project.

Thank you everyone!

Foreword

Leslea J. Hlusko

In this second edition of *A Companion to Biological Anthropology*, Larsen and colleagues have compiled 36 beautifully written chapters that introduce the reader to the latest science, essential concepts, and perspectives spanning the discipline. I have been a biological anthropologist for over 20 years and still found myself enthralled by the interconnections across these chapters. I would love to invite the authors over for dinner and an evening of brainstorming. How interesting it would be to have Sattenspiel and Orbann talking about modern pandemics alongside Stone's knowledge of ancient pathogens. It turns out that we have been living with diseases such as tuberculosis and plague for thousands of years longer than scientists originally thought. This certainly changes one's perspective on how and when the Covid19 pandemic will "end." Let's also bring in Amorim's expertise on ancient DNA, O'Rourke's deep knowledge of human populations, and Beall's classic examples of human environmental adaptation. What a conversation we would have about how pandemics and environmental adaptation shaped the last 100,000 years of human evolution. But it does not stop there. Imagine we also invite Kuzawa and Manis to bring to the conversation their interdisciplinary perspective on today's obesity and cardiovascular disease, which, of course, also calls for invitations to Dufour and Piperata, as nutritional variation is essential to understanding all these observed trends. We also want to consider the role inflammatory response plays in health, well-being, and adaptation, so let us invite Crespo to the dinner. Keep in mind that all of this varies over the course of a lifetime and across species, so we need the life history perspective of Crews and Bogin and the biodiversity perspectives of McGraw, Silcox, and López-Torres. We are going to need a very large dinner table indeed, and we have only just begun the guest list!

Many of the chapter topics are classic, such as taxonomy and adaptation, but the methods applied today are innovative and new. This edition of the *Companion* also includes research genres that were only a pipe dream a decade or two ago, but now, with technological advances, they represent entirely new subdisciplines such as ancient DNA, the microbiome, epigenetics, and genome-wide association studies. The level of technological sophistication within our science always impresses me, but the true heart of biological anthropology is in the meaningful interconnections the anthropologist makes between biology, social science, and humanity.

The past decade has been a watershed moment for the discipline's humanity in ways that extend far beyond the science. The scholarly community pushed to the forefront concerns about who is doing the science and how it is being done. In Chapter 2, Little and Buikstra provide perspective on this, noting that the founders of the discipline in the eighteenth and nineteenth centuries primarily considered race as a valid taxonomic category within humans. This research helped to justify racism within the Unites States and the inequity that continues to exist today (Blakey 1996, 2021; Fuentes 2012). Because of this history, biological anthropologists are, perhaps, especially aware of the social impact of their science. Although there have always been biological anthropologists pushing against racist tropes (e.g., Cobb 1936; Juan Comas 1961; Marks 1995; Jackson 2000; Fuentes 2012), the recent disciplinary shift towards antiracism is notable (as defined by Kendi 2019). I want to highlight some of the recent major events.

In 2021, the flagship association for biological anthropologists in the United States completed the years-long process of changing its name from the American Association of Physical Anthropologists (AAPA) to the American Association of Biological Anthropologists (AABA), distinguishing between the origins of the science that focused on racial distinctions ("physical") and the more interdisciplinary and biological approach employed today. Alongside this name change came a more coordinated effort to communicate the antiracist implications of the science to the public. Pages of peer-reviewed research journals were dedicated to articles about the broader context, advice, and calls-to-action. In 2020, the journal *Human Biology*, the official publication of the American Association of Anthropological Genetics (AAAG), published a special issue on *Race, Racism, and the Genetic Structure of Human Populations* (Malhi 2020). In 2021, the *American Journal of Biological Anthropology* dedicated an issue to the interpretation and communication of biological variation and race (Raff and Mulligan 2021), including an article on how White nationalists use anthropological genetics research to justify their racism (Panofsky et al. 2021),

Changes have also been taking place within the discipline. As Antón et al. (2018) reported that 87 percent of members of the then-AAPA identified as white (an astonishing bias of representation for a discipline aimed at understanding variation), two new cross-institutional training programs had already been developed to reach a broader cohort of students: IDEAS (Increasing Diversity in Evolutionary Anthropological Sciences, Malhi et al. 2019) and SING (Summer Internship for INdigenous peoples in Genomics Consortium, Bardill et al. 2018; Claw et al. 2018). While individual scholars have long made the case that with more diverse perspectives comes a richer science (e.g., Cobb 1936; Jackson 2000; Jackson et al. 2016, 2014; TallBear 2014), over the last few years there has been a flurry of symposia, peer-reviewed journals, and edited volumes dedicated to the topic (e.g., the *American Anthropologists'* Vital Topics Forum: How academic diversity is transforming scientific knowledge in biological anthropology, Bolnick et al. 2019; see also Athreya and Ackermann 2019; Poor and Matthews 2020).

Biological anthropologists are also working to improve academic culture. For example, Clancy, Nelson, and colleagues conducted surveys to quantify sexual harassment in the field (Clancy et al. 2014; Nelson et al. 2017), an important step towards addressing it, and in February 2022, the *American Journal of Human Biology* published a special issue on the theme of #Hackademics: Hacks Towards Success in Academia (Ocobock et al. 2022), articles born out of a series of podcasts from the *Sausage of Science* (https://www.humbio.org/podcasts) that then became fodder for a webinar series hosted by AABA (https://bioanth.org/meetings-and-webinars/aabas-monthly-webinar-series/the-hackademics-series-hacks-for-succeeding-in-academia).

However, there is still much to do and many conversations to be had. As biological anthropologists developed best practices for data-sharing (Turner and Mulligan 2019), colleagues raised the need to more deeply engage with Indigenous data sovereignties (Tsosie et al. 2020). Recent reflections on the ethics of our science have aimed to open up additional discussions (MacClancy and Fuentes 2013; Turner et al. 2018). The new science of ancient DNA raises a swath of ethical issues (Alpaslan-Roodenberg et al. 2021; Tsosie et al. 2021; Wagner et al. 2020), and now, engagement with the descendant communities is considered an essential component of ethically sound research on human DNA, especially within biological anthropology. While the Native American Graves Protection and Repatriation Act (NAGPRA) of 1990 provided a framework for managing the human remains of Indigenous people housed in museum collections (Nash and Colwell 2020), biological anthropologists are now returning to a conversation started by one of the founders of the discipline, W. Montague Cobb, who first noted the disproportionate representations of human remains kept in museum collections, including African Americans (Cobb 1933; Jackson et al. 2016; and see Blakey and Watkins 2022). Biological anthropologists are now much more cognizant of the fact that these biases are primarily the result of social and cultural marginalization (de la Cova 2019).

These academic shifts are hard to capture within a volume like *A Companion of Biological Anthropology*, but this groundswell of change is shaping the biological anthropology of today even more so than did the technological advances of the past decade. While I am in awe at the evolution of biological anthropology since the publication of the 1st edition of the *Companion*, I am already looking forward to where seeing where we will be when it is time for the 3rd edition.

NOTE

1 The official name of the professional organization was changed from the American Association of Physical Anthropologists to the American Association of Biological Anthropologists in 2021. The Association's journal name was changed from the *American Journal of Physical Anthropology* to the *American Journal of Biological Anthropology* in 2022 and its annual publication from the *Yearbook of Physical Anthropology* to the *Yearbook of Biological Anthropology* in 2022.

REFERENCES

Alpaslan-Roodenberg, S., D. Anthony, H. Babiker, et al. "Ethics of DNA Research on Human Remains: Five Globally Applicable Guidelines." *Nature* 599 (2021): 41–46.

Antón, S. C., R. S. Malhi, and A. Fuentes. "Race and Diversity in U.S. Biological Anthropology: A Decade of AAPA Initiatives." *American Journal of Biological Anthropology* 165 (2018): 158–180.

Athreya, S., and R. R. Ackermann. "Colonialism and Narratives of Human Origins in Asia and Africa." In *Interrogating Human Origins: Decolonisation and the Deep Human Past*, edited by Martin Porr and Jacqueline Matthews, 72–95. Routledge, 2019.

Bardill, J., A. C. Bader, N. A. Garrison, D. A. Bolnick, J. A. Raff, A. Walker, and R. S. Malhi. "Summer Internship for INdigenous Peoples in Genomics (SING) Consortium. Advancing the Ethics of Paleogenomics." *Science* 360, no. 6387 (2018): 384–385.

Blakey, M. L. "Skull Doctors Revisited: Intrinsic Social and Political Bias in the History of American Physical Anthropology, with Special Reference to the Work of Aleš Hrdlička." In *Race and Other Misadventures: Essays in Honor of Ashley Montagu in His Ninetieth Year*. Edited by L. T. Reynolds and L. Lieberman, 64–95. Lanham, Maryland: Altamira Press, 1996.

Blakey, M. L. "Understanding Racism in Physical (Biological) Anthropology." *American Journal of Biological Anthropology* 175 (2021): 316–325.

Blakey, M. L., and R. Watkins. "William Montague Cobb: Near the African Diasporic Origins of Activist and Biocultural Anthropology." *The Anatomical Record* 305, no. 4 (2022): 838–848.

Bolnick, D. A., R. W. Smith, and A. Fuentes. "How Academic Diversity Is Transforming Scientific Knowledge in Biological Anthropology." *American Anthropologist* 2 (2019): 464-464.

Clancy, K. B., R. G. Nelson, J. N. Rutherford, and K. Hinde. "Survey of Academic Field Experiences (SAFE): Trainees Report Harassment and Assault." *PloS One* 9, no. 7 (2014): e102172.

Claw, K. G., M. Z. Anderson, R. L. Begay, et al. Summer internship for INdigenous peoples in Genomics (SING) Consortium. "A Framework for Enhancing Ethical Genomic Research with Indigenous Communities." *Nature Communications* 9, no. 1 (2018): 2957.

Cobb, W. M. "Human Materials in American Institutions Available for Anthropology Study." *American Journal of Physical Anthropology* 17, no. 4 (Supplement April–June 1933): 1–45.

Cobb, W. M. "Race and Runners." *The Journal of Health and Physical Education* 7, no. 1 (1936): 3–56.

Comas, J. ""Scientific" Racism Again?" *Current Anthropology* 2, no. 4 (1961): 303–340.

de la Cova, C. "Marginalized Bodies and the Construction of the Robert J. Terry Anatomical Skeletal Collection: A Promised Land Lost." In *Bioarchaeology of Marginalized People*, edited by Madeleine Mant and Alyson Holland, 133–155. Cambridge, Massachusetts: Academic Press, 2019.

Fuentes, A. *Race, Monogamy and Other Lies They Told You: Busting Myths about Human Nature.* Berkeley: University of California Press, 2012.

Jackson, F., L. Jackson, C. Cross, and C. Clarke. "What Could You Do with 400 Years of Biological History on African Americans? Evaluating the Potential Scientific Benefit of Systematic Studies of Dental and Skeletal Materials on African Americans from the 17th Through 20th Centuries." *American Journal of Human Biology* 28, no. 4 (2016): 510–513.

Jackson, F., C. M. Lee, and S. Taylor. "Let Minority-serving Institutions Lead." *Science* 345, no. 6199 (2014): 885.

Jackson, F. L. "Anthropological Measurement: The Mismeasure of African Americans." *The ANNALS of the American Academy of Political and Social Science* 568, no. 1 (2000): 154–171.

Kendi, I. X. *How to Be an Antiracist.* New York: One World, 2019.

MacClancy, J., and A. Fuentes. *Ethics in the Field: Contemporary Challenges.* New York: Berghahn, Oxford, 2013. ISBN 978-0-85745-962-6.

Malhi, R. S. "Contributions to Anti-Racist Science: Introduction to Race, Racism, and the Genetic Structure of Human Populations Special Issue." *Human Biology* 92, no. 3 (2020): 133–134.

Malhi, R. S., S. C. Antón, and A. Fuentes. "Increasing Diversity in Evolutionary Anthropological Sciences – The IDEAS Program." *American Anthropologist* 121, no. 2 (2019): 478–479.

Marks, J. *Human Biodiversity: Genes, Race, and History.* Piscataway, NJ: Aldine Transaction, 1995.

Nash, S. E., and C. Colwell. "NAGPRA at 30: The Effects of Repatriation." *Annual Review of Anthropology* 49 (2020): 225–239.

Nelson, R. G., J. N. Rutherford, K. Hinde, and K. B. H. Clancy. "Signaling Safety: Characterizing Fieldwork Experiences and Their Implications for Career Trajectories." *American Anthropologist* 119, no. 4 (2017): 710–722.h.

Ocobock, C., C. Owens, E. Holdsworth, et al. "# Hackademics: Hacks Toward Success in Academia." *American Journal of Human Biology* 34 (2022): e23653.

Panofsky, A., K. Dasgupta, and N. Iturriaga. "How White Nationalists Mobilize Genetics: From Genetic Ancestry and Human Biodiversity to Counterscience and Metapolitics." *American Journal of Physical Anthropology* 175, no. 2 (2021): 387–398.

Poor, M., and J. M. Matthews, eds. *Interrogating Human Origins: Decolonisation and the Deep Human Past*, 500 pp. Abingdon, Oxon, and New York, NY: Routledge, 2020. ISBN 9780203731659.

Raff, J. A., and C. J. Mulligan. "Race Reconciled II: Interpreting and Communicating Biological Variation and Race in 2021." *American Journal of Physical Anthropology* 175, no. 2 (2021): 313–315.

TallBear, K. "Standing with and Speaking as Faith: A Feminist-Indigenous Approach to Inquiry." *Journal of Research Practice* 10, no. 2 (2014): N17.

Tsosie, K. S., A. Bader, K. Fox, et al. "Ancient DNA Researchers Write Their Own Rules." *Nature* 600, no. 2, December (2021): 37.

Tsosie, K. S., J. M. Yracheta, J. Kolopenuk, and R. W. Smith. "Indigenous Data Sovereignties and Data Sharing in Biological Anthropology." *American Journal Physical Anthropology* 174 (2020): 183–186.

Turner, T. R., and C. J. Mulligan. "Data Sharing in Biological Anthropology: Guiding Principles and Best Practices." *American Journal of Physical Anthropology* 170, no. 1 (2019): 3–4.

Turner, T. R., J. K. Wagner, and G. S. Cabana. "Ethics in Biological Anthropology." *American Journal of Physical Anthropology* 165, no. 4 (2018): 939–951.

Wagner, J. D., C. Colwell, K. G. Claw, et al. "Fostering Responsible Research on Ancient DNA." *American Journal of Human Genetics* 107, no. 2 (2020): 183–195.

CHAPTER 1

The Breadth and Vision of Biological Anthropology

Clark Spencer Larsen

Since the publication of the first edition of *A Companion to Biological Anthropology* in 2010 (Larsen 2010), there have been considerable advances made in biological anthropology[1], the discipline devoted to the study of the evolution and variation of all primates, ancestral and contemporary, nonhuman and human. New and developing knowledge underscores primates' remarkable record of adaptability, resiliency, and success. The temporal, geographic, and biological span is vast, encompassing some 65 million years of evolution, all inhabitable continents, and thousands of genera and species. It is the record of the span of 65 million years that biological anthropologists observe and interpret the extraordinary record of origins and adaptations. Of those 65 million years, early hominins – the ancestor of all of us living today – are represented in the last six to eight million years of primate evolution.

The contributing authors to the new edition of *A Companion to Biological Anthropology* are excited to share with you the many advances made within the broad scope of biological anthropology. All 57 contributing authors involved in preparing contributions to the book are thrilled to be able to present the content of key subareas of the discipline. In my role as both the editor and a contributing author, it is especially exciting to engage readers with new knowledge that is continuing to build on centuries of discovery. You will be reading chapters prepared by leading authorities in biological anthropology, all of whom engage in research and study.

The discipline of biological anthropology owes its origin to a number of pioneers. Franz Boas (1858–1942), the founder of the discipline of anthropology in the United States, was committed to a comprehensive approach to understanding the human condition, both from cultural and biological perspectives. His interest in human biology and behavior played a key role in the development of biological anthropology as it is represented in the United States. It was Boas' vision for the study of the human condition that laid the foundation for the growth and development of biological anthropology as a distinctive and compelling discipline in the broad context of the natural, social, and behavioral sciences. It was also the vision and leadership of two other key pioneering scientists that started the field – Aleš Hrdlička (1869–1943) of the Smithsonian Institution and Earnest Albert

A Companion to Biological Anthropology, Second Edition. Edited by Clark Spencer Larsen.
© 2023 John Wiley & Sons Ltd. Published 2023 by John Wiley & Sons Ltd.

Hooton (1887–1954) of Harvard University (see Little and Buikstra, Chapter 2). Hrdlička founded the professional journal, the *American Journal of Physical Anthropology*, in 1918. More than a century later it was renamed the *American Journal of Biological Anthropology*, reflecting the content and focus of the journal and the modern scientific discipline that it has become. Hrdlička was the driving force in the founding and organization of the discipline's professional society in 1928 (American Association of Physical Anthropologists, now the American Association of Biological Anthropologists). Hooton taught and trained all of the first generation of PhDs who would in turn educate the next generation of professional biological anthropologists. Most of the chapter authors contributing to *A Companion to Biological Anthropology* trace their academic genealogies back to Hooton. Between the two of them, Hrdlička and Hooton engaged with every subject area in biological anthropology. Simply put, it was their collective intellectual vision that laid the foundation for the diverse and growing discipline that we see thriving in the twenty-first century.

As with science in general, much has changed in the field. These changes reflect new interests, building on long-standing concerns, developing new hypotheses, and seeking answers to old and newly emerging questions. As expected in any mature science, paradigms and theoretical perspectives change with new discoveries and new research. Biological anthropology is no exception. The biggest change for the discipline is the shift from description to the application of evolutionary theory and key biological principles, especially beginning in the mid-1950s. It is the energy and commitment of all generations of biological anthropologists, however, that have put this discipline on the path towards discovery and exploration of new subjects, developing an increasingly informed understanding of primates, and addressing hypotheses and answering questions about evolution and variation.

The contributors to this book are the direct beneficiaries of these earlier, remarkable scientists – Hrdlička, Hooton, and all of those that followed – who pioneered areas discussed by Michael Little and Jane Buikstra in their opening chapter on the history of biological anthropology (Chapter 2). Little and Buikstra cover considerable ground, introducing the beginnings and history of key themes in the discipline and the origins of many of the areas discussed in this book, ranging from genetics and genomics, bioarchaeology, and the last 10,000 years of human evolution, the record of the first primates, and the origins of the human lineage.

Biological anthropology is a highly diverse science, both in its temporal breadth and topical scope. The focus on evolution and variation is what gives biological anthropology such a robust approach to the study of humankind, past and present. More than a century-and-a-half ago, the central mechanism underlying evolution – natural selection – was first described by Charles Darwin and Alfred Wallace, working independently of one another (Weiss and Buchanan, Chapter 3). It was the force of natural selection that has shaped variation and evolution. To make sense of the complexity of past and present primates, the development of systematics and taxonomy were well under way by the time Darwin and Wallace thought about evolution. Although taxonomy was originally built on the notion that past and present life is static, Darwin's and Wallace's pioneering work showed that life is dynamic, and that earlier ancestral species gave rise to later descendant species. Today, the reconstruction of phylogeny – evolutionary trees showing ancestral-descendant relationships – serves as the framework for interpreting biology of past and present organisms (Uluutku and Wood, Chapter 4).

The mechanisms that drive evolution are few – natural selection, mutation, genetic drift, and gene flow – but complex in operation (Weiss and Buchanan, Chapter 3; Relethford, Chapter 5; and others in the book). As Relethford points out, these forces interact in many different combinations and often in complex ways. It is the interaction of these evolutionary forces that determines patterns of genetic and phenotypic variation both within and between populations. As the implications of these evolutionary forces became realized in the first half of the twentieth century, a group of early geneticists, especially Sewall Wright, Ronald Fisher, and J. B. S. Haldane, tackled key issues by using mathematics and statistics, founding a new area of study called population genetics (Relethford, Chapter 5).

Population genetics is fundamental to documenting and interpreting patterns of genetic change. Biological anthropologists have been at the forefront of the continued development of this area of study as it applies to humans and nonhuman primates. More than any other discipline, biological anthropology recognizes the importance of the record of DNA, ancient and modern, for interpreting evolutionary change in primates, including humans. The DNA revolution transformed the field of genetics, occasioning the development of genomics, the study of the entire record of DNA at the individual and population levels. Newly discovered genetic markers provide an essential supplement to the rough maps of genetic variation identified using traditional markers (e.g., blood group polymorphisms, PTC tasting, and lactase deficiency) (O'Rourke, Chapter 6). The application of genetics and genomics to the study of dental and skeletal variation has extended back in time to our understanding of the operation of evolutionary forces in earlier human populations. These analyses have also shown that to compartmentalize human variation into discrete groups called "races" is incorrect, inappropriate, and harmful both socially and individually (Caspari, Chapter 7). Although biological anthropologists have long recognized that biological variation in humans cannot be categorized, the race concept based on classification still permeates the public's perception and in various disciplines and some areas of scientific investigation. Simply, the concept of race – types of humans – has engendered discrimination and isolation of most of humanity in profound and harmful ways across the globe. It remains a major threat to human health, wellbeing, and access to fundamental resources.

Boas recognized early in his career that the study of growth and development provides special and important insights into understanding human variation in the context of adaptation and adaptability. Ever since Boas's early studies, biological anthropologists have investigated the entirety of the human life span from conception through senescence and death (Crews and Bogin, Chapter 8). Humans are unique in the way they mature, both prior to and following birth. For example, humans are the only primate to have menopause. Moreover, it is now well recognized that poor health deriving from undernutrition and disease in the youngest stages of growth and development – beginning well prior to birth – predicts poor health in adulthood and earlier death. Indeed, biological anthropologists are at the forefront of documenting undernutrition, exposure to infectious diseases, and poor living conditions globally.

Biological anthropologists are learning that adaptation to extreme environments and the spread of humans into a remarkably wide spectrum of terrestrial habitats in later human evolution have been key to understanding biological variation in today's populations (Beall, Chapter 9). As with the origin of hominins, the origin of *Homo sapiens* was in an equatorial setting in Africa. By at least 200,000 years ago, these earliest incipient modern humans provided the basis for the rapid spread throughout Africa and subsequently across Europe and Asia, including in those regions with extreme conditions – cold, heat, high altitude, ultraviolet radiation, and other circumstances. Biological anthropologists have been leaders in showing how and under what circumstances these adaptations shaped body and limb proportions, facial and dental morphology, nutrition, skin pigmentation, and many other factors that characterize the biology of and variation in living and past humans.

The evolution of humans has also been shaped in many ways by the myriad of infectious diseases that have plagued humanity since the earliest hominins first appeared millions of years ago (Sattenspiel and Orbann, Chapter 10). The kinds of infectious diseases have changed dramatically over time, especially regarding the interaction between various pathogens and social and behavioral structures of human populations. We know, for example, that population concentration and size is a crucial factor in explaining the timing and degree of spread of disease-causing pathogens. That is, large, densely occupied communities provide circumstances that promote the evolution and person-to-person transfer of pathogens. Mechanisms associated with the spread of pathogens have been a focus of study by biological anthropologists for a range of infectious diseases in archaeological, historical, and modern populations. Anthropologists are especially well positioned to contribute to the growing discussion of infectious disease epidemiology owing to their insights into the relationship between pathogens and social and behavioral factors. Newly emerging research in bioarchaeology is revealing the cost of living in large, densely crowded communities in the context of the origins of agriculture, the increasing reliance on domesticated plant carbohydrates, increasing community size and density, permanent residencies in communities, and the burdens of poor health now shared by most populations globally in the twenty-first century. Anthropologists track the record of deep history, documenting the rise in population, especially in the last 10,000 years, and the costs of living in large, agglomerated settings.

Today, considerable effort has been undertaken by biological anthropologists towards the development and understanding of the molecular records of infectious diseases and the pathogens that cause them. As I write this in July 2022, never has there been such a need for understanding the dynamics between pathogens and their human hosts than with the documentation of SARS-CoV-2, the virus that causes COVID-19 and other novel infectious diseases having profoundly negative outcomes for human beings around the world in the twenty-first century. The stakes for health and wellbeing have never been higher. It is truly a life and death concern for many millions around the world. At this writing, more than one million persons have died in the United States and six million globally owing to this disease, beginning in 2020 when COVID-19 was declared a pandemic.

In large measure, much of the world's population has seen a dramatic increase in obesity and cardiovascular disease in clear association with circumstances associated with social inequality and unequal access to resources necessary for health and wellbeing (Kuzawa and Manus, Chapter 11). The rapid rise globally in illnesses relating to dominance of carbohydrates in diets globally has caused an epidemic of cardiovascular disease. The remarkable increases in weight gain in every corner of the globe characterize a worldwide spread of an obesity pandemic.

The growing number of individuals suffering from infectious diseases are linked to the ready movement from person to person in close, crowded living conditions made possible via the growth and increased density of population, and insufficient nutrition and access to necessary resources. These circumstances of population growth have their roots in the origins of agriculture and permanent settlement, which have fueled the growth of population globally from 10 million individuals in the late Pleistocene – mostly widely dispersed, small groups of people to highly sedentary, densely occupied settlements to the mega-cities of today. Along with the trend of overcrowding and increased vulnerability of individuals to infectious disease, both long-standing and newly emerging pathogens are causing challenges to wellbeing. As I write this in July 2022, biological anthropologists are documenting a range of pathogens via the study of ancient DNA (aDNA) recovered from skeletal remains globally, especially about tracking the origin, evolution, and spread of infectious diseases, such as those associated with tuberculosis, venereal diseases, and bubonic plague, also known as the Black Death (Stone, Chapter 12). Important breakthroughs in the study of the aDNA of disease-causing pathogens documented in human remains from archaeological contexts are moving the science of biological anthropology towards the development of a deeper understanding of infectious disease, both long-existing and newly emerging.

Other discoveries from the study of aDNA are also serving to develop an unprecedented knowledge of community and population history, especially in archaeological and past contexts in general (Amorim, Chapter 13). All human populations are structured in their age profiles, which are highly influenced by a preponderance of earlier deaths in some societies and later deaths in others (Konigsberg, Milner, and Boldsen, Chapter 14). Insights into genetic and demographic profiles are also informed by the records of diet and nutrition. In this regard, diet and nutrition have long been a central focus of study in biological anthropology (Dufour and Piperata, Chapter 15). Humans, like nonhuman primates, are omnivorous and have nutritional requirements that are derived from a wide range of foods, including fruits, vegetables, and animal sources of protein. Humans have adopted a remarkable variety of technologies and means of acquiring and processing food that provide the calories and nutrition necessary for survival. Although humans share common nutritional needs and capacities, there nonetheless is an astonishing diversity in the foods humans eat. This diversity suggests that human dietary adaptations have emerged rapidly, and much of it in the recent past. For example, overnutrition – leading to today's obesity epidemic across much of the world – is quite recent in human history. Although the causes of obesity are multifactorial, the availability of an overabundance of various foods, especially plant carbohydrates, combined with the low physical effort needed to acquire these foods, is central to understanding the global pandemic of obesity and the obesogenic environment in the twenty-first century in many places around the globe. This is a novel and new near-universal trend in human evolution, and one that will continue in our increasingly poorly nourished world. In the big picture, adequate food intake and the energy that it provides are essential for normal reproductive and work functions.

As with all animals, humans are continuously evolving. In this regard, the human immune system is a superb example of the record of ongoing evolution (Crespo, Chapter 16). The immune system provides the essential role of the body's defense against pathogens, and as such gives insights into natural selection at the molecular level. As Crespo points out, genetic variation has a dominant influence on the relative degree of susceptibility to a wide range of infectious disease-related pathogens. The record for ongoing evolution is especially abundant in consideration of various responses comparing populations exposed to an increasing diversity of pathogens engendered by increasing connectivity between humans around the globe. This and other evidence reveal the strong record of ongoing evolution as it pertains to infection and infectious diseases.

The study of nonhuman primates has long held a central place in biological anthropology. Research on nonhuman primates is a crucial element for understanding behavior, adaptation, locomotor patterns, and evolution of both nonhuman and human primates. McGraw (Chapter 17) emphasizes that while anthropologists and others have debated the characteristics of the Order Primates – and few diagnostic traits stand out – it is the presence of specialized combinations of features that define primates, making them distinctive from other mammals. The growing consensus is that the central complex of features that distinguish the primates as an order relates to their visual/neural system, appendicular skeleton, and life history. Primates also show a number of trends in anatomy, physiology, and behavior that are either minimized or absent in other mammals. Key to understanding primates is these evolutionary trends, especially in relation to arboreal adaptation.

The study of behavior in nonhuman primates provides a potential pathway for under-standing the origins and evolution of human sociality and behavior (Strier, Chapter 18). A key finding based on a growing record of especially field-related observations and consideration of all primates is their remarkable adaptability. Although the majority of the more than seven hundred species and subspecies of nonhuman primates across the globe are facing extinction to one extent or another, they are nonetheless remarkably flexible, giving the adaptive edge to survival and the ability to navigate challenging circumstances. Virtually all primates spend their time in the company of other members of their social group – primates are highly social. Why are primates social? Although a variety of answers to this question have been forthcoming in primate studies over the last half century, key reasons include protection from predation and competition for food resources. In large part, the size and social unit is a compromise between safety and subsistence issues. Regardless of the characteristics of the social group, social behavior is closely tied to evolu-tionary success. If the study of primate behavior is to continue, then it is becoming increas-ingly important that the world pay close attention to the conservation of primates, especially considering the encroachment into the various habitats globally where nonhuman primates reside often near human populations. As human population grows, so do the threats to the health and wellbeing of nonhuman primates.

As with nonhuman primates, the study of behavior and ecology in humans has become increasingly important in addressing questions regarding adaptation and success. The record of behavioral ecology is centered on the notion that natural selection operating on individual variants is central to understanding diversity in human evolution. Behavioral ecology focuses on a range of issues that gives us insights into adaptive success (O'Connell and Hawkes, Chapter 19). As applied to the study of living societies globally, especially with reference to availability of and success in obtaining resources, the field focusses in part on what foods and food types are selected for in the records of consumption, competition, sexual selection, and life history.

The evolutionary changes in the brains of primates, including humans, provide insights into social and other behaviors. Advanced cognition and intelligence are defining character-istics of the primates. To understand the evolution of the brain and nervous system is to understand the broader picture of primate and human evolution, including sociality, manip-ulative skills, language, and intelligence. Numerous analytical methods have been devel-oped in the study of the evolution of the primate brain and cognitive functions, including comparative methods, endocasts from fossils, communication (including language in humans), and theory of mind. As Miller and Sherwood discuss in Chapter 20, the study of primate brain size and organization, including humans, gives a broad comparative perspec-tive on key functions that characterize specific groups or species of primates and the evolu-tion of a range of behaviors. Importantly, specific areas of the brain and diverse neural substrates offer insights into social and other behaviors. Humans have a distinctive neural anatomy that may provide insights into their social behavior, including social conformity. Interestingly, new advances in the study of neurological function reveals areas of the brain associated with patterns of empathy and the presence of pain in individuals observing others in pain. These and many other behaviors linked to sociality are providing new insights into the human condition. New developments in neurological function are also offering insights into uniquely human behavior, such as language and language-related tasks. Most impor-tantly, biological anthropologist studies of neural anatomy provide new insights into cognitive function having broad implications for hominin cognition. Although much is yet to be learned, several key observations stand out, including similarity of neural organization among the primates in general, but as expected with greater complexity in humans. Only humans have speech and the evolution of the neurological pathways leading to it is an exciting area of investigation. New findings strongly suggest that the neurological basis for language derives from areas of the brain that evolved for reaching and grasping functions.

In the next six chapters, *Companion* contributors outline the details of the intriguing evolutionary record and its context as represented in the hominin past. The growing fossil record gives us insights into the anatomical record, facilitating the development of behavioral inferences. Because this record pertains to fossils, paleontologists rely on key issues that relate to the alteration and preservation of remains of once-living organisms, ranging from early primates to modern humans. As Cabo, Dirkmaat, and Zurek-Ost point out (Chapter 21), it is important to consider the range of circumstances that influence the composition of a fossil record from a specific site or series of sites to determine what is represented. Understanding these circumstances helps to address the questions regarding the degree to which the composition of a set of fossil remains represents the once-living community and the extent to which there has been a loss of key information. Does the fossil assemblage represent life as it once was?

Primate paleontologists have been highly active in the discovery of a fossil record that serves to identify the origins and evolution of the first primates, especially with a focus on the Paleocene and Eocene epochs (ca. 37–65 million years ago). Although the molecular record has provided important understanding of key phylogenetic developments, it is the burgeoning fossil record that gives us a picture of what these early ancestors looked like, what their behaviors may have been, and their relative degree of success and failure. Silcox and López-Torres (Chapter 22) make the argument that the first primates are the plesiadapiforms, a highly diverse and abundant group found throughout Europe, Asia, and North America beginning some 65 million years ago. They suggest that the origin for the Order Primates can be traced to North America, having evolved from an arboreal ancestor. The first modern-looking primates had hallmark characteristics of orbital closure, ocular convergence, and nails instead of claws, and rapidly diversified in the Eocene, providing the basis for all later primate evolution.

Out of this proliferation of Eocene primates came the higher primates of the Old World, the catarrhines (Begun, Chapter 23). This fascinating record is a rich one but focuses on the remarkable sequence dating the earliest catarrhines in the Oligocene epoch, as represented at the Fayum in Egypt. The origin of hominoids is unclear, but the record is best documented from geological deposits dating to at least 20 million years ago in the early Miocene with the fossil primate, *Proconsul*. Following is a new and highly successful adaptive radiation and proliferation of ape-like taxa that were found in Africa, Europe, and Asia. The spread of apes to Europe and Asia by 17 million years ago sets the foundation for the evolution of higher primates and the later appearance of human-like hominins, traditionally called hominids (Simpson, Chapter 24).

One of the most interesting and controversial records of evolution is that of humans and human-like ancestors (Simpson, Chapter 24). Thirty years ago, the record of hominin evolution extended back to just over four million years ago. In the last 20 years, this record has been increased to at least seven million years ago. The record of the first hominins derives from Africa and contains a phylogenetic succession of preaustralopithecines, early australopithecines, and late australopithecines over a period of some six million years. Much of the record pertains to one evolving lineage, diversifying in an adaptive radiation in later australopithecines. The hallmark attribute of the hominins is obligate bipedality associated with the shift from an arboreal to a terrestrial context facilitated by dominance of bipedality as a central locomotor adaptation.

During the evolution of the later australopithecines, there is a concurrent appearance of the genus *Homo*, a larger-brained hominin but having smaller teeth than the australopithecines. It is also during this time that we see the origins of stone tool manufacture and use. Dating to about 2.5 million years ago, these stone tools represent the earliest record of human material culture. Whatever the causes or motivations, increasing reliance on material culture, brain expansion, and complete dedication to a fully terrestrial adaptation signals the beginning of the rise of humans and their remarkable evolutionary success based in part on intelligence.

The appearance of the *Homo* lineage forms the foundation for all the anatomical and behavioral developments linked with humans and humanness (Rightmire, Chapter 25). Beginning with brain expansion, the anatomical package of reduction in tooth size and the masticatory complex, and the appearance of increasingly complex tools and dependence on material culture and associated technology, sets the course for the eventual domination of humans over most of the landscapes they occupy. Soon following the appearance of *Homo erectus* in Africa, hominins migrated out of Africa to Asia and Europe. This hominin was the first to expand its adaptive niche so dramatically, geographically, and ecologically, from tropical to temperate locations where climates were severe, at least on a seasonal basis. The key to this remarkable success lies in the increasing focus on intelligence, dependence on culture and technology, and the ability to adapt to new and novel circumstances ranging from deserts to high altitude settings. In many ways, at this point in hominin evolution, we see the beginnings of their ecological, behavioral, and biological dominance.

It is out of the evolution of the earliest *Homo erectus* in Europe and Asia that we see the rise by 400,000 years ago of distinctive morphological variation, especially in the craniofacial complex (Smith and Karriger, Chapter 26). Their commitment to culture as an adaptive strategy, increase in brain size, and reduction in masticatory size unifies them as a distinctive ancestral-descendant lineage. Predictably, increased habitat diversity is associated with morphological diversity. Post-*Homo erectus* evolution sees the rise of archaic *Homo sapiens* and what Smith and Karriger call *Homo heidelbergensis* (the "Heidelbergs"). Relative to earlier hominins, later hominins show marked brain size expansion and skeletal features, reflecting their tropical adaptation. In Europe, craniofacial changes seen in later *Homo* foreshadow that seen in the Neandertals. In Africa, archaic *Homo sapiens* evolve. However, in contrast to biological and behavioral developments in Europe and Asia, their facial characteristics are decidedly modern. Documented from the site of Herto (Ethiopia), this early modern anatomy is present by at least 160,000 years ago. The record – both fossil and molecular – shows that these earliest modern humans left Africa and migrated to Asia and then to Europe. By the late Pleistocene, these early modern *Homo sapiens* occupied a new frontier, expanding into geographical spaces previously not occupied (e.g., high altitude; see Beall, Chapter 9). Some authorities believe there was a complete replacement of the indigenous Neandertals by these newcomers, whereas others regard this as an example of migration and gene flow. Smith and Karriger (Chapter 26) argue that assimilation is the more likely development whereby much of the anatomical variation we see in living humans in Europe and Asia derives from an African ancestor.

The concluding section of the book focuses on key areas that inform our understanding of mostly Holocene human populations and skeletal and dental biology. Milner and Larsen (Chapter 27) outline developments pertaining to bioarchaeology, the study of human remains from archaeological contents, mostly represented by the last 10,000 years of human evolution. The large samples of skeletal remains in Holocene contexts provide key insights into a population level of understanding of diet, health, lifestyle, and quality of life through a variety of recently developed analytical methods. Similarly, the expanding understanding of human health in recent populations via paleopathology provides new tools for disease diagnosis. Buikstra (Chapter 28) makes the compelling case that the study of ancient pathogens gives a new perspective for understanding infectious diseases in not just past humans, but those living today. Paleopathologists have made extraordinary gains in the development of tools for diagnosis of disease and the placement of disease in interpreting health conditions in regional and global settings. Among these tools is the identification of ancient pathogens via the record of ancient DNA (see Chapter 12). Indeed, it is the population perspective that has made the study of ancient disease such an important part of modern biological anthropology.

Forensic anthropology is an area of expertise that has contributed a key record of knowledge and methods to the legal community, especially as it pertains to the identification of victims of violence and nonviolence circumstances (Ubelaker, Chapter 29). While most of the focus has been on identification pertaining to age, sex, and personage, forensic anthropologists have developed new and compelling approaches to the reconstruction and identification of those recently deceased. As with a number of areas discussed by other authors in this book, a central focus is accuracy in age identification, use of reliable methods, and documentation of the variation in age and senescence in older adults. It is now well understood that older adults age at different rates and that they express increased variation in physical manifestations of senescence (also see Crews and Bogin, Chapter 8). New methods and approaches are rapidly contributing to more accurate means of age estimation, especially for older adults. In addition, ancestry is fundamental to at least initial identification of remains of the deceased.

Biological anthropologists have been especially sensitive to the issue of "race" in public misperceptions of human variation (also see Caspari, Chapter 7). The typologies and categories of race were developed by anthropologists in the nineteenth century based on earlier precedents. Today's biological anthropologists are aware of the public perceptions of the social dimensions of understanding race as a taxonomic record of human variation. That said, biological anthropologists do not classify humans into categories. Rather, today's biological anthropologists recognize that human variation is due to evolutionary forces and other processes associated with climate and environmental circumstances such as heat, cold, and altitude. There are of course geographic tendencies of biological variation discussed throughout the *Companion* volume, all of which are related to the circumstance of evolution and adaptation to local and regional circumstances. Forensic anthropologists have contributed to understanding the underlying biological variation for ancestral identification. New methods are providing important tools for identification of geographical origins, such as stable isotope analysis and inferences drawn from the sources of food and water ingested prior to death (also see this application in Chapter 29 by Ubelaker).

All these areas strongly overlap with and complement the discussions in the final chapters of the book. Individual identifications through analysis of DNA from bones, teeth, and other tissues in ancient settings provide the opening of a new window on to a range of issues that interest biological anthropologists. The new subdiscipline of paleogenetics, sometimes called molecular archaeology, uses a range of techniques developed for the study of biomolecules in living populations and applies that knowledge to the study of ancient biomolecules to past populations (Chapter 13, Amorim). This part of the molecular revolution is possible because of the remarkable advances in molecular biology, including genomic mapping. Like so many areas discussed in this book, biological anthropologists have addressed long-standing issues about humans, primates, and the evolutionary record.

Much of this paleogenetic record pertains to new advances in the study of nuclear DNA, including Y-chromosome sequences for a range of important issues, such as sex identification, familial relationships and social organization, movement of persons, continuity of lineages, and identification of pathogens. Although preservation and contamination issues continue to make the enterprise a challenging one, the developments in sampling and analysis are beginning to allow the kinds of studies not possible even just a few years ago.

Similarly, advances in skeletal and dental chemistry – especially stable isotopes of nitrogen and carbon – have been applied to study of Holocene humans in the last several decades (Schoeninger and Reitsema, Chapter 30). In this regard, research advances provide an unprecedented insight into diet and inferences about dietary ecology, subsistence practices, and nutrition quality. Analysis of some key isotopes of carbon, nitrogen, hydrogen, strontium, and oxygen has given a remarkably detailed picture of relative consumption of specific dietary plants and insights into major shifts in diet, such as those associated with the foraging-to-farming transition, the amount of meat in a diet, and trophic interpretations relating to age-of-weaning and interpretation about the social behavior of mothers and their offspring. Bone chemistry is beginning to provide far more knowledge about the human past than just diet, especially with respect to forensic identification, migratory history and residential movement, environment, gender, and long-term trends in ecological adaptation in a range of nonhuman primates.

The study of the biology of bones and teeth is a crucial endeavor in biological anthropology. Cole, Gosman, and Stout (Chapter 31) make clear the importance of understanding the biology of bone for many of the areas addressed in the book, including paleoanthropology, bioarchaeology, forensic anthropology, and paleopathology. This chapter focuses on current mechanical/structural concepts for understanding the biology of bone, focusing especially on bone as a living tissue and its structural properties. Without an understanding of the underlying developmental processes in bone tissues, these areas of endeavor become in part a mere description. Although growth, development, and process may not be included in any one study in bioarchaeology or paleopathology, the biological anthropologist who studies past or present skeletons, understands bone as a tissue – the skeleton grows, adapts to various circumstances, and maintains itself.

Similarly, the study of teeth has had a central role to play in the study of past and present populations. As so well emphasized by Guatelli-Steinberg (Chapter 32), the enamel of teeth has a vastly different developmental biology than bone. In this regard, enamel forms via a process of enamel matrix deposition and mineralization and is less dynamic than bone. In some ways, teeth are like a living fossil in that only about 4% of the tissue is nonmineral. Thus, it comes as no surprise that teeth tend to endure in paleontological and archaeological contexts, more so than bones. In large part, it is the composition of teeth that facilitate their preservation in many archaeological and paleontological contexts.

The information packed into teeth regarding their growth is highly valuable to the biological anthropologist. In particular, the incremental growth of teeth provides a diary of the development, disturbances during growth, and insight into the pace of growth. The applications of dental growth and biology present a fund of data on when physiological stresses occur and the duration of stress episodes during growth and development.

As the next three chapters reveal, function is a highly significant area of study in biological anthropology. Built on the premise that "form follows function," this general area of inquiry provides a perspective on a range of issues for addressing questions about functional and evolutionary adaptation in primates and humans. With respect to the skull, Wang and Menegaz (Chapter 33) place function within the context of protection of the brain and sensory functions, mastication, respiration, and speech production. Much of the focus in biological anthropology is on functional morphology, especially in relation to mastication, in large part because of the role of diet and dietary reconstruction as they apply to a range of areas of the discipline.

The dentition is central to the study of masticatory function. It is the teeth that meet food and provide a record of kinds of foods eaten and how they are initially processed prior to digestion. In Chapter 34, Schmidt and Ungar present an overview of the various approaches to understanding the role, function, and process of diet and mastication in primates, including issues that biological anthropologists deal with regarding interpreting tooth structure and microwear.

As a number of chapters point out, one of the most significant contributions of biological anthropology is the understanding of function as it pertains to the postcranial skeleton. Function as it relates to everything below the neck is dominated by locomotion (Granatosky and Young, Chapter 35). The primate arboreal adaptation discussed by McGraw (Chapter 17) guides our understanding of the general Bauplan of postcranial skeletal structure, yet it is the range of specializations and adaptations in this general structure that provides the perspective on the evolution of primates over the last 65 million years. Primates are hindlimb dominated, but this is coupled with remarkable mobility of joints for movement in trees and ability to grasp with varying degrees of opposability for holding on to curved surfaces – such as branches. Moreover, all primates climb, including the terrestrial ones. The study of locomotor function in primates presents an important perspective for understanding the very specialized adaptation of the most terrestrial primate – bipedality in humans. This adaptation arose quickly and involved a complete reorientation of the lower limb and back, occasioning a reduction from use of support of four limbs to full dependence on just two limbs.

Pobiner concludes the book with some good news and some challenges regarding teaching and learning of biological anthropology (Chapter 36). The good news: biological anthropology has provided a remarkable record for understanding primate evolution and variation and evolution in general. Pobiner emphasizes facts supporting evolution but are not enough to break the education barrier. Rather, biological anthropologists need to focus on increasing science literacy to provide the public with an understanding of how science works through education. How should biological anthropologists accomplish the goal of more broadly educating the public about science? Pobiner argues that teachers of biological anthropology should use evolution – including the remarkable record of primates – to provide students with a context for understanding why evolution is such an important and strong theory. By focusing on the process of science and placing evolution in its context, students will be far better prepared to understand the meaning of evolution (and themselves) in the natural world. Moreover, the understanding of evolution provides a platform for the student to view human variation as a product of adaptation to conditions both local and regional. This understanding allows the student to think like a biological anthropologist. For example, skin pigmentation and much of biology does not develop in the context of racial categories but as local and regional adaptations to region-specific environments related to heat, cold, exposure to ultraviolet light, and many other conditions and circumstances, leading to the remarkable degree of human variation we see around all of us.

NOTE ON GENERAL ORGANIZATION OF THE BOOK

I have long felt that understanding of biology of the past – derived from the fossil record – is informed by understanding of the biology of the present. Indeed, the founders of evolutionary theory in the nineteenth century had a limited fossil record from which to reconstruct and interpret biological change. In large measure, their ideas were derived from the study of living variation. Therefore, much of the book is organized along the lines of study of the present for informing our understanding of the past. Authors present an historical overview of biological anthropology (Chapter 2) and key aspects of the living, ranging from genetics and phylogeny to behavior and ongoing evolution in humans and primates (Chapters 3 to 11). We then follow with a series of chapters on ancient DNA as pertaining to disease and population history (Chapters 12 and 13), age structure viewed from past and present contexts, nutrition, and foodways (Chapters 14 and 15), ongoing evolution (Chapter 16), and chapters presenting syntheses of the study of living primates (Chapters 17 to 20), of other areas that are broadly applicable to past and living humans, especially regarding the fossil record in particular and the past in general (Chapters 21 to 30), the biology and function of skeletal and dental hard tissues (Chapters 31 to 35), and science education, especially as applied to biological anthropology and evolutionary science in general (Chapter 36). Other sources and perspectives pertaining to the broad scope of biological anthropology are presented in Trevathan (2018) and Cartmill (2018).

NOTE

1 For the better part of a century, the traditional disciplinary term has been *physical anthropology*, used by its founders and commonly presented in textbooks and curricula in the United States. Given the focus on biology and evolutionary science in general, it is increasingly referred to as *biological anthropology*. A key indicator of the shift is represented by the name change in 2021 when the official name of the professional organization was changed from the American Association of Physical Anthropologists to the American Association of Biological Anthropologists. The Association's journal name was changed from the *American Journal of Physical Anthropology* to the *American Journal of Biological Anthropology* in 2022 and its annual publication from the *Yearbook of Physical Anthropology* to the *Yearbook of Biological Anthropology* in 2022.

REFERENCES

Cartmill, M. "Celebrating 100 Years of the *AJPA*: 1918–2018: A Special Centennial Issue of the *American Journal of Physical Anthropology*." *American Journal of Physical Anthropology* 165 (2018): 615–951.

Larsen, C. S., ed. *A Companion to Biological Anthropology*. Chichester: John Wiley & Sons, 2010.

Trevathan, W., ed. *The International Encyclopedia of Biological Anthropology*. Chichester: John Wiley & Sons, 2018.

PART I History

CHAPTER 2

Foundation and History of Biological Anthropology

Michael A. Little and Jane E. Buikstra

EIGHTEENTH AND NINETEENTH CENTURY ORIGINS OF PHYSICAL ANTHROPOLOGY

The fundamental subject matter of biological (formerly physical) anthropology focuses on human origins and human variation. Such interests date back to antiquity, but systematic observations and publications began with the eighteenth century Natural Philosophers of the Enlightenment, such as George-Louis Leclerk, Comte de Buffon (1707–1788) and James Burnett, Lord Monboddo (1714–1799). During this period, human races were defined and various racial classification systems were proposed (Brace 2005: 22 ff.). "Race" as a typological characterization of human variation was to become a dominant theme in physical anthropology until the mid-twentieth century. Classification, an elemental building block of all sciences, was first formalized for humans by Carl von Linné ("Linnaeus" 1707–1778), the great Swedish taxonomist. He identified the close relationships between humans and nonhuman primates, classified *Homo sapiens* as a member of this primate category *Anthropomorpha* (later, *Primates*), and identified several "racial" varieties, both known and mythical (Broberg 1983). Johann Friedrich Blumenbach (1752–1840), the German physician and anatomist, followed Linné's geographic four-fold classification system of human varieties from America, Asia, Africa, and Europe, later adding a fifth variety, Malay, to represent Pacific populations (Gould 1996: 401 ff.). Some identify Blumenbach as a founder of physical anthropology because of his interest in "human varieties" and human craniology (Burns 2003: 29–30; Shapiro 1959).

In the United States, the Enlightenment was represented by several scholar/scientists, e.g., Benjamin Franklin (1709–1790). The one most closely linked to physical anthropology was Samuel Stanhope Smith (1751–1819). Smith, as a natural philosopher and Presbyterian minister, was on the faculty and later President of Princeton University (Brace 2005: 50 ff.). He saw all humans as the same species with continuous variation. "Smith reduced the chief causes of the variation in the human species to three: climate, the state of society, and the manner of living" (Hudnut 1956: 544). His Lamarckian and monogenetic (a single human species origin) view differed from the "fixed-race" and even "separate species origins" – the polygenism typologies of many of his contemporaries.

A very significant figure from Philadelphia who has been deconstructed in recent years is Samuel G. Morton (1799–1851) (Gould 1996: 82 ff.). Morton was a highly respected physician and scientist during his time who made many contributions to paleontology, geology, anatomy, and human craniometry (Brace 2005: 77 ff.; Buikstra 2009; Stanton 1960: 25 ff.). Craniology was his principal contribution to physical anthropology; he had collected more than 900 crania, which he had identified within Blumenbach's five racial varieties. A major work, *Crania Americana* on Native Americans (Morton 1839), was described by Brace (2005: 82) as "… a monumental piece of scholarship…," particularly with Morton's development of a variety of metrics to characterize and measure the dimensions of the skull (Brace 2005: 82). Aleš Hrdlička (1869–1943), who also held Morton in high esteem, had Morton's photograph as the frontispiece of his history and status of physical anthropology and identified him as the "father of American physical anthropology" (Hrdlička 1919).

Gould's (1981, 1996) critique of Samuel Morton was based on his conviction that Morton's calculations of cranial capacity were unconsciously biased because of Morton's belief in racial superiority. Gould's critique, however, has been refuted by Michael (1988) and Lewis and colleagues (2011) in careful restudies of Morton's materials.

Charles R. Darwin's (1809–1882) publication of the *Origin of Species* (1859) and ideas linked to evolution encouraged changed perspectives among ethnologists (and evolutionists) and physical anthropologists. In England, a mid-nineteenth century rift influenced the nascent British Association for the Advancement of Science (BAAS) and probably led to the separation of physical anthropology from ethnology and evolution in both the United Kingdom and the United States (Stocking 1987: 248 ff.).

Physical anthropology or "anthropology," as it was known on the Continent in the mid- to late-1800s, was most highly developed in France and Germany (Stocking 1988), where most of the physical anthropologists were trained through medical studies (Proctor 1988). "Anthropology" in France was established by Paul Broca (1824–1880), a celebrated physician and anatomist who founded the *Société d'Anthopologie de Paris* (SAP) in 1859, *Laboratoire d'Anthropologie* of the *Ècole Practique des Hautes Ètudes* (LA-EPHE) in 1867, and the *Ècole d'Anthropologie* in 1876 (Spencer 1997a). Paul Broca greatly admired Samuel Morton's ideas (Brace 2010). Morton (and Broca) thus indirectly influenced Aleš Hrdlička who studied with Broca's student, Léonce-Pierre Manouvrier (1850–1927), in Paris at the Laboratoire d'Anthropologie in 1896 (Buikstra et al. n.d.). Impressed with the laboratory, Hrdlička unsuccessfully sought to develop a research/teaching institute of physical anthropology according to the French model in the US (Spencer 1979; Stewart 1981).

In Germany, the history of studies in physical anthropology has been badly tarnished by extreme racism, "racial cleansing," and anti-Semitism, beginning in late nineteenth century and the "scientific racism" of the twentieth century (Barkan 1992; Proctor 1988; Spencer 1997b). As in France, physical anthropology was taught in medical schools. The founder of American anthropology, Franz Boas (1858–1942), was trained in physics and geography in Germany during a period of relative liberalism, and experienced little anti-Semitism during his school days, that is, before anti-Semitism began to rise and liberalism declined after 1879 (Cole 1999: 58, 87). His basic training in physical anthropology came in 1881–1883 under the direction of Rudof Virchow (1821–1902); he also studied ethnography with Adolf Bastian (1826–1905) in Berlin. Both Virchow's and Bastian's anti-Darwinian perspectives and Virchow's liberal views on race probably influenced Boas's early ideas (Massin 1996). Academic chairs in physical anthropology were established in Munich in 1886 and Berlin in 1888 (Spencer 1997b: 428).

In England, interests in physical anthropology were held outside medical science and often in paleontology, evolution, and archaeology. Thomas Huxley, a distinguished biologist as well as Darwin's friend and supporter, authored *Evidence as to Man's Place in Nature* (1863), which might be considered the first text in physical anthropology. It included a synthesis of comparative anatomy of human and nonhuman primates, a summary of fossil evidence up to that time, and a review of the natural history of nonhuman primates. Francis Galton (1822–1911), Darwin's cousin and a great biometrician, began conducting body measurements of children in 1873. Arthur Keith (1866–1955), widely respected in the UK and the US, influenced physical anthropology from the nineteenth century to post-World War II physical anthropology, although his ideas largely reflected the nineteenth century. Keith, who spent most of his career at the Royal College of Surgeons in London, studied comparative anatomy of primates, nonhuman primate and human paleontology, primate locomotion, and human evolution (Spencer 1997c).

Twentieth Century Beginnings and The Rise of Professionalism

Physical Anthropology in Europe

While Germany was pre-eminent in physical anthropology at the turn of the twentieth century, there were important figures in France, Switzerland, and England. Léonce-Pierre Manouvrier demonstrated that differences in male and female cranial capacities were simply a function of body size and established skeletal indices that are still in use today (Spencer 1997d). Rudolph Martin (1864–1925), who joined the faculty at the University of Zurich in 1899, published the *Lehrbuch der Anthropologie* (*Handbook of Physical Anthropology*) (Martin 1914), which became a classic reference work and textbook. Spencer (1997b) identified 11 major centers of physical anthropology in German cities at the end of the Weimar Period (1918–1933). The following National Socialist Period of 1933–1945, with the rise of Adolf Hitler and Nazism, was marked by an obsession with "race," racial purity, anti-Semitism, and deplorable atrocities.

English scientists made substantial contributions to comparative primate anatomy in the early part of the twentieth century, including Grafton Elliot Smith (1871–1937) in Manchester and Arthur Keith (1866–1955) in London. Smith was an Egyptologist and a specialist in comparative primate brain anatomy. In 1907, Smith, Frederic Wood Jones (1879–1954), and others studied several thousand Egyptian mummies prior to elevation of the Aswan Dam, thus advancing knowledge of ancient disease (Armelagos 1997; Baker and Judd 2012). Both Smith and Keith played important roles in training and mentoring American physical anthropologists, including T. Wingate Todd (1885–1938) and Earnest A. Hooton (1887–1954). Prior to the twentiethth century, studies of primate behavior included only Keith's casual observations of gibbons in Thailand in the late 1890s. More recently, Sir Solly Zuckerman's (1904–1993) influential book, *The Social Life of Monkeys and Apes* (1932), was published. Much work was done by UK scientists in what is now known as paleoanthropology, including the Piltdown discovery in 1912 and its refutation in 1953 (Weiner 1955); the Swanscombe remains were discovered in the 1930s.

Physical Anthropology in the United States

Three individuals were instrumental in founding physical anthropology during the first half of the twentieth century: Franz Boas, Aleš Hrdlička, and Earnest A. Hooton.

Franz Boas had a broad vision of anthropology as a four-field science and contributed to each of these fields. His research in physical anthropology and biometrics alone led to the publication of more than 180 works that ranged from anthropometrics and osteometrics, to race and racial origins, to environmental influences, and to human growth and development of children (Little 2010). He is best known in anthropology for his study of migrants from Europe to the United States (Boas 1912), but his most significant and lasting research was in child growth (see Figure 2.1).

Aleš Hrdlička, the second of the three, was committed to physical anthropology and determined to advance it as a science (see Figure 2.2). He founded the *American Journal of Physical Anthropology* (*AJPA*) in 1918 and was the principal organizer and first President of the American Association of Physical Anthropologists in 1930 (Little 2018a). His energy and enthusiasm were instrumental in "securing the discipline's identity" and securing a continuing place for it within the broader field of anthropology (Buikstra et al. n.d.; Spencer 1982a: 6).

The third individual, Earnest Hooton, was considerably junior to Boas and Hrdlička. He spent his entire professional career at Harvard University, beginning in 1913 (see Figure 2.3), where he supervised 28 PhD students. Hooton's students dominated the profession and played important roles in developing physical anthropology through the 1970s and early 1980s (Giles 2012).

Boas's primary contributions were in creative and forward-looking research design, Hrdlička's contributions were in a resolute and persistent promotion of the profession, and Hooton's contributions were in training the first generation of physical anthropologists to

Figure 2.1   Franz Boas posing in Inuit garb in Minden, Germany, after his return from Baffin Island in 1985–1986. Courtesy of the American Philosophical Society.

Figure 2.2 The Department of Anthropology at the US National Museum in 1904. Aleš Hrdlička is third from the left. Courtesy of the US National Museum, Smithsonian Institution.

Figure 2.3 Earnest A. Hooton in 1926 about the time that he trained his first PhD student. Courtesy of the Peabody Museum, Harvard University.

fill the expanding faculty of universities around the US. Each of these three prominent anthropologists were either trained in Europe or strongly influenced by European anthropology.

Other important figures from this period were Raymond Pearl (1879–1940), T. Wingate Todd, and Adolph Schultz (1891–1976). Pearl was a Michigan-trained biologist with broad interests in human population biology and strong mathematical training who worked at Johns Hopkins University (Kingsland 1984; Little and Garruto 2010). Pearl contributed to the development of human population biology and also founded two journals that would define this field: *Quarterly Review of Biology* (in 1926) and *Human Biology* (in 1929). Todd established a documented skeletal collection of several thousand individuals (The Hamann Todd Collection) and conducted substantial research on skeletal development and maturation in humans (Kern 2006; Todd 1937). Both Pearl and Todd were Presidents of the American Association of Physical Anthropologists. Schultz was a comparative anatomist trained at the University of Zürich who secured an appointment at Johns Hopkins University as a physical anthropologist in the Department of Anatomy (Erikson 1981). His principal contributions were in comparative primatology and he co-founded the journal, *Folia Primatologica*.

Formative areas of physical anthropology were beginning to emerge, namely child growth and development from Boas's 1880s and 1890s research and his later migrant studies; centers of bone growth and formation, skeletal maturation, and child development from Todd's 1920s and 1930s work; anthropometrics and osteometrics from Manouvrier, Hrdlička, and Martin; comparative primate anatomy and behavior and paleoanthropology from Keith, Schultz, and Hooton in the early 1920s and 1930s; and demography, genetics, epidemiology, and statistics from Pearl throughout the early 1900s. Human population biology was not yet a formal area of study at the beginning of the century, yet Franz Boas's early studies and Pearl's involvement in physical anthropology and editorship of *Human Biology* helped to define this emerging field. During the early twentieth century physical anthropology, Boas and Pearl were major figures in encouraging scientific approaches to inquiry. Field primatology was yet to emerge as an interest to physical anthropologists (Sussman 2007).

Physical Anthropology as a Profession

At the turn of the twentieth century there were virtually no physical anthropologists in US academia. Harvard, with the oldest anthropology program in the US, produced only three PhDs in physical anthropology through 1925. Only two other PhDs were granted in physical anthropology (Pennsylvania and Columbia). During roughly the same period (1900–1925), there were 34 PhDs awarded in archaeology and ethnology at the four PhD degree-granting institutions (Harvard, Pennsylvania, Columbia, and Berkeley) (Spencer, 1982a).

Gradually, physical anthropologists of distinction emerged during the second quarter of the twentieth century, including Theodore D. McCown (1908–1969), Wilton M. Krogman (1903–1987), and W. Montague Cobb (1904–1990). Cobb was the first and only African American physical anthropology PhD trained in the US prior to World War II (Rankin-Hill and Blakey 1994; Watkins 2007).

Early Basic Themes of Inquiry in Physical Anthropology

There are several basic areas or themes of inquiry that characterize the first half of the twentieth century. These include studies of *race, eugenics, human growth and development of children, human origins, primates*, and *skeletal biology*. *Race* as a preoccupation and an essentialist or typological framework for viewing human population variation was largely discarded after World War II (Washburn 1984). The *eugenics* movement began in the nineteenth century, developed in England by Francis Galton (1822–1911). Its impact on human population studies declined in the US during the late 1920s and 1930s (Pearl 1927). Genetics was developed largely outside of physical anthropology in the early twentieth century, whereas early human genetics was closely allied with *eugenics* during this period (Davenport 1921). Franz Boas (1897) had established the tradition of research on *human growth and development in children* in anthropology during the late 1800s (Little 2010; Tanner 1981). Studies of *human origins* and *paleoanthropology* were more highly developed in Europe than in the US, while the origins of New World populations were studied by Hrdlička (1912). Research on *primates* continued into the twentieth century, including the first behavioral studies of nonhuman primates in zoos. Early naturalistic behavior research emerged in the 1930s, with considerable early work by psychologists (Carpenter 1964). Descriptive skeletal biology continued, supplemented by such researchers as Washington Matthews (1843–1905), who explicitly addressed archaeological questions (Buikstra 2006). Studies of ancient diseases such as tuberculosis and syphilis also had nineteenth century roots, carried into the first half of the twentieth century by researchers such as Hrdlička, Stewart, and Williams (Buikstra and Roberts 2012; Buikstra et al. 2012; Powell and Cook 2005).

Race: Prevailing interests during the late 1800s, early 1900s, and between the two world wars were in identifying races through careful anthropometric measurements and morphological observation; determining the effects of race mixture on behavior and biology; and ascertaining origins and history of different racial groups. Races were believed by many to be fixed entities that could be identified as pure groups with some races clearly superior to others in biology and intelligence. These ideas were carried over from nineteenth century beliefs that supported slavery in the US and led to poor treatment of Native Americans.

Eugenics: Eugenics reflected Francis Galton's late nineteenth century Victorian view that "good breeding" would give the "better" races an advantage over the "poorer" or "inferior" ones (Brace 2005: 178; see also Gregory 1919). More broadly, eugenics beliefs centered on improvements in the human species (Marks 1997). Examples of extreme eugenics, including forced sterilization and "racial cleansing," are documented in Gould (1996). The eugenics movement in the US developed during the 1920s when many geneticists and physical anthropologists participated in the movement. Hrdlička (1919), who believed that the growing science of eugenics would essentially be transformed into a form of *applied* anthropology, was critical of eugenics (Spencer 1979). Charles B. Davenport (1866–1944), later president of the AAPA in 1943–1944, was an early proponent of eugenics and supported it enthusiastically. He established the Carnegie Institution-funded Eugenics Record Office at Cold Spring Harbor.

Human Growth and Development of Children: In 1891, Boas conducted the first longitudinal study of the growth of Worcester, Massachusetts schoolchildren. His observations of the growth and likely growth outcomes (Boas 1897) supported his view that race was not fixed but was instead a highly variable process. This research further reinforced his belief in human plasticity. He explored this more than two decades later with a migration study designed to test the assertion by many that the cephalic index of the head was fixed by race and unchanged by the environment. This assertion had also influenced public views about US immigration policy. From measurements of thousands of immigrants from Europe, Boas found that there were generational differences in cephalic index, which were statistically significant (Boas 1912). He also reported that children of immigrants were taller and that children from *large* families with limited resources were shorter than their age cohorts from *small* families with equally limited resources. Although Boas's carefully designed and statistically analyzed studies of growth and of migrants demonstrated the plasticity of race, the impact of these ideas was only appreciated after World War II (Little 2010).

Human Origins: US anthropologists tended to focus on the origins of New World populations, particularly Native Americans from North America. European anthropologists were active in England, France, other parts of Europe, and Asia. Important work was also done in South Africa by Raymond A. Dart (1893–1988), the discoverer of *Australopithecus* in the 1920s (Dart 1925). In East Africa, Louis Leakey (1903–1972) began explorations of human ancestors in the 1930s (Leakey 1931). Hrdlička devoted considerable effort to exploring the Neanderthal origins problem and argued (incorrectly) that Neanderthals were unilineal ancestors to modern *Homo sapiens* (Hrdlička 1927; Spencer and Smith 1981). His major interest, however, was the origin and prehistory of Native Americans (Hrdlička 1912).

Primatology: Considerable work was done in comparative anatomy, paleontology, and naturalistic behavior of primates before World War II. William King Gregory (1876–1970), a dedicated evolutionist, wrote on fish, birds, and mammals, and also on fossil primates, human dentition, and comparative primate anatomy and growth (Schultz 1924). An important publication from the late 1920s was *The Great Apes* (Yerkes and Yerkes 1929), a compilation of knowledge up to that time, although almost nothing was known of primate natural history (Sussman 1997, 2007). C. Raymond Carpenter (1905–1975) was trained as a psychologist. After working with Robert Yerkes as a post-doctoral fellow at Yale, Carpenter studied the behavior of howler monkeys on Barro Colorado Island in Panama. Several years later, in 1937, Carpenter (1964) participated in the famous multidisciplinary study of gibbons in Thailand.

Skeletal Biology: Studies of the human skeleton have been a mainstay of physical anthropology since the mid-nineteenth century, beginning with Morton's craniometric analyses (1839, 1844). Interests in the anatomy of the skeleton were derived from both the need to understand the bases for variation in the human body and to explore human origins. When Aleš Hrdlička was hired by the Smithsonian Institution his skills in skeletal biology were needed to curate a large skeletal sample moved from the Army Medical Museum to the Smithsonian (Little 2018a). A part of Hrdlička's later career at the Smithsonian was devoted to building these skeletal collections. Other areas of skeletal biology are associated with remains uncovered by archaeological excavation or *bioarchaeology*; studies of ancient disease or *paleopathology*; and human remains identification linked to law enforcement or *forensic anthropology*. Hooton's interests in human variation extended to archaeological skeletal populations, including his Pecos Pueblo monograph (Hooton 1930), which illustrated the need to consider change through time in health and demographic patterns. Hooton's students were central players in the description and publication of large series of human remains (Buikstra 2006). Methods and interests in population biology were developed in a range of archaeological settings in North America (Larsen 2012, 2015).

THE SCIENCE MATURES: POST-WORLD WAR II

In 1941, a private foundation was established in the US with substantial funding to support anthropological research and other activities (Lindee and Radin 2016). The Viking Fund Foundation was endowed by Axel Wenner-Gren (1881–1961), a wealthy Swedish industrialist, and directed by Paul Fejos (1897–1963). Fejos was a physician and distinguished film-maker of Hollywood, European, and ethnographic films who led the Foundation for its first 22 years (Dobbs 1963, 1973). Now known as the Wenner-Gren Foundation for Anthropological Research, it was, during the 1940s and 1950s, a vital source of financial and organizational support for anthropology (Szathmáry 1991), which continues today.

In 1945, the Viking Fund/Wenner-Gren Foundation sponsored the Summer Seminars in Physical Anthropology, which were "state of the art" occasions to bring together younger and more senior anthropologists to discuss the most current and exciting research in the profession (Little and Kaplan 2010). Held in New York City, they were organized largely by Sherwood Washburn. Washburn, along with Gabriel Lasker, a new PhD (both trained by Hooton), initiated the *Yearbook of Physical Anthropology* that same year, both to report on the Summer Seminars and to review the important research that had been conducted during the previous year (Lasker was the *Yearbook* editor). The Summer Seminars continued through 1955, whereas the *Yearbook*, as an annual supplement to the *AJPA*, continues to be published.

In June 1950, a watershed symposium was held at the Cold Spring Harbor Institute for Quantitative Biology on Long Island, New York. Organized by Sherwood Washburn and the distinguished population geneticist, Theodosius Dobzhansky (1900–1975), the 15th Cold Spring Harbor Symposium on Quantitative Biology was entitled *The Origin and Evolution of Man* (Warren 1951). The meeting was attended by more than 100 of the most influential anthropologists, geneticists, evolutionary biologists, scientists from the Institute, and students. Of these, 22 were women. Both the Viking Fund/Wenner-Gren Foundation and the Carnegie Corporation funded the conference. In many ways, the symposium signaled the end of the old era of descriptive science, while ushering in modern concepts of evolutionary biology. The talks at the symposium focused more on the population as a unit of evolution than on fixed races, and there was a sense of scientific problem-solving and breadth of inquiry that suggested a change in perspectives and directions for physical anthropology.

The "New Physical Anthropology" of Washburn

About a year after the Cold Spring Harbor Symposium, Sherwood Washburn published a seminal paper on the "New Physical Anthropology" (Washburn 1951), which he later elaborated in a chapter published in the massive Kroeber compendium, *Anthropology Today* (Washburn 1953). Washburn's ideas, built on the Summer Seminars and the 1950 Cold Spring Harbor Symposium, were formative and original. His "new physical anthropology" focused on primate and human evolution and human variation, but with a return to Darwinian evolutionary theory and with genetics as an important unifying perspective (Stini 2010). Also, races were to be studied as populations rather than as essentialist "types," and the more common descriptive studies were to shift to studies employing scientific design and hypothesis testing. These ideas were both a driving force in transforming the profession of physical anthropology and a reflection of changes that were already taking place.

"Race" in the 1950s and 1960s

Despite Washburn's contention that the concept of "race" was inappropriate as a means of studying human variation and that the broader concept of "population" was more productive, the concept of "race" as a more or less concrete and identifiable unit was still fixed in many scientists' minds, e.g., Coon et al. (1950). For example, Boyd (1950) produced a classification of six races according to their blood group genetics. About a decade later, Garn (1961) refined these classifications and identified geographical, local, and micro-races, in a hierarchy of populations and subpopulations. These three works were different from previous efforts at classification in that they attempted to apply contemporary evolutionary, genetic, and ecological principles to the identification of racial population variation around the world.

A year earlier in 1949, Julian Huxley, Thomas Huxley's grandson and then Director General of UNESCO (United Nations Educational, Scientific, and Cultural Organization), recommended that a committee be convened to study and report on race (Marks 2010; Shipman 1994). The *raporteur* for the committee was Ashley Montagu (1905–1915), who was well known for having written a book on race called *Man's Most Dangerous Myth: The Fallacy of Race* (1942). While this group produced a document that attracted outside criticism, following a series of less liberal iterations, a modern revised statement of the UNESCO document was prepared many years later by an AAPA committee chaired by Solomon Katz in 1993 (AAPA Statement 1996; see also Cartmill 1998).

Another significant event was the controversy over Carleton Coon's 1962 book on *The Origin of Races* (1962). He asserted that there were five races – Congoid, Mongoloid, Caucasoid, Capoid, and Australoid – and that all of them crossed the threshold to *Homo sapiens* at different times, which caused a storm of controversy. Stimulated by this controversy, several early 1960s papers were published in *Current Anthropology* by established evolutionary scientists and physical anthropologists Theodosius Dobzhansky, Ernst Mayr, Loring Brace, Juan Comas, and Frank Livingstone, who argued for and against the concept of race as a biological unit of study. In some cases, the older concept of a fixed race was conflated with a more recent view of race-as-population, which confused some of the arguments.

One of the notable exceptions in the contemporary treatment of race is among forensic anthropologists, who are commonly associated with law enforcement identification of human remains. Law enforcement agencies continue to request an identification of race or ancestry, which encourages the use of the concept, whereas some forensic anthropologists argue that even the idea of "ancestry" perpetuates a false concept of "race" (DiGangi and Bethard 2021). Other forensic anthropologists have identified the assignment of an individual to a specific race or ancestral group as an assignation to a "particular socially constructed 'racial' category" (Kennedy 1995; Sauer 1992). This remains a contentious issue.

Increasing Specialization and Development in the 1960s, 1970s, and 1980s

The period of the 1960s through the 1980s was one of considerable training of doctoral students and research in biological anthropology. The National Science Foundation (NSF) had been established in 1950, and science was being promoted in the US, partly as a result of competition with the Soviet Union (Baker and Eveleth 1982). Before World War II, physical anthropologists could, in some sense, be generalists and conduct studies of skeletal biology, measure living populations, and deal with prehistory and current research in human paleontology. During the 1960s, graduate training incorporated increasing specialization and focus on subareas of biological anthropology, including population genetics, living population biology, child growth and development, primatology, paleoanthropology, and skeletal biology, including bioarchaeology, paleopathology, and forensic anthropology.

Population Genetics: A center of human population genetics was the University of Michigan with James V. Neel (1915–2000), the founder of the Department of Human Genetics,

James Spuhler (1917–1992), and Frank B. Livingstone (1928–2005) in the Department of Anthropology. This powerful group of scientists engaged in innovative research and training in anthropological genetics. Livingstone's work on malaria and sickle-cell prevalence in Liberia became a classic example of culture (subsistence) influencing evolution via changes in gene frequencies (Livingstone 1958). As Weiss and Chakraborty (1982: 383) pointed out: "The major thrust of Livingstone's synthesis, namely, the *ongoing* effect of culture in molding human evolution, is a point still largely misunderstood or ignored by many researchers without anthropological training." Identified as the founder of anthropological genetics (Lasker 1994), Spuhler (1951) conducted original research on Native American origins and genetic variations.

Alice Brues (1913–2007), a Hooton student, was a biological anthropologist whose conceptualization of race included elements both of typology and population genetics. She was also marvelously creative and innovative in the modern sphere of biological anthropology. She researched the ABO blood groups, which were one of the polymorphic systems thought to be neutral, that is, not under strong selective pressure (Brues 1954). She demonstrated, however, that the worldwide distribution of these blood groups was not uniform and strongly suggested natural selection.

James Neel also made substantial contributions in anthropological population genetics through his studies of South American tropical forest natives in Brazil and Venezuela, particularly with his work with the Yanomamo (Neel and Salzano 1966). This pioneering multidisciplinary research was done under the aegis of the International Biological Programme IBP Human Adaptability HA projects, in collaboration with Napoleon Chagnon (1938–2019), a sociocultural anthropologist with interests in population, culture, and ecology (Chagnon 1967).

By the late 1970s, population genetics was in a state of transformation. New laboratory methods permitted DNA to be studied directly, replacing the traditional method of determining the genotype from a protein separation phenotype. Both nuclear and mitochondrial DNA studies were being used to establish "precise" phylogenic relationships among the primates, including humans, and the "Mitochondrial Eve" hypothesis on human origins was first presented a decade or so later (Cann et al. 1987). The culmination of the new DNA research was the completion of the Human Genome Project shortly after the turn of the new millennium.

Human Population Biology: The late 1950s and 1960s witnessed a fusion of human ecology, adaptation, and evolution in the scientific maturation of human population biology. Joseph Birdsell (1908–1994) and Paul Baker (1927–2007) in the US and Derek Roberts (1925–2016) in the UK were early pioneers in human ecology, demography, and biogeography (Garruto et al. 2009; Little 2018b; Mai et al. 1981). At this time, anthropologists from the subfields of sociocultural anthropology, archaeology, and biological anthropology united in pursuing a common theoretical perspective – *adaptation to the environment in the context of human ecology* (Vayda and Rappaport 1968). There was also receptivity to integrated, collaborative research, and a rise in international exchange and communication enriched the advancement of this research (Weiner 1977).

In 1964, several distinguished British human biologists published a new text, *Human Biology: An Introduction to Human Evolution, Variation, and Growth* (Harrison et al. 1964). This important book coincided with the initiation of the International Biological Programme (IBP), which was to continue from 1964 through 1976 and to focus on a worldwide study of ecology and human welfare. The human study component of this program was called "human adaptability" (Baker and Weiner 1966); the international head was Joseph Weiner of the UK (Weiner 1965). Studies (Collins and Weiner 1977; Little et al. 1997) centered on multidisciplinary and multinational research, moving human population biology forward in a quantum leap. When the IBP ended in the early 1970s, a new international program (Man and the Biosphere – MaB) was established through UNESCO to continue some of the worldwide ecological research initiated by IBP Human Adaptability projects.

Growth and Development: Major post-war figures in human growth studies were James Tanner (1981), who was working on adolescent growth in the UK, and Wilton Krogman, who established the Philadelphia Center for Research in Child Growth and Development at the University of Pennsylvania in 1947. Several physical anthropologists, including Stanley Garn, conducted studies of longitudinal growth and body composition at the Fels Research Institute in the years following World War II, and Garn later became the leading anthropologist at the University of Michigan Center for Human Growth and Development.

Primatology. There was remarkable expansion of primate studies during the late 1950s and 1960s. The earliest post-war research was conducted by biologists on the Barro Colorado howler monkeys originally studied by C. R. Carpenter; the Japanese set up a colony of Japanese macaques to begin longitudinal studies of this native species and a colony of Rhesis macaques was established on Cayo Santiago, a coastal island near Puerto Rico. Sherwood Washburn led the resurgence of primatology in the US after his observations of baboons in the wild in the mid-1950s (Ribnick 1982). The first study of the social behavior of baboons was conducted by Washburn and DeVore (1961) at the Amboseli Game Reserve in southern Kenya. Washburn was a major influence on the development of primate field biology. By 2007, over 60 percent of the field primatologists active in the US were derived from Washburn's academic lineage (Kelley and Sussman 2007).

A growing knowledge of primate ecology was linked to concerns about the number of endangered primate species in both the Old World and New World tropics. Conservation became an important issue, which led to a practical need to gather information on primate ecology, habitats, diets, and declining land resources (Cowlishaw and Dunbar 2000; Wolfheim 1983). A major trend that began in the 1980s was the reclassification of numerous primate species based on DNA.

Paleoanthropology: By the early 1950s, Australopithecines were clearly accepted as the earliest ancestors of humans and a more modern view of human evolution emerged. Mary Leakey's (1913–1996) and Louis Leakey's (1903–1972) discoveries of *Zinjanthropus* (an Australopithecine) in 1959 (Leakey 1960) and *Homo habilis* in 1964 at Olduvai Gorge in Tanzania placed the Leakeys and East hominids in the spotlight of paleoanthropology (Tobias 2006). The Australopithecines, *Homo habilis* and *Homo erectus* specimens, were found at a number of sites in East Africa throughout the 1960s to 1980s. Work in the Omo Valley in southern Ethiopia began in 1967 with a team of French, American, and Kenyan investigators. An American contingent headed by F. Clark Howell (1925–2007) led to many fossil discoveries (Johanson 2018). Around that time, Richard Leakey, the son of Mary and Louis, discovered the hominid fossil-bearing site of Koobi Fora, on the eastern shore of Lake Turkana in northwest Kenya, and in 1972, Donald Johansen began working with French scientists in Hadar, Ethiopia. Also in Ethiopia, the Awash River Valley project was begun in 1981 and produced specimens from pre-Australopithecines up to early modern *Homo*. In 1974, Mary Leakey's Laetoli discoveries, including those of Australopithecine footprints, added to the accumulating evidence for early hominin evolution in East Africa.

Two major sites outside of Africa became prominent during the 1970s and 1980s. Atapuerca in northern Spain produced rich fossils of archaic *Homo* dated as early as 800,000 years ago. Dmanisi in the Republic of Georgia produced hominids dated to 1.8 million years ago. Both the Spanish and Georgian paleoanthropological sites continue to produce hominin specimens.

Early research in nonhuman primate evolution was conducted by vertebrate paleontologists or by general mammalian anatomists. Since the 1960s, however, Elwyn Simons (1930–2016), of Yale and Duke Universities, had the greatest influence on paleoprimatology. Simons revived the discipline in the early 1960s with his reviews of the primate fossil record. He is responsible for training most primate paleontologists during this period (Fleagle and Hartwig 1997).

Skeletal Biology and Bioarchaeology: Craniology and skeletal biology have been traditional pursuits of biological anthropologists. Considerable early twentieth century effort had been devoted to the "racial-typological model" of skeletal analysis (Armelagos et al. 1982). By the 1970s, papers in skeletal biology had increased to more than half of the published papers in the *American Journal of Physical Anthropology*, and half of these skeletal papers were classified as descriptive rather than analytical in scope (Lovejoy et al. 1982). However, by the late 1960s and early 1970s, scientific papers were dealing increasingly with paleodemography, biomechanics, growth, and skeletal maturation, rather than anatomical description. In addition to these developing areas were new methods of analysis of bone material for dating purposes and dietary analyses (Ubelaker 1982). Studies of craniofacial growth expanded during the 1960s and 1970s, as did work in bone density by use of a variety of X-ray and physical methods (Baker 1961; Garn 1981). The shift from description to understanding past populations and individuals, contextually enriched and from a biocultural perspective, was a fundamental development (Buikstra 1977; Buikstra and Beck 2006; Larsen 2015).

Bioarchaeology (Buikstra 1977) continued an earlier twentieth century tradition that was either collaboration between biological anthropologists and archaeologists or biological anthropologists who had substantial training and field experience in archaeology. Developed as a population biology of the past, more recent developments in the study of individual lives have been heavily influenced by social theories centered on identity (Buikstra et al. 2022). The growth and importance of bioarchaeology within biological anthropology cannot be overestimated. Current papers published in the *American Journal of Physical Anthropology* in skeletal biology and bioarchaeology constitute about 50 percent of the journal's content (report of the Editor-in-Chief, 2020).

Paleopathology: Paleopathology in the US is considered a part of bioarchaeology, although in the UK and elsewhere paleopathology and "osteoarchaeology" are considered to be separate specialties (Grauer 2018; Jarcho 1966). Along with bioarchaeology, paleopathology was revitalized in the post-World War II era along with the associated "New Archaeology" and "New Physical Anthropology." With these new approaches incorporating anthropology, hypothesis testing was applied to investigations of skeletal biology, bioarchaeology, and paleopathology. The medical side of paleopathology was brought into anthropology with the organization of the Paleopathology Association (PPA) by Aiden and Eve Cockburn in 1973 (Roberts et al. 2012). The PPA continues to meet with the AAPA.

Forensic Anthropology: While Aleš Hrdlička testified at trials on medico-legal issues and served as a Federal Bureau of Investigation FBI consultant (Hunt 2006; Ubelaker 2018), modern forensic anthropological skeletal analyses began with Wilton Krogman's (1939) guide on skeletal identification for the FBI and its application in identifying war dead from World War II. Another physical anthropologist who participated in war dead identification was Mildred Trotter (1899–1991), who developed stature estimates from long bones. These activities further stimulated forensic publications by T. Dale Stewart (1901–1997), Harry L. Shapiro (1902–1990), J. Lawrence Angel (1915–1986), and Wilton Krogman (Thompson 1982). Reflecting the growing importance of the field, the 8th Wenner-Gren Summer Seminar in 1955 was devoted to forensic anthropology and was held at the Smithsonian Institution in Washington at the end of the Korean War. After Krogman's (1962) book was published, forensic anthropology began to be recognized as an appropriate applied science in anthropology. The American Academy of Forensic Sciences was founded in 1948 and established a new section on physical anthropology in 1972, which changed its name to the Anthropology Section. This stimulated increased professional identification by many physical anthropologists as forensic anthropologists. Forensic anthropologists are now increasingly involved in the inter-related fields of forensic taphonomy (skeletal assemblages), forensic archaeology, and forensic trauma analysis. These are subfields concerned with the reconstruction of events surrounding death (Dirkmaat et al. 2008).

Journals and Professional Societies

At the end of World War II, two journals, the *American Journal of Physical Anthropology* (*AJPA*) and *Human Biology* (*HB*), were dedicated to physical/biological anthropology. Only one profession society, the AAPA, represented the field. A pre-World War II analysis of the two journals found that the articles in *AJPA* were predominantly anatomical and dealt more with individuals than populations. In contrast, *HB* tended more toward population studies (Goldstein 1940). In 2019, before the Covid-19 pandemic struck, the AAPA was the largest association of biological anthropologists in the world and had a membership of nearly 2000. Reflecting the trend to change the use of "physical anthropology" to "biological anthropology," at the annual business meeting on 14 April 2021, the AAPA membership voted to change its name to the American Association of Biological Anthropologists (AABA). This was followed by renaming the journal as the *American Journal of Biological Anthropology* (*AJBA*). The quarterly journal, *Human Biology*, has been edited by biological anthropologists since shortly after the end of World War II. The annual *Yearbook of Physical Anthropology*, published in 1945 and edited by Gabriel Lasker, reprinted articles from abroad and non-anthropological journals, and served to broaden the topical coverage of the profession (Little and Kaplan 2010).

Table 2.1 lists the largely American journals and societies from the twentieth and into the twenty-first centuries. There are numerous additional societies and their publications outside of the US, some of which are largely international and others with national readerships (Little 2018c). This proliferation of professional societies and specialized journals in the US over the past several decades reflects the continuing division of biological anthropology into subfields that require increasingly specialized training programs.

Gender and Ethnic Diversity in Biological Anthropology

During the first half of the twentieth century, gender and ethnic diversity among those who identified as physical anthropologists was limited. The 84 charter members of the American Association of Physical Anthropologists in 1930 included only two women: Mildred Trotter and Ruth Sawtell Wallis (Powell et al. 2006; Szathmáry 2010; Wilson 2019)

Table 2.1 Founding of some journals and societies in biological/physical anthropology. (Associated societies and journals are linked in parallel columns.)

Year	Journal	Year	Society
1918	*American Journal of Physical Anthropology* (*AJPA*)	1930	American Association of Physical Anthropologists (AAPA)
1945	*Yearbook of Physical Anthropology*	1930	AAPA
2021	*American Journal of Biological Anthropology* (Renamed, formerly *AJPA*)	2021	American Association of Biological Anthropologists (Renamed, formerly AAPA)
1929	*Human Biology*	1974–	Human Biology (Council)
1988	*American Journal of Human Biology*	1988	Human Biology Association
1972	*Journal of Human Evolution*	1972	Physical Anthropology (now Anthropology) Section of the American Academy of Forensic Sciences
1973	*Paleopathology Newsletter*	1973	Paleopathology Association
		1977	American Board of Forensic Anthropology (Diplomate established)
1981	*American Journal of Primatology*	1981	American Society of Primatologists
		1986	Dental Anthropology Association
1992	*Evolutionary Anthropology*		
2003	*Paleoanthropology*	1992	Paleoanthropology Society
		1994	American Association of Anthropological Genetics (Became affiliated with *Human Biology*)
2011	*International Journal of Paleopathology*	1973	Paleopathology Association
2017	*Bioarchaeology International*		
2018	*Forensic Anthropology*		

Figure 2.4 Important women in physical anthropology during the early-to-mid-twentieth century. Left: Mildred Trotter; Right: Alice Brues.

(see Figure 2.4). At that time, Trotter was a young anatomist at Washington University, who was interested in skeletal biology, and Sawtell was a new PhD from Columbia University, who had worked with Hooton and then with Boas studying the growth of children. Most of the charter members were European or European-American men. These two young women constituted only 2.4 percent of the AAPA membership at its beginning, but women members were 9.7 percent a decade later, and by 2014 had risen to about 70 percent of the membership (Wilson 2019). Alice Brues was another pre-World War II PhD (in 1940) who conducted research in skeletal biology, forensic anthropology, and population genetics. She was a distinguished physical anthropologist with a research and academic career that spanned more than 40 years (Sandford 2018).

W. Montague Cobb (see Figure 2.5), an influential African American physical anthropologist and physician, was President of the AAPA (1957–1959), and later became President of the National Association for the Advancement of Colored Persons (NAACP) (1978–1982). Trotter was the first woman to serve as AAPA President and Cobb was the first African American elected as President. Cobb taught at Howard University throughout most of his career: his research productivity was high with numerous papers on anatomy, the health and wellbeing of African Americans, and human rights and equality (Rankin-Hill and Blakey 1994). Another African American, Caroline Bond Day (1886–1948), suffered the dual stigma during the first half of the twentieth century of being a woman and being a mixed race African-American and European-American (see Figure 2.5). She studied mixed-race couples at Radcliffe under Hooton's direction and demonstrated that racially mixed couples did not have children who were in any way aberrant or inferior when compared with like-race couples (Curwood, 2012).

Trudy Turner and her colleagues (2018) prepared a detailed overview of women in biological anthropology from several surveys of AAPA members during the years between 1970 and 2014. They found that women were increasingly employed in academic tenure-track positions during this period of more than 40 years. Although slightly more women than men were in tenure-track faculty positions in 2014 (54.5 percent vs. 45.5 percent), women tended to fall into the lower ranks of assistant and associate professor while more men were in the highest rank (professor). With the high percentage of women

Figure 2.5 African American physical anthropologists from the twentieth century. Top: W. Montagu Cobb; Bottom: Caroline Bond Day.

members of the AAPA at roughly 70 percent (Wilson 2019), and their growing majority in tenured academic positions, gender equity in the profession is moving forward. Race and ethnic diversity in biological anthropology is still low, with 87% of the AAPA members identifying as white (Antón et al. 2018). In order to increase the diversity within the profession, the AAPA established a standing committee (Committee on Diversity, COD) in 2011 with several programs designed to achieve this objective (Antón et al. 2018).

INTO THE TWENTY-FIRST CENTURY

Research, discoveries, and expansion of professionals in biological anthropology in the late twentieth and early twenty-first centuries are testimony to the health and importance of the science. The biological anthropological perspectives that maintain the viability of the science continue to be: (1) a biocultural/biobehavioral approach that can solve scientific problems that are intractable by unidisciplinary social or biological scientists; (2) a theoretical perspective and process applied to humans – *evolution* – whose explanatory power is truly remarkable; (3) an ability to view humans and their biobehavior in deep time and evolutionary perspective and to use this information to foresee problems in contemporary societies; (4) the exploration of human biology and behavior within a population perspective, also an essential element for evolutionary studies; (5) the application of the comparative approaches to human societies, nonhuman primate relatives, and to our evolutionary antecedents; and (6) the applied value of biological anthropology in human health and human variation in DNA, the microbiome, child growth, forensics, and other sciences. Use of these valuable tools, along with application of the scientific method, has enabled biological anthropologists to make substantial progress in its several subfields in the years bracketing the millennium and well into the twenty-first century.

ARCHIVAL AND PUBLISHED SOURCES

Useful bibliographic sources for the history of physical/biological anthropology have been cited in earlier sections of this chapter, and are summarized here. By far the most significant historical research has been done by the late Frank Spencer (Spencer 1982b, 1997e; Boaz and Spencer 1981). His mentor, C. Loring Brace (2005), did substantial work on race, as did Ashley Montagu (1942, 1961, 1972), Stephen Jay Gould (1996), and Pat Shipman (1994). Other sources of biographical information on biological anthropologists can be found in: (1) several autobiographical prefatory articles in the *Annual Review of Anthropology*; (2) *Biographical Memoirs* of the National Academy of Sciences; (3) *festschriften* (volumes in honor of individuals) published by students and colleagues; (4) autobiographical memoirs; (5) obituaries; and (6) unpublished letters, papers, photographs, and other documents at the National Anthropological Archives of the Smithsonian Institution and other institutional archives (Little et al. 1995). Finally, there are several published histories of professional organizations and journals. These include: the American Association of Physical Anthropologists (Alfonso and Little 2005; Comas 1969), the Human Biology Association (Little and James 2005), the *Annals of Human Biology* (Tanner 1999), *Human Biology* (Crawford 2004), and the Wenner-Gren Foundation for Anthropological Research (Lindee and Radin 2016; Szathmáry 1991). There are also histories of subdisciplines of biological anthropology (Buikstra and Roberts 2012). Most recently, Wenda Trevathan and six associates (2018) edited a three volume *International Encyclopedia of Biological Anthropology* that supplements Frank Spencer's (1997e) earlier *History of Physical Anthropology: An Encyclopedia*.

ACKNOWLEDGMENTS

In this brief historical review, we acknowledge, with thanks, those who have already written extensively on the history of biological anthropology. We also recognize the major contributions of the late Robert W. Sussman (1941–2016), who was co-author of the first edition of this chapter. Our gratitude also goes out to Clark Spencer Larsen who invited us to revise this chapter on the history of our profession for the 2nd edition of this volume.

REFERENCES

AAPA Statement. "AAPA Statement on the Biological Aspects of Race." *American Journal of Physical Anthropology* 101 (1996): 569–570.

Alfonso, M. P., and M. A. Little, transl. and eds. "Juan Comas's Summary History of the American Association of Physical Anthropologists 1928–1968." *Yearbook of Physical Anthropology* 48 (2005): 163–195.

Antón, S. C., R. S. Malhi, and A. Fuentes. "Race and Diversity in U.S. Biological Anthropology: A Decade of AAPA Initiatives." *American Journal of Physical Anthropology Yearbook* No. 65, 165 (2018): 158–180.

Armelagos, G. J. "Smith, Sir Grafton Elliot 1871–1937." In *History of Physical Anthropology: An Encyclopedia*. Edited by F. Spencer, 955–957. New York: Garland, 1997.

Armelagos, G. J., D. S.Carlson, and D. P. Van Gerven. "The Theoretical Foundations and Development of Skeletal Biology." In *A History of American Physical Anthropology, 1930–1980*. Edited by F. Spencer, 305–328. New York: Academic Press, 1982.

Baker, P. T. "Human Bone Mineral Variability and Body Composition Estimates." In *Techniques for Measuring Body Composition*. Edited by J. Brožek and A. Henshel, 69–75. Washington, DC: National Academy of Sciences-National Research Council, 1961.

Baker, T. S., and P. B.Eveleth. "The Effects of Funding Patterns on the Development of Physical Anthropology." In *A History of American Physical Anthropology, 1930–1980*. Edited by F. Spencer, 31–48. New York: Academic Press, 1982.

Baker, B. J., and M. A.Judd. "Development of Paleopathology in the Nile Valley." In *The Global History of Paleopathology: Pioneers and Prospect*. Edited by J. E. Buikstra and C. A. R. Roberts, 209–234. Oxford: Oxford University Press, 2012.

Baker, P. T., and J. S. Weiner, eds. *The Biology of Human Adaptability*. London: Clarendon Oxford University Press, 1966.

Barkan, E. *The Retreat of Scientific Racism: Changing Concepts of Race in Britain and the United States Between the World Wars*. Cambridge: Cambridge University Press, 1992.

Boas, F. "The Growth of Children." *Science* 5 (1897): 570–573.

Boas, F. *Changes in the Bodily Form of Descendants of Immigrants*. New York: Columbia University Press, 1912.

Boyd, W. C. *Genetics and the Races of Man*. Boston: Little, Brown, 1950.

Boaz, N. T., and F.Spencer, eds. "1930–1980: Jubilee Issue." *American Journal of Physical Anthropology* 56 (1981): 327–557.

Brace, C. L. *"Race" Is a Four-Letter Word: The Genesis of the Concept*. New York: Oxford University Press, 2005.

Brace, C. L. "Physical Anthropology at the Turn of the Last Century." In *Histories of American Physical Anthropology in the Twentieth Century*. Edited by M. A. Little and K. A. R. Kennedy, 25–53. Lanham, MD: Lexington Books, 2010.

Broberg, G. "*Homo sapiens*: Linnaeus's Classification of Man." In *Linnaeus: The Man and His Work*. Edited by T. Frängsmyr, 156–194. Berkeley: University of California Press, 1983.

Brues, A. M. "Selection and Polymorphism in the ABO Blood Groups." *American Journal of Physical Anthropology* 12 (1954): 559–597.

Buikstra, J. E. "Biocultural Dimensions of Archaeological Study: A Regional Perspective." In *Biocultural Adaptation in Prehistoric America* Edited by R. L. Blakely, 67–84. Southern Anthropological Society Proceedings, No. 11. University, MS: University of Mississippi, 1977.

Buikstra, J. E. "History of Research in Skeletal Biology." In *Handbook of the North American Indians*, vol. *3: Environment, Origins, and Population*. Edited by D. Ubelaker, 67–84. Washington, DC: Smithsonian Institution Press, 2006.

Buikstra, J. E. "Introduction to the 2009 Reprint Edition Crania Americana; or a Comparative View of the Skulls of Various Aboriginal Nations of North and South America: to which is Prefixed an Essay on the Varieties of the Human Species, 1839, by Samuel George Morton." Philadelphia: John Pennington, 2009. www.gustavslibrary.com.

Buikstra, J. E., and L. A.Beck, eds. *Bioarchaelogy: The Contextual Analysis of Human Remains*. Burlington, MA: Academic Press, 2006.

Buikstra, J. E., and C. A. Roberts, eds. *The Global History of Paleopathology: Pioneers and Prospects*. New York: Oxford University Press, 2012.

Buikstra, J. E., J. A. Darling, E. Jones, et al. "'… A Pyramid that Stands on Its Point:' Aleš Hrdlička's Vision of Research in Physical Anthropology." Manuscript on file. n.d.

Buikstra, J. E., D. J.Ortner, and S. McBride-Schreiner. "Aleš Hrdlička 1869–1943: Contributions to Paleopathology." In *The Global History of Paleopathology: Pioneers and Prospects*. Edited by J. E. Buikstra and C. A. Roberts, 174–178. New York: Oxford University Press, 2012.

Buikstra, J. E., S. N. DeWitte, S. C. Agarwal, et al. "21st Century Bioarchaeology: Taking Stock and Moving Forward." *Yearbook of Biological Anthropology*, 178 (2022): 54–114.

Burns, W. E. *Science in the Enlightenment: An Encyclopedia*. Santa Barbara: ABC- CLIO, 2003.

Cann, R. L., M. Stoneking, and A. C. Wilson. "Mitochondrial DNA and Human Evolution." *Nature* 325 (1987): 31–36.

Carpenter, C. R. *Naturalistic Behavior of Non-Human Primates*. University Park, PA: The Pennsylvania State University Press, 1964.

Cartmill, M. "The Status of the Race Concept in Physical Anthropology." *American Anthropologist* 100 (1998): 651–660.

Chagnon, N. A. "Yanomamo – The Fierce People." *Natural History* 77 (1967): 22–31.

Cole, D. *Franz Boas, the Early Years: 1858–1906*. Seattle: University of Washington Press, 1999.

Collins, K. J., and J. S. Weiner, eds. *Human Adaptability: A History and Compendium of Research*. London: Taylor and Francis, 1977.

Comas, J. *Historia Sumaria de la Asociación Americana de Antropólogos Físicos 1928–1968*. Mexico City: Instituto Nacional de Antropologia e Historia, 1969.

Coon, C. S. *The Origin of Races*. New York: Knopf, 1962.

Coon, C. S., S. M. Garn, and J. B. Birdsell. *Races: A Study of the Problems of Race Formation in Man*. Springfield, IL: C.C. Thomas, 1950.

Cowlishaw, G., and R.Dunbar. *Primate Conservation Biology*. Chicago: University of Chicago Press, 2000.

Crawford, M. H. "History of Human Biology 1929–2004." *Human Biology* 76 (2004): 805–815.

Curwood, A. C. "Caroline Bond Day 1889–1948: A Black Woman Outsider Within Physical Anthropology." *Transforming Anthropology* 201 (2012): 79–89.

Dart, R. "*Australopithecus africanus, the Man-Ape of South Africa*." *Nature* 115 (1925): 195–199.

Darwin, C. R. *The Origin of Species by Means of Natural Selection, or the Preservation of Favoured Races in the Struggle for Life*. London: John Murray, 1859.

Davenport, C. B. "Research in Eugenics." *Science* 54, no. 1400 (1921): 391–397.

DiGangi, E. A., and J. D. Bethard. "Uncloaking a Lost Cause: Decolonizing Ancestry Estimation in the United States." *American Journal of Physical Anthropology* 175 (2021): 187–206. https://doi.org/10.1002/ajpa.24212.

Dirkmaat, D. C., L. L.Cabo, S. D. Ousley, and S.Symes. "New Perspectives in Forensic Anthropology." *Yearbook of Physical Anthropology* 51 (2008): 33–52.

Dobbs, J. W. "Eulogy for Paul Fejos 1897–1963." *Current Anthropology* 44 (1963): 405–407.

Dobbs, J. W. *The Several Lives of Paul Fejos: A Hungarian Odyssey*. New York: The Wenner-Gren Foundation, 1973.

Erikson, G. E. "Adolph Hans Schultz, 1981–1976." *American Journal of Physical Anthropology* 56 (1981): 365–371.

Fleagle, J., and W. C. Hartwig. "Paleoprimatology." In *History of Physical Anthropology: An Encyclopedia*, 2 vols. Edited by F. Spencer, 796–808. New York: Garland, 1997.

Garn, S. M. *Human Races*. Springfield, IL: C.C. Thomas, 1961.

Garn, S. M. "The Growth of Growth." *American Journal of Physical Anthropology* 56 (1981): 521–530.

Garruto, R. M., M. A. Little, and G. D. James. "Paul Thornell Baker: February 28, 1927–November 29, 2007." Washington, DC: Biographical Memoirs National Academy of Sciences, 2009.

Giles, E. "Two Faces of Earnest A. Hooton." *Yearbook of Physical Anthropology* 55 (2012): 105–113.

Goldstein, M. S. "Recent Trends in Physical Anthropology." *American Journal of Physical Anthropology* 26 (1940): 191–209.

Gould, S. J. *The Mismeasure of Man*. New York: Norton, 1981.

Gould, S. J. *The Mismeasure of Man, Revised and Expanded*. New York: Norton, 1996.

Grauer, A. L. "A Century of Paleopathology." *American Journal of Physical Anthropology* 165 (2018): 904–914.

Gregory, W. K. "The Galton Society for the Study of the Origin and Evolution of Man." *Science* 49 (1919): 267–268.

Harrison, G. A., J. S. Weiner, J. M. Tanner, and N. A. Barnicot. *Human Biology: An Introduction to Human Evolution, Variation, and Growth*. Oxford: Oxford University Press, 1964.

Hooton, E. A. *The Indians of Pecos Pueblo: A Study of Their Skeletal Remains*. New Haven: Yale University Press, 1930.

Hrdlička, A., with W. H.Holmes, B. Willis, F. E. Wright, and C. N. Fenner. "Early Man in South America." *Bulletin of the Bureau of American Ethnology*, No. 102, 1–405. Washington, DC: Smithsonian Institution, 1912.

Hrdlička, A. *Physical Anthropology: Its Scope and Aims; Its History and Present Status in the United States*. Philadelphia: Wistar Institute, 1919.

Hrdlička, A. "The Neanderthal Phase of Man." *Journal of the Royal Anthropological Institute* 57 (1927): 249–274. (The Thomas Huxley Memorial Lecture, 1926).

Hudnut, W. H., III. "Samuel Stanhope Smith: Enlightened Conservative." *Journal of the History of Ideas* 17 (1956): 540–552.

Hunt, D. "Forensic Anthropology at the Smithsonian Institution." *AnthroNotes* 271 (2006): 6–12.

Huxley, T. H. *Evidence as to Man's Place in Nature*. London: Williams & Norgate, 1863.

Jarcho, S. "The Development and Present Condition of Human Paleopathology." In *Human Paleopathology*. Edited by S. Jarcho, 3–30. New Haven: Yale University Press, 1966.

Johanson, D. C. "Howell, F. Clark." In *The International Encyclopedia of Biological Anthropology*, vol. II. Edited by Wenda Trevathan, 830–831. Hoboken, NJ: Wiley Blackwell, 2018.

Kelley, E. A., and R. W. Sussman. "An Academic Genealogy on the History of American Field Primatology." *American Journal of Physical Anthropology* 132 (2007): 406–425.

Kennedy, K. A. R. "But Professor, Why Teach Race Identification If Races Don't Exist." *Journal of Forensic Sciences* 40 (1995): 797–800.

Kern, K. F. "T. Wingate Todd: Pioneer of Modern American Physical Anthropology." *Kirtlandia* (Cleveland) 55 (2006): 1–42.

Kingsland, S. "Raymond Pearl: On the Frontier in the 1920's. Raymond Pearl Memorial Lecture, 1983." *Human Biology* 56 (1984): 1–18.

Krogman, W. M. "A Guide to the Identification of Human Skeletal Material." *FBI Law Enforcement Bulletin* 3 (1939): 3–31.

Krogman, W. M. *The Human Skeleton in Forensic Medicine.* Springfield, IL: C. C. Thomas, 1962.

Larsen, C. S. "History of Paleopathology in the American Southeast: From Pox to Population." In *Global History of Paleopathology: Pioneers and Prospects.* Edited by J. E. Buikstra and C. A. Roberts, 266–284. New York: Oxford University Press, 2012.

Larsen, C. S. *Bioarchaeology: Interpreting Behavior from the Human Skeleton,* 2nd edn. Cambridge: Cambridge University Press, 2015.

Lasker, G. W. "Place of James Normal Spuhler in the Development of Anthropological Genetics." *Human Biology* 66, no. 4 (1994): 553–566.

Leakey, L. S. B. *Stone Age Cultures of Kenya Colony.* London: Methuen, 1931.

Leakey, L. S. B. "A New Fossil Skull from Olvuvai." *Nature* 185, no. 4685 (1960): 491.

Lewis, J. E., D. DeGusta, M. R. Meyer, et al. "The Mismeasure of Science: Stephen Jay Gould versus Samuel George Morton on Skulls and Bias." *PLoS Biology* 9, no. 6 (2011): e1001071. https://doi.org/10.1371/journal.pbio.1001071.

Lindee, S. M., and J. Radin. "Patrons of the Human Experience: A History of the Wenner- Gren Foundation for Anthropological Research, 1941–2016." *Current Anthropology* 57, no. S14 (2016): S218–S301.

Little, M. A. "Franz Boas's Place in American Physical Anthropology and Its Institutions." In *Histories of American Physical Anthropology in the Twentieth Century.* Edited by M. A. Little and K. A. R. Kennedy, 55–85. Lanham, MD: Lexington Books, 2010.

Little, M. A. "Physical Anthropology in 1918 and the Founding of the U.S. Journal." *American Journal of Physical Anthropology* 165 (2018a): 626–637.

Little, M. A. "Roberts, Derek F." In *The International Encyclopedia of Biological Anthropology,* vol. III. Edited by Wenda Trevathan, 1347–1348. Hoboken, NJ: Wiley Blackwell, 2018b.

Little, M. A. "International Organizations in Biological Anthropology." In *The International Encyclopedia of Biological Anthropology,* vol. II. Edited by W. Trevathan, 885–889. Hoboken, NJ: Wiley Blackwell, 2018c.

Little, M. A., and R. M. Garruto. "Raymond Pearl and the Shaping of Human Biology." *Human Biology* 82 (2010): 77–102.

Little, M. A., and G. D. James. "A Brief History of the Human Biology Association: 1974–2004." *American Journal of Human Biology* 17 (2005): 41–154.

Little, M. A., and B. A. Kaplan. "The Post-War Years: The *Yearbook of Physical Anthropology* and the Summer Seminars." In *Histories of American Physical Anthropology in the Twentieth Century.* Edited by M. A. Little and K. A. R. Kennedy, 155–172. Lanham, MD: Lexington Books, 2010.

Little, M. A., J. E. Buikstra, and F. Spencer. "The Records of Biological Anthropology." In *Preserving the Anthropological Record,* 2nd edn. Edited by S. Silverman and N. J. Parezo, 107–121. New York: Wenner-Gren Foundation, 1995.

Little, M. A., P. W. Leslie, and P. T. Baker. "Multidisciplinary Research of Human Biology and Behavior." In *History of Physical Anthropology: An Encyclopedia.* Edited by F. Spencer, 695–701. New York: Garland, 1997.

Livingstone, F. B. "Anthropological Implications of the Sickle Cell Gene Distribution in West Africa." *American Anthropologist* 60 (1958): 533–562.

Lovejoy, C. O., R. P. Mensforth, and G. J. Armelagos,. "Five Decades of Skeletal Biology as Reflected in the *American Journal of Physical Anthropology.*" In *A History of American Physical Anthropology, 1930–1980.* Edited by Frank Spencer, 329–336. New York: Academic Press, 1982.

Mai, L. L., E. Shanlin, and R. W. Sussman, eds. *The Perception of Evolution: Essays Honoring Joseph B. Birdsell.* Los Angeles: UCLA Publication Services, 1981.

Marks, J. "Eugenics." In *History of Physical Anthropology: An Encyclopedia,* 2 vols. Edited by Frank Spencer, 362–366. New York: Garland, 1997.

Marks, J. "The Two 20th Century Crises of Racial Anthropology." In *Histories of American Physical Anthropology in the Twentieth Century.* Edited by M. A. Little and K. A. R. Kennedy. 187–206. Lanham, MD: Lexington Books, 2010.

Martin, R. *Lehrbuch der Anthropologie in Systematischer Darstellung: Mit Besonderer Berücksichtigung der Anthropologischen Methoden: Für Studierende, Ärzte, und Forschungreisende.* Jena: Fischer, 1914.

Massin, B. "From Virchow to Fischer: Physical Anthropology and 'Modern Race Theories' in Wilhelmine Germany." In *Volksgeist as Method and Ethic: Essays on Boasian Ethnography and the German Anthropological Tradition.* Edited by G. W. Stocking Jr., 79–154. Madison: University of Wisconsin Press, 1996.

Michael, J. S. "A New Look at Morton's Craniological Research." *Current Anthropology* 29 (1988): 349–354.

Montagu, A. *Man's Most Dangerous Myth: The Fallacy of Race.* New York: Columbia University Press, 1942.

Montagu, A. "UNESCO Statements on Race." *Science* 133 (1961): 1632–1633.

Montagu, A. *Statement on Race: Annotated Elaboration and Exposition of the Four Statements on Race Issued by UNESCO.* Oxford: Oxford University Press, 1972.

Morton, S. G. *Crania Americana: Or, a Comparative View of the Skulls of Various Aboriginal Nations of North and South America; To Which Is Prefixed an Essay on the Varieties of the Human Species.* Philadelphia: John Pennington, 1839.

Morton, S. G. *Crania Aegyptiaca; Or, Observations on Egyptian Ethnography, Derived from Anatomy, History, and the Monuments.* Philadelphia: John Pennington, 1844.

Neel, J. V., and F. Salzano. "A Prospectus for Genetic Studies on the American Indian." In *The Biology of Human Adaptability.* Edited by P. T. Baker and J. S. Weiner, 245–274. Oxford: Clarendon Press, 1966.

Pearl, R. "The Biology of Superiority." *The American Mercury* 1247 (1927): 257–266.

Powell, M. L., and D. C. Cook, eds. *The Myth of Syphilis: The Natural History of Treponematosis in North America.* Gainesville: University of Florida Press, 2005.

Powell, M. L., D. C. Cook, G. Bogdan, et al. "Invisible Hands: Women in Bioarchaeology." In *Bioarchaeology: The Contextual Analysis of Human Remains.* Edited by J. E. Buikstra and L. A. Beck, 131–194. Burlington, MA: Academic Press, 2006.

Proctor, R. "From Anthropologie to Rassenkunde in the German Anthropological Tradition." In *Bones, Bodies, Behavior: Essays on Biological Anthropology.* Edited by George W. Stocking Jr., 138–179. Madison: University of Wisconsin Press, 1988.

Rankin-Hill, L. M., and M. L. Blakey. "W. Montague Cobb: Physical Anthropologist, Anatomist, and Activist." *American Anthropologist* 96 (1994): 74–96.

Ribnick, R. "A Short History of Primate Field Studies: Old World Monkeys and Apes." In *A History of American Physical Anthropology, 1930–1980.* Edited by Frank Spencer, 49–73. New York: Academic Press, 1982.

Roberts, C. A., M. L. Powell, and J. E. Buikstra. "T. Aidan Cockburn 1912–1981 and Eve Cockburn 1924–2003." In *The Global History of Paleopathology: Pioneers and Prospects.* Edited by J. E. Buikstra and C. A. Roberts, 32–39. New York: Oxford University Press, 2012.

Sandford, M. K. "Brues, Alice M." In *The International Encyclopedia of Biological Anthropology,* vol. III. Edited by Wenda Trevathan, 284–285. Hoboken, NJ: Wiley Blackwell, 2018.

Sauer, N. J. "Forensic Anthropology and the Concept of Race: If Races Don't Exist, Why Are Forensic Anthropologists So Good at Identifying Them?" *Social Science and Medicine* 34 (1992): 107–111.

Schultz, A. H. "Growth Studies on Primates Bearing upon Man's Evolution." *American Journal of Physical Anthropology* 7 (1924): 149–164.

Shapiro, H. L. "The History and Development of Physical Anthropology." *American Anthropologist* 61 (1959): 371–379.

Shipman, P. *The Evolution of Racism: Human Differences and the Use and Abuse of Science*. New York: Simon & Schuster, 1994.

Spencer, F. "Ales Hrdlicka, M.D., 1869–1943: A Chronicle of the Life and Work of an American Physical Anthropologist." PhD Dissertation. Ann Arbor, MI: University of Michigan, 1979.

Spencer, F. "Introduction." In *A History of American Physical Anthropology, 1930–1980*. Edited by Frank Spencer, 1–10. New York: Academic Press, 1982a.

Spencer, F., ed. *A History of American Physical Anthropology, 1930–1980*. New York: Academic Press, 1982b.

Spencer, F. "Broca, Paul Pierre 1824–1880." In *History of Physical Anthropology: An Encyclopedia*. 2 vols. Edited by F. Spencer, 221–222. New York: Garland, 1997a.

Spencer, F. "Germany." In *History of Physical Anthropology: An Encyclopedia*, 2 vols. Edited by F. Spencer, 423–434. New York: Garland, 1997b.

Spencer, F. "Keith, Sir Arthur 1866–1955." In *History of Physical Anthropology: An Encyclopedia*, 2 vols. Edited by Frank Spencer, 560–562. New York: Garland, 1997c.

Spencer, F. "Manouvrier, Léonce-Pierre 1850–1927." In *History of Physical Anthropology: An Encyclopedia*, 2 vols. Edited by Frank Spencer, 642–643. New York: Garland, 1997d.

Spencer, F., ed. *History of Physical Anthropology: An Encyclopedia*, 2 vols. New York: Garland, 1997e.

Spencer, F., and F. H. Smith. "The Significance of Aleš Hrdlička's "Neanderthal Phase of Man": A Historical and Current Assessment." *American Journal of Physical Anthropology* 56 (1981): 435–459.

Spuhler, J. N. "Some Genetic Variations in American Indians." In *The Physical Anthropology of the American Indian*. Edited by W. S. Laughlin, 177–202. New York: Viking Fund, 1951.

Stanton, W. *The Leopard's Spots: Scientific Attitudes Toward Race in America, 1815–59*. Chicago: University of Chicago Press, 1960.

Stewart, T. D. "Aleš Hrdlička, 1869–1943." *American Journal of Physical Anthropology* 56 (1981): 347–351.

Stini, W. A. "Sherwood L. Washburn and the 'New Physical Anthropology'." In *Histories of American Physical Anthropology in the Twentieth Century*. Edited by M. A. Little and K. A. R. Kennedy, 173–185. Lanham, MD: Lexington Books, 2010.

Stocking, G. W., Jr. *Victorian Anthropology*. New York: The Free Press, 1987.

Stocking, G. W., Jr. "Bones, Bodies, Behavior." In *Bones, Bodies, Behavior: Essays on Biological Anthropology*. Edited by G. W. Stocking Jr., 3–17. Madison: University of Wisconsin Press, 1988.

Sussman, R. W. "Primate Field Studies." In *History of Physical Anthropology: An Encyclopedia*, 2 vols. Edited by Frank Spencer, 842–848. New York: Garland, 1997.

Sussman, R. W. "A Brief History of Primate Field Studies." In *Primates in Perspective*. Edited by C. J. Campbell, A. Fuentes, K. MacKinnon, M. Panger, and S. K. Bearder, 6–10. New York: Oxford University Press, 2007.

Szathmáry, E. J. E. "Reflections on Fifty Years of Anthropology and the Role of the Wenner-Gren Foundation: Biological Anthropology." In *Report for 1990 and 1991: Fiftieth Anniversary Issue*. New York: Wenner-Gren Foundation for Anthropological Research, 1991.

Szathmáry, E. J. E. "The Founding of the American Association of Physical Anthropologists: 1930." In *Histories of American Physical Anthropology in the Twentieth Century*. Edited by M. A. Little and K. A. R. Kennedy, 127–139. Lanham, MD: Lexington Books, 2010.

Tanner, J. M. *A History of the Study of Human Growth*. Cambridge: Cambridge University Press, 1981.

Tanner, J. M. "The Growth and Development of the *Annals of Human Biology*: A 25-year Retrospective." *Annals of Human Biology* 26 (1999): 3–18.

Thompson, D. D. "Forensic Anthropology." In *A History of American Physical Anthropology, 1930–1980*. Edited by Frank Spencer, 357–369. New York: Academic Press, 1982.

Tobias, P. V. "*Homo Habilis* – A Premature Discovery: Remembered by One of Its Founding Fathers, 42 Years Later." In *The First Humans – Origins and Early Evolution of the Genus Homo*, 7–15. Vertebrate Paleobiology and Paleoanthropology Series. Dordrecht: Springer, 2006.

Todd, T. W. *Atlas of Skeletal Maturation*. St. Louis: C.V. Mosby, 1937.

Trevathan, W., ed. *The International Encyclopedia of Biological Anthropology*, 3 vols. Hoboken, NJ: Wiley Blackwell, 2018.

Turner, T. R., R. M. Bernstein, A. B. Taylor, et al. "Participation, Representation, and Shared Experiences of Women Scholars in Biological Anthropology." *American Journal of Physical Anthropology* (Yearbook No. 65) 165 (2018): 126–157.

Ubelaker, D. H. "The Development of American Paleopathology." In *A History of American Physical Anthropology, 1930–1980*. Edited by Frank Spencer, 337–356. New York: Academic Press, 1982.

Ubelaker, D. H. "A History of Forensic Anthropology." *American Journal of Physical Anthropology* 165 (2018): 915–923.

Vayda, A. P., and R. A. Rappaport. "Ecology, Cultural and Noncultural." In *Introduction to Cultural Anthropology: Essays in the Scope and Methods of the Science of Man*. Edited by J. A. Clifton, 476–497. Boston: Houghton Mifflin, 1968.

Warren, K. B., ed. "Origin and Evolution of Man." *Cold Spring Harbor Symposia on Quantitative Biology*, vol. 15. Cold Spring Harbor, NY: The Biological Laboratory, 1951.

Washburn, S. L. "The New Physical Anthropology." *Transactions of the New York Academy of Science* 13 (1951): 298–304.

Washburn, S. L. "The Strategy of Physical Anthropology." In *Anthropology Today: An Encyclopedic Inventory*. Edited by Alfred L. Kroeber, 714–727. Chicago: University of Chicago Press, 1953.

Washburn, S. L. *Review of: A History of Physical Anthropology: 1930–1980*. Edited by F. Spencer. New York: Academic Press, 1984. *Human Biology* 56:393–410.

Washburn, S. L., and I. DeVore. "The Social Life of Baboons." *Scientific American* 204, no. 6 (1961): 63–71.

Watkins, R. "Knowledge from the Margins: W. Montague Cobb's Pioneering Research in Biocultural Anthropology." *American Anthropologist* 109 (2007): 186–196.

Weiner, J. S. *The Piltdown Forgery*. London: Oxford University Press, 1955.

Weiner, J. S. *International Biological Programme Guide to the Human Adaptability Proposals*. London: International Council of Scientific Unions, Special Committee for the IBP, 1965.

Weiner, J. S. "History of the Human Adaptability Section." In *Human Adaptability: A History and Compendium of Research*. Edited by K. J. Collins and J. S. Weiner, 1–31. London: Taylor and Francis, 1977.

Weiss, K. M., and R. Chakraborty. "Genes, Populations, and Disease, 1930–1980: A Problem-Oriented Review." In *A History of American Physical Anthropology, 1930–1980*. Edited by Frank Spencer, 371–404. New York: Academic Press, 1982.

Wilson, E. K. "Women's Experiences in Early Physical Anthropology." *American Journal of Physical Anthropology* 170 (2019): 308–318.

Wolfheim, J. H. *Primates of the World: Distribution, Abundance, and Conservation*. Seattle: University of Washington Press, 1983.

Yerkes, R. M., and A. W. Yerkes. *The Great Apes*. New Haven: Yale University Press, 1929.

Zuckerman, S. *The Social Life of Monkeys and Apes*. New York: Harcourt, Brace, 1932.

PART II The Present and the Living

CHAPTER **3**

Evolution: What It Means and How We Know

*Kenneth M. Weiss and
Anne V. Buchanan*

A MATTER OF TIME

Evolution is change over time, a process that generates a history of relatedness among all living things. The connectedness of life on Earth had been noticed for centuries, but, 150 years ago, Charles Darwin and Alfred Russel Wallace suggested a mechanism, natural selection, to explain how that connectedness, and the functional traits of organisms, could come about. Their brilliantly simple insight made their theory of evolution both new and enduring. Many aspects of evolution are still debated, including the nature and relative importance of selection, but no evolutionary biologist doubts that individuals who can't survive don't survive and that species today have their ancestry in ancient species.

Evolution happens on a vast time scale, but evolutionary changes usually start small and on a much shorter scale. Changes are passed from the cells in which they first arise to their descendant cells, in a process of *inheritance with memory*: what you and your individual cells are today depends on their immediate cellular ancestors. This is because inherited control involves the nucleotide-sequence nature of genes. Cellular memory is encoded by the functional elements in the DNA, and changes in DNA are transmitted to descendant cells. This is memory because organisms and cells die and their traits must be regenerated by their descendants – dramatically so in organisms like humans, who begin life as a single cell, a fertilized egg. It is the accumulated changes from cell to cell, in an unbroken chain that stretches back four billion years to the origins of life on Earth, that has produced the Tree of Life, whose branch tips comprise the species that are alive today.

Organisms as well as genes evolve, and an objective of biology is to understand how the functions and diversity of organisms, as well as their genes, have evolved. The modern theory

A Companion to Biological Anthropology, Second Edition. Edited by Clark Spencer Larsen.
© 2023 John Wiley & Sons Ltd. Published 2023 by John Wiley & Sons Ltd.

of evolution has been formulated around genes, on the assumption that traits are due to, and made by, genes, even if it is organisms that are born, live, and die. If this assumption is right, then the processes that change genes also change organisms. However, this means that we need to pay particular attention to the relationship between genotypes and phenotypes.

Traditionally, the means of genetic change are grouped into four categories. Together they provide a formal mathematical theory of evolution, called *population genetics*. This theory is presented at various levels in many fine textbooks (for instance, Hartl and Clark 2007; Ridley 2004; Templeton 2006) and with special focus on humans (Boyd and Silk 2006; Jobling et al. 2004; Relethford 2003). However, these categories are not as distinct or discretely different as their traditional treatment suggests, and they also depend on the reality of populations as biological units. While the following description keeps the standard categories, we put their names in quotes, to indicate that they are not so neat – an issue to which we will return later.

1. "Mutation": change in the DNA sequence itself, the ultimate source of new variation. Because of inheritance with memory, a mutational change that arises in a cell is (if viable and lucky enough) transmitted to the descendant cells. However, other changes, including modifications that affect the way in which DNA is used without changing its sequence, also occur and are inherited, and many non-DNA aspects of a cell are transmitted as well.

2. "Gene flow": the movement of genes over space from one generation to the next, as individuals choose mates or produce offspring in places other than those where they were born. Typically, most humans and other primates reproduce near their own birthplace, with the fraction diminishing as the distance between natal locales increases. Long-distance migration by land or water mainly seems to have occurred in incursions into areas that were uninhabited by other humans, especially in post-agricultural times beginning roughly 10,000 years ago. Migration on a very large scale is even more recent, but of course it has larger and more immediate effects, especially when the indigenous population is decimated as a result of the immigrant colonization.

3. "Genetic drift": countless factors, including Mendelian parent–offspring transmission, that introduce probabilistic effects on each individual's reproductive success. The factors can be intentional (for instance, choosing to be celibate for cultural reasons) or purely due to environmental happenstance. They are called "chance" because they occur independently of the genotypes they affect. The frequency of a genetic variant (an "allele") from one generation to the next in a given population is always susceptible to change for such probabilistic reasons, which are a predominant source of reproductive variation in any generation. Since each generation is the foundation for the succeeding ones, chance is important in long-term evolution as well.

Some forms of chance are unique events, like lightning strikes, but many involve repeatable events, for which one can assign probabilities. For example, under most circumstances, an *Aa* heterozygote has a 50 percent chance of transmitting its *a* allele to a given offspring. Thus, even among genetically identical individuals in the same environment, who have the same *chance* of reproducing, there can – and usually there will – be differences in their *achieved* reproductive output or their completed family size.

Thus, change in allele frequency does not by itself imply that anything other than chance is involved. Indeed, reproduction always has stochastic aspects. When the observed amount of change is not unusually large in relation to its probabilistic likelihood, we characterize the change as genetic drift. "Unusually" is a subjective term, but it is important because the core of Darwin's and Wallace's theory was about systematic change – change that, by some criterion, is *not* due to chance alone.

4. "Natural selection": when one genetic variant reproduces systematically more than another *because* of some causal factor(s), we say that the variant has higher Darwinian fitness and that natural selection occurs. The phrase "natural selection" implies differences not simply due to chance. From Darwin to the present, natural selection invokes force-like notions of relative inherent value attached to genetic variants. Darwin's basic rationale for his view was that populations typically over-reproduce, forcing a competition among contemporaries that provides opportunity for the worst of them to be weeded out through early mortality or failure to acquire mates or to reproduce, and for the favored to advance through a better survival or reproduction.

Selection can act in various ways. Most commonly, it seems, new mutations that disrupt existing function are usually harmful and removed from the population through "purifying" or "negative" selection. Occasionally, a mutation confers an advantage in the environment in which it arises and increases in frequency through "positive" or "directional" selection. If more than one variant in a system are harmful by themselves, yet their combination in individuals confers some relative advantage, the variants can be maintained in the population through "balancing" selection, also known as "heterosis" or heterozygote advantage. Many or even most traits may, for example, be harmful at the extremes (for instance low and high birthweights) and, to the extent that these trait-values are genetically based, balancing selection maintains genetic variation in the population.

Identifying selecting factors in the environment is usually much more difficult than identifying statistical evidence of selection from genetic variation data. Like reproduction, a selective factor can act probabilistically: individuals with the same *expected* reproductive output (which is greater, say, than that of a competing variant) can have a different number of *achieved* offspring. Again, the individuals are probabilistically equal. Only if, in this sense, genotypes retain their unequal, if probabilistic, fitness values do we attribute the differences to selection. Variants that are probabilistically equivalent are said to be selectively "neutral."

Because selection and drift are both probabilistic, and especially since selection seems generally to be very slow and weak, the distinction between the two is often subjectively based on our judgment of the relative likelihood of an observed change, which is based on some chosen statistical significance test.

When selective differences are very small, the expected offspring sizes between variants would be difficult to detect with statistical significance under most circumstances, even in large samples and especially in small ancestral human demes. A further complication is that natural selection is inherently *relative*. Fitness is not an inherent property of an allele. If conditions change – and they often do – selective differences among the same set of competing alleles can also change: a favored variant may find itself disfavored, or in competition with new mutations that are better than the former competitors. To the extent that conditions are unstable in relation to weak selective differences, selection is much less force-like and deterministic, less certain to drive a population in a predictable direction, more likely to be but one out of several equally "fit" alternatives, and on the whole much closer to the effects of chance alone (for some similar ideas from a population genetics viewpoint, see Lynch 2007).

Contrary to the usual and sometimes unspoken assumption, Malthusian overpopulation does not imply that selection will occur or will be important. Overpopulation provides one way for competing variants to *be* favored by selection, but they may not be. There may not be particularly advantageous variants in the population. Overpopulation could just cause misery for everyone. However, experimental situations in the laboratory or in agriculture show that in most populations there is enough standing genetic variation for deliberate, strong selection to produce a response in the favored direction. Presumably environments could do the same. Antibiotic and pesticide resistance are somewhat artificially accelerated, but rapid major climate change, infectious epidemics, and the like could also produce change that fits the usual Darwinian model well. However, even then, the selective effect may not just favor a single adaptive genotype.

Darwin thought of evolution by natural selection as a very slow, gradualistic, quantitative, force-like deterministic process, which molds organisms to their circumstances. There were problems reconciling this view with the large, sometimes qualitative, variation within or among species, like the number of vertebrae or of teeth. These discrete differences did not seem possible under Darwinian gradualism, where one would expect intermediate states to occur during the process: one cannot have 6 V fingers – which raised a problem for evolutionary explanations of closely related species with different numbers of fingers. Evolutionary ideas were made more perplexing by Gregor Mendel's demonstration, in plants, that inheritance worked through stable, discrete particles (eventually to be called "genes"). In principle, that could explain discontinuous inheritance, for instance different colored peas or even different numbers of fingers, but it was hard to relate to the evolution of continuously varying traits that Darwin thought mostly about.

* * *

These ideas were reconciled by the 1940s in what was known as the "modern evolutionary synthesis." Quantitative traits were understood to be compatible with small contributions from large numbers of discrete Mendelian genes. Such many-gene, or polygenic, traits could also be affected by the environment. This could generate quantitative variation, but it is also possible that, when the quantitative levels of some factor(s) exceed a threshold, a state change – such as in the number of cusps, teeth, or vertebrae – would occur.

On the basis of the understanding that genes control traits, the modern synthesis defined evolution, theoretically, as change in the frequency of genetic variation, and early theorists developed the four basic evolutionary phenomena. The theory was centrally Darwinian in its outlook, stressing the formative power of selection. This view acknowledged chance, mutation, and gene flow – but mainly as statistical noise or as modifiers around the true, selective signal. Then, as now, biologists said such things as "when I see order, I see selection," or "selection fine-tunes a trait," or "if this had no function, it would have been removed by selection, because it has an energy cost to the organism."

These notions are, at best, overstatements of the ubiquity and power of natural selection. The idea that other factors, including drift of various kinds, could also be quite important has arisen and has been debated; it even prevails when it comes to "non-functional" elements in the DNA, which, by definition, must change through chance alone (since there is no function for selection to work on), or through "hitchhiking" along with variation on the same chromosome that is being driven by selection. With a steady march of new knowledge in genetics, it has become less clear just what is functional in the DNA and what is not. However, many or even most biologists resist challenges to the sacrosanct principle – or rather *assumption* – that anything with a function has to have selective value.

Even under this view, however, we are facing new levels of unexpected complexity in the phenogenetic relationships associated with most biological traits, that is, the relationships between genotypes and phenotypes. The indications are that future knowledge will place more emphasis on drift and less on selection at the level of *individual* genetic elements, even when selection is molding the net result – the phenotypes of individuals. Phenotypic variation that is of no interest to natural selection can change by chance alone – a process called phenotypic drift.

Genotypes are only transmitted by individuals with successful phenotypes, whether they succeeded by luck or with selection's help. Competition and drift jointly produce successful function in organisms, which goes by the name "adaptation."

On the shorter time scale of the trees of cellular descent *within* an organism, a rather different kind of evolution occurs. The somatic (body, or non-germline) cells of an organism contain essentially the same genotype, which was inherited in the single fertilized egg cell with which the organism's life began. Mutations do occur and are transmitted from cell to cell. However, change in function within an organism is largely based on change in gene *usage*, not in gene sequence; that is, different tissues use different subsets of the same set of available genes (the others being inactive in that cell). To be differentiated into a tree-like relationship among organs and tissues, gene usage is based on cooperation rather than competition among cells with similar genomes but different gene usage. Cells respond to their environment, which, in an individual, largely involves signaling molecules coded by genes and sent from one type of cell to other cells (hormones are an example). These signals are produced by the sending cell's gene usage and received by receptor molecules coded by genes used by the receiving cells. An organism functions only to the extent that its thousands of genes and their actions interact successfully in such ways during embryogenesis, homeostasis, detection, and response to the outer and inner world.

The distinction is important. Cooperation is what most life, on a continuing and daily basis, is all about. Competition is only a part of the evolutionary story, applying mainly to the accumulation of long-term effects. However, since Darwin, and perhaps due to the transformative nature of his dramatic theory and to the role of social competition in our culture, the appeal of a competitive perspective typically obscures the more important, more prevalent, and at least as vital, cooperative nature of life in the short term.

Population genetics is a rigorous mathematical theory and is key to understanding patterns of genetic variation that we observe today, to designing experimental breeding for the improvement of agriculture, to understanding the ecology and history of infectious diseases, and to much more. It works by extrapolating events at any given time over long periods of time, under its particular assumptions, and, to the extent that such an extrapolation is imprecise, deviation from the theory will occur and the amount of error – usually unknown – will be proportional to the imprecision. This makes it difficult to interpret the *why* and *how* of the evolutionary histories of organisms, even if the *what* can be reconstructed from fossils, present morphology, biology, and genetics.

The four traditional categories of the evolutionary process are not as different as an itemized list would suggest, because the theory depends on the definition (and reality) of "population." As stated earlier, even when a population can be concisely defined, selection and drift are part of a probabilistic spectrum of change. In a similar way, mutation is not the only source of new variations, only of variation in DNA sequences. Recombination and intrusion from outside the population, as well as epigenetic modification of the DNA, which changes its use but not its sequence, also introduce new variations into a population.

Gene flow is not just a sometime process among distinct, isolated populations. Almost all transition from one generation to the next includes the movement of genes from the parents' birthplace to where their children are born. This is true even if the "flow" is between adjacent demes, or lineages within demes, and most demes are not watertight, with stable discrete boundaries. The diffusion of variation is more or less continuous across space, without rigid population boundaries and hence without rigid populations (there are some exceptions, like truly isolated populations). With more gradual change in frequency over space and time, gene flow, and even mutation, are seen as aspects of the same spectrum of change. This is one reason why categories related to humans – "races" for example – are not as rigid, as discrete, or even as easy to define as is often uncritically believed. They are culturally defined concepts designed to chop the more continuous variation into categories.

A gene-centered theory of evolution largely rests on the tacit assumption that genes are closely connected to phenotypes, although phenogenetic connections often prove to be very complex and indirect, weakening simplified notions of evolutionary change and determinism. Categorical concepts can lead to oversimplified thinking and to correspondingly inaccurate conclusions. A more fluid view of evolution and of phenogenetic relationships can help to explain a number of important issues.

THE GENE AS ICON AND METAPHOR

The working assumption in biology, that genes "cause" traits, can have two basic meanings. The first is the mechanistic one, according to which genes code for proteins and proteins make traits. The second is the meaning related to population, whereby genetic variation is associated with variation in relevant traits.

Under this assumption, genes have become iconic metaphors for ultimate causation in life. One hears of genes for language, for upright posture, and so on, but we don't really know what the genetic basis of – or genes "for" – language or upright posture are. In fact, we don't know the genetic basis of most traits, especially traits more complex than those dominated by a single protein – for instance, melanin production related to skin color; hemoglobin genes that may be associated with malarial resistance; or the lactase enzyme that digests milk sugar. We *do* know, however, that, even in these instances, our understanding is incomplete, while environment, chance, and other unidentified contributory factors (including genes) affect the trait.

Similarly, reconstructing evolutionary origins is necessarily indirect, since we cannot observe the past. The degree of indirectness is almost always such that our reconstructions are much more problematic than we would like to admit or be aware of if we didn't recognize the metaphoric use of evolutionary language. Often, without really convincing evidence, we assign selective advantage to present function: "thumbs evolved to manipulate tools" is implicitly intended to mean "hominids with variation in genes for thumbs had more children than hominids without those variants, *because* they were able to use tools." There is a big difference between these sentences and the actual evidence, which is that "thumbs can be used to manipulate tools." The difference is easy to see: given thumbs, we *design* tools that can be manipulated by thumbs. Because we do not know the genetic basis of complex traits like thumbs, when we use evolutionary–genetic rhetoric we are almost forced to explain such traits metaphorically or, worse, to commit the sin of circularity, *assuming* what we want to prove.

Genes-for and selection-for evolutionary stories may get media attention, but they can be poor science. Understanding real evolution is much more challenging. Most of the genetic evidence we actually have is comparative. We compare DNA sequences among individuals within species or between species, and both genetic causation and fitness are statistical in nature, as described earlier. We look for parts of the genome in which the amount of variation statistically suggests that natural selection played a role in its evolution. We can either search the whole genome for such regions, identify the functional elements, and try to determine what their evolutionary history may have been, or we can look for such evidence in candidate genes that we think are involved in a trait of interest. Bioinformatic methods for computer-based analysis of DNA sequence data are rapidly advancing, and we have many tests for statistical signatures of the result of natural selection, such as unusually little or unusually large amounts of change between species, or variation within species, the former perhaps reflecting purifying selection and the latter, positive directional selection. However, building a solid selective explanation is still problematic, especially in terms of a specific selective "force."

The Central Dogma: It Is Not a Dogma Any More, But Is It Central?

Of the many roads that might have been taken, discovery in genetics has gone where the territory is paved. Mendel started us down the genetics road and a series of focused studies, building on his discoveries, gradually led by the mid-twentieth century to an understanding of genes that became known as "the central dogma" of biology – the DNA codes for protein via a messenger RNA (mRNA) intermediate – and this information flows from DNA to protein, but not the other way.

It turns out that, like any dogma, this is an incomplete understanding, a consequence of the road taken. There are other roads on the genetic map. For example, DNA has many other functions beyond coding for proteins, including DNA packaging, protection, and copying, and the differential usage of genes (gene expression) referred to earlier. Because of the expanding understanding of what DNA does, the definition of a "gene" itself has been dizzolving into fuzziness under the microscope of modern molecular technology (e.g., Gerstein et al. 2007). Protein coding remains an important function of DNA, to be sure, but whether it is "central" is debatable. Therefore, when we speak of genes "for thumbs," we need to be careful what we mean.

Another Dogma That Is Not

Evolution by competition is a watchword of our times, but, as noted earlier, biology is predominantly about cooperation, about components interacting at the proper time and place. Internally and externally, cells work through the interaction of proteins with each other and with non-protein substrates, including the RNA and the DNA. These interactions are not incidental. Gene expression is based on cascades of regulatory factors (coded by other genes), on cells interacting with each other via cell-surface receptor molecules detecting external signal molecules, and so on. Similar mechanisms at the gene and cell level are involved in ecological interactions among species and between organisms and their environments on the basis of sensory and neural systems. Since contemporary mechanisms set the stage and determine branchpoints for the future legacy, cooperation is much more important – even on the evolutionary time scale – than is generally credited.

This is not a reference to cooperation in the sense of social behaviors, sharing, and altruism. They are real parts of nature, but a competition-centered evolutionary worldview demands an individual-based selective explanation in terms of (metaphoric or real) genes. Strong Darwinians object to words like "cooperation" as referring to nothing but competition in disguise ("I share only because there's something in it for me"). According to that view, cooperation is a socially loaded term, which seems to be a wishful thinking retreat from cold Darwinian materialism. However, "competition" is equally loaded culturally, and has at least as much potential to mislead.

The Consequences of Evolution By Phenotype

Whole organisms are born, compete, reproduce, and die. It is the traits borne by organisms that are screened through selection. The genetic basis of a trait is only affected indirectly. The slippage between genotype and phenotype adds statistical noise in evolutionary systems. Since most traits are the result of the aggregate contributions of many genes, many genotypes yield similar phenotypes. The effect of natural selection working on phenotypes, on any one of the contributing genes, may be very small. Individually, each allele may essentially be evolving by drift, or nearly so.

With this type of redundancy, a trait can be conserved by selection; but, over time, different genes or alleles can come to be responsible. This is called phenogenetic drift (Weiss and Fullerton 2000). There are many examples. The presence of teeth has been maintained in vertebrates for hundreds of millions of years, but the genetic basis of teeth has changed (Kawasaki et al. 2005).

Some Controversies That Are Not

People, including scientists, enjoy controversy. Whether it is good for good science can be debated, but we can look at some current controversies involving evolution to see the extent to which they are real or exaggerated.

Is speciation adaptive? Darwin felt that his main contribution was the idea that species arise because of *adaptation*: due to natural selection, populations of organisms diverged in the details of their functionality or ecological niche. Leaving aside the problems with the definition of species itself, the basic requirement is reproductive isolation, because that is what allows divergent adaptation to take place.

Darwin essentially felt that adaptation came first, but speciation can occur initially through isolation (individuals never meet to mate, so they never do the latter), with traits diverging subsequently. Chromosomal or other genetic change that interferes with fertilization can lead to the required isolation as much as geographic barriers or distance can, among groups whose other traits and behavior are identical. These changes can arise by chance and by drift, especially in small populations, and need not involve natural selection or new adaptation. Divergent adaptation to environmental conditions may occur later but need not be part of the speciation process itself.

What is "orderly" life? It is widely argued that the orderly appearance of organisms is due to adaptation through natural selection, on the grounds that otherwise only religious explanations could account for such traits. There is some truth to that. For example, really *disorderly* traits seem to be eliminated through natural selection (organisms bearing them simply cannot survive), but there are other ways for orderliness to evolve that are not due to natural selection, or at least not to a simple version of it.

We discussed above how both drift and selection launch one generation probabilistically into the next. Phenotypic drift can occur among variations in which selection has no interest, but, even under the watchful eye of selection, at any given time there may be a range of phenotypes that are equally advantageous. Such traits, and the genes that affect them, are neutral and will change by drift *in relation to each other*. Anthropological examples of phenotypic drift include head shape differences among related primate species (Ackermann and Cheverud 2000); these may not demand adaptive explanation.

Organisms are not just passively screened by the environment and judged more or less fit. They are adaptable and usually exploratory, responding to circumstances; they seek, or *construct*, the circumstances they like. Choosing favorable circumstances is called organismal selection when it is genetically based: organisms that like a given environment from among the ones available to them will aggregate there and mate. Over time, it will appear as if the genes responsible for the preference have been favored by selection, but they need not have had any competitive advantage relatively to the genotypes that aggregated elsewhere as a result of different preferences. The building of suitable micro-environments is called niche construction. Bird nests and human houses are examples.

Now there is a curious fact. Those who hold a strongly selectionist world view rely on the fact that evolutionary time periods are long in order to argue that highly organized traits, like eyes or brains, could have been – *were* – produced through gradual selection. This is because, without long time periods, we would have to accept saltational evolution – the sudden appearance of new, organized traits – which seems implausible. When the weak nature of most selection and the consequent relative importance of drift are raised as a challenge to strong selectionism, a common response is as follows: yes, today's organized traits might be modified slightly here and there by drift, but they must have been driven to their current, highly by the ever-present, always-acting, fine-tuning systematic force of selection. The flaw in this argument is that it assumes that we are living at a special time in the history of life. Instead, selection may *always* have been weak and slow, and, if viewed at *any* given time in the past, then-current traits would have seemed highly organized and adapted. The importance of drift can, and perhaps must, apply back to the history of life, leaving adaptation to be the result of chance much more than is generally believed.

Is life adaptive? In a similar vein, it is said that organisms are obviously suited to their circumstances, which is supposed to show the truth of adaptive–evolutionary explanations. How else could they have got here? Yet the truth of the statement is not as obvious as it may seem. Adaptation is a kind of tautology. If an organism (or at least its ancestors) were not suitable for life, it would not be here today. We can see the reasons why it survives today, but this is not the same as the reasons why it *is* here today. To equate present function to past adaptive selection is a mistake known as the naturalistic fallacy.

We usually cannot know what selective reasons (if any) applied in the past. Classically, Darwinian adaptive evolution certainly occurs and may even be a part of the story most of the time, but selection of a specific type need not have been the key agent, and much less the only one. Enumerating the reasons why an adaptation is good is to make the same mistake as the proponents of the "intelligent design" view in religion. Not all of an organism's functions need to work all that well – all we know is that they have worked *well enough* in the past.

How deterministic is evolution? Darwin was very clear that he viewed natural selection in essentially Newtonian deterministic terms, as a force, or as a law of nature. He said several times that selection detects the "smallest grain in the balance" (meaning the smallest grain on the scale) of competition (Weiss 2004). Yet, when we try to identify the genetic basis of a trait or to detect selection in real time, there is always variation, noise, and subtlety. If selection is typically weak, its existence may be undetectable at *any* given time – and perhaps at *every* time – in the course of a trait's evolution.

Adaptation occurs, but less determinedly, requiring less precision in the screening ability of nature, and it occurs with greater flexibility and tolerance. More organisms have a chance to do well, and populations are not as threatened with poor fitness as they might otherwise be. Chance is *part* of that process. This is a more sanguine and epistemologically more sound view of evolution than an argument about determinism versus chance – selection versus drift – would imply (see, for instance, Lynch 2007).

What is the source of adaptive variation? Over the years, there have been many debates about the source of new variations – numerous enough to serve as fuel for the idea of a "creative" (not creationist!) evolution. In the early twentieth century there were debates as to whether an existing variation, variation plus recombination, or a new mutation was most important. Mutation was thought to be too rare to drive response to changing environments (if those changed rapidly – another unstated assumption?). However, standing variation and its rearrangement or recombination through sexual reproduction readily and steadily present new *combinations* of existing variants to nature, and selection screens whole organisms, not individual genes.

There has been a growing recognition that chromosomal duplication events of various kinds have produced new genes. A duplicate gene is a redundant one and is the potential source of a new function. Correlations between the time of gene duplication events and the appearance of new traits such as body plans have been attributed to this process.

Another debate is about whether adaptive evolution occurs through selected change in the protein-coding regions of the genome or in regions affecting gene regulation, which is a function versus expression debate (see, for instance, Carroll et al. 2005; Hoekstra and Coyne 2007). Many, if not most, proteins are *pleiotropic*: they have many different functions. One idea is that, if the DNA code for a protein suffers mutation, the protein will not function well in all (if in any) of its many uses, and the likely result will be a very unhappy organism. On the other hand, the *expression* of a gene is controlled by numerous short DNA sequences (only a few nucleotides long) near its protein-coding region. When these regulatory sequences are physically bound by other proteins called *transcription factors*, the binding event causes the gene to be used – transcribed into mRNA – or its expression level is altered. Short regulatory sites can arise easily in random sequence among the tens of thousands of bases flanking protein-coding regions, and hence they can come and go by mutation. In any cell that is producing the transcription factor protein itself, such modifications in the regulatory region of other genes could change the time or place of expression of those genes.

Many transcription factors are needed to induce (or repress) the expression of a gene, and the cooperative nature of life is such that many different proteins must interact with each other and with the flanking DNA to accomplish gene expression. This means that *those* genes must already be expressed earlier in the cell in question. This is cooperation in action. However, either by altering the expression of the transcription factor gene itself or by those genes that the transcription factor protein activates, phenotypic change can evolve, and fairly rapidly.

Variation arises in all of these ways. Which one is "more important" is rather a nonquestion – like what is more important, food or water?

Is there too much evidence for selection? Finally, the argument over whether evolution happens by selection or drift, which is sometimes couched as Darwinian versus non-Darwinian evolution, is misplaced. From a neutralist perspective, selected variation is quickly lost or fixed in the population, while neutral variation can stay – drift – around for a long time before being fixed or lost. If so, then most of the variation one sees at any given time, for example in current genetic data, has been evolving neutrally. The argument is important as a way to explain the total *amount* of variation observed among individuals within a species, or accumulated between species. If all the observed variation were being maintained in the population through balancing selection, the amount of over-reproduction needed to compensate for individuals who are eliminated through selection (called the "genetic load") could be beyond sustaining. Individuals would simply be unable to have enough children to ensure that one could survive to replace each parent. However, the weak nature of selection in which most variation is evolving neutrally (or nearly so) at any given time relieves this argument, since change due to drift requires no excess reproduction.

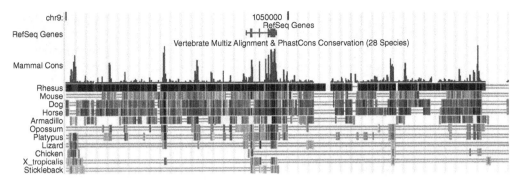

Figure 3.1 Widespread conservation of a non-protein-coding sequence in the human genome. This is a random selection of 100,000 basepairs (0.003 percent) of the human genome starting 1,000,000 nucleotides from the end of chromosome 9. Key: Topline shows basepair position. RefSeq represents exons and introns of known gene (a transcription factor called DMRT2); Mammal Cons shows degree of sequence conservation among mammals. Final lines show positions of conservation in each of many species going back to fish (stickleback).

Yet one question does still pertain, though it is little noticed. If one aligns the genomes of related species, even distant vertebrate species, there is a huge amount of conserved sequence, *in addition to* the protein-coding sequence, across the genome. A randomly chosen segment of just 0.003 percent of the human genome is shown in Figure 3.1. The figure shows the extensive amount of sequence that has been very deeply conserved, even between humans and fish. If not natural selection, then what could conserve this sequence for so long? How is the selective burden, the genetic load, being maintained? This remains a major question for the future.

PHENOGENOMIC VS. PHENOGENETIC EVOLUTION: A RECONCEPTUALIZATION OF EVOLUTION?

The usual idea of evolution is that, if a new mutation helps the organism to outcompete its peers, it steadily rises to high frequency. Yet the fundamentally cooperative aspect of nature seems to be at odds with such a world view. When we examine the evidence for genetic contributions to biological traits, we find that a substantial fraction of variation seems heritable (that is, is passed from parent to offspring, so that relatives resemble each other more than would be expected to happen by chance). Yet intensive searches of the genome identify only modest numbers of genes influencing traits of interest, and variation in those genes accounts for only a fraction of the total heritability (Weiss 2008). It seems that traits are affected by many genes whose individual variation from person to person contributes too little to be identified by available methods, amidst the sea of contributing factors.

A view on the nature of life has been growing under the name of "systems biology." It is a recognition that much of life is about interaction – cooperation – among large numbers of gene products. Networks have alternate pathways and, in systems thinking, it is the *network* of interactions as a whole that is functionally important. This could be the case for complex traits like the mammalian skull or social behavior, to which many genes contribute and each one may contribute in multiple ways.

If a network has a great many factors, hundreds or even thousands, selection's impact on any one of them could be so slight that the variant evolves basically by drift – a point we made earlier. The *trait* could evolve adaptively, being driven in some particular direction, such as toward upright posture, language ability, or useful thumbs. Overall, the genome as a whole will have changed so as to accumulate the variation in the many genes responsible for the trait, but the individual underlying genetic variants may have changed mainly by drift; it would suffice to say that at any time there was an appropriate mix of them to respond to selection. This could be called *phenogenomic* rather than the usual *phenogenetic* evolution. If accurate, it is a picture of evolution very different from the one that has been in place since the discovery of the protein-coding nature genes, in which the focus on function has perhaps inaccurately resulted in a focus on the importance of individual genes as the main factors in evolution.

The Collapse of Possibilities and Oversimplification of Evolution

Looking forward from any given time to the future, there will usually be many comparably viable ways in which a species or an ecosystem can change. Chance will be an essential, even a major part, in the mix of possibilities. Indeed, the mix changes every generation. This greatly limits the power of long-term predictions, but it accurately reflects the nature of life.

Looking backward in time from the present, evolution seems to have taken a much simpler, more direct, or even environmentally directed path. The reason is that all the possibilities have collapsed into one – what actually happened. With a long-term retrospective viewpoint, evolution and its processes can look much simpler, and it may seem easier to assert the values that nature has placed upon the traits of organisms. This, then, leads to a state of confidence about those values today, with all the societal dangers associated with it when the subject is our own species.

Social Misuses of Darwinian Reflexes

Darwinian evolution is a concept so simple and generic as to be easy to invoke, without technical knowledge, as if to assume it were the same as to prove it. Major and sometimes catastrophic consequences have resulted from an uncritically "Darwinian" assertion that life is made of inherently good and bad things engaged in vital competition with each other and that the inherent characteristics of individuals are written in their genes. The ideas of inherent worth, deterministic selection, and identifiable, discrete populations are all abstractions that derive from an assumed theory, and the consequences of that theory may subtly depend on assumptions.

In the case of humans, the obvious and historically ample examples relate to racism and eugenics, in which a group of people in power decide what is good and bad, attribute the same judgment to natural selection, and justify engineering society and interfering with people on the basis of their presumed inherent worth. Behavioral traits, especially intelligence and deviant behavior, are among the favorite targets of these value judgments. Genocide has been a result, and a wise person would always keep in mind the dangers of equating personal views with nature's views, theory with reality, and determinism with probabilism. The temptation to be armchair Darwinians is great; the news media, and even scientists, routinely indulge in drawing speculative value-laden scenarios. Thus, if evolution has been a transformative idea in modern thought, it has also had its downside.

FINALLY, DO GENES MATTER?

If evolution is driven by genetic changes, we can ask, what does it mean, then, to "understand" the evolution of a trait? Do we need to identify every gene? Or every variant in every gene in every population of every species? Is it enough to know just the pattern of gene-by-gene interactions and how they are conserved among species or not, or do we need to identify the specific genotype in each individual? There are no objective answers to these questions, although complete enumeration seems literally impossible. Perhaps, for many purposes, we do not need to know.

Not every question we want to answer, not even every functional or evolutionary question, is a genetic question, even though everything about life involves genes and inheritance in one way or another. For geneticists, understanding the contribution of genes to any given trait may be fascinating and relevant. However, for understanding many aspects of evolution, function, adaptation, and the like, making lists of genes that contribute to a trait may be as irrelevant as enumerating bricks would be for understanding the purpose for which a building was built. In their own place, genes are irreplaceable, but in our evolution not everything of interest is best explained in terms of genes. This is especially true of human behavior, which is largely, if not predominantly, molded by culture.

Darwin was interested in embryology, the way fertilized eggs "evolve" – the earlier use of the term – into adults, but he used comparative embryology to reinforce his main interest: the long-term evolution of adaptations and species. His theory was about phenotypes and it worked, even though his genetic ideas were thoroughly incorrect. Today, too, unless one is a geneticist or interested in mechanisms, the phenotypes of organisms are still the most important aspect of evolution.

However, ever since Darwin changed the focus of biology, the notion of evolutionary change has been restricted to the long term, but, as we have described, evolution also occurs on shorter developmental and ecological time scales (Weiss and Buchanan 2009). There the processes are substantially different from the canon of four factors that have occupied evolutionary thinking for the last century. The picture has been changing because of advances in molecular technologies, which have greatly enhanced what can be learned about these time scales of life.

Since long-term evolution is the accumulation of short-term changes that occur from cell to cell, a perspective that includes the understanding of those short-term changes should illuminate traditional evolutionary studies. In fact, when we look at life on all of its time scales, a set of simple, general principles emerges (Weiss and Buchanan 2009). Beyond Darwin's processes for species evolution, these general principles reflect the many ways in which functional change, the branching divergence of function and species, communication and cooperation, and other characteristics of life operate on scales ranging from those of cells to those of ecosystems. With a broader perspective, an understanding of change and variation in life will continue to challenge and excite our interest for generations to come.

NOTE: "Evolution" and the points discussed in this chapter comprise a vast subject. We cite only a few references, because an exhaustive bibliography would be impossible. These topics and ideas can most profitably be pursued by searching the many sources on the Internet.

REFERENCES

Ackermann, R. R., and J. M. Cheverud. "Phenotypic Covariance Structure in Tamarins (Genus Saguinus): A Comparison of Variation Patterns Using Matrix Correlation and Common Principal Component Analysis." *American Journal of Physical Anthropology* 111, no. 4 (2000): 489–501.

Boyd, R., and J. Silk. *How Humans Evolved.* New York: Norton, 2006.

Carroll, S. B., J. K. Grenier, and S. Weatherbee. *From DNA to Diversity: Molecular Genetics and the Evolution of Animal Design.* Malden, MA: Blackwell, 2005.

Gerstein, M. B., C. Bruce, J. S. Rozowsky, et al. "What Is a Gene, Post-ENCODE? History and Updated Definition." *Genome Research* 17, no. 6 (2007): 669–681.

Hartl, D., and J. A. Clark. *Principles of Population Genetics.* Sunderland, MA: Sinauer, 2007.

Hoekstra, H. E., and J. A. Coyne. "The Locus of Evolution: Evo Devo and the Genetics of Adaptation." *Evolution* 61, no. 5 (2007): 995–1016.

Jobling, M., M. Hurles, and C. Tyler-Smith. *Human Evolutionary Genetics: Origins, Peoples and Disease.* New York: Garland, 2004.

Kawasaki, K., T. Suzuki, and K. M. Weiss. "Phenogenetic Drift in Evolution: The Changing Genetic Basis of Vertebrate Teeth." *Proceedings of the National Academy of Sciences, USA* 102, no. 50 (2005): 18063–18068.

Lynch, M. *The Origin of Genome Architecture.* Sunderland, MA: Sinauer Associates, 2007.

Relethford, J. *The Human Species: An Introduction to Biological Anthropology.* New York: McGraw-Hill, 2003.

Ridley, M. *Evolution.* Malden, MA: Blackwell, 2004.

Templeton, A. *Population Genetics and Microevolutionary Theory.* Hoboken, NJ: John Wiley, 2006.

Weiss, K. M. "The Smallest Grain in the Balance." *Evolutionary Anthropology* 13, no. 4 (2004): 122–126.

Weiss, K. M. "Tilting at Quixotic Trait Loci (QTL): An Evolutionary Perspective on Genetic Causation." *Genetics* 179, no. 4 (2008): 1741–1756.

Weiss, K. M., and A. V. Buchanan. *The Mermaid's Tale: Four Billion Years of Evolution in the Making of Living Things.* Cambridge, MA: Harvard University Press, 2009.

Weiss, K. M., and S. M. Fullerton. "Phenogenetic Drift and the Evolution of Genotype-Phenotype Relationships." *Theoretical Population Biology* 57, no. 3 (2000): 187–195.

CHAPTER 4

Systematics, Taxonomy, and Phylogenetics: Ordering Life, Past and Present

Alexis Uluutku and Bernard Wood

INTRODUCTION

Systematics includes all of the activities involved in the study of the diversity and origins of living and extinct organisms. This review focuses on: (A) identification and comparison of specimens, (B) species-level classification, (C) phylogeny reconstruction, and (D) classification above the level of the species. These activities should be carried out in the order in which they are listed; thus (A) must precede (B), and (A) and (B) must precede (C), etc. The first two, "identification and comparison of specimens" and "species-level classification," constitute what Mayr et al. (1953) referred to as "alpha taxonomy." The fourth activity, "classification above the level of the species," corresponds to the way those authors define "beta taxonomy" (ibid: 19). While some researchers have used (C), phylogenetic reconstruction, to inform (B), species-level taxonomic hypotheses, reversing the order of the analyses is an exercise in circular reasoning.

In biological anthropology, "identification" means making sure a fossil is a primate and deciding what region of the body it comes from. "Comparison" involves recording its morphology as thoroughly and objectively as possible, comparing the specimen with appropriate extant and fossil taxa, and then either assigning it to an existing phenetically coherent group, or to a novel group. "Phenetic coherence" implies that the distributions of the observed morphological characteristics of a group of organisms are sufficiently nonoverlapping with those of other groups that those observations can be used to securely assign individual specimens to the correct group. The second activity, "species-level classification," involves the recognition of those phenetically coherent groups as species and then giving them formal names. The third activity, "phylogeny reconstruction," uses either all of the phenetic evidence, or a subset – as in cladistic analytical methods – to generate relatively simple hypotheses about the relationships among the taxa (for instance, a cladogram), or more complex hypotheses that include specifying ancestors and descendants (for instance, a phylogenetic tree) (Baum and Offner 2008). Phylogeny reconstruction aims to recover what some researchers refer to as the "natural" relationships among taxa (i.e., the branching pattern of the Tree of Life). The fourth activity, "classification above the level of the species," involves using the results of phylogenetic reconstruction to allocate species to a genus, tribe, etc., and then assembling these taxa into a hierarchical classification.

Taxonomy is the study of the principles and theory that inform the process of classification. *Nomenclature*, which straddles classification and taxonomy, includes the principles that should be used when formal names (such as a Linnaean binomial) are assigned to taxa, as well as the rules (priority, synonymy, and the like) and recommendations that govern the application of those principles.

The classification system used by contemporary biologists was developed by Carl Linnaeus (he was not raised to the nobility as Carl von Linné until the 12th edition of the *Systema Naturae*) in the late eighteenth century and is referred to as "Linnaean taxonomy." It is also called the "binomial system" because two (= bi-) of the categories, the genus and the specific name, make up the Latinized name given to each species (e.g., *Homo sapiens*, *Pan troglodytes*).

The system introduced by Linnaeus recognized five basic levels, or categories: kingdom, class, order, genus, and species. Since the introduction of the binomial system, biologists have found that more than five categories are needed to reflect the complexity of the living world. Consequently, Linnaeus's original categories have been supplemented by adding new ones (for instance, the tribe has been inserted between the genus and family) and by adding the prefix "super-" (above), and the prefixes "sub-" and "infra-" (below) to some categories. These additions increase the potential number of taxonomic categories below the level of order to a total of 12 (see Table 4.1). At the heart of the Linnaean hierarchy is its least inclusive category, the species. It comes from the Latin word *specio*, meaning "to look": *specimen* and *inspect* have the same origin.

A group at any level in the Linnaean hierarchy is called a "taxon" (plural "taxa"). The term "taxa" must be distinguished from the various "categories" in the Linnaean hierarchy: *Homo sapiens* is a taxon in the species category. Taxa are the actual groups in nature to which we give names (*Homo sapiens*, Primates). They are then assigned to the appropriate categorical rank in the hierarchy (species, genus, family). The names of taxa function like the names of people; they are a kind of shorthand reference system for the identification of an individual biological entity (species, person). Lower taxa are those in the species and genus categories; higher taxa are in the categories above the level of the genus. When the Linnaean system is applied to a group of related organisms, the resulting scheme is called a "classification" or a "taxonomy" of that group.

There is confusion about the proper use of the terms "diagnosis" and "definition" in relation to taxonomy. Diagnosis is what medical doctors do when they use your symptoms and signs to identify the likely cause of your illness. Diagnosis in taxonomy is a similar exercise. It is a list of the features that (A) permits one taxon to be distinguished from another and (B) facilitates the correct assignment of individual organisms (or specimens) to a taxon. A definition, on the other hand, concentrates on the morphology the members of a taxon have in common. It is a list of the features that binds the organisms of a taxon together; it does not necessarily discriminate one taxon from others (modern humans are bipeds, but without further qualification this attribute does not distinguish us from species in the extinct genus *Australopithecus*).

Table 4.1   List of the categories used in a Linnaean taxonomy. Higher taxa are in bold type

Kingdom
Phylum
Subphylum
Superclass
Class
Subclass
Infraclass
Cohort
Superorder
Order
Suborder
Infraorder
Superfamily
Family
Subfamily
Tribe
Subtribe
Genus
Subgenus
Species
Subspecies

IDENTIFICATION AND COMPARISON

Identification

The first task facing anyone claiming to have found a fossil primate is to make sure the specimen really belongs to a primate and is not the hard-tissue evidence of another type of nonprimate mammal.

The next step is to identify the specimen anatomically as precisely as the preserved morphology allows and then to determine its ontogenetic status. For example, a complete femur is difficult to confuse with a complete humerus, but an undiagnostic piece of longbone shaft or a fragment of tooth enamel may not be so easy to locate on the skeleton or in the tooth row. For parts of the body that are serially homologous (e.g., teeth and vertebrae that have a repetitive resemblance in a series of structures with the same evolutionary origin), researchers must use whatever evidence they can to locate a mandibular molar in the tooth row or a thoracic vertebra to the upper, middle, or lower part of the thoracic spine. Precise anatomical identification is important because it determines which other fossils and which components of the extant comparators should be used to help make decisions about whether the new fossil belongs to an existing species. Once the anatomical part is correctly identified, it can be compared with the same part in the appropriate comparative groups to make sure it is assigned to an existing taxon, or to a new taxon, using the appropriate diagnostic criteria. If the specimen is very scrappy this can be a difficult, sometimes inconclusive, process; better-preserved or more complete specimens are more likely to result in a correct taxonomic assignment than poorly-preserved or fragmentary ones.

It is important to determine the specimen's ontogenetic status, because a newly discovered juvenile fossil primate mandible should be compared with other juvenile mandibles, and not with adult mandibles.

Reassembly and Reconstruction

Bones and teeth that are fragmented but undistorted can be reassembled; researchers sit down with the original pieces and fit them together by hand or they manipulate images of the pieces on a computer screen. If only part of an undistorted fossil bone or tooth has been preserved, the whole can be reconstructed. Reconstruction may involve duplication if the missing piece is a bilateral structure and the other side (called the antimere) is preserved, or it may involve extrapolation if there is no antimere, or if only part of a structure is preserved. In general, the more complete a bone or tooth is and the more contact points there are between the fragments, the more reliable is the reconstruction. More difficult problems are when cracks run through a fossil and the cracks are filled with matrix or if it has been affected by plastic deformation (i.e., the bone has behaved like a plastic material and has permanently deformed when subjected to pressure from rocks fallen from the roof of a cave). If the deformation has affected only one side of a bilateral structure, then the undeformed side can be used to reconstruct the deformed side. If both sides are deformed, then researchers must either painstakingly remove the matrix between the fragments and physically reassemble them or digitally image the fossil and use software programs to estimate and restore the undeformed shape (Lautenschlager 2016). However, the problem with creating "virtual fossils" is that it is easy to forget, especially when looking at the image of an impressively complete fossil on a screen, which parts of the new virtual fossil are "real" and which are reconstructed, and it is all too easy to begin to assume that a reconstructed virtual fossil has the same value as a well-preserved "real" fossil. There is also the problem that if more complete fossils are used to guide reconstructions, there is a danger that the reconstructed fossils regress in the direction of the well-preserved fossils, thus artificially reducing the variation with a fossil taxon. Gunz et al. (2020) and Wu et al. (2021) provide recent examples of the utility of virtual reconstruction.

Relatively few fossil specimens totally escape damage from breakage, loss, erosion, and/ or deformation, processes that result in the loss or distortion of information. The recovery of information through reassembly, restoration, and reconstruction are important early steps in the analysis of a fossil.

Capturing Morphology for Comparison

The morphological characteristics of fossils need to be captured as comprehensively and as objectively as possible. The morphology of a fossil can be divided into two overlapping sets of categories, external and internal, and macroscopic and microscopic.

Information about internal morphology and microstructure can be obtained nondestructively or destructively. Nondestructive techniques employ X-rays (high-energy photons with a very short wavelength), other forms of invisible radiation, and ultrasound (acoustic frequencies above the range audible to the modern human ear, i.e., > 20,000 hertz). Researchers exploit the sophisticated imaging techniques that are used in clinical medicine such as Computed Tomography (CT) and micro-CT. These techniques allow researchers to visualize structures such as the bony labyrinth (Braga et al. 2021; Spoor et al. 2000) hidden within bones, as well as the internal morphology of trabecular bone (Skinner et al. 2015). Synchrotron radiation microtomography (SR-μCT) has been used to recover information about dental microstructure in intact teeth (Le Cabec et al. 2015; Tafforeau and Smith 2007).

Most destructive studies of the microstructure of fossils involve the dentition. For instance, Dean et al. (1993) used a diamond saw to take very thin slices through a tooth and then re-cemented the parts of the tooth crown, adding a thin layer of acrylic cement to make sure that the reassembled tooth had the same linear dimensions as it did before the thin section was removed.

Metrical and Nonmetrical Methods for Capturing Morphology

Two systems of recording morphology are commonly in use. One, called *metrical* or *morphometric* analysis, uses measurements; the other, called *nonmetrical* analysis, records morphology by using presence/absence criteria, or by comparing the fossil with a series of standards, or by characterizing the morphology qualitatively. Examples of nonmetrical traits include the numbers of cusps or roots on a tooth and the presence or absence of markings for cranial venous sinuses.

Measurements are traditionally made between standardized locations, called *landmarks*. Many of these are defined as the places where sutures meet on bones, or where fissures meet on teeth, or are points that can be located with the minimum of ambiguity (for example, the width of the shaft of a well-preserved long bone at 50 percent of its total length), but not all such landmarks have the same evolutionary origin, that is, they are not all homologous. The measurements taken are usually the shortest distance between the points; these are known as chord distances. If the surface between the landmarks is curved, a tape laid between the two points will record the arc distance, and the difference between the chord and arc reflects the degree of curvature. It is also possible to use angles to record morphology. These record the orientation of a structure relative to the sagittal or coronal planes, or to a reference plane such as the Frankfurt Horizontal or the orbital plane.

Recently introduced techniques, usually referred to as geometric morphometrics, collect data in three dimensions. Data capture is not restricted to traditional landmarks, and the use of semi-landmarks between traditional landmarks allows researchers to capture more of the original morphology. The position of each reference point is recorded using a three-dimensional coordinate system and the distances between any two of the recorded points can be recovered if needed. Four types of morphological landmarks are recognized. The first, Type 1, uses an intersection between two structures. For example, bregma, the intersection between the sagittal and coronal sutures on the top of the cranium, is a Type 1 landmark with a high degree of repeatability. Type 2 landmarks are either maxima or minima, such as the most superior and inferior points on the greater trochanter on a femur. Type 3 landmarks depend on a minimum of two Type 1 or Type 2 landmarks. For example, the "middle of the greater trochanter" is a Type 3 landmark that depends on two Type 2 landmarks – the superior and inferior extent of the greater trochanter. The final type of landmark is known as a semi-landmark. For example, the shape of a ridge joining the tips of dentine horns (two Type 2 landmarks) can be captured by a series of landmarks placed digitally at equidistant intervals along the ridge curve by 3D GM software.

The three-dimensional coordinates of Types 1–3 landmarks were initially mostly captured using machines called "digitizers." These machines have a mobile arm with a fine point at the end. The tip is placed on the reference point and the machine automatically records its location in three dimensions (3D). Newer techniques capture data from complex surfaces using laser triangulation, structured light, and laser pulse-based 3D scanning technologies, as well as various imaging modalities that give access to morphology not visible on the surface of a fossil, such as the boundary between the dentine and enamel in an intact tooth crown (Davies et al. 2021), the roots of teeth embedded in the mandible (Kupczik et al. 2019), and the size and shape of the bony labyrinth (Braga et al. 2021). These methods capture 3D data more densely than is possible with digitizers and allow for internal and/or external measurements without damage to the fossil specimens through cutting, drilling, or the use of calipers. Data captured using 3D scanning technologies have the advantage that researchers do not have to decide in advance what landmarks to use; they can place as many as they wish on the digital reconstruction. Traditional landmarks can be located in 3D on the virtual fossils, and semi-landmarks can be used to capture the shape of curved surfaces and ridges between traditional landmarks. Special software programs such as *Morphologika*, http://hyms.fme.googlepages.com/resources, MorphoJ (Klingenberg 2011), and geomorph (Adams et al. 2021) can be used to remove overall size, so that researchers can focus on shape differences.

Comparing Specimens

Observations can be compared one at a time – *univariate analysis* – or by plotting two variables against each other – *bivariate analysis*. It is also possible to analyze many variables simultaneously – *multivariate analysis*. The latter method compares known groups by summarizing multiple variables in the form of a smaller number of factors, or axes. One type of multivariate analysis allows researchers to compute the distance between individuals in multivariate space, and this "multivariate distance" can be used to compare differences between fossils with those observed within, and between, samples from comparative groups. Other multivariate methods are designed to identify clusters of similar fossils by simplifying the patterns of correlation and variance, and a subgroup of multivariate methods allows the form of a structure to be broken down into size and shape components. When analyses are based on traditional linear measurements between reference points, the morphological information they capture is only a small part of the potential information available, and conventional multivariate techniques provide no visual image of how organisms differ in size and shape, and nor do they preserve the spatial relationships among measurements. The new generation of geometric morphometric analytical methods use grids or vector arrows to show how the reference specimen needs to be deformed, or warped, in order to assume the shapes of the specimens with which it is being compared (Weaver and Gunz 2018).

Morphological differences can be resolved into differences in *size* and differences in *shape*. Comparative analyses have been consistent in showing that shape differences are consistently more taxonomically valent than differences in overall size, so a common feature of many metrical methods is scaling the data using a surrogate for overall size, such as the geometric mean. There is, however, a difference between correcting for overall size and removing the "effects" of size. Size and shape are seldom independent, for most of the relationships among metrical variables in organisms are *allometric*. In such a relationship, a change in overall size results in a predictable difference in shape. Thus, in these circumstances, even if isometric size is removed from an analysis, the *effect* of overall size differences on shape (i.e., the allometric component) will not necessarily be removed.

SPECIES-LEVEL CLASSIFICATION

Classifying individual fossils is not a valid endeavor. First, a newly discovered fossil must be assigned to a group and then the group can be classified. If the fossil is within the inferred limits of variation of an existing species, then it can be added to the *hypodigm* – that is, the list of specimens assigned to that species. However, if the specimen falls beyond the range of variation of known species, then it *may* warrant the erection of a new species. The new species must be given an appropriate name, a *holotype* (the *type specimen*) needs to be designated, and then the classification needs to be modified to accommodate it.

What Is a Species?

It may seem counter-intuitive, but biologists have devised many different ways of defining species. Smith (1994) divides contemporary, nontypological, species concepts into *process-related* and *pattern-related*. The former emphasize the processes involved in the generation and maintenance of species boundaries, whereas the latter emphasizes the operations biologists use to demarcate species boundaries.

The three main species concepts in the process category are the *biological species concept* (BSC), the *evolutionary species concept* (ESC), and the *recognition species concept* (RSC). The BSC, as promulgated by Mayr (1942, 1982), defined species as "groups of interbreeding natural populations reproductively isolated from other such groups." There are two problems with the BSC. First, it is a relational definition, in the sense that to delimit one species reference has to be made to at least one other species, and, second, it stresses mechanisms for maintaining reproductive (and hence genetic) isolation, rather than emphasizing the factors that bind the individuals within a species together. The ESC was an attempt by Simpson (1961) to add a temporal dimension to the BSC. Wiley (1978) developed Simpson's concept and defined the ESC as "a single lineage of ancestor-descendant populations which maintain its identity from other such lineages and which has its own evolutionary tendencies and historical fate." Some use the term *chronospecies* to refer to a segment of the type of evolving lineage implied in the ESC definition. The boundaries of the segment can be defined by discontinuities in the fossil record, or a lineage can be subdivided because the fossil sample exceeds the degree and/or the pattern of variation within closely related, living, species. A problem with the ESC is that it assumes pre-existing knowledge of phylogeny, which logically should follow and not precede alpha taxonomy. The third concept in the process category, the RSC, focuses on the factors that promote inter-breeding. Paterson (1985) suggested that under the RSC a species is "the most inclusive population of individual, biparental organisms which shares a common fertilization system." The latter, which he termed the *specific mate recognition system*, or SMRS, comprises the mechanisms organisms use to recognize potential mates and ensure fertilization; this may be a distinctive external morphological feature, a characteristic coloration, a distinctive call, or even an odor. Paterson claims that the RSC is, at least potentially, applicable to the fossil record as long as a species' SMRS fossilizes.

The three main pattern-based species concepts are the *phenetic species concept* (PeSC), the *phylogenetic species concept* (PySC), and the *monophyletic species concept* (MSC). When applied to the fossil record all three are *morphospecies* concepts in that they emphasize different aspects of an organism's morphology. The PeSC as interpreted by Sokal and Crovello (1970) gives equal weight to *all* aspects of the phenotype and uses multivariate analysis to detect clusters of individual specimens that share a similar phenotype. Under the PySC introduced by Cracraft (1983), the emphasis is on those aspects of the phenotype that are diagnostic. According to Nixon and Wheeler (1990), a PySC species is "the smallest aggregation of populations diagnosable by a unique combination of character states." Lastly, under the MSC, the morphological emphasis is narrower still, with species defined not on the basis of unique combinations of characters, but only on uniquely derived characters. The problem with the MSC is that it assumes researchers know which characters are uniquely derived. However, to know this you must have performed a cladistic analysis and to do that you must have already decided on the taxa to include in the analysis. The MSC is thus undermined by circular reasoning.

Eldredge (1993) developed Ghiselin's (1972) proposal that a species taxon should be regarded as an "entity." Eldredge suggested that an individual species taxon has the equivalent of a "life," with a beginning (the result of the speciation process), a middle (that lasts as long as the species persists), and an end (either extinction or participation in another speciation process). In this interpretation, when we observe living species we are looking at the equivalent of a snapshot taken during the course of its life. Biological anthropologists must decide whether a collection of fossils spanning perhaps several hundred thousand or even a million years consists of samples of several different taxa or several samples of the same taxon. One of the many factors that biological anthropologists must take into account in addition to the time represented in their sample is that they have to work with a fossil record that is confined to remains of the hard tissues (bones and teeth). We know from living animals that many uncontested species are difficult to distinguish using bones and teeth (e.g., *Cercopithecus* or *Hylobates* species). Thus, there are reasons to suspect that a hard tissue-bound fossil record is always likely to underestimate the number of species.

In Eldredge's formulation, all species begin at the point of speciation when they and their sister taxon – that is, the other taxon that arose from the same speciation event – arise from a common ancestor. A species may then change during the course of its history (anagenesis), but its existence will come to an end when it either becomes extinct or becomes the common ancestor of daughter taxa. Eldredge also acknowledges the reality that the morphological characteristics of a living, or neontological, species, or of an evolutionary lineage, are never uniformly distributed across its range, and he follows Sewall Wright in recognizing the existence of distinctive local populations, or *demes*. Related demes would share the same SMRS and Eldredge suggests their morphological distinctiveness could, in some cases, justify them being regarded as separate species. He also acknowledges that the same logic could be applied to the *chronospecies* that make up a lineage because the incompleteness of the fossil record suggests that splitting events are more likely to be underestimated than overestimated. Thus, within the fossil record it may be possible to identify several *paleospecies* (*sensu*; Cain 1954) within the equivalent of a neontological biological, or recognition species concept, species. De Queiroz (2007) includes a useful figure (De Queiroz 2007, Figure 1: 882) emphasizing that the various properties researchers have suggested as criteria for recognizing species may arise at different stages in the speciation process. When looking at the gradual change of a metapopulation during a speciation event, all taxonomists, despite their preferred species concept, will see the start of that speciation event as a single species and the end as two separate species. However, due to differences in their applied secondary species criteria (i.e., phenetic distinguishability, monophyly, or ecological niche separation) taxonomists using different species concepts will inevitably place their "cut off" for when one species becomes two at different places along the continuum. De Queiroz (2007) suggests that despite having different secondary species criteria, all species concepts have at least one thing in common: a species is a lineage of a separately evolving metapopulation.

What Happens in Practice?

Most primatologists use either the phylogenetic species concept (although often without specifically acknowledging it) or the evolutionary species concept. If they use the former, they search for the smallest cluster of individual organisms that is diagnosable on the basis of the preserved morphology. Because in the primate fossil record most of that morphology is craniodental, most diagnoses of fossil primate taxa inevitably emphasize craniodental morphology.

What Are the Most Appropriate Comparators?

How different does a new fossil have to be from specimens in the existing fossil record before a researcher can reasonably assume it represents a new species? Once a researcher has been assured that any observed differences are not due to its state of preservation (the effects of plastic deformation or an increase or decrease in size due to matrix-filled cracks or erosion, respectively), ontogeny (comparing a young individual with an old individual), sex (comparing a male with a female), within-species geographical variation, etc., then the decision rests on the range of morphological variation they are prepared to tolerate within a species. In practical terms, paleontologists usually use the extent of size and shape variation within closely related living species as the criterion for judging whether the variation within a collection of fossils merits the fossils being assigned to more than one species (see, for instance, Wood 1991). However, the museum collections used as samples of these contemporary species capture variation at what is effectively an instant in geological time, whereas fossil taxa are usually sampled across geological time. No consensus has been reached about what, if any, "extra" variation needs to be added to the variation observed in the museum collections to make them more comparable to a fossil taxon.

A Very Different Interpretation: Reticulate Evolution

All of the species concepts considered thus far subscribe to a bifurcating model of speciation; one species splits into two, each of those species bifurcates, and so on. In this model, speciation is a process in which most new species arise in geographically isolated subpopulations. This is called "allopatric" speciation, which means speciation in another territory. These subpopulations gradually develop distinctive combinations of genes that eventually result in their carrier's reproductive isolation from the parent population. Proponents of the recognition species concept would argue that this occurs when the new species develops a distinctive specific mate recognition system.

In reticulate evolution, new species arise when two existing species undergo *hybridization*. Under this model, species are seen as components of a complex network, hence the term reticulation. This model of evolution is close to how some researchers interpret evolution in geographically widespread groups like baboons. There are peaks of morphological distinctiveness among contemporary baboon populations; these differences are equivalent to those that in other taxa are interpreted as species differences. The location and nature of these peaks will change over time and new species may form in the hybrid zones between the peaks due to migration, genetic drift, or even natural selection conferring a selective advantage (Jolly 2001).

Nomenclature

The steps involved in naming a new species, genus, or higher taxon are collectively referred to as "nomenclature" and the process is controlled by rules and recommendations set out in the International Code of Zoological Nomenclature, otherwise known as the ICZN, or just "the Code" (Ride et al. 1999). The stipulations in the Code are designed to ensure that everyone who takes part in discussions about issues involving classification and nomenclature do so with a common understanding. They are also designed to make sure that: (a) the names given to new taxa are appropriate; (b) the proposed name has not already been used for an existing taxon (in other words, there is no homonymy); (c) that only one name is given to a taxon (in other words, synonymy is satisfied), and (d) the principle of *priority* is followed (i.e., the name that was used first takes priority and cannot be replaced).

The Code also sets out the conventions used when writing about taxa. Genus and species names are both italicized. The genus name always begins with a capital letter, but in print it can be abbreviated to just the initial letter of the genus name after its first mention. Thus, for our own species, *Homo sapiens*, the abbreviated form is *H. sapiens.* However, when the genus name is used alone, it must always be given in full (*Homo*, not *H.*). The names of the taxa in all the ranks above the genus are not italicized, but they always begin with a capital letter (Table 4.2). Such taxa usually take the root of the name of the earliest validly named genus included within it, with an ending that reflects the rank of the taxon. The informal way to describe the classification of the species *Homo sapiens* in the scheme used here is, in order of decreasing inclusivity, a "hominoid" (superfamily), a "hominid" (family), a "hominine" (subfamily), a "hominin" (tribe), and a "homininan" (subtribe) (see Table 4.2). Thus, *Homo sapiens* is one of several species in the genus *Homo*, which is the only genus in the subtribe Hominina, and one of several genera in the tribe Hominini. An example of a contemporary classification that reflects the molecular (Bradley 2008) and other evidence that points to a close relationship between chimpanzees/bonobos and modern humans is given in Table 4.3, which is typical of taxonomies that recognize the close genetic links between *Pan* and *Homo*. This consensus classification is unsatisfactory in that *Australopithecus* is almost certainly paraphyletic, but it must suffice until we can resolve relationships among hominin taxa more reliably than is presently the case. In Table 4.3, the fossil-only taxa are in bold type.

Phylogeny Reconstruction

Relationships Among Taxa

No matter how many species are recognized in the primate fossil record, researchers must tackle the task of working out how primate species are related. This is because a well-supported hypothesis of relationships is necessary to reconstruct most of the important details of primate evolutionary history.

Hypotheses about the relationships among fossil taxa can be divided into three categories based on their complexity (Baum and Offner 2008; Tattersall and Eldredge 1977). The least complex statement about relationships groups taxa together based on whether they share any novel characteristics. This enables them to be located as "sister taxa" in a hierarchical branching diagram. Such diagrams are called "cladograms" (from the ancient Greek

Table 4.2 Terminology for the higher taxonomic categories immediately involved in the classification of *Homo sapiens*

Category	-ending	For example, for *Homo*	Informal name
Superfamily	-oidea	Hominoidea	hominoid
Family	-idae	Hominidae	hominid
Subfamily	-inae	Homininae	hominine
Tribe	-ini	Hominini	hominin
Subtribe	-ina	Hominina	homininan

Table 4.3 A typical taxonomy that recognizes the close genetic links between *Pan* and *Homo*. The fossil-only taxa are in bold type. This consensus classification is unsatisfactory in that *Australopithecus* is almost certainly paraphyletic, but it must suffice until we can resolve the evolutionary relationships among hominin taxa more reliably than is presently the case

Superfamily Hominoidea
Family Hylobatidae
Genus *Hylobates*
Family Hominidae
Subfamily Ponginae
Genus *Pongo*
Subfamily Gorillinae
Genus *Gorilla*
Subfamily Homininae
Tribe Panini
Genus *Pan*
Tribe Hominini
Subtribe Australopithecina
Genus *Ardipithecus*
Genus *Australopithecus*
Genus *Kenyanthropus*
Genus *Sahelanthropus*
Genus *Orrorin*
Genus *Paranthropus*
Subtribe Hominina
Genus *Homo*

word for branch, *klados*). Note that a cladogram is free of absolute time, unlike a phylogenetic tree. At the nodes linking two sister taxa, common ancestors are implied but not specified. Cladograms are generated using a method called "cladistic analysis" or "cladistics." Remember that even though phylogenetic analysis is often used as a synonym for cladistics, cladistic methods generate cladograms *not* phylogenetic trees. The methods for generating hypotheses of relationships, together with the specialized terminology linked with those methods, were set out by Willi Hennig in the 1950s, but they were not widely adopted until they were published in English (Hennig 1966).

The intermediate category expresses hypotheses about relationships in the form of *phylogenetic* or *phyletic trees*. Phylogenetic trees contain more information than cladograms. As well as specifying the hierarchy of the relationships (in the form of sets of nested taxa), trees place the taxa in ancestor/descendant sequences in absolute time. This category of hypotheses goes beyond those generated using cladistic methods, and they require reliable information about the age of the fossils. Several different phylogenetic trees may be consistent with a single cladogram.

The most complex category of hypothesis about evolutionary relationships is the *evolutionary scenario*. It not only specifies a particular phylogenetic pattern, but also furnishes process-level explanations of why and how evolution took a particular course. Some of these explanations involve factors intrinsic to the taxa themselves (for example, developmental constraints). Others involve factors external to the organism, which are either biological (also known as "biotic") or nonbiological (also known as "abiotic"). Examples of the former include the effects of competition with other animals for resources. Global and regional climate change and changes in paleoenvironments are interrelated examples of potential abiotic influences on human evolutionary history.

Principles of Cladistics

The intrinsic resemblances between any two species can be crudely resolved into three elements called "patristic," "cladistic," and "homoplasic" (Cain 1954).

Patristic similarities are those that reflect relatively remote evolutionary history. In the case of modern humans and chimpanzees, these would include discrete parts of the phenotype – called "character states" – that make them both vertebrates, or mammals, or primates. These patristic features (also called "primitive" or "symplesiomorphic") are useful for generating a hypothesis about the nature of the relationships between a modern human, a chimpanzee, and a snail, but they are incapable of resolving the relationships among, say, modern humans, chimpanzees, and gorillas. In the example given above, the cladistic element of the phenotype is the part that is expressed differently in modern humans, chimpanzees, and gorillas. The shared possession of cladistic (also called "shared-derived" or "synapomorphic") character states can then be used to develop hypotheses about the evolutionary relationships among those taxa. Taxa that share characters inherited from a recent common ancestor belong to the same clade. A pair of linked taxa that are each other's closest relatives based on these shared-derived traits are "sister taxa." A monophyletic group, or clade, comprises all of the descendants of a recent common ancestor. A clade can comprise any number of pairs of sister taxa, as long as they can all be traced back to a common ancestor from which they inherited at least one shared derived character state that is not present in a closely related clade. A "polyphyletic group" is a group that includes taxa belonging to more than one clade. For example, savannah (*Papio*), forest (*Mandrillus*), and mountain (*Theropithecus*) baboons appear, at least from genetic evidence, to be a polyphyletic group, for they did not inherit their long muzzles from their most recent common ancestor. A "paraphyletic group" is a taxonomic grouping that *omits* one or more member(s) of a monophyletic group.

The third type of resemblance is referred to as "homoplasy," and the characters involved are called "homoplasic" or "homoplastic." The three causes of homoplasy are *convergent evolution*, *parallel evolution*, and *character reversal*. Convergent and parallel evolution are the same in principle. Both generate parts of the phenotype that look similar in two taxa, yet those similarities were not inherited from the most recent common ancestor of the taxa. The difference between parallel and convergent evolution is that "parallelism is the production of apparently identical traits by the same generative system and convergence involves the production of similar traits by different generative systems" (Wake 1996: xix). In other words, parallelisms occur in paraphyletic groups where the same character state evolves independently from similar starting points, both genetically and morphologically. Convergences occur in polyphyletic groups, where similar character states evolve from different ancestral states. A character reversal is when a character reverts to its more primitive condition, which gives the false impression that taxa are more closely related than they really are.

There is a fourth, potentially confusing, component to adult morphology. This comprises phenetic features that can alter in size and shape according to how active an individual organism is. For example, some of the phenotype linked with mastication will be modified if the teeth are lost on one side, so that chewing is concentrated on the remaining teeth. Likewise, the thickness of the shafts of long bones will increase if activity levels are chronically high. For instance, the cortical bone of the humerus in the dominant arm/hand of tennis players is thicker than that of the non-dominant side and hockey players on average have a more equal distribution of cortical bone around their femoral shafts than long-distance runners due to their greater range of movement both forwards and backwards as well as side to side (Jones et al. 1977; Saers et al. 2021). These are examples of *plasticity*. Plasticity refers to the ability to change in shape, size, or physiology in response to an extrinsic influence, such as the organism's environment. For example, plasticity in modern humans can be seen when comparing how individuals raised at different latitudes respond differently to hypoxic, low-oxygen, conditions. Some examples of phenotypic plasticity can also be caused by environmentally induced epigenetic effects, where an environmental trigger can change the expression of genes within an organism. This is common in plants, such as the *Arabidopsis*, which alters its response to nutrient levels using this mechanism, but it can also occur in human disease responses (Feinberg 2007; Flavahan et al. 2017). Function-related morphological differences (also known as "homoiologies") are a potential sources of the *character conflict* (the presence of characters consistent with a cladogram that is different from the most parsimonious one) that occurs in many cladistic analyses.

Cladistic Analysis: Where to Begin?

The first decision is what taxa (the cladistic term for each of the taxa included in a cladistic analysis is an "operational taxonomic unit" or OTU) to include in a cladistic analysis. These taxa make up the *ingroup*. The next step is to determine the morphology whose expression will be compared among the OTUs. The cladistic method requires that the phenotype be broken down into morphological units that provide information that is independent of all the other units. In practice, it is difficult to comply with this requirement. It is also in some ways counter-intuitive for, as we shall find, cladistic analysis depends on the fact that a particular branching pattern is supported by more than one character. However, the desirable correlations are those that are due to shared phylogenetic history; the correlations to be avoided are the ones that are due to reasons other than shared recent common ancestry (for instance, descriptive redundancy, homoplasy, or homoiology).

The morphological units are called "characters" and their different morphological expressions, which must vary among at least some of the taxa included in the analysis, are called "character states." Characters must have the same evolutionary and developmental basis among the OTUs included in the cladistic analysis. Character states must also be capable of being assessed objectively. This can be achieved by careful description, but some claim that the only objective way to assess character states is to use size or shape measurements.

Determining a Morphocline

The next task in a cladistic analysis is to determine the sequence of the states of each character, ranging from its most "primitive" expression – that is, its expression in the common ancestor of all the ingroup taxa – to the most "derived," or specialized, expression of that character. This is known as "polarization." Two criteria, "ontogenetic" and "outgroup," can be used to establish which of the character states is the primitive one, which is the most derived, and the sequence of different character states that connects them. The ontogenetic criterion assumes that a character state that more closely resembles the early stages of the ontogeny of an animal will be towards the primitive end of the morphocline. For example, no matter how complex the morphology of a tooth root eventually becomes, early in ontogeny all teeth have a single root. Thus, the ontogenetic criterion suggests that a single root is the primitive condition for the teeth of primates.

The outgroup criterion is based on the assumption of parsimony. This suggests that if any of the character states seen in the ingroup taxa are also seen in one or more closely related outgroup taxa, then that state is likely to have been the primitive condition for the ingroup. Outgroup taxa are chosen because of their previously determined close phylogenetic relationship to the OTUs being investigated as part of the "ingroup," and not on the basis of their phenetic resemblance to the taxa under investigation. Thus, the appropriate outgroup for a study of cetaceans (whales, dolphins, and porpoises) would be another mammal, not a bony fish, and the appropriate outgroup for a cladistic analysis of the living great apes would be one of the taxa in the clade that contains the extant gibbons and siamangs.

Generating and Comparing Cladograms

Once the character states are recorded and their polarity determined, the "topology" or shape of the cladogram can be determined. The two ways to do this are the Hennig method, in which the cladograms are based on a single character's expression across all taxa, and the Wagner method, in which cladograms are generated by comparing the distributions of all the characters, taxon by taxon. As a practical matter, most cladistic studies focus on analyses of all of the characters simultaneously.

There are two main methods for assembling a "consensus cladogram" from the individual character cladograms for the suite of characters used in an analysis of morphology (other methods exist, but they are typically applied to genetic data). The "maximum parsimony" method minimizes the independent acquisition of character states (or homoplasy) and the number of times when character states have to be reversed, so the consensus cladogram will be the cladogram with the fewest character state changes. Maximum likelihood analysis is another variant. The most recent development is Bayesian analysis, which optimizes branch lengths rather than tree length (Dembo et al. 2015). According to the second method – which is the "compatibility method" – the consensus cladogram is the one supported by the largest group of compatible characters (that is characters that result in the same cladogram). Most of the modern cladistic studies dealing with anatomical data focus on parsimony analysis.

Cladograms are conventionally compared using indices, either the "consistency index" (CI) or the "retention index" (RI). The consistency index is calculated so as to represent the minimum number of steps (or character state changes) necessary to explain the distribution of character states in the OTUs being analyzed, divided by the observed number of steps in a cladogram. The retention index is calculated as the maximum number of steps possible on a tree minus the observed number of steps, divided by the maximum number of steps possible on a tree, minus the minimum number of steps calculated from the data. The RI contains additional information about homoplasy compared to the CI and is not inversely related to tree length, as is the CI; both indices have their uses (Farris 1989). The third commonly used measure of the quality and information content of a cladogram, the "rescaled consistency index" (RCI), is the product of the RI and the CI. An index value of 1 suggests a "perfect" fit (that is one with no character conflict) and an index of 0.5 would mean that half the character appearances on the cladogram are due to reasons other than inheritance from the most recent common ancestor (reasons such as homoplasy or homoiology).

Once the shape, or topology, of a cladogram has been determined, the distribution of the character states can then be assessed. The shared primitive characters at the base of the cladogram are known, in Hennigian terminology, as "symplesiomorphies." So-called shared derived characters limited to the smaller, terminal, clades are called "synapomorphies."

Synapomorphies and symplesiomorphies are rank-specific homologies. That is, a synapomorphy that unites three taxa in a monophyletic group will be symplesiomorphic for any monophyletic taxa *within* the group. Unique character states that only appear in one taxon are known as "autapomorphies." As mentioned earlier, character states that arise independently (in other words, they appear in more than one clade, but they are not present in the most recent common ancestor of those clades) are known as "homoplasies."

A "total group" is a monophyletic group that includes every taxon that is more closely related to a living taxon than it is to any other living taxon. Fossil hominins are a total group, for they contain all the taxa more closely related to modern humans than to chimpanzees and bonobos. A "crown group" is the smallest monophyletic group that includes the living taxon in a clade. A "stem group" is a total group minus its crown group. In the case of hominids, the crown group would include modern humans, chimpanzees, bonobos, gorillas, orangutans, and all of their extinct branches leading back to their common ancestor, to the exclusion of extant lesser apes, or any stem taxa after the hominid root. This term is not easily defined within the hominin clade due to modern humans being the only living taxon. If *H. neanderthalensis* were still living, then the crown group for hominins could be easily defined as *H. sapiens, H. neanderthalensis*, and any branching taxa on each of their lineages leading back to the ancestral root of the two species.

CLASSIFICATION

Once hypotheses about the relationships among taxa have been generated – most are generated by using cladistic methods or by applying phenetic methods to 3D data – they can be used to inform the way species are grouped into genera and into higher taxa.

What Is a Genus?

A genus should be both a *clade* and a *grade*. To be a clade, a species grouping must consist of *all* the members of a monophyletic group. It should not contain species belonging to other monophyletic groups and it should not be missing any species that belong to a monophyletic group. To be a grade, all of the species in a species grouping must share the same adaptive regime. A clade is analogous to a *make* of car (all Ford cars share a recent common ancestor, the "Model T," not shared with any other make of car), whereas a grade is analogous to a *type* of car (the SUVs made by Lexus, Porsche, and Land Rover are functionally similar, yet they have different evolutionary histories and therefore have no recent exclusive common ancestor). However, not all species in the same grade have to be in the same genus, for a grade may contain species belonging to more than one monophyletic group or clade. The African apes, plus modern humans, are a clade, but not a grade; baboons are a grade, but not a clade. Others have suggested that genera should be defined by a certain time depth, but that would mean genera would be prone to additional, external, causes of instability. Under this scenario, comparable stipulations should apply to more inclusive taxonomic categories (tribe, family).

How Should Higher Taxa Be Defined?

Higher taxa should also be both clades and grades, and the same criteria that were used to define genera can be used to sort genera into higher taxa. Some researchers insist that cladistic hypotheses should be rigidly reflected in any classifications above the species level, but the problem with this approach is that the results of cladistic analyses are hypotheses and if a new classification had to be generated every time a new cladistic hypothesis was generated, it would result in classifications that are unhelpfully unstable. A particularly difficult classification problem concerns stem taxa, which are notoriously difficult to sort easily into groups that are both grades and clades. Some researchers have proposed using the category of "plesion," which allows taxa to be placed within a taxonomic hierarchy without assigning it a formal rank.

Different Perspectives Can Affect Taxonomic Hypotheses

It is obvious that at each stage in the complicated process just described, researchers can quite legitimately make different decisions and judgments that result in different conclusions about how many species should be recognized and how those species should be assembled into genera and higher taxa. It is often difficult to tell whether disagreements among biological anthropologists about classification are due to genuine differences in the way they interpret a particular part of the primate fossil record or whether they reflect different perspectives about what a species or a genus is.

Usually, close textual analysis of such wrangles reveals that both reasons play a part. Researchers who favor a more "anagenetic," or gradualistic, interpretation of the primate fossil record generally stress the importance of continuities in the fossil record and they tend to opt for fewer species. They are referred to informally as "lumpers." Researchers who favor a more "cladogenetic" – or punctuated equilibrium-based – interpretation of the primate fossil record generally stress the importance of discontinuities within the fossil record and tend to opt for more speciose taxonomic hypotheses. These latter are called "taxic" interpretations and the researchers who favor these interpretations are referred to informally as "splitters."

When all is said and done, taxonomic proposals, phylogenetic reconstructions, and classifications are hypotheses that will inevitably be tested and corroborated or revised as new evidence accumulates and as more effective analytical methods are developed. Such is the nature of science.

ACKNOWLEDGMENT

We are grateful to David Strait for his helpful suggestions.

REFERENCES

Adams, D., M. Collyer, A. Kaliontzopoulou, and E. Baken. "Geomorph: Software for Geometric Morphometric Analyses. R Package Version 4.0." 2021.

Baum, D. A., and S. Offner "Phylogenics and Tree-Thinking." *The American Biology Teacher* 70 (4) (2008): 222–229.

Bradley, B. J. "Reconstructing Phylogenies and Phenotypes: A Molecular View of Human Evolution." *Journal of Anatomy* 212 (2008): 337–353.

Braga, J., C. Samir, A. Fradi, et al. "Cochlear Shape Distinguishes Southern African Early Hominin Taxa with Unique Auditory Ecologies." *Scientific Reports* 11 (2021): 17018.

Cain, A. J. *Animal Species and Evolution.* Princeton: Princeton University Press, 1954.

Cracraft, J. "Species Concepts and Speciation Analysis." In *Current Ornithology.* Edited by R. F. Johnson, vol. 1. New York: Plenum Press, 1983.

Davies, T. W., Z. Alemseged, A. Gidna, et al . "Accessory Cusp Expression at the Enamel-Dentine Junction of Hominin Mandibular Molars." *Peer J* 9 (2021): e11415.

Dembo, M., N. J. Matzke, A. Ø. Mooers, and M. Collard. "Bayesian Analysis of a Morphological Supermatrix Sheds Light on Controversial Fossil Hominin Relationships." *Proceeding of the Royal Society B* 282 (2015): 20150943.

Dean, M. C., A. D. Beynon, J. F. Thackeray, and G. A. Macho. "Histological Reconstruction of Dental Development and Age at Death of a Juvenile *Paranthropus robustus* Specimen, SK 63, from Swartkrans, South Africa." *American Journal of Physical Anthropology* 91 (1993): 401–419.

de Queiroz, K. "Species Concepts and Species Delimitation." *Systematic Biology* 56, no. 6 (2007): 879–886.

Eldredge, N. "What, If Anything, Is a Species?" In *Species, Species Concepts, and Primate Evolution.* Edited by W. H. Kimbel and L. B. Martin, 3–20. New York: Plenum Press, 1993.

Farris, J. S. "The Retention Index and Homoplasy Excess." *Systematic Zoology* 38 (1989): 406–407.

Feinberg, A. P. "Phenotypic Plasticity and the Epigenetics of Human Disease." *Nature* 447 (2007): 433–440.

Flavahan, W. A., E. Gaskell, and B. E. Bernstein. "Epigenetic Plasticity and the Hallmarks of Cancer." *Science* 357 (2017): 6348.

Ghiselin, M. T. "Models in Phylogeny." In *Models in Paleobiology.* Edited by T. J. M. Schopf, 130–145. Freeman: Cooper, 1972.

Hennig, W. *Phylogenetic Systematics.* Chicago: University of Illinois Press, 1966.

Jolly, C. J. "A Proper Study for Mankind: Analogies from the Papionin Monkeys and Their Implications for Human Evolution." *Yearbook of Physical Anthropology* 44 (2001): 177–204.

Jones, H. H., J. D. Priest, W. C. Hayes, et al. "Humeral Hypertrophy in Response to Exercise." *Journal of Bone and Joint Surgery of America* 59 (1977): 204–208.

Klingenberg, C. P. "MorphoJ: An Integrated Software Package for Geometric Morphometrics." *Molecular Ecology Resources* 11 (2011): 353–357.

Kupczik, K., L. K. Delezene, and M. M. Skinner. "Mandibular Molar Root and Pulp Cavity Morphology in *Homo naledi* and Other Plio-Pleistocene Hominins." *Journal of Human Evolution* 130 (2019): 83–95.

Lautenschlager, S. "Reconstructing the Past: Methods and Techniques for the Digital Restoration of Fossils." *Royal Society Open Science* 3 (10) (2016): 160342.

Le Cabec, A., N. Tang, and P. Tafforeau. "Accessing Developmental Information of Fossil Hominin Teeth Using New Synchrotron Microtomography-Based Visualization Techniques of Dental Surfaces and Interfaces." *PLoS One* 10, no. 4 (2015): e0123019.

Mayr, E. *Systematics and the Origin of Species.* New York: Columbia University Press, 1942.

Mayr, E. *The Growth of Biological Thought: Diversity, Evolution and Inheritance.* Cambridge, MA: Harvard University Press, 1982.

Mayr, E., E. G. Linsley, and R. L. Usinger. *Methods and Principles of Systematic Zoology,* 1953.

Nixon, K. C., and Q. D. Wheeler. "An Amplification of the Phylogenetic Species Concept." *Cladistics* 6 (1990): 211–233.

Paterson, H. E. H. "The Recognition Concept of Species." In *Species and Speciation.* Edited by E. Vrba, 21–29. Cambridge, MA: MIT Press, 1985.

Ride, W. D. L., H. G. Cogger, C. Dupuis, et al., eds. *International Code of Zoological Nomenclature.* London: The Natural History Museum, 1999.

Saers, J. P., L. J. DeMars, N. B. Stephens, et al. "Combinations of Trabecular and Cortical Bone Properties Distinguish Various Loading Modalities Between Athletes and Controls." *American Journal of Physical Anthropology* 174 (2021): 434–450.

Simpson, G. G. *Principles of Animal Taxonomy.* New York: Columbia University Press/Oxford University Press, 1961.

Skinner, M. M., N. B. Stephens, Z. J. Tsegai, et al. "Human-like Hand Use in *Australopithecus africanus. Science* 347 (6220) (2015): 395–399.

Smith, A. B. *Systematics and the Fossil Record: Documenting Evolutionary Patterns.* Oxford: Blackwell, 1994.

Sokal, R. R., and T. J. Crovello. "The Biological Species Concept: A Critical Evaluation." *American Naturalist* 104 (1970): 127–153.

Spoor, F., N. Jeffery, and F. Zonneveld. "Using Diagnostic Radiology in Human Evolutionary Studies." *Journal of Anatomy* 197 (2000): 61–76.

Tafforeau, P., and T. M. Smith. "Nondestructive Imaging of Hominoid Dental Microstructure Using Phase Contrast X-Ray Synchrotron Microtomography." *Journal of Human Evolution* 54 (2007): 272–278.

Tattersall, I., and N. Eldredge. "Fact, Theory and Fantasy in Human Paleontology." *American Scientist* 65 (1977): 204–211.

Wake, D. B. "Introduction." In: *Homoplasy, the Recurrence of Similarity in Evolution.* Edited by M. J. Sanderson and L. Hufford, 17–25. San Diego: Academic Press, 1996.

Weaver, T. D., and P. Gunz. "Using Geometric Morphometric Visualizations of Directional Selection Gradients to Investigate Morphological Differentiation." *Evolution* 72 (2018): 838–850.

Wiley, E. O. "The Evolutionary Species Concept Reconsidered." *Systematic Zoology* 27 (1978): 17–25.

Wood, B. A. "A Palaeontological Model for Determining the Limits of Early Hominid Taxonomic Variability." *Palaeontologica Africana* 28 (1991): 71–77.

Wu, X., S. Pei, Y. Cai, et al. "Morphological Description and Evolutionary Significance of 300 ka Hominin Facial Bones from Hualongdong, China." *J. Hum. Evol.* 161 (2021): 103052.

CHAPTER 5

Diversity, Ancestry, and Evolution: The Genetics of Human Populations

John H. Relethford

INTRODUCTION

Population genetics is the mathematical theory of genetic changes in a population from one generation to the next. Like Mendelian genetics, population genetics is also concerned with the transmission of genetic information from one generation to the next – but for the entire breeding population, and not just for a specific pair of mates. The underlying models of population genetics can be applied to all organisms, including humans. The study of the genetics of human populations also incorporates the cultural dimension of human existence. The study of human population genetics today includes research on genetic diversity within and among populations, patterns of genetic ancestry and history in populations, the long-term evolution of the human species, and selection and genetic adaptation.

Population genetics theory looks at genetic change in a population by focusing on the frequency of different alleles (the different forms of a gene or DNA sequence) and on the way these frequencies change over time. Imagine, for example, that you are looking at the frequencies of two alleles, *A* and *B*, for a hypothetical genetic locus. You visit a population and you note that the frequency of the *A* allele is 60 percent and the frequency of the *B* allele is 40 percent. Assume that you come back a generation later to find that the frequencies of these alleles are now 58 percent *A* and 42 percent *B*. A small amount of evolution has taken place – the frequency of *A* has gone down a little bit and the frequency of *B* has gone up. Population genetics looks at the mechanisms by which this type of allele frequency change could take place. Studies of genetic variation within and among populations can then provide data to confirm the mechanism(s) of evolutionary change by comparing reality with theoretical expectations, a standard method of scientific research. The purpose of the present chapter is to review the application of population genetics theory and methods used to study genetic variation in human populations, present and past.

PRINCIPLES OF POPULATION GENETICS

Before looking more closely at how genetic change takes place within populations, it is useful to consider what is meant by a population. In an idealized sense, a population corresponds to a breeding population. In this context the population is usually defined as the local unit within which most mating takes place (keeping in mind that "most" is subjective). For many organisms, including humans, distinct geographic units are often used to delineate populations, such as different towns or villages. This works well in most contexts because, as in the case of many bisexual species, much of human mating is constrained by geography; you are more likely to choose a mate from nearby than one from farther away. Human mate choice can often be more complex, however, and the definition of a population may often have to be reconsidered if one has to deal with other influences on mate choice, such as ethnicity, religion, and social class (among others). In such cases, we often consider a larger population to be subdivided; that is, made up of a number of smaller groups.

What causes genetic change in populations? A principle of population genetics known as the Hardy-Weinberg equilibrium states that, under certain conditions, allele and genotype frequencies will remain constant from one generation to the next. When these conditions are not met, then change can occur in genotype and allele frequencies. One of the conditions of Hardy-Weinberg equilibrium is random mating within the population. When this condition is violated, as, for instance, when significant inbreeding (mating between close relatives) occurs within a population, the genotype frequencies are changed in the next generation. Specifically, inbreeding increases the frequencies of homozygotes and decreases the frequency of heterozygotes relative to the case of complete random mating. (Individuals who have inherited the same allele from both parents are homozygotes and individuals who have inherited a different allele from their parents are heterozygotes.) Deviations from random mating affect only the genotype frequencies, but not the underlying allele frequencies.

Hardy-Weinberg equilibrium assumes no changes in allele frequencies over time (that is, it assumes there is no evolution). Students first learning about Hardy-Weinberg equilibrium often wonder about the importance of learning about a mathematical model that predicts no evolutionary change (Weiss and Kurland 2007). The key point here is to remember that the Hardy-Weinberg equilibrium provides population geneticists with a null model by which they were able to figure out exactly how evolutionary change could occur.

In population genetics, evolution is defined as a change in allele frequencies over time. By examining the assumptions of Hardy-Weinberg equilibrium, population geneticists were able to derive four mechanisms that cause changes in allele frequencies, known as the evolutionary forces:

1. Mutation: random change in the DNA sequence, which is the ultimate source of all new genetic variation (where new alleles come from).
2. Genetic drift: random change in allele frequency due to the sampling effect (the allele frequencies of an offspring generation are not likely to be the same as the parent generation). For example, an allele in the parental generation might be 40 percent but drift to 37 percent due to chance in the offspring generation. The direction of change is random; allele frequencies can drift up or down. Smaller populations are more likely to show the effect of genetic drift than larger populations in a given generation.
3. Natural selection: differences in the survival and reproduction of different genotypes, causing changes in allele frequencies. Some individuals are more likely to survive and reproduce, and therefore pass along their alleles more often. Selection acts on genetic differences in mortality and/or fertility.

4. Gene flow: the mixing of gene pools from different populations due to migration between them. Gene flow tends to make populations more similar to each other genetically. Gene flow can also introduce new alleles into a population.

Hardy-Weinberg equilibrium assumes that there is no mutation, drift, selection, or gene flow, making it a baseline for evaluating possible patterns of evolutionary change.

It is important to remember that the evolutionary forces can interact in many different and often complex ways. For example, a new mutation will often be lost in a small population because of genetic drift, but in some cases a mutation can actually increase dramatically due to genetic drift. To consider another example, genetic differences between populations may increase as a result of genetic drift, but are reduced by gene flow, which leads to little net change. New mutations may also decrease or increase in frequency due to selection. Evolutionary biologists continue to debate the relative impact of drift and selection on genetic variation.

The interaction of evolutionary forces affects the level of genetic diversity within a population. Mutation increases diversity within a population through the introduction of something new (the mutation itself), which was not there before. Gene flow can also increase diversity in a population when new alleles enter it from another population (for instance, a mutation appears in one group and then spreads to another group via gene flow). On the other hand, genetic drift reduces variation because drift will lead over time to alleles becoming fixed (= 100 percent) or extinct (= 0 percent). Either way, the level of genetic diversity will tend to decline over time in a population due to genetic drift. Finally, natural selection can act to increase or decrease genetic variation, depending on initial allele frequencies and on the specific direction of natural selection in a given population.

The interaction of the evolutionary forces also affects the level of variation among populations. (Here, variation is the differences in allele frequencies among populations.) In general, gene flow reduces the genetic difference between a pair of populations because, as populations mix, they become more similar to each other, by analogy with the mixing of different colors of paint. Although gene flow tends to decrease genetic differences among populations, genetic drift tends to increase genetic differences over time, as drift occurs randomly in each population. Natural selection can act to increase or decrease genetic differences among populations, depending on the nature of selection and on differences in environments. In human populations, for example, differences in skin color have increased between some populations because, in our past, darker skin has been selected in populations at or near the equator, whereas lighter skin has been selected in populations further away from the equator.

Although it is mathematically and pedagogically useful to learn about the different evolutionary forces one at a time, we need to remember that the genetic makeup of a population, and the genetic relationship between populations within a species, are the net effect of all of the evolutionary forces acting at the same time. As demographic and/or environmental conditions change, the net balance of the evolutionary forces can also change. Changes in human cultural adaptations can also affect this balance, as illustrated in several examples later in this chapter. See Relethford (2012) for further discussion of the mathematics of human population genetics.

A BRIEF HISTORY OF HUMAN POPULATION GENETICS

The mathematical theory of population genetics developed in the early twentieth century due largely to the work of Sewall Wright, Sir Ronald Fisher, and J. B. S. Haldane (Provine 1971). Population genetics theory provided a link between Darwin's model of natural selection and Mendelian inheritance. These theoretical developments, combined with field studies and laboratory experiments on microevolution, led to a synthesis that combined evolutionary insights from a variety of fields, including zoology, botany, ecology, and paleontology. As population genetics developed, application to human populations also became more common. See Szathmary (2018) for a detailed history of population genetics research, specifically in anthropology, over the past century.

Many initial studies of human populations focused on red blood cell groups, which are genetic traits defined by antibody–antigen reactions on the surface of red blood cells, including well-known systems such as the ABO, Rhesus, and MN blood groups, as well as many others. By the early 1950s, blood group analysis was being used to address questions of population affinity and history (Boyd 1950). These traits were the first discovered genetic markers. (Genetic markers are defined broadly here as genes or DNA sequences whose location can be identified in the genome.)

By the early 1970s, the use of laboratory methods such as electrophoresis (the separation of proteins on the basis of molecular size and electrical charge) had led to the discovery of a large number of red blood cell proteins and enzymes as well as blood plasma proteins showing variation among human populations (Crawford 1973). At the same time, the anthropological nature of studies of human population genetics became more widely apparent and the phrase "anthropological genetics," first coined by Derek Roberts (1965), became more widespread. The scope of investigations in human population genetics was outlined in the classic edited volume *Methods and Theories of Anthropological Genetics* (Crawford and Workman 1973). Several other key works show the continued growth of human population genetics and the vast array of studies resulting from an expanding body of data on blood cell and plasma protein genetic markers (collectively referred to as classical genetic markers). Other key works presented then-emergent approaches in human population genetics, including Morton (1973), Mielke and Crawford (1980), and Crawford and Mielke (1982).

By the late 1980s, the primary focus of human population genetics began to move away from classical genetic markers. With the development of new methods in molecular biology that allowed discovery of a huge number of DNA markers, a more precise view on human genetic variation developed, as seen in more recent reviews of the field (Crawford 2007; O'Rourke 2019). The direct assessment of genetic variation down to the level of specific base pairs was now possible, compared with the classic genetic markers that had provided an indirect view of genetic diversity by focusing on blood group, protein, and enzyme genotypes. In addition, the analysis of DNA markers that are not subject to recombination, such as mitochondrial DNA (inherited only from one's mother) and Y-chromosome DNA (inherited only from father to son), has further revolutionized studies of human migration and ancestry.

Literally millions of new genetic markers are now being described and our species' entire genome is being compared with those of our close relatives, the African apes. Further, the ability to extract ancient DNA (aDNA) from fossils has provided data on human genetic variation in the past, which has helped address questions concerning past evolutionary relationship to other human relatives, such as the Neandertals (Liu et al. 2021).

THE SCOPE OF HUMAN POPULATION GENETICS RESEARCH

There have been several major areas of study in human population genetics. One area is the study of population structure, which looks at the effect of geographic, demographic, and cultural influences on the genetic relationship between individuals and populations. How is a population structured and how does this affect genetic variation? Populations are not typically homogeneous groups within which random mating takes place. Instead, they are frequently subdivided into a number of smaller units. As noted earlier, human populations are frequently subdivided by geographic location, social class, ethnicity, language differences, and other factors, and the study of population structure seeks to determine the genetic impact of these factors. Population structure was a major focus of much early work in anthropological genetics (Crawford and Mielke 1982; Morton 1973).

Another major (though related) area of study is the analysis of population origins and history. That is, what are the ancestral origins of a population? How are populations related to one another over time? Which populations are most closely related to each other and what are the historical reasons for these relationships? Our focus here is on the origin and evolution of populations, and quite often such studies are used to help answer historical and prehistorical questions.

Studies of population structure and history both focus on overall patterns of genetic similarity among groups that reflect the interaction between mutation, gene flow, and genetic drift. Where possible, the objective is to get an estimate of genetic similarity averaged over as many different loci as possible and to look at neutral traits – those not affected by natural selection (or presumed to be unaffected, or minimally affected, by it). Natural selection in this context is noise interfering with the ability of the researcher to discover the signal, which is a picture of population structure or history. For example, one would not want to base interpretations of population affinity on the frequency of the lactase persistence allele that facilitates digestion of milk, which has been selected for in populations with a history of dairy farming. If we find two populations that have a high and similar frequency of the lactase persistence allele and we do not take into account the action of natural selection, we might incorrectly infer that the two populations are related, when in fact they may both have higher frequencies because of a similar adaptation to diet. As another example, consider skin color. Both sub-Saharan Africans and Melanesians have dark skin color, but this common phenotype cannot be used to argue for a close historical connection between the two, because both populations have dark skin color because of adaptation to a similar environment: they live near the equator, where dark skin helps protect against the damaging effects of ultraviolet radiation.

In studies of human population structure and history, we want to exclude such traits because they would distort the signal of population relatedness that we are seeking. In other cases, however, the situation will be reversed, and the objective will be to detect and analyze natural selection. In such cases, what counts as signal and what counts as noise is reversed. Studies of natural selection are interested in the history of a specific trait and in how it originated and evolved rather than the overall genetic history of a population (Relethford 2004a). Several examples of recent natural selection in human populations are described later in this chapter.

In addition to advances in studies of DNA markers, progress has also been made using information on quantitative traits such as craniofacial, dental, and anthropometric measures in a population-genetic context. Analysis of such traits is sometimes ignored in studies of population genetics because these traits are affected by environmental and developmental factors. Although genetic markers are preferred for many studies, analysis of quantitative traits can also be valuable (Relethford 2007). Comparison of patterns of variation in quantitative traits and genetic markers provides information on the relative influence of genetics and environment on quantitative traits. A number of studies have shown that, although quantitative traits are affected by environmental and developmental factors, this influence does not erase patterns of genetic relationship between populations (Relethford 2004a). Thus, quantitative traits can be used successfully in analyses of population structure and history, often in studies of skeletal biology, where adequate samples of ancient DNA may not be available.

All of the areas of research in human population genetics are clearly anthropological in nature, and not just because the species of interest are human beings. The anthropological nature of human population genetics is apparent in every avenue of study. Mate choice, for example, is something that is affected by cultural factors. Marriage preferences and rules affect levels of inbreeding, and sociocultural variables such as ethnicity, religion, and social class (among others) can have a direct genetic impact in terms of inbreeding and gene flow. Culture also affects demography, specifically the size and growth of the population, which in turn can affect the action of genetic drift. Cultural adaptations can change the nature of genetic adaptations, thus having a direct effect on patterns of natural selection; as humans change their cultural and physical environment, they can change the rate and direction of natural selection. In short, human population genetics is yet one more way of looking at the traditional anthropological view of interactions between culture, biology, and nature.

Although much of the underlying genetic and mathematical basis of human population genetics is the same as that of any other organisms, be they fruit flies or guinea pigs, there are also methods that apply specifically to humans. Gene flow, for example, is often much easier to study in human populations because one can simply ask a person about the birthplace of one's parents, whereas tracking gene flow in other species is more complicated. A number of demographic measures (births, deaths, population size) are also often easier to track in human populations, particularly where there are written records.

The specific nature of demographic data from human populations allows additional population genetic methods. One example is migration matrix analysis, where predictions of the balance between gene flow and genetic drift are made on the basis of migration patterns and population size (see Rogers and Harpending 1986). This method allows for the comparison between patterns of genetic variation that are based on recent demographic patterns and those observed from genetic data (e.g., Jorde et al. 1982). Genealogical data are also useful in studies of human population genetics, providing insight into patterns of inbreeding and genetic drift (e.g., Cavalli-Sforza et al. 2004). An additional source of data on human population genetics that is uniquely human is surnames, which can be used to reconstruct inbreeding and population affinities to a limited extent in populations where surname inheritance mimics genetic inheritance (Lasker 1985; Relethford 1988). For example, in some cultures one's last name is inherited through the father's line, analogous to the inheritance in males of the Y chromosome.

The remainder of this chapter focuses on selected examples of some of the past and current studies of human population genetics conducted by anthropologists. These examples are not meant to provide either a comprehensive review of the literature or a detailed examination of selected case studies. Instead, the purpose here is to give a flavor of some of the three major avenues of research in human population genetics: population structure, population history, and natural selection.

EXAMPLES OF STUDIES OF HUMAN POPULATION STRUCTURE

As noted earlier, human populations are not homogenous randomly mating units, but are instead divided into a number of subpopulations. We want to know how much the subpopulations are genetically different and if there is any pattern in genetic differences (such as those reflecting geography, for example). Two measures are of interest in studies of subdivided populations. One is the degree of genetic differentiation among the subpopulations, F_{ST}, where higher values of F_{ST} indicate a greater genetic impact of subdivision (although see Long and Kittles 2003 for a discussion of limitations on inferences based on F_{ST}). The second measure of interest is the pattern of genetic differentiation, usually assessed using a measure of genetic distance (differences among populations) that tells us which subpopulations are most closely related to each other, and by how much.

As noted above, subdivision can occur because of sociocultural factors. For example, studies of human population structure have looked at religion (Crawford et al. 1995), social class (Harrison 1995), and language differences (Friedlaender 1975), among other factors. By far the most widely studied aspect of population structure has been the effect of geographic distance. As shown in numerous studies, geographic distance limits gene flow, such that human populations in many cases tend to be genetically most similar to their geographic neighbors and less similar to populations farther away – a phenomenon known as isolation by distance, which is also seen in many other organisms. Greater amounts of geographic isolation result in greater levels of genetic differentiation among populations. Isolation by distance also results in a correlation between measures of geographic and genetic distance. Some of the many early studies of isolation by distance in human populations are referenced in Jorde (1980), Crawford and Mielke (1982), and Cavalli-Sforza et al. (1994).

EXAMPLES OF STUDIES OF HUMAN POPULATION HISTORY

Genetic data have been used to investigate questions of historical origin for local, regional, continental, and global levels of analysis. (See Rutherford 2017 and Relethford and Bolnick 2018 for general surveys.) Many early studies of population history used classical genetic markers and quantitative traits, most often drawing inferences regarding population origins and affinities from analyses of genetic distance. The rapid discovery of an immense number of DNA markers allowed even greater precision in answering questions of ancestral origin, in part because of their use in tracking mutations across time and space, providing a record of past migrations.

In the past decade, the study of human population history has advanced even farther with studies of ancient DNA, which have provided a direct window into past genetic variation. Before the advent of ancient DNA analysis, events in a population's past were inferred from patterns of present-day (or very recent) variation. We would look at the present to see if an observed variation was compatible with likely past events, such as population expansions, migration, changes in population size, and others. Present-day genetic variation was thus interpreted as "reflections of our past" (Relethford and Bolnick 2018). Obviously, this can get tricky if a number of different models can realistically explain observed variation. Ancient DNA gives us a picture of genetic variation at more than one point in time. This window on the past, combined with the fine-grained assessment of genetic variation (such as DNA sequences), has meant that ancient DNA analysis has provided, and continues to provide, unique insights into past population history. At present, we are still seeing the beginnings of this revolution in the reconstruction of population history.

Many studies of population history focus on the initial origin of populations. One example is the origin of the first Americans. For decades, biological data – including cranial measures, dental measures, classical genetic markers – and archaeological evidence have pointed to an origin in Northeast Asia (Crawford 1998). DNA markers (mitochondrial, Y-chromosome, and autosomal) from present-day populations have confirmed this hypothesis (see Relethford and Bolnick 2018 for a summary). Further, studies of ancient DNA dating back thousands of years ago support genetic continuity between past and present Native Americans and Siberian populations, again reflecting a Northeast Asian origin (Raghavan et al. 2015; Rasmussen et al. 2014). Genetic and archaeological studies continue to seek greater resolution of the movement of humans into the New World, including questions concerning the number, route(s), and timing of migration events. Recent studies of ancient DNA suggest a model of a single wave of migration into Beringia (the region between Siberia and the northwestern part of the Americas). A current view is that human populations remained in Beringia for a period of time, followed by divergence and movement into the Americas around 20,000 years ago (Moreno-Mayar et al. 2018).

Another example of genetics and population history concerns the origin of Polynesian populations. Archaeological evidence shows that humans dispersed out of Southeast Asia eastward into the Pacific starting about 5,000 years ago. Seafaring skills and outrigger canoes allowed the ancestors of modern-day Polynesians to spread rapidly across the Pacific Ocean, settling as far away as New Zealand, Hawaii, and Easter Island. Because the early Polynesians expanded past Melanesia, a region settled tens of thousands of years earlier, the question has arisen as to exactly how fast the Polynesians expanded and if they interbred with Melanesian populations during their expansion. The origin of Polynesians has often been discussed in terms of a rapid expansion with little if any interbreeding (the express train model) versus a slower expansion with more Melanesian gene flow (the slow boat model). Early genetic studies were difficult to resolve, as analyses of mitochondrial DNA supported the express train model and analyses of Y-chromosome DNA supported the slow boat model. One difficulty of mitochondrial DNA and Y-chromosome DNA studies is that they each rely on a single locus and may not always provide a clear picture of overall genetic affinity. More recent studies based on autosomal DNA markers point to the majority of ancestry coming from an expansion out of East Asia from west to east across the Pacific, as well as some mixture with Melanesian populations (Choin et al. 2021; Ioannidis et al. 2021; Kayser et al. 2008; Wollstein et al. 2010). It has also been suggested that the differences between mitochondrial and Y-chromosome DNA might reflect sex differences in migration and Melanesian admixture following an initial Polynesian expansion (Relethford and Bolnick 2018).

Genetic analysis of population history has also been used to investigate hypotheses generated from archaeological evidence. An example is the nature of the spread of agriculture into Europe. The archaeological record shows that agriculture began spreading out of the Middle East into Europe about 9,000 years ago, moving in a northwest direction over the next several thousand years. What was less clear, however, was exactly how this happened. One model (demic diffusion) proposes that farming populations expanded out of the Middle East into Europe, spreading both agriculture and their genes as they mixed with pre-existing populations in Europe. Another model (cultural diffusion) suggests that agriculture spread as a new idea adopted by more and more populations over time, but without the actual movement of populations. Both models account for the spread of agriculture as a new cultural idea, but under the demic diffusion model, both genes and culture spread across Europe, whereas under cultural diffusion only the idea spread. Therefore, the demic diffusion model predicts that genetic traits should show the same geographic pattern (a gradient from southeast to northwest), whereas there would be no correlation with genetics under cultural diffusion. Spatial analysis of allele frequencies of classical genetic markers has shown a gradient from southeast to northwest, paralleling the spread of agriculture and supporting the demic diffusion model (Cavalli-Sforza et al. 1993). However, genetic studies of both classical and DNA markers have also shown that there were also other major migrations that shaped the genetic history of European populations, including migrations from east to west across Eurasia that might be associated with the spread of Indo-European languages. Studies of ancient DNA have been instrumental in showing the complex population history of Europe over many millennia that has involved much more than just an expansion out of the Middle East (De Barros Damgaard et al. 2018; Olalde et al. 2018).

Studies of human population history often look at the admixture of different human groups that come together for a variety of historical reasons; these include, but are not limited to, colonization, slavery, warfare, and trade. The result is admixed populations with complex patterns of ancestry, often from source populations that are widely scattered. The contact of Europeans with native populations in the New World led to varying degrees of mixture between Native American, European, and African populations (Relethford and Bolnick 2018).

One example of admixture analysis has been the study of the population genetics of African American populations. The enslavement and transportation of Africans to the New World led to gene flow between African and European populations. Admixture studies have long used classical genetic markers to estimate the approximate percentage of European ancestry in African American populations, with further insight provided by more recent analysis of DNA markers. Although all of these studies show that the African American genetic diversity has been affected by varying levels of European admixture, they also show that this variation cannot be characterized by a single number for all African Americans. Instead, genetic studies show that there is a great deal of variation in European ancestry, varying not only from one population to the next, but also among individuals within populations (Parra et al. 1998, 2001). More recent DNA analyses show that the level of European ancestry in African Americans varies across individuals from zero to a majority of ancestry (Bryc et al. 2010, 2015). These studies show that a culturally defined group such as African Americans actually encompasses a wide range of genetic histories and that treating African Americans (or any other group) as biologically homogeneous is incorrect.

GLOBAL PATTERNS OF GENETIC VARIATION AND THE ORIGIN OF MODERN HUMANS

An increasing number of studies have looked at the relationship between genetic variation, history, and geography on a global basis, using the findings to make inferences regarding the origin and dispersal of our species (Relethford 2013). Most anthropologists interpret the fossil record as showing an African origin, as the earliest known anatomically modern human forms are found in Africa at least 200,000 years ago, much earlier than elsewhere in the world. (Some recent fossil data suggest that some modern anatomical traits emerged even earlier in Africa.) Over the past two decades, population-genetic analyses have produced several lines of evidence that support an African origin of our species. Analytic methods have been developed that use DNA sequences to reconstruct gene trees, which show the evolutionary history of genetic mutations and how these mutations are related. Gene trees can be used to estimate information on the geographic origin and timing of our most recent common ancestor. In essence, researchers look at the geographic distribution of mutations to infer where the oldest mutations arose (and when). A number of studies have shown an African root (origin) for these gene trees, which is compatible with the idea of an African origin of our species.

An African origin is also compatible with the observation that DNA markers (as well as some quantitative traits) show higher levels of diversity in Africa than elsewhere. These regional differences in diversity have been interpreted as a reflection of the evolutionary history of our species. Under an African origin model, human populations existed for a longer time in Africa than elsewhere, and these populations had more time to accumulate mutations, which led to an increase in genetic diversity over time. Later, when modern human populations began expanding out of Africa, the initially small group of founders who dispersed out of Africa would have had reduced diversity, as small founding groups usually lose diversity because of genetic drift. Thus, modern human populations outside of Africa would have had less time to accumulate as many mutations, and therefore the pattern would be the one we see today, of higher diversity in Africa. Further, there is a geographic pattern of diversity in our species, with levels of genetic diversity decreasing with geographic distance from Africa. This pattern might be due to a series of sequential founding events, whereby new populations split off from older populations as our species dispersed (Ramachandran et al. 2005).

Globally, there is a strong relationship between genetic distance and geographic distance, particularly after adjusting for known routes of migration of early humans (for instance, using the geographic distance associated with movement from Asia to the New World via Siberia rather than a straight-line distance across the oceans). The correlation between genetics and geography is seen in classical genetic markers, DNA markers, and craniometric traits (Relethford 2004b). This relationship is due to a geographic pattern structured by the dispersal of modern humans out of Africa and the limiting effect of geographic distance on gene flow (isolation by distance).

Although by the early 2000s, genetic and fossil evidence pointed to an initial African origin, debate continued as to what happened after modern humans began expanding out of Africa and encountered archaic humans outside of Africa, such as the Neandertals of Europe and the Middle East. For years, some argued for complete replacement of archaic humans by modern humans whereas others suggested some degree of interbreeding, whereby archaic genes were assimilated into the gene pool of modern humans (Smith et al. 2005). In recent years, ancient DNA analysis has settled the question by showing us that there was admixture with non-African archaic human populations such as the Neandertals. For example, the sequencing of a Neandertal genome (Green et al. 2010) revealed that Neandertals interbred with early modern humans before the Neandertals died out. As a consequence, present-day human populations outside of sub-Saharan Africa typically have an average of about two percent Neandertal ancestry. This geographic pattern can be explained by the first modern humans dispersing out of Africa interbreeding with Neandertals in the Middle East after they had left Africa. Thus, all populations expanding into Eurasia and beyond carried Neandertal genes with them.

The genetic history of ancient modern humans has more recently shown even greater complexity, with genetic evidence of ancestry in modern humans that came from the Denisovans, an ancient population that lived in Eastern Asia for which we have ancient DNA but few directly associated fossils. Some present-day human populations have Denisovan ancestry in addition to Neandertal ancestry, whereas some (e.g., western Eurasians) have only Neandertal ancestry, and sub-Saharan Africans have neither. Ancient DNA also shows us that the Neandertals and Denisovans interbred with each other in addition to modern human ancestors. Finally, there is DNA evidence that points to other, thus far unknown, populations (often referred to as ghost populations). It appears that we are converging on a picture of an expansion out of Africa by the first anatomically modern humans, followed by varying low levels of admixture from pre-existing archaic human populations (Liu et al. 2021; Slon et al. 2018).

STUDIES OF RECENT NATURAL SELECTION IN HUMAN POPULATIONS

Studies of the history of specific genes often focus on the role of natural selection, particularly in recent human evolution, where population dispersals, adaptations to widely different environments, and cultural revolutions, such as the origin and spread of agriculture and civilization, could lead to genetic changes in human populations. For example, the dispersal of humans into different environments has led to major differences in human skin color because of varying levels of ultraviolet radiation. In populations at or near the equator, selection has favored darker skin for protection against the damaging effects of too much ultraviolet radiation, such as folate deficiency, sunburn, and skin cancer. For populations whose ancestors dispersed far from the equator, where ultraviolet radiation levels are lower, the problem was that they had too little exposure to ultraviolet radiation, which would have led to a reduction in vitamin-D levels; hence selection for lighter skin (Jablonski and Chaplin 2000).

Genetic responses to changing cultural conditions have also been a focus of studies of natural selection in human populations. A classic example in anthropology is Livingstone's (1958) analysis of the distribution of the sickle cell hemoglobin allele (*S*) in West Africa. Higher frequency of the sickle cell allele is found in populations that have experienced frequent malaria, because individuals with one copy of this allele are resistant to malarial infection and have higher fitness than individuals with either no *S* alleles (normal hemoglobin, but prone to malaria) or two *S* alleles (leading to the genetic disease sickle cell anemia). The case of the sickle cell allele and malaria is a classic example of balancing selection, where having one copy of an allele gives higher fitness than having none or two copies. Livingstone went further in his analysis, outlining the way in which humans changed the environment by bringing horticulture into the area several thousand years ago; this created more favorable conditions for the spread of the mosquito population that carried the malaria parasite. As malaria spread, people with one copy of the *S* allele were selected for, leading to an increase in the frequency of *S*. Thus, cultural change led to environmental change, which in turn led to genetic change.

Another example of recent human evolution through natural selection is lactase persistence in populations with a history of dairy farming. As mammals, humans produce the enzyme lactase to digest milk sugar from breastfeeding. The normal pattern is to cease production of lactase early in life after weaning. In human populations that have become reliant on dairy farming, there has been selection for an allele that allows for the production of lactase throughout adult life, as the ability to digest milk ensures additional nutrition and water. Recent analyses show that different mutations leading to lactase persistence have been selected for in different parts of the world over the past 7,000 years, which is the estimated age of these mutations (Tishkoff et al. 2007).

Diet-related natural selection has also been explored in studies of copy number variants of the salivary amylase gene (*AMY1*), involved in starch digestion. (Copy number variants are repeated sections of the genome.) Perry et al. (2007) found that people from populations with a high-starch diet have more copies of *AMY1* than people in populations with a low-starch diet. This genetic difference might reflect adaptation to diet, although this hypothesis has been questioned (Fernández and Wiley 2017).

As research on molecular genetics continues, we are likely to see an increasing number of examples of recent selection in human evolution. Statistical analysis of the human genome suggests that more of our genome has been shaped by natural selection than was thought to be the case several decades ago. Contrary to the oft-stated view that human evolution no longer occurs, natural selection will continue and, given the huge size of our species, the potential for new mutations with every generation is higher than ever (Hawks et al. 2007). As is the case for the study of population history, continuing research using ancient DNA will undoubtably provide the necessary time depth for assessing past natural selection in human populations more accurately.

CONCLUSION

The study of human population genetics has grown considerably since the 1960s, as has our knowledge of the cultural, demographic, geographic, and ecological factors that affect genetic variation at different levels, ranging from local populations to the entire species. New sources of data have continued to provide new windows on genetic variation, as have new analytic methods and advances in the mathematical theory of genetic change. At present, the field is increasingly focused on the immense amount of data becoming available from the revolution in molecular genetics. The challenge for future generations is to find new and efficient ways of analyzing these data without drowning in them.

REFERENCES

Boyd, W. C. *Genetics and the Races of Man.* Boston: Little, Brown and Company, 1950.

Bryc, K., A. Auton, M. R. Nelson, et al. "Genome-wide Patterns of Population Structure and Admixture in West Africans and African Americans." *Proceedings of the National Academy of Sciences of the United States of America* 107 (2010): 786–791.

Bryc, K., E. Y. Durand, J. M. Macpherson, et al. "The Genetic Ancestry of African Americans, Latinos, and European Americans Across the United States." *American Journal of Human Genetics* 96 (2015): 37–53.

Cavalli-Sforza, L. L., P. Menozzi, and A. Piazza. "Demic Expansions and Human Evolution." *Science* 259 (1993): 639–646.

Cavalli-Sforza, L. L., P. Menozzi, and A. Piazza. *The History and Geography of Human Genes.* Princeton: Princeton University Press, 1994.

Cavalli-Sforza, L. L., A. Moroni, and G. Zei. *Consanguinity, Inbreeding, and Genetic Drift in Italy.* Princeton: Princeton University Press, 2004.

Choin, J., J. Mendoza-Revilla, L. R. Arauna, et al. "Genomic Insights into Population History and Biological Adaptation in Oceania." *Nature* 592 (2021): 583–589.

Crawford, M. H. "The Use of Genetic Markers of the Blood in the Study of the Evolution of Human Populations." In *Methods and Theories of Anthropological Genetics.* Edited by M. H. Crawford and P. L. Workman, 19–38. Albuquerque: University of New Mexico Press, 1973.

Crawford, M. H. *The Origins of Native Americans: Evidence from Anthropological Genetics.* Cambridge: Cambridge University Press, 1998.

Crawford, M. H., ed. *Anthropological Genetics: Theory, Methods and Applications.* Cambridge: Cambridge University Press, 2007.

Crawford, M. H., and J. H. Mielke, eds. *Current Developments in Anthropological Genetics,* Vol. 2. *Ecology and Population Structure.* New York: Plenum Press, 1982.

Crawford, M. H., and P. L. Workman, eds. *Methods and Theories of Anthropological Genetics.* Albuquerque: University of New Mexico Press, 1973.

Crawford, M. H., T. Koertevlyessy, R. Huntsman, et al. "Effects of Religion, Economics, and Geography on Genetic Structure of Fogo Island, Newfoundland." *American Journal of Human Biology* 7 (1995): 437–451.

De Barros Damgaard, P., N. Marchi, S. Rasmussen, et al. "137 Ancient Human Genomes from across the Eurasian Steppes." *Nature* 557 (2018): 369–374.

Fernández, C. I., and A. S. Wiley. "Rethinking the Starch Digestion Hypothesis for *AMY1* Copy Number Variation in Humans." *American Journal of Physical Anthropology* 163 (2017): 645–657.

Friedlaender, J. S. *Patterns of Human Variation: The Demography, Genetics, and Phenetics of Bougainville Islanders.* Cambridge: Harvard University Press, 1975.

Green, R., J. Krause, A. W. Briggs, et al. "A Draft Sequence of the Neandertal Genome." *Science* 328 (2010): 710–722.

Harrison, G. A. *The Human Biology of the English Village.* Oxford: Oxford University Press, 1995.

Hawks, J., E. T. Wang, G. M. Cochran, et al. "Recent Acceleration of Human Adaptive Evolution." *Proceedings of the National Academy of Sciences of the United States of America* 104 (2007): 20753–20758.

Ioannidis, A. G., J. Blanco-Portillo, K. Sandoval, et al. "Paths and Timing of the Peopling of Polynesia Inferred from Genomic Networks." *Nature* 597 (2021): 522–526.

Jablonski, N. G., and G. Chaplin. "The Evolution of Human Skin Coloration." *Journal of Human Evolution* 39 (2000): 57–106.

Jorde, L. B. "The Genetic Structure of Subdivided Human Populations: A Review." In *Current Developments in Anthropological Genetics*, vol. 1. *Theory and Methods*. Edited by J. H. Mielke and M. H. Crawford, 135–208. New York: Plenum Press, 1980.

Jorde, L. B., P. Workman, and A. W. Eriksson. "Genetic Microevolution in the Åland Islands, Finland. In *Current Developments in Anthropological Genetics*, vol. 2. *Ecology and Population Structure*. Edited by M. H. Crawford and J. H. Mielke, 333–366. New York: Plenum Press, 1982.

Kayser, M., O. Lao, K. Saar, et al. "Genome-wide Analysis Indicates More Asian Than Melanesian Ancestry of Polynesians." *American Journal of Human Genetics* 82 (2008): 194–198.

Lasker, G. W. *Surnames and Genetic Structure*. Cambridge: Cambridge University Press, 1985.

Liu, Y., X. Mao, J. Krause, et al. "Insights into Human History from the First Decade of Ancient Human Genomics." *Science* 373 (2021): 1479–1484.

Livingstone, F. B. "Anthropological Implications of Sickle Cell Gene Distribution in West Africa." *American Anthropologist* 60 (1958): 533–562.

Long, J. C., and R. A. Kittles. "Human Genetic Diversity and the Nonexistence of Human Races." *Human Biology* 75 (2003): 449–471.

Mielke, J. H., and M. H. Crawford, eds. *Current Developments in Anthropological Genetics*, vol. 1. *Theory and Methods*. New York: Plenum Press, 1980.

Moreno-Mayar, J. V., B. A. Potter, L. Vinner, et al. "Terminal Pleistocene Alaskan Genome Reveals First Founding Population of Native Americans." *Nature* 553 (2018): 203–207.

Morton, N. E., ed. "Genetic Structure of Populations." In *Population Genetics Monographs*, vol. III. Honolulu: University of Hawaii Press, 1973.

Olalde, I., S. Brace, M. E. Allentoft, et al. "The Beaker Phenomenon and the Genomic Transformation of Northwest Europe." *Nature* 555 (2018): 190–196.

O'Rourke, D. H., ed. *A Companion to Anthropological Genetics*. Hoboken: Wiley-Blackwell, 2019.

Parra, E. J., A. Marcini, J. Akey, et al. "Estimating African American Admixture Proportions by Use of Population-Specific Alleles." *American Journal of Human Genetics* 63 (1998): 1839–1851.

Parra, E., R. A. Kittles, G. Argyropoulos, et al. "Ancestral Proportions and Admixture Dynamics in Geographically Defined African Americans Living in South Carolina." *American Journal of Physical Anthropology* 114 (2001): 18–29.

Perry, G. H., N. J. Dominy, K. G. Claw, et al. "Diet and the Evolution of Human Amylase Gene Copy Number Variation." *Nature Genetics* 39 (2007): 1256–1260.

Provine, W. B. *The Origins of Theoretical Population Genetics*. Chicago: University of Chicago Press, 1971.

Raghavan, M., M. Steinrücken, K. Harris, et al. "Genomic Evidence for the Pleistocene and Recent Population History of Native Americans." *Science* 349 (2015): aab3884. https://doi.org/10.1126/science.aab3884.

Ramachandran, S., O. Deshpande, C. C. Roseman, et al. "Support from the Relationship of Genetic and Geographic Distance in Human Populations for a Serial Founder Effect Originating in Africa." *Proceedings of the National Academy of Sciences of the United States of America* 102 (2005): 15942–15947.

Rasmussen, M., S. L. Anzick, M. R. Waters, et al. "The Genome of a Late Pleistocene Human from a Clovis Burial Site in Western Montana." *Nature* 506 (2014): 225–229.

Relethford, J. H. "Estimation of Kinship and Genetic Distance from Surnames." *Human Biology* 60 (1988): 475–492.

Relethford, J. H. "Boas and Beyond: Migration and Craniometric Variation." *American Journal of Human Biology* 16 (2004a): 379–386.

Relethford, J. H. "Global Patterns of Isolation by Distance Based on Genetic and Morphological Data." *Human Biology* 76 (2004b): 499–513.

Relethford, J. H. "The Use of Quantitative Traits in Anthropological Genetic Studies of Population Structure and History." In *Anthropological Genetics: Theory, Methods and Applications*. Edited by M. H. Crawford, 187–209. Cambridge: Cambridge University Press, 2007.

Relethford, J. H. *Human Population Genetics*. Hoboken: Wiley-Blackwell, 2012.

Relethford, J. H. "Understanding Human Cranial Variation in Light of Modern Human Origins." In *The Origins of Modern Humans: Biology Reconsidered*. Edited by F. H. Smith and J. C. M. Ahern, 321–337. Hoboken: Wiley-Blackwell, 2013.

Relethford, J. H., and D. A. Bolnick. *Reflections of Our Past: How Human History Is Revealed in Our Genes*, 2nd edn. Abingdon, UK: Routledge, 2018.

Roberts, D. F. "Assumption and Fact in Anthropological Genetics." *Journal of the Royal Anthropological Institute of Great Britain and Ireland* 95 (1965): 87–103.

Rogers, A. R., and H. C. Harpending. "Migration and Genetic Drift in Human Populations." *Evolution* 40 (1986): 1312–1327.

Rutherford, A. *A Brief History of Everyone Who Ever Lived: The Human Story Retold Through Our Genes*. New York: The Experiment, 2017.

Slon, V., F. Mafessoni, B. Vernot, et al. "The Genome of the Offspring of a Neanderthal Mother and a Denisovan Father." *Nature* 561 (2018): 113–116.

Smith, F. H., I. Janković, and I. Karavanić. "The Assimilation Model, Modern Human Origins in Europe, and the Extinction of Neandertals." *Quaternary International* 137 (2005): 7–19.

Szathmary, E. J. E. "Exceeding Hrdlicka's Aims: 100 Years of Genetics in Anthropology." *American Journal of Physical Anthropology* 165 (2018): 754–776.

Tishkoff, S. A., F. A. Reed, A. Ranciaro, et al. "Convergent Adaptation of Human Lactase Persistence in Africa and Europe." *Nature Genetics* 39 (2007): 31–40.

Weiss, K. M., and J. A. Kurland. "Going on an Antedate." *Evolutionary Anthropology* 16 (2007): 204–209.

Wollstein, A., O. Lao, C. Becker, et al. "Demographic History of Oceania Inferred from Genome-wide Data." *Current Biology* 20 (2010): 1983–1992.

CHAPTER **6** # Human Population Genomics: Diversity and Adaptation

Dennis H. O'Rourke

INTRODUCTION

Anthropological geneticists have been documenting patterns of genetic variation in the study of population history and human adaptability for over 75 years (Crawford 2007; O'Rourke 2003). Originally this research effort was focused on classical markers typed in human blood samples (O'Rourke 2006), but the field was transformed beginning in the mid-1980s by what has come to be known as the "molecular revolution." The earlier reliance on primary (proteins) or secondary (e.g., blood groups) gene products has given way to a direct assessment of variation in DNA sequences that underlie both the downstream products of genes and various complex phenotypes, including documenting variation in regions of the genome not involved in protein coding.

SOME MOLECULAR BASICS

In a practical sense, the molecular revolution began with Watson and Crick's (1953) discovery of the now well-known double-helical structure of deoxyribonucleic acid (DNA, Figure 6.1). This structural insight made sense of the previously observed equality among the four bases (adenine, thymine, guanine, and cytosine) that were the components of DNA. In any DNA preparation, the amount of adenine (A) always equaled thymine (T), while the concentrations of guanine (G) and cytosine (C) were also equivalent. Given the new insight regarding DNA structure, it became clear that guanine and cytosine were complementary and existed in paired form, as did adenine and thymine. Thus, G and C are paired, as are A and T in any DNA double-stranded sequence. Subsequently, the fact that three adjacent nucleotide bases in a DNA sequence determined a specific amino acid, the building blocks of proteins, helped reveal the molecular and biochemical dynamics of protein synthesis. By the 1980s, more efficient molecular and biochemical methods had been

A Companion to Biological Anthropology, Second Edition. Edited by Clark Spencer Larsen.
© 2023 John Wiley & Sons Ltd. Published 2023 by John Wiley & Sons Ltd.

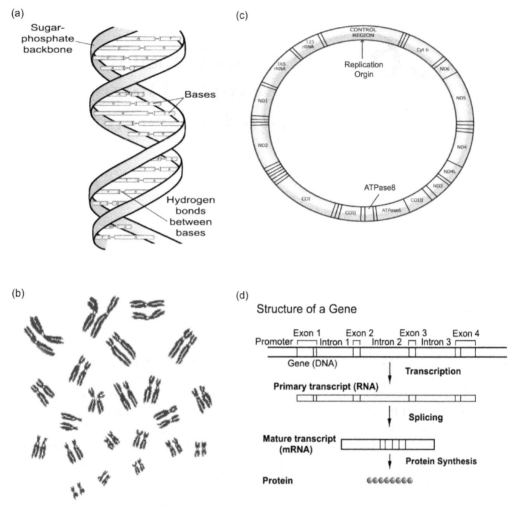

Figure 6.1 (a) Double-stranded DNA indicating complementarity of bases, G-C and T-A. (b) Normal human karyotype showing the full complement of chromosomes in the nucleus during cell division. Each chromosome has already been duplicated, resulting in the "X" shapes of each chromosome. (c) The circular structure of mitochondrial DNA. (d) Gene structure illustrating placement of promoter, exons, and introns in a DNA strand, and the relationship of each to protein synthesis. Figure by R. W. O'Rourke.

developed to isolate DNA from tissue and blood samples, and technological innovations were introduced to facilitate the generation of DNA sequence data and ultimately the documentation of genomic diversity among individuals.

A development that had a particularly important impact in anthropological genetics was the introduction of the Polymerase Chain Reaction (PCR) by Mullis in 1984. PCR emulates a normal cellular function. During cell division, DNA molecules need to be duplicated in order for each new daughter cell to contain the full complement of chromosomes required for normal cellular function. This duplication is accomplished by the "unzipping" of double-stranded DNA into single strands and, under the influence of an enzyme (a polymerase), the complementary nature of DNA bases (A-T and C-G) results in the generation of a new, synthetic strand of DNA complementary to the original strand. This new strand

and the original template strand reestablish the double-stranded structure of the original molecule. PCR performs a very similar series of reactions, first by using heat to dissolve the bonds holding the DNA double-helix together, yielding single-stranded DNA, a process known as denaturation. By designing short DNA fragments of around 20 bases (oligonucleotides) that are complementary to known DNA sequences, the addition of an appropriate polymerase will result in the creation of a new, synthetic strand complementary to an existing single strand.

The PCR process is achieved by three separate steps, each taking place at a specific temperature. First, as already noted, is denaturation, to produce single-stranded DNA templates. The second step is annealing, which takes place at a lower temperature that allows the short oligonucleotide fragments, known as "primers," to bind (anneal) to their complementary sequences on the template strand. The final step, termed extension, involves the introduction of the appropriate polymerase to catalyze the synthesis of the new, complementary strand from the sites of the existing primers. Careful primer design results in the production of two double-stranded DNA molecules that contain the same specific sequence, bounded by the primers. Repeating this three-step procedure through multiple cycles results in a geometric increase in the amount of DNA sequence of interest.

This procedure became the workhorse of molecular genetic labs around the world starting in the 1980s and helped make the molecular revolution accessible to anthropological genetic laboratories. It also made it possible to manipulate and study specific DNA sequences extracted from prehistoric source material, such as skeletal elements, teeth, dental calculus, etc. (De la Fuente et al. 2012; Gilbert et al. 2004; Hofreiter et al. 2001; O'Rourke 2007; Weyrich et al. 2015). Although this DNA (now known as ancient DNA or aDNA) is routinely degraded to a small size and is often acquired in conjunction with enzymatic inhibitors and contaminants, the sensitivity of PCR made it possible to study the genetic variation in prehistoric populations or pathogens directly, rather than relying on indirect methods (see Chapter 12 by Stone and Chapter 13 by Amorim).

THE HUMAN GENOMES

Each individual actually possesses two independent genomes. The nuclear genome located in the nucleus of each cell is comprised of DNA packaged into 23 pairs of linear structures called chromosomes. The full complement of chromosomes is called the karyotype and is shown in Figure 6.1b during cell division. It is biparentally inherited, with half of the genome coming from each parent. It is also quite large with approximately 3 billion base pairs (bp). The second genome is located within the mitochondria, small organelles responsible for cellular metabolism in the cytoplasm of each cell that contain their own unique genome. The mitochondrial genome differs from the nuclear genome in important ways. It is a comparatively small, circular molecule of just over 16,500 base pairs (Figure 6.1c). It is exclusively maternally inherited and is comprised almost entirely of a coding sequence. This contrasts sharply with the nuclear genome, where the majority of the sequence is not involved in coding for the protein product. The mitochondrial genome contains genes involved in electron transport and oxidative phosphorylation (important steps in oxidative metabolism), as well as the ribosomal and transfer RNA genes required to synthesize those proteins. It should be noted that the majority of the genes required for oxidative metabolism are found in the nuclear genome, are synthesized outside the mitochondria, and are later imported into the mitochondria.

Three important aspects of the mitochondrial genome that initially made it so useful to human population geneticists is its high copy number per cell, it is less prone to degradation post-mortem, and has a higher substitution rate compared to the nucleus. Although the nuclear genome is much larger than the mitochondrial genome, there is only one diploid copy of it in each cell. However, each cell may contain many mitochondrial organelles, each with multiple copies of its genome, such that there are typically hundreds to thousands of copies of the mitochondrial genome per cell. This high copy number helps explain why the mtDNA genome has been so widely used in ancient DNA studies (Hagelberg et al. 2015; see Amorim, Chapter 13). Like all organic material, nucleic acids degrade post-mortem. However, the very high number of mtDNA molecules per cell makes it much more likely that at least some proportion of a target sequence of interest will persist for some time after death of the organism. The likelihood it can be accessed, amplified via PCR, and sequenced is greater than is true for the single cellular copy of the nuclear genome. Second, the circular structure of mtDNA seems less prone to post-mortem degradation than the linear nuclear chromosomes (Allentoft et al. 2012). The ring structure of mtDNA may make it less accessible to the degrading effects of exonuclease activity, which enhances the availability of mtDNA sequences in ancient samples in a fashion complementary to the effects of a higher copy number.

The third important property of mtDNA, a higher mutation rate than in the nuclear genome, means the mitochondrial genome evolves at a more rapid rate than does the nuclear genome. This difference in evolutionary rate was once thought to be the result of a lack of molecular editing capability (correcting errors in mtDNA replication, for example), which are well known in the nucleus. However, it is now clear that the mitochondrial genome also has these molecular repair mechanisms (Kazak et al. 2012). Nevertheless, as a result of the elevated evolutionary rate, mtDNA sequences provide insight into population dynamics and evolutionary events in the comparatively recent past. The temporal window into which we can look with mtDNA sequence data is approximately the same as that afforded by archaeology – on the order of centuries or millennia. The slower evolutionary rate of the nuclear genome provides a window into the deeper past. However, in addition to providing a window to the deeper past, the nuclear genome can also reveal more recent population dynamics, such as gene flow and admixture between different populations (Borda et al. 2020) or even recent positive selection (Sabeti et al. 2002).

The uniparental inheritance of mtDNA also means that diversity in this molecule only informs us about the history of maternal lineages. Fortunately, there is an analog in the nuclear genome for paternal lineages, the Y-chromosome. Among other things, Y-chromosome genes are involved in sex determination during embryogenesis and are transmitted from fathers to sons. Thus, while everyone possesses mtDNA inherited from their mothers, only males possess a Y-chromosome in the nuclear genome inherited from their fathers. These two uniparentally inherited genomes therefore permit historical tracking of maternal and paternal lineages, respectively, over time. Because the Y-chromosome is part of the nuclear genome, the two genomes evolve at different rates, occasionally leading to inferred disparities in male and female evolutionary histories.

In addition to being much larger in size than the mtDNA genome, the nuclear genome is also more complex in other ways. The 3 billion plus bases that constitute the nuclear genome are arrayed in 46 linear chromosomes: 23 pairs of autosomes and two sex chromosomes (X and Y). The traditional view is that the DNA sequences that comprise each chromosome define a series of genes that determine the production of protein, or other gene products, important for normal cellular function. In this view, genes are thought of as being arrayed along the chromosomes like "beads on a string." Moreover, the genes were considered to be unitary entities of DNA sequence, with variations arising through changes in nucleotide sequences. The modern view of the genome differs substantially from this historic, traditional characterization.

We now appreciate that the structure of genes is more complex and dynamic than once thought. Genes are DNA sequences that contain both sequences that are involved in the translation of proteins, called exons, and stretches of intervening, noncoding sequence, called introns, that are not involved in the translation of DNA sequence to protein (see Figure 6.1d). The average gene in the human genome has just over eight exonic regions and a comparable number of introns. Both exons and introns are translated during protein synthesis, but the intronic sequences are spliced out of the transcripts prior to translation of the exonic sequences into protein. Indeed, alternative splicing sites within genes and between exons and introns are likely to provide much of the genetic diversity we see in the constellation of proteins produced. This helps explain, in part, why the human genome appears to have only ~20,000 genes, rather than the 100,000 genes hypothesized prior to the sequencing of the human genome (Lander et al. 2001).

Of the known genes, the function of nearly half remains unknown. Moreover, genes tend to be clustered in apparently random sections in the genome, separated by large tracts of noncoding DNA. Indeed, less than 2 percent of the nuclear genomic sequence codes for protein products. A large fraction of the genome (~50 percent) is composed of noncoding repeat sequences. The repeats may be characterized by short (e.g., 2–6 bases, microsatellites), medium (10–70 bases, minisatellites), or long (hundreds to thousands of bases, SINES and LINES) repeat motifs. The shorter repeat motifs are usually repeated in tandem fashion, while the longer repeat motifs are dispersed throughout the genome. Although most of the noncoding sequence, including repeat sequences, is of an unknown function, it is becoming clear that they are likely to be involved in gene regulation and expression. For example, there are substantial stretches of DNA sequence in noncoding regions that are known to be conserved across species. Such conservation of DNA sequences across different individuals and species is typically associated with important cellular functions to the organism. Thus, these conserved noncoding regions (CNRs) are generally thought to be involved in some fundamental regulatory pathway that we have yet to identify. It is known that areas of the genome where coding regions are clustered tend to be bounded by long tracts of GC repeats. The repeated guanine–cytosine base pairs (called CpG islands) are subject to chemical modification, methylation. Methylation is the binding of a methyl group to a cytosine in the DNA sequence. Methylation of multiple cytosines in a sequence can serve to down-regulate gene action, thus the extent of methylation is important in turning genes on and off during periods of development, and is therefore clearly involved in gene regulation and expression. Thus, many of the non-coding regions, repeats, and CNRs alike are involved in basic regulatory functions that we are still learning to appreciate. Such regulatory activity by noncoding regions would contribute to the phenotypic diversity we see as a result of alterations in, for example, growth and development that would not be reflected in protein diversity.

GENOMICS, ADAPTABILITY, AND ANTHROPOLOGY

Genes, Language, and Geography

Anthropological geneticists have long been interested in using patterns of genetic variation to more clearly reconstruct population histories, particularly the population and demographic details of colonizing populations (e.g., Arredi et al. 2007; O'Rourke and Raff 2009;

Tishkiff and Gonder 2007). A major question that has occupied the time and efforts of geneticists interested in reconstructing population histories is whether geography or language plays a greater role in structuring population genetic variation. A strong case for either one can be made, *a priori*, as a significant force in patterning genetic variation.

There is a rich, quantitative area of population genetic theory that predicts that geography should be a dominant factor in the distribution of genetic variation. The logical basis of this is clear. Many demographic studies have demonstrated that individuals tend to select mates that live nearer to them, rather than farther away. If that is generally true, and is a practice followed over time, then individuals residing in geographic proximity will tend to be more closely genetically related than those residing at greater distances. This is known as isolation by distance in population genetics and predicts that geography should be a primary factor in the distribution of genetic variation. It is useful to note that correlations between genetics and geography may also be due to population history. For example, patterns of population expansion, not just mate selection practices, may also result in geographical neighbors being genetically related. A case also can be made for language as a factor in the patterning of genetic variation. It seems intuitively obvious that individuals are more likely to select mates with whom they can easily communicate, that is, who speak the same, or a similar, language. If this is true, then language, and related cultural aspects of mate selection, may be important modifiers of the distribution of genetic variation, independent of geography. Since languages, and language families, also exhibit geographic structure, it has been difficult to unequivocally document the relative importance of either.

In an early study of classical marker variation in Native American populations, Spuhler (1972) argued that the pattern of variation between tribal groups reflected geographic distances between them better than did the distribution of genetic variation between languages or language groups. With the advent of molecular markers, it has become possible to investigate the relative contributions on a finer scale. In most instances, geography does seem to have a greater effect on the distribution of genetic variation than language, but the latter is not without effect.

Hunley and Long (2005) investigated mitochondrial DNA variation in many Native American populations distributed throughout the Americas. They found that irrespective of the language classification system used, language was a worse predictor of genetic affinity than was geography. Later, Novembre and colleagues (Novembre et al. 2008) studied the pattern of variation at over 500,000 Single Nucleotide Polymorphisms (SNPs) distributed across the genome in almost 3,200 individuals from across Europe. Not all of the single nucleotides assayed were equally informative or polymorphic, and the final analysis focused on over 197,000 loci. Similarly, the final sample size of individuals was reduced to just fewer than 1,400 individuals after controlling for those with ancestry outside Europe and with grandparental ancestry from more than one European location. Analyses of the resulting data set show clearly that the pattern of genetic variation in Europe replicates the geography of Europe. Principal Components Analysis, which reduces large data arrays to a smaller set of independent factors, resulted in observed correlations between the first two principal components and latitude and longitude of greater than 0.85. Indeed, using multiple regression methods to predict geographic origin from these genetic data resulted in over 50 percent of individuals being placed within 310 kilometers of their actual place of origin, and over 90 percent within 700 km of their point of origin (Novembre et al. 2008). This is remarkable geographic precision from genetic data on a continental scale.

In a simultaneous and independent study, Lao et al. (2008) reached similar conclusions. These authors also used the Affymetrix 500K SNP chip to assay genetic variation in over

2,500 individuals distributed across 23 European subpopulations. The results of this study found strong correlations between geographic and genetic distances between the European subpopulations, reflecting the strong influence of geography on the genetic structure of the European continent. That the effects of geography are so evident here, despite the lack of overall genetic variation, suggests that the effects of geography on patterns of genetic variation might be even more easily documented in other regions (e.g., Africa, Asia) as large-scale genetic surveys are completed in these continental areas.

It is important to note that the strong role of geography in structuring genetic variation in Europe does not mean that other factors are unimportant. In a worldwide survey of 377 microsatellite loci, Belle and Barbujani (2007) found that while genetic differences between populations more closely reflect geographic distances than linguistic differentiation between them, linguistic diversity did have an observable, although small, effect independent of geography. In the European survey of Novembre et al. (2008), reducing the scale of analysis from continental to a more regional scale resulted in the observation that the distribution of variation in Switzerland corresponded to the distribution of linguistic areas within the country, which, of course, were also correlated with geography.

In comparing studies such as those described above, several issues should be kept in mind. First, the scale of analysis is of considerable importance. It makes a difference whether the geographical scale is regional, continental, or global. For example, Henn et al. (2012) used genome-wide SNP arrays to identify segments of DNA shared between unrelated individuals that were identical by descent (IBD). In a collection of over 20,000 genomes that spanned three continents, these authors found that the level of IBD sharing was significantly different if populations were defined ethnolinguistically rather than by continent of origin. Not surprisingly, greater IBD sharing, and hence more genealogical relatedness, could be identified in smaller regional or ethnolinguistically defined populations than those defined by continent of origin. Even among the former groups, IBD and consanguinity was not uniformly distributed (Henn et al. 2012; Leutenegger et al. 2011).

Second, the type of molecular genetic marker studied can also be important. Lao et al. (2008) and Novembre et al. (2008) assayed variation in a large number of SNPs in European populations. Belle and Barbujani (2007) studied microsatellite (STR) variation. The latter evolves much more rapidly than the former due to different mutational mechanisms. Thus, the nature of the variation being studied, and the evolutionary history of the markers, may be quite different and need to be accommodated in any population level analysis. Nevertheless, analytical methods have been developed to accommodate the different types of molecular markers in population genetic and genomic scale studies. The scope, volume of data, and level of resolution afforded by genomic data is substantially greater than anything that could have been imagined by earlier workers studying genetic variation in classical marker systems.

Genomics, Human Adaptability, and Diet

PUFAs & FADS: Human populations inhabit every ecological region of the globe, from the hot and humid tropics to the cold and arid Arctic. Given the ecological diversity that characterizes human settlement patterns it should come as no surprise that diets across human societies differ dramatically, correlated with the differential availability of resources determined by the local ecology. One of the more extreme environments that human populations have occupied for millennia is the circumarctic regions of the northern hemisphere.

The inhabitants of this high latitude environment in North America, the Inuit, are well documented to subsist on a diet high in protein. These groups have historically relied on sea mammal hunting, such that protein and fatty acids comprise a substantial portion of their diet. The fatty acids are primarily omega-3 polyunsaturated fatty acids (PUFAs). Using scans of Inuit genomes, Fumagalli et al. (2015) detected evidence of natural selection at a number of loci, but the strongest signal of selection and adaptation among the Inuit occurred in a cluster of genes determining fatty acid desaturases (FADS), loci whose function determine PUFA levels. The alleles with the strongest selection signal are also related to other complex phenotypes, including metabolic and anthropometric variation, e.g., height and weight. Fumagalli and colleagues (2015) also analyzed membrane lipids and discovered that the alleles with strong selection signals were involved in fatty acid composition with possible effects on growth hormones. These results suggest that the Inuit, and perhaps other long-time residents of Arctic environments, have genetic adaptations to their PUFA rich diets.

The results of the Fumagalli et al. (2015) study also led to an inference that the selection on the fatty acid desaturases that proved to be adaptive in the Greenlandic Arctic may be a record of past selection in a source population that lived in the Arctic long ago. To investigate this evolutionary hypothesis, Amorim et al. (2017) examined genomic diversity in FADS in other populations, including non-Arctic Native American populations. They showed that the signal of FADS-positive selection is widely observed throughout Indigenous American populations, not just the Arctic. These authors concluded that the shared history of FADS-related selection in diverse populations across diverse ecologies and dietary regimes indicated that selection must have occurred in the ancestral population of people prior to their dispersal and differentiation into the peoples and cultures now present in the Western Hemisphere (Amorim et al. 2017). This local selection episode and its effects on human adaptation must have occurred prior to human migration into North and South America over 18,000 years ago.

Lactase persistance: Human biologists have long known that most human populations follow the general mammalian pattern of losing the ability to digest lactose shortly after weaning. However, a few populations of the world, notably European and some African groups, maintain their ability to digest lactose into adulthood. Exactly how and when this dietary adaptation arose has long been of interest to those studying human adaptation and dietary evolution (Holden and Mace 1997; Simoons 1978).

Lactose is a disaccharide found in milk. It is digested to monosaccharides (simple sugars) more usable in the gut by the enzyme lactase-phlorizin hydrolase (LPH). In most human populations the production of LPH declines following weaning, such that after about age 5 most people can no longer digest the lactose in milk. It has long been observed that the ability to consume milk into adulthood is correlated with a history of herding and dairying (Holden and Mace 1997). Although it seemed obvious that the genetic basis of the ability to continue to digest lactose after childhood must involve variation in the gene encoding lactase (*LCT* located at 2q21) but no such polymorphism had been identified. With the advent of molecular screening, the genetic basis of this important adaptive trait has been clarified (Wooding 2007).

Enattah et al. (2002) demonstrated that while variation in *LCT* sequences were not obviously associated with LPH persistence, a single nucleotide polymorphism in a neighboring gene, *MCM6*, was strongly associated with lactase persistence. This SNP is a C-to-T transition in intron 13 of the *MCM6* gene (C/T-13910) and is located 14 kb (kb = a thousand bases) from *LCT*. Although not located in the *LCT* gene itself, this remote polymorphism appears to have a regulatory effect on *LCT* promoter activity. Curiously, this strong association between marker and lactase persistence is only predictive of lactose digestion phenotype in Europeans, but not for lactase persistent populations elsewhere. In a subsequent study of molecular diversity and lactose absorption phenotypes in East African populations, Tishkoff and colleagues (2007) identified three additional SNPs (G/C-14010, T/G-13915, and C/G-13907), also in the 13th intron of MCM6, associated with LPH persistence in African populations. Of these three SNPs, only the G/C-14010 variant is widely distributed at appreciable frequency in multiple African populations. None of the 43 African populations studied by Tishkoff et al. (2007) possessed the C/T-13910 SNP predictive of lactase persistence in Europeans.

The results of these molecular analyses indicate that the genetic basis for lactase persistence and the adaptation to adult consumption of the nutritionally rich milk of domesticated animals have arisen at least twice. The European and African forms of lactase persistence are the result of separate and independent mutations brought to high frequency by natural selection. Both mutations appear to have regulatory roles on LCT, although they are not found within the lactase gene (LCT) itself. Indeed, both mutations are found within intronic sequences of a neighboring gene. The simple story of selection for persistent lactase production via LCT variants in herding populations is now known to be more complex, with at least two separate molecular bases for the trait in different geographic regions. The picture may be even more complicated, as Enattah and colleagues (2008) identified yet a third genetic variant, a compound allele of two different SNPs (also occurring in MCM6 introns) that is associated with lactase persistence in Middle Eastern populations. Thus, similar but distinct molecular mechanisms may account for three separate and independent origins for lactase persistence in humans.

AMY1 **copy number**: Another example of the molecular underpinnings of dietary evolution is the salivary enzyme amylase and its role in starch hydrolysis. Starch is a significant, and increasing, component of diet in agricultural populations and some arid land small-scale societies but is of lesser significance in tropical forest or arctic populations. Salivary amylase is responsible for starch hydrolysis and is controlled by the gene *AMY1*, known to be characterized by variable copy numbers in humans (Groot et al. 1989).

Perry et al. (2007) demonstrated that the number of *AMY1* copies in individual genomes correlated strongly with the amylase protein level in human saliva, and that individual populations characterized by high starch diets have, on average, more copies of the *AMY1* gene than individuals in populations characterized by low starch diets. These investigators studied three populations with high starch diets (European-Americans, Japanese, and the Hadza) and four populations with low starch diets (Biaka and Mbuti tropical forest groups, Datog pastoralists, and Yakut pastoralist/fishers). Results of the *AMY1* copy number analysis across these populations indicated that the high starch diet populations had significantly more copies of the *AMY1* gene than the low starch populations. The proportion of individuals in the high starch diet populations that had at least six copies of the *AMY1* gene was 70 percent, whereas the comparable figure for the low starch populations was only about 35 percent. Since both the high and low starch diet populations were widely distributed, with both including African and Asian populations, the result is unlikely due to simple models of geography or shared ancestry. Rather, it appears that diet predicts *AMY1* copy number better than geography, suggesting that selection based on dietary starch has driven *AMY1* copy number up in high starch diet populations.

Perry et al. (2007) extended their analysis to chimps and bonobos to clarify the origin of the increased copy number observed in some human populations. In a sample of 15 wild chimpanzees, all exhibited two diploid copies of *AMY1*. Among bonobos, a gain in *AMY1* copy number was observed, but the sequence data suggest the copies may not be functional. Thus, among the great apes tested, which consume only small amounts of starch in their diets, *AMY1* copy number has apparently not expanded as it has in humans, strengthening the inference of copy number expansion as a result of dietary selection. Moreover, sequence diversity in *AMY1* gene sequences suggest that the copy number expansion has occurred in humans within the past 200,000 years or so (Perry et al. 2007). If true, it means that this may be an example of direct selection acting during the time of the evolutionary transition to modern humans.

PTC taste sensitivity: Finally, the ability to taste PTC has long intrigued biological anthropologists and geneticists. This synthetic compound was found to taste bitter to some individuals but was tasteless to others following an accidental laboratory release of the compound (Fox 1932). The taste sensitivity to the compound appeared to be familial and the phenotypes of tasting and nontasting led to the inference of a simple, single, biallelic locus for control of the sensory polymorphism (Wooding 2006). At first, although a genetic system controlling the ability to taste a synthetic compound was puzzling, it ultimately became clear that the compound resembled compounds found in the Brassica family of plants that occasionally acted as thyroid stressors. Thus, the system was viewed as another case of dietary adaptation at the genetic level.

Although R. A. Fisher documented early that the taste polymorphism for PTC also existed in the great apes (Fisher et al. 1939) and inferred an ancient origin for the polymorphism and any associated adaptation, the genetic basis for the taste sensitivity remained elusive. The general model was one of a single locus with two alleles, where one allele conferred the ability to taste PTC (and closely related compounds), while the alternative allele, presumably damaged or nonfunctional, resulted in an inability to taste the compounds. The molecular genetic architecture of the trait was finally elucidated by Kim et al. (2003) and Drayna et al. (2003), who demonstrated that 50–80 percent of variation in PTC taste sensitivity is accounted for by molecular variation at the *TAS2R38* locus. This locus is involved in discrimination of ligands (a molecule that binds to another, typically larger, molecule) in the thiourea group (which includes PTC) and a compound in many cruciferous vegetables (goitrin) (Feeney 2011; Wooding et al. 2010, summarized in Veilleux 2019). The variation at this locus accounting for PTC taste sensitivity derives from two haplotypes, a "taster" and a "nontaster" haplotype, which differ by three SNPs. These two haplotypes are among the five resulting from the three SNPs at *TAS2R38*.

Knowing the molecular genetic basis for PTC taste sensitivity has led to a change in perspective on this sensory polymorphism. Molecular characterization of each haplotype revealed that the "non-taster" variant was not simply a damaged or nonfunctional version of the "taster" haplotype. Rather, the "taster" and "nontaster" haplotypes differ by only three amino acids, and both appear to be fully functional. The "nontaster" haplotype may be the basis for a functional receptor of some family of compounds that does not contain PTC. While no specific ligand for the "nontaster" haplotype has been identified, some plant compounds have been identified that are "tasted" by PTC nontasters, but not by PTC tasters. Further functional studies of a variety of plant compounds and their relationships to taste sensitivity and molecular characterization are required to elucidate more fully the evolutionary history of this interesting sensory and dietary polymorphism (Veilleux 2019).

One additional component to the PTC story has also been clarified by newer molecular genetic studies. Fisher and colleagues (1939), having documented PTC taste sensitivity in the great apes, concluded that the PTC taste polymorphism was of ancient origin, predating the human–ape divergence. Molecular analysis has again refined our understanding of the evolution of this system. While the analysis of *TAS2R38* sequence variation in human populations led to the inference of balancing selection as the origin of the observed variation (Wooding et al. 2004), it cannot account for the PTC taste sensitivity pattern observed in chimpanzees. Like humans, chimps have two PTC taste sensitivity alleles at *TAS2R38*. However, the two alleles are much more similar in chimps than in humans. In chimps, the "nontaster" allele derives from a single SNP in the start codon, changing it from ATG to AGG, and resulting in a nonfunctional protein. This origin of the "nontaster" allele in chimps is quite different from the functional, but still "non-taster" allele in humans, which differs by three amino acid substitutions from the "taster" allele. Thus, Wooding et al. (2004) demonstrated that while humans and chimps both possess "taster" and "nontaster" alleles at *TAS2R38* in roughly equivalent frequencies, the nontaster alleles are quite different in structure and molecular mechanism and indicate that in the primate lineage "nontasting" alleles at this locus have evolved twice independently (Wooding 2006; Wooding et al. 2004).

Population Genomics and Morphological Variation

The role of morphological variation in documenting human population history and evolution is the subject of treatment in other chapters in this volume, so little time or space need be allotted to it here. Interested readers in the analysis of quantitative variation can consult recent review papers in the field (e.g., von Cramon-Taubadel 2019). However, it is worth observing that the metric and meristic variation that has for over a century characterized biological anthropological investigations of human diversity and evolution are now being augmented by genomic analyses. It has often been assumed that metric variation (e.g., stature, weight, cranial and dental metrics, etc.), as well as discrete traits (meristic variants in the crania and dentition), reflected variation in underlying genes affecting morphological development, and therefore were informative analogs for genetic variation (e.g., Cheverud 1982, 1988; Lande 1977; Relethford and Blangero 1990; Roseman and Weaver 2007). Based on heritability estimates, for example, 80 percent of the variation in adult stature may be genetically determined (McEvoy and Visscher 2009; Silventoinen et al. 2003). Certainly, human stature is a complex, multifactorial trait that results from the interaction of alleles at multiple loci, along with environmental variation in diet, prenatal environment, and disease exposure, among others. Recently, the molecular technology afforded by large-scale marker screening and the use of Genome Wide Association Studies (GWAS) has begun to identify some of the specific genes responsible for adult stature.

The first GWAS study of adult stature by Weeden et al. (2007) indicated that common variants in the *HMGA2* gene were associated with variation in stature in both adults and children, but that they accounted for very little of the observed variation in stature. Sanna and colleagues (2008) examined over 2 million SNPs in over 6,500 individuals in Finland and Sardinia to investigate additional sources of genetic variation for stature. These authors identified two linked genes on chromosome 20, *GDF5* (growth differentiation factor 5) and *UQCC* (a ZIC-binding protein suppressed by a fibroblast growth factor), that were found to contribute to variation in adult stature in these samples (Sanna et al. 2008). Both genes have functional roles in growth such that alterations in them could plausibly have effects on not only growth rates and trajectories, but also human adult height. The variants identified by Sanna et al. (2008) are also important to risk for osteoarthritis. Their effects were estimated to have an additive effect on stature of 0.44 cm, a fairly small effect on the overall variation in human stature.

Shortly thereafter, three research groups (Gudbjartsson et al. 2008; Lettre et al. 2008; Weedon et al. 2008) published three additional GWAS on human height that added at least an additional 40 new genomic variants with significant effects on variation in stature. The sample sizes employed in these studies are daunting, ranging from nearly 15,000 to over 30,000 individuals in the initial screening phase (which identified 95 promising variants), to approximately half those sample sizes in the validation stage. Using a SNP chip array to screen over 500,000 markers in each individual, the 54 variants ultimately identified have an average effect size of 0.4 cm on stature (Visscher 2008). Even taken together, this is still a small proportion of variation in adult stature. However, in GWAS, increasing sample sizes routinely led to increases in the number of SNPs found to be significantly associated with complex traits. Recently, Yengo et al. (2018) combined the data from Wood et al.'s (2014) study of genes for human stature and Locke et al.'s (2015) assay for genes contributing to the body mass index (BMI) with a new GWAS of height and BMI using participant data in the UK Biobank for a total sample of over 700,000 individuals of European ancestry. This meta-analysis resulted in the identification of 3,290 and 941 near independent SNPs associated with human stature and BMI, respectively. The genome-wide SNPs identified in this large-scale GWAS explained nearly 25 percent of the variance in human stature and 6 percent of the variance in BMI. The proportion of variance explained in this meta-analysis was substantially greater than those observed in smaller-scale GWAS – a result that is not unexpected. Although confirming the traditional view of stature (and BMI) as a complex character with many underlying genes, identification of such genomic variants for complex traits is important in speeding the discovery of functional gene products involved in the developmental pathways contributing to height, BMI, and other complex phenotypes of interest.

Large genomic scans on large samples is an expensive enterprise, taking such projects beyond the scope of most individual investigators. It is worth noting, however, that the GWAS for height described in the above studies was not always undertaken to investigate the genetic architecture of stature. Rather, the samples were often pooled from earlier studies where genomic screens had been performed to identify disease susceptibility genes for various diseases (Visscher 2008). However, in each of those studies, height had been recorded, permitting a subsequent meta-analysis of the combined genomic data with the recorded statures. This emphasizes for our discipline the potentially fruitful nature of collaborative research with investigators of diverse interests, and the importance of training in statistical and quantitative analyses in the future of biological anthropology. These studies also emphasize the developing capacity to rapidly screen large population samples for ever larger arrays of molecular markers, making it likely that the genetic architecture of complex morphological traits like stature, among others (e.g., BMI, Willer et al. 2009; obesity, Thorleifsson et al. 2009), will succumb to molecular genetic analysis in the foreseeable future, thus providing greater precision and resolution to the historical data on human morphological variation.

Finally, the study of morphological variation in the human dentition has constituted a large proportion of the research into human diversity by bioarchaeologists and biological anthropologists. Dental variation, both metric and discrete traits, have high heritabilities, suggesting that although we know little about the genetic architecture of such traits, they are appropriate analogs to direct measures of genetic variation when genetic or genomic data are unavailable (Irish et al. 2020).

One of the dental characteristics that has been widely studied in global populations is incisor shoveling. This discrete character exhibits lateral ridges of enamel on the lingual surface of maxillary incisors such that when viewed from the occlusal surface the shoveled incisor looks like the blade of a shovel. The distribution of this character is highest in Asian and Indigenous American populations, reaching a frequency of nearly 100 percent in some Native American populations. It is essentially absent in Europeans. This distinct distribution has suggested the action of natural selection on the shoveling trait in Asian and Asian derived populations, but no adaptive function has been associated with the trait.

Kimura et al. (2009) demonstrated that the genetic determinant of incisor shoveling was the ectodysplasin A receptor gene (*EDAR*), which has pleiotropic effects in a number of morphological and developmental pathways, which in addition to incisor shoveling includes sweat gland density and mammary gland ductal branching. Hlusko and colleagues (2018) noted that since both the *EDAR V370A* variant and incisor shoveling are uniquely elevated in populations of North and East Asia and the Americas, the latter could be used as a proxy for the distribution of the *EDAR* variant across a broad geographic region. This is useful since many more populations, both contemporary and ancient, have been studied for the distribution of the shoveling trait than have been characterized genetically for *EDAR* variation. Moreover, the very high frequency of shoveling in Indigenous American populations suggests that the EDAR variant was at an even higher frequency prior to European colonization.

Hlusko et al. (2018) hypothesized that it was selection on the *EDAR V370A* variant in an ancestral population of Indigenous American populations during a period of isolation in Beringia (known as the Beringian Standstill) that resulted in both the elevated frequency of the *EDAR* variant and the shoveling trait. Selection on this variant in an arctic environment makes intuitive sense since it is an environment of reduced UV radiation and, hence, vitamin D-deficient conditions. The role of *EDAR V370A* in increasing ductal branching may have been the substrate for positive selection on the variant as it would result in increasing delivery of critical nutrients to infants via mother's milk in such challenging environments.

The hypothesized selection on the *EDAR V370A* variant in Hlusko et al. (2018) is likely to be related to the documented selection on the FADS gene cluster discussed above, since this genomic region is known to regulate lipid profiles transmitted to mother's milk given the vitamin D-rich diet from consumption of omega-3 fatty acids in modern arctic populations. In this scenario, shoveling of incisors is a byproduct of selection on the *EDAR V370A* variant, which makes the dental discrete trait appropriate as a proxy for *EDAR V370A* frequency estimation in populations for which genetic or genomic data have yet to be generated.

CONCLUSION

The growth of genomic scale analyses has been rapid in recent years. The pace of that growth shows no sign of slowing down; indeed, it continues to increase. Genomic analyses provide a far more robust and detailed understanding of human diversity, gene function, and our evolution than could be imagined not long ago. From the whole genomic SNP arrays now available to the sequencing of whole individual genomes, we have a powerful toolkit to deploy in order to understand gene function, cellular biology at the micro-scale, details of evolutionary adaptive strategies, and how different environments and human behavior affect our history – and our future.

Certainly, genomic analyses hold great promise to more fully enable an understanding of the mechanisms of infectious and chronic diseases, of the underpinning of morphological diversity, and the myriad ways natural selection has molded the human genome. However, with such rapid progress comes new challenges. The size and complexity of genomic databases requires new, more powerful analytical methods. Many have been developed, but as the scale of genomic data becomes greater new and more powerful statistical and bioinformatic methods will also be required. Importantly, ethical issues attendant to genomic data collection and analysis are also growing in importance and complexity. Biological anthropology has much to contribute and much to gain from continuing research in these areas.

Genomics has become an indispensable part of the anthropological geneticist's toolkit. The methods attendant to that enterprise are now equally a part of the discipline, as are the ethical dimensions that must be accommodated. It promises to be an exciting and challenging future.

REFERENCES

Allentoft, M. E., M. Collins, D. Harker, et al. "The Half-Life of DNA in Bone: Measuring Decay Kinetics in 158 Dated Fossils." *Proceedings of the Royal Society B* 279 (2012): 4724–4733.

Amorim, C. E. G., K. Nunes, D. Meyer, et al. "Genetic Signature of Natural Selection in First Americans." *Proceedings of the National Academy Science of the United States of America* 114 (2017): 2195–2199.

Arredi, B., E. S. Poloni, and C. Tyler-Smith. "The Peopling of Europe." In *Anthropological Genetics: Theory, Methods, and Applications.* Edited by M. H. Crawford, 380–408. Cambridge: Cambridge University Press, 2007.

Belle, E. M. S., and G. Barbujani. "Worldwide Analysis of Multiple Microsatellites: Language Diversity Has a Dectectable Influence on DNA Diversity." *American Journal of Physical Anthropology* 133 (2007): 1137–1146.

Borda, V., I. Alvim, M. Mendes, et al. "The Genetic Structure and Adaptation of Andean Highlanders and Amazonians Are Influenced by the Interplay Between Geography and Culture." *Proceedings of the National Academy of Sciences of the United States of America* 117 (2020): 32557–32565.

Cheverud, J. M. "Phenotypic, Genetic, and Environmental Morphological Integration in the Cranium." *Evolution* 36 (1982): 499–516.

Cheverud, J. M. "A Comparison of Genetic and Phenotypic Correlations." *Evolution* 42 (1988): 958–968.

Crawford, M. H., ed. *Anthropological Genetics: Theory, Methods, and Applications.* Cambridge: Cambridge University Press, 2007.

De la Fuente, C., S. Flores, and M. Moraga. "DNA from Human Ancient Bacteria: A Novel Source of Genetic Evidence from Archaeological Dental Calculus." *Archaeometry* 55 (2012): 767–778.

Drayna, D., H. Coon, U. K. Kim, et al. "Genetic Analysis of a Complex Trait in the Utah Genetic Reference Project: A Major Locus for PTC Taste Ability on Chromosome 7q and a Secondary Locus on Chromosome 16p." *Human Genetics* 112 (2003): 567–572.

Enattah, N. S., T. G. K. Jensen, M. Nielsen, et al. "Independent Introduction of Two Lactase-Persistence Alleles into Human Populations Reflects Different History of Adaptation to Milk Culture." *American Journal of Human Genetics* 82 (2008): 57–72.

Enattah, N. S., T. Sahi, E. Savilahti, et al. "Identification of a Variant Associated with Adult-Type Hypolactasia." *Nature Genetics* 30 (2002): 233–237.

Feeney, E. "The Impact of Bitter Perception and Genotypic Variation of TAS2R38 on Food Choice." *Nutrition Bulletin* 36 (2011): 20–33.

Fisher, R. A., E. B. Ford, and J. Huxley. "Taste-Testing the Anthropoid Apes." *Nature* 144 (1939): 750.

Fox, A. L. "The Relationship Between Chemical Constitution and Taste." *Proceedings of the National Academy of Sciences of the United States of America* 18 (1932): 115–120.

Fumagalli, M., I. Moltke, N. Grarup, et al. "Greenlandic Inuit Show Genetic Signatures of Diet and Climate Adaptation." *Science* 349 (2015): 1343–1347.

Gilbert, M. T. P., A. S. Wilson, M. Bunce, et al. "Ancient Mitochondrial DNA from Hair." *Current Biology* 14 (2004): R463–R464.

Groot, P. C., M. J. Blecker, J. C. Pronk, et al. "The Human Alpha-Amylase Multigene Family Consists of Haplotypes with Variable Numbers of Genes." *Genomics* 5 (1989): 29–42.

Gudbjartsson, D. F., Walters, G. B., Thorleifsson, G., et al. "Many Sequence Variants Affecting Diversity of Adult Human Height." *Nature Genetics* 40 (2008): 609–615.

Hagelberg, E., M. Hofreiter, and C. Keyser. "Ancient DNA: The First Three Decades." *Philosophical Transactions of the Royal Society, B* 30 (2015): 20130371. http://dx.doi.org/10.1098/rstb.2013.0371.

Henn, B. M., L. Hon, J. M. Macpherson, et al. "Cryptic Distant Relatives Are Common in Both Isolated and Cosmopolitan Genetic Samples." *PLoS One* 7 (4) (2012): e34267. https://doi.org/10.1371/journal.pone.0034267

Hlusko, L. J., J. P. Carlson, G. Chaplin, et al. "Environmental Selection During the Last Ice Age on the Mother-to-Infant Transmission of Vitamin D and Fatty Acids Through Breast Milk." *Proceedings of the National Academy of Sciences of the United States of America* 115, no. 19 (2018): E4426–E4432.

Hofreiter, M., D. Serre, H. N. Poinar, et al. "Ancient DNA." *Nature Reviews Genetics* 2 (2001): 353–359.

Holden, C., and R. Mace. "Phylogenetic Analysis of the Evolution of Lactose Digestion in Adults." *Human Biology* 69 (1997): 605–628.

Hunley, K., and J. C. Long. "Gene Flow Across Linguistic Boundaries in Native North American Populations." *Proceedings of the National Academy of Sciences of the United States of America* 102 (2005): 1312–1317.

Irish, J. D., A. Morez, L. G. Flink, et al. "Do Dental Nonmetric Traits Actually Work as Proxies for Neutral Genomic Data? Some Answers from Continental- and Global-Level Analyses?" *American Journal of Biological Anthropology* 172 (2020): 347–375.

Kazak, L., A. Reyes, and I. J. Holt. "Minimizing the Damage: Repair Pathways Keep Mitochondrial DNA Intact." *Nature Reviews: Molecular Cell Biology* 13 (2012): 659–671.

Kim, U. K., E. Jorgenson, H. Coon, et al. "Positional Cloning of the Human Quantitative Trait Locus Underlying Taste Sensitivity to Phenylthiocarbamide." *Science* 299 (2003): 1221–1225.

Kimura, R., T. Yamaguchi, M. Takeda, et al. "A Common Variation in EDAR Is a Genetic Determinant of Shovel-Shaped Incisors." *American Journal of Human Genetics* 85 (2009): 528–535.

Lande, R. "Statistical Tests for Natural Selection on Quantitative Characters." *Evolution* 31 (1977): 442–444.

Lander, E. S., L. M. Linton, B. Birren, et al. "Initial Sequencing and Analysis of the Human Genome." *Nature* 409 (2001): 860–921.

Lao, O., T. T. Lu, M. Nothagel, et al. "Correlation Between Genetic and Geographic Structure in Europe." *Current Biology* 18 (2008): 1241–1248.

Lettre, G., A. U. Jackson, C. Gieger, et al. "Identification of Ten Loci Associated with Height Highlights New Biological Pathways in Human Growth." *Nature Genetics* 40 (2008): 584–591.

Leutenegger, A.-L., M. Sahbatou, S. Gazal, et al. "Consanguinity Around the World: What Do the Genomic Data of the HGDP-CEPH Diversity Panel Tell Us?" *European Journal of Human Genetics* 19 (2011): 583–587.

Locke, A. E., B. Kahali, S. I. Berndt, et al. "Genetic Studies of Body Mass Index Yield New Insights for Obesity Biology." *Nature* 518 (2015): 197–206.

McEvoy, B. P., and P. M. Visscher. "Genetics of Human Height." *Economics & Human Biology* 7 (2009): 294–306.

Novembre, J., T. Johnson, K. Bryc, et al. "Genes Mirror Geography Within Europe." *Nature* 456 (2008): 98–101.

O'Rourke, D. H. "Anthroplogical Genetics in the Genomic Era: A Look Back and Ahead." *American Anthropologist* 105 (2003): 101–109.

O'Rourke, D. H. "Classical Marker Variation in Native North Americans." In *Handbook of North American Indians,* Vol. 3. *Environment, Origins and Population.* Edited by D. Ubelaker, 762–776 Washington, DC: Smithsonian Institution, 2006.

O'Rourke, D. H. "Ancient DNA and Its Application to the Reconstruction of Human Evolution and History." In *Anthropological Genetics: Theory, Methods and Applications.* Edited by M. H. Crawford, 210–231 Cambridge: Cambridge University Press, 2007.

O'Rourke, D. H., and J. Raff. (2009). "A Genetic Perspective on American Colonization." *Current Biology* 20 (2009): 202–207.

Perry, G. H., N. J. Dominy, K. G. Claw, et al. "Diet and the Evolution of Human Amylase Gene Copy Number Variation." *Nature Genetics* 39 (2007): 1256–1260.

Relethford, J. H., and J. Blangero. "Detection of Differential Gene Flow from Patterns of Quantitative Variation." *Human Biology* 62 (1990): 5–25.

Roseman, C. C., and T. D.Weaver. "Molecules versus Morphology? Not for the Human Cranium." *BioEssays* 29 (2007): 1185–1188.

Sabeti, P. C., D. E. Reich, J. M. Higgins, et al. "Detecting Recent Positive Selection in the Human Genome from Haplotype Structure." *Nature* 419 (2002): 832–837.

Sanna, S., A. U. Jackson, R. Nagaraja, et al. "Common Variants in the GDF5-UQCC Region Are Associated with Variation in Human Height." *Nature Genetics* 40 (2008): 198–203.

Silventoinen, K., S. Sammalisto, M. Perola, et al. "Heritability of Adult Body Height: A Comparative Study of Twin Cohorts in Eight Countries." *Twin Research* 6 (2003): 399–408.

Simoons, F. J. "The Geographic Hypothesis and Lactose Malabsorption. A Weighing of the Evidence." *American Journal of Digestive Diseases* 23 (1978): 963–980.

Spuhler, J. N. "Genetic, Linguistic, and Geographical Distances in Native North America." In *The Assessment of Population Affinities in Man.* Edited by J. S. Weiner and J. Huizinga, 337–379. Oxford: Clarendon Press, 1972.

Thorleifsson, G., G. B. Walters, D. F. Gudbjartsson, et al. "Genome-Wide Association Yields New Sequence Variants at Seven Loci That Associate with Measures of Obesity." *Nature Genetics* 41 (2009): 18–24.

Tishkiff, S. A, and M. K. Gonder. "Human Origins Within and Out of Africa." In *Anthropological Genetics: Theory, Methods, and Applications.* Edited by M. H. Crawford, 337–379. Cambridge: Cambridge University Press, 2007.

Tishkoff, S. A., F. A. Reed, A. Ranciaro, et al. "Convergent Adaptation of Human Lactase Persistence in Africa and Europe." *Nature Genetics* 39 (2007): 31–40.

Veilleux, C. C. "Sensory Polymorphisms and Dietary Adaptation." In *Companion to Anthropological Genetics.* Edited by D. H. O'Rourke, 233–250. Oxford: Wiley-Blackwell, 2019.

Visscher, P. M. "Sizing up Human Height Variation." *Nature Genetics* 40 (2008): 489–490.

Von Cramon-Taubadel, N. "Evaluating Correspondence in Phenotypic Variation, Genetic Diversity, Geography, and Environmental Factors." In *Companion to Anthropological Genetics.* Edited by D. H. O'Rourke, 89–105. New York: Wiley-Blackwell, 2019.

Watson, J. D. and F. H. C. Crick, "Molecular Structure of Nucleic Acids: A Structure for Deoxyribonucleic Acid." *Nature* 171 (1953): 964–969.

Weeden, M. N., G. Lettre, R. M. Freathy, et al. "A Common Variant of HMGA2 Is Associated with Adult and Childhood Height in the General Population." *Nature Genetics* 39 (2007): 1245–1250.

Weedon, M. N., H. Lango, C. M. Lindgren, et al. "Genome-wide Association Analysis Identifies 20 Loci That Influence Adult Height." *Nature Genetics* 40 (2008): 575–583.

Weyrich, L. S., K. Dobney, and A. Cooper. "Ancient DNA Analysis of Dental Calculus." *Journal of Human Evolution* 79 (2015): 119–124.

Willer, C. J., E. K. Speliotes, R. J. F. Loos, et al. "Six New Loci Associated with Body Mass Index Highlight a Neuronal Influence on Body Weight Regulation." *Nature Genetics* 41 (2009): 25–34.

Wood, A. R., T. Esko, J. Yang, et al. "Defining the Role of Common Variation in the Genomic and Biological Architecture of Adult Human Height." *Nature Genetics* 46 (2014): 1173–1186.

Wooding, S. "Phenylthiocarbamide: A 75-year Adventure in Genetics and Natural Selection." *Genetics* 172 (2006): 2015–2023.

Wooding, S. "Following the Herd." *Nature Genetics* 39 (2007): 7–8.

Wooding, S., U. Kim, M. J. Bamshad, et al. "Natural Selection and Molecular Evolution in PTC, a Bitter-Tase Receptor Gene." *American Journal of Human Genetics* 74 (2004): 637–646.

Wooding, S., H. Gunn, P. Ramos, et al. "Genetics and Bitter Taste Responses to Goitrogen, a Plant Toxin Found in Vegetables. *Chemical Senses* 35 (2010): 685–692.

Yengo, L., J. Sidorenko, K. E. Kemper, et al. "Meta-analysis of Genome-Wide Association Studies for Height and Body Mass Index in ~700,000 Individuals of European Ancestry." *Human Molecular Genetics* 27 (2018): 3641–3649.

CHAPTER 7

Race, Racism, and Racial Thinking: Implications for Biological Anthropology

Rachel Caspari

INTRODUCTION

Over the last century, anthropological discourse about race changed dramatically. Once a core concept in anthropology, it is now widely accepted as the "myth" coined by Ashley Montagu (1942) to denote that race is a social construction with no basis in biology. In *Man's Most Dangerous Myth: The Fallacy of Race*, Montagu (1942) was participating in a long and important history of anti-racist public activism by biological anthropologists, a history that continues to this day (e.g., Fuentes 2022; Marks 2017, and many others). The social constructivist view of race was new in that it not only argued for racial equality, the insignificance of racial differences, and against the type concept, although it did all three. Montagu (1942) made the public case that race did not exist, and since it was a social construction, the word "race" with its biological connotations should be retired in favor of "ethnic groups."

The biological race concept that Montagu attempted to depose, sometimes called the Western race concept, or simply, the race concept, applies the biological category of subspecies to socially constructed races, in the guise of "continental races." Formally constructed in the eighteenth century (Linnaeus 1758), races were defined as part of a biological taxonomy, with essentialized physical and behavioral characteristics that conformed to European prejudices. This taxonomy was later extended to include smaller social groups, so that at the time of Montagu's 1942 publication, some nations, tribes, or religions, such as Jews, were considered races by many. As part of a biological taxonomy, there are assumptions about the nature and cause of perceived differences between groups that are part of the embedded meanings of race. These contribute to the racial thinking discussed in this chapter.

A Companion to Biological Anthropology, Second Edition. Edited by Clark Spencer Larsen.
© 2023 John Wiley & Sons Ltd. Published 2023 by John Wiley & Sons Ltd.

The social constructivist view of race was long in the making in American anthropology. The underpinnings, in terms of the insignificance of racial differences and racial equality in abilities, were discussed by Franz Boas as early as 1894 and had a public impact, influencing the ideas of some progressives including W. E. B DuBois and other Black intellectuals (Levy Zumwalt and Willis 2008). However, calls for the elimination of the race concept post-World War II, if accepted, would strike at the very heart of racism. To anthropologists supporting the social constructivist view, it was understood that the biological race concept itself was not only scientifically invalid, but racist, because it naturalizes or "biologizes" social inequality. As has been well discussed in many venues (e.g., Blakey 1999; Marks 1995), the race concept was born of colonialism, rationalizing European subjugation and exploitation of others through the false belief in the natural (biological) superiority of Europeans. Therefore, the idea that races do not exist in nature was not only biologically supported, it also undermined the very foundation of white supremacy, and this was recognized by some factions within the American anthropological community.

Yet, the social constructivist view of race remained very controversial in biological anthropology until surprisingly recently. Some were overtly racist, but many anthropologists and other scientists argued against the innate inequality of races while accepting (or even arguing for) the existence of biological races. For example, the 1951 UNESCO statement on race (co-authored and cited by Juan Comas (1961) to counter a resurgence of white supremacist scientific racism in the early 1960s) emphasized the lack of evidence for racial differences in intellectual ability or any support for the biological ranking of races but did not engage the race concept itself. As discussed in this chapter, this is because the race concept has been conflated with both social races and the obvious existence of geographic variation. The assumptions about the nature and causes of that variation that are embedded in the race concept were unrecognized. The recent Statement on Race published by the American Association of Physical Anthropologists (Fuentes et al. 2019) may be the first published by biological anthropologists to formally reject the race concept *and its imbedded meanings* regarding the structure of human populations past and present.

The *racial thinking*, the embedded meanings associated with the race concept about the cause and nature of human population differences, are used to "otherize" and validate discrimination against many biologized ethnic/social groups globally, not only the social groups associated with continental races. Therefore, although the Western race concept was created in the colonial context, the rejection of the race concept as an idea applies not only to the social races (e.g., Black, White, Asian, Native American) constructed in that context, but also, more generally, where it has also been used to rationalize subjugation, exploitation, and genocide. While most biological anthropologists reject the Western race concept, specifically the idea that continental groups represent subspecies of humans, racial thinking is far more intractable for reasons explored here. It is a product of systemic racism that is compatible with the psychological essentialism associated with the human mind. However, the culture of biological anthropology is changing along with its demographics (Antón et al. 2018; Bolnick et al. 2019; Fuentes 2019) and while I am optimistic that our ideas of race and racism are evolving, it remains to be seen if the vestiges of the race concept will be fully confronted and eliminated.

Typological thinking about human variation persists in science and society and race continues to be important to biological anthropologists in many ways. This chapter explores three of them. First, the race concept is not dead. The race concept is widely believed, and racial thinking also persists in the public mind and in various scientific studies. In fact, racial thinking may be a part of the human condition, like essentialism itself, and therefore can only be eradicated (or mitigated, if eradication is impossible) through education. Since race and geographic variation are so often conflated, race should be directly addressed when teaching biological variation.

Second, racial thinking may still influence our understanding of human variation, population relationships, and human evolution. Lewontin's seminal work (1972) showed minimal average population structure in the human species, and subsequent studies likewise showed relatively little variation among groups (e.g., Barbujani and Belle 2006; Nei and Roychoudhury 1982; Rosenberg et al. 2002; Serre and Pääbo 2004). This work appeared to drive the final nails in the coffin of the race concept. However, there is debate about the nature of human population structure, and evolutionary trees, rather than networks, are commonly used to denote population relationships, eclipsing the importance of gene flow.

Finally, while social races are not genealogical entities, they have biological dimensions. Phenotypic associations with social races reify the race concept and present a dilemma for forensic anthropology. There are many negative health outcomes associated with race and inequality, of increasing importance to biocultural anthropologists and public health workers. The medical community continues to grapple with race-based medicine that can contribute to poor health outcomes in minority communities and represents one of the most dangerous effects of the perpetuation of the race concept. Unfortunately, because of the primacy of racial thinking, these biological attributes of social groups help to reify the race concept.

THE RACE CONCEPT IS NOT DEAD

The race concept is currently alive and well in the general public, providing fodder for neo-fascists globally (Panofsky et al. 2021), but it has also persisted in biological anthropology until very recently. Although challenged by some anthropologists since the inception of the discipline, it was largely intractable because it lay at the foundation of physical anthropology. In fact, in the early twentieth century, race was used as the *raison d'etre* for the emerging discipline; eugenics and race science were promoted as applied physical anthropology and used by Aleš Hrdlička and others to secure support for the emerging discipline (Blakey 1987; Caspari 2018a).

In the 1960s, seminal papers were published on the nonexistence of human races (Brace 1964; Livingstone 1962), and throughout the next few decades, population genetics increasingly provided evidence against the race concept (Barbujani and Belle 2006; Lewontin 1972; Nei and Roychoudhury 1982; Rosenberg et al. 2002; Serre and Pääbo 2004). Yet, controversy surrounding the existence of human races persisted; less than two decades ago, surveys found that between 20 and 30 percent of American biological anthro-pologists did not reject the biological race concept and in European biological anthropology, more scientists accepted the race concept than in the previous post-war generation (Kaszycka et al. 2009, Lieberman et al. 2004). This may not have been the result of a resurgence of racism in European academia, but rather a lack of critical thinking about race.

Despite a long history of challenges, and increasingly compelling evidence against it, the race concept is surprisingly resistant. If people are not actively taught that races do not exist, the race concept re-emerges. This may be because race is much more than a bad idea about geographic variation; it has psychological and social dimensions that make it a bad idea about geographic variation that is exceptionally difficult to depose. It may be that, left to their own devices, humans think taxonomically and, hence, racially.

Why Won't Race Die? Essentialism and the Psychology of Taxonomy

It may be part of the human condition to construct naïve taxonomies of the natural and social worlds, predisposing us to racial thinking (Atran 1990, 1994; Atran et al. 2002; Gil-White 2001; Hirschfeld 1996, 1998; Hirschfeld and Gelman 1994; Prentice and Miller 2007). Essentialism is a critical component of all such taxonomies. Moreover, the western race concept, by conflating biological and social taxonomies, by fiat "biologizes" social categories (Blakey 1999) may make the western race concept more insidious than other forms of social classification.

Humans create taxonomies of the biological, social, and physical world in similar ways, cross-culturally (Atran 1990, 1994; Atran et al. 2002; Gil-White 2001; Hirschfeld 1996, 1998; Hirschfeld and Gelman 1994; Prentice and Miller 2007). These taxonomies are knowledge structures that allow many inferences to be made (beyond the information given) about constituent categories. Some categories are more inferentially rich than others, allowing stereotypes to form without empirical basis. These categories have been termed "natural kinds," because people believe them to be part of the natural world – "real;" they do not recognize them as mental or cultural constructions (Hirschfeld and Gelman 1994).

It is thought that "natural kinds" are produced through cognitive mechanisms that are specific to particular domains (based on different mental modules); some domains allow people to subconsciously construct naïve theories (and associated inferences) about aspects of the physical world, while competence in another domain governs living things. "Natural kinds" that reflect the biological world have been termed "living kinds," which people learn through different cognitive processes than those used to learn inanimate things or the processes that relate to them (naïve physics). Hirschfeld (1996, 1998) and others (Gil-White 2001; Prentice and Miller 2007) note that in addition to a cognitive domain that governs "living kinds," humans have a separate domain that allows them to easily learn "human kinds" and the traits that make up the essence of a particular kind. These "human kinds" are social categories that are particularly important to a culture; they are thought by members of that culture to be intrinsic to a person's identity. Just as biological categories carry information about the essence of a species, genus, or class, "human kinds" carry information about the "essence" of a type of person – what they are supposed to look like, think like, or act like. The fact that many members of a category do not conform to the stereotype does not dispel the stereotype: this is a hallmark of essentialism.

"Human kinds," then, are groups whose members are believed to share some fundamental essence, considered to be inheritable and relatively unchangeable. In western society and, to some extent, globally, because of cultural interconnection, western dominance, and the legacies of colonialism, "race" is a "human kind" and therefore has a psychological dimension. We may be psychologically, and evolutionarily, disposed to racial thinking.

However, races are also "living kinds." The Western race concept was constructed as a biological taxonomy, based loosely on ideas about geographic variation, variation that has great social meaning because of the history of colonialism and slavery that continues to link differences in power and privilege to geographic ancestry. It developed in part through science in the age of discovery, as racial classifications were developed to make sense of new social groups, effectively "biologizing" relationships between Europeans and other people they encountered, and even relationships between different European groups (Blakey 1999). Incorporated into the natural history tradition, race was a taxonomy of "living kinds," even as it was simultaneously a taxonomy of "human kinds." While race is clearly social, its "naturalness" has been validated by incorporating racial categories into a biological taxonomy.

It is likely that this psychological dimension of race contributes to the persistence of the race concept; in addition to very influential sociopolitical factors, it explains why stereotypes are so difficult to dispel and why racial thinking remains so dominant in science and society. Anthropology's long struggle with the race concept underscores this. In the nineteenth century, Topinard himself, disciple of the polygenist Paul Broca and a major influence on the founders of American physical anthropology, struggled with the type concept. Although he was the pre-eminent student of types and a staunch promoter of the type concept, Topinard recognized that the concept of racial "essence" was undermined by the lack of homogeneity of populations, and that any continuity with supposed once pure racial types was at best "a hypothesis ... convenient for study, impossible to demonstrate."(Topinard 1892) Yet, while he considered races to be an abstraction, Topinard was simultaneously convinced of their reality and of the reality of racial assumptions underlying human variation. As cited by Stocking (1968: 59):

> "We cannot deny them, our mind sees them, our labor separates them out; if in thought we suppress the intermixtures of peoples, their interbreedings, in a flash we see them stand forth – simple, inevitable, a necessary consequence of collective heredity." (Topinard 1885: 202)

Topinard's dilemma (Caspari 2018a), the conflict between the type concept he believed in and the reality he observed, is one shared by many workers and continues to be an obstacle to reconciling race within biological anthropology; racial thinking may be so entrenched that anthropological work that refutes the race concept may be unrecognized even by the workers themselves. Brown and Armelagos (2001) point out a modern example of the same conflict: while Nei and Roychoudhury's (1982) paper undermined racial categorization (they found only 9–11 percent of the total genetic heterozygosity at 86 loci attributable to racial classifications), they nevertheless discuss the evolution of Mongoloid, Caucasoid, and Negroid racial groups. As Brown and Armelagos (2001: 36) put it: "This speaks to the logical disconnect shown by many researchers who simultaneously prove the irrelevance of genetic race and then proceed to discuss the genetic evolution of races."

This psychological dimension of race is of interest to biological anthropologists in several ways. The evolutionary basis of essentialism and race, as a product of mind, is an interesting issue for evolutionary psychologists and has implications for human evolution. It also explains why the race concept does not die and why even when race seems dead it is so easily resurrected. Racial thinking applied to many social groups may explain alterity – the tendency to "otherize." Therefore, although "races" are no longer objects of study, race remains an important topic within biological anthropology that affects us as scientists and educators. Our students may arrive with naïve taxonomies that are at odds with current understandings of human variation and, perhaps more importantly, our understandings of human variation may be influenced by our own naïve taxonomies.

Tree Thinking: Vestige of the Race Concept

The biological race concept is not synonymous with human variation; it is a specific way of interpreting variation consistent with racial thinking. It incorporates essentialism (which, as discussed above, is intrinsic to taxonomies and itself may have a biological basis), biological determinism (a part of essentialized social categories), and the assumption that human intra-specific relationships are tree-like, providing a model that explains the existence of separate essences. Isolation and independent histories are important aspects of the race concept, and these can be tested. This (along with demonstration of the nonconcordance of racial features) led to the demise of the biological race concept, yet tree structures are still often used to depict relationships.

The eighteenth century natural history tradition was descriptive, and the Western race concept developed within it to delineate and describe the primary divisions of humankind (Brace 2005; Caspari 2018b; Marks 1995). While there were debates within science about the number and constituents of the divisions (three, five, or more), there was little question about what they represented: subspecies, or perhaps species. From its very inception, the race concept embodied both essentialism (as discussed above) and biological determinism, the linking of behavioral traits such as intelligence, criminality, industriousness, and other personality traits to the essences of racial categories. The categories and their essences, with both physical and behavioral components believed to be stable and unchanging, were defined by science as natural groups, even as if they were part of a stratified social system.

Isolation is also a component of the race concept. While race concepts held by members of society are rarely deconstructed, scientific explanations of human variation would need to be consistent with the type concept for biological races to be valid. The earliest debates in anthropology were over just how this isolation developed: polygenists argued that races were created separately by God, while monogenists thought they diverged after the creation of Adam and Eve, going their separate ways from Eden, or after the biblical flood (Stanton 1960; Stocking 1968). After the acceptance of Darwinian evolution in the second half of the nineteenth century, these religious ideas were replaced by evolutionary polygenism, which explained racial differences as the product of separate evolutionary histories (Caspari 2010, 2018b, 2018c).

Trees, as the way taxonomic hierarchies are conceived and depicted, express how types can exist – they embody an explanation for the concordance of the physical and behavioral traits that are believed to be the essence of a race. Races have been depicted as clades on an evolutionary tree – as phylogenetic units. Historically, racial trees incorporated and "explained" racist stereotypes as products of separate evolutionary histories; different selection pressures and rates of evolutionary change were thought to affect each separate branch, and branch length could also reflect supposed evolutionary development (see reviews in Caspari 2010, 2018b, 2018c). While tree models, in themselves, do not necessarily represent racism (for instance, short branches have been used to underscore human similarities and the "brotherhood of man," depicting a recent common ancestor of all populations), they are nevertheless reflections of racial thinking – vestiges of the race concept. Branches, whatever their length, imply divergence and isolation, a pattern that does not depict relationships between human populations that are interconnected by gene flow.

Therefore, race is not simply geographic variation or differences between populations; because of the history of the concept and the psychology of racial thinking, race is a taxonomic way of viewing human variation. Because of the relationship between taxonomy and phylogeny, the existence of race in a scientific sense implies that racial differences are phylogenetic – that they can be modeled as a tree. It is telling that the phylogenetic assumption has been used, untested, throughout the history of anthropology; tree models are often used whether or not they are valid (Templeton 1998). Because of the power and prevalence of the race concept, phylogenetic relationships among human populations have often been simply assumed. In the last decade, however, there have been far more complex discussions of the kinds of models best used to represent human genetic diversity; gene flow (although often discussed as "admixture") is represented and has had a large and positive impact on our understanding of human variation past and present (e.g., Hunley et al. 2009, 2016).

CAN DIFFERENCES BETWEEN HUMAN GROUPS BE UNDERSTOOD PHYLOGENETICALLY?

Can tree-thinking be applied to human variation? Can biological differences between populations be explained phylogenetically? There are two issues here. First, do the races of the Western race concept exist in that there are continental groups that can be considered human subspecies? Second lies the deeper issue of whether *racial thinking* is supported by patterns of geographic variation – is there *any* human taxonomy below the species level – can tree structures validly be used to model human population relationships?

Genetics had a strong influence on the changing race concept, especially the population genetics of the modern synthesis that focused on the dynamics of intra-specific evolution. Population geneticists through the years have provided compelling evidence for human unity. Perhaps the most cited scientific challenge to the race concept is Lewontin's (1972) paper emphasizing that very little human genetic variation is attributable to racial or even populational differences. Using Sewall Wright's F-statistic, originally developed to assess inbreeding, Lewontin showed that an assumed hierarchical population structure explained very little of the genetic variation in humans. F_{st}, the proportion of the total variation attributable to between-group genetic differences was very low: about 6 percent for regional differences and 8 percent at the subpopulation level. The vast majority, about 85 percent, of the variation was found within subpopulations. These low levels of interpopulational diversity have been supported by a large number of studies since then (e.g., Barbujani and Belle 2016; Manica et al. 2005; Nei and Roychoudhuri 1982; Rosenberg et al. 2002; Serres and Pääbo 2004). By showing a minimal population structure on several levels, this work undermines the phylogenetic assumption not only on the level of subspecies, but also on the level of populations. This has been underscored by Templeton (1998), who has argued that human populations have such little structure that "treeness" is not demonstrated and phylogenetic models are invalid. A number of more recent studies have underscored the fluidity of populations, showing strong correlations between genetic variation and geographic distance (e.g., Manica et al. 2005), some conforming to an isolation by distance model, with few discrete boundaries between populations (Serre and Pääbo 2004). By challenging the phylogenetic assumption, these studies refute not only the western race concept, but also racial thinking in general.

However, whether there is a phylogenetic pattern to population relationships is still discussed (Hunley et al. 2016). While some workers interpret the correlation of genetic variation with geography as clinal (Serre and Pääbo 2004), other studies have found such correlations consistent with a nested hierarchical pattern (Ramachandran et al. 2005). This underscores a problem pointed out by Long et al. (2009), that the choice of model used in an analysis biases the results. This is the core of a critique of F_{st} that has been challenged as an oversimplification of apportionment of human genetic diversity (Long et al. 2009; Long and Kittles 2003). These authors have argued that, contra to Lewontin (1972), population structure may still explain human diversity, but not the very simple structure assumed in Wright's F_{st} model as used by Lewontin. They highlight several problems. Because F_{st} expresses *average* diversity found between subpopulations, it does not adequately express variation in diversity: some populations may vary a lot, while others very little. Thus, population structure may better explain the diversity among some populations but not others. Moreover, it has been argued that aspects of F_{st} may be circular – that the actual deviance from the population structure assumed in the model affects the apportionment of diversity estimated by F_{st}. Long and Kittles (2003) point out the violated assumption of the evolutionary independence of populations (intrinsic to population structure models – i.e., trees) may have the consequence of increasing the gene identity estimation (the probability of homozygosity) for the total population. Since F_{st} measures the gene identity of subpopulations relative to the total population, this would serve to artificially depress F_{st} measures.

Nevertheless, the conclusions of virtually all studies using various approaches to the assessment of genetic diversity agree that human subspecies do not exist, most on the basis of low levels of diversity and the geographic patterning of that diversity (Relethford 2009; Rosenberg et al. 2002; Serre and Pääbo 2004).

For some, the claim against race has been taken to mean there is no geographically structured biological variation and that any genetic clustering of populations (or classically defined races) indicates that races exist (Reich 2018; Risch et al. 2002) or that it is valid to model them phylogenetically. Thus, studies finding genetic differences among populations are widely circulated (Caspari 2014) and commonly appropriated by neo-fascist hate groups to justify ideas of "racial purity" and white superiority (Panofsky et al. 2021). This is a straw man argument: of course, there are biological differences between myriad human groups. This has always been clear; even the low levels of intergroup variation suggested by Lewontin are significant (Hunley et al. 2009). At issue for the race concept is how important population structure is in characterizing relationships between populations, and whether they should be considered taxonomic.

Genetic studies have underscored the complexities of the causes of human diversity, complexity caused by variation in gene flow and selection that undermines taxonomic assumptions. Since the genetics of populations are based on population histories (including large-scale migrations, population fissioning and reticulation, marriage patterns, and an assortment of other social variables) and natural selection, the apportionment of diversity is extremely variable. This was demonstrated in a 2009 study where the genetic diversity at a number of neutral microsatellite loci was compared to computer simulations of the genetic variation predicted for different demographic models: isolation-by-distance, independent regions, serial fissions, and nested regions (Hunley et al. 2009). Results indicated that none of the models completely fit the data and that a combination of isolation by distance and nested regions seemed to fit the data best. Moreover, while most genetic studies involving the apportionment of human variation have focused on neutral loci, the pattern of spread of recent alleles under selection may also contribute to our understanding of population relationships (Coop et al. 2009; Hawks et al. 2007), including the evolution and spread of mutations of regional adaptive significance. Trees may explain local patterns of diversity for short periods of time, but genetic data to date indicate that there is a broader clinal pattern for both neutral and adaptive genetic variation, which is affected by variable population expansions and population structure. This complexity undermines the taxonomic assumptions of the race concept.

Biological Dimensions of Social Races

Links Between Biological and Social Race

While social races are constantly redefined, they are loosely tied to the impugned and non-existent biological races of the Western race concept. They cannot be truly separated from them; social races are *believed* to be biological races. As discussed below, this has had profound effects, especially in medicine. Moreover, there are biological consequences of racism that affect socially defined racial groups. The conundrum for anthropologists is that recognizing biological dimensions of social races also serves to reify the race concept.

Race and Ancestry

Although we are accustomed to constructing family trees, individual ancestry, like group ancestry, is complex. We tend to think we have a unique individual genealogical ancestry that in turn is conflated with genetic ancestry (Mathieson and Scally 2020; Van Arsdale 2019). These are different things. In fact, only some of our genealogical ancestors from just seven generations ago contribute any genes to us, and our ancestors even a few generations ago are shared by huge numbers of people. Some studies have suggested that most people alive today share *the same set* of genealogical ancestors *only a few millennia ago* – in other words, those ancestors are the only set of people from their generation that have living descendants, and virtually everyone currently on Earth descends from all of them (Chang 1999; Ralph and Coop 2013a, 2013b; Rhode et al. 2004). It is inevitably the case that there is a time in the past when all humans share that set of common ancestors; what is surprising is how recent this ancestry appears to be. We are not equally related to everyone in that set of ancestors, of course; an individual may be connected to some ancestors through numerous ancestor-descendant pathways (generally those in the same geographic area as the individual and their immediate ancestors), while perhaps having only one or a few pathways to ancestors in more distant regions. This pattern is due to both inbreeding and widespread gene flow throughout the human species that is antithetical to the race concept, connecting everyone through a complex network rather than a tree. That pattern of ancestry helps explain why biological races did not develop in humans (Van Arsdale 2019).

Nevertheless, racial thinking affects public and scientific understanding of ancestry in multiple ways (Benn Torres 2020). Few of us know our genealogical history in much detail and it may appear tree-like for the few generations we are aware of. Yet, we extend our family trees, commonly with genetic testing, to identify with real or presumed ancestral groups that are sometimes conflated with social races.

The conflation of social race and ancestry is a particular problem for forensic anthropology, with current debates about whether ancestry is a useful part of the biological profile at all (Albanese and Saunders 2006; Bethard and DiGangi 2020, 2021; Stull et al. 2021). Forensic anthropologists have long argued that race (or ancestry) is important, in part because race (or ancestry) is used as an identifier by law enforcement and others in the medico-legal community within which they work. The use of ancestry has been thought to be an effective tool in individual identification, therefore serving a significant social good. This idea is being challenged. There are arguments about the effectiveness of ancestry assessment (Bethard and DiGangi 2021; Ousley 2009; Sauer 1992; Stull et al. 2021), but the primary argument against the use of ancestry in the biological profile is that this practice reifies race; it biologizes social groups and contributes to systemic racism. It can be argued that perpetuating the race concept is particularly dangerous in the field of law enforcement (Bethard and DiGangi 2021).

As biological anthropology as a discipline came to reject the race concept, forensic anthropology replaced the term "race" with "ancestry." However, by "ancestry" forensic anthropologists really mean social race; they are looking for evidence of social identity. Race and ancestry are not the same, although there may be elements of ancestry associated with social race, and races are *presumed* to be based on shared ancestry. Social race can be thought of as that aspect of ancestry (either real or imagined) that is most important to identity (either self-identity or socially imposed identity). This underlies institutions of hypodescent, such as the "one-drop" rule, so that a "mixed-race" person is assigned the social race of the minority group. There is often a phenotypic component to social races (used in forensic anthropology) and this underscores the "naturalness" or presumed biological basis of the category. People scrutinize each other for clues of racial identity; hence, the slightest African feature could prevent a person from "passing for white" in highly racialized early twentieth century US society. Students sometimes ask why subordinate racial features are "dominant" in mixed race people: they are not. We are just good at looking for them. It may be a part of the human condition that we seek biological cues of social identity.

Perhaps because social races are presumed to be biological races, people often think about their ancestry in terms of "pure races." Thus, a person might speak of their ancestry as "half Black, a quarter White, and a quarter Native American," when speaking of the social races of their grandparents. Of course, each grandparent may also have had mixed ancestry, but this is obscured by the system of racial classification. Racial thinking often occurs even when "race" is not used to define ancestry; more delineated ancestral groups, such as countries or nations, are thought of racially. For example, direct to the consumer genetic testing promotes a racial view of ancestry by encouraging consumers to conceive of reference samples as "pure" source populations (Benn Torres 2020; Bolnick 2008). The vision of ancestry offered, while more refined than continental racial classifications, nevertheless promotes a typological view of human variation that can be easily abused. Applying racist interpretations to the results of ancestry testing has been used to advance ideas of racial purity by white nationalists (Panofsky et al. 2021).

Race therefore obscures ancestry, and ancestry is also racialized. Even when the race concept is rejected, it is common to think of ancestral groups as discrete categories, although this is not true. We understand that for the most part, populations have always been fluid; gene flow is a part of the human condition (Athreya and Ackerman 2019; Fuentes et al. 2019; Wolpoff and Caspari 1997). Franz Weidenreich, an early proponent of multiregional evolution, once argued against race, describing ancient human groups as having multiple ancestors and multiple descendants (Wolpoff and Caspari 1997). This nonracial view of deep ancestry has been borne out with recent genetic data corroborating ubiquitous "mixing" throughout the Pleistocene (Athreya and Ackermann 2019; Slatkin and Racimo 2016). Although Pleistocene populations were smaller and for the most part more isolated than living humans, gene flow was nevertheless common. As geneticists Slatkin and Racimo (2016: 6385) put it: "Admixture among archaic groups and between them and modern humans seems to have occurred whenever they came into geographic proximity." We are all the products of widespread gene flow; yet tree thinking regarding recent human evolution persists and contributes to a reification of race. This racial view of ancestry may have consequences, particularly regarding research into health disparities among different racial groups.

Health Consequences

In May 2022 the American Academy of Pediatrics issued a policy statement against the use of race-based medicine, based on the recognition that race is a social construction (Wright et al 2022). They point out that the biological race concept and its conflation with social race has influenced medical practices to the present day, resulting in deleterious consequences for the health of minority communities, especially African Americans. Many of these medical practices derive from unfounded beliefs that are holdovers from slavery, such as ideas of racial differences in pain tolerance (Hoffman et al. 2016) and that African Americans have "deficient" lung capacity (Lujan and DiCarlo 2018). Similar prejudices led to the expectation that African Americans have larger muscle mass than whites, causing higher normal serum creatine levels. Among other things, these biases have resulted in race-based modifications to diagnostic tests including algorithms used to interpret eGFR tests of kidney function, resulting in inaccurate kidney disease staging and delayed referral for treatment for African Americans (Diao et al. 2021). Lung function assessments are likewise biased; race correction factors of 10–15 percent are programmed into spirometers, affecting the diagnosis and treatment of lung disease, while obscuring environmental causes for racial disparities in lung health (Bhakta et al. 2022; Lujan and DiCarlo 2018). In their policy statement, Wright et al (2022) also draw attention to the race-based modifiers in the clinical algorithm used to assess risk associated with vaginal delivery following cesarian births. The modification indicates a higher risk when applied, so African American women are more likely to be discouraged from attempting vaginal births after cesarians. Globally, unnecessary surgical deliveries are associated with risks to both mothers and offspring, potentially resulting in poor health outcomes for the infants later in life (Rosenberg and Trevathan 2018). The expectation that African Americans might have higher risk appears to be based on antiquated racial ideas about pelvic differences and recent studies indicate that the racial modifier is not useful (Grobman et al. 2021). Nevertheless, it is still used and, in the US non-white women have higher rates of cesarian deliveries and poorer birthing outcomes than their white counterparts. While race-based disparities in maternal health have many causes (some discussed below), race-based medicine may contribute to them. These, and other examples of race-based medicine, contribute to health disparities between social races and demonstrate the dangers associated with the biological race concept.

The American Academy of Pediatrics issued a set of recommendations, most important of which is to critically examine all practices where race-based differences in diagnosis and treatment are recommended, and they encourage others in the medical community to do the same (Wright et al. 2022). American medicine has been slow to recognize that race is not biological, but recent change is very encouraging and is due in large part to the intersection between biological anthropology and medicine, especially through the public health literature (e.g., Tsai et al. 2020). Slowly, the medical community is recognizing that the race concept itself is a major source of racism in the health delivery system.

Race-based medicine reflects some of the many practical dangers of the biological race concept. It also obscures the major cause of real health disparities – differences in the lived experience of members of different social races (Benn Torres and Torres Colon 2015). Indeed, of the ways in which race is relevant to biological anthropology, the biomedical implications of social race may have the largest social importance (Gravlee and Sweet 2008). While races do not exist as genealogical entities, there are significant biological differences between social groups caused by a variety of factors and their inter-relationships. A few factors may relate to genetics and ancestry; there is endogamy within social groups (although this is highly variable), and there are some elements of a partially shared, complex ancestry that may result in observable phenotypic differences between social groups, including those affecting health. Most importantly, however, there are the biological consequences of shared social factors, especially income inequality, discrimination, and systemic racism itself that result in disparate health outcomes for members of different socially defined racial groups.

There is a significant literature on health inequalities among different social races in the US and globally. In the US, African Americans are most disadvantaged (Gravlee 2009). They present significantly higher age-adjusted death rates than whites from a variety of disorders, such as kidney disease, hypertension, diabetes, cardiovascular disease, some forms of cancer, infections, and trauma. These have been linked to a number of social and environmental variables associated with systemic racism. Anthropologists and epidemiologists are focusing on the importance of biocultural interactions, including the biological consequences of poverty, to explain many of these disparities (e.g., Dressler et al. 2005; Gravlee 2009; Schell 1997). Residential and environmental discrimination have been shown to have serious health outcomes including obesity, cardiovascular disease, hypertension, low birth weight, some forms of cancer, tuberculosis, and poisoning from environmental pollutants including heavy metals (Schell 1997; Williams and Collins 2001).

All of these factors interact and have a compounding effect, resulting in disease patterns that have been described as syndemic, where epidemics have their greatest impact on communities with concentrated underlying health problems (Gravlee 2020). COVID-19, a disease that has disproportionately affected poor and minority communities, provides an excellent example of the ways that overlapping epidemics may have a synergistic effect, increasing risk of hospitalization and death from both COVID and the underlying morbidities associated with systemic racism, such as diabetes or cardiovascular disease (Gravlee 2020; Raine et al. 2020).

In addition, the psychosocial effects of racism and discrimination have been associated with negative mental and physical health outcomes, including depression, obesity, cardiovascular disease, and other conditions previously listed (Borrell et al. 2006; Jackson et al. 2018; Kaholokula et al. 2012; Krieger 2004; Nelson 2009).

There is a complex relationship between social race and biology that may be best reflected in the impact of socially defined race on genetic expression. The impact of social trauma, including racism, on epigenetic changes has been the subject of considerable recent research in social and behavioral epigenetics, recently reviewed by Mulligan (2016, 2021). Epigenetic modifications to the genome occur in response to many external stressors, including socially induced trauma, and these changes alter the expression of genes, potentially across generations. There are many studies that indicate that maternal stressors affect the epigenome of offspring (Mulligan 2016, 2021) and it has been shown that some are transferred intergenerationally to a second generation (e.g., Lehrner and Yehuda 2018). Mulligan (2021) points to studies that suggest these modifications may potentially persist even in subsequent generations, known as transgenerational epigenetic inheritance. Thus, social trauma may affect biology for generations.

There is evidence that racial discrimination is a trauma that causes epigenetic changes (Barcelaona DiMendoza et al. 2018), that populations subjected to racism and discrimination accumulate a larger number of epigenetic marks and these changes may be perpetuated into future generations (Mulligan 2021).

Many of the modifications consist of altered DNA methylation, where a methyl group (an epigenetic mark) attaches to a nucleotide that affects the expression of genes and their associated phenotypes. The accumulation of these marks due to trauma may be associated with increased poor health outcomes, but other marks may mitigate risk; some epigenetic modifications may be the result of positive factors associated with healing (Brody et al. 2016; Jackson et al. 2018). Moreover, there is likely to be a feedback loop between the sociocultural environment and health. As Mulligan (2021: 400–401) puts it:

> …. one can imagine a situation in which poverty and homelessness influence DNA methylation changes in genes that lead to an increased risk of depression or other mental illness that further increases the risk of poverty and homelessness … Conversely, positive factors like resilience may modify DNA methylation changes in genes such as those involved in immune function, which would then lead to reduced inflammation, improved health and greater resiliency (Jackson et al. 2018).

Therefore, it is possible that increasing social equality would mitigate some of the detrimental effects of trauma, potentially even historical trauma.

Despite the fact that racial disparities in health may be best understood as the biological consequences of social conditions, racial disparities in health are too often presumed to be the result of genetic factors (Braun 2006; Duster 2005), a consequence of overt racism and the primacy of racial thinking. Because taxonomic meanings of race are so entrenched, many health workers and researchers assume without evidence that racial differences in health outcomes are the consequence of (untested) genetic differences between groups, and, for some, the fact that there are racial differences *is* the evidence for a genetic basis for a condition (Gravlee 2009). As discussed above, there are dangers in uncritically applying a racial-genetic model in medicine. It can obscure actual genetic factors; because of the dominance of racial thinking, those aspects of ancestry not a part of social identity may be unrecognized or ignored. It also overlooks the cultural stressors associated with negative health outcomes. Because race and variation are so often conflated, any biological differences between socially defined racial groups can serve to reify the race concept.

Conclusion

Since its inception, American biological anthropology's turbulent and complex relationship with race has mirrored that of the broader society, with progressive individuals and factions promoting racial equality, even as reactionary forces within the field endorsed segregationist racist agendas. Science is a human activity and social views of race have affected biological anthropology directly as the science of human variation past and present: social views of scientists affect their science, even as the results of science are used to support political agendas. As Haraway (1988) argued decades ago in a feminist context, practice and results of science are situated knowledges; knowledge is situated in the perspectives of the knower. The many identities of practitioners affect their worldviews, and therefore diversity is essential for the growth of intellectual thought and mediation of bias in a discipline. Biological anthropology was dominated by white men for most of its history; Montagu Cobb, one of the few African American biological anthropologists in the first half of the twentieth century, described the field as "lily-white." (Rankin-Hill and Blakey 1994; Watkins 2007). Although systemic racism affects knowledge structures that influence scientists from all backgrounds, for racial thinking in biological anthropology to meaningfully change, the field must diversify.

There are still relatively few People of Color in biological anthropology and they face unique challenges (Nelson 2019). However, the field is in the process of diversifying and the process is accelerating (Antón et al. 2018; Bolnick et al. 2019; Fuentes 2019). The ways biological anthropologists engage with race are also diversifying. Unlike the anti-racism of earlier periods, this engagement not only involves recognition and discussion of our well-recorded and fraught racist history but applies greater emphasis on the effects of systemic racism on the structures of science. Influenced by American anthropology more broadly (Harrison et al. 2010; Mullings 2005) and biological anthropologists (e.g., Blakey and Rankin-Hill 2009), this approach includes, among other things, visiting the ways and by whom science is practiced, the effects of research on marginalized groups, and the often-unrecognized impact of racial thinking on our ideas – in this case how we think about human variation.

While many social scientists consider the race concept irrelevant, focusing on the lived experience of socially defined races, it remains critical to biological anthropology in particular and science in general. The race concept is not dead and is unlikely to die soon. Racial thinking may be a part of the human condition, like essentialism itself, and so is difficult to eradicate. Race and geographic variation continue to be conflated, influencing understandings of biological diversity. While there are clearly differences among populations, the pattern of morphological and genetic variation within our species is not phylogenetic, and genetic studies continue to undermine both the concept of large geographic races and the basis of racial thinking by revealing the complexities of human genetic relationships. Nevertheless, biological race models remain prevalent in science and society, influencing, among other things, the interpretation and treatment of health disparities among socially defined racial groups.

Because of the primacy of racial thinking, the study of populational variation itself may serve to reify race. In the public mind, when the biology of socially defined races is discussed (often in the context of health disparities), or when ancestry is scientifically identified using biological cues, it reinforces the taxonomic assumptions and the biological determinism that are part of the race concept. Since races are unequal social categories, the assumptions that underlie race (biological determinism and separate biological histories), subtly "explain" the social inequality. As "biologized" social categories, social inequality becomes the consequence of inferior biology in the minds of many, the very premise of social Darwinism. Thus, the reification of race gives rise to biological determinism and is, in itself, racist (Blakey 1999). This is a conundrum that faces biological anthropologists and other human biologists today; since the assumptions of race are so deeply embedded, the recognition of the biological attributes of social categories, from health risks associated with poverty and racism to those associated with aspects of an individual's ancestry, may serve to reify race. Although the study of population disparities is of critical importance, reification of race may make social equality even more difficult to achieve. This underscores the importance of an understanding of race, in all its many dimensions, to the study of human variation.

ACKNOWLEDGMENTS

I thank Clark Larsen for the invitation to contribute to this volume and the students and colleagues, too many to name, who have helped me formulate the ideas on race and racism expressed here.

REFERENCES

Albanese, J., and S. R. Saunders. "Is It Possible to Escape Racial Typology in Forensic Identification?" In *Forensic Anthropology and Medicine: Complementary Sciences from Recovery to Cause of Death*. Edited by A. Schmitt, E. Cunha, and J. Pinheiro, 281–316. Humana Press, 2006.

Antón, S. C., R. S. Malhi, and A. Fuentes. "Race and Diversity in U.S. Biological Anthropology: A Decade of AAPA Initiatives." *American Journal of Physical Anthropology* 165, no. S65 (2018): 158–180.

Athreya, S., and R. R. Ackermann. "Colonialism and Narratives of Human Origins in Asia and Africa." In *Interrogating Human Origins: Decolonisation and the Deep Past*. Edited by M. Porr and J. Matthews. London: Routledge, 2019.

Atran, S. *Cognitive Foundation of Natural History*. New York: Cambridge University Press, 1990.

Atran, S. "Core Domains vs. Scientific Theories: Evidence from Systematics and Itza-Maya Folk Biology." In *Mapping The Mind*. Edited by L. Hirschfeld and S. Gelman, 316–340. Cambridge: University of Cambridge Press, 1994.

Atran, S., D. I. Medin, and N. Ross. "Thinking about Biology. Modular Constraints on Categorization and Reasoning in the Everyday Life of Americans." *Maya, and Scientists. Mind & Society* 3, no. 2 (2002): 31–63.

Barbujani, G., and E. M. S. Belle. "Genomic Boundaries Between Human Populations." *Human Heredity* 61 (2006): 15–21.

Barcelona de Mendoza, V., Y. Huang, C. A. Crusto, et al. "Perceived Racial Discrimination and DNA Methylation Among African American Women in the InterGEN Study." *Biological Research for Nursing* 20, no. 2 (2018): 145–152.

Benn Torres, J. "Anthropological Perspectives on Genomic Data, Genetic Ancestry, and Race." *Yearbook of Physical Anthropology* 171, no. S70 (2020): 74–86.

Benn Torres, J., and G. A. Torres Colon. "Racial Experience as an Alternative Operationalization of Race." *Human Biology* 87 (2015): 306–312.

Bethard, J. D., and E. A. DiGangi. "Letter to the Editor – Moving Beyond a Lost Cause: Forensic Anthropology and Ancestry Estimates in the United States." *Journal of Forensic Sciences* 65, no. 5 (2020): 1791–1792.

Bethard, J. D., and E. A. DiGangi. "Uncloaking a Lost Cause: Decolonizing Ancestry Estimation in the United States." *American Journal of Physical Anthropology* 175, no. 2 (2021): 422–326.

Bhakta, N. R., D. A. Kaminsky, C. Bime, et al. "Addressing Race in Pulmonary Function Testing by Aligning Intent and Evidence with Practice and Perception." *Chest* 161, no. 1 (2022): 288–297.

Blakey, M. L. "Skull Doctors: Intrinsic Social and Political Bias in the History of American Physical Anthropology with Special Reference to the Work of Aleš Hrdlička." *Critique of Anthropology* 7, no. 2 (1987): 7–35.

Blakey, M. L. "Scientific Racism and the Biological Concept of Race." *Literature and Psychology* 45, no. 1/2 (1999): 29–43.

Blakey, M. L., and L. M. Rankin-Hill, eds. *The New York African Burial Ground: Unearthing the African Presence in Colonial New York*. Volume 1: *Skeletal Biology of the New York African Burial Ground*. Washington DC: Howard University Press, 2009.

Boas, F. "Human Faculty as Determined by Race." *Proceedings of the American Association for the Advancement of Science* 43 (1894): 301–327.

Bolnick, D. A. "Individual Ancestry Inference and the Reification of Race as a Biological Phenomenon." In *Revisiting Race in a Genomic Age*. Edited by B. Koenig, S. Lee, and S. Richardson, 70–88. New Brunswick, NJ: Rutgers University Press, 2008.

Bolnick, D. A., R. W. A. Smith and A. Fuentes. "How Academic Diversity Is Transforming Scientific Knowledge in Biological Anthropology." *American Anthropologist* 121, no. 2 (2019): 464–464.

Borrell, L. N., C. I. Kiefe, D. R. Williams, et al. "Self-reported Health, Perceived Racial Discrimination, and Skin Color in African Americans in the CARDIA Study." *Social Science & Medicine* 63, no. 6 (2006): 1415–1427.

Brace, C. L. "A Nonracial Approach Towards the Understanding of Human Diversity." In *The Concept of Race*. Edited by M. F. Ashley Montagu, 103–152. New York: Free Press, 1964.

Brace, C. L. "Race Is a Four-Letter Word." In *The Genesis of the Concept*. New York: Oxford University Press, 2005.

Braun, L. "Reifying Human Difference: The Debate on Genetics, Race and Health." *International Journal of Health Services* 36 (2006): 557–573.

Brody, G. H., G. E. Miller, T. Yu, et al. "Supportive Family Environments Ameliorate the Link between Racial Discrimination and Epigenetic Aging: A Replication Across Two Longitudinal Cohorts." *Psychological Science* 27, no. 4 (2016): 530–541.

Brown, R. A., and Armelagos, G. J. "Apportionment of Human Genetic Diversity: A Review." *Evolutionary Anthropology* 10 (2001): 34–40.

Caspari, R. "Deconstructing Race: Race, Racial Thinking and Geographic Variation." In *A Companion to Biological Anthropology*. Edited by C. Larsen, 104–122. Chichester, UK: Wiley-Blackwell, 2010.

Caspari, R. "Review of: 'A Troublesome Inheritance: Genes, Race and Human History' by N. *Wade.*" *American Anthropologist* 116 (2014): 896–897.

Caspari, R. "Race, Then and Now: 1918 Revisited." *American Journal of Physical Anthropology* 165, no. 4 (2018a): 924–938.

Caspari, R. "Race: Conceptual History." In *The International Encyclopedia of Biological Anthropology*. John Wiley and Sons, Inc., 2018b.

Caspari, R. "Polygenism." In *The International Encyclopedia of Biological Anthropology*. John Wiley and Sons, Inc., 2018c.

Chang, J. "Recent Common Ancestors of All Present-Day Individuals." *Advances in Applied Probability* 31 (1999): 1002–1026.

Comas, J. "Scientific Racism Again?" *Current Anthropology* 2 (1961):303–340.

Coop, R., J. K. Pickerell, J. Novembre, et al. "The Role of Geography in Human Adaptation." *Public Library of Science Genetics* 5 (6) (2009): e1000500.

Diao, J. A., L. A. Inker, A. S. Levey, et al. "In Search of a Better Equation – Performance and Equity in Estimates of Kidney Function." *New England Journal of Medicine* 384, no. 5 (2021): 396–399.

Dressler, W. W., K. Oths, and C. C. Gravlee. "Race and Ethnicity in Public Health Research: Models to Explain Health Disparities." *Annual Review of Anthropology* 34, no. 1 (2005): 231–252.

Duster, T. "Race and Reification in Science." *Science* 307 (2005): 1050–1051.

Fuentes, A. "Identities, Experiences, and Beliefs: On Challenging Normativities in Biological Anthropology." *American Anthropologist* 121, no. 2 (2019): 467–469.

Fuentes, A. *Race, Monogamy, and Other Lies They Told You*, 2nd edn. Berkeley: University of California Press, 2022.

Fuentes, A., R. R. Ackermann, S. Athreya, et al. "AAPA Statement on Race and Racism." *American Journal of Physical Anthropology* 169 (2019): 400–402.

Gil-White, Francisco. "Are Ethnic Groups Biological Species to the Human Brain?" *Current Anthropology* 42, no. 4 (2001): 515–553.

Gravlee, C. C. "How Race Becomes Biology: Embodiment of Social Inequality." *American Journal of Physical Anthropology* 139 (2009): 47–57.

Gravlee, C. C. "Systemic Racism, Chronic Health Inequities, and COVID-19: A Syndemic in the Making?" *American Journal of Human Biology* 32, no. 5 (2020): e23482.

Gravlee, C. C., and E. Sweet. "Race, Ethnicity and Racism in Medical Anthropology, 1977–2002." *Medical Anthropology Quarterly* 22 (2008): 27–51.

Grobman, W. A., G. Sandoval, M. M. Rice, et al. "Eunice Kennedy Shriver National Institute of Child Health and Human Development Maternal–Fetal Medicine Units Network. Prediction of Vaginal Birth after Cesarean Delivery in Term Gestations: A Calculator Without Race and Ethnicity." *American Journal of Obstetrics and Gynecology* 225, no. 6 (2021): 664.e1–664.e7.

Haraway, D. "Situated Knowledges: The Science in Feminism and the Privilege of Partial Perspective." *Feminist Studies* 14, no. 3 (1988): 579–599.

Harrison, F. V., ed. *Decolonizing Anthropology: Moving Further Toward an Anthropology for Liberation*. 3rd edn. Arlington, VA: American Anthropological Association, 2010.

Hawks, John, E. T. Wang, G. M. Cochran, et al. "Recent Acceleration in Human Adaptive Evolution." *Proceedings of the National Academy of Sciences USA* 104 (2007): 20753–20758.

Hirschfeld, L. A. *Race in the Making: Cognition, Culture and the Child's Construction of Human Kinds*. Cambridge: MIT Press, 1996.

Hirschfeld, L. A. "Natural Assumptions: Race, Essence and Taxonomies of Human Kinds." *Social Research*, 65 (1998): 331–349.

Hirschfeld, L. A., and S. A. Gelman, eds. *Mapping the Mind: Domain Specificity in Cognition and Culture*. New York: University of Cambridge Press, 1994.

Hoffman, K. M., S. Trawalter, J. R. Axt, and M. N. Oliver. "Racial Bias in Pain Assessment and Treatment Recommendations, and False Beliefs about Biological Differences Between Blacks and Whites." *Proceedings of the National Academy of Sciences USA* 113, no. 16 (2016): 4296–4301.

Hunley, K., M. E. Healy, and J. C. Long. "The Global Pattern of Gene Identity Variation Reveals a History of Long-Range Migrations, Bottlenecks and Local Mate Exchange: Implications for Biological Race." *American Journal of Physical Anthropology* 139 (2009): 35–46.

Hunley, K. L., G. S. Cabana, and J. C. Long. "The Apportionment of Human Diversity Revisited." *American Journal of Physical Anthropology* 160 (2016): 561–569.

Jackson, L., Z. Jackson, and F. Jackson. "Intergenerational Resilience in Response to the Stress and Trauma of Enslavement and Chronic Exposure to Institutionalized Racism." *Journal of Clinical Epigenetics* 4, no. 15 (2018): 10.21767/2472-1158.100100.

Kaholokula, J. K., A. Grandinetti, S. Keller, et al. "Association Between Perceived Racism and Physiological Stress Indices in Native Hawaiians." *Journal of Behavioral Medicine* 35, no. 1 (2012): 27–37.

Kaszycka, K. A., G. Štrkalj, and J. Strzałko. "Current Views of European Anthropologists on Race: Influence of Educational and Ideological Background." *American Anthropologist* 111, no. 1 (2009): 43–56.

Krieger, N., ed. *Embodying Inequality: Epidemiologic Perspectives.* Amityville, NY: Baywood Publishing Company, 2004.

Lehrner, A., and R. Yehuda. "Cultural Trauma and Epigenetic Inheritance." *Development and Psychopathology* 30 (2018): 1763–1777.

Levy Zumwalt, R., and W. S. Willis. "Franz Boas and W. E. B. DuBois at Atlanta University, 1906." *Transactions of the American Philosophical Society* 98, no. 2 (2008): i–iii, vi–viii, 1–83.

Lewontin, R. C. "The Apportionment of Human Diversity." *Evolutionary Biology* 6 (1972): 381–398.

Lieberman, L., K. A. Kaszycka, A. J. Martinez Fuentes, et al. "The Race Concept in Six Regions: Variation Without Consensus." *Collegium Antropologicum* 28, no. 2 (2004): 907–921.

Linnaeus, C. *Systemae Naturae,* 10th edn. Stockholm: Laurentii Salvii, 1758.

Livingstone, Frank B. "On the Non-existence of Human Races." *Current Anthropology* 3, no. 3 (1962): 279–281.

Long, J. C., and R. A. Kittles. "Human Genetic Diversity and the Non-Existence of Human Races." *Human Biology* 75 (2003): 449–471.

Long, J. C., L. Jie, and M. E. Healey. "Human DNA Sequences: More Variation, Less Race." *American Journal of Physical Anthropology* 139 (2009): 23–34.

Lujan, H. L., and S. E. DiCarlo. "Science Reflects History as Society Influences Science: Brief History of 'Race,' 'Race Correction,' and the Spirometer." *Advances in Physiology Education* 42, no. 2 (2018): 163–165.

Manica, A., F. Prugnolle, and F. Balloux. "Geography Is a Better Determinant of Human Genetic Differentiation than Ethnicity." *Human Genetics* 118 (2005): 366–371.

Marks, J. *Human Biodiversity: Genes, Race, and History.* New York: Aldine de Gruyter, 1995.

Marks, J. *Is Science Racist?* Cambridge: Polity Press, 2017.

Mathieson, I., and A. Scally. "What Is Ancestry?" *PLoS Genetics* 16, no. 3 (2020): e1008624.

Montagu, A. *Man's Most Dangerous Myth: The Fallacy of Race.* New York: Columbia University Press, 1942.

Mulligan, C. J. "Early Environments, Stress, and the Epigenetics of Human Health." *Annual Review of Anthropology* 45 (2016): 233–249.

Mulligan, C. J. "Systemic Racism Can Get under Our Skin and into Our Genes." *American Journal of Physical Anthropology* 175, no. 2 (2021): 399–405.

Mullings, L. "Interrogating Racism: Toward an Antiracist Anthropology." *Annual Review of Anthropology* 34, no. 1 (2005): 667–693.

Nei, M., and A. K. Roychoudhury. "Evolutionary Relationships and the Evolution of Human Races." *Evolutionary Biology* 14 (1982): 1–59.

Nelson, R. G. "Adult Health Outcomes and Their Implications for Experiences of Childhood Nutritional Stress in Jamaica." *American Journal of Human Biology* 21, no. 5 (2009): 671–678.

Nelson, R. "Hypervisible and Human." *American Anthropologist* 121, no. 2 (2019): 469–470.

Ousley, S., Jantz, R., and Freid, D. "Understanding Race and Human Variation: Why Forensic Anthropologists are Good at Identifying Race." *American Journal of Physical Anthropology* 139, no. 1 (2009): 68–76.

Panofsky, A., Dasgupta, K., and Itturiaga, N. "How White Nationalists Mobilize Genetics: From Genetic Ancestry and Human Biodiversity to Counterscience and Metapolitics." *American Journal of Physical Anthropology* 175, no. 2 (2021): 387–398.

Prentice, D. A., and D. T. Miller. "Psychological Essentialism of Human Categories." *Current Directions in Psychological Science* 16, no. 4 (2007): 202–206.

Raine, S., A. Liu, J. Mintz, et al. "Racial and Ethnic Disparities in COVID-19 Outcomes: Social Determination of Health." *International Journal of Environmental Research and Public Health* 17, no. 21 (2020): 8115.

Ralph, P., and G. Coop. "The Geography of Recent Genetic Ancestry Across Europe." *PLoS Biology* 11, no. 5 (2013a): e1001555. https://doi.org/10.1371/journal.pbio.1001555.

Ralph, P., and G. Coop. *European Genealogy* (2013b). FAQ: https://gcbias.org/european-genealogy-faq/.

Ramachandran, S., O. Deshpande, C. C. Roseman, et al. "Support from the Relationship of Genetic and Geographic Distance for a Serial Founder Effect Originating in Africa." *Proceedings of the National Academy of Sciences USA* 102 (2005): 15942–15947.

Rankin-Hill, L. M., and Blakey, M. L. "W. Montague Cobb (1904–1990): Physical Anthropologist, Anatomist, and Activist." *American Anthropologist* 96, no. 1 (1994): 74–96.

Reich, D. *Who We Are and How We Got Here: Ancient DNA and the New Science of the Human Past.* New York: Vintage Books, 2018.

Relethford, J. H. "Race and Global Patterns of Phenotypic Variation." *American Journal of Physical Anthroology* 139 (2009): 16–22.

Rhode, D. L. T., S. Olsen, and J. T. Chang. "Modeling the Recent Common Ancestry of All Living Humans." *Nature* 431 (2004): 562–566.

Risch, N., E. Burchard, E. Ziv, and H. Tang. "Categorizations of Humans in Biomedical Research: Genes." *Race and Disease Genome Biology* 3, no. 7 (2002): Comment 2007.1-2007.12.

Rosenberg, K. R., and W. Trevathan. "Evolutionary Perspectives on Cesarean Section." *Evolution, Medicine and Public Health* (2018): 67–81 doi:10.1093/emph/eoy006.

Rosenberg, N. A., J. K. Pritchard, J. L. Weber, et al. "Genetic Structure of Human Populations." *Science* 298 (2002): 2381–2385.

Sauer, N. J. "Forensic Anthropology and the Concept of Race: If Races Don't Exist, Why Are Forensic Anthropologists so Good at Identifying Them?" *Social Science Medicine* 34(2) (1992): 107–111.

Schell, L. M. "Culture as a Stressor: A Revised Model of Biocultural Interaction." *American Journal of Physical Anthropology* 102 (1997): 67–77.

Serre, D., and S. Pääbo. "Evidence for Gradients of Human Genetic Diversity Within and Among Continents." *Genome Research* 14 (2004): 1679–1685.

Slatkin, M., and F. Racimo. "Ancient DNA and Human History." *Proceedings of the National Academy of Sciences* 113, no. 23 (2016): 6380–6387.

Stanton, W. *The Leopard's Spots: Scientific Attitudes Toward Race in America 1815–59.* Chicago: University of Chicago Press, 1960.

Stocking, G. W., Jr. *Race, Culture, and Evolution: Essays on the History of Anthropology.* New York: Free Press, 1968.

Stull, K., E. J. Bartelink, A. R. Klales, et al. "Commentary on: Bethard, JD; DiGangi, EA. Moving Beyond a Lost Cause: Forensic Anthropology and Ancestry Estimates in the United States." *Journal of Forensic Sciences* 66, no. 1 (2021): 417–420.

Templeton, A. R. "Human Races: A Genetic and Evolutionary Perspective." *American Anthropologist* 100 (1998): 632–650.

Topinard. P. *Éléments d'Anthropologie Général.* Paris: Delahaye et Lecrosnier, 1885.

Topinard. P. "On Race in Anthropology." In *This Is Race: An Anthology Selected from the International Literature on the Races of Man.* Edited by E. Count, 171–176. New York: Henry Schuman, 1892, 1950.

Tsai, J., J. P. Cerdeña, R. Khazanchi, et al. "There Is No 'African American Physiology': The Fallacy of Racial Essentialism." *Journal of Internal Medicine* 288, no. 3 (2020): 368–370. http://dx.doi.org/10.1111/joim.13153.

Van Arsdale, A. P. "Population Demography, Ancestry, and the Biological Concept of Race." *Annual Review of Anthropology* 48 (2019): 227–241.

Watkins, R. J. "Knowledge from the Margins: W. Montague Cobb's Pioneering Research in Biocultural Anthropology." *American Anthropologist* 109, no. 1 (2007): 186–196.

Williams, D. R., and C. Collins. "Racial Residential Segregation: A Fundamental Cause of Racial Disparities in Health." *American Journal of Public Health* 93 (2001): 200–208.

Wolpoff, M. H., and R. Caspari. *Race and Human Evolution.* New York: Simon and Schuster, 1997.

Wright, J. L., W. S. Davis, M. M. Joseph, et al. "Eliminating Race-Based Medicine." *Pediatrics* 150, no. 1 (2022): e2022057998.

CHAPTER 8

Human Life History Evolution: Growth, Development, and Senescence

Douglas E. Crews and Barry Bogin

The human lifecycle, which for convenience may be said to begin with fertilization of an ovum by a spermatozoan and to end with death in the ninth or tenth decade, seems long, but human longevity pales with other species, such as giant sequoia trees (*Sequoiadendron giganteum*) that are more than 3,000 years of age and at least one Great Basin bristlecone pine (*Pinus longaeva*) that is nearly 5,000 years old. The transformation of a human fertilized egg cell into an adult with 30 trillion cells, organized into tissues and organ systems capable of artistic and athletic performance from ballet to basketball, as well as intellectual performance ranging from poetry to mathematical proofs, seems wonderous, but is it any more wonderous than the life cycle of mites in the genus *Adactylidium*? A pregnant adult female mite carries several female mite larvae plus a single male larva. These larvae develop within the body of the mother where the male mates with the females. The larvae eat the mother from the inside and females emerge pregnant, ready to start their truncated lifestyle again. Closer to our human "home," as members of the Order Mammalia, the marsupials (pouched mammals such as Australasian kangaroos, wombats, koalas, Tasmanian devils, the American opossums) have remarkable life histories, which may be described as truly "born again." One example are Tammar wallabies (*Notamacropus eugenii*). The mother gestates the fertilized ovum for just 26.5 days – human gestation lasts about 10 times longer, or 266 days. At that time the joey wallabies (the babies) are born the first time via vaginal delivery. The joeys use their partially developed front limbs to crawl from the mother's vagina to her pouch, following a line of saliva that the mother supplied by licking her fur. The newborn joey is, essentially, a partially formed embryo and must develop within the mother's pouch before being born again as an independent youngster. At the time of its first birth the joey weighs 393 +/– 13 mg. By the time the joey leaves the pouch it will weigh about 3 kg – a 10,000-fold increase! Those joeys arriving to the pouch successfully (some are lost in

A Companion to Biological Anthropology, Second Edition. Edited by Clark Spencer Larsen.
© 2023 John Wiley & Sons Ltd. Published 2023 by John Wiley & Sons Ltd.

transit) latch on to a nipple and nurse continuously for about 100 days. During this time, they undergo rapid development of organs and systems including the respiratory system, lymphoid system, and nervous system. At this stage of development, the joey may be described as a fetus and for the next 100 days will detach and reattach to the nipple intermittently but remains in its mother's pouch. During its next phase of development, the joey is born again and may leave the pouch to feed on plant material and return to the pouch to suckle. During this final phase of development, the joey also experiences its most dramatic changes in morphology and growth, and when fully weaned at 300–350 days becomes independent of maternal care.

Despite diversity in growth, development, and aging across species, the human life cycle is unusual. Biological anthropologists and human biologists have long investigated how humans differ from other apes, our closest phylogenetic relatives, other nonhuman primates, and other mammals. Documenting such differences is easy; altricial slow growing offspring, childhood and adolescence stages, late commencement of reproduction, menopause in midlife, survival to ten decades, and maximum life spans of 115+ years (Arking 2006; Bogin 2021; Crews 2003). Determining evolutionary forces underlying these aspects of human life history has proved more difficult. Here, we review the general pattern of human growth and development, reproductive adulthood, aging and senescence, and associated theoretical models for why humans came to be slowly maturing, reproductively successful, and long-lived large-bodied primates.

As described in the biology literature, life history represents a species' multiple adaptations for allocating their limited resources and energy toward growth, maintenance, reproduction, raising offspring, and avoiding death (Bogin 2009; Stearns 1992). However, since energy and effort allocated to one physiological requirement limits its availability for other activities, trade-offs across physiological systems and life history stages are inherent to living systems. Herein we review theories of why birthing slow-maturing altricial offspring became a reproductively successful hominin adaptation, extending to humankind's timing of growth, development, reproductive adulthood, and survival, and correlates of those changes. We first review human growth, development, aging, and life history; these are detailed more fully in Bogin (2021) and Crews (2003, 2019). The second section explores the evolution of hominin biocultural interactions and how these furthered the development of humankind's life history and biobehavioral separation from other apes.

HUMAN LIFE HISTORY

During life all mammals experience at least two post-natal life history stages: infancy and adulthood. Those living in social groups, including many nonhuman primates, frequently show three post-natal life history stages, infant, juvenile, adult (Bogin 2021; Pereira and Fairbanks 1993, 2002). Humans experience four life history stages between birth and adulthood, the infancy and juvenile stages common to many mammals, as well as the novel stages of childhood after infancy and adolescence after the juvenile stage. Life history stages are definable by biological (tooth eruption patterns) and behavioral (feeding) characteristics. Feeding methods are salient demarcations for life history stages. Among most mammals, infants feed mainly via mother's lactation. The infants become juveniles when they cease nursing and must locate, eat, and digest an adult-type diet. This requires adult-like teeth, making first permanent molar tooth eruption a marker of infant–juvenile transition. Juveniles continue growing and may require adult supervision while acquiring local ecological knowledge, but are neither fully grown nor sexually mature. Juvenility reflects a mammalian life history trade-off between growth/development and reproductive activity. The adaptive value of juvenility remains a theoretical question for life history theory (see Bogin 2021; Evans and Harris 2008; Pereira and Fairbanks 1993, 2002). Juveniles mature into reproductive adulthood, a period of sexual maturity during which adults reproduce and care for offspring. Originally, primate life history patterns were modelled using a linear system based on three life history stages: infancy, juvenile, and adult (Figure 8.1: see Smith 1989, 1991). Accumulated evidence now supports a four-stage human life history pattern between birth and adulthood, including childhood and adolescence stages (Figure 8.1: see also Bogin 1988, 2021; Bogin and Smith 1996; Bogin et al. 2018).

Following birth, human life history stages are relatively extended, requiring twice as many years to attain reproductive adulthood than do other apes (Bogin 2021; Thompson and Nelson 2011). Humans gestate only slightly longer (266 days) than other apes (chimpanzee/bonobo ~237 days, gorilla ~257 days, orangutangs ~260 days: average 255 days), suggesting a similar length in their common ancestor and a possible limit on the mother's ability to provide nutrients supporting fetal growth without self-harm. Following birth, humans progress through a month of neonatal development, followed by early infancy to about 12 months, and then later infancy which ends at about 36 months (Bogin et al. 2018). These earliest periods of post-natal human life history span are defined, in large part, by lactation feeding. The age at termination of breast-feeding in traditional, pre-modern societies averaged 30–36 months. In contrast, chimp infancy continues to a mean age of 56 months.

Readers should note that all ages given here are averages, or the typical chronological age at which an event of growth or maturation occurs for boys and girls. The pace of development/maturation for any individual girl or boy, often referred to as her or his developmental tempo (using the musical connotation of the speed at which a piece is played), is variable. Furthermore, girls usually have a faster developmental tempo throughout life than boys. Tempo is influenced by a complex matrix of genomic, nutritional, disease, social, and emotional factors. Particularly relevant in the contemporary discussion about nutrition and obesity, for example, is that it is well known that nutritional status modifies tempo. Starvation slows tempo and obesity accelerates tempo. Variations in developmental tempo during the early periods of life certainly influence the onset of sexual maturation and may have consequences for the onset and pace of senescence and aging later in life.

After feeding by lactation ends chimps immediately enter their juvenile stage. In contrast, human infants transition to the childhood period of growth and development. Human childhood is a period of slow steady growth lasting about four years and is a life history stage shared with no other primate or mammal.

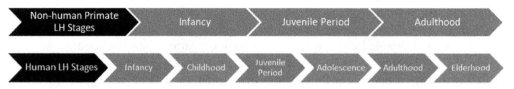

Figure 8.1 Life history stages in human and nonhuman primates. *Source:* M. Clark, E. Lagan, M. O'Hara, M. Hubbe, and D. E. Crews. *Biological Anthropology Laboratory Manual.* Toronto: TopHat Online Publishing, 2021.

The end of the childhood period at about age 6.9 years is characterized by a mature level of bipedal walking and brain volume that is nearly complete, although the organization of the brain and learning will continue for more than four decades. The youngster is now less dependent on older people for feeding due to eruption of the first permanent molar (the M_1 or "6-year molar") and the central incisors. One of the endocrine events that occurs near the end of the childhood stage is adrenarche. This is the post-natal onset of secretion of the androgen hormones dehydroepiandrosterone (DHEA) and DHEA sulfate (DHEA-S) from the adrenal gland. In humans and chimpanzees adrenarche occurs between the ages of 6 and 10 years. In humans, adrenal androgens seemingly cause small amounts of axillary and pubic hair to appear and may be associated with a small acceleration in skeletal growth velocity, the mid-growth spurt in height, and deepening of the voice, changes producing the more "adult-like" physique of the juvenile. Adrenarche may also promote a transition to a more adult-like brain and behavior, called the "5- to 7-year-old shift" by some psychologists, or the shift from the preoperational to concrete operational stage, using the terminology of Piaget. This shift leads to new learning and work capabilities in the older child and juvenile. There is more abstract thinking and inhibition of impulsive behaviors. In traditional societies, older children and juveniles learn and practice important economic and social skills, such as food gathering, food preparation, and "baby-sitting," that is, the care of infants and younger children. In many industrial societies, older children may also engage in these economic–social activities and may enter formal school education (Bogin et al. 2018).

Another event initiating the juvenile stage of human life history is puberty, which we define as an event of relatively short duration (1–2 months). Other researchers consider puberty to be a life history stage of several years' duration, using the words "puberty" and "adolescence" interchangeably. Here we make a distinction between puberty as a life history transition event and adolescence as a life history stage of growth and development. The biological changes of puberty begin in the brain and involve the hypothalamic–pituitary–gonadal axis, its hormones, and their effects on sexual maturation. Puberty leads to a massive increase in sex hormone secretion, which takes the person from the immaturity of the child and early juvenile to the incipient adult-like phenotype of the young adolescent.

The biological, environmental, and sociocultural regulation of puberty is a topic of much current research (Bogin 2021). What is known is that the production of sex hormones results in the maturation of ovaries or testes, secondary sexual characteristics (for example, breasts in females, muscularity in males, and genitalia in both sexes), and a suite of changes in physiological and behavioral characteristics, many of which are sex specific or appear in a different sequence for each sex. One uniquely human characteristic is the adolescent growth spurt. The transition from juvenile to adolescent is marked by a change in skeletal growth rate from deceleration to acceleration. Girls typically experience this growth rate change at about age 10 years and boys at about age 12 years, which is about the same age as the eruption of the second permanent molar tooth. As shown in Figure 8.2 for boys, height growth rate reaches its peak at about age 13–14 years and then decelerates until age 18 or later. Girls peak at a mean age of ~12 years and end growth at ~16 years. Across the range of variation, virtually all early to late maturing girls have a peak adolescent growth rate in the final 9–12 months prior to menarche (first menstruation). The sex steroid hormones underlying menarche are also associated with the sharp decrease in growth velocity of the long bones after the peak. In total, the adolescent stage lasts about six years in both sexes. Boys begin producing motile spermatozoa by about age 13 years, and some notorious cases of fatherhood confirm that those sperm are fertile! Girls

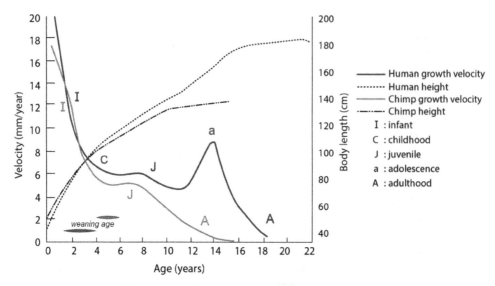

Figure 8.2 Patterns of human and chimpanzee growth. *Source:* M. Clark, E. Lagan, M. O'Hara, M. Hubbe, and D. E. Crews. *Biological Anthropology Laboratory Manual.* Toronto: TopHat Online Publishing, 2021.

experience menarche (first menstruation) between about 12 and 14 years, but do not achieve an adult level of ovulation and fertility until about age 17. Not coincidentally, this is also the age at which the birth canal (internal pelvic dimensions) reaches its mature size. The end of adolescence is marked by eruption of the third, and final, permanent molar, which occurs, on average, between the ages of 19.27 and 20.88 years for European, Bangladeshi, and South African populations (Liversidge 2008). Biologically, young women and men are now adults, but in most societies, it will take more years for them to mature socially, economically, and emotionally and become fully successful reproductive and productive adults (Bogin 2021).

Adulthood may be subdivided into the separate stages of Prime (also referred to as maximum performance age), Transition or degeneration age, and Senescence or old age. The latter two stages, including the menopause of women, are discussed below. The Prime stage of adulthood is characterized by optimal reproductive performance, including success in mating, reproduction, and care of offspring. Prime adults also have a high level of homeostasis, that is, resilience to insults from injury and illness and the ability to maintain cognitive, physical, social, and economic skills to achieve maximum performance. During the transition and senescence stages of adulthood the ability to reproduce usually declines, but contributions to care of offspring may remain high.

Biocultural Reproduction Prior to developing agriculture or metallurgy, humans inhabited every continent on Earth excepting Antarctica. Survival across diverse environments depended on humankind's highly developed sociocultural systems, including bioculturally constructed settings and a life history including economic, social, political, and emotional contributions from pre-reproductive but productive older children, juveniles, and adolescents and post-reproductive "grandparents." This survival strategy likely included communal food procurement, defense, niche construction, and maintenance of microenvironments wherein adults could provision altricial offspring while participating in biocultural reproduction and childcare (see Bogin et al. 2014; Crews 2003). Today, human offspring require parental investment over almost two decades to mature physically and become sufficiently socially adept to not only produce, but to nurture and fledge their off-spring. As part of this life history evolution, human offspring became more dependent on parents and others for their long-term survival and new life history stages evolved in the hominin lineage. From this communal cultural production, language, tool use, future planning, built environments, and biocultural reproduction arose, while the tempo of all latter life history periods slowed.

In biology, cooperative breeding occurs when individuals other than the mother assist in rearing offspring, a behavioral pattern observed among multiple species of insects, birds, fish, and mammals (e.g., wolves and hyenas). Both highly productive and deteriorated environmental settings may favor family living with cooperative foraging and cooperative breeding (Koenig 2017). Among such species, cooperative breeding increases net reproductive output (Bergmüller et al. 2007). In such species and many human groups, but not all, cooperative breeders are close maternal relatives (Clutton-Brock 2016). By helping mothers in caring for their offspring, related helpers increase their inclusive fitness (the genetic material they share with other individuals), thereby increasing representation of their own DNA in the next generation (Hawkes et al. 1997, 1998; Paine and Hawkes 2006).

In contrast to other species, human societies define kinship relations through genetic and social relationships. Humans use language and cultural institutions, such as marriage, divorce, stepparents, and even residence, to define kinship categories, providing an overarching system of culturally categorized relationships across our species. In traditional living societies (foragers, horticulturalist, pastoralists, and pre-industrial agriculturalists) kinship is the central social organizing principle and theme across economic production, social organization, ideology, marriage, and childrearing. All societies, industrial, agrarian, western, eastern, remote, and cosmopolitan, use fictive kinship (apply kinship terms to people unrelated by descent or marriage) in social relationships to establish rights and responsibilities, along with accepted behaviors toward others, including immatures. Addressing a close friend of one's mother using a fictive kinship term ("Aunt Maria") may establish social ties and a pattern of parent-like investment from the fictive relative toward the child. Fictive relatives may be obligated to feed, supervise, protect, or gift a genetically unrelated person and behave toward them according to local cultural rules regarding family members. These types of behaviors go far beyond the cooperative breeding of other animals. Human childrearing patterns are better described as "biocultural reproduction," as the human pattern enhances the social, economic, political, religious, and ideological "fitness" of the social group as much as it contributes to individual genetic fitness (Bogin et al. 2014, Bogin 2021).

Over hominin evolutionary history, biocultural reproduction operated interactively with life history. The evolution of human childhood required provisioning by family and group members. One result was freeing mothers from being the sole caretaker of offspring prior to their independence. Biocultural reproduction and childhood provide women time and energy to rebuild their somas (self-maintenance), sequester resources for reproductive effort at a later time, and build somatic reserves (Bogin 2021; Crews 2003, 2019; Larke and Crews 2006), thereby benefitting reproduction of the local kindred and social group and providing women with greater Reserve Capacity (RC), that is, the sum of resources and energy available to an organism currently not needed to sustain somatic function and maintenance, further slowing the tempo of human life history (see Crews 2003: 77). Examples of somatic RC include energy stores, or lung, kidney, and immune function above current survival needs (Crews 2003, 2019). Within cells, RC helps maintain balance between cellular tissue repair and tumor suppression (see Weinstein and Ciszek 2002). In humans, building of RC begins as early as gestation and continues through infancy and into adulthood. Living in bioculturally constructed niches, with limited external stressors, and a surfeit of nutrients, provides much of humankind opportunities to achieve their lifespan potential (Bogin 2009; Crews 2003, 2007, 2008; Larke and Crews 2006).

LATER LIFE TRANSITION AND SENESCENCE

Early human life is a 20+ year period of canalized growth, development, and maturation, followed by reproductive prime adulthood. Women end their reproduction at about ages 40–50 years, although both sexes may enjoy continued health and well-being through age 60 years and beyond. During early life and prime adulthood, evolved trade-offs, evolutionary compromises, and natural selection tend to favor continued somatic maintenance in iteroparous (multiple birth events over the female lifespan) species providing continuing parental investment to offspring after their birth setting a consistent tempo for life (Crews 2003, 2005, 2008; Hamilton 1964, 1966; Larke and Crews 2006). Conversely, as life continues past this period of maximum reproductive potential, investments in somatic maintenance become less of a priority, as maintaining one's soma at older ages yields trivial fitness benefits, thereby introducing additional variability to the tempo of aging. Fitness benefits decline as age increases, providing an evolutionary model for reduced cellular and DNA repair, senescent changes across systems, increasing infectious and chronic conditions, and increased cell cycle arrest with age. As we outlive our reproductive capabilities, selection for systems maintaining one's soma declines and dysregulation proceeds, for some rapidly, for others slowly, but all cells, organs, and systems eventually show senescent phenotypes. A senescent life history stage and phenotype are unusual across lifeforms. Most mammals succumb to extrinsic causes (predation, accidents, disease, starvation) well before experiencing senescence.

From birth through adolescence, energetic resources are strategically invested into growing and developing a reproductive adult to replicate the immortal germline (see Crews 2019; Drenos et al. 2004; Kirkwood 1977, 1990). Among iteroparous species with high parental investment post-reproduction, evolution promotes maintenance of adult somas as multiple offspring require longer support than do semelparous (single birthing event over the life span) species without extensive parental investment. Among species experiencing high lifelong extrinsic mortality, selection against senescent biology is low and few organisms survive sufficiently long to show reduced fitness. Conversely, with low extrinsic mortality, selection against senescent changes will be stronger as longer life may improve fitness significantly. As a rule, natural selection acts against processes that reduce total lifetime fitness. However, it is unlikely that natural selection generally influences length of post-reproductive life, as older organisms do not greatly influence the fitness of others nor do they retain significant reproductive ability to influence selective pressures (see Stearns 1992). However, eventually all individuals die. Natural selection is only partly responsible for timing of deaths as a general outcome of selection on other life history variables. In addition to reflecting genetic propensities and phylogenetic inertia, individual length of life reflects multiple intrinsic properties: maternal and generational factors, internal stressors, somatic capacities built during life, quality of one's genome, and which of multiple extrinsic stressors they experienced during life. These set the tempo of one's individual life course. Evolution of childhood and adolescence provided humans with greater time for building stable reproductive somas with significant RC. Living in bioculturally constructed niches and social settings contributed to new life history stages during hominin evolution, while socioculturally constructed lifeways provided adequate resources and support for long-term growth of offspring, likely accounting for significant proportions of our current longevity (Bogin 2009; Crews 2003, 2007, 2008; Larke and Crews 2006).

Late Life and Senescence   As late as 40 thousand years ago few humans may have lived past about their 40th birthday (see Caspari and Lee 2004), leaving few to experience menopause, i.e., "…the sudden or gradual cessation of the menstrual cycle subsequent to the loss of ovarian function…" (see Bogin 2021). As a general concept, we may define the later life portion of human life spans as commencing once most women have experienced menopause, approximately aged 50 in today's settings. Prior to 40 thousand years ago, it is likely that only a small proportion of women achieved this life history stage, with few men surviving as long either. Nor is 50 years achieved by any nonhuman primates in their natural environments. Significant proportions surviving into their sixth decade is a phenomenon of modern *Homo sapiens* secondary to biocultural evolution and life in bioculturally constructed niches (Crews 2007, 2008, 2019).

Worldwide in the twenty-first century, most men and women survive to their 60th birthday, with over 75 percent of Japanese men and 88 percent of women surviving to 70 years, while 29 and 59 percent respectively survive to 85 years; conversely, in India only 41 percent of men and 47 percent of women survive to age 70 (Crews 2021). Estimated ages in modern foraging/hunting populations suggest those surviving to 20 years are likely to survive into their fifth and sixth decades of life (see Carey and Judge 2001; Hawkes et al. 1997, 1998). Since 40 KYA, most human groups are likely to have included some persons aged 50+ years, but it is unlikely many survived past 60, ages to which many do not survive today. Unfortunately, without actual birth and death dates, survival probabilities in the past and among many of today's foraging populations are not fully reliable. Still, demographic analyses among populations currently relying on hunting, gathering, foraging, and/or horticultural resource acquisition suggest a modal age at death of around 70 years among adults (see Gurven and Kaplan 2007). Their life expectancy at birth is shorter due to relatively high infant and childhood mortality, with only 57–67 percent of births surviving to 15 years (Gurven and Kaplan 2007). Among Tsimane, life expectancy at birth was 43 years 1950–1989; in 2002 it was closer to 53 years (Gurven et al. 2017), similar to survival patterns in nineteenth century Europe (Gurven et al. 2017). Of those surviving 15 years, among traditional hunter-gatherers 64 percent survived 45 years, forager horticulturalists 61 percent, and acculturated hunter-gatherers 79 percent (see Gurven and Kaplan 2007). Women surviving to post-reproductive life (45+ years) experienced about 2 to 2.5 additional decades of life (Gurven and Kaplan 2007). Such results in contemporary settings suggest among our more recent ancestors (circa post-40 KYA) adult survival likely averaged about 5–6 decades, with those surviving to age 45 years perhaps enjoying as much as 20+ more years of life.

Among contemporary populations, life expectancy exceeds 85 years only among women in Sweden and Japan (Crews 2021; Larke and Crews 2006). This survival pattern suggests that a late-life senescent LH phase is expressed by humans in built environments of the late twentieth and early twenty-first centuries. Such data also suggest that biocultural evolution, lifestyles, and constructed niches have had greater influences on recent increases in human survival than have genetic modifications. Indeed, life expectancy is a statistical term, and strongly relies on neonatal/infant/child survival. When the rate of neonatal/infant/child mortality is high, life expectancy (average age at death) of the entire population is low. The increase in life expectancy among many human populations during the twentieth century was due, primarily, to reductions in neonatal/infant/child death caused by infectious disease, contaminated water, and poor sanitation (Bogin 2001). Nevertheless, high survival probabilities to ages 70+ years in the contemporary world and for some human groups in the past suggest that a post-reproductive period, characterized by investments of remaining RC into somatic maintenance, survival, and into younger generations is a human LH characteristic (Figure 8.1, Bogin and Smith 1996; Hawkes et al. 1998).

After about age 70, the senescent LH phase includes exponentially increasing risks of mortality, decreasing reproductive capability among men and cessation of ovulation among women in their sixth decade. Concurrently, physiological, neurological, and structural systems show declines from optima achieved during prime adulthood as dividing and nondividing cells succumb to external and internal stressors (see Arking 2006; Austad 1997b; Rose 1991; Rose et al. 2005). As a biological process, senescence reflects multiple somawide alterations. Loss of cells and cell cycle arrest lead to declining tissue and organ functionality. These reduce physiological abilities to mount responses to stressors, push somatic function away from previous homeostatic equilibria, and thereby reduce the likelihood of additional reproductive effort, while increasing one's probability of death (see Arking 2006).

Among lifeforms surviving sufficiently long, senescence is cumulative, increasing organismal vulnerability to challenges; progressive with gradual functional and somatic losses; intrinsic, not due to external factors; and deleterious, reducing function and increasing mortality over time (Arking 2006). Senescence is not a chronological process dependent on time, rather it occurs in biological time as measured by DNA transcription and cell cycles (Arking 2006). Other measures of biological time are physiological biomarkers, cascades of metabolic events, disintegration of physiological pathways, and cumulative alterations in gene expression and cellular proteomes (Arking 2006; Hayflick 2007). Contrary to growth and development, senescence reflects losses of attained competencies, organismal integration, and abilities to perceive and receive signals modulating cellular function (Finch and Rose 1995). Human senescence reflects processes and mechanisms observed across earthly organisms, including worms, insects, and rodents. Major differences separating these species lifespans from humankind's are our primate heritage of slow life histories, extended offspring care, sociality, and our biocultural adaptations.

Menopause As women survive through their fifth decade, they experience declining fecundity (the biological capability for producing offspring) and eventually complete cessation of ovulation. Across modern industrialized settings the tempo of reproductive decline and cessation may differ significantly. European-descent women show average ages at menopause between 50 and 52 years, while women in Latin America, Indonesia, Singapore, and Pakistan tend to experience natural menopause several years earlier, with reports of 47–48 years among Filipino and Malay and 45 years in Maya women (reviewed by Gold 2011). Among Bangladeshi sedentees, age at menopause was earlier (45.8 years) than among Bangladeshi migrants (47.5 years) and women of European origin in London (49.1 years), but above the 43.6 years previously reported for Bangladesh (see Murphy et al. 2012). Overall, women in urban areas tend toward later natural menopause than those in rural settings. Differences in ages at natural menopause reflect variation across individuals and populations in genetic, socioeconomic, environmental, familial, racial/ethnic, lifestyle, parity, maternal ages, oral contraceptives use, occupational, physical activity, and malnourishment (see Gold 2011). Findings clearly indicating age at menopause and tempo of reproductive cessation are responsive to sociocultural influences.

Evolved trade-offs and allometric constraints on size of ovaries and number of primary oocytes may underlie declining reproduction with age among large-bodied mammals (see Austad 1994; Graham 1979; Leidy 1994; Packer et al. 1998; Tully and Lambert 2011). Previously, it was suggested that human reproductive decline and menopause were unique among mammals (Hawkes et al. 1997, 1998; Pavelka et al. 1991). However, oocyte depletion appears universal among aging female mammals (Austad 1997a; Graham 1979; Leidy 1994; Packer et al. 1998). Most mammals surviving beyond 35 years, including killer whales (*Orcinus orca*), short-finned pilot whales (*Globicephala macrorhynchus*), Beluga whales (*Delphinapterus leucas*), and narwhals (*Monodon monoceros*), show declining reproduction and individuals living past 50 years in the wild experiencing menopause (Brent et al. 2015; Ellis et al. 2018). As described by Austad (1994, 1997b), reproductive decline with increasing age is likely to be a plesiomorphic mammalian and primate LH trait (see also Packer et al. 1998). A major reason menopause is seldom seen among most female mammals is their limited survival past 50 years, when most women are post-menopausal (see Crews 2003: 114). There are reports of captive, but not wild-living, long-lived chimpanzee females reproducing into their mid-50s (Thompson et al. 2007), although most die during their third and fourth decades (see Hawkes et al. 2009).

Decreased circulating estrogen and progesterone, lack of ovulation, and increased follicle-stimulating hormone characterize human menopause. Menopause also presages senescent age-related changes within multiple physiological systems. Decreased estrogen associates significantly with the presence of cardiovascular diseases, hypertension, bone loss, and cancer. Many female cell and tissue types increase and decrease in response to patterns of reproductive hormones, including vaginal and uterine tissues, which show hyperplasia during puberty and hypoplasia following menopause (Arking 2006). Menopause is followed by increased susceptible to circulatory diseases and cancers of reproductive tissues. Those who experience early natural menopause (before age 44) show higher mortality rates than those with natural menopause at 50–54 years (Snowden et al. 1989). Reproductive senescence is also reflected as reduced homeostatic control across interacting systems promoting additional alterations across the soma. For example, prior to menopause, women show only slightly higher bone loss than do same-aged men. After menopause, their rate of bone loss is two to three times that of same-age men (Stini 1990). Consequently, elderly women experience osteoporosis and hip fractures at three to four times the rate of same-age men. Declining bone mineral content, along with increasing arteriosclerosis as people age, provide additional examples of biological senescence (Arking 2006; Crews 2008). Where women remain physically active following menopause, they show fewer declines in their physiological and physical functioning with age. Conversely, bone loss, arteriosclerosis, and frailty generally progress more rapidly among the less active. Such observations suggest maintenance of physical activity may reduce detrimental impacts of menopause on late-life physiology.

CHRONIC CONDITIONS AND LATE LIFE

Generally, encompassing our third through sixth decades, one's reproductive prime adulthood is a period of maximum health, physical fitness, and energetic capabilities. It is also a time when we are best equipped to obtain resources to sustain our own wellbeing and that of our offspring. However, physiological, functional, and physical abilities begin declining during the latter years of reproductive adulthood. Still, in modern constructed environments, most individuals survive more than sufficiently long to reproduce and fledge offspring, while retaining sufficient physiological capacity to survive into their eighth decade. Unfortunately, over our later years, we also experience multiple chronic and degenerative conditions, reflecting underlying senescent changes in cellular and organ biology, lifelong wear and tear, and somatic damage (see Tchkonia and Kirkland 2018; Zenin et al. 2019). Multiple chronic/degenerative conditions occur secondary to the inherent biology of life. These tend to reflect long-term evolutionary trade-offs and compromises interacting with our environmental settings and exposures, sociocultural factors, interactions with others, and lifestyle choices. Today, variation among individuals and across populations in their genomic attributes, environments, sociocultural systems, and lifeways underlie broad variability in late life health and survival. Given multiple pathways by which our genomes, microbiomes, epigenomes, and somas have interacted with and responded to our environments and stressor exposures, over time we all experience chronic degenerative and senescent biological processes, illnesses, cellular losses and breakdowns, and physiological alterations as we age.

Across most populations today, chronic and degenerative conditions lead morbidity and mortality statistics. Frequencies of these conditions, particularly types of cancer, chronic conditions, and infectious/parasitic exposures (e.g., HIV, COVID-19, SARS, malaria, helminths) vary widely across environments and sociocultural settings. Multiple factors, including local genomic and epigenome variants, contribute to population variation in disease risks and individual survival times. Some are likely to influence rates and patterns of senescence, others pathogen susceptibility and lifespan, but not directly rates of senescence (see Passarino et al. 2016; Tchkonia and Kirkland 2018; Zenin et al. 2019). Many well-established high risk genomic factors, such as BRCA 1 and 2 alleles, breast cancer, apolipoprotein E*4, hyperlipidemia, cardiovascular disease, Alzheimer's disease, mutated mismatch repair genes, Lynch syndrome colorectal cancer, mutated LDL-receptor, and familial hypercholesterolemia, limit lifespan, but may not alter one's rate of senescence or cell-cycle arrest. Conversely, there are rare conditions wherein specific mutations determine a premature aging phenotype, such as Hutchinson-Gilford (childhood) and Werner progeria (adulthood), comprising fewer than 400 known cases. Overall, genomic predispositions to chronic and constitutional conditions are relatively rare, and only about 25 percent of observed lifespan variations appear to reflect genomic factors (Passarino et al. 2016). Thus, most of our risk for mortality during life reflects environmental, sociocultural, and lifestyle factors and conditions such as Lynch syndrome. Some of these may occur early in life but only express as chronic conditions and low resilience during later life.

Skeletal Senescence As described briefly here, bones lose calcium and minerals as age increases. Loss of bone mineral density (BMD) leads to a less interstitial matrix, osteoporosis, increasingly brittle and porous bone, and greater breakage risk. Low BMD increases risk for hip and other fractures. These in turn may reduce mobility and promote bed confinement, low physical activity, muscular atrophy, additional fractures, bed sores, secondary infections, and death (see Cummings and Nevitt 1989). Low BMD and osteoporosis also may underlie vertebral collapse and spinal compression, leading to additional loss of mobility. Degenerative joint disease increases with age, most often affecting our weight-bearing joints as articular cartilage on our knee joints is lost, eburnation of articulating bone occurs, and calcification and buildup of bone spurs follow. Finally, age-related loss of lean body mass (i.e., muscle and bone) and decreasing height secondary to loss of BMD in the spine and knees may lead to inflammation and stiffness of joints, contributing to osteoarthritis and phenotypic frailty.

With age and bipedality comes osteoarthritis (OA: joint pain, cartilage loss, bone spurs, eburnation) of major weight-bearing and frequently used joints. This often is aggravated by concurrent osteoporosis (low bone mineral density). Jointly, these reduce mobility and strength, and compromise self-care as assessed by abilities to complete basic Activities of Daily Living (ADLs: Katz et al. 1963) and Instrumental Activities of Daily Living (IADLs: Brock et al. 1990; Miles and Brody 1994). Osteoarthritis becomes common after age 50, but may occur at much younger ages, and is almost universal after 70 years (Clark et al. 2019; Kim and Jazwinski 2015). Osteoarthritis begins as cartilage lubricating and protecting joints are lost and bones begin articulating with bony surfaces, leading to bony spurs, and eventually eburnation, a process aggravated by previous injuries. Cumulatively, senescent alterations weaken bones, reduce skeletal integrity, and increase risks for falls, fractures, accidents, frailty, and death.

Physiological Senescence With increasing age, cells senesce. Their function and output decline secondary to mutations and stressors altering their genome. Some die, some continue functioning, others survive to experience senescence and cell-cycle arrest (Arking 2006; van Deursen 2014). Concurrently, physiological, neurological, skeletal, and reproductive systems decline in function and stressor response capabilities. Cellular senescence and cell-cycle arrest may not reflect the end of cellular activity. Arrest may reflect a state of low activity as arrested cells continue showing diverse internal states indicative of continued activity (see van Deursen 2014; Kumari and Jat 2020).

Arteriosclerosis and Atherosclerosis Arteriosclerosis, specifically atherosclerosis, is a chronic degenerative condition characterized by arterial narrowing secondary to plaque accumulation: a composite of cell debris, lipids, amyloid, cross-linked collagen, elastin, and other components adhering to artery walls. Atherosclerosis is so common it exemplifies a senescing phenotype (Arking 2006; Machado-Oliveira et al. 2020). Humans have experienced atherosclerosis at least since Egyptians were mummifying their dead. Additionally, arteriosclerosis is observed in nonhuman primates, including both captive and feral chimpanzees, possibly representing a shared senescent process across long-lived primates.

Among United States residents aged 70+ years, over 50 percent show amyloid deposits in their arteries. This coincides with half of all United States heart failure cases and 90 percent of all deaths occurring at ages 70+ years, making atherosclerosis a disease of elders (Strait and Lakatta's 2012) and suggesting that heart failure may be a senescent process. As an intrinsic, cumulative, and debilitating condition, atherosclerosis is influenced by genomic predispositions and aggravated by atherogenic environments. Atherosclerosis elevates blood pressure and contributes to mortality from heart disease and stroke, the leading and sixth highest causes of death in the US in 2020 (Ahmad and Anderson 2021).

Neurological Senescence and Dementia Dementia represents a heterogeneous assortment of conditions affecting the brain and central nervous system. Senescent brain cells and age-related neurological conditions, including Parkinson's and Alzheimer's diseases, are significantly related. Across diagnosed dementias, chronic inflammatory processes apparently underlie neurological deterioration (see Swenson et al. 2019). Effectiveness of macrophage and microglia in modulating CNS neuronal repair and regeneration decreases as age increases, as does peripheral immune system activity (Swenson et al. 2019), suggesting that cellular senescence alters cognitive function. As terminally differentiated nondividing cells, neurons accumulate age-related alterations and show irreversible cell-cycle arrest and senescence with increasing age. Via paracrine activity, they also may influence cells without senescent biomarkers to exhibit senescent phenotypes (Swenson et al. 2019). Multiple types of diagnosed dementias exist: Alzheimer's dementia (AD), Parkinson's dementia, vascular dementias, pharmacological and alcohol-induced dementias, and non-Alzheimer's senile dementias. All show similar symptoms, namely reduced cognitive function, loss of time and space orientation, muscular control, and long- and short-term memory, and impaired neurological abilities, with language, attention, memory, and higher-order executive functions being most affected. Dementia is a general dysfunctional endpoint resulting from variable age-related neurological alterations in primate brains that often co-occur with strokes. For all dementias, vascular and neurological sites wherein alterations occur determine disablement and specificity of individual dysfunction. During normal aging without dementia, neurons also show alterations in molecular signaling patterns, as overall cell numbers remain relatively stable; conversely, neurodegenerative dementias may associate with neuronal loss (Swenson et al. 2019).

Interestingly, dementias do not necessarily show familial aggregation or suggest private familial alleles. Still, multiple loci harbor mutations predisposing to AD and its familial forms: Apolipoprotein E*4 chromosome 19, presenilins 1 and 2 chromosomes 14 and 1, mutated amyloid precursor proteins, and amyloid beta (Aβ) protein chromosome 21. Most dementia risk likely reflects environmental exposures, lifestyle attributes, and biological fragility. Alzheimer's dementia shows both early-onset forms, initiating symptoms before 65 years and late-onset ones occurring at later ages. Familial dementia also shows both early- and late-onset forms. Because dementias, particularly AD, continually increase in frequency as age increases, one hypothesis is that all who live sufficiently long will experience dementia. Based on the 2010 US census, at 65–74 years 3.0 percent suffered from AD; this rate increased to 17.6 percent among those aged 75–84 years, and to 32.3 percent in those 84 years and older (Hebert 2003). In general, women exhibit higher prevalences of AD than men, accounting for two-thirds of all diagnosed cases in the United States and are diagnosed at slightly later ages than men (Beam et al. 2018). Continually increasing in frequency with age, dementias are among the leading causes of morbidity and mortality among older adults worldwide. In the USA, AD is currently the eighth leading cause of death (Ahmad and Anderson 2021). Although the suggestion is we will all suffer AD if we survive sufficiently long, many people, about half, do not experience dementia during their lives.

Frailty Frailty is an observable phenotype composed of multiple assessments indicating limited physical and functional capabilities (see review, Walston and Bandeen-Roche 2015). Developed originally by Fried and colleagues (2001, 2005) and Rockwood et al. (2005), frailty indices commonly include physical assessments of strength, mobility, endurance, and physical activity. The original index included recent unintentional weight loss of ten-plus pounds, slow walking speed, self-reported exhaustion, weakness, and low physical activity (Fried et al. 2001). Frailty indices reflect lifelong outcomes of physical and sociocultural stressors encountered and altered somatic capabilities, which also increase with age, peaking at the oldest ages (see Crews 2005, 2022; Walston 2005).

Everyone experiences multiple stressors over their lives. Even in utero and during growth and development our tissues, organs, and bones respond to stressors, e.g., malnutrition, lifestyle and social settings, oxygen intake, and trauma. In stressful settings those surviving to early childhood may already show signs of frailty: poor skeletal growth, short height, low bone density or organ size, and health issues. With age, indicators of frailty increase in scope, severity, and prevalence, cellular losses and malfunctions progress and our mobility, physical, and task performance abilities are hampered (Crews 2021). Not only seniors, but people with physical limitations, those with congenital issues and injuries also may show high frailty. Human frailty may be an example of evolutionary inertia (Fried et al. 2005). Frailty indices provide clinically recognizable and valid assessments of current functional abilities and reveal variability in capabilities across age, sex, social, environmental, and cultural settings (Crews 2021).

CONCLUSION

A major difference between human longevity and the longevity of other primates and animals is humankind's reliance on biocultural reproduction in socioculturally constructed niches to provide a microenvironment capable of supporting secondarily altricial offspring. Socioculturally constructed niches allowed hominins to avoid many extrinsic stressors and develop multiple kinship relationships based on both genetically and socially defined roles, promoting biocultural reproduction, a special form of cooperative breeding. Thereby, enhancing hominin reproductive output and favoring genomic variants promoting slow inter- and extra-uterine growth and development. Incipient reliance on sociocultural interactions within hominin social groups provided the early life opportunities to build somatic capacity. This capacity ultimately led to insertion of human childhood and adolescence phases into our life history pattern and today underlies our extended growth, development, and life spans.

Combined, constructed niches, extended preadult growth and development periods, and sociocultural developments largely explain why a higher percentage of modern human young, and likely the young of earlier hominins, survive to a longer reproductive adulthood than any other primate species. Our life history pattern, requiring offspring to experience two additional stages, stretches our lives out, which likely accounts for much of our extended longevity. Additionally, bioculturally enhanced residential settings and foraging skills have likely provided an improved nutritional base supporting extended periods of dependency during growth. Over time, investments in prereproductive young allowed evolving hominins to build larger, stronger, and healthier somas while also contributing to their development of biological, behavioral, and cultural resilience prior to achieving sexual maturity (Bogin 2009; Crews 2003). Early life investments in somatic, cognitive, and emotional reserves – jointly contributing to hominin reserve capacity (RC) – likely led to improved adult health, fitness, and longevity, characteristics most fully represented among today's humans living in bioculturally constructed niches. Extended post-reproductive lives among women and late-life survival of men are derivatives of our evolved early-life propensity to grow slowly over two-plus decades, build and develop the RC needed to reproduce over an extended span, and survive till our last offspring matures. Today, in less stressful and bioculturally built environments, we have sufficient energetic, economic, social, educational, and emotional inputs to build RC not only during growth and development, but throughout our prime reproductive adult years, jointly providing opportunities to maintain our somas into late life. This is a period now extending to twice the maximum age observed among other great apes.

Prior to the advent of modern constructed settings, in the environment of evolutionary adaptation, opportunities to build RC were probably hampered by lower energetic inputs, higher intrinsic and extrinsic mortality, and few survivors past their fourth decade. The advent of modern human life histories reflects our ancestors' increasing reliance on culturally constructed biobehavioral niches that provided less uncertain and more benign living environments. This shift extended opportunities to attain nutritious foods, increase our period of growth and development, acquire extensive RC during growth, development, and prime adulthood, and ultimately shifted our life history tempo to support a vigorous and healthy post-reproductive life (see also Bogin 2021; Crews 2019, 2021; Drenos et al. 2006; Sterling 2020).

Senescence occurs as genetic, protein, cellular, tissue, organ, and organ systems maintaining our somas begin to fail. Thus, biological senescence is an outcome of event-driven deleterious processes affecting all organs and bodily systems, that incrementally and continually increase one's probability of death. Residing in protected environments less exposed to multiple extrinsic stressors and causes of death reduces event frequencies, slows rates of dysfunction, reduces investment to repair damage, and thereby allows increased Reserve Capacity sufficient to maintain somatic stability into late life. Although not dependent on chronological time, senescent changes accumulate over an organism's life span and are thus age-related (Arking 2006), partly because early life history events pace the timing of later events and senescence (Crews 2003, 2019), and partly because loss of function is dependent upon cellular processes of replication and differentiation occurring in biological time (Arking 2006). One hallmark of human senescence is the variable patterning and timing of specific events and its variable tempo in relation to chronological age across human settings and societies.

Keys to understanding human life history and life spans likely are evolution of biocultural reproduction and development of culturally constructed niches and residences. By reducing extrinsic stressors and mortality, these developments allowed humans to evolve new life history phases, build stronger more resilient somas, and retain physical, cognitive, and emotional RC into late life. Across all existent human populations, a majority of humans live sufficiently long to reproduce and fledge offspring, grow old, develop diseases specific to aging and related conditions, including frailty and allostatic load, that ultimately hamper individual physical capabilities and limit life span. We also live sufficiently long to meet our grand- and great-grandchildren and die of old age in our eighth and later decades of life.

REFERENCES

Ahmad, F. B., and R. N. Anderson. "The Leading Causes of Death in the US for 2020." *JAMA* 325, no. 18 (2021): 1829–1830.

Arking, R. *The Biology of Aging: Observations and Principles*, 3rd edn. New York: Oxford University Press, 2006.

Austad, S. N. "Menopause – An Evolutionary Perspective." *Experimental Gerontology* 29 (1994): 255–263.

Austad, S. N. "Comparative Aging and Life Histories in Mammals." *Experimental Gerontology* 32 (1997a): 23–38.

Austad, S. N. *Why We Age: What Science Is Discovering about the Body's Journey Through Life*. New York: John Wiley and Sons, 1997b.

Beam, C. R., C. Kaneshiro, J. Y. Jang, et al. "Differences Between Women and Men in Incidence Rates of Dementia and Alzheimer's Disease." *Journal of Alzheimer's Disease* 64 (2018): 1077–1083.

Bergmüller, R., R. A. Johnstone, A. F. Russell, et al. "Integrating Cooperative Breeding into Theoretical Concepts of Cooperation." *Behavioral Processes* 76 (2007): 61–72.

Bogin, B. *Patterns of Human Growth*. Cambridge: Cambridge University Press, 1988.

Bogin, B. *The Growth of Humanity*. New York: Wiley-Liss, 2001.

Bogin, B. "Childhood, Adolescence, and Longevity: A Multilevel Model of the Evolution of Reserve Capacity in Human Life History." *American Journal of Human Biology* 21 (2009): 567–577.

Bogin, B. *Patterns of Human Growth*, 3rd edn. Cambridge: Cambridge University Press, 2021.

Bogin, B., and B. H. Smith. "Evolution of the Human Life Cycle." *American Journal of Human Biology* 8 (1996): 703–716.

Bogin, B., J. Bragg, C. Kuzawa, et al. "Humans Are Not Cooperative Breeders but Practice Biocultural Reproduction." *American Journal of Human Biology* 41 (2014): 368–380.

Bogin, B., C. Varea, M. Hermanussen, et al. "Human Life Course Biology: A Centennial Perspective of Scholarship on the Human Pattern of Physical Growth and Its Place in Human Biocultural Evolution." *American Journal of Physical Anthropology* 165 (2018): 834–854.

Brent, L. J. N., D. W. Franks, D. W. Foster, et al. "Ecological Knowledge, Leadership, and the Evolution of Menopause in Killer Whales." *Current Biology* 25 (2015): 746–750.

Brock, D.B., J. M. Guralnik, and J. A. Brody . "Demography and Epidemiology of Aging in the United States." In *Handbook of the Biology of Aging*. Edited by E. L. Schneider and J. E. Rose , 3–23. San Diego: Academic Press, Inc., 1990.

Carey, J. R., and D. S. Judge. "Life Span Extension in Humans Is Self-Reinforcing: A General Theory of Longevity." *Population and Development Review* 27 (2001): 411–436.

Caspari, R., and S.-H. Lee. "Older Age Becomes Common Late in Human Evolution." *Proceedings of the National Academy of Sciences of the United States of America* 101 (2004): 10895–10900.

Clark, M., E. Lagan, M. O'Hara, et al. *Biological Anthropology Laboratory Manual*. Toronto: TopHat, 2021.

Clutton-Brock, T. H. *Mammal Societies*. Hoboken: Wiley-Blackwell, 2016.

Crews, D. E. *Human Senescence: Evolutionary and Biocultural Perspectives*. New York: Cambridge University Press, 2003.

Crews, D. E. "Artificial Environments and an Aging Population: Designing for Age-Related Functional Loss." *Journal of Physiological Anthropology and Applied Human Sciences* 24 (2005): 103–109.

Crews, D. E. "Senescence, Aging, and Disease." *Journal of Physiological Anthropology* 26 (2007): 365–372.

Crews, D. E. "Co-evolution of Human Culture, Mating Strategies and Longevity." In *Aging Related Problems in Past and Present Populations*. Edited by C. Susanne and E. Bodzsar, 9–29. Budapest: Eötvös University Press, 2008.

Crews, D. E. "Senescence." In *Encyclopedia of Evolutionary Psychological Sciences*. Edited by T. K. Shackelford and V. A. Weekes-Shackelford, 7018–7031. New York: Springer Publishing, 2021.

Crews, D. E. "Aging, Frailty, and Design of Built Environments." *Journal of Physiological Anthropology* 41 (2022): Article number: 2.

Cummings, S. R., and M. C. Nevitt. "A Hypothesis: The Cause of Hip Fractures." *Journals of Gerontology* 44 (1989): M107–M111.

Drenos, F., R. G. J. Westendorp, and T. B. L. Kirkwood. "Trade-Off Mediated Effects on the Genetics of Human Survival Caused by Increasingly Benign Living Conditions." *Biogerontology* 7 (2006): 287–295.

Ellis, S., D. W. Nattrass S. Franks, et al. "Analyses of Ovarian Activity Reveal Repeated Evolution of Post-Reproductive Lifespans in Toothed Whales." *Scientific Reports* 8 (2018): 12833.

Evans, K. E., and S. Harris. "Adolescence in Male African Elephants, Loxodonta Africana and the Importance of Sociality." *Animal Behaviour* 76 (2008): 779–787.

Finch, C. E., and M. R. Rose. "Hormones and Physiological Architecture of Life History Evolution." *Quarterly Review of Biology* 70 (1995): 1–52.

Fried, L. P., C. M. Tangen, J. D. Walston, et al. "Frailty in Older Adults: Evidence of a Phenotype." *Journals of Gerontology Series A* 56 (2001): M146–M156.

Fried, L. P., E. C. Walston J. D. Hadley, et al. "From Bedside to Bench: Research Agenda for Frailty." *Science of Aging Knowledge Environment* 31 (2005): pe24.

Gold, E. B. "The Timing of the Age at Which Natural Menopause Occurs." *Obstetrics and Gynecology Clinics of North America* 38 (2011): 425–440.

Graham, C. E. "Reproductive Senescence in Female Non-human Primates." In *Aging in Non-human Primates*. Edited by D. M. Bowden, 183–209. New York: Van Nostrand Reinhold, 1979.

Gurven, M., and H. Kaplan. "Longevity Among Hunter-Gatherers: A Cross-Cultural Examination." *Population and Development Review* 33 (2007): 321–365.

Gurven, M., J. Stieglitz, B. Trumble, et al. "The Tsimane Health and Life History Project: Integrating Anthropology and Biomedicine." *Evolutionary Anthropology* 26 (2017): 54–73.

Hamilton, W. D. "The Genetical Evolution of Social Behavior. II." *Journal of Theoretical Biology* 7 (1964): 1–16.

Hamilton, W. D. "The Moulding of Senescence by Natural Selection." *Journal of Theoretical Biology* 12 (1966): 12–45.

Hawkes, K., J. F. O'Connell, and N. G. Blurton Jones. "Hazda Women's Time Allocation, Offspring Provisioning, and the Evolution of Long Postmenopausal Life Span." *Current Anthropology* 48 (1997): 551–577.

Hawkes, K., J. F. Jones, N. O'Connell, G. Blurton, et al. "Grandmothering, Menopause, and the Evolution of Human Life Histories." *Proceedings of the National Academy of Sciences of the United States of America* 95 (1998): 1336–1339.

Hawkes, K., K. R. Smith, and S. L. Robinson. "Mortality and Fertility Rates in Humans and Chimpanzees: How Within-Species Variation Complicates Cross-Species Comparisons." *American Journal of Human Biology* 21 (2009): 578–586.

Hayflick, L. "Biological Aging Is No Longer an Unsolved Problem." *Annals of the New York Academy of Sciences* 1100 (2007): 1–13.

Hebert, L. E., J. Weuve, P. A. Scheer, et al. "Alzheimer Disease in the United States (2010–2050) Estimated Using the 2010 Census." *Neurology* 80 (2013): 1778–1783.

Katz, S. A., A. B. Moskowitz, R. W. Ford, et al. "Studies of Illness in the Aged. The Index of ADL: A Standardized Measure of Biological and Psychosocial Function." *Journal of the American Medical Association* 185 (1963): 94–101.

Kim, S., and S. M. Jazwinski. "Quantitative Measures of Healthy Aging and Biological Age." *Healthy Aging Research* 4 (2015): 26.

Kirkwood, T. B. L. "Evolution of Ageing." *Nature* 270 (1977): 301–304.

Kirkwood, T. B. L. "The Disposable Soma Theory of Aging." In *Genetic Effects on Aging II*. Edited by D. E. Harrison, 9–19. Telford, PA: The Telford Press, Inc. 1990.

Koenig, W. D. "What Drives Cooperative Breeding?" *PLoS Biology* 5, no. 6 (2017): e2002965.

Kumari, R., and P. Jat. "Mechanisms of Cellular Senescence: Cell Cycle Arrest and Senescence Associated Secretory Phenotype." *Frontiers in Cell and Developmental Biology* 9 (2020): 64559329; March 2021.

Larke, A., and D. E. Crews. "Parental Investment, Late Reproduction, and Increased Reserve Capacity Are Associated with Longevity in Humans." *Journal of Physiological Anthropology* 25 (2006): 119–131.

Leidy, L. E. "Biological Aspects of Menopause: Across the Lifespan." *Annual Review of Anthropology* 23 (1994): 231–253.

Liversidge H. M. "Timing of Human Mandibular Third Molar Formation." *Annals of Human Biology* 35 (2008): 294–321.

Machado-Oliveira, G., C. Ramos, A. R. A. Marques, et al. "Cell Senescence, Multiple Organelle Dysfunction and Atherosclerosis." *Cells* 9, no. 10 (2020): 2146.

Miles, T., and J. Brody. "Aging as a Worldwide Phenomenon." In *Biological Anthropology and Aging: Perspectives on Human Variation Over the Life Span*. Edited by D. E. Crews and R. M. Garutto, 3–15. New York: Oxford University Press, 1994.

Murphy, L., L. Begum, K. Sievert, et al. "Life Course Effects on Age at Menopause among Bangladeshi Sedentees and Migrants to the UK." *American Journal of Human Biology* 25 (2012): 83–93.

Packer, C., M. Tatar, and A. Collin. "Reproductive Cessation in Female Mammals." *Nature* 392 (1998): 807–810.

Paine, R. R., and K. Hawkes. "The Evolution of Human Life History." In *The Evolution of Human Life History*. Edited by K. Hawkes and R. R. Paine, 95–126. Santa Fe: University of New Mexico Press, 2006.

Passarino, G., F. De Rango, and A. Montesanto. "Human Longevity: Genetics or Lifestyle? It Takes Two to Tango." *Immunity and Ageing* 13 (2016): 12.

Pavelka, M., S. McDonald, and L. Fedigan. "Menopause: A Comparative Life History Perspective." *Yearbook of Physical Anthropology* 34 (1991): 13–38.

M. E. Pereira, and L. A. Fairbanks. *Juvenile Primates: Life History, Development, and Behaviour.* New York: Oxford University Press, 1993.

Pereira, M. E., and L. A. Fairbanks. *Juvenile Primates: Life History, Development and Behavior, with a New Foreword.* New York: Oxford University Press, 2002.

Rockwood, K., X. Song, C. MacKnight, et al. "A Global Clinical Measure of Fitness and Frailty in Elderly People." *Canadian Medical Association Journal* 173 (2005): 489–495.

Rose, M. R. *Evolutionary Biology of Aging.* New York: Oxford University Press, 1991.

Rose, M. R., C. L. Rauser, and L. D. Mueller. "Late Life: A New Frontier for Physiology." *Physiological and Biochemical Zoology* 78 (2005): 869–878.

Smith, B. H. "Growth and Development and Its Significance for Early Hominid Behaviour." *OSSA* 14 (1989): 63–96.

Smith, B. H. "Age at Weaning Approximates Age of Emergence of the First Permanent Molar in Non-Human Primates." *American Journal of Physical Anthropology,* Suppl. 12 (1991): 163–164.

Snowden, D. A., R. L. Beeson, G. L. Dane, et al. "Is Early Natural Menopause a Biologic Marker of Health and Aging?" *American Journal of Public Health* 79 (1989): 709–714.

Stearns, S. C. *The Evolution of Life Histories.* Oxford: Oxford University Press, 1992.

Sterling, R. *What Is Health? Allostasis and the Evolution of Human Design.* Cambridge, MA: The MIT Press, 2020.

Stini, W. A. "Changing Patterns of Morbidity and Mortality and the Challenge to Heath Care Delivery Systems of the Future." *Collegium Anthropologicum* 14 (1990): 189–195.

Strait, J. A., and E. G. Lakatta. "Aging-Associated Cardiovascular Changes and Their Relationship to Heart Failure." *Heart Failure Clinics* 8 (2012): 143–164.

Swenson, B. L., C. F. Meyera, T. J. Bussianb, et al. "Senescence in Aging and Disorders of the Central Nervous System." *Translational Medicine of Aging* 3 (2019): 17–25.

Tchkonia, T., and J. L. Kirkland. "Aging, Cell Senescence, and Chronic Disease. Emerging Therapeutic Strategies." *JAMA* 320, no. 13 (2018): 1319–1320.

Thompson, E. M., J. H. Pusey, A. E. Jones, et al. "Aging and Fertility Patterns in Wild Chimpanzees Provide Insights into the Evolution of Menopause." *Current Biology* 17 (2007): 2150–2156.

Thompson, J. L., and A. J. Nelson. "Middle Childhood and Modern Human Origins." *Human Nature* 22 (2011): 249–280.

Tully, T., and A. Lambert. "The Evolution of Post-reproductive Life Span as an Insurance Against Indeterminacy." *Evolution* 65 (2011): 3013–3020.

van Deursen, J.M. "The role of senescent cells in aging." *Nature* 509 (2014): 439-446.

Walston, J. D. "Biological Markers and the Molecular Biology of Frailty." In *Longevity and Frailty.* Edited by J. R. Carey, J.-M. Robine, and Y. Christen, 39–56. New York: Springer-Verlag, 2005.

Walston, J. D., and K. Bandeen-Roche. "Frailty: A Tale of Two Concepts." *BMC Medicine* 13 (2015): 1–3.

Weinstein, B., and D. Ciszek. "The Reserve-Capacity Hypothesis: Evolutionary Origins and Modern Implications of the Trade-Off Between Tumor-Suppression and Tissue-Repair." *Experimental Gerontology* 37 (2002): 615–627.

Zenin, A., Y. Sharapov, P.A. Telford, S. Tsepilov, P.A. Telford, et al. "Identification of 12 Genetic Loci Associated with Human Healthspan." *Communications Biology* 2 (2019): 41.

CHAPTER 9

Climate-Related Human Biological Variation

Cynthia M. Beall

The impressive worldwide variation in human biology prompts biological anthropologists to ask why it exists and how it came about. Answers come from applying evolutionary principles: variation arises from evolution, adaptation, and life history (Gluckman et al. 2009, 2019; Pomeroy et al. 2021; Washburn 1951; Wells et al. 2019). That deceptively simple response glosses over many complexities of how populations and individuals change over time. Anthropologists have approached these questions by examining the effects of stressful environments, such as climate extremes exerting physiological stresses that elicit biological responses, adaptations, and human variation.

Global and local approaches to answering the "why" and "how" questions have emerged. The global survey approach applies correlation-regression analyses of the variation in human biology and climate variables: with a, often temperature or a surrogate variable (Katzmarzyk and Leonard 1998; Pomeroy et al. 2021; Roberts 1973). Body size, morphology, development, and metabolism vary clinally across geographic space. The International Biological Program of the 1960s and 1970s took a local approach using case studies of communities in stressful environments (Baker and Weiner 1966; Harrison 1966). In the genomic era (since the first sequencing of a human genome; see International Human Genome Sequencing Consortium 2001), research straddles and extends the two approaches. Research in this era compares variation across populations by analyzing clines in allele frequencies, signals of selection, and intrapopulation variation (Coop et al. 2010; Fan et al. 2016; Reich 2018; Tishkoff 2015; Werren et al. 2021).

Both global and local approaches acknowledge the role of behavior and culture in buffering people from climate. The widely used phrase "adaptation to the environment" is the process or state of achieving better function than an alternative and usually refers to biological responses occurring when behavioral buffering is inadequate. The study of adaptation to climate rests on the concept of homeostasis – a compensatory physiological mechanism maintaining a dynamic narrow range of internal characteristics, such as core temperature or the partial pressure of oxygen in arterial blood, under widely varying

A Companion to Biological Anthropology, Second Edition. Edited by Clark Spencer Larsen.
© 2023 John Wiley & Sons Ltd. Published 2023 by John Wiley & Sons Ltd.

environmental circumstances. We recognize multiple modes of adaptation, including genetic, developmental, and acclimatization. Populations adapt over a range of time frames and may do so on an ongoing basis or more than once and in more than one way. Progress in identifying the modes of adaptation has been slow, partly due to our limited understanding of how genetics, the environment, and individual life history influence the traits of interest. The genetic mode of adaptation occurs when a heritable trait increases in frequency over generations, owing to natural selection due to the fact that the resulting form of the trait confers higher reproductive success. The developmental mode refers to "an irreversible trait acquired during the process of growth and development that reflects cellular or organ system plasticity in response to early … exposure" (Brutsaert 2016: 102). The acclimatization mode of adaptation consists of immediate (seconds to weeks or months) physiological processes that reverse when the stress is removed. Cultural adaptation refers to behaviors, practices, or technologies that buffer individuals from stress or improve their biological response. It is challenging to determine whether an intriguing biological characteristic (phenotype) is an adaptation and, if so, by what mode it arose. One approach uses "migrant models" comparing populations with different exposure histories to distinguish among the various modes of adaptation (Baker 1969; Harrison 1966; Lasker 1969; Kiyamu et al. 2015; McGarvey 1991; Moore 2021; Smith et al. 2021; Zamudio et al. 1995). Nuanced models combining genetic and developmental approaches, such as predictive adaptive developmental origins and predictive adaptive response models, acknowledge the intertwined genetic and developmental origins of traits (Gluckman et al. 2009, 2019). New methods for collecting biological traits and population genetics and genomics analyses expand the tools available to detect adaptations.

This chapter briefly describes the current understanding of climate and human variation using global and local approaches, and considers the emerging topics of epigenetic analyses and climate change. It characterizes stresses, describes human biological variation, and presents evidence for modes of adaptation.

CLIMATE

"Climate in a narrow sense is usually defined as the average weather, or more rigorously, as the statistical description in terms of the mean and variability of relevant quantities over a time ranging from months to thousands or millions of years" (IPCC (Intergovernmental Panel on Climate Change) 2012). Anthropologists operationalize climate broadly to include temperature and humidity, ultraviolet radiation (UVR) intensity, and altitude above sea level. Derek Roberts explained why climate interests evolutionary biologists. "Climate tends to remain constant over long periods of time (by comparison with organism lifespan); consequently, selection pressures operate in the same direction generation after generation. Macroclimatic factors usually change rather slowly over wide areas, except where altitude is involved…. Hence characters that vary with climate tend to show clinal variation, by contrast to the variation that is produced in response to other types of environmental variation. Moreover, climatic gradients occur in parallel in different continents so that intercontinental comparisons can be made, and if populations long separated genetically show parallel morphological gradients, the case that they are associated with climate is strengthened" (Roberts 1973: 34–35). Subsequent scholars built on this perspective using new types of data and models.

TEMPERATURE

Thermal stress, like all stresses, can be described in terms of magnitude, frequency, and duration. Combinations of these features suggest a variety of responses. For instance, the response to a rare, fleeting heat wave may differ from the response to daily walking in the sun, heavy seasonal agriculture work in humid heat, or lifelong exposure to ambient temperatures above 25 °C (77 °F) (Ioannou et al. 2021).

Thermoneutrality refers to the ambient temperature at which a nude, inactive adult maintains core temperature without engaging behavioral and biological thermoregulation. The thermoneutral range is approximately 25–27 °C (77–80 °F). Maintaining core temperature within a narrow range represents thermal homeostasis. The core–shell–environment model of thermoregulation explains how people lose heat to the environment when core and skin temperatures are higher than ambient temperatures and vice versa when ambient temperatures are high. Consider the body core (organs) as the source of heat generation and the cooler shell (fat and skin) as the section of the body through which heat passes to the body surface and the environment. Cold temperatures can establish a temperature gradient from a warm core to a cooler shell to the cold environment and result in heat loss from the core. A warm environment can do the opposite and raise core temperature. Behavior buffers may maintain core temperature; for example: physical activity, heating, fans and air conditioning. If these measures fail to maintain homeostasis, biological thermoregulation is engaged. For example, the constriction of blood vessels from the warm core to the cooler shell restricts heat loss; metabolism, shivering, and nonshivering thermogenesis increase heat production in cold climates. In contrast, blood vessels vasodilate and heart rate rises to increase blood flow to the body surface in hot environments; the heat required to evaporate sweat also reduces body temperature.

The average human core temperature is 37 °C (98.6 °F) with a range from 36.2 to 37.5 °C (97.2 to 99.5 °F). Unexpectedly, two recent studies suggested that core temperature may not be a static trait. One reported that the average core temperature in the United States decreased by 0.05 °C/decade over the past two centuries. Another study found that the average core temperature of lowland Bolivian forager farmers decreased even faster: ~ 0.05 °C/year over the past two decades (Gurven et al. 2020; Protsiv et al. 2020).

An enduring research method introduced in the 1950s is to plot the mean values of certain traits of indigenous populations against temperature measured by mean annual temperature. Heavier bodies and shorter legs characterized samples from colder climates collected both before and after 1950 (Figure 9.1A and B) (Katzmarzyk and Leonard 1998). These findings confirm Bergmann's and Allen's rules in people. In 1847, German biologist Carl Bergmann observed that birds and mammals in cold regions were bulkier than individuals of the same species in warm regions. In 1877, American ornithologist Joel Asaph Allen added that animals in cold regions had shorter limbs than animals adapted to warm climates. American anthropologist Howells (1960: 118) explained the reason for these observations: "As an animal of a given shape gets larger, its inner bulk increases faster than its outer surface, so the ratio of heat produced to heat dissipated is higher in larger individuals." Data kindly provided by the authors of the 1998 paper illustrate this phenomenon. The five samples living in the coldest climate (average mean annual temperature of –13.9 °C (7 °F)) were compared with the nine samples living in the warmest climates (average mean annual temperature of 28.2 °C (83 °F)). The cold climate samples had an average ratio of weight to body surface

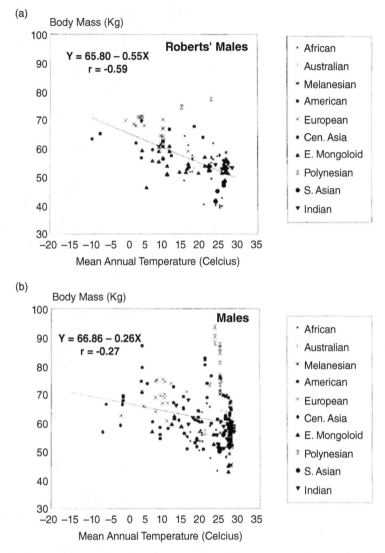

Figure 9.1   Body mass of men plotted against mean annual temperature using studies published before (top) and after (bottom) 1950. (Katzmarzyk and Leonard 1998)

area of ~ 38 kg/m^2 compared with 33 kg/m^2 for the hot climate samples. The samples residing in the cold climate had approximately 15 percent larger "inner bulk" – and heat generating potential – relative to their body surface area. The local studies described in Figure 9.1 the increased influence of non-climatic factors.

Other authors used a variety of climate measures, including maximum and minimum annual temperatures, year-to-year volatility of mean annual temperature, maximum relative humidity, net primary productivity, and annual precipitation, and confirmed the general principle of morphological adaptation to temperature (Pomeroy et al. 2021). Some studies found that a few geographical and ecological factors explained almost 50 percent of the between population variation based on height. This is remarkable because many factors influence body size (Bernstein 2010; Little 2020; Mummert et al. 2011).

The pattern of larger bodies occurring at higher and colder latitudes has a deep history over the past million years in the genus *Homo*, including among Neandertals and other Pleistocene hominins (Will et al. 2021). The long existence of the height cline is noteworthy because ancient DNA (aDNA) evidence showed that our ancestors moved long distances around the Old World, including in and out of zones with different temperatures (Reich 2018). This implies that populations can adapt quickly to temperature changes via acclimatization or developmental adaptation to local climate alone or in concert with natural selection.

How do the larger bodies and shorter legs in colder climates come about? A cline of allele frequencies shows a high frequency of variants associated with short stature in southern Europe that slowly transitions to a high frequency of alleles associated with tall stature in the North, providing evidence of natural selection (Lango Allen et al. 2010; Turchin et al. 2012). However, genetic drift in the form of serial founder effects could account for the cline (Berg et al. 2019; Hruschka et al. 2015; Turchin et al. 2012). The serial founder effect refers to the net effect on genetic variation when a population gives rise to another population with less genetic variation and that population, in turn, gives rise to another with even less variation. Over time, the repeated founder events randomly reduce genetic variation, and later populations have fewer genetic variants than the parent population. In this case, the reduction in genetic variation related to height does not appear to be random. The serial founder effect and natural selection may both account for the finding (Berg et al. 2019; Sohail et al. 2019). An aDNA analysis concluded that taller height among Northern Europeans resulted partly from the migration of populations with tall alleles followed by selection for taller height (Mathieson et al. 2015).

Alternatively, developmental plasticity may connect climate to phenotype without genetic changes. The range of body sizes could reflect the range of possible phenotypes for height arising from one gene pool. Body size can change dramatically in a single generation. For instance, Maya children growing up in the US average nearly 12 cm (~ 4½ in) taller than those growing up in Guatemala and had proportionately longer legs, showing that "height and body proportions are sensitive indicators of the quality of the environment for growth" (Bogin et al. 2002: 753). Temperature, along with public health factors, may be one of many environmental contributors to growth. This example does not exclude genetic contributions to the range of human height, although it reminds us of the complexity of quantitative traits. Genes with large effects contribute to stature in some populations. For example, the very short stature of low-latitude African rainforest hunter-gatherers is partly attributable to a high frequency of one variant at the hyaluronidase 2 *HYAL2* locus (Perry et al. 2014; Zoccolillo et al. 2020).

Global studies do not consider the actual exposure to heat or cold that elicits behavioral and biological responses. Turning from global clines and correlations to local studies by comparing populations adapting to climate stress provides a more realistic, nuanced assessment of thermal stress.

Heat exposure occurs when a high environmental temperature imposes a physiological load or physical exertion increases the metabolic rate. The evolutionary history of heat stress may extend to ~ 2 million years ago, when *Homo erectus* foraged and engaged in persistence hunting (when hunters pursue prey until it is exhausted) in the open landscape of East Africa. Lieberman explains that "…humans have a specially elaborated system of cutaneous sweat glands that differs in several important respects from other mammals, including those that also sweat" (Lieberman 2015: 105). The Engrailed Homeobox 1 (*EN1*) transcription factor plays a role in sweat gland formation and has variants specific to humans

(Aldea et al. 2021). The capacity to substantially increase sweat output may correlate with the requirement of replacing lost water.

Cold exposure occurs when low air or water temperature results in heat loss from the warm body to the cooler environment. Skin temperature falls and may lead to a fall in core temperature. The evolutionary history of cold exposure stretches back to *H. erectus*, which was found 1.8 mya in Dmanisi, Georgia, at 41°N latitude, where the mean annual temperature was ~ 11 °C (52 °F) (Lordkipanidze et al. 2013). By 45,000 years ago, *Homo sapiens* lived above the Arctic Circle (66.7°N) (Pitulko et al. 2016). Cold exposure varies widely from whole body overnight cold exposure in hot deserts by Aborigines in the Australian outback to hours-long immersion in cold water by Korean and Japanese diving women, to peripheral (feet and hands) cold exposure during hunting and fishing.

Types of cold responses include raising metabolism (e.g., Alacaluf Native Americans of South America), insulating the core by vasoconstriction (e.g., coastal Aborigines of Australia), allowing the core temperature to drift downward (e.g., Kalahari San), and combinations thereof. Diving women in Japan and Korea are traditionally known for having high basal metabolic rates (BMRs) and effective vascular adaptations to prevent heat loss to cold water. When the divers replaced the traditional cotton bathing suit with wetsuits buffering them from the cold, BMR fell to that predicted by age and body size (Hong 1973; Hong and Rahn 1967). These findings suggest that restudies of other classic local adaptations are warranted.

Genome scans reveal signals of selection at loci related to sensing moderate cold, increasing muscle tone and energy output, and increasing nonshivering thermogenesis in brown adipose tissue. More than a half dozen loci are associated with latitude and brown adipose tissue thermogenesis (Sellayah 2019). For example, there is a cline for increasing the frequency of derived variants at the Transient Receptor Potential Cation Channel Subfamily M Member 8 (*TRPM8*) locus from less than 10 percent among African samples to over 80 percent in Northern European samples (Iftinca and Altier 2020; Key et al. 2018). A high frequency of variants at loci involved in metabolic heat generation occurs among Inuit people from Greenland. The cold-adapted variants moved into that population through interbreeding with archaic Neandertals and Denisovans (Racimo et al. 2017).

Physiological traits vary with temperature. Comparing populations, heat generation measured as basal and resting metabolic rates increased with lower temperatures (Leonard et al. 2002; Roberts 1973). In a cold-water stress test, people with certain Actinin Alpha 3 (*ACTN3*) variants maintained a higher core temperature by generating more heat in skeletal muscles (Wyckelsma et al. 2021). Shivering in the cold generates heat (Ocobock 2016). Nonshivering thermogenesis generates heat in brown adipose tissue. The mechanism involves molecules, called uncoupling proteins, in the mitochondria of brown adipose tissue that short-circuit the respiratory chain producing ATP and produce heat instead. Variants of genes encoding uncoupling proteins 1 and 3 (*UCP1* and *UCP3*) increase protein expression. The allele frequencies of these genes form a cline from 0 percent near the equator to 40 percent at higher latitudes and colder temperatures (Figure 9.2) (Hancock et al. 2011). *UCP1* variants associated with brown adipose tissue thermogenesis also vary inversely with temperature (Nishimura et al. 2017). Nishimura and colleagues (2017) tested the change in oxygen consumption (to measure metabolic heat generation) by a group of Japanese male students clad in t-shirts and shorts who sat quietly through a 90-minute exposure to 16 °C (61 °F). Students with one particular variant exhibited a four-fold higher increase in oxygen consumption than the others, suggesting that the cline in variants reflects a cline in adaptive response. Other work on brown adipose tissue thermogenesis suggested the

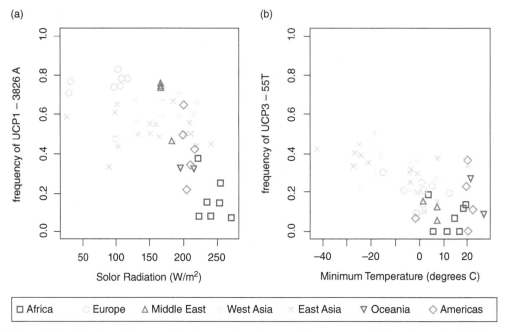

Figure 9.2   Clinal variation in allele frequencies of uncoupling proteins. (Hancock, et al. 2011)

existence of seasonal acclimatization among residents of temperate regions of the US (Niclou and Ocobock 2021) and of developmental adaptation among Siberian reindeer herders (Levy et al. 2021; Levy and Leonard 2021).

Heat stress elicits responses that limit a rise in core temperature. The responses include an increase in heart rate and blood flow to the body surface and heat dissipation to the environment. Sweat evaporation has a cooling effect because body heat provides the energy. Sweating is not effective when the vapor pressure of water on the skin is close to the dew point, the temperature at which the relative humidity is 100 percent of the air. Acclimatization to heat stress is reflected by smaller increases in heart rate and enabled by a more rapid onset of sweating (Lee et al. 2019). Our capacity to sweat as much as one liter of water per hour increases the risk of dehydration. As a result, conserving water is another challenge in hot environments. One study that requires replication reported findings consistent with selection based on genes associated with thyroid function. Variants of thyroid binding globulin (TBG) with signals of selection dampened swings in metabolism (and thus caloric expenditure) in the laboratory among desert-dwelling Australian aborigines exposed to 39 °C (~ 102 °F) (Malaspinas et al. 2016; Qi et al. 2014).

Elevated mortality rates during cold snaps or heat waves reveal that heat and cold stress adaptations can fail. People with lower socioeconomic status have a higher risk of thermal-related mortality, which suggests the influence of behavioral factors (Berko et al. 2014; Min et al. 2021). Young and old individuals are particularly vulnerable (O'Neill and Ebi 2009).

ULTRAVIOLET RADIATION

"The UVR [ultraviolet radiation] content of sunlight is relevant to human biology because different wavelengths of UVR have diverse effects on different biochemical pathways in the body, and these effects have an impact on health and reproductive success" (Beall et al.

2012: 205). UVR penetrates the outer layers of the skin, where melanin and other molecules either reflect or absorb radiation. UVB (ultraviolet B radiation) initiates the photoconversion of a precursor molecule to previtamin D. After that occurs in the skin, the liver and the kidney metabolize previtamin D to produce active vitamin D. Synthesis was the primary source throughout human evolution because few foods apart from oily fish and animal liver provide vitamin D. Vitamin D contributes to calcium and phosphorous homeostasis, bone metabolism, and immune and endocrine function (Dusso et al. 2005). Vitamin D deficiency increases vulnerability to infections, cancers, and cardiovascular disease. Severe deficiency can cause poor bone calcification (rickets in children, osteomalacia in adults) (Gil et al. 2018; Holick 2017; Pike and Christakos 2017). Some UVR is needed; however, too much UVR can physically damage skin, cause mutations, suppress the immune system, and destroy nutrients circulating in the blood. The nutrients vulnerable to photo destruction include folate (vitamin B9) and vitamin D itself (Lucock et al. 2018).

The average annual ultraviolet radiation or variability across the year describes its magnitude, frequency, and duration. Annual UVR energy is maximal near the equator and declines at higher and lower latitudes (Figure 9.3A) (Jablonski and Chaplin 2010a, 2010b). High UVR levels remain relatively stable throughout the year near the equator; in contrast, UVR fluctuates around lower levels at higher latitudes (Figure 9.3B) (Jablonski and Chaplin 2000). For example, the mean UVB level is more than four times higher in equatorial Yemen than in high-latitude Norway (https://apps.who.int/gho/data/view.main.35300, accessed November 1, 2021). Ultraviolet A penetrates the dermis to degrade vitamin D and folate in circulation. Thus, the climate stress from UVR at high latitudes is vitamin D deficiency during months when little or no UVB reaches the Earth's surface, while the stress near the Equator is related to photodamage to many systems throughout the year. A global cline in skin color – darkest near the equator and gradually lightening moving north or south away from the equator – evolved in response to the gradual variation in UVR (Figure 9.3C) (Jablonski and Chaplin 2000).

People make two types of melanin: red/yellow pheomelanin makes up approximately ¼ of our melanin and brown/black eumelanin makes up the rest (Del Bino et al. 2015). Pheomelanin readily degrades upon UVR exposure and releases reactive oxygen species that damage DNA and proteins. Discussion of skin color variation generally centers on eumelanin because it can be photoprotective (Del Bino et al. 2015). Melanin granule synthesis and packaging into organelles known as melanosomes occurs in cells called melanocytes located at the base of the epidermis. Melanosomes are transferred to cells called keratinocytes that make up most of the epidermis. Melanosomes full of UVA-absorbing melanin pigment reduce photodamage by clustering above the nuclei in keratinocytes. The number of pigment granules and the sizes and shapes of melanosomes in keratinocytes influence skin color. An individual's melanin content varies with genotype and exposure to sunlight (acclimatization in the form of sun-tanning).

Dark skin absorbs a high proportion of incident UVR, leaving a small proportion to penetrate the epidermis and initiate the photoconversion to previtamin D. Light skin absorbs a small proportion "… and incrementally lighter pigmentation maximizes penetration of UVR into the skin under conditions of highly seasonal or mostly low UVR outside of the tropics" (Beall et al. 2012: 220).

Skin pigmentation is a quantitative polygenic adaptive trait with solidly established genotype associations (Werren et al. 2021). Figure 9.4 illustrates variation over the range from low skin melanin content to high content variation for two populations and the overlap between them to emphasize the quantitative nature of this trait (Crawford et al. 2017; Hernandez-Pacheco et al. 2017; Shriver and Parra 2000).

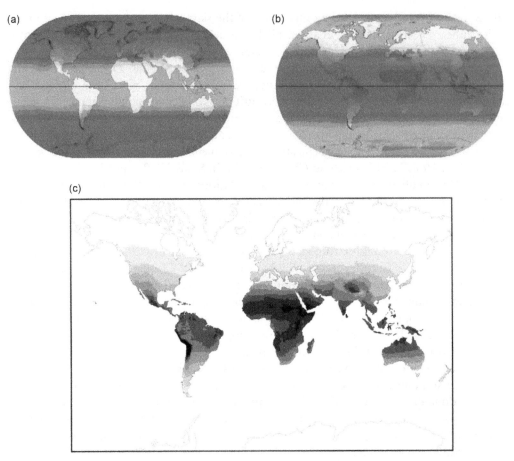

Figure 9.3   Global variation in UVR radiation intensity and variability and skin color (Jablonski and Chaplin 2000, 2010a, 2010b).

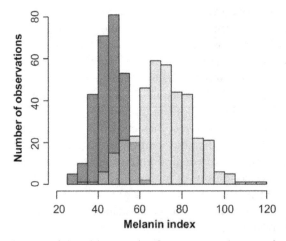

Figure 9.4   The distribution of the melanin index for Hispanics/Latinos from Puerto Rico (blue) and African American (yellow) samples, and the overlap of observations (brown); the *y*-axis represents the number of observations. (Hernandez-Pacheco, et al. 2017)

Regarding the polygenic nature of this trait, more than one hundred pigment-related loci have human phenotypes (Baxter 2019) and some have hundreds of known DNA sequence variants (genecards.com accessed November 1, 2021). Some loci have large effects, and others have small effects on melanin content (Ju and Mathieson 2021). The vast genetic variation underlies the potential for phenotypic variation in skin color and natural selection. Genes and variants arose at different times in the past and show individual patterns of global spread. Old World populations have had both dark and light skin color variants for at least one million years (Crawford et al. 2017). Different combinations of light and dark variants occur together in populations and result in a smooth cline for skin color (Figure 9.3C). The microevolutionary histories of four genes encoding melanocyte or melanosome membrane proteins illustrate the variety.

The major facilitator superfamily domain containing 12 (MFSD12) gene encodes a protein that transports molecules into melanosomes (Adelmann et al. 2020). A variant of MFSD12 results in a very high melanin content and very dark skin. It arose approximately 500,000 years ago in East Africa and spread to Southern India, Melanesia, and Australia (Crawford et al. 2017).

The *OCA2* melanosomal transmembrane protein locus encodes a melanosome membrane protein influencing melanin synthesis (Wiriyasermkul et al. 2020). A geographically localized *OCA2* variant came under selection approximately 15,000 years ago and underlies light skin in NE Asia (Yang et al. 2016).

The solute carrier family 24-member 5 (*SLC24A5*) locus encodes a melanocyte membrane protein influencing melanin synthesis (Wilson et al. 2013). *SLC24A5* was polymorphic for light and dark alleles a million years ago in South Africa. The lightly melanized variant came under selection in Eurasia approximately 30,000 years ago, followed by a strong selective sweep between 6,000 and 5,000 years in Europe, where it is now fixed or nearly fixed. The recent selection for light skin is noteworthy because it suggests that highly melanized populations thrived at high latitudes in Eurasia until recently. The light variant appeared in India in the past 5,000 years and was reintroduced to East Africa approximately 2,000 years ago, where it remains under selection (Crawford et al. 2017; Wilde et al. 2014). In contrast to the localized *OCA2* variant for light skin in Asia, *SLC24A5* variants for light skin are widespread. Notably, the light variants at *OCA2* and *SLC24A5* show that Northern Asian and Northern European populations evolved light skin color independently.

The melanocortin 1 receptor (*MC1R*) gene encodes a melanocyte receptor protein that initiates the synthesis of pheomelanin and eumelanin and contributes to DNA repair. Europeans are highly polymorphic at the locus. The *MC1R* variants include one associated with a combination of red hair, very lightly melanized (primarily pheomelanin) skin, and a high risk of melanoma. In contrast, Africans show slight variation at this locus (Makova and Norton 2005). The highest frequency (10–12 percent) of the recessive variants for red hair and fair skin occur in very high latitude populations, such as the United Kingdom, with a low annual UVR (Morgan et al. 2018).

The trade-off between vitamin D synthesis and folate degradation may have emerged nearly two million years ago with early *Homo erectus*, the first hominin to spend significant amounts of time unclothed in year-round hot and open equatorial grasslands, rather than in forests. The resulting heat stress may have selected for the loss of fur, enabling evaporation of sweat and exposing skin with little melanin to continuously high annual UVR (Jablonski 2010a, 2010b; Lieberman 2015). Those hominins presumably could tan; however, tanned skin offers less protection against UVR damage than skin with a constitutively high melanin content. Furthermore, DNA damage is the signal for tanning. This scenario suggests that deeply melanized skin evolved quickly, and lightly melanized skin evolved later as *Homo erectus* and subsequent *Homo* groups expanded north into higher latitudes with progressively less annual UVR.

How does variation in skin melanin content contribute to differential survival and reproduction? Hypotheses based on logical reasoning prevail because we do not have direct biological tests of the hypothesis of a selective advantage of the local adaptations in skin color under various UVR exposures.

Global variation in skin color arises from the convergence of ultraviolet radiation influences on both folate and vitamin D levels. In turn, those levels are associated with reproductive success (Franasiak et al. 2017; Tamura and Picciano 2006).

The vitamin D-folate hypothesis suggests that the role of light skin at higher latitudes is to enable sufficient vitamin D synthesis to maintain DNA integrity, bone health, and reproductive function (Franasiak et al. 2017; Jablonski and Chaplin 2010a, 2010b; Luk et al. 2012). During the 1700s and 1800s in England, the misshapen pelves of women with rickets, indicative of severe vitamin D deficiency, was a common cause of obstructed labor and maternal and child death (Loudon 1986). However, the lack of earlier evidence of vitamin D deficiency weakens that hypothesis. The vitamin D-folate hypothesis also hypothesizes that high melanin content protects circulating folates from photodegradation by UVB. "Natural selection has, thus, affected varied genetic and physiological mechanisms to protect folate and 5-MTHF [the form of folate vulnerable to photo destruction] in the face of high UVR. The primary role of constitutive dark skin colour in hominin and modern human evolution is that of a natural sunscreen to conserve folate" (Jablonski and Chaplin 2017: 3). Folates play a direct role in synthesizing and repairing DNA, DNA methylation, and male and female reproduction (Tamura and Picciano 2006).

Debate continues as to whether skin cancer mortality drove selection for high melanin content at equatorial latitudes. The skin-cancer hypothesis explains why high melanin content reduces vulnerability to DNA damage leading to sunburn, which increases the risk of cutaneous malignant melanoma, the deadliest form of skin cancer (Greaves 2014a, 2014b; Osborne and Hames 2014). Some authors explain that deaths due to melanoma occur mainly during the post-reproductive years and therefore would not influence reproductive success (Jablonski and Chaplin 2014). Others counter that post-reproductive people contribute to the survival and reproduction of their younger relatives (Osborne and Hames 2014). Other counter-arguments note that pre-reproductive deaths from skin cancer do occur. In the US, 1 in 230 males and 1 in 156 females develop melanoma before the age of 45 (American Cancer Society 2021).

Less well-supported is the skin barrier hypothesis arguing that high melanin content reduces vulnerability to dehydration and sunburn (Elias and Williams 2016). The skin forms microbiome, chemical, and immune system barriers in addition to a physical barrier (Eyerich et al. 2018). Surprisingly, these hypotheses do not incorporate perspectives from photoimmunology. Ultraviolet radiation suppresses many immune functions (Bernard et al. 2019; Del Bino et al. 2018) and thus may influence morbidity and mortality.

Vitamin D exerts its effects by binding with the vitamin D receptor, a transcription factor that induces the transcription of hundreds of genes with many functions (Hanel and Carlberg 2020). The vitamin D receptor gene (*VDR*) has a latitudinal cline (Tiosano, et al. 2016). *VDR* polymorphisms have been associated with the risk of polycystic ovary syndrome and female idiopathic infertility (Djurovic et al. 2020; Reis et al. 2017). The folate synthesis gene methylenetetrahydrofolate reductase (*MTHFR*) shows clines with UVR. *MTHFR* regulates bioavailable folate; its variants are associated with different serum levels (Hiraoka and Kagawa 2017), risk of coronary heart disease (Lao et al. 2008), osteoporosis (Agueda et al. 2008), and infertility (Bezold et al. 2001; Callejón et al. 2007; Reyes-Engel et al. 2002).

Much remains to be learned about adaptation to UVR and its biological effects. For example, recent work detected a role for dietary antioxidants among the factors described here (Lucock et al. 2022).

HIGH-ALTITUDE HYPOXIA

The air we breathe supplies the oxygen required for our mitochondria to produce the energy necessary for life via aerobic respiration. At sea level (0 m altitude) and on top of Mt. Everest (8,848 m, 29,032 ft), oxygen makes up 21 percent of the air; that is, 1 liter of air contains 0.21 liter of oxygen at all altitudes. Ascending from sea level to higher altitudes, the air column shortens and weighs less, causing the barometric pressure to fall. As a result, the air is less dense and has fewer total molecules in a liter of air, with components in the usual proportion. Imagine a trip from New Orleans, Louisiana, at 0 m to Denver, Colorado (1,500 m, 5,280 ft), followed by a day trip to Leadville, Colorado (3,000 m, 10,141 ft), and another day trip to Pike's Peak, Colorado (4,300 m, 14,115 ft). At Denver, Leadville, and Pike's Peak, the amount of oxygen in a lungful of air will be approximately 84, 69, and 60 percent of that in New Orleans (Figure 9.5).

The decrease in the partial pressure of oxygen lessens the pressure difference between the air and the lungs' alveoli. In turn, the oxygen pressure difference between the alveoli and the blood flowing around them lessens, diffusion lessens, and this effect ripples along the oxygen delivery cascade (Figure 9.6). Less than the "usual" (near sea level where we evolved) oxygen availability owing to lower pressure is called hypobaric hypoxia, referred to simply as hypoxia. That is, hypoxia stresses most biological systems and elicits responses that offset the stress to varying degrees. Scientific convention considers 2,500 m to be the threshold at which responses are engaged, although very large samples have revealed small responses at lower altitudes (Staub et al. 2020). High-altitude hypoxia stress can be characterized by its magnitude (altitude above sea level), frequency e.g., once, occasional, regular, seasonal and duration (acute - days to weeks or months - chronic lifelong, or generational exposure.

Unlike temperature and ultraviolet radiation, behavior buffering of the climate stress due to oxygen levels was not traditionally possible and, even now, it is used only under specific

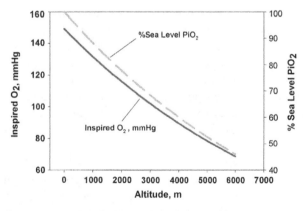

Figure 9.5 Ambient oxygen levels, measured by the partial pressure of oxygen (solid line) or as a percent of sea-level values (dashed line), decrease with increasing altitude, a situation called high-altitude or hypobaric hypoxia. The atmosphere contains ≈ 21 percent of oxygen at all altitudes. (Beall 2007)

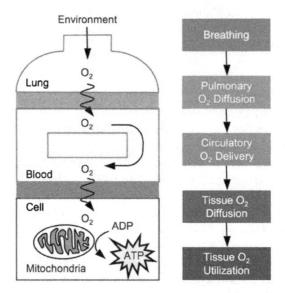

Figure 9.6   Oxygen is transported from atmospheric air to the mitochondria of tissue cells along a pathway with several diffusive and convective steps. The steps in this oxygen cascade are breathing, oxygen diffusion across the blood–gas interface, circulation of oxygen throughout the body, oxygen diffusion across the blood–tissue interface to the mitochondria, and oxygen utilization to generate ATP by oxidative phosphorylation. (Storz, et al. 2010)

circumstances. The use of oxygen tanks remains confined to medicine and high-altitude expeditions. The distribution of hypoxic stress does not follow a global latitudinal pattern as does that of temperature and ultraviolet radiation. Instead, the Andean, East African, and Tibetan plateaus are the home of indigenous populations with millennia of residence and the opportunity for selection and the other evolutionary forces to act. Studies on adaptation to high altitude often compare local populations living at very different altitudes to obtain the largest contrast in stress. Another approach compares populations living on different plateaus to obtain contrasts in microevolutionary history. In addition to hypoxic stress, high-altitude areas experience more ultraviolet and cold stress than lowland areas at the same latitudes.

In contrast to ultraviolet and thermal stress that changes magnitude slowly with latitude, highlands occur on the landscape abruptly and discontinuously. The founders of the high-land populations shared an ancient conserved oxygen homeostasis system consisting of genes encoding oxygen sensors, transcription factors called hypoxia inducible factors (HIFs), and target genes encoding proteins functioning to maintain cellular oxygen levels (Semenza 2012). Each continental population of upward migrants experienced hypoxia after a unique evolutionary history of adapting to other stresses at low altitudes. This may help to explain why Andean, East African, and Tibetan highland populations have different suites of responses.

The acclimatization of people from low altitude regions visiting high altitude areas for days to weeks provides evidence of the "unselected" responses not modified by evolutionary forces over generations of chronic, lifelong exposure. The extent to which the indigenous populations depart from the unselected responses suggests the possibility of other modes of adaptation. Specific responses to acute hypoxia occur in seconds: a plunge in the oxygen saturation of hemoglobin, an increased drive to breathe (called the hypoxic ventilatory response), and an increase in minute ventilation compared to the low altitude baseline (Beall et al. 1997; West et al. 2013). Other responses occur within minutes: vasoconstriction (narrowing) of the blood vessels to the lung and vasodilation (widening) of those to the brain and other organs (Fatemian et al. 2016; Rhodes 2005; Wolff et al. 2002; Xu and Lamanna 2006). Pulmonary vasoconstriction remains while cerebral vasodilation returns to baseline during the first week (Beall and Strohl 2021). The ventilatory responses return to the pre-exposure baseline over months (Powell et al. 1998). Within hours and days of exposure, oxygen homeostasis genes increase the transcription of proteins, stimulating the production of more red blood cells, the absorption and transport of iron, and the synthesis of iron-containing hemoglobin. These and other responses may contribute to the elevated basal metabolic rate that returns to baseline after approximately three weeks (Butterfield et al. 1992; Grover 1963; Mawson et al. 2000). These responses enable more or less usual, but not maximal, function. Maximal aerobic work capacity, a measure of the maximum amount of oxygen an individual can use during exercise, falls immediately and remains low. During the first weeks at altitude, acutely exposed lowlanders metabolize more oxygen to support vital processes and have a smaller capacity to meet the increased oxygen demands of physical work. Early visitors and settlers to the high-altitude plateaus would have mounted these responses, which provided the phenotypic variation for natural selection.

The East African Plateau   The earliest evidence of accessing the East African highlands comes from sites dated to 47,000–31,000 years ago (ya) at 3,500 m (Ossendorf et al. 2019). The earliest evidence of permanent settlement dates to approximately 5,000 ya (Aldenderfer 2003). The Amhara ethnic group inhabits the plateau in northeast Ethiopia that was settled approximately 5,000 ya. According to historical records, the Oromo ethnic group migrated to the plateau in southern Ethiopia approximately 500 ya. The two ethnic groups are genetically closely related yet show different patterns of adaptation. The more recent arrivals at high altitude qualitatively resemble acutely exposed individuals. Oromo men and women have lower saturation and higher hemoglobin concentrations than their low-altitude counterparts (Alkorta-Aranburu et al. 2012; Lundgrin et al. 2013). The Amhara, with the longer residence, resemble unstressed lowlanders, although not completely. They have slightly lower oxygen saturation and an unelevated hemoglobin concentration. A partial explanation for the lower hemoglobin concentration may be higher levels of the hepcidin protein that inhibits iron absorption from the gut and may limit the synthesis of iron-requiring hemoglobin molecules. The assumption is that 500 years is not sufficient for evolutionary forces to influence oxygen delivery phenotypes among the Oromo, while over 5,000 years, phenotypic effects have evolved among the Amhara. Unelevated hemoglobin concentrations, compared to elevated ones, are beneficial because they do not raise blood viscosity and stress the cardiovascular system.

As with adaptation to temperature and UVR stress, genomic studies have included tests of hypotheses about genetic adaptations to hypoxia. The genomic studies of Amhara and Oromo populations require replication and, thus, interpretation of the results is tentative. Genome-wide association studies (GWAS) found associations with lower hemoglobin concentrations and higher hepcidin levels among Amhara (Alkorta-Aranburu et al. 2012; Lundgrin et al. 2013). GWAS detected no genome-wide significant associations in the Oromo samples. However, the Oromo exhibited evidence of altitude differences in DNA methylation (Alkorta-Aranburu et al. 2012).

The Tibetan Plateau   Archaeological evidence indicated the presence of humans on the Tibetan Plateau approximately 45,000–30,000 years ago (Zhang et al. 2018) and permanent occupation by humans starting approximately 12,000–7,400 ya (Meyer et al. 2017). Archaeological and genetic evidence indicated that ascent to the plateau likely occurred from the Northeast and probably took longer than that to the East African Plateau because the Tibetan Plateau is higher and ringed with barriers, including the Himalayas. The early populations arrived at altitude after exposure to varying degrees of heat, cold, UVR, and different types of food and disease while expanding from northeast Africa to northeast Asia. In addition, the gene pool likely reflected bouts of random genetic drift and genetic immigration since splitting with the ancestors of the African populations. For instance, Tibetans show evidence of the introgression of an oxygen homeostasis gene variant from archaic hominins called Denisovans, first found in a cave in Siberia (Huerta-Sanchez et al. 2014).

Compared to temporarily exposed lowlanders, Tibetan highlanders have low saturation and unelevated hemoglobin concentrations in the expected sea-level range (similar to Amhara). Two loci in the oxygen homeostasis pathway, one of which is from the Denisovans, are associated with an unelevated hemoglobin concentration. They are Egl-9 family hypoxia inducible factor 1 (*EGLN1*), encoding a cellular oxygen sensor called PHD2, and endothelial PAS domain protein 1 (*EPAS1*), encoding a protein that is part of the transcription factor HIF2 (Jeong et al. 2018). Notably, the associations of *EGLN1* and *EPAS1* with elevated hemoglobin concentrations have been replicated many times, strengthening confidence in the finding (Beall and Strohl 2021). Recent evidence indicates that the unelevated hemoglobin concentration of Tibetans results from dilution by a large plasma volume rather than a lower total mass of hemoglobin (Stembridge et al. 2019).

Other distinctive Tibetan phenotypes include less vasoconstriction of the lungs and no vasodilation of cerebral blood flow, a brisk drive to breathe, and a high minute ventilation (Groves et al. 1993; Hoit et al. 2006). Tibetans have the BMR and work capacity expected for their age, sex, and body size (Beall et al. 1996; Huang et al. 1992). This results in a minimum and maximum capacity to deliver oxygen similar to that of lowlanders at low altitudes.

Some genotypes and phenotypes are associated with reproductive success among Tibetans. Phenotypes associated with reproductive success include higher uterine artery blood flow during pregnancy, which correlates with heavier birthweights (Browne et al. 2015). Heavier babies have a greater chance of survival. Among post-reproductive Tibetan women, an unelevated hemoglobin concentration is associated with a higher chance of their pregnancies resulting in livebirths (Cho et al. 2017).

The Andean Plateau   People first accessed the Andean Plateau approximately 13,000 ya (Rademaker et al. 2014). These people descended from ancestors that migrated from NE Asia through Beringia and North America and halfway down South America. They would have had another unique history of adaptation to changing environments and evolutionary processes. The earliest permanent residences date to approximately 7,000 ya (Haas et al. 2017). Compared with lowlanders acutely exposed for days to weeks, Andean highlanders have a low drive to breath, low minute ventilation, very large lung volumes, elevated hemoglobin concentration, vasoconstriction of blood vessels to the lungs and vasodilation of those to the brain (Beall and Strohl 2021). Similar to that of Tibetans, their BMR and physical work capacity are predicted by age, sex, and body weight (Beall and Strohl 2021; Brutsaert 2016).

The explanation for a distinctive trait of Andean highlanders, a large lung volume, became apparent in a study using a "migrant model" comparing residents and migrants from one altitude to another. Based on the model, differences between high-altitude residents and upward migrants in the mean values are interpreted as evidence of a trait associated with good function. The study compared two samples of individuals of highland Andean ancestry born and raised at high and low altitudes with two samples of individuals of lowland European ancestry also born and raised at high and low altitudes. Both Andean and European individuals had larger lung volumes measured as Forced Vital Capacity (FVC) if they grew up at high altitudes. However, a larger effect among those of Andean descent indicated that both developmental exposure to hypoxia and genetic ancestry contributed to the notably large FVC (Brutsaert et al. 1999).

The genomes of Andean highlanders have revealed intriguing associations with adaptive phenotypes. Variants in the *EGLN1* loci encoding a cellular oxygen sensor are associated with maximal exercise capacity (Brutsaert et al. 2019). Two oxygen homeostasis-related genes, *PRKAA1* and *EDN*, are associated with uterine artery diameter and birthweight, and are likely to be linked to reproductive success (Bigham et al. 2014).

Population Comparisons   Andean and Tibetan highlanders living at the same altitude differ quantitatively with respect to numerous traits, thus leading to the hypothesis that there are at least two successful patterns of adaptation to the same stress. More evidence from East Africa may support a hypothesis of three successful patterns. Compared with Tibetans, Andean highlanders have significantly (7–9 percent) higher hemoglobin concentrations, approximately 20 percent lower drive to breathe and minute ventilation, 18 percent lower cerebral blood flow, and lower uterine artery blood flow. Despite these quantitative differences at some points in the oxygen delivery process, the Tibetan and Andean highlanders share similar traits considered integrated functional measures: healthy birthweight and expected-for-age-and-sex physical work capacity (Beall and Strohl 2021).

Emerging Topic

The science of epigenetics deals with molecular processes that change gene expression "… in the context of the same DNA sequence" (Cavalli and Heard 2019: 489). The processes can arise from one's behavior and environment. Epigenetic processes remain poorly studied in the context of adaptation to the environment. However, future work is likely to turn to this intriguing area for an understanding of the mechanisms of adaptation. For example, UVB damages DNA by adding molecules in ways that increase the risk of skin cancer and immune suppression (Johann To Berens and Molinier 2020; Prasad and Katiyar 2017). Another example addresses hypoxia. Adults who grew up at high altitudes exhibit different epigenetic patterns from those acutely exposed or unexposed, implying different gene expression levels. Andean highlanders with different *EPAS1* variants had different epigenetic modifications. These findings suggest the benefits of adding epigenetic analyses to genotype–phenotype association studies (Childebayeva et al., 2019a, 2019b, 2021a, 2021b).

Climate Change

Our understanding of past climate change obtained from the geologic record is coarse-grained compared with the year-to-year information available for the past few centuries. The Intergovernmental Panel on Climate Change (IPCC) defines climate change as "A change in the state of the climate that can be identified (e.g., by using statistical tests) by changes in the mean and/or the variability of its properties and that persists for an extended period, typically decades or longer" (IPCC (Intergovernmental Panel on Climate Change) 2012). Biological anthropologists know little about biological adaptation to climate change; however, past works provide some insights.

The global surface temperature rose approximately 7 °C (about 13 °F) in the past 24,000 years (Figure 9.7) (Marcott and Shakun 2021). The goal of the 2015 Paris Agreement on climate change was "to limit global warming to well below 2, preferably to 1.5 °C (about 3.6 and 2.7 °F, respectively), compared to preindustrial levels" (https://unfccc.int/process-and-meetings/the-paris-agreement/the-paris-agreement). A change of that size carries implications for human biology, adaptation, evolution, and health.

Warming will not occur uniformly; modeling efforts consistently report that human populations will experience abrupt changes in the magnitude, duration, and frequency of heat, cold, water availability, and ultraviolet radiation (Raymond et al. 2020). Central Asia is the only area of the world likely to experience more cold events. The number of extreme cold events will fall elsewhere, and heat events will increase in magnitude, frequency, and duration. For instance, children under 10 years of age in 2020 may experience a fourfold increase in the number of lifetime extreme heat events (Thiery et al. 2021). Mortality rises during heat waves, despite the buffers of technology and modern conveniences found in high- and middle-income countries (Alahmad et al. 2020; Chen et al. 2018). Furthermore, areas with combined heat and humidity that are beyond human thermal tolerance (usually cited as 35 °C (95 °F) wet-bulb temperature) already exist in tropical areas and will increase (Pal and Eltahir 2016; Raymond et al. 2020). Examples of institutional adaptations include the Israeli Defense Force regimes for acclimatizing to heat (Yanovich et al. 2020), the France National Heatwave Plan (Plan National Canicule available at https://ghhin.org/resources/plan-national-canicule-2017), and the [US] National Integrated Heat Health Information System (Keith et al. 2021).

Climate warming has knock-on effects for other stressors, including effects on the ozone layer and ultraviolet radiation. The ultraviolet radiation index will decrease by

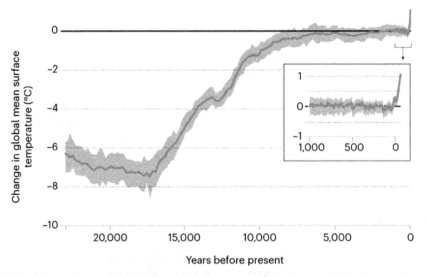

Figure 9.7 Changes in the global mean surface temperature over the past 24,000 years relative to the average for the preindustrial period of the past millennium (1,000–1,850). (Marcott and Shakun 2021)

9 percent in latitudes above 60 °N, including parts of Alaska, Canada, Greenland, Scandinavia, and Russia. It will increase by 4 percent in the tropics (Hegglen and Shepherd 2009). These changes have implications for vulnerability to vitamin D deficiency at high latitudes, skin cancers, and other health consequences of high ultraviolet radiation in the tropics.

Climate change will alter the water supply for human and agricultural use, including precipitation, ground, and surface sources; "the quantity and quality of our water are woven into the intersections between human health, culture, and human biology, just as they are for food" (Rosinger and Brewis 2020). Water needs decreased throughout the evolution of the genus *Homo* (Pontzer et al. 2021; Hora et al. 2019). Water sufficiency is an important emerging area of research.

We have both vulnerabilities and strengths. Some vulnerabilities are part of our evolutionary heritage, such as the vulnerability of kidneys to prolonged heat stress and dehydration (Barraclough et al. 2017; de Lorenzo and Liaño 2017). Can we anticipate how to buffer ourselves behaviorally and biologically from the multiple anticipated stresses?

Conservation biologists use the concept of genomic vulnerability to climate change. It refers to the difference between a population's current allele frequencies and those in locales where populations are already well adapted (Hoffmann et al. 2021). The concept may have limited use among human populations because variants at individual loci typically explain a small percentage of the variance in complex traits and because multiple loci are usually involved. However, as noted above, some variants have large quantitative effects on traits. Information on the reaction norms of such traits could help plan behavioral responses or identify particularly vulnerable individuals.

Phenotypic vulnerability refers to the existing range of variations that may increase the risk of a poor response to abrupt stress. Higher levels of UVR damage could increase the risk of skin cancer among populations with light skin color, for example. The prevalence of chronic diseases may increase the risk of a poor outcome if many are ill with diseases interfering with thermoregulation (Barraclough et al. 2017; de Lorenzo and Liaño 2017). The vulnerability may arise from limited energy resources. For instance, acclimatization to heat, cold, and high altitude have metabolic energy costs requiring calories (Green et al. 1992; Mawson et al. 2000; Ocobock 2016).

Demographic vulnerability could arise from the size or age–sex composition of a population. For instance, children and the elderly are among the most vulnerable to extreme thermal stress (Smith 2019). Natural selection may favor children with more effective responses. The globally growing number of people over 60 or 80 years of age directs attention to offsetting age-related changes such as loss of melanocytes or sweat glands that may hobble adaptation (Gildner and Levy 2021).

Human biological strengths in the face of climate change include the modes of adaptation, plasticity, acclimation (acclimatization arising from deliberate laboratory exposure), cross-adaptation, and preconditioning. Cross-adaptation refers to exposure and acclimatization to stress that benefits from exposure to a different stress. Prior heat and cold acclimatization may benefit the response to acute high-altitude hypoxia (Gibson et al. 2017). For example, Australian Aborigines adapted to daytime hot desert conditions and night-time temperatures below freezing. Evidence that the *TRPM8* locus senses both warm and cool stresses suggests avenues for exploring cross-adaptation there and elsewhere (Iftinca and Altier 2020). Preconditioning refers to exposure and acclimatization to a stress that provides benefits upon re-exposure. For instance, recent prior exposure to high altitudes decreases the risk of acute mountain sickness upon subsequent exposure (Muza et al. 2010). Preconditioning may become helpful in the context of abrupt extreme climate events.

The relevant outcomes of the trade-offs among vulnerabilities and strengths from an evolutionary standpoint are survival and reproduction. The human adaptability standpoint adds homeostasis and functional outcomes, while a health perspective incorporates wellbeing as a valued outcome. Climate change introduces an urgent research agenda in biological anthropology. Adding to the urgency is that indigenous populations with many generations of exposure to these conditions are shrinking in numbers, owing to migration, urbanization, and climate change. A vanishing reservoir of human behavioral and biological adaptation to the environment may be lost to science unless we act soon.

CONCLUSION

This chapter addressed human biological variation from the standpoint of adaptation to climate. The environmental stresses of temperature and ultraviolet radiation vary slowly across geographical space, and biological variation corresponds in ways that apparently improve survival and reproduction. Global analyses demonstrating progressively larger body size with colder temperatures or lower skin melanization with lower UVB have been replicated using a variety of approaches. Research on adaptation to high-altitude hypoxia has generally taken the local approach, identified different adaptations on different continents, and included phenotypes associated with function and reproductive success. There has been some success in identifying the genetic bases of adaptive phenotypes. Concepts of adaptation are changing as anthropology moves away from the typological thinking underlying the "modes of adaptation" model to population thinking and acknowledging that traits and their variation emerge from multiple pathways. Studies of adaptation to climate usually report data from living people. Incorporating evidence from paleoanthropology, on the one hand, and from cellular and molecular biology, on the other hand, can yield a better understanding of the reasons and mechanisms of human biological variation and its relation to climate. Climate change already stresses human biology and this will most likely increase in the future.

REFERENCES

Adelmann, C. H., A. K. Traunbauer, B. Chen, et al. "MFSD12 Mediates the Import of Cysteine into Melanosomes and Lysosomes." *Nature* 588, no. 7839 (2020): 699–704.

Agueda, L., M. Bustamante, S. Jurado, et al. "A Haplotype-Based Analysis of the LRP5 Gene in Relation to Osteoporosis Phenotypes in Spanish Postmenopausal Women." *Journal of Bone and Mineral Research: The Official Journal of the American Society for Bone and Mineral Research* 23, no. 12 (2008): 1954–1963.

Alahmad, B., H. Khraishah, A. F. Shakarchi, et al. "Cardiovascular Mortality and Exposure to Heat in an Inherently Hot Region: Implications for Climate Change." *Circulation* 141, no. 15 (2020): 1271–1273.

Aldea, D., Y. Atsuta, B. Kokalari, et al. "Repeated Mutation of a Developmental Enhancer Contributed to Human Thermoregulatory Evolution." *Proceedings of the National Academy of Sciences of the United States of America* 118, no. 16 (2021).

Aldenderfer, M. S. "Moving up in the World; Archaeologists Seek to Understand How and When People Came to Occupy the Andean and Tibetan Plateaus." *American Scientist* 91 (2003): 542–549.

Alkorta-Aranburu, G., C. M. Beall, D. B. Witonsky, et al. "The Genetic Architecture of Adaptations to High Altitude in Ethiopia." *PLoS Genetics* 8, no. 12 (2012): e1003110.

American Cancer Society. *Cancer Facts & Figures 2021.* Atlanta: American Cancer Society, 2021.

Baker, P. T., and J. S. Weiner, eds. "The Biology of Human Adaptability." In *Symposium on the Biology of Populations of Anthropological Importance.* Oxford: Clarendon Press, 1966.

Barraclough, K. A., G. A. Blashki, S. G. Holt, and J. W. M. Agar. "Climate Change and Kidney Disease – Threats and Opportunities." *Kidney International* 92, no. 3 (2017): 526–530.

Baker, P. T. "Human Adaptation to High Altitude." *Science* 163, 1149 (1969): 1156.

Baxter, L. L., D. E. Watkins-Chow, W. J. Pavan, et al. "A Curated Gene List for Expanding the Horizons of Pigmentation Biology." *Pigment Cell Melanoma Research* 32, no. 3 (2019): 348–358.

Beall, C. M., and K. P. Strohl. "Adaptations to High-Altitude Hypoxia." In *Oxford Research Encyclopedia of Anthropology.* Edited by M. Aldenderfer. Oxford: Oxford University Press, 2021.

Beall, C. M. "Two Routes to Functional Adaptation: Tibetan and Andean High-altitude Natives." *Proceedings of the National Academy of Sciences* 104, Suppl. 1 (2007): 8655.

Beall, C. M., G. M. Brittenham, K. P. Strohl, et al. "Ventilation and Hypoxic Ventilatory Response of Tibetan and Aymara High Altitude Natives." *American Journal of Physical Anthropology* 104 (1997): 427–447.

Beall, C. M., J. Henry, C. Worthman, and M. C. Goldstein. "Basal Metabolic Rate and Dietary Seasonality Among Tibetan Nomads." *American Journal of Human Biology: The Official Journal of the Human Biology Council* 8 (1996): 361–370.

Beall, C. M., N. G. Jablonski, and A. T. Steegmann. "Human Adaptation to Climate: Temperature, Ultraviolet Radiation, and Altitude." In *Human Biology: An Evolutionary and Biocultural Perspective.* Edited by S. Stinson, B. Bogin, and D. O'Rourke, 177–250. Hoboken, NJ: John Wiley & Sons, Inc., 2012.

Berg, J. J., A. Harpak, N. Sinnott-Armstrong, et al. "Reduced Signal for Polygenic Adaptation of Height in UK Biobank." *Elife* 8 (2019).

Berko, J., D. D. Ingram, S. Saha, et al. "Deaths Attributed to Heat, Cold, and Other Weather Events in the United States, 2006–2010." *National Health Statistics Report* 76 (2014): 1–15.

Bernard, J. J., R. L. Gallo, and J. Krutmann. "Photoimmunology: How Ultraviolet Radiation Affects the Immune System." *Nature Reviews. Immunology* 19, no. 11 (2019): 688–701.

Bernstein, R. M. "The Big and Small of It: How Body Size Evolves." *American Journal of Physical Anthropology* 143, no. Suppl. 51 (2010): 46–62.

Bezold, G., M. Lange, and R. U. Peter. "Homozygous Methylenetetrahydrofolate Reductase C677T Mutation and Male Infertility." *The New England Journal of Medicine* 344, no. 15 (2001): 1172–1173.

Bigham, A. W., C. G. Julian, M. J. Wilson, et al. "Maternal PRKAA1 and EDNRA Genotypes Are Associated with Birth Weight, and PRKAA1 with Uterine Artery Diameter and Metabolic Homeostasis at High Altitude." *Physiological Genomics* 46, no. 18 (2014): 687–697.

Bogin, B., P. Smith, A. B. Orden, et al. "Rapid Change in Height and Body Proportions of Maya American Children." *American Journal of Human Biology: The Official Journal of the Human Biology Council* 14, no. 6 (2002): 753–761.

Browne, V. A., C. G. Julian, L. Toledo-Jaldin, et al. "Uterine Artery Blood Flow, Fetal Hypoxia and Fetal Growth." *Philosophical Transactions of the Royal Society of London. Series B, Biological Sciences* 370, no. 1663 (2015): 20140068.

Brutsaert, T. "Why Are High Altitude Natives so Strong at High Altitude? Nature vs. Nurture: Genetic Factors vs. Growth and Development." *Advances in Experimental Medicine and Biology* 903 (2016): 101–112.

Brutsaert, T. D., R. Soria, E. Caceres, et al. "Effect of Developmental and Ancestral High Altitude Exposure on Chest Morphology and Pulmonary Function in Andean and European/North American Natives." *American Journal of Human Biology* 11 (1999): 385–395.

Brutsaert, T. D., M. Kiyamu, G. Elias Revollendo, et al. "Association of EGLN1 Gene with High Aerobic Capacity of Peruvian Quechua at High Altitude." *Proceedings of the National Academy of Sciences of the United States of America* 116, no. 48 (2019): 24006–24011.

Butterfield, G. E., J. Gates, S. Fleming, et al. "Increased Energy Intake Minimizes Weight Loss in Men at High Altitude." *Journal of Applied Physiology* 72, no. 5 (1992): 1741–1748.

Callejón, G., A. Mayor-Olea, A. J. Jiménez, et al. "Genotypes of the C677T and A1298C Polymorphisms of the MTHFR Gene as a Cause of Human Spontaneous Embryo Loss." *Human Reproduction (Oxford, England)* 22, no. 12 (2007): 3249–3254.

Cavalli, G., and E. Heard. "Advances in Epigenetics Link Genetics to the Environment and Disease." *Nature* 571, no. 7766 (2019): 489–499.

Chen, R., P. Yin, L. Wang, et al. "Association Between Ambient Temperature and Mortality Risk and Burden: Time Series Study in 272 Main Chinese Cities." *BMJ* 363 (2018): k4306.

Childebayeva, A., T. Harman, J. Weinstein, et al. "DNA Methylation Changes Are Associated with an Incremental Ascent to High Altitude." *Frontiers in Genetics* 10 (2019a): 1062.

Childebayeva, A., T. R. Jones, J. M. Goodrich, et al. "LINE-1 and EPAS1 DNA Methylation Associations with high-altitude exposure." *Epigenetics* 14, no. 1 (2019b): 1–15.

Childebayeva, A., J. M. Goodrich, F. Leon-Velarde, et al. "Genome-Wide Epigenetic Signatures of Adaptive Developmental Plasticity in the Andes." *Genome Biology and Evolution* 13 no. 2 (2021a).

Childebayeva, A., T. Harman, J. Weinstein, et al. "Genome-Wide DNA Methylation Changes Associated with High-Altitude Acclimatization During an Everest Base Camp Trek." *Frontiers in Physiology* 12 (2021b): 660906.

Cho, J. I., B. Basnyat, C. Jeong, et al. "Ethnically Tibetan Women in Nepal with Low Hemoglobin Concentration Have Better Reproductive Outcomes." *Evol. Med. Public Health* 2017, no. 1 (2017): 82–96.

Coop, G., D. Witonsky, A. Di Rienzo, and J. K. Pritchard. "Using Environmental Correlations to Identify Loci Underlying Local Adaptation." *Genetics* 185, no. 4 (2010): 1411–1423.

Crawford, N. G., D. E. Kelly, E. B. Hansen, et al. "Loci Associated with Skin Pigmentation Identified in African Populations." *Science* 358, no. 6365 (2017): eaan 8433.

de Lorenzo, A., and F. Liaño. "High Temperatures and Nephrology: The Climate Change Problem." *Nefrologia* 37, no. 5 (2017): 492–500.

Del Bino, S., S. Ito, J. Sok, et al. "Chemical Analysis of Constitutive Pigmentation of Human Epidermis Reveals Constant Eumelanin to Pheomelanin Ratio." *Pigment Cell & Melanoma Research* 28, no. 6 (2015): 707–717.

Del Bino, S., C. Duval, and F. Bernerd. "Clinical and Biological Characterization of Skin Pigmentation Diversity and Its Consequences on UV Impact." *International Journal of Molecular Sciences* 19, no. 9 (2018).

Djurovic, J., G. Stamenkovic, J. Todorovic, et al. "Polymorphisms and Haplotypes in VDR Gene Are Associated with Female Idiopathic Infertility." *Human Fertility (Cambridge)* 23, no. 2 (2020): 101–110.

Dusso, A. S., A. J. Brown, and E. Slatopolsky. "Vitamin D." *American Journal of Physiology. Renal Physiology* 289, no. 1 (2005): F8–28.

Elias, P. M., and M. L. Williams. "Basis for the Gain and Subsequent Dilution of Epidermal Pigmentation During Human Evolution: The Barrier and Metabolic Conservation Hypotheses Revisited." *American Journal of Physical Anthropology* 161, no. 2 (2016): 189–207.

Eyerich, S., K. Eyerich, C. Traidl-Hoffmann, and T. Biedermann. "Cutaneous Barriers and Skin Immunity: Differentiating a Connected Network." *Trends in Immunology* 39, no. 4 (2018): 315–327.

Fan, S., M. E. Hansen, Y. Lo, and S. A. Tishkoff. "Going Global by Adapting Local: A Review of Recent Human Adaptation." *Science* 354, no. 6308 (2016): 54–59.

Fatemian, M., M. Herigstad, Q. P. Croft, et al. "Determinants of Ventilation and Pulmonary Artery Pressure During Early Acclimatization to Hypoxia in Humans." *The Journal of Physiology* 594, no. 5 (2016): 1197–1213.

Franasiak, J. M., E. E. Lara, and A. Pellicer. "Vitamin D in Human Reproduction." *Current Opinion in Obstetrics & Gynecology* 29, no. 4 (2017): 189–194.

Gibson, O. R., L. Taylor, P. W. Watt, and N. S. Maxwell. "Cross-Adaptation: Heat and Cold Adaptation to Improve Physiological and Cellular Responses to Hypoxia." *Sports Medicine* 47, no. 9 (2017): 1751–1768.

Gil, Á., J. Plaza-Diaz, and M. D. Mesa. "Vitamin D: Classic and Novel Actions." *Annals of Nutrition & Metabolism* 72, no. 2 (2018): 87–95.

Gildner, T. E., and S. B. Levy. "Intersecting Vulnerabilities in Human Biology: Synergistic Interactions between Climate Change and Increasing Obesity Rates." *American Journal of Human Biology: The Official Journal of the Human Biology Council* 33, no. 2 (2021): e23460.

Gluckman, P. D., M. A. Hanson, P. Bateson, et al. "Towards a New Developmental Synthesis: Adaptive Developmental Plasticity and Human Disease." *Lancet* 373, no. 9675 (2009): 1654–1657.

Gluckman, P. D., M. A. Hanson, and F. M. Low. "Evolutionary and Developmental Mismatches Are Consequences of Adaptive Developmental Plasticity in Humans and Have Implications for Later Disease Risk." *Philosophical Transactions of the Royal Society of London. Series B, Biological Sciences* 374, no. 1770 (2019): 20180109.

Greaves, M. "Response to Jablonski and Chaplin." *Proceedings of Biologial Science* 281, no. 1789 (2014a): 20140940.

Greaves, M. "Was Skin Cancer a Selective Force for Black Pigmentation in Early Hominin Evolution?" *Proceedings of Biological Science* 281, no.1781 (2014b): 20132955.

Green, H. J., J. R. Sutton, E. E. Wolfel, et al. "Altitude Acclimatization and Energy Metabolic Adaptations in Skeletal Muscle During Exercise." *Journal of Applied Physiology* 73, no. 6 (1992): 2701–2708.

Grover, R. F. "Basal Oxygen Uptake of Man at High Altitude." *Journal of Applied Physiology: Respiratory, Environmental and Exercise Physiology* 18, no. 5 (1963): 909–912.

Groves, B. M., T. Droma, J. R. Sutton, et al. "Minimal Hypoxic Pulmonary Hypertension in Normal Tibetans at 3,658 m." *Journal of Applied Physiology: Respiratory, Environmental and Exercise Physiology* 74, no. 1 (1993): 312–318.

Gurven, M., T. S. Kraft, S. Alami, et al. "Rapidly Declining Body Temperature in a Tropical Human Population." *Science Advances* 6 no. 44 (2020).

Haas, R., I. C. Stefanescu, A. Garcia-Putnam, et al. "Humans Permanently Occupied the Andean Highlands by at Least 7 Ka." *Royal Society Open Science* 4, no. 6 (2017): 170331.

Hancock, A. M., V. J. Clark, Y. Qian, and A. Di Rienzo. "Population Genetic Analysis of the Uncoupling Proteins Supports a Role for UCP3 in Human Cold Resistance." *Molecular Biology and Evolution* 28, no. 1 (2011): 601–614.

Hanel, A., and C. Carlberg, "Skin Colour and Vitamin D: An Update." *Experimental Dermatology* 29, no.9 (2020): 864–875.

Harrison, G. A. "Human Adaptability with Reference to the IBP Proposals for High Altitude Research." In *The Biology of Human Adaptability*. Edited by P. T. Baker and J. S. Weiner, 509–519. Oxford: Clarendon Press, 1966.

Hegglin, M. I., and T. G. Shepherd. "Large Climate-Induced Changes in Ultraviolet Index and Stratosphere-to-Troposphere Ozone Flux." *Nature Geoscience* 2 (2009): 687–691.

Hernandez-Pacheco, N., C. Flores, S. Alonso, et al. "Identification of a Novel Locus Associated with Skin Colour in African-Admixed Populations." *Scientific Reports* 7, no. 1 (2017): 44548.

Hiraoka, M., and Y. Kagawa. "Genetic Polymorphisms and Folate Status." *Congenital Anomalies* 57, no. 5 (2017): 142–149.

Hoffmann, A. A., A. R. Weeks, and C. M. Sgrò. "Opportunities and Challenges in Assessing Climate Change Vulnerability Through Genomics." *Cell* 184, no. 6 (2021): 1420–1425.

Hoit, B. D., N. D. Dalton, S. C. Erzurum, et al. "Nitric Oxide and Cardiopulmonary Hemodynamics in Tibetan Highlanders." *Journal of Applied Physiology* 99 (2006): 1796–1801.

Holick, M. F. "Ultraviolet B Radiation: The Vitamin D Connection." *Advances in Experimental Medicine and Biology* 996 (2017): 137–154.

Hong, S. K. "Pattern of Cold Adaptation in Women Divers of Korea (Ama)." *Federation Proceedings* 32, no. 5 (1973): 1614–1622.

Hong, S. K., and H. Rahn. "The Diving Women of Korea and Japan." *Scientific American* 216, no. 5 (1967): 34–43.

Hora, M., H. Pontzer, C. M. Wall-Scheffler, et al. "Dehydration and persistence hunting in *Homo erectus*." *Journal of Human Evolution* 138 (2020): 102682.

Howells, W. W. "The Distribution of Man." *Scientific American* 203 (1960):113–130.

Hruschka, D. J., C. Hadley, A. A. Brewis, and C. M. Stojanowski. "Genetic Population Structure Accounts for Contemporary Ecogeographic Patterns in Tropic and Subtropic-Dwelling Humans." *PLoS One* 10, no. 3 (2015): e0122301.

Huang, S. Y., S. Sun, T. Droma, et al. "Internal Carotid Arterial Flow Velocity During Exercise in Tibetan and Han Residents of Lhasa (3,658 M)." *Journal of Applied Physiology: Respiratory, Environmental and Exercise Physiology* 73, no. 6 (1992): 2638–2642.

Huerta-Sanchez, E., X. Jin, Z. Asan, et al. "Altitude Adaptation in Tibetans Caused by Introgression of Denisovan-like DNA." *Nature* 512, no. 7513 (2014): 194–197.

Iftinca, M., and C. Altier. "The Cool Things to Know About TRPM8!" *Channels (Austin)* 14, no. 1 (2020): 413–420.

International Human Genome Sequencing Consortium. "Initial Sequencing and Analysis of the Human Genome." *Nature* 409, no. 6822 (2001): 860–921.

Ioannou, L. G., L. Tsoutsoubi, K. Mantzios, et al. "The Impacts of Sun Exposure on Worker Physiology and Cognition: Multi-Country Evidence and Interventions." *International Journal of Environmental Research and Public Health* 18 no. 14 (2021).

IPCC (Intergovernmental Panel on Climate Change). *Managing the Risks of Extreme Events and Disasters to Advance Climate Change Adaptation.* Edited by C. B. Field, V. Barros, T. F. Stocker, et al., 555–564. Cambridge, UK: Cambridge University Press, 2012.

Jablonski, N. G. "The Naked Truth." *Scientific American* 302, no. 2 (2010a): 42–49.

Jablonski, N. G. "Colloquium Paper: Human Skin Pigmentation as an Adaptation to UV Radiation." *Proceedings of the National Academy of Sciences* 107 Suppl. 2 (2010b): 8962–8968.

Jablonski, N. G., and G. Chaplin. "The Evolution of Human Skin Coloration." *Journal of Human Evolution* 39, no. 1 (2000): 57–106.

Jablonski, N. G., and G. Chaplin. "Skin Cancer Was Not a Potent Selective Force in the Evolution of Protective Pigmentation in Early Hominins." *Proceedings. Biological Sciences* 281, no. 1789 (2014): 20140517.

Jablonski, N. G., and G. Chaplin. "The Colours of Humanity: The Evolution of Pigmentation in the Human Lineage." *Philosophical Transactions of the Royal Society of London. Series B, Biological Sciences* 372, no. 1724 (2017).

Jeong, C., D. B. Witonsky, B. Basnyat, et al. "Detecting past and Ongoing Natural Selection Among Ethnically Tibetan Women at High Altitude in Nepal." *PLoS Genetics* 14, no. 9 (2018): e1007650.

Johann To Berens, P., and J. Molinier. "Formation and Recognition of UV-Induced DNA Damage Within Genome Complexity." *International Journal of Molecular Sciences* 21, no. 18 (2020).

Ju, D., and I. Mathieson. "The Evolution of Skin Pigmentation-Associated Variation in West Eurasia." *Proceedings of the National Academy of Sciences of the United States of America* 118, no. 1 (2021).

Katzmarzyk, P. T., and W. R. Leonard. "Climatic Influences on Human Body Size and Proportions: Ecological Adaptations and Secular Trends." *American Journal of Physical Anthropology* 106, no. 4 (1998): 483–503.

Keith, L., S. Meerow, D. M. Hondula, et al. "Deploy Heat Officers, Policies and Metrics. *Nature* 598, no. 7879 (2021): 29–31.

Key, F. M., M. A. Abdul-Aziz, R. Mundry, et al. "Human Local Adaptation of the TRPM8 Cold Receptor Along a Latitudinal Cline." *PLoS Genetics* 14, no. 5 (2018): e1007298.

Kiyamu, M., M. Rivera-Chira, and T. D. Brutsaert. "Aerobic Capacity of Peruvian Quechua: A Test of the Developmental Adaptation Hypothesis." *American Journal of Physical Anthropology* 156, no. 3 (2015): 363–373.

Lango Allen, H., K. Estrada, G. Lettre, et al. "Hundreds of Variants Clustered in Genomic Loci and Biological Pathways Affect Human Height." *Nature* 467, no. 7317 (2010): 832–838.

Lao, O., I. Dupanloup, G. Barbujani, et al. "The Mediterranean Paradox for Susceptibility Factors in Coronary Heart Disease Extends to Genetics." *Annals of Human Genetics* 72, Pt 1 (2008): 48–56.

Lasker, G. W. "Human Biological Adaptability." *Science* 166 (1969): 1480-1486.

Lee, B. J., O. R. Gibson, C. D. Thake, et al. "Editorial: Cross Adaptation and Cross Tolerance in Human Health and Disease." *Frontiers in Physiology* 9, no. 1827 (2019).

Leonard, W. R., M. V. Sorensen, V. A. Galloway, et al. "Climatic Influences on Basal Metabolic Rates Among Circumpolar Populations." *American Journal of Human Biology: The Official Journal of the Human Biology Council* 14, no. 5 (2002): 609–620.

Levy, S. B., and W. R. Leonard. "The Evolutionary Significance of Human Brown Adipose Tissue: Integrating the Timescales of Adaptation." *Evolutionary Anthropology* 31 (2021): 75–91.

Levy, S. B., T. M. Klimova, R. N. Zakharova, et al. "Evidence for a Sensitive Period of Plasticity in Brown Adipose Tissue During Early Childhood Among Indigenous Siberians." *American Journal of Physical Anthropology* 175, no. 4 (2021): 834–846.

Lieberman, D. E. "Human Locomotion and Heat Loss: An Evolutionary Perspective." *Comprehensive Physiology* 5, no. 1 (2015): 99–117.

Little, M. A. "Evolutionary Strategies for Body Size." *Frontiers in Endocrinology* 11 (2020): 107.

Lordkipanidze, D., M. S. Ponce de León, A. Margvelashvili, et al. "A Complete Skull from Dmanisi, Georgia, and the Evolutionary Biology of Early Homo." *Science* 342, no. 6156 (2013): 326–331.

Loudon, I. "Deaths in Childbed from the Eighteenth Century to 1935." *Medical History* 30, no. 1 (1986): 1–41.

Lucock, M., P. Jones, C. Martin, et al. "Photobiology of Vitamins." *Nutrition Reviews* 76, no. 7 (2018): 512–525.

Lucock, M. D., P. R. Jones, M. Veysey, et al. "Biophysical Evidence to Support and Extend the Vitamin D-folate Hypothesis as a Paradigm for the Evolution of Human Skin Pigmentation." *American Journal of Human Biology: The Official Journal of the Human Biology Council* 34, no. 4 (2022): e23667.

Luk, J., S. Torrealday, G. N. Perry, and L. Pal. "Relevance of Vitamin D in Reproduction." *Human Reproduction (Oxford, England)* 27, no. 10 (2012): 3015–3027.

Lundgrin, E. L., A. J. Janocha, C. D. Koch, et al. "Plasma Hepcidin of Ethiopian Highlanders with Steady-State Hypoxia." *Blood* 122, no. 11 (2013): 1989–1991.

Makova, K., and H. Norton. "Worldwide Polymorphism at the MC1R Locus and Normal Pigmentation Variation in Humans." *Peptides* 26, no. 10 (2005): 1901–1908.

Malaspinas, A. S., M. C. Westaway, C. Muller, et al. "A Genomic History of Aboriginal Australia." *Nature* 538, no. 7624 (2016): 207–214.

Marcott, S. A., and J. D. Shakun. "Global Temperature Changes Mapped Across the Past 24,000 Years." *Nature* 599, no. 7884 (2021): 208–209.

Mathieson, I., I. Lazaridis, N. Rohland, et al. "Genome-Wide Patterns of Selection in 230 Ancient Eurasians." *Nature* 528, no. 7583 (2015): 499–503.

Mawson, J., B. Braun, P. Rock, et al. "Women at Altitude: Energy Requirement at 4,300 M." *Journal of Applied Physiology: Respiratory, Environmental and Exercise Physiology* 88 (2000): 272–281.

McGarvey, S. T. "Obesity in Samoans and a Perspective on Its Etiology in Polynesians." *The American Journal of Clinical Nutrition* 53, no. 6 Suppl. (1991): 1586s–1594s.

Meyer, M. C., M. S. Aldenderfer, Z. Wang, et al. "Permanent Human Occupation of the Central Tibetan Plateau in the Early Holocene." *Science* 355, no. 6320 (2017): 64–67.

Min, J. Y., H. S. Lee, Y. S. Choi, et al. "Association Between Income Levels and Prevalence of Heat- and Cold-Related Illnesses in Korean Adults." *BMC Public Health* 21, no. 1 (2021): 1264.

Moore, L. G. "Hypoxia and Reproductive Health: Reproductive Challenges at High Altitude: Fertility." *Pregnancy and Neonatal Well-Being.* Reproduction 161, no. 1 (2021): F81–f90.

Morgan, M. D., E. Pairo-Castineira, K. Rawlik, et al. "Genome-Wide Study of Hair Colour in UK Biobank Explains Most of the SNP Heritability." *Nature Communications* 9, no. 1 (2018): 5271.

Mummert, A., E. Esche, J. Robinson, and G. J. Armelagos. "Stature and Robusticity during the Agricultural Transition: Evidence from the Bioarchaeological Record." *Economics and Human Biology* 9, no. 3 (2011): 284–301.

Muza, S. R., B. A. Beidleman, and C. S. Fulco. "Altitude Preexposure Recommendations for Inducing Acclimatization." *High Altitude Medicine & Biology* 11, no. 2 (2010): 87–92.

Niclou, A., and C. Ocobock. "Weather Permitting: Increased Seasonal Efficiency of Nonshivering Thermogenesis Through Brown Adipose Tissue Activation in the Winter." *American Journal of Human Biology* 34 no. 6 (2021): e23716.

Nishimura, T., T. Katsumura, M. Motoi, et al. "Experimental Evidence Reveals the UCP1 Genotype Changes the Oxygen Consumption Attributed to Non-shivering Thermogenesis in Humans." *Scientific Reports* 7, no. 1 (2017): 5570.

Ocobock, C. "Human Energy Expenditure, Allocation, and Interactions in Natural Temperate, Hot, and Cold Environments." *American Journal of Physical Anthropology* 161, no. 4 (2016): 667–675.

O'Neill, M. S., and K. L. Ebi. "Temperature Extremes and Health: Impacts of Climate Variability and Change in the United States." *Journal of Occupational Environmental Medicine* 51 no. 1 (2009): 13–25.

Osborne, D. L., and R. Hames. "A Life History Perspective on Skin Cancer and the Evolution of Skin Pigmentation." *American Journal of Physical Anthropology* 153, no. 1 (2014): 1–8.

Ossendorf, G., A. R. Groos, T. Bromm, et al. "Middle Stone Age Foragers Resided in High Elevations of the Glaciated Bale Mountains." *Ethiopia. Science* 365, no. 6453 (2019): 583–587.

Pal, J. S., and E. A. B. Eltahir. "Future Temperature in Southwest Asia Projected to Exceed a Threshold for Human Adaptability." *Nature Climate Change* 6 (February 2016): 197200.

Perry, G. H., M. Foll, J. C. Grenier, et al. "Adaptive, Convergent Origins of the Pygmy Phenotype in African Rainforest Hunter-Gatherers." *Proceedings of the National Academy of Sciences of the United States of America* 111, no. 35 (2014): E3596–603.

Pike, J. W., and S. Christakos. "Biology and Mechanisms of Action of the Vitamin D Hormone." *Endocrinology and Metabolism Clinics of North America* 46, no. 4 (2017): 815–843.

Pitulko, V. V., A. N. Tikhonov, E. Y. Pavlova, et al. "Paleoanthropology. Early Human Presence in the Arctic: Evidence from 45,000-year-old Mammoth Remains." *Science* 351, no. 6270 (2016): 260–263.

Pomeroy, E., J. T. Stock, and J. C. K. Wells. "Population History and Ecology, in Addition to Climate, Influence Human Stature and Body Proportions." *Scientific Reports* 11, no. 1 (2021): 274.

Pontzer, H., M. H. Brown, B. M. Wood, et al. "Evolution of Water Conservation in Humans. *Current Biology* 31, no. 8 (2021): 1804–1810.e5.

Powell, F. L., W. K. Milsom, and G. S. Mitchell. "Time Domains of the Hypoxic Ventilatory Response." *Respiration Physiology* 112, no. 2 (1998): 123–134.

Prasad, R., and S. K. Katiyar. "Crosstalk Among UV-Induced Inflammatory Mediators, DNA Damage and Epigenetic Regulators Facilitates Suppression of the Immune System." *Photochemistry and Photobiology* 93, no. 4 (2017): 930–936.

Protsiv, M., C. Ley, J. Lankester, et al. "Decreasing Human Body Temperature in the United States since the Industrial Revolution." *Elife* 9 (2020).

Qi, X., W. L. Chan, R. J. Read, et al. "Temperature-Responsive Release of Thyroxine and Its Environmental Adaptation in Australians." *Proceedings. Biological Sciences/The Royal Society* 281, no. 1779 (2014): 20132747.

Racimo, F., D. Gokhman, M. Fumagalli, et al. "Archaic Adaptive Introgression in TBX15/WARS2." *Molecular Biology and Evolution* 34, no. 3 (2017): 509–524.

Rademaker, K., G. Hodgins, K. Moore, et al. "Paleoindian Settlement of the High-Altitude Peruvian Andes." *Science* 346, no. 6208 (2014): 466–469.

Raymond, C., T. Matthews, and R. M. Horton. "The Emergence of Heat and Humidity Too Severe for Human Tolerance." *Science Advances* 6, no. 19 (2020): eaaw1838.

Reich, D. A. *Who We Are and How We Got Here. Ancient DNA and the New Science of the Human Past.* Oxford: Oxford University Press, 2018.

Reis, G. V., N. A. Gontijo, K. F. Rodrigues, et al. "Vitamin D Receptor Polymorphisms and the Polycystic Ovary Syndrome: A Systematic Review." *The Journal of Obstetrics and Gynaecology Research* 43, no. 3 (2017): 436–446.

Reyes-Engel, A., E. Muñoz, M. J. Gaitan, et al. "Implications on Human Fertility of the 677C–>T and 1298A–>C Polymorphisms of the MTHFR Gene: Consequences of a Possible Genetic Selection." *Molecular Human Reproduction* 8, no. 10 (2002): 952–957.

Rhodes, J. "Comparative Physiology of Hypoxic Pulmonary Hypertension: Historical Clues from Brisket Disease." *Journal of Applied Physiology* 98, no. 3 (2005): 1092–1100.

Roberts, D. F. "*Climate and Human Variability. An Addison-Wesley Module in Anthropoloogy No. 34.*" Reading, MA: Addison-Wesley Publishing Co, 1973.

Rosinger, A. Y., and A. Brewis. "Life and Death: Toward a Human Biology of Water." *American Journal of Human Biology: The Official Journal of the Human Biology Council* 32, no. 1 (2020): e23361.

Sellayah, D. "The Impact of Early Human Migration on Brown Adipose Tissue Evolution and Its Relevance to the Modern Obesity Pandemic." *Journal of the Endocrine Society* 3, no. 2 (2019): 372–386.

Semenza, G. L. "Hypoxia-Inducible Factors in Physiology and Medicine. *Cell (Cambridge)* 148, no. 3 (2012): 399–408.

Shriver, M. D., and E. J. Parra. "Comparison of Narrow-Band Reflectance Spectroscopy and Tristimulus Colorimetry for Measurements of Skin and Hair Color in Persons of Different Biological Ancestry." *American Journal of Physical Anthropology* 112, no. 1 (2000): 17–27.

Smith, C. J. "Pediatric Thermoregulation: Considerations in the Face of Global Climate Change." *Nutrients* 11 (2019): 9.

Smith, N., L. L. Sievert, S. Muttukrishna, et al. "Mismatch: A Comparative Study of Vitamin D Status in British-Bangladeshi Migrants." *Evolution and Medical Public Health* 9, no. 1 (2021): 164–173.

Sohail, M., R. M. Maier, A. Ganna, et al. "Polygenic Adaptation on Height Is Overestimated Due to Uncorrected Stratification in Genome-Wide Association Studies." *Elife* 8 (2019).

Staub, K., M. Haeusler, N. Bender, et al. "Hemoglobin Concentration of Young Men at Residential Altitudes between 200 and 2000 masl Mirrors Switzerland's Topography." *Blood* 135, no.13 (2020): 1066–1069.

Stembridge, M., A. M. Williams, C. Gasho, et al. "The Overlooked Significance of Plasma Volume for Successful Adaptation to High Altitude in Sherpa and Andean Natives." *Proceedings of the National Academy of Sciences of the United States of America* 116, no. 33 (2019): 16177–16179.

Storz, J. F., G. R. Scott, and Z. A. Cheviron. "Phenotypic Plasticity and Genetic Adaptation to High-Altitude Hypoxia in Vertebrates." *The Journal of Experimental Biology* 213, Part 24 (2010): 4125–4136.

Tamura, T., and M. F. Picciano. "Folate and Human Reproduction." *The American Journal of Clinical Nutrition* 83, no. 5 (2006): 993–1016.

Thiery, W., S. Lange, J. Rogelj, et al. "Intergenerational Inequities in Exposure to Climate Extremes." *Science* 374, no. 6564 (2021): 158–160.

Tiosano, D., L. Audi, S. Climer, et al. "Latitudinal Clines of the Human Vitamin D Receptor and Skin Color Genes." *G3 (Bethesda)* 6, no. 5 (2016): 1251–1266.

Tishkoff, S. "GENETICS. Strength in small numbers." *Science* 349, no. 6254 (2015): 1282–1283.

Turchin, M. C., C. W. Chiang, C. D. Palmer, et al. "Evidence of Widespread Selection on Standing Variation in Europe at Height-Associated SNPs." *Nature Genetics* 44, no. 9 (2012): 1015–1019.

Washburn, S. L. "The New Physical Anthropology." *Transactions of the New York Academy of Sciences* 13, no. 7 (1951): 298–304.

Wells, J. C., M. A. Saunders, A. S. Lea, et al. "Beyond Bergmann's Rule: Global Variability in Human Body Composition Is Associated with Annual Average Precipitation and Annual Temperature Volatility." *American Journal of Physical Anthropology* 170, no. 1 (2019): 75–87.

Werren, E. A., O. Garcia, and A. W. Bigham. "Identifying Adaptive Alleles in the Human Genome: From Selection Mapping to Functional Validation." *Human Genetics* 140, no. 2 (2021): 241–276.

West, J. B., R. B. Schoene, A. M. Luks, and J. S. Milledge. *High Altitude Medicine and Physiology*, 5th edn. Boca Raton, FL: CRC Press, 2013.

Wilde, S., A. Timpson, K. Kirsanow, et al. "Direct Evidence for Positive Selection of Skin, Hair, and Eye Pigmentation in Europeans During the Last 5,000 Y." *Proceedings of the National Academy of Sciences of the United States of America* 111, no. 13 (2014): 4832–4837.

Will, M., M. Krapp, J. T. Stock, and A. Manica. "Different Environmental Variables Predict Body and Brain Size Evolution in Homo." *Nature Communications* 12, no. 1 (2021): 4116.

Wilson, S., R. S. Ginger, T. Dadd, et al. "NCKX5, a Natural Regulator of Human Skin Colour Variation, Regulates the Expression of Key Pigment Genes MC1R and alpha-MSH and Alters Cholesterol Homeostasis in Normal Human Melanocytes." *Advances in Experimental Medicine and Biology* 961 (2013): 95–107.

Wiriyasermkul, P., S. Moriyama, and S. Nagamori. "Membrane Transport Proteins in Melanosomes: Regulation of Ions for Pigmentation." *Biochim. Biophys. Acta Biomembr.*, 1862, no. 12 (2020): 183318.

Wolff, C. B., P. Barry, and D. J. Collier. "Cardiovascular and Respiratory Adjustments at Altitude Sustain Cerebral Oxygen Delivery – Severinghaus Revisited." *Comparative Biochemistry and Physiology. Part A, Molecular & Integrative Physiology* 132, no. 1 (2002): 221–229.

Wyckelsma, V. L., T. Venckunas, P. J. Houweling, et al. "Loss of α-Actinin-3 During Human Evolution Provides Superior Cold Resilience and Muscle Heat Generation. *American Journal of Human Genetics* 108, no. 3 (2021): 446–457.

Xu, K., and J. C. Lamanna. "Chronic Hypoxia and the Cerebral Circulation." *Journal of Applied Physiology: Respiratory, Environmental and Exercise Physiology* 100, no. 2 ((1985) 2006): 725–730.

Yang, Z., H. Zhong, J. Chen, et al. "A Genetic Mechanism for Convergent Skin Lightening During Recent Human Evolution." *Molecular Biology and Evolution* 33, no. 5 (2016): 1177–1187.

Yanovich, R., I. Ketko, and N. Charkoudian. "Sex Differences in Human Thermoregulation: Relevance for 2020 and Beyond." *Physiology (Bethesda)* 35, no. 3 (2020): 177–184.

Zamudio, S., S. K. Palmer, T. Droma, et al. "Effect of Altitude on Uterine Artery Blood Flow During Normal Pregnancy." *Journal of Applied Physiology* 79, no. 1 (1995): 7–14.

Zhang, X. L., B. B. Ha, S. J. Wang, et al. "The Earliest Human Occupation of the High-Altitude Tibetan Plateau 40 Thousand to 30 Thousand Years Ago." *Science* 362, no. 6418 (2018): 1049–1051.

Zoccolillo, M., C. Moia, S. Comincini, et al. "Identification of Novel Genetic Variants Associated with Short Stature in a Baka Pygmies Population." *Human Genetics* 139, no. 11 (2020): 1471–1483.

CHAPTER **10** Infectious Disease and Epidemiology: Dealing with the Present and Preparing for Future New Epidemics

Lisa Sattenspiel and Carolyn Orbann

In the first edition of this book, the infectious disease chapter began with a discussion of a new disease called severe acute respiratory syndrome (SARS), caused by a brand-new coronavirus, SARS-CoV-1, that emerged in 2003. Fast forward almost 20 years and we are dealing with yet another brand-new coronavirus, SARS-CoV-2, that has spread throughout the world. So far, this virus and the disease it causes, COVID-19, have killed more Americans than died in another notorious pandemic, the 1918 influenza pandemic[1]. We have watched as the death toll mounted, schools shut down, borders closed and travel stopped, and work for many people was either moved completely online or was put on hold. This pandemic began in late 2019 or early 2020 in most parts of the world and at the time of writing (February 2022) it is still not clear when it will end. Where did it come from? Why are so many people dying from infectious disease outbreaks now? How can these outbreaks be controlled more effectively? What does the future hold for us?

A chapter like this cannot answer all these questions, but it can help you to understand how scientists are trying to find their answers. To do this, we will focus on major issues that are at the center of research in infectious diseases today: (1) the evolution of new pathogens and how that process is affected by global climate change, (2) approaches that have been used to control and deal with recent epidemics, and (3) strategies to communicate effectively about infectious disease issues. These are not the only concerns related to infectious diseases in the twenty-first century, but due to space limitations we have chosen to center our discussions on these issues.

The roots of the field of epidemiology, the study of the transmission, distribution, and control of diseases, most likely extend back into prehistory, but the modern discipline really

A Companion to Biological Anthropology, Second Edition. Edited by Clark Spencer Larsen.
© 2023 John Wiley & Sons Ltd. Published 2023 by John Wiley & Sons Ltd.

got its start during the latter part of the nineteenth century, after the acceptance of the germ theory of disease. Much of the credit for this theory is given to Louis Pasteur, who showed in the 1860s that disease could be produced after certain microorganisms (germs) were introduced into the body. His theory was the culmination of several earlier ideas. For example, an important concept was the Hippocratic idea that disease resulted from an imbalance in essential elements in the body (the bodily humors of phlegm, yellow bile, blood, and black bile), as well as the recognition that health is strongly influenced by climate and the environment. Modern epidemiology was also influenced by the concept of contagion, or the belief that diseases can be transferred from person to person via invisible particles in the air, an idea that was formalized by Girolamo Fracastoro in the sixteenth century.

The work of John Snow, who conducted one of the first detailed studies linking a particular environmental risk factor to the development of disease, is often considered the beginning of modern epidemiology. Snow plotted deaths during an 1854 cholera outbreak on a map of London and was able to show convincingly that these deaths were connected to water coming from one source. He was not able to isolate the real cause of cholera, however. An Italian, Filippo Pacini, first discovered the causal bacterium that same year, but his work was ignored by scientists. It was not until 1884 when Robert Koch isolated the bacterium, *Vibrio cholerae*, in pure culture that the scientific world began to accept it as the cause, although the actual causal relationship was not formally proven until 1959, when the toxin that is responsible for the disease was discovered (Lippi and Gotuzzo 2014). Koch's work, which resulted in a set of guidelines for determining the link between a specific pathogen and a disease (called Koch's postulates) solidified the role of Pasteur's germ theory of disease in modern epidemiology.

Initially epidemiology centered on the study of infectious disease epidemics. As the application of germ theory and improved sanitation led to more effective control of epidemics, reduced mortality, especially among children, and increased life expectancy, emphasis shifted to the study of chronic and noninfectious health conditions, such as cancer or heart disease. For a while, in the high-income countries of the world, infectious diseases were thought to be a thing of the past. Consequently, active research on infectious diseases declined, at least until the HIV/AIDS pandemic emerged. Now with the emergence and worldwide spread of many new pathogens, including SARS-CoV-2, as well as resurgent pathogens such as drug-resistant tuberculosis, epidemiologists are expending renewed energy on understanding the distribution, spread, and control of infectious diseases.

Why do we have so many new diseases now? One major reason is that life in the twenty-first century is marked by significant increases in rates of worldwide travel and trade and increased interactions among individuals who were once isolated from one another because of distance and cultural barriers such as differing languages. As a result, diseases like COVID-19 can spread through global networks in a matter of weeks or days, and, in addition, there are new opportunities for the evolution and spread of emerging pathogens. For example, the pressures of global markets may encourage the growth of poultry farms, leading to increased contact between poultry and humans and setting the stage for the evolution of new strains of avian influenza that become capable of infecting humans. Other attributes of modern life also contribute to the evolution of new pathogens, especially global climate change, overpopulation, deforestation, social and economic inequalities, and globalization of markets. Scientists studying infectious diseases are playing increasingly important roles in modern endeavors to continue improving the health and wellbeing of all populations.

Anthropologists and epidemiologists have worked in parallel and in collaboration for much of the twentieth and twenty-first centuries, sharing conceptual and theoretical affinities, qualitative and quantitative methods, and an interest in international health, but at the same time they have retained boundaries and some healthy skepticism about each other's research (Janes et al. 1986; Trostle 2006). In this chapter, we focus on important questions related to present-day infectious diseases, but biological anthropologists have made relatively few contributions; rather, most of the work has been done by disease ecologists, epidemiologists, and culturally oriented medical anthropologists (recent examples of the last include Ennis-McMillan and Hedges 2020; Farmer 2020; Gomez-Temesio 2018; Singer and Rylko-Bauer 2021). Given the nature of this volume, however, we highlight whenever possible the work of biological anthropologists and illustrate ways in which biological anthropology can use epidemiological theory and methods to address questions of interest.

One area related to infectious diseases of humans that has been a long-standing focus in biological anthropology is the study of disease in prehistoric populations, made possible by analyses of skeletal remains. This type of work is covered in Chapters 11, 26, and 27 of this book; to avoid duplication we limit our discussion to historical and modern populations. It is worth noting, however, that the study of skeletal remains in an archaeological context has led biological anthropologists to expand Omran's (1971) classic model of the epidemiological transition, a model of great importance to scientists studying health and disease in present-day populations. In its original formulation, Omran focused on data from preindustrial Western Europe, Japan, Chile, and Ceylon (Sri Lanka). Biological anthropologists have addressed a number of weaknesses in the model and extended it back to the Paleolithic to offer a framework for understanding how major shifts in social and demographic conditions have shaped human disease patterns from prehistory to the present (Barrett et al. 1998; Harper and Armelagos 2010). For example, the progressive reliance on food production during the Neolithic period led to increased social complexity and stratification, larger population sizes and density, growing sedentism, and widening trade networks that increased rates of contact among humans from different communities and facilitated the spread of new types of pathogens between humans and from animals to humans. Social inequalities have mediated all epidemiological transitions in human history, resulting in higher burdens of disease and death among relatively less affluent people within societies, as well as between societies.

A growing number of biological anthropologists focus on epidemiology in more recent historic and modern populations. Many of the classic disease studies by biological anthropologists centered on the epidemiology of chronic diseases, including diabetes in native communities in North America (see, for example, Neel 1962; Szathmáry 1994). Much of the recent research in epidemiological approaches within biological anthropology (including our own) has focused on infectious diseases, however. Within a historical context, for example, recent studies have considered the impact of several epidemics in Gibraltar and Malta (e.g., Sawchuk and Tripp 2021), the 1918 influenza pandemic and other early twentieth century disease outbreaks in Newfoundland, Labrador, and Alaska (e.g., Mamelund et al. 2013; van Doren and Sattenspiel 2021), and a variety of epidemics in historical Quebec (e.g., Bruckner et al. 2018). Examples of recent epidemiological studies in contemporary human groups include Hurtado and colleagues' (2008) studies of helminths in the Ache of Paraguay; Littleton and King's (2008) analysis of the political ecology of tuberculosis in New Zealand; Gurven et al.'s (2007) study of mortality in the Tsimane Amerindians of Bolivia; and Dinkel et al.'s (2019) and Houck et al.'s (2019) studies of the relationship between water improvements and usage on health in small-scale societies. In addition, the entire September/October 2020 issue of the *American Journal of Human Biology* (Volume 32, number 5) centers on biological anthropologists' contributions to understanding and dealing with the COVID-19 pandemic.

To illustrate in more depth how biological anthropology can aid in the study of infectious diseases, we turn now to the discussion of our three chosen topics: (1) newly emerging infectious diseases and climate change, with mosquito-borne diseases used to illustrate the problem; (2) understanding and controlling the spread of recent epidemics, including COVID-19 and the 2014–16 Ebola epidemic, and dealing with the growing problem of vaccine hesitancy; and (3) how to prepare for future epidemics by communicating more effectively to the public the risks and strategies that might control them.

Newly Emerging Infectious Diseases: Sources, Detection, and Climate Change

The phrase "emerging infectious disease" refers to diseases that either are new to a population or show an increase in the number of cases, in association with a rapid expansion of their range (Morse 1993). While media attention to emerging infections has generated panic and a tendency to connect this phrase with exotic and frightening viruses such as Ebola or SARS-CoV-2, the phrase is appropriately applied to many commonplace diseases such as influenza, which have ebbed and flowed over the course of human history. The phrase came into fashion in the 1990s, in the wake of the HIV/AIDS epidemic, which demonstrated that infectious diseases were not a feature of the past, but an ever-present and inevitable aspect of everyday life.

A significant proportion of new human infectious diseases begin as zoonoses, or diseases of other animals that become capable of infecting humans. Many of these diseases originate in the tropical regions of the world following environmental or human behavioral change and increased human interactions with wildlife or domesticated animals that interact with wildlife (Cunningham et al. 2017; Petrovan et al. 2021). Human diseases that have emerged from wildlife in the twenty-first century include SARS (severe acute respiratory syndrome), MERS (Middle Eastern Respiratory Syndrome), new strains of avian influenza, and many others. Bats appear to be reservoirs (natural sources) for many zoonotic viruses (Cunningham et al. 2017), as are non-human primates and rodents (Petrovan et al. 2021). Human interactions with these reservoirs likely provide the necessary opportunities for a shift from the reservoir to a human host. Examples of factors that influence these opportunities are changes in land-use patterns, agricultural intensification, loss of natural hosts of vectors due to urbanization and other human activities (which can force the vectors to bite humans more regularly), and recreational or subsistence activities that increase rates of contact between humans and wildlife. Biological anthropology as a discipline stresses a strong understanding of both human biology and the role and importance of these types of behaviors for human existence; thus, this is one important area where biological anthropologists contribute to the study of infectious disease origins and spread (see, for example, Amoroso and Nunn 2021; Herrera et al. 2020).

Infectious diseases spread through a population in multiple ways. Some pass directly from person-to-person, some are transmitted through contaminated water or soil, and many are spread by means of a vector, or living organism that transfers a pathogen from one human to another or from other animals to humans (WHO 2020). The most common vectors are insects (e.g., mosquitoes, ticks, fleas, etc.). Diseases transmitted by means of vectors are referred to as vector-borne diseases. Vectors are implicated in some of the most serious human infectious diseases, including malaria (*Anopheles* mosquitoes), dengue fever (*Aedes* mosquitoes), yellow fever (*Aedes* mosquitoes), and African trypanosomiasis (sleeping sickness) (tsetse flies) (WHO 2020).

One of the big questions associated with newly emerging diseases is how to detect their presence. Since they are new, it can be difficult to recognize them until there are a substantial number of cases, by which time an epidemic is likely to have taken hold and begun to spread. Such was the case with the 2016 Zika epidemic in Brazil. The disease itself was first reported in Nigeria in the early 1950s (Plourde and Bloch 2016), although it was uncommon until recent outbreaks in the Pacific and the Americas in the mid-2010s (Musso and Gubler 2016). The epidemic in Brazil is thought to have begun in 2013 or 2014, but it remained undetected and circulated for over a year and a half before it was connected to severe cases of microcephaly in newborns, a new manifestation of the disease. By that time, it had already spread to over 40 countries, leading the World Health Organization to declare a public emergency at the beginning of February in 2016, and it has continued to circulate in some parts of the world (Faria et al. 2017; Grubaugh et al. 2019; Lowe et al. 2018).

It is generally acknowledged that the recognition of novel pathogens can only be achieved at the community level due to the difficulty at larger geographic scales of conducting the intense surveillance needed to detect a rare pathogen. Globally, however, many regions with the highest potential to be sources for new pathogens struggle, even at the community level, with insufficient disease surveillance capabilities, laboratory facilities, and trained personnel needed for the identifications. Furthermore, ill individuals may be most comfortable first turning to local healers and may either avoid or not have access to biomedical clinics and hospitals until they have already spread a pathogen to others. This delay may also limit the information about a new pathogen that comes to the attention of biomedical practitioners, making it more difficult for a new pathogen to be recognized by organizations such as the WHO. Good communication between biomedical and traditional practitioners can help to facilitate quicker identification of significant new pathogens – another potential role for biological anthropologists, who can use their anthropological training as well as their understanding of biological issues to communicate effectively with both parties.

Most of the efforts to detect new pathogens focus on molecular techniques such as PCR and whole genome sequencing (see Bird and Mazet 2018 for a review of these methods). Another approach, sentinel surveillance systems, relies on observations of specific types of animals to warn of potential human problems (e.g., die-offs of rodents in the southwestern US can signal potential plague outbreaks). Syndromic surveillance methods, which analyze daily reports of general practitioners for unusual human illness patterns, are used in some countries (e.g., Randrianasolo et al. 2010). Computer models can analyze potential risk situations such as climatic changes, spillover of infections from other animals to humans (e.g., cases of avian influenza in human farmers), or spatial variation in characteristics known to influence the risk for a particular disease. In recent years, in an attempt to better gauge risks for the spread of COVID-19, bioaerosol sampling has been conducted in high traffic situations such as airports, and wastewater near communities has been sampled to detect and identify new variants of SARS-CoV-2, the virus causing COVID-19 (Oeschger et al. 2021; Sims and Kasprzyk-Hordern 2020).

These techniques all aid in detecting new pathogens, but the fact remains that there really is no way to know for sure where and when the next pathogen capable of causing another human pandemic will evolve. As the history of SARS-CoV-2 has shown, when faced with a *new* pathogen, even the most basic biological characteristics of the pathogen and its interaction with the host cannot be understood until a significant number of people have already become infected. In addition, the response of humans to a new pathogen is complex and impossible to predict. Nonetheless, these new techniques and increased recognition of the potential threats of new pathogens have led to better communication and collaboration among health authorities and governments worldwide, which will help to ensure rapid responses to pathogens of the future.

The Impact of Climate Change

New pathogens are evolving all the time, but the world is facing a major environmental problem, climate change, that is likely to result in significant new shifts in human interactions with potential pathogens, other hosts of those pathogens, and disease vectors such as mosquitoes that facilitate transmission of the pathogens among humans. Here we briefly mention the most important consequences of climate change on the distribution, transmission, and prevalence of human infectious diseases. The breadth of pathogen diversity is such that space does not allow consideration of this topic for all kinds of human diseases. Consequently, we limit our discussion here to the effects of climate change on vector-borne diseases such as malaria and dengue fever. Vector-borne diseases are responsible for over 17 percent of all cases of infectious disease in humans and cause over 700,000 deaths worldwide every year (WHO 2020) and, in addition, have clear ties to both environmental and social factors. Readers interested in more in-depth discussions of the impacts of climate change on vector-borne and other kinds of diseases than can be presented here are encouraged to consult some of the many recent reviews of this topic (e.g., Bartlow et al. 2019; Ellwanger et al. 2020).

Many of the changes expected to occur in vector-borne diseases following climate change will result from adjustments in vector characteristics that influence their ability to effectively transfer pathogens from one human to another. These characteristics include rates of vector survival, biting rates, rate of development, and length of the vector reproductive period. Almost all these characteristics are sensitive to variations in temperature, rainfall, and humidity, with most showing maximum values at intermediate levels of the climate variables (Mordecai et al. 2019). For example, many mosquitoes have a well-defined temperature range that is ideal for their survivorship. If temperatures rise too far above or too far below this range, survivorship drops.

Computer models have been developed to explore the impacts of defined climate changes (e.g., Colón-González et al. 2021; Mordecai et al. 2019; Ryan et al. 2019) and these provide some insight into what we might expect to happen with vector-borne diseases as the global climate warms. Some of these studies and observations of present disease and vector distributions indicate that the distribution of malaria in East Africa is shifting toward higher altitudes, which are becoming warm enough to allow survival of the mosquito vector, and there are suggestions that transmission in lower altitudes could be lessened due to poorer survivorship of the malaria vector in hotter temperatures.

As another example, because of warmer temperatures in southern Europe, *Aedes aegypti* mosquitoes (the vector of dengue fever, yellow fever, Zika virus, and other diseases) are increasing their range into that region and may even overtake *Anopheles* mosquitoes (the malaria vector) in some areas. This means that in these areas the diseases transmitted by *Aedes* mosquitoes may become much more problematic. In addition, due to less suitable conditions for survivorship of the malaria vector as well as competition between the two types of vectors (*Aedes* and *Anopheles* mosquitoes), there may be further reductions in malaria in these regions (Mordecai et al. 2020). An additional consideration is that *Aedes* mosquitoes bite during the day (when bug spray is a preferred prevention strategy), while *Anopheles* mosquitoes bite at night (when bed nets are more effective). Thus, a shift in the predominant mosquito species means the types of public health efforts most effective could change due to the differing ecology of dengue fever, yellow fever, and Zika virus as well as the *Aedes* vector (Mordecai et al. 2020), leaving populations with inadequate strategies and resources to deal with the new disease risks (Colón-González et al. 2021). Another complication is that in such a situation, communications about how to prevent the disease may be outdated and focus on the prior species of mosquito that was most prevalent rather than the newly predominant mosquitoes, a situation that was observed during the 2016 Zika epidemic (Kristin Hedges, personal communication, January 4, 2022). In addition, the limited prior exposure of these populations to malaria may mean that they have few of the genetic adaptations to malaria (e.g., carriers of sickle cell hemoglobin) observed in areas with long-standing exposure to the disease and they may also have limited levels of immunity built up from exposure at young ages.

Changes are also likely to occur in the pathogens themselves as well as in environmental conditions that affect disease transmission rates. Most pathogens go through some of their life stages within their vectors (i.e., the vectors are not just conduits for them to get from one human to another but are necessary for the pathogen to complete its life cycle). Changes in temperature, humidity, and rainfall can alter the reproduction rate of a pathogen in its vector and/or host and can also change the length of time it takes for a newly infected host to become infectious and be able to transmit the pathogen to a new vector and ultimately another host. Changes in these climatic variables can also influence the length of transmission season, allowing for more or fewer generations of the vector and/or the pathogen in a given year, and environmental shifts can lead to changes in the number and/or distribution of vector breeding sites. For example, environmental shifts can lead to increased rainfall, which can cause increases in standing water, prime breeding locations for many types of mosquitoes.

Finally, many changes in the human environment can occur due to climate change. If drought occurs, humans may need more water storage containers; these are prime breeding locations for *Aedes* mosquitoes. Extreme climate events can lead to a destabilization of infrastructure related to sanitation and public health, especially in regions with inadequate infrastructure to begin with. Deforestation and habitat fragmentation often accompany climate change – these can upset the natural cycles of disease that occur in wild animals and result in increased human risk as vectors and pathogens seek alternate hosts. This process is exacerbated by increasing encroachment of humans on wildlife habitat, agricultural intensification and land use changes, mining, dam building, urbanization-related destruction of the natural environment, increased hunting and consumption of wild game (which also reduces the availability of an important source of protein in low-resource populations), and a growing international trade of animals and animal products. It is important to note, however, that some of these changes may have some positive consequences for a region. In particular, mining, dam building, and urbanization often result in improvements in the local road system and water supplies, which can make it easier to access medical facilities and clean water (although often these upgrades do not come with funds to maintain them beyond the short term and may result in more problems down the line). It is essential to carefully assess the overall consequences, both negative and positive, of human impacts on the environment in attempts to determine the ultimate impacts of climate change[2].

UNDERSTANDING AND CONTROLLING INFECTIOUS DISEASE

Small pre-agricultural human populations were likely troubled primarily by parasites or environmentally acquired infections rather than the kinds of infectious diseases most prominent in high-income countries today. As human groups increased in size, new opportunities arose for pathogens that are transmitted directly from individual to individual, from domesticated animals to the human population, or through the detritus associated with larger more sedentary human populations. Diseases like measles, influenza, and polio can circulate regularly if a supply of susceptible hosts is available. Humans have responded to the threat of infectious disease outbreaks with both technological solutions, like vaccines and medications, and behavioral changes designed to control outbreaks of disease, like quarantine or avoidance behaviors.

Before an infectious disease can be controlled, basic information about it must be understood, including the means of transmission, how a pathogen can be transmitted to others, the probability that transmission occurs, how long an infected person is likely to be sick, and what, if any, treatments work to manage symptoms or cure the disease. In the scientific approach used in biomedicine it is understood that diseases are caused by specific pathogens. The human–pathogen environment is envisioned as an ecosystem containing environment, host, and infectious agent. This framework, known as the socioecological model, allows scientists to think about specific parts of the disease process and their effects on population-level outcomes. For example, influenza transmission from person to person is highly impacted by season and by social behaviors and cultural structures. The disease spreads more readily in winter because people spend more time indoors where they share more air. Influenza also spreads in family and other co-habiting groups more frequently because their contacts are stronger (they spend more time together, often closer together than groups of strangers).

Another way to consider infectious disease is with a One Health model, which looks more closely at the connection of human, animal, and environment. A One Health model might look at the way that influenza circulates in wild and domestic bird populations and how and when it is likely to move into human populations in order to apply appropriate public health measures. In both of these models, successful control of infectious disease requires consideration of both biological and sociocultural factors.

One of the most effective ways to stop an outbreak of infectious disease is to deny the pathogen access to susceptible hosts. This can be achieved through methods like vaccination, which reduce the numbers of susceptible people, or movement controls like quarantine, isolation, and border control. Social norms, including stigmas (Brewis et al. 2020) and emotions such as disgust related to the consequences of infections (Cepon-Robins et al. 2021), can also influence disease control by discouraging mixing of infectious and susceptible individuals or encouraging self-moderating of risky behavior. For example, sneezing directly into another person's face is a risky behavior in terms of pathogen transfer and is also seen as a violation of social norms. In this way, culture can promote behaviors that limit disease spread. Note, however, that stigmas may further isolate vulnerable populations and often become morally coded so that people with certain types of infectious disease become shunned or scapegoated. Stigma can also be implicated in reduced use of health care resources by people who have or fear they have stigmatized conditions.

Border closure, travel restriction, quarantine, and isolation have all been in use for centuries. Quarantine is the enforced separation of a group of people whose disease status is unknown; isolation is the process of separating out an infected (and presumably infectious) person and keeping them from passing the contagion along to others in their community. Quarantines are recorded as far back as the twelfth century in Venice as a measure to prevent disease from spreading due to contact with traders from other parts of the world (McDonald 1951). They were common throughout the Mediterranean and British Isles in the sixteenth through ninetenth centuries and became a standard way that countries controlled the spread of disease from other locations. The quarantine period is determined by disease attributes – typically it should last long enough to confirm that someone is not infected before allowing them to mix within a larger population. Isolation is enforced during the time a sick person could possibly transmit a pathogen, which can vary widely depending on the disease. Border controls are typically intended to prevent the entrance of infected people into a susceptible community, but often are not implemented in time to totally prevent pathogen spread. Each of these actions can be effective in slowing the pace of new infections and can be very useful, particularly in cases where medical options are limited and prevention is of vital importance.

Recent outbreaks of new infectious diseases have varied in size, but all have had severe morbidity and mortality effects, severe economic effects, or both. In the remainder of this section, we use case studies of COVID-19 and Ebola to illustrate some specific tools used in the control of infectious disease and how anthropological thought has and can continue to contribute to infectious disease control.

COVID-19

COVID-19 is clearly the most significant infectious disease to emerge in recent history. As of this writing, the pandemic is entering its third year and has caused widespread mortality, morbidity, and economic disruption. The WHO estimates over 430 million cases and nearly 6 million deaths worldwide as of late February 2022 (WHO 2022). The disease was first detected in China in late 2019, and quickly spread to Europe and North America in early 2020; by April 2020 it had been detected in most countries around the world.

COVID-19 causes respiratory symptoms, including a cough and fever. The risk of mortality is highest among people over age 50 (as of late February 2022, over 93 percent of COVID-19 deaths in the US were among people in this age group) (CDC 2022). Disparities in COVID-19 deaths have also been recorded by gender (Bambra et al. 2021), racial and ethnic identities (both in the US and in other countries) (Bentley 2020; Gross et al. 2020), and disability status (Bosworth et al. 2021). Disparities are largely driven by social features, such as access to care, insurance coverage, and employment in public facing jobs or other workplaces where distancing or working from home is not possible. Some people have also reported experiencing long COVID, in which symptoms continue for several months past the initial infection (Callard and Perego 2021).

In the earliest days of the pandemic, most countries attempted to control spread by first imposing travel restrictions, including cancellation of flights, mass-transit, and individual domestic travel. This typically was followed by lockdowns, during which schools, businesses, and public places were closed. People were advised to work from home and avoid nonessential movement in their communities. These movement restrictions were often coupled with mandated wearing of masks, testing protocols, and other nonpharmaceutical interventions (NPIs) designed to increase understanding of the spread of COVID-19 and prevent new infections.

The NIH announced the first Phase I trial of a viable vaccine candidate in March 2020 (NIH 2020), only weeks after the viral genetic sequence was released to the international community. By late 2020, the US government was close to giving emergency approval to a vaccine. This represents the fastest development of a vaccine for an infectious disease to date, and while it is a significant achievement, the speed also contributed to the problem of vaccine hesitancy for specific parts of the population (Kim et al. 2020).

Even as vaccines were being made available to frontline workers, issues of vaccine equity arose. Within the US, native English-speaking people with higher incomes, health insurance, and better access to health care were likely to get vaccinated earliest (Crane et al. 2021). Internet access was almost always necessary to book vaccine appointments, so people with low technical literacy or lack of high-speed Internet were less likely to be able to successfully book vaccine appointments. Other factors, like work schedules, transportation access, and childcare availability also played a role in people's ability to make use of vaccines.

Globally, issues of vaccine equity were even more significant. High-income nations purchased billions of doses of vaccines, sometimes more than was required to vaccinate their entire populations. Middle- and low-income nations have had challenges getting doses even for frontline healthcare workers. As of February 2022, the WHO COVID dashboard indicates that most African nations continue to have much lower rates of vaccination than the rest of the world. Measures to increase equity have been recommended, including developing internal infrastructure related to vaccine storage and distribution in low- and middle-income nations, the relaxation of patents covering the vaccines so that more manufacturers can start production, and calling on high-income nations to hold off on distributing boosters until more people can get their first set of doses (The Lancet Infectious Diseases 2021).

Many anthropological journals released special issues on COVID-19 in which they shared the ways that anthropological methodologies might be useful for researchers working with populations during the pandemic (e.g., *American Journal of Human Biology*, Volume 32 (5): "Human Biologists Confront the COVID-19 Pandemic" and *Open Anthropological Research*, Volume 1 (1) special issue: "Pathogenic Politics: Life, Death, and Social Responses to the COVID-19 Pandemic"). Anthropological research has also directly addressed issues like systemic racism, structural inequalities, and the relationship between patients and health systems in the context of the pandemic (e.g., *Medical Anthropology*, Volume 39 (5): "COVID-19 and other Crises: On Risk and Repercussion"), as well as how anthropologists can leverage the strengths of the field during health emergencies like COVID-19 (Ali 2020; Gray et al. 2020).

Ebola

Prior to the emergence of COVID-19, Ebola was one emerging infectious disease of concern to the international infectious disease community. Identified in the 1970s, Ebola is related to other viruses that cause hemorrhagic disease and it infects humans, nonhuman primates, and possibly other animal species. It has been reported primarily in West African nations and is likely to have a wild reservoir in bats (Leendertz et al. 2016), though its specific reservoir species is still unknown. Ebola spreads through bodily fluids and transmission often occurs during care-giving or mortuary practices, like washing a body, cleaning body fluids, or otherwise coming into direct contact with an infected person (Rewar and Mirdha 2014).

Sporadic outbreaks of Ebola have been recorded since its discovery, but the long and widespread epidemic of 2014–2016 was of greatest concern to international health authorities and one case in particular where anthropologists were able to contribute to control efforts. Travel restrictions were widely implemented and prevented or limited travel from

West Africa to other parts of the world, but the epidemic ultimately spread to 10 countries and caused the deaths of over 11,000 people (Kamorudeen et al. 2020). Domestic travel controls in countries hardest hit by the outbreak were implemented incompletely and often encountered local resistance. Additionally, protocols were put in place to ensure safe burials and handling of potentially infectious materials, like used hospital supplies. These precautions, recommended by health workers, also encountered resistance as local communities often were not included in planning processes and their concerns were not considered by international health actors.

Clearly, control of Ebola is important, as the pace of outbreaks has been increasing since the 1990s, and the numbers of people impacted is also increasing (Rugarabamu et al. 2020). At the same time, global health professionals found that they were having increasing difficulty implementing control programs because they had not established a strong working relationship with affected communities. Anthropologists helped to identify major communication barriers that were limiting adherence to NPI (non-pharmaceutical intervention) policies and suggested alternative and amended policies that were more consistent with local norms (Venables and Pellecchia 2017). Almost as importantly, anthropologists were able to illuminate ways that global health practitioners were themselves underprepared for dealing with the social and emotional aspects of a deadly pandemic (Moran 2017).

Anthropologists' work on Ebola was notable because it provides a blueprint for how to successfully incorporate anthropological methods at a larger than usual scale in a health emergency. One important development was the use of rapid ethnographic assessments to help in control efforts. Infectious disease outbreaks are often fast moving and information is needed quickly to be useful. The Ebola Response Anthropology Platform, developed in 2014, is one example of how to implement a resource that is accessible and up to date for use by health workers (Martineau et al. 2017). This platform was later developed into the Epidemic Response Anthropology Platform (http://archive.ids.ac.uk/epr/index.html), an expanded site that contains resources for public health professionals for a variety of infectious disease scenarios. Both platforms include cultural information, research studies, and recommendations on topics like mortuary practices, communication, and tools for health workers to improve their cultural competency skills.

Since the end of the 2014–2016 pandemic, anthropologists have continued to work with Ebola survivors on topics like stigma (Minor 2017; Smith-Morris 2017) and resistance to ongoing public health work in affected areas (Fairhead 2016). Two FDA-approved vaccines for Ebola are now available, but like the COVID-19 vaccine, resistance to vaccination is emerging and is now a priority for social scientists in global public health.

Vaccine Hesitancy

Vaccine hesitancy, the decision to delay or forgo recommended vaccinations, is a major obstacle to the control of infectious disease, and this phenomenon is not new. In fact, resistance to vaccines goes back as far as the development of the earliest smallpox vaccines (Schwartz 2012). Prior to the COVID-19 pandemic, the incidence of vaccine-preventable illnesses was increasing worldwide, with notable outbreaks of measles, pertussis, mumps, and the continuing persistence of polio (Kubin 2019). In the US, recent outbreaks have been driven by spread in groups of people who were unvaccinated by choice, sometimes spilling over into the public through breakthrough infections.

Hesitancy toward vaccines started as a kind of outspoken avoidance of vaccines (Schwartz 2012), but these behaviors sometimes manifest as public protests (Leask 2020) and may occasionally include violence (Berman 2021). In many places, vaccine hesitancy has a longer history among underserved communities or within populations that suffered previous medical harms. Vaccine hesitancy has gained adherents among specific social groups, including higher-income, high-education people and people concerned with government intrusion, or who question the role of big pharma in vaccine design and production (Dubé et al. 2014). The ideas and attitudes that underly these behaviors are complex and varied. That is, not everyone who is hesitant has the same reasons for being hesitant, and anthropologists can and have played an important role in deepening the understanding of these beliefs and behaviors (e.g., Dubé et al. 2015; Sobo 2016). The Communivax program, which will be discussed further below, is one way that anthropologists are using their strengths to address the problem of COVID-19 vaccine hesitancy.

SCIENCE COMMUNICATION

Communication about infectious disease has traditionally been left to public health and community health workers, or to specialists in communication. However, anthropologists have increasingly found it important to get more involved in communicating their work to the public (Manderson 1998). The Ebola epidemic illustrated the potential role that anthropologists have as interlocutors between people trying to survive an epidemic and the global health practitioners trying to help them. During this epidemic, anthropologists were able to identify communication barriers and suggest ways to improve communication and cooperation between international health workers and local communities experiencing the epidemic. This can help with acceptance of health policies and practices.

During COVID-19, a wide array of experts on the 1918 influenza pandemic were called on to draw parallels and share lessons from that pandemic that might apply today. In this case, anthropologists were able to provide historical and cultural context to COVID-19 by sharing information about the use of interventions like masking and closure orders in the past. This helps the public see public health actions as being effective and having past precedent, which can assist in adherence and acceptance of these measures. Conversely, anthropologists studying vaccine hesitancy or inequities in the health care system have valuable expertise that has been used to help design vaccination campaigns, for example the Communivax program (https://www.communivax.org), a multidisciplinary coalition aiming to increase vaccine equity in the US. Communivax is a "national coalition of social scientists, public health experts, and community advocates" working together to advance the cause of vaccine equity. They have sites in five states in which multidisciplinary groups work to listen to community concerns about vaccines and help design vaccine programs that are responsive to the needs of local communities. They pay special attention to underserved populations and have published a number of reports on their work with specific culture and language groups, as well as providing ready-to-use tools on their website.

Communicating one's findings to the public is increasingly recognized as an important part of being a scientist and academic (Ocobock and Lynn 2020). Individual anthropologists have cultivated strong web-presences and have used their platforms to share research, both their own and that of colleagues across disciplines. More importantly, anthropologists must strive to build structures that bridge the divide between the public and paywalled scientific literature. New genres of communication have provided avenues for engagement with a wider public interested in anthropological issues, who may not have the access or ability to dig into the peer-reviewed literature. Anthropological professional associations sponsor discipline-oriented podcasts (e.g., *This Anthro Life* and *The Sausage of Science*), many of which have featured one or more episodes on infectious disease and health. The Wenner Gren Foundation's *Sapiens* magazine has a website, teaching tools, and podcasts, and has engaged with topics on infectious disease. It also has a robust presence on social media. Given the clear communication failures during the COVID-19 and Ebola epidemics, communication needs to be included in infection control planning, and the anthropological community can and has played an important role.

Humans are highly social animals and, as such, we will always provide good opportunities for the transmission of infectious diseases. Further population growth, coupled with more intensive use of natural resources and climate change, will likely make the issue of infectious disease more severe. Communication between the public and the scientists who study infectious disease is essential for successful control of future epidemics that will inevitably occur. We hope the lessons we have learned when dealing with the COVID-19, Ebola, and other recent epidemics will provide guidance for when we must face the next new epidemic.

NOTE

1 It is important to note that the size of the US population in 1918 was only one third of what it is today, and so the mortality *rate* now is only a fraction of the rate observed in 1918.
2 Gurven et al. (2007) present an excellent anthropological example of how the health of human populations may be impacted by changes in access to healthcare resources.

REFERENCES

Ali, I. "Anthropology in Emergencies: The Roles of Anthropologists During the COVID-19 Pandemic." *Practicing Anthropology* 42, no. 3 (2020): 16–22.

Amoroso, C. R., and C. L. Nunn. "Epidemiological Transitions in Human Evolution and the Richness of Viruses, Helminths, and Protozoa." *Evolution, Medicine, and Public Health* 2021 (2021): 139–148. https://doi.org/10.1093/emph/eoab009.

Bambra, C., V. Albani, and P. Franklin. "COVID-19 and the Gender Health Paradox." *Scandinavian Journal of Public Health* 49, no. 1 (2021): 17–26. https://doi.org/10.1177/1403494820975604.

Barrett, R., C. W. Kuzawa, T. McDade, et al. "Emerging and Re-Emerging Infectious Diseases: The Third Epidemiologic Transition." *Annual Review of Anthropology* 27 (1998): 247–271.

Bartlow, A. W., C. Manore, C. Xu, et al. "Forecasting Zoonotic Infectious Disease Response to Climate Change: Mosquito Vectors and a Changing Environment." *Veterinary Sciences* 6, no. 40 (2019): https://doi.org/10.3390/vetsci6020040.

Bentley, G. R. "Don't Blame the BAME: Ethnic and Structural Inequalities in Susceptibilities to COVID-19." *American Journal of Human Biology* 32, no. 5 (2020): e23478. https://doi.org/10.1002/ajhb.23478.

Berman, J. M., "When Antivaccine Sentiment Turned Violent: The Montréal Vaccine Riot of 1885." *Canadian Medical Association Journal* 193, no. 14 (2021): E490–E492. https://doi.org/10.1503/cmaj.202820.

Bird, B. H., and J. A. K. Mazet. "Detection of Emerging Zoonotic Pathogens: An Integrated One Health Approach." *Annual Review of Animal Biosciences* 6 (2018): 121–139. https://doi.org/10.1146/annurev-animal-030117-014628.

Bosworth, M. L., D. Ayoubkhani, V. Nafilyan, et al. "Deaths Involving COVID-19 by Self-Reported Disability Status during the First Two Waves of the COVID-19 Pandemic in England: A Retrospective, Population-Based Cohort Study." *Lancet Public Health* 6, no. 11 (2021): https://doi.org/10.1016/S2468-2667(21)00206-1.

Brewis, A., A. Wutich, and P. Mahdavi. "Stigma, Pandemics, and Human Biology: Looking Back, Looking Forward." *American Journal of Human Biology* 32, no. 5 (2020): e23480. https://doi.org/10.1002/ajhb.23480.

Bruckner, T. A., S. Gailey, S. Hallman, et al. "Epidemic Cycles and Environmental Pressure in Colonial Quebec." *American Journal of Human Biology* 30, no. 5 (2018): e23155. https://doi.org/10.1002/ajhb.23155.

Callard, F., and E. Perego. "How and Why Patients Made Long Covid." *Social Science & Medicine* 268 (2021): 113426. https://doi.org/10.1016/j.socscimed.2020.113426.

Centers for Disease Control and Prevention (CDC). COVID Data Tracker. *Electronic document,* 2022. https://covid.cdc.gov/covid-data-tracker/#demographics.

Cepon-Robins, T. J., A. D. Blackwell, T. E. Gildner, et al. "Pathogen Disgust Sensitivity Protects Against Infection in a High Pathogen Environment." *Proceedings of the National Academy of Sciences, USA* 118, no. 8 (2021): e2018552118. https://doi.org/10.1073/pnas.2018552118.

Colón-González, F. J., M. O. Sewe, A. M. Tompkins, et al. "Projecting the Risk of Mosquito-Borne Diseases in a Warmer and More Populated World: A Multi-Model, Multi-Scenario Intercomparison Modelling Study." *Lancet Planetary Health* 5 (2021): e404–e414. https://doi.org/10.1016/S2542-5196(21)00132-7.

Crane, M. A., R. R. Faden, and J. A. Romley. "Disparities in County COVID-19 Vaccination Rates Linked to Disadvantage and Hesitancy." *Health Affairs* 40, no. 11 (2021): 1792–1796. https://doi.org/10.1377/hlthaff.2021.01092.

Cunningham, A. A., P. Daszak, and J. L. N. Wood. "One Health, Emerging Infectious Diseases, and Wildlife: Two Decades of Progress?" *Philosophical Transactions of the Royal Society B* 372 (2017): 20160167. http://dx.doi.org/10.1098/rstb.2016.0167.

Dinkel, K. A., M. E. Costa, T. S. Kraft, et al. "Relationship of Sanitation, Water Boiling, and Mosquito Nets to Health Biomarkers in a Rural Subsistence Population." *American Journal of Human Biology* 32, no. 1 (2019): e23356. https://doi.org/10.1002/ajhb.23356.

Dubé, E., D. Gagnon, E. Nickels, et al. "Mapping Vaccine Hesitancy – Country-Specific Characteristics of a Global Phenomenon." *Vaccine* 32, no. 49 (2014): 6649–6654. https://doi.org/10.1016/j.vaccine.2014.09.039.

Dubé, E., M. Vivion, and N. E. MacDonald. "Vaccine Hesitancy, Vaccine Refusal and the Anti-Vaccine Movement: Influence, Impact and Implications." *Expert Review of Vaccines* 14, no. 1 (2015): 99–117. https://doi.org/10.1586/14760584.2015.964212.

Ellwanger, J. H., B. Kulmann-Leal, V. L. Kaminski, et al. "Beyond Diversity Loss and Climate Change: Impacts of Amazon Deforestation on Infectious Diseases and Public Health." *Annals of the Brazilian Academy of Sciences* 92, no. 1 (2020): e20191375. https://doi.org/10.1590/0001-2765202020191375.

Ennis-McMillan, M. C., and K. Hedges. "Pandemic Perspectives: Responding to COVID-19." *Open Anthropology* 8, no. 1 (2020). https://www.americananthro.org/StayInformed/OAArticleDetail.aspx?ItemNumber=25631.

Fairhead, J. "Understanding Social Resistance to the Ebola Response in the Forest Region of the Republic of Guinea: An Anthropological Perspective." *African Studies Review* 59, no. 3 (2016): 7–31. https://doi.org/10.1017/asr.2016.87.

Faria, N. R., J. Quick, I. M. Claro, et al. "Establishment and Cryptic Transmission of Zika Virus in Brazil and the Americas." *Nature* 546 (2017): 406–410. https://doi.org/10.1038/nature22401.

Farmer, P. *Fever, Feuds, and Diamonds: Ebola and the Ravages of History.* New York: Farrar, Strauss, and Giroux, 2020.

Gomez-Temesio, V. "Outliving Death: Ebola, Zombies, and the Politics of Saving Lives." *American Anthropologist* 120, no. 4 (2018): 738–751. https://doi.org/10.1111/aman.13126.

Gray, D., D. Himmelgreen, and N. Romero-Daza. "Anthropological Engagement with COVID-19." *Human Organization* 79, no. 4 (2020): 247–249.

Gross, C. P., U. R. Essien, S. Pasha, et al. "Racial and Ethnic Disparities in Population-Level Covid-19 Mortality." *Journal of General Internal Medicine* 35, no. 10 (2020): 3097–3099. https://doi.org/10.1007/s11606-020-06081-w.

Grubaugh, N. D., S. Saraf, K. Gangavarapu, et al. "Travel Surveillance and Genomics Uncover a Hidden Zika Outbreak during the Waning Epidemic." *Cell* 178 (2019): 1057–1071. https://doi.org/10.1016/j.cell.2019.07.018.

Gurven, M., H. Kaplan, and A. Zelada Supa. "Mortality Experience of Tsimane Amerindians of Bolivia: Regional Variation and Temporal Trends." *American Journal of Human Biology* 19 (2007): 376–398. https://doi.org/10.1002/ajhb.20600.

Harper, K., and G. Armelagos. "The Changing Disease-Scape in the Third Epidemiological Transition." *International Journal of Environmental Research and Public Health* 7 (2010): 675–697. https://doi.org/10.3390/ijerph7020675.

Herrera, J. P., N. R. Wickenkamp, M. Turpin, et al. "Effects of Land Use, Habitat Characteristics, and Small Mammal Community Composition on Leptospira Prevalence in Northeast Madagascar." *PLoS Neglected Tropical Diseases* 14, no. 12 (2020): e0008946. https://doi.org/10.1371/journal.pntd.0008946.

Houck, K. M., E. Terán, J. Ochoa, et al. "Drinking Water Improvements and Rates of Urinary and Gastrointestinal Infections in Galápagos, Ecuador: Assessing Household and Community Factors." *American Journal of Human Biology* 32, no. 1 (2019): e23358. https://doi.org/10.1002/ajhb.23358.

Hurtado, A. M., M. A. Frey, I. Hurtado, et al. "The Role of Helminthes in Human Evolution: Implications for Global Health in the Twenty-First Century." In *Medicine and Evolution: Current Applications, Future Prospects.* Edited by S. Elton and P. O'Higgins, 151–178. New York: Taylor and Francis, 2008.

Janes, C. R., R. Stall, and S. M. Gifford, eds. *Anthropology and Epidemiology: Interdisciplinary Approaches to the Study of Health and Disease*, Dordrecht/Boston: D. Reidel, 1986.

Kamorudeen, R. T., K. A. Adedokun, and A. O. Olarinmoye. "Ebola Outbreak in West Africa, 2014–2016: Epidemic Timeline, Differential Diagnoses, Determining Factors, and Lessons for Future Response." *Journal of Infection and Public Health* 13, no. 7 (2020): 956–962. https://doi.org/10.1016/j.jiph.2020.03.014.

Kim, Y. C., B. Dema, and A. Reyes-Sandoval. "COVID-19 Vaccines: Breaking Record Times to First-in-Human Trials." *NPJ Vaccines* 5 (2020): 34. https://doi.org/10.1038/s41541-020-0188-3.

Kubin, L. "Is There a Resurgence of Vaccine Preventable Diseases in the US?" *Journal of Pediatric Nursing* 44 (2019): 115–118. https://doi.org/10.1016/j.pedn.2018.11.011.

Leask, J. "Vaccines – Lessons from Three Centuries of Protest." *Nature* 585, no. 7826 (2020): 499–502. https://doi.org/10.1038/d41586-020-02671-0.

Leendertz, S. A. J., J. F. Gogarten, A. Düx, et al. "Assessing the Evidence Supporting Fruit Bats as the Primary Reservoirs for Ebola Viruses." *EcoHealth* 131 (2016): 18–25. https://doi.org/10.1007/s10393-015-1053-0.

Lippi, D., and E. Gotuzzo. "The Greatest Steps Towards the Discovery of Vibrio Cholerae." *Clinical Microbiology and Infection* 20 (2014): 191–195. https://doi.org/10.1111/1469-0691.12390.

Littleton, J., and R. King. "The Political Ecology of Tuberculosis in Auckland: An Interdisciplinary Focus." In *Multiplying and Dividing: Tuberculosis in Canada and Aotearoa New Zealand.* Edited by J. Littleton, J. Parks, D. A. Herring, and T. Farmer, Research in Anthropology and Linguistics 3(3):43–53. New Zealand: University of Auckland, Department of Anthropology. Electronic document, 2008, https://www.researchgate.net/publication/37986664_Multiplying_and_dividing_tuberculosis_in_Canada_and_Aotearoa_New_Zealand.

Lowe, R., C. Varcellos, P. Brasil, et al. "The Zika Virus Epidemic in Brazil: From Discovery to Future Implications." *International Journal of Environmental Research in Public Health* 15 (2018): 96. https://doi.org/10.3390/ijerph15010096.

Mamelund, S. E., L. Sattenspiel, and J. Dimka. "Influenza Associated Mortality during the 1918-19 Influenza Pandemic in Alaska and Labrador: A Comparison." *Social Science History* 37, no. 2 (2013): 177–229. https://doi.org/10.1215/01455532-2074420.

Manderson, L., "Applying Medical Anthropology in the Control of Infectious Disease." *Tropical Medicine & International Health* 3, no. 12 (1998): 1020–1027. https://doi.org/10.1046/j.1365-3156.1998.00334.x.

Martineau, F., A. Wilkinson, and M. Parker. "Epistemologies of Ebola: Reflections on the Experience of the Ebola Response Anthropology Platform." *Anthropological Quarterly* 90, no. 2 (2017): 475–494. 10.1353/anq.2017.0027.

McDonald, J. C. "The History of Quarantine in Britain During the 19th Century." *Bulletin of the History of Medicine* 25, no. 1 (1951): 22–44. https://www.jstor.org/stable/44443588.

Minor, O. M. "Ebola and Accusation: Gender and Stigma in Sierra Leone's Ebola Response." *Anthropology in Action* 24, no. 2 (2017): 25–35. https://doi.org/10.3167/aia.2017.240204.

Moran, M. H. "Missing Bodies and Secret Funerals: The Production of 'Safe and Dignified Burials' in the Liberian Ebola Crisis." *Anthropological Quarterly* 90, no. 2 (2017): 399–421. https://doi.org/10.1353/anq.2017.0024.

Mordecai, E. A., J. M. Caldwell, M. K. Grossman, et al. "Thermal Biology of Mosquito-Borne Disease." *Ecology Letters* 22 (2019): 1690–1708. https://doi.org/10.1111/ele.13335.

Mordecai, E. A., S. J. Ryan, J. M. Caldwell, et al. "Climate Change Could Shift Disease Burden from Malaria to Arboviruses in Africa." *Lancet Planetary Health* 4 (2020): e416–e423. https://doi.org/10.1016/S2542-5196(20)30178-9.

Morse, S. S., ed. *Emerging Viruses*, Oxford: Oxford University Press, 1993.

Musso, D., and D. J. Gubler. "Zika Virus." *Clinical Microbiology Reviews* 29, no. 3 (2016): 487–524. https://doi.org/10.1128/CMR.00072-15.

National Institutes of Health (NIH). *NIH Clinical Trial of Investigational Vaccine for COVID-19 Begins.* Electronic Document, 2020. https://www.nih.gov/news-events/news-releases/nih-clinical-trial-investigational-vaccine-covid-19-begins.

Neel, J. V. "Diabetes Mellitus: A 'Thrifty' Genotype Rendered Detrimental by Progress?" *American Journal of Human Genetics* 14 (1962): 353–362.

Ocobock, C., and C. D. Lynn. "Human Biology is a Matter of Life or Death: Effective Science Communication for COVID-19 Research." *American Journal of Human Biology* 32 (2020): e23472. https://doi.org/10.1002/ajhb.23472.

Oeschger, T.M., D. S. McCloskey, R. M. Buchmann, et al. "Early Warning Diagnostics for Emerging Infectious Diseases in Developing into Late-Stage Pandemics." *Accounts of Chemical Research* 54 (2021): 3656–3666. https://doi.org/10.1021/acs.accounts.1c00383.

Omran, A. R. "The Epidemiological Transition." *Millbank Memorial Fund Quarterly* 49 (1971): 509–538.

Petrovan, S. O., D. C. Aldridge, H. Bartlett, et al. "Post COVID-19: A Solution Scan of Options for Preventing Future Zoonotic Epidemics." *Biological Reviews* 96 (2021): 2694–2715. http://dx.doi.org/10.1111/brv.12774.

Plourde, A. R., and E. M. Bloch. "A Literature Review of Zika Virus." *Emerging Infectious Diseases* 22, no. 7 (2016): 1185–1192. http://dx.doi.org/10.3201/eid2207.151990.

Randrianasolo, L., Y. Raoelina, M. Ratsitorahina, et al. "Sentinel Surveillance System for Early Outbreak Detection in Madagascar." *BMC Public Health* 10 (2010): 31. http://www.biomedcentral.com/1471-2458/10/31.

Rewar, S., and D. Mirdha. "Transmission of Ebola Virus Disease: An Overview." *Annals of Global Health* 80, no. 6 (2014): 444–451. http://dx.doi.org/10.1016/j.aogh.2015.02.005.

Rugarabamu, S., L. Mboera, M. Rweyemamu, et al. "Forty-Two Years of Responding to Ebola Virus Outbreaks in Sub-Saharan Africa: A Review." *BMJ Global Health* 5, no. 3 (2020): e001955. http://dx.doi.org/10.1136/bmjgh-2019-001955.

Ryan, S. J., C. J. Carlson, E. A. Mordecai, et al. "Global Expansion and Redistribution of Aedes-Borne Virus Transmission Risk with Climate Change." *PLoS Neglected Tropical Diseases* 13, no. 3 (2019): e007213. https://doi.org/10.1371/journal.pntd.0007213.

Sawchuk, L. A., and L. Tripp. "Managing an Epidemic in Imperfect Times: Encampment and Immunity Passes in 19th Century Gibraltar." *BMJ Global Health* 6 (2021): 006713. http://dx.doi.org/10.1136/bmjgh-2021-006713.

Schwartz, J. L. "New Media, Old Messages: Themes in the History of Vaccine Hesitancy and Refusal." *AMA Journal of Ethics* 14, no. 1 (2012): 50–55.

Sims, N., and B. Kasprzyk-Hordern. "Future Perspectives of Wastewater-Based Epidemiology: Monitoring Infectious Disease Spread and Resistance to the Community Level." *Environment International* 139 (2020): 105689. https://doi.org/10.1016/j.envint.2020.105689.

Singer, M., and B. Rylko-Bauer. "The Syndemics and Structural Violence of the COVID Pandemic: Anthropological Insights on a Crisis." *Open Anthropological Research* 1 (2021): 7–32. https://doi.org/10.1515/opan-2020-0100.

Smith-Morris, C. "Epidemiological Placism in Public Health Emergencies: Ebola in Two Dallas Neighborhoods." *Social Science & Medicine* 179 (2017): 106–114. http://dx.doi.org/10.1016/j.socscimed.2017.02.036.

Sobo, E. J. "Theorizing (Vaccine) Refusal: Through the Looking Glass." *Cultural Anthropology* 31, no. 3 (2016): 342–350. http://dx.doi.org/10.14506/ca31.3.04.

Szathmáry, E. J. E. "Non-Insulin Dependent Diabetes Mellitus among Aboriginal North Americans." *Annual Review of Anthropology* 23 (1994): 457–482.

The Lancet Infectious Diseases. "COVID-19 Vaccine Equity and Booster Doses." *Lancet Infectious Diseases* 21 (2021): 743. https://doi.org/10.1016/S1473-3099(21)00486-2.

Trostle, J. A. *Epidemiology and Culture*, Cambridge: Cambridge University Press, 2006.

van Doren, T. P., and L. Sattenspiel. "The 1918 Influenza Pandemic Did Not Accelerate Tuberculosis Mortality Decline in Early-Twentieth Century Newfoundland: Investigating Historical and Social Explanations." *American Journal of Physical Anthropology* 176, no. 2 (2021): 179–191. http://dx.doi.org/10.1002/ajpa.24332.

Venables, E., and U. Pellecchia. "Engaging Anthropology in an Ebola Outbreak: Case Studies from West Africa." *Anthropology in Action* 24, no. 2 (2017): 1–8. https://doi.org/10.3167/aia.2017.240201.

World Health Organization (WHO). *Vector-Borne Diseases. Electronic Document*, 2020. https://www.who.int/news-room/fact-sheets/detail/vector-borne-diseases.

World Health Organization (WHO). *WHO Coronavirus (COVID-19) Dashboard. Electronic Document*, 2022, https://covid19.who.int.

CHAPTER 11

Evolutionary Insights into the Social and Environmental Drivers of Health Inequality: The Example of the Global Epidemic of Overweight and Cardiovascular Diseases

Christopher W. Kuzawa and Melissa B. Manus

Evolutionary Insights into Obesity and CVD: Moving Beyond "Thrifty Genes" as Adaptations to Famine

Cardiovascular diseases (CVDs) like hypertension, diabetes, heart attack, and stroke are now the leading causes of premature death globally, which has been tied to the rapid global rise of overweight and obesity as major public health issues. As individuals gain excess weight, this can lead to a constellation of metabolic disruptions that include elevated blood pressure, insulin resistance, poor glucose control and diabetes, changes in cholesterol profiles, and inflammation (Jayedi et al. 2020). These in turn elevate risk for outcomes like heart attack, stroke, and renal failure. In 2016, it was estimated that nearly two billion adults were overweight or obese, with those numbers projected to increase to nearly three billion by 2025 (Collaboration 2016). This represents a tripling of obesity prevalence – and a correspondingly rapid rise in the burden of CVDs – in recent generations.

A Companion to Biological Anthropology, Second Edition. Edited by Clark Spencer Larsen.

Sixty years ago, Neel (1962) proposed an evolutionary explanation to shed light on the rapid modern emergence of widespread obesity and metabolic diseases. He argued that, prior to the domestication of crops and development of agricultural subsistence, human ancestors would have been faced with cycles of "feast" and "famine" that would have selected for a genetic capacity to deposit body fat. Given what he perceived to be the unpredictable nature of food availability in natural ecologies, Neel suggested that a "thrifty" metabolism that efficiently stores excess dietary energy as stored fat when food was abundant would have provided a survival edge during later periods of shortage. By this reasoning, genes contributing to metabolic traits that encourage fat deposition during periods of nutritional abundance would have allowed survival during subsequent periods of famine, and thus become more common in the human gene pool. These genetic traits that evolved as adaptations to periodic food shortage are now thrust into modern environments in which there is often a persistent surplus of calorie-dense foods, thus leading to cumulative weight gain.

The idea that humans are adapted to cycles of feast–famine has intuitive appeal and continues to be cited widely in textbooks and the medical literature focused on the causes of obesity (Moini 2020; Wadden et al. 2018). Despite this, there is little evidence to support the idea that famine was an important force of selection on human metabolism during much of hominin evolution (Benyshek and Watson 2006; Kuzawa 2010). One line of evidence comes from ecological studies among contemporary hunter–gatherers, who do not rely on industrialized market-based food economies and share presumed dietary and lifestyle similarities with ancestral hominin populations. Anthropological research shows that these groups use a wide and flexible array of foraged and hunted foods, including "fallback foods" that may be used as backup food sources when more favorable foods are scarce. Elaborate forms of food sharing and cooperation are also hallmarks of social organization in modern human foragers and are assumed to have been important among hominin ancestors pursuing a similar foraging strategy. The breadth and flexibility of the human diet, combined with the universal practice of food sharing, would have provided important insurance against extreme or periodic food shortages in early foragers.

In fact, the routine threat of feast–famine cycles is believed to have emerged more recently with the rise of agriculture and reliance upon a smaller variety of more intensively harvested crops. This is supported by skeletal evidence from archaeological sites that straddle the origins of agriculture, which generally point to a deterioration in health as hunter–gatherers adopted a sedentary, agricultural lifestyle (Cohen et al. 1984; Larsen 1995). Finally, there is no evidence that contemporary foragers living a traditional lifestyle, and with a traditional foraged diet, put on excess fat during periods of abundance as Neel's theory presumes. Indeed, most studies of contemporary foragers report that these populations tend to be very lean, even when healthy and well-nourished (Howell 2010).

In this chapter we review current research that is helping revise understandings of the evolutionary forces and processes that are contributing to the rise of overweight and metabolic disease. To that end, we first review recent updates to our understanding of the role of diet and activity – reflecting the major influences on energy intake and expenditure – to these conditions, with work increasingly pointing to the primacy of diet and diet composition as major influences on weight gain. We then discuss newer evidence that one's risk for gaining excess weight, and the metabolic and health impacts triggered by that weight gain, may be modified by a range of biological but nongenetic processes that include developmental plasticity, epigenetic sensitivity, and the gut microbiome. These environmentally sensitive pathways can modify one's risk for gaining weight, while also altering how biological systems respond to that weight gain to drive disease development. As we will discuss, these newer understandings of contributing pathways demonstrate biological sensitivities that interact with, and come to embody, the cumulative impact of the environments that we inhabit and experience. They influence disease risk in the exposed generation, but can in some instances also have nongenetic but biological effects on development that may be transmitted to offspring to influence disease risk across multiple generations.

These newly appreciated domains of biology not only help explain the rise of obesity generally, but also clarify why these conditions differentially impact lower socioeconomic or minoritized subgroups in high income societies. They also shed light on the common tendency for lower- and middle-income countries (LMICs) to be particularly hard hit with a rapid increase in CVD in the span of a mere generation or two in response to lifestyle and diet transition. We conclude with a discussion of some of the historical and policy developments that have played an important role in shaping contemporary diets, and associated social and health inequities. This review underscores the need to prioritize structural and policy change, rather than targeting individual behavior, if we hope to reduce the mismatch between our evolved biology and modern lifestyle and attenuate the public health impact of these conditions.

Background Primer: Why High Heritabilities for a Trait Tell us Nothing About the Causes of Inequality in the Burden of Disease Between Groups

In this chapter, we have the task of explaining differences in disease risk through time, as environments change rapidly, or between groups that are faced with markedly distinct environments and experiences. At the outset, it is important to point out the common but erroneous tendency to view group-level health inequality as tracing to genes rather than to differences in experiences. As a common example of this, in the United States, Americans with African ancestry tend to have higher rates of hypertension compared to Americans with predominantly European or Asian family backgrounds. Through the years, many physicians and medical researchers have assumed – incorrectly – that this difference has a genetic basis (Pickering 2001). In fact, Wilson and Grim (1991) went so far as to propose that this predisposition may have resulted from the African slave trade itself. Their idea is that the high mortality related to salt-depletion during captivity on the long sea voyage would have increased survival of those individuals with salt-retaining genes, which would now increase genetic hypertension risk in today's salt-rich environment among their descendants. This so-called "slavery hypertension hypothesis" has been widely discussed in medical textbooks despite having little basis in the peer-reviewed scientific literature (Kaufman and Hall 2003), while historical, evolutionary, and biological evidence all soundly undermine its premise (Armelagos 2005; Poston et al. 2001). This is one example of how assumptions about the genetic basis of a health condition can conflate genes and ethnicity or socially defined race and, in doing so, obscure the role of social and physical environments in structuring health inequities.

How does the idea that genes contribute to health *inequality* prove insufficient? On the one hand, genes and genetic heritability clearly influence *all* aspects of human biology and disease risk to varying degrees. With the example of hypertension, studies typically calculate heritabilities for blood pressure of 0.5–0.6, which indicates that genetic variants account for 50–60 percent of the variance in these traits within any given population (Snieder et al. 2003).

Because genes and environments collectively explain all trait variance, these heritabilities also imply that the other 40–50 percent of variance in these traits trace to the environment. Although informative about the biological contributions to a disease in a specific population, the way that heritabilities are calculated limits their utility for inferring the causes of differences in disease burden *between* groups. Heritabilities are calculated by comparing traits in closely related individuals, such as parents and offspring, or by comparing the strength of correlations between a trait in mono- versus dizygotic twins. Such studies can only detect an impact of the range of environmental variation that distinguishes such closely related individuals. As a helpful thought experiment, it is in theory possible for a trait like blood pressure to have nearly 100 percent heritability *within* two groups (owing to the fact that environments and experiences within each group are largely shared and similar between individuals), but for differences in the average experiences and environments *between* those groups to drive even large group-level inequalities in disease burden. This hypothetical example illustrates why it is important to not interpret evidence for high heritabilities for a disease (a within-group measure) as evidence that genes likely drive inequalities in that disease (a between-group measure).

Additional problems with assuming that genes underlie health disparities come from the way that individuals are categorized, which almost always reflects cultural, socioeconomic, and historical forces rather than an objective grounding in genetic ancestry. Again using the US as an illustration, the "race" to which an individual is labeled is based largely upon social criteria that have little grounding in genetics, such as the tendency to see any evidence of admixture of African ancestry as a basis for labeling that individual as Black or African American, even if the majority of their genes are descended from European ancestors (the so-called "one drop rule" or hypodescent; Harris 1964). Further, the true genetic ancestry of people deemed non-White is often obfuscated by the use of phenotypic traits to determine race. This is particularly salient in the example of using skin color, a characteristic that exists on a spectrum, to group people of varied ancestry into broad racial categories like Black or Brown. However, while there is generally little evidence for genetic contributions to major health inequalities related to conditions like weight gain and metabolic disease, there is an extensive and ever-growing public health literature documenting the importance of *social determinants* of these health patterns (Braveman et al. 2011). For example, we know that chronic activation of stress physiology has myriad effects, from influencing regulation of immunity and inflammation, to mobilizing glucose, elevating blood pressure, altering patterns of fat deposition, and even affecting appetite and caloric intake. As such, when experiences of chronic stress vary by dimensions of experience, like social status, gender, sexuality, or socially imposed race, this can contribute to persistent health differences across these groups.

In this chapter, we are concerned primarily with the evolved, biological mechanisms that link human social and environmental experiences to weight gain, and that also influence how weight gain negatively impacts health through effects on outcomes like diabetes and heart disease. We approach weight gain as a biological response to environmental inputs that is influenced, but not primarily driven by, genes. As we will see, recent research has started to provide a firmer foundation for understanding the evolutionary roots of weight gain and CVDs. As an example of one line of this work, there is growing evidence that the dietary environment matters; for example, the quantity of calories may be more important to weight gain than levels of physical activity or energy expenditure. In turn, evolutionary perspectives are showing how the composition of our diet, such as the relative proportions of fats, carbohydrates, and protein, may be particularly important as an influence on how much we eat. We will further see that there are multiple biological means, operating for instance through maternal nutrients or hormones during pregnancy or through the gut microbiome, by which weight gain in one generation can increase risk for similar adverse health outcomes in future generations. Understanding these pathways and their evolution helps us to understand the complex biological processes that link inequalities in metabolic and chronic disease burden to social, political, and economic realities that shape diet, lifestyle, and experience.

Beyond Thrifty Genes: Newer Evolutionary Perspectives into the Rise of Weight Gain and CVD

Is Dietary Intake or Physical Activity More Important to Weight Gain?

Because each gram of fat represents 9 kcal of stored energy, weight gain requires that the calories consumed exceed those expended on other body functions. Thus, research into the origins of obesity has been dominated by an energetic model in which rising food intake, reduced energy expenditure, or both, are assumed to drive chronic energy excess, leading to weight gain (Ulijaszek and Lofink 2006). Although there have been debates about the relative importance of changing intake and expenditure to weight gain, recent work has led to the surprising insight that total energy expenditure (TEE) looks almost identical in populations from widely varied settings. Using the doubly labeled water method, studies show similar TEE across relatively sedentary populations from high income subsets of the US, but also in rural settings and among highly active hunter–gatherers (Pontzer et al. 2012; Urlacher et al. 2021). What this work shows is that, despite remarkable differences in the level of physical activity and calories burned through exercise, the *total* energy expended by these populations is basically the same. This work underscores that physical activity is just one of the many functions to which energy is allocated in the body, and that increases in activity tend to be matched by proportionate decreases in other functions, with no net change in total expenditure.

Based upon these findings, it has recently been argued that it is excess caloric intake – above the total expenditure on the body's functions – that drives excess weight gain. If this model is correct, what accounts for individual or group-level differences in how many calories are consumed? On the one hand, we know that experiences like stress can motivate appetite and increase intake (Adam and Epel 2007). It is widely appreciated that the availability of inexpensive, high calorie foods is likely to be important (Popkin et al. 2012), and recent work is showing how recent shifts in the composition of the diet in particular may play a key role. Work in a range of species has shown that animals often eat to reach a target level of protein intake (Mayntz et al. 2005). As the composition of the diet shifts, and especially as the concentration of protein versus other macronutrients changes, this means that individuals will need to eat more or less of that food to reach the same protein target. Experiments in which humans were given diets of varying nutrient composition generally support the idea that they tend to eat to meet protein requirements (Gosby et al. 2011; Simpson et al. 2003; Skov et al. 1999). For instance, in one experiment, human volunteers were fed foods that were either high or low in protein (Simpson et al. 2003). On the low protein diet, they ended up eating more total calories than on their regular diet, and with findings the opposite on the high protein diet. These findings support a model in which people will tend to eat more as the protein content of their diet goes down, which could help explain why high fat or high carbohydrate foods tend to be associated with larger portion sizes and increased total energy intake (Martinez Steele et al. 2018). As we will return to later, this work points to the wide availability and affordability of highly caloric but low protein foods, and the policies that reinforce this availability, as a potentially important culprit in population differences in weight gain.

The Developmental Origins of Health and Disease (DOHaD) Framework

Excess weight gain has public health relevance owing to the many adverse health effects that it can trigger. As individuals gain weight, skeletal muscle and other tissues may become insulin resistant, which elevates glucose levels and increases the risk for type 2 (adult-onset) diabetes. Weight gain is also associated with other biological changes like elevated blood pressure, which can contribute directly to the risk of heart attack and stroke. Adipose tissue can also harbor immune cells called macrophages, which secrete signals that trigger inflammation throughout the body. Inflammation is an important means by which the body defends itself against infection, and is also crucial to other processes like repairing tissues or organs. However, when chronically elevated, inflammation can carry costs in the form of oxidative damage and aging.

These various examples illustrate why gaining excess weight tends to increase risk for a wide range of chronic degenerative diseases, most notably including cardiovascular diseases (CVDs). In recent decades it has become clear that the biological response of the body to weight gain, and the intensity of the biological changes that are induced, may be modified in response to one's nutrition much earlier in the lifecycle, and even prior to birth. Starting in the late 1980s, the British epidemiologist David Barker and his colleagues started to show that risk for CVDs not only is elevated by being overweight as an adult – which we have known for some time – but also in relation to being born small or thin (Barker et al. 1989). Barker showed that an individual's risk for conditions like diabetes, hypertension, heart attacks, and stroke relates inversely to their birth weight. Because nutrition is a major influence on fetal growth rate, they hypothesized that the level of prenatal nutrition might influence long-term risk for developing chronic diseases by altering development of organs like the liver and kidneys. Since then, experiments in species like rats and sheep have shown that restricting the diet during fetal development can replicate many of these findings. Collectively this work on the "developmental origins of health and disease" (DOHaD) has shown that the so-called "diseases of overnutrition" are also linked to lower nutrition experienced prior to birth or early in infancy (Benyshek et al. 2001; Gluckman and Hanson 2006).

Consistent with this general framework, in human studies there is evidence that the risks of adverse health outcomes that accompany weight gain and obesity tend to be more pronounced among individuals who experienced reduced nutrition and slow fetal growth during prenatal life. As an analog to Neel's thrifty genotype, Hales and Barker (1992) proposed that prenatal undernutrition could thus induce a "thrifty phenotype," operating not through inherited genes but through developmental responses to *in utero* conditions of undernutrition that persist into later life to influence risk for weight gain and conditions like diabetes. This set of findings inspired more general speculation that the fetus might use maternal nutrition as a "cue" to predict the level of nutrition that it is likely to experience after birth: if conditions are similar to those predictions, this would result in favorable health, but in the event that postnatal conditions exceed those expectations this could then lead to a distinct form of "mismatch" – this type based not in genes but in development – that elevates risk for metabolic disease (Bateson 2001; Gluckman and Hanson 2004).

Much like the original thrifty genotype hypothesis, this hypothesis has an intuitive appeal and has generated much discussion and interest in both the scientific and popular literatures. Also like the thrifty genotype, tests of the hypothesis have generally not supported it

(Lea et al. 2017). Studies have shown, for instance, that experiencing poor nutrition early in life has negative consequences for later health and genetic fitness, irrespective of whether favorable or lean conditions are experienced. This is not what we would expect if early undernutrition increased one's ability to thrive in lean conditions later. Instead, it suggests that biological adaptations to early nutritional insufficiency may be primarily geared toward surviving early life conditions (Kuzawa and Quinn 2009), or alternatively that early under-nutrition simply impairs development in nonadaptive ways that have lingering, adverse effects on later function and health (Hayward et al. 2013).

Irrespective of whether these effects are adaptive in some sense, what is clear is that the biological and health consequences of rapid weight gain will tend to vary inversely in rela-tion to one's weight at birth. This means that socioeconomic conditions that juxtapose rapid childhood or adult weight gain with poor early life nutrition can lead to a particularly rapid rise of chronic diseases like CVD. This can occur, for instance, because the causes of infancy undernutrition in many LMICs tend to relate to issues like water quality and risk for infectious diseases like diarrheal illnesses that are the major causes of nutritional stress at this age (Kuzawa 2007). As immune systems gradually develop and are better capable of pro-tecting against these pathogens by childhood, these nutritional impacts are greatly reduced. At the same time, exposure to higher fat or low protein diets may increase the potential for weight gain, even among individuals whose growth faltered due to infections earlier in life. In this way, the broader adoption of so-called "Western" diets, or those common in the Global North, that are high in carbohydrates and fats may lead to an especially rapid rise in chronic metabolic disease in populations in the Global South.

In addition to the effects of undernutrition as an amplifier of the negative health impacts of rapid weight gain, there are also distinct and arguably even more important effects of being born at the other end of the birth weight distribution – being born larger than normal. This is in fact one important means by which overweight and obesity in one gen-eration can elevate risk for developing those same outcomes in the next generation. This works through a process of nongenetic but biological inheritance. When a mother is over-weight or obese during pregnancy, she will tend to have elevated glucose during pregnancy. This increases delivery of glucose across the placenta, which stimulates fetal growth and increases the size and body fat of the newborn. Exposure to high levels of glucose in utero also has the effect of modifying that individual's metabolism to increase their own risk of excess postnatal weight gain and obesity. In this way, conditions that increase the chances of obesity in one generation can lead to increased risk of obesity in the next – not simply because they inherit a similar obesogenic postnatal environment, but also because they are exposed to an obesogenic intrauterine environment in which glucose levels are dysregulated and unusually high.

The Role of the Microbiome

Another factor that influences how the body responds to a particular diet or lifestyle is the gut microbiome (GM), the collection of microorganisms (and their genes) that inhabit the human gut. The GM mediates interactions with myriad factors in the environment and dietary differences between individuals are linked to marked variation in the GM. In an experimental study that introduced different diets to study participants, researchers detected variation in microbial community composition and gene expression between indi-viduals consuming plant-based and animal-based diets (David et al. 2014). Global compar-ative studies report similar results. Tanzanians who practice a hunter–gatherer subsistence strategy harbor different gut microbial communities than individuals living in the USA, including an increased capacity for digesting plant carbohydrates (Smits et al. 2017). The ability to adjust the GM's composition in response to dietary changes may reflect the importance of dietary flexibility for survival in ancestral hominin lifeways. If fluctuations in food availability and quality are buffered by a GM that responds to changing environmental conditions, then plasticity in the composition and function of the GM may have played a considerable role in the evolution of human dietary flexibility (Amato et al. 2019).

How does the GM affect the relationship between host dietary variation, energy, and weight gain? Since certain aspects of our diet directly feed the GM, changes to what we eat can also alter our microbial communities. For example, dietary fiber is a key compound that serves as a carbon source for gut microbes, yet is significantly reduced in Western-style diets that are increasingly being adopted globally. Reduced dietary fiber leads to considerable differences in GM composition and diversity (De Filippo et al. 2010; Obregon-Tito et al. 2015), some of which can only be reversed if both dietary fiber *and* specific microbial taxa are reintroduced into the gut (Sonnenburg et al. 2016). This suggests a mismatch scenario in which gut microbes do not receive the dietary inputs that are required to maintain a balanced community, leading to a disturbed state of *dysbiosis*. Experimental studies in animal models support this notion. Mice fed a soybean oil-infused diet exhibited marked changes in their GM, including an enrichment in microbial taxa and metabolic pathways that are associated with atherosclerosis and CVD in humans (Korach-Rechtman et al. 2020). Similarly, a high-fat/low-fiber diet led to compositional changes in the GM of pigs, including elevated abundances of microbial taxa that are linked to type 2 diabetes (Heinritz et al. 2016). This mismatch-induced dysbiosis may contribute to the elevated incidence of obesity and metabolic syndrome in Global North populations who consume a low fiber/ high fat diet (Howarth et al. 2001), as well as populations in other parts of the world whose exposure to a Western-style diet is increasing (Agyemang et al. 2015; Luhar et al. 2020; Wu et al. 2021).

As microbes break down compounds in our diet, they also extract energy that may be stored by the host in adipose tissue (Bäckhed et al. 2004). There is growing evidence that the elevated energy harvest that is associated with obesity is in part modulated by the GM. In seminal work by Turnbaugh et al. (2006), germ-free mice (that lack their own GM) received gut microbes either from obese or lean mice. The mice who received microbes from obese donors gained significantly more weight than their counterparts, despite no increase in food consumption. The GM's effect on host energy and weight gain is largely mediated by bioactive nutrients, including short-chain fatty acids (SCFAs) that are produced during microbial fermentation of dietary compounds. Certain SCFAs can activate a pathway in the liver that improves glycemic control (den Besten et al. 2013), while others can induce obesity and insulin resistance (Perry et al. 2016). Altered SCFA profiles have been detected in obese humans compared to lean individuals (see Angelakis et al. 2012), which is intriguing given that SCFAs can both stimulate (Larraufie et al. 2018) and suppress (Frost et al. 2014) host appetite. If the diversity of dietary components helps shape GM activity and host energy balance, then a thorough understanding of disparities in obesity and metabolic syndrome must consider the drivers of variation in food access, availability, and consumption, which we discuss in more detail below.

Since the GM plays an important role in regulating our physiology and metabolism, many researchers are now interested in understanding how we first acquire our microbes in early life. In line with the DOHaD model, there is evidence that early life environments, beginning *in utero*, affect both short- and long-term health outcomes related to the GM (Amato et al. 2021). A key finding from studies of the vertical (mother to fetus or infant) transmission of microbe-mediated phenotypes is that pregnant individuals display decreased

GM diversity in the third trimester of pregnancy. In a study that transplanted microbes from individuals in their first and third trimesters of pregnancy into healthy germ-free mice, those who received the third trimester GM displayed insulin resistance and adiposity (Koren et al. 2012). Intriguingly, individuals in this study with prepregnancy obesity experienced the most dramatic reduction in microbial diversity in the third trimester. This suggests a cascade of effects through which an individual's physiology and nutritional environment influences their GM during pregnancy, which can then directly affect their offspring's GM. There is also evidence that maternal metabolites, such as folate produced by Bifidobacteria, can influence the epigenetics of fetal intestinal cells and adipocytes, which in turn shapes the expression of genes that influence lipid metabolism and fat storage (Mischke and Plösch 2013). Further, maternal microbes continue to shape the assembly of the infant GM during infancy and childhood (Asnicar et al. 2017; Ferretti et al. 2018; Korpela et al. 2018; Lou et al. 2021): for instance, offspring of overweight or obese mothers have been shown to have altered GM composition (Collado et al. 2010; Kalliomäki et al. 2008), including lower levels of beneficial bacteria that predict reduced weight gain among children (Luoto et al. 2011).

THE SOCIAL, POLITICAL, HISTORICAL, AND ECONOMIC DETERMINANTS OF CONTEMPORARY DIET AND LIFESTYLE

Our discussion of the biology of obesity has focused on pathways that result in weight gain and that alter the body's biological response to that weight gain. In general, work is highlighting the importance of diet composition to caloric intake and weight gain, which has variable effects that are modified by factors like prenatal experiences and the gut microbiome. This work is emphasizing the importance of shifts in diet composition, which tend to stray from the types of low-fat/high-fiber foods typically available to foraging populations in natural ecologies, and increasingly include refined nutrients like simple sugars and saturated fats. Collectively, this dietary change is driving mismatches between contemporary food environments and our evolved metabolism and physiology, leading to greater total caloric intake and increased weight gain. Importantly, these mismatches also extend to more recently described physiological pathways that mediate our interactions with the surrounding environment, including developmental plasticity, epigenetic sensitivity, and the malleability of the gut microbiome. In light of these factors, we next turn to what drives variation in diet across individuals and populations. We explore some of the historical and political dimensions of this question in the United States, where the ongoing epidemic of overweight and obesity is intricately linked to agricultural and food policies as well as systemic inequities. This review highlights the need for structural, policy-based changes rather than a focus on modifying individual behavior related to diet or physical activity.

Since 1933, the US government has shaped agriculture, rural development, and nutrition programs (Ayazi and Elsheikh 2015) through the Farm Bill, which influences agricultural production by providing subsidies to farmers who grow certain crops. As a result, 96 percent of cropland in the US is dedicated to growing only eight main crops, with corn and soybeans accounting for roughly 60 percent of that crop area (Jackson et al. 2009). This leads to the mass production of soybean oil and high-fructose corn syrup (HFCS), which are then used extensively in inexpensive, high-fat/high-sugar food items, including soft drinks, frozen meals, condiments, canned goods, desserts, and cereals. Experimental studies in rats show that a diet high in HFCS leads to weight gain, an increase in adiposity, and elevated circulating triglyceride levels (Bocarsly et al. 2010), just as a maternal diet high in HFCS can contribute to obesity in offspring (Kisioglu and Nergiz-Unal 2020). There is also evidence that HFCS-sweetened beverages can change lipid profiles in ways that elevate CVD risk (Stanhope et al. 2015). Furthermore, subsidized corn production has led to wide availability of cheap feed for livestock, in turn resulting in easily accessible, low-cost meats that are high in fat and thus an important influence on weight gain. While meat was likely to be a critical protein source for human ancestors, and continues to be an important food item both nutritionally and culturally in many contemporary populations, the overconsumption of processed, high-fat meat is associated with elevated BMI (body mass index), waist circumference, obesity (Wang and Beydoun 2009), and type 2 diabetes (Fung et al. 2004; Vang et al. 2008). The global demand for processed meat is also rising, and fast-food chains like Kentucky Fried Chicken, Taco Bell, and McDonald's, or locally inspired emulators, are increasingly present in many African and Asian nations. Alongside changing economies and increased sedentism, accessibility of these foods, coupled with strategic marketing of the Western lifestyle, has undoubtedly contributed to the increase of obesity and metabolic disorders in the Global South (Agyemang et al. 2015; Luhar et al. 2020; Wu et al. 2021). In fact, a comparative study of 170 countries found that meat consumption was the largest predictor of overweight and obesity, independent of physical inactivity or total calorie consumption (You and Henneberg 2016).

It is crucial to emphasize that the diets that individuals eat are often dictated by structural forces and barriers, whether monetary or otherwise. In the US, wide availability of high-fat/high-sugar foods, coupled with a paucity of fresh nutritious options, are powerful contributors to inequalities in weight gain and related disease risk. "Food deserts" – areas where there is limited (or sometimes, no) availability of fresh foods – are disproportionately concentrated in low-income communities of color in the US (Block et al. 2004; Morland et al. 2002). One contributor to the emergence of food deserts was geographic and economic segregation along racial lines in the 1970s and 1980s (Alwitt et al. 1997; Guy et al. 2004). As wealthy and middle-class families moved out of cities and into the suburbs, larger supermarket chains followed. Smaller grocery stores in inner-city settings struggled to compete, causing many to close and allowing fast-food chains and convenience stores to take their place. Moreover, policies that reduce people's educational, economic, and employment opportunities limit their purchasing power, further de-incentivizing supermarkets from investing in their neighborhoods (Zenk et al. 2005). As one example, a study in the highly segregated city of New Orleans found that predominantly black neighborhoods had six times more fast-food restaurants per square mile than did white neighborhoods (Block et al. 2004). One result is that individuals in food deserts face increased exposure to obesogenic environments, including diets rich in processed, energy-dense foods and factory-farmed meats (Drewnowski and Specter 2004).

Even in areas where fresh foods are available, barriers to access can also affect people's diets. This may include limited financial resources for purchasing fresh foods, lack of a personal vehicle and/or dependence on public transportation to travel to the supermarket, or constraints on free time to be used for shopping and cooking (Rose and Richards 2004). Further, structural barriers to engaging in physical activity can also contribute to poor health outcomes. This can include a lack of public resources like sidewalks, green spaces, or streetlamps, as well as increased police presence that makes it unsafe for minoritized groups to play outdoors.

Critically, though barriers to healthy diets and active lifestyles are structural, people with obesity and metabolic disorders are often blamed for individual shortcomings, such as poor decision making or "bad genes." Instead, as we have discussed, a constellation of social, structural, and biological (but nongenetic) determinants contributes to the experience of minoritized groups living in obesogenic environments. Moving forward, it is imperative that interdisciplinary research across medicine, public health, and policymaking addresses the structural and social determinants of food environments, dietary variation, and subsequent weight gain.

Conclusion

Overweight and obesity, and the related conditions of cardiovascular diseases, rose to global prominence as causes of morbidity and mortality in the short span of several generations. This points to the overwhelming role of environments and experiences, and the mismatch between our evolved genomes and current environments, as the cause of these patterns. While early formulations of evolutionary explanations for the rise of overweight and obesity assumed that humans are afflicted by genetic adaptations to past feast–famine conditions, current work is pointing instead to a likely mismatch between ancestral and contemporary diets as important to excess caloric intake and weight gain (Figure 11.1). There is also evidence that experiences early in life, even beginning prior to birth, can influence our tendency to put on weight while also moderating the adverse health impacts of weight gain. This is seen in the finding that weight gain has more adverse effects on health among individuals who experienced reduced nutrition or growth faltering prior to birth or during infancy. This could be an especially important factor in LMICs, where common

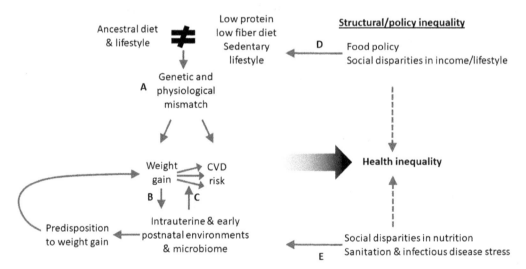

Figure 11.1   The main drivers of gene-environment mismatch and pathways of biological plasticity that contribute to the rapid modern rise and social disparities in obesity and related metabolic diseases. A. The discordance between ancestral and contemporary diets and lifestyles can result in mismatches with the human genome and microbiome. B. These mismatches promote adult weight gain that can influence a person's risk for CVD. Maternal weight gain, glucose, and related alterations in the gut microbiome can then influence the biology and health of offspring. C: Pre- and post-natal influences on physiology and the microbiome may also alter the metabolic and health impacts of any weight that is gained. D. Structural inequalities underpin the dietary and lifestyle mismatches that contribute to adult weight gain. E. Structural inequalities also directly shape early life nutritional and infectious disease environments that influence early patterns of developmental/epigenetic/microbial plasticity (*Source*: Kuzawa and Manus).

underweight and lower birth weight may be followed by rapid weight gain as energy dense foods are increasingly consumed later in childhood or adulthood. In addition, overweight or obese mothers are more likely to have elevated glucose during pregnancy, which can lead to the opposing problem of babies that are born larger than is healthy, which can increase the risk of gaining weight during childhood and beyond. We also see how the gut microbiome is shaped by dietary mismatches that also influence how likely we are to gain excess weight, with some evidence for similar intergenerational pathways linking maternal experiences to disease predisposition in the next generation.

In contemporary populations, the availability of specific food types is often powerfully shaped by food policies. In the United States, those policies reward production of foods that are high in calories but low in protein and fiber. This reduces the cost of obesogenic diets and encourages weight gain across society. Because all human populations inhabit environments that are shaped by social, political, and economic forces, these factors operate as a prism through which our changing lifestyles are refracted – patterning harmful exposures and opportunities for healthy behaviors, including access to healthy diets and opportunities to lead a physically active lifestyle. An evolutionary perspective thus emphasizes the crucial importance of structural solutions, rather than targeting individual behavior, if we hope to reduce the burden of common chronic diseases.

REFERENCES

Adam, T. C., and E. S. Epel. "Stress, Eating and the Reward System." *Physiology and Behavior* 91, no. 4 (2007): 449–458.

Agyemang, C., S. Boatemaa, G. A. Frempong, and A. Aikins. "Obesity in Sub-Saharan Africa." In *Metabolic Syndrome: A Comprehensive Textbook*. Edited by R. S. Ahima, 1–13. Switzerland: Springer International, 2016.

Alwitt, L. F., and D. Thomas. "Retail Stores in Poor Urban Neighborhoods." *Journal of Consumer Affairs* 31, no. 1 (1997): 139–164.

Amato, K. R., T. Jeyakumar, H. Poinar, et al. "Shifting Climates, Foods, and Diseases: The Human Microbiome Through Evolution." *Bioessays* 41, no. 10 (2019): e1900034.

Amato, K. R., M. C. Arrieta, M. B. Azad, et al. "The Human Gut Microbiome and Health Inequities." *Proceedings of the National Academy of Sciences of the United States of America* 118, no. 25 (2021).

Angelakis, E., F. Armougom, M. Million, et al. "The Relationship Between Gut Microbiota and Weight Gain in Humans." *Future Microbiology* 7, no. 1 (2012): 91–109.

Armelagos, G. J. "The Slavery Hypertension Hypothesis – Natural Selection and Scientific Investigation: A Commentary." *Transforming Anthropology* 13, no. 2 (2005): 119–124.

Asnicar, F., S. Manara, M. Zolfo, et al. "Studying Vertical Microbiome Transmission from Mothers to Infants by Strain-Level Metagenomic Profiling." *mSystems* 2, no. 1 (2017).

Ayazi, H., and E. Elsheikh. "The US Farm Bill: Corporate Power and Structural Racialization in the US Food System." Haas Institute, Berkeley University of California, 2015.

Bäckhed, F., H. Ding, T. Wang, et al. "The Gut Microbiota as an Environmental Factor that Regulates Fat Storage." *Proceedings of the National Academy of Sciences* 101, no. 44 (2004): 15718–15723.

Barker, D. J., C. Osmond, J. Golding, et al. "Growth in Utero, Blood Pressure in Childhood and Adult Life, and Mortality from Cardiovascular Disease." *BMJ* 298, no. 6673 (1989): 564–567.

Bateson, P. "Fetal Experience and Good Adult Design." *International Journal of Epidemiology* 30, no. 5 (2001): 928–934.

Benyshek, D. C., J. F. Martin, and C. S. Johnston. "A Reconsideration of the Origins of the Type 2 Diabetes Epidemic Among Native Americans and the Implications for Intervention Policy." *Medical Anthropology* 20, no. 1 (2001): 25–64.

Benyshek, D. C., and J. T. Watson. "Exploring the Thrifty Genotype's Food-Shortage Assumptions: A Cross-Cultural Comparison of Ethnographic Accounts of Food Security Among Foraging and Agricultural Societies." *American Journal of Physical Anthropology* 131, no. 1 (2006): 120–126.

Block, J. P., R. A. Scribner, and K. B. DeSalvo. "Fast Food, Race/Ethnicity, and Income: A Geographic Analysis." *American Journal of Preventive Medicine* 27, no. 3 (2004): 211–217.

Bocarsly, M. E., E. S. Powell, N. M. Avena, et al. "High-Fructose Corn Syrup Causes Characteristics of Obesity in Rats: Increased Body Weight, Body Fat and Triglyceride Levels." *Pharmacology Biochemistry and Behavior* 97, no. 1 (2010): 101–106.

Braveman, P., S. Egerter, and D. R. Williams. "The Social Determinants of Health: Coming of Age." *Annual Review of Public Health* 32 (2011): 381–398.

Cohen, M. N., and G. J. Armelagos. *Paleopathology at the Origins of Agriculture*. New York: Academic Press, 1984.

Collaboration, N. C. D., and R. Factor. "Trends in Adult Body-Mass Index in 200 Countries from 1975 to 2014: A Pooled Analysis of 1698 Population-Based Measurement Studies with 19.2 Million Participants." *Lancet* 387, no. 10026 (2016): 1377–1396.

Collado, M. C., E. Isolauri, K. Laitinen, et al. "Effect of Mother's Weight on Infant's Microbiota Acquisition, Composition, and Activity during Early Infancy: A Prospective Follow-Up Study Initiated in Early Pregnancy." *The American Journal of Clinical Nutrition* 92, no. 5 (2010): 1023–1030.

David, L. A., C. F. Maurice, R. N. Carmody, et al. "Diet Rapidly and Reproducibly Alters the Human Gut Microbiome." *Nature* 505, no. 7484 (2014): 559–563.

De Filippo, C., D. Cavalieri, M. Di Paola, et al. "Impact of Diet in Shaping Gut Microbiota Revealed by a Comparative Study in Children from Europe and Rural Africa." *Proceedings of the National Academy of Sciences of the United States of America* 107, no. 33 (2010): 14691–14696.

den Besten, G., K. Lange, R. Havinga, et al. "Gut-Derived Short-Chain Fatty Acids are Vividly Assimilated into Host Carbohydrates and Lipids." *American Journal of Physiology – Gastrointestinal and Liver Physiology* 305, no. 12 (2013): G900–G910.

Drewnowski, Adam, and S. E. Specter. "Poverty and Obesity: The Role of Energy Density and Energy Costs." *The American Journal of Clinical Nutrition* 79, no. 1 (2004): 6–16.

Ferretti, P., E. Pasolli, A. Tett, et al. "Mother-to-infant Microbial Transmission from Different Body Sites Shapes the Developing Infant Gut Microbiome." *Cell Host & Microbe* 24, no. 1 (2018): 133–145.e5.

Frost, G., M. L. Sleeth, M. Sahuri-Arisoylu, et al. "The Short-Chain Fatty Acid Acetate Reduces Appetite via a Central Homeostatic Mechanism." *Nature Communications* 5, no. 1 (2014): 3611.

Fung, T. T., M. Schulze, JoA. E. Manson, et al. "Dietary Patterns, Meat Intake, and the Risk of Type 2 Diabetes in Women." *Archives of Internal Medicine* 164, no. 20 (2004): 2235–2240.

Gluckman, P., and M. Hanson. "Echoes of the Past: Evolution, Development, Health and Disease." *Discovery Medicine* 4, no. 24 (2004): 401–407.

Gluckman, P. D., and M. A. Hanson. *Developmental Origins of Health and Disease*. Cambridge: Cambridge University Press, 2006.

Gosby, A. K., A. D. Conigrave, N. S. Lau, et al. "Testing Protein Leverage in Lean Humans: A Randomised Controlled Experimental Study." *PLoS One* 6, no. 10 (2011): e25929.

Guy, C., G. Clarke, and H. Eyre. "Food Retail Change and the Growth of Food Deserts: A Case Study of Cardiff." *International Journal of Retail & Distribution Management* 32, no. 2 (2004): 72–88.

Hales, C. N., and D. J. Barker. "Type 2 (Non-insulin-Dependent) Diabetes Mellitus: The Thrifty Phenotype Hypothesis." *Diabetologia* 35, no. 7 (1992): 595–601.

Harris, M. *Patterns of Race in the Americas*. New York: Walker, 1964.

Hayward, A. D., I. J. Rickard, and V. Lummaa. "Influence of Early-Life Nutrition on Mortality and Reproductive Success During a Subsequent Famine in a Preindustrial Population." *Proceedings of the National Academy of Sciences of the United States of America* 110, no. 34 (2013): 13886–13891.

Heinritz, S. N., E. Weiss, M. Eklund, et al. "Intestinal Microbiota and Microbial Metabolites Are Changed in a Pig Model Fed a High-Fat/Low-Fiber or a Low-Fat/High-Fiber Diet." *PLoS One* 11, no. 4 (2016): e0154329.

Howarth, N. C., E. Saltzman, and S. B. Roberts. "Dietary Fiber and Weight Regulation." *Nutrition Reviews* 59, no. 5 (2001): 129–139.

Howell, N. *Life Histories of the Dobe! Kung*. Berkeley: University of California Press, 2010.

Jackson, R. J., R. Minjares, K. S. Naumoff, et al. "Agriculture Policy Is Health Policy." *Journal of Hunger & Environmental Nutrition* 4, no. 3–4 (2009): 393–408.

Jayedi, A., A. Rashidy-Pour, S. Soltani, et al. "Adult Weight Gain and the Risk of Cardiovascular Disease: A Systematic Review and Dose-Response Meta-analysis of Prospective Cohort Studies." *European Journal of Clinical Nutrition* 74, no. 9 (2020): 1263–1275.

Kalliomäki, M., M. C. Collado, S. Salminen, et al. "Early Differences in Fecal Microbiota Composition in Children May Predict Overweight." *The American Journal of Clinical Nutrition* 87, no. 3 (2008): 534–538.

Kaufman, J. S., and S. A. Hall. "The Slavery Hypertension Hypothesis: Dissemination and Appeal of a Modern Race Theory." *Epidemiology* 14, no. 1 (2003): 111–118.

Kisioglu, B., and R. Nergiz-Unal. "Potential Effect of Maternal Dietary Sucrose or Fructose Syrup on CD36, Leptin, and Ghrelin-Mediated Fetal Programming of Obesity." *Nutritional Neuroscience* 23, no. 3 (2020): 210–220.

Korach-Rechtman, H., O. Rom, L. Mazouz, et al. "Soybean Oil Modulates the Gut Microbiota Associated with Atherogenic Biomarkers." *Microorganisms* 8, no. 4 (2020): 486.

Koren, O., J. K. Goodrich, T. C. Cullender, et al. "Host Remodeling of the Gut Microbiome and Metabolic Changes During Pregnancy." *Cell* 150, no. 3 (2012): 470–480.

Korpela, K., P. Costea, L. P. Coelho, et al. "Selective Maternal Seeding and Environment Shape the Human Gut Microbiome." *Genome Research* 28, no. 4 (2018): 561–568.

Kuzawa, C. W. "The Developmental Origins of Adult Health: Intergenerational Inertia in Adaptation and Disease." In *Evolutionary Medicine and Health: New Perspectives.* Edited by W. Trevathan, E. Smith, and J. McKenna, 325–349. New York: Oxford University Press, 2007.

Kuzawa, C. W. "Beyond Feast–Famine: Brain Evolution, Human Life History, and the Metabolic Syndrome." In *Human Evolutionary Biology.* Edited by M. Muehlenbein. Cambridge: Cambridge University Press, 2010.

Kuzawa, C. W., and E. A. Quinn. "Developmental Origins of Adult Function and Health: Evolutionary Hypotheses." *Annual Review of Anthropology* 38 (2009): 131–147.

Larraufie, P., C. Martin-Gallausiaux, N. Lapaque, et al. "SCFAs Strongly Stimulate PYY Production in Human Enteroendocrine Cells." *Scientific Reports* 8, no. 1 (2018): 74.

Larsen, C. S. "Biological Changes in Human Populations with Agriculture." *Annual Review of Anthropology* 24 (1995): 185–213.

Lea, A. J., J. Tung, E. A. Archie, et al. "Developmental Plasticity: Bridging Research in Evolution and Human Health." *Evolution, Medicine, and Public Health* 2017, no. 1 (2017): 162–175.

Lou, Y. C., M. R. Olm, S. Diamond, et al. "Infant Gut Strain Persistence Is Associated with Maternal Origin, Phylogeny, and Traits Including Surface Adhesion and Iron Acquisition." *Cell Reports Medicine* (2021): 100393.

Luhar, S., I. M. Timæus, R. Jones, et al. "Forecasting the Prevalence of Overweight and Obesity in India to 2040." *PLoS One* 15, no. 2 (2020): e0229438.

Luoto, R., M. Kalliomäki, K. Laitinen, et al. "Initial Dietary and Microbiological Environments Deviate in Normal-Weight Compared to Overweight Children at 10 Years of Age." *Journal of Pediatric Gastroenterology and Nutrition* 52, no. 1 (2011): 90–95.

Martinez Steele, E., D. Raubenheimer, S. J. Simpson, et al. "Ultra-processed Foods, Protein Leverage and Energy Intake in the USA." *Public Health Nutrition* 21, no. 1 (2018): 114–124.

Mayntz, D., D. Raubenheimer, M. Salomon, et al. "Nutrient-Specific Foraging in Invertebrate Predators." *Science* 307, no. 5706 (2005): 111–113.

Mischke, M., and T. Plösch. "More than Just a Gut Instinct – The Potential Interplay Between a Baby's Nutrition, Its Gut Microbiome, and the Epigenome." *American Journal of Physiology – Regulatory, Integrative and Comparative Physiology* 304, no. 12 (2013): R1065–R1069.

Moini, J. *Global Health Complications of Obesity.* Waltham: Elsevier, 2020.

Morland, K., S. Wing, R. A. Diez, et al. "Neighborhood Characteristics Associated with the Location of Food Stores and Food Service Places." *American Journal of Preventive Medicine* 22, no. 1 (2002): 23–29.

Neel, J. V. "Diabetes Mellitus: A 'Thrifty' Genotype Rendered Detrimental by 'Progress'?" *American Journal of Human Genetics* 14 (1962): 353–362.

Obregon-Tito, A. J., R. Y. Tito, J. Metcalf, et al. "Subsistence Strategies in Traditional Societies Distinguish Gut Microbiomes." *Nature Communications* 6 (2015): 6505.

Perry, R. J., L. Peng, N. A., et al. "Acetate Mediates a Microbiome–Brain–β-cell Axis to Promote Metabolic Syndrome." *Nature* 534, no. 7606 (2016): 213–217.

Pickering, T. G. "Why Is Hypertension More Common in African Americans?" *Journal of Clinical Hypertension (Greenwich)* 3, no. 1 (2001): 50–52.

Pontzer, H., D. A. Raichlen, B. M. Wood, et al. "Hunter-Gatherer Energetics and Human Obesity." *PLoS One* 7, no. 7 (2012): e40503.

Popkin, B. M., L. S. Adair, and S. W. Ng. "Global Nutrition Transition and the Pandemic of Obesity in Developing Countries." *Nutrition Reviews* 70, no. 1 (2012): 3–21.

Poston, W. S., V. N. Pavlik, D. J. Hyman, et al. "Genetic Bottlenecks, Perceived Racism, and Hypertension Risk Among African Americans and First-Generation African Immigrants." *Journal of Human Hypertension* 15, no. 5 (2001): 341–351.

Rose, D., and R. Richards. "Food Store Access and Household Fruit and Vegetable Use Among Participants in the US Food Stamp Program." *Public Health Nutrition* 7, no. 8 (2004): 1081–1088.

Simpson, S. J., R. Batley, and D. Raubenheimer. "Geometric Analysis of Macronutrient Intake in Humans: The Power of Protein?" *Appetite* 41, no. 2 (2003): 123–140.

Skov, A. R., S. Toubro, B. Ronn, et al. "Randomized Trial on Protein vs Carbohydrate in Ad Libitum Fat Reduced Diet for the Treatment of Obesity." *International Journal of Obesity Related Metabolism Disorders* 23, no. 5 (1999): 528–536.

Smits, S. A., J. Leach, E. D. Sonnenburg, et al. "Seasonal Cycling in the Gut Microbiome of the Hadza Hunter–Gatherers of Tanzania." *Science* 357, no. 6353 (2017): 802.

Snieder, H., G. A. Harshfield, and F. A. Treiber. "Heritability of Blood Pressure and Hemodynamics in African- and European-American Youth." *Hypertension* 41, no. 6 (2003): 1196–1201.

Sonnenburg, E. D., S. A. Smits, M. Tikhonov, et al. "Diet-Induced Extinctions in the Gut Microbiota Compound over Generations." *Nature* 529, no. 7585 (2016): 212–215.

Stanhope, K. L., V. Medici, A. A. Bremer, et al. "A Dose-Response Study of Consuming High-Fructose Corn Syrup-Sweetened Beverages on Lipid/Lipoprotein Risk Factors for Cardiovascular Disease in Young Adults." *The American Journal of Clinical Nutrition* 101, no. 6 (2015): 1144–1154.

Turnbaugh, P, J., R. E. Ley, M. A. Mahowald, et al. "An Obesity-Associated Gut Microbiome with Increased Capacity for Energy Harvest." *Nature* 444, no. 7122 (2006): 1027–1031.

Ulijaszek, S. J., and H. LofinkH. "Obesity in Biocultural Perspective." *Annual Review of Anthropology* 35 (2006): 337–360.

Urlacher, S. S., J. J. Snodgrass, L. R. Dugas, et al. "Childhood Daily Energy Expenditure Does Not Decrease with Market Integration and Is Not Related to Adiposity in Amazonia." *Journal of Nutrition* 151, no. 3 (2021): 695–704.

Vang, A., P. N. Singh, J. W. Lee, et al. "Meats, Processed Meats, Obesity, Weight Gain and Occurrence of Diabetes Among Adults: Findings from Adventist Health Studies." *Annals of Nutrition and Metabolism* 52, no. 2 (2008): 96–104.

Wadden, T. A., and G. A. Bray, eds. *Handbook of Obesity Treatment*. Guilford Publications, 2018.

Wang, Y., and M. A. Beydoun. "Meat Consumption Is Associated with Obesity and Central Obesity Among US Adults." *International Journal of Obesity* 33, no. 6 (2009): 621–628.

Wilson, T. W., and C. E. Grim "Biohistory of Slavery and Blood Pressure Differences in Blacks Today. A Hypothesis." *Hypertension* 17, no. 1 Suppl. (1991): I122–128.

Wu, Y., L. Wang, J. Zhu, et al. "Growing Fast Food Consumption and Obesity in Asia: Challenges and Implications." *Social Science & Medicine* 269 (2021): 113601.

You, W., and M. Henneberg. "Meat Consumption Providing a Surplus Energy in Modern Diet Contributes to Obesity Prevalence: An Ecological Analysis." *BMC Nutrition* 2, no. 1 (2016): 22.

Zenk, Shannon N., A. J. Schulz, B. A. Israel, et al. "Neighborhood Racial Composition, Neighborhood Poverty, and the Spatial Accessibility of Supermarkets in Metropolitan Detroit." *American Journal of Public Health* 95, no. 4 (2005): 660–667.

CHAPTER 12 Ancient DNA and Disease

Anne Stone

INTRODUCTION AND BACKGROUND

While SARS-Cov2 is currently at the forefront of attention because of the COVID-19 pandemic, it is one of many pathogens to make the jump into humans during our evolutionary history. How and when pandemics begin, how pathogens adapt over time, and how human actions and adaptations affect pathogen spread are some of the interesting questions that can be examined using ancient DNA methods and data. What is ancient DNA? A basic definition is simply degraded DNA. Ancient DNA may be thousands of years old with significant degradation from environmental exposure, as is typical for DNA from archaeological samples, or it may be only a few years old yet fragmented and damaged, such as found in formalin-fixed paraffin embedded medical samples. In both cases, standard DNA analyses are generally not successful. Over the past two decades, technological developments in DNA recovery, enrichment, and sequencing have enabled the analysis of ancient pathogen genome sequences and revolutionized our understanding of many ancient pathogens and their effects on human populations. Significant challenges for retrieving ancient pathogen DNA remain, however. These include DNA preservation, which can depend on the burial environment, as well as pathogen load and location in the body. Distinguishing pathogens from close relatives ubiquitous in the environment or identifying a now extinct (or now commensal) pathogen as causing disease are additional challenges. Finally, ancient DNA data have to be placed in an evolutionary context, and thus an additional challenge for research is that sufficient modern pathogen data, as well as information about pathogen ecology and population dynamics, are needed.

METHODS

At death, pathogen DNA is only a small subset of the DNA found in an individual and degradation reduces this endogenous DNA even further. How can we retrieve pathogen DNA from an individual? First, a decision has to be made about where to sample. Common

A Companion to Biological Anthropology, Second Edition. Edited by Clark Spencer Larsen.
© 2023 John Wiley & Sons Ltd. Published 2023 by John Wiley & Sons Ltd.

sources for DNA analyses of pathogens include bone (particularly near lesions if present), the tooth pulp (for systemic pathogens), coprolites (for parasites and gut microbiomes), and dental calculus (for oral microbiomes). Next, ancient DNA research should be undertaken in a clean room with dedicated equipment to reduce the likelihood of contamination by modern sources of DNA (Cooper and Poinar 2000; Malmstrom et al. 2007; Pilli et al. 2013). Early attempts to recover pathogen DNA from ancient contexts used fairly standard DNA extraction methods followed by polymerase chain reaction (PCR) analyses and then Sanger sequencing (Stone and Ozga 2019). These recovered small fragments of the genome that typically were not amenable to answering the interesting questions posed above. Instead, these studies usually focused on confirming the identification of a pathogen, such as *Mycobacterium tuberculosis* or *Treponema pallidum*, thought to have caused a specific paleopathological lesion (in these examples, causing the diseases tuberculosis and syphilis, respectively) (e.g., Donoghue et al. 2005; Salo et al. 1994; Taylor et al. 1996). PCR uses polymerase and primers to copy a specific locus in the genome so that it can be further analyzed, but because ancient DNA is fragmented and usually < 100 base pairs in length, it must target very small regions. As a result, many sequenced PCR fragments must be pieced together to examine a gene or region of interest. PCR can be used to piece together the genomes of viruses, which are small. For example, RNA from the 1918 influenza pandemic was recovered from formalin-fixed lung tissue and from lung tissue of an individual buried in permafrost using reverse transcribed PCR (rtPCR), and all eight gene segments comprising the genome were recovered (Tumpey et al. 2005).

However, newer methods of DNA recovery and sequencing have revolutionized the field and facilitated the analysis of ancient pathogen genome sequences (see Orlando et al. 2021, for an in-depth review). Briefly, these methods include extraction methods, such as that by Dabney et al. (2013), which have been refined to recover small fragments of DNA <70 bp in size. In addition, the extracted DNA is typically used to make a library, which effectively immortalizes the sample since it can be amplified for multiple uses. The DNA fragments in the library can be single or double stranded, and in both cases have an adaptor and an index ligated to each end. The index or "barcode" is used to distinguish one sample from another if multiple libraries are pooled for subsequent analyses, while the adaptors are a specific sequence used for library amplification and sequencing. The choice of single vs. double stranded library construction is based generally on the preservation characteristics of the DNA and cost. Specifically, double stranded libraries are cheaper and often faster to construct, while single stranded libraries can facilitate DNA recovery of samples that are particularly degraded (Carøe et al. 2018; Gansauge et al. 2017).

Once a library is made, it can be sequenced directly (known as shotgun sequencing) using Next Generation Sequencing (NGS) technology. Shotgun sequencing gives the user DNA reads that are generally reflective of the overall DNA composition of the sample. For ancient samples, this can be a problem since the overwhelming majority of DNA will likely be from bacteria and viruses in the burial environment rather than from the host or a pathogen in the host. Shotgun sequencing is most successfully used for samples from exceptional contexts, such as permafrost or an intact, protected context (such as a crypt) (Orlando et al. 2013; Sabin et al. 2020a; Schuenemann et al. 2013). It is also useful for screening a sample for pathogen DNA and for microbiome DNA. Since most samples do not contain high proportions of pathogen DNA relative to environmental DNA, capture, also known as targeted enrichment, is the method used to target specific DNA of interest, increasing the amount sequenced. This requires the use of DNA or RNA baits that bind to complementary sequences in the DNA extract. These are then "fished out" or captured such that the DNA sequences of interest are enriched among the reads that are obtained with NGS.

Regardless of whether shotgun sequencing or enrichment is used, the resulting sequencing reads are first analyzed using bioinformatic programs that sort reads by their index sequences, trim away adaptors and indexes, remove duplicates that result from library construction or enrichment steps, and assess read quality and damage. Next, the sequences that pass quality checkpoints are mapped to reference sequences or assembled using de novo methods. In the case of shotgun sequencing, the initial analyses could include using programs such as MALT (Vagene et al. 2018) for taxonomic assignment. These use many reference sequences to determine where reads best map, and that then put them in "taxonomic bins" for further analyses. These can then be used to characterize the taxa present in the microbiome of dental calculus or coprolites or identify the proportion of DNA from a specific pathogen in the sample. Such analyses can also reveal the presence of an unexpected pathogen and thus guide the design of baits for subsequent capture. In particular, capture may be required to recover more reads in order to increase the depth of coverage of that pathogen genome (i.e., the average number of sequence reads that cover a site in the genome), as well as the coverage of the genome (i.e., the percentage of the total genome that is covered by mapped reads). Ideally, greater than 5–10× depth of coverage as well as 90–95 percent genome coverage is obtained since such data enable better statistical support in subsequent analyses. While most DNA analyses of ancient pathogens use mapping to reconstruct genome sequences, occasionally de novo assembly can be used. This makes no assumption about the genome structure (which can be useful for pathogens with inserted or deleted regions or with different plasmids when compared to the modern reference), but it also requires a greater depth of coverage (>30–50×). For example, Schuenemann et al. (2013) used de novo assembly to generate a >100× genome sequence of *Mycobacterium leprae* from a well-preserved medieval Danish individual.

Additional analyses of the resulting data depend upon the questions of interest to the researcher (for examples, see Bos et al. 2019; Orlando et al. 2021; Stone and Ozga 2019; Warinner et al. 2015, 2017). For microbiome analyses, these can include an assessment of community structure, functional diversity, or even genome reconstructions of specific taxa. If focusing on a specific pathogen, phylogenetic analyses, assessments of diversity, and tests of selection may be of interest. The following case examples illustrate the range of questions and analyses used to address them.

APPLICATIONS

The Microbiome   The pathogenic and commensal microorganisms on and within a human host are collectively referred to as the microbiome, and many studies have revealed its importance for health as well as its influence on disease when perturbed (e.g., Davenport et al. 2017; Gilbert et al. 2018; Goodrich et al. 2017; Sedghi et al. 2021). In the archaeological record, there are two primary sources of microbiome data: dental calculus preserves DNA of the oral microbiome, while coprolites and latrine sediments provide a window into the gut microbiome (e.g., Adler et al. 2013; Sabin et al. 2020b; Tito et al. 2012; Warinner et al. 2014). Early ancient microbiome research often used PCR to amplify 16S ribosomal RNA (rRNA) segments that were then sequenced using NGS in order to identify the microbes present. However, this method limits data recovery since fragments >200 bp are generally needed for amplification of the 16S rRNA variable regions, and it misses species that have mismatches to the primer sequences or that do not have the 16S rRNA gene at all. Shotgun sequencing (i.e., shotgun metagenomics) solves these problems though mapping small fragments to specific taxa may be challenging and the cost can be high (Jacobson et al. 2020; Velsko et al. 2017; Warinner et al. 2017).

Ancient DNA analyses of the oral microbiome have focused on how it has changed over human evolutionary history, the extent to which it reflects the environment (including diet), and the taxa linked to disease, particularly periodontal disease. Dental calculus preserves both host and oral microbiome DNA (Black et al. 2011; De la Fuente et al. 2012; Mann et al. 2018; Ozga et al. 2016; Warinner et al. 2014). Identification of pathogens in the oral microbiome has included members of the so-called "red-complex" of bacteria (*Porphyromonas gingivalis, Tannerella forsythia, Treponema denticola*) that have been linked by some studies to periodontal disease, though recent research has also questioned this linkage (Rocas et al. 2001; Socransky et al. 1998; Velsko et al. 2019). Bravo-Lopez et al. (2020) screened 53 tooth and dental calculus samples for pathogens using shotgun sequencing. After identifying the taxa present, they used capture to recover partial genomes (~8 percent) of *T. forsythia* from seven Pre-Hispanic and five Colonial period individuals from central Mexico. Their analyses showed that Colonial period *T. forsythia* sequences clustered with those recovered from ancient Europeans (from the United Kingdom and Germany) and with two modern sequences from the United States. The Pre-Hispanic *T. forsythia* sequences grouped together and diverged separately, likely reflecting the separation of American and Eurasian populations in the late Pleistocene prior to the expansion of first peoples into the Americas (Willerslev and Meltzer 2021). Additional studies could reveal whether the *T. forsythia* biogeography mirrors that of human populations and whether pre-contact strains were replaced or are still found today. In addition, studies of primate dental calculus microbiomes (including great apes, humans, and Neandertals) point to the presence of red complex taxa as a common component, so further research may help us understand when and if these do indeed act as pathogens and the characteristics and drivers of oral microbiome dysbiosis (Fellows Yates et al. 2021; Jacobson et al. 2020; Ozga et al. 2019; Weyrich et al. 2017).

In addition to "normal" components of the microbiome, dental calculus may also incorporate pathogens found in the nose and throat, such as respiratory pathogens (Eerkens et al. 2018; Fotakis et al. 2020). For example, Fotakis et al. (2020) obtained *M. leprae* genomic and proteomic data from the dental calculus of a sixteenth century individual from Trondheim, Norway. The data show that this woman, who had some skeletal changes perhaps consistent with the early stages of Hansen's disease (or leprosy), had a strain of *M. leprae* belonging to branch 3 and related to other ancient strains from Northern Europe as well as modern strains currently found in the Americas. How often pathogens are incorporated into dental calculus and under what conditions are not yet clear.

Tuberculosis   Some pathogens, including those causing the mycobacterial diseases tuberculosis (TB) and Hansen's disease, as well as treponemal diseases such as yaws, bejel, and syphilis, can result in characteristic changes to the skeleton in those with chronic disease. The recovery and analysis of ancient TB DNA are facilitated by focusing on such individuals, but can be challenging because of the many species of environmental mycobacteria found in soil and water that can contaminate samples. TB can be caused by any of the members of the *Mycobacterium tuberculosis* complex (MTBC), which affects a range of mammals. Today, most human cases are caused by *M. tuberculosis*, which was the leading cause of death by a single pathogen worldwide prior to the SARS-CoV2 pandemic (CDC https://www.cdc.gov/globalhealth/newsroom/topics/tb/index.html). Tuberculosis (TB) was long thought to be an ancient disease, perhaps dating to the time when cattle were domesticated, since *M. bovis* is a close relative within the MTBC (Cockburn 1963). However, genetic analyses of modern MTBC strains shows that the TB strains affecting domesticated animals are derived when compared with human strains (Brosch et al. 2000; Hershberg et al. 2008). Research examining the diversity of modern strains suggested that TB may have been present prior to the Neolithic and even during the expansion of our species out of Africa (Comas et al. 2013; Hughes et al. 2002). Ancient DNA analyses have aided in calibrating the molecular clock to obtain a more accurate estimate of the time to the most recent common ancestor (TMRCA) of *M. tuberculosis* and other members of the MTBC. These analyses point to a more recent origin (Bos et al. 2014; Sabin et al. 2020a; Vågene et al. 2022) roughly 3000–6000 years ago.

One major puzzle about the geographic distribution of ancient TB strains was the cause of TB in the Americas prior to European contact, as well as its apparent first appearance in South America, where the oldest cases have been documented in the archaeological record (Buikstra 1999; Roberts and Buikstra 2003; Stone et al. 2009). Initial assessment of an infected Peruvian mummy using PCR of the IS6110 repeat element found that this was indeed present, indicating the presence of a member of the MTBC (Salo et al. 1994). The identity of this MTBC member was not revealed until 2014, when Bos et al. recovered three ancient genomes from three ~800–1000-year-old sites in the Osmore River Valley of Peru. This research showed that these cases were caused by *M. pinnipedii*, a type of TB affecting southern hemisphere seals and sea lions. In addition, these data offered the first good calibration of the MTBC phylogeny and pointed to the TMRCA of *M. tuberculosis* (including human and animal strains) 3000–6000 years ago. Subsequent analyses of individuals from further inland in the Osmore River Valley and in the highlands of Colombia indicate that the ancient *M. pinnipedii* strains were not only present at sites near the coast and suggest that human-to-human transmission likely occurred (Vågene et al. 2022). These studies explain the source of TB in South America and why it appears there first, but additional research is needed to examine the history of TB in North America before contact as well as the turnover of these strains to European *M. tuberculosis* lineage 4 strains after contact.

The Plague   Most pathogens do not leave clear indicators of disease on the skeleton, but they may leave archaeological indicators such as mass graves when many people die over a short time period. *Vibrio cholerae*, variola virus, and *Yersinia pestis*, causing cholera, smallpox, and the plague, respectively, are examples of pathogens that have caused major pandemics. Ancient DNA analyses have focused particularly on *Y. pestis*, showing that it caused both the Justinian plague (541–549 AD) and the Black Death (1346–1353 AD) as well as the third plague pandemic in the twentieth century (Bos et al. 2011; Schuenemann et al. 2011; Wagner et al. 2014). This was also the first ancient pathogen investigated using the new capture and NGS methods. Specifically, in 2011, DNA was recovered from the tooth pulp of individuals buried in the East Smithfield Black Death plague pits in London. *Y. pestis* DNA was first recovered from the pPCP1 virulence-associated plasmid followed soon thereafter by the rest of the genome (Bos et al. 2011; Schuenemann et al. 2011). These studies found that while the Black Death was caused by a now extinct strain of *Y. pestis*, it did not appear to be appreciably different from modern strains. The severe impact of this plague pandemic is likely due to the introduction of what appeared to be a new pathogen combined with changes in transmission (i.e., affected by shifts in vectors and trade routes), susceptibility, and frailty resulting from the proceeding famine and comorbidities (e.g., Dean et al. 2018; DeWitte 2015; DeWitte and Wood 2008; Immel et al. 2021). The Black Death strains examined in subsequent research show that this was a very rapid spread with few differences among strains (Bramanti et al. 2021; Spyrou et al. 2019).

After the Black Death, periodic outbreaks occurred over a period of about 500 years (fourteenth to nineteenth centuries AD). However, there is debate about whether these stemmed from local reservoirs or reintroductions from the east (Bos et al. 2016; Bramanti et al. 2021; Namouchi et al. 2018; Schmid et al. 2015; Seifert et al. 2016; Spyrou et al. 2016). These outbreaks became less severe over time, perhaps due to decreased human susceptibility as well as changes in the pathogen itself (Immel et al. 2021; Susat et al. 2020). For example, Susat et al. (2020) found that two seventeenth century *Y. pestis* genomes from Riga each had two types of pPCP1 plasmids, with the pla gene and without it, at an approximately 1:10 ratio, and they suggest that this could account for a decline in virulence. Bramanti et al. (2021) also note a decrease in pla copy number in other post-Black Death strains. However, it is unclear how low copy number of pla affects virulence, but research suggests that the pla gene is required for bubonic plague (Sebbane et al. 2020; Zimbler et al. 2015).

The Black Death was not, in fact, the first time that plague affected Europe. The Justinianic Plague started the first historically recorded pandemic (sixth–eighth centuries AD), but ancient DNA analyses show earlier cases in the late Neolithic and early Bronze ages that shed light on the evolution of *Y. pestis* from *Y. pseudotuberculosis*. Specifically, *Y. pestis* was identified in DNA sequences (retrieved from tooth pulp) of late Neolithic and early Bronze Age individuals from central Asia and the Caucasus (including Siberia, Armenia, and Russia) and Europe (including Germany, Sweden, Poland, Estonia, Lithuania, Russia, and Croatia) (Andrades Valtueña et al. 2017; Rascovan et al. 2019; Rasmussen et al. 2015; Spyrou et al. 2018). The genome sequences of these strains showed that the Late Neolithic/Bronze Age *Y. pestis* strains are diverse with many lacking the murine toxin gene (ymt), which enables *Y. pestis* to survive in the gut of fleas that have a broad range of mammalian hosts, including humans (Bland et al. 2021). This gene is one requirement for the bubonic form of the disease, suggesting that the main types of plague affecting these early individuals were septicemic and pneumonic. However, Spyrou et al. (2018) found strains in Late Bronze Age (~3800 BP) individuals from the Samara region of modern-day Russia that do have the ymt gene, as well as some other changes needed for adapting to fleas and increasing virulence in humans (though not the derived version of the pla gene in the PCP1 plasmid). These strains appear to be at the base of the branch in the phylogeny leading to the strains causing historical pandemics, including the first recorded pandemic, the plague of Justinian.

Ancient DNA analyses also provide insight into the dynamics of the first plague pandemic, showing that it was independent of subsequent pandemics (Feldman et al. 2016; Harbeck et al. 2013; Wagner et al. 2014). The Justinianic plague (AD 541–544) kicked off the first pandemic, which then lasted for another two hundred years. Interestingly, some strains from the later years of the first pandemic also show changes consistent with reduced virulence like the later second pandemic strains (Bramanti et al. 2021; Keller et al. 2019). *Y. pestis* is the most intensively studied pathogen from ancient individuals, but, at present, these data are from Western and Central Eurasia and a better understanding of the evolution of *Y. pestis* from *Y. pseudotuberculosis*, as well as the reach and impact of the plague pandemics in Africa and East Asia, are particularly needed.

Conclusions

Ancient DNA analyses of pathogens provide new insights into their evolution as well as our understanding of human disease patterns over time. For example, there have been significant debates about the antiquity of specific pathogens as well as the pace and pattern of the first epidemiological transition after the shift to agriculture (Cohen and Armelagos 1984; Gage and DeWitte 2009; Pearce-Duvet 2006; Stone 2020) that ancient DNA studies can help address. This research also offers the opportunity to examine the process of pathogen adaption when there is a "jump" into humans and to observe the evolution of human immune loci in response. Taking advantage of these opportunities for research, however, should not result in taking advantage of or ignoring living, descendant communities by discounting their concerns. There are many examples of diseases that can be stigmatizing, such as Hansen's disease, HIV/AIDS, and syphilis, and there are many reasons why communities may be troubled by specific research. Ancient DNA research must be collaborative and researchers must engage descendent communities and other stakeholders with respect (Bardill et al. 2018; Wagner et al. 2020). While scientists interested in ancient pathogens typically have some expertise in anthropology, evolutionary biology, population genetics, biostatistics, human genetics, bioinformatics, and/or pathogen genetics, the research benefits from collaboration with other scholars from different perspectives and backgrounds, including clinicians, ecologists, historians, and indigenous scholars, since pathogens can impact many facets of human life (and human actions can affect pathogen dynamics in turn).

Challenges remain for ancient DNA analyses of many pathogens. Specifically, the majority of aDNA data from pathogens are from European contexts, giving a biased view of their biogeography and evolution. Biodiversity is greater in warmer, wetter places on our planet (Brown 2014), and despite our lack of information about ancient pathogens from such regions of the world, it is likely that many originated there. In addition, our knowledge is biased against those pathogens that are less likely to preserve, such as single-stranded RNA viruses, or that are poorly understand (or absent) in modern contexts. New methods may help address some of these issues, though not all.

Ancient DNA research has progressed significantly in the last 35 years with the technical advances of molecular genetics and bioinformatics, and it holds great promise for addressing many long-standing questions about pathogen evolutionary histories and their impact on humans.

REFERENCES

Adler, C. J., K. Dobney, L. S. Weyrich, et al. "Sequencing Ancient Calcified Dental Plaque Shows Changes in Oral Microbiota with Dietary Shifts of the Neolithic and Industrial Revolutions." *Nature Genetics* 45, no. 4 (2013): 450–455, 455e451.

Andrades Valtuena, A., A. Mittnik, F. M. Key, et al. "The Stone Age Plague and Its Persistence in Eurasia." *Current Biology: CB* 27, no. 23 (2017): 3683–3691, e3688.

Bardill, J., A. C. Bader, N. A. Garrison, et al. "Advancing the Ethics of Paleogenomics." *Science* 360, no. 6387 (2018): 384–385.

Black, J., S. Kerr, L. Henebry-Delfon, and J. G. Lorenz. "Dental Calculus as an Alternate Source of Mitochondrial DNA for Analysis of Skeletal Remains." *SCA Proceedings* 25 (2011): 1–7.

Bland, D. M., A. Miarinjara, C. F. Bosio, et al. "Acquisition of Yersinia Murine Toxin Enabled *Yersinia pestis* to Expand the Range of Mammalian Hosts that Sustain Flea-Borne Plague." *PLoS Pathogens* 17, no. 10 (2021): e1009995.

Bos, K. I., V. J. Schuenemann, G. B. Golding, et al. "A Draft Genome of *Yersinia pestis* from Victims of the Black Death." *Nature* 478, no. 7370 (2011): 506–510.

Bos, K. I., K. M. Harkins, A. Herbig, et al. "Pre-Columbian Mycobacterial Genomes Reveal Seals as a Source of New World Human Tuberculosis." *Nature* 514 (2014): 494–497.

Bos, K. I., A. Herbig, J. Sahl, et al. "Eighteenth Century *Yersinia pestis* Genomes Reveal the Long-Term Persistence of an Historical Plague Focus." *Elife* 5 (2016): e12994.

Bos, K. I., D. Kuhnert, A. Herbig, et al. "Paleomicrobiology: Diagnosis and Evolution of Ancient Pathogens." *Annual Review of Microbiology* 73 (2019): 639–666.

Bramanti, B., Wu, Y., Yang, R., et al. "Assessing the Origins of the European Plagues Following the Black Death: A Synthesis of Genomic, Historical, and Ecological Information." *Proceedings of the National Academy of Sciences of the United States of America* 118, no. 36 (2021): e2101940118.

Bravo-Lopez, M., V. Villa-Islas, C. Rocha Arriaga, et al. "Paleogenomic Insights into the Red Complex Bacteria *Tannerella forsythia* in Pre-Hispanic and Colonial Individuals from Mexico." *Philosophical Transactions of the Royal Society of London Series B, Biological Sciences* 375, no. 1812 (2020): 20190580.

Brosch, R, S. V. Gordon, A. Pym, et al. "Comparative Genomics of the Mycobacteria." *International Journal of Medical Microbiology* 290, no. 2 (2000): 143–152.

Brown, J. H. "Why Are There So Many Species in the Tropics?" *Journal of Biogeography* 41, no. 1 (2014): 8–22.

Buikstra, J. E. "Paleoepidemiology of Tuberculosis in the Americas." In *Tuberculosis: Past and Present. Budapest-Szeged: Golden Book – TB Foundation.* Edited by G. Palfi, O. Dutour, J. Deak, and I. Hutas, 479–494. Szeged: Golden Book Publishers, Budapest: Tuberculosis Foundation, 1999.

Carøe, C., S. Gopalakrishnan, L. Vinner, et al. "Single-Tube Library Preparation for Degraded DNA." *Methods in Ecology and Evolution* 9 (2018): 410–419.

Cockburn, A. *The Evolution and Eradication of Infectious Diseases.* Baltimore: Johns Hopkins Press, 1963.

Cohen, M. N., and G. J. Armelagos. *Paleopathology at the Origins of Agriculture.* Orlando, FL: Academic Press, 1984.

Comas, I., M. Coscolla, T. Luo, et al. "Out-of-Africa Migration and Neolithic Coexpansion of *Mycobacterium Tuberculosis* with Modern Humans." *Nature Genetics* 45, no. 10 (2013): 1176–1182.

Cooper, A., and H. N. Poinar. "Ancient DNA: Do It Right or Not at All." *Science* 289 (2000): 1139.

Dabney, J., M. Knapp, I. Glocke, et al. "Complete Mitochondrial Genome Sequence of a Middle Pleistocene Cave Bear Reconstructed from Ultrashort DNA Fragments." *Proceedings of the National Academy of Sciences of the United States of America* 110, no. 39 (2013): 15758–15763.

Davenport, E. R., J. G. Sanders, S. J. Song, et al. "The Human Microbiome in Evolution." *BMC Biology* 15, no. 1 (2017): 127.

Dean, K. R., F. Krauer, L. Walloe, et al. "Human Ectoparasites and the Spread of Plague in Europe During the Second Pandemic." *Proceedings of the National Academy of Sciences of the United States of America* 115, no. 6 (2018): 1304–1309.

De la Fuente, C., S. Flores, and M. Moraga. "DNA from Human Ancient Bacteria: A Novel Source of Genetic Evidence from Archaeological Dental Calculus." *Archaeometry* 55, no. 4 (2012): 766–778.

DeWitte, S. N. "Setting the Stage for Medieval Plague: Pre-black Death Trends in Survival and Mortality." *American Journal of Physical Anthropology* 158, no. 3 (2015): 441–451.

DeWitte, S. N., and J. W. Wood. "Selectivity of Black Death Mortality with Respect to Preexisting Health." *Proceedings of the National Academy of Sciences of the United States of America* 105, no. 5 (2008): 1436–1441.

Donoghue, H. D., A. Marcsik, C. Matheson, et al. "Co-infection of *Mycobacterium Tuberculosis* and *Mycobacterium Leprae* in Human Archaeological Samples: A Possible Explanation for the Historical Decline of Leprosy." *Proceedings. Biological Sciences/The Royal Society* 272, no. 1561 (2005): 389–394.

Eerkens, J. W., R. V. Nichols, G. G. R. Murray, et al. "A Probable Prehistoric Case of Meningococcal Disease from San Francisco Bay: Next Generation Sequencing of Neisseria Meningitidis from Dental Calculus and Osteological Evidence." *International Journal of Paleopathology* 22 (2018): 173–180.

Feldman, M., M. Harbeck, M. Keller, et al. "A High-Coverage *Yersinia pestis* Genome from a Sixth-Century Justinianic Plague Victim." *Molecular Biology and Evolution* 33, no. 11 (2016): 2911–2923.

Fellows Yates, J. A., I. M. Velsko, F. Aron, et al. "The Evolution and Changing Ecology of the African Hominid Oral Microbiome." *Proceedings of the National Academy of Sciences of the United States of America* 118 (2021): 20.

Fotakis, A. K., S. D. Denham, M. Mackie, et al. "Multi-omic Detection of *Mycobacterium Leprae* in Archaeological Human Dental Calculus." *Philosophical Transactions of the Royal Society of London Series B, Biological Sciences* 375, no. 1812 (2020): 20190584.

Gage, T. B., and S. DeWitte. "What Do We Know about the Agricultural Demographic Transition?" *Current Anthropology* 50, no. 5 (2009): 649–655.

Gansauge, M. T., T. Gerber, I. Glocke, et al. "Single-stranded DNA Library Preparation from Highly Degraded DNA Using T4 DNA Ligase." *Nucleic Acids Research* 45, no. 10 (2017): e79.

Gilbert, J. A., M. J. Blaser, J. G. Caporaso, et al. "Current Understanding of the Human Microbiome." *Nature Medicine* 24, no. 4 (2018): 392–400.

Goodrich, J. K., E. R. Davenport, A. G. Clark, and R. E. Ley. "The Relationship Between the Human Genome and Microbiome Comes into View." *Annual Review of Genetics* 51 (2017): 413–433.

Harbeck, M., L. Seifert, S. Hansch, et al. "*Yersinia pestis* DNA from Skeletal Remains from the 6(th) Century AD Reveals Insights into Justinianic Plague." *PLoS Pathogens* 9, no. 5 (2013): e1003349.

Hershberg, R., M. Lipatov, P. M. Small, et al. "High Functional Diversity in *Mycobacterium Tuberculosis* Driven by Genetic Drift and Human Demography." *PLoS Biology* 6, no. 12 (2008): e311.

Hughes, A. L., R. Friedman, and M. Murray. "Genomewide Pattern of Synonymous Nucleotide Substitution in Two Complete Genomes of *Mycobacterium Tuberculosis*." *Emerging Infectious Diseases* 8, no. 11 (2002): 1342–1346.

Immel, A., F. M. Key, A. Szolek, et al. "Analysis of Genomic DNA from Medieval Plague Victims Suggests Long-Term Effect of *Yersinia pestis* on Human Immunity Genes." *Molecular Biology and Evolution* 38, no. 10 (2021): 4059–4076.

Jacobson, D. K., T. P. Honap, C. Monroe, et al. "Functional Diversity of Microbial Ecologies Estimated from Ancient Human Coprolites and Dental Calculus." *Philosophical Transactions of the Royal Society of London Series B, Biological Sciences* 375, no. 1812 (2020): 20190586.

Keller, M., M. A. Spyrou, C. L. Scheib, et al. "Ancient *Yersinia pestis* Genomes from Across Western Europe Reveal Early Diversification during the First Pandemic (541–750)." *Proceedings of the National Academy of Sciences of the United States of America* 116, no. 25 (2019): 12363–12372.

Malmstrom, H., E. M. Svensson, M. T. Gilbert, et al. "More on Contamination: The Use of Asymmetric Molecular Behavior to Identify Authentic Ancient Human DNA." *Molecular Biology and Evolution* 24, no. 4 (2007): 998–1004.

Mann, A. E., S. Sabin, K. Ziesemer, et al. "Differential Preservation of Endogenous Human and Microbial DNA in Dental Calculus and Dentin." *Scientific Reports* 8, no. 1 (2018): 9822.

Namouchi, A., M. Guellil, O. Kersten, et al. "Integrative Approach Using *Yersinia pestis* Genomes to Revisit the Historical Landscape of Plague during the Medieval Period." *Proceedings of the National Academy of Sciences of the United States of America* 115, no. 50 (2018): E11790–E11797.

Orlando, L., R. Allaby, P. Skoglund, et al. "Ancient DNA Analysis." *Nature Reviews Methods Primers* 1, 14 (2021).

Orlando, L., A. Ginolhac, G. Zhang, et al. "Recalibrating Equus Evolution Using the Genome Sequence of an Early Middle Pleistocene Horse." *Nature* 499, no. 7456 (2013): 74–78.

Ozga, A. T., I. Gilby, R. S. Nockerts, et al. "Oral Microbiome Diversity in Chimpanzees from Gombe National Park." *Scientific Reports* 9, no. 1 (2019): 17354.

Ozga, A. T., M. A. Nieves-Colon, T. P. Honap, et al. "Successful Enrichment and Recovery of Whole Mitochondrial Genomes from Ancient Human Dental Calculus." *American Journal of Physical Anthropology* 160, no. 2 (2016):220–228.

Pearce-Duvet, J. M. "The Origin of Human Pathogens: Evaluating the Role of Agriculture and Domestic Animals in the Evolution of Human Disease." *Biological Reviews of the Cambridge Philosophical Society* 81, no. 3 (2006): 369–382.

Pilli, E., A. Modi, C. Serpico, et al. "Monitoring DNA Contamination in Handled vs. Directly Excavated Ancient Human Skeletal Remains." *PLoS One* 8, no. 1 (2013): e52524.

Rascovan, N., K. G. Sjogren, K. Kristiansen, et al. "Emergence and Spread of Basal Lineages of *Yersinia pestis* during the Neolithic Decline." *Cell* 176, nos. 1–2 (2019): 295–305 e210.

Rasmussen, S., M. E. Allentoft, K. Nielsen, et al. "Early Divergent Strains of *Yersinia pestis* in Eurasia 5,000 Years Ago." *Cell* 163, no. 3 (2015): 571–582.

Roberts, C., and J. E. Buikstra. *The Bioarchaeology of Tuberculosis. A Global View on a Reemerging Disease*. Gainesville: University Press of Florida. 343 pp., 2003.

Rocas, I. N., J. F. Siqueira, Jr., K. R. Santos, and A. M. Coelho. "'Red Complex' (Bacteroides Forsythus, Porphyromonas Gingivalis, and Treponema Denticola) in Endodontic Infections: A Molecular Approach." *Oral Surgery, Oral Medicine, Oral Pathology, Oral Radiology, and Endodontics* 91, no. 4 (2001): 468–471.

Sabin, S., A. Herbig, A. J. Vagene, et al. "A Seventeenth-Century *Mycobacterium Tuberculosis* Genome Supports a Neolithic Emergence of the Mycobacterium Tuberculosis Complex." *Genome Biology* 21, no. 1 (2020a): 201.

Sabin, S., H. Y. Yeh, A. Pluskowski, A., et al. "Estimating Molecular Preservation of the Intestinal Microbiome via Metagenomic Analyses of Latrine Sediments from Two Medieval Cities." *Philosophical Transactions of the Royal Society of London Series B, Biological Sciences* 375, no. 1812 (2020b): 20190576.

Salo, W. L., Aufderheide, A. C., Buikstra, and T. A. Holcomb. "Identification of *Mycobaterium Tuberculosis* DNA in a Pre-Columbian Peruvian Mummy." *Proceedings of the National Academy of Sciences of the United States of America* 91 (1994): 2091–2094.

Schmid, B. V., U. Buntgen, W. R. Easterday, et al. "Climate-Driven Introduction of the Black Death and Successive Plague Reintroductions into Europe." *Proceedings of the National Academy of Sciences of the United States of America* 112, no. 10 (2015): 3020–3025.

Schuenemann, V. J., K. Bos, S. DeWitte, et al. "Targeted Enrichment of Ancient Pathogens Yielding the pPCP1 Plasmid of *Yersinia pestis* from Victims of the Black Death." *Proceedings of the National Academy of Sciences of the United States of America* 108, no. 38 (2011): E746–E752.

Schuenemann, V. J., P. Singh, T. A. Mendum, et al. "Genome-wide Comparison of Medieval and Modern *Mycobacterium Leprae*." *Science* 341, no. 6142 (2013): 179–183.

Sebbane, F., V. N. Uversky, and A. P. Anisimov. "*Yersinia pestis* Plasminogen Activator." *Biomolecules* 10 (2020): 11.

Sedghi, L., V. DiMassa, A. Harrington, et al. "The Oral Microbiome: Role of Key Organisms and Complex Networks in Oral Health and Disease." *Periodontology 2000* 87, no. 1 (2021): 107–131.

Seifert, L., I. Wiechmann, M. Harbeck, et al. "Genotyping *Yersinia pestis* in Historical Plague: Evidence for Long-Term Persistence of *Y. pestis* in Europe from the 14th to the 17th Century." *PloS One* 11, no. 1 (2016): e0145194.

Socransky, S. S., A. D. Haffajee, M. A. Cugini, et al. "Microbial Complexes in Subgingival Plaque." *Journal of Clinical Periodontology* 25, no. 2 (1998): 134–144.

Spyrou, M. A., R. I. Tukhbatova, M. Feldman, et al. "Historical *Y. pestis* Genomes Reveal the European Black Death as the Source of Ancient and Modern Plague Pandemics." *Cell Host & Microbe* 19, no. 6 (2016): 874–881.

Spyrou, M. A., R. I. Tukhbatova, C. C. Wang, et al. "Analysis of 3800-year-old *Yersinia pestis* Genomes Suggests Bronze Age Origin for Bubonic Plague." *Nature Communications* 9, no. 1 (2018): 2234.

Spyrou, M. A., M. Keller, R. I. Tukhbatova, et al. "Phylogeography of the Second Plague Pandemic Revealed Through Analysis of Historical *Yersinia pestis* Genomes." *Nature Communications* 10, no. 1 (2019): 4470.

Stone, A. C. "Getting Sick in the Neolithic." *Nature Ecology and Evolution* 4, no. 3 (2020): 286–287.

Stone, A. C., and A. T. Ozga. "Ancient DNA in the Study of Ancient Disease." In *Ortner's Identification of Pathological Conditions in Human Skeletal Remains*, 3rd edn. Edited by J. E. Buikstra, 183–210. London, UK: Academic Press, 2019.

Stone, A. C., A. K. Wilbur, J. E. Buikstra, and C. A. Roberts. "Tuberculosis and Leprosy in Perspective." *American Journal of Physical Anthropology* 140, no. Suppl. 49 (2009): 66–94.

Susat, J., J. H. Bonczarowska, E. Petersone-Gordina, et al. "*Yersinia pestis* Strains from Latvia Show Depletion of the Pla Virulence Gene at the End of the Second Plague Pandemic." *Scientific Reports* 10, no. 1 (2020): 14628.

Taylor, G. M., M. Crossey, J. Saldanha, and T. Waldron. "DNA from *Mycobacterium Tuberculosis* Identified in Mediaeval Human Skeletal Remains Using Polymerase Chain Reaction." *Journal of Archaeological Science* 23 (1996): 789–798.

Tito, R. Y., D. Knights, J. Metcalf, et al. "Insights from Characterizing Extinct Human Gut Microbiomes." *PloS One* 7, no. 12 (2012): e51146.

Tumpey, T. M., C. F. Basler, P. V. Aguilar, et al. "Characterization of the Reconstructed 1918 Spanish Influenza Pandemic Virus." *Science* 310, no. 5745 (2005): 77–80.

Vagene, A. J., A. Herbig, M. G. Campana, et al. "*Salmonella Enterica* Genomes from Victims of a Major Sixteenth-Century Epidemic in Mexico." *Nature Ecology and Evolution* 2 (2018): 520–528.

Vågene, Å. J, T. P. Honap, K. M. Harkins, M. S. Rosenberg, K. Griffen, F. Cárdenas-Arroyo, L. P. Leguizamón, J. Arnett, J. E. Buikstra, A. Herbig, J. Krause, A. C. Stone, and K. I. Bos. "Geographically Dispersed Zoonotic Tuberculosis in Pre-Contact New World Human Populations." *Nature Communications* 13: 1195. https://doi.org/10.1038/s41467-022-28562-8.

Velsko, I. M., K. A. Overmyer, C. Speller, et al. "The Dental Calculus Metabolome in Modern and Historic Samples." *Metabolomics* 13, no. 11 (2017): 134.

Velsko, I. M., J. A. Fellows Yates, F. Aron, et al. "Microbial Differences Between Dental Plaque and Historic Dental Calculus Are Related to Oral Biofilm Maturation Stage." *Microbiome* 7, no. 1 (2019): 102.

Wagner, D. M., J. Klunk, M. Harbeck, et al. "*Yersinia pestis* and the Plague of Justinian 541–543 AD: A Genomic Analysis." *The Lancet Infectious Diseases* 14, no. 4 (2014): 319–326.

Wagner, J. K., C. Colwell, K. G. Claw, et al. "Fostering Responsible Research on Ancient DNA." *American Journal of Human Genetics* 107, no. 2 (2020): 183–195.

Warinner, C., J. F. Rodrigues, R. Vyas, et al. "Pathogens and Host Immunity in the Ancient Human Oral Cavity." *Nature Genetics* 46, no. 4 (2014): 336–344.

Warinner, C., C. Speller, M. J. Collins, and C. M. Lewis, Jr, "Ancient Human Microbiomes." *Journal of Human Evolution* 79 (2015): 125–136.

Warinner, C., A. Herbig, A. Mann, et al. "A Robust Framework for Microbial Archaeology." *Annual Review of Genomics and Human Genetics* 18, no. 1 (2017): 321–356.

Weyrich, L. S., S. Duchene, J. Soubrier, et al. "Reconstructing Neandertal Behavior Diet, and Disease Using Ancient DNA from Dental Calculus." *Nature* 544 (2017): 357–361.

Willerslev, E., and D. J. Meltzer. "Peopling of the Americas as Inferred from Ancient Genomics." *Nature* 594, no. 7863 (2021): 356–364.

Zimbler, D. L., J. A. Schroeder, J. L. Eddy, and W. W. Lathem. "Early Emergence of *Yersinia pestis* as a Severe Respiratory Pathogen." *Nature Communications* 6 (2015): 7487.

CHAPTER 13 Paleogenomics: Ancient DNA in Biological Anthropology

C. Eduardo Guerra Amorim

INTRODUCTION

In recent years, novel technology for obtaining DNA molecules from archaeological material, museum specimens, and sediments has opened up new horizons within the genomic sciences, culminating in the development of the field of paleogenomics. Compared to traditional population genetic datasets, composed of a single time point, ancient DNA (aDNA) enables the direct assessment of genetic diversity in different time transects and allows for the recovery of lost genetic lineages. In biological anthropology, aDNA has been used – together with population genetics methods (see Chapter 6) – to infer human migration routes, characterize past population structure, reconstruct phenotypes of ancient and archaic humans, determine biological sex from human remains, and infer biological relatedness in ancient communities. This chapter discusses the techniques used to obtain aDNA from archaeological material, the analytical methods used in paleogenomics, and the applications of aDNA data in biological anthropology. The focus of this chapter is human aDNA. For a detailed discussion of the uses of aDNA for the study of ancient pathogens see Chapter 12.

One common question we hear from students being introduced to aDNA is "how old does DNA need to be to be considered ancient?" In practice, many scholars use the term "ancient DNA" to denote the DNA of organisms that died decades to millions of years ago. At the time of this chapter, the oldest specimen from which DNA has been recovered is a 1.6-million-year-old mammoth (van der Valk et al. 2021). Human aDNA has been successfully recovered from *Homo sapiens* remains dated from a few hundred up to 45,000 years ago (Fu et al. 2016; Liu et al. 2021), as well as from archaic humans (Green et al. 2010; Reich et al. 2010). Although the label "ancient DNA" has a clear temporal meaning, the term is, in fact, more related to the condition of the DNA molecule than to its age. Below, the characteristics of aDNA and its differences from DNA obtained from fresh tissues are discussed.

A Companion to Biological Anthropology, Second Edition. Edited by Clark Spencer Larsen.
© 2023 John Wiley & Sons Ltd. Published 2023 by John Wiley & Sons Ltd.

THE CHARACTERISTICS OF ANCIENT DNA

In humans, DNA is found in the cell nucleus and the mitochondria. After the death of an individual, DNA molecules start to degrade due to the effect of the environment – temperature, water, and oxygen – and due to spontaneous damage. As a result, aDNA molecules found in archaeological specimens are fragmented into shorter DNA stretches. The length of these aDNA fragments is very variable and depends on several factors, including the age of the sample, its preservation status, and the environmental conditions in which the specimen is found or stored. In general, the mean aDNA molecule length observed in sequencing experiments is between 40 and 150 base pairs (Knapp and Hofreiter 2010). Shorter DNA molecules may exist in the same sample, but the sequencing of very short fragments, typically smaller than 30 base pairs, is often challenging and thus these extremely short molecules are often not identified in aDNA studies.

In addition to being fragmented, aDNA molecules also reveal a peculiar characteristic that clearly contrasts with DNA obtained from fresh tissues and living organisms – that is, aDNA exhibits an accumulation of specific types of mutations toward the ends of the DNA fragment (Dabney et al. 2013). Those mutations are identified in sequencing experiments as an excess of C-to-T and G-to-A mutations, where A stands for adenine, C for cytosine, G for guanine, and T for thymine. These are the four bases that compose DNA. These types of mutations are common in living organisms and happen in specific DNA sequence contexts known as CpG sites. Because of the random nature of DNA mutations, we would expect C-to-T and G-to-A mutations (also known as transitions) to happen anywhere along the extent of a DNA molecule in a living organism. In aDNA molecules, however, transitions happen more often in the ends (Dabney et al. 2013). This spontaneous mutation bias results in the typical aDNA damage signature depicted in Figure 13.1a, known as the post-mortem damage pattern.

The existence of post-mortem damage in aDNA molecules has at least two important implications in paleogenomics. The first one is that aDNA data are biased toward an excess of transitions (i.e., C-to-T and G-to-A mutations). In other words, aDNA datasets present errors relative to those containing DNA sequences obtained from fresh, present-day samples. In practice, these errors, if uncorrected, will result in the misspecification of the genetic diversity of the studied individuals, which could then lead to biases in the

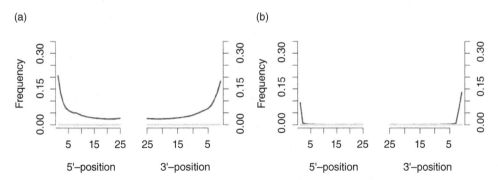

Figure 13.1 Damage profile of the terminal nucleotides of two samples treated in different ways during genomic library preparation: (a) no UDG treatment and (b) partially UDG-treated. The frequencies (*y*-axis) of nucleotide misincorporation are plotted as a function of the distance (*x*-axis) from the ends of the sequencing read. In this plot, C-to-T and G-to-A misincorporations are shown in black. Other types are shown in grey.

interpretation of the data in aDNA studies. While these sorts of errors are undesirable, an excess of transitions at the ends of the sequencing reads is indicative of the authenticity of aDNA samples – this being the second key implication of post-mortem aDNA damage in paleogenomics studies. In other words, the very existence of this type of signature in aDNA and its absence in DNA data obtained from fresh tissues are used to confirm that the DNA extracted from an archaeological specimen is indeed aDNA, as opposed to contamination resulting from the handling of the remains by living humans in the laboratory or in the field.

In order to address the issues resulting from post-mortem damage, when analyzing aDNA, one may (a) exclude C-to-T and G-to-A transitions from their dataset, (b) use probabilistic models to infer the DNA sequence on a given locus while controlling for post-mortem damage (Hofmanová et al. 2016), or (c) use uracil–DNA–glycosylase (UDG) to chemically fix these mutations (Briggs et al. 2010). However, because post-mortem damage is utilized for the authentication of aDNA samples, as mentioned in the previous paragraph, full UDG treatment may not be an optimal choice, as it can completely erase the aDNA signature from the sequences being analyzed. As an alternate solution, partial UDG treatment protocols have been developed, according to which post-mortem damage is eliminated in the interior of the DNA molecules, while it is kept in its terminal regions (Figure 13.1b, Rohland et al. 2015). One may then computationally "trim" the ends of the sequencing reads, where the great majority of the transitions resulting from post-mortem damage are found. In doing so, any variants observed in the internal part of the sequencing read can be included in the dataset, regardless of whether they are transitions or not. Given that aDNA data usually contains a great amount of missing data, partial UDG treatment is often preferable over the option of excluding C-to-T and G-to-A transitions from the dataset. However, UDG treatment (full or partial) should be avoided when DNA preservation is precarious because it tends to decrease the DNA concentration in a sample.

DNA degradation also results in the complete loss of some of the DNA molecules available in samples. Because of that, aDNA sequencing data usually present a large amount of missing data and a low depth of coverage, i.e., the average number of sequencing reads covering a base pair in the genome. It is not rare to see aDNA sequencing data with a depth of coverage of 1× or less (Amorim et al. 2018; Clemente et al. 2021; Margaryan et al. 2020; Maróti et al. 2022 – to cite a few). In the cases in which a locus is covered by a single sequencing read, it is technically impossible to call a diploid genotype. As a consequence, heterozygous loci (i.e., those in which two different alleles are observed) are miscalled as homozygous. This introduces additional biases in aDNA data analysis. To address this issue, aDNA data is often analyzed in a "pseudo-haploid" format. This means that aDNA data are computationally made homozygous, usually by selecting a random allele at each heterozygous locus. This is obviously not needed for the mtDNA and Y-chromosome, as these loci are haploid by nature. For some population genetic inference methods, when comparing aDNA with present-day DNA data, it is important to have the whole dataset in the pseudo-haploid format. Alternatively, one may impute diploid genotypes using a reference dataset comprising high-quality DNA sequences. However, it is still unclear whether imputation methods perform well with aDNA data due to its typically low coverage and the presence of post-mortem damage.

Because DNA is usually found in low concentrations due to DNA degradation, contaminant DNA from modern sources may be present in relatively high amounts in the samples under analysis. Contamination may also bias research conclusions and should be assessed in each sample in every study. Low levels of contamination, typically less than 5 percent, are usually tolerated. However, any research conclusions based on contaminated samples should be considered with caution. Contamination in aDNA samples is commonly identi-fied using haploid loci such as the mtDNA and the X-chromosome in XY males. Roughly speaking, these methods are based on the identification of heterozygous sites in the data, which should not be observed for haploid genetic loci. Other methods leverage information from post-mortem damage patterns in order to isolate reads of interest from present-day contaminants.

Another type of contaminant is non-human DNA molecules mixed in the sample. These can be ancient pathogens and environmental microbes, and they can be filtered from the dataset with the use of computational techniques. These techniques, for instance, align sequencing reads for a given sample against a human reference genome and filter out the sequencing reads that do not map to the reference genome. The sequencing reads that do map to the reference genome, and are thus not filtered out, are referred to as endogenous DNA. The endogenous DNA content is indicative of the preservation status of the sample, and after initial screening, it is taken into account for the inclusion of a sample in an aDNA study. There is no consensus on the acceptable threshold of endogenous DNA content in a sample for its inclusion in a study. However, this is often factored in when deciding what type of sequencing strategy is best performed with a given sample.

In order to prevent contamination, aDNA is usually analyzed in aDNA-dedicated clean laboratories, where positive pressure is present, the air is HEPA-filtered, and surfaces are routinely cleaned with bleach and UV light (Fulton and Shapiro 2019). These aDNA-dedicated laboratories are typically located far from other genetic and molecular biology laboratories where, for instance, DNA from fresh tissues is handled. Personnel should also use personal protective equipment such as lab coats or coveralls, shoe covers, gloves, face shields, and facemask. In addition, one should avoid going to an aDNA lab if one has recently been in other DNA laboratories.

OBTAINING DNA FROM ARCHAEOLOGICAL MATERIAL

Ancient DNA molecules can be obtained from organic remains such as teeth, bones, soft tissues like skin, and coprolites. DNA can also be obtained from objects used by humans or from the soil. The two most common aDNA sources are teeth and bones, in particular the petrous portion (*pars petrosa*) of the temporal bone ("petrous bone" hereafter). The petrous bone is one of the densest bones in the human body and is considered the optimal source of DNA for paleogenomics studies due to its high endogenous DNA yield (Pinhasi et al. 2015). The amount of human aDNA available in the petrous bone is very variable and depends on the preservation of the sample and its exposure to weather conditions. In general, tooth samples present a lower DNA yield relative to the petrous bone. However, because teeth are vascularized, they are the prime material for recov-ering both ancient pathogen and human endogenous DNA (see Chapter 12). Once bone or tooth samples are obtained, they need to be pulverized. Then DNA can be extracted from tooth/bone powder in the laboratory using protocols designed for these types of tissues, which partially differ from those designed for extraction of DNA from blood or buccal swab. Minimally invasive techniques are available for reducing the damage caused during sampling, which may be detrimental to other archaeological and anthropological analyses, such as those based on bone/tooth morphology and stable isotope characterization.

Ethical considerations when dealing with DNA obtained from human remains include, but are not limited to, reducing damage to the remains and engaging the stakeholder communities in the scientific process (Fleskes et al. 2022). Traditional notions of informed consent in biomedical research with human subjects and corresponding legislation often do not directly translate to paleogenomics research, even when the materials being analyzed are human remains. Moreover, it is often challenging to identify who are the present-day communities that descend from the ancient individuals being studied. In the United States of America, official regulations, such as the Native American Graves Protection and Repatriation Act (NAGPRA), outline the characteristics of descendent or culturally affiliated Indigenous communities. Scholars must be aware of the consequences of their study for these communities and carefully examine the results of open data sharing, considering its potential social harms and political implications. For a detailed view of the ethical issues involving paleogenomics research, see Fleskes et al. (2022) and references therein.

PALEOGENOMICS APPLICATIONS IN BIOLOGICAL ANTHROPOLOGY

To date, more than six thousand ancient human genomes have been reconstructed, mostly from Europe and Asia (Liu et al. 2021). These genomes have been analyzed together with present-day human genetic data for different applications in biological anthropology. These include, for instance, the inference of past human migrations and the interactions between modern and archaic humans. Ancient DNA data has also been used to examine local adaptation events and to characterize phenotypic evolution in modern humans. More importantly, aDNA allowed, for the first time, the direct assessment of some important hypotheses of human evolution that were developed years before, based on genetic data from present-day people, morphology, historical texts, and archaeology. The uses of aDNA in biological anthropology are unlimited. This chapter focuses on four main applications that are most relevant to the field of biological anthropology. Additional examples and applications can be found in the literature (reviewed by Irving-Pease et al. 2021; Liu et al. 2021; Marciniak and Perry 2017).

Characterizing Ancient Human Migration and Population Structure

Early paleogenomics studies revealed that part of the genetic ancestry of human populations from the past was not seen in present-day people (Bramanti et al. 2009; Liu et al. 2021). These data highlighted major population turnover events across the globe and have shown that admixture has been pervasive throughout human history. In Europe, for instance, hunter-gatherer populations were partially replaced by Neolithic farmers with origins in the Near East (Goldberg et al. 2017; Hofmanová et al. 2016). At the beginning of the Bronze Age, Europe witnessed an additional major demographic change. This change is related to the spread of the Yamnaya Steppe pastoralist culture on the continent, and it is likely associated with the emergence of the Indo-European languages (Haak et al. 2015). The Steppe migration had a great impact throughout Europe, with varying levels of replacement of the local genetic ancestry depending on the specific region (Clemente et al. 2021; Haak et al. 2015; Liu et al. 2021), in some cases replacing approximately 90 percent of the local gene pool (Olalde et al. 2018). Interestingly, genetic evidence from aDNA shows that the Steppe migration was strongly male-biased (Clemente et al. 2021; Goldberg et al. 2017).

Because aDNA provides direct evidence of demographic shifts and population turnovers, paleogenomic data can shed light on the dating of demographic events associated with the peopling of different regions of the globe. In a study involving 89 ancient South American individuals, Nakatsuka et al. (2020) were able to detect a clear population structure separating northern and southern populations from the region that encompasses the Andes and the Pacific Coast of South America. The age of the remains corresponding to each individual was inferred from radiocarbon dating and was used to build a time-series dataset that revealed that the observed North–South population structure must have emerged at some time between 4,200 and 5,800 years before the present. The dating of this demographic shift, inferred from the combined analysis of aDNA and radiocarbon dates, roughly corresponds to the onset of the late preceramic period, which is associated with a shift toward a stronger reliance on agriculture in the region. Authors hypothesize that a greater reliance on plant cultivation could have, for instance, contributed to reduced mobility and therefore reduced gene flow between the North and the South (Nakatsuka et al. 2020).

Non-human DNA has also a place in biological anthropology. When humans migrate, they bring together crops, domesticated animals, and pathogens. Coanalysis of dog and human aDNA has revealed, for instance, that the dog population history mirrors that of humans (Bergström et al. 2020). Because of this intimate relationship between dogs and humans, dog aDNA data have been used to characterize human history and migration. For instance, Feuerborn et al. (2021) used dog aDNA to infer the origins and timing of major trading events between northwestern Siberia and populations living in distant regions. According to this study, amongst the populations that seem to have traded with northwestern Siberians is the Near East, suggesting a wide continental trading network involving peoples from different geographical origins (Feuerborn et al. 2021). Ancient DNA evidence also points to the origins of domesticated dogs approximately 23,000 years before the present (Perri et al. 2021), shedding light on the dating of major prehistoric events, even in the absence of direct genetic evidence from humans.

More recent population replacement and admixture events have also been evidenced with ancient DNA. These include, for instance, key events during the post-classical era that are associated with the origins of some of the modern European nations (Amorim et al. 2018; Margaryan et al. 2020; Maróti et al. 2022). A common subject in these studies is whether historical migrations inferred from the archaeological record indeed correspond to the movement of people across regions or are a result of cultural diffusion that does not involve the migration of people. One can imagine, for instance, that two populations could present similar material cultures, even though they descend from independent groups (Olalde et al. 2018). Genetic evidence provides the means to directly assess these questions by allowing for testing the hypothesis of genetic continuity between geographically distant populations. For instance, genetic data has validated the historical hypothesis that Huns and Avars originated in present-day Mongolia and that they are related to Asian Hun groups, such as the Xiongnus (Maróti et al. 2022). In another study, for instance, the origin of the barbarian group known as the Longobards, which had previously only been described in historical texts (Paul the Deacon 2011), was suggested as being in northern Europe with the analysis of aDNA (Amorim et al. 2018). This work corroborated the idea of long-distance migrations during the so-called "Barbarian Invasions" and revealed complex interactions between the migrant Longobards and the local populations, including Romans (Amorim et al. 2018). In sum, aDNA studies with historical period samples may furnish evidence of long-distance migration – sometimes involving cross-continental dispersal – and may provide a means to assess existing hypotheses of human history based on written and archaeological records.

Assessing Biological Relatedness in Archaeological Contexts

Initially, aDNA studies focused on generating data for one or a couple of individuals per archaeological site (Veeramah 2018). Dense population sampling in paleogenomics studies is hindered, in part, because of the inherent challenges of aDNA analysis, compromised sample preservation, and ethical concerns related to the destruction of the archaeological material. While these datasets with reduced sample sizes per time period, region, and culture are very useful for reconstructing human history, they say little to nothing about more local and fine-scale processes. Around the year 2015, we start to see human aDNA studies including larger sample sizes per archaeological site (Veeramah 2018). A few examples of such studies following this denser sampling approach are the studies by Amorim et al. (2018), Mathieson et al. (2015), and Yaka et al. (2021), where sample sizes are in the range of tens. This shift from a sparser to a denser sampling strategy has opened up new doors in paleogenomics research and furnished the opportunity for interdisciplinary collaborations to address novel questions in human history and evolution (Veeramah 2018). One example of a research question that is possible to be addressed with denser sampling is the inference of biological relatedness, or kinship, between pairs of individuals. Assessing kinship in archaeological contexts can provide unique insights into the social habits of past human communities. In this chapter, "kinship" refers to "biological kinship," which is the phenomenon in which two individuals share genetic loci that are inherited from a common ancestor (synonym to "biological relatedness"). While other types of kinship exist, genetic data have little or no relationship with it.

Initial attempts to infer kinship with aDNA focused on the mitochondrial DNA (mtDNA) and were based on amplification by the Polymerase Chain Reaction (PCR) (reviewed in Vai et al. 2020). Because each human cell contains a very large number of mitochondria, in the order of hundreds to thousands, amplification of mtDNA from human remains is relatively more successful than that of nuclear loci. More details about the use of mtDNA in human population genetics analyses are described in Chapter 6 by O'Rouke. For kinship inference, specifically, mtDNA is used to establish maternal relationships between individuals. However, these relationships are rather unspecific because two unrelated individuals may share an mtDNA haplotype. Because of this, kinship is not always possible to be confirmed with mtDNA analysis. In some cases, at best, mtDNA data can be used to rule out maternal relationships when individuals do not share the same mtDNA haplotype.

A more efficient approach to infer biological relatedness with aDNA data is based on Next Generation Sequencing (NGS). High-throughput sequencing platforms, in a timely and cost-effective manner, generate data for billions of DNA fragments per sequencing run. As a result, multiple genetic markers can be analyzed for a large number of individuals and used for biological kinship inference in biological anthropology studies. There are two main types of data generated through NGS platforms. One is whole-genome sequencing, commonly referred to as "shotgun sequencing," and the other is target capture enrichment. The latter consists of sequencing selected loci in the genome that are known to present a genetic variant (single nucleotide polymorphism, or SNP) in at least one human population worldwide. The number of SNPs analyzed in human paleogenomic studies varies, but the most widely used SNP set consists of ~1.2 million loci (Fu et al. 2015; Mathieson et al. 2015). This SNP set is known in the literature as the "1240K" dataset. It was developed with the intent of capturing global human genetic variation, and it has been widely used in biological anthropology.

Statistical methods to infer kinship are based on the sharing of genetic variants by identity-by-descent (IBD). IBD means that two individuals inherit an allele from the same ancestor in the past. The probability of IBD between two individuals is proportional to the degree to which two individuals are related. Its patterns across the genome – i.e., the proportion of loci in which zero, one, or two alleles are shared – are indicative of the type of relationship between them. For instance, full siblings are expected to share one and two alleles in IBD in 50 and 25 percent of the loci across their genomes, respectively. In the remaining 25 percent portion of their genome, full siblings are expected to share no allele by IBD. In contrast, a parent and child share only one allele in IBD in 100 percent of their genome. The same can be calculated for every other possible lineal and collateral bond between two individuals (Vai et al. 2020). In paleogenomics studies, these IBD allele-sharing patterns can be analyzed across multiple individuals in a population and used for the inference of pedigrees potentially involving multiple generations (Amorim et al. 2018). Thus, using methods to infer IBD, one can gain an insight into how related two individuals are and reconstruct the exact biological relationship between them, if a sufficient number of genetic markers are covered in both of them. It is estimated that ~ 50 SNPs have a similar informative power to that of 10 STRs, which are genetic markers commonly used in forensics analyses (Amorim and Pereira 2005). However, in practice, more accurate inferences can be made with a hundred thousand SNPs.

In inferring biological relatedness with aDNA, one should be aware of the problems introduced by low coverage sequences. Traditional NGS-based methods to infer kinship were meant to be applied on diploid sequences and, as mentioned above, aDNA is usually analyzed as pseudo-haploid data. Several methods have been developed more recently to infer IBD patterns with low-coverage data. These include software such as *READ* (Monroy Kuhn et al. 2018) and *lcmlkin* (Lipatov et al. 2015). Most of these methods rely on population genetics datasets, often from present-day individuals, to infer the allele frequencies used to calculate the probabilities of IBD (Vai et al. 2020). Up to third-degree relatedness may be detected by some methods, even with low coverage data (Lipatov et al. 2015).

Ancient DNA has been successfully used to infer kinship between individuals in Early Medieval graveyards in Europe, showing that graves with biologically related individuals more often shared elements of mortuary practice than those with unrelated individuals (Amorim et al. 2018; O'Sullivan et al. 2018). Similarly, Sánchez-Quinto et al. (2019) have analyzed the genomes of 24 ancient individuals from five European megalithic tombs of the fourth millennium BC. Their data show close kin relationships among individuals buried within the same megalith and, in some cases, even among individuals from different megaliths, and suggest these funerary monuments were associated with patrilineal kindred groups. Interestingly, Amorim et al. (2018) reconstructed four pedigrees in a medieval archaeological site in present-day Hungary and observed one single instance in which a pedigree completely lacked adult women, suggesting varying funerary practices depending on both sex and kinship status. Ancient DNA evidence has also been used to study funerary practice in Neolithic villages in Anatolia dated to the ninth to seventh millennia BC (Yaka et al. 2021). Results show contrasting funerary practices across time, where parent–offspring co-burials were common in the earlier societies and rare in the more recent ones. In another study, kinship inference based on aDNA was used to characterize Viking burials, revealing that Viking expeditions often involved biologically related individuals (Margaryan et al. 2020). This study also identified two instances where closely related individuals were excavated from sites located hundreds of kilometers apart from each other, illustrating the high mobility of individuals during the Viking Age. Studies such as these highlight the key role biological kinship played in burial organization, mortuary practice, and other social aspects of past human communities.

Inferring Social Organization and Local Population Histories

Genetic data can be combined with the written record, linguistic, stable isotope, and other archaeological data into an interdisciplinary framework in order to provide a more nuanced picture of the social organization and cultural habits of past human populations. This does not mean that genetic variation underlies variation in culture, but rather that it can be leveraged alongside other types of data to furnish insights into how biological relatedness between individuals and populations might have shaped certain habits of past human societies, in particular those related to the mortuary practice. For instance, Amorim et al. (2018) have generated data for over 60 individuals from two cemeteries associated with the Longobard culture (Paul the Deacon 2011), located in western Hungary and northern Italy and dated to the sixth century AD. These data were combined with mobility and diet stable isotopes, as well as a detailed description of grave goods, to provide a better picture of their social organization and history, including aspects that were not described in the written record. For instance, genetic data evidenced that these Longobard populations were composed of people with two distinct genetic ancestries: one associated with southern European populations (such as the one seen in present-day Italians) and the other with northern European populations (such as the one seen in present-day Norwegians). The latter was associated with specific grave furnishing, including weapons, pottery, and beads, whereas most of the graves bearing individuals with southern European ancestry were devoid of such grave goods and mostly contained common articles such as clothing items and coins. The grave structure was also clearly distinct between groups. Northern European genetic ancestry was associated with deeper graves with ledge walls, while graves for individuals with a major southern European ancestry component were relatively shallower and did not present structured or adorned walls. Dietary stable isotopes indicated that individuals with northern European ancestry had access to relatively higher amounts of protein than the others. Additionally, strontium stable isotope signatures suggested adults from both groups were not locals, but instead recent immigrants. Altogether, these data pointed to the existence of a structured, mobile population containing two groups with distinct genetic origins, diet, and culture. Approaches such as this, leveraging information from multiple sources in addition to aDNA data, require the collaboration of people with different expertise, which can be challenging. Moreover, a dense aDNA sampling strategy is not always possible due to the challenges that are inherent to aDNA. However, they can prove extremely valuable, especially when the studied group did not leave any written record and when archaeological data are scarce.

Local Adaptation and Phenotypic Reconstruction

Ancient DNA offers the opportunity to directly measure allele frequency changes associated with events of local adaptation, additionally providing a better notion of the timing of such events. Ancient DNA also aids in reconstructing the phenotypes of ancient and archaic humans, even when the phenotype per se is not directly observed. One of the first studies to take advantage of the full potential of aDNA to characterize local adaptation in humans used the 1240K SNPs to identify targets of natural selection in Europe (Mathieson et al. 2015). Amongst the genetic loci identified by the study as targets of natural selection are genes associated with variation in pigmentation and height, resistance against pathogens, and diet. The strongest natural selection signal in this study was found in a genetic variant associated with lactase persistence (Mathieson et al. 2015). Similar observations were made in posterior studies with aDNA and present-day populations (Marciniak and Perry 2017; Margaryan et al. 2020), highlighting the importance of diet as a key element in recent human evolution.

Genetic diversity underlying human phenotypic variation has been leveraged from aDNA datasets to offer a better picture of our ancestors (Clemente et al. 2021; Margaryan et al. 2020; Olalde et al. 2014). Skin, hair, and eye pigmentation are among the most common phenotypes that are reconstructed using aDNA because their genetic architecture is relatively well-known and dominated by mutations with large effects. However, the extent to which these reconstructions are accurate remains uncertain (Irving-Pease et al. 2021), at least in part due to the fact that the genetic architecture of these traits can vary across populations and time (Duncan et al. 2019; Marciniak et al. 2022). To assess the potential of predicting phenotype from aDNA, height has been inferred from bone measurements in over a thousand individuals and then compared to the predicted height based on genetic variants (Cox et al. 2019). Although height is a polygenic characteristic thought to be determined by a number of genetic variants with small effects and a strong influence from the environment, this study concluded that the height of an ancient individual can be partially predicted by aDNA (Cox et al. 2019). In addition to genetic effects, these results also highlight shifts in height that are more likely to be environmentally driven. Being one of the first studies to attempt combining phenotypic and genetic data from ancient humans, this research provided a model for interpreting phenotypic changes predicted from aDNA data. In a more recent study, the discrepancy between predicted and measured height in over 150 prehistoric Europeans was used to infer the impact of subsistence shifts on human health in the past (Marciniak et al. 2022). Combining osteological stature measurements with aDNA data, Marciniak et al. (2022) have found that early European farmers were relatively shorter than expected based on genetic variation. Authors hypothesize that this is likely to be the result of poorer nutrition and an increased infectious disease burden associated with agriculture.

Beyond phenotypic predictions of ancient *Homo sapiens*, attempts have been made in order to characterize the phenotypic diversity of archaic humans using genetic data. For instance, Gokhman et al. (2020) used aDNA to reconstruct the skeletal morphology and facial anatomy of Denisovans. This enigmatic archaic human, distinct from *Homo neanderthalensis* and *Homo sapiens*, was initially described solely based on its DNA extracted from the pinky bone and a few molars of a young female who lived around 41 thousand years ago (Reich et al. 2010). Because of the incomplete fossil record available for this specimen, scholars were left wondering, for over a decade, about what Denisovans looked like. To solve this enigma, Gokhman et al. (2020) inferred the DNA methylation map of Denisovans from post-mortem DNA damage patterns observed in aDNA. DNA methylation is one of the types of epigenetic changes that can affect phenotypic diversity through the regulation of gene expression. Results of this work showed that, for instance, Denisovans presented an elongated face and a wide pelvis, similar to Neanderthals, as well as unique characteristics such as an increased dental arch and lateral cranial expansion (Gokhman et al. 2020). This study illustrates the potential of paleogenomics for the reconstruction of phenotypes of ancient and archaic humans, even those phenotypes that do not survive in the fossil record.

Another aspect of human evolution that began to be studied with the advent of paleogenomics is the detection of adaptive archaic introgression in humans (Green et al. 2010; Marciniak and Perry 2017; Reich et al. 2010). Genetic introgression from archaic into anatomically modern humans is shown to have had a great impact on human adaptation to environmental pressures and is widespread in European, Asian, and Melanesian populations (Racimo et al. 2015). Candidate genes implicated in adaptive introgression involve traits such as high-altitude adaptation, resistance against pathogens, muscular function, pigmentation, and metabolism, among others (Marciniak and Perry 2017; Racimo et al. 2015). Because these archaic humans inhabited their environments for thousands of years before the worldwide dispersal of anatomically modern humans, the introgression of alleles associated with locally adapted phenotypes is thought to have promoted fast-paced local adaptation of humans to novel environments.

Because aDNA allows for the direct assessment of allele frequencies in the past, it has been proposed that time-series aDNA datasets should shed new light on the strength and timing of selective events that happened in the human lineage (Dehasque et al. 2020). For instance, observed allele frequency changes – directly measured using aDNA data – suggested an increase in the frequency of lactase persistence around 4,000–4,500 years ago in Eurasia (Mathieson et al. 2015), corresponding to the arrival of the Steppe pastoralist migrations in Europe (Haak et al. 2015). Despite the great promise of aDNA for the timing of evolutionary events and the dynamics of complex trait evolution (Dehasque et al. 2020; Irving-Pease et al. 2021), the small sample sizes that are typically obtained in aDNA studies may be an obstacle to the implementation of methods based on time-series data.

CONCLUSIONS

From providing the means to recover lost genetic lineages to aiding in the reconstruction of ancient and archaic human phenotypes, aDNA has revolutionized the way that we can study the human past. This chapter summarizes the challenges and some of the main applications of the study of aDNA in biological anthropology. Genomic data for thousands of ancient individuals are now available, and this number is rapidly increasing with the advent of more efficient and cost-effective DNA extraction and sequencing techniques. The future of aDNA studies is very promising. More robust statistical methods, together with the generation of an increasing amount of ancient genomic data, will shed new light on important aspects of human evolution, history, and health. A few recent advances in paleogenomics are the study of the ancient proteome based on dental calculus (Scott et al. 2022) and the possibility of imputing the complete DNA sequence of ancient genomes from low-coverage data (Rubinacci et al. 2021).

Despite the promises of further development of the field, paleogenomics faces key challenges. One main challenge is the ethical concerns related to the identification and engagement of descendant communities and stakeholders, to the social and political consequences of genetic research, and, in some cases, to the lack of acknowledgment of Indigenous peoples' sovereignty over data and human remains. Additionally, paleogenomics currently suffers from an underrepresentation of non-European genomes in study sets. This lack of diversity results in a biased and incomplete notion of human evolution and can limit the reach of potential biomedical applications of aDNA data. The lack of communication among geneticists, archaeologists, and social scientists may further hinder the development of the field; however, recent studies that take an interdisciplinary approach have pointed to a potential paradigm shift that should propel the field of paleogenomics into novel venues. As we, as a community, overcome these challenges, we should ensure a more equitable and ethical future for paleogenomics. Because this discipline is a relatively young field of inquiry, we can expect significant transformations in the years to come. These transformations should have profound consequences for anthropological genetics and the study of human evolution more broadly.

REFERENCES

Amorim, A., and L. Pereira. "Pros and Cons in the Use of SNPs in Forensic Kinship Investigation: A Comparative Analysis with STRs." *Forensic Science International* 150, no. 1 (2005): 17–21.

Amorim, C. E. G., S. Vai, C. Posth, et al. "Understanding 6th-Century Barbarian Social Organization and Migration through Paleogenomics." *Nature Communications* 9, no. 1 (2018): 3547.

Bergström, A., L. Frantz, R. Schmidt, et al. "Origins and Genetic Legacy of Prehistoric Dogs." *Science* 370, no. 6516 (2020): 557–564.

Bramanti, B., M. G. Thomas, W. Haak, et al. "Genetic Discontinuity Between Local Hunter-Gatherers and Central Europe's First Farmers." *Science* 326, no. 5949 (2009): 137–140.

Briggs, A. W., U. Stenzel, M. Meyer, et al. "Removal of Deaminated Cytosines and Detection of In Vivo Methylation in Ancient DNA." *Nucleic Acids Research* 38, no. 6 (2010): e87.

Clemente, F., M. Unterländer, O. Dolgova, et al. "The Genomic History of the Aegean Palatial Civilizations." *Cell* 184, no. 10 (2021): 2565–86.e21.

Cox, S. L., C. B. Ruff, R. M. Maier, and I. Mathieson. "Genetic Contributions to Variation in Human Stature in Prehistoric Europe." *Proceedings of the National Academy of Sciences of the United States of America* 116, no 43 (2019): 21484–21492.

Dabney, J., M. Meyer, and S. Pääbo. "Ancient DNA Damage." *Cold Spring Harbor Perspectives in Biology* 5, no. 7 (2013): a012567.

Dehasque, M., M. C. Ávila-Arcos, D. Díez-Del-Molino, et al. "Inference of Natural Selection from Ancient DNA." *Evolution Letters* 4, no. 2 (2020): 94–108.

Duncan, L., H. Shen, B. Gelaye, et al. "Analysis of Polygenic Risk Score Usage and Performance in Diverse Human Populations." *Nature Communications* 10, no. 1 (2019): 3328.

Feuerborn, T. R., A. Carmagnini, R. J. Losey, et al. "Modern Siberian Dog Ancestry Was Shaped by Several Thousand Years of Eurasian-Wide Trade and Human Dispersal." *Proceedings of the National Academy of Sciences of the United States of America* 118, no. 39 (2021): e2100338118.

Fleskes, R. E., A. C. Bader, K. S. Tsosie, et al. "Ethical Guidance in Human Paleogenomics: New and Ongoing Perspectives." *Annual Review of Genomics and Human Genetics* 23, no. 1 (2022): 627–652.

Fu, Q., M. Hajdinjak, O. T. Moldovan, et al. "An Early Modern Human from Romania with a Recent Neanderthal Ancestor." *Nature* 524, no. 7564 (2015): 216–219.

Fu, Q., C. Posth, M. Hajdinjak, et al. "The Genetic History of Ice Age Europe." *Nature* 534, no. 7606 (2016): 200–205.

Fulton, T. L., and B. Shapiro. "Setting up an Ancient DNA Laboratory." *Methods in Molecular Biology* 1963 (2019): 1–13.

Gokhman, D., N. Mishol, M. de Manuel, et al. "Reconstructing Denisovan Anatomy Using DNA Methylation Maps." *Cell* 179, no. 1 (2020): 180–192.e10.

Goldberg, A., T. Günther, N. A. Rosenberg, and M. Jakobsson. "Ancient X Chromosomes Reveal Contrasting Sex Bias in Neolithic and Bronze Age Eurasian Migrations." *Proceedings of the National Academy of Sciences of the United States of America* 114, no. 10 (2017): 2657–2662.

Green, R. E., J. Krause, A. W. Briggs, et al. "A Draft Sequence of the Neandertal Genome." *Science* 328, no. 5979 (2010): 710–722.

Haak, W., I. Lazaridis, N. Patterson, et al. "Massive Migration from the Steppe Was a Source for Indo-European Languages in Europe." *Nature* 522, no. 7555 (2015): 207–211.

Hofmanová, Z., S. Kreutzer, G. Hellenthal, et al. "Early Farmers from Across Europe Directly Descended from Neolithic Aegeans." *Proceedings of the National Academy of Sciences of the United States of America* 113, no. 25 (2016): 6886–6891.

Irving-Pease, E. K., R. Muktupavela, M. Dannemann, and F. Racimo. "Quantitative Human Paleogenetics: What Can Ancient DNA Tell Us About Complex Trait Evolution?" *Frontiers in Genetics* 12 (August 2021): 703541.

Knapp, M., and M. Hofreiter. "Next Generation Sequencing of Ancient DNA: Requirements, Strategies and Perspectives." *Genes* 1, no. 2 (2010): 227–243.

Lipatov, M., K. Sanjeev, R. Patro, and K. Veeramah. "Maximum Likelihood Estimation of Biological Relatedness from Low Coverage Sequencing Data." *bioRxiv* (2015): https://doi.org/10.1101/023374.

Liu, Y., X. Mao, J. Krause, and Q. Fu. "Insights into Human History from the First Decade of Ancient Human Genomics." *Science* 373, no. 6562 (2021): 1479–1484.

Marciniak, S., C. M. Bergey, A. M. Silva, et al. "An Integrative Skeletal and Paleogenomic Analysis of Stature Variation Suggests Relatively Reduced Health for Early European Farmers." *Proceedings of the National Academy of Sciences of the United States of America* 119, no. 15 (2022): e2106743119.

Marciniak, S., and G. H. Perry. "Harnessing Ancient Genomes to Study the History of Human Adaptation." *Nature Reviews Genetics* 18, no. 11 (2017): 659–674.

Margaryan, A., D. J. Lawson, M. Sikora, et al. "Population Genomics of the Viking World." *Nature* 585, no. 7825 (2020): 390–396.

Maróti, Z., E. Neparáczki, O. Schütz, et al. "The Genetic Origin of Huns, Avars, and Conquering Hungarians." *Current Biology* S0960-9822, no. 22 (2022): 00732–1.

Mathieson, I., I. Lazaridis, N. Rohland, et al. "Genome-Wide Patterns of Selection in 230 Ancient Eurasians." *Nature* 528, no. 7583 (2015): 499–503.

Monroy Kuhn, J. M., M. Jakobsson, and T. Günther. "Estimating Genetic Kin Relationships in Prehistoric Populations." *PloS One* 13, no. 4 (2018): e0195491.

Nakatsuka, N., I. Lazaridis, C. Barbieri, et al. "A Paleogenomic Reconstruction of the Deep Population History of the Andes." *Cell* 181, no. 5 (2020): 1131–45.e21.

Olalde, I., M. E. Allentoft, F. Sánchez-Quinto, et al. "Derived Immune and Ancestral Pigmentation Alleles in a 7,000-Year-Old Mesolithic European." *Nature* 507, no. 7491 (2014): 225–228.

Olalde, I., S. Brace, M. E. Allentoft, et al. "The Beaker Phenomenon and the Genomic Transformation of Northwest Europe." *Nature* 555, no. 7695 (2018): 190–196.

O'Sullivan, N., C. Posth, V. Coia, et al. "Ancient Genome-Wide Analyses Infer Kinship Structure in an Early Medieval Alemannic Graveyard." *Science Advances* 4, no. 9 (2018): eaao1026.

Paul the Deacon. *History of the Lombards.* Philadelphia, PA: University of Pennsylvania Press, 2011.

Perri, A. R., T. R. Feuerborn, L. A. F. Frantz, et al. "Dog Domestication and the Dual Dispersal of People and Dogs into the Americas." *Proceedings of the National Academy of Sciences of the United States of America* 118, no. 6 (2021): e2010083118.

Pinhasi, R., D. Fernandes, K. Sirak, et al. "Optimal Ancient DNA Yields from the Inner Ear Part of the Human Petrous Bone." *PloS One* 10, no. 6 (2015): e0129102.

Racimo, F., S. Sankararaman, R. Nielsen, and E. Huerta-Sánchez. "Evidence for Archaic Adaptive Introgression in Humans." *Nature Reviews. Genetics* 16, no. 6 (2015): 359–371.

Reich, D., R. E. Green, M. Kircher, et al. "Genetic History of an Archaic Hominin Group from Denisova Cave in Siberia." *Nature* 468, no. 7327 (2010): 1053–1060.

Rohland, N., E. Harney, S. Mallick, et al. "Partial Uracil–DNA–Glycosylase Treatment for Screening of Ancient DNA." *Philosophical Transactions of the Royal Society B: Biological Sciences* 370, no. 1660 (2015): 20130624.

Rubinacci, S., D. M. Ribeiro, R. J. Hofmeister, and O. Delaneau. "Efficient Phasing and Imputation of Low-Coverage Sequencing Data Using Large Reference Panels." *Nature Genetics* 53, no. 1 (2021): 120–126.

Sánchez-Quinto, F., H. Malmström, M. Fraser, et al. "Megalithic Tombs in Western and Northern Neolithic Europe Were Linked to a Kindred Society." *Proceedings of the National Academy of Sciences of the United States of America* 116, no. 19 (2019): 9469–9474.

Scott, A., S. Reinhold, T. Hermes, et al. "Emergence and Intensification of Dairying in the Caucasus and Eurasian Steppes." *Nature Ecology & Evolution* 6, no. 6 (2022): 813–822.

Vai, S., C. E. G. Amorim, M. Lari, and D. Caramelli. "Kinship Determination in Archeological Contexts through DNA Analysis." *Frontiers in Ecology and Evolution* 4, no. 9 (2020): eaao1262.

Van der Valk, T., P. Pečnerová D. Díez-Del-Molino, et al. "Million-Year-Old DNA Sheds Light on the Genomic History of Mammoths." *Nature* 591, no. 7849 (2021): 265–269.

Veeramah, K. R. "The Importance of Fine-Scale Studies for Integrating Paleogenomics and Archaeology." *Current Opinion in Genetics & Development* 53 (2018): 83–89.

Yaka, R., I. Mapelli, D. Kaptan, et al. "Variable Kinship Patterns in Neolithic Anatolia Revealed by Ancient Genomes." *Current Biology* 31, no. 11 (2021): 2455–68.e18.

CHAPTER 14 Demography, Including Paleodemography

*Lyle W. Konigsberg,
George R. Milner, and
Jesper L. Boldsen*

Demography is the study of a group's age and sex structure. "Group," although vague, is intentionally used because we may study a species, a village, a large sociopolitical unit, such as a nation, or a population, although what constitutes a population is often ambiguous as well. In biological anthropology, demography may refer to nonhuman primates or to humans, although in this chapter we focus on the latter. By prefixing "paleo" to demography, we refer to the demography of past groups, generally understood to pertain to work with archaeological skeletons, but also to studies of sites and radiocarbon dates when monitoring regional population growth (or decline). While skeletal analyses often cover relatively recent periods in human history (DeWitte 2010, 2012; DeWitte and Hughes-Morey 2012), they may focus on earlier time horizons, such as the Neolithic (Bocquet-Appel 2011; Bocquet-Appel and Naji 2006; Eshed et al. 2004), and even as far back as those of our hominin ancestors (Bocquet-Appel and Arsuaga 1999; Caspari and Lee 2004; Mann 1975).

In this chapter, we focus primarily on the life table and its continuous form, known as a hazard or survivorship model. The life table can be thought of as a spreadsheet of deaths. Some attribute the first life table to John Graunt (1662), such as Ciecka (2008: 66), who notes that Graunt "engaged in a great deal of guess work because age at death was unrecorded and because London's population was growing in an un-quantified manner due to migration." The first true life table, however, can be attributed to Halley (1693). It was a complete life table in that it showed survivorship in yearly intervals. In bioanthropology, it is more common to see abridged life tables (Shryock and Siegel 1976: 249), which typically feature age intervals in years of 0–1, 1–5, 5–10, and so on in five-year intervals. Life tables can also be classified as generation or current tables (Dublin and Spiegelman 1941), or more often cohort versus period life tables. In cohort life tables, a birth cohort is followed through time, while in a period life table, deaths during a certain period are used to

A Companion to Biological Anthropology, Second Edition. Edited by Clark Spencer Larsen.
© 2023 John Wiley & Sons Ltd. Published 2023 by John Wiley & Sons Ltd.

construct the life table. In that instance, no single cohort might experience precisely what is captured by the life table parameters because living conditions, such as diseases and their treatment, change over time.

AN ABRIDGED LIFE TABLE

Table 14.1 shows an abridged life table, which for the moment is assumed to be a cohort life table. We simulated 500 deaths using a model life table from Séguy and Buchet (2013), the details of which are described in the Appendix. The first two columns in Table 14.1, labelled "open" and "close," represent the beginning and ending of age intervals. The third column, designated "$_wD_x$", represents the number of deaths within each age interval. The complete notation for the first four intervals is $_1D_0, _4D_1, _5D_5, _5D_{10}$, and for the last interval is $_{15}D_{75}$, assuming nobody lives beyond the age of 90, or, more generally, $_wD_x$ or $_nD_x$, where x is the start of the interval and w or n is the interval width ("close" minus "open"). The bottom of the third column shows the sum of deaths; in this instance, the 500 simulated individuals. The fourth column, labelled l_x, gives survivorship to the beginning ("open") of each age interval. This column begins at the "radix," which here is the total number of deaths. Other values can be used for the radix. For example, had we divided all the numbers in column 4 by 500 the column could be interpreted as the probability of surviving to the beginning of the age interval. Because survivorship refers to survivors at the start of the age interval, there is no notation to the left; in other words, the first four values are l_0, l_1, l_5, and l_{10}. The fifth column, labelled $_wq_x$ (the complete notation for the first four intervals is $_1q_0$, $_4q_1, _5q_5$, and $_5q_{10}$), is the age-specific probability of death in the age interval. In other words, it is the probability of an individual alive at age x dying before the end of the interval at $x + w$. It is equal to $_wD_x/l_x$, the number of deaths in an interval divided by the number of individuals entering the interval, where l_x uses the radix equal to the sum of the D_x values.

Column 6, labelled $_wL_x$, contains the person-years lived in an age interval of a given width (w), and is one of the more difficult calculations to follow. As a historical note, $_wL_x$ is the only life table function given by Halley (1693). The calculation is based on the idea that individuals who die in an interval are uniformly distributed across the age interval. Consequently, individuals who die in the interval contribute half the width of the age interval, while individuals who survive contribute the full interval width. For example, for $_5L_5$ we have $l_5 - l_{10} = 320 - 289 = 31$ individuals who contribute $w/2 = 2.5$ years, while $l_{10} = 289$ individuals contribute 5 years. This gives $_5L_5 = (l_5 - l_{10}) \times w/2 + l_{10}w = (l_5 + l_{10})/2 \times w$ so that $_5L_5$ is the average of l_5 and l_{10} times the age interval width. Having uniform ages at death is not a good assumption for the young, but it is made for simplicity's sake. Column 8, T_x, is "the **total years to be lived** (person years) by those reaching age X until all are dead" (Weiss 1973: 37, emphasis in the original). It lists the person-years to be lived at the opening of an age interval and beyond and can be found by summing the $_wL_x$ values from the bottom up. Note that $T_0 = 9,877.5$, the sum from the bottom of column 6. Dividing T_x by the corresponding l_x gives the average years yet to be lived at the opening of the age interval; that is, life expectancy as given in column 9 as e_x. We see that $e_{75} = 7.5$, which is logical given that everyone dies by 90 in the example, a uniform distribution of ages at death is assumed between 75 and 90, and $(90 - 75)/2 = 7.5$. The 10th column shows the person-years to be lived in an interval divided by the total person-years to be lived by the 500 individuals. The symbol $_wc_x$ is for the proportion of the living population in the age interval. The 11th column shows the products of the 10th column entries with the midpoint of each age interval. The sum of this column is an estimate of the mean age in the living (MAL). The mean age at death (MAD) is the same as the life expectancy at birth (the first entry of 19.76 in the 9th column). The crude death rate, the number of deaths (at any age) per annum divided by the mid-year population size, is shown as $d = 0.051$, which is the inverse of the mean age at death (life expectancy at birth). As zero population growth is assumed, the intrinsic rate of increase (r) is zero, so the crude birth rate is also 0.051 ($r = b - d$).

Not mentioned so far, but relevant to the later discussion of hazards analysis, is the central mortality rate, shown as $_wm_x$ in column 7. While in the abridged life table, as well as in the complete yearly life table, age is placed into ordered "bins," age is really a continuous variable that could be measured in years, months, days, or even shorter intervals. The hazard rate when applied to the continuous variable of age at death is the instantaneous rate of death, and as such it can be greater than 1.0, unlike the age-specific probability of death ($_wq_x$). The central mortality rate is assumed to be a constant throughout the age interval. The simplest calculation, and the one used here, assumes that survivorship is linear throughout the age interval. The central mortality rate can be estimated as (Keyfitz 1985: 35)

$$_wm_x = \frac{l_x - l_{x+w}}{_wL_x} \tag{14.1}$$

where w is the age interval width. More simply, the central mortality rate can be obtained by solving Equation 1 from Greville (1943):

$$_wm_x = \frac{2\,_wq_x}{w(2 - _wq_x)} \tag{14.2}$$

For both young and old age intervals, the assumption of a linear decline in survivorship is problematic. In the first edition of Coale and Demeny (1966), a linear decline in survivorship was assumed when calculating $_5L_5$ through $_5L_{75}$, though in the second edition (Coale and Demeny 1983) they give $_5L_x = 2.6 \times l_x + 2.4 \times l_{x+5}$ for x from 5 to 75. Weiss (1973: 37) uses $_1L_0 = 0.35 \times l_0 + 0.65 \times l_1$ and $_4L_1 = 1.361 \times l_1 + 2.639 \times l_5$ from some of the values in Coale and Demeny (1966: 20). Both equations represent curvilinear decreasing values for survivorship. The life table in Table 14.1 is simplified by assuming a linear decrease in survivorship for all age intervals.

Fertility for The Abridged Life Table

For the moment we can treat Table 14.1 as a period life table, instead of a cohort life table, for a stable population. A stable population is one that has fixed fertility and mortality schedules and "that neither gains nor loses by migration" (Coale 1972: 3). With sufficient time, such populations reach a fixed age distribution. Weiss (1975: 56) states that "...we can at least be reasonably confident of average vital rates determined from ostensibly minimally disturbed populations." We can further simplify by assuming that the population is stationary; in other words, crude birth and death rates are equal so that the population size is neither shrinking nor expanding. A stationary population is thus a special case of a stable population, the characteristics of which are discussed in Keyfitz (1985).

Under the condition that Table 14.1 is a stationary period life table, we can extend it to the one in Table 14.2 to consider fertility, following Weiss (1973). The first column has five-year age intervals starting at 15 years and ending with the interval 45–50, capturing the age span during which females are fertile. The second column is the l_x column from

Table 14.1 A stationary life table

1 open	2 close	3 $_wD_x$	4 l_x	5 $_wq_x$	6 $_wL_x$	7 $_wm_x$	8 T_x	9 $\overset{\circ}{e}_x$	10 $_wc_x$	11 years
0	1	115	500	0.2300	442.5	0.2599	9877.5	19.76	0.0448	0.022
1	5	65	385	0.1688	1410.0	0.0461	9435.0	24.51	0.1427	0.428
5	10	31	320	0.0969	1522.5	0.0204	8025.0	25.08	0.1541	1.156
10	15	33	289	0.1142	1362.5	0.0242	6502.5	22.50	0.1379	1.724
15	20	46	256	0.1797	1165.0	0.0395	5140.0	20.08	0.1179	2.064
20	25	41	210	0.1952	947.5	0.0433	3975.0	18.93	0.0959	2.158
25	30	31	169	0.1834	767.5	0.0404	3027.5	17.91	0.0777	2.137
30	35	23	138	0.1667	632.5	0.0364	2260.0	16.38	0.0640	2.081
35	40	27	115	0.2348	507.5	0.0532	1627.5	14.15	0.0514	1.927
40	45	27	88	0.3068	372.5	0.0725	1120.0	12.73	0.0377	1.603
45	50	20	61	0.3279	255.0	0.0784	747.5	12.25	0.0258	1.226
50	55	14	41	0.3415	170.0	0.0824	492.5	12.01	0.0172	0.904
55	60	9	27	0.3333	112.5	0.0800	322.5	11.94	0.0114	0.655
60	65	6	18	0.3333	75.0	0.0800	210.0	11.67	0.0076	0.475
65	70	3	12	0.2500	52.5	0.0571	135.0	11.25	0.0053	0.359
70	75	3	9	0.3333	37.5	0.0800	82.5	9.17	0.0038	0.275
75	90	6	6	1.0000	45.0	0.1333	45.0	7.50	0.0046	0.376
		500			9877.5					

MAL = 19.57

MAD = 19.76

b = 0.051

d = 0.051

r = 0

Table 14.2 Calculation of fertility

1 Age	2 l_x	3 $_5L_x$	4 K_x	5 $K_x \times {_5}L_x$	6 $FB = K_x \times \bar{B}$	7 $_5L_x \times FB$	8 Years
15	0.5120	2.3300	0.64199	1.496	0.061	0.141	2.48
20	0.4200	1.8950	1.73859	3.295	0.164	0.312	7.01
25	0.3380	1.5350	1.74068	2.672	0.165	0.253	6.95
30	0.2760	1.2650	1.41042	1.784	0.133	0.169	5.49
35	0.2300	1.0150	0.98137	0.996	0.093	0.094	3.53
40	0.1760	0.7450	0.40670	0.303	0.038	0.029	1.22
45	0.1220	0.3050	0.08418	0.026	0.008	0.002	0.12
			ave(B) = 0.095		0.663		
					TFR = 3.31	NRR = 1.00	T = 26.79

Table 14.1, but here divided by 500 so that $l_0 = 1.000$; in other words, the radix is 1.000. The third column, L_x, is calculated as in Table 14.1. The fourth column, $_5K_x$, lists age-specific fertility rates from Weiss' (1973) populations in his Table 12. Age-specific fertility rates are the observed number of births to women in a five-year interval divided by the observed number of woman-years in that interval (Wood 1994: 25). These are annual rates, so they need to be multiplied by the five-year widths to get the rates per interval. Column 5 is the product $K_x \times {_5}L_x$ combining fertility with mortality. The inverse of the sum of the column is the "'mean' fertility rate" (Weiss 1973: 31). Column 6 contains the products of K_x (column 4) with the "mean" fertility rate, which Weiss (1973) refers to as "FB" for "female births." The sum of column 6 multiplied by five for the interval width gives the Total Fertility Rate, "the expected number of offspring ever born to a randomly selected woman who survives to the end of the reproductive span" (Wood 1994: 27). Column 7 is the product of $_5L_x$ and FB, and its sum is the net reproduction rate (NRR) (Shryock and Siegel 1976: 315): "a measure of the number of daughters that a cohort of newborn girl babies will bear during their lifetime assuming a fixed schedule of age-specific fertility rates and a fixed set of mortality rates." Because we have assumed a stationary life table, the NRR = 1. Column 8, labelled "Years," is the product of the entries in column 7 with the midpoint of the age interval. The sum of this column is the generation length, which is the "mean age of mothers at the birth of their daughters" (Shryock and Siegel 1976: 317).

A Nonstationary Life Table

In Table 14.3 the life table, in contrast to the Table 14.1 cohort life table, represents a period life table with an intrinsic rate of increase of $r = 0.02$. The main calculations follow Asch (1976: Table 5), though some calculations are also given in Carrier (1958) and Bennett (1973). We need to be aware that there are two ways of making calculations that include non-zero population growth (or decline). One way uses "annual compounding." If we start with a population of $N_0 = 100$ and an intrinsic rate of increase of $r = 0.02$ (a 2 percent

Table 14.3 Life table with an intrinsic rate of increase of 0.02

r =	0.02										
1	2	3	4	5	6	7	8	9	10	11	12
open	close	$_wD_x$	e^{ra}	$_wD_xe^{ra}$	l_x	$_wL_x$	T_x	e_x	$_wL_xe^{-ra}$	$_wc_x$	Years
0	1	115	1.01005	116.1558	807.9511	749.9	23177.6	28.69	742.41	0.0483	0.024
1	5	65	1.061837	69.01938	691.7953	2629.1	22427.7	32.42	2476.03	0.1611	0.483
5	10	31	1.161834	36.01686	622.776	3023.8	19798.5	31.79	2602.64	0.1694	1.270
10	15	33	1.284025	42.37284	586.7591	2827.9	16774.7	28.59	2202.34	0.1433	1.792
15	20	46	1.419068	65.27711	544.3863	2558.7	13946.8	25.62	1803.11	0.1173	2.054
20	25	41	1.568312	64.3008	479.1091	2234.8	11388.1	23.77	1424.97	0.0927	2.087
25	30	31	1.733253	53.73084	414.8083	1939.7	9153.3	22.07	1119.12	0.0728	2.003
30	35	23	1.915541	44.05744	361.0775	1695.2	7213.6	19.98	884.99	0.0576	1.872
35	40	27	2.117	57.159	317.0201	1442.2	5518.4	17.41	681.25	0.0443	1.663
40	45	27	2.339647	63.17047	259.8611	1141.4	4076.2	15.69	487.84	0.0317	1.349
45	50	20	2.58571	51.71419	196.6906	854.2	2934.8	14.92	330.34	0.0215	1.021
50	55	14	2.857651	40.00712	144.9764	624.9	2080.6	14.35	218.66	0.0142	0.747
55	60	9	3.158193	28.42374	104.9693	453.8	1455.7	13.87	143.69	0.0094	0.538
60	65	6	3.490343	20.94206	76.54556	330.4	1002.0	13.09	94.65	0.0062	0.385
65	70	3	3.857426	11.57228	55.6035	249.1	671.6	12.08	64.57	0.0042	0.284
70	75	3	4.263115	12.78934	44.03122	188.2	422.5	9.60	44.14	0.0029	0.208
75	90	6	5.20698	31.24188	31.24188	234.3	234.3	7.50	45.00	0.0029	0.242
		500		807.9511		23177.6			15365.77		

MAL = 18.02
MAD = 19.63
b = 0.053
d = 0.033

increase), the population size N_t at $t = 50$ years later is $N_{50} = N_0(1 + r)^{50} \cong 269.16$. This gives a doubling time of about 35.00 years. This method is used by Moore et al. (1975) and Swedlund and Armelagos (1976: 52), among others. Carrier (1958) and Bennett (1973) divide the number of deaths by powers of $1 - r$. A similar method is continuous compounding where $N_{50} = N_0 \exp(r \times 50) \cong 271.83$, which gives a doubling time of about 34.66 years. The difference between annual compounding and continuous compounding is trivial for relatively short periods of time. We use the latter simply because it extends easily to hazard models where age is a continuous variable.

The first three columns of Table 14.3 are the same as in Table 14.1. The fourth column in Table 14.3 pertains to population growth, and is $\exp(ra)$, where a is the middle of the age interval, the average of "open" and "close" (the first two columns), and $r = 0.02$. This column deals with a growing population (positive value of r) where individuals in older age intervals came from smaller birth cohorts than those in younger age intervals. The number of deaths consequently must be adjusted upward in later age intervals. The fifth column shows these adjusted numbers of deaths as $_wD_x \exp(ra)$, which is exactly equal to $_wD_x / \exp(-ra)$. Such is not the case for "annual compounding," where $_wD_x(1 + r)^a$ is only approximately equal to $_wD_x / (1 - r)^a$. Note that the sum of the numbers of deaths has now increased and serves as the first number in the survivorship column (column 6). Columns 6 through 9 in Table 14.3 are calculated, as were columns 4, 6, 8, and 9 in Table 14.1. Column 10 in Table 14.3 is $_wL_x \exp(-ra)$, which is the same as column 7 divided by column 4 from this table. Column 11, the living age distribution, lists the elements of column 10 divided by its sum. The 12th column, "years," has the elements from column 11 times the midpoint of the age intervals. The sum of column 12 is an estimate of the mean age in the living population (MAL). The crude birth rate is estimated by the sum of column 5 divided by the sum of column 7. The crude death rate is then $b - r$. From the crude death rate, MAL, and growth rate, we can find the MAD using Equation (14.14), below.

LIFE TABLES FROM EXTANT ANTHROPOLOGICAL SAMPLES

For an extant group it may be possible to obtain information on ages-at-death, although generally it is more common to have census information on the living (a cross-sectional sample). Either way, it would be unusual to have vital registration information; that is, records of date of birth for an accurate census or both the dates of birth and death for ages-at-death. Unlike national census or death records, anthropological samples tend to be small and subject to stochastic (random) effects. Both problems often require some form of smoothing to calculate a life table.

Wood (1987: 179), for example, comments that for the Gainj, a group from the highlands of Papua New Guinea, "age- and sex-specific life tables have been estimated by the Brass two-parameter logit method." The Brass (1971) two-parameter logit model assumes that there is a common shape for human survivorship. Consequently, observed survivorship values beyond $l_0 = 1.0$ can be converted to logits:

$$\ln\left(\frac{1 - l_x}{l_x}\right) \tag{14.3}$$

as is also done in Brass' Table 4. Others invert so that the term in parentheses is $l_x / (1 - l_x)$. Brass multiplied his logits by one-half, but this unnecessary step was taken to look up values in an old set of statistical tables. The two parameters in Brass' model are the intercept and slope from a linear regression of the observed survivorship logits on Brass' logits. If y are the estimated logits, as in Equation (14.3), from predicting the sample logits from Brass' logits, then the estimated survivorships are $l_x = 1/(1 + \exp(y_x))$. Brass' two-parameter logit model is not always sufficient to fit survivorship. For example, it does not give a good fit to the life table in Table 14.1. Ewbank et al. (1983) give a four-parameter logit model that uses a different standard life table from that of Brass for ages below 15 years. In addition to the intercept and slope in Brass' two-parameter logit model, the Ewbank model contains a parameter κ that adjusts survivorship at younger ages and λ that adjusts survivorship at older ages. As shown in Figure 14.1A, the Brass two-parameter model does not fit the Table 14.1 life table as well as the Ewbank four-parameter model.

Single census life table estimates for anthropological samples are made additionally difficult because growth rates may be unknown. The samples might not be drawn from stable populations because fertility and mortality schedules have changed, there is immigration or emigration, or both. Weiss (1973: 20) gives an example of calculating survivorship for the Guarani of Brazil from a single census and assuming a stationary population. Under this assumption, survivorship can be found from the decrease in the number of individuals when moving from one age interval to the next older one of equal width. Because of small sample size and stochastic variation, subtracting the number of individuals in the older age interval from the adjacent younger age interval can yield negative numbers. To correct for this, Weiss smoothed the data using running averages (moving averages or rolling means). Doing so replaces individual values with the mean of a "window" of values, usually three of them, leaving the first and last values unchanged. This method of "rolling means" was previously often used in paleodemography to smooth the number of skeletons in age intervals (e.g., Palkovich 1981).

A single census with a previous population size some known number of years earlier can be used to fit a stable, but non-stationary, life table. If there are two censuses separated by a known number of years, a non-stable life table can be estimated (Gage et al. 1984, 1986).

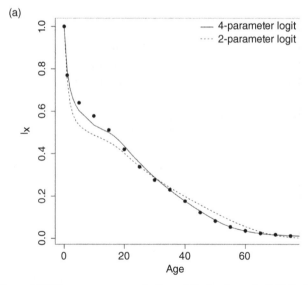

Figure 14.1A A Brass (1971) two-parameter logit and Ewbank et al. (1983) four-parameter logit fit to survivorship.

Hazard Models

A hazard model generalizes the life table so that age is a continuous variable. The survivorship, in column 4 of Table 14.1, could have been written using a radix of 1.0. Survivorship then starts at $l_0 = 1.0$, proceeds through $l_{75} = 6/500 = 0.012$, and ends with $l_{90} = 0.0$. In a hazard model there is a continuous hazard of death, and survivorship is likewise a continuous function. One of the first hazard models was from Gompertz (1825), who intended his function to apply to adults. The Gompertz function can be fitted to Table 14.1, starting at age 15 and continuing to 90. The Gompertz function is

$$\mu(t) = a_3 \exp(b_3(t - 15)) \tag{14.4}$$

where the minus 15 allows the function, in this instance, to start at age zero. The subscript numbering follows that from the Siler model (Gage 1988, 1991; Gage and Dyke 1986; Siler 1979). The log Gompertz hazard forms a straight line, but we will work in the original scale. The survival function from the Gompertz hazard is

$$S(t) = \exp\left[\frac{a_3}{b_3}(1 - \exp(b_3(t - 15)))\right] \tag{14.5}$$

where the function, and others to follow, are from Wood et al. (2002). Holman (2003) provides a plethora of hazard models, the survival functions, and the probability density functions. The probability density functions are the continuous density functions for ages-at-death, which, like any proper probability density function, integrate to 1.0. Hazard functions can be fit using maximum likelihood and survival functions. The parameters a_3 and b_3 (Equation 14.5) are searched across until the maximum log-likelihood is found, as we show in the R code available at http://faculty.las.illinois.edu/lylek/Demog/Demography.html. Figure 14.1B shows the Gompertz survivorship and the l_x values from the life table between ages 15 to 75 years. Makeham (1860) added an additional term to the hazard function, yielding

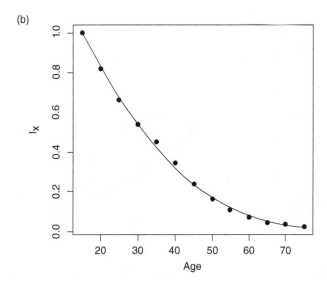

Figure 14.1B   A Gompertz survivorship model fit from ages 15 to 75.

$$\mu(t) = a_2 + a_3 \exp(b_3(t - 15)) \tag{14.6}$$

but given the good fit of the Gompertz function the additional term is unnecessary for current purposes.

The Siler hazard function (Gage 1988; Gage and Dyke 1986; Siler 1979) is intended to cover the entire human lifespan, and is written as

$$\mu(t) = a_1 \exp(-b_1 t) + a_2 + a_3 \exp(b_3 t) \tag{14.7}$$

where the first component is a negative Gompertz function that represents decreasing mortality during early life, the a_2 component represents a constant hazard and the third component is a Gompertz function that represents increasing mortality with old age. Together the constant hazard and the old age Gompertz function are a Makeham hazard. The constant hazard is often not necessary to fit the model, and indeed this is the case in Figure 14.1C, which shows the life table l_x and the Siler survivorship without the a_2 parameter. Wood et al. (2002) describe a mixed-Makeham model that can also be fitted to the life table data from Table 14.1. This would ordinally be a five-parameter model like the Siler, but in the case of fitting the life table data from Table 14.1 we used a four-parameter model. The first term is a mixture parameter while the next three terms are for a Makeham model for individuals at high risk of death and the last two terms are for a Gompertz model representing mortality in low-risk individuals. As the mixed model gives a fit that is nearly identical to the Siler model without the constant term (see Figure 14.1D), we use the latter model.

We hasten to add that there is an interpretive complication in paleodemographic reconstructions. Differences in mortality profiles derived from archaeological skeletons that accumulated over time, often several centuries or more, are commonly interpreted as mainly reflecting overall fertility, not mortality. If one has adequate samples of skeletons, a challenge in itself, both population growth and the age-independent Siler component, a_2, affect the mortality profile. Because population growth over centuries must have approximated zero (balanced fertility and mortality rates), age-independent mortality contributes potentially meaningful variation among samples in skeletal age distributions.

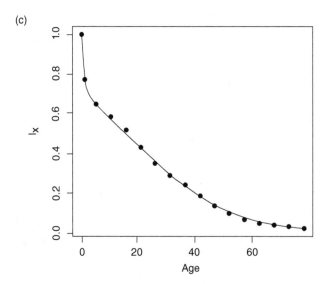

Figure 14.1C   A negative and positive Gompertz survivorship (Siler model less the a_2 parameter) fit from ages zero to 75.

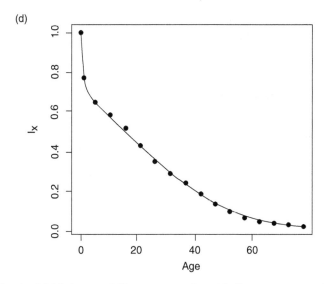

Figure 14.1D   A mixed Makeham and Gompertz survivorship fit to age zero to 75.

In our model fitting we have assumed that there is no under-enumeration of any age class; consequently, we can use the survivorship data to fit the models. We did this using maximum likelihood estimation as done previously. The very young are commonly under-enumerated in paleodemographic samples, affecting subsequent survivorship values but not mortality values (Moore et al. 1975). It is for this reason that Gage (1988) recommends using mortality functions to fit hazard models if there is reason to suspect that the young are underenumerated. As the simulated data are from a model life table, there is no under-enumeration and the survivorship function can be used to fit the hazard model.

Nonstationary Use of a Hazard Model

One benefit of hazard models is they can be extended to nonstationary cases. We would say that they can be "easily" extended, but calculus is required and, more specifically, the use of integrals. We do this in R (R Core Team 2022) using the "integrate" function. The crude birth rate is (Keyfitz 1985: 79)

$$b = \frac{1}{\int_0^\omega \exp(-rt)S(t)dt} \tag{14.8}$$

where $S(t)$ is the survivorship to age t from the hazard model, ω is the maximum possible age, and r is the intrinsic rate of increase. Table 14.3 gives a crude birth rate of 0.053, while Equation (14.8) gives an identical value of 0.053. The crude death rate is

$$d = \frac{\int_0^\omega \exp(-rt)\mu(t)S(t)dt}{\int_0^\omega \exp(-rt)S(t)dt} \tag{14.9}$$

although it can be found more simply as $d = b - r$, giving 0.033. The distribution of age in the living is (Keyfitz 1985: 78)

$$c(t) = b\exp(-rt)S(t) \tag{14.10}$$

so that the mean age in the living is

$$\bar{a}_L = b\int_0^\omega t\exp(-rt)S(t)dt \tag{14.11}$$

Equation (14.11) gives 18.15 years versus 18.02 in Table 14.3. The distribution of ages at death is

$$f(t) = \frac{\exp(-rt)\mu(t)S(t)}{\int_0^\omega \exp(-rt)\mu(t)S(t)dt} \tag{14.12}$$

so the mean age at death is

$$\bar{a}_D = \frac{\int_0^\omega t\exp(-rt)\mu(t)S(t)dt}{\int_0^\omega \exp(-rt)\mu(t)S(t)dt} \tag{14.13}$$

which is 19.30 versus 19.63 in Table 14.3.

The mean age-at-death can also be obtained from the third equation in Sattenspiel and Harpending's (1983) appendix as

$$\bar{a}_D = \frac{1 - r\times\bar{a}_L}{d} \tag{14.14}$$

Unfortunately, Horowitz and colleagues' paper (1988) contains typographical errors, so their Equation 9, with some simplification and substitution, reads as

$$\bar{a}_D = \frac{1 - r\times\bar{a}_L}{(r-d)(1-r/(r-d))} \tag{14.15}$$

where it should have read as

$$\bar{a}_D = \frac{r\times\bar{a}_L - 1}{(r-d)(1-r/(r-d))} \tag{14.16}$$

which simplifies to Equation (14.14).

Sattenspiel and Harpending (1983) importantly noted that when the intrinsic rate of increase is unknown, the inverse of the mean age-at-death is much closer to the crude birth rate than to the crude death rate. As the intrinsic rate of increase is generally unknown in paleodemographic settings, this means that the inverse of the mean age-at-death tells us more about fertility than mortality. Paleodemographers had previously assumed the reverse: the mean age-at-death was more informative about mortality than about fertility. While Johansson and Horowitz (1986) and Horowitz et al. (1988) argued against Sattenspiel and Harpending's (1983) finding, there does appear to be a stronger relationship between the inverse of the mean age-at-death and crude birth rate. Buikstra et al. (1986) also used the Coale and Demeny (1966) model "West" life tables to show there was a stronger relationship between the inverse of mean age-at-death and the crude birth rate.

DEMOGRAPHIC ESTIMATORS

To this point, we have blithely assumed that ages-at-death are known. This is a problematic assumption in the absence of vital records and it certainly causes difficulties for paleodemographic studies. Bocquet and Masset (1977) suggested using the ratio $D_{5-14}/D_{20-\omega}$, where the capital Ds represent the number of deaths in the given intervals, in place of paleodemographic estimates derived from abridged life tables. The advantage of this ratio is that it excludes individuals under age five years that may be underenumerated and it only requires making decisions about relatively well-defined age thresholds, avoiding the problem of inaccurate and biased adult age estimates. Later Bocquet-Appel and Bacro (1997) referred to a similar ratio as the "juvenility index." Proportions were considered in Buikstra et al. (1986), but both these and the "juvenility index" were found wanting by Paine and Harpending (1996). Bocquet-Appel (2002, 2011) used a proportion he referred to as "P", $D_{5-19}/D_{5-\omega}$, interpreted as indicating an increase in fertility with the Neolithic transition. Paine and Boldsen (2002) used a death rate ratio, defined as $1-[S(18)/S(5)]^{1/13}$ divided by $1-[S(5)/S(2)]^{1/3}$, to show an increase from the Mesolithic to the Iron Age and then a decrease to the late medieval period. They interpreted this as indicating a decrease in the span between epidemics during the Iron Age. More recently, McFadden and Oxenham (2018) have used what they refer to as the D_{0-14}/D ratio as an estimator for the Total Fertility Rate. As this is the number of deaths between ages 0 and 14 divided by the total number of deaths, it is a proportion, not a ratio. McFadden and Oxenham (2019) argue that the proportion is resistant to underenumeration and age misestimation, the reason researchers such as Bocquet and Masset (1977) used demographic estimators rather than abridged life tables as much as 40 years earlier. Because of unknown, indeed unknowable, sampling issues with archaeological skeletons, such indicators are only interpretable as general tendencies in large numbers of cemetery samples.

ARE RELIABLE ABRIDGED LIFE TABLES OR HAZARD MODEL PARAMETERS POSSIBLE IN PALEODEMOGRAPHY?

Shortly after paleodemography began to gain traction, Petersen (1975: 232) delivered a cutting remark on the still-developing field when he wrote that "the direct evidence on the mortality of ancient man depends mainly on skeletal remains, from which rather little can be deduced with reasonable certainty." Although this critique has rightly been viewed as comments from an expert in one field venturing into another discipline, the response was not helped by Armelagos and colleagues (1975: 461) writing that Petersen "should have focused less on techniques for ageing skeletal material." Ignoring a problem that continues to vex researchers does not make it go away. Shortly thereafter Howell (1976) called for uniformitarianism in paleodemography, noting that skeletal data should not show large departures from what is known about the structure of anthropological populations. From that perspective, the paleodemographic reconstruction for Libben (Lovejoy et al. 1977) called for continued "research on techniques of aging and sexing skeletons" (Howell 1982: 269). The Libben life table showed much lower survival estimates at older ages than was the case for model life tables. Meindl et al. (2008) have since re-examined the Libben analysis and found a number of complicating factors in comparing this site to the demography of extant anthropological populations. Nevertheless, their estimates still indicated that few adults at Libben had survived into their sixth decade or beyond, a common finding (and we would argue an erroneous one) in paleodemographic work.

Bocquet-Appel and Masset (1982) in their "Farewell to Paleodemography" levelled several critiques against the reliability of life tables generated from skeletons. Their article's title suggested a retreat from the field, but four decades later the paper is more properly viewed as a clarion call for a paradigm shift, much of which involved Bocquet-Appel's own work (Bocquet-Appel 1994, 2002, 2005, 2011; Bocquet-Appel and Bacro 2008). One of their main critiques involved the way ages were estimated using reference sample skeletons. Ages were tabulated against ordered skeletal stages in a reference sample, with the end result being that the age distribution for a paleodemographic (target) sample tended to recapitulate the age distribution of the reference sample. Mensforth (1990) referred to this problem as "age mimicry." Several authors (Aykroyd et al. 1997, 1999; Hoppa and Vaupel 2002; Konigsberg and Frankenberg 1992; Konigsberg et al. 1997), as well as Bocquet-Appel and Masset (1982) in their original article, noted that "age mimicry" arose because the causality was reversed in the original reference work. Ordinal skeletal stages depend on age, not vice versa. Our bones look older because we get older, not that we get older because our bones look older. This problem of using reversed causality had been noted in the fisheries literature (Kimura 1977) and it was largely solved by Kimura and Chikuni (1987). Their method failed to take account of sampling variance due to small reference sample sizes, but Hoenig and Heisey (1987), using a similar method, accounted for this problem.

As originally applied in paleodemography, the solution was to find a life table structure that best reproduced the distribution of skeletal stages using information from the reference sample (Bocquet-Appel and Bacro 1997; Konigsberg and Frankenberg 1992). The problem could then be framed as one of maximum likelihood estimation. The "Rostock Manifesto" (Hoppa and Vaupel 2002) extended this approach by estimating hazard parameters that best approximated the count of skeletal stages, again using the reference sample. An immediate problem with this approach was the reliance on a single age indicator. Holman et al. (2002) developed a method that used multiple age indicators, while Boldsen et al. (2002) developed "transition analysis" also based on multiple age indicators. An advantage of this method is that it controlled for correlations between age indicators that existed even after the effect of age had been removed. The method has proved useful, but not ideal (Bullock et al. 2013; Getz 2020; Godde and Hens 2012, 2015; Jooste et al. 2016; Milner and Boldsen 2012; Sironi and Taroni 2015). Caussinus and Courgeau (2010) and Séguy et al. (2013) have developed a novel Bayesian estimation method for obtaining life tables. Although Gowland and Chamberlain (2002) had previously applied Bayesian age estimation to perinatal remains, their method used the likelihood (information on bone stages against age in a reference collection) and a prior age distribution to estimate the "posterior" age distribution. The method from Caussinus and Courgeau (2010) and Séguy et al. (2013) uses multiple updating of the prior to obtain the "posterior" age distribution, but as presently developed it still relies on a single age indicator.

APPLICATIONS IN PALEODEMOGRAPHY

We can only scratch the surface here. Much more detail can be found in Boldsen et al. (2022). Some of the most useful applications in paleodemography have come from using the Cox (1972) proportional hazard method. Godde et al. (2020) write the model as

$$h(t) = h_0(t)\exp(b_1x_1 + b_2x_2 + \ldots + b_px_p) \tag{14.17}$$

where $h_0(t)$ is a baseline hazard at age t, the x values are covariates (such as sex or cemeteries formed during epidemic versus epidemic-free periods), and the b values are regression coefficients. Rearranging slightly shows why this is referred to as a proportional hazards model:

$$\frac{h(t)}{h_0(t)} = \exp(b_1x_1 + b_2x_2 + \ldots + b_px_p) \tag{14.18}$$

Taking the logarithms of both sides shows the relationship to regression analysis:

$$\ln(h(t)) - \ln(h_0(t)) = b_1x_1 + b_2x_2 + \ldots + b_px_p \tag{14.19}$$

Using the Cox proportional hazards method Godde et al. (2020) demonstrated that for individuals who died during the Black Death there was a significant effect for individuals with skeletal markers of "frailty," but not for sex. DeWitte (DeWitte 2010, 2014; DeWitte and Hughes-Morey 2012) has used the proportional hazards model in several different analyses of medieval people.

Two other fruitful areas in paleodemography have been in the use of "cementochronology" (Naji et al. 2016) and in differentiating attritional from catastrophic death assemblages (Bocquet-Appel and Arsuaga 1999; de Castro et al. 2004; Gowland and Chamberlain 2005; Margerison and Knüsel 2002). The former makes use of annual lines in tooth cementum, which surrounds tooth roots. The accuracy of cementochronology continues to be debated; if accurate, age estimation then becomes a matter of counting lines and adding them to the age of root formation. The question of whether a death assemblage formed through gradual attrition or a catastrophic event is a matter of whether the life table or hazard model results approximate the ages in a normal accumulation of deaths or those in a living population. The distinction boils down to whether deaths were largely independent of age, which can occur in mass disasters, or not.

Although there have been advances in how data are handled, such as hazards models, there still remains a need for better age-informative skeletal indicators. Inaccurate and biased skeletal age estimates, especially for adults, continue to plague paleodemographic work. This state of affairs underscores the importance of the Séguy and colleagues (2013) approach because some sense can finally be made of data collected with widely used age-estimation methods. Fortunately, there are promising developments in adult age estimation that, when implemented, will allow that aspect of paleodemographic work to catch up with analytical developments (Milner et al. 2021). Doing so will permit our understanding of demography to be extended from relatively recent times into the deep past.

CONCLUSIONS

Like much of biological anthropology, demography is inherently mathematical, including both algebra and calculus. To circumvent calculation difficulties, we provide R code (R

Core Team 2022) at http://faculty.las.illinois.edu/lylek/Demog/Demography.html. This code can be pasted into R (https://cran.r-project.org) or RStudio (https://www.rstudio.com/products/rstudio/download).

In this chapter we began with a stationary abridged life table. This is essentially a spreadsheet of deaths categorized into age classes (consequently "abridged" rather than having yearly intervals). "Stationary" refers to a sample where fertility and mortality are balanced so that the population stays a constant size. From this point of departure, we showed how various measures of fertility can be constructed, and we then turned to nonstationary life tables where the population is growing or decreasing in size. This led to a discussion of hazard models where age is measured on a continuous scale. Finally, we considered some applications in paleodemography where ages are unknown and must be estimated.

While we focused on calculations, they are only part of the story. Meaningful interpretations of anthropological data only come about through a careful consideration of sample origins (not just size) and cultural and social contexts. In short, numbers alone do not speak for themselves. They are, however, a solid basis for furthering our understanding of the human experience and how we got to where we are today.

APPENDIX

The simulated data on counts of deaths in age intervals for Table 14.1 came from a model life table using Séguy and Buchet's (2013) regression of the log of the probability of death in the first year of life on the log of Bocquet-Appel's (2002) P, deaths between ages 5 and 19 divided by all deaths over five years. We used a value of $P = 0.1$ and a growth rate of 0.0 (no change in group size over time) from Séguy and Buchet's (2013: 129) Table 8.3. Subsequent age-specific probabilities of death were obtained from Séguy and Buchet's (2013: 132) Table 8.5. The 500 deaths were simulated through 500 random uniform variates between zero and one, which were then compared to survivorship.

REFERENCES

Armelagos, G. J., L. Krader, N. McArthur, et al. "On a Demographer's View of Prehistoric Demography." *Current Anthropology* 16, no. 3 (1975): 461–464.

Asch, D. *The Middle Woodland Population of the Lower Illinois Valley: A Study in Paleodemographic Methods.* Evanston, IL: Northwestern Archaeological Program, 1976.

Aykroyd, R., D. Lucy, A. M. Pollard, et al. "Regression Analysis in Adult Age Estimation." *American Journal of Physical Anthropology* 104, no. 2 (1997): 259–265.

Aykroyd, R. G., D. Lucy, A. M. Pollard, et al. "Nasty, Brutish, but Not Necessarily Short: A Reconsideration of the Statistical Methods Used to Calculate Age at Death from Adult Human Skeletal and Dental Age Indicators." *American Antiquity* 64, no. 1 (1999): 55–70.

Bennett, K. A. "On the Estimation of Some Demographic Characteristics on a Prehistoric Population from the American Southwest." *American Journal of Physical Anthropology* 39 (1973): 223–231.

Bocquet, J.-P., and C. Masset. "Estimateurs En Paléodémographie." *L'Homme* 17, no. 4 (1977): 65–90.

Bocquet-Appel, J.-P. "Estimating the Average for an Unknown Age Distribution in Anthropology." In *Statistical Tools in Human Biology.* Edited by S. Borgognini-Tarli, M. Di Bacco, and E. Pacciani, 197–202. Singapore: World Scientific, 1994.

Bocquet-Appel, J.-P. "Paleoanthropological Traces of a Neolithic Demographic Transition." *Current Anthropology* 43, no. 4 (2002): 637–650.

Bocquet-Appel, J.-P. "La Paléodemographie." In *Objets Et Méthodes En Paléoanthropologie.* Edited by O. Dutour, J.-J. Hublin, and B. Vandermeersch, 271–313. Paris: CTHS, Comité des travaux historiques et scientifiques, 2005.

Bocquet-Appel, J.-P. "When the World's Population Took Off: The Springboard of the Neolithic Demographic Transition." *Science* 333, no. 6042 (2011): 560–561. https://doi.org/10.1126/science.1208880.

Bocquet-Appel, J.-P., and J. L. Arsuaga. "Age Distributions of Hominid Samples at Atapuerca (SH) and Krapina Could Indicate Accumulation by Catastrophe." *Journal of Archaeological Science* 26, no. 3 (1999): 327–338.

Bocquet-Appel, J.-P., and J. N. Bacro. "Brief Communication: Estimates of Some Demographic Parameters in a Neolithic Rock-Cut Chamber (Approximately 2000 BC) Using Iterative Techniques for Aging and Demographic Estimators." *American Journal of Physical Anthropology* 102, no. 4 (1997): 569–575.

Bocquet-Appel, J.-P., and J. N. Bacro. "Estimation of an Age Distribution with Its Confidence Intervals Using an Iterative Bayesian Procedure and a Bootstrap Sampling Approach." In *Recent Advances in Paleodemography.* Edited by J.-P. Bocquet-Appel, 63–82. Dordrecht, The Netherlands: Springer, 2008.

Bocquet-Appel, J.-P., and C. Masset. "Farewell to Paleodemography." *Journal of Human Evolution* 11, no. 4 (1982): 321–333.

Bocquet-Appel, J.-P., and S. Naji. "Testing the Hypothesis of a Worldwide Neolithic Demographic Transition." *Current Anthropology* 47, no. 2 (2006): 341–365.

Boldsen, J. L., G. R. Milner, and S. D. Ousley. "Paleodemography: From Archaeology and Skeletal Age Estimation to Life in the Past." *American Journal of Biological Anthropology (Yearbook of Biological Anthropology)* 178, Suppl. 74, (2022): 115-150.

Boldsen, J. L., G. R. Milner, L. W. Konigsberg, et al. "Transition Analysis: A New Method for Estimating Age from Skeletons." In *Paleodemography: Age Distributions from Skeletal Samples.* Edited by R. D. Hoppa and J. W. Vaupel, 73–106. New York, NY: Cambridge University Press, 2002.

Brass, W. "On the Scale of Mortality." In *Biological Aspects of Demography.* Edited by W. Brass, 69–110. London, UK: Taylor & Francis, 1971.

Buikstra, J. E., L. W. Konigsberg, and J. Bullington. "Fertility and the Development of Agriculture in the Prehistoric Midwest." *American Antiquity* 51, no. 3 (1986): 528–546.

Bullock, M., L. Márquez, P. Hernández, et al. "Paleodemographic Age-at-Death Distributions of Two Mexican Skeletal Collections: A Comparison of Transition Analysis and Traditional Aging Methods." *American Journal of Physical Anthropology* 152, no. 1 (2013): 67–78. https://doi.org/10.1002/ajpa.22329.

Carrier, N. H. "A Note on the Estimation of Mortality and Other Population Characteristics Given Deaths by Age." *Population Studies* 12, no. 2 (1958): 149–163.

Caspari, R., and S. H. Lee. "Older Age Becomes Common Late in Human Evolution." *Proceedings of the National Academy of Sciences* 101, no. 30 (2004): 10895–10900. https://doi.org/10.1073/pnas.0402857101.

Caussinus, H., and D. Courgeau. "Estimating Age Without Measuring It: A New Method in Paleodemography." *Population* 65, no. 1 (2010): 117–144. https://doi.org/10.3917/pope.1001.0117.

Ciecka, J. E. "Edmond Halley's Life Table and Its Uses." *Journal of Legal Economics* 15, no. 1 (2008): 65–74.

Coale, A. J. *The Growth and Structure of Human Populations: A Mathematical Investigation.* Princeton, NJ: Princeton University Press, 1972.

Coale, A. J., and P. Demeny. *Regional Model Life Tables and Stable Populations.* Princeton, NJ: Princeton University Press, 1966.

Coale, A. J., and P. Demeny. *Regional Model Life Tables and Stable Populations, 2nd edn.* New York: Academic Press, 1983.

Cox, D. R. "Regression Models and Life-Tables." *Journal of the Royal Statistical Society: Series B (Methodological)* 34, no. 2 (1972): 187–202.

de Castro, J. M. B., M. Martinón-Torres, M. Lozano, et al. "Paleodemography of the Atapuerca: Sima de Los Huesos Hominin Sample: A Revision and New Approaches to the Paleodemography of the European Middle Pleistocene Population." *Journal of Anthropological Research* 60, no. 1 (2004): 5–26.

DeWitte, S. N. "Sex Differentials in Frailty in Medieval England." *American Journal of Physical Anthropology* 143, no. 2 (2010): 285–297. https://doi.org/10.1002/ajpa.21316.

DeWitte, S. N. "Sex Differences in Periodontal Disease in Catastrophic and Attritional Assemblages from Medieval London." *American Journal of Physical Anthropology* 149, no. 3 (2012): 405–416. https://doi.org/10.1002/ajpa.22138.

DeWitte, S. N. "Mortality Risk and Survival in the Aftermath of the Medieval Black Death." *PLoS One* 9, no. 5 (2014): e96513. https://doi.org/10.1371/journal.pone.0096513.

DeWitte, S. N., and G. Hughes-Morey. "Stature and Frailty During the Black Death: The Effect of Stature on Risks of Epidemic Mortality in London, AD 1348–1350." *Journal of Archaeological Science* 39, no. 5 (2012): 1412–1419. https://doi.org/10.1016/j.jas.2012.01.019.

Dublin, L. I., and M. Spiegelman. "Current Versus Generation Life Tables." *Human Biology* 13, no. 4 (1941): 439–458.

Eshed, V., A. Gopher, T. B. Gage, et al. "Has the Transition to Agriculture Reshaped the Demographic Structure of Prehistoric Populations? New Evidence from the Levant." *American Journal of Physical Anthropology* 124, no. 4 (2004): 315–329. https://doi.org/10.1002/ajpa.10332.

Ewbank, D. C., J. C. Gomez de Leon, and M. A. Stoto. "A Reducible Four-Parameter System of Model Life Tables." *Population Studies* 37, no. 1 (1983): 105–127.

Gage, T. B. "Mathematical Hazard Models of Mortality: An Alternative to Model Life Tables." *American Journal of Physical Anthropology* 76, no. 4 (1988): 429–441.

Gage, T. B. "Causes of Death and the Components of Mortality: Testing the Biological Interpretations of a Competing Hazards Model." *American Journal of Human Biology* 3, no. 3 (1991): 289–300.

Gage, T. B., and B. Dyke. "Parameterizing Abridged Mortality Tables: The Siler Three-Component Hazard Model." *Human Biology* 58, no. 2 (1986): 275–291.

Gage, T. B., B. Dyke, and J. W. Maccleur. "Estimating Mortality Level for Small Populations: An Evaluation of a Pair of Two-Census Methods." *Population Studies* 40, no. 2 (1986): 263–273.

Gage, T. B., B. Dyke, and P. Riviere. "Estimating Mortality from Two Censuses: An Application to the Trio of Surinam." *Human Biology* 56, no. 3 (1984): 489–501.

Getz, S. M. "The Use of Transition Analysis in Skeletal Age Estimation." *WIREs Forensic Science* 2, no. 6 (2020): 1–11, e1378. https://doi.org/10.1002/wfs2.1378.

Godde, K., and S. M. Hens. "Age-at-Death Estimation in an Italian Historical Sample: A Test of the Suchey-Brooks and Transition Analysis Methods." *American Journal of Physical Anthropology* 149, no. 2 (2012): 259–265. https://doi.org/10.1002/ajpa.22126.

Godde, K., and S. M. Hens. "Modeling Senescence Changes of the Pubic Symphysis in Historic I Talian Populations: A Comparison of the R. Ostock and Forensic Approaches to Aging Using Transition Analysis." *American Journal of Physical Anthropology* 156, no. 3 (2015): 466–473. https://doi.org/10.1002/ajpa.22671.

Godde, K., V. Pasillas, and A. Sanchez. "Survival Analysis of the Black Death: Social Inequality of Women and the Perils of Life and Death in Medieval London." *American Journal of Physical Anthropology* 173, no. 1 (2020): 168–178. https://doi.org/10.1002/ajpa.24081.

Gompertz, B. "On the Nature of the Function Expressive of the Law of Human Mortality, and on a New Mode of Determining the Value of Life Contingencies." *Philosophical Transactions of the Royal Society of London (Series A)* 115 (1825): 513–583.

Gowland, R. L., and A. T. Chamberlain. "A Bayesian Approach to Ageing Perinatal Skeletal Material from Archaeological Sites: Implications for the Evidence for Infanticide in Roman-Britain." *Journal of Archaeological Science* 29, no. 6 (2002): 677–685. https://doi.org/10.1006/jasc.2001.0776.

Gowland, R. L., and A. T. Chamberlain. "Detecting Plague: Palaeodemographic Characterisation of a Catastrophic Death Assemblage." *Antiquity* 79, no. 303 (2005): 146–157. https://doi.org/10.1017/S0003598X00113766.

Graunt, J. *Natural and Political Observations Mentioned in a Following Index, and Made upon the Bills of Mortality.* London, UK: Thos. Roycroft, 1662.

Greville, T. N. E. "Short Methods of Constructing Abridged Life Tables." *Record of the American Institute of Actuaries* 32, no. 65 (1943): 29–43.

Halley, E. "An Estimate of the Degrees of the Mortality of Mankind; Drawn from Curious Tables of the Births and Funerals at the City of Breslaw; with an Attempt to Ascertain the Price of Annuities upon Lives." *Philosophical Transactions of the Royal Society of London* 17, no. 196 (1693): 596–610.

Hoenig, J. M., and D. M. Heisey. "Use of a Log-Linear Model with the EM Algorithm to Correct Estimates of Stock Composition and Convert Length to Age." *Transactions of the American Fisheries Society* 116, no. 2 (1987): 232–243.

Holman, D. J. *Mle: A Programming Language for Building Likelihood Models. Version 2.1, vol. 2: Reference Manual*, 2003. Accessed September 9, 2022: http://faculty.washington.edu/djholman/mle.

Holman, D. J., J. W. Wood, and K. A. O'Connor. "Estimating Age-at-Death Distributions from Skeletal Samples: Multivariate Latent-Trait Approach." In *Paleodemography: Age Distribution from Skeletal Samples*. Edited by R. D. Hoppa and J. W. Vaupel, 193–221. New York, NY: Cambridge University Press, 2002.

Hoppa, R. D., and J. W. Vaupel. "The Rostock Manifesto for Paleodemography: The Way from Stage to Age." In *Paleodemography: Age Distributions from Skeletal Samples*. Edited by R. D. Hoppa and J. W. Vaupel, 1–8. New York: Cambridge University Press, 2002.

Horowitz, S., G. Armelagos, and K. Wachter. "On Generating Birth Rates from Skeletal Populations." *American Journal of Physical Anthropology* 76, no. 2 (1988): 189–196.

Howell, N. "Toward a Uniformitarian Theory of Human Paleodemography." In *The Demographic Evolution of Human Populations*. Edited by R. H. Ward and K. M. Weiss, 25–40. New York: Academic Press, 1976.

Howell, N. "Village Composition Implied by a Paleodemographic Life Table: The Libben Site." *American Journal of Physical Anthropology* 59, no. 3 (1982): 263–269.

Johansson, S. R., and S. Horowitz. "Estimating Mortality in Skeletal Populations: Influence of the Growth Rate on the Interpretation of Levels and Trends During the Transition to Agriculture." *American Journal of Physical Anthropology* 71, no. 2 (1986): 233–250.

Jooste, N., E. L'Abbé, S. Pretorius, et al. "Validation of Transition Analysis as a Method of Adult Age Estimation in a Modern South African Sample." *Forensic Science International* 266 (2016): 580. e1–580, e7. https://doi.org/10.1016/j.forsciint.2016.05.020.

Keyfitz, N. *Applied Mathematical Demography*, 2nd edn. New York, NY: Springer-Verlag, 1985.

Kimura, D. K. "Statistical Assessment of the Age-Length Key." *Journal of the Fisheries Research Board of Canada* 34, no. 3 (1977): 317–324.

Kimura, D. K., and S. Chikuni. "Mixtures of Empirical Distributions: An Iterative Application of the Age-Length Key." *Biometrics* 43, no. 1 (1987): 23–35.

Konigsberg, L. W., and S. R. Frankenberg. "Estimation of Age Structure in Anthropological Demography." *American Journal of Physical Anthropology* 89, no. 2 (1992): 235–256.

Konigsberg, L. W., S. R. Frankenberg, and R. B. Walker. "Regress What on What?: Paleodemographic Age Estimation as a Calibration Problem." In *Integrating Archaeological Demography: Multidisciplinary Approaches to Prehistoric Population*. Edited by R. R. Paine, 64–88. Carbondale, IL: SIU Press, 1997.

Lovejoy, C. O., R. S. Meindl, T. R. Pryzbeck, et al. "Paleodemography of the Libben Site, Ottawa County, Ohio." *Science* 198, no. 4314 (1977): 291–293.

Makeham, W. M. "On the Law of Mortality and the Construction of Annuity Tables." *Journal of the Institute of Actuaries* 8, no. 6 (1860): 301–310.

Mann, A. *Paleodemographic Aspects of the South African Australopithecines*, vol. 1. Philadelphia: Pennsylvania Publication in Anthropology, 1975.

Margerison, B. J., and C. J. Knüsel. "Paleodemographic Comparison of a Catastrophic and an Attritional Death Assemblage." *American Journal of Physical Anthropology* 119, no. 2 (2002): 134–143. https://doi.org/10.1002/ajpa.10082.

McFadden, C., and M. F. Oxenham. "The D0-14/D Ratio: A New Paleodemographic Index and Equation for Estimating Total Fertility Rates." *American Journal of Physical Anthropology* 165, no. 3 (2018): 471–479. https://doi.org/10.1002/ajpa.23365.

McFadden, C., and M. F. Oxenham. "The Impacts of Underenumeration and Age Estimation Error on the D0–14/D Ratio and Palaeodemographic Measures." *Journal of Archaeological Science: Reports* 23 (2019): 57–61. https://doi.org/10.1016/j.jasrep.2018.10.033.

Meindl, R. S., R. P. Mensforth, and C. O. Lovejoy. "Method and Theory in Paleodemography, with Application to a Hunting, Fishing, and Gathering Village from the Eastern Woodlands of North America." In *Biological Anthropology of the Human Skeleton*, 2nd edn. Edited by M. A. Katzenberg and S. R. Saunders, 601–617. Hoboken, NJ: John Wiley & Sons, 2008.

Mensforth, R. P. "Paleodemography of the Carlston Annis (Bt-5) Late Archaic Skeletal Population." *American Journal of Physical Anthropology* 82, no. 1 (1990): 81–99.

Milner, G. R., and J. L. Boldsen. "Transition Analysis: A Validation Study with Known-Age Modern American Skeletons." *American Journal of Physical Anthropology* 148, no. 1 (2012): 98–110. https://doi.org/10.1002/ajpa.22047.

Milner, G. R., J. L. Boldsen, S. D. Ousley, et al. (2021). "Great Expectations: The Rise, Fall, and Resurrection of Adult Skeletal Age Estimation." *In Remodeling Forensic Skeletal Age*. Edited by B. F. B. Algee-Hewitt and J. Kim, 139–154. London: Academic Press.

Moore, J. A., A. C. Swedlund, and G. J. Armelagos. 1975. "The Use of Life Tables in Paleodemography." In *Population Studies in Archaeology and Biological Anthropology: A Symposium*. Edited by A. C. Swedlund, 57–70. Washington, DC: Society for American Archaeology.

Naji, S., T. Colard, J. Blondiaux, et al. "Cementochronology, to Cut or Not to Cut?" *International Journal of Paleopathology* 15 (2016): 113–119. https://doi.org/10.1016/j.ijpp.2014.05.003.

Paine, R. R., and J. L. Boldsen. "Linking Age-at-Death Distributions and Ancient Dynamics: A Case Study." In *Paleodemography: Age Distributions from Skeletal Samples*. Edited by R. D. Hoppa and J. W. Vaupel, 169–180. New York, NY: Cambridge University Press, 2002.

Paine, R. R., and H. C. Harpending. "Assessing the Reliability of Paleodemographic Fertility Estimators Using Simulated Skeletal Distributions." *American Journal of Physical Anthropology* 101, no. 2 (1996): 151–159.

Palkovich, A. M. "Demography and Disease Patterns in A Protohistoric Plains Group: A Study of the Mobridge Site (39WW1)." *Plains Anthropologist* 26, no. 94 (1981): 71–84. https://doi.org/10.1080/2052546.1981.11909054.

Petersen, W. "A Demographer's View of Prehistoric Demography [And Comments and Replies]." *Current Anthropology* 16, no. 2 (1975): 227–245.

R Core Team. *R: A Language and Environment for Statistical Computing*. Vienna, Austria: R. Foundation for Statistical Computing, 2022. https://www.R-project.org/.

Sattenspiel, L., and H. Harpending. "Stable Populations and Skeletal Age." *American Antiquity* 48, no. 3 (1983): 489–498.

Séguy, I., and L. Buchet. *Handbook of Paleodemography*. New York, NY: Springer International Publishing, 2013.

Séguy, I., H. Caussinus, D. Courgeau, et al. "Estimating the Age Structure of A Buried Adult Population: A New Statistical Approach Applied to Archaeological Digs in France." *American Journal of Physical Anthropology* 150, no. 2 (2013): 170–183. https://doi.org/10.1002/ajpa.22187.

Shryock, H. S., and J. S. Siegel. *The Methods and Materials of Demography*. New York, NY: Academic Press, Inc., 1976.

Siler, W. "A Competing-Risk Model for Animal Mortality." *Ecology* 60, no. 4 (1979): 750–757.

Sironi, E., and F. Taroni. "Bayesian Networks for the Age Classification of Living Individuals: A Study on Transition Analysis." *Journal of Forensic Science and Medicine* 1, no. 2 (2015): 124. https://doi.org/10.4103/2349-5014.162785.

Swedlund, A. C., and G. L. Armelagos. *Demographic Anthropology*. Dubuque, IA: Wm. C. Brown, 1976.

Weiss, K. M. *Demographic Models for Anthropology*, vol. 27. *Memoirs of the Society for American Archaeology*, Washington, DC: Society for American Archaeology, 1973.

Weiss, K. M. "Demographic Disturbance and the Use of Life Tables in Anthropology." In *Population Studies in Archaeology and Biological Anthropology: A Symposium*. Edited by A. C. Swedlund, 46–56. Washington, DC: Society for American Archaeology, 1975.

Wood, J. W. "The Genetic Demography of the Gainj of Papua New Guinea. 2. Determinants of Effective Population Size." *The American Naturalist* 129, no. 2 (1987): 165–187.

Wood, J. W. *Dynamics of Human Reproduction: Biology, Biometry, Demography.* New York, NY: Aldine de Gruyter, 1994.

Wood, J. W., D. L. Holman, K. A. O'Connor, et al. "Mortality Models for Paleodemography." In *Paleodemography: Age Distributions from Skeletal Samples.* Edited by R. D. Hoppa and J. W. Vaupel, 129–168. New York: Cambridge University Press, 2002.

CHAPTER 15

Nutritional Anthropology: Contemporary Themes in Food, Diet, and Nutrition

*Darna L. Dufour and
Barbara A. Piperata*

INTRODUCTION

Nutritional anthropology encompasses a wide range of interests in food, diet, and nutrition. Biological anthropologists approach the subject from both evolutionary and biocultural perspectives. In the former, they are particularly interested in understanding how diet shaped the evolution of the genus *Homo* and, in the latter, how inter-relationships between diet and environmental factors (physical, biological, social, and cultural) shape the nutritional health of individuals and populations.

Foods, of course, are the plants and animals considered edible and chosen for consumption by a given population. They are always a subset of all the plants and animals in any environment, and in historic and contemporary populations are imbued with meaning. Diet refers to what is consumed and provides the majority of an individual's or population's energy (calories) and nutrients. Nutrition is a broadly defined term. In biological anthropology, it is short for nutritional status, i.e., the biological condition of the organism with respect to diet. Hence it includes things like child growth, over- and undernutrition, and nutrient deficiencies.

Nutritional anthropology developed from two separate, but complimentary, threads. One was anthropologists' long-standing interest in the diets of ancestral populations. Indeed, when Raymond Dart "discovered" the Taung child in 1924, he immediately suspected that it had a diet different from that of other apes (Sponheimer and Dufour 2009). The Harris and Ross (1987) volume, *Food and Evolution: Toward a Theory of Human Food Habits*, was a major contribution that brought together researchers from

A Companion to Biological Anthropology, Second Edition. Edited by Clark Spencer Larsen.
© 2023 John Wiley & Sons Ltd. Published 2023 by John Wiley & Sons Ltd.

across the discipline to demonstrate that diets were not static and that biological and nutritional requirements were rooted in our evolutionary background. The subtitle of the book indicates the continuing interest in food habits within cultural anthropology, but the editors (Harris and Ross) make it clear that this interest should "not obscure" the material realities of diet.

The second thread was the deeply rooted interest of anthropologists in the food and food-related behavior of the peoples they studied. The classic example is Richard's (1939) study, *Land, Labour and Diet in Northern Rhodesia*, a study that systematically emphasized the inter-relationship of food and cultural/social processes. In the 1940s the war effort in both the USA and Europe sparked interest in understanding both what people were willing to eat from a social point of view, i.e., their food habits, and what their food needs actually were from a biological point of view. Margaret Mead is well known for her research on the former. In the early 1970s, a group of anthropologists doing food and nutritionally related research in the USA formed an interest group within the Society for Medical Anthropology of the American Anthropological Association (Wilson 2002). The rostering of the group within medical anthropology is noteworthy as it demonstrated the emphasis on health-related aspects of nutrition, not just food habits, i.e., it linked food habits to biological outcomes.

These two threads have continued to frame core assumptions within nutritional anthropology: (1) evolutionary history matters; (2) diets change over time; (3) the foods people consume have social meaning but are also related to biological outcomes. In this essay we will consider examples of research by biological anthropologists that demonstrate current understanding of these core assumptions. First, we will focus on studies that attempt to understand diet in our evolutionary past, specifically the Paleolithic period of human evolution and the Neolithic, i.e., the transition to agriculture. Second, we will consider foods, diets, and nutrition in contemporary populations, including the transitions in diet that accompany economic changes and globalization, the problems of food insecurity that plague many groups, ongoing increases in overweight and obesity across the globe, and infant feeding. In ending, we will briefly note an exciting new direction in research: the relationship of diet to the gut microbiome.

FOODS AND DIETS IN PAST POPULATIONS

What did our ancestors eat? How did those foods shape the evolution of the genus *Homo*? Does our evolutionary heritage matter in terms of our current nutritional requirements and health? These are important questions because diet has long been considered a driving force in human evolution. They are also difficult questions to answer and ones we may never be able to answer with the precision desired (Ungar 2007). Here we consider three issues that have received much attention. The first is the relationship of diet to the increases in body size and especially brain size (encephalization) that characterize the early evolution of our lineage, the genus *Homo*. The second is the transition from hunting–gathering to agriculture and its impact on human diet and health. The third is the relevance of ancestral diets to modern health concerns.

Early Evolution of Diet and the Question of a Larger Body and Brain Size

Our understanding of the diets of early hominins (humans and their direct ancestors) comes from the fossils themselves, the archaeological record, and the conceptual frameworks developed to interpret various lines of evidence. Early hominins, like the Austrolopithecines, lived in Africa about 4 mya (millions of years ago). Fossil teeth of these animals provide important clues to diet. One clue is the morphology of their dentition, which indicates an omnivorous diet. A second clue comes from the microscopic wear patterns on their teeth (dental microwear), which suggests a diet dominated by soft fruits or other foods of similar texture (Ungar 2012). A third clue comes from the chemical elements in foods that have become incorporated into dental enamel. One of these elements is carbon. The analysis of carbon isotopes (different forms of carbon) indicates that early hominins had relatively broad diets that included both forest-derived foods, like fruits, as well as savannah plants like grasses and sedges, and/or the animals that ate those grasses and sedges (Sponheimer et al. 2013). This method of analysis relies on the fact that some plants use the C_3 photosynthetic pathway (trees, shrubs, bushes, herbs) while others use the C_4 photosynthetic pathway (grasses and sedges). The method cannot tell us exactly what plants were consumed, nor can it distinguish diets based solely on C_4 plants from those that included animals, like zebras, that ate those C_4 grasses and sedges (Sponheimer et al. 2013).

Later fossil hominins assigned to the genus *Homo*, and referred to as early *Homo*, are characterized by a larger average body size and most significantly a notably larger brain size (Antón et al. 2014). They include a number of different species, of which one of the best known is *Homo erectus* (about 1.8 mya). For *Homo erectus* we have fossilized remains, an archaeological record containing evidence of the foods assumed to have been part of the diet, as well as the artifacts used to process those foods. The fossilized remains of teeth are still indicative of an omnivorous diet, but the dentition is smaller and less robust than that of early hominins, like the Australopithecines. This suggests *Homo erectus* consumed a different diet. The dental microwear suggests a more mixed diet (Ungar 2012). The carbon isotope data indicate a greater emphasis on grasses and sedges, and/or the animals consuming those plants (Sponheimer 2013). The archaeological record for sites occupied by early *Homo*, including *Homo erectus*, provides evidence of the consumption of animals in the form of butchery marks on animal bones, as well as percussion marks to break long bones and access marrow (Blumenschine and Pobiner 2007). The record also contains evidence of plant consumption in the form of wear marks on stone tools consistent with the processing of roots/tubers, grasses, and sedges (Lemorini et al. 2014). Remains of the plants themselves were not preserved; they rarely are. This archaeological evidence is consistent with the isotopic evidence showing a shift toward C_4 plants.

Can we link the expanded brain and body size observed in early *Homo*, especially *Homo erectus*, to the changes in diet? To answer this question, scholars have developed conceptual frameworks to integrate nutritional requirements with evidence in the fossil and archaeological records. In essence they argue that the morphological changes observed in early *Homo* would have required a higher quality diet – that is, a diet that was more energy and nutrient dense (i.e., calories and nutrients per unit weight). One of the conceptual frameworks is Leonard and Robertson's (1994) comparison of human diets and energy requirements with those of other primates. Using diets of contemporary hunter–gatherers as a proxy for the subsistence strategy of early *Homo*, they assessed diet quality of both humans and contemporary nonhuman primates in terms of energy and nutrient density and found that humans have a higher quality diet than expected for a primate of their size. They suggest that the higher quality diet of humans was linked to the high metabolic (energy) cost of the large human brain, a trait that appeared early in the evolution of the genus *Homo*.

Another influential conceptual framework for linking diet with body/brain size in early *Homo* is Aiello and Wheeler's (1995) "expensive tissue hypothesis." They reasoned that since brain tissue has a high metabolic cost, highly encephalized animals like humans should have a higher-than-expected basal metabolic rate (BMR) for their body size, and since humans do not, something else must have changed in the course of evolution. They posited that a reduction in the size (and hence metabolic cost) of the gastrointestinal tract would have allowed more energy for brain function and hence compensated for the increase in brain size. Further, they argued that the reduction in the size of the gut would have required the adoption of a high-quality diet such as one that contained animal products, nuts, and tubers because a smaller gut would not provide the space necessary for processing bulky, nutrient poor foods like leaves and stems.

A third influential framework is Wrangham's (2017) "cooking hypothesis." Wrangham argues that meat was a smaller part of the diet of early *Homo*, and that the process of cooking, especially the cooking of roots/tubers, was the basis of the improved diet quality responsible for the increased body and brain size. Why cooking? Because cooking can increase the digestibility and hence energy value of foods. It seems obvious that cooking became important at some point in our evolutionary history since all human groups cook at least some of their food. The unresolved question is when the advent of cooking occurred. Although Wrangham has consistently associated cooking with the morphological changes in early *Homo*, the archaeological evidence for the regular use of fire post-dates those morphological changes.

Lastly, Broadhurst et al. (2002) also argue for the necessity of a high-quality diet to support the evolution of the large brain in *Homo*, but focus on a single type of food: aquatic foods. Their argument rests on the fact that the brain is composed almost entirely of two polyunsaturated fatty acids, arachidonic acid (AA) and docosahexaenoic acid (DHA), which are more abundant in aquatic than terrestrial food chains. They hypothesize that AA and DHA could have been limiting to the development of a large brain in *Homo* unless marine-based dietary sources of AA and DHA were available.

In summary, for the diets of early *Homo* we have various lines of evidence, most of which are not very specific. Taken together, however, they suggest that humans evolved as omnivores on a diet higher in quality than that of the Australopithecines and our nearest living relatives, the apes. This higher quality diet coincided with the increases in body and brain size evident in early *Homo*, suggesting that this higher quality diet was a driving force in the increase in body size and encephalization. Although the consumption of animal tissues is often assumed to play a central role in this higher quality diet, a recent analysis of the zoo-archaeological record by Barr et al. (2022) calls this interpretation into question. There is much we still need to know.

From Wild Foods to Domesticated Crops and Animals

The transition from gathering wild plants and hunting animals for food in the Paleolithic (Old Stone Age) to farming domesticated plants and animals was a major shift in subsistence strategies. This early period of plant and animal domestication is commonly referred to as the Neolithic (New Stone Age) and sometimes as the Neolithic Revolution because it was a dramatic change from the millions of years humans had spent as hunter gatherers, and was accompanied by significant changes in diet, settlement patterns, lifestyle, and population size.

The transition to farming (both plants and animals) included three food crops that now provide over **60** percent of the food energy in human diets (FAO n.d.): wheat, rice, and maize (corn). These crops, along with other plants, were domesticated independently in different parts of the world. Wheat, barley, and lentils were domesticated in the Near East about **10,000** years ago (Brown et al. 2009). Rice (paddy rice) was domesticated in China about 8,000 years ago (Zong et al. 2007), and maize and squash were domesticated in Mesoamerica at about the same time (Piperno et al. 2009). Animals like cattle, sheep, and goats were also domesticated in the Near East around the same time as food plants. Pigs were domesticated in China around the same time as paddy rice.

The process of domestication was no doubt slow and, as would be expected, certain wild plants were relied on before they were domesticated. For example, in the Levant (Near East) there is archaeological evidence in the form of stone tools used to pound wild seeds as early as 14,000 BC (Eshed et al. 2004), well before seeds like wheat and barley were considered domesticated. The adoption of domesticated plants and animals, could, however, be quite rapid. For example, in coastal Britain carbon isotopes in bone collagen indicate a rapid change from diets based on wild marine resources to domesticated plants and animals between about 5,200–4,500 years ago, a period of only 700 years (Richards et al. 2003). Archaeological evidence of plant remains indicates that the plants were predominately wheat and barley (McClatchie et al. 2014), plants that were domesticated in the Near East and then spread west across Europe to Britain.

The major question biological anthropologists ask is, how did the dietary changes associated with the transition to farming affect human health? Evidence for changes in the actual foods consumed comes largely from plant remains at archaeological sites. Evidence for changes in health comes from human skeletal remains. Some of the main health indicators are dental caries, skeletal markers of infectious disease, and nonspecific indicators of stress (cribra orbitalia and porotic hyperostosis). Health is also assessed in terms of adult stature, which is a proxy for child growth, itself an indicator of the combined effect of dietary adequacy and infectious disease experience.

Most, but not all, studies have shown an association between the transition to farming and declines in health (Cohen and Armelagos 1984; Larsen 2006; Mummert et al. 2011). Some of the studies showing little or no change in health were associated with longer periods of transition (Mummert et al. 2011), suggesting that the gradual nature of the transition allowed for a period of adjustment. This was the case in the Levant, where the transition to farming occurred over a period of about 20,000 years. In this region the main difference in health was increased evidence of infectious disease, which was attributed to the increased population density that occurred with the more sedentary lifestyle and, perhaps, the proximity to domesticated animals (Eshed et al. 2010). It is also clear that the agricultural transition could affect the health of children as well as adult males and females differently. For example, in the Levant, male life expectancy increased while female life expectancy decreased (Eshed et al. 2010).

The actual role of specific foods in the diet in the transition to agriculture is hazy. The assumption is that dietary diversity decreased, but there is little actual evidence to demonstrate that. There is, however, compelling evidence that foods associated with the adoption of agriculture and animal husbandry acted as selective forces shaping human genetic variation. For example, Tishkoff and colleagues (2007) identified several genetic variants in African pastoralists that allowed adults to digest lactose (milk sugar). The most common variant originated in Africa in the past 2,700–6,800 years and is consistent with the archaeological evidence of the spread of pastoralism in Kenya and Tanzania 3,300 to 4,500 years ago (Ambrose 1998). This is a clear example of recent genetic change due to selective pressure from a dietary element (lactose), and hence human adaptation to the diet.

The second example is the work of Perry et al. (2007) on the gene coding for amylase, an enzyme required for starch digestion. They found that human populations historically reliant on starchy staple foods (e.g., maize, millet, rice, sorghum, tubers, and wheat) had more copies of the amylase gene, and, hence, produced more of the enzyme, than groups more dependent on animal products (e.g., pastoralists). This suggests that human populations may have enhanced their ability to digest carbohydrates in the recent past.

Linking Ancestral to Modern Diets

In 1985 Eaton and Konner made ancestral diets relevant to modern health concerns in an influential paper entitled "Paleolithic nutrition: A consideration of its nature and current implications." It was the first in a series of papers arguing that we are genetically adapted to the characteristics of Paleolithic diets – diets based on minimally processed wild foods – and, hence, not well-matched to the diets and lifestyles that began with the transition to farming. This mismatch is argued to negatively impact our health and contribute to diet-related chronic disease. Eaton and Konner (1985) described the diets of pre-agricultural *Homo* as higher in nutrients including protein, especially animal protein, calcium, vitamin C, and dietary fiber, and lower in saturated fats and sodium than many processed foods in our contemporary diets.

The Paleolithic diet model is based largely on the diets of known hunter–gatherer populations like the !Kung San, Hadza, Australian Aborigines, Inuit, and Tasaday. Unfortunately, our understanding of the diets of these groups is limited, and they are unrepresentative of the ecological and geographic variation of preagricultural human populations. These limitations acknowledged, the Paleolithic diet is a model of the pattern of nutrient intake expected on a wild food diet, and this pattern is different than that of a diet based on plants and animals grown on factory farms and industrially processed.

The idea that Paleolithic-type diets are more healthy than modern diets has captured the imaginations of many people and led to the popularity of "paleo diet" regimes. It has also stimulated medical studies designed to evaluate the effects of a Paleolithic-style diet on chronic disease risk. While most studies to date have looked at these effects over a relatively short period of time, many have demonstrated beneficial effects on markers of chronic non-communicable diseases, like cardio-vascular disease and diabetes (see the review in Ghaedi et al. 2019). Further, within anthropology the Paleolithic diet model has stimulated a re-thinking of the evolution of the human diet. For example, Ulijaszek (2002) uses primate diets and foraging behaviors as a "template" for understanding human preference for sweet tasting and high fat foods. He argues that our taste for sugar is linked to our evolutionary heritage of frugivory (fruit eating), particularly the consumption of ripe fruits, which are highly palatable foods for large primates. Regarding dietary fat, he argues that hominins would have selected foods that maximized energy intake, like higher fat foods.

FOODS, DIET, AND NUTRITION IN CONTEMPORARY POPULATIONS

Biological anthropologists have examined a variety of different, but inter-related topics, in the food, diet, and nutrition of contemporary populations. Here we will consider four. First, human diets have changed over time. That is clear. Few populations still produce all their own food in their own local ecosystem by foraging, hunting/fishing, agriculture, and/or pastoralism. Most buy at least some foods in local marketplaces, and these markets are invariably connected to global trade networks dominated by industrialized food products. These trade networks overcome local limiting factors, such as lack of arable land and seasonal variation in agricultural potential, and, coupled with industrialized food production systems, have served to generally increase food availability globally year-round. How else, for example, could residents of Siberia enjoy strawberries in January? However, this modern globalized food system has also disrupted local food production, especially of staple food crops, and encouraged people to rely on markets. Further, economic crises can disrupt trade, as happened with the global economic crisis of 2008, and the corona virus pandemic of 2020–2022, leaving some populations vulnerable to food insecurity.

Second, is the larger problem of food insecurity itself, a problem that is not only the result of global crises, but an outcome of the inequitable distribution of food at global, national, and local levels. In some places people do not have enough to eat. They talk of difficulties getting access to food, having to eat less, having to eat less-desirable foods, and not being able to satisfy their hunger (Moreno-Black and Guerrón-Montero 2005). In other places food is very available and some people suffer from overnutrition and obesity. Third, is the much talked about problem of obesity. The popular press paints a picture of everyone being obese, but this portrait is less accurate for the food insecure and not completely accurate for the food secure. Fourth, is the fact that the very first food in the diets of infants, milk, exemplifies our mammalian heritage. For most of our evolutionary history that milk was human milk, a food we do not completely understand. Only later, as infants mature, do their diets begin to mirror those of the contemporary populations to which they belong.

Dietary Changes in Contemporary Populations

A model developed to explain the phenomenon of dietary change is known as the Nutrition Transition (Popkin et al. 2011). According to this model, economic development along with the industrialization of food production and expansion of global trade networks has led to an increased consumption of highly processed carbohydrates, vegetable oils, simple sugars, and animal source foods, and a decrease in the consumption of roots/tubers and grains like millet. These dietary changes, and concomitant decreases in physical activity, have contributed to an increase in the global prevalence of overweight/obesity and associated diet-related chronic disease such as hypertension and diabetes. The Nutrition Transition model has shaped thinking about dietary change, and anthropologists have applied it to understanding dietary shifts in local populations living in a variety of geographic and economic contexts.

One example is research in Colombia, a rapidly developing country where the Nutrition Transition model would predict dietary changes, and an increase in overweight/obesity. Research between 1990–1995 and 2008 documented an increased prevalence of overweight/obesity in urban women (Olszowy et al. 2012). The question then is, how did diet change over this same time interval? Dufour et al. (2015) studied the diets of low-income women who purchased food in local markets and had a diet based on rice, processed grains (e.g., bread, crackers), potatoes, plantains, beans, fruits, and beef. Data on dietary intake collected using direct observation and 24-hour recalls indicated no change in overall dietary composition, except for an increase in vegetable oil as a percent of total dietary energy, a change predicted by the Nutrition Transition model. However, the model also predicts an increase in animal source foods and sugared beverages, which researchers did not observe. The authors of the Colombian study point to economic constraints on food purchases as a potential explanation for the minimal dietary change observed.

Nutritional transitions look different in rural populations, which historically produced all, or most, of their own food. In these populations, overweight/obesity are usually absent, and the incorporation of purchased foods into the diet is often gradual. Dietary changes tend to go hand in hand with other lifestyle changes, such as reductions in the physical work of local food production and increased reliance on markets. Below we provide two examples of the early stages of nutrition transitions in rural populations.

The first example is the Hadza of Tanzania. Known historically as hunter–gatherers, the Hadza have increased their reliance on market foods in the past 10–20 years. In 2005, Pollom et al. (2021) found that residents of "bush camps" subsisted on a diet consisting primarily of wild plants (e.g., roots/tubers, baobab fruit, stone fruits, berries, figs, legumes) and game meat (e.g., birds, rodents, impala, kudu, dik dik). In contrast, the residents of "villages" had a mixed diet that included wild plant and animal foods, as well as grains such as maize, barley, and wheat, which they obtained from markets and/or donations. By 2017, both groups were consuming mixed diets, but residents of bush camps continued to consume more wild foods. Data on the height and weight of children 0–17 years of age indicated growth improved in both groups, i.e., children were taller, but not heavier, in comparison to international standards (WHO Multicentre Growth Reference Study Group 2006). It is unclear if the improved growth was attributable to an increase in total food intake or the nutritional qualities of the foods consumed because researchers knew the types, but not the amounts, of food consumed.

The second example is from research with rural riverine communities, *Ribeirinhos*, in the eastern Brazilian Amazon (Piperata et al. 2011a, 2011b). In 2002, the Ribeirinho diet was largely (87 percent of food energy) based on locally produced foods, including bitter manioc (cassava), fruits (including the palm fruit açaí), and fish, but also included some (13 percent) purchased foods such as beans and crackers. Dietary data from 2009 indicated a greater consumption of food energy from purchased, nonlocal foods, including vegetable oil, beans, rice, processed wheat products (crackers), and processed canned meats. Indeed, the calories in the diet from purchased foods tripled. These changes coincided with increases in income and declines in agricultural production and associated physical work. The changes in diet and physical activity were associated with modest increases in the child growth (males) and body fatness in both children and adults. It is noteworthy that, although the types of foods in the diet changed, actual dietary energy intake declined. In fact, in this setting, the early stage of the nutrition transition could be characterized as one of food instability rather than excess.

In summary, the examples here show that changes in diet in local populations are variable, and not all are consistent with predictions of the Nutrition Transition model. The urban Colombian example demonstrates the increased prevalence of overweight/obesity expected, but it is dissociated from changes in the types of foods consumed. In the rural populations, diets shifted away from roots/tubers and toward grains, and especially more processed grains, changes in keeping with the model. However, changes in anthropometry were modest, and there was no indication of increases in overweight/obesity.

Food Security for Some, Food Insecurity for Others

Food security refers to the ability to obtain sufficient food. The inability to obtain sufficient food, i.e., being food insecure, has far-reaching biological as well social consequences. Unfortunately, the number of food insecure people in the world is large, an estimated 30 percent of the global population in 2020. While it is true that the majority (96 percent) of the food insecure live in lower income countries (FAO et al. 2021), food insecurity is also a reality for some citizens of high-income countries. In the USA, for example, an estimated 14 percent of children live in food insecure homes (Coleman-Jensen et al. 2020).

What exactly is food security? The most oft cited definition is that of the Rome Declaration on World Food Security: "*Food security exists when all people, at all times, have physical and economic access to sufficient, safe and nutritious food to meet their dietary needs and food preferences for an active and healthy life*" (FAO 1996). Food insecurity is understood as the absence of one or more of these conditions. As conceptualized by the FAO et al. (2013), food security has four dimensions: *availability, access, utilization,* and *stability.* The availability dimension is concerned with food production, food stocks, and trade. The access dimension recognizes that while food may be available, it may not be physically, economically, or socially accessible. The third dimension, utilization, is complex and has two components. One is food utilization itself, specifically food choice, preparation, and distribution within the household. These food-related behaviors capture the strategies people use to cope when they are unable to access sufficient food to meet their dietary needs and/or preferences. The other component of utilization includes the health outcomes that are a function of the biological utilization of food. Most often these are defined in terms of nutritional status. The final dimension, stability, adds a time element to the other three dimensions and refers to the constancy of food at global, national, local, and household scales.

The magnitude and pervasiveness of food insecurity has inspired a growing body of scholarship on the relationship between food insecurity and human health. Dominating this research are large surveys that measure food insecurity in the access dimension specifically in terms of economic access to food (see the review by Piperata and Dufour 2021). For children, these surveys offer inconclusive evidence of the linkages between food insecurity and health assessed as physical growth, although the expectation is that food insecurity negatively impacts growth. For adult women the data are more limited but consistent: in low-income countries food insecurity is associated with underweight and anemia, while in some middle-income countries it is associated with overweight and anemia.

Biological anthropologists have been particularly interested in how people cope with food insecurity and identifying the pathways linking food insecurity and health. Here we provide examples of this work. We limit our examples to the food-related components of the utilization domain: food choice, food preparation, and intra-household food distribution.

Food choice under conditions of food insecurity was addressed by Dufour et al. (1997) in their study among urban Colombian women who lived in a state of chronic income uncertainty due to reliance on work in the informal economy. When money was in short supply, they altered meal composition. A common strategy was substituting eggs, or even less expensive chicken feet, for more valued meat, and omitting vegetables. The choice of eggs did not necessarily affect the protein or energy content of the diet, but the choice of chicken feet did reduce protein intake. For most women these meal alterations were intermittent and were not associated with nutritional status.

Food preparation methods are also opportunities for managing inadequate access to food. One method is food-stretching. Hampshire et al. (2009) describe the stretching of the dietary staple, *boule,* during the 2004–2005 food crisis in Niger. *Boule* is a porridge of millet, water, sugar, and curdled milk, and as food insecurity worsened, women increased the water-to-millet ratio and/or eliminated the sugar and milk. Piperata et al. (2020) reported that Nicaraguan mothers altered the staple dish, *gallo pinto* (rice, beans, fried onion), by increasing the ratio of rice-to-beans when money was inadequate. In both cases the stretching lowers dietary quality, which can have health consequences.

The distribution of food within the household is a third component of utilization. A common assumption is that adults, particularly mothers, buffer children from food insecurity by eating less than their share. One example of buffering is Leonard's (1991) study in highland Peru where he documented adults buffering children in the pre-harvest food scarcity season and its positive association with children's nutritional status and level of physical activity. A second example is Piperata et al.'s (2013) study of mother–child pairs in rural

Amazonian communities. They demonstrated that children's energy and protein intakes were more adequate than those of their mothers, and that younger children were buffered more than older children. Interestingly, they also showed that buffering was most evident when households had some food but not enough to meet the needs of all members, and less pronounced when food supplies were extremely low (severe food insecurity) or adequate (food secure).

In summary, food security is a complex, multidimensional construct. Most of the food security–health literature has been focused on the access dimension, specifically economic access, and a very limited range of health outcomes, specifically nutritional status. Research on the utilization dimension is still underexplored but has provided insights into the pathways linking food insecurity to health. As the number of food-insecure people continues to rise, anthropologists working in affected communities worldwide will be witness to the impacts on individuals and households and well-positioned to draw attention to the problem, as well as to inform interventions.

Overnutrition and Obesity

Obesity is a new phenomenon in human evolutionary history (Ulijaszek and Lofink 2006). From a purely biological view, obesity, a body mass index > 30, is simply the result of a history of positive energy balance – that is, a history of food intake exceeding energy needs. From an anthropological vantage point, the current situation raises interesting questions. Why at this point in history and in so many different places are so many people obese? What is it about our current environment that has made this possible and/or inevitable? What factors in our evolutionary past may have predisposed us to responding to our current environment in a manner that results in obesity?

A key assumption that has guided the search for answers to these questions is that, for most of our history, humans have lived in and adapted to environments in which food availability fluctuated. Under such conditions, there would have been selection for fat storage in times of food abundance. James Neel (1962) formalized this idea as the "thrifty gene" hypothesis. It is now clear that the genetic predisposition to obesity is complex and that there is significant population variation (Qasim et al. 2018). It is also clear that environmental factors are critical because the development of obesity requires that food be regularly available, as well as easily accessible in terms of physical effort and/or money. In addition, cultural norms also need to permit, or encourage, overeating relative to need. The first two conditions, regular availability and easy access, are assumed to be novel from an evolutionary point of view and have been labelled "obesogenic" environments (Swinburn et al. 1999). These environments are found in high-income countries and increasingly in low-and-middle-income countries. In these environments, industrially processed foods have become more pervasive (Lang and Heasman 2015: 28). These foods tend to be energy dense (i.e., high in calories per unit weight), which makes them easy to overconsume relative to need (Ulijaszek 2007). Hence, the consumption of these kinds of foods is often assumed to be a causal factor in the development of obesity.

Lieberman (2006) argues that optimal foraging theory can help make sense of the current obesogenic environment. Optimal foraging theory posits that an organism will forage in a way that maximizes their food energy intake per unit time (Macarthur and Pianka 1966). If maximizing energy intake is our evolutionary heritage and access to food in modern environments requires little human energy expenditure (e.g., drive your car to the grocery store), it makes sense that we are becoming more obese. Indeed, Ulijaszek (2007) has referred to obesity as a "disorder of convenience." However, as Mintz (1985) reminds us in his classic work on the history of sugar consumption, foods are social things. Hence, in an obesogenic environment, we are not just foraging optimally, we are responding to the socially defined qualities of foods, i.e., markers of status and identity. The association of foods with social status is clear in ethnographic accounts of modernization. For example, *Ribeirinho* populations in the Amazon want to eat beef and not just the fish that was traditionally the basis of their diet (Murrieta 1998). In the high Andes, rural children "cry for bread" – the white wheat bread purchased at the market and consumed by people in town – and show distain for the homegrown barley gruel that was part of their traditional diet (Weismantel 1989).

In summary, our understanding of the occurrence of obesity in contemporary societies is incomplete. The concept of obesogenic environments is a helpful starting point, but narrow. Anthropological insights into factors like social norms and food-related behaviors can add an important dimension to our understanding of these kinds of environments.

Infant Diets: The Transition from Human Milk to Family Foods

In all human societies, parents must choose how to feed their infants. Whether mothers breastfeed or bottle feed with human milk substitutes and how they pattern those feedings are not arbitrary decisions. Rather, they are decisions in keeping with local customs (Van Esterik 2002). Similarly, the kinds of weaning foods mothers introduce, when they introduce them, and how frequently they feed them are not arbitrary decisions but are shaped by local food availability, household food security, beliefs about the healthfulness of foods, as well as the broader social, cultural, and environmental context in which infant feeding is imbedded (Macharia et al. 2018; Pelto and Armar-Klemesu 2011; Thompson et al. 2020).

Biological anthropologists have been interested in many aspects of infant and young child feeding. Here we will highlight current understanding of evolutionary aspects and the characteristics of the foods in infant diets. These foods, as well as the feeding practices associated with them, have health consequences because adequate nutrition during infancy and early childhood is crucial for optimum growth and development (Black et al. 2013).

From an evolutionary perspective, humans are like other mammals in that they breastfeed their newborns. However, humans, unlike almost all other mammals and most other primates, also have a relatively long period of weaning during which liquid and solid foods are gradually added to the breast milk diet. It is a major period of transition referred to as complementary feeding and generally occurs between about 6 and 24 months of age. The beginning, at about 6 months of age, is the point at which human milk alone is no longer adequate to meet infants' needs, but the infant is not developmentally ready to consume the foods in the family diet. The evolution of this pattern of a relatively short period of exclusive breast feeding followed by a long period of complementary feeding is hypothesized to have evolved early in the genus *Homo* to lessen the energetic cost of breast feeding for the mother and thus increase fitness (Sellen 2007). Exactly what complementary foods mothers may have chosen or how they might have prepared them to make them suitable for infants is not known. Pelto et al. (2010) have posited that in the Paleolithic, mothers would have premasticated (i.e., pre-chewed) foods in the adult diet and then fed them to infants.

Human Milk, The First Food   The guiding assumption is that human milk was optimized to meet infants' biological needs during evolution (Hinde and German 2012; Sellen 2007). It is a complex fluid that contains all the elements required for infant growth and development (Dror and Allen 2018). These elements include macronutrients (carbohydrates, fats, proteins) and micronutrients (vitamins and minerals), as well as an array of bioactive components that promote infant growth and development.

The macro- and micronutrient composition of human milk is similar in all populations, despite variations in maternal nutritional status (Black et al. 2008; Prentice et al. 1995). Of the macronutrients, fats are the most variable component in terms of total amounts, as well as the types of fatty acids (Ballard and Morrow 2013). For example, research with Filipino women demonstrated that DHA, a type of fatty acid, was higher in women who consumed fish more regularly (Quinn and Kuzawa 2012). The authors did not measure infant outcomes, but it is well known that DHA is important in neurological growth.

The bioactive components of human milk are less well understood. These components include growth factors like IGF-1 (insulin-like growth factor), immunological factors like maternal antibodies, and human milk oligosaccharides (HMOs), which are carbohydrates that support growth of the infant gut microbiome. One goal of current research is to identify factors associated with population variation in bioactive components and define how these components are related to infant growth and health. For example, Miller (2018) compared concentrations of four anti-inflammatory proteins, i.e., proteins with immune-related functions, in the milk of mothers living in two very different environments, urban USA and rural Kenya. Concentrations of the four proteins differed significantly between the two populations, suggesting differences in local disease ecologies. One of them, TGF-β2, was consistently associated with infant growth in length in both populations. A second example comes from the research of Davis et al. (2017) in The Gambia. They found that certain HMOs in the milk of Gambian mothers was associated with lower rates of morbidity in their infants. The authors proposed that the HMOs enhanced the gut microbiome that protected against gastrointestinal infection and that lower rates of infection would be associated with better growth.

Complementary Foods, The Second Foods   Complementary foods, especially those fed in the 6–12-month age range, are soft-textured foods like homemade porridges or industrially produced purees and strained foods. In low-income countries, particularly under conditions of food insecurity, the first complementary foods are typically porridges made from locally available cereal grains. In Ghana, for example, these porridges are often based on millet, a dominant grain crop (Pelto and Armar-Klemesu 2011). These kinds of porridges are usually thin and watery, and hence low in energy and nutrient density. They are suboptimal from a nutritional point of view and, further, are associated with increased illness, especially from diarrheal diseases due to food contamination (Dewey and Adu-Afarwuah 2008). The combination of suboptimal dietary quality and illness events contributes to growth faltering, i.e., failure of infants to meet expectations for growth in length and weight (Onyango et al. 2014). Intervention studies that provided high-quality complementary food supplements (e.g., chickpea, soy, or peanut-based therapeutic foods) have demonstrated improvements in infant growth, indicating that the quality of the typical diet was suboptimal (Panjwani and Heidkamp 2017).

In high-income countries, complementary foods are typically industrially produced, pasteurized, and quality is more in keeping with infant nutritional requirements. Hence, infant growth in length and weight tends to follow expectations. However, there is concern that some industrially produced complementary foods are too energy dense, as they contain high amounts of sugars, saturated fat, and protein, and could lead to overweight/obesity. Although this issue is not fully resolved, current data do not support the idea (Thompson 2020).

In summary, infant feeding is at once an ancient mammalian adaptation and a reflection of contemporary contexts and diets. Research on milk composition continues to deepen our understanding of the bioactive components, their variation among human populations, and their effects on infant health. The quality of complementary foods, which reflects the quality of the adult diet, is equally critical for normal growth and development. Although the quality of infant foods themselves is important, anthropological studies show that infant "feeding" is a process that cannot be divorced from the larger social, cultural, and environmental contexts in which it occurs.

EMERGING THEME: DIET AND GUT MICROBIOME

A new and exciting research area for nutritional anthropology is the human gut microbiome, i.e., the colonies of microbes, especially bacteria, that populate the gastrointestinal tract, primarily the large intestine. The gut microbiome is largely shaped by diet because the foods ingested provide the major source of energy for bacterial colonies. The metabolic activities of the gut microbiota, in turn, have consequences for human health (Chow et al. 2010).

The effect of human milk on the infant gut microbiome is a good example. At birth, the infant gut is microbe free – a *tabula rasa*. It is only through contact with the environment, including food, that the gut microbiome is seeded and subsequently develops. A diet of human milk is important to this development because it contains HMOs. In fact, HMOs make up the third largest component of breastmilk, surpassed only by lactose (milk sugar) and fat (Bode 2012). Despite their abundance in breastmilk, HMOs cannot be digested by the infant. Rather, they are the sustenance of a group of bacteria called *bifidobacteria* known to support newborn nutrient absorption, as well as intestinal immune system maturation and brain development (Nijman et al. 2018).

Determining the effects of diverse diets on the microbiomes of children and adults across human populations is an area of active research, and an arena where anthropologists, in collaboration with microbiologists and other scientists, are making important contributions. Good examples are the studies of Schnorr et al. (2014) in Africa and Obregon-Tito et al. (2015) and Stagaman et al. (2018) in South America.

SUMMARY AND CONCLUDING THOUGHTS

Humans evolved as omnivores over a period of more than 2 million years. Omnivory, as a dietary strategy, provided enormous flexibility and allowed humans to thrive on a wide variety of plant and animal foods. Although in most instances we do not know exactly what these plant and animal foods were, they must have varied from place to place depending on local ecological conditions, and that variation no doubt increased as *Homo* migrated out of Africa and into Europe, Asia, and eventually the Americas.

Between about 7,000 and 10,000 years ago, humans began to add domesticated plants and animals to their wild food diets. The transition to agriculture is considered a revolutionary change in diet, as well as lifestyle. It was, however, based on many of the foods that had been part of the hunter–gatherer diets in the Paleolithic. The revolutionary aspect was intensification of dependence on a limited range of these previously wild foods. The addition of a new type of food, animal milks, occurred in some populations and was accompanied by genetic changes that allowed adults to digest lactose.

More recently, the past 200 years or so, food production and processing has become increasingly industrialized. That is, foods have been increasingly mass produced on factory farms, and extensively processed in factories into a variety of new forms. In essence it is another revolution in diet. Highly processed foods tend to be energy dense, nutrient poor, and seemingly high in variety, although many are based on a small number of the same plants domesticated thousands of years ago. For example, today we consume not only fresh corn kernels and the same corn meal that could be produced with an ancient grinding stone, but also corn oil, corn starch, corn syrup, corn chips, corn flakes, and high-fructose corn syrup. These industrially processed foods, along with changes in lifestyles, have led to nutrition transitions in contemporary populations, and are associated with negative health outcomes such as obesity and diet-related chronic disease. At the same time, food insecurity, as well as undernutrition, persist in some populations. The appearance of obesity in so many populations is novel in evolutionary terms. Determinants are multiple, but the idea of obesogenic environments is a useful framework for thinking about the potential contributions of the environmental context as well as factors like social norms, local food availability, and household food security. These same kinds of factors influence the complementary foods used in infants' diets because those diets reflect adult diets. In contrast, the initial diet of infants is assumed to be an ancient mammalian adaptation that has not changed over millions of years. New research on milk composition is expanding our understanding of the complexity of human milk and how it functions to support infant growth and development.

Finally, research on the gut microbiome is adding new dimensions to our understanding of dietary change, and the health impact of those changes. It is interesting to consider how this new focus on the gut takes us back to earlier conversations regarding the importance of changes in gut size and anatomy in the evolution of our species.

REFERENCES

Aiello, L. C., and P. Wheeler. "The Expensive Tissue Hypothesis." *Current Anthropology* 36, no. 2 (1995): 199–221.

Ambrose, S. H. "Chronology of the Later Stone Age and Food Production in East Africa." *Journal of Archaeological Science* 25 (1998): 377–392.

Antón, S. C., R. Potts, and L. C. Aiello. "Evolution of Early *Homo*: An Integrated Biological Perspective." *Science* 344 (2014): 1236828.

Ballard, O., and A. L. Morrow. "Human Milk Composition: Nutrients and Bioactive Factors." *Pediatric Clinics of North America* 60 (2013): 49–74.

Barr, W. A., B. Pobiner, J. Rowan, et al. "No Sustained Increase in Zooarchaeological Evidence for Carnivory after the Appearance of *Homo Erectus*." *Proceedings of the National Academy of Sciences* 119, no. 5 (2022): e2115540119. https://doi.org/10.1073/pnas.2115540119.

Black, R. E., L. H. Allen, Z. A. Bhutta, et al. "Maternal and Child Undernutrition: Global and Regional Exposures and Health Consequences." *Lancet* 371 (2008): 243–260.

Black, R. E., C. G. Victora, S. P. Walker, et al. "Maternal and Child Undernutrition and Overweight in Low-Income and Middle-Income Countries." *Lancet* 382 (2013): 427–451.

Blumenschine, R. J., and B. L. Pobiner. "Zooarchaeology and the Ecology of Oldowan Hominin Carnivory," In *Evolution of the Human Diet: The Known, the Unknown, and the Unknowable.* Edited by P. S. Ungar, 167–190. New York: Oxford University Press, 2007.

Bode, L. "Human Milk Oligosaccharides: Every Baby Needs a Sugar Mama." *Glycobiology* 22, no. 9 (2012): 1147–1162.

Broadhurst, C. L., Y. Wang, M. A. Crawford, et al. "Brain-Specific Lipids from Marine, Lacustrine, or Terrestrial Food Resources: Potential Impact on Early African *Homo Sapiens*." *Comparative Biochemistry and Physiology, B, Biochemistry & Molecular Biology* 131 (2002): 653–673.

Brown, T. A., M. K. Jones, W. Powell, et al. "The Complex Origins of Domesticated Crops in the Fertile Crescent." *Trends in Ecology and Evolution* 24 (2009): 103–109.

Chow, J., S. M. Lee, Y. Shen, et al. "Host-Bacterial Symbiosis in Health and Disease." *Advances in Immunology* 107 (2010): 243–274.

Cohen, M. N., and G. J. Armelagos, eds. *Paleopathology at the Origins of Agriculture.* Orlando: Academic Press, 1984.

Coleman-Jensen, A., M. P. Rabbitt, C. A. Gregory, et al. "Household Food Security in the United States in 2019." *ERR-275, U.S. Department of Agriculture, Economic Research Service,* 2020.

Davis, J. C. C., Z. T. Lewis, S. Krishnan et al. "Growth and Morbidity of Gambian Infants Are Influenced by Maternal Milk Oligosaccharides and Infant Gut Microbiota." *Scientific Reports* 7 (2017): 40466.

Dewey, K. G., and S. Adu-Afarwuah. "Systematic Review of the Efficacy and Effectiveness of Complementary Feeding Interventions in Developing Countries." *Maternal and Child Nutrition* 4 (2008): 24–85.

Dror, D. K., and L. H. Allen. "Overview of Nutrients in Human Milk." *Advances in Nutrition* 9 (2018): 278S–294S.

Dufour, D. L., L. K. Staten, J. C. Reina, et al. "Living on the Edge: Dietary Strategies of Economically Impoverished Women in Calí, Colombia." *American Journal of Physical Anthropology* 102, no. 1 (1997): 5–15.

Dufour, D. L., R. L. Bender, and J. C. Reina. "Local Trends in Diet in Urban Colombia, 1990–1995 to 2008: Little Evidence of a Nutrition Transition Among Low-Income Women." *American Journal of Human Biology* 27 (2015): 106–115.

Eaton, S. B., and M. Konner. "Paleolithic Nutrition: A Consideration of Its Nature and Current Implications." *New England Journal of Medicine* 312 (1985): 283–289.

Eshed, V., A. Gopher, T. B. Gage, et al. "Has the Transition to Agriculture Reshaped the Demographic Structure of Prehistoric Populations? New Evidence from the Levant." *American Journal of Physical Anthropology* 124 (2004): 315–329.

Eshed, V., A. Gopher, R. Pinhasi, et al. "Paleopathology and the Origin of Agriculture in the Levant." *American Journal of Physical Anthropology* 143 (2010): 121–133.

FAO. "Rome Declaration on World Food Security and World Food Summit Plan of Action." *World Food Summit* 13–17 November 1996. Rome, FAO, 1996. http://www.fao.org/3/w3613e/w3613e00.htm.

FAO. "*What Do People Eat?*" n.d. https://www.fao.org/3/u8480e/u8480e07.htm.

FAO, IFAD, UNICEF, et al. "*The State of Food Insecurity in the World: The Multiple Dimensions of Food Security.*" Rome, FAO, 2013. http://www.fao.org/3/a-i3434e.pdf.

FAO, IFAD, UNICEF, et al. "*The State of Food Security and Nutrition in the World: Transforming Food Systems for Food Security, Improved Nutrition and Affordable Healthy Diets for All.*" Rome, FAO, 2021. https://doi.org/10.4060/cb4474en.

Ghaedi, E., M. Mohammadi, H. Mohammadi, et al. "Effects of a Paleolithic Diet on Cardiovascular Disease Risk Factors: A Systematic Review and Meta-Analysis of Randomized Controlled Trials." *Advances in Nutrition* 10 (2019): 634–646.

Hampshire, K. R., C. Panter-Brick, K. Kilpatrick, et al. "Saving Lives, Preserving Livelihoods: Understanding Risk, Decision-Making and Child Health in a Food Crisis." *Social Science & Medicine* 68 (2009): 758–765.

Harris, M., and E. B. Ross, eds. *Food and Evolution: Toward a Theory of Human Food Habits.* Philadelphia: Temple University Press, 1987.

Hinde, L., and J. B. German. "Food in an Evolutionary Context: Insights from Mother's Milk." *Journal of the Science of Food and Agriculture* 92 (2012): 2219–2223.

Lang, T., and M. Heasman. *Food Wars: The Global Battle of Mouths, Minds and Markets.* London: Earthscan Books, 2015.

Larsen, C. S. "The Agricultural Revolution as Environmental Catastrophe: Implications for Health and Lifestyle in the Holocene." *Quaternary International* 150 (2006): 12–20.

Lemorini, C., T. W. Plummer, D. R. Braun, et al. "Old Stones' Song: Use-Wear Experiments and Analysis of the Oldowan Quartz and Quartzite Assemblage from Kanjera South (Kenya)." *Journal of Human Evolution* 72 (2014): 10–25.

Leonard, W. R. "Household-Level Strategies for Protecting Children from Seasonal Food Scarcity." *Social Science & Medicine* 33, no. 10 (1991): 1127–1133.

Leonard, W. R., and M. L. Robertson. "Evolutionary Perspectives on Human Nutrition: The Influence of Brain and Body Size on Diet and Metabolism." *American Journal of Human Biology* 6 (1994): 77–88.

Lieberman, L. S. "Evolutionary and Anthropological Perspectives on Optimal Foraging in Obesogenic Environments." *Appetite* 47 (2006): 3–9.

Macarthur, R. H., and E. R. Pianka. "On Optimal Use of a Patchy Environment." *American Naturalist* 100 (1966): 603–609.

Macharia, T. N., S. Ochola, M. K. Mutua, et al. "Association Between Household Food Security and Infant Feeding Practices in Urban Informal Settlements in Nairobi, Kenya." *Journal of Developmental Origins of Health and Disease* 9, no. 1 (2018): 20–29. https://doi.org/10.1017/S2040174417001064.

McClatchie, M., A. Bogaard, S. College, et al. "Neolithic Farming in North-Western Europe: Archaeobotanical Evidence from Ireland." *Journal of Archaeological Science* 51 (2014): 206e215.

Miller, E. M. "Ecological Immunity of Human Milk: Life History Perspectives from the United States and Kenya." *American Journal of Physical Anthropology* 167 (2018): 389–399.

Mintz, S. *Sweetness and Power: The Place of Sugar in Modern History.* New York: Viking, 1985.

Moreno-Black, G., and C. Guerrón-Montero. "Speaking of Hunger and Coping with Food Insecurity: Experiences in the Afro-Ecuadorian Highlands." *Ecology of Food and Nutrition* 44 (2005): 391–420.

Mummert, A., E. Esche, J. Robinson, et al. "Stature and Robusticity During the Agricultural Transition: Evidence from the Bioarchaeological Record." *Economics & Human Biology* 9 (2011): 284–301.

Murrieta, R. S. S. "O Dilema do Papa-Chibé: Consumo Alimentar, Nutrição e Práticas de Intervenção na Ilha de Ituqui, Baixo Amazonas, Pará." *Revista de Antropologia* 41, no. 1 (1998): 97–150.

Neel, J. V. "Diabetes Mellitus: A "Thrifty" Genotype Rendered Detrimental by "Progress?" *American Journal Human Genetics* 14 (1962): 353–362.

Nijman, R. M., Y. Liu, A. Bunyatratchata, et al. "Characterization and Quantification of Oligosaccharides in Human Milk and Infant Formula." *Journal of Agricultural and Food Chemistry* 66, no. 26 (2018): 6851–6859.

Obregon-Tito, A. J., R. Y. Tito, J. Metcalf, et al. "Subsistence Strategies in Traditional Societies Distinguish Gut Microbiomes." *Nature Communications* 6 (2015): 6505.

Olszowy, K. M., D. L. Dufour, R. L. Bender, et al. "Socioeconomic Status, Stature, and Obesity in Women: 20-Year Trends in Urban Colombia." *American Journal of Human Biology* 24 (2012): 602–610.

Onyango, A. W., E. Borghi, M. de Onis et al. "Complementary Feeding and Attained Linear Growth Among 6–23 Month Old Children." *Public Health Nutrition* 17 (2014): 1975–1983.

Panjwani, A., and R. Heidkamp. "Complementary Feeding Interventions Have a Small but Significant Impact on Linear and Ponderal Growth of Children in Low- and Middle-Income Countries: A Systematic Review and Meta-Analysis." *Journal of Nutrition* 147 (2017): 2169S–78S.

Pelto, G. H., and M. Armar-Klemesu. "Balancing Nurturance, Cost and Time: Complementary Feeding in Accra, Ghana." *Maternal & Child Nutrition* 7, no. S3 (2011): 66–81.

Pelto, G. H., Y. Zhang and H. P. Habicht. "Premastication: The Second Arm of Infant and Young Child Feeding for Health and Survival?" *Maternal & Child Nutrition* 6 (2010): 4–18.

Perry, G. H., N. J. Dominy, K. G. Claw, et al. "Diet and the Evolution of Human Amylase Gene Copy Number Variation." *Nature Genetics* 39 (2007): 1256–1260.

Piperata, B. A., and D. L. Dufour. "Food Insecurity, Nutritional Inequality, and Maternal–Child Health: A Role for Biocultural Scholarship in Filling Knowledge Gaps." *Annual Review of Anthropology* 50 (2021): 75–92. https://doi.org/10.1146/annurev-anthro-101819-110317.

Piperata, B. A., J. E. Spence, P. Da-Gloria, et al. "The Nutrition Transition in Amazonia: Rapid Economic Change and Its Impact on Growth and Development in *Ribeirinhos*." *American Journal of Physical Anthropology* 146 (2011a): 1–13.

Piperata, B. A., S. A. Ivanova, P. Da-Gloria, et al. "Nutrition in Transition: Dietary Patterns of Rural Amazonian Women During a Period of Economic Change." *American Journal of Human Biology* 23 (2011b): 458–469.

Piperata, B. A., K. K. Schmeer, C. Hadley, et al. "Dietary Inequalities of Mother–Child Pairs in the Rural Amazon: Evidence of Maternal-Child Buffering?" *Social Science & Medicine* 96 (2013): 183–191.

Piperata, B. A., M. Salazar, K. K. Schmeer, et al. "Tranquility Is a Child with a Full Belly: Pathways Linking Food Insecurity and Maternal Mental Distress in Nicaragua." *Ecology of Food and Nutrition* 59, no. 1 (2020): 79–103.

Piperno, D. R., A. J. Ranere, I. Holst, et al. "Starch Grain and Phytolith Evidence for Early Ninth Millennium B.P. Maize from the Central Balsas River Valley, Mexico." *Proceedings of the National Academy of Sciences* 106 (2009): 5019–5024.

Pollom, T. R., C. L. Cross, K. N. Herlosky, et al. "Effects of a Mixed-Subsistence Diet on the Growth of Hadza Children." *American Journal of Human Biology* 33 (2021): e23455.

Popkin, B. M., L. S. Adair, and S. W. Ng. "Global Nutrition Transition and the Pandemic of Obesity in Developing Countries." *Nutrition Reviews* 70 (2011): 3–21.

Prentice, A. M., and A. Prentice. "Evolutionary and Environmental Influences on Human Lactation." *Proceedings of the Nutrition Society* 54 (1995): 391–400.

Qasim, A., M. Turcotte, R. J. de Souza, et al. "On the Origin of Obesity: Identifying the Biological, Environmental and Cultural Drivers of Genetic Risk Among Human Populations." *Obesity Reviews* 19 (2018): 121–149.

Quinn, E. A., and C. W. Kuzawa. "A Dose–Response Relationship Between Fish Consumption and Human Milk DHA Content Among Filipino Women in Cebu City, Philippines." *Acta Pædiatrica* 101 (2012): 39–e445.

Richards, A. I. *Land, Labour and Diet in Northern Rhodesia: An Economic Study of the Bemba Tribe.* New York: Oxford University Press, 1939.

Richards, M. P., R. J. Schulting, and R. E. Hedges. "Archaeology: Sharp Shift in Diet at Onset of Neolithic." *Nature* 425 (2003): 366–366.

Schnorr, S. L., M. Candela, S. Rampelli, et al. "Gut Microbiome of the Hadza Hunter-Gatherers." *Nature Communications* 5 (2014): 3654.

Sellen, D. W. "Evolution of Infant and Young Child Feeding: Implications for Contemporary Public Health." *Annual Review of Nutrition* 27 (2007): 123–148.

Sponheimer, M., and D. L. Dufour. "Increased Dietary Breadth in Early Hominin Evolution: Revisiting Arguments and Evidence with a Focus on Biogeochemical Contributions." In *The Evolution of Hominin Diets: Integrating Approaches to the Study of Paleolithic Subsistence.* Edited by J. J. Hublin and M. P. Richards, 229–240. New York: Springer Science + Business Media B.V., 2009.

Sponheimer, M., Z. Alemseged, T. E. Cerling, et al. "Isotopic Evidence of Early Hominin Diets." *Proceedings of the National Academy of Science* 110 (2013): 10513–10518.

Stagaman, K., T. J. Cepon-Robins, M. A. Liebert, et al. "Market Integration Predicts Human Gut Microbiome Attributes Across a Gradient of Economic Development." *Msystems* 3, no. 1 (2018): e00122–17.

Swinburn, B. A., G. Egger, and F. Raza. "Dissecting Obesogenic Environments: The Development and Application of a Framework for Identifying and Prioritizing Environmental Interventions for Obesity." *Preventive Medicine* 29 (1999): 563–570.

Thompson, A. L. "Evaluating the Pathways Linking Complementary Feeding Practices to Obesity in Early Life." *Nutrition Reviews* 78, no. S2 (2020): 13–24.

Tishkoff, S. A., F. A. Reed, A. Ranciaro et al. "Convergent Adaptation of Human Lactase Persistence in Africa and Europe." *Nature Genetics* 39 (2007): 31–40.

Ulijaszek, S. J. "Human Eating Behaviour in an Evolutionary Ecological Context." *Proceedings of the Nutrition Society* 61 (2002): 517–526.

Ulijaszek, S. J. "Obesity: A Disorder of Convenience." *Obesity Reviews* 8, no. S1 (2007): 183–187.

Ulijaszek, S. J., and H. Lofink. "Obesity in Biocultural Perspective." *Annual Review of Anthroplogy* 35 (2006): 337–360.

Ungar, P. S. "Limits to Knowledge on the Evolution of Hominin Diet." In *Evolution of the Human Diet: The Known, the Unknown, and the Unknowable.* Edited by P. S. Ungar, 395–408. New York: Oxford University Press, 2007.

Ungar, P. S. "Dental Evidence for the Reconstruction of Diet in African Early *Homo*." *Current Anthropology* 53 (2012): S318–S329.

Van Esterik, P. "Contemporary Trends in Infant Feeding Research." *Annual Review of Anthropology* 31 (2002): 257–278.

Weismantel, M. J. "The Children Cry for Bread: Hegemony and the Transformation of Consumption." In *The Social Economy of Consumption*. Edited by B. Orlove and J. J. Ruitz, 85–99. New York: The University Press of America, 1989.

WHO Multicentre Growth Reference Study Group. "WHO Child Growth Standards Based on Length/Height, Weight and Age." *Acta Pædiatrica Suppl.* 450 (2006): 76–85.

Wilson, C. S. "Reasons for Eating: Personal Experiences in Nutrition and Anthropology." *Appetite* 38 (2002): 63–67.

Wrangham, R. W. "Control of Fire in the Paleolithic. Evaluating the Cooking Hypothesis." *Current Anthropology* 58 (2017): 303–313.

Zong, Y., Z. Chen, J. B. Innes, et al. "Fire and Flood Management of Coastal Swamp Enabled First Rice Paddy Cultivation in East China." *Nature* 449 (2007): 459–463.

Fabian Crespo

INTRODUCTION

In the first edition of Companion to Biological Anthropology, Lorena Madrigal and Jessica Willoughby (2010) explored the concept of *ongoing evolution in humans* with a special focus on how different evolutionary forces (natural selection, genetic drift, and gene flow) affected human evolution (Madrigal and Willoughby 2010). One of the emerging questions that the authors asked was *How do we detect if natural selection has acted on the human species?* Madrigal and Willoughby described the several ways that can be used to detect natural selection. One way is to explore changes in population frequencies of genetic polymorphisms that have a functional impact on an organism. The authors suggested that if the distribution of genetic polymorphisms in a population is the result of natural selection, then we should find a cline associated with different biological roles (i.e., differential mortality or differential fertility) and probably associated with different environmental contexts. One of the genetic polymorphisms analyzed by Madrigal and Willoughby is associated with a chemokine receptor 5 (CCR5-Δ32) and how its interaction with infectious diseases could be correlated with a selective process impacting our immune system in recent human history.

The immune system is constantly trained and reshaped by biological, ecological, and social factors. If the environment changes, then the immune system will try to adjust, and if possible, maintain homeostasis. Simply put, the immunological competence of an individual is a reflection of its biological, environmental, and social history, especially where different factors (biotic and abiotic) play a significant role in constantly reshaping the immune response and immune competence (Crespo and Lawrenz 2014). The immune system must maintain a delicate and complex balance because deficient responses may result in increased susceptibility to pathogens while excessive ones may result in pathologic consequences to the host. In this chapter, we revisit the ongoing evolution in humans utilizing the immune system as a model to show that we are still evolving, and we must continue evolving in order to adjust to different physiological, environmental, and social circumstances. This chapter focusses on the human immune system and explores how admixture between early humans and Neanderthals could have reshaped our immune responses. The chapter re-examines how different infectious diseases have influenced CCR5-Δ32 allele distribution in human populations; how over-reactive or abnormal immune responses observed today could be the legacy of past infectious diseases; and finally, to propose how the study of ancient human remains helps us to reconstruct changes in skeletal inflammatory phenotypes in past populations and explore the ongoing evolution of our immune system.

IMMUNOGENETICS, NEANDERTHALS, AND MODERN HUMANS

The immune system is involved in the body's defense against pathogens. Therefore, it is not surprising that genes within the immune system provide some of the best-documented evidence of natural selection at the molecular level (Hughes 2008). For example, twin studies showed that there was a significant host genetic influence on susceptibility to different diseases such as tuberculosis and poliomyelitis (Hill 1999). Human genetic variation, especially related to the immune system, exerts a major influence on the course of disease caused by different pathogens. The strength of the pathogen hypothesis when trying to explain the diversity at the molecular level observed in the immune system could be associated with the apparent explosion in infectious disease diversity in the last 10,000 years, clearly marked by a major transitional stage for the evolutionary forces acting on human populations (Baum and Bar Gal 2003), especially as humans made the transition from hunting and gathering to life in settled agricultural communities (Armelagos et al. 1998; Larsen 2006). For example, genes associated with the human leukocyte antigen system – HLA are among the most variable gene family in our species, where HLA alleles codify for immune cell membrane proteins that are involved in the display of cell-associated antigens to lymphocytes (T cells) allowing the immune system to recognize self or nonself proteins (Abbas and Lichtman 2005). An emerging question when testing ongoing evolution in the human immune system is *Did a differential macroscale pathogen distribution shape a different immune genetic make-up in different human populations?* It seems that the answer is "yes," especially from lessons that we are learning from genes of the major histocompatibility complex (HLA in humans) (Parham 2005).

Human populations exposed to higher diversity of pathogens display higher genetic diversity of the HLA genes than can be expected under a neutral model or no selection (Guegan et al. 2008). Pathogens that occur in tropical and temperate zones are generally directly transmitted viruses, bacteria, and fungi, which are internal to the host and therefore little affected by environmental variability. In contrast, pathogens with external stages (helminth worms, vector-transmitted pathogens, and reservoir-borne diseases) are more strongly influenced by environmental conditions (Guegan et al. 2008). Thus, it could be hypothesized that the immune response that will be mounted will be different depending on latitude. The rapid expansion of human populations can be traced back to 50,000 years ago and accelerated after the agriculture explosion to 10,000 years ago. Both phenomenon or processes are (evolutionary speaking) recent events (Cochran and Harpending 2009). Interestingly, decades ago it was proposed that, in general, proteins from the immune system evolve faster than other proteins (Hughes 1997; Murphy 1993), suggesting that natural selection could have played (or constantly plays) a "recent" role in shaping the genetic make-up of the human immune system. Fascinating research in recent decades suggests that admixture with other hominin species could have also had an impact on the evolution of our immune system.

After the first Neanderthal DNA (short sequence of a hypervariable part of the mtDNA control region) was published in 1997, a new window was opened to study the DNA from our ancestors and other hominins (Krings et al. 1997). Subsequently, a team of researchers revealed the first draft of the Neanderthal genome. When analyzing DNA mutations (nucleotide substitutions) that change the protein-coding capacity of genes, they found a gene that codes for a protein modulator of the immune response that carried the ancestral form in the Neanderthal ("chimpanzee-like" DNA sequence) but presents new amino acid substitutions that are fixed in contemporary human populations (Green et al. 2010). One year later, another team explored the possibility that our immune system was also shaped by admixture with archaic humans, suggesting that modern humans acquired the HLA-B*73 allele from archaic ones (Denisovans) in Asia around 50,000 years ago, along with other HLA alleles (B*07, B*51, C*07:02, and C*16:02) (Abi-Rached et al. 2011). More recent investigations have increased the number of Neanderthal's single nucleotide polymorphisms (SNPs) that were detected in human genomes, such as IL-18 (cytokine involved in innate responses against bacteria) and Toll-like receptors (TLRs), which play a role in microbe recognition (Dannemann et al. 2016; Sankararaman et al. 2014). Aligned with these findings, it was proposed that the persistence of such functional polymorphisms might have conferred modern humans with an acquired advantageous immune-related genetic variation, a process called adaptive introgression (Ségurel and Quintana-Murci 2014).

Using modern DNA from 52 populations, researchers studied the caspase-12 polymorphic gene, where caspases are directly involved in apoptosis and other nonapoptotic functions crucial for the expression of immune proteins. A caspase-12 polymorphic gene presents two alternatives, namely active (ancestral) and inactive (recent or derived), where those who carry the inactive form are more resistant to severe sepsis and avoid overreactive immune responses against bacterial infections. It was proposed that the inactive form arose and evolved in Africa around 100,000–500,000 years ago and was probably exposed to positive selection beginning around 60,000–100,000 years ago due to the advantageous phenotype offered by this inactive form when decreasing the possibility of sepsis during more frequent exposure and prevalence of bacterial infections (Xue et al. 2006)

A different group of researchers gave us more evidence on the potential evolutionary impact of admixture between archaic hominins on the recent evolution of our immune system. Remarkably, these studies included not only genomic analysis but immune gene expression (transcriptional level) in human populations with European or African descent from two different countries: Canada and Belgium (Nédélec et al. 2016; Quach et al. 2016). One study used RNA sequencing to characterize immune activation of TLRs in monocytes exposed to bacterial lipopolysaccharides in 200 individuals with self-reported African or European ancestry living in Belgium. The results showed significant differences in transcriptional responses to immune stimulation, where individuals with European ancestry showed a decreased expression of pro-inflammatory genes. The researchers detected a Neandertal genetic signature in modern Europeans that could be potentially associated with admixture of both populations in the Pleistocene, where Neandertal populations introduced regulatory variants that decreased hyperinflammatory responses in European genomes that could have facilitated immunological adaptation for pathogenic microbial ecologies in European environments (Quach et al. 2016). The second study, using a similar methodological approach, compared transcriptional responses of macrophages from individuals of European and African ancestry living in Canada when cells were exposed to live bacteria. The results shows that some genetic variants account for the differences in innate immune responses observed in both populations. It was observed that the stronger inflammatory response was generated in cells from individuals of African descent. The authors proposed that one explanation is that after modern human populations migrated out of Africa during the Pleistocene they were exposed to lower pathogen levels (or perhaps to different pathogenic microbiota), thus reducing the need for strong pro-inflammatory responses (Nédélec et al. 2016). As observed by Quach and colleagues, this study revealed the potential introgression of Neanderthal genetic variants that may have contributed to reshaping the immunogenetic identity and evolution of ancient European populations.

Another study explored introgressed immunogenetic variants in present day human genomes. Again, a cluster of different TLRs showed unusually high allele frequencies (with some haplotypes very similar to those found in Neanderthal genomes), suggesting that there were recurrent introgressions in modern humans moving into European environments, which immediately underwent local positive selection (Dannemann et al. 2016). Importantly, these studies suggest that the admixture between ancient hominin populations generated descendant populations in Europe with more strongly regulated inflammatory responses, whereas African populations retained more robust inflammatory responses, showing the ongoing evolutionary process of the immune system in association with different microbial pathogenic landscapes.

For the current circumstances, the COVID-19 pandemic is showing us another potential immunogenetic legacy of the admixture between modern and archaic hominins thousands of years ago. In this regard, Hugo Zeberg and Svante Pääbo (2020, 2021) observed two contrasting results where different genetic variants (in different chromosomes) were probably inherited by past admixtures with Neanderthals and their dissimilar genetic risk for severe COVID-19 (Zeberg and Pääbo 2021, 2020). First, exploring the COVID-19 Host Genetics Initiative database, they found that a genetic locus in chromosome 3 has a significant association with developing severe COVID-19. In addition, they found evidence that these genetic variants could have entered human populations via gene flow from Neanderthals or Denisovans around 40,000–60,000 years ago (Zeberg and Pääbo 2020). This Neanderthal derived genetic locus shows a high frequency (30 percent) in South Asia but is almost absent in East Asia. Using this genomic evidence, the researchers are trying to unveil the recent heterogenous evolutionary history of this locus, which shows alternative positive selection (or genetic drift?) and negative selection depending on the geographical region and is probably related to exposure to different pathogens (Zeberg and Pääbo 2020). Conversely, the same authors, using data from the Genetics of Mortality in the Critical Care Consortium, found that a different genetic variant localized in chromosome 12 (and potentially inherited from admixture with Neanderthals) offers protection against severe COVID-19. This genetic locus encodes proteins that activate enzymes that break down viral RNA and is found in populations in Asia, Europe, and America, which in some cases exceed 50 percent. The researchers proposed that this genetic variant offered some selective immunological advantage and is probably not only related to coronaviruses (SARS-Cov-2 is a recent phenomenon) but to other RNA viruses as well, such as West Nile virus or hepatitis C virus, proving a recent and complex evolution of our immune system (Zeberg and Pääbo 2021).

However, the observed differences associated with inflammatory gene expression (e.g., after pathogen exposure) across continental groups or populations does not solely imply that all differences are simply genetically inherited, as many other developmental, behavioral, and social inputs influence the regulation of inflammation. Moreover, the evolution of a single immunogenetic locus, such as CCR5-Δ32, is far more complex, showing that this chemokine receptor probably had multiple selective factors that varied in time and space.

Infectious Diseases and Recent Evolution of the Human Immune System: Revisiting the Complex History of CCR5-Δ32

Plague pandemics are usually described as three major pandemics, where the second plague pandemic that probably started around 1347 (see the discussion for an earlier start in Green 2020) is well recognized because of its first outbreak or wave, known as the "Black Death." The Black Death pandemic was probably the first semi-global phenomenon, and the mortality caused by this pandemic can be considered as one of the highest of any global catastrophe known to humankind, with an estimate of 40 to 60 percent of all people in Europe, the Middle East, and North Africa (Green 2014).

A catastrophic event with a high mortality, such as the Black Death, can be seen as a process or phenomenon that will change the species culturally and biologically. Although we cannot know exactly how many individuals were exposed and survived, still from an evolutionary perspective, an infectious disease that generates such high mortality can be associated with a natural selection process or because of the changes in population size via genetic drift. If natural selection or genetic drift (as well as gene flow) acted during and after the pandemic, then changes in allele frequencies within a population, especially alleles related to the immune system, should be detected. Using skeletal information when exploring different osteological markers that inform about individual frailty, it was shown that in some medieval populations, Black Death did not kill indiscriminately, suggesting that the pandemic was selective with respect to frailty (DeWitte and Wood 2008).

As presented in the previous edition of the book by Madrigal and Willoughby, the CCR5-Δ32 high-frequency function-altering deletion in some human populations remains a matter of intense debate (Madrigal and Willoughby 2010). The CCR5 protein is used by the human immunodeficiency virus (HIV) to gain access into immune cells (T-lymphocytes), but the CCR5-Δ32 variant offers resistance to HIV (Liu et al. 1996). The CCR5-Δ32 variant is older than HIV infection in humans, and HIV infection cannot be used as the primary factor to explain the high frequencies observed across Eurasia. Therefore, bubonic plague (second pandemic), especially Black Death, was one of the first candidates to explain the recent evolutionary changes in Δ32 frequencies (Stephens et al. 1998). A. Galvani and M. Slatkin developed a genetic model that considers the temporal pattern and age-dependent nature of plague and smallpox (with a higher prevalence in children) and concluded that the recent evolution of CCR5-Δ32 variant is consistent with an allele conferring dominant resistance to smallpox (Galvani and Slatkin 2003). Interestingly, plague has not been a significant source of mortality (especially in Europe) for the last 250 years. However, smallpox has a more chronic selective pressure, probably for more than 2,000 years, and after smallpox eradication the emergence of HIV infection continued the selective pressure for CCR5-Δ32 (Galvani and Slatkin 2003). The hypothesis for CCR5-Δ32 recent positive selection due to the protective effect against smallpox was also associated with Viking expansion between the eighth and tenth centuries (Lucotte 2002). The hypothesis that Black Death or smallpox were the main (primary) selective forces for the evolution of the CCR5-Δ32 allele was challenged by Duncan and colleagues, who asserted that (considering the older age for the emergence of the Δ32 allele) sporadic epidemics of hemorrhagic fever (viral infection) could have generated and kept the high allele frequency before the arrival of Black Death or smallpox (Duncan et al. 2005).

Two questions emerge in the study of the evolution of a genetic variant or allele, namely, *When did the mutation that ended in the new genetic variant happen?* and *Does the new genetic variant have a functional impact?* (This last question is crucial when exploring any potential role of natural selection.) Two investigations used different genetic models to determine the origin of the CCR5-Δ32 allele and revealed significant differences: 700 years ago with a 95 percent confidence interval of 275–1,875 years (Stephens et al. 1998) or 2,000 years ago with an interval from 375 to 4,800 years (Libert et al. 1998). Both challenged the idea that the increase of the allele frequency was due to a single selective event around the fourteenth century (the Black Death outbreak). If natural selection was the evolutionary force behind the high CCR5-Δ32 allele frequency in Europe, then the selective force should have started much earlier. In the early twentieth century, other scholars joined the exploration of the recent natural selection hypothesis for the protective CCR5-Δ32 allele. Sabeti and colleagues expanded the genetic analysis and estimated the origin of the allele to around 5,000 years ago. They concluded that there is no genetic evidence supporting strong recent selection for this allele but explained that the lack of support does not exclude the possibility of selection for the allele or locus (Sabeti et al. 2005). However, results of the study of ancient DNA from 2,900-year-old skeletal samples from different sites in Germany and Italy revealed that this chemokine allele was already prevalent among ancient Europeans, providing more evidence to exclude Black Death (or the whole second plague pandemic) as the major force for the rapid increase in the CCR5-Δ32 allele frequency in European populations (Hummel et al. 2005). Another argument against the Black Death outbreak as the primary selective force was that the gradient that (hypothetically) Black Death mortality generated dropped in the opposite direction from present-day genotype frequencies for CCR5-Δ32 (Cohn and Weaver 2006). A comparative analysis of human ancient DNA (eleventh to fourteenth centuries) and human contemporary DNA in Poland (affected by plague in the Middle Ages) implies, again, that the allele frequency in medieval Poland predates the medieval plague pandemic (Zawicki and Witas 2008). Similarly, analysis of ancient DNA from individuals interred in a medieval German cemetery confirms the presence of a more ancient origin for the CCR5-Δ32 allele, suggesting that the allele frequency probably remained unchanged in Central Europe over the last millennium (Bouwman et al. 2017).

Exploring the functional (protective) role of the CCR5-Δ32 allele, Joan Mecsas and colleagues also challenged the idea that plague was the selective force when they infected both normal and CCR5-deficient mice with the bacterium causative of plague. They found no difference in either bacterial growth or survival time between the two groups (Mecsas et al. 2004). These experiments were conducted in a nonhuman animal model, and although we cannot rule out pathogenic differences between mice and humans, this evidence shows no evidence for the role of the selective power of plague on the CCR5-Δ32 frequency increase in European populations. However, comparison of the CCR5-Δ32 allele contemporary frequency in Lopar (island of Rab) and Komiža (island of Vis), two isolated island communities in Croatia, reached different conclusions. Historical records show that the island of Rab was affected by a plague epidemic in 1449 and 1456, but the island of Vis was spared those major epidemics (Smoljanović et al. 2006). The frequency of CCR5-Δ32 allele is significantly lower in Vis when compared to Rab, suggesting that the plague epidemic could have exerted some positive selective pressure for the allele frequency in Rab. The authors also argued that other infectious diseases may have played a role. In consideration that both populations are confined to isolated island communities, we cannot rule out the effect of genetic drift to reduce the allele frequency in Vis (Smoljanović et al. 2006). Tollenaere and colleagues also explored the potential protective effects of the CCR5 variant in black rats from Madagascar (the rodent that is considered today's main *Yersinia pestis* reservoir in the island). The authors compared CCR5 genotypes of dying and surviving plague-infected rats and analyzed the allele frequency in rats from plague-focus areas compared to plague-free areas. Their results show a higher prevalence of the allele variant in resistant animals and higher frequencies of the allele in plague-focus areas, suggesting (at least in black rats) the potential correlation between CCR5 genotypes and plague resistance (Tollenaere et al. 2008).

Knowing the origin and age of the HIV protective CCR5-Δ32 allele is important for us to start the discussion on the temporality of the evolutionary factor/s that drove the high allele frequency in European populations. However, as proposed by Hedrick and Verelli, an earlier age predating plague or smallpox epidemics should not rule out the CCR5-Δ32 allele adaptive or protective value against those infectious diseases, conferring, as it happens, with HIV today (Hedrick and Verrelli 2006). We should also consider that the CCR5-Δ32 allele might represent an unusual selected variant because it results in a nonfunctional genetic variant with a selective advantage. The selective advantage is likely to be associated with resistance to more than one infectious disease (Hedrick and Verrelli 2006). In this regard, the CCR5-Δ32 allele frequency varied (and still varies) among human populations. The effects and involvement of this allele in different infectious diseases are also complex and varied, which should not be generalized or oversimplified (Ellwanger et al. 2020). We must also consider that the immune competence of the host (immune resistance or susceptibility) is not solely determined by the genetics of the host or the genetics of the microbial pathogen or determined by a single genetic variant. That is, the construction and ongoing evolution of the immune competence of the host is also a reflection of the complex interaction of genetic, epigenetic, environmental, and social factors.

Today's Inflammatory Phenotypes as Legacies of Past Infectious Diseases?

As discussed above, the immune system plays a fundamental role in protecting us from pathogens. Many of its mechanisms, particularly inflammation, are also major contributors to tissue damage and disease, especially when those responses are exaggerated or directed against our own cells or their components. In fact, inflammatory responses need to achieve an optimal balance in their anti- and pro-inflammatory mechanisms, largely because deficient responses may result in increased susceptibility to pathogens, whereas excessive responses may result in heightened inflammation and pathologic consequences to the host. Immune and inflammatory responses are known to be regulated by multiple genes and proteins among which cytokines, the soluble mediators of the immune system, play a very important role (Cronkite and Strutt 2018; Smale and Natoli 2014). Indeed, genetic defects or polymorphisms in cytokine genes often influence the strength of immune/inflammatory responses and susceptibility of individuals to certain pathogens. Pathogens usually try to overcome the host immune response by different mechanisms, including immune suppression. At the population level, some hosts will be able to mount a stronger immune response commonly associated with hyper-inflammation and therefore overcome the immune suppression generated by pathogens. However, under these circumstances, the surviving population could face the negative and pathological consequences of a hyper-inflammatory phenotype as legacy of the selective process against microbial pathogens. It was proposed that the persistence and increasing prevalence of conditions or diseases associated with pathological inflammation is an enigmatic aspect of the human diversified immune responses. In this regard, these conditions or diseases could be partially linked to the roles of some immune genes and proteins against pathogenic microbes that underwent a strong natural selection in humans (Brinkworth 2017; Brinkworth and Barreiro 2014).

It cannot be overstated that diversity in the immune system can be associated with the apparent explosion in infectious disease variety in the last 10,000 years. This event is associated with a major change in subsistence as humans made the transition from mobile hunter–gatherers to settled small agricultural communities. Changes in our biology and behavior likely led to the emergence of new diseases, where the spatial distribution of different pathogens has been shaped by subsistence strategies, migration, and other anthropogenic factors. Several ecological factors likely played an important role in determining pathogen distribution and consequently shaping the evolution of immune responses of human populations. It was proposed that antimicrobial hereditary immunity in all modern populations reflects the ongoing co-evolutionary process with a myriad of different pathogens (Karlsson et al. 2014; Rumyantsev 2011). Consequently, the immunological profile of an individual or population still reflects the evolutionary history of that individual or population. From an evolutionary perspective, disease or abnormal inflammatory responses can be produced by a mismatch between the evolutionary history of an individual or population and the environment in which they live today (Gluckman et al. 2009). For example, inflammation under specific conditions or pathogenic insults usually has a protective mechanism. However, if it is still present when those conditions are absent or change, excessive or undesired inflammation can be considered pathogenic (Okin and Medzhitov 2012). An over-reactive immune system is part of a natural process, largely because the immune system may be driven to self-destruction or over-reaction through the ever-changing strategies of the pathogens it is attempting to deter. This is especially the case where some pathogens may cause chronic disease because "long-term" disturbances on the body machinery persist even after the pathogen is gone (Ewald 2002). Thus, the self-destructive or over-reactive immune response could be still the legacy of different past pathogenic experiences.

An interesting example of this kind of response has emerged from the recent co-evolution between leprosy and TLRs (Hart and Tapping 2012; Krutzik et al. 2003). Leprosy is considered to be one of the oldest infectious diseases and has probably been endemic to nonhuman primates for millions of years, and it appears that the Hansen's disease (modern clinical denomination) pathogen *Mycobacterium leprae* has infected humans or human ancestors during the last 100,000 years (Han and Silva 2014). However, recent evidence suggests that it chronically infected humans no longer than 5,000 years ago (Schuenemann et al. 2013). The TLR1 locus, which is linked to protection against leprosy, is significantly differentiated in human populations (Wong et al. 2010). The protective dysfunctional 602S allele is rare in Africa but is dominant among individuals of European descent (Wong et al. 2010). Therefore, in the context of medieval endemic leprosy in Europe, this infectious disease probably contributed to reshape the allele frequency of one of the TLR genes in European populations during the selective process, leading to successful antimicrobial immunity. Nevertheless, it is important to also consider that the recent evolution of the immune system could have been shaped by the co-existence of more than one infectious disease (synergistically or counter-synergistically). Innovative studies on leprosy and psoriasis can help us to understand changes in the immunological profile of populations over time – what is called an "*immunological shift*." As with leprosy, psoriasis is a human disease. It is a hereditary inflammatory skin disease with higher prevalence in populations with northern European ancestry (Gudjonsson and Elder 2007). Interestingly, areas in which psoriasis is currently highly prevalent overlap with most geographical areas of past leprosy epidemics. It has been suggested that the exacerbated inflammatory response present in psoriasis (called by some scholars "psoriasis genotype") could have reduced the clinical progression of leprosy. This observation leads to the argument that the "psoriasis genotype" expanded in different human populations under the selective pressure of historical leprosy epidemics (Bassukas et al. 2012). Moreover, latent infections may create a polarized cytokine environment and develop a prolonged state of cross-protection when the host faces different pathogens (Barton et al. 2007). For example, *in vitro* experimental findings suggests that chronic exposure to the tuberculosis pathogen (*Mycobacterium tuberculosis*) or leprosy pathogen (Hansen's disease, *M. leprae*) can permanently shift inflammatory responses that can affect systemically other inflammatory processes (Crespo et al. 2017). A recent study on leprosy explored the association between childhood nonspecific osteological markers of stress and leprosy immunity in Medieval England, finding that immune processes were likely to be more influenced by maternal and early physiological stress than environmental factors later in life (Filipek-Ogden 2014).

The study and identification of genetic factors influencing variation in the immune system is still in the initial steps. At this point, we cannot rule out some genetic polymorphisms in immune-related genes having been selected and evolved to maintain some levels of developmental and ecological plasticity (Lagou et al. 2018; Liston and Goris 2018). Moreover, attempts to identify the genetic or environmental influence on variation of immune responses revealed that parameters of immune innate responses are more controlled by genetic factors than those of adaptive responses (Patin et al. 2018). Thus, although genetics plays a significant role in individual heterogeneity of immune responses, most of the variation observed at the population level cannot be fully explained by the genetics of the immune system (Barreiro and Quintana-Murci 2020).

Clearly, then, the immune system presents a high degree of plasticity, and marked fluctuations in the immune response occur as a reaction to environmental and social factors during an individual's lifetime (French et al. 2009). Ecological immunology helps us to study and explore the dynamic nature of the immune response (McDade 2003, 2005b), showing that we cannot extrapolate genetic and experimental data without carefully considering social and ecological factors. Ecological immunology reveals that shaping the immunological phenotype of an individual starts early in life (McDade 2005a; McDade et al. 2010). Therefore, when feasible, there is a clear need for consideration of early ecological and social contexts for the life of each individual. Another emerging factor potentially involved in the evolution of the immune system is epigenetic variation, where DNA methylation has been shown to alter the immune responses to infection (Barreiro and Quintana-Murci 2020). Social and environmental factors during early development can also influence DNA methylation and modify the expression of inflammatory genes in young adulthood (McDade et al. 2017). Importantly, it has already been proposed that the epigenetics of host–pathogen interactions not only impact life-history traits in the host during a single generation but may also have transgenerational consequences, adding another crucial factor to the ongoing evolution of the immune system in humans (Gómez-Díaz et al. 2012; Jablonka 2017).

The ongoing evolution of the immune system should not be restricted to genetic and physiological factors. Rather, it should also consider the complex interaction of social and environmental factors that can influence functional changes of the immune system over generations. As proposed for the study of human health, we should incorporate a *syndemics* approach that will consider historical contexts and interactions that are not readily apparent, allowing us to connect bioecological and social environments that will determine differential health outcomes (Singer et al. 2021, 2017). We should extrapolate the syndemics approach when exploring the evolution of the immune system, and perhaps reconceptualize a more comprehensive concept of *immune competence* rather than immunity. Moreover, the interaction of different disciplines, such as immunology, bioarchaeology, and history, provides a unique opportunity to take syndemics into the past – *paleosyndemics* – and helps to unveil the ever-evolving nature of the immune system (Larsen and Crespo 2022).

FUTURE RESEARCH

As presented in previous sections of this chapter, ancient and contemporary DNA analysis of human populations proved the ongoing evolution of humans, especially for our immune systems. Ancient DNA analysis is a powerful tool that allows us to reconstruct ancient immunological genotypes and how they changed over generations. The emerging question here is "*Can we reconstruct ancient immunological phenotypes using skeletal samples and test how they changed over generations?*"

Most diseases that involve chronic inflammation start at a local site, but ultimately involve many other organs owing to long-term activation of the immune system (Straub 2011; Straub and Schradin 2016). Immune and inflammatory responses are confined to local tissues or organs, but when inflammation is chronic and strong, there can be a spillover of pro-inflammatory proteins and activated cells that significantly affect systemic responses, leading in some cases to chronic inflammatory systemic diseases (i.e., rheumatoid arthritis; systemic lupus, multiple sclerosis). In recent decades, various disciplines have grappled with understanding the underlying mechanisms and ultimate ongoing evolution of chronic inflammation in humans (Buckley 2011; Medzhitov 2008; Straub 2012), but longitudinal studies in human populations face substantial logistical barriers, such as sampling and recording of immunological responses along the life course of an individual. At the same time, bioarchaeology is expanding the analysis of past populations and moving beyond simplistic interpretations of skeletal lesions as markers of ill health as well as considering what those markers might really tell us about underlying physiological processes, such as inflammation and immune responses.

In recent decades, the study of the interplay between immune and skeletal systems motivated the emergence of a new discipline, osteoimmunology (Arron and Choi 2000; Lorenzo et al. 2011; Nakashima and Takayanagi 2009). Biological anthropologists proposed that osteoimmunology should be considered one of the new frontiers in bioarchaeology (Gosman et al. 2011; Klaus 2014). As expressed by Haagen Klaus, chronic infections promote long-term inflammatory responses, and wherever inflammatory conditions or diseases occur, systemic impacts on bone develop on some level (Klaus 2014).

Using a systemic perspective for each individual, we propose that the expression of chronic inflammatory processes in skeletal tissues are far from simple and do not adhere to the generally stagnant and isolated conception that one local inflammatory lesion cannot be separate from the whole organism (a local inflammatory process can influence a distant inflammatory process and vice versa). Consequently, we must consider that chronic skeletal inflammatory processes that have a different cause or origin (infection, trauma) are still interconnected through systemic immune responses. The first steps into this area were made by bioarchaeologists DeWitte and Bekvalac, who observed associations between periodontitis, periostosis, and early life stress in a Medieval English skeletal sample. They provocatively considered that an abnormally heightened immune response connected these disparate conditions (DeWitte and Bekvalac 2011).

Aligned with this rationale, it can be proposed that systemic stress (i.e., chronic infection) can generate systemic inflammation, leaving a mark on local and distant persistent

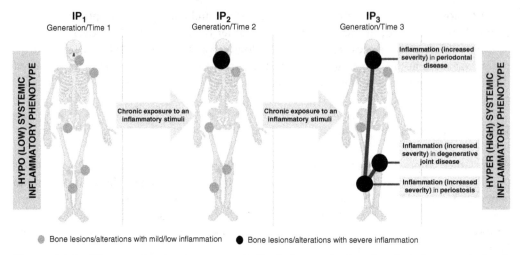

Figure 16.1 Diagram showing how systemically, before and after chronic inflammatory insult (chronically over generations), different bone lesions could increase bone alteration or resorption, informing about a hyper- or hypo-inflammatory phenotype (IP). (Modified from Crespo 2020).

infections, such as periodontitis and periostosis. Therefore, we can predict an elevated lesion severity and correlation between most inflammatory lesions in individuals (populations) that were exposed to a chronic inflammatory insult. Moreover, from an evolutionary perspective, and to test ongoing evolution of our immune system, we can predict changes in skeletal inflammatory phenotypes through different generations if the chronic inflammatory insult/s persist over time (Figure 16.1).

The key concept behind this newly proposed skeletal inflammatory index (SINDEX) is to consider as many inflammatory lesions as possible, related to infections or not, and to use different criteria to quantify the severity of the inflammatory process in each lesion or bone alteration (not only presence/absence) in order to reconstruct more comprehensive skeletal inflammatory phenotypes (Crespo 2020). If feasible, it is also proposed that this inflammatory index should include an ancient proteomic analysis (expression of inflammatory proteins) and an osteoimmunological analysis (experimental *in vitro* analysis) to explore cross-talk between immunity and bone cells (Crespo 2018, 2020). Biological anthropology will be a unique protagonist when reconstructing SINDEX and comparing the evolutionary process between populations in time and space. The integration of different disciplines will help us to recognize that past populations experienced complex heterogeneous biosocial landscapes, consequently allowing us to predict the development of equally heterogeneous and constantly evolving immunological landscapes. SINDEX will provide another piece to study the complex evolutionary history of inflammatory responses, where, as presented in this chapter, selective processes at the genetic level, admixture with ancient populations, co-evolution with infectious diseases, and ecological and social factors, all act in concert to continually shape our immune system.

ACKNOWLEDGMENTS

I thank Clark Spencer Larsen for the invitation to contribute to the new edition of this volume. I also thank Sharon DeWitte, Molly Zuckerman, Kathryn Marklein, and Haagen Klaus for their help when trying to design and extrapolate the reconstruction of skeletal inflammatory phenotypes in archaeological samples and to study how to score changes in skeletal inflammatory processes in past populations. I thank all comments from an anonymous reviewer that helped to improve the final version of this chapter.

REFERENCES

Abbas, A. K., and A. H. Lichtman. *Cellular and Molecular Immunology*, 5th edn. Philadelphia: Elsiever Saunders, 2005.

Abi-Rached, L., M. J. Jobin, S. Kulkarni, et al. "The Shaping of Modern Human Immune Systems by Multiregional Admixture with Archaic Humans." *Science* 334 (2011): 89–94.

Armelagos, G. J., K. C. Barnes, and J. Lin. "Disease in Human Evolution: The Reemergence of Infectious Disease in the Third Epidemiological Transition." In *Anthropology Explored*. Edited by R. Osterweis Selig and M. London, 96–106. Washington, DC: Smithsonian Institution Press, 1998.

Arron, J. R., and Y. Choi. "Bone Versus Immune System." *Nature* 408 (2000): 535–536.

Barreiro, L. B., and L. Quintana-Murci. "Evolutionary and Population (Epi)genetics of Immunity to Infection." *Human Genetics* 139 (2020): 723–732.

Barton, E. S., D. W. White, J. S. Cathelyn, et al. "Herpesvirus Latency Confers Symbiotic Protection from Bacterial Infection." *Nature* 447 (2007): 326–329.

Bassukas, I. D., G. Gaitanis, and M. Hundeiker. "Leprosy and the Natural Selection for Psoriasis." *Medical Hypotheses* 78 (2012): 183–190.

Baum, J., and G. K. Bar Gal. "The Emergence and Co-evolution of Human Pathogens." In *Emerging Pathogens: Archaeology, Ecology and Evolution of Infectious Diseases*. Edited by C. Greenblatt and M. Spigelman, 67–78. New York: Oxford University Press, 2003.

Bouwman, A., N. Shved, G. Akgül, et al. "Ancient DNA Investigation of a Medieval German Cemetery Confirms Long-Term Stability of CCR5-Δ32 Allele Frequencies in Central Europe." *Human Biology* 89 (2017): 119–124, 116.

Brinkworth, J. F. "Infectious Disease and the Diversification of the Human Genome." *Human Biology* 89 (2017): 47–65.

Brinkworth, J. F., and L. B. Barreiro. "The Contribution of Natural Selection to Present-Day Susceptibility to Chronic Inflammatory and Autoimmune Disease." *Current Opinion in Immunology* 31 (2014): 66–78.

Buckley, C. D. "Why Does Chronic Inflammation Persist: An Unexpected Role for Fibroblasts." *Immunology Letters* 138 (2011): 12–14.

Cochran, G., and H. Harpending. *The 10,000 Year Explosion: How Civilization Accelerated Human Evolution*. New York: Basic Books Publisher, 2009.

Cohn, S. K., Jr., and L. T. Weaver. "The Black Death and AIDS: CCR5-Delta32 in Genetics and History." *QJM: An International Journal of Medicine* 99 (2006): 497–503.

Crespo, F. "A Biocultural Approach to Reconstruct Immune Competence in past Populations: Searching for A New Dialogue between Immunology and Bioarchaeology." *American Journal of Physical Anthropology* 165 (2018): 56.

Crespo, F. Reconstructing Immune Competence in Skeletal Samples: A Theoretical and Methodological Approach. In *Theoretical Approaches in Bioarchaeology*. Edited by C. Cheverko, J. Prince-Buitenhuys, and M. Hubbe, 76–92. New York: Routledge Press, 2020.

Crespo, F., C. K. Klaes, A. E. Switala, and S. N. DeWitte. "Do Leprosy and Tuberculosis Generate a Systemic Inflammatory Shift? Setting the Ground for a New Dialogue between Experimental Immunology and Bioarchaeology." *American Journal of Physical Anthropology* 162 (2017): 143–156.

Crespo, F., and M. B. Lawrenz. "Heterogeneous Immunological Landscape and Medieval Plague: An Invitation to a New Dialogue between Historians and Immunologists." *The Medieval Globe* 1 (2014): 229–257.

Cronkite, D. A., and T. M. Strutt. "The Regulation of Inflammation by Innate and Adaptive Lymphocytes." *Journal of Immunology Research* 2018 (2018): 1467538-1467538.

Dannemann, M., A. M. Andrés, and J. Kelso. "Introgression of Neandertal- and Denisovan-like Haplotypes Contributes to Adaptive Variation in Human Toll-Like Receptors." *American Journal of Human Genetics* 98 (2016): 22–33.

DeWitte, S. N., and J. Bekvalac. "The Association Between Periodontal Disease and Periosteal Lesions in the St. Mary Graces Cemetery, London, England A.D. 1350–1538." *American Journal of Physical Anthropology* 146 (2011): 609–618.

DeWitte, S. N., and J. W. Wood. "Selectivity of Black Death Mortality with Respect to Preexisting Health." *Proceedings of the National Academy of Sciences* 105 (2008): 1436–1441.

Duncan, S. R., S. Scott, and C. J. Duncan. "Reappraisal of the Historical Selective Pressures for the CCR5-Δ32 Mutation." *Journal of Medical Genetics* 42 (2005): 205–208.

Ellwanger, J. H., B. Kulmann-Leal, V. de Lima Kaminski, et al. "Beyond HIV Infection: Neglected and Varied Impacts of CCR5 and CCR5Δ32 on Viral Diseases." *Virus Research* 286 (2020): 198040.

Ewald, P. *Plague Time: The New Germ Theory of Disease*. New York: Anchor Books, 2002.

Filipek-Ogden, K. L. "Ill-Fated? Exploring Bioarchaeological Links Between Childhood Non-Specific Indicators of Stress and Leprosy Immunity in Medieval England." *American Journal of Physical Anthropology* 153 (2014): 117.

French, S. S., M. C. Moore, and G. E. Demas. "Ecological Immunology: The Organism in Context." *Integrative Comparative Biology* 49 (2009): 246–253.

Galvani, A. P., and M. Slatkin. "Evaluating Plague and Smallpox as Historical Selective Pressures for the CCR5-Δ32 HIV-Resistance Allele." *Proceedings of the National Academy of Sciences* 100 (2003): 15276–15279.

Gluckman, P., A. Beedle, and M. Hanson. *Principles of Evolutionary Medicine*. New York: Oxford University Press, 2009.

Gómez-Díaz, E., M. Jordà, M. A. Peinado, et al. "Epigenetics of Host–Pathogen Interactions: The Road Ahead and the Road Behind." *PLoS Pathogens* 8 (2012): e1003007.

Gosman, J. H., S. D. Stout, and C. S. Larsen. "Skeletal Biology over the Life Span: A View from the Surfaces." *American Journal of Physical Anthropology* 146 (2011): 86–98.

Green, M. H. "Editor's Introduction to Pandemic Disease in the Medieval World: Rethinking the Black Death." *The Medieval Globe* 1 (2014): 9–26.

Green, M. H. "The Four Black Deaths." *The American Historical Review* 125 (2020): 1601–1631.

Green, R. E., J. Krause, A. W. Briggs, et al. "A Draft Sequence of the Neandertal Genome." *Science* 328 (2010): 710–722.

Gudjonsson, J. E., and J. T. Elder. "Psoriasis: Epidemiology." *Clinical Dermatology* 25 (2007): 535–546.

Guegan, J.-F., F. Prugnolle, and F. Thomas. "Global Spatial Patterns of Infectious Diseases and Human Evolution." In *Evolution in Health and Disease*. Edited by S. Stearns and J. Koella, 19–29. New York: Oxford University Press, 2008.

Han, X. Y., and F. J. Silva. "On the Age of Leprosy." *PLoS Neglected Tropical Diseases* 8 (2014): e2544.

Hart, B. E., and R. I. Tapping. "Genetic Diversity of Toll-Like Receptors and Immunity to M. Leprae Infection." *Journal of Tropical Medicine* (2012): 415057. doi: 10.1155/2012/415057.

Hedrick, P. W., and B. C. Verrelli. "'Ground Truth' for Selection on CCR5-Delta32." *Trends in Genetics* 22 (2006): 293–296.

Hill, A. "Genetics and Genomics of Infectious Disease Susceptibility." *British Medical Bulletin* 55 (1999): 401–413.

Hughes, A. L. "Rapid Evolution of Immunoglobulin Superfamily C2 Domains Expressed in Immune System Cells." *Molecular Biology and Evolution* 14 (1997): 1–5.

Hughes, A. L. "Vertebrate Immune System: Evolution." In *Handbook of Human Molecular Evolution*. Edited by D. Cooper and H. Kehrer-Sawatzki, vol. 2, 1063–1067. Indianapolis, IN: John Wiley & Sons Ltd, 2008.

Hummel, S., D. Schmidt, B. Kremeyer, et al. "Detection of the CCR5-Delta32 HIV Resistance Gene in Bronze Age Skeletons." *Genes and Immunity* 6 (2005): 371–374.

Jablonka, E. "The Evolutionary Implications of Epigenetic Inheritance." *Interface Focus* 7 (2017): 20160135.

Karlsson, E. K., D. P. Kwiatkowski, and P. C. Sabeti. "Natural Selection and Infectious Disease in Human Populations." *Nature Review Genetics* 15 (2014): 379–393.

Klaus, H. D. "Frontiers in the Bioarchaeology of Stress and Disease: Cross-Disciplinary Perspectives from Pathophysiology, Human Biology, and Epidemiology." *American Journal of Physical Anthropology* 155 (2014): 294–308.

Krings, M., A. Stone, R. W. Schmitz, et al. "Neandertal DNA Sequences and the Origin of Modern Humans." *Cell* 90, no. 1 (1997): 19–30.

Krutzik, S. R., M. T. Ochoa, P. A. Sieling, et al. "Activation and Regulation of Toll-Like Receptors 2 and 1 in Human Leprosy." *Nature Medicine* 9 (2003): 525–532.

Lagou, V., J. E. Garcia-Perez, I. Smets, et al. "Genetic Architecture of Adaptive Immune System Identifies Key Immune Regulators." *Cell Reports* 25 (2018): 798–810.

Larsen, C. S. "The Agricultural Revolution as Environmental Catastrophe: Implications for Health and Lifestyle in the Holocene." *Quaternary International* 150 (2006): 12–20.

Larsen, C. S., and F. Crespo. "Paleosyndemics: A Bioarchaeological and Biosocial Approach to Study Infectious Diseases in the Past." *Centaurus* 64, no. 1 (2022): 181–196.

Libert, F., P. Cochaux, G. Beckman, et al. "The Delta CCR5 Mutation Conferring Protection against HIV-1 in Caucasian Populations Has a Single and Recent Origin in Northeastern Europe." *Human Molecular Genetics* 7 (1998): 399–406.

Liston, A., and A. Goris. "The Origins of Diversity in Human Immunity." *Nature Immunology* 19 (2018): 209–210.

Liu, R., W. A. Paxton, S. Choe, et al. "Homozygous Defect in HIV-1 Coreceptor Accounts for Resistance of Some Multiply-Exposed Individuals to HIV-1 Infection." *Cell* 86 (1996): 367–377.

Lorenzo, J., Y. Choi, M. Horowitz, et al. "Overview: The Developing Field of Osteoimmunology." In *Osteoimmunology*. Edited by J. Lorenzo, Y. Choi, M. Horowitz, and H. Takayanagi, 1–5. Cambridge, MA: Elsevier–Academic Press, 2011.

Lucotte, G. "Frequencies of 32 Base Pair Deletion of the (Delta 32) Allele of the CCR5 HIV-1 Co-receptor Gene in Caucasians: A Comparative Analysis." *Infections Genetics Evolution* 1 (2002): 201–205.

Madrigal, L., and J. Willoughby. Ongoing Evolution in Humans. In *A Companion to Biological Anthropology*. Edited by C. S. Larsen, 207–221. Hoboken, NJ: Blackwell Publishing, 2010.

McDade, T. W. "Life History Theory and the Immune System: Steps Toward a Human Ecological Immunology." *American Journal of Physical Anthropology Supplement* 37 (2003): 100–125.

McDade, T. W. "Life History, Maintenance, and the Early Origins of Immune Function." *American Journal of Human Biology* 17 (2005a): 81–94.

McDade, T. W. "The Ecologies of the Human Immune Function." *Annual Review of Anthropology* 34 (2005b): 495–521.

McDade, T. W., J. Rutherford, L. Adair, et al. "Early Origins of Inflammation: Microbial Exposures in Infancy Predict Lower Levels of C-Reactive Arotein in Adulthood." *Proceedings of Biological Sciences* 277 (2010): 1129–1137.

McDade, T. W., C. Ryan, M. J. Jones, et al. "Social and Physical Environments Early in Development Predict DNA Methylation of Inflammatory Genes in Young Adulthood." *Proceedings of the National Academy of Sciences USA* 114 (2017): 7611–7616.

Mecsas, J., G. Franklin, W. A. Kuziel, et al. "CCR5 Mutation and Plague Protection." *Nature* 427 (2004): 606-606.

Medzhitov, R. "Origin and Physiological Roles of Inflammation." *Nature* 454 (2008): 428–435.

Murphy, P. M. "Molecular Mimicry and the Generation of Host Defense Protein Diversity." *Cell* 72 (1993): 823–826.

Nakashima, T., and H. Takayanagi. "Osteoimmunology: Crosstalk Between the Immune and Bone Systems." *Journal of Clinical Immunology* 29 (2009): 555–567.

Nédélec, Y., J. Sanz, G. Baharian, et al. "Genetic Ancestry and Natural Selection Drive Population Differences in Immune Responses to Pathogens." *Cell* 167 (2016): 657–669.e621.

Okin, D., and R. Medzhitov. "Evolution of Inflammatory Diseases." *Current Biology* 22 (2012): R733–740.

Parham, P. "MHC Class I Molecules and KIRs in Human History, Health and Survival." *Nature Review Immunology* 5 (2005): 201–214.

Patin, E., M. Hasan, and The Milieu Interieur Consortium. "Natural Variation in the Parameters of Innate Immune Cells Is Preferentially Driven by Genetic Factors." *Nature Immunology* 19 (2018): 302–314.

Quach, H., M. Rotival, J. Pothlichet, et al. "Genetic Adaptation and Neandertal Admixture Shaped the Immune System of Human Populations." *Cell* 167 (2016): 643–656.e617.

Rumyantsev, S. "Selection for Hereditary Immunity to Infections During the Evolution of Humankind." *Webmed Central Human Biology* 2, no. 12 (2011): WMC001026.

Sabeti, P. C., E. Walsh, S. F. Schaffner, et al. "The Case for Selection at CCR5-Δ32." *PLoS Biology* 3 (2005): e378.

Sankararaman, S., S. Mallick, M. Dannemann, et al. "The Genomic Landscape of Neanderthal Ancestry in Present-Day Humans." *Nature* 507 (2014): 354–357.

Schuenemann, V. J., P. Singh, T. A. Mendum, et al. "Genome-Wide Comparison of Medieval and Modern Mycobacterium Leprae." *Science* 341 (2013): 179–183.

Ségurel, L., and L. Quintana-Murci. "Preserving Immune Diversity Through Ancient Inheritance and Admixture." *Current Opinion in Immunology* 30 (2014): 79–84.

Singer, M., N. Bulled, B. Ostrach, et al. "Syndemics and the Biosocial Conception of Health." *The Lancet* 389 (2017): 941–950.

Singer, M., N. Bulled, B. Ostrach, et al. "Syndemics: A Cross-Disciplinary Approach to Complex Epidemic Events like COVID-19." *Annual Review of Anthropology* 50 (2021): 41–58.

Smale, S. T., and G. Natoli. "Transcriptional Control of Inflammatory Responses." *Cold Spring Harbor Perspectives in Biology* 6 (2014): 10.1101/cshperspect.a016261.

Smoljanović, M., S. Ristić, and C. Hayward. "Historic Exposure to Plague and Present-Day Frequency of CCR5del32 in Two Isolated Island Communities of Dalmatia, Croatia." *Croatian Medical Journal* 47 (2006): 579–584.

Stephens, J. C., D. E. Reich, D. B. Goldstein, et al. "Dating the Origin of the CCR5-Delta32 AIDS-Resistance Allele by the Coalescence of Haplotypes." *American Journal of Human Genetics* 62 (1998): 1507–1515.

Straub, R. H. "Concepts of Evolutionary Medicine and Energy Regulation Contribute to the Etiology of Systemic Chronic Inflammatory Diseases." *Brain Behavior Immunity* 25 (2011): 1–5.

Straub, R. H. "Evolutionary Medicine and Chronic Inflammatory State – Known and New Concepts in Pathophysiology." *Journal of Molecular Medicine* 90 (2012): 523–534.

Straub, R. H., and C. Schradin. "Chronic Inflammatory Systemic Diseases: An Evolutionary Trade-Off Between Acutely Beneficial but Chronically Harmful Programs." *Evolution Medicine and Public Health* 2016 (2016): 37–51.

Tollenaere, C., L. Rahalison, M. Ranjalahy, et al. "CCR5 Polymorphism and Plague Resistance in Natural Populations of the Black Rat in Madagascar." *Infection Genetics and Evolution* 8 (2008): 891–897.

Wong, S. H., S. Gochhait, D. Malhotra, et al. "Leprosy and the Adaptation of Human Toll-Like Receptor 1." *PLoS Pathogens* 6 (2010): e1000979.

Xue, Y., A. Daly, B. Yngvadottir, et al. "Spread of an Inactive Form of Caspase-12 in Humans Is Due to Recent Positive Selection." *American Journal of Human Genetics* 78 (2006): 659–670.

Zawicki, P., and H. W. Witas. "HIV-1 Protecting CCR5-Delta32 Allele in Medieval Poland." *Infection Genetics and Evolution* 8 (2008): 146–151.

Zeberg, H., and S. Pääbo. "The Major Genetic Risk Factor for Severe COVID-19 Is Inherited from Neanderthals." *Nature* 587 (2020): 610–612.

Zeberg, H., and S. Pääbo. "A Genomic Region Associated with Protection Against Severe COVID-19 Is Inherited from Neandertals." *Proceedings of the National Academy of Sciences* 118 (2021): e2026309118.

CHAPTER 17 Primates Defined

W. Scott McGraw

Unguiculate, claviculate placental mammals, with orbits encircled by bone; three kinds of teeth, at least one time of life; brain always with a posterior lobe and calcarine fissure; the innermost digit of at least one pair of extremities opposable; hallux with a flat nail or none; a well-developed caecum; penis pendulous; testes scrotal; always two pectoral mammae

(Mivart 1873)

Although probably more intensely studied than any other mammalian order, the classification and nomenclature of the Primate has been, and to some extent still is, a matter for adverse comment, for strong differences of opinion, and in some respects even for despair

(Hill 1953: 20)

In fact, it is not easy to give a clear-cut definition of the order as a whole ... and there is no single distinguishing feature which characterizes them all .... While many other mammalian order can be defined by conspicuous specializations of a positive kind which readily mark them off from one another, the Primates ... are to be mainly distinguished from other orders by a negative feature – their lack of specialization

(Le Gros Clark 1959: 42)

... the order Primates must be defined, not by the shared inheritance of any particular anatomical features, but by an inborn tendency to evolve in a monkey-like direction

(Cartmill 2018: 3)

DEFINING ISSUES

Groups of organisms are typically classified by a single or set of uniquely shared traits. Primates are among the most well-known animals; however, compiling a list of their distinctive characters is challenging. The main obstacle is the fact that lemurs, lorises, tarsiers, monkeys, and apes possess a modest number of specialized features and those they do have

A Companion to Biological Anthropology, Second Edition. Edited by Clark Spencer Larsen.
© 2023 John Wiley & Sons Ltd. Published 2023 by John Wiley & Sons Ltd.

are often shared with other mammals. Most mammal groups have acquired enough unique modifications to make distinguishing one group from another relatively straightforward. This is not the case with primates; viewed from a comparative mammalian perspective, humans and their relatives display a modest number of uniquely defining traits. Nevertheless, while individual diagnostic traits are relatively few, specialized *combinations* of features readily distinguish primates from other mammals. Among the most important *feature complexes* are those pertaining to the visual/neural system, the appendicular skeleton, and life history, and it is the interaction of features within these complexes that sets primates apart from other mammalian groups (Ross and Martin 2007). In addition, primates display several dramatic trends in anatomy, physiology and behavior that are less pronounced or absent in other mammalian groups. Understanding the direction, magnitude, and significance of these trends is central to defining primates. This chapter reviews the most important characters, character complexes and trends that characterize members of the primate order.

Modern and Archaic Primates

Class Mammalia contains about 6,400 living species arranged into approximately 26 orders (Wilson and Reeder 2005). Linnaeus was the initial architect of this ordering and the first order he created – the Primates (meaning "of the first rank") – began with four genera: *Homo* (humans, plus a form known as troglodytes), *Simia* (monkeys and tarsiers), *Lemur* (lemurs and lorises), and *Vespertilio* (bats).[1] Bats have since been relegated to their own order (Chiroptera); however, the basic gradistic scheme recognized by Linnaeus – lemur–monkey–ape – remains today. Linnaeus' original criteria for defining primates consisted of two characters: *Dentes primores superiors iv paralleli; mamammae pectorals ii*, i.e., (1) upper front teeth four in number, parallel and (2) two pectoral mammary glands. The suite of features used to distinguish primates from other mammals has grown in the last 250 years; however, the group bracketed by Linnaeus' definition has remained relatively stable during that time (Gregory 1910; Hill 1953).

The fossil record of primate evolution extends at least 65 million years BP. Many authorities contend the best candidate for the ancestor of modern primates lies within or near a group of early mammals known as plesiadapiformes (Bloch and Boyer 2002; Chester et al. 2015; Gingerich 1976; Silcox et al. 2015, 2017; Szalay 1968). The plesiadapiformes were a diverse and successful radiation that flourished throughout the 10 million years of Paleocene and into the first few million years of the Eocene epochs. They are suitable candidates for ancestral primates because their tooth cusp morphology was more similar to modern primates than the dentition of other Paleocene mammals. Although their dental anatomy makes them good potential ancestors, plesiadapiformes lack many features found in subsequent "true primates." For this reason, most authorities do not place plesiadapiformes within the order Primates, but instead refer to them as *Archaic* primates in recognition of their role as precursors of true primates. Mammals meeting the minimum requirements for primate status are called *Euprimates*, or "primates of modern aspect" to emphasize their possession of all features found in modern primates (Simons 1972). Several spectacular finds have fueled debate about the relationship between Archaic primates and Euprimates and exactly which taxa constitute the first members of the primate order. The stakes are significant because they bear directly on the priority given to features that bracket the Order as well as where we draw the primate–non-primate boundary. Some authorities maintain that because plesiadapiformes share derived features with modern primates, they should be included within the Order (Bloch et al. 2007; Chester et al. 2015; Silcox 2007; Silcox et al. 2007, 2015, 2017). Others contend that because these basal forms did not possess all features found in modern forms (Euprimates), they cannot be considered as true primates (Kirk et al. 2003; Soligo and Martin 2006; Tavare et al. 2002) and/or they are in fact more closely related to Dermoptera (colugos) (Beard 1990, 1993; Kay et al. 1990, 1992; Ni et al. 2013). Part of the problem is the difficulty of applying a definition of modern primates to the fossil record, a point Osman Hill made explicit nearly 60 years ago: "The level at which the distinguishing line is drawn between Primates and non-Primates depends on what definition is given to that order ... the inclusion of such a fossil family as the Plesiadapidae involves the discarding of some classic Primate diagnostic features" (Hill 1953: 5). This chapter attempts to resolve none of these issues and proceeds from the position that while the plesiadapiformes represent the most likely group from which modern primates arose, the definition of primates pertains to monophyletic Euprimates and their descendants. Readers interested in a discussion of plesiadapiformes and primate origins should consult Chapter 22 by Silcox and López-Torres.

PRIMITIVE EUTHERIAN MAMMALS: BASELINE FOR CHARACTERS, COMPLEXES, AND TRENDS

Descriptions of primates often begin with statements similar to the following: primates are generalized mammals that have retained a primitive body plan with comparatively few modifications. The statement is accurate; by and large, modern primates preserve a primitive anatomical configuration consisting of many ancestral features, and they are not as specialized as many other mammalian groups such as, for example, whales and porpoises (Cetaceans), seals and walruses (Pinnipeds), bats (Chiropterans), pangolins (Pholidontans), or aardvarks (Tubulidentans). How do we know this? The answer comes from appreciating the anatomical diversity of living (extant) mammals and comparing this diversity to that found in the extinct animals from which modern forms evolved. The fossil record provides the referential baseline for highlighting which descendants have become most specialized and which are anatomically more conservative.

Mammals with placentas are known as Eutherian mammals. Eutherian mammals comprise the great majority of Class Mammalia and are distinct from two other major mammalian groups: those that lay eggs, the monotremes (Prototheria), and those with pouches, the marsupials (Metatheria). Excavations from Upper Jurassic and Lower Cretaceous-aged deposits in China have yielded exquisitely preserved fossils that provide critical information about the structure of early mammals, including the oldest and most primitive eutherians (Hu et al. 2009; Ji et al. 2002; Luo et al. 2011). These discoveries reveal that early eutherians were tiny, quadrupedal, agile, scansorial animals whose diets consisted largely of insects. These shrew-sized animals had long tails, long, pointed snouts, small brains, five digits on their hands and feet, and claws on the tips of their digits. Studies of their limb structure suggest that these precursors of modern mammals were well adapted to climbing and could move with ease amid small branches in arboreal habitats.

Many descendants of this or some similarly configured early mammal became specialized to move in environments other than trees. Primates did not. Primates are, and always have been, an arboreal radiation and many features that distinguish them from other mammalian groups are adaptations for life in the canopy. Making a living in the trees is difficult and dangerous, so selection should favor traits that decrease the risk of falling and increase the chances of finding food while avoiding predators. Although primates have solved the problems of moving in arboreal habitats in a number of ways, a core of generalized features related to limb mobility and overall agility – inherited from the primitive ancestor – is found in all primates and accounts for some of their most striking differences from other mammals. It should be emphasized that while these limb adaptations facilitate an arboreal existence, adoption of an arboreal lifestyle does not require them. There are highly successful arboreal mammals such as squirrels, sloths, pangolins, and possums that lack many of these features and are, obviously, not primates. Thus, while arboreality alone cannot explain the evolution of primate features, it is almost certainly the case that many characteristics of primates are associated in some fashion with the adaptive landscape of trees (Cartmill 1972; Jones 1916; Kay 2018; Le Gros Clark 1959; Sussman 1991).

The Primate Bauplan

Postcranial Features

Hands and Feet   Primitive eutherian mammals had five digits on their hands and feet and primates retain five digits on their cheiridia.[2] Although pendactyly is an ancient mammalian feature retained in a number of extant mammal groups, primate hands and feet are distinguished by a major difference: an enhanced ability to grasp. This grasping or prehensile ability is brought about by a combination of features. First, the fingers and toes (or rays) of primates are characterized by increased mobility and the ability to act independently of one another. Second, primate rays tend to be longer relative to the rest of the hand and foot (respectively) and this increased length, combined with an enhanced ability to flex or bend the fingers, promotes effective grasping. Third, the digits of most mammals with five digits tend to be oriented in a single plane. In primates, however, the first digits on the hand and feet are not in the same plane with the other toes and fingers. Instead, the fleshy surfaces at the tips of the hallux (big toe) and pollex (thumb) lie, to varying degrees, at angles to the remaining digits. Because the hallux and pollex are divergent and lie in different planes from the other digits, they can be more easily brought into contact with, or be opposed to, the rest of the foot or hand. Because primates use their hands for so many activities, an opposable thumb combined with comparatively long and independently moving fingers is one of the most important primate characteristics. For example, unlike most mammals that bring their mouth to their food, primates tend to use their hands to bring their food to their mouth (Napier 1993). Grasping feet with opposable big toes are useful for moving through the trees and are found in all primates except one: humans.[3] "Acquirement of prehensility of the hands and feet and of 'opposability' of the thumb and big toe are among the most striking and important evolutionary trends of the primates (Napier and Napier 1967: 10)."

Nails Instead of Claws   The tips (apices) of the fingers and toes in primates differ in several important ways from those of other living mammals and from those of the eutherian ancestors. Early mammals had claws on their digits, but primates have replaced claws with flattened nails.[4] Also, the apices of primate fingers and toes are characterized by soft-tissue expansions containing enriched nerve endings and capillary beds resulting in a widening of the cheiridial tip. These expanded, apical tufts, in combination with the replacement of claws with nails, provide primates with an enhanced sense of touch and the ability to grasp branches using a friction grip rather than one involving clawed contact/penetration. The appearance of nails in the fossil record is central to identifying the first primates of modern aspect, but the adaptive significance of claw loss continues to be debated (Soligo and Muller 1999). A growing consensus is that claws enable their possessor to grasp and ascend/descend relatively large vertical supports, an important arboreal challenge for small-bodied quadrupeds.

Forearm Mobility   The forearm is that portion of the upper limb between the elbow and the wrist. In primitive Eutherians, the two bones of the forearm – the radius and ulna – were unfused. These bones have become fused or greatly reduced, with the ulna becoming a splint attached to the radius and the latter becoming the principal weight-bearing member in a number of mammalian groups, but in primates they remain large and unfused. Radio-ulnar fusion significantly limits the range of motion below the elbow and, therefore, by retaining unfused forelimb bones, primates can more easily rotate their forearms and hands about their long axis so as to contact the ground substrate (a process known as pronation) or to position the palm face up (referred to as supination) than most other mammals. The capacity for flexible, rotatory movement of the hands is important for grasping branches, for collecting, inspecting and opening different foods, and for grooming conspecifics. In addition, the two bones of the leg (the portion of the lower limb between the knee and ankle) known as the tibia and fibula remain unfused in all living primates except tarsiers. In other mammals, these bones are frequently fused or the fibula is reduced.

Clavicle   The clavicle or collar bone is an S-shaped bone that runs between the manubrium (top of the breast bone) and scapula (shoulder blade) and to which attach several muscles that move the arm. The clavicle acts as a strut that helps stabilize the shoulder area while providing for a great range of motion. A clavicle was present in the primitive mammalian ancestor but this bone has been lost in many descendent groups. Primates have retained a clavicle and, in doing so, are afforded great mobility at the shoulder and, more generally, of the entire upper limb. A high degree of forelimb flexibility is important for animals that move in environments with discontinuous supports (trees) and that require enhanced manipulative abilities for obtaining food. The significance of clavicles (and claws) was so profound as to prompt Mivart (1873) to begin his famous definition of primates with these features (see the introductory quote).

Quadrupedal Idiosyncrasies   Many mammals move on the ground or in the trees by placing weight on their four limbs in a locomotor mode known as quadrupedalism. Most primates also move quadrupedally; however, the quadrupedal locomotion of primates is different from that of virtually all other mammalian quadrupeds in at least three ways (Larson 2017). First, primates practice an uncommon kind of gait (the order or sequence in which the limbs contact the substrate). During walking, most primates employ a diagonal sequence gait (i.e., a foot touches the ground followed by the opposite hand, followed by the other foot) whereas most non-primates use a lateral-sequence gait (i.e., a foot touches the ground, followed by the hand on the same side, followed by the other foot). Second, compared to other mammals, primates tend to protract their arms, reaching them further forward, when the forelimbs contact the substrate. This feature, in combination with an increased limb length, may have evolved as a means of increasing speed without increasing stride frequency. Finally, primates experience lower substrate reaction forces in the forelimbs than the hindlimbs when they land, a characteristic likely to be related to the greater manipulative role of primate forelimbs. This combination of quadrupedal peculiarities is likely to be the product of successful invasion of the small branch niche and was probably a key innovation in the radiation of primates (Larson et al. 2000; Schmitt and Lemelin 2002).

Truncal Erectness   Primates have evolved an array of locomotor adaptations that include quadrupedalism, forelimb suspension, knuckle-walking, vertical clinging and leaping, and bipedality. Despite this diversity in locomotor strategies, primates are all characterized by a common postural element – a tendency for the trunk to be oriented more upright so that the long axis of the vertebral column is more perpendicular to the ground. In locomotor modes such as brachiation, vertical clinging and leaping, and bipedalism, the trunk is maintained in an erect or semi-erect position, but even primates that move quadrupedally usually adopt upright postures when feeding, resting, or socializing. This tendency for primates to adopt upright postures required modification of several skeletal regions, and one obvious benefit of these changes is that doing so liberated the hands from a purely supportive role to one involving more explorative and manipulative activities.

FEATURES OF THE SKULL

Decreased Reliance on Olfaction   In most mammalian groups, the sense of smell is the principal mechanism for obtaining information related to feeding, mating, predator avoidance, and communication. Primates are still "smelling animals," but, compared to other mammals, primates have decreased their reliance on olfaction in favor of increased visual acuity. Animals with a highly developed sense of smell are characterized by features including a projecting snout and enlargement of those neural regions – the olfactory bulbs – responsible for processing chemical signals. Increased facial prognathism can be achieved via forward projection of bones in the nasal region; expansion of the nasal cavity provides more surface area for nasal turbinates. Turbinates provide the platform for the tissues and neural cells (epithelium) involved in capturing chemical signals: the more surface area for turbinates, the better the ability to smell. The progressive shortening of the snout in primates, therefore, almost certainly reflects a relaxed emphasis on the sense of smell. In addition to reducing the size of structures that capture smells, primates have reduced that part of the neural circuitry that transmits chemical signals from olfactory cells in the nasal cavity to the brain. These switching stations for smell are known as olfactory bulbs and there is a strong correlation across primates between the size of the olfactory bulbs and reliance on olfactory communication (Nero and Heymann 2015). Prosimians, particularly nocturnal forms that communicate with various scent glands, have relatively large olfactory bulbs while monkeys, apes, and humans have more diminutive bulbs.

Orbital Frontation and Convergence   The eyeballs sit within bony structures known as orbits. The orbits of primitive mammals, and those of many non-primate mammals today, are positioned on the sides of the skull, which results in expansive, lateral visual fields, or enhanced peripheral vision. In primates, the orbits and their contents have undergone two significant changes: they have migrated toward the front of the skull, a process known as orbital convergence, and the orbital apertures have become more vertically oriented (i.e., have tilted to align with the long axis of the cranium), a process known as orbital frontation (Noble et al. 2000). The forward and vertical shifts in eye socket orientation bring the visual fields from the sides of the skull forward so that the fields overlap. In so doing, both eyes are able to focus on the same object or area, a feature known as binocular vision. This results in stereopsis or the ability to see in three dimensions. Primates have the greatest orbital convergence and largest binocular visual fields of all mammals (Heesy 2004, 2005). The ability to see in three dimensions and judge distances is particularly important for animals that make their living within the structurally discontinuous environments of trees.

Other mammals such as carnivores and bats also have highly convergent orbits, but the particular combination of high orbital convergence, greatly enlarged brains, and a modified visual system is seen only in primates (Ross and Martin 2007).

Post-orbital Bars   In many mammals, the bony socket housing the eyeball does not form a complete ring, i.e., the lateral aspect of the orbital margin remains open. A number of mammalian groups – including primates – have evolved a bar of bone on the orbit's lateral aspect so that the eyeball is surrounded by a complete ring. What purpose does this additional bar serve? The reorientation (frontation and convergence) of the orbits facilitates binocular vision, a trait that should have adaptive value for animals living in trees and requiring acute depth perception. A progressive shifting of the orbits from the sides to the front of the skull changes how chewing muscles act on the orbits when they are being used. Recent comparative analyses suggest that the forward migration of the orbits makes them susceptible to deformation by a powerful masticatory muscle known as the temporalis. These studies suggest that the post-orbital bar functions as a strut to reinforce or stiffen the orbital cavity, preventing the orbital margin from being deformed by the chewing musculature. In other words, the post-orbital bar may prevent disruption of normal visual functions in mammals with highly convergent orbits. Post-orbital bars are found in a number of mammalian groups; however, because this is a derived feature of Euprimates (relative to Archaic primates), an animal cannot be considered a primate if it lacks a post-orbital bar.

Petrosal Bulla   The middle ear of mammals contains three bones: the incus, malleus, and stapes. These bones are housed in a bubble-like outgrowth of bone known as an auditory bulla, which protects the base of the inner and middle ear. In most mammals, the auditory bulla is formed from the tympanic bone or it is not encased by bone at all; in primates, however, the auditory bulla is derived from the petrous (petrosal) part of the temporal bone. A petrosal bulla is considered the only feature of the basicranium unique to primates (Rasmussen 2002) and its recognition in the fossil record has figured prominently in the classification of Euprimates (Cartmill 2018; Silcox et al. 2017).

Dentition   Primate teeth are characterized by a combination of trends generally not found in other mammals. Primate teeth are functionally differentiated into four types, known as incisors, canines, premolars, and molars. While most primates have at least one of each tooth *type*, primates have reduced the total *number* of teeth in their mouth, a process known as dental reduction. The primitive Eutherian (placental mammal) dental formula is 3–1–4–3, meaning that each quadrant of the mouth contained three incisors, one canine, four premolars and three molars. Living primates have lost at least one incisor and at least one premolar in each of the four mouth quadrants. While there is a diversity of dental formulae within the primate Order, all primates have fewer teeth than their mammalian ancestors and fewer teeth generally than most non-primate mammals. Primate teeth also tend to be less specialized than those of other mammals. Primates are best described as omnivores, capable of eating a variety of food items including fruit pulp, leaves, seeds, nuts, meat, insects, bark, and tree exudate. Primates have evolved adaptations to help facilitate the processing of specific food types; no primate, however, has evolved teeth so specialized that they are capable of processing only a single food type. On the contrary: primate teeth are comparatively generalized and designed for processing foods across a range of sizes, shapes, and mechanical properties.

Brain Expansion   One of the most significant features distinguishing primates from other mammals is brain size: primates have very large brains for their body size. The average primate brain is approximately 2.3 times larger than that of non-primate mammals of similar body size. That portion of the brain that has expanded the most is the outermost layer, known as the neocortex (Latin for "new bark"), and it is this region that is responsible for higher cognitive functions, including the coordination of sensory perception with motor commands and spatial reasoning. All mammals possess a neocortex, but that of primates is both enlarged and characterized by many convolutions, wrinkles, and fissures, all of which provide additional surface areas. The neocortex of humans, for example, comprises nearly 80 percent of total brain volume. Because the development and maintenance of brain tissue is metabolically costly (the brains of nonhuman primates consume approximately 8–9 percent of the total energy budget while the human brain, even at rest, consumes 20–25 percent of the energy budget), the tremendous expansion in brain (neocortex) size must have provided a significant adaptive advantage for primates.

The primate brain is characterized by additional changes, beyond great neocortical expansion. Compared to other mammals, primates have decreased their reliance on smell and reduced the size of those neural regions that process olfactory signals. As primates became more reliant on vision, those regions of the brain responsible for transmitting and interpreting visual signals and integrating them with motor commands expanded and became more sophisticated. These regions are known as the primary visual cortex and lateral geniculate nucleus. Recent comparative analyses have demonstrated a strong association between the size of these brain structures and the degree of binocularity or stereopsis across primates. This evidence suggests that the increase in brain size among primates is strongly associated with enhanced visual specialization (Barton 2004; Ross and Martin 2007). In addition, primates are the only eutherian mammals capable of trichromatic color vision (Bowmaker 1998; Leonhardt et al. 2008). The selective pressures responsible for increased brain expansion continue to be debated. Most authorities contend that the large brains of primates are a consequence of ecological factors, especially those related to diet (Clutton-Brock and Harvey 1980; DeCasien et al. 2017; Harvey et al. 1980; Martin 1984; Milton 1981; Powell et al. 2017) or pressures associated with increased sociality (Cheney and Seyfarth 1990; Dunbar 1992; Dunbar and Schultz 2007; Jolly 1966).

LIFE HISTORY AND REPRODUCTION

Prolongation of Prenatal and Postnatal Life   Primates are distinguished from other mammals by a combination of trends related to reproduction and life history. First, the gestation period of primates tends to be longer than those in other mammals of equivalent body size and fetal nourishment is more efficient. Many mammals give birth to multiple offspring, a practice not found in the majority of primates. Primates have reduced the number of offspring they produce while increasing the amount of care given to individuals. This results in decreased levels of infant mortality among primates. Compared to most mammals, primates are born developmentally advanced, or precocial. Nevertheless, they are completely dependent on parental (usually maternal) care for long periods of time. The extended period of infant dependency helps establish strong bonds between mother and infant and it is during this period that young primates acquire much of the knowledge they need to survive. After infancy, primates typically are characterized by long periods of growth during the juvenile period. The length of this period is strongly associated with species longevity: those primates that live longer take longer to reach adulthood. The length of the adult period is also comparatively long in primates. This combination of extended infant, juvenile, and adult periods means that primates tend to live longer lives than other mammals of equivalent body size. For example, the average lifespan for a five kg dog is 12 years while that of a similarly sized primate is upwards of 25 years. Primates with comparatively short life spans tend to reach adulthood sooner. Large primates tend to reach maturity later and live longer than smaller primates. Comparative analyses have also revealed associations between the lengths of the prenatal and postnatal periods and patterns of brain growth (Leigh 2004).

Development of Complex Social Systems   Like many other organisms, primates live in groups. What distinguishes the group-living of primates is the tendency for individuals within groups to form differentiated social relationships. A large percentage of the daily, monthly and lifetime activity budget of most primates is devoted to learning and cultivating relationships with other group members. One of the most fascinating aspects of primate sociality is the diversity of ways individuals are arranged within social systems and the selective pressures responsible for this diversity (Kappeler and van Schaik 2002). Primates can be found living in (1) single-male/multi-female groups, (2) single-female/multi-male groups, (3) multi-male/multi-female groups, (4) male–female pairs, (5) fission–fusion communities, and (6) multi-level societies containing one-male units within multi-male/multi-female groups. Importantly, a species' social system does not necessarily correspond to its mating system (Henzi 1988). For example, throughout most of the year, Blue monkeys (*Cercopithecus mitis*) live in single-male, multi-female groups; during the breeding system, however, these polygynous groups may be invaded by extra-group males, resulting in a polygynandrous mating system in which members of both sexes mate with multiple individuals of the opposite sex (Cords 2002).

Behavioral Flexibility   Primates are characterized by big brains and high levels of intelligence. The high intelligence of primates is manifest in many ways across the order: primates solve complex ecological problems, they readily distinguish relatives from non-relatives, they devise mechanisms for deception, they show capacities for symbolic thought (a prerequisite for language), they have a concept of self, they develop friendships, and they make and use tools in innumerable ways. Like other mammals, much of a primate's knowledge base is hard wired or inherited genetically. What distinguishes primates from many other mammals, however, is the quantity of information that is obtained through learning: many basic survival skills are acquired via observation of and learning from other group members. The fact that so much critical information is *not* innate underscores the importance of the mother–infant bond for transmitting important social and ecological skills. One of the most intriguing developments in this arena concerns the extent to which socially transmitted behaviors vary in space and time. Several decades of research indicate that some behavioral variation between primate groups cannot be accounted for genetically or as responses to local ecological conditions, but rather is due to differences in learned behavior (e.g., Watson et al. 2018; Whiten and de Waal 2018). Comparative studies of chimpanzees, orangutans, gorillas, and several monkey species have highlighted group differences in tool use and other cultural traditions rooted in social learning (Krutzen et al. 2011; Luncz et al. 2012). Recognition of this has forced anthropologists to rethink what features are uniquely human.

CLASSIFICATION: GRADES VS. CLADES

Modern taxonomy strives to have classifications that reflect patterns of ancestry and descent, grouping animals strictly on the basis only of shared derived traits. This approach is known as cladistic classification, with resultant groups called clades. Older classification schemes grouped animals on the basis of similarity, with groups known as grades. For example, in the old scheme, humans would be classified as one group and great apes as another based on overall similarity (i.e., an ape grade and a human grade). The modern, gradistic classification scheme recognizes that chimpanzees and humans share a common ancestor (e.g., comprising the Hominini clade), and therefore does not recognize a great ape group, exclusive of humans, in its classification. Understanding the distinction between gradistic (classifying based on similarity, or level of complexity) and cladistic (classifying based on shared derived features) classifications will become apparent shortly.

The basic features presented in the preceding sections are characteristics that distinguish primates from non-primate mammals. Within the Order, members can be grouped according to overall levels of complexity, shared features, and biogeography. In the older classification based on overall similarity, the Order Primates is divided into two suborders, called Prosimii and Anthropoidea. The prosimian–anthropoid division is a *gradistic* one that separates lower primates from higher primates based on levels or grades of morphological complexity (similarity). The prosimian grade contains lemurs, lorises, galagos, and tarsiers. Because these primates lack many of the derived features found in monkeys and apes, they are said to occupy a level of specialization most similar to the earliest true primates (Euprimates) found in the fossil record. Living prosimians, or lower primates, are recognized by their retention of ancestral features combined with the *absence* of more specialized features found in higher primates. Prosimians are evolutionarily successful mammals characterized by a stage of morphological complexity similar to that seen in the first true primates approximately 50 million years ago. The other primate grade – Anthropoidea – contains monkeys, apes, and humans. These primates, like prosimians, also possess the minimum requirements for admission to the primate Order; however, they have evolved additional features resulting in greater divergence from the first Euprimates. Their suite of derived features not only unites anthropoids, but also results in a more advanced level of complexity. For this reason, anthropoids are said to have achieved a stage of evolutionary development beyond the prosimian grade.

The prosimian–anthropoid classification makes no attempt to establish ancestor-descendant relationships; it is a means of dividing primates based on overall morphological similarity (Fleagle 2013). An alternative scheme is to sort primates according to lines of descent. Descendants of a single common ancestor are said to comprise a monophyletic group. If primate classification were neat and tidy, members of Anthropoidea and Prosimii would each be descended from a common ancestor (i.e., each would be monophyletic). This may be the case for anthropoids, and a growing body of fossil evidence suggests that the ancestor shared by all monkeys and apes emerged in India or North Africa approximately 45–50 million years ago (Beard 2016; Seiffert 2012; Williams et al. 2010). The members within Prosimii, in contrast, are believed to have been descended from two ancestors. That is, Prosimii is paraphyletic. The primates preventing prosimian monophyly are tarsiers. Tarsiers (the genera *Tarsius*, *Carlito*, and *Cephalopachus*) are small, nocturnal primates found in the forests of southeast Asia (Wright et al. 2003). These enigmatic primates possess a number of features that ally them with prosimians but are absent in anthropoids. Such features are primitive (ancestral) for primates and include an unfused mandibular symphysis, grooming claw on the second digit of the foot, multiple nipples, and a bicornuate uterus. A newly discovered feature concerns the pathway of a nerve known as the chorda tympani involved in the sense of taste. In prosimians, this nerve passes over a muscle – the tensor tympani – that tightens the eardrum (tympanic membrane), while in anthropoids, the nerve passes below the muscle (Maier 2008).

In addition to sharing primitive features with other prosimians, tarsiers share several derived features with anthropoids, suggesting phyletic affinities between them. Features shared by tarsiers and anthropoids – and to the exclusion of other non-tarsier

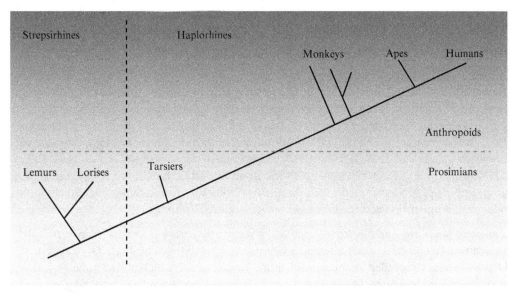

Figure 17.1 Alternative schemes for dividing the primate order. The prosimian/anthropoid division emphasizes general stages – or grades – of evolution. The alternative classification emphasizes descent from common ancestors and divides primates into two monophyletic groups: Strepsirhines and Haplorhines.

prosimians – include a mobile upper lip, lack of a tapetum lucidum (reflective layer of retinal cells facilitating night vision), a hemochorial placenta, nose covered by skin (vs. naked, wet rhinarium), reduced nasal turbinates, a reduced sphenoethmoid (or olfactory) recess, novel features of the auditory bulla including the presence of an accessory middle ear chamber, partial closing off by bone of the connection between the orbit and the chewing muscles (i.e., partial post-orbital closure), blood supply to the brain via the promontory branch of the internal carotid artery, and similar dental proportions.[5]

The fact that tarsiers possess shared derived features with anthropoids (while all other prosimians do not) implies that tarsiers are descended from a different ancestor than that which gave rise to lemurs, lorises, and galagos. All current genetic data support a Tarsier–Anthropoid clade (Perelman et al., 2011; Springer et al. 2012). Thus, despite shared organizational (gradistic) similarities, prosimians cannot be a monophyletic group because one group, the tarsier, has a different ancestor. In the alternative classificatory scheme that emphasizes shared descent from a common ancestor, the non-tarsier prosimians (lemurs, lorises, and galagos) are placed in a clade known as Strepsirrhini, while tarsiers are grouped with anthropoids in a clade known as Haplorhini. The pivotal primates in the higher-order division of the Order are the tarsiers and their evolutionary position continues to be a source of exploration and debate (Kawashima et al. 2013; Smith et al. 2013). The key features associated with the Strepsirrhine and Haplorhine clades are reviewed below (Figure 17.1).

STREPSIRRHINE FEATURES AND DISTRIBUTION

Strepsirrhines possess the primitive primate features such as a simple post-orbital bar, two mobile bones in the forearm, and five digits. They also retain a number of primitive mammalian features that have been lost in anthropoids. These include:

Prognathic Face and Reliance on Olfaction   The sense of smell is still well-developed in strepsirrhines. Most stepsirrhines have projecting nasal bones that provide more surface area for the nasal turbinates and specialized neural cells that detect olfactory signals in the environment.

Rhinarium   The skin on the end of the nose of most mammals differs from normal skin by being wet, hairless, and containing specialized glands for receiving chemical signals. This wet, naked region is called a rhinarium and is involved in the collection of olfactory cues from the environment. The rhinarium communicates with the brain via an intimate connection with the vomeronasal (Jacobson's) organ housed in the roof of the mouth (Hill 1972). This communication is facilitated by a cleft in an immobile (anchored to the underlying gum) upper lip. Most mammals, including strepsirrhines, possess a rhinarium and an immobile, clefted upper lip, features that have been lost in haplorhines.

Tapetum Lucidum and Nocturnality   Most strepsirrhines are nocturnal (active at night). In addition to enlarged orbits, the night vision in strepsirrhines is facilitated by a specialized layer of retinal cells called a tapetum lucidum ("eye-shine"), which allows enhanced vision even when light levels are quite low. A tapetum is found in many living mammal groups and is likely to be a primitive mammalian character.

In addition to these primitive traits, the strepsirrhine clade is defined by several derived characteristics including:

Toothcomb   In strepsirrhines, the incisors and canines of the mandible (lower jaw) are elongated, parallel, and project forward much like the tines on a fork or a comb. This structure, called a toothcomb, is used for grooming and feeding in several strepsirrhine species.

Maxillary Incisors   The front teeth (incisors) in the upper jaw (maxilla) of strepsirrhines are distinctive in that they are small, vertically oriented, and separated in the midline (median) by a gap.

Toilet Claw   Strepsirhines possess a claw on the second digit of their feet that is used for grooming purposes.

The members of the strepsirrhine clade are the lemurs, lorises, and galagos (Table 17.1). Ancestors of living stepsirrhines ranged widely throughout the Old and New Worlds; today, however, they are restricted to Asia, Africa, and Madagascar. There are seven families of living stepsirrhines. The five families of lemurs are found only on the island of Madagascar and include some of the world's rarest and most endangered primates (Mittermeier et al. 2008). Each lemur family is characterized by a number of anatomical and behavioral idiosyncrasies (Mittermeier et al. 1994; Tattersall 1982). The galagids, or bush babies, are confined to Africa while members of the lorisids are found in both Africa (potto, angwantibo) and Asia (slender loris, slow loris).

HAPLORHINE FEATURES AND DISTRIBUTION

Haplorhines also possess the minimum primate characteristics described above, but have lost several primitive mammalian features retained by Strepsirrhines, many of which are associated with a decreased reliance on smell and increased reliance on vision. Neither a nasal rhinarium nor a tapetum lucidum is present in haplorhines, which also show reduced facial prognathism, have smaller olfactory bulbs, and possess fewer turbinates in their nasal cavity. An increased reliance on vision is reflected in more frontated and convergent orbits.

Table 17.1   The diversity of living primates

Order Primates			

Suborder Strepsirhini			

Family Cheirogalidae			
	Microcebus	mouse lemur	Madagascar
	Allocebus	hairy-eared dwarf lemur	Madagascar
	Mirza	giant mouse lemur	Madagascar
	Cheriogaleus	greater dwarf lemur	Madagascar
	Phaner	fork-marked lemur	Madagascar
Family Lepilemuridae			
	Lepilemur	sportive lemurs	Madagascar
Family Lemuridae			
	Hapalemur	bamboo lemur	Madagascar
	Prolemur	greater bamboo lemur	Madagascar
	Lemur	ring-tailed lemur	Madagascar
	Eulemur	brown lemur	Madagascar
	Varecia	ruffed lemur	Madagascar
Family Indriidae			
	Avahi	avahi	Madagascar
	Propithecus	sifaka	Madagascar
	Indri	indri	Madagascar
Family Daubentoniidae			
	Daubentonia	aye-aye	Madagascar
Family Loridae			
	Loris	slender loris	Asia
	Nycticebus	slow loris	Asia
	Arctocebus	angwantibo	Africa
	Perodicticus	potto	Africa
Family Galagidae			
	Galagoides	dwarf galago	Africa
	Galago	lesser galago/ bushbaby	Africa
	Sciurocheirus	squirrel galago	Africa
	Eoticus	needle-clawed bushbaby	Africa
	Sciurocheirus	Allen's galago	Africa
	Otolemur	greater galago	Africa

(Continued)

Table 17.1 *(Continued)*

Order Primates

Suborder Haplorhini

Infraorder Tarsiiformes
Family Tarsiidae

	Tarsius	tarsiers	Asia
	Cephalopachus	Western tarsiers	Asia
	Carlito	Philippine tarsiers	Asia

Infraorder Platyrrhini
Family Cebidae

	Cebus	gracile capuchins	Neotropics
	Sapajus	robust capuchins	Neotropics
	Saimiri	squirrel monkeys	Neotropics

Subfamily Callitrichinae

	Leontopithecus	golden lion tamarins	Neotropics
	Saguinus	tamarins	Neotropics
	Callithrix	Atlantic marmosets	Neotropics
	Mico	Amazonian marmosets	Neotropics
	Callimico	Goeldi's marmoset	Neotropics
	Cebuella	pygmy marmoset	Neotropics
	Callibella	Roosmalens' dwarf marmoset	Neotropics

Family Pitheciidae

	Pithecia	sakis	Neotropics
	Chiropotes	bearded sakis	Neotropics
	Cacajao	uakaris	Neotropics

Subfamily Aotinae

	Aotus	owl monkeys	Neotropics

Subfamily Callicebinae

	Callicebus	titi monkeys	Neotropics

Family Atelidae

	Alouatta	howler monkeys	Neotropics
	Ateles	spider monkeys	Neotropics
	Brachyteles	woolly spider monkeys	Neotropics
	Lagothrix	woolly monkeys	Neotropics
	Oreonax	yellow-tailed woolly monkey	Neotropics

(Continued)

Table 17.1 *(Continued)*

Order Primates

Suborder Haplorhini

Infraorder Catarrhini

Family Cercopithecoidea

Subfamily Cercopithecinae

Macaca	macaques	Asia (Africa)
Lophocebus	arboreal mangabeys	Africa
Cercocebus	terrestrial mangabeys	Africa
Rungwecebus	Kipunji mangabey	Africa
Mandrillus	mandrills and drills	Africa
Papio	baboons	Africa
Theropithecus	gelada	Africa
Allenopithecus	swamp monkey	Africa
Miopithecus	talapoin monkeys	Africa
Erythrocebus	patas monkeys	Africa
Cercopithecus	guenons	Africa
Allochrocebus	terrestrial guenons	Africa
Chlorocebus	vervets/green monkeys	Africa

Subfamily Colobinae

Nasalis	proboscis monkey	Asia
Presbytis	surilis	Asia
Simias	pig-tailed langurs	Asia
Pygathrix	douc langusr	Asia
Rhinopithecus	snub-nosed monkeys	Asia
Semnopithecus	Indian or gray langurs	Asia
Trachypithecus	Luntung	Asia
Procolobus	olive colobus	Africa
Piliocolobus	red colobus monkeys	Africa
Colobus	black and white colobus monkeys	Africa

Family Hylobatidae

Hoolock	hoolock gibbons	Asia
Hylobates	lar or white-handed gibbons	Asia
Nomascus	concolor or black-crested gibbons	Asia
Symphalangus	siamangs	Asia

Family Hominida

Pongo	orangutans	Asia
Pan	chimpanzee, bonobo	Africa
Gorilla	gorillas	Africa
Homo	humans	global

Source: Website of IUCN/SSC Primate Specialist Group (http://www.primate-sg.org/diversity.htm).

Compared to strepsirrhines, haplorhines are characterized by increased brain size, increased body size, and more conservative dentition, at least in lacking a tooth comb. In addition to these trends and departures from the primitive condition, haplorhines are distinguished by several derived features, as follows.

Fused Mandible   In strepsirrhines and tarsiers, the right and left halves of the mandible are connected by cartilage and remain unfused. In all haplorhines except tarsiers, the halves fuse at the midline, resulting in a rigid mandible.

Fused Frontal Bones   Among strepsirrhines and tarsiers, the right and left halves of the frontal bone are not fused and the bones usually remain unfused throughout adulthood. In all haplorhines except tarsiers, the right and left halves fuse at the midline, obliterating the metopic suture and forming a single frontal bone.

Post-orbital Closure   In addition to a post-orbital bar, haplorhines have walled off the back of the orbital cavity with contributions from the frontal, zygomatic, and sphenoid bones. This results in a condition known as post-orbital closure. Tarsiers display partial post-orbital closure.

Diurnality and Color Vision   With two exceptions (tarsiers and owl monkeys), haplorhine primates are active during daylight hours, i.e., they are diurnal. Most haplorhines have three kinds of cones that permit trichromatic color vision. Strepsirrhines, by contrast, are generally able to see only in varying shades of black and white.

Uterus   Haplorhines have a single-chambered uterus. The tarsier is exceptional in that it has a bicornate uterus like that found among strepsirrhines.

Blood to Brain   The brain is supplied by branches of the internal carotid artery (ICA). One branch of the ICA passes through the stapes (stirrup) bone in the middle ear. A stapedial branch of the ICA is a primitive feature for mammals and all strepsrrihines retain one throughout adulthood. Among haplorhines, a stapedial branch is fetally present; however, this artery becomes obliterated and lost during development. In tarsiers, monkeys, and apes, the major source of blood to the brain is via another branch of the ICA known as the promontory artery (Ankel-Simons 2000).

Living members of the Haplorhine clade consist of the Tarsioidea (with three genera of living tarsiers), Platyrrhini (New World monkeys), and Catarrhini (Old World monkeys and apes) (Table 17.1). The platyrrhine monkeys are found in the Neotropics (South and Central America) while living non-human catarrhines are found in Africa, Asia, and are marginally present in Europe. In addition to the basic biogeographic distinction, platyrrhines are distinguished from catarrhines by several features. The nostrils of New World monkeys are flat, widely spaced, and point sideways (platyrrhine means *broad nosed*). In catarrhines, the nostrils are more closely approximated and converge toward the midline. Platyrrhines have one more premolar in each oral quadrant than do catarrhines and most New World monkeys have a dental formula of 2133.[6] The bones in the temporal region of platyrrhines display a zygomatic-parietal articulation, while in catarrhines the frontal and sphenoid articulate thus precluding a zygomatic-parietal articulation. Platyrrhines do not possess the long, bony tube that exits the ear cavity in catarrhines; among platyrrhines, this feature is a simple ring. Platyrrhines range in body size from about 100 grams (pygmy marmosets) to over 11 kilograms (male Mexican black howler monkey) (Smith and Jungers 1997). All platyrrhines are predominantly arboreal and some have evolved specialized adaptations for movement in the trees, including secondarily derived claws for clinging (the callitrichids) and prehensile tails (the atelines).

The catarrhines are divided into Cercopithecoidea (Old World monkeys) and Hominoidea (apes and humans) (Table 17.1). It is not necessary to say Old World apes because apes have never existed anywhere but in the Old World. The superfamily Hominoidea is comprised of the lesser apes (gibbons and siamangs) and the great apes (chimpanzees, gorillas, orangutans, humans). All hominoids are distinguished from cercopithecoids by features including relatively larger brains, simple molars, absence of a tail, broader nose and face, and numerous postcranial adaptations for suspension and climbing, including short trunks, long forelimbs, mobile shoulder joints, and long fingers. The lesser apes are monkey-sized and their weights range between 5.5 kg (pileated gibbon) and 12 kg (siamang). Great apes are much larger and include the largest living primate, the gorilla, which can weigh upwards of 200 kg (Smith and Jungers 1997).

Members of the Family Cercopithecoidea are distinguished from apes by their possession of a tail, bilophodont molars, narrower faces, and longer trunks. The family is divided into two subfamilies: Cercopithecinae, omnivorous monkeys whose diets are usually dominated by fruit, and Colobinae, the leaf eating monkeys. Field studies have shown that the fruit-eating vs. leaf-eating designation obscures significant dietary variation within each group; however, several features that distinguish the two cercopithecoid subfamilies are functionally related to the requirements of obtaining and processing fruits versus leaves. Colobine monkeys possess complex, multichambered (ruminant) stomachs, molars with high shearing crests, narrow incisors, deep jaws, reduced (or absent) thumbs, shortened nasal bones, and greater leaping capabilities. Cercopithecine monkeys have cheek pouches, wider incisors, shallow jaws, greater pollical opposability, and limbs of more equal size (Fleagle 2013; Schultz 1969; Strasser and Delson 1987). The smallest cercopithecoids (talapoin monkeys) weigh just over 1 kg while the largest (mandrills and some baboons) weigh over 35 kg (Smith and Jungers 1997).

A NOTE ON CONSERVATION

As researchers continue to explore the features that bound the Primate order, the contents of the order expand as well. Depending on the source referenced (Wilson and Reeder 2005, IUCN, ITIS, Mittermeier et al. 2013), there are currently between 500 and 700 species of living primates and the number continues to rise: 39 lemur species have been described since 2000 (Mittermeier et al. 2008). Such increases might suggest that the planet's population of non-human primates is growing, but the reverse is very much the case. While the number of primate taxa has grown, the number of individuals occupying them is falling sharply. Expansion of the primate roster is not the result of growing populations or the discovery of new ones, but rather due to the recognition of "cryptic" diversity within existing taxa (e.g., elevating subspecies to full species). Arguments of taxonomic inflation notwithstanding (e.g., Meiri and Mace 2007; Tattersall 2007), the world's primates are disappearing because most cannot withstand the pace of human activities (Estrada et al. 2017). Two factors on the rise in tropical regions – habitat loss and hunting – are most responsible for the increasing number of taxa at risk of disappearing. Given primates' reliance on trees, the continued loss of forest as a consequence of agricultural expansion, wood harvesting, and livestock farming/ranching is a death knell for many taxa. Table 17.2 provides a summary of threatened taxa in each region; the trajectory of these data is not encouraging. Indeed, a comparison of these data with those in the 2010 version of this table (McGraw 2010) underscores how much the number of threatened taxa has increased over the last decade (Estrada et al. 2017). Seventy percent of species are in decline and 60 percent are now

Table 17.2 Summary of primate taxa threatened within each major biogeographic region

Region	Genera	Species/Subspecies	% Threatened
Africa	27	107	58.8%
Asia	20	132	72.5%
Madagascar	15	108	93.8%
Neotropics	22	176	62.8%

Source: Website of IUCN/SSC Primate Specialist Group (http://www.primate-sg.org/summary_primate_threat_status//).

threatened with extinction. Aggressive, coordinated, targeted efforts are needed to halt this trend, and to that end, various actions plans identifying specific threats and outlining detailed recommendations at priority sites have been assembled to save the most imperiled taxa (e.g., IUCN SSC Primate Specialist Group 2020; Linder et al. 2021; Schwitzer et al. 2013). As we strive to understand the world's lemurs, lorises, monkeys, and apes, let us hope that these "last-ditch" efforts will not be required to save our primate relatives in the coming years.

Summary

Living primates include forms commonly referred to as lemurs, lorises, galagos, tarsiers, monkeys, apes, and humans. Based on an understanding of the fossil record of early mammals and features found in living non-primate mammals, morphologists can identify those features that unite primates. Compared to many other mammalian groups, primates have not diverged significantly from the primitive mammalian condition and retain a generalized, unspecialized morphology. Many "specializations" of primates are present in other mammalian groups. Although the list of distinctly primate features is not extensive, the group is distinguished via unique *suites of features* combined with several important *trends* in anatomy and behavior that are less pronounced or absent in other mammalian groups. Many features are related to the demands of arboreal living and include an increased reliance on vision (vs. olfaction), enhanced brain power, and skeletal adaptations that facilitate movement through the trees.

The unique combination of primitive and derived features that are found in members of the primate Order include: decreased reliance on smell, reduced facial prognathism, reduction in the size of nasal turbinates and olfactory bulbs, increased reliance on vision, enhanced orbital frontation and orbital convergence, brain expansion (especially of the neocortex), generalized flexible limb structure, retention of a clavicle, grasping hands and feet with enhanced manipulative abilities, replacement of claws by nails, tendency for an upright posture, a prolonged gestation period, longer periods of infant dependency, extended juvenile and adult periods, development of varied and complex social organizations emphasizing individual relationships, and an increased capacity for culture and learning.

The Order Primates can be divided in several ways. A gradistic classification emphasizing an overall level of organization places lemurs, lorises, galagos, and tarsiers in the suborder Prosimii. Higher primates, or anthropoids, include monkeys, apes, and humans. These forms have become more specialized compared to the first Euprimates. Because tarsiers share several features with anthropoids, prosimians cannot be considered monophyletic given that their members are not descended from a single common ancestor. A second means of classifying primates emphasizing shared descent from a common ancestor also exists and, in this scheme, primates are divided into two monophyletic clades: the Strepsirrhini containing lemurs, lorises, and galagos and the Haplorrhini containing tarsiers, monkeys, apes, and humans. In addition to features primitive to all primates, Strepshrrhines retain other primitive mammalian features including a tapetum lucidum, rhinarium, and a greater reliance on olfaction. Derived features of strepsrrhines include a grooming claw on the second pedal digit and a tooth comb. The derived features and trends found in Haplorrhines include a fused mandible, fused frontal bones, post-orbital closure, blood supply to the brain via a promontory branch of the internal carotid artery, a single-chambered uterus, and an enlarged brain. Strepsirhines are found only in the Old World and include the lemurs of Madagascar, the galagos of Africa, and the lorises present in both Africa and Asia. Haplorrhines are found in both the New and Old World. Tarsiers are restricted to southeast Asia. Aside from humans, the only Haplorrhines in the New World are monkeys: monkeys of the New World are referred to as Platyrrhines. Old World Haplorrhines are known as Catarrhines and this group includes monkeys (Family Cercopithecoidea) and apes (Family Hominoidea).

ACKNOWLEDGMENTS

Thanks to Richard Kay, Michael Plavcan, Walter Hartwig, Pierre Lemelin, John Fleagle, Randall Susman, Matt Cartmill, Larissa Swedell, and Clark Larsen who provided valuable comments on an earlier version of this manuscript.

NOTES

1 Linneaus' ability to correctly group closely related organisms was remarkable for its time. His *Lemur* genus contained prosimians as well as what we now refer to as *Cynocephalus volans*, a species of flying lemur. Flying lemurs are not lemurs (nor do they fly) and they are now placed in their own Order, Dermoptera. However, recent molecular studies have shown that they are the closest living relatives of primates (Janecka et al. 2007).

2 A handful of primates, including spider monkeys, wooly spider monkeys and colobus monkeys have greatly reduced or absent thumbs. The adaptive significance of pollical reduction is unclear.

3 Humans have realigned their hallux with the other toes in order to facilitate our unique locomotor mode of bipedality.

4 Several primate groups have secondarily evolved claws. These include the callitrichids (marmosets and tamarins) of the Neotropics and the bizarre, yet spectacular, aye-aye of Madagascar.

5 To further complicate matters, tarsiers are unique in several respects. They have a unique dental formula (2-1-3-3/1-1-3-3), have claws on both the second and third digits (only) of their feet, and are the only totally animalivorous (diet consisting entirely of insects or fauna) primate.

6 The callitrichines (except Callimico) have lost a molar and have a dental formula of 2-1-3-2.

REFERENCES

Ankel-Simons, F. *Primate Anatomy*, 2nd edn. New York: Academic Press, 2000.
Barton, R. A. "Binocularity and Brain Evolution in Primates." *PNAS* 101 (2004): 10113–10115.

Beard, K. C. "Gliding Behavior and Palaecology of the Alleged Primate Family Paromomyidae (Mammalia, Dermoptera)." *Nature* 345 (1990): 340–341.

Beard, K. C. "Phylogenetic Systematics of the Primatomorpha, with Special Reference to Dermoptera." In *Mammal Phylogeny: Placentals.* Edited by F. S. Szalay, M. C. McKenna, and M. J. Novacek, 129–150. New York: Springer-Verlag, 1993.

Beard, K. C. "Out of Asia: Anthropoid Origins and the Colonization of Africa." *Annual Review of Anthropology* 45 (2016): 199–213.

Bloch, J. I., and D. M. Boyer. "Grasping Primate Origins." *Science* 298 (2002): 1606–1610.

Bloch, J. I., M. T. Silcox, D. M. Boyer, and E. J. Sargis. "New Paleocene Skeletons and the Relationship of Plesiadapiforms to Crown-Clade Primates." *PNAS* 104 (2007): 1159–1164.

Bowmaker, J. K. "Evolution of Colour Vision in Vertebrates." *Eye* 125 (1998): 541–547.

Cartmill, M.. "Arboreal Adaptations and the Origin of the Primates." In *Functional and Evolutionary Biology of the Primates.* Edited by R. H. Tuttle, 97–122. Chicago: Aldine-Atherton, 1972.

Cartmill, M. "Primates: Conceptual History." In *The International Encyclopedia of Biological Anthropology.* Edited by W. Trevathan, 1–7. New York: John Wiley & Sons, Inc., 2018.

Cheney, D. L., and R. M. Seyfarth. *How Monkeys See the World.* Chicago: University of Chicago Press, 1990.

Chester, S. G. B., J. I. Blocj, D. M. Boyer, and W. A. Clemens. "Oldest Known Euarchontan Tarsals and Affinities of Paleocene *Purgatorius* to Primates." *Proceedings of the National Academy of Sciences of the United States of America* 112 (2015): 1487–1492.

Clutton-Brock, T. H., and P. H. Harvey. "Primates, Brains and Ecology." *Journal of Zoology* 190 (London) (1980): 309–323.

Cords, M. "When are There Influxes in Blue Monkey Groups?" In *The Guenons: Diversity and Adaptation in African Monkeys.* Edited by M. Glenn and M. Cords, 189–201. New York: Kluwer: Academic/Plenum Press, 2002.

DeCasien, A. R., S. A. Williams, and J. P. Higham. "Primate Brain Size Is Predicted by Diet but Not Sociality." *Nature Ecology and Evolution* 1 (2017): 0112.

Dunbar, R. I. M. "Neocortex Size as a Constraint on Group Size in Primates." *Journal of Human Evolution* 22 (1992): 469–493.

Dunbar, R. I. M., and S. Shultz. "Evolution in the Social Brain." *Science* 317 (2007): 1344–1347.

Estrada, A., P. A. Garber, A. B. Rylands, et al. "Impending Extinction Crisis of the World's Primates: Why Primates Matter." *Science Advances* 3 (2017): e1600946.

Fleagle, J. G. *Primate Adaptation and Evolution,* 3rd edn. New York: Academic Press, 2013.

Gingerich, P. D. "Cranial Anatomy and Evolution of Early Tertiary Plesiadapidae (Mammalia, Primates)." *University of Michigan Papers on Paleontology* 15 (1976): 1–141.

Gregory, W. K. "The Orders of Mammals." *Bulletin of the American Museum of Natural History* 27 (1910): 1–524.

Harvey, P. H., T. H. Clutton-Brock, and G. M. Mace. "Brain Size and Ecology in Small Mammals and Primates." *Proceedings of the National Academy of Sciences of the United States of America* 77 (1980): 4387–4389.

Heesy, C. P. "On the Relationship Between Orbit Orientation and Binocular Visual Field Overlap in Mammals." *Anatomical Record Part A* 281A (2004): 1104–1110.

Heesy, C. P. "Function of the Mammalian Postorbital Bar." *Journal of Morphology* 264 (2005): 363–380.

Henzi, S. P. "Many Males Do Not a Multimale Troop Make." *Folia Primatologica* 51 (1988): 165–168.

Hill, W. C. *Primates: Comparative Anatomy and Taxonomy I – Strepsirhini.* Edinburgh: Edinburgh University Press, 1953.

Hill, W. C. *Evolutionary Biology of the Primates.* New York: Academic Press, 1972.

Hu, Y., J. Meng, C. Li, and Y. Wang. "New Basal Eutherian Mammal from the Early Cretaceous Jehol Biota, Liaoning, China." *Proceedings of the Royal Society, B* 277 (2009): 220–236.

IUCN SSC Primate Specialist Group. *Regional Action Plan for the Conservation of Western Chimpanzees (Pan Troglodytes Verus) 2020–2030.* Gland, Switzerland: IUCN, 2020.

Janecka, J. E., W. Miller, T. H. Pringle, et al. "Molecular and Genomic Data Identify the Closest Living Relative of Primates." *Science* 318 (2007): 792–794.

Ji, Q., Z.-X. Luo, C.-X. Yuan, et al. "The Earliest Known Eutherian Mammal." *Nature* 416 (2002): 816–822.

Jolly, A. "Lemur Social Behavior and Primate Intelligence." *Science* 153 (1966): 501–506.

Jones, F. W. *Arboreal Man.* London: E. Arnold, 1916.

Kappeler, P. M., and C. P. van Schaik. "Evolution of Primate Social Systems." *International Journal of Primatology* 23 (2002): 707–740.

Kawashima, T., R. W. Thorington, Jr., K. Murakami, and F. Sato. "Evolutionary Anatomy and Phyletic Implication of the Extrinsic Cardiac Nervous System in the Philippine Tarsier (*Tarsius Syrichta*, Primates) in Comparisons with Strepsirrhines and New World Monkeys." *The Anatomical Record* 296 (2013): 798–806.

Kay, R. F. "100 Years of Primate Paleontology." *American Journal of Physical Anthropology* 165 (2018): 652–676.

Kay, R. F., R. W. Thorington, and P. Hounde. "Eocene Plesiadapiform Shows Affinities with Flying Lemurs Not Primates." *Nature* 345 (1990): 342–344.

Kay, R. F., J. G. M. Thewissen, and A. D. Yoder. "Cranial Anatomy of *Ignacius Graybullianus* and the Affinities of the Plesiadapiformes." *American Journal of Physical Anthropology* 89 (1992): 477–498.

Kirk, E. C., M. Cartmill, R. F. Kay, and P. Lemelin. "Comment on "Grasping Primate Origins." *Science* 300 (2003): 741b.

Krutzen, M., E. P. Willems, and C. P. van Schaik. "Culture and Geographic Variation in Orangutan Behavior." *Current Biology* 21 (2011): 1808–1812.

Larson, S. G. "Nonhuman Primate Locomotion." *American Journal of Physical Anthropology* 165 (2017): 705–725.

Larson, S. G., D. Schmitt, P. Lemelin, and M. Hamrick. "Uniqueness of Primate Forelimb Posture During Quadrupedal Locomotion." *American Journal of Physical Anthropology* 112 (2000): 87–101.

Le Gros Clark, W. E. *The Antecedents of Man.* Edinburgh: Edinburgh University Press, 1959.

Leigh, S. R. "Brain Growth, Life History and Cognition in Primate and Human Evolution." *American Journal of Primatology* 62 (2004): 139–164.

Leonhardt, S. D., J. Tung, J. B. Camden, M. Neal, and C. M. Drea. "Seeing Red: Behavioral Evidence of Trichromatic Color Vision in Strepsirrhine Primates." *Behavioral Ecology* 20 (2008): 1–12.

Linder, J. M., D. T. Cronin, N. Ting, et al. *Red Colobus (Piliocolobus) Conservation Action Plan 2021–2026.* Gland, Switzerland: IUCN, 2021.

Luncz, L. V., R. Mundry, and C. Boesch. "Evidence for Cultural Differences Between Neighboring Chimpanzee Communities." *Current Biology* 22 (2012): 922–926.

Luo, Z.-X., C.-X. Yuan, G.-J. Meng, and Q. Ji. "A Jurassic Eutherian Mammal and Divergence of Marsupials and Placentals." *Nature* 476 (2011): 442–445.

Maier, W. Epitensoric Position of the Chorda Tympani in Anthropoidea: A New Synamomorphic Character, with Remarks on the Fissure Glaseri in Primates. In *Mammalian Evolutionary Morphology: A Tribute to Frederick S. Szalay.* Edited by E. J. Sargis and M. Dagosto, 347–360. New York: Springer Science + Business B.V., 2008.

Martin, R. D. "Body Size, Brain Size and Feeding Strategies." In *Food Acquisition and Processing in Primates.* Edited by D. J. Chivers, B. A. Wood, and A. Bilsborough, 73–103. New York: Plenum Press, 1984.

McGraw, W. S. "Primates Defined." In *A Companion to Biological Anthropology.* Edited by C. S. Larsen, 222–242. West Sussex, UK: Wiley Blackwell, 2010.

Meiri, S., and G. M. Mace. "New Taxonomy and the Origin of Species." *PLoS Biology* 5, no. 7 (2007): 1385–1386.

Milton, K. "Distribution Patterns of Tropical Plant Foods as an Evolutionary Stimulus to Primate Mental Development." *American Anthropologist* 83 (1981): 534–548.

Mittermeier, R. A., I. Tattersall, B. Konstant, et al. *Lemurs of Madagascar.* Washington, DC: Conservation International, 1994.

Mittermeier, R., J. Ganzhorn, W. Konstant, et al. "Rasoloarison (2008) Lemur Diversity in Madagascar." *International Journal of Primatology* 29 (2008): 1607–1656.

Mittermeier, R. A., A. B. Rylands, and D. E. Wilson, eds. *Handbook of the Mammals of the World: 3. Primates.* Barcelona, Spain: Lynx Edicions, 2013.

Mivart, G. J., St. "On *Lepilemur* and *Cheirogaleus* and on the Zoological Rank of the Lemuroidea." *Proceedings of the Zoological Society of London* (1873): 484–510.

Napier, J. *Hands*. Princeton: Princeton University Press, 1993.

Napier, J. R., and P. H. Napier. *A Handbook of Living Primates*. New York: Academic Press, 1967.

Nero, O., and E. W. Heymann. "Led by the Nose: Olfaction in Primate Feeding Ecology." *Evolutionary Anthropology* 24 (2015): 137–148.

Ni, X. J., D. L. Gebo, M. Dagosto, et al. "The Oldest Known Primate Skeleton and Early Haplorrhine Evolution." *Science* 352 (2013): 673–677.

Noble, V. E., E. M. Kowalski, and M. J. Ravosa. "Orbit Orientation and the Function of the Mammalian Postorbital Bar." *Journal of Zoology* 250 (2000): 405–418.

Perelman, P., W. E. Johnson, C. Roos, et al. "A Molecular Phylogeny of Living Primates." *PloS Genetics* 7, no. 3 (2011): e1001342.

Powell, L. E., K. Isler, and R. A. Barton. "Re-evaluating the Link Between Brain Size and Behavioral Ecology in Primates." *Proceedings of the Royal Society, B* 284 (2017): 20171765.

Rasmussen, D. T. "The Origin of Primates." In *The Primate Fossil Record*. Edited by W. C. Hartwig, 5–9. Cambridge: Cambridge University Press, 2002.

Ross, C. F., and R. D. Martin. "The Role of Vision in the Origin and Evolution of Primates." In *Evolution of Nervous Systems*, vol. 4. The Evolution of Primate Nervous Systems. Edited by T. M. Preuss and J. Kaas, 59–78. Oxford: Elsevier, 2007.

Schmitt, D., and P. Lemelin. "Origins of Primate Locomotion: Gait Mechanics of the Woolly Opossum." *American Journal of Physical Anthropology* 118 (2002): 231–238.

Schultz, A. H. *The Life of Primates*. New York: Universe Books, 1969.

Schwitzer, C., R. A. Mittermeier, N. Davies, et al., eds. *Lemurs of Madagascar: A Strategy for Their Conservation 2013–2016*, 185. Bristol, UK: IUCN SSC Primate Specialist Group, Bristol Conservation and Science Foundation, and Conservation International, 2013.

Seiffert, E. R. "Early Primate Evolution in Afro-Arabia." *Evolutionary Anthropology* 21 (2012): 239–253.

Silcox, M. T. "Primate Taxonomy, Plesiadapiformes, and Approaches to Primate Origins." In *Primate Origins: Adaptations and Evolution*. Edited by M. J. Ravosa and M. Dagosto, 143–178. New York: Springer, 2007.

Silcox, M. T., D. M. Boyer, J. I. Bloch, and E. J. Sargis. "Revisiting the Adaptive Origins of Primates (Again)." *Journal of Human Evolution* 53 (2007): 321–324.

Silcox, M. T., E. J. Sargis, J. I. Bloch, and D. M. Boyer. "Primate Origins and Supraordinal Relationships: Morphological Evidence." In *Handbook of Paleoanthropology*, 2nd edn. Edited by W. Henke and I. Tattersall, 1053–1081. Berlin: Springer-Verlag, 2015.

Silcox, M. T., J. I. Bloch, D. M. Boyer, et al. "The Evolutionary Radiation of the Plesiadapiformes." *Evolutionary Anthropology* 26 (2017): 74–94.

Simons, E. *Primate Evolution*. New York: Macmillan, 1972.

Smith, R. J., and W. L. Jungers. "Body Mass in Comparative Primatology." *Journal of Human Evolution* 32 (1997): 523–559.

Smith, T. D., V. B. Deleon, and A. L. Rosenberger. "At Birth, Tarsiers Lack a Postorbital Septum." *The Anatomical Record* 296 (2013): 365–377.

Soligo, C., and R. D. Martin. "Adaptive Origins of Primate Revisited." *Journal of Human Evolution* 50 (2006): 414–430.

Soligo, C., and A. E. Muller. "Nails and Claws in Primate Evolution." *Journal of Human Evolution* 36 (1999): 97–114.

Springer, M. S., R. W. Meredith, J. Gatesy, et al. "Macroevolutionary Dynamics and Historical Biogeography of Primate Diversification Inferred from a Species Supermatrix." *PloS One* 7, no. 11 (2012): e49521.

Strasser, E., and E. Delson. "Cladistic Analysis of Cercopithecid Relationships." *Journal of Human Evolution* 16 (1987): 81–99.

Sussman, R. "Primate Origins and the Evolution of Angiosperms." *American Journal of Primatology* 23 (1991): 209–233.

Szalay, F. S. "The Beginnings of Primates." *Evolution* 22 (1968): 19–36.

Tattersall, I. *The Primates of Madagascar*. New York: Columbia University Press, 1982.

Tattersall, I. "Madagascar's Lemurs: Cryptic Diversity or Taxonomic Inflation?" *Evolutionary Anthropology* 16 (2007): 12–23.

Tavare, S., C. R. Marshall, O. Will, et al. "Using the Fossil Record to Estimate the Age of the Last Common Ancestor of Extant Primates." *Nature* 416 (2002): 726–729.

Watson, S. K., J. Botting, A. Whiten, and E. van de Waal. "Culture and Selective Social Learning in Wild and Captive Primates." In *Evolution of Primate Social Cognition. Interdisciplinary Evolution Research*. Edited by L. Di Paolo, F. Di Vincenzo, and F. De Petrillo, 211–230. Cham, Switzerland: Springer, 2018. https://doi.org/10.1007/978-3-319-93776-2_14.

Whiten, A., and E. van de Waal. "The Pervasive Role of Social Learning in Primate Lifetime Development." *Behavioral Ecology and Sociobiology* 72 (2018): 80. https://doi.org/10.1007/s00265-018-2489-3.

Williams, B. A., R. F. Kay, and E. C. Kirk. "New Perspectives on Anthropoid Origins." *Proceedings of the National Academy of Sciences of the United States of America* 107 (2010): 4797–4804.

Wilson, D. E., and D. M. Reeder. *Mammal Species of the World: A Taxonomic and Geographic Reference*, 3rd edn. Baltimore, Maryland: Johns Hopkins University Press, 2005.

Wright, P. C., E. L. Simon, and S. Gursky. *Tarsier: Past, Present and Future*. New Brunswick: Rutgers University Press, 2003.

CHAPTER 18

Primate Behavior, Social Flexibility, and Conservation

Karen B. Strier

INTRODUCTION

The behavior of nonhuman primates holds a special interest for biological anthropologists because our closest living relatives provide comparative perspectives into the origins of human sociality. Pioneering field studies include those conducted on mantled howler monkeys (*Alouatta palliata*) in Panama in the early 1930s (Carpenter 1934) and on Japanese macaques (*Macaca fuscata*) at various locations since the mid-1950s (Imanishi 1960). Subsequently, research focused more explicitly on particular primates with either ecological or phylogenetic affinities with hominins. Savanna-dwelling, semi-terrestrial baboons (*Papio anubis*) were among the first of these research subjects because the ecological selection pressures that shape their social adaptations were also thought to resemble those of human ancestors occupying similar habitats (Washburn and DeVore 1961; Figure 18.1). The great apes, which include chimpanzees (*Pan troglodytes*: Goodall 1971), gorillas (*Gorilla gorilla*: Fossey 1983), and orangutans (*Pongo pygmaeus*: Galdikas 1995), were also targeted early on because of the behavioral continuities that could be expected to persist as a result of our shared common ancestry.

Baboons and the great apes, which also include bonobos (*Pan paniscus*), continue to be among the most intensively studied primates, and long-term research on these taxa from multiple study sites continues to provide invaluable insights that inform our understanding of human behavioral evolution. Nowadays, however, most biological anthropologists also appreciate the value of broader, more comprehensive comparisons that take into account the diversity of social patterns exhibited across the Order Primates. Indeed, these broader comparative analyses have brought into focus the effects of ecology and phylogeny on social behavior, and are stimulating new investigations into the ways in which other factors contribute to both inter- and intraspecific behavioral variation (Strier 2009). Not surprisingly, with >60 percent of the more than 700 species and subspecies of primates recognized today currently threatened with extinction, there is growing appreciation for the importance of understanding intraspecific behavioral flexibility (e.g., Riley 2020; Strier 2017). Indeed, the ability of primates to adjust their behavior under diverse local ecological and demographic

Figure 18.1   Yellow baboons (*Papio cynocephalus*) accompanied by the author in Amboseli National Park, Kenya, a savanna woodland habitat. *Source:* Karen B. Strier, All rights reserved©.

conditions has direct implications for their adaptive potential in the anthropogenic landscapes in which many of them now live, as well as for the development of effective conservation and management efforts on their behalf (McLennan et al. 2017; Strier 2018).

Methodological advances, such as the use of field experiments to investigate cognitive capabilities for solving ecological and social problems (e.g., Cheney and Seyfarth 1990) and the development of noninvasive procedures for measuring hormones (e.g., Ziegler and Wittwer 2005), genetic relationships (e.g., Di Fiore 2003), and gut microbiomes (e.g., Amato et al. 2019) have provided essential tools for evaluating the mechanisms and consequences of primate behavior (Setchell and Curtis 2011). At the same time, ethnoprimatological approaches have emphasized the complexity of human-nonhuman primate interactions and the impact of these interactions on primate behavior, biology, and conservation (Ellwanger 2017; Fuentes 2012). Even earlier, however, observational studies were enhanced by the widespread adoption of systematic methods of behavioral sampling, which made it possible to control for potential observer biases and compare the behavior of individuals within and between groups of the same and different species (Altmann 1974). These methods have helped to transform the study of primate behavior from a largely descriptive endeavor into the more rigorous, quantitative science that it is today.

Although many important discoveries about primates have come from captive studies, in this overview of primate social patterns I will emphasize findings from field studies because of the insights they provide into how ecological and demographic variables influence behavior. I begin by describing the basic characteristics of primate groups, which include their size and composition, and the degree to which group members maintain cohesive or fluid associations with one another (Kappeler 2019). Much of the variation in group size and grouping patterns can be explained by local ecological or demographic conditions, which differ between species as well as across populations of the same species and within populations over time. Other characteristics, such as whether groups are comprised of extended networks of female or male kin or unrelated adults, tend to cluster differently within phylogenetic clades (Di Fiore and Rendall 1994) and coincide with other basic life history traits related to maturation and reproductive rates (Lee and Kappeler 2003). Distinguishing behavioral adaptations from traits that are shared among closely related species requires the use of phylogenetic controls, which are now widely employed in comparative analyses (Nunn and Barton 2001). Yet even phylogenetically conservative traits, such as dispersal patterns, can vary in response to local conditions (Moore 1984).

In the second section of this chapter, I consider the various social options that different types of groups provide and the extent to which observed social patterns are consistent with or deviate from predictions based on evolutionary and ecological theories. In principle, social behavior should be subject to the same kinds of selection pressures as other types of traits, and therefore behavior patterns that enhance fitness, or an individual's genetic contribution to future generations, should be favored over those that do not. Competition and cooperation over access to limited resources, such as food or mates, should dictate whether groups are comprised of biological kin or nonkin and the types of relationships that these individuals maintain with one another. In practice, however, it is difficult to evaluate the fitness consequences of behavior without long-term demographic and genetic data. In addition, because primates adjust their behavior in response to local conditions and as a result of their individual experiences, many researchers now regard their social flexibility to be an adaptation that distinguishes primates from other animals with more conservative – and predictable – behavioral repertoires (Barrett and Henzi 2005).

It is not surprising that primates exhibit such high levels of phenotypic plasticity in their social lives considering the long length of their life spans compared to most other mammals of similar body size. Primate life spans generally scale with body size within phylogenetic clades, but most primates live long enough to experience a variety of social and ecological conditions over the course of their lives. The ability to respond to fluctuating conditions and unpredictable events has obvious advantages, but it also requires enhanced cognitive abilities that have been associated with the correspondingly large size of primate brains. One hypothesis for the expansion of the neocortex, where most higher-level thought processes occur, relates directly to the social flexibility required to keep track of multiple social relationships and social networks as the sizes of their groups increase (Dunbar 2003). Enhanced cognitive abilities include the facility to learn, and long lives and group living provide the necessary time and contexts in which life-long social learning can occur.

In the final section of this chapter, I turn to some of the greatest challenges for contemporary and future studies of primate behavior. These challenges begin and end with the precarious status of so many primates, which can be attributed to human activities that are threatening primate habitats and populations at an unprecedented pace (Estrada et al. 2017). The urgency of conservation concerns has become a driving force behind the growth of primate field research and has influenced the directions that many of our research questions now take (Cowlishaw and Dunbar 2000; Wich and Marshall 2016). Ironically, however, the same human activities that are altering primate habitats and endangering their populations are also inadvertently creating unique opportunities to investigate how primates respond to different types of environmental change. Studies that are sensitive to the behavioral variation within and between populations can therefore provide insights into the adaptive potentials of primates and the ways in which their social flexibility can contribute to their future survival in a rapidly changing world (Strier 2021a).

CHARACTERISTICS OF SOCIAL GROUPS

Most primates spend all or most of their lives in the company of other members of their species. Their groups vary in size and composition, which can range from small families consisting of a single adult male and female with dependent offspring, to mixed sex and age classes of tens or even hundreds of individuals, to multilevel societies in which one-male units with multiple females associate with one another and bachelor males within larger clans and even larger troops or herds (Swedell 2012). Even when adults are most frequently encountered on their own or with dependent young, as is the case for orangutans, they are still members of larger communities comprised of familiar individuals that interact with one another differently than they do with strangers (van Schaik 2004). Both the quality of social interactions and the amount of time individuals spend together distinguish social groups from aggregations of individuals that form for their mutual safety from predators or because of their mutual attraction to concentrated resources.

Predator pressures tend to favor larger groups over smaller ones because the chances of detecting and ultimately avoiding a predator are usually improved by the presence of extra ears and eyes. Some researchers regard the safety that group-living provides as the foundation for the evolution of primate sociality in general (Hart and Sussman 2009). However, competition for access to food resources can exert an opposing force on group size if preferred foods, such as energy-rich fruits, are distributed in small patches that cannot feed as many individuals as would benefit by associating together if protection from predators was the only factor involved. Often, the ideal group size for many primates is a compromise between these safety and subsistence concerns (van Schaik 1983).

Primates cope with the problem of competition at small food patches either by living alone or in small, cohesive groups that can feed together without conflict, or by living in large, fluid communities, known as fission–fusion societies, in which party sizes shrink and swell according to the sizes of food patches available at any particular time. The maintenance of large, cohesive groups, by contrast, usually requires the capacity to switch to more abundant, but less preferred foods, such as leaves, grasses, or herbaceous vegetation, when large, preferred fruit patches are scarce. Although most primates consume a combination of fruit, which is prized for its readily digestible energy, and either insects or leaves, which are rich in protein, they vary in their morphological and physiological capabilities to process foods whose high-fiber content make them more difficult than fruit to digest (Lambert and Rothman 2015). Even with the physical traits needed to process low-quality foods, the nutritional costs of diet switching should only be tolerated when they are outweighed by the benefits of staying together instead of fissioning. High-predation risks represent one such benefit of remaining together; cooperating with other group members to defend high-quality food patches from other groups of conspecifics represents another (Wrangham 1980).

When cooperation over food is involved, females are usually found living in groups with their kin. To understand the power of food over females, it helps to step back a bit and consider the differences between male and female reproductive potential, or the number of offspring each is physically capable of producing over the course of their lives. Obviously, both males and females need to survive in order to reproduce, but only females bear the time and energetic burdens of gestation and lactation (Altmann 1980). The time devoted to pregnancy and, with some notable exceptions, nursing sets biological limits on the maximum number of offspring that females can produce. These limits do not apply to males, whose reproductive potentials are limited by their access to fertile females and the number of fertilizations they achieve. In a small number of primates, such as marmosets (*Callithrix* spp.) and tamarins (*Saguinus* spp.), females can conceive again soon after giving birth, and can therefore be nursing one set of offspring while they are pregnant with the next. However, these are also unusual primates because males and other group members do much of the infant carrying, providing some relief from the energetic burdens that other lactating mothers who carry their infants must bear on their own.

There is little that female primates can do to reduce the time that gestation and lactation require without compromising their offsprings' survival, but they can offset the high energetic demands of these vital activities by satisfying their nutritional needs. Better-fed females tend to have longer reproductive life spans, faster reproductive rates, and healthier offspring compared to poorly-fed females, and the amount and quality of food that a female consumes affects her nutritional status. The energetic costs of female reproduction make food a limiting resource on female reproductive success, in much the same way that fertilizable females are a limiting resource for males. If cooperation with group members provides access to more and better food in competitive confrontations against other groups, then females may fare better by cooperating with kin, with whom they also share some proportion of their genes.

These biological sex differences explain why the distribution of food is thought to influence whether females distribute themselves alone or in groups, and why the distribution of fertile females dictates the optimal distribution and behavior patterns of males (Emlen and Oring 1977; Wrangham 1979). When the distribution of food favors or permits females to live together, it may be possible for a single male to defend a group of females, or the foods that attracts them, resulting in what is referred to as either female-defense or resource-defense polygyny, respectively. However, as the size of female groups or the number of groups in an area increase, pressure from unattached males in the neighborhood to join or take over a female group can make it difficult for a single male to repel intruders and retain his position for very long. One solution to this dilemma is to gain the females' support by proving one's superiority as an ally in defending food resources or in preventing other conspecifics from harassing females and their infants. Another solution is to join forces with one or more male allies. For the same genetic reasons that cooperation among females is more likely to involve close biological relatives, male kin are often one anothers' allies of choice.

Cooperating with male kin is also an alternative when females maintain fluid, fission–fusion dynamics that result in their foraging at least some of the time on their own. The amount of time females spend by themselves or with one another and the density of females within an area determine the feasibility of male options, which range from associating with a single female, to monitoring multiple independent females simultaneously, to cooperating with other males to monopolize a larger number of females than he could on his own.

The effects of predators in general, and of food on females and of females on males, can explain some of the variation in the number of adults of each sex that primate groups contain, whether groups with multiple adults of the same sex are biological kin or not, and the degree of cohesiveness or fluidity in their associations (Foley and Lee 1989). However, the boundaries between these so-called group "types" are often blurred in different ways. For example, a single species can have more than one type of group, such as in the case of mountain gorillas (*Gorilla gorilla*), where unimale and multimale groups live side-by-side in the same population. The composition of any group can change due to specific demographic events, such as deaths or the immigration or emigration of individuals, and as a result of more encompassing demographic conditions, such as fluctuations in adult sex ratios within the local population. Because of these dynamics, a single individual can spend different times of his or her life in different types of groups (Robbins 2001).

Similarly, although some species are more likely, on average, to occur in certain types of groups, fluctuations in the distribution of food resources and local demographic conditions can lead to differences in their normative grouping patterns. For example, when I first started studying northern muriqui monkeys (*Brachyteles hypoxanthus*) in 1982, the

22 members in my main study group traveled together as a cohesive, multimale, multifemale unit. Within 15 years, the group had grown to more than 2½ times its initial size, and grouping patterns had shifted to more fluid, fission–fusion associations, which have persisted ever since as both the group and the population have continued to grow (Strier 2021b). Some of the same individuals that were present in 1982 were responsible for this behavioral change, but other, younger, individuals have never experienced life in a cohesive group, and therefore have never had the opportunity to see and interact with all members of their group on a daily basis.

SOCIAL OPTIONS

The frequencies with which group members associate and interact with one another vary within different groups as well as between groups of different types. To decipher the strength and quality of their relationships with one another, we rely on systematic observations, which can then be used to calculate the proportion of time individuals spend in close proximity and the rates and directionality of their affiliative and agonistic interactions. Primate spatial associations are rarely random, and just as in humans, most primates spend more of their time with close friends, family, or mates than with other individuals when they have the chance. Even when pursuing their own activities, higher rates of proximity imply a higher level of tolerance, and generally lead to higher rates of affiliative interactions, such as grooming or embracing. When the pattern of initiating and maintaining spatial and affiliative interactions between pairs of individuals is symmetrical, we can infer that the relationship is mutually beneficial to both, whereas asymmetrical effort implies that one individual stands to benefit more from the relationship than the other. Variation in age, sex, health and reproductive conditions, and social rank contribute to the asymmetries in primate social relationships, which can change over the course of each individual's lifetime.

Maintaining close spatial and affiliative relationships is useful whenever having allies nearby increases the chances of gaining their support in aggressive interactions with other group members. In many cercopithecines, for example, females spend their lives in their natal groups, surrounded by their female relatives. Females can be individually ranked based on whether they win or lose in agonistic interactions with other females in their matrilines, and matrilines can be ranked relative to one another. Cultivating allies that are likely to come to one's aid if the need should arise can be a good social investment, particularly in hierarchical societies where encounters with higher-ranking females, as well as with males, can pose risks. Females with close social bonds have higher offspring survivorship than females that are less socially integrated in their groups (Silk et al. 2009). Not surprisingly, though, the importance of maintaining allies is proportional to the levels of within group competition. In societies with female dispersal and egalitarian relationships, such as those of northern muriquis, the threat of being targeted for aggression by another group member is slim, and social relationships among females are less differentiated than they are in matrilocal, hierarchical societies (Strier 2011).

Dispersal patterns determine the extent to which extended kin are available as potential social partners and allies (Strier 2008). Whether males, females, or both sexes disperse from their natal groups varies with phylogeny and with local ecological and demographic conditions. For example, although male-biased dispersal with female philopatry characterizes most cercopithecines, some colobines, white-faced capuchin monkeys (*Cebus imitator*) and many lemurs, female-biased dispersal with male philopatry is found in chimpanzees and bonobos, as well as the New World atelines, which include spider monkeys (*Ateles* spp.), woolly monkeys (*Lagothrix* spp.), and muriquis. In other primates, such as gorillas, howler monkeys, callitrichines, and several prosimians, bisexual dispersal is more common. However, many of these species also exhibit variation in their dispersal patterns that reflect local demographic conditions. For example, extended matrilines have been observed in red howler monkeys (*Alouatta seniculus*, Pope 2000) and buffy-headed marmosets (*Callithrix flaviceps*, Ferrari and Digby 1996) when demographic conditions result in the retention of daughters in their natal groups. Similarly, although female western gorillas typically disperse from their natal groups, genetic evidence indicates that many remain in their natal neighborhoods, where the potential for future interactions among female kin persist (Bradley et al. 2007).

Females that remain in their natal groups have the opportunity to bias their affiliative interactions and agonistic support in favor of their kin, but whether they do so depends on the relative fitness costs and benefits involved. Among female Japanese macaques, there appears to be a "relatedness threshold," and distantly related kin that fall below this threshold are generally not favored over unrelated females (Chapais 2001). However, we do not yet understand whether this threshold reflects a limit on the ability of primates to recognize distant kin or the minimal fitness gains that would accrue by helping more distant relatives. In both rhesus macaques (*Macaca mulatta*) and yellow baboons (*Papio cynocephalus*), females favor close maternal kin over close paternal kin, which are themselves favored over nonkin (Widdig 2007). Familiarity is known to play an important role in kin recognition, but other mechanisms of phenotypic matching using chemical cues may also be involved.

Examples of kin-biased relationships among males in patrilocal societies are not as clear-cut as those among females in matrilocal societies, perhaps because fertilizations cannot be shared in the same way as food. In the patrilocal societies of chimpanzees, for example, males maintain hierarchical relationships with one another, and genetic studies have shown that higher-ranking males achieve more fertilizations than females. However, there is no evidence that paternally related male kin associate or affiliate preferentially with one another relative to other males within their communities in the same way that maternally related female macaques and baboons do in their matrilocal societies (Langergraber et al. 2007).

Although the persistence of life-long associations and alliances with same-sexed kin requires co-residence in the same natal groups, both males and females can maintain some associations with kin if they transfer into the same groups with paternal kin in their age cohorts, or into the same groups that older maternal or paternal kin have previously joined. Related males that disperse together sometimes form cooperative alliances against other males, even if the fitness benefits of doing so are indirect. Coalitions between related male red howler monkeys (*Alouatta seniculus*) are more successful in defending groups of females than single males or coalitions among unrelated males, even though genetic data have shown that often only one of the males sires the infants in their group (Pope 1990). Equally high levels of reproductive skew occur when pairs of related male moustached tamarins (*Saguinus mystax*) cooperate in defending a single breeding female and caring for her offspring in their group (Huck et al. 2005).

The reproductive monopolies that the dominant male in multimale groups of red howler monkeys and moustached tamarins are known to achieve illustrate how misleading it can be to assume that mating systems are accurately reflected by the number of adults in a group. Both males and females in pair-bonded societies have been observed to engage in extra-pair copulations, and genetic studies of fork-marked lemurs (*Phaner furcifer*) have shown that not all of the infants are sired by their mother's so-called mate (Shülke et al. 2004). In multimale groups of western lowland gorillas, paternity is biased heavily, but not entirely, in favor of alpha silverback males (Bradley et al. 2005). In the matrilineal, multimale societies of yellow baboons (*Papio cynocephalus*), paternity can be strongly skewed in favor of some, but not all, alpha males, depending on the length of time an alpha male can retain his status and how stable or unstable male group membership is during these times (Altmann et al. 1996). Demographic conditions affect the number of male challengers, and male competitive abilities vary individually and as their physical and social skills change with age.

A male's physical condition and social skills affect not only his relationships with other males but also his attractiveness to females as mates. Male olive baboons (*Papio anubis*) that invest time and energy in befriending females can improve their chances of being chosen as preferred mating partners (Smuts 1985). In many other primates, a male's ability to provide protection extends beyond females and can make the difference between saving and losing an infant to infanticide before it is weaned. The risks of infanticide are predicted to be high whenever a male without any genetic relationship to an infant can increase his chances of fertilizing the mother by interrupting lactation and its inhibitory effect on ovulation (Hrdy 1977). These conditions are ripe when a new, unrelated male takes over an established group with females that are nursing infants sired by his predecessor. In some species, such as mountain gorillas, female groups may disintegrate when a silverback dies or is ousted by a marauding male, but in others, such as Hanuman langurs (*Semnopithecus entellus*), females may mate and conceive their next infant with the same male whose aggression led to her previous infant's death but who is more likely to protect than to harm his own progeny (Borries et al. 1999). Nonetheless, high rates of male replacements can result in fewer surviving offspring, affecting both female fitness and, potentially, group sizes, as simulations in white-faced capuchin monkeys (*Cebus imitator*) have shown (Fedigan et al. 2021).

Females can reduce the risks of losing their infants to male aggression by confusing males about their potential paternity (Hrdy 1981). Mating with multiple males is not always an option if only one male is present, nor is it always advantageous, especially if male qualities vary and the costs of conceiving with a less preferred male are high. However, when multiple males are available and conception probabilities are low, then the protection that promiscuity can provide for her infant should, theoretically, offset other risks. Although we do not yet know whether male primates can recognize their own offspring, or what cues they rely on to do so, male yellow baboons have been found to support their juvenile offspring over non-offspring in agonistic interactions, and appear to bias their support based on the frequencies with which they mated with the infant's mother during her most fertile times (Buchan et al. 2003).

It is easier to assess conception probabilities in some primates than others. In baboons and chimpanzees, for example, females have patches of skin on their rumps that visually inflate and deflate in response to hormonal fluctuations associated with their ovarian cycles. In most primates, however, males must rely on pheromonal or behavioral cues to assess a female's reproductive condition. Although females cannot manipulate the pheromonal signals they emit any more than they can control their sexual swellings, they can – and do – alter their behavior to encourage or discourage the attentions of males. A number of field studies, conducted by measuring hormone levels in urine or more commonly fecal samples collected noninvasively from females in the wild, have shown that many female primates mate with different partners at times in their cycles when the chances of conception are low.

The decoupling of sex from reproduction *per se* was long thought to be one of the hallmarks of human relationships, yet we now know that sex can serve important social functions in other primates as well. In bonobos, for example, relatedness among philopatric males should reduce the risks of male infanticide and therefore minimize the benefits of promiscuous mating that confuse paternity in primates where males pose threats to unrelated females and infants. Instead, the high frequencies and contexts with which female bonobos engage in sexual interactions with both males and one another suggest that sex may function to ease social tensions in their societies (Clay and de Waal 2015).

FUTURE CHALLENGES

The growth of primate field studies over the last half a century has brought new insights into the diversity of primate social patterns from which our own sociality evolved (Strier 2018). The initial emphases on ecological and phylogenetic determinants of behavior have been refined as new empirical data have been incorporated into theories of behavioral evolution. Contemporary approaches to primate sociality are increasingly sensitive to the effects of local demographic conditions (Struhsaker 2008) and are attentive to the underlying hormonal and physiological mechanisms and developmental processes that regulate behavior (Thierry 2008). Although the focus of most behavioral studies continues to be on individuals and their interactions within groups and communities, there is increasing greater recognition that primate groups and communities are situated within populations whose dynamics and histories should not be ignored (Henzi and Barrett 2005; Strier 2009). These histories, along with contemporary conservation concerns, have also stimulated closer scrutiny of the effects of past and ongoing anthropogenic activities and interactions with primates on local primate populations and their communities (Dore et al. 2017; McLennan et al. 2017).

Expanding our comparative analyses to include populations represents a significant departure from past conventions that focused on identifying normative, species-specific patterns. It is also an important next step in the process of interpreting intraspecific variation relative to the interspecific variation upon which anthropological interest in primates was initially based. For example, comparisons of different populations of chimpanzees have revealed a combination of consistent social patterns, such as male philopatry, and differences, which include the associations between males and females and the levels of aggression exhibited between communities (Boesch et al. 2008). Our ability to distinguish phylogenetically conservative behavior patterns from more labile ones requires these types of within-species comparisons as much as it requires between-species comparisons.

Populations are also of critical importance to assessing the conservation status of endangered species. We know that large, continuous populations are less vulnerable to extinction because their size buffers them from demographic fluctuations, including high mortality caused by unpredictable events, such as epidemics, droughts, or devastating storms, and from the genetic risks that arise from the loss of alleles due to genetic drift and inbreeding depression in small, isolated populations. Human activities, such as habitat fragmentation, hunting, logging, and other forms of disturbances, are often a result of global consumerism (Estrada et al. 2019), yet they negatively impact the size, composition, and connectivity of primate populations, and thus their demographic and genetic structures, at local scales. When these populations become too small and isolated from one another, their long-term viabilities are severely compromised. Even primates inhabiting the most remote, undisturbed areas are not immune from the effects of global climate change, which are predicted to transform many habitats that are currently suitable for primates into ones that can no longer support them (Stewart et al. 2020).

Conservation efforts to protect primates and their habitats can produce promising results if they are implemented in time. Some of the most compelling success stories have involved primatologists, who have used their discoveries about the behavior of primates to attract attention to the conservation cause. Results have included the establishment of the Ranomafana National Park in Madagascar, which is now a sanctuary for at least 12 species of lemurs in addition to other endangered wildlife (Wright 1992), and the reintroduction of captive-bred golden lion tamarins (*Leontopithecus rosalia*) into what remains of their native habitat in southeastern Brazil (Kleiman and Rylands 2002; Ruiz-Miranda et al.

2019). In another protected fragment of Brazil's Atlantic Forest, one population of northern muriquis grew from about 50 individuals to over 350 individuals in less than 35 years (Strier 2021b), in large part thanks to the commitment to conservation made by the owners of the forest.

The muriquis' population recovery has been fascinating to follow because it has given us glimpses into which of their behavior patterns are most susceptible to change. In addition to adopting fluid, fission–fusion dynamics, they also began to spend increasing amounts of their time on the ground. We presumed that the expansion of their vertical niche was initially driven by demographic pressures and ultimately became established as a new behavioral tradition, which has spread among the male-biased social networks in their patrilocal society (Tabacow et al. 2009). Yet, perhaps because they still have ecological options, the unusual affiliative, peaceful egalitarian relationships among group members have not yet shown any signs of change (Strier 2021b).

While such an extreme type of social transformation may seem implausible, this is exactly what happened, although in the opposite direction, in one troop of olive baboons at the Masai Mara Reserve in Kenya after all of the troop's most aggressive male members died from disease (Sapolsky and Share 2004). The surviving males in the troop were among the most pacifistic and their interactions with one another and with females became measurably more affiliative once the composition of their group had changed.

The effects of local demographic and ecological events on social patterns may have even more significant consequences in small, isolated populations because they lack access to immigrants that can import their own behavior along with their genes. For example, while the peaceful tradition that has become established in the baboon troop could potentially be reversed by the immigration of more aggressive males from other troops in their population, any future shift in the muriquis' breeding sex ratios will be entirely dependent on the number of males and females that are born and survive within the borders of the forest that supports their isolated population (Figure 18.2).

Figure 18.2 Adult male northern muriquis (*Brachyteles hypoxanthus*) at the Reserva Particular Patrimônio Natural Feliciano Miguel Abdala, in Caratinga, Minas Gerais, Brazil. Low rates of intra-group aggression and strong affiliative associations among philopatric males characterize social relationships in their egalitarian society. Photo by Carla B. Possamai/Muriqui Project of Caratinga, All rights reserved©.

As populations of other primates become more fragmented and their habitats become increasingly altered, opportunities to identify the underlying causes of their behavioral differences will become even more numerous than they are today. Longitudinal studies can provide historical perspectives on the processes that lead to behavioral changes over time, and therefore contribute, along with comparative studies of multiple populations, to a better understanding of behavioral plasticity and intraspecific variation in behavior. Nonetheless, although flexible behavior patterns may permit primates to occupy disturbed, fragmented habitats, they are still highly vulnerable to regional threats, such as the outbreak of sylvatic yellow fever that caused severe mortality in many populations of brown howler monkeys (*Alouatta guariba*; Bicca-Marques et al. 2020) as well as in recovering populations of other primates including the golden lion tamarins and northern muriquis (Dietz et al. 2019; Strier et al. 2019). Even greater uncertainties can be anticipated as primates are impacted by the effects of climate change on both local and global scales (Meyer and Pie 2021; Zhang et al. 2019).

The integration of comparative knowledge of intraspecific and interspecific variations in primate social patterns is essential to evaluating conservation priorities and developing informed management programs for the most threatened populations and species. However, we also now recognize that our conservation efforts are unlikely to succeed unless we can also address the underlying threats to primate survival that we humans continue to pose. Insights from anthropology, which have been critical to advances in ethnoprimatology, are increasingly relevant for understanding and addressing the human dimensions of primate conservation (Dore et al. 2017; Riley 2020; Strier 2014). These insights have also contributed to heightened concern and attention to the ethical impacts on both the primates we study and seek to conserve and the human communities that are affected by these efforts (Bezanson and McNamara 2019; Bezanson et al. 2013; Riley and Bezanson 2018). Ultimately, the potential for future generations of primatologists to answer questions about human social evolution will be dependent on securing a future for the primates and the clues about our shared ancestry that they hold.

ACKNOWLEDGMENTS

I am grateful to Clark Larsen for the invitation to contribute to this volume. I also thank Jon Marks for comments on the first edition of this chapter, and Jon and Michelle Bezanson for their comments on the present edition.

REFERENCES

Altmann, J. "Observational Study of Behavior: Sampling Methods." *Behaviour* 49 (1974): 227–267.

Altmann, J. *Baboon Mothers and Infants*. Cambridge: Harvard University Press, 1980.

Altmann, J., S. C. Alberts, S. A. Haines, et al. "Behavior Predicts Genetic Structure in a Wild Primate Group." *Proceedings of the National Academy of Sciences* 93 (1996): 5797–5801.

Amato, K. R., E. K. Mallott, D. McDonald, et al. "Convergence of Human and Old World Monkey Gut Microbiomes Demonstrates the Importance of Human Ecology over Phylogeny." *Genome Biology* 20, no. 1 (2019): 201. https://doi.org/10.1186/s13059-019-1807-z.

Barrett, L., and P. Henzi, The Social Nature of Primate Cognition. *Proceedings of the Royal Society B* 272 (2005): 1865–1875.

Bezanson, M., and A. McNamara. "The What and Where of Primate Field Research May Be Failing Primate Conservation." *Evolutionary Anthropology* 28, no. 4 (2019): 166–178.

Bezanson, M., R. Stowe, and S. M. Watts. "Reducing the Ecological Impact of Field Research." *American Journal of Primatology* 75 (2013): 1–9.

Bicca-Marques, J. C., Ó. M. Chaves, and G. P. Hass. "Howler Monkey Tolerance to Habitat Shrinking." *Lifetime Warranty or Death Sentence? American Journal of Primatology* 82 (2020): e23089. https://doi.org/10.1002/ajp.23089.

Boesch, C., C. Crockford, I. Herbinger, et al. "Intergroup Conflicts Among Chimpanzees in Täi National Park: Lethal Violence and the Female Perspective." *American Journal of Primatology* 70 (2008): 519–532.

Borries, C., K. Launhardt, C. Epplen, et al. "Males as Infant Protectors in Hanuman Langurs (*Presbytis Entellus*) Living in Multimale Groups – Defence Pattern, Paternity and Sexual Behaviour." *Behavioral Ecology and Sociobiology* 46 (1999): 350–356.

Bradley, B. J., M. M. Robbins, E. A. Williamson, et al. "Mountain Gorilla Tug-of-War: Silverbacks Have Limited Control over Reproduction in Multimale Groups." *Proceedings of the National Academy of Sciences* 102 (2005): 9418–9423.

Bradley, B. J., D. M. Doran-Sheehy, and L., Vigilant. "Potential for Female Kin Associations in Wild Western Gorillas Despite Female Dispersal." *Proceedings of the Royal Society B* 274 (2007): 2179–2185.

Buchan, J. C., S. C. Alberts, J. B. Silk, and J. Altmann. "True Paternal Care in a Multi-male Primate Society." *Nature* 425 (2003): 179–181.

Carpenter, C. R. "A Field Study of the Behavior and Social Relations of Howling Monkeys." *Comparative Psychological Monographs* 48 (1934): 1–168.

Chapais, B. "Primate Nepotism: What Is the Explanatory Value of Kin Selection?" *International Journal of Primatology* 22 (2001): 203–229.

Cheney, D., and R. Seyfarth. *How Monkeys See the World*. Chicago: University of Chicago Press, 1990.

Clay, Z., and F. B. M. de Waal. "Sex and Strife: Post-Conflict Sexual Contacts in Bonobos." *Behaviour* 152, no. 3–4 (2015): 313–334. https://doi.org/10.1163/1568539X-00003155.

Cowlishaw, G., and R. I. M. Dunbar. *Primate Conservation Biology*. Chicago: University of Chicago Press, 2000.

Di Fiore, A. "Molecular Genetic Approaches to the Study of Primate Behavior, Social Organization, and Reproduction." *Yearbook of Physical Anthropology* 37 (2003): 62–99.

Di Fiore, A., and D., Rendall. "Evolution of Social Organization: A Reappraisal for Primates by Using Phylogenetic Methods." *Proceedings of the National Academy of Sciences* 91 (1994): 9941–9945.

Dietz, J. M., S. J. Hankerson, B. R. Alexandre, et al. "Yellow Fever in Brazil Threatens Successful Recovery of Endangered Golden Lion Tamarins." *Scientific Reports* 9 (2019): e12926. https://doi.org/10.1038/s41598-019-49199-6.

Dore, K. M., E. P. Riley, and A. Fuentes, eds. *Ethnoprimatology: A Practical Guide to Research at the Human–Nonhuman Primate Interface*. New York: Cambridge University Press, 2017.

Dunbar, R. I. M. "The Social Brain: Mind, Language, and Society in Evolutionary Perspective." *Annual Review of Anthropology* 32 (2003): 163–181.

Ellwanger, A. L. "Ethnoprimatology." In *The International Encyclopedia of Primatology*. Edited by M. Bezanson, K. C. MacKinnon, E. Riley, et al., 2017. https://doi.org/10.1002/9781119179313.wbprim0178.

Emlen, S., and L. Oring. "Ecology, Sexual Selection and the Evolution of Mating Systems." *Science* 197 (1977): 215–223.

Estrada, A., P. A. Garber, A. B. Rylands, et al. "Impending Extinction Crisis of the World's Primates: Why Primates Matter." *Science Advances* 3, no. 1 (2017): e1600946. 10.1126/sciadv.1600946.

Estrada, A, P. A. Garber, and A. Chaudhary. "Expanding Global Commodities Trade and Consumption Place the World's Primates at Risk of Extinction." *Peer Journal* 7 (2019): e7068. 10.7717/peerj.7068.

Fedigan, L. M., J. D. Hogan, F. A. Campos, et al. "Costs of Male Infanticide for Female Capuchins: When Does an Adaptive Male Reproductive Strategy Become Costly for Females and Detrimental to Population Viability?" *American Journal of Physical Anthropology* 176, no. 3 (2021): 349–360.

Ferrari, S. F., and L. J. Digby. "Wild *Callithrix* Groups: Stable Extended Families?" *American Journal of Primatology* 38 (1996): 19–27.

Foley, R. A., and P. C. Lee. "Finite Social Space, Evolutionary Pathways, and Reconstructing Hominid Behavior." *Science* 243 (1989): 901–906.

Fossey, D. *Gorillas in the Mist*. Boston: Houghton Mifflin Company, 1983.

Fuentes, A. "Ethnoprimatology and the Anthropology of the Human-Primate Interface." *Annual Review of Anthropology* 41 (2012): 101–117.

Galdikas, B. M. F. *Reflections of Eden: My Years with the Orangutans of Borneo*. Boston: Little, Brown and Company, 1995.

Goodall, J. *In the Shadow of Man*. London: Collins, 1971.

Hart, D., and R. W. Sussman. *Man the Hunted: Primates, Predators, and Human Evolution*. New York: Westview Press, 2009.

Henzi, S. P., and L. Barrett. "The Historical Socioecology of Savannah Baboons (*Papio Hamadryas*)." *Journal of Zoology, London* 265 (2005): 215–226.

Hrdy, S. B. *The Langurs of Abu*. Cambridge: Harvard University Press, 1977.

Hrdy, S. B. *The Woman That Never Evolved*. Cambridge: Harvard University Press, 1981.

Huck, M., P. Lottker, U. R. Bohle, and E. W. Heymann. "Paternity and Kinship Patterns in Polyandrous Moustached Tamarins (*Saguinus Mystax*)." *American Journal of Physical Anthropology* 127 (2005): 449–464.

Imanishi, K. "Social Organization of Subhuman Primates in Their Natural Habitat." *Current Anthropology* 1 (1960): 393–407.

Kappeler, P. M. "A Framework for Studying Social Complexity." *Behavioral Ecology and Sociobiology* 73, no. 1 (2019): 13.

Kleiman, D. G., and A. B. Rylands, eds. *Lion Tamarins: Biology and Conservation*. Washington, DC: Smithsonian Institution Press, 2002.

Lambert, J. E., and J. M. Rothman. "Fallback Foods, Optimal Diets, and Nutritional Targets: Primate Responses to Varying Food Availability and Quality." *Annual Review of Anthropology* 44, no. 1 (2015): 493–512.

Langergraber, K. E., J. C. Mitani, and L. Vigilant, "The Limited Impact of Kinship on Cooperation in Wild Chimpanzees." *Proceedings of the National Academy of Sciences* 104 (2007): 7786–7790.

Lee, P. C., and P. M. Kappeler. "Socioecological Correlates of Phenotypic Plasticity of Primate Life Histories." In *Primate Life Histories and Socioecology*. Edited by Peter M. Kappeler and Michael E. Pereira, 41–65. Cambridge: Cambridge University Press, 2003.

McLennan, M. R., N. Spagnoletti, and K. J. Hockings. "The Implications of Primate Behavioral Flexibility for Sustainable Human–Primate Coexistence in Anthropogenic Habitats." *International Journal of Primatology* 38, no. 2 (2017): 105–121.

Meyer, A., and M. Pie. "Climate Change Estimates Surpass Rates of Climatic Niche Evolution in Primates." *International Journal of Primatology* 43 (2021): 40–56. 10.1007/s10764-021-00253-z.

Moore, J. "Female Transfer in Primates." *International Journal of Primatology* 5 (1984): 537–589.

Nunn, C. L., and R. A. Barton. "Comparative Methods for Studying Primate Adaptation and Allometry." *Evolutionary Anthropology* 10 (2001): 81–98.

Pope, T. R. "The Reproductive Consequences of Male Cooperation in the Red Howler Monkey: Paternity Exclusion in Multi-Male and Single-Male Troops Using Genetic Markers." *Behavioral Ecology and Sociobiology* 27 (1990): 439–446.

Pope, T. R. "Reproductive Success Increases with Degree of Kinship in Cooperative Coalitions of Female Red Howler Monkeys (*Alouatta Seniculus*)." *Behavioral Ecology and Sociobiology* 48 (2000): 253–267.

Riley, E. P. *The Promise of Contemporary Primatology*. New York: Routledge, 2020.

Riley, E. P., and M. Bezanson. "Ethics of Primate Fieldwork: Toward an Ethically Engaged Primatology." *Annual Reviews of Anthropology* 47 (2018): 493–512.

Robbins, M. M. "Variation in the Social System of Mountain Gorillas: The Male Perspective." In *Mountain Gorillas*. Edited by M. M. Robbins, P. Sicotte, and K. J. Stewart, 29–58. Cambridge: Cambridge University Press, 2001.

Ruiz-Miranda, C. R., M. M. de Morais, Jr, L. A. Dietz, et al. "Estimating Population Sizes to Evaluate Progress in Conservation of Endangered Golden Lion Tamarins (*Leontopithecus Rosalia*)." *PLoS One* 14, no. 6 (2019): e0216664. https://doi.org/10.1371/journal.pone.0216664.

Sapolsky, R. M., and L. J. Share. "A Pacific Culture Among Wild Baboons: Its Emergence and Transmission." *PLoS Biology* 2 (2004): 534–541.

Schülke, O., P. M. Kappeler, and H. Zischler. "Small Testes Size Despite High Extra-Pair Paternity in the Pair-Living Nocturnal Primate *Phaner Furcifer*." *Behavioral Ecology and Sociobiology* 55 (2004): 293–301.

Setchell, J. M., and D. J. Curtis, eds. *Field and Laboratory Methods in Primatology: A Practical Guide.* 2nd edn. Cambridge: Cambridge University Press, 2011.

Silk, J. B., J. C. Beehner, T. J. Bergman, et al., "The Benefits of Social Capital: Close Social Bonds Among Female Baboons Enhance Offspring Survival." *Proceedings of the Royal Society B,* 276, no. 1670 (2009): 3099–3104. doi: 10.1098/rspb.2009.0681.

Smuts, B. B. *Sex and Friendship in Baboons.* New York: Aldine, 1985.

Stewart, B. M., S. E. Turner, and H. D. Matthew. "Climate Change Impacts on Potential Future Ranges of Non-human Primate Species." *Climatic Change* 162 (2020): 2301–2318. https://doi.org/10.1007/s10584-020-02776-5.

Strier, K. B. "The Effects of Kin on Primate Life Histories." *Annual Review of Anthropology* 37 (2008): 21–36.

Strier, K. B. "Seeing the Forest Through the Trees: Mechanisms of Primate Behavioral Diversity from Individuals to Populations and Beyond." *Current Anthropology* 50 (2009): 213–228.

Strier, K. B. "Social Plasticity and Demographic Variation in Primates." In *The Origins and Nature of Cooperation and Altruism in Non-human and Human Primates.* Edited by R. W. Sussman and C. R. Cloninger, 179–192. New York: Springer, 2011.

Strier, K. B., ed. *Primate Ethnographies.* London: Routledge, 2014.

Strier, K. B. "What Does Variation in Primate Behavior Mean?" *American Journal of Physical Anthropology* 162, no. S63 (2017): 4–14.

Strier, K. B. "Primate Social Behavior." *American Journal of Physical Anthropology* 165, no. 4 (2018): 801–812.

Strier, K. B. *Primate Behavioral Ecology,* 6th edn. London: Routledge, 2021a.

Strier, K. B. "The Limits of Resilience." *Primates* 62 (2021b): 861–868.

Strier, K. B., F. P. Tabacow, C. B. Possamai, et al. "Status of the Northern Muriqui (*Brachyteles Hypoxanthus*) in the Time of Yellow Fever." *Primates* 60, no. 1 (2019): 21–28. 10.1007/s10329-018-0701-8.

Struhsaker, T. T. "Demographic Variability in Monkeys: Implications for Theory and Conservation." *International Journal of Primatology* 29 (2008): 19–34.

Swedell, L. "Primate Sociality and Social Systems." *Nature Education Knowledge* 3, no. 10 (2012): 84. https://www.nature.com/scitable/knowledge/library/primate-sociality-and-social-systems-58068905.

Tabacow, F. P., S. L. Mendes, and K. B. Strier. "Spread of a Terrestrial Tradition in an Arboreal Primate." *American Anthropologist* 111 (2009): 238–249.

Thierry, B. "Primate Socioecology, the Lost Dream of Ecological Determinism." *Evolutionary Anthropology* 17 (2008): 93–96.

van Schaik, C. P. "Why Are Diurnal Primates Living in Groups?" *Behaviour* 87 (1983): 120–144.

van Schaik, C. P. *Among Orangutans: Red Apes and the Rise of Human Culture.* Cambridge, MA: Harvard University Press, 2004.

Washburn, S. L., and I. DeVore. "The Social Life of Baboons." *Scientific American* 204 (1961): 62–71.

Wich, S. A., and A. J. Marshall, eds. *An Introduction to Primate Conservation.* New York: Oxford University Press, 2016.

Widdig, A. "Paternal Kin Discrimination: The Evidence and Likely Mechanisms." *Biological Reviews* 82 (2007): 319–334.

Wrangham, R. W. "On the Evolution of Ape Social Systems." *Social Science Information* 18 (1979): 335–368.

Wrangham, R. W. "An Ecological Model of Female-Bonded Primate Groups." *Behaviour* 75 (1980): 262–299.

Wright, P. C. "Primate Ecology, Rainforest Conservation, and Economic Development: Building a National Park in Madagascar." *Evolutionary Anthropology* 1 (1992): 25–33.

Zhang, L., E. I. Ameca, G. Cowlishaw, et al. "Global Assessment of Primate Vulnerability to Extreme Climatic Events." *Nature Climate Change* 9 (2019): 554–561. doi: 10.1038/s41558-019-0508-7; and authors' correction. http://10.1038/s41558-019-0577-7.

Ziegler, T. E., and D. J. Wittwer. "Fecal Steroid Research in the Field and Laboratory: Improved Methods for Storage, Transport, Processing, and Analysis." *American Journal of Primatology* 67 (2005): 159–174.

CHAPTER 19

Behavioral Ecology: Background and Illustrative Example

James F. O'Connell and
Kristen Hawkes

Behavioral ecology (BE), also called *evolutionary ecology*, is a field of study based on the idea that a continuous process of natural selection among individual variants explains both the diversity of living things and their adaptive intricacy. Here we provide background on the overall enterprise and then review its treatment of one of the most fundamental problems in human evolution, the development of a distinctive pattern of life history, one that structures all aspects of our behavior from the Early Pleistocene onward.

BACKGROUND

Behavioral ecologists are concerned with *phenotypes*, the observable characteristics of individuals that result from the interaction of their genotypes with their developmental and socioecological environments. This strategy has been called the *phenotypic gambit*. While population genetics necessarily underlies BE, the genetics of most observed phenotypic variations remain poorly known. Behavioral ecologists assume that whatever the molecular pathways, a history of natural selection on small heritable variations has designed individuals' morphology, physiology, and behavior to serve their contribution to descendent gene pools, i.e., their *inclusive fitness* (Grafen 1991).

Recognizing that the world is infinitely complex, most behavioral ecologists focus on just a few aspects of phenotypic variation at a time. The usual process is to build simple models that identify a likely fitness-related *goal*, the *decision variable* associated with achieving it, the *tradeoffs* connected with the decision variable, the *currencies* in which those tradeoffs are measured, and the *constraints* that limit the actor's response, thus generating contingent hypotheses that can be assessed empirically. The models themselves are tautologies, always true by definition; it is hypotheses drawn from them that are tested. At risk in any

A Companion to Biological Anthropology, Second Edition. Edited by Clark Spencer Larsen.
© 2023 John Wiley & Sons Ltd. Published 2023 by John Wiley & Sons Ltd.

analysis are situationally specific propositions, not only about the fitness-related behavioral goal but also about currencies, tradeoffs, and constraints. When observations are inconsistent with hypotheses, the latter must be reassessed.

Fitness-related goals and tradeoffs have been seen by some as proxies for actual fitness, but behavioral ecologists usually seek to explain more immediate fitness-related goals and tradeoffs in phenotypic variants. Actual fitness itself, the relative representation of variants in future generations, is always subject to chance and ever-changing circumstances. As emphasized in George Williams' (1966) *Adaptation and Natural Selection*, the useful focus in behavioral ecology is on *design* for fitness because that results from a history of selection in the past.

Explanations for variation can take several forms. Following Niko Tinbergen (1963), behavioral ecologists identify four. Full explanation for any observed variation would require attention to all of them but they are not competing alternatives. Each entails different research agendas, different lines of evidence, and – especially important – answers to one are not answers to the others. *Proximate* explanations focus on the immediate triggers and machinery for an individual's tendency and capacity to do certain things in certain contexts. *Ontogenetic* explanations pertain to the development of those capacities and tendencies as individuals mature and experience their socioecologies. *Phylogenetic* explanations seek the deeper evolutionary genealogy of capacities and tendencies of interest: when in evolutionary history they emerged to persist and be shared among descendants of their common ancestors. Tinbergen called a fourth category *survival* explanations. These are concerned with the fitness *effects* of behavioral variation, appealing explicitly to natural selection: why those tendencies and capacities resulted in more descendants and so shifted descendant populations from the ancestral condition. These explanations are typically framed in terms of the model form outlined above, identifying likely fitness-related goals and tradeoffs, which then provide a series of contingent hypotheses amenable to test. BE explanations for phenotypic variation in physiology, morphology, and behavior are *functional* or *adaptive* in this sense. While fitness-related considerations are the primary focus in these analyses, phylogenetic, ontogenetic, and even proximate factors may sometimes be relevant for identifying constraints and the fitness-related costs and benefits of available alternatives.

Behavioral ecology emerged as a self-identified field of study beginning in the 1960s (Parker 2006). Comprehensive reviews of its form and development have been provided in several volumes edited by John Krebs and Nicholas Davies entitled *Behavioural Ecology: An Evolutionary Approach* (1978, 1984, 1991, 1997), which comprise chapters by specialists; and who also wrote a widely used student text, *An Introduction to Behavioural Ecology* (first edition by Krebs and Davies 1981 and fourth edition co-authored with Stuart West: Davies et al. 2012).

Applications in the study of human behavior began early in the development of the field (e.g., Chagnon and Irons 1979; Wilmsen 1973). Colleagues have distinguished a *human* behavioral ecology (e.g., Borgerhoff Mulder 1991; Cronk et al. 2000; Hames 2014; Nettle et al. 2013; Smith and Winterhalder 1992; Winterhalder and Smith 2000), with topical coverage now including resource choice, competition, ownership, parental effort, sexual selection, cooperation, sharing, collective action, and life history. Archaeological applications have focused on subsistence, technology, habitat modification, colonization processes, demography, agricultural origins, hereditary inequality, and material signaling of social identity (Bird and O'Connell 2006). Paleoanthropological treatments remain limited but are promising (see below).

Review of all this work or even a significant part of it is well beyond this chapter. Instead, we identify a broad problem in human evolutionary history, show how we and others have attacked it from a BE perspective, and indicate how it might be further pursued going forward. The goal is to illustrate the scale of approach possible as well as the benefits for situating the exercise in evolutionary/behavioral ecology rather than a narrower *human* behavioral ecology.

EVOLUTION OF HUMAN LIFE HISTORY

We use the definition of life history employed in evolutionary/behavioral ecology: age-specific fertility and age-specific mortality across the lifespan. Those features are evident in population age structures. The problem can be framed by a selective summary of differences between our closest living relatives, members of genus *Pan* – best studied in chimpanzees (*Pan troglodytes*) (Muller et al. 2017) – and human hunter–gatherers, especially the Tanzanian Hadza (Blurton Jones 2016; Marlowe 2010) who occupy the closest modern analog for ecologies in which genus *Homo* evolved.

Chimpanzees live in communities that may include more than 100 members but are encountered in much smaller parties varying in age/sex composition. Infants begin to pick food for themselves while they are carried along by their still-nursing mothers and become independent feeders at four to five years. While diets are broadly similar between the sexes, adult males also hunt and consume small animals. Sexual maturity is about age 12 when females usually leave their natal community. While females solicit copulations with multiple mates, males aggressively coerce female preferences (van Schaik and Janson 2000). Adolescent males gain paternities on just-maturing females as adult males prefer older mates, the highest ranked male monopolizing access to older females when conception is most likely (Muller et al. 2020). Lifespans seldom exceed 45 years. Aging faster than humans, females usually die before menopause.

Most living hunter–gatherers are also part of larger communities, usually numbering several hundred members, but are typically encountered in smaller, often changing, coresident clusters commonly numbering 25–50 individuals of mixed ages and sexes (Kelly 2013). Like chimpanzees, these break into smaller parties throughout the day. Unlike chimpanzees, nuclear families – one adult male and female and their children – are core components of residential clusters and are often identified as units of common economic and reproductive interest. Food acquisition among adults is structured by gender, females generally targeting plants and small game, males pursuing larger prey (Bliege Bird et al. 2009). Products of men's hunting are shared widely within local groups; those of women's foraging much less so. Juveniles are weaned at ages 2–4 years, well before they reach nutritional independence. Though they may contribute part of their own nutritional needs as early as age five, they are routinely provisioned by adults, including but not limited to close kin. Even as adults, people do not acquire all they eat or eat all they acquire. Females bear their first offspring at about age 18, with age-specific fertility declining to zero before 50 (Blurton Jones 2016; Hill and Hurtado 1996; Howell 1979). First offspring is later in males and some men win paternities well into their sixties. Though life expectancy at birth in the best-known populations averages less than 40 years, lifespans are much longer than in chimpanzees. In these same hunter–gatherer populations, those reaching age 45 enjoy on average an additional 20 years of life. As in all other human populations, child-bearing ends by about 45 but women remain physically active well past that threshold.

It is commonly assumed that the modern chimpanzee pattern represents something close to the ancestral hominin condition, prevalent before chimpanzee and modern human lineages diverged about 5–8 million years ago (5–8 Ma) and persisting in descendant hominins until the evolution of genus *Homo* 2–3 Ma. It is further assumed that at least some elements of the human pattern, notably later maturity, longer lifespans, and nuclear family social organization began to develop about two million years ago, prompted by long-term increases in aridity and seasonality in African hominin homelands (Antón et al. 2014). The question is how to account for the emergence of that pattern. The argument most widely favored, called the *hunting hypothesis*, holds that changes in climate and environment restricted tropical forests and fostered the spread of savannas, increasing the abundance of prey not previously taken by hominins, notably large ungulates (Washburn and Lancaster 1968). A *sexual division of labor* developed as ancestral males hunted newly available large animal prey and brought them to a home base to share with mates and offspring in exchange for relatively exclusive sexual access. Provisioning enabled mothers to raise more offspring; hunting favored larger brains and delayed maturity for more learning and practice of skills that benefited from improved cognitive capabilities. Nuclear families were a product of these developments. Archaeological evidence of access to large ungulates through some combination of hunting and aggressive scavenging, roughly coincident with the emergence of large-bodied, large-brained *Homo*, is seen to offer strong support for the overall hypothesis (Isaac 1978). Versions of this argument have been the predominant model of early human evolution for the last six decades (Alger et al. 2020; Hill 1982; Kaplan et al. 2000; Washburn and Lancaster 1968).

Behavioral ecologists have critiqued these ideas along several lines, drawing on aspects of hunter–gatherer ethnography, life history theory, and related formal modeling, as well as the integration of the results with hominin fossil and archaeological evidence. Five lines of evidence and argument are salient.

Food Choice

Formal models collectively called *optimal foraging theory* (prey and patch choice, marginal value) are central here. Models most widely cited are deterministic, ignoring variance and assuming that a forager's fitness-related goal is to maximize the average rate of nutrient acquisition, although risk-sensitive foraging models have also been useful (Stephens and Krebs 1986). Analysts employing the classic models hypothesize that hunter–gatherers choose among foraging sites and potential prey to meet that mean rate maximizing goal. Charnov's (1976) version of the basic prey or optimal diet model is the one most frequently employed in anthropology. It makes the simplifying assumption that foragers encounter potential prey of various types at random in an otherwise undifferentiated environment. Prey are ranked by average rate of energy gain during the time required to pursue, collect, and process them for consumption. At each encounter with a food item, foragers decide whether to *handle* it or continue to search for one of higher rank, a decision based on their familiarity with the environment and assessment of those options. Declines in encounter rates for high-ranked prey prompt the forager to handle a broader range of resources, adding them to the diet in order by rank to the point that returns from handling the next lowest ranked item fall below those expected from continuing to search for and handle higher ranked ones. Changes in encounter rates may result from shifts in the intensity of forager predation or environmental variation independent of forager action. Among the potentially counter-intuitive implications are: (1) prey choice depends on the encounter rates for higher ranked prey and is independent of the abundance of lower ranked items; (2) investments in search efficiency are advantageous when diets are narrow, those in handling technology when diets are broad – as more different types of resources are added to the diet, more time is spent handling, raising payoffs for handling efficiency and technological diversification (Hawkes and O'Connell 1992)

Ethnographic research has shown that foraging women are concerned with their daily production; sensitive to hungry children, they tend to target resources for which success is reliable (Hawkes 1991, 1992). Children's size and strength affect their foraging capacities: they take resources that adults usually pass by because their slower walking speeds reduce their encounter rates with high-ranked prey (Bird and Bliege Bird 2002). Mothers sometimes take advantage of their children's abilities by choosing resources that provide *team* returns greater than those they could earn by maximizing their own personal return rates (Blurton Jones et al. 1994; Hawkes et al. 1995).

Men's choices often do not fit this pattern. Data from the Hadza are especially relevant here. During an 11-month observation period (September 1985 to July 1986), Hadza men devoted 20-fold more time to the pursuit of large game (adult weights >40 kg) rather than small, even though their success rates for the former average one animal acquired every 30 hunter-days versus two of every three hunter-days for the latter (Hawkes et al. 1991). The average body size of their large prey – 5 to >100 times greater than the small ones – meant that far more meat was acquired on average *annually* because of the hunters' big game emphasis. However, their sporadic success rate meant that meat from big game was often unavailable to their families and other co-resident group members for days, occasionally weeks at a time. This counters a key element of the hunting hypothesis that men's focus on large animal prey is an effective day-to-day provisioning strategy. Moreover, most of the meat from a hunter's kill went to consumers other than his own family while that eaten by his own household often came from kills made by other hunters, a further challenge to the idea that this focus represents an effective form of *paternal* provisioning (Hawkes et al. 2001a, 2001b; cf. Hawkes et al. 2014; Wood and Marlowe 2014).

The wide sharing of big animal carcasses can be explained by Nicholas Blurton Jones's (1987) behavioral ecology defendability model of *tolerated theft*. The model identifies the difference in utility that the same share will have to different individuals depending on how much they have already claimed. Once any claimants have some, the next shares are worth less to them than to those without. Costs of not allowing other members of the local group to claim shares of large-package, divisible resources they value more would be more than they are worth.

As Blurton Jones noted, widespread observations of sharing are commonly seen as risk reduction for the group or as a form of reciprocal exchange among individuals – "I give to you now when I'm successful so you will repay me later when fortunes are reversed." Hadza data show that even with wide sharing, the risk of having no meat remains substantial. Children must eat nearly every day to thrive, yet the 1985–1986 data show that even with as many as 8–10 active hunters in a camp enjoying frequent but generally unsuccessful encounters with big game, "no meat" periods of a week or more were not uncommon. The exchange hypothesis is also countered by Hadza data and other hunter–gatherer sharing data sets as well (Hawkes et al. 2001a; Kaplan and Hill 1985), showing that shares go to consumers regardless of whether they have given to the successful hunter in the past or are likely to do so in the future. Moreover, hunters who are more successful spend more time hunting, continuing to supply more that will be claimed by others.

This begs the obvious question: why did Hadza men devote so much time to big game hunting to the near-complete exclusion of many other foraging opportunities? If we assume a hunter's fitness-related goal is to feed his own household, then the choice between largely ignoring small animals and focusing on big ones takes the form familiarly known in game theory as the *prisoner's dilemma* (Hawkes 1992, 1993; Hawkes et al. 1991). There is more overall when more hunters target big game, but a hunter does better for his family to take smaller prey he could keep exclusively for them. Since shares of big game are claimed by all, those carcasses are like public goods, engaging long-recognized problems of collective action (Olson 1965). A hunter prioritizing food for his own household does better by spending his limited time on things he can keep for them alone while they also consume public goods supplied by others.

LIFE HISTORY

Recall those aspects of female reproduction that together distinguish humans, not just from chimpanzees and other primates but from all other mammals: long post-menopausal lifespans, weaning well before offspring are nutritionally independent, and stacking juvenile dependents. It is generally recognized that food provided by others covers the nutritional shortfall of those still-dependent juveniles, a practice now often called *cooperative breeding* (Hrdy 2009). As indicated, mid-1980s observations among the Hadza show that men's big game hunting does not meet this provisioning need in the modern environments most like those in which the early stages of human evolution unfolded. The absence in earlier times of the powerful bow and arrow technology used by the Hadza probably made meeting this goal even more unlikely.

Parallel observations further suggest that the critical provisioning role is filled by grand-mothers. Post-menopausal Hadza women are active, effective foragers into their seventies (Hawkes et al. 1989). They acquire high-value plant foods at daily low-variance rates equal to those achieved by childbearing-age women but with higher overall production because they spend more time at it. Their effect on grandchildren's nutritional welfare is evident: those children's weight gains correlate with mother's time spent foraging, except when mother has a newborn and her foraging effort is reduced. At those times, children's weight gains correlate with their grandmother's foraging effort (Hawkes et al. 1997). Older Hadza women's residence locations show them choosing to go where their productivity contributes most to dependent grandchildren; demographic analysis shows the substantial effects that living grandmothers have on children's survival (Blurton Jones 2016). All this directs analytic attention to multi-generational sets of closely related, interdependent women. This is a common pattern not just among hunter–gatherers but in a wide range of historical and modern societies (Sear 2016).

The economic productivity of foraging women past their childbearing years plus the fact that post-menopausal lifespans are ubiquitous features of living human populations makes explaining our longevity an important issue. Why did it evolve? While female fertility ends about the same age in humans and great apes, great apes age faster than humans and usually die while still cycling. Post-menopausal lifespans are not a consequence of public health institutions and modern medicine. In the demographically best-studied hunter–gatherer societies, all remote from those advantages, life expectancy at birth falls well below 40 years due to the short lives of many babies and children. However, girls who reach adulthood are much more likely than not to outlive their fertility.

Charnov's (1991, 1993; Charnov and Berrigan 1993) mammalian life history model provides a framework for addressing the question of why human longevity evolved. The model identifies adult mortality as the main determinant of other aspects of life history. Broadly speaking, when adult mortality is lower, selection favors variants that delay maturity to gain the benefits of growing longer to reach a larger adult size with greater productive capacity. However, that delay risks dying before reproducing. The greater that risk, the more selection favors variants for beginning fertility earlier, at a smaller body size. Charnov built his model informed by accumulating life history data across the class Mammalia, showing that lower adult mortality and later age at first offspring are correlated with each other as well as with lower rates of baby production. In taxa that mature later, mothers invest more in a singleton or litter before bearing the next one. Humans conform to this pattern of greater longevity paired with later maturity. Adult lifespans are longer and age at first birth later in humans than in great apes. But *unlike* them and other primates, as well as most other mammals, human females have a distinctive post-fertile life stage. Also, *unlike* them, later first birth in humans is not paired with longer birth intervals. Human intervals are shorter and weaning earlier compared to our great ape cousins.

The *grandmother hypothesis* (Hawkes and Coxworth 2013; Hawkes et al. 1998) suggests a possible explanation. Imagine an environmental change that spread habitats which favored resources that could give reliably high returns to adult foragers but not to infants and juveniles too small to exploit them. Mothers that committed to those habitats would have to provision their dependent offspring. That would lengthen their birth intervals and reduce their fertility. However, older females nearing the end of their own fertility would still be earning high reliable returns. Not bearing new offspring, their productivity could subsidize dependent grandchildren. Reliable subsidies would make selection favor mothers investing less in each offspring themselves and moving to next pregnancy sooner. More vigorous older females subsidizing more grandchildren would leave more descendants. Slower aging and greater peri- and post-menopausal vigor would spread in succeeding generations. Limitations on habitat choice imposed by youngsters' foraging capabilities would be relaxed, opening access to habitats previously unavailable to ancestral populations.

Roots, tubers, and corms (collectively *geophytes*) are among the resources this scenario suggests may have been exploited more intensively across this transition. Their abundance and distribution were favored in the highly seasonal arid and semi-arid settings that became more common over the last several million years. Many of them store water and carbohydrates that allow their persistence through periods of seasonal stress. This makes them potentially attractive to a wide range of consumers. A history of selection has given geophytes tactics to defend themselves, including living well below the ground surface, having a high fiber content, and accumulating chemical compounds that make them difficult to digest, in some cases even poisoning potential consumers. These qualities discourage many of those consumers, including great apes and human juveniles, but are readily circumvented with simple technologies, including sturdy digging sticks and cooking. Many taxa, even those that are heavily defended, are exploited by human foragers worldwide at rates high enough to support both the collector and 1–2 others. In the Hadza case, geophytes are key to mothers' and grandmothers' provisioning efforts year-round, especially during resource-poor dry seasons (Crittenden 2009; Hawkes et al. 1997).

MAMMALIAN BRAIN SCALING AND INFANT DEVELOPMENT

The proposal that grandmothers' foraging productivity drove the evolution of human longevity and with it longer developmental duration and shorter birth intervals has other consequences implied by regularities across the mammals and by comparative studies of primate infants. Barbara Finlay and colleagues (e.g., Finlay and Uchiyama 2017) have found aston-ishing regularity in the sequence of neuro-developmental events across the wide mamma-lian range of variation in brain size. Final brain size depends on the duration of development: when that lengthens, brains expand. Components that finish developing later are larger fractions of that final size. With adult mortality setting the duration of development in Charnov's mammal model, the size and scaling regularities in mammalian neural ontogeny exposed by Finlay and colleagues are the foundation for seeing shifts in ancestral hominin brain size as markers of changes in longevity.

If the evolution of human longevity *was* propelled by grandmother effects, then as lon-gevity and the duration of development increased and brain size expanded, mothers were shortening birth intervals. Shorter intervals were part of a shift in our evolution away from the independent mothering of other great apes. Sarah Hrdy (2009) has highlighted the survival challenges that shift posed for ancestral infants. While great ape infants are already feeding themselves and become fully independent at it before their mothers bear the next offspring, ancestral infants in our lineage found their mothers' attention elsewhere while they were still entirely dependent on adults for survival. Other ape babies need not actively attract attention and engagement since they have their mother's full commitment. If ances-tral infants in our radiation faced these novel survival challenges with brains that were maturing more slowly, then strong cumulative selection for the distinctive *social* precocious-ness so evident in otherwise helpless human babies came along with the evolution of our grandmothering life history (Hawkes 2020).

MODELING OUTCOMES

An obvious question is whether the evolutionary scenario outlined above is realistic; that is, whether the proposed provisioning model could lead to the transition from a chimpanzee-like life history that might approximate the ancestral hominin pattern to the one characteristic of modern humans. Charnov's mammal model aimed to explain the evolution of female life histories. Quantitative modeling exercises building on it have assumed the allometries he identified and used them to explore the sufficiency of grandmother effects to derive human-like longevity from a great ape-like ancestral condition. These exercises have entailed several mathematical forms and stipulations about key variables, including mortality, conception, and mutation rates, and have shown that it can (Chan et al. 2017; Kim et al. 2012, 2019). Among the more important findings are that: (1) the addition of grandmothers' subsidies for dependents can extend longevity under a wide range of circumstances, (2) grandmother effects both increase longevity and also maintain the end of female fertility before 50 years when both are allowed to vary, and (3) depending on mutation rates that affect longevity, the transition from a great ape-like to a modern human-like life history may be complete from within tens of thousands of years to more than a million.

Note that these are two-sex models, opening the door to the sexual conflict and sexual selection that behavioral ecologists expect in sexually reproducing organisms. Across the mammals, females develop a finite set of oocytes very early in life, then lose them continu-ously. Mammalian males, on the other hand, continue to produce sperm throughout adult-hood. Consequently, as aging slows and the fraction of post-menopausal females expands with grandmothering, the fraction of older, still-fertile males grows as well. That shifts the sex ratio in the fertile ages from a female bias that is typical of mammals including chimpan-zees to a male bias. Across well-studied hunter–gatherer populations, pair bonds are shorter where paternity opportunities are greater (Blurton Jones et al. 2000). Formal modeling and observations among a wide array of species show that when mating sex ratios are female-biased males gain more descendants by competing for each available paternity, but when the mating pool is male-biased, the increased competition favors mate guarding (Coxworth et al. 2015). Male strategies that claim and guard a mate usually win more paternities (Loo et al. 2017). Pair-bonded nuclear families typical of humans are an outcome.

APPLICATION TO THE PALEOANTHROPOLOGICAL RECORD

This requires evidence of changes in (1) hominin life history, (2) climate and environment of the sort flagged as essential elements of the grandmother hypothesis, and (3) hominin subsistence indicating the use of resources that younger juveniles cannot take for themselves but that adults can gather reliably at relatively high rates.

Brain sizes in the earliest known hominins, *Ardipithecus ramidus* (4.4–4.2 Ma), *Australopithecus anamensis* (4.2–3.8 Ma), and *Au. afarensis* (3.9–2.9 Ma), overlap those of modern chimpanzees: 300–500 cc. versus 300–450 cc. for the latter (Cofran 2018; Du et al. 2018; Haile-Selassie et al. 2019), implying similar adult life expectancies for all four. The earliest available brain size values for *Australopithecus*-derived *Homo*, 2.1–1.8 Ma, are nearly all in the 600–800 cc. range, indicating an increase in longevity in this lineage by this time. Data on early human age at maturity and weaning age are patchier but so far consistent with the grandmother variant of Charnov's model: maturity delayed relative to the chimpanzee pattern by 1.8 Ma (Dean 2016) and weaning age reduced by 2.0 Ma (Tacial et al. 2019). Although fully modern human life histories are not indicated, these data imply that the shift toward the human pattern had begun by 2.1–1.8 Ma, coincident with the earliest evidence for *H. erectus*, the first clear-cut representative of genus *Homo*. Significant from the perspective of the Charnov model, *H. erectus* is also estimated to have been 20–50 percent heavier than its Late Pliocene and Early Pleistocene antecedents (Ruff et al. 2018). How much earlier the transition began is unclear: a date just before 2.1 Ma is possible and so is one of up to 2.8 Ma, the earliest age assigned to pre-*erectus Homo* based on (contested) mandibular data (Villmoare et al. 2015; cf. Hawks et al. 2015). New data on human brain sizes >2.1 Ma should help resolve this issue.

Over the past several million years, major changes in climate have been driven by shifts in Earth's orbital geometry. Knowledge of the timing of these shifts paired with geological and biological proxies for climate change point to multimillennial periods of markedly high aridity and seasonality every few hundred thousand years from 5.0 Ma onward (Potts and Faith 2015). Those dated 2.7–2.5 Ma were especially dramatic and may have been the trigger that promoted departure from the chimpanzee and earlier hominin life history pattern. Why that transition should have occurred then rather than with earlier pulses in aridity and seasonality, at least one similar in scale, requires explanation, but none is immediately obvious. Nevertheless, the expected match between climate and life history change may be indicated.

Tracking the use of plant foods in the past, particularly geophytes that juveniles cannot take for themselves, is a difficult task, especially for the early Pleistocene. Recent developments in plant microfossil analysis may produce relevant data but have not yet done so (Hather 2016).

Archaeological evidence for human consumption of large ungulates, central to the hunting hypothesis, first appears in North and East Africa as early as 2.5 Ma (Pobiner 2020; Thompson et al. 2019). It becomes markedly more abundant after 2.0 Ma, but whether this shows a real change in early human diets is disputed: it may be a function of larger archaeological sample sizes rather than an index of more meat consumption (Barr et al. 2022). Archaeological data from 2.0 to 1.6 Ma show that early humans (probably *H. erectus*) acquired large animals in complete or nearly complete condition at this time, mainly during dry seasons (Linares Matás and Clark 2021; O'Connell et al. 1999, 2002). Whether earlier, non-*erectus* hominins could have done the same is unclear. Archaeo-faunal data from 2.5 to 2.0 Ma may reflect infrequent passive scavenging of large ungulate kills made and abandoned in heavily ravaged condition by those other predators. If so, the nutritional returns would have been minor (Blumenschine 1987; O'Connell et al. 1988).

If the apparent 2.0–1.9 Ma threshold is real, then it implies a significant increase in big game hunting and aggressive scavenging success after, possibly well after, the transition toward human life histories began. This change in large carcass access might have been a consequence of the life history shift but could not have been its cause. Even if it began in earnest coincident with that shift, it still might not have been the determining factor. The day-to-day unreliability of Hadza big game hunting in a modern setting like that in which the initial life history change began indicates the need for caution in drawing that inference.

This brings us back to the question raised above: if big game hunting is as unreliable as the 1985–1986 Hadza data indicate and most of the meat goes to non-family members, why do men devote so much time to it, to the near-complete exclusion of attention to small game they could take more consistently *and* keep for their own households? And why did post-2.0 Ma *Homo* do something similar, as suggested by the large archaeo-faunal assemblages from Olduvai and other East African localities, when comparatively limited early Pleistocene weaponry and the presence of a more diverse large carnivore guild (van Valkenburgh 2001) would have made the practice even less reliable and more dangerous than it is for the Hadza?

An argument for the Hadza appeals to sexual selection: successful hunters intermittently provide large quantities of a highly valued, widely shared resource, making them favored members of their communities, deserving of respect and deference (Hawkes 2004; Hawkes and Bliege Bird 2002; Smith 2004). The fact that big game hunting and aggressive interaction with large carnivores are dangerous further enhances the appeal of successful hunters as attractive allies and potentially formidable competitors. In short, men's status competition is the game and large ungulate hunting and aggressive scavenging an especially important venue in which to play it. Bonanzas that are widely consumed are a consequence, an important collective good supplied by that competition. The private fitness benefit for individual hunters, what Olson (1965) called a selective incentive, is *credit* for supplying that collective good. The fitness-related benefit is *not* improved differential welfare of the hunter's own offspring but the advantage he gains in mating competition (Blurton Jones 2016; Loo et al. 2020). Preference for younger females accompanied the evolution of post-menopausal longevity (Muller et al. 2020). Hunting reputations earn others' deference to the proprietary mate guarding that allows better hunters to claim and hold fertile wives through more of their adulthood (Blurton Jones 2016).

The same rationale applies in the Early Pleistocene. Post-menopausal longevity changed the fertile-age sex ratio from female- to male-biased, favoring a shift in male strategies from multiple mating to mate guarding. With more males competing, proprietary claims depended on others' deference. A reputation for success in acquiring big game meat – a highly valued, widely shared resource – earned that deference. By this reading of the evidence, longer lifespans driven by peri- and post-menopausal women's reliable foraging productivity ultimately led to the formation of nuclear families. Increased attention to big game hunting and scavenging was a product of that life history transition, not its cause (Coxworth et al. 2015). Instead of paternal provisioning, big game hunting was favored in ancestral populations as the socioecology of our evolution increased paternity competition, making others' deference to proprietary mating claims the effective way our male ancestors left more descendants (Loo et al. 2020).

SUMMARY

Evolutionary/behavioral ecology has become a well-established, productive framework for explaining phenotypic variation including among humans. The example reviewed here illustrates its form and the gains available from taking advantage of its reach. In addressing one of the most important problems in our own evolution, it draws on research in mammalian life history and neural ontogeny, sexual selection and mating strategies, social and economic behavior, quantitative modeling grounded in those fields, modern hunter–gatherer ethnography and chimpanzee ethology, and the fossil and archaeological records of hominin morphology and behavior from the late Pliocene onward. That broad reach exposes evolutionary regularities in phenotypic variation not evident in a more narrowly defined *human* behavioral ecology.

In the process, it has yielded unexpected findings, among them: that one can develop theoretically and empirically well-grounded *expectations* about patterning in features of life history and brain development rather than simply relying on discovering them in an inevitably incomplete fossil record; that contrary to conventional wisdom, brain size has not necessarily been a direct focus of selection in the hominin line but more likely a product of extended longevity; that post-menopausal women are critical players in the economics of foraging societies and probably have been since the Early Pleistocene – this in contrast to their invisible status in most hunter–gatherer ethnographies and nearly all models of human evolution; that big game hunting is not necessarily the reliable family provisioning strategy commonly assumed; that nuclear families are not the units of common economic and reproductive interest that paleoanthropologists and others take for granted; and that their emergence may have had more to do with the male mating competition aspect of sexual selection than is generally recognized.

We expect this expansion in perspective driven by evolutionary/behavioral ecology to continue – not just in reference to life history, neural development, and social appetites, but to an ever-widening range of problems in human ecology and evolution.

ACKNOWLEDGMENTS

Nicholas Blurton Jones and Eric Charnov, two anonymous reviewers and members of the University of Utah Archaeological Center discussion group, offered useful comments.

REFERENCES

Alger, I., P. L. Hooper, D. Cox, et al. "Paternal Provisioning Results from Ecological Change." *Proceedings of the National Academy of Sciences (USA)* 117 (2020): 10746–10754.

Antón, S. C., R. Potts, and L. C. Aiello. "Evolution of Early *Homo*: An Integrated Biological Perspective." *Science* 345 (2014): 1236828.

Barr, W. A., B. Pobiner, J. Rowan, et al. "No Sustained Increase in Zooarchaeological Evidence for Carnivory after the Appearance of *Homo erectus*." *Proceedings of the National Academy of Sciences (USA)* 119 (2022): e2115540119.

Bird, D. W., and R. Bliege Bird. "Children on the Reef." *Human Nature* 13 (2002): 269–297.

Bird, D. W., and J. F. O'Connell. "Behavioral Ecology and Archaeology." *Journal of Archaeological Research* 14 (2006): 143–188.

Bliege Bird, R., B. F. Codding, and D. B. Bird. "What Explains Differences in Men's and Women's Production? Determinants of Gendered Foraging Inequalities among Mardu." *Human Nature* 20 (2009): 105–129.

Blumenschine, R. J. "Characteristics of an Early Hominid Scavenging Niche." *Current Anthropology* 28 (1987): 383–407.

Blurton Jones, N. G. "Tolerated Theft, Suggestions About the Ecology and Evolution of Sharing, Hoarding and Scrounging." *Social Science Information* 26 (1987): 31–54.

Blurton Jones, N. G. *Demography and Evolutionary Ecology of Hadza Hunter-Gatherers.* Cambridge, UK: Cambridge University Press, 2016.

Blurton Jones, N. G., K. Hawkes, and P. Draper. "Foraging Returns of !Kung Adults and Children: Why Didn't !Kung Children Forage?" *Journal of Anthropological Research* 50 (1994): 217–248.

Blurton Jones, N. G., F. Marlowe, K. Hawkes, et al. "Hunter-Gatherer Divorce Rates and the Paternal Provisioning Theory of Human Monogamy." In *Adaptation and Human Behavior: An Anthropological Perspective.* Edited by L. Cronk, N. Chagnon, and W. Irons, 65–84. New York: Aldine de Gruyter, 2000.

Borgerhoff Mulder, M. "Human Behavioural Ecology." In *Behavioural Ecology: An Evolutionary Approach*, 3rd edn. Edited by J. R. Krebs and N. B. Davies, 69–98. Oxford: Blackwell, 1991.

Chagnon, N. A., and W. Irons. *Evolutionary Biology and Human Social Behavior: An Anthropological Perspective.* London: Duxbury Press, 1979.

Chan, M. H., K. Hawkes, and P. S. Kim. "Modelling the Evolution of Traits in a Two-Sex Population, with an Application to Grandmothering." *Bulletin of Mathematical Biology* 79 (2017): 2132–2148.

Charnov, E. L. "Optimal Foraging: Attack Strategy of a Mantid." *American Naturalist* 110 (1976): 141–151.

Charnov, E. L. "Evolution of Life History Variation Among Female Mammals." *Proceedings of the National Academy of Sciences (USA)* 88 (1991): 1134–1137.

Charnov, E. L. *Life History Invariants: Some Explorations of Symmetry in Evolutionary Ecology.* Oxford: Oxford University Press, 1993.

Charnov, E. L., and D. Berrigan. "Why Do Female Primates Have Such Long Lifespans and So Few Babies? *Or* Life in the Slow Lane." *Evolutionary Anthropology* 1 (1993): 191–194.

Cofran, Z. "Brain Size Growth in Wild and Captive Chimpanzees." *American Journal of Physical Anthropology* 80 (2018): 22876.

Coxworth, J. E., P. S. Kim, J. S. McQueen, et al. "Grandmothering Life Histories and Human Pair Bonding." *Proceedings of the National Academy of Sciences (USA)* 112 (2015): 11806–11811.

Crittenden, A. N. "Allomaternal Care and Juvenile Foraging Among the Hadza: Implications for the Evolution of Cooperative Breeding in Humans." PhD dissertation, University of California, San Diego, 2009.

Cronk, L., N. A. Chagnon, and W. Irons. *Adaptation and Human Behavior: An Anthropological Perspective.* New York: Aldine de Gruyter, 2000.

Davies, N. B., J. R. Krebs, and S. A. West. *An Introduction to Behavioural Ecology*, 4th edn. Oxford: Wiley-Blackwell, 2012.

Dean, M. C. "Measures of Maturation in Early Fossil Hominins: Events at the First Transition from Australopiths to Early *Homo*." *Philosophical Transactions of the Royal Society B* 371 (2016): 20150234.

Du, A., A. M. Zipkin, K. G. Hatala, et al. "Pattern and Process in Hominin Brain Size Evolution are Scale-Dependent." *Proceedings of the Royal Society B* 285 (2018): 20172738.

Finlay, B. L., and R. Uchiyama. "The Timing of Brain Maturation, Early Experience, and the Human Social Niche." In *Evolution of Nervous Systems*, 2nd edn., vol. 3. Edited by J. Cass, 123–148. Oxford: Elsevier, 2017.

Grafen, A. "Modeling in Behavioural Ecology." In *Behavioural Ecology: An Evolutionary Approach*, 3rd edn. Edited by J. R. Krebs and N. B. Davies, 5–31. Oxford: Blackwell Scientific, 1991.

Haile-Selassie, Y., S. M. Melillo, A. Vazzana, et al. "A 3.8-million-year-old Hominin Cranium from Woranso-Mille, Ethiopia." *Nature* 573 (2019): 214–219.

Hames, R. "Diversity in Human Behavioral Ecology." *Human Nature* 25 (2014): 443–447.

Hather, J. G. *Archaeological Parenchyma*. New York: Routledge, 2016.

Hawkes, K. "Showing Off: Tests of an Hypothesis about Men's Foraging Goals." *Ethology and Sociobiology* 12 (1991): 29–54.

Hawkes, K. "Sharing and Collective Action." In *Evolutionary Ecology and Human Behavior*. Edited by E. A. Smith and B. Winterhalder, 269–300. New York: Aldine de Gruyter, 1992.

Hawkes, K. "Why Hunter-Gatherers Work: An Ancient Version of the Problem of Public Goods." *Current Anthropology* 34 (1993): 341–361.

Hawkes, K. "Mating, Parenting and the Evolution of Human Pair Bonds." In *Kinship and Behavior in Primates*. Edited by B. Chapais and C. Berman, 443–473. Oxford: Oxford University Press, 2004.

Hawkes, K. "Cognitive Consequences of Our Grandmothering Life History: Cultural Learning Begins in Infancy." *Philosophical Transactions of the Royal Society B* 375 (2020): 20190501.

Hawkes, K., and R. Bliege Bird. "Showing Off, Handicap Signaling and the Evolution of Men's Work." *Evolutionary Anthropology* 11 (2002): 58–67.

Hawkes, K., and J. E. Coxworth. "Grandmothers and the Evolution of Human Longevity: A Review of Findings and Future Directions." *Evolutionary Anthropology* 22 (2013): 294–302.

Hawkes, K., and J. F. O'Connell. "On Optimal Foraging Models and Subsistence Transitions." *Current Anthropology* 33 (1992): 63–65.

Hawkes, K., J. F. O'Connell, and N. G. Blurton Jones. "Hardworking Hadza Grandmothers." In *Comparative Socioecology: The Behavioural Ecology of Humans and Other Mammals*. Edited by V. Standen and R. A. Foley, 341–366. London: Basil Blackwell, 1989.

Hawkes, K., J. F. O'Connell, and N. G. Blurton Jones. "Hunting Income Patterns Among the Hadza: Big Game, Common Goods, Foraging Goals and the Evolution of the Human Diet." *Philosophical Transactions of the Royal Society B* 334 (1991): 243–251.

Hawkes, K., J. F. O'Connell, and N. G. Blurton Jones. "Hadza Children's Foraging: Juvenile Dependency, Social Arrangements and Mobility Among Hunter-Gatherers." *Current Anthropology* 36 (1995): 688–700.

Hawkes, K., J. F. O'Connell, and N. G. Blurton Jones. "Hadza Women's Time Allocation, Offspring Provisioning and the Evolution of Post-menopausal Lifespans." *Current Anthropology* 38 (1997): 551–577.

Hawkes, K., J. F. O'Connell, N. G. Blurton Jones, et al. "Grandmothering, Menopause, and the Evolution of Human Life Histories." *Proceedings of the National Academy of Sciences (USA)* 95 (1998): 1336–1339.

Hawkes, K., J. F. O'Connell, and N. G. Blurton Jones. "Hadza Meat Sharing." *Evolution and Human Behavior* 22 (2001a): 113–142.

Hawkes, K., J. F. O'Connell, and N. G. Blurton Jones. "Hunting and Nuclear Families: Some Lessons from the Hadza about Men's Work." *Current Anthropology* 42 (2001b): 681–709.

Hawkes, K., J. F. O'Connell, and N. G. Blurton Jones. "More Lessons from the Hadza about Men's Work." *Human Nature* 25 (2014): 596–619.

Hawks, J., D. J. de Ruiter, and L. R. Berger. "Comment on 'Early *Homo* at 2.8 Ma from Ledi-Geraru, Ethiopia.'" *Science* 348 (2015): 1326.

Hill, K. "Hunting and Human Evolution." *Journal of Human Evolution* 11 (1982): 521–544.

Hill, K., and A. M. Hurtado. *Ache Life History: The Ecology and Demography of a Foraging People*. New York: Aldine Transaction, 1996.

Howell, N. *Demography of the Dobe !Kung*. New York: Academic Press, 1979.

Hrdy, S. B. *Mothers and Others: The Evolutionary Origins of Mutual Understanding*. Cambridge, MA: Belknap Press, 2009.

Isaac, G. Ll. "The Food Sharing Behavior of Protohuman Hominids." *Scientific American* 238, no. 4 (1978): 90–108.

Kaplan, H., and K. Hill. "Aché Food Sharing: Tests of Some Explanatory Hypotheses." *Current Anthropology* 26 (1985): 223–245.

Kaplan, H., K. Hill, J. Lancaster, et al. "A Theory of Human Life History Evolution: Diet, Intelligence, and Longevity." *Evolutionary Anthropology* 9 (2000): 156–185.

Kelly, R. L. *The Lifeways of Hunter-Gatherers: The Foraging Spectrum*. Cambridge, UK: Cambridge University Press, 2013.

Kim, P. S., J. E. Coxworth, and K. Hawkes. "Increased Longevity Evolves from Grandmothering." *Proceedings of the Royal Society B* 279 (2012): 4880–4884.

Kim, P. S., J. S. McQueen, and K. Hawkes. "Why Does Women's Fertility End in Mid-life? Grandmothering and Age at Last Birth." *Journal of Theoretical Biology* 461 (2019): 84–91.

Krebs, J. R., and N. B. Davies, eds. *Behavioural Ecology: An Evolutionary Approach*. Oxford: Blackwell Scientific, 1978 (later editions 1984, 1991, 1997).

Krebs, J. R., and N. B. Davies. *An Introduction to Behavioural Ecology*. Oxford: Blackwell, 1981 (later editions 1987, 1993, fourth edition Davies et al. 2012).

Linares-Matás, G. J., and J. Clark. "Seasonality and Oldowan Behavioral Variability in East Africa." *Journal of Human Evolution* 164 (2021): 103070.

Loo, S. L., K. Hawkes, and P. S. Kim. "Evolution of Male Strategies with Sex-Ratio-Dependent Pay-offs: Connecting Pair Bonds with Grandmothering." *Philosophical Transactions of the Royal Society B* 372 (2017): 20170041.

Loo, S. L., M. D. Weight, K. Hawkes, et al. "Why Males Compete Rather than Care, with an Application to Supplying Collective Goods." *Bulletin of Mathematical Biology* 82 (2020): 125.

Marlowe, F. *The Hadza Hunter-Gatherers of Tanzania*. Berkeley: University of California Press, 2010.

Muller, M. N., R. W. Wrangham, and D. R. Pilbeam, eds. *Chimpanzees and Human Evolution*. Cambridge, MA: Belknap Press, 2017.

Muller, M. N., N. G. Blurton Jones, F. Colchero, et al. "Sexual Dimorphism in Chimpanzee (*Pan troglodytes schweinfurthii*) and Human Age-specific Fertility." *Journal of Human Evolution* 144 (2020): 102795.

Nettle, D., M. A. Gibson, D. W. Lawson, et al. "Human Behavioral Ecology: Current Research and Future Prospects." *Behavioral Ecology* 24 (2013): 1031–1040.

O'Connell, J. F., K. Hawkes, and N. G. Blurton Jones. "Hadza Scavenging: Implications for Plio-Pleistocene Hominid Subsistence." *Current Anthropology* 29 (1988): 356–363.

O'Connell, J. F., K. Hawkes, and N. G. Blurton Jones. "Grandmothering and the Evolution of *Homo erectus*." *Journal of Human Evolution* 36 (1999): 461–485.

O'Connell, J. F., K. Hawkes, K. D. Lupo, et al. "Male Strategies and Plio-Pelistocene Archaeology." *Journal of Human Evolution* 43 (2002): 832–872.

Olson, M. *The Logic of Collective Action: Public Goods and the Theory of Groups*. Cambridge, MA: Harvard University Press, 1965.

Parker, G. A. "Behavioural Ecology: Natural History as Science." In *Essays in Animal Behaviour: Celebrating 50 Years of Animal Behaviour*. Edited by J. R. Lucas and L.W. Simmons, 23–56. Amsterdam: Elsevier, 2006.

Pobiner, B. L. "The Zooarchaeology and Paleoecology of Early Hominin Scavenging." *Evolutionary Anthropology* 29 (2020): 68–82.

Potts, R., and J. T. Faith. "Alternating High and Low Climate Variability: The Context of Natural Selection and Speciation in Plio-Pleistocene Hominin Evolution." *Journal of Human Evolution* 87 (2015): 5–20.

Ruff, C. B., M. L. Burgess, N. Squyres, et al. "Lower Limb Articular Scaling and Body Mass Estimation in Pliocene and Pleistocene Hominins." *Journal of Human Evolution* 115 (2018): 85–111.

Sear, R. "Beyond the Nuclear Family: An Evolutionary Perspective on Parenting." *Current Opinion in Psychology* 7 (2016): 98–103.

Smith, E. A. "Why Do Good Hunters Have Higher Reproductive Success?" *Human Nature* 15 (2004): 343–364.

Smith, E. A., and B. Winterhalder. *Evolutionary Ecology and Human Behavior*. New York: Aldine de Gruyter, 1992.

Stephens, D., and J. R. Krebs. *Foraging Theory*. Princeton: Princeton University Press, 1986.

Tacail, T., J. E. Martin, F. Arnaud-Godet, et al. "Calcium Isotopic Patterns in Enamel Reflect Different Nursing Behaviors Among South African Early Hominins." *Science Advances* 5 (2019): eaax3250.

Thompson, J., S. Carvalho, C. Marean, et al. "Origins of the Human Predatory Pattern: The Transition to Large Animal Exploitation by Early Hominins." *Current Anthropology* 60 (2019): 1–23.

Tinbergen, N. "On Aims and Methods of Ethology." *Zeitschrift für Tierpsychologie* 20 (1963): 410–433.

van Schaik, C. P., and C. H. Janson, eds. *Infanticide by Males and Its Implications*. Cambridge, UK: Cambridge University Press, 2000.

van Valkenburgh, B. "The Dog-Eat-Dog World of Carnivores: A Review of Past and Present Carnivore Community Dynamics." In *Meat-Eating and Human Evolution*. Edited by C. Stanford and H. T. Bunn, 101–121. Oxford: Oxford University Press, 2001.

Villmoore, B., W. H. Kimbel, C. Seyoum, et al. "Early *Homo* at 2.8 Ma from Ledi-Geraru, Ethiopia." *Science* 347 (2015): 1352–1355.

Washburn, S. L., and C. S. Lancaster. "The Evolution of Hunting." In *Man the Hunter*. Edited by R. B. Lee and I. DeVore, 293–303. Chicago: Aldine, 1968.

Williams, G. C. *Adaptation and Natural Selection: A Critique of Some Current Evolutionary Thought*. Princeton: Princeton University Press, 1966.

Wilmsen, E. N. "Interaction, Spacing Behavior, and the Organization of Hunting Bands." *Journal of Anthropological Research* 29 (1973): 1–31.

Winterhalder, B., and E. A. Smith. "Analyzing Adaptive Strategies: Human Behavioral Ecology at Twenty-Five." *Evolutionary Anthropology* 9 (2000): 51–72.

Wood, B. M., and F. W. Marlowe. "Toward a Reality Based Understanding of Hadza Men's Work." *Human Nature* 25 (2014): 620–630.

CHAPTER 20

Brain, Cognition, and Behavior in Humans and Other Primates

Elaine N. Miller and
Chet C. Sherwood

SECTION 1: MEASUREMENT OF BRAINS

Absolute Brain Size, Encephalization, and Neocorticalization

Nonhuman primate brains can be as tiny as the 2-gram brain of mouse lemurs or as big as the 500-gram brain of gorillas (Stephan et al. 1981). Because brain size is tightly linked to body size, comparative neuroscientists often use methods to examine relative brain size, or "encephalization." Encephalization refers to how much larger a species' brain size is relative to what would be expected for their body size based on the typical brain–body relationship for a comparative phylogenetic group (Jerison 1973). For example, primates are characterized by a high degree of encephalization compared to other mammals, meaning they have relatively large brains for their body sizes. From the earliest stages of prenatal development, a fetal primate has approximately twice the brain mass of a nonprimate fetus (Count 1947; Halley 2016). Notably, the rate of fetal brain growth is similar between primates and other mammals, indicating that primate fetal encephalization may be mostly attributed to a relatively slower rate of early somatic growth, causing the developing body to be proportionally small compared to the brain (Halley 2017; Sacher and Staffeldt 1974).

Three major grade shifts have occurred throughout primate evolution concerning relative brain size. First, strepsirrhines have brains that are approximately double in mass than would be expected for a mammal of the same body size; second, anthropoids have brains that are up to two times greater in mass than would be expected for a strepsirrhine of the same body size; third, modern humans demonstrate an exceptionally high degree of encephalization, with a brain up to four times greater in mass than would be expected for an anthropoid of the same body size (Halley and Deacon 2017). There is ongoing debate about the evolutionary drivers of relative brain size variation. The highly social lifestyle observed in many primate species is thought to impact encephalization, but more recent studies point to

A Companion to Biological Anthropology, Second Edition. Edited by Clark Spencer Larsen.
© 2023 John Wiley & Sons Ltd. Published 2023 by John Wiley & Sons Ltd.

ecological or dietary correlates; specifically, that frugivores tend to have larger relative brain sizes (DeCasien et al. 2017). Particular hypotheses have been put forth to explain how humans evolved to be exceptionally encephalized. The expensive tissue hypothesis proposes that humans increased the quality of their diet and reduced the size of high-energy consuming digestive organs to afford the metabolic needs of a large brain (Aiello and Wheeler 1995). Another hypothesis proposes that the exceptional degree of human encephalization is a result of developing unique skills in social cognition and the capacity for culture (Herrmann et al. 2007).

Although the concept of encephalization has long held significant influence in evolutionary neuroscience by providing a simple means of comparison for a wide range of species, it fails to consider size variation between parts of the brain such as the neocortex, thalamus, cerebellum, and brainstem. More recent studies have analyzed structures within the brain to compare species. Notably, primates have an enlarged neocortex relative to other brain parts (Barton and Harvey 2000; Finlay and Darlington 1995), which is thought to contribute to behavioral and cognitive functions. The neocortex includes primary sensory and motor areas, higher-order sensory and motor areas (which receive and process information from primary areas), and association areas. Cortical association areas function to integrate multimodal information from primary areas and higher-order secondary areas for advanced cognitive processes. One way in which an expanded neocortex can change brain function is by increasing the number of direct synaptic connections from the cerebral cortex to subcortical structures. For example, in humans, neurons of the motor cortex make more direct synaptic connections to neurons in the brainstem nucleus that controls muscles of the larynx (nucleus ambiguus) than has been observed in other primates. This rewiring of brain parts is believed to facilitate better vocal control for speech production in humans (Simonyan and Horwitz, 2011).

Gray Matter, White Matter, and Wrinkles

In larger mammalian brains, like those observed in large-bodied primates, the distance between brain areas increases, which introduces new challenges to coordinating neuronal signaling between functionally linked regions. In primates, white matter, which contains myelinated axon fiber bundles, hyperscales to the rest of the brain (i.e the volume of white matter increases at a disproportionately greater rate compared to the rest of the brain) (Barton and Harvey 2000). Although larger brains have a higher proportion of white matter compared to gray matter (Rilling and Insel 1999; Zhang and Sejnowski 2000), the cost of slower neurotransmission across long distances is still significant (Rilling and Van Den Heuvel 2018). To compensate, larger brains tend to have a higher proportion of wider axons with a more rapid conduction velocity, but these make only a small fraction of the total axons (Phillips et al. 2015; Wang et al. 2008). Another way to maintain efficient processing in a large brain is by simple reorganization of networks. Large brains have evolved small-world networks, with predominantly short-range local connections, made up of a few nodes, that can reach other networks in a few steps via a select few long-range projections. These long-range connections increase efficiency of communication by acting as shortcuts between nodes (Bassett and Bullmore 2006; Watts and Strogatz 1998).

Dynamics of gray matter growth relative to white matter have been theorized to influence folding patterns of the cerebral cortex (Mota and Herculano-Houzel 2015; Van Essen 1997). Gyrification refers to a high degree of cortical folding, which can be observed as the occurrence of wrinkling patterns on the outside of the cerebrum. Among primates, gyrification predictably increases as brain size increases (Zilles et al. 1989). Human cortical gyrification is generally in the range of what would be predicted for a primate of our brain size, with the exception of the prefrontal cortex, which is more gyrified than expected (Rilling and Insel 1999).

SECTION 2: PRIMATE BRAINS

Olfaction in Primate Brains

Early primates were small-bodied, nocturnal, and solitary creatures that evolved to fill the fine-branch niche in tropical forest habitats. With a new lifestyle came new adaptations and changes in brain organization. For example, over the course of evolution in the haplorrhine lineage, reliance on olfactory cues waned, resulting in the reduction of the olfactory bulb (Baron et al. 1983; Stephan and Andy 1964). Catarrhines effectively lost a functional vomernasal organ and accessory olfactory bulb, structures involved in detecting the water-soluble compounds used in sociosexual communication (Smith et al. 2001). However, some argue that primates remain olfactory-oriented to an extent that is underappreciated, as the number of olfactory bulb neurons in monkeys, apes, and humans is comparable to that of highly olfactory-oriented mammals (Ribeiro et al. 2014). Nevertheless, among the sensory modalities, it is undisputed that primates have remarkable visual adaptations that have changed how they see and interact with their environment.

Color Vision in Primate Brains

The visual pathway begins with the retina, which sits along the back of the eyeball. The retina contains rods, which are sensitive to low-light conditions, and cones, which contain particular opsin proteins that are sensitive to different wavelengths or colors. Early nocturnal primates, like other mammals, probably had a rod-dominated retina and were dichromatic, meaning they had a retina with only two color opsins: one that detects short wavelengths and the other that detects medium–long wavelengths. Of considerable importance to retinal evolution in primates is the acquisition of trichromacy. In some primate lineages, trichromatic vision, which enables further discrimination of colors between the red–green range, has evolved through opsin gene duplication events or heterozygous opsin alleles on the X chromosome. The common ancestor of catarrhines evolved routine trichromatic vision through opsin gene duplication. Similarly, the platyrrhine howler monkeys (*Alouatta*) also acquired trichromatic vision through an independent opsin gene duplication event. Other platyrrhine species have evolved polymorphisms for the medium–long opsin on the X chromosome. With two X chromosomes, females can be heterozygous at this locus and have trichromatic vision (Jacobs 2008). Similarly, several diurnal lemur taxa show variation in X-linked opsin alleles to enable trichromatic vision in females (Jacobs et al. 2017).

The evolution of trichromatic vision is believed to have transformed life for primates by allowing them to detect ripe fruits, vibrant flowers, and young protein-rich leaves that vary in shades of red, green, and yellow. Haplorrhines further refined high-acuity color vision for fine-grained spatial discrimination by developing a fovea, which is a depression in the center of the retina that is densely packed with cones (Bringmann et al. 2018).

Visually-Guided Reaching in Primate Brains

Beyond seeing in three colors, other visual adaptations enabled success in the fine-branch niche for early primates by providing advantages for moving in forest canopies and foraging for animal and plant foods. As primates have forward-facing eyes, each retina receives input from both the left and right visual hemifields with substantial binocular overlap from the center of the visual field. Visual input is carried from the optic nerve to the lateral geniculate nucleus (LGN) of the thalamus and then to cortical layer IV of the primary visual cortex (V1). The axons of the optic nerve in primates leave the retina and before reaching the LGN are crossed such that the visual cortex of each hemisphere receives information from both eyes. This particular organization of crossing optic fibers enables stereoscopic depth perception. From V1, visual information can be further processed in either the ventral stream, which takes place in the temporal cortex, or dorsal stream, which takes place in the posterior parietal cortex (PPC) (Mishkin et al. 1983; Ungerleider and Mishkin 1982). The ventral stream functions to process perception of an object's features such as its color, size, and shape, and is involved in facial recognition. The dorsal stream functions to drive motor movements for skilled actions to engage with objects (Goodale and Milner 1992).

One of the first anatomical areas to process visual information in the dorsal stream is the middle temporal area (MT), which is believed to be a unique innovation of primate brains that is important for visual motion processing (Allman and Kaas 1971; Krubitzer and Kass 1990). MT, and other visual areas, make connections to the PPC (Baizer et al. 1991) and the PPC makes connections with the frontal cortex to form parietal-frontal networks (Kaas and Stepniewska 2016). These connections drive visually guided reaching and grasping behaviors that aid primates in obtaining food resources as they collect fruit and leaves or hunt for prey (Goodale and Milner 1992). For example, in macaques, it has been shown that the lateral intraparietal area shifts gaze to fields of interest through its connections to the frontal eye fields (Blatt et al. 1990; Colby et al. 1996). The caudomedial intraparietal area drives reach movements through its connections to the dorsal premotor area (Batista et al. 1999; Caminiti et al. 1996). There are multiple parietal–frontal connections that facilitate grasping movements (Gharbawie et al. 2011), but the connections between the anterior intraparietal area and ventral premotor area make up the primary network for grasping action (Luppino et al. 1999; Sakata et al. 1995) (Figure 20.1). These parietal–frontal networks are unique in primates as most mammals have few, relatively small, cortical areas that are homologous to the numerous and expanded primate posterior parietal and premotor cortices (Krubitzer 2009; Remple et al. 2007; Wu et al. 2000).

Learning and Problem Solving in Primate Brains

As parietal–frontal networks evolved in primates, the prefrontal cortex (PFC) appears to have expanded. Early primates evolved a novel set of prefrontal areas and anthropoids further expanded the PFC with additional areas (Preuss and Goldman-Rakic, 1991a, 1991b, 1991c). At the onset of primate evolution, stem euprimates emerged with two novel prefrontal areas: the granular orbitofrontal cortex and the caudal PFC. The granular orbitofrontal cortex is specialized in tracking the changes in value of predicted outcomes, which allows primates to optimize decision-making (Rhodes and Murray 2013; Rudebeck et al. 2013). The caudal PFC, including the frontal eye fields, was initially defined by its role in controlling eye movements, but now has been shown to play a role in searching and attending to valuable items in chaotic surroundings (Armstrong and Moore 2007). Anthropoids further expanded the prefrontal areas of the neocortex that are involved with rapid learning and problem solving (Browning et al. 2007; Bussey et al. 2001, 2002).

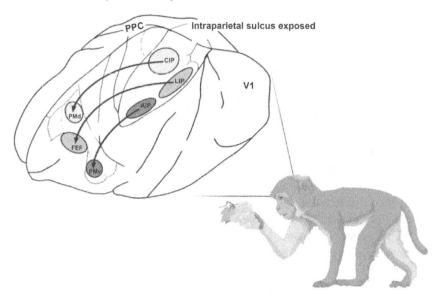

Figure 20.1   Parietal-frontal networks that control visually-guided reaching and grasping. Macaque monkey gazing, reaching, and grasping for grapes and macaque monkey brain with arrows that show connections between the posterior parietal cortex and frontal cortex. The caudomedial intraparietal area (CIP) and dorsal premotor area (PMd) shown in light gray are specialized for reach movements, lateral intraparietal area (LIP), and frontal eye fields (FEF) shown in medium gray are specialized for gaze, and anterior intraparietal area (AIP) and ventral premotor area (PMv) shown in dark gray are specialized for grasp movements. Image of macaque monkey gazing, reaching, and grasping for grapes created in BioRender. Image of parietal-frontal networks is modified from J. H. Kaas, H. X. Qi, and I. Stepniewska, "Evolution of Parietal-Frontal Networks in Primates," in *Evolution of Nervous Systems*, Edited by Jon H. Kaas, 287–295. London: Academic Press, 2017.

SECTION 3: THE HUMAN BRAIN

Hominin Fossil Endocasts

Unfortunately, brains and other soft tissues do not fossilize. Therefore, neuroscientists rely on methods of paleoneurology to cautiously glean information regarding neuroanatomical changes of the deep past from the size, shape, and impressions made inside fossil crania of extinct species. Apart from two exceptions (*Homo naledi* and *Homo floresiensis*) known to date, cranial capacity has gradually increased over the course of hominin evolution since the human lineage split from a common ancestor with chimpanzees and bonobos (Du et al. 2018).

Modern humans and Neandertals exhibit the largest endocranial volumes among hominins, which range in size from ~1,000 to 1,800 cc. Modern humans have a globular cranium unlike Neandertals who have a long, low cranium. Morphometric analyses demonstrate that human endocranial globularity is related to expansion of parietal and cerebellar regions (Pereira-Pedro et al. 2020). This is likely to be a genetically regulated phenotype; recent studies show that modern humans that carry certain introgressed Neandertal genetic variants tend to have a less globular brain shape (Gunz et al. 2019).

Endocasts from archaic hominins and some early members of the genus *Homo* display postorbital constriction (narrowing of the neurocranium behind the eye sockets) and deep temporal fossae (concavity in the area of cranium that covers the temporal lobe), which suggests relatively less endocranial space for the frontal lobe. In contrast, endocasts from modern humans and Neandertals demonstrate wider prefrontal areas evidenced by broader anterior cranial fossae at Broca's cap (area of cranium that covers Broca's area) (Bruner and Holloway 2010). Additionally, the crania of modern humans have bulging frontal squama (area of cranium that is referred to as the forehead) (Bruner et al. 2013). As the overall frontal lobe size of modern humans is unexceptional when scaled to overall brain size (Semendeferi et al. 1997, 2002), the wide prefrontal area and anterior fossae are thought to be associated with a redistribution of structures within the frontal lobe volume.

Additional hypotheses regarding cortical reorganization have emerged from interpreting the location of sulcal impressions on endocasts. For example, the lunate sulcus of *Australopithecus africanus* has been described as posteriorly positioned relative to that of chimpanzees, suggesting that the occipital lobe was reduced in size and the parietal association cortex was expanded. With this evidence, some have concluded that cortical reorganization was occurring before brain size increased substantially (Holloway et al. 2004). However, other analyses challenge this view. For example, Gunz et al. (2020) argue for an ape-like positioned lunate sulcus in DIK1-1, a three-year-old *Australopithecus afarensis* (Gunz et al. 2020).

Specialization of Human Brain Development

Comparative studies have shown that modern humans are exceptionally encephalized compared to other primates and the majority of hominins. This leads to questions regarding how such large brains develop. Humans and other primates undergo the same course of neurodevelopmental events (e.g., generation of neurons, myelination of neurons, and synapse formation/elimination) that are common to all vertebrate species, but the onset, peak, and completion of these milestones and the timing of birth relative to brain development varies widely (Workman et al. 2013). For highly encephalized humans, fetal development requires only a few weeks longer than chimpanzees and a few months longer than rhesus macaques. At birth, humans have larger brains compared to other primates, approximately twice the size of newborn great apes (Sakai et al. 2013; Sherwood and Gómez-Robles 2017). Despite spending more time *in utero* and having larger brains at birth, humans are born in a relatively underdeveloped state neurologically compared to other primates, which makes human infants especially dependent on caregivers (Trevathan and Rosenberg 2016). After birth, humans maintain a longer period of postnatal accelerated brain growth compared to other primates, during which time white matter volume expansion and myelination are primarily occurring (Halley 2017; Sakai et al. 2012, 2013). In all mammals, the brain continues to develop after birth, which allows for sensory stimuli to shape various neural circuits from the visual system to complex cognitive networks. In humans, this is the time when individuals acquire the capacity for sensory-dependent functions such as joint attention and acquisition of first words (Sherwood and Gómez-Robles 2017).

Two human-specific gene variants have recently garnered considerable interest for their involvement in human cortical development: *ARHGAP11B* and *NOTCH2NLB*. Both of these genes were duplicated in the human lineage and evolved new functions that affect neocortical development. *ARHGAP11B* was detected as a partial paralog to *ARHGAP11A* and is expressed in human neural stem cells. Functional assays in which *ARHGAP11B* was expressed in mouse neural stem cells resulted in a thicker proliferative zone in the fetal brain and increased mitoses to generate a greater number of cells. *ARHGAP11B* expression also led to increased folding of the cortical plate (Florio et al. 2015). *NOTCH2NLB* has been shown to maintain progenitor status in neural stem cells and produced a greater abundance of cortical neurons (Fiddes et al. 2018; Suzuki et al. 2018). The various mechanisms that increase overall brain size through enlarging the pool of proliferating neurons are key to understanding how evolution has acted to shape brain architecture and connectivity in humans.

Composition of the Human Brain

With the human brain being the largest of all primates, it predictably contains the greatest number of neurons (Herculano-Houzel et al. 2015). With ~ 16 billion neurons in the human cerebral cortex, it has been interpreted by some that the sheer magnitude of neurons in human brains forms the neural basis for the emergence of unique cognitive capacities (Herculano-Houzel 2009, 2011). Complicating this argument is the observation that at least one species has been reported to have nearly three-fold more cortical neurons than humans – the long-finned pilot whale who has 29–46 billion neurons in the cerebral cortex (Mortensen et al. 2014). It is therefore more probable that distinct cognitive capacities arise from a combination of factors including neuron numbers, as well as variation in other traits like cellular morphologies, gene and protein expression profiles, and connectivity patterns.

As the human brain is the largest of the primates and contains the most neurons, further studies have investigated the organization of cortical and subcortical areas. Humans have expanded association areas in terms of the proportion of total cortical volume. Morphometric studies have identified four "hotspots" in the association areas as regions of greatest expansion in the human brain compared to the brains of other species, including chimpanzees and macaque monkeys: inferior parietal cortex, superior and middle temporal cortex, lateral anterior PFC, as well as dorsomedial frontal cortex (Van Essen and Dierker 2007; Wei et al. 2019) (Figure 20.2). Of all the association areas, the PFC has attracted considerable attention because of its critical role in primate evolution. Volumetric studies based on architectonic delineations show that monkeys, apes, and humans display grade-level changes in PFC size relative to other parts of the brain, and that prefrontal white matter volumes are expanded in humans compared to great apes, gibbons, and cercopithecid monkeys (Passingham and Smaers 2014; Smaers et al. 2017). There is ongoing debate about whether the expansion of human cortical association areas is an expected outcome of brain scaling effects, or whether enlargement of certain association regions is beyond what is predictable for a primate of human brain size (Barton and Montgomery 2019; Smaers et al. 2017).

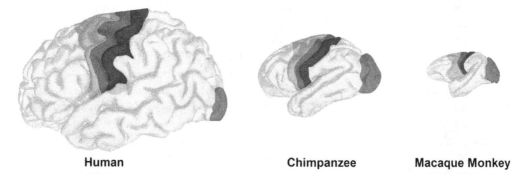

Human   **Chimpanzee**   **Macaque Monkey**

Figure 20.2 Association areas are expanded in human brains compared to chimpanzees and rhesus macaques. Cortical areas are shaded: primary somatosensory cortex (darkest gray), primary motor cortex (medium dark gray), primary visual cortex (medium gray), premotor cortex (light gray), primary auditory cortex (lightest gray). Unshaded cortex represents association areas.

In addition to size variation in cortical areas, there is also growing evidence for significant variation in subcortical structures between humans and other species. The hippocampus, which is critical for memory formation, is conserved across species in its general structure, but the human hippocampus is considerably larger than would be predicted for an ape of human brain volume (Barger et al. 2014). Further investigation has demonstrated that only specific subregions of the human hippocampal formation, including CA3, subiculum, and adjacent rhinal cortex, are relatively larger compared to other anthropoids. These volumetric changes in hippocampal subregions have been speculated to enhance the capacity for episodic memory and imagining oneself in different points of time, which is critical as one plans for the future (Vanier et al. 2019).

The amygdala can be subdivided into several nuclei, with four being most critical in social and emotional function: the lateral nucleus, basal nucleus, accessory basal nucleus, and central nucleus. In humans, the lateral nucleus is especially large while the basal and central nuclei are comparatively small, and the accessory basal nucleus falls within the range of what is expected for great apes. These changes in amygdala volume have been hypothesized to be linked to sociality in humans. The corticobasolateral area of the amygdala, which includes the expansive lateral nucleus, positively scales with social group size across primates and has been shown to be affected in social disorders in human patients (Barger et al. 2007).

Differences have also been observed in the size of nuclei that compose the dorsal thalamus. For example, mediodorsal thalamic nuclei are highly connected to association cortices and accordingly are relatively large and contain disproportionately more neurons in humans compared to apes (Armstrong 2012).

Sociality, Empathy, and Imitation

Understanding the neural substrates associated with a social lifestyle is key to defining how primates, and humans in particular, are adapted for living in large groups, sharing resources, and cooperating. Although many primates display social behaviors, modern humans are characterized by their extremely prosocial way of life and cultural practices. It has been hypothesized that a key subcortical structure called the striatum plays a critical role in promoting the evolution of human affiliative behaviors. The human striatum as a whole is smaller in size relative to what would be expected for an anthropoid of human brain size (Barger et al. 2014). However, humans are distinct from other primates as they display a higher degree of striatal dopaminergic innervation and a lower degree of striatal cholinergic innervation. These changes in the human striatal neurochemical profile might be associated with greater social conformity behaviors because the striatum is a key node in the social reward network (Hirter et al. 2021; Raghanti et al. 2018).

A major benefit of social living is acquiring information from the experience of others through functions such as empathy. The anterior insula and the anterior cingulate cortex are two key regions that allow an individual to experience empathic emotional understanding (Fan et al. 2011). For example, the anterior insula encodes disgust in an individual who is simply observing another individual express disgust (Krolak-Salmon et al. 2003; Phillips et al. 1997). This mechanism allows an observer to have a viscerosensory (i.e., interoceptive) model based on another individual's experience. Furthermore, humans experience pain when they observe a loved one experience pain. This empathic response activates the anterior insula and anterior cingulate cortex while the other components of the pain network remain inactivated (Singer et al. 2004). Notably, the anterior insula and cingulate cortex are both regions that contain large, spindle-shaped cells called Von Economo neurons (VENs) (Von Economo 1926) that are more numerous in humans compared to other primates (Allman et al. 2011). Although VENs have been described in several species

(Raghanti et al. 2015), they appear to be especially critical for social understanding because their selective degeneration in human patients with frontotemporal dementia leads to a profound loss of empathy while sparing other cognitive abilities (Pasquini et al. 2020).

Beyond the acquisition of knowledge or experience of empathy, an individual can imitate conspecifics by learning to perform actions from the observation of others. Humans and chimpanzees tend to imitate, or precisely copy actions, whereas other primates, such as macaques, are known to emulate the product at the endpoint of action. Imitation involves the "mirror system", which is a network of frontal, parietal, and temporal brain areas that respond to observed and performed actions. In macaques and chimpanzees, this circuitry largely includes frontal–temporal connections whereas humans have more robust fontal–parietal and temporal–parietal connections. Notably, in both humans and chimpanzees these connections reach the inferior temporal cortex, whereas only in humans these connections are extended to reach the superior parietal cortex (Hecht et al. 2013).

Language

The human brain is remarkably specialized for speech and the syntactic properties of language. Classic hypotheses regarding the neural substrates associated with human language production and comprehension focus on two important nodes in the network: Broca's area in the inferior frontal gyrus and Wernicke's area in the posterior superior temporal lobe. Comparative studies have shown that Broca's and Wernicke's homologs are present in nonhuman primates, including apes and rhesus macaques (Rilling 2014). Compared to chimpanzees, Broca's area in humans is more enlarged than Wernicke's area (Sherwood et al. 2012), which might be related to increasing the neural resources devoted to syntax functions that create meaning from the ordering of words. Neuroimaging methods that allow for analysis of pathways in the brain have revealed that the arcuate fasciculus, the bundle of white matter axons that project between Broca's area and Wernicke's area, is common to anthropoid primates, but there are some pronounced differences among species. In macaques, projections of the arcuate fasciculus reach only the superior temporal sulcus, while in chimpanzees these projections extend further ventrally in some individuals to also reach the middle temporal gyrus. In humans, the arcuate fasciculus extends ventrally to the middle temporal gyrus and continue to reach ventrally into the inferior temporal gyrus (Rilling et al. 2008) (Figure 20.3). This area of the ventrolateral temporal cortex that is uniquely connected to the language network in humans is associated with semantic processing important for attaching meanings to words (Binder et al. 2009).

Brain areas associated with language display hemispheric specializations in function and structure. The majority of people demonstrate left-lateralized activity during language-related tasks (Frost et al. 1999). Furthermore, in humans, connections between Broca's area and temporal language areas tend to be stronger in the left hemisphere compared to the homologous tracts in chimpanzees and rhesus macaques (Rilling et al. 2008). This lateralized organization likely evolved to prioritize intra-hemispheric connections between language areas in order to minimize conduction delays. In humans, Broca's area is characterized by a lower global connection strength to other brain regions compared to chimpanzees, but also a relatively higher connection strength with other language areas (Ardesch et al. 2019). This finding reflects the specializations of the human brain connectome to enhance the performance of complex cognitive functions such as language.

Understanding the genomic basis of human language evolution has been an area of exciting research and the gene *FOXP2* has attracted considerable attention. *FOXP2* encodes a transcription factor that is crucial to the development of speech motor control

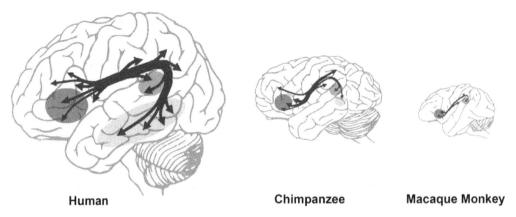

Human   **Chimpanzee**   **Macaque Monkey**

Figure 20.3 Humans show unique connectivity patterns between language areas. Black arrows represent the arcuate fasciculus – the white matter tract that connects prefrontal language areas to temporal language areas. Dark gray regions represent Broca's area (human) or Broca's homolog (chimpanzee and rhesus macaque). Medium gray regions represent a portion of Wernicke's area (human) or Wernicke's homolog (chimpanzee and rhesus macaque). Light gray regions represent middle and inferior temporal gyri (human) and middle temporal gyrus (chimpanzee). Images of language networks are modified from J. K. Rilling, M. F. Glasser, T. M. Preuss, et al., "The Evolution of the Arcuate Fasciculus Revealed with Comparative DTI," *Nature Neuroscience*, 11 (2008): 426–428.

in humans, and has also been shown to be involved in vocalization in mice, as well as song learning in birds (Chabout et al. 2016; Lai et al. 2001; Xiao et al. 2021). Humans have evolved a novel *FOXP2* variant that is characterized by two fixed, nonsynonymous mutations and is associated with changes in the development and structure of the cortex, basal ganglia, and cerebellum that affects orofacial motor control (Enard et al. 2009). The derived version of *FOXP2* has also been observed in Neandertals and Denisovans, indicating that certain aspects of brain plasticity important for the acquisition of speech and language may have been shared by several late hominin species (Krause et al. 2007; Meyer et al. 2012).

CONCLUSION

Biological anthropologists and neuroscientists have uncovered fascinating neural features that distinguish primates from other species. This has led to a greater understanding of how primates navigate their world and perform unique cognitive functions. With continued exploration, we will continue to answer questions about how variation IN brain size, structure, cellular composition, and connectivity patterns enable the traits that make primates, and especially humans, stand out in the animal kingdom.

REFERENCES

Aiello, L. C., and P. Wheeler. "The Expensive-Tissue Hypothesis: The Brain and the Digestive System in Human and Primate Evolution." *Current Anthropology* 36 (1995): 199–221.

Allman, J. M., and J. H. Kaas. "A Representation of the Visual Field in the Caudal Third of the Middle Temporal Gyrus of the Owl Monkey (*Aotus trivirgatus*)." *Brain Research* 31 (1971): 85–105.

Allman, J. M., N. A. Tetreault, A. Y. Hakeem, et al. "The von Economo Neurons in the Frontoinsular and Anterior Cingulate Cortex." *Annals of the New York Academy of Sciences* 1225 (2011): 59–71.

Ardesch, D. J., L. H. Scholtens, L. Li, et al. "Evolutionary Expansion of Connectivity Between Multimodal Association Areas in the Human Brain Compared with Chimpanzees." *Proceedings of the National Academy of Sciences* 116 (2019): 7101–7106.

Armstrong, E. "Limbic Thalamus: Anterior and Mediodorsal Nuclei." In *The Human Nervous System*. Edited by George Paxinos, 469–481. San Diego: Academic Press, 2012.

Armstrong, K. M., and T. Moore. "Rapid Enhancement of Visual Cortical Response Discriminability by Microstimulation of the Frontal Eye Field." *Proceedings of the National Academy of Sciences* 104 (2007): 9499–9504.

Baizer, J. S., L. G. Ungerleider, and R. Desimone. "Organization of Visual Inputs to the Inferior Temporal and Posterior Parietal Cortex in Macaques." *Journal of Neuroscience* 11 (1991): 168–190.

Barger, N., K. L. Hanson, K. Teffer, et al. "Evidence for Evolutionary Specialization in Human Limbic Structures." *Frontiers in Human Neuroscience* 8 (2014): 1–17.

Barger, N., L. Stefanacci, and K. Semendeferi. "A Comparative Volumetric Analysis of the Amygdaloid Complex and Basolateral Division in the Human and Ape Brain." *American Journal of Physical Anthropology* 134 (2007): 392–403.

Baron, G., H. D. Frahm, K. P. Bhatnagar, et al. "Comparison of Brain Structure Volumes in Insectivora and Primates. III. Main Olfactory Bulb (MOB)." *Journal fur Hirnforschung* 24 (1983): 551–568.

Barton, R. A., and P. H. Harvey. "Mosaic Evolution of Brain Structure in Mammals." *Nature* 405 (2000): 1055–1058.

Barton, R. A., and S. H. Montgomery. "Proportional versus Relative Size as Metrics in Human Brain Evolution." *Proceedings of the National Academy of Sciences* 116 (2019): 3–4.

Bassett, D. S., and E. D. Bullmore. "Small-World Brain Networks." *The Neuroscientist* 12 (2006): 512–523.

Batista, A. P., C. A. Buneo, L. H. Snyder, et al. "Reach Plans in Eye-Centered Coordinates." *Science* 285 (1999): 257–260.

Binder, J. R., R. H. Desai, W. W. Graves, et al. "Where Is the Semantic System? A Critical Review and Meta-analysis of 120 Functional Neuroimaging Studies." *Cerebral Cortex* 19 (2009): 2767–2796.

Blatt, G. J., R. A. Andersen, and G. R. Stoner. "Visual Receptive Field Organization and Cortico-cortical Connections of the Lateral Intraparietal Area (Area LIP) in the Macaque." *Journal of Comparative Neurology* 299 (1990): 421–445.

Bringmann, A., S. Syrbe, K. Görner, et al. "The Primate Fovea: Structure, Function and Development." *Progress in Retinal and Eye Research* 66 (2018): 49–84.

Browning, P. G., A. Easton, and D. Gaffan. "Frontal–Temporal Disconnection Abolishes Object Discrimination Learning Set in Macaque Monkeys." *Cerebral Cortex* 17 (2007): 859–864.

Bruner, E., S. Athreya, J. M. de la Cuetara, et al. "Geometric Variation of the Frontal Squama in the Genus *Homo*: Frontal Bulging and the Origin of Modern Human Morphology." *American Journal of Physical Anthropology* 150 (2013): 313–323.

Bruner, E., and R. L. Holloway. "A Bivariate Approach to the Widening of the Frontal Lobes in the Genus *Homo*." *Journal of Human Evolution* 58 (2010): 138–146.

Bussey, T. J., S. P. Wise, and E. A. Murray. "The Role of Ventral and Orbital Prefrontal Cortex in Conditional Visuomotor Learning and Strategy Use in Rhesus Monkeys (*Macaca mulatta*)." *Behavioral Neuroscience* 115 (2001): 971–982.

Bussey, T. J., S. P. Wise, and E. A. Murray. "Interaction of Ventral and Orbital Prefrontal Cortex with Inferotemporal Cortex in Conditional Visuomotor Learning." *Behavioral Neuroscience* 116 (2002): 703–715.

Caminiti, R., S. Ferraina, and P. B. Johnson. "The Sources of Visual Information to the Primate Frontal Lobe: A Novel Role for the Superior Parietal Lobule." *Cerebral Cortex* 6 (1996): 319–328.

Chabout, J., A. Sarkar, S. R. Patel, et al. "A Foxp2 Mutation Implicated in Human Speech Deficits Alters Sequencing of Ultrasonic Vocalizations in Adult Male Mice." *Frontiers in Behavioral Neuroscience* 10 (2016): 197.

Colby, C. L., J. R. Duhamel, and M. E. Goldberg. "Visual, Presaccadic, and Cognitive Activation of Single Neurons in Monkey Lateral Intraparietal Area." *Journal of Neurophysiology* 76 (1996): 2841–2852.

Count, E. W. "Brain and Body Weight in Man: Their Antecedents in Growth and Evolution: A Study in Dynamic Somatometry." *Annals of the New York Academy of Sciences* 46 (1947): 993–1122.

DeCasien, A. R., S. A. Williams, and J. P. Higham. "Primate Brain Size Is Predicted by Diet but Not Sociality." *Nature Ecology & Evolution* 1 (2017): 1–7.

Du, A., A. M. Zipkin, K. G. Hatala, et al. Pattern and Process in Hominin Brain Size Evolution Are Scale-Dependent. *Proceedings of the Royal Society B: Biological Sciences* 285 (2018): 20172738.

Enard, W., S. Gehre, K. Hammerschmidt, et al. "A Humanized Version of Foxp2 Affects Cortico-basal Ganglia Circuits in Mice." *Cell* 137 (2009): 961–971.

Fan, Y., N. W. Duncan, M. de Greck, et al. "Is There a Core Neural Network in Empathy? An fMRI Based Quantitative Meta-analysis." *Neuroscience & Biobehavioral Reviews* 35 (2011): 903–911.

Fiddes, I. T., G. A. Lodewijk, M. Mooring, et al. "Human-specific NOTCH2NL Genes Affect Notch Signaling and Cortical Neurogenesis." *Cell* 173 (2018): 1356–1369.

Finlay, B. L., and R. B. Darlington. "Linked Regularities in the Development and Evolution of Mammalian Brains." *Science* 268 (1995): 1578–1584.

Florio, M., M. Albert, E. Taverna, et al. "Human-Specific Gene ARHGAP11B Promotes Basal Progenitor Amplification and Neocortex Expansion." *Science* 347 (2015): 1465–1470.

Frost, J. A., J. R. Binder, J. A. Springer, et al. "Language Processing Is Strongly Left Lateralized in Both Sexes: Evidence from Functional MRI." *Brain* 122 (1999): 199–208.

Gharbawie, O. A., I. Stepniewska, H. Qi, et al. "Multiple Parietal–Frontal Pathways Mediate Grasping in Macaque Monkeys." *Journal of Neuroscience* 31 (2011): 11660–11677.

Goodale, M. A., and A. D. Milner. "Separate Visual Pathways for Perception and Action." *Trends in Neurosciences* 15 (1992): 20–25.

Gunz, P., A. K. Tilot, K. Wittfeld, et al. "Neandertal Introgression Sheds Light on Modern Human Endocranial Globularity." *Current Biology* 29 (2019): 120–127.

Gunz, P., S. Neubauer, D. Falk, et al. "*Australopithecus afarensis* Endocasts Suggest Ape-Like Brain Organization and Prolonged Brain Growth." *Science Advances* 6 (2020): 14 eaaz4729.

Halley, A. C. "Prenatal Brain–Body Allometry in Mammals." *Brain, Behavior & Evolution* 88 (2016): 14–24.

Halley, A. C. "Minimal Variation in Eutherian Brain Growth Rates During Fetal Neurogenesis." *Proceedings of the Royal Society B: Biological Sciences* 284 (2017): 20170219.

Halley, A. C., and T. W. Deacon. "The Developmental Basis of Evolutionary Trends in Primate Encephalization." In *Evolution of Nervous Systems*. Edited by Jon H. Kaas, 149–160. London: Academic Press, 2017.

Hecht, E. E., D. A. Gutman, T. M. Preuss, et al. "Process versus Product in Social Learning: Comparative Diffusion Tensor Imaging of Neural Systems for Action Execution–Observation Matching in Macaques, Chimpanzees, and Humans." *Cerebral Cortex* 23 (2013): 1014–1024.

Herculano-Houzel, S. "The Human Brain in Numbers: A Linearly Scaled-up Primate Brain." *Frontiers in Human Neuroscience* 3 (2009): 1–10.

Herculano-Houzel, S. "Brains Matter, Bodies Maybe Not: The Case for Examining Neuron Numbers Irrespective of Body Size." *Annals of the New York Academy of Sciences* 1225 (2011): 191–199.

Herculano-Houzel, S., K. Catania, P. R. Manger, et al. "Mammalian Brains Are Made of These: A Dataset of the Numbers and Densities of Neuronal and Nonneuronal Cells in the Brain of Glires, Primates, Scandentia, Eulipotyphlans, Afrotherians and Artiodactyls, and Their Relationship with Body Mass." *Brain, Behavior & Evolution* 86 (2015): 145–163.

Herrmann, E., J. Call, M. V. Hernández-Lloreda, et al. "Humans Have Evolved Specialized Skills of Social Cognition: The Cultural Intelligence Hypothesis." *Science* 317 (2007): 1360–1366.

Hirter, K. N., E. N. Miller, C. D. Stimpson, et al. "The Nucleus Accumbens and Ventral Pallidum Exhibit Greater Dopaminergic Innervation in Humans Compared to Other Primates." *Brain Structure & Function* 226 (2021): 1909–1923.

Holloway, R. L., R. J. Clarke, and P. V. Tobias. "Posterior Lunate Sulcus in *Australopithecus africanus*: Was Dart Right?" *Comptes Rendus Palevol* 3 (2004): 287–293.

Jacobs, G. H. "Primate Color Vision: A Comparative Perspective." *Visual Neuroscience* 25 (2008): 619–633.

Jacobs, R. L., T. S. MacFie, A. N. Spriggs, et al. "Novel Opsin Gene Variation in Large-Bodied, Diurnal Lemurs." *Biology Letters* 13 (2017): 20170050.

Jerison, H. J. *Evolution of the Brain and Intelligence.* New York and London: Academic Press, 1973.

Kaas, J. H., and I. Stepniewska. "Evolution of Posterior Parietal Cortex and Parietal-Frontal Networks for Specific Actions in Primates." *Journal of Comparative Neurology* 524 (2016): 595–608.

Kaas, J. H., H. X. Qi, and I. Stepniewska. "Evolution of Parietal-Frontal Networks in Primates." In *Evolution of Nervous Systems,* Edited by Jon H. Kaas, 287–295. London: Academic Press, 2017.

Krause, J., C. Lalueza-Fox, L. Orlando, et al. "The Derived FOXP2 Variant of Modern Humans Was Shared with Neandertals." *Current Biology* 17 (2007): 1908–1912.

Krolak-Salmon, P., M. A. Hénaff, J. Isnard, et al. "An Attention Modulated Response to Disgust in Human Ventral Anterior Insula." *Annals of Neurology: Official Journal of the American Neurological Association and the Child Neurology Society* 53 (2003): 446–453.

Krubitzer, L. "In Search of a Unifying Theory of Complex Brain Evolution." *Annals of the New York Academy of Sciences* 1156 (2009): 44–67.

Krubitzer, L. A., and J. H. Kass. "Cortical Connections of MT in Four Species of Primates: Areal, Modular, and Retinotopic Patterns." *Visual Neuroscience* 5 (1990): 165–204.

Lai, C. S., S. E. Fisher, J. A. Hurst, et al. "A Forkhead-Domain Gene is Mutated in a Severe Speech and Language Disorder." *Nature* 413 (2001): 519–523.

Luppino, G., A. Murata, P. Govoni, et al. "Largely Segregated Parietofrontal Connections Linking Rostral Intraparietal Cortex (Areas AIP and VIP) and the Ventral Premotor Cortex (Areas F5 and F4)." *Experimental Brain Research* 128 (1999): 181–187.

Meyer, M., M. Kircher, M. T. Gansauge, et al. "A High-Coverage Genome Sequence from an Archaic Denisovan Individual." *Science* 338 (2012): 222–226.

Mishkin, M., L. G. Ungerleider, and K. A. Macko. "Object Vision and Spatial Vision: Two Cortical Pathways." *Trends in Neurosciences* 6 (1983): 414–417.

Mortensen, H. S., B. Pakkenberg, M. Dam, et al. "Quantitative Relationships in Delphinid Neocortex." *Frontiers in Neuroanatomy* 8 (2014): 1–10.

Mota, B., and S. Herculano-Houzel. "Cortical Folding Scales Universally with Surface Area and Thickness, Not Number of Neurons." *Science* 349 (2015): 74–77.

Pasquini, L., A. L. Nana, G. Toller, et al. "Salience Network Atrophy Links Neuron Type-Specific Pathobiology to Loss of Empathy in Frontotemporal Dementia." *Cerebral Cortex* 30 (2020): 5387–5399.

Passingham, R. E., and J. B. Smaers. "Is the Prefrontal Cortex Especially Enlarged in the Human Brain? Allometric Relations and Remapping Factors." *Brain, Behavior & Evolution* 84 (2014): 156–166.

Pereira-Pedro, A. S., E. Bruner, P. Gunz, et al. "A Morphometric Comparison of the Parietal Lobe in Modern Humans and Neanderthals." *Journal of Human Evolution* 142 (2020): 102770.

Phillips, M. L., A. W. Young, C. Senior, et al. "A Specific Neural Substrate for Perceiving Facial Expressions of Disgust." *Nature* 389 (1997): 495–498.

Phillips, K. A., C. D. Stimpson, J. B. Smaers, et al. The Corpus Callosum in Primates: Processing Speed of Axons and the Evolution of Hemispheric Asymmetry. *Proceedings of the Royal Society B: Biological Sciences* 282 (2015): 20151535.

Preuss, T. M., and P. S. Goldman-Rakic. "Myelo- and Cytoarchitecture of the Granular Frontal Cortex and Surrounding Regions in the Strepsirhine Primate Galago and the Anthropoid Primate *Macaca*." *Journal of Comparative Neurology* 310 (1991a): 429–474.

Preuss, T. M., and P. S. Goldman-Rakic. "Ipsilateral Cortical Connections of Granular Frontal Cortex in the Strepsirhine Primate Galago, with Comparative Comments on Anthropoid Primates." *Journal of Comparative Neurology* 310 (1991b): 507–549.

Preuss, T. M., and P. S. Goldman-Rakic. "Architectonics of the Parietal and Temporal Association Cortex in the Strepsirhine Primate Galago Compared to the Anthropoid Primate *Macaca*." *Journal of Comparative Neurology* 310 (1991c): 475–506.

Raghanti, M. A., L. B. Spurlock, F. R. Treichler, et al. "An Analysis of von Economo Neurons in the Cerebral Cortex of Cetaceans, Artiodactyls, and Perissodactyls." *Brain Structure & Function* 220 (2015): 2303–2314.

Raghanti, M. A., M. K. Edler, A. R. Stephenson, et al. A Neurochemical Hypothesis for the Origin of Hominids. *Proceedings of the National Academy of Sciences* 115 (2018): E1108–E1116.

Remple, M. S., J. L. Reed, I. Stepniewska, et al. "The Organization of Frontoparietal Cortex in the Tree Shrew (*Tupaia Belangeri*): II. Connectional Evidence for a Frontal–Posterior Parietal Network." *Journal of Comparative Neurology* 501 (2007): 121–149.

Rhodes, S. E., and E. A. Murray. "Differential Effects of Amygdala, Orbital Prefrontal Cortex, and Prelimbic Cortex Lesions on Goal-Directed Behavior in Rhesus Macaques." *Journal of Neuroscience* 33 (2013): 3380–3389.

Ribeiro, P.F., P. R. Manger, K. C. Catania, et al. "Greater Addition of Neurons to the Olfactory Bulb than to the Cerebral Cortex of Eulipotyphlans but Not Rodents, Afrotherians or Primates." *Frontiers in Neuroanatomy* 8 (2014): 1–12.

Rilling, J. K. "Comparative Primate Neurobiology and the Evolution of Brain Language Systems." *Current Opinion in Neurobiology* 28 (2014): 10–14.

Rilling, J. K., and T. R. Insel. "The Primate Neocortex in Comparative Perspective Using Magnetic Resonance Imaging." *Journal of Human Evolution* 37 (1999): 191–223.

Rilling, J. K., and M. P. Van Den Heuvel. "Comparative Primate Connectomics." *Brain, Behavior & Evolution* 91 (2018): 170–179.

Rilling, J. K., M. F. Glasser, T. M. Preuss, et al. "The Evolution of the Arcuate Fasciculus Revealed with Comparative DTI." *Nature Neuroscience* 11 (2008): 426–428.

Rudebeck, P. H., R. C. Saunders, A. T. Prescott, et al. "Prefrontal Mechanisms of Behavioral Flexibility, Emotion Regulation and Value Updating." *Nature Neuroscience* 16 (2013): 1140–1145.

Sacher, G. A., and E. F. Staffeldt. "Relation of Gestation Time to Brain Weight for Placental Mammals: Implications for the Theory of Vertebrate Growth." *The American Naturalist* 108 (1974): 593–615.

Sakai, T., S. Hirata, K. Fuwa, et al. "Fetal Brain Development in Chimpanzees versus Humans." *Current Biology* 22 (2012): 791–792.

Sakai, T., M. Matsui, A. Mikami, et al. "Developmental Patterns of Chimpanzee Cerebral Tissues Provide Important Clues for Understanding the Remarkable Enlargement of the Human Brain." *Proceedings of the Royal Society B: Biological Sciences* 280 (2013): 20122398.

Sakata, H., M. Taira, A. Murata, et al. "Neural Mechanisms of Visual Guidance of Hand Action in the Parietal Cortex of the Monkey." *Cerebral Cortex* 5 (1995): 429–438.

Semendeferi, K., H. Damasio, R. Frank, et al. "The Evolution of the Frontal Lobes: A Volumetric Analysis Based on Three-Dimensional Reconstructions of Magnetic Resonance Scans of Human and Ape Brains." *Journal of Human Evolution* 32 (1997): 375–388.

Semendeferi, K., A. Lu, N. Schenker, et al. "Humans and Great Apes Share a Large Frontal Cortex." *Nature Neuroscience* 5 (2002): 272–276.

Sherwood, C. C., and A. Gómez-Robles. "Brain Plasticity and Human Evolution." *Annual Review of Anthropology* 46 (2017): 399–419.

Sherwood, C. C., A. L. Bauernfeind, S. Bianchi, et al. "Human Brain Evolution Writ Large and Small." *Progress in Brain Research* 195 (2012): 237–254.

Simonyan, K., and B. Horwitz. "Laryngeal Motor Cortex and Control of Speech in Humans." *The Neuroscientist* 17 (2011): 197–208.

Singer, T., B. Seymour, J. O'Doherty, et al. "Empathy for Pain Involves the Affective but Not Sensory Components of Pain." *Science* 303 (2004): 1157–1162.

Smaers, J. B., A. Gómez-Robles, A. N. Parks, et al. "Exceptional Evolutionary Expansion of Prefrontal Cortex in Great Apes and Humans." *Current Biology* 27 (2017): 714–720.

Smith, T. D., M. I. Siegel, and K. P. Bhatnagar. "Reappraisal of the Vomeronasal System of Catarrhine Primates: Ontogeny, Morphology, Functionality, and Persisting Questions." *The Anatomical Record* 265 (2001): 176–192.

Stephan, H., and O. J. Andy. "Quantitative Comparisons of Brain Structures from Insectivores to Primates." *American Zoologist* 4 (1964): 59–74.

Stephan, H., H. Frahm, and G. Baron. "New and Revised Data on Volumes of Brain Structures in Insectivores and Primates." *Folia Primatologica* 35 (1981): 1–29.

Suzuki, I. K., D. Gacquer, R. Van Heurck, et al. "Human-Specific NOTCH2NL Genes Expand Cortical Neurogenesis Through Delta/Notch Regulation." *Cell* 173 (2018): 1370–1384.

Trevathan, W. R., and K. R. Rosenberg. "Human Evolution and the Helpless Infant." In *Costly and Cute: Helpless Infants and Human Evolution*. Edited by Wenda R. Trevathan and Karen R. Rosenberg, 1–28. Albuquerque: University of N. M. Press, 2016.

Ungerleider, L. G., and M. Mishkin. "Two Cortical Visual Systems." In *Analysis of Visual Behavior.* Edited by David J. Ingle, Melvyn A. Goodale, and J. W. Mansfield Richard, 549–586. Cambridge: MIT Press, 1982.

Van Essen, D. C. "A Tension-Based Theory of Morphogenesis and Compact Wiring in the Central Nervous System." *Nature* 385 (1997): 313–318.

Van Essen, D. C., and D. L. Dierker. "Surface-Based and Probabilistic Atlases of Primate Cerebral Cortex." *Neuron* 56 (2007): 209–225.

Vanier, D. R., C. C. Sherwood, and J. B. Smaers. "Distinct Patterns of Hippocampal and Neocortical Evolution in Primates." *Brain, Behavior & Evolution* 93 (2019): 171–181.

Von Economo, C. F. "Eine Neue Art Spezialzellen des *Lobus cinguli* und *Lobus insulae*." *Zeitschrift für die gesamte Neurologie und Psychiatrie* 100 (1926): 706–712.

Wang, S. S. H., J. R. Shultz, M. J. Burish, et al. "Functional Trade-offs in White Matter Axonal Scaling." *Journal of Neuroscience* 28 (2008): 4047–4056.

Watts, D. J., and S. H. Strogatz. "Collective Dynamics of 'Small-World' Networks." *Nature* 393 (1998): 440–442.

Wei, Y., S. C. de Lange, L. H. Scholtens, et al. "Genetic Mapping and Evolutionary Analysis of Human-Expanded Cognitive Networks." *Nature Communications* 10 (2019): 1–11.

Workman, A. D., C. J. Charvet, B. Clancy, et al. "Modeling Transformations of Neurodevelopmental Sequences Across Mammalian Species." *Journal of Neuroscience* 33 (2013): 7368–7383.

Wu, C. W. H., N. P. Bichot, and J. H. Kaas. "Converging Evidence from Microstimulation, Architecture, and Connections for Multiple Motor Areas in the Frontal and Cingulate Cortex of Prosimian Primates." *Journal of Comparative Neurology* 423 (2000): 140–177.

Xiao, L., D. P. Merullo, T. M. Koch, et al. "Expression of FoxP2 in the Basal Ganglia Regulates Vocal Motor Sequences in the Adult Songbird." *Nature Communications* 12 (2021): 1–18.

Zhang, K., and T. J. Sejnowski. A Universal Scaling Law Between Gray Matter and White Matter of Cerebral Cortex. *Proceedings of the National Academy of Sciences* 97 (2000): 5621–5626.

Zilles, K., E. Armstrong, K. H. Moser, et al. "Gyrification in the Cerebral Cortex of Primates." *Brain, Behavior & Evolution* 34 (1989): 143–150.

PART **III**   **The Past and the Dead**

CHAPTER 21

Taphonomy and Biological Anthropology

Luis L. Cabo, Dennis C. Dirkmaat, and Andrea M. Zurek-Ost

Assemblage formation, alteration, and preservation are central issues to most biological anthropology interpretations regarding past populations or forensic settings. When considering demographic, behavioral, or biological community interaction patterns, we must ponder to what extent the composition of the recovered assemblage reflects that of the actual living community, and how much of it is the result of the differential deposition and degradation processes that the deposit experienced through time. When trying to date an assemblage, it is key to know if it was originally deposited at the recovery location or instead represents a secondary deposit transported there from another, older location by water or other transport agents or processes. One must also assess whether the whole assemblage is likely to have been deposited very rapidly, even as a single event, and thus represents a cross-section of a single, contemporary population, or if it instead may be the result of slow accumulation through maybe tens of millennia, containing an admixture of remains from individuals from very different times, generations, and even populations. In all forensic, paleontological, and bioarchaeological settings, the first step of bone trauma interpretation is determining which alterations were likely inflicted around the time of death and which ones occurred much later, when the organic matrix of the bone has been significantly degraded. The second task is determining which alterations are likely to have been inflicted by humans and which ones can be better explained as the action of nonhuman, natural degradation processes and agents.

In short, it is indeed hard to find examples of any forensic, archaeological, or evolutionary applications relating to biological anthropology that do not require prior inference on deposit formation and preservation issues.

Taphonomy is the scientific discipline that addresses these types of issues, focusing on the study of all processes, agents, and transformations affecting an organism from the time of its death and deposition to the time that its preserved remains reach the analyst's desk. In this chapter, we will review some examples of its main, primary applications in biological anthropology, how they came into being within biological anthropology, and how they have helped to transform and revitalize the discipline. We will also highlight some taphonomic literature to introduce and delve deeper into a variety of aspects of the field.

The Origin Story of Taphonomy

It is almost mandatory to start any review of taphonomy by mentioning that the term was coined by the Russian paleontologist Ivan Efremov (1908–1972) to describe the branch of paleontology devoted to "the study of the transition (in all its details) of animal remains from the biosphere into the lithosphere" (Efremov 1940: 85).

Not including plant remains in this definition is likely to have been an accident as, at least in the English translation of the original Russian article, botany is mentioned alongside zoology early in the paper. That omission hints at something that even the most superficial examination of the structure of the paper can confirm rather unequivocally: that Efremov did not intend that mid-text sentence as a formal definition of the field. Maybe for that reason, though it does provide a superbly concise overall description of the field as understood today, it does not work well as a standalone definition, and requires some clarifications to prevent common misinterpretations. For example, its mention of the transition to the lithosphere as the apparent endpoint may lead to the interpretation that lithification (the formation of true fossils via the substitution of all organic tissues with rock materials) is the primary target of the field. Were that to be the case, it would diminish the potential relevance of taphonomy for biological anthropology, as heavily lithified hominin assemblages are more the exception than the rule.

However, this is one of those cases in which one must follow the proverbial admonition to read the fine print, as the seemingly humble parenthetical "in all its details" is probably the most important part of that definition. Indeed, Efremov (1940) was entirely devoted to showing how the study of fossil formations cannot be limited to fossil diagenesis narrowly understood as the study of sedimentation and lithification processes, but must incorporate the study of all embedding processes, from the manner of death to decomposition, dismemberment, transport, and all remaining alterations suffered by the assemblage before and after interment.

Efremov's scientific background and the historical context in which his 1940 paper was written are essential to understanding its scope, and with it that of taphonomy as originally conceived. The first relevant element is that the creation of taphonomy was far from Efremov's main focus or contribution to paleontology, and the new field was conceived more as a tool than as an end. Both before and after his 1940 taphonomy paper, his main line of research focused on Permian terrestrial vertebrate faunas. In the three years before his seminal 1940 taphonomy paper, he had proposed the first classification of the Permian assemblages of land vertebrates from Eastern Europe (Golubev 2000, and references therein). He would keep improving this classification and remain a key contributor to the paleontology of that period for the rest of his career. Thus, taphonomy was originally conceived from the perspective of vertebrate paleontology, deeply influencing both the scope of taphonomy and its later intimate relationship with biological anthropology.

In the broader context of paleontology, the decades preceding Efremov's 1940 article had been profoundly impacted by the discovery of lagerstätten, such as the Burgess Shale fauna. Broadly speaking, lagerstätten (singular *lagerstätte*) are deposits showing exceptional fossil preservations, resulting in either large accumulations of well-preserved mineralized skeletal elements (*konzentrat-lagerstätten*) or the fossilization of soft tissues preserving their anatomical and even histological structures in delicate detail (*konservat-lagerstätten*) (Allison 1988). The Burgess Shale is a Middle Cambrian (~530 Ma) konservat-lagerstätte discovered in the Canadian Rockies in 1909, which had an extraordinary impact on bringing the importance of understanding assemblage formation and preservation processes to the forefront of paleontological research. Gould (1989) provides a detailed, delightful, and very accessible in-depth discussion of all matters relating to the Burgess Shale.

Before the Burgess Shale, trilobites were thought to absolutely dominate benthic and pelagic faunas during the first half of the Cambrian. Trilobites are extinct arthropods with sclerotized exoskeletons that typically represented over three-quarters of the species in most previously known Early and Middle Cambrian assemblages. In the Burgess Shale deposits only 37 percent of the recovered taxa are arthropods, including a notable representation of lightly sclerotized nontrilobite species, many from previously unknown arthropod classes (Morris 1979). Contrary to the image of the period portrayed by previous sites, around 80 percent of the Burgess Shale fauna was soft-bodied, revealing a previously unknown, fascinating, Cambrian diversity in groups such as polychaeta, priapulids, or sponges. In sum, the Burgess Shale provided a startling demonstration of the impact of preservation biases on palaeoecological reconstruction.

Most of the resulting research on those and other similar invertebrate deposits representing early aquatic environments targeted two processes that were very familiar to early twentieth century geologists following the chemistry revolution and the advances in stratigraphy and sedimentology of the second half of the previous century: sedimentation and chemical preservation (fossil diagenesis) processes.

The central argument in Efremov (1940), and thus the main impetus for the definition of taphonomy, is that the approach based primarily on those two elements (sedimentology and diagenesis) is neither sufficient nor appropriate for the study of terrestrial vertebrate deposits. After commenting on the incompleteness of the fossil record and the impact of preservation biases, Efremov introduces the interplay of complex processes that would become some of the central areas of taphonomic research in later decades: manner of death (necrology), disarticulation and transport processes, and time resolution issues derived from mode of deposition and burial.

If sedimentology and fossil diagenesis did not suffice to understand assemblages, then what fields should be invoked to complement them? Efremov (1940) was particularly open in recognizing that, in his proposal of taphonomy as a new scientific field, he was not creating any new methodologies, but simply advocating for the integration of already existing ones into a cohesive discipline. He was also very candid in detailing the sources of his ideas and rationale, crediting two German paleontologists, namely Johannes Weigelt and Rudolf Ritcher.

Weigelt (1890–1948) defined biostratinomy (originally *biostratanomy*) in 1919 as a discipline that studied all changes and processes of an organism from its death to its initial interment (Jablonski and Fairbridge 1979). In 1927 he published what may arguably be considered the first taphonomy monograph, translated into English as *Recent Vertebrate Carcasses and Their Paleobiological Implications* (Weigelt 1989). Rudolf Richter (1881–1956) proposed the discipline of actualistic paleontology (*Aktuo-paläontologie*) in 1928 as a science devoted to the study of current-day modes of formation of future fossils, in the broadest sense (Jablonski and Fairbridge 1979). Richter's actualistic paleontology overlaps widely with Weigelt's biostratinomy, but Richter's construct offered a much more rigorous, articulated, and scientific rationale, solidly anchored in the classic uniformitarianism of

Hutton and Lyell. Efremov (1940) recognized the value of Richter's view by devoting a very large portion of his paper to comprehensively explaining and discussing it.

In summary, as originally proposed by Efremov (1940), taphonomy was a discipline primarily defined by the scope and needs of vertebrate paleontologists studying terrestrial faunas and focusing on site formation processes. The main goal behind this perspective was controlling preservation biases in palaeoecological reconstruction, relying on two major components: (i) biostratinomy, focusing on all processes from death to deposition, and (ii) diagenesis, the classic approach focusing on physical and chemical alteration after burial.

A Slow Start in the West

Aside from defining taphonomy and its scope with admirable clarity and depth, Efremov (1940) listed several specific lines of research that he considered key to advancing taphonomy as a scientific field. In the years immediately following that publication, the end of World War II marked the start of what Norman D. Newell (1987) called the golden age of paleobiology, characterized by an abundance of funds for scientific research (first directly resulting from the war effort and later further stimulated by the Sputnik launches) and the fruits of the evolutionary synthesis, which brought together paleontology, genetics, and systematic biology.

However, Efremov's proposed agenda of field-advancing studies remained largely untouched in the West by the early 1960s, with the bulk of what nowadays would be considered taphonomic studies still focusing on the diagenetic context of invertebrate faunas, examined from the traditional diagenetic scope combining geochemistry and sedimentology. A very notable exception is Johnson (1960), who examined the formation of shallow-water marine assemblages from an actualistic and, basically, fully taphonomic approach, but without using the term *taphonomy* or citing Efremov's or Richter's work. In his 1961 review of the state of paleontology at the time, George Gaylord Simpson mentioned biostratinomy and taphonomy only to comment that "it may be a little premature to designate as distinct sciences fields in which, unfortunately, there is as yet little concrete accomplishment" (Simpson 1961: 1683). That dismal situation would start to change the following year with the publication of Olson (1962), a landmark that Dodson (1980) considered the first real introduction of Efremov's ideas in the USA. Like Efremov, Everett C. Olson specialized in Permian vertebrate communities. The volume includes a section on taphonomy, including that of terrestrial vertebrate faunas (Olson 1962: 134–139).

Olson's dissemination efforts seem to have rendered mixed initial results, because monographs published in subsequent years by some of his colleagues at the Field Museum did contain sections on the biostratinomy of vertebrate deposits, but still no mention of the term *taphonomy* or Efremov. Olson (1962: 134) noted how the term *taphonomy* had been scarcely used in the anglophone literature by 1962 and the paleoecologist David R. Lawrence repeated the same remark, in almost the exact same terms, almost a decade later (Lawrence 1971: 595). Most biostratinomic interpretations published in English before 1969 were still much more conjectural than empirical, lacking the actualistic scope central to Efremov's conception. The most notable exception came from German paleontology.

The year1962 witnessed the publication of a second landmark contribution to taphonomy, this time applied to marine environments, with the publication by German zoologist Wilhelm Schäfer of *Aktuo-Paläontologie: nach Studien in der Nordsee*, later translated into English as *Ecology and Palaeoecology of Marine Environments* (Schäfer 1972). Schäfer applied the fruits of three decades of Richter's actualistic vision to the study of current mortality, accumulation, and embedding patterns and processes in extant ecosystems of the North Sea. This introduced the concept of biofacies and related all those elements to species habitat and ecology. Schäfer's rationale and approach to link taphonomy and ecology are still relevant today. Indeed, Schäfer (1972) may be one of the more illuminating references to understanding some of the main elements of the original conception of taphonomy.

C. K. Brain (1967a, 1967b) published what may be the first two clear contributions to taphonomy from biological anthropology, although the term taphonomy was not referenced. Brain (1967a) demonstrated how some bone fragments with acute points or sharp edges, which had been considered as potential hominin-made tools, were actually natural artifacts (*pseudotools*) created by environmental factors such as sun exposure, eolic and sedimentological abrasion, and trampling. Brain (1967b) published a second study in which he examined skeletal representation patterns in a systematically collected faunal assemblage generated by an extant Hottentot community. This built on earlier work by Dale Guthrie (1967), who suggested that some mammal bones had a tendency to preserve better than others. Brain observed that the relative frequency with which each anatomical feature appeared in the bone assemblage simply reflected how resistant they were to natural degradation rather than human consumption or utilization patterns, finding marked differences between the patterns observed in the contemporary human assemblage and South African australopithecine sites (Brain 1967b, 1969, 1972, 2007).

According to Dodson (1980: 6), Lawrence (1968) represents the first appearance of the term *taphonomy* in the title of an article in a major Western journal. The study compared species representation in a living community of aquatic invertebrates versus that of the death assemblage collected from it (one of the types of studies proposed in Efremov 1940). Still, it was not until the very end of the decade that Voorhies (1969) published what probably represents the first Western publication, which clearly checks all boxes of taphonomy as proposed by Efremov (1940), including citation and discussion of his work. The study addressed a fully taphonomic question: reconstructing the depositional origin of a Pliocene vertebrate deposit, focusing squarely on the mechanisms of deposition of the type of terrestrial vertebrate accumulations that had inspired Efremov to propose the new field. Voorhies (1969) comprehensively discussed and recognized Efremov (1940) and Schäfer (1972) as key reference sources for the design of the study and, even more importantly, complemented the field and laboratory observations of the deposit with a set of experiments to test the hypothesis that the bone accumulation had been created by fluvial transport.

Aside from the type of materials addressed in the Voorhies (1969) study, and its actualistic scope, assemblage formation by water transport in terrestrial environments was one of the subjects explicitly mentioned in Efremov (1940) as one of the key areas in need of actualistic research. More importantly, Voorhies (1969) came to be more than a historical landmark and represents the first English study to fully embrace Efremov's (1940) subjects, materials, hypotheses, methods, and scope. Unlike most of the Efremov- or Richter-inspired studies discussed above, Voorhies (1969) had a very strong, immediate impact on the development and popularization of taphonomy, inspiring a flurry of follow-up studies on the depositional characteristics derived from water transport during the 1970s and 1980s.

Biological Anthropology and the Development of Modern Taphonomy

Following Voorhies (1969) and Brain (1967a, 1967b, 1969), the volume of taphonomy studies would explode in the 1970s, as the field underwent an adaptive radiation that would result in the definition of most broad study areas that we recognize today as classic taphonomic subjects in vertebrate paleontology, zooarchaeology, and biological anthropology. This growth spurt continued during the 1980s, as taphonomy gradually merged into those disciplines, not only as a useful tool, but as one of their essential components. Biological anthropology was at the front and center of that process, first through contributions to and from human paleontology, and later from zooarchaeology and bioarchaeology.

Part of that leadership is explained by attempts to refute Shotwell (1955) in his support of Raymond Dart's series of papers on his proposed osteodontokeratic culture (Dart 1949; Dart and Wolberg 1971; Mason et al. 1958; Wolberg 1970). These studies provided the nascent 1970s taphonomy with a set of highly visible, contested hypotheses to address, as well as an opportunity to showcase how Efremov's taphonomic approach provided the most effective tools and scope to do so by highlighting the interpretation errors rendered by some of the earlier approaches.

Shotwell (1955) had proposed that taxa representing proximal (i.e., local) communities would appear as more anatomically complete in an assemblage than those representing distal communities, which had been transported to the deposit from distant locations. Voorhies (1969) pointed to a diverse number of taphonomic sources of bias that would invalidate that view, demonstrating how actualistic sampling and experimental designs could be used to factor the effects of biostratinomic processes into quantitative interpretations.

Biostratinomy was also at the heart of Dart's osteodontokeratic culture hypothesis. Raymond Arthur Dart (1893–1988) studied the first australopithecine fossil, the famed Taung's Child from the homonymous site in South Africa, and defined the genus *Australopithecus*, alongside the species *Au. africanus* (Dart 1925). In his first description of the Taung remains (Dart 1925: 197), Dart already hypothesized that the combination of bipedalism and reduced canine size suggested that *Au. africanus* was a toolmaker. In his view, the release of the hands from their locomotory function indicated that they had adapted to complex manipulation. The loss of the large canines seen in other primate species suggested that *Au. africanus* had other defensive and offensive weapons, in the form of some sort of tool culture (Dart 1925, 1934).

However, the question of the inflicting tools remained since no lithic industry appeared associated with the australopithecine remains. During his work at Makapansgat, Dart thought he had found those tools in the faunal assemblage itself: he interpreted some bone fracture patterns of baboon skulls and surface alterations as intentional modifications, and thus altered bones as part of the australopithecine toolkit. To Dart, this was evidence that australopithecines were not only mighty hunters, but creatures viciously inclined toward interpersonal violence and cannibalism (Brain 1972).

This led to his proposal of an *osteodontokeratic* (*bone, teeth, and antler*) australopithecine culture in a long series of articles (Dart and Wolberg 1971, and references therein). Dart's complex osteodontokeratic construct faced criticism from the beginning. Contemporary reviews of the most relevant arguments for and against Dart's construct formulated up to the mid-1970s (e.g., Read-Martin et al. 1975; Wolberg 1970) reveal that most falsification attempts followed what we can term *the faunal analysis approach*.

Traditionally, the study of faunal remains from archaeological sites was largely segregated from that of vertebrate paleontology, being alternatively described as zooarchaeology, archaeozoology, osteoarchaeology, or ethnozoology (Olsen and Olsen 1981). The commonality between the studies spanning all of these different scopes was that they all could be grouped under the broader, more inclusive, and noncontroversial umbrella of *faunal analysis*, addressing a common set of topics that Lyman (1982: 179) characterized as "subsistence, diet, economy, hunting practices, butchery practices, seasonality, domestication, paleoenvironments, bone artifacts, and taxonomic identity."

Methodologically, most traditional faunal analysis approaches had been characterized by a focus on taxonomic identification and skeletal part representation, with the main classic references being essentially identification guides, annotated with some general comments on basic interpretations of species or skeletal part frequencies (e.g., Chaplin 1971; Cornwall 1956; Olsen 1971). The necessity of taxon identification resulted in many pre-1980s faunal analyses presenting as taxonomic "laundry lists" (but see Lyman 2015). In many cases, only a subset of the total assemblage was considered. Authors such as Olsen (1961) recommended methods to select only those taxa, skeletal elements, and individual specimens deemed subjectively relevant for identification and interpretation, thus introducing sampling biases into faunal analyses (Lyman 1979). The discipline was young, and zooarchaeologists were themselves in the process of learning how to learn, or as some historians of science have described it, learning how to see, the information that would prove to be useful in studies of bone surface modification.

Highly quantitative approaches during this time tended to add refined frequency analyses of taxonomic, demographic, and skeletal part representation, and in some cases also econometric or body-size estimates based on regression models when seeking to address a variety of explicit questions beyond species representation (Lyman 1982). Other studies that may be considered relevant to Dart's hypothesis were focused on whether the assemblage or some of its elements had been deposited and/or modified by humans or by other agents and natural processes.

Nevertheless, studies were based primarily on laboratory examinations of the assemblage, akin to what in the forensic anthropology field has been termed the *box of bones approach* (Cabo and Dirkmaat in press; Dirkmaat and Cabo 2016). In this scenario, analysts are the recipients of a box of bones to examine, without input into the context, including sampling and excavation designs. Consequently, key information was missing for both depositional context and, importantly, the specific hypotheses derived from it. Within this framework, the interpretation of whether an element or assemblage reflected human activities or natural processes was often based on broad contextual assumptions, potential activity markers, or ethnoarchaeological analogs. This model-centered approach (rather than a hypothesis-centered approach, such as that employed in actualistic taphonomy) can result in the propagation of untested aprioristic assumptions from one site to the next.

Dart's osteodontokeratic construct was built on the classic model of seeking confirmatory information in support of an initial formal hypothesis, seeking to increase internal consistency rather than testability. To young biological anthropologists, Dart's osteodontokeratic culture may sound like just a historical curiosity that inspired the opening scene of Stanley Kubrick's *2001: A Space Odyssey* in 1968, or the "killer ape" theories that resurface periodically in different forms. However, in the early 1970s, it was still a seriously debated theory in human paleontology (Brain 1972, 2007; Dart and Wolberg 1971; Wolberg 1970). While up to that point most attempts to debunk it had relied on offering alternative hypotheses from a faunal analysis scope (Wolberg 1970), studies such as Voorhies (1969) or Brain (1967a, 1967b, 1969) showcased a different approach to that sort of site formation questions, by presenting not only suitable hypotheses, but via experimental and actualistic sampling strategies to test them. Other authors soon joined them in that approach. Anna K. ("Kay") Behrensmeyer and biological anthropologist Noel T. Boaz had soon followed Voorhies' (1969) lead with their own flume experiments on water transport (Behrensmeyer 1975; Boaz and Behrensmeyer 1976), discussing potential water transport markers beyond sorting.

There are very good arguments to support Behrensmeyer's candidacy as the most important contributor to the development of modern taphonomy, as evidenced by her ground-breaking work during the 1970s and 1980s. She studied the geology of paleontological sites from a wide variety of chronologies early in her career, ultimately becoming the Research Curator in Paleobiology at the National Museum of Natural History within the Smithsonian Institution in 1981. There she founded a multidisciplinary program devoted to the evolution of land ecosystems and continues to contribute to taphonomy and paleo-anthropology to this day.

Her interest in water transport derives from her East Turkana studies, where she attempted to explain the depositional origin of deposits (Behrensmeyer 1975). She quickly expanded her studies to the recognition and analysis of taphonomic signatures left by other depositional agents and processes in terrestrial environments. In 1974, she assisted Diane Gifford-Gonzalez on an actualistic study following the evolution of a modern human-generated assemblage from deposition to burial, documenting the signatures of a variety of taphonomic processes, such as transport, trampling, and mode of burial. She also noted the interactions between all of the processes and the precise characterization of the sedimentological setting (Gifford and Behrensmeyer 1977; Gifford-Gonzalez 1977). Soon after, Behrensmeyer (1978) published a bone weathering scale that is still widely used.

These two sets of studies brought the paleontological taphonomy and sedimentology traditions into the same subjects and approaches at which Brain had arrived from his paleo-anthropological scope. They reflected actualistic comparisons with *ethnological analogs* (Gifford-Gonzalez 1989) provided by assemblages from modern human populations with traditional, preindustrial economies (Brain 1967b, 1969; Gifford and Behrensmeyer 1977; Gifford-Gonzalez 1977) and bone surface modification by natural agents (Behrensmeyer 1978; Brain 1967a). Even more importantly, the intersection of both subjects (humans as taphonomic agents and bone modification) in human paleontology introduced a completely new element to Efremov's original conception of taphonomy, as a field primarily aimed at removing preservation biases from palaeoecological interpretation.

In July 1976, Behrensmeyer, alongside Andrew Hill, C. K. Brain, and Alan Walker, organized the Wenner-Gren symposium *Taphonomy and Vertebrate Paleoecology, With Special Reference to the Late Cenozoic of Sub-Saharan Africa*, at the Burg Wartenstein Center in the Austrian Alps. This meeting was extremely influential for popularizing taphonomy, through the success and wide dissemination of the volume compiling the symposium's talks, *Fossils in the Making* (Behrensmeyer and Hill 1980). It brought together researchers who approached taphonomy from classic paleontology, as well as from paleoanthropology and zooarchaeology, from a variety of different regions.

During this time, taphonomy also saw significant methodological advances. In the early 1970s, Richard G. Klein developed robust sampling and analytical methodologies for quantitative assemblage analyses and ethnoarchaeological comparisons. Those methods became the backbone of his influential volume, co-authored with Kathryn Cruz-Uribe, *The Analysis of Animal Bones from Archaeological Sites* (Klein and Cruz-Uribe 1984), which introduced many students of the 1980s to rigorous quantitative faunal analysis methods and, especially, to computer applications for that purpose. The term *taphonomy*, however, was not employed in the body of any of those contributions, even when citing Voorhies (1969) (see Klein 1976).

Pat Shipman and Jane E. Phillips (1976, 1977), challenged Dart's interpretation of the Makapansgat assemblage on the basis of their study, which combined actualistic data on animal behavior, taxonomic and skeletal part representation, fracture (breakage), and surface modification patterns of deposits formed by modern hyenas at the Awash

National Park in Ethiopia (Shipman and Phillips 1976; Shipman and Phillips-Conroy 1977). They were also able to examine the ecological, behavioral, and biostratinomic aspects of assemblages generated under drought conditions (Shipman 1975). They compared the Makapansgat specimens proposed to represent hominin tools directly with those in their natural, carnivore-produced assemblage. They concluded that both the breakage patterns and surface modifications (polishing) were indistinguishable (Shipman and Phillips-Conroy 1977).

Before the 1970s were over, Behrensmeyer addressed yet another key subject in Efremov's (1940) list of research areas by examining the differences between the actual composition of an extant terrestrial faunal community and its death assemblage (Behrensmeyer et al. 1979). Behrensmeyer et al. (1979) is an actualistic study of an extant mammal community from the Amboseli National Park in Kenya. Following a spatial transect design, they studied species representation of carcasses found on the surface. The study found that approximately one-quarter of the species in the community was missing from the bone assemblage, and estimated abundances differed significantly from the actual community composition, with clear biases linked to body size. The authors also examined transport and accumulation mechanisms, and the spatial and skeletal representation patterns derived from them.

The dozens of citations that Behrensmeyer et al. (1979) had accumulated by 1985 serve to illustrate the explosive growth and diversification of applications and study areas that vertebrate taphonomy experienced in the 1980s. Between 1979 and 1985, literature covered a whole set of typical taphonomic problems that Behrensmeyer (1984: 562) proposed as "the identification of specific processes that leave marks on organic remains, the circumstances that preserve some species but not others in fossil assemblages, the transport of organic remains, and 'time-averaging,' or the amount of time represented in single fossil samples."

This adaptive radiation originally ignited by the 1970s taphonomic studies served to link to paleoanthropology and paleontology. Soon after, the conversion of zooarchaeology into the taphonomic gospel finally set modern vertebrate taphonomy into full throttle.

1980s–1990s: The Rise of Modern Zooarchaeology and the Information Gains Approach

Many of the first generation of zooarchaeologists in North America were professionally trained biologists or paleontologists, and research questions often focused on advances in quantitative methodologies – particularly those related to which quantitative units were most appropriate for measuring taxonomic abundances (Lyman 2008, 2016). The earliest journal article which we have been able to find and access which applies taphonomic studies to a classic modern-human archaeological site, mentions the field by name, and references taphonomic literature belongs to Noe-Nygaard (1977). While earlier studies on butchery and marrow extraction exist (e.g., Guilday et al. 1962), the explicit tie between analysis of tool marks from intentional disarticulation and the term taphonomy anticipated what would become a flourishing area of study in the discipline.

We have already discussed some early actualistic studies on the natural disarticulation, dispersion, and modification of modern fauna carcasses by authors such as Behrensmeyer et al. (1979), Shipman and Phillips (1976), and Shipman and Phillips-Conroy (1977). They were immediately followed by a flurry of studies on terrestrial carcass decomposition, disarticulation, animal modification, and dispersal during the 1980s (e.g., Andrews and Cook 1985, 1985; Berger 1983; Haynes 1988; Hill and Behrensmeyer 1984; Richardson 1980).

The study of hyena deposits is particularly useful in illustrating the evolution of taphonomic carnivore studies. Surface marks and breakage patterns are important considerations when trying to distinguish between assemblages generated by humans and those generated by carnivores, particularly hyenas. Hyenas break bones, typically long bone ends, to extract marrow by crushing them under the pressure of their amazing bite force, while humans do so by percussion, typically to long bone shafts. In biomechanical terms, hyenas crush bone through static loads (sustained pressure), while humans use dynamic loads (sudden impacts), which result in different fracture dynamics. Among the latter, the study of highly diagnostic byproducts such as toothmarks, cutmarks, or impact notches, benefit enormously from the use of microscopy.

Another major contributor to the development of modern vertebrate taphonomy, Pat Shipman, revolutionized bone modification research through her introduction and popularization of scanning electron microscopy protocols as a tool to assess the origin and nature of surface marks on bone (Potts and Shipman 1981; Shipman 1981a). Through the 1980s, Shipman joined other authors in expanding the application of her methods to differentiate between cutmarks and pseudo-cutmarks (Olsen and Shipman 1988; Shipman and Rose 1984) and between cutmarks and bone modification patterns derived from a growing array of cultural practices.

Shipman also contributed decisively to the growing list of influential reviews and volumes that helped to popularize taphonomy among a wider audience during the early 1980s (Behrensmeyer and Hill 1980; Binford 1981; Brain 1981; Gifford 1981) with her *Life History of a Fossil* (Shipman 1981b). This can be considered as the first introductory volume to taphonomy. It was written in a manner that made it accessible to a wider audience of students and professionals from almost any field. This combination of factors, with increasing overlap into archaeological subjects, resulted in the integration of taphonomy into zooarchaeology, consolidating zooarchaeology and transforming it into the discipline we recognize today. Lyman (1987) mentions taphonomy by name and provides a spectacular, in-depth discussion of the intimate relationship between taphonomy and modern zooarchaeology, and, importantly, includes a comprehensive and extremely informative bibliography list.

Taphonomy also witnessed a conceptual evolution during the 1980s. With a much broader list of practitioners and deeper knowledge base now accumulated, more theoretical papers discussing conceptual underpinnings joined the literature. The most important conceptual innovation of taphonomy during that time was the acknowledgment that taphonomy was not just focused on identifying biases and information losses, but also interpreting information gains. In 1985, Anna K. Behrensmeyer and Susan Kidwell proposed a new working definition of taphonomy as "the study of processes of preservation and how they affect information in the fossil record. This encompasses not only information loss and bias, but also the more positive contributions that taphonomy is now making to the study of organisms and environments through time" (Behrensmeyer and Kidwell 1985: 105).

The information-based definition of taphonomy (Behrensmeyer and Kidwell 1985) is far from Susan Kidwell's only contribution during those years. Alongside Behrensmeyer, she may be the only author who contributed most decisively to the development of modern taphonomy's deeper conceptual framework, with a long list of contributions on various aspects of taphonomic inference that were invariably characterized by a special depth and insight (e.g., Kidwell 1985, 1986; Kidwell and Behrensmeyer 1988).

All of these developments led taphonomy to emerge during the 1990s as an almost fully mature field. Some authors even cheered in their titles that "taphonomy has come of age!" (Allison 1991). The 1990s witnessed an ever-accelerating growth in the field, which reaped some spectacular fruits of the work carried out during the previous two decades, further enhancing its visibility. Still, the event that most clearly signaled the full maturity of the field would likely have to be the publication of Lyman's *Vertebrate Taphonomy* (Lyman 1994).

The explosive growth and diversification of taphonomy from the 1970s had raised some new problems. One of the most important of these was a diminishing cohesiveness in terminology, methodological structure, and precise definitions. Arriving at taphonomy from the highly quantitative zooarchaeological tradition, Lee Lyman (1982, 1987) addressed those inconsistencies for more than a decade. His comprehensive effort to standardize terminology and quantitative indices, as well as to delineate and coherently organize the subfields, study areas, and methods of taphonomy, and define, as he would later put it "what taphonomy is" (Lyman 2010), crystallized in the monumental book (Lyman 1994). His work was the first full-blown textbook on taphonomy, which became something akin to the Bible to many 1990s graduate students. This work presented taphonomy not just as an application of paleontological techniques that could be useful to other fields and chronologies, but as an integral part of biological anthropology and zooarchaeology. It presented taphonomy as a mature scientific field that was an essential component of a variety of disciplines, rather than as a set of techniques and applications. Since this publication, the maturity of taphonomy has been reflected in such works as Rogers et al. (2007), Sincerbox and DiGangi (2018), Fernández-Jalvo and Andrews (2016), and Noto (2011), as well as Sahle et al.'s discussion of equifinality and crocodiles as taphonomic agents (2017), and even in the creation of a taphonomy board game (Martindale and Weiss 2020).

FORENSIC TAPHONOMY AND FUTURE RESEARCH

Forensic anthropology was a late adopter of taphonomy, with the first two important monographs on forensic taphonomy appearing in the late 1990s and early 2000s (Haglund and Sorg 1997, 2002). In its defense, forensic anthropology remains a rather young field itself. Even though biological anthropologists were sporadically involved in the analysis of human remains for forensic investigation purposes since the early twentieth century, we can trace the establishment of forensic anthropology as a distinct, viable discipline to the early 1970s (Dirkmaat et al. 2008). Thus, modern forensic anthropology developed at nearly the same time as modern vertebrate taphonomy.

The reservation of a special section to the subject of forensic taphonomy is partly due to personal bias (the authors are forensic practitioners), but also because (i) there are few other scientific fields in which taphonomy has had such a transformational impact and (ii) we honestly believe that forensic taphonomy has a special role to play in the future of the field of taphonomy.

Originally, forensic anthropology was defined exclusively as a laboratory field, with the primary focus of aiding in victim identification. The first applications of taphonomy to forensic anthropology, as conceived by Marcie Sorg and Bill Haglund, date back to the 1980s, and were related to decomposition and scavenger modifications to forensic human remains (Sorg et al. 2012). However, the first article with the word *taphonomy* in its title, abstract, or keywords in the *Journal of Forensic Sciences* would not appear until 1989, and only five other papers included the term during the following five years (Haglund et al. 1989; Haglund and Sorg 1997). It would be the progressive introduction of forensic archaeology, with the detailed contextual field (scene) information that it brought to the table, that would allow for a full integration of taphonomy into forensic anthropology, and thus the birth of forensic taphonomy during the 1990s (Cabo and Dirkmaat 2015, in press; Dirkmaat and Cabo 2016; Dirkmaat et al. 2008; Sorg et al. 2012).

The adoption of forensic taphonomy represented a true paradigm shift in forensic anthropology, as it brought about a decisive change to its study goals, objectives, and materials. The introduction of taphonomic inference transformed forensic anthropology from an applied field exclusively devoted to aiding in victim identification, into a scientific field that, in addition, sought to reconstruct the events surrounding death and deposition, operating with a rigorous research component (Beary and Lyman 2012; Cabo and Dirkmaat 2015, in press; Dirkmaat et al. 2008). Haglund and Sorg (1997) defined forensic taphonomy as "the use of models, approaches, and analyses in forensic contexts to estimate the time since death, reconstruct the circumstances before and after deposition, and discriminate the products of human behavior from those created by the Earth's biological, physical, chemical, and geological subsystems" (Haglund and Sorg 1997).

Questions posed to an investigator at an outdoor scene represent a familiar set of subjects, such as site formation and deposition processes, including transport, human versus animal agency, natural versus artificial bone modification, behavioral and cultural patterns of modification, and quantitative taphonomy questions. Every single inference in modern forensic anthropology, other than victim identity, refers to classic taphonomic issues.

However, forensic taphonomy contains a key novel trait that distinguishes it from classic taphonomy as approached from other fields. While taphonomic applications in paleoecology, paleontology, paleoanthropology, and archaeology seek to reconstruct past environments, forensic taphonomy also seeks to reconstruct past events and conditions that transpired, but in current environments. This means that, while at archaeological or paleontological sites we are exclusively interested in the environmental information captured in the sedimentological medium, at an outdoor forensic case scene we are also interested in *all* elements, factors, and conditions of the current environment (flora, fauna, soils, slope, shade, etc.). Forensic taphonomy is actualistic, not in the uniformitarian, comparative sense, but in and of itself; each forensic anthropology case is a natural experiment examining the death, decomposition, disarticulation, dispersion, and modification of large vertebrate "carcasses" under known contextual and environmental conditions. Importantly, these natural experiments are (unfortunately) continuously replicated across locations and climate regimes spanning entire continents and, carefully documented under the appropriate recovery protocols (Dirkmaat 2012; Dirkmaat and Adovasio 1997; Dirkmaat and Cabo 2016; Dirkmaat et al. 2008), contain a wealth of information impossible to match in traditional research.

Classic actualistic taphonomy studies are still alive and well. This includes initiatives such as that of the INCUAPA-CONICET from the Universidad Nacional del Centro de la Provincia in Buenos Aires, Argentina. The INCUAPA team has been conducting both observational and experimental research on a wide variety of interrelated taphonomic agents and processes, from experiments on water transport or weathering under controlled conditions, to carnivore feeding behavior studies at a local zoo. They have also constructed actualistic sampling designs targeting carnivore and rodent accumulations, preservation biases, and carcass disarticulation and dispersal along transects in different patterns throughout a variety of environments (Gutiérrez et al. 2018; and references therein).

The information retrievable from these studies and, importantly, information that can be brought to bear to address a wide variety of hypotheses regarding past taphonomic events at that scene, pales in comparison to the depth and breadth of information standardly retrieved from a properly approached and processed outdoor forensic scene – effectively an actualistic taphonomic study. Information is obtained from the earliest of the times in the taphonomic interval (around the time of death) and into extended timeframes. It is primarily for these reasons that forensic taphonomy has unparalleled transformative potential to advance taphonomic inference.

Perhaps the best example of that potential comes from modern forensic bone trauma analysis. Fracture analysis in taphonomy has traditionally relied on breakage patterns and overall fracture morphology (e.g., Johnson 1985; Villa and Mahieu 1991). The demanding evidentiary standards of criminal justice has led to the utilization of microscopic techniques to infer the fracture dynamics by precisely identifying the distribution of tension and compression failure areas, as well as some inferences on the timing of the fracture (*peri-* or *post-mortem*) based on changes of the mechanical properties of bone and its biomechanical reaction under stress as it gradually loses its viscoelastic properties during decomposition (Dirkmaat et al. 2008; Symes et al. 2012, 2021). These forensic techniques permit the reconstruction of the exact direction of forces and strains that combine to create the fracture (i.e., the exact manner and direction in which the bone bent and broke), as well as inferences regarding postural reconstructions. An analysis of the *Au. sediba* Malapa assemblage in South Africa (L'Abbe et al. 2015) serves to illustrate the promise of these techniques for paleoanthropological inference. Based on geological information, it had been hypothesized that the depositional process behind the Malapa assemblage was a natural trap (Dirks et al. 2010). The forensic trauma analysis techniques of the broken upper limb bones suggested that the two *Au. sediba* individuals displayed peri-mortem fractures that were highly consistent with a fall from height, and also that one of them was *necessarily* alive, awake, and actively bracing themselves during the fall at the time of impact (L'Abbé et al. 2015).

Thus, we firmly believe that a larger interest and participation in forensic taphonomy of taphonomists from other fields, as well as from researchers from other areas, such as systems ecology, entomology, and molecular biology, could have a transformative impact in the future development of taphonomy.

FINAL THOUGHTS

Using a historical approach to outline a scientific field has some risks and inconveniences, the main one being that it is impossible to do justice to all relevant contributors. We are sure we have unfairly omitted many authors who contributed decisively to the development of taphonomy during its formative years, from the early 1960s to the early 1990s. Although we have tried to avoid it, the attention devoted to particular subfields and authors is also irremediably biased by our personal experiences, background, and memories. In our review we did not even touch upon some important areas of taphonomic research, such as fire alteration or domestication studies. For those of us who still remember those not so ancient times during which it was possible to have read basically all existing volumes and key references in taphonomy, the current impossibility to even list them is probably the best testament to the explosive and fruitful development of taphonomy during the last five decades.

However, while fully aware of all its risks and shortcomings, when pondering what might be the best approach to outlining the field of taphonomy for the audience of *A Companion to Biological Anthropology*, we still decided to settle for a historical approach. Looking back at key landmarks gives us a perspective of both the approaches that were more successful to advance the field, and the mistakes and obstacles that slowed its advancement, and, with it, a view of what to avoid and seek in the future.

In our historical review of taphonomy, we found some recurring themes. The first is how the incorporation of the actualistic, hypothesis-centered approach repeatedly solved previous analytical problems and misinterpretations – from Dart's hypothesis to faunal interpretations in zooarchaeology, pseudo-tools, pseudo-cutmarks, or hunting versus scavenging questions. With the vast body of literature now available for comparisons and interpretations, it is important to remember that taphonomy, as with any science, is defined by its methods and scope rather than simply by the gradual accumulation of a body of knowledge. Thus, it is crucial to continue to stress the actualistic approach and to base our interpretations on testable hypotheses.

A second major recurring theme is the importance of a fluid communication between fields. C. K. Brain or the zooarchaeologists of the 1970s were aware of the sampling biases outlined by Efremov three decades earlier, and were trying to address them on their own, while largely unaware of the advances already made by paleontologists, including human paleontologists. It was not until initiatives such as the Burg Wartenstein meeting started bringing together paleoanthropologists from different regions that volumes such as Behrensmeyer and Hill (1980), Binford (1981), Brain (1981), or Shipman (1981a, 1981b) started introducing the field to a wider audience in the early 1980s, and the analysis of bone modification started addressing hypotheses increasingly intersecting archaeological matters (e.g., Bonnichsen and Sorg 1989; Gifford-Gonzalez 1989; Hill and Behrensmeyer 1985; Shipman et al. 1981; Shipman and Rose 1983). Only then did researchers working on archaeological chronologies start to fully benefit from the advances in taphonomy of the previous three decades. Thus, the history of taphonomy also teaches us that it is crucial to prevent the atomization of the field into separate, poorly interconnected lines and traditions.

This risk is further exacerbated today by a third recurring theme in taphonomy, namely the need to rely on more than one line of evidence, and breaking the problem into a set of simple testable hypotheses that require examination from different approaches, materials, and independent information sources. This adds an additional subdivision between researchers approaching taphonomy from paleontology, paleoanthropology, archaeology, or forensic anthropology, as the increased sophistication of analytical techniques promotes ever higher levels of specialization in different subjects, techniques, and materials. We believe that maintaining a common core of literature, relevant to all subfields and approaches, is the first step in preventing the atomization of taphonomy and ensuring its future growth as a cohesive field. We feel that the classic references listed in this chapter are the best starting point to build that core.

Even though taphonomy has spectacular applications to social sciences such as archaeology and paleoecology, as a scientific field, taphonomy has one foot in biology and the other in geology, including paleontology and sedimentology. While it plays an integral role in modern biological anthropology, the most fruitful taphonomic experimentations and developments have systematically emerged at the intersection of different disciplines.

REFERENCES

Allison, P. A. "Konservat-Lagerstätten: Cause and Classification." *Paleobiology* 14, no. 4 (1988): 331–344.

Allison, P. A. "Taphonomy Has Come of Age!" *Palaios* 6, no. 4 (1991): 345–346.

Andrews, P., and J. Cook. "Natural Modifications to Bones in a Temperate Setting." *Man* 20, no. 4 (1985): 675–691.

Beary, M. O., and R. L. Lyman. "The Use of Taphonomy in Forensic Anthropology: Past Trends and Future Prospects." In *A Companion to Forensic Anthropology*. Edited by D. C. Dirkmaat, 499–527. Hoboken, NJ: John Wiley & Sons, 2012.

Behrensmeyer, A. K. "The Taphonomy and Paleoecology of Plio-Pleistocene Vertebrate Assemblages East of Lake Rudolf, Kenya." *Bulletin of the Museum of Comparative Zoology Harvard* 146 (1975): 473–578.

Behrensmeyer, A. K. "Taphonomic and Ecologic Information from Bone Weathering." *Paleobiology* 4, no. 2 (1978): 150–162.

Behrensmeyer, A. K. "Taphonomy and the Fossil Record." *American Science* 72, no. 6 (1984): 558–566.

Behrensmeyer, A. K., and A. P. Hill. *Fossils in the Making: Vertebrate Taphonomy and Paleoecology.* Chicago, IL: University of Chicago Press, 1980.

Behrensmeyer, A. K., and S. M. Kidwell. "Taphonomy's Contributions to Paleobiology." *Paleobiology* 11, no. 1 (1985): 105–119.

Behrensmeyer, A. K., D. Western, and D. E. Dechant Boaz. "New Perspectives in Vertebrate Paleoecology from a Recent Bone Assemblage." *Paleobiology* 5, no. 1 (1979): 12–21.

Berger, J. "Ecology and Catastrophic Mortality in Wild Horses: Implications for Interpreting Fossil Assemblages." *Science* 220, no. 4604 (1983): 1403–1404.

Binford, L. R. *Bones: Ancient Men and Modern Myths.* Cambridge, MA: Academic Press, 1981.

Boaz, N. T., and A. K. Behrensmeyer. "Hominid Taphonomy: Transport of Human Skeletal Parts in an Artificial Fluviatile Environment." *American Journal of Physical Anthropology* 45 (1976): 53–60.

Bonnichsen, R., and M. Sorg. *Bone Modification.* Institute for Quaternary Studies, University of Maine. Orono, ME: University of Maine Press, 1989.

Brain, C. K. "Bone Weathering and the Problem of Bone Pseudo-tools." *South African Journal of Science* 63, no. 3 (1967a): 97–99.

Brain, C. K. "Hottentot Food Remains and Their Bearing on the Interpretation of Fossil Bone Assemblages." *Scientific Papers of the Namib Desert Research Station* 32 (1967b): 1–11.

Brain, C. K. "The Contribution of Namib Desert Hottentots to an Understanding of Australopithecine Bone Accumulations." *Scientific Papers of the Namib Desert Research Station* 39 (1969): 13–22.

Brain, C. K. "An Attempt to Reconstruct the Behaviour of Australopithecines: The Evidence for Interpersonal Violence." *Africa Zoology* 7, no. 1 (1972): 379–401.

Brain, C. K. *The Hunters or the Hunted? An Introduction to African Cave Taphonomy.* Chicago, IL: University of Chicago Press, 1981.

Brain, C. K. "Fifty Years of Fun with Fossils: Some Cave Taphonomy-Related Ideas and Concepts that Emerged Between 1953 and 2003." In *Breathing Life into Fossils: Taphonomic Studies in Honor of CK (Bob) Brain.* Edited by T. Pickering, K. Schick, and N. Toth, 1–24. Bloomington, IN: Stone Age Institute Press, 2007.

Cabo, L. L., and D. C. Dirkmaat. Forensic Archaeology in the United States. In *Forensic Archaeology: A Global Perspective.* Edited by W. M. Groen, N. Marquez-Grant, and R. Janaway, 255–270. Hoboken, NJ: John Wiley & Sons, 2015.

Cabo, L. L., and D. C. Dirkmaat. "A View of Forensic Taphonomy as A Present and Future Discipline." In *Haglund and Sorg's Forensic Taphonomy: 21st Century Advances and Regional Variation.* Edited by M. H. Sorg and W. D. Haglund. Boca Raton, FL: CRC Press, in press.

Chaplin, R. E. *The Study of Animal Bones from Archaeological Sites.* London, UK: Seminar Press, 1971.

Cornwall, I. W. *Bones for the Archaeologist.* New York, NY: Macmillan, 1956.

Dart, R.A. "*Australopithecus Africanus*: The Man-Ape of South Africa." *Nature* 115, no. 2884 (1925): 195–199.

Dart, R. A. "The Dentition of Australopithecus Africanus." *Folia Anatomica Japonica* 12, no. 4 (1934): 207–221.

Dart, R. A. "The Predatory Implemental Technique of the Australopithecines." *American Journal of Physical Anthropology* 7 (1949): 1–16.

Dart, R. A., and D. L. Wolberg. "On the Osteodontokeratic Culture of the Australopithecinae." *Current Anthropology* 12, no. 2 (1971): 233–236.

Dirkmaat, D. C. "Documenting Context at the Outdoor Scene: Why Bother." In *A Companion to Forensic Anthropology.* Edited by D. C. Dirkmaat, 48–65. Hoboken, NJ: John Wiley & Sons, 2012.

Dirkmaat, D. C., and J. M. Adovasio. "The Role of Archaeology in the Recovery and Interpretation of Human Remains from an Outdoor Forensic Setting." In *Taphonomy: The Postmortem Fate of Human Remains.* Edited by W. D. Haglund and M. H. Sorg, 39–64. Boca Raton, FL: CRC Press, 1997.

Dirkmaat, D. C., and L. L. Cabo. "Forensic Archaeology and Forensic Taphonomy: Basic Considerations on How to Properly Process and Interpret the Outdoor Forensic Scene." *Academic Forensic Pathology* 6, no. 3 (2016): 439–454.

Dirkmaat, D. C., L. L Cabo, S. D. Ousley, et al. "New Perspectives in Forensic Anthropology." *American Journal of Physical Anthropology* 137, no. S47 (2008): 33–52.

Dirks, P. H., J. M. Kibii, B. F. Kuhn, et al. "Geological Setting and Age of *Australopithecus Sediba* from Southern Africa." *Science* 328, no. 5975 (2010): 205–208.

Dodson, P. "Vertebrate Burials." *Paleobiology* 6, no. 1 (1980): 6–8.

Efremov, I. A. "Taphonomy: A New Branch of Paleontology." *Pan-American Geology* 74, no. 2 (1940): 81–93.

Fernández-Jalvo, Y., and P. Andrews. *Atlas of Taphonomic Identifications: 1001+ Images of Fossil and Recent Mammal Bone Modification.* Berlin: Springer, 2016.

Gifford, D. P. "Taphonomy and Paleoecology: A Critical Review of Archaeology's Sister Disciplines." In *Advances in Archaeological Method and Theory, vol. 3.* Edited by M. B. Schiffer, 365–438. Cambridge, MA: Academic Press, 1981.

Gifford, D. P., and A. K. Behrensmeyer. "Observed Depositional Events at a Modern Human Occupation Site in Kenya." *Quaternary Research* 8, no. 3 (1977): 245–266.

Gifford-Gonzalez, D. P. *Observations of Modern Human Settlements as an Aid to Archaeological Interpretation. PhD Dissertation.* Berkeley: University of California, 1977.

Gifford-Gonzalez, D. "Ethnographic Analogues for Interpreting Modified Bones: Some Cases from East Africa." In *Bone Modification.* Edited by R Bonnichsen and M. Sorg, 179–246. Orono, ME: Institute for Quaternary Studies, University of Maine, 1989.

Golubev, V. K. "The Faunal Assemblages of Permian Terrestrial Vertebrates from Eastern Europe." *Paleontology Journal* 34, Suppl. 2 (2000): S211–S224.

Gould, S. J. *Wonderful Life: The Burgess Shale and the Nature of History.* New York, NY: W. W. Norton & Company, 1989.

Guilday, J. E., P. W. Parmalee, and D. P. Tanner. "Aboriginal Butchering Techniques at the Eschelman Site (36LA12), Lancaster County, Pennsylvania." *Pennsylvania Archaeologist* 32 (1962): 59–83.

Guthrie, R. D. "Differential Preservation and Recovery of Pleistocene Large Mammal Remains in Alaska." *Journal of Paleontology* 41 (1967): 243–246.

Gutiérrez, M. A., D. J. Rafuse, M. C. Álvarez, et al. "Ten Years of Actualistic Taphonomic Research in the Pampas Region of Argentina: Contributions to Regional Archaeology." *Quaternary International* 492 (2018): 40–52.

Haglund, W. D., and M. H. Sorg. *Forensic Taphonomy: The Postmortem Fate of Human Remains.* Boca Raton, FL: CRC Press, 1997.

Haglund, W. D., and M. H. Sorg. *Advances in Forensic Taphonomy: Method, Theory, and Archaeological Perspectives.* Boca Raton, FL: CRC Press, 2002.

Haglund, W. D., D. T. Reay, and D. R. Swindler. "Canid Scavenging/Disarticulation Sequence of Human Remains in the Pacific Northwest." *Journal of Forensic Sciences* 34, no. 3 (1989): 587–606.

Haynes, G. "Longitudinal Studies of African Elephant Death and Bone Deposits." *Journal of Archaeology Sciences* 15, no. 2 (1988): 131–157.

Hill, A., and A. K. Behrensmeyer. "Disarticulation Patterns of Some Modern East African Mammals." *Paleobiology* 10, no. 3 (1984): 366–376.

Hill, A., and A. K. Behrensmeyer. "Natural Disarticulation and Bison Butchery." *American Antiquity* 50, no. 1 (1985): 141–145.

Jablonski, D., and R. W. Fairbridge, eds. (1979). *The Encyclopedia of Paleontology.* Stroudsburg, PA: Dowden, Hutchinson & Ross.

Johnson, E. "Current Developments in Bone Technology." In *Advances in Archaeological Method and Theory, vol. 8.* Edited by M. B. Schiffer, 157–235. Cambridge, MA: Academic Press, 1985.

Johnson, R. G. "Models and Methods for Analysis of the Mode of Formation of Fossil Assemblages." *Geological Society of American Bulletin* 71, no. 7 (1960): 1075–1086.

Kidwell, S. M. "Palaeobiological and Sedimentological Implications of Fossil Concentrations." *Nature* 318, no. 6045 (1985): 457–460.

Kidwell, S. M. "Models for Fossil Concentrations: Paleobiologic Implications." *Paleobiology* 12, no. 1 (1986): 6–24.

Kidwell, S. M., and A. K. Behrensmeyer. "Overview: Ecological and Evolutionary Implications of Taphonomic Processes." *Palaeogeography Palaeoclimatology Palaeoecology* 63, no. 1–3: 1–13 (1988).

Klein, R. G. "The Mammalian Fauna of the Klasies River Mouth Sites, Southern Cape Province, South Africa." *S. Afr. Archaeol. Bull.* 31, no. 123/124 (1976): 75–98.

Klein, R. G., and K. Cruz-Uribe. *The Analysis of Animal Bones from Archeological Sites.* Chicago, IL: University of Chicago Press, 1984.

L'Abbé, E. N., S. A. Symes, J. T. Pokines, et al. "Evidence of Fatal Skeletal Injuries on Malapa Hominins 1 and 2." *Scientific Reports* 5, no. 1 (2015): 1–11.

Lawrence, D. R. "Taphonomy and Information Losses in Fossil Communities." *Geological Society of American Bulletin* 79, no. 10 (1968): 1315–1330.

Lawrence, D. R. "The Nature and Structure of Paleoecology." *Journal of Paleontology* 45, no. 4 (1971): 593–607.

Lyman, R. "Faunal Analysis: An Outline of Method." *Northwest Anthropology Research Notes* 13, no. 1 (1979): 22–35.

Lyman, R. L. "Nomenclature in Faunal Studies: A Response to Olsen and Olsen." *American Antiquity* 47, no. 1 (1982): 179–180.

Lyman, R. L. "Zooarchaeology and Taphonomy: A General Consideration." *Journal of Ethnobiology* 7, no. 1 (1987): 93–117.

Lyman, R. L. *Vertebrate Taphonomy.* Cambridge, UK: Cambridge University Press, 1994.

Lyman, R. L. *Quantitative Paleozoology.* Cambridge, UK: Cambridge University Press, 2008.

Lyman, R. L. "What Taphonomy Is, What It Isn't, and Why Taphonomists Should Care About the Difference." *Journal of Taphon.* 8, no. 1 (2010): 1–16.

Lyman, R. L. "The History of 'Laundry Lists' in North American Zooarchaeology." *Journal of Anthropology Archaeology* 39 (2015): 42–50.

Lyman, R. L. *Theodore E. White and the Development of Zooarchaeology in North America.* Lincoln, NE: University of Nebraska Press, 2016.

Martindale, R. C., and A. M. Weiss. "'Taphonomy: Dead and Fossilized': A New Board Game Designed to Teach College Undergraduate Students about the Process of Fossilization." *Journal of Geoscience Education* 68 (2020): 265–285.

Mason, R. J., R. A. Dart, and J. W. Kitching. "Bone Tools at the Kalkbank Middle Stone Age Site and the Makapansgat Australopithecine Locality, Central Transvaal." *South African Archaeological Bulletin* 13, no. 51 (1958): 85–116.

Morris, S. C. "The Burgess Shale (Middle Cambrian) Fauna." *Annual Review of Ecology and Systematics* 10, no. 1 (1979): 327–349.

Newell, N. D. "Paleobiology's Golden Age." *Palaios* 2, no. 3 (1987): 305–309.

Noe-Nygaard, N. "Butchering and Marrow Fracturing as a Taphonomic Factor in Archaeological Deposits." *Paleobiology* 3, no. 2 (1977): 218–237.

Noto, C. R. "Hierarchical Control of Terrestrial Vertebrate Taphonomy over Space and Time: Discussion of Mechanisms and Implications for Vertebrate Paleobiology. Discussion of Mechanisms and Implications for Vertebrate Paleobiology." In *Taphonomy: Process and Bias Through Time.* Edited by P. A. Allison and D. J. Bottjer, 287–336. London, UK: Springer, 2011.

Olsen, S. J. "The Relative Value of Fragmentary Mammalian Remains." *American Antiquity* 26, no. 4 (1961): 538–540.

Olsen, S. J. *Zooarchaeology: Animal Bones in Archaeology and Their Interpretation.* Boston, MA: Addison-Wesley Publishing Company, 1971.

Olsen, S. L., and J. W. Olsen. "A Comment on Nomenclature in Faunal Studies." *American Antiquity* 46, no. 1 (1981): 192–194.

Olsen, S. L., and P. Shipman. "Surface Modification on Bone: Trampling versus Butchery." *Journal of Archaeological Sciences* 15, no. 5 (1988): 535–553.

Olson, E. C. "Late Permian Terrestrial Vertebrates, USA and USSR." *Transactions of the American Philosophical Society* 52, no. 2 (1962): 1–224.

Potts, R., and P. Shipman. "Cutmarks Made by Stone Tools on Bones from Olduvai Gorge, Tanzania." *Nature* 291, no. 5816 (1981): 577–580.

Read-Martin, C. E., D. W. Read, E. Aguirre, et al. "Australopithecine Scavenging and Human Evolution: An Approach from Faunal Analysis [and Comments and Reply]." *Current Anthropology* 16, no. 3 (1975): 359–368.

Richardson, P. R. "Carnivore Damage to Antelope Bones and Its Archaeological Implications." *Palaeontology Africa* 23 (1980): 109–125.

Rogers, R. R., D. A. Eberth, and A. R. Fiorillo, eds. *Bonebeds: Genesis, Analysis, and Paleobiological Research*. Chicago, IL: University of Chicago Press, 2007.

Sahle, Y., S. El Zaatari, and T. D. White. "Hominid Butchers and Biting Crocodiles in the African Plio-Pleistocene." *Pnas* 114, no. 50 (2017): 13164–13169.

Schäfer, W. *Ecology and Palaeoecology of Marine Environments*. Chicago, IL: Chicago University Press, 1972.

Shipman, P. "Implications of Drought for Vertebrate Fossil Assemblages." *Nature* 257, no. 5528 (1975): 667–668.

Shipman, P. "Applications of Scanning Electron Microscopy to Taphonomic Problems." *Annals of the New York Academy of Sciences* 376, no. 1 (1981a): 357–385.

Shipman, P. *Life History of a Fossil: An Introduction to Taphonomy and Paleoecology*. Boston, MA: Harvard University Press, 1981b.

Shipman, P., and J. E. Phillips. "Scavenging by Hominids and Other Carnivores." *Current Anthropology* 17, no. 1 (1976): 170–172.

Shipman, P., and J. Phillips-Conroy. "Hominid Tool-Making versus Carnivore Scavenging." *American Journal of Physical Anthropology* 46, no. 1 (1977): 77–86.

Shipman, P., and J. J. Rose. "Early Hominid Hunting, Butchering, and Carcass-Processing Behaviors: Approaches to the Fossil Record." *Journal of Anthropology Archaeology* 2, no. 1 (1983): 57–98.

Shipman, P., and J. J. Rose. "Cutmark Mimics on Modern and Fossil Bovid Bones." *Current Anthropology* 25, no. 1 (1984): 116–117.

Shipman, P., W. Bosler, K. L. Davis, et al. "Butchering of Giant Geladas at an Acheulian Site [and Comments and Reply]." *Current Anthropology* 22, no. 3 (1981): 257–268.

Shotwell, J. A. "An Approach to the Paleoecology of Mammals." *Ecology* 36, no. 2 (1955): 327–337.

Simpson, G. G. "Some Problems of Vertebrate Paleontology: The Study of Fossil Vertebrates Elucidates the General Principles of Evolutionary Biology." *Science* 133, no. 3465 (1961): 1679–1689.

Sincerbox, S. N., and E. A. DiGangi. *Forensic Taphonomy and Ecology of North American Scavengers*. Cambridge, MA: Academic Press, 2018.

Sorg, M. H., W. D. Haglund, and J. A. Wren. "Current Research in Forensic Taphonomy." In *A Companion to Forensic Anthropology*. Edited by D. C. Dirkmaat, 477–498. Hoboken, NJ: John Wiley & Sons, 2012.

Symes, S. A., N. Ericka, E. N. C. L'Abbé, et al. "Bone in Medicolegal Investigations." In *A Companion to Forensic Anthropology*. Edited by D. C. Dirkmaat, 340–389. Hoboken, NJ: John Wiley & Sons, 2012.

Symes, S. A., E. N. L'Abbé, K. E. Stull, et al. "Taphonomy and the Timing of Bone Fractures in Trauma Analysis." In *Manual of Forensic Taphonomy*. Edited by J. T. Pokines, E. N. L'Abbe, and S. A. Symes, 341–365. Boca Raton, FL: CRC Press, 2021.

Villa, P., and E. Mahieu. "Breakage Patterns of Human Long Bones." *Journal of Human Evolution* 21 (1991): 27–48.

Voorhies, M. R. "Taphonomy and Population Dynamics of an Early Pliocene Vertebrate Fauna, Knox County, Nebraska." In *Contributions to Geology Special Paper*, vol. 1. Laramie, WY: University of Wyoming Press, 1969.

Weigelt, J. *Recent Vertebrate Carcasses and Their Paleobiological Implications*. Chicago, IL: University of Chicago Press, 1989.

Wolberg, D. L. "The Hypothesized Osteodontokeratic Culture of the Australopithecinae: A Look at the Evidence and the Opinions." *Current Anthropology* 11, no. 1 (1970): 23–37.

CHAPTER 22

Primate Origins: The Earliest Primates and Euprimates and Their Role in the Evolution of the Order

Mary T. Silcox and Sergi López-Torres

INTRODUCTION

The extinction of the non-avian dinosaurs at the Cretaceous-Paleogene (K-Pg) boundary approximately 66 million years ago heralded the start of a fundamental shift in the vertebrate ecosystem that has often been called the "Beginning of the Age of Mammals" (e.g., Rose 2006). Within a relatively short time frame following the extinction event (O'Leary et al. 2013), placental mammals are inferred to have radiated into diverse new niches. Although these shifts constituted the first steps in creating a familiar world, many of the mammals that were successful in the first epoch following the extinction event represent groups whose relationships (if any) with modern orders of mammals remain in debate. These groups are sometimes referred to as "archaic" because they lack the specializations characteristic of modern taxa (e.g., Rose 2006). Whether or not this is a fair characterization, it is clear that relating groups such as "Condylarthra" (a wastebasket for early ungulates), Creodonta (carnivorous forms of debatable relation to modern carnivorans), and Mesonychia (carnivorous taxa that had been thought to be ancestors of early whales but probably are not) to the modern mammalian orders is challenging.

Not so, however, with taxa that begin to appear at the beginning of the next geologic epoch, the Eocene. Within a relatively short timeframe, inarguable members of modern groups such as Perissodactyla (odd-toed ungulates such as horses) and Artiodactyla (even-toed ancestors of deer and cows) appear in deposits across the northern continents (i.e., Laurasia), likely in association with a transient warming event called the Paleocene–Eocene

Thermal Maximum (PETM; e.g., Gingerich 2006). To a time-traveler, the world would still have seemed strange (e.g., the earliest known horses were the size of a housecat and had four toes on the front foot and three on the back; Rose 2006), but with more hints of familiarity than if they had visited the preceding Paleocene epoch.

What of the fossil record for Primates? Inarguable members of the order (called here Euprimates following Hoffstetter 1977) form part of the fauna whose spread across Laurasia has been tied to the PETM (Gingerich 2006), although technically the oldest known likely euprimate is slightly older (*Altiatlasius* from the late Paleocene of Morocco; Sigé et al. 1990). Within the first one–two million years of the Eocene, two groups of euprimates, the Adapoidea and the Omomyoidea, had begun to radiate in parts of North America, Europe, and Asia (Dunn et al. 2016; Godinot 2015; Morse et al. 2019; see Table 22.1), with the former also appearing in the middle Eocene of Africa (Godinot et al. 2018). When known, these adapoids and omomyoids have all the hallmarks of "proper" primates, including convergent orbits with postorbital bars, nails on most digits (e.g., see Rose 1994: figure 3), and brains with some expansion of the neocortex and proportionally small olfactory bulbs (Harrington et al. 2016, 2020; Ramdarshan and Orliac 2016). There is really no debate about the primate status of adapoids and omomyoids, although (as discussed below) their ultimate fate in primate phylogeny is still a source of some dispute.

What is still very much in debate is the source of Euprimates, both phylogenetically and biogeographically, and the adaptive basis for the origin of Primates as an order. In particular, there is a diverse array of "archaic" taxa that make up part of the Paleocene fauna (extending in some cases into the Eocene) who have been linked to Primates. These potential stem Primates, often referred to as "Plesiadapiformes", underwent their own radiation in the ~ 10-million-year period between the extinction of the dinosaurs and the first appearance of the Euprimates (Silcox et al. 2017).

In this chapter we will provide an overview of the fossil record for the key early euprimate groups, and for the plesiadapiforms, and we will discuss how this record relates to Primate Origins and to the origins of Strepsirrhini and Anthropoidea.

EARLY EUPRIMATES

Adapoidea

Adapis was the first fossil primate to be named (Cuvier 1812), although the reference in its name to Apis, the sacred Egyptian bull, implies some initial confusion about its identity. For most anthropologists, the image they have of adapoids probably originates with one of the great classic works in Paleoprimatology, Gregory's 1920 monograph on *Notharctus*, an extremely well documented genus from the early Eocene of North America. The impression given by *Notharctus* is that adapoids were larger than their contemporary omomyoids, with lemur-like adaptations for arboreal quadrupedalism with some leaping, an omnivorous diet, and a diurnal activity period. This perspective over-simplifies the impressive diversity of adapoids currently known, including over 100 species (Godinot 2015), with body masses (~100–6,900 g; Soligo 2006) that overlap the omomyoid range, and an impressive diversity of adaptations in terms of activity period, locomotion, and diet. As one example, the European *Caenopithecus* was a folivorous, slow arboreal quadruped with loris-like postcranial features (Seiffert et al. 2015). Adapoids also provide the oldest evidence of sexual dimorphism in the primate fossil record (Alexander 1994; Krishtalka et al. 1990), differing in this way from most known strespsirrhines.

Table 22.1 Classification of Early Primates. Plesiadapiforms follow the taxonomic framework in Silcox et al. (2017), adapoids as in Godinot (1998, 2015), and omomyoids as in Godinot (2015). Some additions were made necessary by recent discoveries (Chavasseau et al. 2019; Dunn et al. 2016; Ni et al. 2016)

Primates

Purgatoriidae (North America)

Micromomyidae (North America, ?Asia)

Microsyopidae (North America, Europe)

Toliapinidae (Europe)

Picromomyidae (North America)

Paromomyoidea

Paromomyidae (North America, Europe, Asia)

Palaechthonidae (North America, ?Asia)

Picrodontidae (North America)

Plesiadapoidea

Plesiadapidae (North America, Europe)

Carpolestidae (North America, Asia)

Saxonellidae (North America, Europe)

Adapoidea

Notharctidae

Notharctinae (North America, Europe)

Cercamoniinae (Europe)

Adapidae

Caenopithecinae (North America, Europe, Asia, Africa)

Adapinae (Europe)

Asiadapidae (Asia)

Ekgmowechashalidae (North America, Asia)

Sivaladapidae

Hoanghoniinae (Asia)

Sivaladapinae (Asia)

Anthradapinae (Asia)

Omomyoidea

Omomyidae

Omomyinae (North America, Asia)

Anaptomorphinae (North America)

Microchoeridae

Microchoerinae (Europe, Asia)

Primitive adapoids and omomyoids are very similar dentally, although adapoids do possess two apparently derived features of the dentition that allows them to be distinguished (the loss of the postmetaconule crista on the upper molars and the presence of a buccally shifted hypoconulid on the lower first and second molars; see Rose 1994: figures 1 and 2). Discoveries of postcranial material of primitive adapoids and omomyoids from India, which may constitute the oldest (~54.5 mya) well preserved skeletal remains for Euprimates (Dunn et al. 2016), also suggest that the two groups may have also been similar postcranially at their inception. Although the Indian specimens show adaptations for arboreal quadrupedalism, they lack features for leaping, which is somewhat surprising since that locomotor mode is often inferred to be primitive for Euprimates (e.g., Silcox et al. 2015).

Most large-scale analyses find that adapoids exist as a series of branches off the strepsirrhine stem (e.g., Seiffert et al. 2015, 2018). As discussed below, an alternative, minority view would consider them haplorhines rather than strepsirrhines, with relevance to anthropoid origins rather than strepsirrhine evolution (Franzen et al. 2009; Gingerich et al. 2010). In recent years, the geographic scope of the family has expanded considerably, with discoveries in Egypt, Namibia, India, Vietnam, Thailand and Myanmar (e.g., Beard et al. 2007; Chaimanee et al. 2008; Chavasseau et al. 2019; Godinot et al. 2018; Rose et al. 2009; Seiffert et al. 2018), demonstrating that adapoids were broadly distributed not only in Laurasia, but also in Africa. The temporal range of the superfamily is also incredibly long, stretching from the earliest Eocene in Europe and North America (see Figure 22.1 and Godinot 2015) around 56 mya (Dunn et al. 2016) to the Miocene of China at about 8 million years ago (Pan and Wu 1986; Wu and Pan 1985). As such, Adapoidea is arguably the longest-lived primate superfamily. The North American record includes literally thousands of specimens of the genus *Cantius*, which provides one of the best-documented examples of gradual evolution in the fossil record (O'Leary 2021). The latest occurring

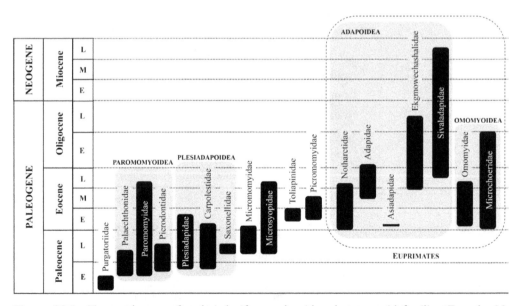

Figure 22.1 Temporal ranges for plesiadapiform, adapoid and omomyoid families. E: early; M: middle; L: late. Approximate age ranges based on Godinot (1978), Wu and Pan (1985), Gingerich (1986), Pan and Wu (1986), Wilson (1986), Beard et al. (1994), Köhler and Moyà-Solà (1999), Seiffert (2007); Hooker (2010, 2012), Marigó et al. (2013), Samuels et al. (2015); Dunn et al. (2016), Silcox et al. (2017), and Rust (2018). Source: Sergi López-Torres

endemic North American primate, *Ekgmowechashala philotau*, is now considered to be an adapoid, persisting until ~ 26 mya (Samuels et al. 2015).

The most complete specimen of a fossil primate known also pertains to an adapoid, *Darwinius massillae*, from the middle Eocene (~47 mya) Lagerstätten deposits of Messel, Germany. Among the extraordinary discoveries possible from the *Darwinius* skeleton is the first evidence of stomach contents for a fossil primate (Franzen and Wilde 2003), consisting of fruit and leaves. Interestingly, no evidence of insect remains were found, even though they are common elements of Messel stomach contents. The *Darwinius* skeleton (aka "Ida") pertained to a subadult of perhaps just over 1 year old (López-Torres et al. 2015) that is assumed to be female based on the lack of an os baculum (Franzen et al. 2009). Adaptively, *Darwinius* is inferred to have been a nocturnal arboreal quadruped, without particular specializations for leaping (Franzen et al. 2009). Interpretation of the *Darwinius* skeleton has brought debates about the role of adapoids in the larger picture of primate evolution into sharp relief (see below; Gingerich et al. 2010; Williams et al. 2010b).

Omomyoidea

Traditionally, omomyoids have been viewed as tarsier-like, in contrast to the lemur-like adapoids. However, the current knowledge of omomyoid biology shows that they were not uniformly tarsier-like, but instead filled a wider range of adaptive niches, with many forms being more similar to present-day bushbabies (Gunnell and Rose 2002). Omomyoids are characterized by having large orbits, a tubular ectotympanic (a feature seen in tarsiers and catarrhines), and a short snout, and were generally small in body mass (22 g – 2.5 kg; Fleagle 2013; Strait 2001). The large orbits in omomyoids are interpreted as adaptations to nocturnality, even though the earliest members of this group were reconstructed as diurnal, visually oriented predators, making nocturnality likely to be a derived adaptation of later-occurring omomyoids (Ankel-Simons and Rasmussen 2008; Godinot 2015; Ni et al. 2004). Most omomyoids are also characterized by having large incisors and small canines, but there are some notable exceptions, such as *Washakius*, which had small anterior teeth (Covert and Williams 1991). The postcranial skeleton of most omomyoids shows hallmarks of leaping behaviour; however, there is a significant diversity in modes of locomotion, ranging from the *Cheirogaleus*-like type of generalized arboreal quadrupedalism of the most primitive forms to tarsier-like extreme leapers (Boyer et al. 2013; Dunn et al. 2016; Godinot 2015). As in modern strepsirrhines and tarsiers (and likely some adapoids; Koenigswald et al. 2012), some omomyoids (including the very primitive *Teilhardina brandti*) also had a grooming claw (Boyer et al. 2018).

There are over 120 species of omomyoids found across North America, Europe, and Asia. The rich North American dental record includes evidence of the evolution of one genus (*Tetonius*) into another (*Pseudotetonius*), which represents a compelling example of gradual evolution (Rose and Bown 1984). With respect to diet, most omomyoids were either strict insectivores or were omnivores (Strait 2001), but the evolution of larger taxa after the extinction of large-bodied adapoids by the late middle Eocene (Jones et al. 2014) brought more folivorous behaviours to the fore (Covert 1986). As mentioned earlier, during the early Eocene, primitive adapoids and omomyoids were very similar dentally (Rose 1994; Rose and Bown 1991). However, omomyoids can be distinguished from adapoids by a slight mesiodistal compression of the lower antemolar series. This compression occurs due to the relatively more reduced canine and first lower premolar (p1), loss of one root from the second lower premolar (p2), and compaction of the third and fourth lower premolars (p3–4) (Rose 1994).

The question of the relationships of omomyoids with modern-day tarsiers has sparked considerable debate, with some authors considering that, due to the lack of clear features linking omomyoids to tarsiers, omomyoids should be considered a separate group from Tarsiiformes, for which the name Omomyiformes is sometimes used (Godinot 2015; Williams et al. 2010a). Some cladistic analyses recover omomyoids as stem haplorhines (e.g., Holroyd and Strait 2008; Ni et al. 2004), but most large-scale phylogenetic analyses find that omomyoids exist as a series of branches off the tarsiiform stem (Morse et al. 2019; Ni et al. 2016; Seiffert et al. 2015, 2018), favouring historical osteological interpretations tying omomyoids to tarsiers (e.g., Cope 1882; Stehlin 1916). As such, omomyoids might represent a paraphyletic grouping (Godinot 2015). Alternatively, some have viewed omomyoids as a monophyletic sister group to adapoids (Martin 1990). The omomyoid temporal range (see Figure 22.1) stretches from the earliest Eocene of Wyoming around 56 mya (*Teilhardina brandti*; Gingerich 1993; Morse et al. 2019; Rose et al. 2011), appearing around the same time as adapoids as part of the PETM fauna (Gingerich 2006), to the early Oligocene of Catalonia, Spain, around 31 mya (*Pseudoloris godinoti*; Köhler and Moyà-Solà 1999).

Possible Stem Primates (Plesiadapiforms)

While there is no real debate about the primate status of adapoids and omomyoids, whether any earlier taxa can be considered primates is still in question. The earliest forms that have been linked to Primates belong to the family Purgatoriidae and the genus *Purgatorius* (Wilson Mantilla et al. 2021). The purgatoriids comprise but one of 11 families that are clustered together as "plesiadapiforms" (Silcox et al. 2017). The oldest well-dated material for *Purgatorius* comes from northeastern Montana and is likely to be within 105–139 kya of the K–Pg boundary; a possible Cretaceous record (Van Valen and Sloan 1965) is from a fauna that is now considered to be of mixed age (Wilson Mantilla et al. 2021) and in any case is not particularly diagnostic (i.e., it consists of a single fragmented molar). Therefore, there is no clear evidence of coexistence of primates with any nonavian dinosaurs. Quantitative analysis of the dentition of the earliest purgatoriids (Wilson Mantilla et al. 2021) show that they already had features consistent with omnivory and frugivory. Indeed, plesiadapiforms generally share with euprimates a similar overall pattern of molar dental morphology, with relatively low trigonids and broad talonid basins (e.g., see Rose 1994: figure 1).

Known from across Laurasia (Beard and Wang 1995; Russell 1964; Silcox and Gunnell 2008), nine of the 11 plesiadapiform families originate in the Paleocene (see Figure 22.1 and Table 22.1), forming part of the archaic fauna alluded to in the Introduction. In North America some families became extinct near the Paleocene–Eocene boundary in what could be considered the first major primate extinction event, the basis of which is still in debate (Prufrock et al. 2016). However, several families do survive the Paleocene–Eocene boundary and coexist with euprimates, with two families being documented only in the Eocene (Toliapinidae and Picromomyidae; see Figure 22.1). There are large collections of some plesiadapiform families known from the Paleocene and Eocene of North America. Indeed, the members of one family, the Plesiadapidae, are used as critical index taxa in North American Paleocene biostratigraphy (Gingerich 1976). Another Paleocene family, the Carpolestidae, provides a nice example of directional adaptive evolution in the increasing size and elaboration of its large, mitten-like fourth premolar through time (Rose 1977: figure 1). The carpolestid p4 also serves as one of several examples of the ways in which the dentitions of plesiadapiforms exceed the adaptive boundaries of modern euprimates, being more similar to that tooth in Mesozoic multituberculates and some modern marsupials (recognized by Simpson 1933 as a particular adaptive type, the "plagiaulacoid" dentition). Other examples include the peculiar enlarged m1 of picrodontid plesiadapiforms, which is similar to the fig-eating bat genus *Ariteus* (Burger 2013), and the pointed p4 of paromomyid plesiadapiforms, which has been likened to the specialized puncturing teeth of modern petaurid marsupials (Gingerich 1974).

In general, plesiadapiforms were small mammals – indeed the group includes several contenders for the smallest primate, with *Toliapina vinealis* in particular being a strong candidate with an estimated body mass of only ~ 6.6 g (Hooker et al. 1999; Silcox et al. 2017). The largest plesiadapiform weighed only ~ 3.5 kg (*Megadelphus lundeliusi*; Silcox et al. 2017). All plesiadapiforms are characterized by enlarged upper and lower incisors. Although this would have given them a somewhat rodent-like appearance, the incisors lack the restricted enamel of rodent incisors, and were not ever-growing.

Much of the fossil record of plesiadapiforms is dental, but at least some postcranial material is known for seven of the 11 families (Silcox et al. 2017). What is arguably the oldest primate skeleton pertains to the plesiadapiform *Torrejonia wilsoni* (Chester et al. 2017, 2019) from the early Paleocene of New Mexico. This species would have had highly mobile ankle joints and habitually flexed fore and hind limbs, consistent with nonleaping arboreality. Indeed, all plesiadapiforms known from postcranial material were nonleaping arborealists, but with a diversity of locomotor behaviours within that general framework. For example, the genus *Plesiadapis* is sometimes treated as a good proxy for the entire plesiadapiform radiation, since it has been well known from cranial, postcranial, and dental material for more than 50 years (e.g., see Russell 1964). This approach is problematic, however, in under-representing the diversity of plesiadapiforms generally, and even plesiadapids specifically. *Plesiadapis* would likely have been more specialized for moving on large vertical supports than other plesiadapiforms, with *Plesiadapis cookei* in particular showing adaptations for suspensory behavior such as very deep manual unguals (Boyer and Gingerich 2019). However, other members of the family were better adapted for manual grasping (suggesting greater use of smaller supports), as evidenced by variation in humeral anatomy and hand proportions (Bloch and Boyer 2007). One of the best represented plesiadapiforms postcranially is *Carpolestes simpsoni*, known from a remarkably complete partial skeleton, which demonstrates that the species had a divergent big toe with a flat nail (Bloch and Boyer 2002). If this represents a trait shared with the common ancestor to euprimates it would form some of the most compelling evidence for the primate affinities of plesiadapiforms (see the discussion below).

There are at least some cranial remains known for members of all but four families of plesiadapiforms (Silcox et al. 2017). These specimens demonstrate a quite different Bauplan from the euprimate cranium (Figure 22.2), with orbits that face fairly far laterally, no complete postorbital bars, and quite long snouts (Bloch et al. 2016; Bloch and Silcox 2006; Kay et al. 1990; Russell 1964; Silcox et al. 2020). The makeup of the auditory bulla in plesiadapiforms remains a matter of debate. While the paromomyid plesiadapiform *Ignacius* had a nonpetrosal bulla (probably formed from an entotympanic element; Bloch and Silcox 2001; Kay et al. 1990; Silcox 2003) and microsyopids may not have had a bulla (Silcox et al. 2020), some other families (Carpolestidae, Plesiadapidae, Micromomyidae) show continuity between at least part of the bulla and the petrosal (Bloch and Silcox 2006; Bloch et al. 2016; Boyer et al. 2012; Russell 1964) and so might exhibit the distinctively primate-like feature of a petrosal bulla. The endocasts of plesiadapiforms indicate that the brain had not yet evolved a euprimate-like expansion of the neocortex, with notably larger olfactory

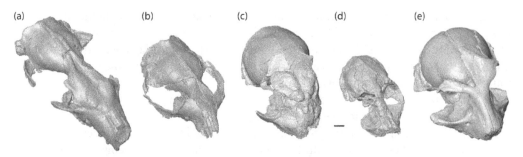

Figure 22.2   Reconstructions of crania in oblique dorsal view based on high-resolution X-ray microCT data. (A) *Microsyops annectens* (UW 12362); (B) *Ignacius graybullianus* (USNM 421608); (C) *Smilodectes gracilis* (USNM UM 32773); (D) *Necrolemur antiquus* (MaPhQ 289); (E) *Rooneyia viejaensis* (TMM 406887). Scale bar = 5 mm. Source: Mary T. Silcox.

bulbs relative to the overall size of the brain compared to even the most primitive euprimates (Gingerich and Gunnell 2005; Orliac et al. 2014; Silcox et al. 2009, 2010).

But Are They Primates?

Of course, the million-dollar question for plesiadapiforms is whether they can be considered members of our order. Two papers published in *Nature* in 1990 (Beard 1990; Kay et al. 1990) seemed to tell a compelling tale of nonprimate affinities for one group of plesiadapiforms, the Paromomyidae, based on apparent cranial and postcranial similarities to the modern Southeast Asian gliding mammals of the order Dermoptera (i.e., colugos or "flying lemurs"), which even led to the suggestion that paromomyids may have been gliders (Beard 1990). Subsequently, more complete discoveries (Bloch and Silcox 2001; Bloch et al. 2007), as well as the study of the cranial material with modern high-resolution X-ray CT (Silcox 2003), have brought these conclusions into question. With better-associated postcranial material, it is now clear that paromomyids were not gliders (Boyer and Bloch 2008), but were instead callitrichine-like, active arborealists capable of bounding behaviours (Bloch et al. 2007; Boyer and Bloch 2008).

In some analyses incorporating these new discoveries (e.g., Bloch et al. 2007; Chester et al. 2017; Silcox 2008), plesiadapiforms fall out as more closely related to primates than are any other taxa – as such, they could be considered stem primates. However, in others, they fall out as euarchontans (i.e., members of the group including Primates, Dermoptera, and Scandentia [treeshrews]) but not as stem primates per se (e.g., Ni et al. 2016). We have argued (Silcox et al. 2017) that analyses explicitly designed to answer questions about plesiadapiform relationships are more likely to produce correct answers about plesiadapiform relationships than analyses designed with other purposes in mind, because they include characters and taxa that are critical to form correct inferences about the primitive states of plesiadapiform groups. While we (unsurprisingly) continue to hold that view, we do also offer another observation. The fossil record for nonprimate members of Euarchonta continues to be extremely poor (Silcox et al. 2005). Therefore, reconstructing relationships on the euarchontan stem is very challenging, since it is effectively mixing highly derived modern taxa (colugos and treeshrews) that have been evolving away from their common ancestor with primates for probably at least 65 million years (Upham et al. 2019), with forms much less removed from the euarchontan common ancestor. Until we know more about primitive euarchontans, the relationships of plesiadapiforms are likely to continue to be contentious.

A different approach to the question of the primate status of plesiadapiforms is to compare what we know of the group to definitions of Primates based on characters that are either universally present in living members of the order, or have been deduced to have been present in their common ancestor. Such an approach was taken, for example, by Martin (1968) and Cartmill (1972, 1974). It is certainly true that plesiadapiforms lack some of the features that would appear on such a list, including, for example, the postorbital bar, nails on most digits, and convergent orbits. Certainly, a concept of "Primates" that excludes plesiadapiforms is easier to define, both in a formal taxonomic sense and adaptively. However, as our knowledge of both plesiadapiforms and early primates has grown, these lines have begun to blur. As one example, a distinctive primate trait, pedal grasping, can now be inferred to have evolved through a series of steps in the course of plesiadapiform evolution (Bloch et al. 2007; Sargis et al. 2007). Similarly, an enlarged brain (relative to body mass) is often cited as a distinctively primate trait (e.g., Cartmill 1992), but as our knowledge of endocranial anatomy in early euprimates has grown it has become increasingly clear that primitive forms were less encephalized than would be expected from the modern record (Harrington et al. 2020). Simply put, an approach that requires taxa to have all of a list of defining traits becomes problematic as more intermediate forms are found.

For these reasons, we will continue to argue that the best evidence that exists supports the inference that plesiadapiforms were indeed primates, with some primitive features compared to modern members of the order, but sharing features of the dentition associated with omnivory, and the postcranium associated with a primate-like mode of arboreality (i.e., see Bloch et al. 2007: figure 5).

Looking Backwards and Looking Forwards

Explaining Primate Origins

There are several scenarios that attempt to explain coordinated shifts in primate traits through the lens of overarching changes in the primate niche. Historically (e.g., Le Gros Clark 1959), the key to such change was thought to be the transition to arboreality. However, this model is now widely discredited because there is solid evidence that the ancestors of primates of modern aspect were already arboreal (Szalay and Drawhorn 1980). Arboreality in and of itself cannot explain many primate features (Cartmill 1974) and early primates show arboreal characteristics long before other primate traits appear (Chester et al. 2015, 2017, 2019). Four ecological scenarios that variously emphasize particular behaviours arose out of the ashes of the arboreality hypothesis and continue to frame many discussions about Primate Origins: (1) visual predation (Cartmill 1974, 1992), which emphasizes visually directed capture of prey (primarily insects) as the catalyst to shifting the primate niche; (2) grasp-leaping locomotor behaviours, preceded by a shift toward greater consumption of plant material (including fruit, leaves, nectar, gums, etc.), emphasizing a sequence of adaptive changes that eventually led to the unique suite of specializations seen in primates (Szalay 1968); (3) terminal branch feeding, tying more intense use of angiosperm resources, like fruit and flowers, to major adaptive shifts in primate evolution (Sussman 1991), perhaps through diffuse coevolution between primates and fruiting trees; and (4) a combination involving terminal branch feeding being followed by visual predation (Rasmussen 1990). The sequence of change in characters in primitive primates is most consistent with the terminal branch feeding hypothesis (Bloch et al. 2007; Silcox et al. 2015; Silcox and López-Torres 2017). However, this conclusion fails to provide a clear explanation for the unique visual system in primates (but see Changizi and Shimojo 2008) or to consider shifts in ecology between plesiadapiforms and euprimates (e.g., to incorporate more leaping), demonstrating that more work needs to be done to explain both primate and euprimate origins.

The Origins of Anthropoidea and Strepsirrhini

The origins of anthropoids have been a matter of extensive discussion in the literature. The main contenders for the anthropoid stem have been (1) the Eosimiiformes and (2) the Adapoidea. These two models lead to different perspectives on what the earliest anthropoids should look like – more tarsier-like in the first case and more like early definitive anthropoids in the second.

Eosimiiforms include two families of middle Eocene to early Oligocene primates: the Eosimiidae and the Afrotarsiidae. Eosimiids were a family of diminutive primates from the middle Eocene of China and Myanmar (Beard et al. 1994; Jaeger et al. 1999) and the Oligocene of Pakistan (Marivaux et al. 2005) that are very tarsier-like in morphology, but with some traits, such as vertically implanted incisors, obliquely oriented premolar roots, and a deep mandible, that are more anthropoid-like. The most broadly accepted view is that eosimiids are stem anthropoids (Beard et al. 1994; Kay et al. 1997; Marivaux et al. 2005; Williams et al. 2010a), which is supported by comprehensive phylogenetic analyses (e.g., Bajpai et al. 2008; Rose et al. 2009). In light of the widespread acceptance of the relationship between modern tarsiers and anthropoids, eosimiids are, perhaps, close to what one might predict an anthropoid ancestor might look like. However, other authors disagree with this placement (e.g., Godinot 1994; Gunnell and Miller 2001), in part because of the deep morphological chasm between members of this group and unquestionable early anthropoids from the Fayum of Egypt (Gunnell and Miller 2001). Afrotarsiids, also from the Fayum, have been interpreted by some as being anthropoids closely related to the Asian taxa (Beard 2016), despite their name being more suggestive of tarsier affinities, and having originally been described as tarsiids (Simons and Bown 1985).

Most contemporary authors have supported a closer relationship of adapoids to strepsirrhines (i.e., Adapoid–Strepsirrhine Hypothesis; see Dagosto 1988; Gregory 1920; Hoffstetter 1977; Kay et al. 1997), but the Adapoid–Anthropoid Hypothesis has a long history in the literature on this subject (e.g., Bloch et al. 1997; Gingerich and Schoeninger 1977; Rasmussen and Simons 1988; Wortman 1903–1904), and gained some attention recently in the context of the description of *Darwinius*, as mentioned above (Franzen et al. 2009; Gingerich et al. 2010). The authors argued that its short rostrum, deep mandibular ramus, partially fused mandible, vertical and spatulate incisors, talus with a steep talofibular facet, apparently absent grooming claw (but see Koenigswald et al. 2012), lack of a tooth-comb, mediolaterally compressed cuneiform, and long fourth pedal digit supported ties with halporhines and anthropoids (Franzen et al. 2009; Gingerich et al. 2010). However, the short rostrum, symphyseal fusion, and deep mandible have evolved many times in primate evolution, and other characters could be interpreted as primitive for euprimates (Williams et al. 2010b). For example, as mentioned above, the omomyoid *Washakius* is known to have small anterior teeth, somewhat similar to that of adapoids and anthropoids (Covert and Williams 1991). This suggests that this feature might actually be a plesiomorphic trait of the euprimate ancestor, and anthropoids simply inherited this primitive trait. Additionally, grooming claws are well documented in other adapoids (Boyer et al. 2018; Maiolino et al. 2012). The Adapoid–Strepsirrhine Hypothesis is supported by most recent large-scale phylogenetic analyses (e.g., Ni et al. 2016; Seiffert et al. 2015, 2018). However, it is important to note that despite the consistent support for adapoids as stem strepsirrhines, adapoids do lack many of the typical strepsirrhine features, like the toothcomb. The oldest evidence of a toothcomb in the fossil record is found in the early late Eocene stem lorisoid *Karanisia* (Seiffert et al. 2003), making it the first known primate that actually looks like a modern strepsirrhine, implying a large gap in the known record of early strepsirrhine evolution between adapoids primitive enough to be strepsirrhine ancestors and the first definitive member of the group.

REFERENCES

Alexander, J. P. "Sexual Dimorphism in Notharctid Primates." *Folia Primatologica* 63 (1994): 59–62.

Ankel-Simons, F., and D. T. Rasmussen. "Diurnality, Nocturnality, and the Evolution of Primate Visual Systems." *Yearbook of Physical Anthropology* 51 (2008): 100–117.

Bajpai, S., R. F. Kay, B. A. Williams, et al. "The Oldest Asian Record of Anthropoidea." *Proceedings of the National Academy of Sciences, USA* 105 (2008): 11093–11098.

Beard, K. C. "Gliding Behavior and Palaecology of the Alleged Primate Family Paromomyidae (Mammalia, Dermoptera)." *Nature* 345 (1990): 340–341.

Beard, K. C. "Out of Asia: Anthropoid Origins and the Colonization of Africa." *Annual Review of Anthropology* 45 (2016): 199–213.

Beard, K. C., and J. Wang. "The First Asian Plesiadapoids." *Annals of the Carnegie Museum* 64 (1995): 1–33.

Beard, K. C., T. Qi, M. R. Dawson, B. Wang, and C. Li. "A Diverse New Primate Fauna from Middle Eocene Fissure Fillings in Northeastern China." *Nature* 368 (1994): 604–609.

Beard, K. C., L. Marivaux, S. T. Tun, et al. "New Sivaladapid Primates from the Eocene Pondaung Formation of Myanmar and the Anthropoid Status of Amphipithecidae." *Bulletin of the Carnegie Museum of Natural History* 39 (2007): 67–76.

Bloch, J. I., and D. M. Boyer. "Grasping Primate Origins." *Science* 298 (2002): 1606–1610.

Bloch, J. I., and D. M. Boyer. "New Skeletons of Paleocene–Eocene Plesiadapiformes: A Diversity of Arboreal Positional Behaviors in Early Primates." In *Primate Origins: Adaptations and Evolution*. Edited by M. J. Ravosa and M. Dagosto, 535–581. New York: Springer, 2007.

Bloch, J. I., and M. T. Silcox. "New Basicrania of Paleocene-Eocene *Ignacius*: Re-evaluation of the Plesiadapiform–Dermopteran Link." *American Journal of Physical Anthropology* 116 (2001): 184–198.

Bloch, J. I., and M. T. Silcox. "Cranial Anatomy of the Paleocene Plesiadapiforms *Carpolestes simpsoni* (Mammalia, Primates) Using Ultra High-Resolution X-ray Computed Tomography, and the Relationships of Plesiadapiforms to Euprimates." *Journal of Human Evolution* 50 (2006): 1–35.

Bloch, J. I., D. C. Fisher, P. D. Gingerich, et al. "Cladistic Analysis and Anthropoid Origins." *Science* 278 (1997): 2134–2136.

Bloch, J. I., M. T. Silcox, D. M. Boyer, and E. J. Sargis. "New Paleocene Skeletons and the Relationship of 'Plesiadapiforms' to Crown Clade Primates." *Proceedings of the National Academy of Sciences, USA* 104 (2007): 1159–1164.

Bloch, J. I., S. G. B. Chester, and M. T. Silcox. "Cranial Anatomy of Paleogene Micromomyidae and Implications for Early Primate Evolution." *Journal of Human Evolution* 96 (2016): 58–81.

Boyer, D. M., and J. I. Bloch. "Evaluating the Mitten-Gliding Hypothesis for Paromomyidae and Micromomyidae (Mammalia, 'Plesiadapiformes') Using Comparative Functional Morphology of New Paleogene Skeletons." In *Mammalian Evolutionary Morphology: A Tribute to Frederick S. Szalay*. Edited by M. Dagosto and E. J. Sargis, 231–279. New York: Springer-Verlag, 2008.

Boyer, D. M., and P. D. Gingerich. "Skeleton of Late Paleocene *Plesiadapis cookei* (Mammalia, Euarchonta): Life History, Locomotion, and Phylogenetic Relationships." *University of Michigan Papers on Paleontology* 38 (2019): 1–269.

Boyer, D. M., C. S. Scott, and R. C. Fox. "New Craniodental Material of *Pronothodectes gaoi* Fox (Mammalia, 'Plesiadapiformes') and Relationships Among Members of Plesiadapidae." *American Journal of Physical Anthropology* 147 (2012): 511–550.

Boyer, D. M., E. R. Seiffert, J. T. Gladman, and J. I. Bloch. "Evolution and Allometry of Calcaneal Elongation in Living and Extinct Primates." *PLoS One* 8 (2013): e67792.

Boyer, M., S. A. Maiolino, P. A. Holroyd, et al. "Oldest Evidence for Grooming Claws in Euprimates." *Journal of Human Evolution* 122 (2018): 1–22.

Burger, B. J. "A New Species of the Archaic Primate *Zanycteris* from the Late Paleocene of Western Colorado and the Phylogenetic Position of the Family Picrodontidae." *Peer Journal* 1 (2013): e191.

Cartmill, M. "Arboreal Adaptations and the Origin of the Order Primates." In *The Functional and Evolutionary Biology of Primates*. Edited by R. Tuttle, 97–122. Chicago: Aldine, 1972.

Cartmill, M. "Rethinking Primate Origins." *Science* 184 (1974): 436–443.

Cartmill, M. "New Views on Primate Origins." *Evolutionary Anthropology* 1 (1992): 105–111.

Chaimanee, Y., C. Yamee, P. Tian, et al. "First Middle Miocene Sivaladapid Primate from Thailand." *Journal of Human Evolution* 54 (2008): 434–443.

Changizi, M. A., and S. Shimojo. "'X-ray Vision' and the Evolution of Forward-Facing Eyes." *Journal of Theoretical Biology* 254 (2008): 756–767.

Chavasseau, O., Y. Chaimanee, S. Ducrocq, et al. "A New Primate from the Late Eocene of Vietnam Illuminates Unexpected Strepsirrhine Diversity and Evolution in Southeast Asia." *Scientific Reports* 9 (2019): 1–11.

Chester, S. G. B, J. I. Bloch, D. M. Boyer, and W. A. Clemens. "Oldest Known Euarchontan Tarsals and Affinities of Paleocene *Purgatorius* to Primates." *Proceedings of the National Academy of Sciences, USA* 112 (2015): 1487–1492.

Chester, S. G. B., T. E. Williamson, J. I. Bloch, et al. "Oldest Skeleton of a Plesiadapiform Provides Additional Evidence for an Exclusively Arboreal Radiation of Stem Primates in the Palaeocene." *Royal Society Open Science* 4 (2017): 170329.

Chester, S. G. B, T. E. Williamson, M. T. Silcox, et al. "Skeletal Morphology of the Early Paleocene Plesiadapiform *Torrejonia wilsoni* (Euarchonta, Palaechthonidae)." *Journal of Human Evolution* 128 (2019): 76–92.

Cope, E. D. "Contributions to the History of the Vertebrata of the Lower Eocene of Wyoming and New Mexico, Made During 1881." *Proceedings of the American Philosophical Society* 20 (1882): 139–197.

Covert, H. H. "Biology of Early Cenozoic Primates." In *Comparative Primate Biology. Volume I: Systematics, Evolution and Anatomy*. Edited by D. R. Swindler and J. Erwin, 335–359. New York: Alan R. Liss, Inc, 1986.

Covert, H. H., and B. A. Williams. "The Anterior Lower Dentition of *Washakius insignis* and Adapid-Anthropoidean Affinities." *Journal of Human Evolution* 21 (1991): 463–467.

Cuvier, G., *Recherches sur les ossements fossiles de quadrupèdes (I)*. Paris: Librairie Déterville, 1812.

Dagosto, M. "Implications of Postcranial Evidence for the Origins of Euprimates." *Journal of Human Evolution* 17 (1988): 35–56.

Dunn, R. H., K. D. Rose, R. S. Rana, et al. "New Euprimate Postcrania from the Early Eocene of Gujarat, India, and the Strepsirrhine–Haplorhine Divergence." *Journal of Human Evolution* 99 (2016): 25–51.

Fleagle, J. G. *Primate Adaptation and Evolution*, 3rd edn. London: Academic Press, 2013.

Franzen, J. L., and V. Wilde. "First Gut Content of a Fossil Primate." *Journal of Human Evolution* 44 (2003): 373–378.

Franzen, J. L., P. D. Gingerich, J. Habersetzer, et al. "Complete Primate Skeleton from the Middle Eocene of Messel in Germany: Morphology and Paleobiology." *PLoS One* 4 (2009): e5723.

Gingerich, P. D. "Function of Pointed Premolars in *Phenacolemur* and Other Mammals." *Journal of Dental Research* 53 (1974): 497.

Gingerich, P. D. "Cranial Anatomy and Evolution of Early Tertiary Plesiadapidae (Mammalia, Primates)." *University of Michigan Papers on Paleontology* 15 (1976): 1–141.

Gingerich, P. D. "Early Eocene *Cantius torresi* – Oldest Primate of Modern Aspect from North America." *Nature* 319 (1986): 319–321.

Gingerich, P. D. "Early Eocene *Teilhardina brandti*: Oldest Omomyid Primate from North America." *Contributions from the Museum of Paleontology, University of Michigan* 28 (1993): 321–326.

Gingerich, P. D. "Environment and Evolution Through the Paleocene–Eocene Thermal Maximum." *Trends in Ecology & Evolution* 21 (2006): 246–253.

Gingerich, P. D., and G. F. Gunnell. "Brain of *Plesiadapis cookei* (Mammalia, Proprimates): Surface Morphology and Encephalization Compared to Those of Primates and Dermoptera." *Contributions from the Museum of Paleontology, University of Michigan* 31 (2005): 185–195.

Gingerich, P. D., and M. Schoeninger. "The Fossil Record and Primate Phylogeny." *Journal of Human Evolution* 6 (1977): 483–505.

Gingerich, P. D., J. L. Franzen, J. Habersetzer, et al. "2010 *Darwinius masillae* is a Haplorhine-Reply to Williams et al." *Journal of Human Evolution* 59 (2010): 574–579.

Godinot, M. "Un Nouvel Adapidé (Primate) de l'Eocène Inférieur de Provence." *Comptes Rendus de l'Académie des Sciences, Série D* 286 (1978): 1869–1872.

Godinot, M. "Early North African Primates and Their Significance for the Origin of Simiiformes (= Anthropoidea)." In *Anthropoid Origins*. Edited by J. G. Fleagle and R. F. Kay, 235–296. New York: Plenum Press, 1994.

Godinot, M. "A Summary of Adapiform Systematics and Phylogeny." *Folia Primatologica* 69 (1998): 218–249.

Godinot, M. "Fossil Record of the Primates from the Paleocene to the Oligocene." *Handbook of Paleoanthropology* 2 (2015): 1137–1259.

Godinot, M., B. Senut, and M. Pickford. "Primitive Adapidae from Namibia Sheds Light on the Early Primate Radiation in Africa." *Communications of the Geological Survey of Namibia* 18 (2018): 140–162.

Gregory, W. K. "On the Structure and Relations of *Notharctus*, an American Eocene Primate." *Memoirs of the American Museum of Natural History* 3 (1920): 49–243.

Gunnell, G. F., and E. R. Miller. "Origin of Anthropoidea: Dental Evidence and Recognition of Early Anthropoids in the Fossil Record, with Comments on the Asian Anthropoid Radiation." *American Journal of Physical Anthropology* 114 (2001): 177–191.

Gunnell, G. F., and K. D. Rose. "Tarsiiformes: Evolutionary History and Adaptation." In *The Primate Fossil Record*. Edited by W. C. Hartwig, 45–82. Cambridge: Cambridge University Press, 2002.

Harrington, A. R., M. T. Silcox, G. S. Yapuncich, et al. "First Virtual Endocasts of Adapiform Primates." *Journal of Human Evolution* 99 (2016): 52–78.

Harrington, A. R., G. S. Yapuncich, and D. M. Boyer. "The Digital Endocast of *Necrolemur antiquus*." *Palaeovertebrata* 43 (2020): e1.

Hoffstetter, R. "Phylogénie des primates: confrontation des résultats obtenus par les diverses voies d'approche du problème." *Bulletins et Mémoires de la Societé d'Anthropologie de Paris* 4 (1977): 327–346.

Holroyd, P. A., and S. G. Strait. "New Data on *Loveina* (Primates: Omomyidae) from the Early Eocene Wasatch Formation and Implications for Washakiin Relationships." In *Elwyn Simons: A Search for Origins*. Edited by J. G. Fleagle and C. C. Gilbert, 243–257. New York: Springer Science+Business Media, 2008.

Hooker, J. J. "The 'Grande Coupure' in the Hampshire Basin, UK: Taxonomy and Stratigraphy of the Mammals on Either Side of This Major Palaeogene Faunal Turnover." In *Micropalaeontology, Sedimentary Environments and Stratigraphy: A Tribute to Dennis Curry (1912–2001)*. Edited by J. E. Whittaker and M. B. Hart, 147–215. London: The Micropalaeontological Society, 2010.

Hooker, J. J. "A New Omomyid Primate from the Earliest Eocene of Southern England: First Phase of Microchoerine Evolution." *Acta Palaeontologica Polonica* 57 (2012): 449–462.

Hooker, J. J., D. E. Russell, and A. Phélizon. "A New Family of Plesiadapiformes (Mammalia) from the Old World Lower Paleogene." *Palaeontology* 42 (1999): 377–407.

Jaeger, J.-J., T. Thein, M. Benammi, et al. "A New Primate from the Middle Eocene of Myanmar and the Asian Early Origin of Anthropoids." *Science* 286 (1999): 528–530.

Jones, K. E., K. D. Rose, and J. M. G. Perry. "Body Size and Premolar Evolution in the Early–Middle Eocene Euprimates of Wyoming." *American Journal of Physical Anthropology* 153 (2014): 15–28.

Kay, R. F., R. W. Thorington, Jr, and P. Houde. "Eocene Plesiadapiforms Shows Affinities with Flying Lemurs Not Primates." *Nature* 345 (1990): 342–344.

Kay, R. F., C. F. Ross, and B. A. Williams. "Anthropoid Origins." *Science* 275 (1997): 797–804.

Koenigswald, W. von, J. Habersetzer, and P. D. Gingerich. "Pedal Distal Phalanges of the Eocene Adapoids *Europolemur* and *Darwinius* Compared to Phalanges of *Notharctus* and Other Primates." *Palaeobiodiversity and Palaeoenvironments* 92 (2012): 539–565.

Köhler, M., and S. Moyà-Solà. "A Finding of Oligocene Primates on the European Continent." *Proceedings of the National Academy of Sciences, USA* 96 (1999):14664–14667.

Krishtalka, L., R. K. Stucky, and K. C. Beard. "The Earliest Fossil Evidence for Sexual Dimorphism in Primates." *Proceedings of the National Academy of Sciences, USA* 87 (1990): 5223–5226.

Le Gros Clark, W. E. *The Antecedents of Man*. Chicago: Quadrangle Books, 1959.

López-Torres, S., M. A. Schillaci, and M. T. Silcox. "Life History of the Most Complete Fossil Primate Skeleton: Exploring Growth Models for *Darwinius*." *Royal Society Open Science* 2 (2015): 150340.

Maiolino, S., D. M. Boyer, J. I. Bloch, et al. "Evidence for a Grooming Claw in a North American Adapiform Primate: Implications for Anthropoid Origins." *PLoS One* 7 (2012): e29135.

Marigó, J., R. Minwer-Barakat, and S. Moyà-Solà. "*Nievesia sossisensis*, a New Anchomomyin (Adapiformes, Primates) from the Early Late Eocene of the Southern Pyrenees (Catalonia, Spain)." *Journal of Human Evolution* 64 (2013): 473–485.

Marivaux, L., P.-O. Antoine, S. R. H. Baqri, et al. "Anthropoid Primates from the Oligocene of Pakistan (Bugti Hills): Data on Early Anthropoid Evolution and Biogeography." *Proceedings of the National Academy of Sciences, USA* 102 (2005): 8436–8441.

Martin, R. D. "Towards a New Definition of Primates." *Man* 3 (1968): 377–401.

Martin, R. D. *Primate Origins and Evolution: A Phylogenetic Reconstruction*. Princeton: Princeton University Press, 1990.

Morse, P. E., S. G. B. Chester, D. M. Boyer, et al. "New Fossils, Systematics, and Biogeography of the Oldest Known Crown Primate *Teilhardina* from the Earliest Eocene of Asia, Europe, and North America." *Journal of Human Evolution* 128 (2019): 103–131.

Ni, X., L. Qiang, L. Lüzhou, and K. C. Beard. "Oligocene Primates from China Reveal Divergence between African and Asian Primate Evolution." *Science* 352 (2016): 673–677.

Ni, X., Y. Wang, H. Yaoming, and L. Chuankui. "A Euprimate Skull from the Early Eocene of China." *Nature* 427 (2004): 65–68.

O'Leary, M. A. "A Dense Sample of Fossil Primates (Adapiformes, Notharctidae, Notharctinae) from the Early Eocene Willwood Formation, Wyoming: Documentation of Gradual Change in Tooth Area and Shape Through Time." *American Journal of Physical Anthropology* 174 (2021): 728–743.

O'Leary, M. A., J. I. Bloch, J. J. Flynn, et al. "The Placental Mammal Ancestor and the Post–K-Pg Radiation of Placentals." *Science* 339 (2013): 662–667.

Orliac, M. J., S. Ladevèze, P. D. Gingerich, et al. "Endocranial Morphology of Palaeocene *Plesiadapis tricuspidens* and Evolution of the Early Primate Brain." *Proceedings of the Royal Society B* 281 (2014): 20132792.

Pan, Y., and R. Wu. "A New Species of *Sinoadapis* from the Lufeng Hominoid Locality." *Acta Anthropologica Sinica* 5 (1986): 31–40.

Prufrock, K. A., S. López-Torres, M. T. Silcox, and D. M. Boyer. "Surfaces and Spaces: Trouble-Shooting the Study of Dietary Niche Space Overlap Between North American Stem Primates and Rodents." *Surface Topography: Metrology and Properties* 4 (2016): 024005.

Ramdarshan, A., and M. J. Orliac. "Endocranial Morphology of *Microchoerus erinaceus* (Euprimates, Tarsiiformes) and Early Evolution of the Euprimates Brain." *American Journal of Physical Anthropology* 159 (2016): 5–16.

Rasmussen, D. T. "Primate Origins: Lessons from a Neotropical Marsupial." *American Journal of Primatology* 22 (1990): 263–277.

Rasmussen, D. T., and E. L. Simons. "New Specimens of *Oligopithecus savagei*, Early Oligocene Primate from the Fayum, Egypt." *Folia Primatologica* 51 (1988): 182–208.

Rose, K. D. "Evolution of Carpolestid Primates and Chronology of the North American Middle and Late Paleocene." *Journal of Vertebrate Paleontology* 51 (1977): 536–542.

Rose, K. D. "The Earliest Primates." *Evolutionary Anthropology* 3 (1994): 159–173.

Rose, K. D. *The Beginning of the Age of Mammals*. Baltimore, MD: Johns Hopkins University Press, 2006.

Rose, K. D., and T. M. Bown. "Gradual Phyletic Evolution at the Generic Level in Early Eocene Omomyid Primates." *Nature* 309 (1984): 250–252.

Rose, K. D., and T. M. Bown. "Additional Fossil Evidence on the Differentiation of the Earliest Euprimates." *Proceedings of the National Academy of Sciences, USA* 88 (1991): 98–101.

Rose, K. D., R. S. Rana, A. Sahni, et al. "Early Eocene Primates from Gujarat, India." *Journal of Human Evolution* 56 (2009): 366–404.

Rose, K. D., S. G. B. Chester, R. H. Dunn, et al. "New Fossils of the Oldest North American euprimate *Teilhardina brandti* (Omomyidae) from the Paleocene–Eocene Thermal Maximum." *American Journal of Physical Anthropology* 146 (2011): 281–305.

Russell, D. E. "Les mammifères Paléocènes d'Europe." *Mémoires du Muséum d'Histoire Naturelle, Série C* 13 (1964): 1–324.

Rust, K. "An Investigation of the Phylogenetic Affinities of Sivaladapidae within Adapoidea." MA Thesis, CUNY Hunter College, New York, 2018.

Samuels, J. X., L. B. Albright, and T. J. Fremd. "The Last Fossil Primate in North America, New Material of the Enigmatic *Ekgmowechashala* from the Arikareean of Oregon." *American Journal of Physical Anthropology* 158 (2015): 43–54.

Sargis, E. J., D. M. Boyer, J. I. Bloch, and M. T. Silcox. "Evolution of Pedal Grasping in Primates." *Journal of Human Evolution* 53 (2007): 103–107.

Seiffert, E. R. "Early Evolution and Biogeography of Lorisiform Strepsirrhines." *American Journal of Primatology* 69 (2007): 27–35.

Seiffert, E. R., E. L. Simons, and Y. Attia. "Fossil Evidence for an Ancient Divergence of Lorises and Galagos." *Nature* 422 (2003): 421–424.

Seiffert, E. R., L. Costeur, and D. M. Boyer. "Primate Tarsal Bones from Egerkingen, Switzerland, Attributable to the Middle Eocene Adapiform *Caenopithecus lemuroides*." *Peer Journal* 3 (2015): e1036.

Seiffert, E. R., D. M. Boyer, J. G. Fleagle, et al. "New Adapiform Primate Fossils from the Late Eocene of Egypt." *Historical Biology* 30 (2018): 204–226.

Sigé, B., J.-J. Jaeger, J. Sudre, and M. Vianey-Liaud. "*Altiatlasius koulchii* n. gen. et sp., primate omomyidé du paléocène supérieur du Maroc, et les origines des euprimates." *Palaeontographica* 212 (1990): 1–24.

Silcox, M. T. "New Discoveries on the Middle Ear Anatomy of *Ignacius graybullianus* (Paromomyidae, Primates) from Ultra High Resolution X-ray Computed Tomography." *Journal of Human Evolution* 44 (2003): 73–86.

Silcox, M. T. "The Biogeographic Origins of Primates and Euprimates: East, West, North, or South of Eden?" In *Mammalian Evolutionary Morphology: A Tribute to Frederick S. Szalay*. Edited by M. Dagosto and E. J. Sargis, 199–231. New York: Springer-Verlag, 2008.

Silcox, M. T., and G. F. Gunnell. "Plesiadapiformes." In *Evolution of Tertiary Mammals of North America Vol. 2: Small Mammals, Xenarthrans, and Marine Mammals*. Edited by C. M. Janis, G. F. Gunnell, and M. D. Uhen, 207–238. Cambridge: Cambridge University Press, 2008.

Silcox, M. T., and S. López-Torres. "Major Questions in the Study of Primate Origins." *Annual Review of Earth and Planetary Sciences* 45 (2017): 113–137.

Silcox, M. T., J. I. Bloch, E. J. Sargis, and D. M. Boyer. "Euarchonta." In *The Rise of Placental Mammals: Origins and Relationships of the Major Extant Clades*. Edited by K. D. Rose and J. D. Archibald, 127–144. Baltimore: Johns Hopkins University Press, 2005.

Silcox, M. T., C. K. Dalmyn, and J. I. Bloch. "Virtual Endocast of *Ignacius graybullianus* (Paromomyidae, Primates) and Brain Evolution in Early Primates." *Proceedings of the National Academy of Sciences USA* 106 (2009): 10987–10992.

Silcox, M. T., A. E. Benham, and J. Bloch. "Endocasts of *Microsyops* (Microsyopidae, Primates) and the Evolution of the Brain in Primitive Primates." *Journal of Human Evolution* 58 (2010): 505–521.

Silcox, M. T., E. J. Sargis, J. I. Bloch, and D. M. Boyer. "Primate Origins and Supraordinal Relationships: Morphological Evidence." In *Handbook of Palaeoanthropology*, 2nd edn. Edited by W. Henke and I. Tattersall, 1053–1081. London: Springer, 2015.

Silcox, M. T., J. I. Bloch, D. M. Boyer, et al. "The Evolutionary Radiation of Plesiadapiforms." *Evolutionary Anthropology* 26 (2017): 74–94.

Silcox, M.T., G. F. Gunnell, and J. I. Bloch. "Cranial Anatomy of *Microsyops annectens* (Microsyopidae, Euarchonta, Mammalia) from the Middle Eocene of Northwestern Wyoming." *Journal of Paleontology* 94 (2020): 979–1006.

Simons, E. L., and T. M. Bown. "*Afrotarsius chatrathi*, First Tarsiiform Primate (? Tarsiidae) from Africa." *Nature* 313 (1985): 475–477.

Simpson, G. G. "The 'Plagiaulacoid' Type of Mammalian Dentition. A Study of Convergence." *Journal of Mammalogy* 14 (1933): 97–107.

Soligo, C. "Correlates of Body Mass Evolution in Primates." *American Journal of Physical Anthropology* 130 (2006): 283–293.

Stehlin, H. G. "Die Säugetiere des schweizerischen Eocaens: Critischer Catalog der Materialien." *Abhandlungen der Schweizerischen Paläontologischen Gesellschaft* 41 (1916): 1299–1552.

Strait, S. G. "Dietary Reconstruction of Small-Bodied Omomyoid Primates." *Journal of Vertebrate Paleontology* 21 (2001): 322–334.

Sussman, R. W. "Primate Origins and the Evolution of Angiosperms." *American Journal of Primatology* 23 (1991): 209–223.

Szalay, F. S. "The Beginnings of Primates." *Evolution* 22 (1968): 19–36.

Szalay, F. S., and G. Drawhorn. "Evolution and Diversification of the Archonta in an Arboreal Milieu." In *Comparative Biology and Evolutionary Relationships of Tree Shrews*. Edited by W. Patrick Luckett, 133–169. New York: Plenum Press, 1980.

Upham, N. S., J. A. Esselstyn, and W. Jetz. "Inferring the Mammal Tree: Species-Level Sets of Phylogenies for Questions in Ecology, Evolution, and Conservation." *PLoS Biology* 17 (2019): e3000494.

Van Valen, L., and R. E. Sloan. "The Earliest Primates." *Science* 150 (1965): 743–745.

Williams, B. A., R. F. Kay, and E. C. Kirk. New Perspectives on Anthropoid Origins. *Proceedings of the National Academy of Sciences, USA* 107 (2010a): 4797–4804.

Williams, B. A., R. F. Kay, E. C. Kirk, and C. F. Ross. "*Darwinius masillae* is a Strepsirrhine – A Reply to Franzen et al." (2009) *Journal of Human Evolution* 59 (2010b): 567–573.

Wilson, J. A. "Stratigraphic Occurrence and Correlation of Early Tertiary Vertebrate Faunas, Trans-Pecos Texas: Agua Fria-Green Valley Areas." *Journal of Vertebrate Paleontology* 6 (1986): 350–373.

Wilson Mantilla, G. P., S. G. B. Chester, W. A. Clemens, et al. "Earliest Palaeocene purgatoriids and the Initial Radiation of Stem Primates." *Royal Society Open Science* 8 (2021): 210050.

Wortman, J. L. "Studies of Eocene Mammalia in the Marsh Collection, Peabody Museum, Part II, Primates." *American Journal of Science* 15 (16: 345–368;17: 23–33,133–140, 203–214 1903–1904): 163–176,399–414, 419–436.

Wu, R., and Y. Pan. "A New Adapid Genus from the Miocene of Lufeng." *Acta Anthropologica Sinica* 4 (1985): 1–6.

CHAPTER 23 Catarrhine Origins and Evolution

David R. Begun

INTRODUCTION

The history of paleoprimatology effectively begins in the early nineteenth century with the discovery of a fossil from the gypsum quarries of Paris. Georges Cuvier, whom many consider the founder of vertebrate paleontology, described an odd-looking skull with cresty teeth and a long snout, *Adapis parisiensis*, which he considered to be a primitive artiodactyl (even-toed ungulates like cows, pigs, and deer). It was the first fossil primate ever published, though not as such. In Cuvier's defense, the teeth of *Adapis* resemble those of artiodactyls from the same time period – the Eocene. In the Eocene primates and artiodactyls were not so far removed from their common ancestor so, if you have never seen a fossil primate you might mistake one for an artiodactyl.

In 1836 *Pliopithecus*, a fossil that no one could deny was a primate, was described from a site in France (Begun 2002a). Throughout the remainder of the nineteenth century, fossils linked to living Old World monkeys and apes[1] were described from South Asia, Egypt, and Europe (Begun 2002a, 2002b; Kelley 2002; Rasmussen 2002). In the twentieth century, our knowledge of fossil catarrhines expanded to include new sites in sub-Saharan Africa, Asia, and Europe. Table 23.1 lists the fossil catarrhines included in this review and their geological ages. The classification of living catarrhines adopted in this chapter is in Table 23.2.

THE EARLIEST CATARRHINES

The largest collection of early catarrhines comes from the Fayum deposits of Egypt, from which early primates have been described for more than 100 years (Harrison 2013; Rasmussen 2002). *Propliopithecus* was the first catarrhine described from Fayum. Since then, a spectacular diversity of primates has been discovered (Beard 2013; Rasmussen 2002, 2007; Seiffert 2012). *Proplioithecus* was originally viewed as a small ape related to gibbons,

A Companion to Biological Anthropology, Second Edition. Edited by Clark Spencer Larsen.
© 2023 John Wiley & Sons Ltd. Published 2023 by John Wiley & Sons Ltd.

Table 23.1   Fossil catarrhines and their geological ages and geographic distributions

Taxon	Age	Country/Region
Catopithecus	Late Eocene, 35.5–36 Ma[a]	Egypt
Oligopithecus	Late Eocene, 34–35 Ma	Egypt
Aegyptopithecus	Early Oligocene, 33–33.5 Ma	Egypt
Propliopithecus	Early Oligocene, 33–34 Ma	Egypt
Saadanius	Late Oligocene, 28–29 Ma	Saudi Arabia
Pliopithecus[b]	Middle–Late Miocene, 16–10 Ma	Europe
Epipliopithecus	Middle Miocene, 14 Ma	Slovakia
Anapithecus	Late Miocene, 10 Ma	Hungary, Austria, Germany
Pliobates	Late Miocene, 10.6 Ma	Spain (Catalonia)
Rukwapithecus	Late Oligocene, 26 Ma	Tanzania
Kamoyapithecus	Late Oligocene, 26 Ma	Kenya
Dendropithecus	Early Miocene, 20–17 Ma	Kenya
Rangwapithecus	Early Miocene, 20–17 Ma	Kenya
Limnopithecus[c]	Early Miocene, 20–17 Ma	Kenya
Micropithecus	Early Miocene, 20–17 Ma	Kenya, Uganda
Proconsul	Early Miocene, 20–19 Ma	Kenya, Uganda
Ekembo	Early Miocene, 19–17 Ma	Kenya
Afropithecus	Early Miocene, 17 Ma	Kenya
Morotopithecus	Early or Middle Miocene, 20–15 Ma?	Uganda
Heliopithecus	Early Miocene, 17.5 Ma	Saudi Arabia
Griphopithecus	Latest Early Miocene, 16–16.5 Ma	Germany, Slovakia, Turkey
Equatorius	Middle Miocene, 15 Ma	Kenya
Nacholapithecus	Middle Miocene, 15 Ma	Kenya
Kenyapithecus	Middle Miocene, 15–16 Ma	Kenya, Turkey
Nakalipithecus	Late Miocene, 9.8 Ma	Kenya
Chororapithecus	Late Miocene, 8 Ma	Ethiopia
Samburupithecus	Late Miocene, 9.6 Ma	Kenya
Sivapithecus	Middle/Late Miocene, 12.5–7 Ma	India, Pakistan, Nepal
Khoratpithecus	Late Miocene, 11–9 Ma	Thailand, Manmar
Ankarapithecus	Late Miocene, 10 Ma	Turkey
Indopithecus	Late Miocene, 6.5 Ma	India
Gigantopithecus	Pleistocene, 1–0.3 Ma	China
Dryopithecus	Middle/Late Miocene, 12.5–11.9 Ma	France, Spain, Austria
Pierolapithecus	Middle Miocene, 11.9 Ma	Spain
Anoiapithecus	Middle Miocene, 11.9 Ma	Spain
Danuvius	Late Miocene, 11.6 Ma	Germany
Hispanopithecus	Late Miocene, 10–9.5 Ma	Spain
Rudapithecus	Late Miocene, 10 Ma	Hungary
Neopithecus	Late Miocene, ~10 Ma	Germany

(Continued)

Table 23.1   *(Continued)*

Taxon	Age	Country/Region
Udabnopithecus	Late Miocene, 8.5 Ma	Georgia
Ouranopithecus	Late Miocene, 9.5 Ma	Greece
Graecopithecus	Late Miocene, 7.2 Ma	Greece, Bulgaria
Lufengpithecus	Late Miocene, 9 Ma	China
Oreopithecus	Late Miocene, 8–6.7 Ma	Italy
Nyanzapithecus	Middle/Late Miocene, 18–9.8 Ma	Kenya
Sahelanthropus	Late Miocene, 6–7 Ma	Chad
Orrorin	Late Miocene, 6 Ma	Kenya
Ardipithecus	Late Miocene/Early Pliocene, 5.7–4.4 Ma	Ethiopia
Nsungwepithecus	Late Oligocene, 26 Ma	Tanzania
Alophia	Early Miocene, 22 Ma	Kenya
Prohylobates	Early Miocene, ~19 Ma	Egypt
Zaltanpithecus	Middle Miocene, ~15 Ma	Libya
Noropithecus	Early Miocene, >17.2–14.5 Ma	Kenya
Victoriapithecus[d]	Early/Middle Miocene, 19–12.5 Ma	Kenya, Uganda
Mesopithecus	Late Miocene–Pliocene, 8–5 m	Europe, Iran, Afghanistan

[a] Ma Mega-annum, or million years.
[b] Other pliopithecoid genera are known from Europe and Asia.
[c] A number of small East African Early and Middle Miocene catarrhines are not listed here. See Harrison (2010) for a more complete list.
[d] Discussion of the numerous fossil cercopithecoids is restricted to a few key species. See Benefit and McCrossin (2002) and Jablonski (2002) for more details.

Table 23.2   Taxonomy of living catarrhine genera. The cercopithecid taxonomy is simplified for clarity

Infraorder Catarrhini
    Superfamily Hominoidea
        Family Hominidae
            Subfamily Homininae
                Genus *Homo* (humans)
                Genus *Gorilla* (gorillas)
                Genus *Pan* (chimpanzees and bonobos)
            Subfamily Ponginae
                Genus *Pongo* (orangutans)
            Family Hylobatidae
                Genera *Hylobates, Nomascus, Hoolock* (gibbons)
                Genus *Symphalangus* (siamangs)
    Superfamily Cercopithecoidea
        Family Cercopithecidae
            Subfamily Cercopithecinae
                Genera *Papio, Macaca, Cercocebus, Cercopithecus, Theropithecus* (baboons, macaques, mangabeys, guenons, geladas)
            Subfamily Colobinae
                Genera *Colobus, Semnopithecus, Nasalis* (colobus, langurs, odd nosed monkeys)

by way of *Pliopithecus*. More recent discoveries have shown, however, that the story is quite different and more complicated. The Fayum catarrhines are distinguished from other Fayum primates in details of their dental anatomy, but mainly in having only two premolars on each side of each jaw (a dental quadrant). This is the most obvious difference between catarrhines and the other major group of anthropoids, the platyrrhines or New World monkeys, which have three premolars per quadrant.

The best known Fayum catarrhine is *Aegyptopithecus*, with multiple crania, mandibles, and limb bones preserved (Rasmussen 2002; Seiffert 2012). It was the size of a small monkey or gibbon, about six kilograms. *Aegyptopithecus* has a hominoid-like dentition, with two premolars, upper molars with four cusps (as in many other primates), and lower molars with five cusps and grooves forming a Y-5 pattern (Figure 23.1). Though a "dental ape," *Aegyptopithecus* is not a hominoid but a catarrhine that predates the divergence of Old World monkeys and apes. Old World monkeys have more recently evolved specialized molars (see below) while hominoids retain the ancient pattern.

Beyond the Y-5 lower molar morphology, not much else ties *Aegyptopithecus* to more advanced catarrhines. *Aegyptopithecus* is a good example of a missing link – a transitional form between prosimians, which still exist today, and living catarrhines. Like all anthropoids (and tarsiers), *Aegyptopithecus* has a bony wall separating the orbits posteriorly. However, it

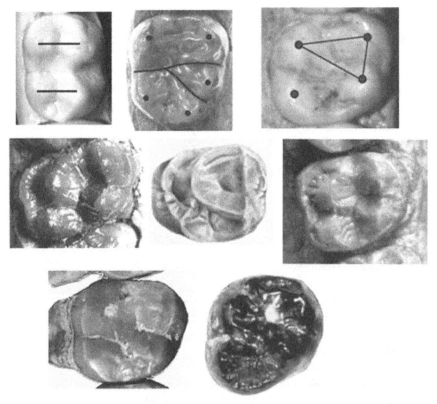

Figure 23.1   Extinct and living catarrhine molars. From left to right, top row, baboon lower molar, *Rudapithecus* lower molar, chimpanzee upper molar; middle row, *Aegyptoppithecus*, *Epipliopithecus*, *Proconsul* upper molars; lower row, *Griphopithecus*, *Rudapithecus* upper molar. The trigon and hypocone are illustrated on the chimpanzee upper molar. Images are not to scale. *Aegyptopipthecus* modified from Rasmussen (2002); *Epipliopithecus* modified from Zapfe (1960); *Proconsul* modified from Harrison (2002); *Griphopithecus* modified from Kelley (2002).

is more like prosimians in other attributes of the skull – for instance the size of the snout, which is large, and of the brain, which is small. This probably reflects behaviors more characteristic of living prosimians than catarrhines, including a greater reliance on the sense of smell and a simpler social organization. It also lacked a bony ear tube found in all living catarrhines (see below). Nevertheless, *Aegyptopithecus* was like all living catarrhines in being active during the day (diurnal), which we can tell from the size of their eye sockets. We suspect that they lived in social groups, as opposed to being solitary, as in many prosimians, because they are sexually dimorphic in body mass and canine dimensions, two attributes commonly associated with social catarrhines.

While the brain of *Aegyptopithecus*, known indirectly from the interior of the brain case, is similar in size to that of prosimians of the same body size, in a few details it is more advanced. For example, the frontal lobes, responsible for many higher-level cognitive functions, including the mediation of complex social interactions, are intermediate in size between those of living prosimians and catarrhines. The olfactory lobes, responsible for the sense of smell, are relatively small compared with prosimians, which suggests that the sense of smell was less developed than in prosimians and more like catarrhines (Begun and Kordos 2004; Simons et al. 2007).

The limbs of *Aegyptopithecus* are relatively short and stout, unlike the elongated and often relatively slender limbs of catarrhines (Beard 2013; Rasmussen 2002). The skeleton of *Aegyptopithecus* suggests that it was a cautious climber, spending most of its time in the trees. One primitive feature in *Aegyptopithecus* is the entepicondylar foramen, a hole in the lower end of the humerus (upper arm bone) through which a nerve and blood vessels pass. Most mammals have this foramen, but it has been lost in living catarrhines.

Other Fayum anthropoids have a less secure claim to catarrhine status. *Catopithecus* and *Oligopithecus* are more primitive than *Aegyptopithecus*. They are small, weighing about 500 g, the size of the smallest living anthropoids (Beard 2013; Harrison 2013; Rasmussen 2007; Seiffert 2012). *Catopithecus*, the better known of the two, is sexually dimorphic in body mass and canine size, like *Aegyptopithecus*. Both *Catopithecus* and *Oligopithecus* have teeth that are difficult to distinguish from those of prosimians, though they do have only two premolars per quadrant. They also lack mandibular symphysis fusion, which means that each side of their lower jaw remains separate during life. In all other anthropoids the two sides of the mandible are fused together. The catarrhine status of *Catopithecus* and *Oligopithecus* is still debated.

Saadanius, about 28–29 Ma, from Saudia Arabia, partially bridges the gap between *Aegyptopithecus* and more modern catarrhines. The ancestors of *Saadanius* dispersed into Saudi Arabia, which was still part of Africa at the time, from northern Africa (the Arabian and African plates began to separate around 25 Ma). *Saadanius* resembles *Aegyptopithecus* in the development of the snout but shares with living catarrhines a tubular ectotympanic, the bony canal mentioned earlier leading from the ear drum inside the ear to the outer ear hole (or external auditory meatus). This suggests that *Saadanius* is closer to the divergence of Old World monkeys and apes than are the propliopithecoids (Harrison 2013; Zalmout et al., 2010).

The Pliopithecoidea

There is a substantial gap in time and space between the propliopithecoids and the next most primitive catarrhine group, the pliopithecoids. Pliopithecoids are a diverse and successful group of catarrhines that ranged from Spain to China between about 18 to 9 Ma (Begun 2002a). They resemble living anthropoids in the anatomy of the skull and limbs, but their claim to catarrhine status is still mostly confined to their dental formula, which has two premolars in each quadrant. Their teeth are more modern looking than those of *Aegyptopithecus*. One difference is the development of cingula – ridges of enamel that run along the cheek side of lower molars and the tongue side of the upper molars. *Aegyptopithecus* has broad, shelf-like cingula while *Pliopithecus* has thinner, ridge-like *cingula*, more like those of the earliest apes (Figure 23.1).

Unlike propliopithecoids and most noncatarrhine primates, pliopithecoids have ectotympanic tubes but they are only partially ossified (that is, the tube was probably present but partly composed of cartilage, which does not preserve in fossils). A partial tube might be an intermediate condition, although *Saadanius*, which is otherwise more primitive, has a complete tube. In pliopithecoids the partial tube might instead be a unique variation.

Many pliopithecoid species are known, but here the focus is on the best-known taxon, *Epipliopithecus*, of which three partial skeletons were found at a site in Slovakia (Zapfe 1960). The face of *Epipliopithecus* is shorter and the brain larger and more modern anthropoid-like than in *Aegyptopithecus* (Begun and Kordos 2004). The teeth of *Epipliopithecus* are more modern, most like the teeth of living catarrhines that mainly consume soft fruits (Figure 23.1). However, they retain well-developed cingula, not found in the teeth of living apes. The canines are sexually dimorphic, but the degree of body mass dimorphism is not known. The fact that pliopithecoids are often found in large numbers suggests that they lived in large groups.

Epipliopithecus is most like living New World monkeys in having relatively long and slender limbs, long and flexible backs, and strongly grasping hands and feet, indicating that they were arboreal. Unlike living catarrhines but like *Aegyptopithecus*, *Epipliopithecus* has an entepicondylar foramen. Other large samples of pliopithecoids are known from Spain, Austria, Hungary and China (Alba et al. 2010; Begun 2002a). A small, pliopithecoid-sized catarrhine, *Pliobates cataloniae* from Catalonia (Spain), was initially described as a hominoid (Alba et al. 2015). However, *Pliobates* retains a primitive dentition and an incompletely ossified ectotympanic, and is positioned among more primitive catarrhines in the analysis of Nengo et al. (2017).

Pliopithecoids represent another step in catarrhine evolution. They are monkey-like in overall anatomy but superficially gibbon-like in their skull, resembling living catarrhines more than propliopithecoids. Pliopithecoids branched off from Old World monkeys, apes, and humans before Old World monkeys and hominoids branched off from one another (see Figure 23.2). Since Old World monkeys and hominoids probably diverged at least 30 Ma (Pozzi et al. 2014), pliopithecoids must have diverged before 30 Ma, and since catarrhines are only known from Africa at that time, the pliopithecoids probably came from Africa as well. Their early history is unknown until about 18 Ma when they appear in China and soon after in Europe; this is what may be called a "ghost lineage," which is uncommon among primates.

The Hominoidea

Early Apes in Africa

Hominoid origins are difficult to pinpoint in the fossil record. Two African sites between 25 and 26 Ma contain fragments of the earliest known possible hominoids. *Kamoyapithecus* from Kenya and *Rukwapithecus* from Tanzania resemble *Aegyptopithecus* (Leakey et al. 1995; Stevens et al. 2013). The upper molars of *Kamoyapithecus* are broad with well-developed cingula, but they are larger. A few details of the lower teeth of *Rukwapithecus*

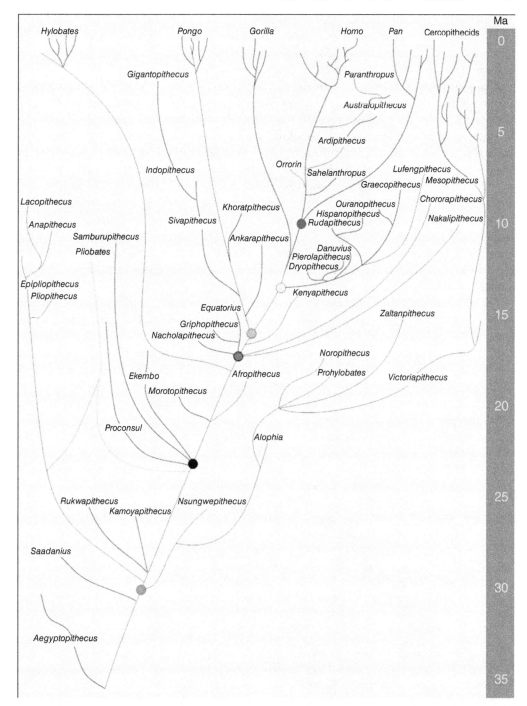

Figure 23.2   A phylogeny of many of the taxa discussed in the text. The phylogeny depicted here represents one scenario of catarrhine evolution consistent with the text. Portions of this scenario differ from other hypotheses (see Alba 2012; Harrison 2010; Almécija et al. 2021). *Anoiapithecus*, closely related to *Pierolapithecus* and *Dryopithecus*, is omitted for space limitations. *Aegyptopithecus* and *Saadanius* are early stem catarrhines. The pliopithecoids branch off next, radiating into a plethora of taxa, only some of which are represented here. The position of *Pliobates* is unclear, the dotted lines representing the two most likely possibilities, that it is either a stem hominoid or a pliopithecoid. The crown catarrhines begin with the divergence of the cercopithecoids and the hominoids (blue circle).

suggest it might be a hominoid. More specimens of both are needed to confirm their hominoid status. The oldest fossils that most researchers more confidently attribute to the Hominoidea are assigned to the genera *Ekembo* and *Proconsul*, from early Miocene deposits in Kenya (Begun 2015; Harrison 2010; McNulty et al. 2015).

Ekembo is the best known of the many fossil apes from the early Miocene of East Africa. The closely related genus *Proconsul* is a bit older on average and is also known from many sites, but generally less well preserved. *Ekembo* and *Proconsul* were components of a diverse and successful group, which lasted roughly 12 million years, from about 22 to 10.5 Ma, though it is mostly known from the early Miocene, becoming rare after about 17.5 Ma (Begun 2015; McNulty et al. 2015). There are three widely recognized species of *Proconsul* and two of *Ekembo*, ranging from the size of a female baboon (about 10 kg) to that of a female gorilla (about 80 kg). Many other fossil catarrhines, perhaps related to *Ekembo* and *Proconsul*, lived at the same time in East Africa (Table 23.1; see also Harrison 2010 and Begun 2015 for more comprehensive lists), but I will focus here on *Ekembo*, as it is the best known and represents a plausible candidate for the earliest known hominoid. *Ekembo* has the definitive catarrhine characters of two premolars, a complete ectotympanic tube, and a humerus without an entepicondylar foramen.

The richest collection of *Ekembo* sites is from Rusinga Island, in Lake Victoria, western Kenya. Over a century of research has led to the discovery of well-preserved crania, mandibles, and partial skeletons (Begun 2015; Harrison 2010; McNulty et al. 2015; Walker 1997; Walker and Teaford 1989). *Ekembo* has a short face and a large brain in comparison with earlier catarrhines. The brain and body mass are within the size ranges of papionins (baboons and their relatives). *Ekembo*'s relative brain size (the size of the brain once body mass is taken into account) is close to that of gibbons and siamangs (hylobatids) as well, which are otherwise smaller in body mass (Begun and Kordos 2004). *Ekembo*'s cognitive capabilities were probably comparable to those of the most intelligent living monkeys. Old World monkeys are highly intelligent and generally form complexly organized groups. They are very adaptable and able to exploit a wide range of resources. *Ekembo* was probably similar and had achieved a monkey-like grade or level of behavioral complexity.

The molars of *Ekembo* have low, cone-shaped cusps and small basins, suggesting a diet of soft fruits. *Ekembo* lacks the specialized front teeth, molar crests, or enlarged molars of later,

Figure 23.2 (Continued) *Rukwapithecus* and *Kamoyapithecus* may be stem hominoids. The relationship between them is unresolved so they are depicted here as branching off together. Undoubted hominoids diverge into multiple lineages beginning with *Proconsul* before 22 Ma, representing the first major radiation of hominoids (black circle). Following the divergence of the hylobatids around 18 Ma, a second radiation of hominoids begins some time before 17 Ma with the dispersal of apes into Eurasia (red circle). The remnants of this radiation persist into the late Miocene with *Samburupithecus*, *Chororapithecus*, and *Nakalipithecus*. The third radiation of hominoids is that of crown hominids (great apes and humans) (green circle). The pongines branch off first, probably at least 16 million years ago. Stem hominines represent a fourth hominoid radiation in Europe and possibly Asia with *Lufengpithecus* (yellow circle). Crown hominines appear as *Gorilla* diverges from the *Pan-Homo* clade. Hominins (humans and fossil relatives postdating the divergence of *Pan*) represent the fifth great radiation of hominoids, beginning in the late Miocene and continuing well into the Pleistocene (purple circle). Circling back to the cercopithecoids, following a sparce record until about 20 Ma, stem cercopithecoids radiate, but only one taxon, *Victoriapithecus*, is well known. There is a gap between the youngest *Victoriapithecus* at about 15 Ma and the oldest crown cercopithecoid, the long-lived primitive colobine *Mesopithecus*. Cercopithecines and colobines radiate broadly during the late Miocene and into the Plio-Pleistocene. The branches at the end of each living catarrhine clade represent multiple known taxa or hypothetical taxa yet to be discovered.

more specialized hominoids. The jaws are also relatively slender and were incapable of resisting the powerful chewing forces needed to consume hard or tough foods, as in many later apes.

More of the skeleton of *Ekembo* is known than in any other fossil ape. *Ekembo* has a narrow and deep thorax, like most quadrupeds including monkeys, and its limbs are positioned beneath the body. *Ekembo* and living monkeys are described as pronograde quadrupeds, with arms and legs of equal length and a backbone oriented parallel to the substrate (in the case of *Ekembo*, usually a branch). This is the type of limb orientation of most mammals familiar to us all (dogs, cats, horses, cows, sheep, and the like). However, unlike most pronograde mammals, *Ekembo* and primates generally walk on the palms of their hands (palmigrade) and the soles of their feet, in contrast to the digitigrade locomotion of most other mammals, walking on their toes rather than their palms. This almost certainly results from the arboreal heritage of primates, most of which remain largely arboreal to this day. Modern apes and humans differ in that, unlike monkeys, the arms are positioned on the side of the trunk. This is possible because in modern hominoids the thorax is broad and flat, allowing the shoulder blade (scapula) to move from the side of the thorax (as in pronograde quadrupeds) to the back. Instead of facing down as in a typical pronograde quadruped, the shoulder joint in hominoids faces out, shifting the arms from beneath the body to the side. This position gives modern apes a more mobile arm and allows them to swing below branches with ease. Humans retain modern ape-like arm position despite our commitment to life on the ground. It gives us our highly mobile arms, which are useful for carrying and throwing (among many other manipulative capacities). There are a few ape-like features in *Ekembo*, the most obvious of which is the presence of a coccyx or tail bone in place of an external tail. *Ekembo* also had powerfully gripping hands and feet. The hips and wrists of *Ekembo* show indications of higher levels of mobility than in monkeys, and are more like those of apes.

Ekembo is a primitive or stem ape, which means that it is more closely related to living apes and humans than it is to Old World monkeys, but not specifically related to any single living ape lineage. It is at the stem of the radiation of apes but not in the crown – that is, not in those parts of the radiation that led to each living ape. In other words, *Ekembo* is an extinct side-branch of the early hominoids, but one that probably looks like the common ancestor of apes and humans.

As noted, many other fossil catarrhines lived around the same time as *Proconsul* and *Ekembo*. They were broadly similar in anatomy, though often with unique dental specializations. They include *Limnopithecus*, *Lomorupithecus*, *Kogolepithecus*, *Micropithecus*, *Rangwapithecus*, *Simiolus*, *Dendropithecus*, *Turkanapithecus*, and *Kalepithecus*. Often fragmentary in preservation and primitive in morphology, it is difficult to decide which if any among these other taxa are actually hominoids and which are stem catarrhines. For this reason, they are not included in Figure 23.2. Together with *Ekembo*, *Proconsul*, and two more taxa described next (*Morotopithecus* and *Afropithecus*), they represent the first great radiation of Miocene catarrhines. We cannot be sure which, if any, of these fossil taxa are related to later, more modern apes, but *Ekembo* currently seems to be the best candidate.

Morotopithecus is a contemporary of *Proconsul* and *Ekembo* that may provide us with additional clues about great ape origins. It is from Uganda and is dated to about 19 Ma (MacLatchy 2004; MacLatchy et al. 2019). *Morotopithecus* specimens include a partial face, femur, scapula, and a lower back (lumbar) vertebra. The face and teeth are broadly like those of *Afropithecus* and suggest a similar diet (see below). However, based on the postcrania, which are interpreted by some as more ape-like (a short, stiff back and more mobile limbs), *Morotopithecus* has been called an early great ape, that is, specifically in the great ape line after it diverged from the hylobatids (Maclatchy 2004.) However, other researchers question this interpretation, suggesting that the anatomy is not especially ape-like or that certain attributes may have evolved in parallel with great apes (Begun 2015; Nakatsukasa 2008). If *Morotopithecus* is a great ape instead of a stem hominoid like *Ekembo* and *Afropithecus*, it means that great apes (hominids) origins are much older than generally accepted. Given the uncertainties about the postcranial anatomy and its more primitive craniodental morphology, *Morotopithecus* is best considered to be another early stem ape.

Afropithecus is another large fossil ape (close in size to *Morotopithecus* and the largest species of *Proconsul* and *Ekembo*) known from ~17 Ma sites in Kenya. *Afropithecus* has distinctive thick incisors and canines and powerfully built jaws. The chewing muscles are large, indicative of a very powerful bite, allowing *Afropithecus* to consume foods with tough or hard outer coverings – a dietary strategy known as "hard-object feeding" (Leakey and Walker 1997). Studies of the internal anatomy of *Afropithecus* teeth reveal that it grew more slowly than *Ekembo* and was in this way more like great apes, which grow more slowly and take longer to reach maturity than do monkeys (Smith et al. 2003). This has profound implications concerning the biology of apes compared with that of monkeys (see below). While some researchers have concluded that *Afropithecus* and *Morotopithecus* are in the same taxon, differences in craniodental and postcranial anatomy support the genus-level distinction adopted here (Maclatchy 2004; MacLatchy et al. 2019).

The face of *Afropithecus* is longer and wider than in *Ekembo* due to the presence of large chewing muscles and robust front teeth. The lower jaw is built to withstand powerful chewing forces. The front of the cranium, which is smooth in *Ekembo*, is marked by strong ridges and is deeply constricted behind the orbits (postorbital constriction). This and the massive face indicate large chewing muscles in *Afropithecus*, much stronger than in *Ekembo*. However, the limbs of *Afropithecus* were like those of *Ekembo*, more like monkeys than apes.

The main differences between *Afropithecus* and *Ekembo* are in dietary strategy and growth, changes that may have allowed *Afropithecus* or one of its descendants to expand into Eurasia. In both cases, these changes may signal a greater degree of adaptability. *Afropithecus*, with its powerful jaws and large teeth, was able to exploit a wider range of foods than *Ekembo*, including foods that were inaccessible to *Ekembo* because the outer coverings were too difficult for the teeth to penetrate. This may have allowed *Afropithecus* to range beyond the areas in which *Ekembo* could survive and may have given its descendants an adaptive advantage in the more seasonal and variable environments of Eurasia. In addition, the slower rate of growth in *Afropithecus* is associated in living apes with a larger brain and an extended period of infant dependency, which affords more time to learn about the social and ecological environment. This is a major distinction from other primates, accounting for much of the cognitive superiority of apes compared with monkeys. We do not know to what extent *Afropithecus* resembled the great apes in behavior, but we can speculate that it may have been just different enough to exploit environments into which *Proconsul* and *Ekembo* could not expand.

Around 17 Ma, an ape from Saudi Arabia called *Heliopithecus* was the first to leave Africa. The Arabian Peninsula, which by this time had separated from the African plate, was much more humid than today. Like African early Miocene apes, *Heliopithecus* was probably a forest-dweller. It is only known from a crushed upper jaw and a few isolated teeth, resembling *Afropithecus*. Shortly afterwards a new type of hominoid appears in the eastern Mediterranean and Europe.

Expansion into Eurasia

Around 17 Ma, early apes from Africa/Arabia expanded their range into Eurasia. They are first documented in Germany, at about 16.5 Ma, just before the beginning of the middle Miocene and somewhat later in Anatolia, the Asian part of Turkey (Begun et al. 2003; Heizmann and Begun 2001). These apes, known as *Griphopithecus*, differ from their African predecessors in their more modern-looking dentition, with reduced cingula, thickly enameled molars, and broad cusps that wear flat (Kelley 2002; see Figure 23.1). These attributes suggest a diet heavy in abrasives. A thick layer of enamel may also be related to forceful crushing and grinding. We find similar-looking molars in later fossil apes, and in most hominins (humans and all taxa more closely related to humans than to chimpanzees). Modern orangutans and some New World monkeys have similar teeth. *Griphopithecus* may have eaten hard/tough objects and foods with grit, possibly from more terrestrial sources, indicating a change in diet and habitat use from early Miocene apes.

Griphopithecus is known mostly from isolated teeth, but a few jaw and limb fragments have been described. The jaws also point to a diet that required heavy mastication, and the limb fragments indicate a skeleton like that of *Ekembo* and *Afropithecus*, a generalized arboreal quadruped without any of the enhanced suspensory abilities of living hominoids (Ersoy et al. 2008). A similar genus, *Equatorius*, from Kenya, is about 15 Ma (Ward and Duren 2002). Another taxon in this group is *Nacholapithecus*, also from Kenya at about 15.5 Ma. It resembles the others dentally but is better known postcranially. Most telling are the enlarged elbow and wrist joints, which are not known in other middle Miocene apes. Although enlarged, these joints look like *Ekembo* and not like living apes, in which the joints are modified in shape to allow modern apes to effortlessly hang from branches, which *Ekembo* did not do. The combination of large joints that retain primitive morphology is difficult to interpret, but it may be a sign of more modern ape-like use of the forelimbs. *Nacholapithecus* probably used its forelimbs for climbing more than early Miocene apes but without the hanging component of living apes (Nakatsukasa and Kunimatsu 2009). Finally, a closely related form, *Kenyapithecus*, appears in Kenya and possibly Turkey, at around 13.5 Ma (Kelley et al. 2008; McCrossin and Benefit et al. 1997). It has subtle indications of a more modern upper jaw and elbow that may presage the next phase of ape evolution (Begun, 1992, 2015).

The impressive diversity of middle Miocene taxa shows that the area extending from Europe to East Africa was inhabited by a successful radiation of more modern-looking apes, endowed with powerful jaws and thickly enameled teeth. This could be the core area from which the ancestors of the living great apes arose. By around 12.5 Ma we find the earliest members of each of the living groups of great apes: the pongines (orangutans and their fossil relatives) and the hominines (African apes, humans, and their fossil relatives). The earliest hominines and pongines are only known from Eurasia, and it is likely that they evolved on that continent.

Pongines

The oldest known pongines are about 12.7 Ma, from the Chinji Formation in India and Pakistan. These and other specimens from the Indian subcontinent, dated to between 12.7 and 7 Ma, belong to the genus *Sivapithecus* (Kelley 2002, 2005). *Sivapithecus* has been known since the nineteenth century, but until the 1980s its place in ape and human evolution was not well understood. *Sivapithecus* has large molars with broad, flat cusps and thick enamel, and its jaws are powerfully built. Overall, the jaws and the back teeth resemble fossil humans such as *Australopithecus*, but also *Griphopithecus*. A well-preserved face of *Sivapithecus* reveals that it is closely related to living orangutans (Pilbeam 1982). Among the unique features shared between *Pongo* and *Sivapithecus* are tall, narrow eye sockets (orbits), separated by a narrow space between them, and a very elongated and concave face. The front part of the upper jaw, the premaxilla, which holds the incisor teeth, is elongated, horizontal, and continuous with the floor of the nasal cavity. These highly distinctive features, shared exclusively between *Sivapithecus* and *Pongo*, are strong evidence that *Sivapithecus* is a fossil relative of the orangutan (Kelley 2002). While the oldest known *Sivapithecus* is about 12.7 Ma, genetic evidence suggests that pongines and hominines may have diverged before 16 Ma (Pozzi et al. 2014).

Sivapithecus was well adapted to feeding on a diversity of foods types. It was probably capable of generating more power in its jaws than modern chimpanzees, which may have allowed it to exploit foods with hard or tough outer coverings, perhaps in times of food scarcity. This effective dental adaptation allowed *Sivapithecus* and its relatives to survive for more than 6 Ma in Asia. They have been found as far west as Turkey (*Ankarapithecus*) and as far south and east as Thailand (*Khoratpithecus*) (Begun 2005; Chaimanee et al. 2004). A large relative of *Sivapithecus*, *Indopithecus*, is known from sites in India that are about 6.5 Ma. *Indopithecus* may be ancestral to *Gigantopithecus*, the largest primate ever to have lived. *Gigantopithecus* survived until about 300,000 years ago and lived contemporaneously with fossil humans (*Homo erectus*) in China (Kelley 2002; Zhang and Harrison 2017). A recent analysis of fossil proteins confirmed the relationship of *Gigantopithecus* to *Pongo* (Welker et al. 2019).

Unlike the face, the limbs of *Sivapithecus* are not especially orangutan-like (Madar et al. 2002). *Sivapithecus* probably had a body type generally like that of apes, with a broad chest and arms hanging from the side rather than supporting the body from below, but it was not a suspensory ape. *Sivapithecus* probably spent more time on the ground, possibly engaging in a modified form of knuckle-walking (Begun and Kivell 2011), though it was probably an excellent climber. *Sivapithecus* grew like modern great apes, with a lengthy period of maturation, dependence on parents, and a large and slowly growing brain (Kelley 2004).

Hominines

While pongines were evolving in Asia, hominines were evolving in Europe. The oldest known hominine, *Dryopithecus*, is found in sites in France, Spain, and Austria dating to between about 12.5 and 11.9 Ma (Begun 2002b; Casanovas-Vilar et al. 2011). Like *Sivapithecus*, the role of *Dryopithecus* in ape and human evolution was not clear until better specimens were discovered.

Discoveries of fossil apes in Spain, Germany, Hungary, and Greece have greatly expanded our knowledge of ape evolution. Spectacular discoveries in Catalonia (northern Spain) include partial skeletons of two genera and well-preserved cranial remains of a third (Alba 2012). Dated to between 12.5 and 11.9 Ma, *Dryopithecus*, *Anoiapithecus*, and *Pierolapithecus* are the most primitive members of the dryopithecins, an early hominine clade (Begun 2015.) The most informative specimen is a partial skeleton of *Pierolapithecus* (Moyà-Solà et al. 2004). The vertebrae and ribs indicate an ape-like body form, and the wrists and hands show that this animal was a strong climber with highly mobile limbs, as in living apes. *Pierolapithecus* was orthograde (more upright backbone, walking with modified hand postures) and at least partly suspensory, as in modern apes.

Pierolapithecus is fundamentally different from early and middle Miocene apes, representing a huge step in the evolution of ape modernity. Later dryopithecins take this even further. The jaws and teeth of *Dryopithecus*, *Anoiapithecus*, and *Pierolapithecus* resemble those of chimpanzees. The structure of the teeth, with their thin enamel and widely spaced cusps, was adapted to a diet of soft fruits, as in living chimpanzees. The jaws are slenderer than in *Sivapithecus*, as are all the muscle attachment sites, indicating that dryopithecins were not hard object feeders.

A partial skeleton and additional teeth and limb remains of another dryopithecin, *Danuvius*, are known from a site in Bavaria, Germany (Böhme et al. 2019). Bones of the forearm and shin (ulna and tibia, respectively) are nearly complete, telling us that *Danuvius* was suspensory and probably adopted bipedal postures in the trees, a new form of positional behavior called **extended limb clambering**. Vertebrae indicate a broad ribcage and a short back as in modern apes (see below).

Later dryopithecins, after 10 Ma, are even more modern-looking. Dozens of dryopithecin fossils of *Rudapithecus* have been described from the 10 Ma site of Rudabánya, Hungary (Kordos and Begun 2001, 2002). *Rudapithecus* had a chimpanzee-sized brain, the first direct fossil evidence of modern great ape brain size (Begun and Kordos 2004; Gunz et al. 2020). The face of *Rudapithecus* is like that of African apes. The premaxilla is raised above the level of the palate (stepped subnasal fossa), as in African apes. The face is tilted downward as in hominines. In pongines the face is tilted upward. *Rudapithecus* grew at great ape rates, which is consistent with its large brain and means that *Rudapithecus* and relatives behaved probably more like modern great apes (Smith et al. 2019). Along with *Sivapithecus* and its relatives, these are the first modern great apes. Their adaptations set the stage for the evolution of living great apes and humans.

Two partial skeletons of *Hispanopithecus*, a contemporary of *Rudapithecus* from Spain, have ape attributes even more modern than *Pierolapithecus* (Moyà-Solà and Köhler 1996; Alba 2012). The lumbar vertebrae are more modern, and along with a well-preserved pelvis of *Rudapithecus*, show that these apes had a shorter back than monkeys, *Ekembo*, and *Nacholapithecus* (the only fossils in which the lumbar number can be assessed), like gibbons and humans, though not as short as in great apes (Susanna et al. 2014; Ward et al. 2019). Both *Rudapithecus* and *Hispanopithecus* have mobile wrists and long, curved phalanges with prominent attachments for strong muscles, all reliable indicators of suspensory positional behavior. In short, *Hispanopithecus* and *Rudapithecus* are the first apes we know of with modern ape jaws, teeth, brains, and bodies.

Other dryopithecins, *Ouranopithecus* and *Graecopithecus*, are found in Greece, Bulgaria, and Turkey, ranging in age between 9.5 and 7.2 Ma (Bonis and Koufos 1994; Fuss et al. 2017; Güleç et al. 2007). A well-preserved face, upper jaws, and mandibles tell us that, like *Rudapithecus*, *Ouranopithecus* has an African ape-like skull, but its jaws and teeth are much larger and more robust than in other dryopithecins, mirroring the differences between *Australopithecus* and *Paranthropus*. *Graecopithecus*, the youngest of these dryopithecins, inhabited a dry, open habitat, unlike that of older dryopithecins (Böhme et al. 2017; Fuss et al. 2017). The ability of *Graecopithecus* to survive under these conditions attests to the ecological diversity of European Miocene hominines, which may account for their ability to disperse back into Africa (Begun 2015; Begun et al. 2012).

Lufengpithecus, from sites in China dated to between 9 and 6 Ma, was long thought to be a pongine, but it may be more closely related to European late Miocene apes or it may be an independent lineage (Begun 2015; Ji et al. 2013). It lacks the distinctive morphology of the face of *Sivapithecus* and *Pongo*, resembling *Rudapithecus* in its face, front teeth, and limb morphology. If *Lufengpithecus* is a hominine, this extends the range of the earliest hominines from Spain to China, essentially the entire expanse of Eurasia.

Chororapithecus, *Nakalipithecus*, and *Samburupithecus* are fossil apes from Kenya and Ethiopia dated to between 9.6 to 10 Ma (Ishida and Pickford 1997; Kunimatsu et al. 2007; Suwa et al. 2007). They are thought by some to be more closely related to living hominines than any Eurasian ape. Unfortunately, they are poorly preserved, but where comparisons are possible, they share attributes with African early and middle Miocene apes. They are more likely to be remnants of the radiation of early and middle Miocene African hominoids than anything else.

Oreopithecus

Oreopithecus is a hominoid from Italy dated to between 6.7 and 8 Ma (Begun 2015). The combination of unique dental morphology, a primitive skull and a skeleton mixing primitive and advanced attributes make it hard to place. *Oreopithecus* may be a member of a lineage from Africa that diverged before hominines and pongines separated (Begun 2015; Nengo 2017).

THE CERCOPITHECOIDEA

Based on genetic evidence, it is estimated that hominoids and cercopithecoids diverged from one another before 30 Ma, but the oldest known widely accepted Old World monkey fossils date to about 22 Ma. One fossil, a jaw fragment with one molar from the *Rukwapithecus* site, *Nsungwepithecus*, may be the oldest known Old World monkey at about 25 Ma (Stevens et al. 2013). More fossils are needed to confirm this attribution.

Alophe is a primitive Old World monkey from a 22 Ma site in Kenya (Rasmussen et al. 2019). Like modern cercopithecoids, its molar cusps are arranged in two transverse pairs (Figure 23.1). Unlike modern cercopithecoids, the paired cusps are not joined by the sharp crests that form "lophs" and produce the bilophodont morphology of modern Old World monkeys. Bilophodont molars, unique to Old World monkeys among anthropoids, allow them to efficiently slice fibrous foods such as leaves and also to crush seeds. Old World monkeys also have more evolved digestive systems than apes, allowing them to extract nutrients from relatively nutrient-poor foods like leaves.

Noropithecus, *Prohylobates*, and *Zaltanpithecus* are early cercopithecoids from North and East Africa showing varying degrees of bilophodonty, but represented only by fragmentary fossils (Miller et al. 2009; Rasmussen et al. 2019; Stevens et al. 2013). By far the best known early cercopithecoid is *Victoriapithecus*, from sites in Kenya and Uganda (Benefit and McCrossin 2002). *Victoriapithecus* is a stem cercopithecoid, not specifically related to either of the main groups of living cercopithecoids, the colobines and the cercopithecines. In *Victoriapithecus* the molar lophs are less completely formed than in living forms, but are more developed than in the earliest cercopithecoids (Benefit and McCrossin 2002).

Victoriapithecus has a relatively large snout and small brain, resembling *Aegyptopithecus*, though it is not so primitive. Its body plan is essentially monkey-like, with arms and legs of equal length, and a back positioned parallel to the ground or to branches (pronograde, see above). *Victoriapithecus* first appears in the early Miocene, becoming more common in the middle Miocene. In the late Miocene, more modern Old World monkeys evolve in Eurasia and Africa. *Microcolobus* is the oldest modern monkey, a member of the colobines or leaf-eating monkeys (Benefit and Pickford 1986). *Mesopithecus*, a colobine as well, is the first known monkey to disperse into Eurasia, and would become highly successful for millions of years (Jablonski 2002). *Mesopithecus* became widespread in Europe and Asia after 10 Ma, as the climate became drier and more seasonal. *Mesopithecus* was better equipped to cope with the climate changes occurring during the Miocene in Europe and survived there while the apes died out. *Mesopithecus* is known from many fossils and was a typical-looking monkey from head to toe. It probably spent more time on the ground than most monkeys, especially colobines, do today.

Many other Miocene Old World monkeys are known, varying in size and anatomy. All the major subgroups of Old World monkeys evolve in the Pliocene and early Pleistocene (starting around 5.1 Ma). Fossil species range in size from the smallest living Old World monkeys (~1 kg) to the size of small gorillas (~70 kg) (Delson et al. 2000). Many develop impressive specializations to exploit a wide range of resources, especially in open country settings in East Africa, where many Old World monkeys are found in association with early human sites. The radiation of Old World monkeys is among the most impressive among primates or any other mammal family, which attests to their flexibility and adaptability. There were probably more monkeys in the Pliocene, both in numbers of individuals and species diversity, than apes in the Miocene. They were more terrestrial early on, and the largely arboreal nature of the group today is a relatively recent development.

Summary and Conclusions

The fossil record allows us to unravel the evolutionary transformation from prosimian to catarrhine (Figure 23.2). *Aegyptopithecus* is a transitional form, with a snout and a brain more prosimian than anthropoid. *Ekembo* had clearly made the transition to a catarrhine grade of organization, but they were more monkey-like than ape-like in most attributes. *Afropithecus* evolved a more modern dentition and pattern of growth and development, which may have allowed it or its descendants to expand its range into Eurasia. Once in Eurasia, the descendants of this pioneering ape experienced a series of adaptive radiations: first a centralized core group of apes ranging from central Europe to east Africa, with powerful jaws and thickly enameled teeth; and then two branches, one in Asia, the pongines, and one in Europe, the hominines. As these evolutionary events unfolded, the basic attributes of the living great apes and of the ancestors of humans were developing in the context of the ecological conditions of Europe and Asia. The seasonal and variable ecology selected for a hominid pattern of behavior, large brains, complex social relations, and elaborate strategies of foraging and reproductive biology. As the environment of Eurasia became increasingly seasonal and drier, apes were replaced by monkeys, which, after a lengthy period of slow evolution in Africa, explode on the scene. By 7 Ma the evidence of apes in Europe, like the climate, dries up, while the monkeys live on. The apes that survived moved south, tracking the milder conditions, becoming the founding populations of pongines in southeast Asia and hominines in Africa (Begun et al. 2012; see Alba 2012 and Almécija et al. 2021 for alternative interpretations). Most hominoids remain confined to tropical forests today. One lineage, evolved beyond the trends initiated in the Miocene (orthogrady, suspension, bigger brains, slower growth), developing a more terrestrial, eventually bipedal lifestyle, perhaps with the ability to range across a wider range of environments and exploit a greater diversity of resources. This is, of course, our own lineage. Aside from humans, the most successful descendants of the fossil catarrhines are the Old World monkeys.

NOTE

1   In this chapter apes refers to all taxa more closely related to each other than to the next closest taxon, the Old World monkeys (Cercopithecoidea) (Figure 23.2). It is used synonymously with hominoid (Hominoidea). In the past "apes" has sometimes been used to include taxa with ape-like attributes that predate the divergence of cercopithecoids and hominoids, such as *Aegyptopithecus*, referred to as a "dental ape" because it shares the primitive catarrhine molar cusp pattern with hominoids (see text for a further discussion).

REFERENCES

Alba, D. M. "Fossil Apes from the Vallès-Penedès Basin." *Evolutionary Anthropology* 21 (2012): 254–269.

Alba, D. M., S. Moyà-Solà, A. Malgosa, et al. "A New Species of Pliopithecus Gervais, 1849 (Primates: Pliopithecidae) from the Middle Miocene (MN8) of Abocador de Can Mata (els Hostalets de Pierola, Catalonia, Spain)." *American Journal of Biological Anthropology* 141 (2010): 52–75.

Alba, D. M., S. Almécija, D. DeMiguel, et al. "Miocene Small-Bodied Ape from Eurasia Sheds Light on Hominoid Evolution." *Science* 350 (2015): aab2625.

Almécija, S., A. S. Hammond, N. E. Thompson, et al. "Fossil Apes and Human Evolution." *Science* 372 (2021): 587.

Beard, K.C. "Anthropoid Origins." In *A Companion to Paleoanthropology*. Edited by D. R. Begun, 358–375. New York: Blackwell Publishing Ltd, 2013.

Begun, D. R. "Phyletic Diversity and Locomotion in Primitive European Hominids." *Am. J. Phys. Anthropol.* 87 (1992): 311-340.

Begun, D. "Fossil Record of Miocene Hominoids." In *Handbook of Paleoanthropology*. Edited by W. Henke and I. Tattersall, 1261–1332. Berlin, Heidelberg: Springer, 2015.

Begun, D. R. "The Pliopithecoidea." In *The Primate Fossil Record*. Edited by W. C. Hartwig, 221–240. Cambridge: Cambridge University Press, 2002a.

Begun, D. R. "European Hominoids." In *The Primate Fossil Record*. Edited by W. C. Hartwig, 339–368. Cambridge: Cambridge University Press, 2002b.

Begun, D. R. "*Sivapithecus* Is East and *Dryopithecus* Is West, and Never the Twain Shall Meet." *Anthropological Sciences* 113 (2005): 53–64.

Begun, D. R., and T. L. Kivell. "Knuckle-Walking in *Sivapithecus*? The Combined Effects of Homology and Homoplasy with Possible Implications for Pongine Dispersals." *Journal of Human Evolution* 60 (2011): 158–170.

Begun, D. R., and L. Kordos. "Cranial Evidence of the Evolution of Intelligence in Fossil Apes." In *The Evolution of Thought: Evolutionary Origins of Great Ape Intelligence*. Edited by A. E. Russon and D. R. Begun, 260–279. Cambridge: Cambridge University Press, 2004.

Begun, D. R., E. Güleç, and D. Geraads. "Dispersal Patterns of Eurasian Hominoids: Implications from Turkey." *Deinsea* 10 (2003): 23–39.

Begun, D. R., M. C. Nargolwalla, and L. Kordos. "European Miocene Hominids and the Origin of the African Ape and Human Clade." *Evolutionary Anthropology* 21 (2012): 10–23.

Benefit, B. R., and M. L. McCrossin. "The Victoriapithecidae, Cercopithecoidea." In *The Primate Fossil Record*. Edited by W. C. Hartwig, 241–253. Cambridge: Cambridge University Press, 2002.

Benefit, B. R., and M. Pickford. "Miocene Fossil Cercopithecoids from Kenya." *American Journal of Physical Anthropology* 69 (1986): 441–464.

Böhme, M., N. Spassov, et al. "Messinian Age and Savannah Environment of the Possible Hominin Graecopithecus from Europe." *PLoS One* 12 no. 5 (2017): e0177347.

Böhme, M., N. Spassov, J. Fuss, et al. "A New Miocene Ape and Locomotion in the Ancestor of Great Apes and Humans." *Nature* 575 (2019): 489–493.

Bonis, L. de, and G. Koufos. "Our Ancestors' Ancestor: *Ouranopithecus* Is a Greek Link in Human Ancestry." *Evolution Anthropology* 3 (1994): 75–83.

Casanovas-Vilar, I., D. M. Alba, M. Garcés, et al. "Updated Chronology for the Miocene Hominoid Radiation in Western Eurasia." *Proceedings of the National Academy of Sciences* 108 (2011): 5554–5559.

Chaimanee, Y., V. Suteethorn, J. Pratueng, et al. "A New Orang-Utan Relative from the Late Miocene of Thailand." *Nature* 427 (2004): 439–441.

Delson, E., C. J. Terranova, W. L. Jungers, et al. "Body Mass in Cercopithecidae (Primates, Mammalia): Estimation and Scaling in Extinct and Extant Taxa." *American Museum of Natural History, Anthropological Papers* 83 (2000): 1–159.

Ersoy, A., J. Kelley, P. Andrews, and B. Alpagut. "Hominoid Phalanges from the Middle Miocene Site of Paşalar, Turkey." *Journal of Human Evolution* 54 (2008): 518–529.

Fuss, J., N. Spassov, D. R. Begun, and M. Böhme. "Potential Hominin Affinities of *Graecopithecus* from the Late Miocene of Europe." *PLoS One* 12 (2017): e0177127.

Güleç, E., A. Sevim, C. Pehlevan, and F. Kaya. "A New Great Ape from the Late Miocene of Turkey." *Anthropological Sciences* 115 (2007): 153–158.

Gunz, P., S. Kozakowski, S. Neubauer, et al. "Skull Reconstruction of the Late Miocene Ape *Rudapithecus hungaricus* from Rudabánya, Hungary." *Journal of Human Evolution* 138 (2020): 102687.

Harrison, T. *Late Oligocene to Middle Miocene Catarrhines from Afro-Arabia. The Primate Fossil Record.* Edited by W. C. Hartwig, 311–338. Cambridge: Cambridge University Press, 2002.

Harrison, T. "Chapter 24. Dendropithecoidea, Proconsuloidea, and Hominoidea (Catarrhini, Primates)." In *Cenozoic Mammals of Africa.* Edited by L. Werdelin and W. J. Sanders, 429–469. Berkeley: University of California Press, 2010.

Harrison, T. "Catarrhine Origins." In *A Companion to Paleoanthropology.* Edited by D. R. Begun, 376–396. New York: Wiley-Blackwell, 2013.

Heizmann, E., and D. R. Begun. "The Oldest European Hominoid." *Journal of Human Evolution* 41 (2001): 465–481.

Ishida, H., and M. Pickford. "A New Late Miocene Hominoid from Kenya: *Samburupithecus kiptalami* gen. et sp. nov." *C. R. Academy of Sciences Paris* 325 (1997): 823–829.

Jablonski, N. G. "Fossil Old World Monkeys: The Late Neogene." In *The Primate Fossil Record,* Edited by W. C. Hartwig, 255–299. Cambridge: Cambridge University Press, 2002.

Jablonski, N. G., and S. R. Frost. "Cercopithecoidea." In *Cenozoic Mammals of Africa.* Edited by L. Werdelin and W. L. Sanders, 393–428. Berkeley: University of California Press, 2010.

Ji, X., N. Jablonski, D. Su, et al. "Juvenile Hominoid Cranium from the Terminal Miocene of Yunnan, China." *Chinese Science Bulletin* (2013): 1–9.

Kelley, J. "The Hominoid Radiation in Asia." In *The Primate Fossil Record.* Edited by W. C. Hartwig, 369–384. Cambridge: Cambridge University Press, 2002.

Kelley, J. "Life History and Cognitive Evolution in the Apes." In *The Evolution of Thought: Evolutionary Origins of Great Ape Intelligence.* Edited by A. E. Russon and D. R. Begun, 280–297. Cambridge: Cambridge University Press, 2004.

Kelley, J. "Twenty-five Years Contemplating *Sivapithecus* Taxonomy." In *Interpreting the Past: Essays on Human, Primate, and Mammal Evolution in Honor of David Pilbeam.* Edited by D. R. Pilbeam, D. Lieberman, R. J. Smith, and J. Kelley, 123–143. Boston: Brill Academic Publishers, 2005.

Kelley, J., P. Andrews, and B. Alpagut. "A New Hominoid Species from the Middle Miocene site of Paşalar, Turkey." *Journal of Human Evolution* 54 (2008): 455–479.

Kordos, L., and D. R. Begun. "A New Cranium of *Dryopithecus* from Rudabánya, Hungary." *Journal of Human Evolution* 41 (2001): 689–700.

Kordos, L., and D. R. Begun. "Rudabánya: A Late Miocene Subtropical Swamp Deposit with Evidence of the Origin of the African Apes and Humans." *Evolutionary Anthropology* 11 (2002): 45–57.

Kunimatsu, Y., M. Nakatsukasa, Y. Sawada, et al. "A New Late Miocene Great Ape from Kenya and Its Implications for the Origins of African Great Apes and Humans." *Proceedings of the National Academy of Sciences* 104 (2007): 19220–19225.

Leakey, M., and A. Walker. "*Afropithecus*: Function and Phylogeny." In *Function, Phylogeny and Fossils: Miocene Hominoid Evolution and Adaptations.* Edited by D. R. Begun, C. V. Ward, and M. D. Rose, 225–239. New York: Plenum Publishing Co, 1997.

Leakey, M. G., P. S. Ungar, and A. Walker. "A New Genus of Large Primate from the Late Oligocene of Lothidok, Turkana District, Kenya." *Journal of Human Evolution* 28 (1995): 519–531.

Maclatchy, L. "The Oldest Ape." *Evolutionary Anthropology* 13 (2004): 90–103.

MacLatchy, L., J. Rossie, A. Houssaye, et al. "New Hominoid Fossils from Moroto II, Uganda and Their Bearing on the Taxonomic and Adaptive Status of Morotopithecus Bishopi." *Journal of Human Evolution* 132 (2019): 227–246.

Madar, S. I., M. D. Rose, J. Kelley, et al., "New *Sivapithecus* Postcranial Specimens from the Siwaliks of Pakistan." *Journal of Human Evolution* 42 (2002): 705–752.

McCrossin, M. L., and B. R. Benefit. "On the Relationships and Adaptations of *Kenyapithecus*, a Large-Bodied Hominoid from the Middle Miocene of Eastern Africa." In *Function, Phylogeny and Fossils: Miocene Hominoid Origins and Adaptations.* Edited by D. R. Begun, C. V. Ward, and M. D. Rose, 241–267. New York: Plenum Press, 1997.

McNulty, K. P., D. R. Begun, J. Kelley, et al. "A Systematic Revision of *Proconsul* with a New Genus of Early Miocene Hominoid." *Journal of Human Evolution* 84 (2015): 42–61.

Miller, E. R., B. R. Benefit, M. L. McCrossin, et al. "Systematics of Early and Middle Miocene Old World Monkeys." *Journal of Human Evolution* 57 (2009): 195–211.

Moyà-Solà, S. and M. Köhler. "A *Dryopithecus* Skeleton and the Origins of Great Ape Locomotion." *Nature* 379 (1996): 156–159.

Moyà-Solà, S., M. Köhler, D. M. Alba, et al. "*Pierolapithecus catalaunicus*, a New Middle Miocene Great Ape from Spain." *Science* 306 (2004): 1339–1344.

Nakatsukasa, M. "Comparative Study of Moroto Vertebral Specimens." *Journal of Human Evolution* 55 (2008): 581–588.

Nakatsukasa, M., and Y. Kunimatsu. "*Nacholapithecus* and Its Importance for Understanding Hominoid Evolution." *Evolutionary of Anthropology* 18 (2009): 103–119.

Nengo, I., P. Tafforeau, C. C. Gilbert, et al. "New Infant Cranium from the African Miocene Sheds Light on Ape Evolution." *Nature* 548 (2017): 169–174.

Pilbeam, D. R. "New Hominoid Skull Material from the Miocene of Pakistan." *Nature* 295 (1982): 232–234.

Pozzi, L., J. A. Hodgson, A. S. Burrell, et al. "Primate Phylogenetic Relationships and Divergence Dates Inferred from Complete Mitochondrial Genomes." *Molecular Phylogenetics and Evolution* 75 (2014): 165–183.

Rasmussen, D. T. "Early Catarrhines of the African Eocene and Oligocene." In *The Primate Fossil Record*. Edited by W. C. Hartwig, 203–220. Cambridge: Cambridge University Press, 2002.

Rasmussen, D. T. "Fossil Record of the Primates from the Paleocene to the Oligocene." In *Handbook of Palaeoanthropology, Volume 2: Primate Evolution and Human Origins*. Edited by W. H. Henke and I. Tattersall, 889–920. Berlin: Springer, 2007.

Rasmussen, D. T., A. R. Friscia, M. Gutierrez, et al. "Primitive Old World Monkey from the Earliest Miocene of Kenya and the Evolution of Cercopithecoid Bilophodonty." *Proceedings of the National Academy of Sciences – PNAS* 116, no. 13 (2019): 6051–6056.

Roos, C., M. Kothe, D. M. Alba, et al. "The Evolutionary Radiation of Macaques out of Africa: Evidence from Mitogenome Divergence Times and the Fossil Record." *Journal of Human Evolution* 133 (2019): 114–132.

Rossie, J. B., C. C. Gilbert, and A. Hill. "Early Cercopithecid Monkeys from the Tugen Hills, Kenya." *Proceedings of the National Academy of Sciences* 110, no. 15 (2013): 5818–5822.

Seiffert, E. R. "Early Primate Evolution in Afro-Arabia." *Evolution Anthropology* 21 (2012): 239–253.

Simons, E. L., E. R. Seiffert, T. M. Ryan, and Y. Attia. "A Remarkable Female Cranium of the Early Oligocene Anthropoid *Aegyptopithecus zeuxis* (Catarrhini, Propliopithecidae)." *Proceedings of the National Academy of Sciences* 104 (2007): 8731–8736.

Smith, T. M., L. B. Martin, and M. G. Leakey. "Enamel Thickness, Microstructure and Development in Afropithecus Turkanensis." *Journal of Human Evolution* 44 (2003): 283–306.

Smith, T. M., P. Tafforeau, J. Pouech, and D. R. Begun. "Enamel Thickness and Dental Development in Rudapithecus Hungaricus." *Journal of Human Evolution* 136 (2019): 102649.

Stevens, N. J., E. R. Seiffert, P. M. O'Connor, et al. "Palaeontological Evidence for an Oligocene Divergence Between Old World Monkeys and Apes." *Nature* 497 (2013): 611–614.

Susanna, I., D.M. Alba, S. Almécija, and S. Moyà-Solà. "The Vertebral Remains of the Late Miocene Great Ape *Hispanopithecus laietanus* from Can Llobateres 2 (Vallès-Penedès Basin, NE Iberian Peninsula)." *Journal of Human Evolution* 73 (2014): 15–34.

Suwa, G., R. T. Kono, S. Katoh, et al. "A New Species of Great Ape from the Late Miocene Epoch in Ethiopia." *Nature* 448 (2007): 921–924.

Walker, A. "*Proconsul*: Function and Phylogeny." In *Function, Phylogeny and Fossils: Miocene Hominoid Evolution and Adaptations*. Edited by D. R. Begun, C. V. Ward, and M. D. Rose, 209–224. New York: Plenum Publishing Company, 1997.

Walker, A., and M. F. Teaford. "The Hunt for *Proconsul*." *Scientific American* 260 (1989): 76–82.

Ward, S. C., and D. L. Duren. "Middle and Late Miocene African Hominoids." In *The Primate Fossil Record*. Edited by W. C. Hartwig, 385–397. Cambridge: Cambridge University Press, 2002.

Ward, C. V., A. S. Hammond, J. M. Plavcan, and D. R. Begun. "A Late Miocene Hominid Partial Pelvis from Hungary." *Journal of Human Evolution* 136 (2019): 102645.

Welker, F., J. Ramos Madrigal, M. Kuhlwilm, et al. "Enamel Proteome Shows That *Gigantopithecus* Was an Early Diverging Pongine." *Nature* 576 (2019): 262–265.

Zalmout, I. S., W. J. Sanders, L. M. MacLatchy, et al. "New Oligocene Primate from Saudi Arabia and the Divergence of Apes and Old World Monkeys." *Nature* 466 (2010): 360–364.

Zapfe, H. "Die Primatenfunde aus der Miozänen Spaltenfüllung von Neudorf an der March (Dévinská Nová Ves), Tschechoslovakei. Mit anhang: Der Primtenfund aus dem Miozän von Klein Hadersdorf in Niederosterreich." *Schweizerische Paleontologische Abhandlungen* 78 (1960): 1–293.

Zhang, Y., and T. Harrison. "*Gigantopithecus blacki*: A Giant Ape from the Pleistocene of Asia Revisited." *American Journal of Physical Anthropology* 162 (2017): 153–177.

24 The Human Journey Begins: Origins and Diversity in Early Hominins

Scott W. Simpson

Paleontological field research conducted during recent decades has led to the discovery of many new hominin fossils that document the remarkable taxonomic diversity and distinctive paleobiology of our earliest ancestors. Hominins include humans, our ancestors, and our many extinct relatives that all shared a common ancestor separate from our closest living relatives – the chimpanzees and bonobos – about 7–10 million years ago (Ma). In very broad terms, we can organize our ancestors into three phases: the earliest hominins, the australopiths, and the rise of *Homo*. These can be loosely considered as time-successive groups that evolved in Africa (Figure 24.1) and span the last 7 million years with each exhibiting distinctive adaptations and geographical distributions. The earliest hominins exhibit adaptations to some degree of terrestrial bipedality and a craniodental anatomy to a generalized diet that arose before 7 Ma and were replaced by the australopiths about 4.2 Ma. The australopiths are competent terrestrial bipeds, have craniodental adaptations to eating a coarse or hard diet, are small brained and went extinct after 1 Ma. The australopiths coexisted with the earliest *Homo* that appeared prior to 2.8 Ma. The australopiths did not share a singular adaptation and these can be grouped into more generalized and specialized taxa. Here, we will focus on the earlier hominins including the australopiths. The origins and evolution of the genus *Homo* will be covered elsewhere in this volume.

BEFORE THE AUSTRALOPITHS: THE HOMININ FOSSIL RECORD BEFORE 4.2 MA

The earliest hominins include three groups (*Sahelanthropus*, *Orrorin*, and *Ardipithecus*) dated between 7 and 4.3 Ma. These fossils are identifiable as hominins (humans and our extinct relatives that shared a common ancestor separate from the chimpanzees) by

A Companion to Biological Anthropology, Second Edition. Edited by Clark Spencer Larsen.
© 2023 John Wiley & Sons Ltd. Published 2023 by John Wiley & Sons Ltd.

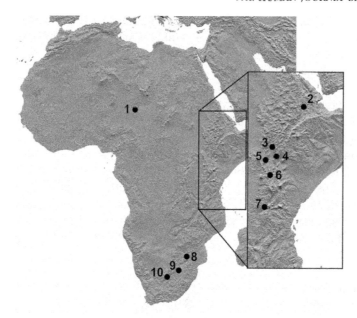

Figure 24.1 Locations of major hominin localities. 1 = Toros Menalla & Koro Toros, Chad; 2 = Afar, Ethiopia (Middle Awash, Gona, Woranso Mille, Hadar, Galili); 3 = Omo, Ethiopia; 4 = East Turkana, Kenya; 5 = West Turkana, Kenya (Lothagam); 6 = Tugen Hills, Kenya; 7 = Laetoli & Olduvai Gorge, Tanzania; 8 = Makapansgat, South Africa; 9 = Sterkfontein, Swartkrans, Drimolen, Gladysvale, South Africa; and 10 = Taung, South Africa. The Konso, Ethiopia locality is slightly east of Omo, Ethiopia (3).

exhibiting the two signature adaptations of our lineage: a smaller, nonsectorial maxillary canine and evidence of adaptations to terrestrial bipedality. Where it can be measured, their brain and body size approximate those of modern chimpanzees.

Sahelanthropus tchadensis *(Brunet et al. 1996, 2002)*
Sahelanthropus tchadensis is currently the oldest identified hominin, known from a collection of dentognathic fossils from the now hyper-arid Toros-Menalla area of northern Chad and dated to between 7.2 and 6.8 Ma (Lebatard et al. 2008). The type specimen is a distorted but nearly complete cranium with a brain size of 360–370 ml, or about the same size as a modern chimpanzee. These fossils, including three partial mandibles, exhibit a smaller, nonsectorial canine with apical wear, and reduced subnasal prognathism with a very thick supraorbital torus (Brunet et al. 2002, 2005; Guy et al. 2005; Zollikofer et al. 2005).

The evidence for bipedalism is inferred from the inferiorly oriented foramen magnum and basicranial anatomy. Like later bipedal hominins and unlike apes, the plane of the foramen magnum opening is oriented inferiorly, allowing the head to be positioned atop a vertical spine. A functionally ambiguous partial femur and two ulnae have also been attributed to this species (Macchiarelli et al. 2020, although see also Daver et al. 2022).

Orrorin tugenensis *(Senut et al. 2001)*
The 5.7–6.0 Ma (Sawada et al. 2002) species *Orrorin tugenensis* is documented by a series of dentognathic and post-cranial fossils (Senut et al. 2001) from the Tugen Hills and Lukeino in Kenya. The large triangular maxillary canine has a disto-lingually facing wear facet described as "almost sectorial" (Senut et al. 2001: 140) and the molar crown enamel has an intermediate thickness (Pickford and Senut 2005) similar to that of *Ardipithecus* (see

below) and *Sahelanthropus*. Perhaps the most significant fossils of *Orrorin* are three proximal femora (Galik et al. 2004; Pickford et al. 2002). One (BAR 1002′00) has a complete femoral head and neck, anatomy necessary to reconstruct locomotor behavior indicating adaptations to some form of bipedality.

Ardipithecus kadabba *(Haile-Selassie et al. 2004)*

These 5.8–5.2 Ma *Ardipithecus kadabba* fossils from the Afar Depression of Ethiopia are broadly similar to the previously named 4.8-4.3 Ma *Ar. ramidus* (*see below*) although being 1.0–1.5 million years older. These fossils are from the Middle Awash (Haile-Selassie and WoldeGabriel 2009) and Gona (Simpson et al. 2015) study areas and include dental and post-cranial remains. Significantly, a pedal proximal phalanx exhibits anatomy seen in bipedal hominins that experience hyperdorsiflexion at the metatarsophalangeal joint while walking. The triangular maxillary canine (ASK-VP-3/400) and the mandibular third premolar (from a different individual) show that the C/P3 complex was primitive but not sectorial (honing) as in the living apes.

Ardipithecus ramidus *(White et al. 1994, 1995)*

Beginning in the 1990s, the discovery of 4.8-4.3 Ma fossils in the Middle Awash (White et al. 1994) and the Gona (Semaw et al. 2005; Simpson et al. 2019) study areas in Ethiopia provided the first substantial evidence for a hominin older than 4 Ma. These fossils led to the naming of a new genus ("*Ardipithecus*," combining the local Afar word for "ground" and Greek word for "ape") and species ("*ramidus*," from the word "root" in the Afar language). A 4.41–4.48 Ma mandibular fragment (Deino et al. 2002; Hill 1985) from the Tugen Hills of Kenya may also be reasonably assignable to *Ar. ramidus* (White et al. 2009).

In addition to the usual collection of isolated elements, this sample includes three partial skeletons including "Ardi" (ARA-VP-6/500). Relative to the later australopiths, this small-brained hominin (Figure 24.2) has smaller molar teeth with thinner enamel, larger canines, and a more anteriorly (relative to apes) positioned foramen magnum. Detailed descriptions of the fossils (Lovejoy et al. 2009a, 2009b, 2009c; Simpson et al. 2019; Suwa et al. 2009a, 2009b; White et al. 2009, 2015) indicate advanced but incomplete adaptations to terrestrial bipedality (pelvis, lateral foot) while retaining climbing adaptations (long forelimbs, hamstring muscle function, grasping big toe). Body size is estimated to have been about 50 kg with limited skeletal size sexual dimorphism present – about the same as the extant chimpanzees. The anterior teeth lack the ape-like C/P3 honing complex and the magnitude of canine size sexual dimorphism is no greater than that observed in humans (Suwa et al. 2009b, 2021).

LATE MIOCENE AND EARLY PLIOCENE HOMININ EVOLUTION OVERVIEW

These three late Miocene taxa had non-sectorial canines, were bipeds to some degree, and had a significant temporal and spatial distribution across north-central and eastern Africa. *Sahelanthropus* and most of the *Orrorin* fossils were found in perilacustrine environments with significantly open (wooded grassland) habitats (Pickford and Senut 2001; Vignaud et al. 2002) whereas *Ar. kadabba* was more commonly found in wooded or forested habitats (Haile-Selassie and WoldeGabriel 2009; Simpson et al. 2015). This indicates that the hominins (either as a single lineage or multiple independent lineages that adopted bipedality and canine reduction) were, soon after diverging from the chimpanzee–human last common ancestor, widely dispersed across Africa and capable of exploiting a diversity of habitats. Ecological reconstructions of the three *Ar. ramidus* localities include forests to

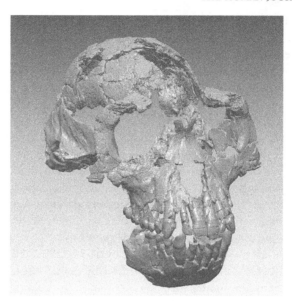

Figure 24.2   Virtual reconstruction of the 4.4 Ma composite skull of *Ardipithecus ramidus* (ARA-VP-6/500 & ARA-VP-1/500) recovered from the Aramis area, Ethiopia. Image provided by Gen Suwa and the Middle Awash research team.

more open habitats in the Tugen Hills (Pickford and Senut 2001; Pickford et al. 2004), humid, cool, grassy woodlands at Aramis (WoldeGabriel et al. 2009), and woodland to grassy woodland at Gona (Levin et al. 2008, 2022; Semaw et al. 2005). The vast majority of terrestrial mammals were grazing (grass-eating) herbivores at Gona and the Middle Awash areas although the hominins have a carbon isotopic signature indicating a diet including grassy woodland resources (Cerling et al. 2013; Suwa et al. 2009b).

While similarities in anatomy, such as similarities in tooth crown dimensions and enamel thickness, link the two *Ardipithecus* species (Haile-Selassie and WoldeGabriel 2009) into a coherent phyletic group, the relatedness of these three genera remains unclear. Aside from the issues of biological variation due to broad spatial and temporal distribution is the unfortunate fact that the three samples tend to document different portions of their anatomy, making direct comparisons difficult. For example, bipedalism is proposed for all three groups although each species' locomotion is inferred from a different part of the skeleton, thus rendering difficult our understanding to both the degree of adaptation to bipedality as well as the nature of their bipedalism. Where the anatomy does overlap (e.g., maxillary canine), only preliminary descriptions have been published to date, thus precluding formal comparisons between the samples. While Haile-Selassie and colleagues (2004) raised the possibility that all three taxa are part of a single lineage, until further studies are conducted (e.g., Macchiarelli et al. 2020), it is reasonable and useful to retain the separate taxonomic names.

What is the Significance of Bipedality and Canine Reduction?

The anatomical and behavior transition to bipedality by hominins required significant reorganization of the musculoskeletal system that is unique among mammals. These changes decreased their capacity to exploit arboreal resources – the historical adaptive niche of the apes – reflecting a transition of dietary focus with decreased reliance on the protection offered by trees from terrestrial predators. Therefore, the challenges imposed by terrestrial bipedality must have been overcome by the resulting increase in fitness and survivorship of the ancient hominins that adopted these behaviors. While it is most parsimonious to suggest bipedality only arose once and would unite these early hominins into a single phylogenetic unit (i.e., hominins), multiple independent origins of bipedalism are possible with early hominins having polyphyletic origins.

The loss of the large, sectorial canine in hominin male documents changes in male–male competition for dominance and reproductive and resource access that is characteristic of the great apes and many monkeys. These competitions are often mediated by biting so a reduction in canine size suggests novel behaviors were adopted by hominins that altered the nature of male intrasexual competition. This, in tandem with female mate choice of males, is crucial to these behavioral changes as females may have mated preferentially with males lacking the behaviors and anatomy associated with aggression.

A model where males provision females (Lovejoy 1981, 2009, 2014) attempts to link fitness, anatomy, and behavior. Provisioning of food by males – best pursued bipedally – builds strong bonds between mating pairs (as is common in other pair-bonded mammals and birds) and has the benefit of ensuring paternity and a reproductive return on these paternal investments. Female choice of mates and pair-bonding is central in this model and competition by males for reproductive access to females with hidden signs of ovulation (unique in humans) is perhaps best achieved by emphasizing intersexual social bonds rather than male–male physical competition as in many other primates.

The Early Australopiths: 4.2–2.95 Ma

Hominins from this period have been recovered from the East African Rift System (EARS) in Kenya and Ethiopia, South Africa, and from the Djurab Desert in Chad. Characteristics that unite these small-brained hominins, that will be collectively called australopiths (derived from the genus name *Australopithecus* that means "southern apes") to distinguish them from the older *Ardipithecus*, include an increase in size of the post-canine teeth with thicker occlusal enamel, a trend of decreasing size of the canines, a broader midface, and further musculoskeletal adaptations to bipedality. Previously, the two best-known early australopiths, *Australopithecus anamensis* and *Au. afarensis*, were considered time-successive species representing a single anagenetic lineage (Haile-Selassie et al. 2010; Kimbel et al. 2006) that could be derived from *Ar. ramidus* and ended with the radiation into the specialized robust australopiths and *Homo*. The discovery of additional australopith and australopith-like hominins (*Au. bahrelghazali*, *Au. deyiremeda*, *Kenyanthropus platyops*), and the enigmatic 3.4 Ma partial foot skeleton from the Woranso-Mille study area in Ethiopia, has demonstrated that hominin diversity and evolution were more complex and interesting than first suggested.

Australopithecus anamensis *(Leakey et al. 1995)*

Australopithecus anamensis fossils have been recovered from Kenya (4.17–4.07 Ma Kanapoi and ca. 3.9 Ma Allia Bay deposits in the Turkana Basin (Leakey et al. 1995; Ward et al. 2001, 2017)) and Ethiopia (4.2–4.1 Ma Asa Issie, Middle Awash study area (White et al. 2006), 3.8 Ma cranium from the Woranso-Mille study area (Haile-Selassie 2021; Haile-Selassie et al. 2019), associated teeth from Fejej (Ward 2014) with some additional teeth provisionally assigned to *Au. anamensis* from the Mulu Basin (also known as Galili, 3.9–3.8 Ma) (Haile-Selassie and Asfaw 2000)).

This species has thick-enamelled and larger post-canine teeth and robust mandibles with a distinctive receding symphysis (~ "chin") with parallel tooth rows. The few post-cranial fossils (Ward et al. 2001, 2020; White et al. 2006) indicate an adaptation to terrestrial bipedality although additional fossils are needed to better understand the full scope of the changes to their musculoskeletal system. The presence of larger and smaller elements (Ward et al., 2017) may indicate a greater degree of body size sexual dimorphism than in *Ar. ramidus*.

The habitats occupied by these hominins appears to have been "closed to grassy woodlands" (White et al. 2006: 885) at Asa Issie and more open habitats near a "large, slow-moving body of water" (Field 2017: 1) in Kenya with a nearby gallery forest (Leakey et al. 1995). The carbon isotopic signal from the teeth of the 4.4 Ma *Ar. ramidus* from the Middle Awash area and that of *Ar. ramidus* may reflect similar diets (Levin et al. 2015; although see Quinn 2019) of leaves and fruits despite marked differences in dental size and proportions.

Australopithecus afarensis *(Johanson et al. 1978)*

Field research in the 3.4–2.95 Ma Hadar study area in the Afar region of Ethiopia has yielded many well-preserved fossils including partial skeletons, of which "Lucy" (A. L. 288-1) is the best known, as well as a rich collection of bones from at least 13 individuals at the A. L. 333 site, ranging in age from young adolescents to older adults (see *American Journal of Physical Anthropology* 1982, volume 57(4) for descriptions of the 1973–1977 collections; Kimbel and Delzene, 2009; Kimbel et al. 2004). A juvenile "Selam" (DIK-1-1) (Alemseged et al. 2006) partial skeleton from the nearby Dikika study area is a significant contribution to our understanding of *Au. afarensis* development. More recent finds from Ethiopia, such as the A. L. 444-1 skull (Kimbel et al. 2004) from Hadar, the well-preserved 3.4 Ma mandibles and teeth from Maka in the Middle Awash Study area (White et al. 2000), the partial skeleton (KSD-VP-1/1) and dentognathic remains from Woranso-Mille (Haile-Selassie et al. 2010, 2016a; Haile-Selassie and Su 2016; Melillo et al. 2021) have broadened our knowledge of the species. More recent discoveries in the highlands of Kenya (Mbua et al. 2016) further broadens the range and habitats of the species.

In 1974, Mary Leakey and her team recovered a number of primitive 3.85–3.63 Ma hominin fossils including a well-preserved mandible (L. H. [Laetoli Hominid] 4) (Harrison 2011; Leakey and Harris 1987) from Laetoli, Tanzania. Undoubtedly the most important fossils from Laetoli are the 3.66 Ma multiple hominin trackways preserved in a solidified volcanic tuff. These footprints clearly demonstrate a modern-like gait pattern. Comparison of the Laetoli and Hadar fossils suggested that they shared many similarities, which were all attributed to a newly named species, *Australopithecus afarensis*. The combination of the Tanzanian trackways and the Ethiopian post-crania indicated that this ancient hominin was fully bipedal. Curiously, recent research (McNutt et al. 2021) has recognized two distinct footprint forms and gait patterns between the different trackways at Laetoli, suggesting that a second unidentified bipedal hominin may also have been present at the site.

Australopithecus deyiremeda *(Haile-Selassie et al. 2015)*

Hominin diversity increased with the announcement of a series of 3.5–3.3 Ma fossils from the Woranso-Mille study in Ethiopia. While demonstrably an australopith (thick-enamelled post-canine teeth), it differed from the synchronic and sympatric *Au. afarensis* by having smaller maxillary post-canine teeth with very thick enamel and more anterior origins of the zygomatic root and mandibular ramus. It is distinguishable from *Kenyanthropus platyops* (see below) by details of facial anatomy with a more anterior position of the maxillary incisors (Haile-Selassie et al. 2015; Spoor et al. 2016). Some of its anatomy (e.g., mandibular corpus robusticity) is shared with later *Homo* and *Paranthropus*. It is difficult to determine if it bears any phyletic relation to these taxa although it does highlight the possibility of homoplasy (independent acquisition of characters) in the hominins.

Kenyanthropus platyops *(Leakey et al. 2001)*

These 3.5–3.2 Ma fossils attributed to *Kenyanthropus platyops* ("flat-faced human from Kenya") were discovered at Lomekwi on the west side of Lake Turkana in Kenya. The type specimen is a highly fragmented and distorted, but mostly complete, cranium (KNM-WT 40000) (Leakey et al. 2001). The cranium, although similar in size to both *Au. afarensis* and *Au. africanus*, exhibits a number of traits (such as flattened midface, less facial prognathism, a transversely and sagittally flattened subnasal clivus, a small external auditory meatus, and tooth proportions) that distinguish it from either species to the extent that the recognition both of a new species and of a new genus was proposed. Unfortunately, the postfossilization deformation of the holotype cranium obscures anatomical details of the face and vault to a degree such that reservations about its taxonomic distinctiveness have been raised (White 2003). Ecologically, *K. platyops* seems to overlap with the Ethiopian *Au. afarensis* habitat types, although it may have lived in somewhat wetter and more vegetated zones (Villaseñor et al. 2020).

A number of other hominin remains were recovered from Lomekwi that could represent this species (although they have not been assigned to *K. platyops*) or another group (Skinner et al. 2020). Significantly, the oldest stone tools of the Lomekwian type have been found in nearby sediments (Harmand et al. 2015).

Australopithecus africanus *(Dart 1925)*

Australopithecus africanus ("the southern ape of Africa") was the first truly ancient hominin known when it was discovered in 1924. At a time when the large-brained, primitive-jawed "Piltdown"-based model of human evolution was dominant, Dart's announcement of a small-brained juvenile fossil skull from the site of Taung in South Africa ran counter to expectations, both by its anatomy (small brain and less "ape-like" teeth) and where it was found. At that time Asia – and not southern Africa – was widely considered to be the home of the earliest hominins. Since the 1920s, hundreds of fossils assigned to *Au. africanus* have been recovered from karstic caves in South Africa, most notably from the sites of Sterkfontein (Members 2 and 4), Makapansgat, and Gladysvale. Most of these underground caverns were accessible via vertical shafts that had trees and shrubs at their openings on the otherwise grassy landscape that provided resting and feeding spots for terrestrial (Brain 1981) and avian (Berger and Clarke 1995) predators. Recent research (Granger et al. 2022) has redated the hominin-rich Member 4 and Jacovec Cavern at Sterkfontein to 3.7–3.4 Ma, indicating that the *Au. africanus* sample is much older than previously thought (2.6–2.0 Ma) and coexisted in time with the earlier australopiths. These newly proposed earlier dates for the South African have been challenged (Frost et al. 2022) with the biochronological data supporting an age less than 2.8 Ma.

The *Au. africanus* collections are extensive and include multiple male, female, and juvenile crania and mandibles; hundreds of teeth; and post-crania – notably the small-bodied Sts 14 and the larger-bodied Stw 431 partial skeletons. The crania have small-brained (435–560 ml) globular vaults with a prognathic face and larger molar and premolar teeth and smaller canines. The chewing muscles can be large, but they are not hypertrophied to the extent observed in the "robust" australopiths (e.g., *P. robustus*, *P. aethiopicus*, *P. boisei*). These individuals are fully adapted to bipedalism with requisite pelvic and vertebral specializations, a valgus knee, and a permanently adducted great toe. In many anatomical details, their post-crania are similar to those of the more northern *Au. afarensis*, although *Au. africanus* exhibits larger post-canine teeth and smaller canines. It is possible that the Member 4 fossils represent two species (Clarke and Kuman 2019; Lockwood and Tobias 2002).

Australopithecus prometheus *(Dart 1948)*
A partial hominin foot (Stw 573 "Little Foot") was reconstructed from fossils recovered from the cave breccia of Sterkfontein Member 2 (Clarke 2019). Following extensive and difficult excavation, a nearly complete hominin skeleton of that individual was recovered. While the specimen exhibits many similarities to the *Au. africanus* fossils from other deposits at Sterkfontein, it was assigned to the previously named taxon *Au. prometheus* based on anatomical details of the cranium (Clarke and Kuman 2019) and suggested simi-larities to fossils recovered from Makapansgat. The preferred date of the breccia is 3.67 Ma (Granger et al. 2015) based on cosmogenic dating. There is professional disagreement about the fossil's age (Bruxelles et al. 2019; Herries and Shaw 2011; Frost et al. 2022) and distinctiveness (Price 2018), such that the anatomical differences do not warrant separation from *Au. africanus* (Rak et al. 2021) or that the taxon name *Au. prometheus* is invalid for technical reasons (Berger and Hawks 2019). The contentious redating of the *Au. africa-nus*-bearing deposits at Sterkfontein to between 3.7–3.4 Ma (Granger et al. 2022) and acceptance of the older dates for Member 2 may be possible support for including these and other specimens from Sterkfontein and Makapansgat (e.g., StW 505, StW 252, MLD1) into a single taxon. Alternatively, this could be evidence of taxic diversity and sympatry that is evident at Woranso-Mille, Ethiopia (*Au. afarensis* and *Au. deyiremeda*).

Australopithecus bahrelghazali (*Brunet et al. 1996*)
Australopithecus bahrelghazali is notable for expanding the range of australopiths beyond eastern and South Africa into the paleo-Lake Chad basin in North–Central Africa. Recent geochronological analyses (Lebatard et al. 2008) suggest an age near 3.6 Ma for the now hyper-arid Koro Toro area in the Djurab Desert of Chad. Unfortunately, this taxon has few known specimens, including an anterior mandible fragment nicknamed "Abel" (KT 12/H1) and associated maxillary P3 (KT 12/H2) and two additional mandibles. While some aspects of its anatomy distinguish it from other hominins (Guy et al. 2008), it is possible to be a regional variant of *Au. afarensis* (Kimbel et al. 2006).

The habitats sampled at Koro Toro were dominated by tropical C_4 grasses and grazing her-bivores (alcelaphine and antilopine bovids, notochoerine suids, equids) (Zazzo et al. 2000).

Taxon indeterminate – "Burtele Foot" (Haile-Selassie et al. 2012)
A 3.4–3.3 Ma partial hominin foot was discovered at the Burtele locality within the Woranso-Mille, Ethiopia, study area (Haile-Selassie et al. 2012). While teeth found in the same area are demonstrably australopith (*Au. deyiremeda*), the foot is unlike any australo-pith foot known by retaining a grasping hallux and unusual metatarsal lengths. Only the older *Ardipithecus* fossils have a grasping hallux although they are larger in size. This fossil was a bipedal hominin as it was regularly dorsiflexed at the lateral metatarsophalangeal joints as in all hominins.

The implications for this are that this foot demonstrates that a more arboreally adept hominin was occupying the same landscape as the terrestrial biped *Au. afarensis* and pre-sumed biped *Au. deyiremeda*, providing evidence of unexpected locomotor and phyletic diversity.

EARLY AUSTRALOPITHS OVERVIEW

In the period between 4.3 and 4.1 Ma, a new type of small-brained, bipedal hominin arose – the australopith – that differed from the earlier hominins and are known from EARS and North–Central Africa and southern Africa prior to 3.0 Ma. They are distinguishable from the older *Ardipithecus* by an increase in the size and enamel thickness of the post-canine teeth and continuing reduction of maxillary canine crown size. The australopiths also differ by further anatomical refinement of bipedal locomotion and perhaps an increase in body size sexual dimorphism.

Currently, *Au. anamensis* is the only species recognized between 4.2 and 3.9 Ma (although see Haile-Selassie et al. (2019) for possibility of overlap with early *Au. afarensis*). In Ethiopia there is close spatial and temporal proximity and ecological similarity between *Ar. ramidus* and *Au. anamensis* (White et al. 2006), suggesting an *in situ* transition between the species despite numerous anatomical differences. However, the possibility of an allopatric origin of *Au. anamensis* with a subsequent invasion into the Afar region cannot be ruled out.

Five hominin species are currently identified between 3.8 and 2.9 Ma: *Au. afarensis, Au. africanus, Au. deyiremeda, Au. bahrelghazali*, and *K. platyops* (six species if the Burtele foot is a distinct group). While anatomical differences between *Au. anamensis, Au. afarensis*, and *Au. africanus* are evident, the distinctiveness is primarily a matter of degree rather than of fundamental differences in form and adaptation. Organizing the fossils of *Au. anamensis* and *Au. afarensis* in chronological order (Kanapoi→Allia Bay→Laetoli→Hadar) strongly suggests phyletic relatedness and evolutionary anagenesis (Kimbel et al. 2006). In such circumstances, the species boundary may be a product of the sequence of discovery and sample composition. The discovery of additional, chronologically intermediate, fossils has blurred the species' boundary even further (Haile-Selassie 2008). More recent discoveries suggest that these two species overlapped in time, challenging the hypothesis of anagenesis (Haile-Selassie et al. 2019).

The possible redating of the *Au. africanus*-bearing Sterkfontein deposits (Granger et al. 2022) to 3.7–3.4 Ma may lead to a reconsideration of the phyletic role of this species as well as the biogeography of the early australopiths. *Australopithecus africanus* exhibits a broadly similar adaptive complex with the other early australopiths, although some traits appear to link *Au. africanus* with the younger *P. robustus* (Lockwood and Tobias 1999), and the younger age originally suggested for this species (2.6–2.0 Ma) lent credence to this proposal. Cave infilling is a complex process and difficult to reconstruct, leading to differing interpretations (Sewell et al. 2022). The absence of volcanism in the region requires use of multiple dating approaches including the cosmogenic nuclide approach (Granger et al. 2015, 2022). While in some ways this redating may simplify our understanding of the early australopiths, additional research must continue on the karstic deposits to reconcile alternative dating methods such as biochronology (Frost et al. 2022), U/Pb dating, and paleomagnetism that have previously supported the 2.6–2.0 Ma ages.

Although the *K. platyops* holotype cranium is crushed and distorted, it is considered to retain enough distinctive anatomy to allow it to be reliably distinguished from other hominins. This led to two phyletic proposals about *K. platyops*: first, that it was phyletically distinct from the contemporary and near-sympatric *Au. afarensis* and second, it was uniquely ancestral to *Homo rudolfensis* – a taxon that includes the larger-brained, flatter-faced, approximately 1.9 Ma KNM-ER 1470 cranium. However, other researchers (for example, White 2003) suggested that the magnitude of distortion of the cranium introduced by significant amount of fragmentation rendered its original shape difficult to assess.

The fact that *Kenyanthropus* and *Au. deyiremeda* (Spoor et al. 2016), in addition to *Au. afarensis*, *Au. bahrelghazali*, *Au. africanus*, and the "Burtele foot," are distinct taxa has significant implications for our understanding of hominin diversity, adaptations, and distribution in the middle Pliocene EARS, Chadian basin, and southern Africa. It also raises the question of phyletic origins (where and when did they originate, and who are their ancestors) and ecological niche partitioning (Haile-Selassie et al. 2016b).

The middle Pliocene hominins in the EARS appear to occupy more mixed woodland and grassland habitats (Villaseñor et al. 2020) or very open habitats such as Laetoli (Harrison 2011). While carnivory and the use and manufacture of stone tools was widely considered to coincide with the origins of the genus *Homo*, recent discoveries of pre-Oldowan tools (Harmand et al. 2015) and cut-marked bone (McPherron et al. 2010) may push these behaviors back to 3.3–3.4 Ma, suggesting an australopith-grade hominin had these capacities. The early cut-marked bones are compelling, although some suggest that the marks were due to crocodile biting and not stone tools (Sahle et al. 2017). Currently, no early australopith has been found in association with the stone tools or with evidence of carnivory.

THE LATER AUSTRALOPITHS: 3.0–<1.0 MA

These australopiths are known from the EARS and the karstic caves in South Africa. They range from more generalized forms (*Au. sediba*) to taxa exhibiting significant masticatory specializations (*Paranthropus aethiopicus*, *P. boisei*, *P. robustus*) that are colloquially called "robust" australopiths[1]. Although *Au. garhi* also exhibits these craniodental traits, it has not been characterized as a "robust" australopith. All of these small-brained hominins are terrestrial bipeds with large, thick-enamelled post-canine teeth, robust mandibles, and evidence of hypertrophy of the chewing muscles. These fossils were recovered in more open environments occupied by grazing herbivores.

Australopithecus garhi *(Asfaw et al. 1999)*
This enigmatic 2.5 Ma cranium from the Hata Member in the Middle Awash (Ethiopia) project area defies simple phyletic allocation. This cranium is clearly *Australopithecus* due to its small brain size (about 450 ml) and thick-enamelled, very large crowned post-canine dentition; yet it also contains some characters found in later *Homo*, such as similar canine/post-canine tooth proportions and a rounded anterior alveolar margin. The type specimen is unique in possessing a canine with a large occlusal area and unusual morphology. A major contributing factor to the lack of understanding of this species is the paucity of hominin fossils from this period. While other hominin fossils were found at the same level, they have not been assigned to *Au. garhi*; therefore, a complete sense of the species' degree of anatomical variation is unknown. Also found at this stratigraphic level were cut-marked bones and stone tools, suggesting some degree of carnivory. These fossils were recovered in a perilacustrine zone with edaphic grasslands, occupied by a diversity of grazing bovids (de Heinzelin et al. 1999).

One of the proposed phyletic possibilities of this species was for it to be a transitional taxon between *Australopithecus afarensis* and early *Homo*. However, similarly aged deposits from the Middle Awash study area have yielded additional, more gracile hominin fossils, which are not assignable to *Au. garhi* as the latter is currently defined – a fact that raises the possibility that multiple taxa were present in the Afar Depression about 2.5 Ma.

Australopithecus sediba *(Berger et al. 2010)*

Additional investigations of the karstic caves in the Malapa site of South Africa has yielded two partial skeletons (Berger et al. 2010) dated to ca. 2.0 Ma (Dirks et al. 2010) that add significantly to our understanding of the later nonrobust australopiths. The original descriptions focused on its mixture of derived or *Homo*-like features (aspects of pelvic morphology, humeral-femoral length ratio) and primitive features (overall body plan, small brain, cranial anatomy, larger thick-enamelled teeth) highlighting the complexity and diversity of earlier hominin evolution. The lower limb shows some unexpected anatomy, perhaps reflecting a distinctive gait pattern (DeSilva et al. 2013).

The phyletic relationship of *Au. sediba* with other hominins is unclear, although it is most likely linked in some way to *Au. africanus* (Kimbel and Rak 2017).

Paranthropus robustus *(Broom 1938)*

The discovery of ancient hominins in South Africa prompted others – notably Robert Broom – to look for hominin fossils in the karstic caves. Broom's discoveries at the site known as Kromdraai led to the naming of a new species, *Paranthropus robustus*, in 1938. Subsequently, the name of the genus *Paranthropus* was considered to be a junior synonym to *Australopithecus*. More recently, the consensus view recognizes the distinctiveness of the species and its original generic name is now adopted for the group. The fossils from the cave sites of Kromdraai, Swartkrans, Gondolin, and Drimolen (Keyser 2000) have depositional histories and a preservational quality similar to those of the *Au. africanus* fossils.

Significant fossil collections are known, especially from Swartkrans, consisting primarily of dentognathic remains. *Paranthropus robustus* is readily distinguishable from the older *Au. africanus* through the enlargement of their post-canine teeth, the reduction of their canines and incisors, a flatter, less prognathic face, and the hypertrophied temporalis muscle that commonly form a boney sagittal crest atop the small-brained (less than 550 ml) cranial vault (Rak et al. 2021). The thick-enamelled teeth generally wear flat. Unfortunately, few undistorted post-crania are known.

The dating of these sites suffers from the same limitations as the other South African cave sites, although a review of the data (Herries and Adams 2013) has suggested that this hominin is found in deposits dated between ca. 2 Ma and perhaps less than 1 Ma, with more recent research indicating an earlier first appearance datum of 2.22 Ma at Swartkrans (Kuman et al. 2021).

Paranthropus aethiopicus *(Arambourg and Coppens 1968)*

This species was named on the basis of an edentulous mandible from the Shungura Formation sediments that outcrop along the Omo River in southern Ethiopia that are part of the Lake Turkana basin spanning Kenya and Ethiopia. This approximately 2.3 Ma mandible has a very thick corpus and a buttressed symphysis, with large post-canine tooth roots and small anterior tooth alveoli. Poorly known and often overlooked, the species languished until the recovery in 1985 of the KNM-WT 17000 cranium (Walker et al. 1986). This small-brained (410 ml) cranium, nicknamed "Black skull," is distinctive for its large post-canine dentition, unflexed cranial base, prognathic lower midface, and large sagittal crest. Unfortunately, the species is still poorly represented by fossils (primarily dental remains) and is known only from the 2.7–2.3 Ma Turkana basin deposits.

Paranthropus boisei *(Leakey 1959)*

In 1959 at Olduvai Gorge, Tanzania, Mary Leakey discovered a well-preserved 1.8 Ma cranium, (Olduvai Hominid 5 [OH-5]). This iconic specimen was the first major discovery of a hominin in eastern Africa and had the resulting effect of stimulating hominin paleontological research in the EARS. Initially the cranium was assigned to the newly created genus *Zinjanthropus*. It was subsequently allocated to *Australopithecus*, although currently it is most commonly assigned to *Paranthropus*. The OH-5 cranium (Tobias 1967) has among the largest hominin post-canine teeth known; very small, vertically implanted canines and incisors; a tall but not prognathic lower midface; anteriorly positioned and laterally flaring zygomatic arches; prominent sagittal and nuchal crests; and a small brain size. Additional *P. boisei* fossils dated between 2.3 and 1.34 Ma have been recovered from Olduvai Gorge, the Turkana basin deposits in Ethiopia and Kenya, the well-preserved 1.4 Ma skull from the southern Ethiopia site of Konso (Suwa et al. 1997) (Figure 24.3), and Malawi in the southern portion of the East African Rift (Kullmer et al. 1999). Unfortunately, few post-crania of this species are available (although see Dominguez-Rodrigo et al. 2013; Richmond et al. 2020), so details of its species' stature, bodily form, and body size dimorphism remain poorly known.

THE LATER AUSTRALOPITHS: OVERVIEW

Between 3.0 and 2.6 Ma, a hominin radiation occurred (Suwa et al. 1996), leading to the origins of *Homo* and the robust australopiths. Although where in Africa this speciation event occurred is currently unknown, the event itself resulted in at least two (and probably

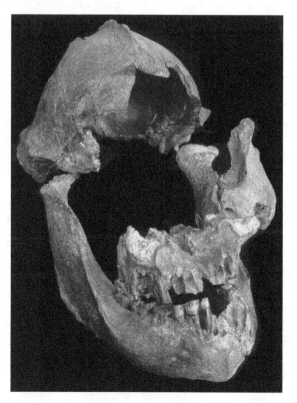

Figure 24.3   The 1.4 Ma *Paranthropus boisei* skull (KGA10-525) from Konso, Ethiopia. Image provided by Gen Suwa and the Konso Project research team.

more) lineages that exhibited fundamental differences in adaptation and that rapidly spread throughout Africa. These two adaptive roles are characterized by the elaboration and enlargement of the dentognathic structures – namely in the "robust" australopiths and *Au. garhi* – and by a lineage (the genus *Homo*) that ultimately reduced its tooth crown dimensions and enlarged its brain.

Australopithecus afarensis seems to be a reasonable stem hominin from which the eastern African robust lineages (*P. aethiopicus*→*P. boisei*), *Au. garhi*, and the early *Homo* lineage arose, although the simplicity of this model has been undercut by the possible redating of *Au. africanus* and the discovery of new taxa. Resolving the phyletic position of the South African australopiths (*Au. africanus*, *Au. sediba*, and *P. robustus*) to both each other and the eastern African has been especially difficult. *Australopithecus africanus*, while a likely ancestor of *Au. sediba*, has been identified variously as the LCA of the robust and *Homo* lineages, replacing *Au. afarensis* in this role (Skelton et al. 1986), or as uniquely ancestral to the robust lineage (Johanson and White 1979, although see Villmoare and Kimbel 2011). The phyletic role of *Au. africanus* is made especially difficult by disagreements as to whether it represents one species or two (Clarke and Kuman 2019) and the unresolved age of the Sterkfontein deposits.

The robust australopiths include *Paranthropus robustus*, *P. aethiopicus*, and *P. boisei*, who share a common dentognathic adaptation (large, thick-enamelled molars and premolars, large and robust mandibular corpora with tall rami, reduced incisors and canines, "dished" faces, laterally projecting and anteriorly positioned zygomatic arches, sagittal crests, and small brains). Dentognathic evidence in these taxa indicates a dietary preference for an abrasive, lower-quality herbivorous diet requiring intense masticatory preparation with an increased reliance on C4 plants such as tropical grasses and sedges, occurring about 2.37 Ma (Wynn et al. 2020). This is probably an adaptation to open terrestrial habitats, which were expanding in Africa throughout the latter half of the Pliocene and early Pleistocene. *Australopithecus garhi* also exhibits similar dental and cranial adaptations as the robust australopiths yet lacks the distinctive facial morphology (Rak et al. 2021). indicating an independent acquisition of these characters. Similar adaptations to occupying open habitats are also seen at that time in other nonrobust hominins and fauna, including suid, bovid, and monkey species.

By approximately 2.3 Ma, changes in dental morphology and facial architecture are evident that distinguish *P. aethiopicus* from *P. boisei* (Suwa et al. 1996). Phyletically, it appears that these eastern African "robust" australopiths are part of a single, continuous lineage that probably arose from *Au. afarensis*. The origins of the South African *P. robustus* are more obscure. The South African fossils defy the standard contention that more and better-preserved fossils will resolve these issues (Haile-Selassie et al. 2016b), as many fossils are known of this species but there is no consensus on phyletic origins or taxonomic diversity. A clarification of the stratigraphy and dating of all of these cave sites should help to resolve these issues. *Paranthropus robustus* has been variously identified as part of a monophyletic robust australopith radiation assigned to the genus *Paranthropus* that includes the eastern African *P. aethiopicus* and *P. boisei*, or as a separate and independently derived robust australopith species. Similarity with the eastern African forms suggests a common phyletic origin (*Paranthropus*) and adaptation. However, differences in anatomical detail, such as tooth morphology and craniofacial anatomy, may indicate that these are adaptive parallelisms that arose independently in two areas (southern Africa and the East African Rift) rather than shared specializations that occurred in two places (southern Africa and the East African Rift).

Multiple hominin species (*Homo*, "robust" australopiths, and later australopiths)' and Oldowan stone tools and evidence of carnivory are known from a number of sites in South Africa (such as Swartkrans, Drimolen, and perhaps Gladysvale) (Herries et al. 2020, although see recent research by Zannolli and colleagues 2022, which questions the assignment of some teeth to *Homo*, notably at Drimolen) and in eastern Africa (Olduvai Gorge, Turkana Basin, and Konso), indicating that the different hominin species had the potential for encounters in their shared home ranges across a span that lasted at least 0.5 million years. It is tempting to think that the dentognathic specializations of the "robust" australopiths is a response to reducing competition for dietary resources by niche partitioning with the sympatric stone tool-using, more carnivorous *Homo*. The robust australopiths, unlike *Homo*, did not expand out of Africa despite the absence of insurmountable physical barriers. This biogeographical history suggests strong differences in adaptive ability and perhaps dietary preferences between *Homo* and the "robust" australopiths, as the latter had less capacity to invade and exploit novel habitats.

The extinction of the robust australopiths occurred after 1.0 Ma in South Africa and somewhat earlier (~1.3 Ma) in eastern Africa. There is little evidence to indicate a widespread turnover in open-adapted fauna at this time, which suggests that the extinction of the "robust" australopiths may not have been the consequence of environmental changes. Was their demise a consequence of competition with *Homo*? Their protracted sympatry suggests that this may not be the case. However, as the technical sophistication of *Homo erectus* improved, its members may have been able to adapt behaviorally to an increasing diversity of environments, whereas the "robust" australopiths' capacity to modify their behavior and anatomy may have been insufficient in the face of the pervasive adaptive abilities of *Homo*.

OVERVIEW AND SUMMARY

To us, understanding what it means to be human is very straightforward and reflects our daily experiences. We are large-brained, bipedal, tool-using individuals belonging to a single species who are highly social and live across the Earth in dense, complex societies that share knowledge through a symbols-based language. Significantly, there is no other species similar to us alive today. Our current situation is the product of millions of years of evolution and adaptation, including a diversity of now extinct relatives. How we got here is not very intuitive as our small-brained arboreal ancestors had to reorganize their musculoskeletal system while adopting terrestrial bipedality and changing how they could exploit their landscape. These differences require us to take a longer look at the complex paths our ancestors and near relatives took during the past seven or so million years. Fortunately, paleoanthropological field research has produced the fossil and archeological evidence that documents this historical journey. We know now that our origins date back to well before 6 Ma and the earliest adaptations were bipedality and novel social behaviors. Sometimes these synchronic and sympatric species could be very similar in overall adaptive pattern (e.g., *Au. afarensis* and *Au. deyiremeda*) or display very different dietary specializations and behavioral capacities (e.g., *Homo erectus* [see Chapter 25 on evolution of the genus *Homo*] and *P. boisei*). Overall, there were many different ways to be a hominin that differ greatly from our recent history. The behaviors so central to our current condition, such as tool use and language, arose late in our evolution and were not a part of our origins. Knowledge of the behaviors and adaptations of our early ancestors is insufficient to predict the diversity and adaptive paths of our ancestors. Our lineage did not follow a straight adaptive path from a small-brained, bipedally inexpert woodland ape to large-brained, socially complex, technologically dependent modern humans.

The transition to the australopith pattern appears to occur between 4.4 and 4.2 Ma and is readily identifiable through changes in canine form and larger and thicker enameled postcanine teeth. The adaptive motivation for this transition is unclear, although changes in the dentition and masticatory muscles appear to be linked with diet as thickened occlusal enamel and enlarged post-canine teeth seem to be associated with tougher consistency or with harder, more brittle foodstuffs (Teaford and Ungar 2000), although the relationship between tooth morphology and dietary consistency is more complex than initially proposed (Ungar, Grine and Teaford 2008). Current evidence regarding locomotion adaptations in *Ar. ramidus* and *Au. anamensis* support a broader model of changing land use between these taxa at about 4.2 Ma. The australopith dental morphotype continues, with minor changes (Kimbel et al. 2006), until about 2.9 Ma, which is then followed by a phyletic radiation that resulted in multiple taxa elaborating upon this adaptive complex with even larger and thicker enameled post-canine teeth (*Au. africanus*, *P. robustus*, *Au. garhi*, *P. aethiopicus*, and *P. boisei*). In addition, at some time between 2.9 and 2.6 Ma (or earlier), a new lineage (or lineages) arose that adopted stone tool use and manufacture, increased carnivory, lacked extreme post-canine megadontia, and subsequently enlarged their brains and dispersed across the Old World. The factors leading to this origin and radiation of *Homo* are currently unknown but are of significant interest to all humans.

FUTURE RESEARCH

Even with the many recent advances, substantial and substantive questions about the early stages of human evolution remain. Biomolecular estimates of the divergence dates of the African ape lineages (gorilla–chimpanzee/human: about 9–7 Ma; chimpanzee–human: 7–5 Ma) (Scally et al. 2012) still require support from the fossil record, although it is clear that hominins arose in Africa. Of the few fossil apes known between 5 and 10 million years in Africa and Europe, *Chororapithecus* (Suwa et al. 2007); *Samburupithecus* (Ishida and Pickford 1997); Hominoidea *gen. et sp. indet.* (Pickford et al. 2008); and *Ouranopithecus* (Koufos and de Bonis 2005) (see Almécija et al. 2021 and elsewhere in this volume for a more thorough review), none appears to be a possible hominin ancestor. In addition, the near-complete absence of chimpanzee-like (McBrearty and Jablonski 2005) and gorilla-like (or gorilloid: *Chororapithecus*, Suwa et al. 2007, or *Nakalipithecus*, Almécija et al. 2021) fossils is a major gap in our understanding of when, where, and in what habitats our closest relatives evolved. The biogeography of the earliest hominins remains poorly known and requires paleontological prospecting in new areas throughout Africa – work that is best identified through the use of remote imaging and geospatial data analysis (Conroy et al. 2009).

Fossils still form the foundation of all of these studies. Our generation may be experiencing a "golden age" of field discoveries; however, this may not last long, due to the depletion of the most easily accessible fossils (White 2004). Even extensive and well-preserved fossil collections, like those of *Au. afarensis* from Hadar, are insufficient to address fully the issues of growth and populational variation. Thus, to further our understanding of our ancestors, we must be more intensive in our surveys for additional fossils and more ambitious in the development of novel means of assessing their biology.

NOTE

1 If the robust australopiths were monophyletic (originated from a single common ancestor), then the group can all be accommodated in the genus *Paranthropus*. Some researchers (e.g., Rak et al. 2021) recognize the possibility that the east and South African robust australopiths may be polyphyletic and adopted the more conservative taxonomy and include them within the genus *Australopithecus*.

REFERENCES

Alemseged, Z., F. Spoor, W. H. Kimbel, et al. "A Juvenile Early Hominin Skeleton from Dikika, Ethiopia." *Nature* 443 (2006): 296–301.

Almécija, S., A. S. Hammond, N. E. Thompson, et al. "Fossil Apes and Human Evolution." *Science* 372 (2021): eabb4363.

Arambourg, C., and Y. Coppens. "Découverte d'un Australopithécien Nouveau dans les Gisements de l'Omo (Éthiopie)." *South African Journal of Science* 64 (1968): 58–59.

Asfaw, B., T. White, O. Lovejoy, et al. "*Australopithecus garhi*: A New Species of Early Hominid from Ethiopia." *Science* 284 (1999): 629–635.

Berger, L. R., and R. J. Clarke. "Eagle Involvement in Accumulation of the Taung Child Fauna." *Journal of Human Evolution* 29 (1995): 275–299.

Berger, L. R., and J. Hawks. "*Australopithecus prometheus* Is a Nomen Nudum." *American Journal of Physical Anthropology* 168 (2019): 383–387.

Berger, L. R., D. J. de Ruiter, S. E. Churchill, et al. "*Australopithecus sediba*: A New Species of *Homo*-Like Australopith from South Africa." *Science* 328 (2010): 195–204.

Brain, C. K. *The Hunters or the Hunted? An Introduction to African Cave Taphonomy.* Chicago, IL: University of Chicago Press, 1981.

Broom, R. "The Pleistocene Anthropoid Apes of South Africa." *Nature* 142 (1938): 377–379.

Brunet, M., A. Beauvilain, Y. Coppens, et al. "*Australopithecus bahrelghazali*, une Nouvelle Espèce d'Hominidé Ancien de la Région de Koro Toro (Tchad)." *Comptes Rendus de l'Académie des Sciences – Series IIA – Earth and Planetary Science* 322 (1996): 907–913.

Brunet, M., F. Guy, D. Pilbeam, et al. "A New Hominid from the Upper Miocene of Chad, Central Africa." *Nature* 418 (2002): 145–151.

Brunet, M., J.-R. Boisserie, D. Ahounta, et al. "*Sahelanthropus tchadensis*: The Facts." *South African Journal of Science* 100 (2005): 443–445.

Bruxelles, L., D. J. Stratford, R. Maire, et al. "A Multiscale Stratigraphic Investigation of the Context of StW 573 'Little Foot' and Member 2, Sterkfontein Caves, South Africa." *Journal of Human Evolution* 133 (2019): 78–98.

Cerling, T., F. K. Manthi, E. Mbua, et al. "Stable Isotope-Based Diet Reconstructions of Turkana Basin Hominins." *Proceedings of the National Academy of Sciences USA* 110 (2013): 10501–10506.

Clarke, R. J. "Excavation, Reconstruction and Taphonomy of the StW 573 *Australopithecus prometheus* Skeleton from Sterkfontein Caves, South Africa." *Journal of Human Evolution* 127 (2019): 41–53.

Clarke, R. J., and K. Kuman. "The Skull of StW 573, a 3.57 Ma *Australopithecus prometheus* Skeleton from Sterkfontein Caves, South Africa." *Journal of Human Evolution* 134 (2019): 102634.

Conroy, G. C., R. L. Anemone, J. van Regenmorter, et al. "Google Earth, GIS, and the Great Divide: A New and Simple Method for Sharing Paleontological Data." *Journal of Human Evolution* 55 (2009): 751–755.

Dart, R. A. "*Australopithecus africanus*: The Man–Ape of South Africa." *Nature* 115 (1925): 195–199.

Dart, R. A. "The Makapansgat Proto-Human *Australopithecus prometheus*." *American Journal of Physical Anthropology* 6 (1948): 259–284.

Daver, G., F. Guy, H. T. Mackaye, et al. "Postcranial Evidence of Late Miocene Hominin Bipedalism in Chad." *Nature* 609 (2022): 94–100.

de Heinzelin, J., J. D. Clark, T. D. White, et al. "Environment and Behavior of 2.5-Million-Year-Old Bouri Hominids." *Science* 284 (1999): 625–629.

Deino, A. L., L. Tauxe, M. Monaghan, et al. "^{40}Ar/^{39}Ar Geochronology and Paleomagnetic Stratigraphy of the Lukeino and Lower Chemeron Formations at Tabarin and Kapcheberek, Tugen Hills, Kenya." *Journal of Human Evolution* 42 (2002): 117–140.

DeSilva, J. M., K. G. Holt, S. E. Churchill, et al. "The Lower Limb and Mechanics of Walking in *Australopithecus sediba*." *Science* 340 (2013): 1232999.

Dirks, P. H. G. M., J. M. Kibii, B. F. Kuhn, et al. "Geological Setting and Age of *Australopithecus sediba* from Southern Africa." *Science* 328 (2010): 205–208.

Domínguez-Rodrigo, M., T. R. Pickering, E. Baquedana, et al. "First Partial Skeleton of a 1.34-Million-Year-Old *Paranthropus boisei* from Bed II, Olduvai Gorge, Tanzania." *PloS One* 8 (2013): e80347.

Field, D. J. "Preliminary Paleoecological Insights from the Pliocene Avifauna of Kanapoi, Kenya: Implications for the Ecology of *Australopithecus anamensis*." *Journal of Human Evolution* 140 (2017): 102384.

Frost, S. R., White, F. J., Reda, H. G., et al. "Biochronology of South African Hominin-Bearing Sites: A Reassessment Using Cercopithecid Primates." *Proceedings of the National Academy of Sciences, USA.* 119, no. 45 (2022): e2210627119 https://doi.org/10.1073/pnas.2210627119

Galik, K., B. Senut, M. Pickford, et al. "External and Internal Morphology of the BAR 1002"00 *Orrorin tugenensis* Femur." *Science* 305 (2004): 1450–1453.

Granger, D. E., R. J. Gibbon, K. Kuman, et al. "New Cosmogenic Burial Ages for Sterkfontein Member 2 *Australopithecus* and Member 5 Oldowan." *Nature* 522 (2015): 85–88.

Granger, D. E., D. Stratford, L. Bruxelles, et al. "Cosmogenic Nuclide Dating of *Australopithecus* at Sterkfontein, South Africa." *Proceedings of the National Academy of Sciences USA* 119, no. 27 (2022): 2123516119. https://doi.org/10.1073/pnas.2123516119.

Guy, F., D. E. Lieberman, D. Pilbeam, et al. "Morphological Affinities of the *Sahelanthropus tchadensis* (Late Miocene Hominid from Chad) Cranium." *Proceedings of the National Academy of Sciences USA* 102 (2005): 18836–18841.

Guy, F., H.-T. Mackaye, A. Likius, et al. "Symphyseal Shape Variation in Extant and Fossil Hominoids and the Symphysis of *Australopithecus bahrelghazali*." *Journal of Human Evolution* 55 (2008): 37–47.

Haile-Selassie, Y. "New Early Pliocene Hominid Fossils from the Woranso-Mille (Central Afar, Ethiopia) and the Question of Phyletic Evolution in Early *Australopithecus*." *Journal of Vertebrate Paleontology* 28, Suppl. 3 (2008): 87A.

Haile-Selassie, Y. "From Trees to Ground: The Significance of *Australopithecus anamensis* in Human Evolution." *Journal of Anthropological Research* 77 (2021): https://doi.org/10.1086/716743.

Haile-Selassie, Y, and B. Asfaw. "A Newly Discovered Early Pliocene Hominid Bearing Paleoentological Site in the Mulu Basin, Ethiopia." *American Journal of Physical Anthropology* 111, no. S30 (2000): 70.

Haile-Selassie, Y., and D. F. Su, eds. *The Postcranial Anatomy of Australopithecus afarensis*. Dordrecht: Springer, 2016.

Haile-Selassie, Y., and G. WoldeGabriel, eds. *Ardipithecus kadabba: Late Miocene Evidence from the Middle Awash, Ethiopia*. Berkeley: University of California Press, 2009.

Haile-Selassie, Y., G. Suwa, and T. D. White. "Late Miocene Teeth from Middle Awash, Ethiopia, and Early Hominid Dental Evolution." *Science* 303 (2004): 1503–1505.

Haile-Selassie, Y., B. Z. Saylor, Deino, A., et al. "New Hominid Fossils from Woranso-Mille (Central Afar, Ethiopia) and Taxonomy of Early *Australopithecus*." *American Journal of Physical Anthropology* 141 (2010): 406–417.

Haile-Selassie, Y., B. Z. Saylor, A. Deino, et al. "A New Hominin Foot from Ethiopia Shows Multiple Pliocene Bipedal Adaptations." *Nature* 483 (2012): 565–570.

Haile-Selassie, Y., L. Gilbert, S. M. Melillo, et al. "New Species from Ethiopia Further Expands Middle Pliocene Hominin Diversity." *Nature* 521 (2015): 483–488.

Haile-Selassie, Y., S. M. Melillo, T. W. Ryan, et al. "Dentognathic Remains of *Australopithecus afarensis* from Neferaytu (Woranso-Mille, Ethiopia): Comparative Description, Geology, and Paleoecological Context." *Journal of Human Evolution* 100 (2016a): 35–53.

Haile-Selassie, Y., S. M. Melillo, and D. Su. "The Pliocene Hominin Diversity Conundrum: Do More Fossils Mean Less Clarity?" *Proceedings of the National Academy of Sciences USA* 113 (2016b): 6364–6371.

Haile-Selassie, Y., S. M. Melillo, A. Vazzana, et al. "A 3.8-Million-Year-Old Hominin Cranium from Woranso-Mille, Ethiopia." *Nature* (2019). https://doi.org/10.1038/s41586-019-1513-8.

Harmand, S., J. E. Lewis, G. S. Feibel, et al. "3.3-Million-Year-Old Stone Tools from Lomekwi 3, West Turkana, Kenya." *Nature* 521 (2015): 310–315.

Harrison, T., ed. *Paleontology and Geology of Laetoli: Human Evolution in Context*. Dordrecht: Springer, 2011.

Herries, A. I. R., and J. W. Adams. "Clarifying the Context, Dating and Age Range of the Gondolin Hominins and *Paranthropus* in South Africa." *Journal of Human Evolution* 65 (2013): 676–681.

Herries, A. I. R., and J. Shaw. "Palaeomagnetic Analysis of the Sterkfontein Palaeocave Deposits: Implications for the Age of the Hominin Fossils and Stone Tool Industries." *Journal of Human Evolution* 60 (2011): 523–539.

Herries, A. I. R., J. M. Martin, A. B. Leece, et al. "Contemporaneity of *Australopithecus, Paranthropus,* and Early *Homo erectus* in South Africa." *Science* 368 (2020): eaaw7293.

Hill, A. "Early Hominid from Baringo, Kenya." *Nature* 315 (1985): 222–224.

Ishida, H., and M. Pickford. "A New Late Miocene Hominoid from Kenya: *Samburupithecus kiptalami* gen. et sp. nov." *Comptes-Rendus Earth and Planetary Sciences* 325 (1997): 823–829.

Johanson, D. C., and T. D. White. "A Systematic Assessment of Early African Hominids." *Science* 203 (1979): 321–329.

Johanson, D. C., T. D. White, and Y. Coppens. "A New Species of the Genus *Australopithecus* (Primates: Hominidae) from the Pliocene of Eastern Africa." *Kirtlandia* 28 (1978): 1–11.

Keyser, A. "The Drimolen Skull: The Most Complete Australopithecine Cranium and Mandible to Date." *South African Journal of Science* 96 (2000): 189–193.

Kimbel, W. H., and L. K. Delezene. "'Lucy' Redux: A Review of Research on *Australopithecus afarensis.*" *Yearbook of Physical Anthropology* 52 (2009): 2–48.

Kimbel, W. H., and Y. Rak. "*Australopithecus sediba* and the Emergence of *Homo*: Questionable Evidence from the Cranium of the Juvenile Holotype MH 1." *Journal of Human Evolution* 107 (2017): 94–106.

Kimbel, W. H., Y. Rak, and D. C. Johanson. *The Skull of Australopithecus afarensis.* Oxford: Oxford University Press, 2004.

Kimbel, W. H., C. A. Lockwood, C. V. Ward, et al. "Was *Australopithecus anamensis* Ancestral to *A. afarensis?* A Case of Anagenesis in the Hominin Fossil Record." *Journal of Human Evolution* 51 (2006): 134–152.

Koufos, G. D., and L. de Bonis. "The Late Miocene Hominoids *Ouranopithecus* and *Graecopithecus.* Implications about Their Relationships and Taxonomy." *Annales de Paléontolgie* 91 (2005): 227–240.

Kullmer, O., O. Sandrock, R. Abel, et al. "The First *Paranthropus* from the Malawi Rift." *Journal of Human Evolution* 37 (1999): 121–127.

Kuman, K., D. E. Granger, R. J. Gibbon, et al. "A New Absolute Age from Swartkrans Cave for the Oldest Occurrences of *Paranthropus robustus* and Oldowan Stone Tools in South Africa." *Journal of Human Evolution* 156 (2021): 103000.

Leakey, L. S. B. "A New Fossil Skull from Olduvai." *Nature* 184 (1959): 491–493.

Leakey, M. D., and J. M. Harris, eds. *Laetoli: A Pliocene Site in Northern Tanzania.* Oxford: Clarendon, 1987.

Leakey, M. G., C. S. Feibel, I. McDougall, and A. C. Walker. "New Four-Million-Year-Old Hominid Species from Kanapoi and Allia Bay, Kenya." *Nature* 376 (1995): 565–571.

Leakey, M. G., F. Spoor, F. H. Brown, et al. "New Hominin Genus from Eastern Africa Shows Diverse Middle Pliocene Lineages." *Nature* 410 (2001): 433–440.

Lebatard, A.-E., D. L. Bourlès, P. Duringer, et al. "Cosmogenic Nuclide Dating of *Sahelanthropus tchadensis* and *Australopithecus bahrelghazali*: Mio-Pliocene Hominids from Chad." *Proceedings of the National Academy of Sciences* 105 (2008): 3226–3231.

Levin, N. E., S. W. Simpson, J. Quade, et al. "Herbivore Enamel and Soil Carbon Isotopic Composition and the Environmental Context of *Ardipithecus* at Gona, Ethiopia." In *The Geology of Early Humans in the Horn of Africa.* Edited by J. Quade and J. Wynn, 215–234. Boulder, CO: Geological Society of America Special Paper 446, 2008.

Levin, N. E., Y. Haile-Selassie, S. R. Frost, et al. "Dietary Change Among Hominins and Cercopithecids in Ethiopia During the Early Pliocene." *Proceedings of the National Academy of Sciences USA* (2015). https://doi.org/10.1073/pnas.1424982112.

Levin, N. E., S. W. Simpson, J. Quade, et al. "The 6-Million-Year Record of Ecological and Environmental Change at Gona, Afar Region, Ethiopia." In *African Paleoecology and Human Evolution.* Edited by S. Reynolds and R. Bobe, 197–213. Cambridge, UK: Cambridge University Press, 2022.

Lockwood, C. A., and P. V. Tobias. "A Large Male Hominin Cranium from Sterkfontein, South Africa, and the status of *Australopithecus africanus.*" *Journal of Human Evolution* 36 (1999): 637–685.

Lovejoy, C. O. "The Origin of Man." *Science* 211 (1981): 341–350.

Lovejoy, C. O. "Reexamining Human Origins in Light of *Ardipithecus* ramidus." *Science* 326 (2009): 74e1–e8.

Lovejoy, C. O. "*Ardipithecus* and Early Human Evolution in Light of Twenty-First-Century Developmental Biology." *Journal of Anthropological Research* 70 (2014): 337–363.

Lovejoy, C. O., B. Latimer, G. Suwa, et al. "Combining, Prehension and Propulsion: The Foot of *Ardipithecus ramidus.*" *Science* 326 (2009a): 72e1–e8.

Lovejoy, C. O., S. W. Simpson, T. D. White, et al. "Careful Climbing in the Miocene: The Forelimbs of *Ardipithecus ramidus* and Humans Are Primitive." *Science* 326 (2009b): 70e1–e8.

Lovejoy, C. O., G. Suwa, L. Spurlock, et al. "The Pelvis and Femur of *Ardipithecus ramidus*: The Emergence of Upright Walking." *Science* 326 (2009c): 71e1–e6.

Macchiarelli, R., A. Bergeret-Medina, D. Marchi, et al. "Nature and Relationships of *Sahelanthropus tchadensis.*" *Journal of Human Evolution* 149 (2020): 102898.

Mbua, E., S. Kusaka, Kunimatsu, Y., et al. "Kantis: A New *Australopithecus* Site on the Shoulders of the Rift Valley, Kenya." *Journal of Human Evolution* 94 (2016): 28–44.

McBrearty, S., and N. G. Jablonski. "First Fossil Chimpanzee." *Nature* 437 (2005): 105–108.

McNutt, E. J., K. G. Hatala, C. Miller, et al. "Footprint Evidence of Early Hominin Locomotor Diversity at Laetoli, Tanzania." *Nature* 600 (2021): 468–471.

McPherron, S. P., Z. Alemseged, C. W. Marean, et al. "Evidence for Stone-Tool-Assisted Consumption of Animal Tissues before 3.39 Million Years Ago at Dikika, Ethiopia." *Nature* 466 (2010): 857–860.

Melillo, S. M., L. Gibert, B. Z. Saylor, et al. "New Pliocene Hominin Remains from the Leado Dido'a Area of Woranso-Mille, Ethiopia." *Journal of Human Evolution* 153 (2021): 102956.

Pickford, M., and B. Senut. "The Geological and Faunal Context of Late Miocene Hominid Remains from Lukeino, Kenya." *Comptes Rendus de l'Académie des Sciences* 332 (2001) : 145–152.

Pickford, M., and B. Senut. "Hominoid Teeth with Chimpanzee- and Gorilla-Like Features from the Miocene of Kenya: Implications for the Chronology of Ape-Human Divergence and Biogeography of Miocene Hominoids." *Anthropological Science* 113 (2005): 95–102.

Pickford, M., B. Senut, D. Gommery, et al. "Bipedalism in *Orrorin tugenensis* Revealed by Its Femora." *Comptes Rendus Palevol* 1 (2002): 1–13.

Pickford, M., B. Senut, and C. Mourer-Chauviré. "Early Pliocene Tragulidae and Peafowls in the Rift Valley, Kenya: Evidence for Rainforest in East Africa." *Compte Rendus Paleovol* 3 (2004): 179–189.

Pickford, M., B. Senut, J. Morales, et al. "First Hominoid from the Late Miocene of Niger." *South African Journal of Science* 104 (2008): 337–340.

Price, M. "Identity of Little Foot Fossil Stirs Controversy." *Science* (2018). doi: 10.1126/science.aaw3406; https://www.science.org/content/article/identity-little-foot-fossil-stirs-controversy.

Quinn, R. L. "Isotopic Equifinity and Rethinking the Diet of *Australopithecus anamensis.*" *American Journal of Physical Anthropology* 169 (2019): 403–421.

Rak, Y., W. H. Kimbel, J. Moggi-Cecchi, et al. "The DNH 7 Skull of *Australopithecus robustus* from Drimolen (Main Quarry), South Africa." *Journal of Human Evolution* 151 (2021): 102913.

Richmond, B. G., D. J. Green, M. R. Lague, et al. "The Upper Limb of *Paranthropus boisei* from Ileret, Kenya." *Journal of Human Evolution* 141 (2020): 102727.

Sahle, Y., S. El Zaatari, and T. D. White "Hominid Butchers and Biting Crocodiles in the African Plio-Pleistocene." *Proceedings of the National Academy of Sciences USA* 114 (2017): 13164–13169. https://doi.org/10.1073/pnas.1716317114.

Sawada, Y., M. Pickford, B. Senut, et al. "The Age of *Orrorin tugenensis*, an Early Hominid from the Tugen Hills, Kenya." *Comptes Rendus Palevol* 1 (2002): 293–303.

Scally, A., J. Y. Dutheil, L. W. Hillier, et al. "Insights into the Hominid Evolution from the Gorilla Genome Sequence." *Nature* 483 (2012): 169–175.

Semaw, S., S. W. Simpson, J. Quade, et al. "Early Pliocene Hominids and Their Environments from Gona, Ethiopia." *Nature* 433 (2005): 301–305.

Senut, B., M. Pickford, D. Gommery, et al. "First Hominid from the Miocene (Lukeino Formation, Kenya)." *Comptes Rendus de l'Académie des Sciences – Series IIA – Earth and Planetary Science* 332 (2001): 137–144.

Sewell, L. C., J. M. Kibii, and S. C. Reynolds. "The Paleoenvironments of Sterkfontein." In *African Paleocology and Hominin Evolution*. Edited by S. C. Reynolds and R. Bobe, 92–101. Cambridge, UK: Cambridge University Press, 2022.

Simpson, S. W., L. Kleinsasser, J. Quade, et al. "Late Miocene Hominin Teeth from the Gona Paleoanthropological Research Project Area, Afar, Ethiopia." *Journal of Human Evolution* 81 (2015): 68–82.

Simpson, S. W., N. E. Levin, J. Quade, et al. "*Ardipithecus ramidus* Postcrania from the Gona Project Area, Afar Regional State, Ethiopia." *Journal of Human Evolution* 129 (2019): 1–45.

Skelton, R. R., H. M. McHenry, and G. M. Drawhorn. "Phylogenetic Analysis of Early Hominids." *Current Anthropology* 27 (1986): 21–43.

Skinner, M. M., M. G. Leakey, L. N. Leakey, et al. "Hominin Dental Remains from the Pliocene Localities at Lomekwi, Kenya (1982–2009)." *Journal of Human Evolution* 145 (2020): 102820.

Spoor, F., M. G. Leakey, and P. O. O'Higgins. "Middle Pliocene Hominin Diversity: *Australopithecus deyiremeda* and *Kenyanthropus platyops*." *Philosophical Transactions of the Royal Society B* 371 (2016): 20150231.

Suwa, G., T. D. White, and F. C. Howell. "Mandibular Postcanine Dentition from the Shungura Formation, Ethiopia: Crown Morphology, Taxonomic Allocations, and Plio-Pleistocene Hominid Evolution." *American Journal of Physical Anthropology* 101 (1996): 247–282.

Suwa, G., B. Asfaw, Y. Beyene, et al. "The First Skull of *Australopithecus boisei*." *Nature* 389 (1997): 489–492.

Suwa, G., R. T. Kono, S. Katoh, et al. "A New Species of Great Ape from the Late Miocene Epoch in Ethiopia." *Nature* 448 (2007): 921–924.

Suwa, G., B. Asfaw, R. T. Kono, et al. "The *Ardipithecus ramidus* Skull and Its Implications for Hominid Origins." *Science* 326 (2009a): 68e1–7.

Suwa, G., R. T. Kono, S. W. Simpson, et al. "Paleobiological Implications of the *Ardipithecus ramidus* Dentition." *Science* 326 (2009b): 94–99.

Suwa, G., T. Sasaki, S. Semaw, et al. "Canine Sexual Dimorphism in *Ardipithecus ramidus* Was Nearly Human-Like." *Proceedings of the National Academy of Sciences USA* 118 (2021): e2116630118.

Teaford, M. F., and P. S. Ungar "Diet and the Evolution of the Earliest Human Ancestors." *Proceedings of the National Academy of Sciences USA* 94 (2000): 13506–13511.

Tobias, P. V. *Olduvai Gorge, Volume 2: The Cranium and Maxillary Dentition of Australopithecus (Zinjanthropus) boisei*. Cambridge, UK: Cambridge University Press, 1967.

Ungar, P. S., F. E. Grine, and M. F. Teaford "Dental Microwear and Diet of the Plio-Pleistocene hominin *Paranthrous boisei*." *PLoS One* 3 (2008): e2044. doi.org/10.1371/journal.pone.0002044.

Vignaud, P., P. Duringer, H. T. Mackaye, et al. "Geology and Palaeontology of the Upper Miocene Toros–Menalla Hominid Locality, Chad." *Nature* 418 (2002): 152–155.

Villaseñor, A., R. Bobe, and A. K. Behrensmeyer. "Middle Pliocene Hominin Distribution Patterns in Eastern Africa." *Journal of Human Evolution* 147 (2020): 102356.

Villmoare, B. A., and W. H. Kimbel. CT-Based Study of Internal Structure of the Anterior Pillar in Extinct Hominins and Its Implications for the Phylogeny of Robust *Australopithecus*. *Proceedings of the National Academy of Sciences USA* 108 (2011): 16200–16205.

Walker, A., R. E. Leakey, J. M. Harris, et al. "2.5-Myr *Australopithecus boisei* from West of Lake Turkana, Kenya." *Nature* 322 (1986): 517–522.

Ward, C., M. G. Leakey, and A. Walker. "Morphology of *Australopithecus anamensis* from Kanapoi and Allia Bay, Kenya." *Journal of Human Evolution* 41 (2001): 255–368.

Ward, C. V. "Taxonomic Affinity of the Pliocene Hominin Fossils from Fejej., Ethiopia." *Journal of Human Evolution* 73 (2014): 98–102.

Ward, C. V., J. M. Plavcan, and F. K. Manthi. "New Fossils of *Australopithecus anamensis* from Kanapoi, West Turkana, Kenya (2012–2015)." *Journal of Human Evolution* 140 2017 (2020): 102368. https://doi.org/10.1016/j.jhevol.2017.07.008.

White, T. D. "Early Hominids – Diversity or Distortion." *Science* 299 (2003): 1994–1997.

White, T. D. "Managing Paleoanthropology's Nonrenewable Resources: A View from Afar." *Comptes Rendus Paleovol* 3 (2004): 339–349.

White, T. D., G. Suwa, and B. Asfaw. "*Australopithecus ramidus*, a New Species of Early Hominid from Aramis, Ethiopia." *Nature* 371 (1994): 306–312.

White, T. D., G. Suwa, and B. Asfaw. "Corrigendum: *Australopithecus ramidus*, a New Species of Early Hominid from Aramis, Ethiopia." *Nature* 375 (1995): 88.

White, T. D., G. Suwa, S. W. Simpson, et al. "Jaws and Teeth of *Australopithecus afarensis* from Maka, Middle Awash, Ethiopia." *American Journal of Physical Anthropology* 111 (2000): 45–68.

White, T. D., G. WoldeGabriel, B. Asfaw, et al. "Asa Issie, Aramis and the Origin of *Australopithecus*." *Nature* 440 (2006): 883–889.

White, T. D., B. Asfaw, Y. Beyene, et al. "*Ardipithecus ramidus* and the Paleobiology of Early Hominids." *Science* 326 (2009): 75–86.

White, T. D., C. O. Lovejoy, B. Asfaw, et al. "Neither Chimpanzee nor Human, *Ardipithecus* Reveals the Surprising Ancestry of Both." *Proceedings of the National Academy of Science* 112 (2015): 4877–4884.

WoldeGabriel, G., S. H. Ambrose, D. Barboni, et al. "The Geological, Isotopic, Botanical, Invertebrate, and Lower Vertebrate Surroundings of *Ardipithecus ramidus*." *Science* 326 (2009): 65e1–5.

Wynn, J. G., Z. Alemseged, R. Bobe, et al. "Isotopic Evidence for the Timing of the Dietary Shift Towards C4 Foods in Eastern African *Paranthropus*." *Proceedings of the National Academy of Sciences USA* 117 (2020): 21978–21984.

Zannolli, C., T. W. Davies, R. Joannes-Boyau, et al. "Dental Data Challenge the Ubiquitous Presence of *Homo* in the Cradle of Humankind." *Proceedings of the National Academy of Sciences USA* 119 (2022): e2111212119.

Zazzo, A., H. Bocherens, M. Brunet, et al. "Herbivore Paleodiet and Paleoenvironmental Changes in Chad During the Pliocene Using Stable Isotope Ratios of Tooth Enamel Carbonate." *Paleobiology* 26 (2000): 294–309.

Zollikofer, C. P. E., M. S. Ponce de Leon, D. E. Lieberman, et al. "Virtual Cranial Reconstruction of *Sahelanthropus tchadensis*." *Nature* 434 (2005): 755–759.

CHAPTER **25** Early *Homo*: Systematics, Paleobiology, and the First Out-of-Africa Dispersals

G. Philip Rightmire

INTRODUCTION

Humans evolved in Africa over millions of years. This history is revealed through fossils and artifacts, application of the geosciences, and analysis of ancient DNA and proteins. An impressive suite of modern technologies can now be used to compare the anatomy of the hominins, date the sites, reconstruct paleoenvironments, assay paleodiet, and trace population ancestry. Relative to an antecedent species of *Australopithecus*, *Homo* is characterized by an increase in encephalization, reduction of the posterior dentition, larger body size, greater mobility, and the capacity to make tools and process food.

The most ancient fossils that show *Homo*-like features are a ca. 2.8 Ma old hemi-mandible and a ca. 2.3 Ma old maxilla from the Afar region of Ethiopia. To date, information from the period prior to ca. 2.1 Ma ago is limited to the dentognathic complex. We know little about facial form and nothing of the neurocranium or cranial base. By 2.0 Ma ago, representatives of *Homo* were becoming relatively abundant in eastern and in southern Africa. The fossil inventory includes nearly complete crania and mandibles along with a scattering of post-cranial remains. A fragile consensus holds that at least three species of *Homo* can be identified in the late Pliocene and early Pleistocene records.

Before 2.0 Ma ago, hominins were dispersing from Africa into the Levant, across the Arabian Peninsula, and eastward into Asia. It is widely accepted that the first populations to leave Africa were representatives of *Homo*, but the biology of these early travelers is poorly understood. *Homo erectus* emerging in eastern Africa has been regarded as the species anatomically and behaviorally best equipped to adapt to novel Eurasian landscapes, but new evidence offers alternatives to this hypothesis.

A Companion to Biological Anthropology, Second Edition. Edited by Clark Spencer Larsen.
© 2023 John Wiley & Sons Ltd. Published 2023 by John Wiley & Sons Ltd.

Important problems have still to be resolved. Fossils are scarce and there is much variation among the available skulls, teeth, and post-cranial elements. The sources of this variation, and how it should be partitioned within and between populations, are unclear. The proper taxonomic attributions of even relatively well-preserved adult specimens remain contentious, and it is hardly surprising that experienced workers have not been able to agree on just where species boundaries lie. In addition to systematics, there are questions about life history, ranging behavior, energetics, and other aspects of early hominin biology. Answers to these questions bear not only on the emergence of *Homo* but also on the first out-of-Africa dispersals and the evolution of *H. erectus*.

EARLIEST *HOMO*

Early *Homo* specimens from African localities are listed in Table 25.1. The mandible from Ledi-Geraru, partial maxilla from Hadar, ancient skull fragments and teeth from the Omo-Turkana Basin, and damaged hemi-mandibles from Uraha in Malawi share some traits with species of *Australopithecus*, but derived morphology said to be diagnostic for *Homo* can also be identified (Grine et al. 2019; Kimbel et al. 1997; Schrenk et al. 2007; Villmoore et al. 2015). Additional specimens from the Omo-Turkana Basin are not so old but are more

Table 25.1 Early *Homo* fossils from Eastern and Southern Africa

	Crania and partial crania	Mandibles	Partial skeletons and isolated elements	Stratigraphic provenience/ dating (Ma)
East Africa				
Ledi-Geraru		LD 350–1		2.8–2.75
Hadar	AL 666–1			Kada Hadar, 2.33
Omo	L894–1	Omo 75–69–14		Shungura G
Turkana Basin	KNM-ER 1470, 1590, 1805, 1813, 3732, 62000	KNM-ER 817, 1482, 1483, 1501, 1502, 1801, 1802, 1805, 3734, 60000	pelvic bone, femora, talus, partial skeleton	Upper Burgi, KBS, ca. 2.09–1.75
Olduvai Gorge	OH 7, 13, 16, 24, 65	OH 7, 13, 37	hand, foot, ulna, tibia, fibula, partial skeleton	Bed I, Bed II, ca. 1.9–1.65
Malawi				
Uraha		HCRP-U18–501		Chiwando Beds, ca. 2.5–1.5?
South Africa				
Swartkrans	SK 847	SK 45		Member 1, 2.25–1.7

numerous and, in some cases, quite complete. The KNM-ER 1470 braincase is relatively large and globular in form and coupled with a tall but subnasally flattened face. The KNM-ER 1813 cranium is much smaller, with a more prognathic face (Antón 2012; Benazzi et al. 2014; Wood 1991). These individuals have become iconic for two distinct "morphs" frequently, but not universally, attributed to *Homo rudolfensis* and *Homo habilis*.

Further to the south, joining hemi-mandibles have been discovered at Uraha in the Malawi Rift. Correlations with faunal assemblages in East Africa point to a maximum age of 2.5 to 2.3 Ma (Zanolli et al. 2019), but the Uraha fossil might also be substantially younger. The UR 501 mandible is very robust but *Homo*-like, while some tooth crown and root features approach the *Paranthropus* condition. Size of the corpus and morphology of the cheek teeth suggest similarities with KNM-ER 1802, a specimen that has been referred to *H. rudolfensis*.

Fossils from Swartkrans in South Africa include the SK 847 partial face and left temporal bone. Flowstones underlying the bones have U–Pb ages of ca. 2.25 Ma, while the capping speleothem is dated to ca. 1.80 Ma (Pickering et al. 2011). There has been disagreement as to how the fossils should be identified. SK 847 has been described as *H. habilis*, but other workers find parallels with the KNM-ER 3733 *H. erectus* cranium from Kenya. These attributions are questioned by Grine et al. (2009), who suggest that the Swartkrans hominin may represent an unnamed species of *Homo*.

Homo habilis

A case can be made for lumping all of the East African early *Homo* specimens together, as one highly dimorphic lineage (Suwa et al. 2007; Tobias 1991). However, there is substantial agreement that the resulting hypodigm displays so much variation that partitioning is warranted, and the fossils are usually assigned to several species. One is *H. habilis*, named in 1964 to accommodate the (then) newly discovered remains from Beds I and II at Olduvai Gorge in Tanzania (Leakey et al. 1964). The ca. 1.8 Ma old parietal bones, damaged mandible, and hand bones of OH 7, along with the ca. 1.65 Ma old partial skull of OH 13, suggested that *H. habilis* could be distinguished from *Australopithecus* by possessing a larger brain and bucco-lingually narrow premolar and molar teeth. The hand is robust with curved proximal and middle phalanges, but resembles *H. sapiens* in its metacarpo-phalangeal joints and broad terminal phalanges. Further fieldwork at Olduvai and in the Omo-Turkana Basin has expanded the *H. habilis* inventory to include the KNM-ER 1805 partial skull, the OH 24 and KNM-ER 1813 crania (Tobias 1991; Wood 1991), the OH 65 maxilla (Blumenschine et al. 2003; Clarke 2012), the OH 62 fragmentary skeleton (Johanson et al. 1987), and a partial skeleton from Koobi Fora (Wood 1992). Fragmentary specimens from the Omo region may also share affinities with this group (Grine et al. 2019).

The brain of *H. habilis* has been characterized as larger than in australopiths but small relative to that of other *Homo* species. This assumption now seems incorrect. Spoor et al. (2015) obtain volume (ECV) estimates from CT-based reconstructions of the OH 7 parietal endocranial surface, known to be strongly correlated with brain size. Predicted ECVs range from 729 ml to 824 ml, with a mean value of 779 ml. This result substantially exceeds previous estimates, and OH 7 is far more voluminous than OH 13 (650 ml), OH 24 (590 ml), and KNM-ER 1813 (509 ml). *Homo habilis* is comparable to some individuals referred to as *H. erectus*.

Facial size is an important attribute distinguishing hominin taxa. Most notably in *Paranthropus* but also in *Australopithecus*, the facial skeleton tends to be large in relation to the braincase. In *Homo*, the size of the masticatory system is reduced, while encephalization is increased. This relationship can be tracked with the geometric mean (GM) (Coleman 2008). Here, 10 linear dimensions are used to construct a measure of overall size for the face (GM_{face}), and eight measurements allow a similar assessment for the neurocranium and base (GM_{vault}). Two of the *H. habilis* crania provide the necessary data. For OH 24, GM_{face} = 42.2 and GM_{vault} = 84.5. Quantified in this way, facial size is 49.9 percent of braincase size. For KNM-ER 1813, this ratio is 52.8 percent. These individuals have face-to-braincase ratios that are reduced in comparison to those for *Paranthropus boisei* (OH 5 = 64.3 percent) and *Australopithecus africanus* (Sts 5 = 57.5 percent).

In KNM-ER 1813, the nasal region is more prominent relative to the zygomatic arches than in *Australopithecus*. The nasal sill is slightly guttered to either side of an anterior nasal spine. Also, the maxillary clivus is convex in KNM-ER 1813, rather than transversely flattened. Prognathism can be quantified by angles measured in the midsagittal plane. The clivus angle (Lordkipanidze et al. 2013) is determined by the nasospinale-prosthion chord and the alveolar plane. KNM-ER 1813 and OH 65 have similar angles (42° and 41°), registering slightly greater prognathism than in AL 666–1 (47°) but less than in *Australopithecus africanus* (Sts 5 = 36°, Sts 71 = 35°).

The OH 7 mandible suggests that *H. habilis* possessed primitive gnathic morphology more similar to that of *A. afarensis* than to *H. erectus* (Spoor et al. 2015). The relatively long and narrow dental arcade is indicative of a subnasally prognathic face. As modeled from the mandible, the OH 7 palate resembles that of KNM-ER 1813, but the two individuals lie "at the extreme boundaries of the intraspecific shape differences" found in pair-wise comparisons within extant human and great ape populations (Spoor et al. 2015: 84). Whether these differences can be attributed to sex dimorphism within *H. habilis* is presently unknown.

Two partial skeletons have been referred to *H. habilis*. Both OH 62 (Johanson et al. 1987) and KNM-ER 3735 (Leakey et al. 1989) are quite incomplete, leading to uncertainty about limb proportions. OH 62 appears to have femoral/humeral strength proportions that are more like those of a chimpanzee than a modern human (Ruff 2009). KNM-ER 3735 may also evince relatively greater upper limb mechanical loading (Haeusler and McHenry 2004; Ruff 2009), and several features of the forelimb have been taken to imply enhanced climbing abilities (Leakey et al. 1989).

The ca. 1.9 Ma old KNM-ER 5881 post-cranial remains clearly represent early *Homo*, but species identification is uncertain. The ilium is well enough preserved to demonstrate that the anterior border conforms to a human-like sigmoidal pattern. There is a distinct iliac pillar, more pronounced than the weak buttresses of *Australopithecus*. The large femoral head and antero-posteriorly expanded neck ally KNM-ER 5881 with African *Homo*. However, the femoral shaft differs from that of other fossils, with the exception of OH 62 and probably KNM-ER 3735. The relatively small size of the ilium and femur and the anatomical features shared with OH 62 appear to strengthen an argument for linking KNM-ER 5881 with *H. habilis* (Ward et al. 2015).

The OH 8 partial foot is routinely attributed to *H. habilis*. The specimen offers convincing evidence that the first metatarsal was adducted. The Olduvai foot also preserves a largely human-like pattern of metatarsal robusticity and torsion, indicating the presence of a transverse tarsal arch (Aiello and Dean 1990; Pontzer et al. 2010). Venkadesan et al. (2020) model the arch of OH 8 as an elastic shell, revealing curvature that is clearly human-like and would have enabled effective walking and running. The talus of OH 8 has been characterized as more ape-like (Harcourt-Smith and Aiello 2004), but given the derived features of the midfoot, the significance of this finding remains unclear.

Body mass bears on encephalization, ranging behavior, and energy expenditure. Ruff et al. (2018) use the femoral head and tibial plateau to predict mean body masses of 49.3

kg for *A. afarensis*, 39.3 kg for *A. africanus*, 45.9 kg for *P. boisei*, and 55.8 kg for early *Homo*. This result anticipates the work of Püschel et al. (2021), who document an evolutionary trend toward smaller body mass prior to the emergence of *Homo*, but an increase in size after this event. It follows that early *Homo* would have required additional energy, likely obtained by consumption of a higher quality diet including meat as well as plant material. Access to more diverse food sources would have been facilitated by the ability to range over longer distances (Antón et al. 2014; Pontzer 2012).

Homo rudolfensis

Homo rudolfensis was named by Valery Alexeev in 1986, with KNM-ER 1470 later designated as the type. This ca. 2.06 Ma old cranium presents facial features that are *Australopithecus*-like, and the cheek teeth may have been quite large. However, a voluminous braincase places KNM-ER 1470 with *Homo* and has been taken as a feature distinguishing *H. rudolfensis* from *H. habilis*. The hypodigm was expanded by Wood (1992) to encompass the KNM-ER 1590 and KNM-ER 3732 partial crania, along with the KNM-ER 1482 and KNM-ER 1802 mandibles. More recent discoveries include the KNM-ER 60000 adult mandible and the KNM-ER 62000 juvenile face. Reconstruction and analysis of the latter have prompted Leakey et al. (2012) to exclude the KNM-ER 1802 mandible from *H. rudolfensis*, based on a mismatch in dental arcade shape. The robust UR 501 mandible from Malawi should also be set aside, as neutron microtomography scanning reveals that the enamel-dentine junction in P_4, M_1, and M_2 may be closer in form to South African *Australopithecus* than to early *Homo* (Zanolli et al. 2019).

KNM-ER 1470 has routinely been emphasized in comparisons with specimens such as OH 13, OH 24, and KNM-ER 1813. This practice has sustained the impression that *H. rudolfensis* is big-brained compared to *H. habilis*. The neurocranium is indeed relatively large and rounded, lacking either supratoral hollowing on the frontal bone or nuchal muscular impressions on the rear of the vault. However, the ECV of 750 ml does not place KNM-ER 1470 outside the range observed for *H. habilis*.

For KNM-ER 1470, GM_{face} = 53.84, GM_{vault} = 93.56, and the facial size is 57.5 percent of the braincase size. This ratio is greater than in *H. habilis* and matches that of *A. africanus*, although KNM-ER 1470 does not approach the condition seen in hyper-robust *P. boisei*.

As has been emphasized, the face of KNM-ER 1470 is quite orthognathic. Angles measuring prominence of the subnasal region in relation to the bimaxillary chord are the highest recorded for any specimen of early *Homo*, indicating extreme flattening in the transverse plane. Alveolar prognathism as judged by the slope of the nasomaxillary clivus in relation to the alveolar plane is much reduced (Leakey et al. 2012; Lordkipanidze et al. 2013). In both its transverse and sagittal profiles, the face of KNM-ER 1470 clearly differs from the more projecting face of KNM-ER 1813.

The KNM-ER 1470 palate is broad and relatively short (Wood 1991). Tooth crowns are not preserved, but the size and placement of the incisor and canine roots suggest a maxilla that is flattened anteriorly. Because of damage, the shape of the dental arcade cannot be documented with much confidence. More information is provided by the KNM-ER 62000 juvenile. In its transversely flat midface and highly orthognathic profile, KNM-ER 62000 shows a "striking similarity to KNM-ER 1470" (Leakey et al. 2012). Bone is missing from the incisor and canine alveolar walls, but even when this minor truncation is accounted for, the clivus is short and nearly vertical. In occlusal view, a well-defined P^3 jugum marks the "corner" between the anterior and lateral surfaces of the maxillary alveolar process, and the palate is U-shaped rather than elongated as in *H. habilis* (Spoor et al. 2015).

VARIATION IN THE AFRICAN ASSEMBLAGES

The first fossils attributed to *H. habilis* were found over a half century ago, and the ensuing debate over the validity of this taxon is well documented. Continuing discoveries have greatly expanded the record for early *Homo* and many researchers now envision a radiation of *Homo* species beginning in Africa well before 2.0 Ma ago. However, as presently constituted, the hypodigms for *H. habilis* and particularly for *H. rudolfensis* remain small and in many respects inadequate (Antón 2012; Antón et al. 2014; Grine et al. 2019; Wood and Leakey 2011). There is much variation among individuals and it has been difficult to identify characters that are diagnostic. The composition of hypodigms has shifted repeatedly, as varying emphasis is placed on characters such as brain size, facial prognathism, mandibular form, and dental morphology.

As detailed by Tobias (1991), brain size distinguishes early *Homo* from *Australopithecus*. ECV is less useful in sorting the *Homo* fossils into distinct lineages. Given their reconstruction of OH 7, Spoor et al. (2015) find little evidence for interspecific diversification in brain size. Recent reviews reflect this conclusion, reporting ECV as one character varying among *Homo* "morphs" but giving greater taxonomic weight to facial form and the dental arcade (Antón 2012; Antón et al. 2014; Wood and Boyle 2016).

Facial proportions differ among species of *Australopithecus* and *Homo*. In *A. afarensis* and *A. africanus*, the face is relatively broad at the level of the cheek bones. The incomplete face of early *Homo* from Swartkrans (SK 847) appears to be similar. In OH 24, the midfacial (bimaxillary) and upper facial (biorbital) breadths are about equal, whereas for KNM-ER 1813, the upper face is broader than the midface. In KNM-ER 1470, the biorbital breadth clearly exceeds the bimaxillary dimension. These observations do not support the often-stated claim that a wide midface distinguishes *H. rudolfensis* from *H. habilis* (Wood 1992; Wood and Boyle 2016).

WESTERN ASIA

Hominin remains from Dmanisi are listed in Table 25.2. The fossils are dated to 1.78–1.77 Ma, while crude stone flakes and manuports confirm an earlier human presence ca. 1.85 Ma ago (Ferring et al. 2011). It has been claimed that several taxa must be documented at the site (Bermúdez de Castro et al. 2014), but resampling analyses and other evidence refute this view and support the hypothesis that the five individuals are drawn from a single population (Lordkipanidze et al. 2013; Rightmire et al. 2008). Within-group variation is substantial but appears to reflect age differences, facial remodeling associated with dental attrition, and sex dimorphism (Margvelashvili et al. 2013, 2016; Rightmire et al. 2019; Zollikofer et al., 2014). Stratigraphic evidence demonstrates that the assemblage accumulated in an extremely brief interval of time (Ferring et al. 2011), making Dmanisi the clearest example on record of a *Homo* deme from the Early Pleistocene.

The Dmanisi individuals combine remarkably small brains (mean ECV = 634 ml) with robust faces. D2280 is the largest of the crania, bearing a thickened supraorbital torus and a strongly flexed occipital bone. This specimen resembles early African *H. erectus*. Skull 2 (D2282/D211) is a young adult, with M3s coming into full occlusion. Its delicate supraorbital torus, small mastoid process, smooth occipital, and gracile mandible are in keeping with female status (Figure 25.1).

Table 25.2 Skulls and postcranial remains from Dmanisi

Crania and partial crania	Mandibles	Partial skeletons and isolated elements	Stratigraphic provenience/ dating (Ma)
D2280, D2282, D2700, D3444, D4500	D211, D2600, D2735, D3900	vertebrae, ribs, clavicles, scapula, humeri, femora, tibia, foot bones of several individuals	Stratum B1, 1.77–1.78

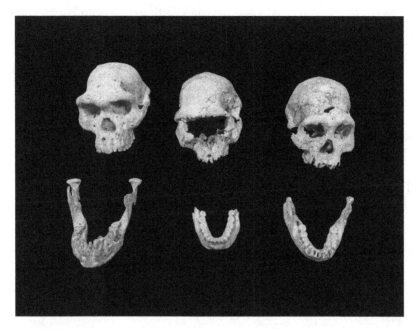

Figure 25.1 Three skulls from Dmanisi. (A) Skull 5 is likely a robust adult male with sagittal keeling, strong mastoid cresting, a massive face, and a very large mandible. (B) Skull 2 is likely a female with a more globular vault, reduced cresting, and a smaller face. (C) Skull 3 is a subadult. Further growth would not have greatly altered its morphology. This Dmanisi cranium resembles KNM-ER 1813.

Skull 3 (D2700/D2735) is a late subadult with its M^3 crown erupted and the root half formed. D2700 is comparable in globularity, supraorbital development, post-orbital narrowing, and rounding of the posterior braincase to KNM-ER 1813 (Figure 25.2). The face is diminutive in comparison to that of *H. erectus* but similar in midsagittal profile, orbital proportions, and palate shape to individuals referred to *H. habilis*. D2735 shares many features with the small, but very robust, mandible of OH 13. Indeed, if skull 3 had been found with the East African fossils, these specimens would almost certainly have been attributed to the same taxon.

Skull 4 (D3444/D3900) is a small, edentulous adult with projecting supraorbital tori, cranial cresting, and a blunt occipital transverse torus. Although there is advanced alveolar bone atrophy associated with tooth loss, the face is robust, with large orbits and deep malar bones. The D3900 mandibular body is highly attenuated, reflecting advanced age.

Skull 5 (D4500/D2600) is almost certainly an adult male (Figure 25.1). The cranium is low, relatively broad, less globular than those of other early *Homo*, and carries massive crests and tori. GM_{face}/GM_{vault} is 56.1, close to that of KNM-ER 1470 and Sterkfontein *Australopithecus*. Lower facial prognathism is comparable to that of D2700, KNM-ER 1813, and OH 65. The palate is slightly more elongated ("primitive") than AL 666–1, but both fossils share dentognathic traits with *H. habilis*. In supraorbital projection, facial profile, midfacial breadths, and clivus angle, D4500 also resembles the SK 847 partial cranium from Swartkrans.

Post-cranial remains from Dmanisi include the femur, patella, tibia, and partial foot of a single adult individual. Relative to the estimated body mass, the Dmanisi hind limb is longer than that of African apes and the AL 288–1 ("Lucy") *A. afarensis* skeleton (Pontzer et al. 2010). The first metatarsal is robust and fully adducted, and the transverse tarsal arch exhibits pronounced curvature (Venkadesan et al. 2020). In its size and overall morphology, the Dmanisi talus is comparable to that of African *H. erectus* and later *Homo*, with a trochlea that is broad and flat, suggesting an ankle joint with increased surface area for transmitting joint reaction forces associated with walking and running.

Homo erectus in Africa

Skulls and postcranial remains attributed to *H. erectus* are known from localities in North Africa, the Upper and Middle Awash regions of Ethiopia, the Omo-Turkana Basin, Olduvai Gorge, Olorgesailie in Tanzania, and in South Africa (Table 25.3). The most ancient specimen is from Drimolen in South Africa, dated at 2.04 to 1.95 Ma, (Herries et al. 2020). The DNH 134 cranium is subadult, lacks the entire face and base, and retains little diagnostic architecture. Identification as *H. erectus* remains tentative, and DNH 134 might well represent earlier *Homo* as documented nearby at Swartkrans. The KNM-ER 2598 occipital fragment from Koobi Fora is > 1.85 Ma old (Hammond et al. 2021). Its morphology can be matched in *H. erectus* and also in D2280 and D4500.

The KNM-ER 3733 cranium from Koobi Fora (Wood 1991) is ca. 1.63 Ma in age (Lepre and Kent 2015). With an ECV of 848 ml, KNM-ER 3733 has a larger brain than earlier *Homo*. The vault is relatively long and low with pronounced postorbital narrowing and a flexed occipital bone (Figure 25.2). KNM-ER 3733 is slightly less globular than OH 24 or KNM-ER 1470 but comparable in form to D2280 from Dmanisi. The prominent supraorbital torus is arched over the orbits, frontal midline keeling is evident, and a mound-like transverse torus is well developed near the occipital midline.

The KNM-ER 3733 facial skeleton is larger (GM_{face} = 53.5) than in earlier *Homo* and is set well forward from the anterior cranial fossa. The neurocranium is also large (GM_{vault} = 98.6), resulting in a face-to-vault ratio (54.3 percent), comparable to *H. habilis*, D2700, and D3444. The nasal sill is smooth and carries an anterior spine. Although the front of the maxilla has been damaged, it is possible to estimate the clivus angle as 44°. The palate is demonstrably quite short, narrow, and deep, differing from the longer and shallower palate of KNM-ER 1813.

Other crania provide useful information. The ca. 1.55 Ma old DAN5/P1 partial cranium from Gona is quite small, with an arching supraorbital torus, prominent temporal lines, and moderate postorbital narrowing (Semaw et al. 2020). In sagittal profile, the occipital is rounded, and there is little development of an occipital transverse torus. Of the face, only the lower portion is preserved. The nasal floor passes smoothly on to the flattened maxillary clivus, and prognathism is reduced relative to *H. habilis*. The form of the braincase suggests that this individual is female. DAN5/P1 resembles several of the gracile crania from Dmanisi, the ca. 1.55 Ma old KNM-ER 42700 subadult from Ileret (Neubauer et al. 2018) and the small ca. 0.94 Ma old KNM-OL 45500 specimen from Olorgesailie (Potts et al. 2004). A second, larger cranium from Gona retains portions of a thickened supraorbital

Table 25.3   Localities yielding fossils attributed to *Homo erectus*[1]

	Crania	Mandibles	Postcranial bones
Southeast Asia			
Trinil	Trinil 2		femur, femoral fragments
Sangiran	Sangiran 2, 4, 10, 12, 17, 27, 31, Skull IX	Sangiran 1b, 8, 9, 22, BK 7905, BK 8606	femora
Ngandong	Nandong 1, 3, 6, 7, 10, 11, 12		tibia A, tibia B
Sambungmacan	Sambungmacan 1, 3, 4		tibia
Ngawi	Ngawi 1		
Mojokerto	Perning 1		
China			
Zhoukoudian	Skulls II, III, V, X, XI, XII	A II, B I, G I, H I, H IV, K I, M II, PA 86	clavicle, humeri, femora, tibia
Gongwangling	PA 1051–6		
Chenjiawo		PA 102	
Hexian	PA 830		
Yunxian	EV 9001, 9002		
Tangshan	Nanjing 1, 2		
North Africa			
Ternifine	Ternifine 4	Ternifine 1, 2, 3	
Eastern Africa			
Bouri	BOU-VP-2/66		
Gona	DAN5/P1, BSN12/P1		vertebra, pelvis
Konso		KGA10–1	
Buia	UA-31		pelvic bone
Koobi Fora and Ileret	KNM-ER 730, 2598, 3733, 3883 42700	KNM-ER 730, 820, 992	femora, tibia, talus, partial skeletons
Nariokotome	KNM-WT 15000A	KNM-WT 15000B	skeleton
Olorgesailie	KNM-OL 45500		
Olduvai Gorge	OH 9, OH 12	OH 22, OH 23, OH 51	pelvic bone, femur
South Africa			
Drimolen	DNH 134		
Swartkrans		SK 15	

[1] Listing is incomplete, as many fragmentary specimens are omitted.

torus and a parietal sagittal keel. BSN12/P1 is comparable to more robust and possibly male African *H. erectus* fossils such as OH 9 (Rightmire 1990), BOU-VP-2/66 from Daka (Asfaw et al. 2008), and UA-31 from Buia (Macchiarelli et al. 2004).

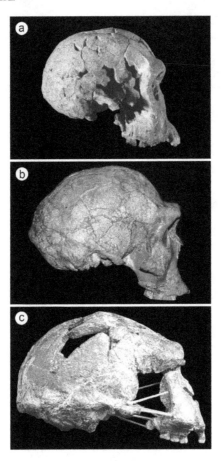

Figure 25.2   Lateral views of crania referred to *Homo habilis* (KNM-ER 1813) and *Homo erectus* (KNM-ER 3733, Sangiran 17). (A) KNM-ER 1813 has a brain volume of only 509 ml but differs from australopiths in its rounded vault, less massive face, and generally smaller cheek teeth. (B) KNM-ER 3733 has an ECV of 848 ml. The vault is relatively low with prominent supraorbital tori, an angled occipital, and a prominent nasal saddle. (C) Sangiran 17 has an ECV 1004 ml, an elongated cranium with an expanded nuchal plane, and robust facial bones. Face size relative to the neurocranium is reduced compared to earlier African *Homo erectus*.

The KNM-ER 992 mandible shows little indication of a bony chin. A flattened post-incisive planum is bounded below by a strong superior transverse torus. On the external aspect of the corpus, the lateral prominence is maximally thickened at the level of M_2/M_3. Corpus robusticity in this region is lower than in *H. habilis* but greater than in KNM-ER 730 and comparable to several of the *H. erectus* mandibles from Java.

Locomotor habits of early *H. erectus* are revealed by the tracks of at least 20 individuals preserved near Ileret and dated to ca. 1.5 Ma ago (Hatala et al. 2016). Many of these traces show fine detail, indicating that they were hardened and then covered rapidly with sediment. The prints provide the oldest direct evidence for a human-like medial transfer of body weight while walking, where the foot acts as a rigid lever with toe-off through the hallux and second toe.

A nearly complete subadult skeleton from Nariokotome provides further insight into body form for one early representative of *H. erectus*. Given a likely age at death of only 7.6 to 8.8 years (Dean and Smith 2009), KNM-WT 15000 is surprisingly tall and linear, with a relatively small bi-iliac diameter and long legs. Ruff and Burgess (2015) use modern African great apes as growth models, estimating an adult body mass of ca. 82 kg. While high, this result for KNM-WT 15000 may not be unusually large when compared to other *H. erectus* from East Africa.

The BSN49/P27 pelvis collected at Gona has been referred to as *H. erectus* (Simpson et al. 2008). However, the postcranial material is not associated with a skull or teeth, and there remains a possibility that it documents a taxon other than *Homo*. Apparently female, the pelvis is quite small but has a relatively large bi-iliac diameter. The size of the acetabulum indicates that the body mass must be much reduced in comparison to the Nariokotome boy. This suggests a remarkably high level of sex dimorphism.

The average body mass for *H. erectus* exceeds that of *H. habilis.* Ruff et al. (2018) calculate 73 kg as an average for KNM-WT 15000 and OH 28. It can be argued that this increase relative to early *Homo* reflects a change in diet. Along with foraging for plants and fruit, *H. erectus* probably consumed more meat and bone marrow (Patterson et al. 2019). Such high protein foods and fat would have facilitated expansion of the larger and hence energetically more "expensive" brain (Aiello and Wheeler 1995). Also, body proportions and other musculoskeletal specializations can be read to show that *H. erectus* was capable of endurance running. The ability to run over long distances at a moderate pace would have been advantageous to early hominin scavengers or hunters (Bramble and Lieberman 2004).

Along with the tracks of *H. erectus*, the Ileret sites preserve traces left by many animals (Roach et al. 2018). Although this community includes numerous water-dependent species, the hominins show a pattern of association with marginal lacustrine habitats that is not apparent for the other vertebrates. Given the evidence for increasing carnivorousness with the emergence of *H. erectus* (Patterson et al. 2019), lake margin grasslands may have been important for hunting while also providing access to aquatic plants, fish, shellfish, and turtles.

Homo erectus in Asia

The first fossils attributed to *H. erectus* were found by Eugene Dubois, who sailed to the East Indies to search for the missing link. Shortly after starting to excavate at Trinil in 1891, Dubois' workers came across a skullcap, and later a complete femur. Many more specimens from Mojokerto, Sangiran, Ngawi, Ngandong, and Sambungmacan have since been added to this inventory (Table 25.3).

Within the Sangiran region, some fossils were found in the lower Grenzbank/Sangiran stratigraphic levels, but most are derived from the overlying Bapang Formation. Many researchers have accepted an age of ca. 1.7 Ma for the earliest remains, but some $^{40}Ar/^{39}Ar$ dates on samples collected from the lowermost Bapang Formation center around 0.88 Ma. The latter are consistent with magnetostratigraphy, implying a "short chronology" for the Sangiran sequence (Hyodo et al. 2011). Matsu'ura et al. (2020) report U-Pb and fission-track dates that confirm this chronology, setting ca. 1.27 Ma as the maximum age for the hominins and ca. 0.79 Ma as the age of the youngest fossil-bearing sediments.

The ancient Sangiran 4 cranium is damaged, but estimated ECV (ca. 900 ml) is comparable to early African *H. erectus*. The braincase is low rather than globular, quite massively constructed, and presents a mound-like parietal keel with parasagittal depressions. These characters are shared with skull 5 from Dmanisi. The younger Sangiran 17 cranium is complete, with an ECV of 1004 ml. Sangiran 17 is larger than KNM-ER 3733 and has a much thicker supraorbital torus and a more strongly flexed occipital (Figure 25.2). The face is wide with massive cheek bones, a broad but shallow palate, and relatively small teeth. Face-to-braincase size is reduced relative to that of KNM-ER 3733.

Kaifu et al. (2008, 2013) describe the more robust Grenzbank/Sangiran crania as "primitive" in comparison to the gracile specimens from the same stratigraphic zone, but there is overlap in the expression of most features. Mandibles from these deposits also display much variation in corpus height and thickness, as well as the development of lateral prominences. Sangiran 9 exhibits the relatively narrow, elongated dental arcade that is characteristic of *H. habilis*, whereas Sangiran 1 and Sangiran 22 have more open, parabolic arcades as in African *H. erectus*. Kaifu et al. (2013) attribute this high level of variation to sex dimorphism.

Teeth from Yuanmou in China that may belong to *H. erectus* are ca. 1.7 Ma in age (Zhu et al. 2008). Additional cranial and dentognathic material is known from Lantian (Gongwangling and Chenjiawo), Hexian, Yunxian, Nanjing (Tangshan), and Meipu (Wu and Poirer 1995; Xing et al. 2021). Certainly, the most famous Chinese locality is Zhoukoudian, where excavations of a karstic fissure revealed fossils including complete braincases, mandibles, teeth, and postcranial elements. Shen et al. (2009) report cosmogenic $^{26}Al/^{10}Be$ ages for the lower strata of Locality 1 as 0.68 to 0.78 Ma, while the upper levels date to 0.40 Ma. As is well known, nearly all of the original specimens were lost. Fortunately, Franz Weidenreich's monographs and carefully made casts provide a very detailed anatomical record. The Zhoukoudian crania are relatively large and display the prominent supraorbital tori and low, angular vault profiles that are associated with Middle Pleistocene populations of *H. erectus*. Baab (2010) notes that the Zhoukoudian crania differ from the Sangiran specimens in their frontal and occipital widths and in prominence of crests in the mastoid region, concluding that there is significant regional differentiation among populations of Asian *H. erectus*.

Homo in the Middle Pleistocene

Skulls that differ from *H. erectus* are known from Middle Pleistocene localities at Irhoud in Morocco, Bodo, Herto, and Omo (Kibish) in Ethiopia, Ndutu and Laetoli in Tanzania, Broken Hill in Zambia, and at Florisbad and Elandsfontein in South Africa (Table 25.4). ECVs are large (≥ 1100 ml). Relative to *H. erectus*, there is an increase in cranial height, breadth of the frontal bone, and globularity of the parieto-occipital region. In Bodo, Broken Hill, and Elandsfontein, the supraorbital torus is partitioned into medial and lateral segments. Nevertheless, the torus remains very massive. There is no reduction in overall face size in relation to *H. erectus*, and the facial skeleton is "hafted" to the braincase in such a way as to accentuate facial projection (Lieberman 2011). Other individuals including Irhoud 2, Irhoud 10, Irhoud 11, Herto, Omo 1, and Laetoli 18 display more modern morphology.

Dates of ca. 600 Ka for Bodo, ca. 195 Ka for Omo 1, and ca. 155 Ka for Herto suggest an evolutionary sequence in Africa from archaic *H. heidelbergensis*/*H. rhodesiensis* toward anatomically modern *H. sapiens*. This scenario is called into question by a date of ca. 299 Ka for the Broken Hill cranium (Grün et al. 2020), placing this specimen at a time when intermediate morphology might be expected. However, the massive face and low braincase of Broken Hill appear archaic, and there are few of the derived traits that would be expected in modern populations (Rightmire 2017). An alternative hypothesis is that the evolutionary roots of *H. sapiens* predate Omo 1 and Herto and extend further back into the Middle Pleistocene. This view is supported by the age of ca. 315 Ka obtained for the Jebel Irhoud fossils, which possess more derived traits than Broken Hill (Hublin et al. 2017). African populations seem to have displayed much morphological variation in this interval, perhaps denoting the presence of distinct lineages.

Middle Pleistocene fossils from the Rising Star cave system in South Africa add to this apparent diversity. Partial skulls, teeth, axial and limb elements, a nearly complete adult

Table 25.4   *Homo* fossils from Middle Pleistocene localities in Africa

	Crania and partial crania	Mandibles	Partial skeletons and isolated elements	Stratigraphic provenience/ dating (Ka)
North Africa				
Jebel Irhoud	Irhoud 1,2,10	Irhoud 3,11	ribs, humerus, prox. femur, fibula	ca. 315
East Africa				
Bodo	Bodo 1,2			ca. 600
Herto	BOU-VP-16/1, 16/2,16/5			160–154
Omo KHS	Omo 1	Omo 1	partial skeleton	Kibish Formation, ca. 195
Omo PHS	Omo 2			Kibish Formation
Baringo		KNM-BK 67, 8518		Kapthurin Formation
Ndutu	Ndutu 1			
Laetoli	LH 18			
Broken Hill	E686		femur, tibia?	ca. 299
South Africa				
Dinaledi	DNH 1,2,3,4,5	DNH 1, UW 101–377	partial skeletons	335–236
Lesedi	LES 1	LES 1	partial skeletons	
Florisbad	Florisbad 1			ca. 259?
Elandsfontein	Elandsfontein (or Saldanha) 1			1000–700?

hand, and a foot from Dinaledi are referred to *Homo naledi* by Berger et al. (2015). At least 15 individuals are represented, and the Dinaledi assemblage is 335 to 236 Ka in age (Dirks et al. 2017). Additional material including a cranium has been recovered from a second depository within the same cave complex (Hawks et al. 2017).

The DH1 cranium has an ECV of 555 ml (Holloway et al. 2018). The supraorbital torus is thin and shelf-like, and the contour of the frontal suggests a globular shape. There is slight parietal bossing and the vault lacks strong ectocranial relief. DH1 differs from *H. erectus* and resembles modern humans in displaying a raised external occipital protuberance. The mandibular fossa is situated almost entirely underneath the vault. The midface gives the impression of gracility. A little of the entrance to the nasal cavity is preserved and there is a prominent anterior nasal spine. The subnasal region is flattened in the coronal plane and is moderately prognathic. Palate shape is parabolic as in later humans.

The nearly complete mandible is quite robust. When the jaw is viewed from the side, it is apparent that corpus height increases anteriorly, to reach a maximum at the symphysis. The symphysis itself is vertical and flattened. On its internal aspect, there is hollowing below the alveolar margin but little indication of the shelving post-incisive planum characteristic of archaic *Homo*. The teeth of *H. naledi* are small in comparison to samples of *H. habilis* and *H. erectus* and more similar in their dimensions to later human populations.

H. naledi couples a small brain with primitive postcranial features. The cranially oriented shoulder joint and australopith-like humerus depart sharply from the morphology present in other Middle Pleistocene humans and *H. sapiens*. The wrist and thumb point to enhanced manipulative ability relative to australopiths, but the relatively long, curved fingers indicate frequent use of the hand during climbing and suspension in an arboreal environment. At the same time, *Homo naledi* possessed an absolutely long lower limb. The foot differs only slightly from modern humans in having a reduced medial longitudinal arch and a gracile calcaneal tuber. Also, the proximal pedal phalanges are curved as in some apes and OW monkeys (Harcourt-Smith et al. 2015). *Homo naledi* was probably capable of striding on the ground but had a locomotor repertoire differing from that of contemporary humans.

WHERE DO WE STAND?

Our knowledge of earliest *Homo* is far from complete. *Homo habilis* is documented by damaged skulls, teeth, and partial skeletons, but this assemblage is in many respects inadequate. Wood and Boyle (2016) express "moderate confidence" in the taxonomic distinctiveness of *H. habilis*, but the precise makeup of the hypodigm has shifted repeatedly. Variation is substantial, and the differences in arcade form between OH 7 and KNM-ER 1813 stretch the limits observed in extant human and great ape populations. Also, cranial and dentognathic differentiation between *H. habilis* and early African *H. erectus* is incomplete (Baab 2016; Mori and Harvati 2019; Suwa et al. 2007).

A key question is the extent to which differences can reasonably be interpreted as evidence for taxonomic diversity, rather than as the variation to be expected within populations. Here, Dmanisi offers a unique guide. The five skulls exhibit a high level of morphological variability, suggesting that changes due to growth, senescence, and sex dimorphism are marked within this paleodeme. Skull 1 and skull 2 are like African *H. erectus*, while other specimens resemble early *Homo* from the Turkana Basin and Olduvai Gorge. The low braincase and massive face of skull 5 are unmatched in the hominin record (Rightmire et al. 2017). It is difficult to read this evidence as supporting the recognition of three or more species of *Homo* in the eastern Rift Valley and perhaps another in South Africa.

Evidence from genetics bears critically on these issues. Admixture has long shaped patterns of variation in humans. Genomic comparisons document multiple interbreeding events involving Neanderthals, Denisovans, and recent humans, and it has been possible to extend such analyses further back in time. Rogers et al. (2020) postulate an ancient episode of intermixture, in which the "neandersovan" antecedents to Neanderthals and Denisovans interbred with a "superarchaic" population, ca. 2.3 Ma or ca. 1.9 Ma ago. These models allow the superarchaics to have evolved either in Africa or from the first hominins dispersing into Eurasia.

Mapping this genetic history on to phylogeny as inferred from fossils is difficult. It is not known what species of *Homo* the "superarchaics" might represent, but the role of gene exchange in shaping ancient populations is increasingly acknowledged. Reticulate evolution, defined as the mixing of lineages, may have "driven evolutionary innovation in our hominin ancestors and perhaps contributed to bursts of exceptional phenotypic diversification" (Ackermann et al. 2019). Introgressive hybridization implies the blurring of species boundaries, so it is not surprising that defining *Homo* taxa has been problematic.

The origin of *H. erectus* remains unclear. If the DNH 134 juvenile and the KNM-ER 2598 occipital fragment are set aside, the most ancient fossil securely identified as *H. erectus* is the KNM-ER 3733 cranium, dated at ca. 1.63 Ma. One hypothesis holds that *H. erectus* originated in eastern Africa, probably from *H. habilis*. Bands of this new species then ventured beyond Africa, leaving traces of their passing in the Sinai, the Jordan Valley, and the Caucasus. From sites such as Dmanisi, the hominins would have spread across Asia to the Far East. This scenario implies that differences between African *H. erectus* and the Dmanisi people reflect geographic distance, adaptation to new environments, and drift in small isolates.

A problem with this "African origins" hypothesis is that the Dmanisi fossils predate KNM-ER 3733 by ca. 150,000 years. It is apparent that the southern Caucasus was occupied even earlier, ca. 1.85 Ma ago. An alternative view holds that small-brained, pre-*erectus* *Homo* dispersed from Africa into western Asia prior to 2.0 Ma ago. These populations later evolved the cranial characters and body build that define *H. erectus*. This "Asian origins" hypothesis allows the possibility that *H. erectus* emerging in western Eurasia later returned to Africa.

After dispersing across much of the Old World, *H. erectus* persisted longer in some geographic areas than others. At localities in China, the species survived until perhaps 350,000 years ago. At Ngandong in Java, the fossils are ca. 117,000 to 108,000 years old (Rizal et al. 2019). The pattern documented for the Far East contrasts with that in Africa, where *H. erectus* disappears from the record much earlier. This suggests that a western branch of the species likely gave rise to later people, and it is in Africa and Europe where more advanced hominins make their first appearance.

ACKNOWLEDGMENTS

Colleagues at numerous museums and universities have allowed me access to hominin fossils in their care, and I am very grateful for this help. The Leakey Foundation, the National Science Foundation, and the American School of Prehistoric Research (Harvard University) have funded much of the research on which this chapter is based.

REFERENCES

Ackermann, R. R., M. L. Arnold, M. D. Baiz, et al. "Hybridization in Human Evolution: Insights from Other Organisms." *Evolutionary Anthropology* 28 (2019): 189–209.

Aiello, L. C., and M. C. Dean. *An Introduction to Human Evolutionary Anatomy.* London: Academic Press, 1990.

Aiello, L. C., and P. Wheeler. "The Expensive-Tissue Hypothesis: The Brain and the Digestive System in Human and Primate Evolution." *Current Anthropology* 36 (1995): 199–221.

Antón, S. C. "Early *Homo*. Who, When and Where." *Current Anthropology* 53 (2012): S278–S298.

Antón, S. C., R. Potts, and L. C. Aiello. "Evolution of Early *Homo*: An Integrated Biological Perspective." *Science* 345 (2014): 1236828.

Asfaw, B., W. H. Gilbert, and G. D. Richards. "*Homo erectus* Cranial Anatomy." In *Homo erectus. Pleistocene Evidence from the Middle Awash, Ethiopia.* Edited by W. H. Gilbert and B. Asfaw, 265–328. Berkeley: University of California Press, 2008.

Baab, K. L. "Cranial Shape in Asian *Homo erectus*: Geographic, Anagenetic, and Size-Related Variation." In *Asian Paleoanthropology: From Africa to China and Beyond.* Edited by C. J. Norton and D. R. Braun, 57–79. Heidelberg: Springer, 2010.

Baab, K. L. "The Role of Neurocranial Shape in Defining the Boundaries of an Expanded *Homo erectus* Hypodigm." *Journal of Human Evolution* 92 (2016): 1–21.

Benazzi, S., G. Gruppioni, D. S. Strait, et al. "Virtual Reconstruction of KNM-ER 1813 *Homo habilis* Cranium." *American Journal of Physical Anthropology* 153 (2014): 154–160.

Berger, L. R., J. Hawks, D. J. de Ruiter, et al. "*Homo naledi*, a New Species of the Genus *Homo* from the Dinaledi Chamber, South Africa." *eLife* 4 (2015): 09560 (1–35).

Bermúdez de Castro, J. M., M. Martinón-Torres, M. J. Sier, et al. "On the Variability of the Dmanisi Mandibles." *PLoS One* 9 (2014): 88212–88212.

Blumenschine, R. J., C. R. Peters, F. T. Masao, et al. "Late Pliocene *Homo* and Hominid Land Use from Western Olduvai Gorge, Tanzania." *Science* 299 (2003): 1217–1221.

Bramble, D. M., and D. E. Lieberman. "Endurance Running and the Evolution of *Homo*." *Nature* 432 (2004): 345–352.

Clarke, R. J. "A *Homo habilis* Maxilla and Other Newly Discovered Hominid Fossils from Olduvai Gorge, Tanzania." *Journal of Human Evolution* 63 (2012): 418–428.

Coleman, M. N. "What Does Geometric Mean, Mean Geometrically? Assessing the Utility of Geometric Mean and Other Size Variables in Studies of Skull Allometry." *American Journal of Physical Anthropology* 135 (2008): 404–415.

Dean, M. C., and B. H. Smith. "Growth and Development of the Nariokotome Youth, KNM-WT 15000." In *The First Humans: Origin and Early Evolution of the Genus Homo*. Edited by F. E. Grine, J. G. Fleagle, and R. E. Leakey, 101–120. Heidelberg: Springer, 2009.

Dirks, P., E. M. Roberts, H. Hilbert-Wolf, et al. "The Age of *Homo naledi* and Associated Sediments in the Rising Star Cave, South Africa." *eLife* 6, no. 24231 (2017): 1–59.

Ferring, R., O. Oms, J. Agusti, et al. "Earliest Human Occupations at Dmanisi (Georgian Caucasus) Dated to 1.85–1.78 Ma." *Proceedings of the National Academy of Sciences* 108 (2011): 10432–10436.

Grine, F. E., H. F. Smith, C. P. Heesy, et al. "Phenetic Affinities of Plio-Pleistocene *Homo* Fossils from South Africa: Molar Cusp Proportions." In *The First Humans: Origin and Early Evolution of the Genus Homo*. Edited by F. E. Grine, J. G. Fleagle, and R. E. Leakey, 49–62. Heidelberg: Springer, 2009.

Grine, F. E., M. G. Leakey, P. N. Gathogo, et al. "Complete Permanent Mandibular Dentition of Early *Homo* from the Upper Burgi Member of the Koobi Fora Formation, Ileret, Kenya." *Journal of Human Evolution* 131 (2019): 152–175.

Grün, R., A. Pike, F. McDermott, et al. "Dating the Skull from Broken Hill, Zambia, and Its Position in Human Evolution." *Nature* 580 (2020): 372–381.

Haeusler, M., and H. M. McHenry. "Body Proportions of *Homo habilis* Reviewed." *Journal of Human Evolution* 46 (2004): 433–465.

Hammond, A. S., S. S. Mavuso, M. Biernat, et al. "New Hominin Remains and Revised Context from the Earliest *Homo Erectus* Locality in East Turkana, Kenya." *Nature Communications* 12, no. 1939 (2021): 1–12.

Harcourt-Smith, W., and L. C. Aiello. "Fossils, Feet and the Evolution of Human Bipedal Locomotion." *Journal of Anatomy* 204 (2004): 403–416.

Harcourt-Smith, W., Z. Throckmorton, K. A. Congdon, et al. "The Foot of *Homo naledi*." *Nature Communications* 6, no. 8432 (2015): 1–8.

Hatala, K. G., N. T. Roach, K. R. Ostrofsky, et al. "Footprints Reveal Direct Evidence of Group Behavior and Locomotion in *Homo erectus*." *Scientific Reports* 6, no. 28766 (2016): 1–9.

Hawks, J., M. Elliott, P. Schmid, et al. "New Fossil Remains of *Homo Naledi* from the Lesedi Chamber, South Africa." *eLife* 6 (2017): 24232 (1–63).

Herries, A. I. R., J. M. Martin, A. B. Leece, et al. "Contemporaneity of *Australopithecus, Paranthropus*, and Early *Homo erectus* in South Africa." *Science* 368 (2020): 1–19.

Holloway, R. L., S. D. Hurst, H. M. Garvin, et al. "Endocast Morphology of *Homo naledi* from the Dinaledi Chamber, South Africa." *Proceedings of the National Academy of Sciences* 115 (2018): 5738–5743.

Hublin, J. J., A. Ben-Ncer, S. E. Bailey, et al. "New Fossils from Jebel Irhoud, Morocco and the Pan-African Origin of *Homo sapiens*." *Nature* 546 (2017): 289–292.

Hyodo, M., S. Matsu'ura, Y. Kamishima, et al. "High-Resolution Record of the Matuyama-Brunhes Transition Constrains the Age of Javanese *Homo erectus* in the Sangiran Dome, Indonesia." *Proceedings of the National Academy of Sciences* 108 (2011): 19563–19568.

Johanson, D. C., F. T. Masao, G. G. Eck, et al. "New Partial Skeleton of *Homo habilis* from Olduvai Gorge, Tanzania." *Nature* 327 (1987): 205–209.

Kaifu, Y., F. Aziz, E. Indriati, et al. "Cranial Morphology of Javanese *Homo erectus*: New Evidence for Continuous Evolution, Specialization, and Terminal Extinction." *Journal of Human Evolution* 55 (2008): 551–580.

Kaifu, Y., E. Setiyabudi, I. Kurniawan, et al. "Evolution of Indonesian *Homo erectus* in the Early Pleistocene: Significance of Sangiran 17." In *Homo erectus in Indonesia*. Edited by F. Aziz and H. Baba, 65–91. Bandung: Centre for Geological Survey, 2013.

Kimbel, W. H., D. C. Johanson, and Y. Rak. "Systematic Assessment of a Maxilla of *Homo* from Hadar, Ethiopia." *American Journal of Physical Anthropology* 103 (1997): 235–262.

Leakey, L. S. B., P. V. Tobias, and J. R. Napier. "A New Species of the Genus *Homo* from Olduvai Gorge." *Nature* 202 (1964): 7–9.

Leakey, M. G., F. Spoor, M. C. Dean, et al. "New Fossils from Koobi Fora in Northern Kenya Confirm Taxonomic Diversity in Early *Homo*." *Nature* 488 (2012): 201–204.

Leakey, R. E., A. Walker, C. V. Ward, et al. "A Partial Skeleton of a Gracile Hominid from the Upper Burgi Member of the Koobi Fora Formation, East Lake Turkana, Kenya." In *Hominidae: Proceedings of the 2nd International Congress of Human Palaeontology*. Edited by G. Giacobini, 167–173. Milan: Jaca, 1989.

Lepre, C. J., and D. V. Kent. "Chronostratigraphy of KNM-ER 3733 and Other Area 104 Hominins from Koobi Fora." *Journal of Human Evolution* 86 (2015): 99–111.

Lieberman, D. E. *The Evolution of the Human Head*. Cambridge: Belknap (Harvard University), 2011.

Lordkipanidze, D., M. S. Ponce de León, A. Margvelashvili, et al. "A Complete Skull from Dmanisi, Georgia and the Evolutionary Biology of Early *Homo*." *Science* 342 (2013): 326–331.

Macchiarelli, R., L. Bondioli, M. Chech, et al. "The Late Early Pleistocene Human Remains from Buia, Danakil Depression, Eritrea." *Rivista Italiana di Paleontologia e Stratigrafia* 110 (2004): 133–144.

Margvelashvili, A., C. P. E. Zollikofer, D. Lordkipanidze, et al. "Tooth Wear and Dentoalveolar Remodeling Are Key Factors of Morphological Variation in the Dmanisi Mandibles." *Proceedings of the National Academy of Sciences* 110 (2013): 17278–17283.

Margvelashvili, A., C. P. E. Zollikofer, D. Lordkipanidze, et al. "Comparative Analysis of Dentognathic Pathologies in the Dmanisi Mandibles." *American Journal of Physical Anthropology* 160 (2016): 229–253.

Matsu'ura, S., M. Kondo, T. Danhara, et al. "Age Control of the First Appearance Datum for Javanese *Homo erectus* in the Sangiran Area." *Science* 367 (2020): 210–214.

Mori, T., and K. Harvati. "Basicranial Ontogeny Comparison in *Pan Troglodytes* and *Homo sapiens* and Its Use for Developmental Stage Definition of KNM-ER 42700." *American Journal of Physical Anthropology* 17 (2019): 579–594.

Neubauer, S., P. Gunz, L. Leakey, et al. "Reconstruction, Endocranial Form and Taxonomic Affinity of the Early *Homo* Calvaria KNM-ER 42700." *Journal of Human Evolution* 121 (2018): 25–39.

Patterson, D. B., D. R. Braun, K. Allen, et al. "Comparative Isotopic Evidence from East Turkana Supports a Dietary Shift Within the Genus *Homo*." *Nature Ecology and Evolution* 3 (2019): 1048–1056.

Pickering, R., J. D. Kramers, P. J. Hancox, et al. "Contemporary Flowstone Development Links Early Hominin Bearing Cave Deposits in South Africa." *Earth and Planetary Science Letters* 306 (2011): 23–32.

Pontzer, H. "Ecological Energetics in Early *Homo*." *Current Anthropology* 53 (2012): S346–S358.

Pontzer, H., C. Rolian, G. P. Rightmire, et al. "Locomotor Anatomy and Biomechanics of the Dmanisi Hominins." *Journal of Human Evolution* 58 (2010): 492–504.

Potts, R., A. K. Behrensmeyer, A. Deino, et al. "Small Mid-Pleistocene Hominin Associated with East African Acheulean Technology." *Science* 305 (2004): 75–78.

Püschel, H. P., O. C. Bertrand, J. E. O'Reilly, et al. "Divergence-Time Estimates for Hominins Provide Insight into Encephalization and Body Mass Trends in Human Evolution." *Nature Ecology and Evolution* 5 (2021): 808–819.

Rightmire, G. P. *The Evolution of Homo erectus. Comparative Anatomical Studies of an Extinct Human Species.* Cambridge: Cambridge University Press, 1990.

Rightmire, G. P. Middle Pleistocene *Homo* Crania from Broken Hill and Petralona: Morphology, Metric Comparisons, and Evolutionary Relationships. In *Human Paleontology and Prehistory: Contributions in Honor of Yoel Rak.* Edited by A. Marom and E. Hovers, 145–159. Heidelberg: Springer 2017.

Rightmire, G. P., A. P. Van Arsdale, and D. Lordkipanidze. "Variation in the Mandibles from Dmanisi, Georgia." *Journal of Human Evolution* 54 (2008): 904–908.

Rightmire, G. P., M. S. Ponce de León, D. Lordkipanidze, et al. "Skull 5 from Dmanisi: Descriptive Anatomy, Comparative Studies, and Evolutionary Significance." *Journal of Human Evolution* 104 (2017): 50–79.

Rightmire, G. P., A. Margvelashvili, D. Lordkipanidze, et al. "Variation among the Dmanisi Hominins: Multiple Taxa or One Species?" *American Journal of Physical Anthropology* 168 (2019): 481–495.

Rizal, Y., K. E. Westaway, Y. Zaim, et al. "Last Appearance of *Homo erectus* at Ngandong, Java, 117,000 to 108,000 Years Ago." *Nature* 577 (2019): 381–385.

Roach, N. T., A. Du, K. G. Hatala, et al. "Pleistocene Animal Communities of a 1.5 Million-Year-Old Lake Margin Grassland and Their Relationship to *Homo erectus* Paleoecology." *Journal of Human Evolution* 122 (2018): 70–83.

Rogers, A. R., N. S. Harris, and A. A. Achenbach. "Neanderthal–Denisovan Ancestors Interbred with a Distantly Related Hominin." *Science Advances* 6 (2020): 5483.

Ruff, C. B. "Relative Limb Strength and Locomotion in *Homo Habilis*." *American Journal of Physical Anthropology* 138 (2009): 90–100.

Ruff, C. B., and M. L. Burgess. "How Much More Would KNM-WT 15000 Have Grown?" *Journal of Human Evolution* 80 (2015): 744–782.

Ruff, C. B., M. L. Burgess, N. Squyres, et al. "Lower Limb Articular Scaling and Body Mass Estimation in Pliocene and Pleistocene Hominins." *Journal of Human Evolution* 115 (2018): 85–111.

Schrenk, F., O. Kullmer, and T. Bromage. The Earliest Putative *Homo* Fossils. In *Handbook of Paleoanthropology, Volume 3: Phylogeny of Hominids.* Edited by W. Henke and I. Tattersall, 1611–1631. Berlin: Springer, 2007.

Semaw, S., M. J. Rogers, S. W. Simpson, et al. "Co-Occurrence of Acheulean and Oldowan Artifacts with *Homo erectus* Cranial Fossils from Gona, Afar, Ethiopia." *Science Advances* 4694, no. 1–8 (2020).

Shen, G., X. Gao, B. Gao, et al. "Age of Zhoukoudian *Homo erectus* Determined with $^{22}Al/^{10}Be$ Burial Dating." *Nature* 458 (2009): 198–200.

Simpson, S. W., J. Quade, N. E. Levin, et al. "A Female *Homo erectus* Pelvis from Gona, Ethiopia." *Science* 322 (2008): 1089–1092.

Spoor, F., P. Gunz, S. Neubauer, et al. "Reconstructed *Homo habilis* Type OH 7 Suggests Deep-Rooted Species Diversity in Early *Homo*." *Nature* 519 (2015): 83–89.

Suwa, G., B. Asfaw, Y. Haile-Selassie, et al. "Early Pleistocene *Homo erectus* Fossils from Konso, Southern Ethiopia." *Anthropological Science* 115 (2007): 133–151.

Tobias, P. V. *Olduvai Gorge, Volume 4: The Skulls, Endocasts and Teeth of Homo habilis.* Cambridge: Cambridge University Press, 1991.

Venkadesan, M., A. Yawar, C. M. Eng, et al. "Stiffness of the Human Foot and Evolution of the Transverse Arch." *Nature* 579 (2020): 97–100.

Villmoare, B., W. H. Kimbel, C. Seyoum, et al. "Early *Homo* at 2.8 Ma from Ledi-Geraru, Afar, Ethiopia." *Science* 347 (2015): 1352–1355.

Ward, C. V., C. S. Feibel, A. S. Hammond, et al. "Associated Ilium and Femur from Koobi Fora, Kenya, and Postcranial Diversity in Early *Homo*." *Journal of Human Evolution* 81 (2015): 48–67.

Wood, B. *Koobi Fora Research Project,* Volume 4: *Hominid Cranial Remains.* Oxford: Clarendon Press, 1991.

Wood, B. "Origin and Evolution of the Genus *Homo*." *Nature* 355 (1992): 783–790.

Wood, B. A., and E. Boyle. "Hominin Taxic Diversity: Fact or Fantasy?" *American Journal of Physical Anthropology* 159, Suppl. 61 (2016): S37–78.

Wood, B., and M. Leakey. "The Omo-Turkana Basin Fossil Hominins and Their Contribution to Our Understanding of Human Evolution in Africa." *Evolutionary Anthropology* 20 (2011): 264–292.

Wu, X. Z., and F. E. Poirer. *Human Evolution in China. A Metric Description of the Fossils and A Review of the Sites.* Oxford: Oxford University Press, 1995.

Xing, S., M. Martinón-Torres, C. Deng, et al. "Early Pleistocene Hominin Teeth from Meipu, Southern China." *Journal of Human Evolution* 151, no. 102924 (2021): 1–18.

Zanolli, C., M. M. Skinner, F. Schrenk, et al. "The Internal Structural Organization of the Post-canine Dentition of the Initial Early Pleistocene HCRP-U18-501 Hominin Mandible from Malawi." *European Society for the Study of Human Evolution*, Liège, 2019.

Zhu, R., R. Potts, Y. Pan, et al. "Early Evidence of the Genus *Homo* in East Asia." *Journal of Human Evolution* 55 (2008): 1075–1085.

Zollifofer, C. P. E., M. S. Ponce de León, A. Margvelashvili, et al. "Response to Comment on a Complete Skull from Dmanisi, Georgia, and the Evolutionary Biology of Early *Homo*." *Science* 344 (2014): 362–363.

CHAPTER **26**

Panmixis in Middle and Late Pleistocene Human Subspecies: The Genetic/Genomic Revolution in Paleoanthropology

Fred H. Smith and
Whitney M. Karriger

Data from recent years have substantially changed scientific understanding of Middle and Late Pleistocene human evolution. Some are new fossil discoveries but more significant are advances in chronology and analysis of ancient DNA. This time frame witnessed a complex pattern of migration within and out of Africa. During the final 600,000 years (600 ky) of the Pleistocene, regional populations became increasingly differentiated. Additionally, there was at least one major "out of Africa" migration. This post-Erectine migration reflects the spread of modern human anatomical form at some time between ~ 150 kya (thousand years ago) and ~ 100 kya, but genetic data suggest modern genes radiate from Africa around 50 kya. These movements extended throughout Africa and ultimately the remainder of the Earth (Bräuer 2015; Trinkaus 2005). Whether this phenomenon represented the spread of a new species, which replaced archaic *Homo* groups throughout Eurasia, or a novel population of a polytypic single species, continues to be debated. In either case, a complex pattern of interaction between migrant and indigenous populations characterized this part of the human evolutionary record, much as it has more recently.

By 400 kya humans in Europe, Africa, and Asia exhibited prominent regional morphological differences. These humans were still similar across the continents in having expanded brains and brain cases compared to Erectines (Figure 26.1). They also retained many primitive (ancestral) features: lower crania, prognathic faces, prominent supraorbital tori, receding mandibular symphyses with no "chin," large anterior teeth, and robust postcrania.

A Companion to Biological Anthropology, Second Edition. Edited by Clark Spencer Larsen.
© 2023 John Wiley & Sons Ltd. Published 2023 by John Wiley & Sons Ltd.

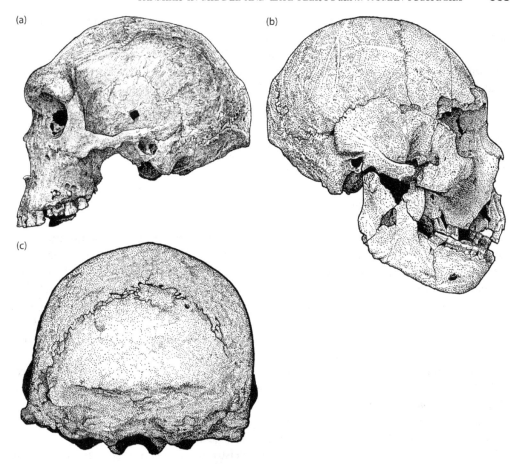

(a)

(b)

(c)

Figure 26.1   Heidelberg specimens from Kabwe (Kabwe 1), Zambia (left); Sima de los Huesos 5 cranium (AT 700) articulated with a mandible from the same site (AT 888 + AT 721), Spain (right); and Petralona (rear view), Greece (bottom left).

However, there are also differences in body shape and details of craniofacial anatomy from region to region. By 100 kya, regional differentiation was clearly established, including the distinctive Neandertals in Europe and much of Asia; early modern people in Africa and the Levant; possibly late Erectines in Australasia; some form of archaic *Homo* in eastern Asia; and several isolates with unusual or primitive morphology in various regions. For many paleoanthropologists, there could be at least six species coexisting in the later Pleistocene.

THE SPECIES ISSUE

There are many ways to define a species in biology (Holliday 2003), but in paleontology the Evolutionary Species Concept (ESC – Simpson 1961) is the most robust. An ES is defined when morphological groupings can be established that are separated from other groups by distinctive morphological gaps. The ESC extends these morphological patterns over time, identifying an evolutionary lineage that has its own unique evolutionary fate. The ESC might seem to incorporate reproductive exclusivity over time, but its basis is entirely morphological. Identifying species in paleontology generally is based in cladistics, which uses patterns of derived (apomorphic) and shared derived (synapomorphic) morphological features to define taxa. While this is a robust methodology, the judicious use of phenetic data can be pivotal in many cases (see Cartmill and Smith 2022).

The Biological Species Concept (BSC; Mayr 1963) defines species based on reproductive isolation. This often occurs when peripheral populations of a species become physically isolated from the body of that species. In such small, marginal populations, environmental stresses are greater, and genetic changes are more likely to become established. Thus, the biology of these populations may develop significant differences from the species' main body. While the BSC is often used, it actually works well only for some extant organisms, including mammals, and complications are common. Consequently, paleontologists generally do not apply the BSC to fossil data even though reproductive exclusivity is often implied. However, recent advances in ancient DNA analysis shed light on species identification during later human biological history, reducing the need to rely on morphology alone.

How much speciosity is expected in specific mammalian lineages depends on three factors: geographic range, adaptive pattern, and body size. Mammals that are more likely to speciate are those with large ranges covering multiple ecological zones, those in the tropics compared to those in higher latitudes, and those with ranges extending to islands (Foley 1991). Foley (1991) notes that lineages with broad adaptive strategies show reduced speciosity and argues that, compared to earlier hominins, Erectines and later *Homo* exploited a much wider range of dietary resources, including significant amounts of meat. Another study asserts the probable high habitat tolerance of Middle and Late Pleistocene hominins, based on a canid analogy, significantly limited hominin speciation (Arcadi 2006). Combined with the more complex technological capabilities of *Homo* (Klein 2009), Middle/Late Pleistocene *Homo* emerge as consummate generalists. Compared to specialized species, generalized species exploit wider geographic and ecological ranges, show more intraspecific variation, and exhibit less of a tendency to split (see Cartmill and Smith 2022).

The cultural capabilities of Middle and Late Pleistocene *Homo* bear special mention. In the modern world, culture is seen more as a specializing agent, promoting separation between groups (Klein 2009). However, as White (1949) emphasized many years ago, culture is also a means of adaptation that defines a unique all-encompassing resource exploitation strategy. Culture as an adaptive mechanism further defines humans as the consummate generalist and it is logical that this generalist adaptive strategy would have limited the speciosity of the Middle and Late Pleistocene hominins.

Species diversity in mammals is tied to body mass, with larger forms exhibiting less taxonomic diversity. Conroy (2002) found that mammals similar in body size to early *Homo* are not speciose. He argues that recognition of more than two synchronic species in early *Homo* would put the human lineage at odds with the pattern for similar-sized mammals.

Holliday and colleagues (Holliday 2006; Holliday et al. 2014) showed that mammalian lineages need to be separated for at least 2 million years to become fully reproductively isolated. Since the divergence times for none of the Late and most Middle Pleistocene hominin lineages of interest here are this old, it is unlikely these groups would have been reproductively isolated from each other – an assertion supported by genetic analyses.

THE GENETIC/GENOMIC REVOLUTION

Advances in ancient DNA recovery and analysis techniques have revolutionized how we understand genetic relationships among extinct hominins. While this revolution technically began with the sequencing of Neandertal mitochondrial DNA (mtDNA), the more significant impact came with the first Neandertal draft genome by Green and colleagues in 2010. MtDNA revealed no Neandertal contribution to modern humans, but there were some clues that Neandertals and early moderns were exchanging genes (see Cartmill and Smith 2022). The genomic data demonstrated that Neandertals contributed on average 1–4 percent of the genetic material in living Eurasians but did not contribute to modern Africans (Green et al. 2010). These results were challenged, but the conclusions of the 2010 paper were verified later (e.g., Prüfer et al. 2014, 2017). Subsequently, it was determined that although each individual Eurasian received about 2 percent of their genetic material from Neandertals, between 35 and 70 percent of the Neandertal genome existed in modern Eurasians (Vernot and Akey 2014). Small amounts of Neandertal genetic material have been found in living Africans, reflecting introgression with Eurasians during the last 20 kya (Chen et al. 2020). Early modern humans also contributed genes to late Neandertal populations (Hubisz et al. 2020).

In Asia, the enigmatic Denisovans, represented by only a mandible and nondiagnostic fragments (see Cartmill and Smith 2022) contributed as much as 6 percent to various populations, especially in Southeast Asia, Tibet, and Papua-New Guinea (Browning et al. 2018; Prüfer et al. 2014). Also "ghost lineages" – lineages not currently associated with a morphologically described hominin – are represented in the genetic record and contribute to modern and other archaic human groups (Prüfer et al. 2014; Rogers et al. 2020). These "ghosts" may actually be known hominins, such as east Asian archaics (Dali, Maba, etc.), Heidelbergs, *Homo floresiensis* or another isolate, or even *Homo erectus* (Hubisz et al. 2020; Rogers et al. 2020). Genetic exchange among these archaic groups (Schaefer et al. 2021) created an interconnected web throughout the Middle and Late Pleistocene of the Old World.

HEIDELBERGS AND THE ORIGIN OF REGIONAL HUMAN DIVERSITY

African post-Erectine humans are represented by remains from a geographically diverse series of sites. Many paleoanthropologists place these remains in *Homo heidelbergensis*, but not all agree. Africa may yield the earliest Heidelbergs, but dating of the African Heidelberg sites is difficult. Among the oldest are Bodo and Saldanha at ca. 600 kya (Klein et al. 2006). Broad estimates for most other specimens are 300–600 kya.

The most informative site is Kabwe, or Broken Hill, in Zambia, which produced a complete cranium (Kabwe 1), a second maxilla, and a series of postcrania. Despite strong chemical homogeneity, the association among the remains is not certain (see Cartmill and Smith 2022). The Kabwe 1 cranium (Figure 26.1), like others of this group, combines primitive and advanced (compared to Erectines) cranial features. The face is large and exhibits Erectine-like total facial prognathism, or prognathism in both the mid- and lateral face. Advanced features include a cranial capacity that is 30 percent larger than Erectines, likely reflecting a significant shift in brain-to-body size patterning (Ruff et al. 1997). Changes in the nose and palate are shared with other members of later *Homo* (Rightmire 2008). Postcrania have both primitive and more modern features (Pearson 2013). The most complete specimen, a tibia, is relatively long, indicating body proportions reflecting a warm environment. Other African Heidelbergs exhibit large anterior teeth, reduced posterior teeth, and chinless mandibles. All specimens have relatively large supraorbital tori and low, broad crania.

Heidelbergs also range all over Europe. Most date between 300 and 600 kya, but slightly earlier and later dates are known (see Cartmill and Smith 2022). These European

Heidelbergs share some features with their African counterparts, such as their shared derived features compared to Erectines in increased cranial capacity and expanded neurocrania (Figure 26.1), as well as shared primitive retentions (prominent supraorbital tori, total facial prognathism, absence of chins) (Rightmire 2008, 2015). However, the two samples differ in some details. For example, European forms often exhibit features that are precursors to Neandertal morphology, such as incipient suprainiac fossae and occipital bunning, and infraorbital morphology. Aspects of the postcrania from Boxgrove and Sima de los Huesos suggest body forms were more cold-adapted than African forms (Arsuaga et al. 1999; Trinkaus et al. 1999). Based on synapomorphies, European Heidelbergs are clearly Neandertal ancestors (Arsuaga at al 2014; Dean et al. 1998; Rightmire 2015; Wolpoff 1999). Certain Asian specimens are best considered Heidelbergs as well (see Cartmill and Smith 2022).

It is difficult to determine the ultimate origin of the Heidelbergs. Some hold that Heidelbergs evolved from Erectines in different regions of the Old World (Athreya 2019; Wolpoff 1999) through gene flow among regional lineages of humans – in other words, multiregional evolution. However, genetics suggest that Heidelbergs spread out of Africa around 650 kya (Schaefer 2021; Templeton 2005). This is an intriguing idea, but the current fossil record can neither support nor refute it.

Do Heidelbergs form a cohesive species separate from other *Homo*? Can the African and European Heidelbergs be accommodated in one species? Some have argued that African forms should be placed in a separate species from European Heidelbergs, with the latter (*H. heidelbergensis*) being ancestral to Neandertals and the former (*H. rhodesiensis*) to modern humans in Africa (Bermúdez de Castro et al. 1997). However, the morphometric similarities among the African and European Heidelbergs argue against this dual species model (Rightmire 2008, 2015). While the consensus is that *H. heidelbergensis* is the valid taxon for these humans, it has not been defined using specific apomorphies. Rightmire (2013, 2015) has marshaled the characteristic features for *H. heidelbergensis*, but, as he notes, these features are a mosaic of traits shared either with more primitive or more derived forms of *Homo*. While the concept of *H. heidelbergensis* plays an important role in the quest for "bushiness" in human evolution, its existence as a distinctly defined taxon is contentious.

ISOLATES: NEW PLAYERS

Recent decades have witnessed the realization that some "populations" of hominins do not fit morphologically in their time frame. This perspective emerged with the human remains from Flores, *Homo floresiensis*. These extremely small-brained hominins with relatively primitive crania and mandibles were probably the result of accidental arrival and subsequent isolation on Flores and are considered a separate species of our genus (Aiello 2015). The same scenario may also explain other specimens (e.g., Callao Cave in the Philippines). More ancient examples of fossils with unexpectedly primitive anatomy for their time frame include Gran Dolina (Spain), Ceprano (Italy), and Rising Star (South Africa). Ceprano was first described as an Erectine, then as *Homo antecessor*, and now as a late surviving group of more primitive humans at about 400 kya (Manzi et al. 2011). Rising Star yields a large sample of remains exhibiting Erectine or earlier *Homo* morphology at 230–330 kya (Berger et al. 2017). Finally, the enigmatic fossils from the Gran Dolina site are now interpreted as an early incursion of *Homo* into Europe that became isolated and did not contribute to later human evolution (Bermúdez de Castro et al. 2017).

It seems clear that there were pockets of hominins who were not part of the major lines of human evolution, although some may represent the genetic "ghost lineages." Whether each of these should have their own species designations is a debatable question. These fossils clearly complicate our understanding of human evolution, but such complications provide a more complete picture of our biological past.

Neandertals and Their "Contemporaries"

Neandertals are the best known and most intensely studied fossil humans. They are found in all but northern-most Europe and in western and central Asia. An impressive amount is known about their anatomy, behavior, adaptive pattern, and genome. In Europe, there is consensus that Neandertals gradually emerge from European Heidelbergs, but there is disagreement whether they emerged by accretion over time in isolation (Dean et al. 1998) or as the European lineage in the multiregional perspective (Wolpoff 1999). Both viewpoints agree that the boundary between European Heidelbergs and Neandertals is rather arbitrary. Arsuaga and colleagues (2014) assert the Sima de los Huesos hominins should be classified in the same taxon as the Neandertals. However, the Sima sample also exhibits features not characteristic of Neandertals. Thus, there is value in maintaining them in the Heidlebergs, while recognizing that European Heidelbergs are ancestral to Neandertals.

A case can be made that the hominins from the site of Ehringsdorf (Germany) represent the earliest sample of unequivocal Neandertals at 210 kya, and a series of sites between 200 and 100 kya exclusively yield Neandertals. Higham and colleagues (2014) assert that Neandertals (and their archaeological contexts) disappear in Europe between 41 and 39 kya. This conclusion is based on the fact that new techniques applied to radiocarbon dating keep pushing Neandertal fossil and archaeological sites further back in time (see Cartmill and Smith 2022).

As mentioned above, some Neandertal features derive from their Heidelberg ancestry, including their large faces, chinless mandibles, pronounced supraorbital tori, low cranial vaults, and large anterior teeth (Figure 26.2). In other ways, Neandertals are derived compared to Heidelbergs. Neandertals exhibit expanded brains, resulting in the cranial vault being expanded, the maximum breadth being higher relative to the cranial base, and the brain case having a characteristic oval shape when viewed from the rear (Figure 26.2). Other distinctive features include the form of the temporal bone, the inferior projection of the occipitomastoid region of the cranial base, the presence of suprainiac fossae on the occipital, the formation of occipital bunning on the rear of the cranium, and a series of mandibular details (Harvati 2015). Neandertals also have large nasal openings, oblique lower cheek margins, and lack canine fosse (Figure 26.2). The most distinctive proposed Neandertal apomorphy is their facial prognathism. Neandertals exhibit prognathism along the midline of the face, but the lateral face is less forwardly projecting. One view holds that the facial midline is moved forward relative to the lateral face, constituting an apomorphic condition (Rak 1986). Another view is that the lateral face retreats relative to the facial midline, defining an intermediate stage between the total facial prognathism of earlier humans and the orthognathism of modern humans (Trinkaus 2006). Midfacial prognathism is related to cold adaptation, because elongating the nasal chamber provides for warming and humidifying inhaled air that is crucial for efficient respiration (Yokley et al. 2018).

Neandertals also have distinctive postcranial features, mostly primitive retentions. For example, the thick cortical bone of Neandertal long bones reflects a pattern of heavy loading, relating to locomotor and other activities. Most significant is their overall body form. Neandertals had a barrel-shaped, broad thorax, and relatively short distal limb segments (Holliday 1997; Ruff et al. 2002). These features indicate a cold-adapted body form, evolved

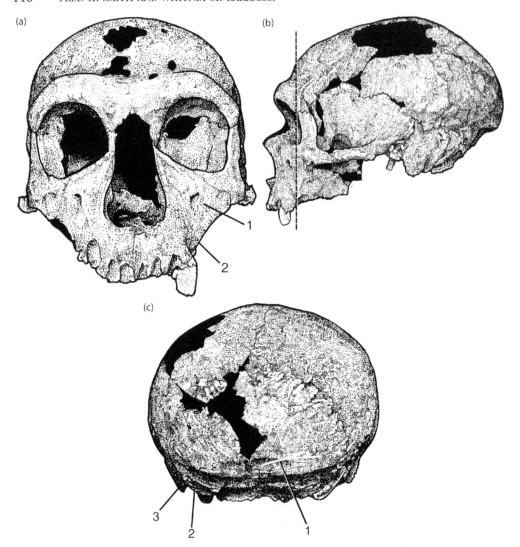

Figure 26.2   Neandertal cranial morphology. La Chapelle-aux-Saints, France – front, side, and rear views. Frontal view: 1. absence of a canine fossa; 2. oblique lower cheek (zygomaticoalveolar) margin. Side view: the vertical line approximates the front of the brain and illustrates the typical Neandertal midline facial prognathism. Rear view: 1. suprainiac fossa; 2. occipitomastoid crest; 3. small mastoid process.

to enhance heat conservation. In fact, Neandertal body form has been called "hyper-arctic" because it appears even more adapted to cold conditions than cold-adapted living people.

Neandertals in Asia are known from the Levant extending into Iraq and the Caucasus region. Near Eastern Neandertals exhibit the distinctive features noted for European Neandertals except they have higher cranial vaults, lack occipital bunning, and do not show as extreme a pattern of distal element shortening in the arm. The morphology of fossils in Central Asia is fundamentally Neandertal, an identity that is revealed in the genetics. MtDNA from Teshik Tash, as well as subadult limb bones from the Okladnikov Cave, reveal the presence of uniquely Neandertal sequences (Krause et al. 2007). A genome from the Chagyrskaya Cave also demonstrates a Neandertal presence (Mafessoni et al. 2020). Thus, Neandertal influences reached farther east than traditionally has been accepted. This is supported by the presence of Neandertal features in the Xuchang hominins from China (Li et al. 2017).

In East Asia, the human fossil record has increased significantly in the past two decades. It includes archaic folk that are distinct from Neandertals. Xuchang, for example, is not a Neandertal although it exhibits some Neandertal characteristics. The Harbin cranium and a series of others (Rosenberg and Wu 2013) are also relatively primitive but are certainly not Neandertals. While they share features with Chinese Erectines, it is unclear if they primarily evolved from Erectines in China (Rosenberg and Wu 2013; Wolpoff 1999) or derived from a Heidelberg expansion into East Asia. The Jinniushan skull, for example, has an archaic cranial vault and a cranial capacity comparable to other late archaic peoples. The face is gracile but appears relatively flat (total facial prognathism), with a broad nose and interorbital area. Detailed analysis of body form for Jinniushan shows a wide trunk, large body mass, and short limbs, suggesting cold adaptation similar to Neandertals (Rosenberg et al. 2006).

ARCHAIC HUMAN ADAPTATION IN HIGHER LATITUDES

Neandertals and higher latitude archaic Asians are adapted for life in the cold but not just in terms of anatomy. Based on analogy with modern circumpolar populations, Neandertals likely had significantly higher basal metabolism rates (BMR) than more equatorial populations, due in part to the effects of temperature and day lengths on thyroid function (Leonard et al. 2002). The combination of a bulky body build and generation of more internal heat would seem to be key to high latitude archaic hominin survival. Some form of body covering and other cultural and biological factors provided additional buffering.

A large body and elevated BMR are energetically expensive. One model calculates that adult Neandertals would have required a BMR 18 and 15 percent higher than in males and females of recent peoples with similar ecologies (Frohle et al. 2013). Although plants were also consumed, there is evidence from stable-isotope studies and archaeology that Neandertals obtained most of their calories and protein from meat, a diet also rich in fat (Kuhn and Steiner 2006; Richards et al. 2000; Speth 2012).

The total energy budget of an organism is expended on normal maintenance or survival activities, growth and development, and reproduction (Sorenson and Leonard 2001). Given their adaptation, maintenance or survival demands would have required almost all of the energy the Neandertal diet could provide, leaving precious little energy for reproduction. Thus, it is likely that Neandertals had lower long-term fertility rates than modern humans, which translated into very small populations sizes. This is supported by archaeological evidence (Holliday et al. 2014; Mellars and French 2011) and genetic evidence. Analyses of mitochondrial and nuclear DNA of Neandertals and Denisovans (Mafessoni et al. 2020; Prüfer 2014, 2017). indicate extremely low levels of genetic diversity, reflecting small population sizes. Thus, Neandertals and other archaic folk were very rare on the landscape (Churchill 2014; Smith 2013), a fact that certainly impacted their evolutionary fate.

AFRICA AND THE ORIGIN OF MODERN HUMANS

While European Heidelbergs gave rise to Neandertals, the descendants of African Heidelbergs are characterized by reduced faces that approach orthognathism, a modern-like cheek region, canine fossa, and a smaller nasal opening. However, brain cases are still primitive, with low cranial vaults and pronounced supraorbital tori. The single known mandible lacks a chin (Hublin et al. 2017). Cranial capacity is virtually identical to the European Neandertal mean (Cartmill and Smith 2022). These African Heidelberg descendants are found at a smattering of sites throughout Africa, including Florisbad, Ngaloba, Eliye

Springs, Guomde, Omo Kibish 2, and Jebel Irhoud and date from 315 to ~ 190 kya (Bräuer 2015; Cartmill and Smith 2022). There are almost no postcranial elements or teeth, but the cranial mosaic indicates evolution toward modern human morphology. This sample has been assigned to the species *Homo helmei* (see Stringer 1994) but is more informally known as the African Transitional Group (ATG).

Whereas the ATG is widely spread in Africa, the earliest evidence of modern humans is more restricted. However, based on the distribution of the ATG and genetic data, recent studies suggest that all of Africa contributed to modern human origins (Hublin et al. 2017; Scerri et al. 2018; Stringer 2016). Three sites in East Africa yield evidence of the earliest modern anatomy. Herto (Ethiopia) has several crania that date between 154 and 160 kya. The most complete adult (Herto 1) exhibits a high, rounded cranial vault, a modern face, and a rear vault contour that shows a maximum breadth high on the parietals like recent humans (Figure 26.3). The face is modern and orthognathic but still has a supraorbital torus (White et al. 2003). The fragmentary Omo 1 skull from the Omo Kibish site KHS

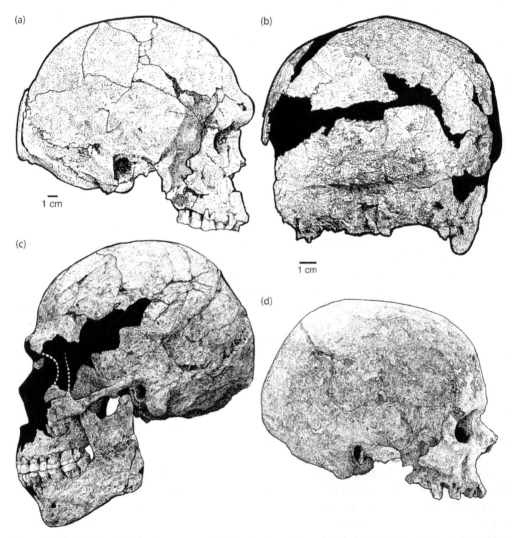

Figure 26.3 Early modern human crania/skulls from Herto (Herto 1), Ethiopia (top left); Omo Kibish 1 (rear view), Ethiopia (top right); Skhūl 5, Israel (bottom left); and Cro-Magnon 1, France (bottom right).

clearly shows modern cranial form, a chin, and a modern face. The fragmentary postcranial skeleton is described as modern and relatively tall (Pearson et al. 2008). The latter suggests a tropical body form, but there is not enough data to be certain of this. The Omo 1 skeleton was excavated just above the Nakaa'kire tuff, dated to 196 ± 2 kya (Brown and Fuller 2008). While the skeleton is likely close to this age, it could be younger. Finally, the Singa cranium (Sudan) exhibits a modern overall form and dates between 133 and 160 kya (Stringer et al. 1985).

THE MODERN HUMAN RADIATION

From East Africa, modern humans spread throughout Africa and ultimately into Eurasia. The first extensive evidence of modern human morphology outside Africa is from the sites of Skhūl and Qafzeh in southwest Asia (Franciscus and Holliday 2013). These sites yield an informative sample of skeletal remains associated with Mousterian tools, very similar to those associated with European and Asian Neandertals. A good "summary estimate" for the dates of the Skhūl/Qafzeh sample is 80–100 kya (Franciscus and Holliday 2013). The total morphology of the specimens is essentially modern. The crania have a vault shape similar to early modern Africans, even in the maintenance of a supraorbital torus in most adults (Figure 26.3) (Franciscus and Holliday 2013). There are also relatively complete mandibles, which show the development of chins and other modern human features (Rak et al. 2002). The postcrania are modern and the body form is linear with relatively long distal limb segments similar to recent African populations adapted to a more tropical climate. However, one individual (Skhūl 5) is somewhat more like Neandertals in body form, and this along with other features may mean that the biological boundary between Neandertals and early moderns in western Asia is more porous than promoters of multiple species argue. In fact, morphometric analysis of crania indicates the likelihood of a small degree of interbreeding between early moderns and Neandertals in the Near East (Thackeray et al. 2005).

Two sites may show modern human morphology at earlier dates in Eurasia. An adult maxilla from Misliya Cave (Israel) exhibits morphology similar to some of the Skhūl hominins. Dating of tooth enamel places Misliya 1 between 177 and 194 kya, while the dentine of the same tooth and the crust adhering directly to the maxilla have yielded a minimum age of 70.2 ± 1.6 kya (Hershkovitz et al. 2018). The Apidima 1 partial posterior cranium from Greece dates to ~ 210 kya and may be the oldest known modern human. Harvati and colleagues (2019) find that Apidima 1's vault shape falls into the modern human range and argue that it represents an early incursion of modern humans into Europe. This is a possibility, but it requires additional evidence.

Early dates of 80–125 kya have been claimed for several sites in China, but accuracy of these dates has been seriously challenged (Sun et al. 2021). Fragmentary remains from Zhiren Cave (Zhirendong) comprising a mandibular symphysis and two lower molars exhibit modern and archaic features (especially on the mandible fragment) and underlie flowstone with a uranium-series date of > 100 kya (Liu et al. 2010). However, this date probably suffers from the same uncertainties. The earliest well-dated modern specimen from mainland East Asia is the 39–43 kya Tianyuan 1 skeleton, which preserves a partial mandible and some 30 postcranial elements (Shang and Trinkaus 2010) exhibiting modern features. Based on partially reconstructed elements, Tianyuan 1 also appears to a have lower limb form that indicates a relatively tropical ancestry. Shang and colleagues (2007) conclude that substantial gene flow from early modern populations to the south and west likely explains the origin of modern populations in this region, but they also note that the Tianyuan 1 specimen preserves a few features that reflect some local archaic contributions in China. Thus, it is not certain if modern humans reached eastern mainland Asia earlier than ~ 40 kya, but it is possible.

In Australasia, controversial dates on the Willandra Lakes (Lake Mungo) 3 skeleton and some archaeological sites indicate people could have reached Greater Australia (Sahulland) by 62–65 kya (Clarkson et al. 2017; Thorne et al. 1999), but others argue that a more reasonable time frame is 35–40 kya (Allen and O'Connell 2020). Extant Australian and Papuan genomes indicate that they split from Eurasians between 51 and 72 kya and from each other between 25 and 40 kya (Malaspinas et al. 2016). This latter split provides additional support for the younger dates. The same study concludes that Australian/Papuans mixed with an unknown archaic population before they split, yielding further evidence for widespread introgression between archaic and early modern humans.

The earliest Australians are modern people morphologically (Durband and Westaway 2013) and the Willandra Lakes 3 skeleton suggests a relatively linear body build. Early Australians exhibit considerable variability, with the Willandra Lakes 50 cranium having morphology that is somewhat primitive and may reflect influence from archaic Australasians (Wolpoff and Lee 2014). The oldest known modern specimen from Sundaland is the Niah Cave (Borneo) juvenile, dated to at least 35 kya (Barker et al. 2007), although a tibia fragment from the Tabon cave (Palawan Island) dates to 47 kya, but with a large error range (Corny et al. 2016). The Sundaland specimens are also modern and there is no evidence of post-Erectine archaic specimens here except possibly the Ngandong people.

Modern humans probably arrived in Europe about 45 kya or slightly earlier, based on the Bacho Kiro site in Bulgaria, where fragmentary modern fossils are dated to ~ 47–44 kya (Fewlass et al. 2020). Thus, Europe is a late frontier for early modern people. The earliest more complete fossil remains are from Peştera cu Oase (Romania) and comprise a fundamentally modern cranium and mandible dated to between 37 and 42 kya (Trinkaus et al. 2013). These are followed in age by specimens from several sites, including Zlatý Kůň, Mladeč, Cioclovina, Muierii, Kostenki, and Ust'-Ishim, all older than 30 kya (see Cartmill and Smith 2022). Early modern Europeans (EME) are modern in skull form and are overall more similar to early modern West Asians and Africans than to the indigenous Neandertals (Figure 26.3). EME also lack supraorbital tori, which are present in earlier moderns from Asia and Africa. Additionally, the EME body form also differs from Neandertals in being more linear with longer distal limb segments, suggesting an origin for EME in warmer environs (Holliday 1997). These morphological differences have long been interpreted as reflecting a migration of modern people into Europe, ultimately replacing the Neandertals. However, a strong argument can be made that there is some continuity with Neandertals in certain morphological details, but not in overall morphological form (Cartmill and Smith 2022).

THE PATTERN OF MODERN HUMAN ORIGINS

From the mid-1980s, two models dominated discussions of modern human origins. The Recent African Origins model (RAO) posited that modern humans were a species distinct from all archaic humans and that these archaics were almost (if not totally) replaced by expanding modern humans. The RAO gained support from recent human genetics and the mtDNA extracted from Neandertals (see Relethford 2001). The Multiregional Evolution model (MRE) argued that modern human characteristics evolved in different areas of the

Old World and then spread by gene flow. These features coalesced at different times in different regions, depending on the pattern of gene flow, local selective environment, and genetic drift. Thus, there was no specific region where modern human biology originated and contributions by archaic peoples might be as much as 50 percent (Wolpoff et al. 2004). Some geneticists suggested that not all genetic data supported complete replacement of archaics and the "mostly out of Africa" model emerged (see Relethford 2001; Templeton 2005). However, this and other models had relatively minor impacts.

With the publication of the first Neandertal genome (Green et al. 2010), things changed – at least somewhat. Various studies demonstrated that Neandertals, Denisovans, and other archaic groups regularly exchanged genes with each other and with early modern humans. The contribution of these archaic hominin groups was relatively small, seemingly always below 10 percent, but many contributions were significant. Based on this introgression, the Middle and Late Pleistocene evolution of humans has been presented as a braided stream process, where groups split off and often rejoin over time. This model is particularly supported by scholars working in China, where arguments for continuity have a long history (Athreya 2019; Athreya and Wu 2017; Rosenberg and Wu 2013). Recent assessments have argued that all parts of Africa contributed to the emergence of modern humans (Scerri et al. 2018). Both of these developments support the original ideas presented in Weidenreich's "trellis" model, the basis of the MRE (see Cartmill and Smith 2022; Wolpoff 1999). However, Africa is still seen as the origin of modern humans (Scerri et al. 2018) and the RAO still explains that origin and radiation.

ASSIMILATION

The Assimilation model (AM) was developed in the late 1980s (Smith et al. 1989). It agrees with the RAO that the preponderance of evidence indicates the origin of modern human morphology in Africa. However, the AM accepts introgression between expanding modern populations and the archaic Eurasians they encountered. The AM differs from the MRE by positing that the archaic contribution to modern populations was always small, and thus continuity would only be seen in limited anatomical details. The AM agrees with the MRE that Neandertals and other archaic hominins should be classified in *Homo sapiens*. The AM was initially developed on the basis of morphological features, not genetics, and the degree to which morphological features reflect introgression continues to be debated (see Cartmill and Smith 2022). In Europe, such features as occipital bunning, supraorbital form, midfacial projection, cold-adapted limb proportions of the Lagar Velho child and other features are argued to reflect the continuity in anatomical details the AM advocates. Opponents generally consider such features to be non-homologous between Neandertals and early modern humans. While these objections can be countered (Cartmill and Smith 2022), uncertainty persists. Regardless, the genetic/genomic data affirm the basic tenants of the AM (Figure 26.4).

There are two explanations for the paucity of archaic contributions to modern people. The first is selection against archaic contributions, both genetic and morphological. Neandertals have long been considered less intelligent than modern humans, and it was this inferiority that led to their demise. Early modern humans certainly possessed a more sophisticated cultural complex than the Neandertals (Klein 2009), but recent research shows the difference between them is not qualitative, nor even as quantitative as once thought (Villa and Roebroeks 2014). Negative genetic selection against Neandertal alleles seems to occur in the first 10 generations after hybridization (Petr et al. 2019), although this has been challenged. Most early modern genomes show a 2–3 percent Neandertal contribution – about

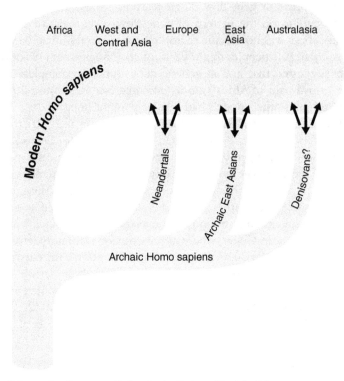

Figure 26.4 Schematic diagram of the Assimilation Model. The arrows represent gene flow, although modern gene flow into archaics is demonstrated only for Neandertals. Archaic humans were also exchanging genes with each other, but this is not represented here. (Drawing by Graphic Design, Illinois State University).

the same as in living Eurasians (see Cartmill and Smith 2022). However, the genome from Peştera cu Oase (Romania) indicates a 6–9 percent Neandertal contribution (Fu et al. 2015). Southeast Central Europe also shows the strongest indication of Neandertal morphological contributions to early modern Europeans (Cartmill and Smith 2022). Whether the additional Neandertal genes were lost here through selection or genetic drift is uncertain.

While early generation selection certainly targeted Neandertals in interaction with early moderns, the paleodemographic factors are more significant. Neandertals were clearly "thin on the ground," and there are convincing reasons to accept that early modern human populations were much larger (Churchill 2014; Holliday et al. 2014; Smith 2013). Their small population densities are almost certainly the main reason Neandertals (and probably other archaic Eurasians) did not have greater impacts on early modern humans. Nevertheless, Neandertal influences, as well as those of Denisovans and other archaic people, were far from insignificant.

Subspecies Not Species

Based on these factors, the argument that post-Erectine humans represent a single lineage (species) is much more robust than it was 10 years ago. Neandertals (and other archaic populations) are regional human groups with distinctive sets of anatomical and genetic features, but they are not unequivocally different species as they systematically exchange genes.

These hominins and modern humans conform to the textbook definition of subspecies as defined by Mayr (1963). Anthropologists have argued for some time that living humans do not conform to the biological concept of race (see Larsen 2020) and genetic studies show that living humans have truncated genetic diversity compared to other wide-ranging mammalian species. The fact is that all living humans (*Homo sapiens sapiens*) evolved from Late Pleistocene African hominins. In Europe and Asia, early modern humans exchanged relatively small but adaptively significant genetic material with Neandertals and other morphologically undefined hominin groups.

To see regional differentiation of humans that equates to separate subspecies, one has to go to the fossil record. It is the Neandertals (*H. sapiens neanderthalensis*), the Ngandong people, archaic East Asians, and possibly others that reflect the original regional Eurasian adaptations of humans. These earlier subspecies are extinct morphologically, but not in the classic sense of the concept. Rather they have been assimilated into a larger human subspecies – us. This "extinction" through assimilation (cf. Levin 2002) has been, and continues to be, a common theme in recent human history. The evidence suggests it likely explains the evolutionary history of Middle and Late Pleistocene humans as well.

REFERENCES

Aiello, L. "Homo Floresiensis." In *Handbook of Paleoanthropology*, 2nd edn. Edited by W. Henke and I. Tattersall, 2281–2297. Berlin, Heidelberg: Springer, 2015.

Allen, J., and J. O'Connell. "A Different Paradigm for the Initial Colonisation of Sahul." *Archaeology in Oceania* 55 (2020): 1–14.

Arcadi, A. "Species Resilience in Pleistocene Hominids that Traveled Far and Ate Widely: An Analogy to the Wolf-Like Canids." *Journal of Human Evolution* 51 (2006): 383–394.

Arsuaga, J., C. Lorenzo, J. Carretero, et al. "A Complete Human Pelvis from the Middle Pleistocene of Spain." *Nature* 399 (1999): 255–258.

Arsuaga, J. L., I. Martínez, L. Arnold, et al. "Neandertal Roots: Cranial and Chronological Evidence from Sima de los Huesos." *Science* 344 (2014): 1358–1363.

Athreya, S. "Braided Streams: Evolutionary Dynamics Among Pleistocene Hominins in East Asia." *Capeia*, (2019): 20190930.008. capeia.com/paleobiology.

Athreya, S., and X. Wu. "A Multivariate Assessment of the Dali Hominin Cranium from China: Morphological Affinities and Implications for Pleistocene Evolution in East Asia." *American Journal of Physical Anthropology* 164 (2017): 679–701.

Barker, G., H. Barton, M. Bird, et al. "The 'Human Revolution' in Lowland Tropical Southeast Asia: The Antiquity and Behavior of Anatomically Modern Humans at Niah Cave (Sarawak, Borneo)." *Journal of Human Evolution* 52 (2007): 243–261.

Berger, L., J. Hawks, P. Dirks, et al. "*Homo naledi* and Pleistocene Hominin Evolution in Subequatorial Africa." *eLife* 6 (2017): e24234. 10.7554/eLife.24234.

Bermúdez de Castro, J., J. Arsuaga, E. Carbonell, et al. "A Hominid from the Lower Pleistocene of Atapuerca, Spain: Possible Ancestor to Neandertals and Modern Humans." *Science* 276 (1997): 1392–1395.

Bermúdez de Castro, J., M. Martinón-Torres, J. L. Arsuaga, and E. Carbonell. "Twentieth Anniversary of *Homo antecessor* (1997–2017): A Review." *Evolutionary Anthropology* 26 (2017): 157–171.

Bräuer, G. "Origin of Modern Humans." In *Handbook of Paleoanthropology*, 2nd edn. Edited by W. Henke and I. Tattersall, 2299–2330. Berlin, Heidelberg: Springer, 2015.

Brown, F., and C. Fuller. "Stratigraphy and Tephra of the Kibish Formation, Southwestern Ethiopia." *Journal of Human Evolution* 55 (2008): 366–403.

Browning, S., B. Browning, Y. Zhou, et al. "Analysis of Human Sequence Data Reveals Two Pulses of Archaic Denisovan Admixture." *Cell* 173 (2018): 53–61.

Cartmill, M., and F. H. Smith. *The Human Lineage*, 2nd edn. Hoboken: Wiley-Blackwell, 2022.

Chen, L., A. Wolf, W. Fu, et al. "Identifying and Interpreting Apparent Neanderthal Ancestry in African Individuals." *Cell* 180 (2020): 677–687.

Churchill, S. *Thin on the Ground. Neandertal Biology, Archaeology, and Ecology*. Ames, Iowa: Wiley-Blackwell, 2014.

Clarkson, C., Z. Jacobs, B. Marwick, et al. "Human Occupation of Northern Australia by 65,000 Years Ago." *Nature* 547 (2017): 306–310.

Conroy, G. "Speciosity in the Early *Homo* Lineage: Too Many, Too Few, or Just about Right?" *Journal of Human Evolution* 43 (2002): 759–766.

Corny, J., A. Garong, F. Semah, et al. "Paleoanthropological Significance and Morphological Variability of the Human Bones and Teeth from Tabon Cave." *Quaternary International* 416 (2016): 210–218.

Dean, D., J. Hublin, R. Holloway, and R. Ziegler. "On the Phylogenetic Position of the Pre Neandertal Specimen from Reilingen, Germany." *Journal of Human Evolution* 34 (1998): 485–508.

Durband, A., and M. Westaway. "Perspectives on the Origins of Modern Australians." In *The Origins of Modern Humans. Biology Reconsidered*. Edited by F. H. Smith and J. C. M. Ahern, 123–150. Hoboken: Wiley-Blackwell, 2013.

Fewlass, H., S. Talamo, L. Wacker, et al. "A ^{14}C Chronology for the Middle to Upper Palaeolithic Transition at Bacho Kiro Cave, Bulgaria." *Nature Ecology and Evolution* 4 (2020): 794-801.

Foley, R. "How Many Species of Hominid Should There Be?" *Journal of Human Evolution* 20 (1991): 413–427.

Franciscus, R., and T. Holliday. "Crossroads of the Old World: Late Hominin Evolution in Western Asia." In *The Origins of Modern Humans. Biology Reconsidered*. Edited by F. H. Smith and J. C. M. Ahern, 45–88. Hoboken, NJ: Wiley-Blackwell, 2013.

Froehle, A., T. Yokley, and S. Churchill. "Energetics and the Origin of Modern Humans." In *The Origins of Modern Humans. Biology Reconsidered*. Edited by F. H. Smith and J. C. M. Ahern, 285–320. Hoboken, NJ: Wiley-Blackwell, 2013.

Fu, Q., M. Hajdinjak, O. Moldovan, et al. "An Early Modern Human from Romania with a Recent Neanderthal Ancestor." *Nature* 524 (2015): 216–219.

Green, R., J. Krause, A. Briggs, et al. "A Draft Sequence of the Neandertal Genome." *Science* 328 (2010): 710–725.

Harvati, K. "Neanderthals and Their Contemporaries." In *Handbook of Paleoanthropology*, 2nd edn. Edited by W. Henke and I. Tattersall, 2244–2279. Berlin, Heidelberg: Springer, 2015.

Harvati, K., C. Röding, A. Bosman, et al. "Apidima Cave Fossils Provide Earliest Evidence of *Homo sapiens* in Eurasia." *Nature* 571 (2019): 500–504.

Hershkovitz, I., G. Weber, R. Quam, et al. "The Earliest Modern Humans Outside Africa." *Science* 359 (2018): 456–459.

Higham, T., K. Douka, R. Wood, et al. "The Timing and Spatiotemporal Patterning of Neanderthal Disappearance." *Nature* 512 (2014): 306–309.

Holliday, T. "Postcranial Evidence of Cold Adaptation in European Neandertals." *American Journal of Physical Anthropology* 104 (1997): 245–258.

Holliday, T. "Species Concepts, Reticulation, and Human Evolution." *Current Anthropology* 44 (2003): 653–673.

Holliday, T. "Neanderthals and Modern Humans: An Example of a Mammalian Syngameon?" In *Neanderthals Revisited: New Approaches and Perspectives*. Edited by K. Harvati and T. Harrison, 281–297. Dordrecht: Springer, 2006.

Holliday, T., J. Gautney, and L. Friedl. "Right for the Wrong Reasons: Reflections on Modern Human Origins in the Post-Neanderthal Genome Era." *Current Anthropology* 55 (2014): 696–724.

Hubisz, M., A. Williams, and A. Siepel. "Mapping Gene Flow Between Ancient Hominins Through Demography-Aware Inference of the Ancestral Recombination Graph." *PLoS Genetics* 16 (2020): e1008895.

Hublin, J.-J., A. Ben-Ncer, S. Bailey, et al. "New Fossils from Jebel Irhoud, Morocco and the Pan African Origin of *Homo sapiens*." *Nature* 546 (2017): 289–292.

Klein, R. *The Human Career. Human Biological and Cultural Origins*, 3rd edn. Chicago: University of Chicago Press, 2009.

Klein, R., G. Avery, K. Cruz-Uribe, and Y. Steele. "The Mammalian Fauna Associated with an Archaic Hominin Skullcap and Later Acheulean Artifacts at Elandsfontein, Western Cape Province, South Africa." *Journal of Human Evolution* 52 (2006): 164–186.

Krause, J., L. Orlando, D. Serre, et al. "Neandertals in Central Asia and Siberia." *Nature* 442 (2007): 902–904.

Kuhn, S., and M. Steiner. "What's a Mother to Do? The Division of Labor among Neandertals and Modern Humans in Eurasia." *Current Anthropology* 47 (2006): 953–980.

Larsen, C. S. *Our Origins: Discovering Biological Anthropology*, 5th edn. New York: W. W. Norton, 2020.

Leonard, W., M. Sørensen, V. Galloway, et al. "Climatic Influences on Basal Metabolic Rates Among Circumpolar Populations." *American Journal of Human Biology* 14 (2002): 609–620.

Levin, D. "Hybridization and Extinction." *American Scientist* 90 (2002): 254–261.

Li, Z., X. Wu, l. Zhou, et al. "Late Pleistocene Archaic Human Crania from Xuchang, China." *Science* 355 (2017): 969–972.

Liu, W., C. Jin, Y. Zhang, et al. "Human Remains from Zhirendong, South China, and Modern Human Emergence in East Asia." *Proceedings of the National Academy of Sciences* 107 (2010): 19201–19206.

Mafessoni, F., S. Grote, C. de Filippo, et al. "A High-Coverage Neandertal Genome from Chagyrskaya Cave." *Proceedings of the National Academy of Sciences* 117 (2020): 15132–15136.

Malaspinas, A.-S., M. Westaway, C. Muller, et al. "A Genomic History of Aboriginal Australia." *Nature* 538 (2016): 207–214.

Manzi, G., D. Margi, and M. Palombo. "Early-Middle Pleistocene Environmental Changes and Human Evolution in the Italian Peninsula." *Quaternary Science Review* 30 (2011): 1420–1438.

Mayr, E. *Animal Species and Evolution*. Cambridge: Harvard University Press, 1963.

Mellars, P., and J. French. "Tenfold Population Increase in Western Europe at the Neandertal-to-Modern Human Transition." *Science* 333 (2011): 623–627.

Pearson, O. "Africa: The Cradle of Modern People." In *The Origins of Modern Humans Biology Reconsidered*. Edited by F. H. Smith and J. C. M. Ahern, 1–43. Hoboken, NJ: Wiley-Blackwell, 2013.

Pearson, O., D. Royer, F. Grine, and J. Fleagle. "A Description of the Omo 1 Postcranial Skeleton, Including Newly Discovered Fossils." *Journal of Human Evolution* 55 (2008): 421–437.

Petr, M., S. Pääbo, J. Kelso, and B. Vernot. "Limits of Long-Term Selection Against Neandertal Introgression." *Proceedings of the National Academy of Sciences* 116 (2019): 1639–1644.

Prüfer, K., F. Racimo, N. Patterson, et al. "The Complete Genome Sequence of a Neanderthal from the Altai Mountains." *Nature* 505 (2014): 43–49.

Prüfer, K., C. de Filippo, S. Grote, et al. "A High-Coverage Neandertal Genome from Vindija Cave in Croatia." *Science* 358 (2017): 655–658.

Rak, Y. "The Neanderthal: A New Look at an Old Face." *Journal of Human Evolution* 15 (1986): 151–164.

Rak, Y., A. Ginzburg, and E. Geffen. "Does *Homo neanderthalensis* Play a Role in Modern Human Ancestry? The Mandibular Evidence." *American Journal of Physical Anthropology* 119 (2002): 199–204.

Relethford, J. *Genetics and the Search for Modern Human Origins*. New York: Wiley-Liss, 2001.

Richards, M., P. Pettitt, E. Trinkaus, et al. "Neanderthal Diet at Vindija and Neanderthal Predation: The Evidence from Stable Isotopes." *Proceedings of the National Academy of Sciences* 97 (2000): 7663–7666.

Rightmire, G. P. "*Homo* in the Middle Pleistocene: Hypodigms, Variation, and Species Recognition." *Evolutionary Anthropology* 17 (2008): 8–21.

Rightmire, G. P. "*Homo erectus* and Middle Pleistocene Hominins: Brain Size, Skull Form, and Species Recognition." *Journal of Human Evolution* 65 (2013): 223–252.

Rightmire, G. P. "Later Middle Pleistocene *Homo*." In *Handbook of Paleoanthropology*, 2nd edn. Edited by W. Henke and I. Tattersall, 2221–2242. Berlin, Heidelberg: Springer, 2015.

Rogers, A., N. Harris, and A. Achenbach. "Neanderthal–Denisovan Ancestors Interbred with a Distantly Related Hominin." *Science Advances* 6 (2020): eaay5483.

Rosenberg, K., and X. Wu. "A River Runs Through It: Modern Human Origins in East Asia." In *The Origins of Modern Humans. Biology Reconsidered*. Edited by F. H. Smith and J. C. M. Ahern, 89–121. Hoboken, NJ: Wiley-Blackwell, 2013.

Rosenberg, K., Z. Lü, and C. Ruff. "Body Size, Body Form and Encephalization in a Middle Pleistocene Archaic Human from Northern China." *Proceedings of the National Academy of Sciences* 103 (2006): 3352–3556.

Ruff, C., E. Trinkaus, and T. Holliday. "Body Mass and Encephalization in Pleistocene *Homo*." *Nature* 387 (1997): 173–176.

Ruff, C., E. Trinkaus, and T. Holliday. "Body Proportions and Size." In *Portrait of the Artist as a Young Child. The Gravettian Human Skeleton from the Abrigo Do Lagar Velho and Its Archaeological Context*. Edited by J. Zilhão and E. Trinkaus, 365–391. Lisbon: *Trabalhos de Arqueologia* Number 22, 2002.

Scerri, E., M. Thomas, A. Manica, et al. "Did Our Species Evolve in Subdivided Populations Across Africa, and Why Does It Matter?" *Trends in Ecology and Evolution* 33 (2018): 582–594.

Schaefer, N., B. Shapiro, and R. Green. "An Ancestral Recombination Graph of Ancient Human, Neandertal and Denisovan Genes." *Science Advances* 7 (2021): eabc0776.

Shang, H., and E. Trinkaus. *The Early Modern Human from Tianyuan Cave, China*. College Station: Texas A&M Press, 2010.

Shang, H., H. Tong, F. Zhang, et al. "An Early Modern Human from Tianyuan Cave, Zhoukoudian, China." *Proceedings of the National Academy of Sciences* 104 (2007): 6573–6578.

Simpson, G. G. *Principles of Animal Taxonomy*. New York: Columbia University Press, 1961.

Smith, F. H. "The Fate of the Neandertals." *Journal of Anthropological Research* 69 (2013): 167–200.

Smith, F. H., A. Falsetti, and S. Donnelly. "Modern Human Origins." *Yearbook of Physical Anthropology* 32 (1989): 35–68.

Sorensen, M. and W. Leonard. "Neandertal Energetics and Foraging Efficiency." *Journal of Human Evolution* 40 (2001): 483–495.

Speth, J., "Middle Palaeolithic Subsistence in the Near East: Zooarchaeological Perspectives – Past, Present and Future." *Before Farming 2012/2 article* 1: 1–45.

Stringer, C. B. "Out of Africa: A Personal History." In *Origins of Anatomically Modern Humans*. Edited by M. Nitecki and D. Nitecki, 149–174. New York: Plenum, 1994.

Stringer, C. B. "The Origin and Evolution of *Homo sapiens*." *Philosophical Transactions of the Royal Society of London, Series B* 371 (2016): 20150237.

Stringer, C. B., L. Cornish, and P. Stuart-Macadam. "Preparation and Further Study of the Singa Skull from the Sudan." *Bulletin of the British Museum of Natural History (Geology)* 38 (1985): 347–358.

Sun, X., S. Wen, C. Lu, et al. "Ancient DNA and Multimethod Dating Confirm the Late Arrival of Anatomically Modern Humans in Southern China." *Proceedings of the National Academy of Sciences* 118 (2021): e2019158118.

Templeton, A. "Haplotype Trees and Modern Human Origins." *Yearbook of Physical Anthropology* 48 (2005): 33–59.

Thackeray, F., B. Maureille, B. Vandermeersch, et al. "Morphometric Comparisons Between Neanderthals and 'Anatomically Modern' *Homo sapiens* from Europe and the Near East." *Annals of the Transvaal Museum* 42 (2005): 47–51.

Thorne, A., R. Grün, G. Mortimer, et al. "Australia's Oldest Human Remains: Age of the Lake Mungo 3 Skeleton." *Journal of Human Evolution* 36 (1999): 591–612.

Trinkaus, E. "Early Modern Humans." *Annual Review of Anthropology* 34 (2005): 207–230.

Trinkaus, E. "Modern Human versus Neandertal Evolutionary Distinctiveness." *Current Anthropology* 47 (2006): 597–620.

Trinkaus, E., C. Stringer, C. Ruff, et al. "Diaphyseal Cross-Sectional Geometry of the Boxgrove 1 Middle Pleistocene Human Tibia." *Journal of Human Evolution* 37 (1999): 1–25.

Trinkaus, E., S. Constantin, and J. Zilhão, eds. *Life and Death at the Peştera cu Oase. A Setting for Modern Human Emergence in Europe*. Oxford: Oxford University Press, 2013.

Vernot, B., and J. Akey. "Resurrecting Surviving Neandertal Lineages from Modern Human Genomes." *Science* 343 (2014): 1017–1021.

Villa, P., and W. Roebroeks. "Neandertal Demise: An Archaeological Analysis of the Modern Human Superiority Complex." *PLoS One* 9 (2014): e96424.

White, L. A. *The Science of Culture: A Study of Man and Civilization*. New York: Farrar, Straus and Cudahy, 1949.

White, T. D., B. Asfaw, D. DeGusta, et al. "Pleistocene *Homo Sapiens* from Middle Awash, Ethiopia." *Nature* 423 (2003): 742–747.

Wolpoff, M. *Paleoanthropology*, 2nd edn. New York: McGraw–Hill, 1999.

Wolpoff, M., and S.-H. Lee. "WLH 50: How Australia Informs the Worldwide Pattern of Pleistocene Human Evolution." *PaleoAnthropology* 2014 (2014): 505–564.

Wolpoff, M., B. Mannheim, A. Mann, et al. "Why Not the Neandertals?" *World Archaeology* 36 (2004): 527–546.

Yokley, T., N. Holton, and F. H. Smith. "Cold Adaptation and the Neandertal Face." *PaleoAnthropology* 2018 (2018): A39.

CHAPTER **27**

Bioarchaeology: Transformations in Lifestyle, Morbidity, and Mortality

George R. Milner and Clark Spencer Larsen

INTRODUCTION

Bioarchaeology, a highly contextualized study of human remains embedded in their cultural and natural settings (Buikstra and Beck 2006; Buikstra et al. 2022; Larsen 2015), is a multidisciplinary study of past human biological variation that draws upon allied fields in the natural, social, and medical sciences, as well as the humanities. For decades, the term has designated a focus on human skeletons and mummified soft tissue, along with associated funerary material (Buikstra 1977; Buikstra and Beck 2006; Buikstra et al. 2022; Charles 2013; Larsen 2015). In the United Kingdom, it is also applied to studies of all manner of biological remains from archaeological sites, a use that predates by several years the singular emphasis on human remains. Appropriately enough for a volume on biological anthropology, this chapter focuses on how human remains enhance our knowledge about the lives of past people, and hence provide a deep temporal context for a better understanding of the world as it exists today. There is, however, much more to bioarchaeology, including studies of the social and ritual significance of mortuary activities (Charles 2013; Goldstein 2006; Zakrzewski 2015).

Bioarchaeology provides a perspective on how our ancestors dealt, successfully or not, with challenges resulting from greater population size and density, aggregation into larger settlements, institutionalization of socioeconomic distinctions, increased interregional contact, and an intensification of food production with concomitant alterations of environmental settings. These transformations in how people lived left distinctive skeletal signatures revealing information about workload, infectious disease, nutritional deficiencies, trauma, and population structure.

Present conditions are a consequence of lengthy histories rooted deep in the past. By focusing on the lives of long-deceased people, bioarchaeological research adds a unique dimension to our understanding of global diversity in the human experience and how we got to where we are today. Although this research covers many aspects of human behavior that leave indelible imprints on skeletons, here we emphasize topics that resonate in the twenty-first century. They include population structure and change, migration, disease, inequality, and conflict.

BIOARCHAEOLOGY

Bioarchaeologists direct most of their attention to human remains from the Holocene. Although the last 10,000 years is short relative to seven million years of hominin evolution, it encompasses major changes in how people lived, notably the development of agricultural economies and organizationally complex societies. These transitions were accompanied by anthropogenic transformations in natural settings, population growth, and profound alterations in lifestyle and wellbeing.

As a coherent field of study, bioarchaeology dates back to the 1970s when there was a marked uptick in research on human remains from archaeological contexts, much of which was directed toward understanding life in the past as distinct from measuring bones and assigning crania to idealized types (Angel 1971; Armelagos et al. 1982; Buikstra 1976, 1977; Ubelaker 1974). This shift followed on the heels of an upheaval in archaeology, the New Archaeology of the 1960s and 1970s, when research emphasis turned from the description and classification of stone tools, pottery, and architecture to a concern with human behavior. This sea change set the stage for moving skeletons from archaeological site-report appendices, an afterthought to the real purpose of the work, to their being an integral part of research designs from the outset.

There is a rather obvious overlap between studies of human remains and mortuary contexts. In combination, they are informative about age and gender roles, funerary participant activities and intentions, social organization, and belief systems. Nevertheless, bioarchaeology has been criticized for an overemphasis on its "bio," or skeletal, component (Goldstein 2006). Yet such concerns, at least when centered solely on mortuary studies, are themselves too narrowly defined. The bigger objective is furthering an understanding of the entire life experiences of people in the past. Reaching that goal requires the adoption of a holistic community and regional-level perspective that incorporates inferences from a wide variety of archaeological contexts, not just what can be learned from graves, their locations, and their contents, or, indeed, bones alone.

Sampling Skeletons

Case reports of single, or perhaps a few, skeletons have always been an important part of bioarchaeology. This is especially true of paleopathology, where the identification of specific diseases, such as tuberculosis, has long been of interest (Buikstra 2019; see also Chapter 28). Much of this work focuses on outliers, a useful entrée into what lies behind the diversity of what might be found in skeletal samples. Archaeological samples are typically small – rarely numbering more than a few hundred skeletons – so infrequently occurring pathological processes, social positions, or life histories might be represented by only a few individuals, and perhaps only one of them (Stodder and Palkovich 2012). Occasionally, these remains are of known historical figures, providing an opportunity to integrate physical and documentary evidence (Knüsel et al. 2010). However, the lives of quite ordinary people are also of great interest (Mant et al. 2021; Zakrzewski 2015). They provide integrated perspectives on what people as individuals experienced, as distinct from general tendencies in skeletal or dental markers of ill-health, activity patterns, and the like, as understood through analyses of entire skeletal samples. Quite aside from what can be learned from such studies, individual life histories are important when disseminating research findings because they capture the public's attention in ways that reams of statistical data do not.

Bioarchaeological studies often focus on groups of skeletons from a cemetery or other such context. Much like the situation with other archaeological remains, inferences drawn from skeletons are based on small samples relative to the number of people who ever lived. In fact, what is known about the past is disproportionately derived from a relatively few contextually well-characterized skeletal series (e.g., Boldsen 2005a, 2005b, 2007; Klaus and Toyne 2016; Larsen et al. 2019; Milner et al. 1991).

Skeletal samples are typically derived from burials that collectively span generations or even centuries. Occasionally, however, they consist of deaths from specific events, such as battles or outbreaks of disease. Regardless of a skeletal sample's origin, defining the precise segment of society that might be represented requires a firm grasp of the archaeological context. Because cemeteries are often used by many generations of people, one must establish whether socioeconomic changes were sufficiently great to have fundamentally altered the conditions of life during the period when the skeletons accumulated.

Human remains from archaeological settings are a highly selected sample of the people who were once alive (Milner et al. 2019). That is true even when all skeletons came from a single settlement and every person was interred in one cemetery. Sample selection starts with death itself because everyone of a given age does not experience the same risk of dying. Skeletal samples are weighted toward people who, for their age, were the sickest or most prone to injury because of their behavior or occupation (DeWitte and Stojanowski 2015; Wood et al. 1992). For example, a severely malnourished person, everything else being equal, was more likely to die than someone of the same age who had access to a plentiful and nutritionally complete diet. Other deficiencies in samples come about through differential bone preservation; varied excavator skill; field project objectives where the excavation of human remains can be a low priority; and institutional curation practices, such as a retention of crania in favor of postcranial remains. Old collections, in particular, can consist of remains that from the field onward underwent a selection process that favored pathological specimens or, alternatively, supposedly representative remains, the latter reducing variation that might have once existed in the excavated skeletons.

It follows that one of the first challenges bioarchaeologists face is the definition of what precisely is studied. As with other areas of biological anthropology, designing research – that is, being able to derive reliable inferences from available evidence – requires coordination among the questions guiding the work, methods employed, and samples examined. Sample size is also a concern. Archaeological skeletal series tend to be small, with only a minority consisting of more than several hundred individuals. However, despite problems posed by relatively few skeletons, a more challenging issue is establishing the appropriateness of the sample for the research question(s) being asked. The difficulty boils down to whether skeletons – the dead – are representative of the once-living people needed to address the research goals (Saunders et al. 1995).

Uncertainty over what a group of skeletons represents highlights a rather slippery use of "population" in bioarchaeology (Boldsen et al. 2022). As a contrast to case studies, population is appropriate if it is understood that its use merely refers to inferences drawn from many skeletons, not just a handful of them. Defining what a skeletal sample represents temporally, geographically, and socially is challenging. Doing so might start with determining if the age and sex composition of the sample approximates what would be expected of the deaths that would normally accumulate over time, but the process must rapidly progress to a detailed consideration of the archaeological context. A partially excavated cemetery could mask important variation if graves were spatially segregated for any number of reasons, such as by social position. Completely excavated cemeteries could still be biased samples of a site's inhabitants if more than one burial ground was in simultaneous use. Even if the individuals who died within a particular settlement are adequately sampled, they might not be representative of those who made up the society as a whole.

In short, numerous skeletons are not necessarily an unbiased sample drawn from a group of individuals with readily defined temporal, geographical, and social boundaries. An example of where it is possible to establish who was interred is a cemetery in one of the short-lived seventeenth century Spanish missions on the south Atlantic coast of the United States (Larsen 1990; Thomas 2008). The skeletons were from a geographically circumscribed group of individuals who were members of a single tribe prior to the Spaniards' arrival. Yet not everyone was likely to have become a convert, and hence admitted to the mission cemetery. Later in the mission period the situation is even more complicated because once-separate communities coalesced and tribal affinities changed, resulting in shifts in local group composition and identity (Stojanowski 2009).

It's All about Context

Research results and their interpretation must be embedded within an appropriate cultural setting. Regardless of a particular study's objective – among others, clarifying population structure, disease experiences, and habitual activities – skeletons are interpreted in light of their archaeological context and, when available for the historic period, written sources. Delineating the appropriate cultural context can be a formidable challenge when there is little control over the sampling strategy (e.g., the sites or parts of them excavated), yet interpretations depend on knowledge about the representativeness of skeletons with regard to the group of people from which they were drawn.

There is a need to strengthen a community-level focus to characterize life experiences in the past. Community, however, is an imprecise concept that must be tailored to the realities of the research question(s) being addressed. Because culturally well-characterized skeletal samples are generally from single cemeteries, community refers to people who were predominately from one location, although the area's spatial extent might be large, perhaps encompassing more than a single settlement. The key point is that these people maintained social, political, or economic associations with one another. In small-scale societies, many, and perhaps all, members of a community shared real or fictive kin relationships (e.g., Pilloud and Larsen 2011). That would not have been true of large and organizationally complex societies where other social and economic mechanisms knit together multiple kin groups, although clusters of related people might be detectable in the arrangement of cemetery space.

Characterizing the conditions under which community members actually lived is essential, as opposed to simply referring to broad societal categories, such as hunter-gatherer, or to region-specific archaeological cultures. Çatalhöyük in Turkey, for example, illustrates the diversity in adaptations to dynamic ever-changing village life and subsistence practices within a Neolithic existence (Larsen et al. 2019). The paths to agricultural economies were long and varied, and so too were how people lived, as shown by their skeletons.

It cannot be stressed enough that skeletal samples typically reflect local social and natural settings. They are not necessarily representative of what took place more widely, no matter how narrowly defined the cultural category. For example, considerable mortality from repeated ambushes of small numbers of people in one late prehistoric village in the North American Midwest – one-third of the adults were killed in such attacks – was not necessarily typical of what took place in other contemporaneous, geographically proximate, and culturally similar societies (Milner et al. 1991).

Research Foci

Once bioarchaeological research began to gain traction, accelerating in the 1980s, the field diversified into various areas of specialization (Larsen 2015). They include topics as diverse as population structure (paleodemography); disease and trauma (paleopathology and paleoepidemiology); activity-associated modifications of bone structure (biomechanics); diet and migration (stable isotopes and trace elements); and biological relatedness as understood through skeletal morphology, dental characteristics, and ancient DNA (biodistance). Increasingly sophisticated analyses require greater quantitative skills and specific laboratory expertise, and hence an evolution in graduate student training.

Many researchers conducting different kinds of analyses have resulted in an explosion in the number of bioarchaeological publications. This growth and, more importantly, what has been learned about past people are remarkable advances in biological anthropology. In fact, our understanding of human adaptation, biological relatedness, health, diet, and life-style variation has advanced in ways that were not dreamed of just a few decades ago, but the new-found knowledge comes at a price. The integration of work to describe life in the past can suffer from a proliferation of narrowly defined areas of expertise. That leads to tightly focused papers on specific aspects of skeletal morphology or bone composition where both archaeological context and complementary research are given short shrift.

It is not easy to balance cutting-edge statistical and laboratory expertise, familiarity with field methods, a secure grasp of cultural and natural contexts, and an appreciation for why the research is undertaken in the first place. An example of such a research endeavor focuses on the medieval Danish village of Tirup, where explicit questions have been matched to appropriate samples and innovative methods (Boldsen 2005a, 2005b, 2007). One solution is the development of long-term projects featuring interdisciplinary teams that address not only what took place in individual communities but how and why life experiences changed over great periods of time, such as has been done at Neolithic Çatalhöyük (Larsen et al. 2019).

Research Objectives

Much of bioarchaeological research has focused on documenting trends in morbidity and mortality associated with major shifts in ways of life. Of particular concern are the effects on human wellbeing and lifestyles associated with the transition from foraging to farming and the development of complex societies, especially those featuring urban settings (Cohen and Armelagos 1984a; Steckel et al. 2019; Steckel and Rose 2002).

Research on human remains was initially dominated by comparisons of skeletons from individual sites, with skeletal samples regarded as exemplars of particular ways of life defined by some combination of subsistence strategy and sociopolitical organization, notably hunter-gatherer and subsistence agriculturalist. There was variable, but generally limited, control over specific community contexts. Little attention was directed toward how people actually lived in specific cultural and natural settings when classifying skeletal collections as representative of particular societal categories, such as hunter-gatherers, or by archaeological period or culture. Doing so failed to recognize the profound societal and environmental differences that existed among groups classified in such a manner. Nor did it adequately capture variation in the processes that lay behind the evolution of sociopolitical and economic systems. For example, the transition from fully hunter-gatherer to agricultural subsistence systems was long and varied wherever it took place independent of similar developments elsewhere in the world (Smith 2001).

As a means of discovering patterning among differences in life experiences that once existed, data have been compiled from large and diverse skeletal samples (Steckel et al. 2019; Steckel and Rose 2002). This work provides broad-brush characterizations of long-term trends in human biology. Many samples are needed to detect underlying tendencies because variation, not underlying sameness, should be regarded as the default within societal or archaeological categories, no matter how narrowly they might be defined.

Tightly focused and integrative community-level analyses are an alternative to general pictures of life in the past. At the community level, there is command over the details of social, economic, and environmental settings that complement skeletally derived information on age-at-death distributions, disease experience, and activity patterns. Such work highlights the complexity of human responses to ever-changing social and natural settings, as well as the diversity of life within a particular cultural category, such as the Neolithic at Çatalhöyük (Larsen et al. 2019). Multiple near-contemporaneous and culturally well-characterized communities can be investigated to identify variation within and among different segments of society, as has been done for heavy metal exposure and its relationship to social position and settlement type in medieval Denmark and northern Germany (Rasmussen et al. 2020, 2015).

Moving Forward

At this point, two approaches appear to be the especially promising. They include analyses of large numbers of communities to delineate the general outline of health, behavior, and other topics over great periods of time or large geographical areas. The second involves studies of individual and regionally based communities that provide a rich record of responses to constantly changing local conditions affecting, among others, pathogen transmission, dietary adequacy, workload, and movement across long and short distances. Research questions, although focused on furthering our understanding of the human experience, necessarily change as the scale of investigation shifts from one to many communities.

With regard to the grand narrative of human existence, comparisons of just a few sites regarded as emblematic of dramatically different ways of life should be replaced by compilations of large and diverse samples. After all, a central goal of biological anthropology is the development of an understanding of human variation. Treating a skeletal sample as representative of a category such as hunter-gatherer, an all too common approach, implies a uniformity in life experience that simply did not exist. Further progress will entail developing summary measures with a demonstrable relationship to selected features of past societies. They must accommodate shortcomings having to do with the size and biased nature of archaeological samples, as well as the requirements of extracting comparable and reliable information from mortality samples. To date, that has been done most effectively with age-distribution data that can be readily obtained from numerous studies. Notable among them are ratios consisting of two age ranges interpreted as capturing changes in fertility or age-independent mortality related to major changes in ways of life (Bocquet-Appel 2002; Bocquet-Appel et al. 2008; Paine and Boldsen 2002).

At the other end of the scale are analyses that feature a substantial and direct articulation between both skeletons and other archaeological materials, along with historical sources when available. There is a need to consider various aspects of life from different datasets because explanatory variables are unlikely to be found in solely one dimension, such as diet, sedentism, or population density (Larsen et al. 2019). Cemetery samples, after all, are local samples of deaths of people whose life histories were largely determined by local circumstances and events. The rich contextual detail serves as a counterpoint to broad-brush appraisals of general trends in human existence.

How We Got to Today

Population

Patterning in age-at-death in large and well-characterized skeletal samples provides perspectives on population structure and change that cannot be obtained from other sources. At the outset, it must be said that humans, like our primate relatives, share similarities in their life histories. What are of paleodemographic interest are the details of variation among past human groups that are related to cultural and environmental challenges to survival. Despite its potential contributions to our understanding of the human experience, the decades-long development of paleodemography has been marked by controversy. Considerable effort, which has met with mixed success, has centered on the development of age-estimation methods capable of accurate and unbiased estimates, as well as how to extract reliable information from age-at-death distributions (Bocquet-Appel and Masset 1982; Boldsen et al. 2022; Frankenberg and Konigsberg 2006; Konigsberg and Frankenberg 1994; Milner et al. 2019).

One of the more obvious questions that could be asked about age-at-death distributions is whether people in the distant past ever lived to old age (Boldsen et al. 2022; Howell 1982; Milner et al. 2019). Quite aside from an inherent interest in tracking changes in human longevity, the issue highlights a debate over the veracity of data, and hence the inferences drawn from them. Most paleodemographic studies indicate that there was considerable early adult mortality, and few peopled survived past the age of 50 years. The issue here is not life expectancy at birth, which was relatively short because of high childhood, especially infant, mortality, but how long people could be expected to live once they reached adulthood. If almost all adults died during their prime productive and reproductive years, as the overwhelming majority of paleodemographic studies indicate, critical household functions must have been frequently disrupted, with attendant increases in mortality for dependents. Few elderly people were available to help with childcare and serve as repositories of cultural knowledge. Their rarity calls into question the evolutionary significance of lengthy post-reproductive female life, the Grandmother Hypothesis (Blurton Jones et al. 2002; Hawkes et al. 1998). There is, however, an alternative explanation: the lack of skeletons said to have been from individuals older than about 50 years is a problem with skeletal age estimation. An underestimation of the ages of elderly individuals effectively hides any people who indeed lived that long, while it simultaneously inflates the number of young adults who are thought to have died.

Fortunately, quantitative methods are on the horizon that are capable of providing accurate and unbiased estimates of age throughout adulthood (Milner et al. 2021). Much remains to be learned about old-age mortality in the past, but it is likely some people lived beyond the age of 50 in the preindustrial world, notably in the small-scale societies that dominated most of the Holocene. Longer lives than anticipated from oddly truncated paleodemographic results are indicated by mortality distributions generated from ages based on transition analysis and experience, both of which permit estimates into the upper reaches of adulthood (Boldsen et al. 2022; Bullock et al. 2013; Dangvard Pedersen et al. 2020; Milner and Ferrell 2011; Wilson 2014). These paleodemographic findings are reasonably consistent with ethnographic data and demographic models, a major reason for well-deserved skepticism about skeletal age distributions (Blurton Jones et al. 2002). In short, common perceptions about the length of adult life in the distant past must be reassessed using methods that yield unbiased results.

Lifting our gaze from the structure of individual communities to the long trajectory of population growth, age-at-death data from many settings worldwide provide a perspective on the overall pace of change at regional and continental scales. Numerous skeletal samples are needed because the experiences of separate groups of people would have varied greatly, as is also true of the excavation, preservation, and reporting of human remains.

A ratio of immature skeletons relative to all skeletons, excluding those who died during the first several years of life, displays a sharp increase in early agricultural (Neolithic) societies (Bocquet-Appel 2002, 2011; Bocquet-Appel et al. 2008; Kohler and Reese 2014). It has long been recognized that where agricultural economies developed independently there was a lengthy transition spanning thousands of years separating foraging peoples from those who relied mostly on agriculture (Smith 2001). The skeletal indicator – usually interpreted as a measure of fertility, but also indicative of age-independent mortality – indicates this transformation in human existence involved, at least in part, step-like changes in the process. That is, it was not entirely, or perhaps even mostly, a gradual accumulation of incremental adjustments in how people lived. A halting process featuring periods of stasis interspersed with comparatively rapid change is consistent with Wood's (1998) MaB Rachet evolutionary model for population growth and technological innovation in preindustrial societies, which emphasizes average wellbeing and its demographic consequences. However, when viewed in terms of the entirety of hominin evolution – a process spanning several million years – agricultural societies arose both extraordinarily late and quickly. Once again, characterizations of what took place depend on one's temporal frame of reference.

Migration

People have always moved across short or long distances, one consequence being continual change in community composition. Primarily through analyses of stable isotopes, nonlocal as opposed to local people have been identified in skeletal samples (e.g., Katzenberg and Waters-Rist 2019; Knudson et al. 2012; Price et al. 2011). Although it is possible to identify people who came from somewhere other than the immediate vicinity of a cemetery, it is much harder to determine their birthplace. Doing so requires comprehensive knowledge of local and regional geochemistry, including the possible complicating effects of modern agricultural contaminants (Thomsen et al. 2021). A single site, however, tells only part of the migration story. In-migration can be identified, but not net-migration (movement both in and out). Furthermore, isotopically nonlocal people might have been members of a widely distributed, but socially cohesive, community.

Existing work, especially with stable isotopes, has made progress in showing who moved, but little has been done to identify how many did so and what happened to them afterwards. Estimating how many people moved involves not only numerous individual life histories defined through bone chemistry, but also the definition of the boundaries of the community from which the skeletons were drawn. Knowledge of migration outcomes with regard to health – for example, whether migrants experienced higher mortality than locally born people – requires estimating the risk of dying of both groups of people. If large enough samples can be obtained, a challenge in itself, one way to structure research about the health consequences for migrants relative to local people would be to adapt what has already been done for injuries (see Boldsen et al. 2015). The relative risk of dying for a group identified by a skeletal (or cultural) marker, such as a chemical indicator for migrants, can be contrasted with the remainder of the sample.

Çatalhöyük in Anatolia is one place where skeletal remains have contributed to knowledge about how households were structured, with implications about the movement of people. In this Neolithic village where the dead were interred in living spaces, heritable dental morphology, stable isotopes, and mitochondrial DNA indicate that households often consisted of biologically unrelated people (Chyleński et al. 2019; Larsen et al. 2019). This finding is supported by nuclear DNA, although community members in Neolithic settlements elsewhere in the region were often genetically related to one another (Yaka et al. 2021). Differences among otherwise similar Anatolian sites underscore the diversity in how people structured their lives and, indeed, the situationally expedient manner in which they coped with challenges to survival. Skeletons from several sites indicate greater movement as people increasingly relied on agriculture with its attendant changes in village life (Yaka et al. 2021).

Disease Experience

Furthering an understanding of the health of past peoples and its societal consequences involves recognizing specific pathological conditions in skeletal samples, estimating their prevalence among different segments of past communities, and identifying their social and biological effects. That is not as easy as it might sound because mortality samples present significant interpretive challenges for researchers interested in the lives of people in the past (DeWitte and Stojanowski 2015; Wood et al. 1992). Disease prevalence will be underestimated to the extent that bony lesions might not appear on skeletons or they are not distinctive. However, conditions acquired during a lifetime, such as tuberculosis, also push frequencies of affected skeletons in the other direction because the frailest members of each age group are the ones most likely to enter the mortality sample. Healthy people tend to survive to older ages when they too eventually die, perhaps with some illness acquired in later life that affects the skeleton.

There is a great potential, as yet largely unrealized, for adding a public health dimension to the long-standing archaeological interest in how communities were organized and functioned. Doing so – that is, moving toward paleoepidemiology – requires going beyond simple counts of skeletons with lesions (Milner and Boldsen 2017). Objectives include quantifying the experiences of various segments of communities that are identifiable by sex, social position, and pathological conditions. For example, in medieval to early modern Denmark male survivors of cranial vault trauma had a higher risk of dying than uninjured men (Boldsen et al. 2015). Healed cranial trauma serves as a proxy for something that cannot be directly observed in skeletons, namely the debilitating consequences of traumatic brain injuries. Long-lasting effects on adult mortality related to poor health experienced early in life – for skeletons, it might be marked by developmental defects in tooth enamel – have also been identified (Armelagos et al. 2009; Boldsen 2007).

Ever since the early 1980s, it has been generally believed that the transition to agriculture was accompanied by greater illness and earlier death, and another such decline in the human condition occurred with the development of societies centered on large settlements where people were concentrated (Cohen and Armelagos 1984b). Quite apart from logical and methodological problems with a universally applicable stepwise decline-in-health model, the empirical evidence indicates a more complex story. One example is the interdisciplinary work at Çatalhöyük where mobility, workload, diets, infectious diseases, and injuries varied over time as the Neolithic community responded to altered environmental conditions, subsistence-related activities, and settlement size (Larsen et al. 2019). A long, halting, and nonlinear process that over millennia resulted in a transformation in how people fed themselves, and everything that came with it, is consistent with accumulating evidence for a highly varied picture of health in past populations. Nevertheless, people who lived in large and densely packed communities and relied on domesticated plants and animals experienced challenges from infectious diseases that their mobile forager forebearers did not.

Inequality

Bioarchaeology is well situated to track inequalities among community members as societies underwent a transition from small acephalous groups to the heavily populated and organizationally complex states of the last several millennia. The latter featured a division and specialization of labor, hierarchical control of decision-making, institutions that reinforced inequality, differential access to the means of survival such as food and shelter, and residential segregation into more or less salubrious settings. These changes in the human experience are potentially measurable in archaeological skeletons through their effects on workload, pathogen exposure, dietary adequacy, injury patterns, and mortality (Larsen 2015; Mant et al. 2021). One aspect of inequality that has attracted recent bioarchaeological attention is violence. Violence experienced by certain segments of communities reflects how societies were structured, including differential rights, opportunities to redress wrongs, and access to the levers of power (Martin and Harrod 2015).

Contact between Indigenous societies and colonizing nation-states highlights what can happen when there are great disparities in power among different groups of people. Native Americans, for example, were concentrated in seventeenth century Spanish missions in the North American Southeast, where their labor was appropriated for the production of food, among other activities, required to support the newcomers (Larsen et al. 2001). In comparison to precontact settings, there was a dietary shift to less meat and more maize, an increase in dental caries accompanying a greater consumption of carbohydrate-rich food, more childhood developmental disruptions of tooth enamel, and a higher frequency of bony lesions attributable to infectious disease and poor nutrition. Long bone cross-sectional geometric properties indicate that the labor required of people changed over the course of the seventeenth century. Greater mobility is indicated for a number of males, consistent with historical sources that indicate only some men took part in long-distance travel.

Of great interest is when during the long course of human existence shifts in the material conditions of life were sufficiently great to leave detectable traces on the bodies of people of different social status. However, obtaining large and temporally equivalent samples for comparisons of low- and high-status people is difficult because social positions are often marked by separate burial locations, especially in organizationally complex societies.

Given the scattered nature of skeletal collections, especially problems with properly matching low- and high-status samples, we have only an inexact appreciation of how and when human health and wellbeing were affected by the evolution of organizationally complex societies. When looking at published results from around the world, however, it is our impression that with increasing sociopolitical complexity there is a disjunction between archaeological measures of inequality and skeletal evidence of the same. The former includes, among others, the form and location of residential structures, symbols of authority, and the quantity of elaborate objects fashioned from nonlocal materials. The skeletal evidence mainly consists of indicators of diet, disease, and trauma. For convenience, here we use as a short-hand the chiefdom societal category that is deeply embedded in anthropological studies. For archaeological materials, there are widespread, unambiguous, and consistent signs of social differentiation in the diverse societies classified as chiefdoms. For archaeological skeletons that is not always the case. To some extent, the discrepancy reflects limitations in skeletal analyses. Dietary composition, for example, estimated from isotopic studies that measure the classes of food routinely consumed (meat as well as C_3 versus C_4 photosynthetic pathway plants) might not capture the most relevant status-related distinctions, such as unequal access to food during hard times. Nevertheless, the weight of evidence, although far from ideal, indicates that from an evolutionary perspective hierarchical differentiation routinely occurred in how people distinguished themselves through signs of high rank, including arti-facts and architecture, before significant differences arose in access to the means of sus-taining life as measured by experience with infectious diseases and nutritional disorders.

Warfare

Prior to the 1990s, intergroup conflict was rarely a subject of concerted archaeological inves-tigation (Keeley 1996; LeBlanc 2020). For the small-scale societies of the distant past, skeletons provide an important means of assessing both the existence and severity of warfare. Human remains complement archaeological evidence of intergroup conflict, such as weapons, artwork, and defensive structures, notably walls around settlements. Bioarchaeological studies provide a way to determine how warfare was conducted, estimate its impact on com-munities, and identify who was most likely to become a victim (Holst et al. 2018; Knüsel and Smith 2014; Milner et al. 1991; Milner and Ferrell 2011; Schroeder et al. 2019; Willey 1990; Willey and Emerson 1993).

Semi-sedentary hunter–gatherers (Mesolithic) and village farmers (Neolithic) were often embroiled in intergroup fighting, although its intensity varied over time and space (Keeley 1996; Milner 1999; Smith et al. 2020). It is clear that the members of small mobile hunter–gatherer groups were also killed, but too few skeletons are preserved to provide a satisfac-tory picture about the prevalence of such conflict. The overall picture from archaeological sites resembles what might be expected from descriptions of warfare in historical and eth-nographic sources. Massacres of numerous people took place along with more frequent ambushes, each consisting of one or a few targets of opportunity. Both could result in con-siderable mortality, either all at once or cumulatively over time.

A 700-year-old cemetery in the North American Midwest, Norris Farms, provides one of the clearest views of the effect of ambushes on prehistoric village agriculturalists (Milner et al. 1991; Milner and Ferrell 2011). Mostly adults were killed, about one-third of them, with the sexes falling victim in roughly equal proportions. At the time of their deaths, many victims were suffering from conditions that reduced their capacity to fight or flee. When several victims were buried in a single grave, they tended to be of the same sex, presumably reflecting the composition of work parties overwhelmed by their attackers. Differential preservation and scavenger damage show that the amount of time between death and dis-covery varied greatly, which would have reflected an attack's location relative to the village. The few adults who survived were women, probably because they spent more of their time close to the village than men. Their skeletons indicate that victims sometimes managed to struggle home before succumbing to wounds or exposure.

A mass attack resulting in the deaths of many villagers took place several decades later at Crow Creek in the northern Plains (Willey 1990; Willey and Emerson 1993). The remains of hundreds of people – men, women, and children – were damaged by scavenging animals and, later, the disarticulated bones were picked up and buried in a defensive ditch surrounding the village. Some of these people showed signs of having survived earlier attacks, presumably ambushes much like what the Norris Farms villagers experienced. Archaeological evidence indicates that the Crow Creek villagers were situationally vulnerable because their palisade was being replaced when they were attacked.

Although these examples provide vivid pictures of the nature of conflict among village agriculturalists, it is also clear from the bulk of archaeological, including skeletal, information that these events did not take place everywhere, even among roughly contemporaneous and culturally similar groups in the North American Midwest and Plains (Milner et al. 2013). In fact, the weight of evidence indicates there was considerable temporal and geographical variability in the extent to which warfare was a feature of life in such societies in North America, Europe, and elsewhere. The distant past was neither a state of Hobbesian Warre nor a Rousseauian Eden, despite what the public, and some scholars, stubbornly persist in believing.

Conflict-related contexts can provide much more information than just how fighting was conducted. One such example is the first century AD Iron Age site of Alken Enge in Denmark (Holst et al. 2018). Disarticulated, weapon-damaged, and scavenger-gnawed bones of over 80 individuals, mainly young adults and mostly, or entirely, males, were deposited unceremoniously along with a few weapons in a wetland. Several times that number of people are probably represented by scattered bones at the site, since only part of it has been excavated. This unsuccessful war party must have been drawn from multiple settlements because its size is larger than what could have been mustered from archaeologically known Iron Age villages in the region. In northern Germania, well beyond the reach of Romans, there was apparently sufficient integration among communities to assemble militarily formidable groups, although things did not always go well for them.

Ancient DNA can provide entirely new perspectives on life in the past, such as what has been provided by 15 people of both sexes ranging from children to adults who had been killed and carefully buried together at Koszyce, a Neolithic site in Poland (Schroeder et al. 2019). Members of several nuclear families, part of a larger descent group, were represented, indicating that such closely related people were the basis of residential groups. There are rarely situations where it is possible to identify relationships among people who were alive at precisely the same time. In this instance, it could be done because an episode of violence was followed by group burial.

CONCLUSIONS

Although skeletons from archaeological settings are the central focus of bioarchaeological studies, they are not the primary reason for the research. The work is undertaken to enrich our appreciation of the diversity of the human experience, notably adaptive and behavioral variation, as understood through contextualized studies of life during the Holocene.

It is only natural that research questions have changed over the years, often in tandem with the development of methods that have grown in sophistication (Buikstra et al. 2022; Larsen 2015). Despite such advances, to reach its full potential bioarchaeology must tackle major challenges that, for convenience, might be divided into research needs and human resources. Among the former are developing rigorous quantitative methods to estimate past population characteristics, including their composition (see Chapter 13) and disease experience (see Chapter 11) from mortality samples, as well as expanding temporal and geographical coverages to document and interpret the variation that surely existed. Once again, we return to the central role of cultural context, namely the archaeological and historical source materials essential for the interpretation of skeletal findings. The second challenge is a need for greater diversity, inclusion, and equity among practitioners. Also essential is involving and listening to communities with a vested interest in what research findings can say about our shared human experience. Meeting these two challenges will do much to further our understanding of the long history of our species' existence and how we arrived at the world of today.

ACKNOWLEDGMENTS

We are grateful to M. Anne Katzenberg and Sonia Zakrzewski whose thoughtful comments sharpened this chapter.

REFERENCES

Angel, J. L. *The People of Lerna*. Princeton, NJ: American School of Classical Studies at Athens, 1971.

Armelagos, G. J., D. S. Carlson, and D. P. Van Gerven. "The Theoretical Foundations and Development of Skeletal Biology." In *A History of American Physical Anthropology, 1930–1980*. Edited by F. Spencer, 305–328. New York: Academic Press, 1982.

Armelagos, G. J., A. H. Goodman, K. N. Harper, and M. L. Blakey. "Enamel Hypoplasia and Early Mortality: Bioarcheological Support for the Barker Hypothesis." *Evolutionary Anthropology* 18 (2009): 261–271.

Blurton Jones, N. G., K. Hawkes, and J. F. O'Connell. "Antiquity of Postreproductive Life: Are There Modern Impacts on Hunter-Gatherer Postreproductive Life Spans?" *American Journal of Human Biology* 14 (2002): 184–205.

Bocquet-Appel, J.-P. "Paleoanthropological Traces of a Neolithic Demographic Transition." *Current Anthropology* 43 (2002): 637–650.

Bocquet-Appel, J.-P. "When the World's Population Took Off: The Springboard of the Neolithic Demographic Transition." *Science* 333 (2011): 560–561.

Bocquet-Appel, J.-P., and C. Masset. "Farewell to Paleodemography." *Journal of Human Evolution* 11 (1982): 321–333.

Bocquet-Appel, J.-P., S. Naji, and M. Bandy. "Demographic and Health Changes During the Transition to Agriculture in North America." In *Recent Advances in Palaeodemography*. Edited by J.-P. Bocquet-Appel, 277–292. Dordrecht: Springer, 2008.

Boldsen, J. L. "Analysis of Dental Attrition and Mortality in the Medieval Village of Tirup, Denmark." *American Journal of Physical Anthropology* 126 (2005a): 169–176.

Boldsen, J. L. "Leprosy and Mortality in the Medieval Danish Village of Tirup." *American Journal of Physical Anthropology* 126 (2005b): 159–168.

Boldsen, J. L. "Early Childhood Stress and Adult Age Mortality – A Study of Dental Enamel Hypoplasia in the Medieval Danish Village of Tirup." *American Journal of Physical Anthropology* 132 (2007): 59–66.

Boldsen, J. L., G. R. Milner, and S. Weise. "Cranial Vault Trauma and Selective Mortality in Medieval to Early Modern Denmark." *Proceedings of the National Academy of Sciences, USA* 112 (2015): 1721–1726.

Boldsen, J. L., G. R. Milner, and S. D. Ousley. "Paleodemography: From Archaeology and Skeletal Age Estimation to Life in the Past." *Yearbook of Biological Anthropology* 178, Suppl. 74 (2022): 115–150.

Buikstra, J. E. *Hopewell in the Lower Illinois Valley.* Scientific Papers, 2. Evanston: Northwestern University Archeological Program, 1976.

Buikstra, J. E. "Biocultural Implications of Archeological Study: A Regional Perspective." In *Biocultural Adaptation in Prehistoric America.* Edited by R. L. Blakely, 67–84. Athens: University of Georgia Press, 1977.

Buikstra, J. E., ed. *Ortner's Identification of Pathological Conditions in Human Skeletal Remains,* 3rd edn. London: Academic Press, 2019.

Buikstra, J. E., and L. A. Beck, eds. *Bioarchaeology: The Contextual Analysis of Human Remains.* Amsterdam: Academic Press, 2006.

Buikstra, J. E., S. N. DeWitte, S. C. Agarwal, et al. "Twenty-First Century Bioarchaeology: Taking Stock and Moving Forward." *Yearbook of Biological Anthropology* 178, Suppl. 74 (2022): 54–114.

Bullock, M., L. Márquez, P. Hernández, et al. "Paleodemographic Age-at-Death Distributions of Two Mexican Skeletal Collections: A Comparison of Transition Analysis and Traditional Aging Methods." *American Journal of Physical Anthropology* 152 (2013): 67–78.

Charles, D. K. "Grave Concerns: The Intersection of Biological and Social Approaches to the Archaeology of Cemeteries". In *The Dead Tell Tales: Essays in Honor of Jane E. Buikstra.* Edited by M. C. Lozada and B. O'Donnabhain, 16–23. Monograph, 76. Los Angeles: Cotsen Institute of Archaeology Press, 2013.

Chyleński, M., E. Ehler, M. Somel, et al. "Ancient Mitochondrial Genomes Reveal the Absence of Maternal Kinship in the Burials of Çatalhöyük People and Their Genetic Affinities." *Genes* 10 (2019): 207.

Cohen, M. N., and G. J. Armelagos, eds. *Paleopathology at the Origins of Agriculture.* Orlando: Academic Press, 1984a.

Cohen, M. N., and G. J. Armelagos. "Paleopathology at the Origins of Agriculture: Editor's Summation." In *Paleopathology at the Origins of Agriculture.* Edited by M. N. Cohen and G. J. Armelagos, 585–601. Orlando: Academic Press, 1984b.

Dangvard Pedersen, D., P. Tarp, M. Søvsø, et al. "A Millennium of Population Change in Pre-Modern Danish Ribe." *Anthropologischer Anzeiger* 77 (2020): 13–25.

DeWitte, S. N., and C. M. Stojanowski. "The Osteological Paradox 20 Years Later: Past Perspectives, Future Directions." *Journal of Archaeological Research* 23 (2015): 397–450.

Frankenberg, S. R., and L. W. Konigsberg. "A Brief History of Paleodemography from Hooton to Hazards Analysis." In *Bioarchaeology: The Contextual Analysis of Human Remains.* Edited by J. E. Buikstra and L. A. Beck, 227–261. Amsterdam: Academic Press, 2006.

Goldstein, L. G. "Mortuary Analysis and Bioarchaeology." In *Bioarchaeology: The Contextual Analysis of Human Remains.* Edited by J. E. Buikstra and L. A. Beck, 375–387. Amsterdam: Academic Press, 2006.

Hawkes, K., J. F. O'Connell, N. G. Blurton Jones, et al. "Grandmothering, Menopause, and the Evolution of Human Life Histories." *Proceedings of the National Academy of Sciences, USA* 95 (1998): 1336–1339.

Holst, M. K., J. Heinemeicr, E. Hertz, et al. "Direct Evidence of a Large Northern European Roman Period Martial Event and Postbattle Corpse Manipulation." *Proceedings of the National Academy of Sciences, USA* 115 (2018): 5920–5925.

Howell, N. "Village Composition Implied by a Paleodemographic Life Table: The Libben Site." *American Journal of Physical Anthropology* 59 (1982): 263–269.

Katzenberg, M. A., and A. L. Waters-Rist. "Stable Isotope Analysis: A Tool for Studying Past Diet, Demography, and Life History." In *Biological Anthropology of the Human Skeleton,* 3rd edn. Edited by M. A. Katzenberg and A. L. Grauer, 469–504. Hoboken, NJ: Wiley-Blackwell, 2019.

Keeley, L. H. *War Before Civilization.* Oxford: Oxford University Press, 1996.

Klaus, H. D., and J. M. Toyne, eds. *Ritual Violence in the Ancient Andes: Reconstructing Sacrifice on the North Coast of Peru.* Austin: University of Texas Press, 2016.

Knudson, K. J., W. J. Pestle, C. Torres-Rouff, et al. "Assessing the Life History of an Andean Traveler Through Biogeochemistry: Stable and Radiogenic Isotope Analyses of Archaeological Human Remains from Northern Chile." *International Journal of Osteoarchaeology* 22 (2012): 435–451.

Knüsel, C. J., and M. J. Smith, eds. *The Routledge Handbook of the Bioarchaeology of Human Conflict.* New York: Routledge, 2014.

Knüsel, C. J., C. M. Batt, G. Cook, et al. "The Identity of the St Bees Lady, Cumbria: An Osteobiographical Approach." *Medieval Archaeology* 54 (2010): 271–311.

Kohler, T. A., and K. M. Reese. "Long and Spatially Variable Neolithic Demographic Transition in the North American Southwest." *Proceedings of the National Academy of Sciences, USA* 111 (2014): 10101–10106.

Konigsberg, L. W., and S. R. Frankenberg. "Paleodemography: 'Not Quite Dead'." *Evolutionary Anthropology* 3 (1994): 92–105.

Larsen, C. S., ed. *The Archaeology of Mission Santa Catalina de Guale: 2. Biocultural Interpretations of a Population in Transition.* Anthropological Papers, 68. New York: American Museum of Natural History, 1990.

Larsen, C. S. *Bioarchaeology: Interpreting Behavior from the Human Skeleton,* 2nd edn. Cambridge: Cambridge University Press, 2015.

Larsen, C. S., M. C. Griffin, D. L. Hutchinson, et al. "Frontiers of Contact: Bioarchaeology of Spanish Florida." *Journal of World Prehistory* 15 (2001): 69–123.

Larsen, C. S., C. J. Knüsel, S. D. Haddow, et al. "Bioarchaeology of Neolithic Çatalhöyük Reveals Fundamental Transitions in Health, Mobility, and Lifestyle in Early Farmers." *Proceedings of the National Academy of Sciences, USA* 116 (2019): 12615–12623.

LeBlanc, S. "The Origins of Warfare and Violence." In *The Cambridge World History of Violence,* Vol. 1. Edited by G. G. Fagan, L. Fibiger, M. Hudson, and M. Trundle, 39–57. Cambridge: Cambridge University Press, 2020.

Mant, M., C. de la Cova, and M. B. Brickley. "Intersectionality and Trauma Analysis in Bioarchaeology." *American Journal of Physical Anthropology* 174 (2021): 583–594.

Martin, D. L., and R. P. Harrod. "Bioarchaeological Contributions to the Study of Violence." *Yearbook of Physical Anthropology* 156 (2015): 116–145.

Milner, G. R. "Warfare in Prehistoric and Early Historic Eastern North America." *Journal of Archaeological Research* 7 (1999): 105–151.

Milner, G. R., and J. L. Boldsen. "Life Not Death: Epidemiology from Skeletons." *International Journal of Paleopathology* 17 (2017): 26–39.

Milner, G. R., and R. J. Ferrell. "Conflict and Death in a Late Prehistoric Community in the American Midwest." *Anthropologischer Anzeiger* 68 (2011): 415–436.

Milner, G. R., E. Anderson, and V. G. Smith. "Warfare in Late Prehistoric West-Central Illinois." *American Antiquity* 56 (1991): 581–603.

Milner, G. R., G. Chaplin, and E. Zavodny. "Conflict and Societal Change in Late Prehistoric Eastern North America." *Evolutionary Anthropology* 22 (2013): 96–102.

Milner, G. R., J. W. Wood, and J. L. Boldsen. "Paleodemography: Problems, Progress, and Potential." In *Biological Anthropology of the Human Skeleton,* 3rd edn. Edited by M. A. Katzenberg and A. L. Grauer, 593–633. Hoboken, NJ: Wiley-Blackwell, 2019.

Milner, G. R., J. L. Boldsen, S. D. Ousley, et al. "Great Expectations: The Rise, Fall, and Resurrection of Adult Skeletal Age Estimation." In *Remodeling Forensic Skeletal Age.* Edited by B. F. B. Algee-Hewitt and J. Kim, 139–154. London: Academic Press, 2021.

Paine, R. R., and J. L. Boldsen. "Linking Age-at-Death Distributions and Ancient Population Dynamics: A Case Study." In *Paleodemography: Age Distributions from Skeletal Samples.* Edited by R. D. Hoppa and J. W. Vaupel, 169–180. Cambridge: Cambridge University Press, 2002.

Pilloud, M. A., and C. S. Larsen. "'Official' and 'Practical' Kin: Inferring Social and Community Structure from Dental Phenotype at Neolithic Çatalhöyük, Turkey." *American Journal of Physical Anthropology* 145 (2011): 519–530.

Price, T. D., K. M. Frei, L. E. Wright, et al. "Who Was in Harold Bluetooth's Army? Strontium Isotope Investigation of the Cemetery at the Viking Age Fortress at Trelleborg, Denmark." *Antiquity* 85 (2011): 476–489.

Rasmussen, K. L., L. Skytte, A. J. Jensen, et al. "Comparison of Mercury and Lead Levels in the Bones of Rural and Urban Populations in Southern Denmark and Northern Germany during the Middle Ages." *Journal of Archaeological Science: Reports* 3 (2015): 358–370.

Rasmussen, K. L., G. R. Milner, T. Delbey, et al. "Copper Exposure in Medieval and Post-Medieval Denmark and Northern Germany: Its Relationship to Residence Location and Social Position." *Heritage Science* 8 (2020): 18.

Saunders, S. R., A. Herring, L. A. Sawchuk, et al. "The Nineteenth-Century Cemetery at St. Thomas' Anglican Church, Belleville: Skeletal Remains, Parish Records and Censuses." In *Grave Reflections: Portraying the Past Through Cemetery Studies.* Edited by S. R. Saunders and A. Herring, 93–117. Toronto: Canadian Scholars' Press, 1995.

Schroeder, H., A. Margaryan, M. Szmyt, et al. "Unraveling Ancestry, Kinship, and Violence in a Late Neolithic Mass Grave." *Proceedings of the National Academy of Sciences, USA* 116 (2019): 10705–10710.

Smith, B. D. "Low-Level Food Production." *Journal of Archaeological Research* 9 (2001): 1–43.

Smith, M., R. J. Schulting, and L. Fibiger. "Settled Lives, Unsettled Times: Neolithic Violence in Europe." In *Cambridge World History of Violence.* Edited by G. Fagan, L. Fibiger, M. Hudson, and M. Trundle, 79–98. Cambridge: Cambridge University Press, 2020.

Steckel, R. H., and J. C. Rose, eds. *The Backbone of History: Health and Nutrition in the Western Hemisphere.* Cambridge: Cambridge University Press, 2002.

Steckel, R. H., C. S. Larsen, C. A. Roberts, and J. Baten, eds. *The Backbone of Europe: Health, Diet, Work, and Violence over Two Millennia.* Cambridge: Cambridge University Press, 2019.

Stodder, A. L. W., and A. M. Palkovich, eds. *The Bioarchaeology of Individuals.* Gainesville: University Press of Florida, 2012.

Stojanowski, C. M. "Bridging Histories: The Bioarchaeology of Identity in Postcontact Florida." In *Bioarchaeology and Identity in the Americas.* Edited by K. J. Knudson and C. M. Stojanowski, 59–81. Gainesville: University Press of Florida, 2009.

Thomas, D. H., ed. *Native American Landscapes of St. Catherines Island, Georgia,* 3 vols. Anthropological Papers, 88. New York: American Museum of Natural History, 2008.

Thomsen, E., R. Andreasen, and T. L. Rasmussen. "Homogeneous Glacial Landscapes Can Have High Local Variability in Strontium Isotope Signatures: Implications for Prehistoric Migration Studies." *Frontiers of Ecology and Evolution* 8 (2021): 588318.

Ubelaker, D. H. *"Reconstruction of Demographic Profiles from Ossuary Skeletal Samples: A Case Study from the Tidewater Potomac."* In *Smithsonian Contributions to Anthropology,* vol. 18. Washington, DC: Smithsonian Institution Press, 1974.

Willey, P. S. *Prehistoric Warfare on the Great Plains: Skeletal Analysis of the Crow Creek Massacre Victims.* New York: Garland, 1990.

Willey, P. S., and T. E. Emerson. "The Osteology and Archaeology of the Crow Creek Massacre." *Plains Anthropologist* 38 (1993): 227–269.

Wilson, J. J. "Paradox and Promise: Research on the Role of Recent Advances in Paleodemography and Paleoepidemiology to the Study of 'Health' in Precolumbian Societies." *American Journal of Physical Anthropology* 155 (2014): 268–280.

Wood, J. W. "A Theory of Preindustrial Population Dynamics." *Current Anthropology* 39 (1998): 99–135.

Wood, J. W., G. R. Milner, H. C. Harpending, and K. M. Weiss. "The Osteological Paradox: Problems of Inferring Prehistoric Health from Skeletal Samples." *Current Anthropology* 33 (1992): 343–370.

Yaka, R., I Mapelli, D. Kaptan, et al. "Variable Kinship Patterns in Neolithic Anatolia Revealed by Ancient Genomes." *Current Biology* 31 (2021): 1–14.

Zakrzewski, S. "'Behind Every Mask There Is a Face, and Behind That a Story.' Egyptian Bioarchaeology and Ancient Identities." In *Egyptian Bioarchaeology: Humans, Animals, and the Environment.* Edited by S. Ikram, J. Kaiser, and R. Walker, 157–167. Leiden: Sidestone Press, 2015.

CHAPTER 28

Paleopathology: A Twenty-first Century Perspective

Jane E. Buikstra

INTRODUCTION

In studying ancient disease, bioanthropologists focus on two lines of evidence – primary and secondary (Roberts 2002: 3). The former includes skeletal remains, mummified tissues, and clinical studies of pathological conditions. Secondary sources encompass iconographic representations, documents, archaeologically recovered non-primary materials, and ethnographic information from traditional living groups. This chapter will emphasize primary sources, while also including products of human alimentary processes (coprolites/colon contents) and ancient organisms associated with remains (microorganisms/parasites).

Frequently attributed to the French physician and Egyptologist, Sir Marc Armand Ruffer, the term "paleopathology" was coined by the American physician, Robert Wilson Schufeldt, in an 1892 article published in *Popular Science Monthly*. Schufeldt emphasized a broad-based paleopathology: the study of pathological conditions in any extinct or fossil organism (Cook and Powell 2006). Over time, however, the subject and its practitioners have increasingly focused upon the human condition. As noted later in this chapter, however, animal paleopathology has seen renewed interest, and an inclusive "ONE Paleopathology" approach has been proposed.

"Paleopathology" is frequently glossed as "the study of ancient disease," a seemingly elegant and straightforward characterization that nonetheless requires clarification of the terms "disease" and "ancient." "Disease" is generally defined as "an impairment of health or a condition of abnormal functioning" (wordnet. princeton.edu/perl/webwn). Thus, paleopathologists study not only infectious diseases, but also myriad other conditions that affect health, such as the arthropathies (diseases of joints), congenital anomalies, circulatory, endocrine, growth (dysplasias), hematological and metabolic disorders, oral pathologies, neoplastic conditions, and trauma. Length constraints necessarily limit discussion here to recent advances in studying ancient disease, referring the interested reader to excellent comprehensive texts by Aufderheide and Rodríguez-Martín (1998), Buikstra (2019), and Roberts and Manchester (2005).

A Companion to Biological Anthropology, Second Edition. Edited by Clark Spencer Larsen.
© 2023 John Wiley & Sons Ltd. Published 2023 by John Wiley & Sons Ltd.

The term "ancient" might imply that paleopathology focuses exclusively upon archaeological and historical contexts. This is not the case. As the Paleopathology Association motto states, "*Mortui viventes docent*" – the dead teach the living, symbolizing the growing number of examples wherein the deep time perspective offered by paleopathology meaningfully informs contemporary medical science. The following transdisciplinary[1] examples illustrate this point.

TRANSDISCIPLINARITY IN PALEOPATHOLOGY

The third decade of the twenty-first century will no doubt be known as the gateway to the "COVID-19 Era," a result of the pandemic caused by the SARS CoV-2 virus. We have much to learn from past pandemics as we engage with our contemporary example (DeWitte 2016, 2019; DeWitte and Wissler 2022). One important lesson is that pandemics should be conceptualized as long-term processes, whose impact is tempered by prior conditions, with outcomes that can vary significantly, depending upon political, economic, and environmental factors. Public health measures that ensure effective responses and health care delivery can figure as heavily as biomedical advances, such as vaccine development. Morbidity and mortality directly depend upon individuals mounting effective immune responses, which are heavily influenced by life history stressors that begin in the womb. Proactive initiatives to reduce global poverty and to encourage trust in responsible leadership and science would also be significant steps in protecting humankind from pandemics that will doubtless threaten our future.

Twentieth century archival tissue samples and frozen remains from the 1918–1919 "Spanish 'flu" pandemic, which killed an estimated 40–50 million people, have served to anchor ancient DNA (aDNA) studies of the deadly, causative virus. Results indicate that this influenza strain is intermediate between mammals and birds, having been transmitted to mammals only shortly before 1918. Such pioneering paleopathological research led to complete sequencing and facilitated the development of antiviral drugs and vaccines (Drancourt and Raoult 2005; Reid et al. 1999).

Archaeological skeletons have been studied to assess whether abnormal bone loss (osteopenia) and bone loss leading to increased risk of fractures (osteoporosis) are very recent phenomena attributable to contemporary lifestyles or if today's patterns extend into deep time (Brickley et al. 2020). Bioarchaeological and historical evidence for nineteenth century London, for example, identifies patterns of age-related bone loss and osteoporosis being similar to today (Brickley 2002). By contrast, Medieval (eleventh–sixteenth century) remains from North Yorkshire, United Kingdom, present age-related bone loss distinctly different from more recent historical and contemporary models (Agarwal et al. 2004). These and other comparative studies help inform our contemporary perspective on osteopenia and osteoporosis (https://asu.zoom.us/j/4524736341https://asu.zoom.us/j/4524736341https://asu.zoom.us/j/4524736341). They also assist us in appreciating variability across our species (Agarwal 2021).

Similarly, evaluating the nature of past neoplastic processes, especially for malignant conditions (cancers) holds potential for assessing the degree to which cancer is a recent phenomenon. Such knowledge will help us consider how today's lifestyle choices, environmental conditions, and industrialization have fostered an increasingly carcinogenic world (Kirkpatrick et al. 2018). Presently, however, there is little consensus on the manner in which cancer rates in the past should be estimated; this important topic requires further thought and refining (Marques 2022; Marques et al. 2021). Thus, while today's medical science would be usefully informed concerning cancer risk in the past, the important paleo-pathological research topic is still a subject of debate.

American Indian tribes, such as the Omaha, are interested in how recent dietary changes have affected their risk of disease. The Omaha Tribe and physical anthropologist Karl Reinhard have collaborated in research centered upon ancestral Omaha human remains. The Omaha have been particularly interested in Reinhard and colleagues' dietary and activity reconstructions, indicating that the current high diabetes rates among the Omaha result from recent changes in lifestyle (Reinhard et al. 2012).

Expanding upon Ruffer's 1911 studies of blood vessels in ancient Egyptian mummies, the Horus Study Team (Thompson et al. 2013) has investigated atherosclerosis in a global sample of mummies. The researchers conclude that this condition was common in ancient peoples, including preindustrial hunter-gatherers. The paleopathological finding that atherosclerosis is not a modern disease raises issues concerning measures for reducing risk in contemporary groups and well illustrates the importance of using the archaeological record as a natural laboratory for investigating predisposing factors.

Studies of climate change, such as those reported by Robbins Schug (2020), frequently use health as a measure of resilience. These studies illustrate the diversity of human responses to major stressors, including the sequelae of climate change. As they document myriad biocultural responses, they also reaffirm that there are no easy solutions to the challenges attendant to climate change. Neither violence nor migrations are inevitable outcomes. Resilience responses depend upon numerous factors, as relevant to researchers as they are to policy-makers.

These are but a few examples that illustrate why studying disease in deep time has relevance for contemporary global health. The remainder of this chapter focuses upon recent developments in the study of ancient diseases, beginning by briefly embedding today's research in historical contexts and then considering both invasive and noninvasive methods for observing disease in human remains, including standardized gross descriptions, computerization, imaging, histology, and molecular approaches. Following a discussion of three specific, bone-seeking infectious diseases in a co-evolutionary perspective, an example of recent changes in disease diagnosis is considered, followed by global comparative evaluations of population health, which are based primarily upon markers of nonspecific stress. We next address the rapidly developing field of mummy science and the related topic of paleo-parasitology. Other subjects of salience, including animal disease, disability and identity, violence, and ethics are also considered. We then briefly consider the way interdisciplinary communication and collaboration are encouraged through professional associations, journals, and congresses and close by exploring likely future directions for paleopathology.

History

Although eighteenth century Renaissance scholars identified diseases in excavated bones of animals such as elephants, amphibians, cave bears, hyenas, as well as humans, the first systematic studies of ancient disease date to the nineteenth century (Aufderheide and Rodríguez-Martín 1998; Cook and Powell 2006), primarily as initiatives by medical doctors and anatomists who were focused upon documenting human morphological variation. Trauma, cranial deformation, arthropathies, infectious disease, congenital anomalies, and tumors were, however, reported by the end of the nineteenth century (Buikstra 2006). Among the first systematic studies that focused specifically upon disease in ancient communities were those of Joseph Jones, who explored evidence for syphilis in pre-Columbian American remains (Cook and Powell 2006). At the turn of the twentieth century, Sir Marc Armand Ruffer (1859–1917) commenced pioneering studies of Egyptian materials, including mummified remains, which set a high standard for future researchers (Sandison 1967). For much of the subsequent half century, however, there were few significant advances in the study of ancient disease. Medical historian Saul Jarcho (1966) criticized paleopathologists for failing to (1) develop deep syntheses, (2) generate truly significant contributions, (3) promote communication between medical scientists and anthropologists, (4) advance the scientific study of mummies, and (5) create systematic data retrieval systems, registries, or topical indices. The profession has responded to such concerns, as demonstrated in contemporary paleopathology, discussed in the remainder of this chapter.

Striking A Balance: Case Studies, Disease Diagnosis, and Population Health in Comparative Perspective

Studies of ancient disease fall into four categories: (1) methodological and technological advances; (2) case studies, which are detailed descriptions of individual or small numbers of remains with the goal of providing new information to facilitate differential diagnoses or to provide new evidence concerning temporal or geographic distributions in the past; (3) specific diseases, including identification, comparisons across time and space, and host–parasite co-evolution; and (4) population health, consisting of characterizations and comparisons. Each will be considered in turn, first considering the relative value of these four subjects, in response to recent critiques.

Armelagos and van Gerven (2003) and Armelagos (2003) have argued for a problem-oriented paleopathology, explicitly contrasting this approach with a field driven by biomedical or clinical interests in disease diagnoses and distributions in time and space. Similarly, they assert that technical advances have encouraged method-driven approaches and that description is all too common (categories 1–3 above). They favor biocultural studies of population health (category 4 above). In this chapter, we advocate for balance and rigor (Appleby et al. 2015; Buikstra 2017), noting the remarkable impact of methodological advances in imaging, histology, and especially molecular approaches. As Mays (2009) has argued, case studies have an important role in paleopathology if they extend knowledge of a condition by time or space, contribute substantially to ongoing debate in the field, hold local historical or cultural significance, or provide key information concerning a condition not well described in current texts. A model case study by Lagia et al. (2007) of a documented case of thalassemia from Greece fulfills most of Mays' criteria. The study of ancient rare diseases, illustrated in a series of papers organized by Julia Gresky and Emmanuele Petiti (2021), demonstrates a rigorous approach that bridges case studies and population-based approaches.

Assumptions and Methodologies

In interpreting ancient disease, certain assumptions about the relationship between ancient and modern conditions are necessary, specifically that the two are sufficiently similar for a contemporary label to be used. In certain cases, this is easily justified, as in healed fractures and benign tumors. In less obvious examples, a rigorous protocol for observation and interpretation of abnormal tissue changes must be applied.

Studies of ancient disease necessarily begin with distinguishing evidence of pathology from postmortem (taphonomic) changes. Next, using standard terminology, paleopathologists generate descriptions of abnormal changes observed grossly, through imaging techniques, and by invasive methods, such as histology and molecular biology. Comprehensive protocols applying standardized terminology to gross observations have been advanced by Buikstra and Ubelaker (1994) and modified by Brickley and McKinley (2004) and the "History of Health in Europe" Project (Roberts et al. 2019; Steckel et al. 2019). Databases that facilitate data recording and analysis have been developed from such protocols. For example, the Repatriation Office of the National Museum of Natural History has developed a comprehensive data entry system based on that of Buikstra and Ubelaker (1994). This relational database (*Osteoware*), freely available, includes a module on pathology (https://naturalhistory.si.edu/research/anthropology/programs/repatriation-office/osteoware). In the UK, more than 17,000 skeletons held by the Museum of London have been entered into the Wellcome Osteological Research Database (or WORD, https://www.museumoflondon.org.uk/collections/other-collection-databases-and-libraries/centre-human-bioarchaeology/osteological-database). Pathology is part of this comprehensive database, which emphasizes both description and subsequent classification as congenital, infectious, joint disease, traumatic, metabolic, endocrine, neoplastic, or circulatory (White 2008).

In developing differential diagnoses, paleopathologists commonly follow either a clinical, case-based approach or an epidemiological strategy. The former is illustrated in paleopathology texts; the latter take several forms. In adapting clinical evidence, as Mays (2018; see also Klaus 2017; Klaus and Lynnerup 2019; Lynnerup and Klaus 2019) emphasizes, pattern-matching with images or descriptions is widely used in differential diagnoses, but understanding pathophysiological processes is essential. One epidemiological perspective involves explicitly adding demographic and contextual lines of evidence to differential diagnoses, including pattern fit and key diagram models (Buikstra et al. 2017). The first is suitable for conditions that have high population prevalence, such as treponemal disease in ancient North America; the second is appropriate for relatively rare conditions, such as ancient tuberculosis. Researchers have also explicitly adapted epidemiological models to discussion of disease prevalence (Pinhasi and Turner 2008; Waldron 2007).

Noninvasive methods available to enhance diagnostic specificity include sophisticated imaging strategies drawn from the biomedical sciences, a tradition begun with the study of human and animal mummies within a year after Röntgen's development of the X-ray in 1895 (Aufderheide 2003). X-ray radiography (flat screen) continues to be used to investigate disease in ancient bones and mummified materials, having been joined by other methods, including computerized tomography (CT) and magnetic resonance imaging (MRI) (Villa et al. 2019). Micro-CT is also appropriate for the study of materials less than 14 cm in diameter, providing pixel images in the micrometer range (Saab et al. 2008). Brain tissue from the mummy Nakht has been explored through both CT and Micro-CT scans (Chhem 2008), for example, while sixteenth century rheumatoid arthritis has been identified in a mummy from Italy through CT (Ciranni et al. 2002).

In imaging mummies, experimentation with MRI is a welcome advancement. Thus far, results have been mixed, as basic MRI techniques require rehydration of desiccated tissues and are inappropriate for dry bone. Recently, however, MRI studies of dry brain tissue (Karlik et al. 2007) and full mummies (Rühli et al. 2007) using ultra-short-echo time (UTE-MRI) suggest that MRI may be adapted to studies in paleopathology. MRI can be considered a complement to CT, having potential to isolate the nature of mummification methods in ancient Egyptian remains and appearing to function quite well in imaging

Korean mummies from fifteenth–nineteenth century Joseon Dynasty tombs (Giovannetti et al. 2016; Shin et al. 2010).

The challenge in applying such high-tech approaches, however, is to move past the exploratory phase to the generation of new knowledge of past disease in a rigorous, scientific manner, addressing issues relating to health in past societies. As O'Brien et al. (2009) discovered in their survey of CT studies, 65 percent were driven by curiosity rather than clearly articulated research questions or hypotheses. Disappointingly, a third of the authors failed to describe their protocols in sufficient detail for the results to be reproduced by other workers.

Another noninvasive method for studying mummies is endoscopy, whereby a flexible fiberglass tube with a lens at the distal end is inserted through a small aperture (~2 cm in diameter) into the body. Images are transmitted both to the operator and a video screen. Endoscopic methods have been used to identify various conditions, including true disease remnants such as hydatid cysts and pneumoconiosis, along with artifacts of the embalming process. Although this method is considered noninvasive, it may require creating a small incision in the skin through which the tube is inserted. In addition, there is the risk of damaging brittle tissues as the endoscope traverses the body (Aufderheide 2003; Lynnerup 2019).

Two invasive methods, paleohistology and ancient DNA (aDNA) analysis, also enhance current studies in paleopathology. Histological methods were first applied to the study of early disease during in the nineteenth century, with the term "paleohistology" coined by Moodie (1923a). While these early methods favored decalcification and embedding bone in paraffin, contemporary techniques for hard tissues utilize different embedding agents such as epoxy resins and light microscopy (Schultz 2011). This approach has been employed in case studies of various diseases that disrupt remodeling processes, such as osteomyelitis, tumors, osteopetrosis, metabolic diseases, infectious diseases, and Paget's disease, as well as for population-based inferences (Crowder and Stout 2011; Grupe and Garland 1993; Stout et al. 2019). Histological studies of desiccated soft tissues complement osteological investigations. As summarized by Aufderheide (2003: 373–374), diagnoses of various conditions, unapproachable in skeletonized remains, have been strengthened through paleohistological study of mummified soft tissues, including anthracosis, cirrhosis, colon adenocarconima, pneumonia, and silicate pneumoconiosis.

Molecular methods have produced significant results in the study of ancient pathogen DNA. Researchers have reported aDNA for the pathogens that cause Chagas' disease, influenza, leprosy, malaria, plague, bilharzia, syphilis, trench fever, tuberculosis, typhoid fever, and various endo- and ecto-parasites (Nieves-Colón and Stone 2019; Orlando et al. 2021; Stone and Ozga 2019).

INFECTIOUS DISEASE AND HUMAN HOST–PATHOGEN RELATIONSHIPS

Did Columbus discover venereal syphilis along with the riches of the Americas, returning with it to Europe at the wane of the fifteenth century? When this question, a seeming preoccupation of paleopathologists and the public alike, was posed to eminent paleopathologist Donald Ortner (2005: xix–xx), he opined that he would rather focus upon how the treponematoses inform our understanding of human host/pathogen co-evolution, emphasizing that ancient human remains provide a "powerful source of information."

Host–pathogen co-evolution has indeed emerged center stage in the study of infectious diseases. With the "molecular revolution" has come a new appreciation for the intricate balance struck by pathogens and how they may evolve new adaptive mechanisms over time. Here, we concentrate upon three of the infectious diseases that affect bone and have long co-evolved with our species: treponematosis, tuberculosis, and leprosy. Rather than describing bony changes, as these are thoroughly described in paleopathology texts, this discussion will emphasize current knowledge concerning the history of these diseases in relationship to the human condition.

A recent, multiscalar synthesis of information relevant to the natural history of treponematosis (Baker et al. 2020) moves beyond the perennial preoccupation of origins to address broad evolutionary questions while also encouraging researchers to focus upon the individual impact of these infections across the broad landscape of human history. Importantly, the authors conclude that pathophysiological syphilis, yaws, and bejel (endemic syphilis) are caused by a single species of pathogen, *Treponema pallidum*. While the recovery of ancient treponemal DNA remains challenging, high-throughput methods have, for example, permitted the reconstruction of four ancient, highly diverse genomes from early Modern Europe, including syphilis, yaws, and an unknown genome (Majander et al. 2020). Majander and colleagues argue for a pre-Colombian presence of *T. pallidum* in Europe.

A spectacular development has been the generation of phylogenetic models that push the origins of *M. tuberculosis* into deep time, perhaps 35,000 to 2.5–30 mya, with the human pathogen being older than *M. bovis* (Brosch et al. 2002; Gagneux and Small 2007). Prevailing wisdom had been that the zoonotic, bovine form adapted to humans from intensified animal husbandry in the Eastern Mediterranean approximately 10,000 years ago, an assertion supported by considerable archaeological evidence (Roberts and Buikstra 2003). Startling is twenty-first century evidence that human–*M. tuberculosis* (or a progenitor strain) relationships developed in Africa with an archaic human species, moving then to South and Southeast Asia. Sometime during this process, selection for a virulent form led to the European strain that moved thence from Europe during the Era of Exploration across the globe, swamping the indigenous American *M. tuberculosis*, which had entered the hemisphere transmitted to human by seals, who acquired the pathogen in Africa and transmitted it to coastal communities in eastern South America (Bos et al. 2014).

While an African origin for tuberculosis is now accepted (Stone and Ozga 2019; Stone et al. 2009), the course taken by leprosy is far less clear. There appears to have an ancient division between two species, *M. leprae* and *M. lepromatosis*, with divergence times estimated to be around 14 million years ago. *M. lepromatosis* is found today in the Americas and has not been identified in archaeological materials, thus leaving its history enigmatic. Variation in contemporary and ancient *M. leprae* genomes is much better documented than the American form (Krause-Kyora et al. 2018; Schuenemann et al. 2018, Stone and Ogza 2019). Considerable genomic diversity in Medieval Europe has led Schuenemann and co-workers (2018) to propose either a western Eurasian origin for leprosy or multiple introductions from varied sources. Still unresolved is a possible co-evolutionary relationship between tuberculosis and leprosy, especially the proposed cross-immunity between the two diseases with the rise of tuberculosis in Europe during Medieval times (Mancheser 1984; Roberts 2020).

METABOLIC DISEASE

The metabolic diseases, including rickets, osteomalacia, scurvy, the anemias, Paget's disease, and osteopetrosis, require the full set of paleopathological skills for recognition, differential diagnosis, and interpretation. The limited set of ways bones can respond to genetic and external challenges is fully represented, as skeletal structures may resorb, change shape, coarsen, and add bone in abnormal ways. Conditions may express differently based upon age at insult, while one biological sex may be more at risk than the other. Pattern matching will not resolve alternative diagnoses; the researcher must be knowledgeable about the pathophysiology of each disease, along with detailed familiarity with archaeological and historical contexts. That said, important steps have been taken to resolve thorny issues of differential diagnosis and rigorous ways to interpret cranial porosities, as exemplified in recent contributions by Brickley (2018), Mays and Brickley (2018), Brickley and Mays (2019), Brickley et al. (2020), and Crandall and Klaus (2014). Along with methodological advancements, studies are addressing important issues about childhood health. Why did rickets, for example, increase markedly in post-medieval Europe? Other problem-oriented studies have identified adults who died suffering from scurvy, such as sailors, workhouse inmates during the Great Irish Potato Famine, and early European colonists in North America (Mays 2014).

GLOBAL HEALTH

The 1984 landmark publication *Paleopathology at the Origins of Agriculture* (Cohen and Armelagos 1984) wedded archaeological interest in exploring the mechanisms that stimulated agricultural intensification with the study of "nonspecific indicators of stress" in temporally sequential, regionally derived skeletal series that represented the requisite time periods. Such indicators include developmental enamel defects, stunting, cortical thickness of long bones, cribra orbitalia, porotic hyperostosis, periosteal reactions on long bones, trauma, osteoarthritis, and oral pathology.

This comparative study concluded that health in many parts of the globe health was compromised with this significant shift in subsistence strategy, and the editors asserted that agricultural intensification had been stimulated by stress and need rather than choice and invention. Subsequent research (Cohen and Crane-Kramer 2007) reaffirmed 1984 conclusions and expanded the earlier database from primarily European and Western Hemisphere sequences to include further samples from Africa and Southeast Asia. Thus, data drawn from paleopathology were used in global tests of theoretical models for the intensification of food production.

A second significant effort at global comparisons, influenced by the Cohen and Armelagos study, has been the Global History of Health Project, focused first on the Western Hemisphere (Steckel and Rose 2002) and then extended to Europe (Steckel et al. 2019). In this case, two economic historians – Richard Steckel and Joerg Baten – and numerous bioarchaeologists joined forces to evaluate the quality of human life through the study of skeletal attributes similar to those recorded by Cohen's bioarchaeological colleagues.

The Global History of Health Project has focused upon collecting extensive data sets that measured qualitative factors such as climate, political complexity, location, and subsistence, along with skeletal data reflecting nonspecific stress. As the project pertains to the Western Hemisphere, a "health index" was proposed, as a quantitative comparative measure based upon rating each skeletal variable on a scale of 0–100. The results of this study argue that throughout the history of the human condition, health has declined. In the closing chapter, the authors conclude that life *became* "nasty, brutish and short" for the typical person with the rise of agriculture, government, and urbanization (Steckel and Rose 2002: 573).

The European component of the Global History of Health Project accumulated a massive, standard set of health-related data on 15,119 skeletons dating between 300 and 1900 CE (Steckel et al. 2019). Data were partitioned by age, sex, social status, urban vs. rural, occupation, environment, and topography. The health index was refined to measure quality adjusted life-years. Surprisingly, the authors discovered health improvement during the Early Medieval Period (500–1000 CE), with declining health status thereafter, which they (Baten et al. 2019) attribute to the long-term impact of the Justinian Plague. Thus, there was no observable "urban [health] penalty" during the Early Medieval period. Less surprising is their discovery of the health-related impacts of social inequality in urban areas, as those with higher incomes presented fewer indicators of childhood health insults and survived. As with the Western Hemisphere project, coastal regions appeared more salubrious; farmers present more skeletal evidence of occupational stress than craftsmen during the Early Medieval Period. During the High and Late Medieval Periods 1000–1500 CE violence declined first in cities when compared to rural regions. Baten et al. (2019: 392) conclude that "the histories of health, nutrition, workload, and violence show a multifaceted picture of European development over the last two millennia, with more positive aspects represented by the movement from violence to personal security, and a dramatic decline in health and nutritional quality (negative). The latter trend was remarkably reversed during the late 19th century."

The approaches taken by these projects have excited critique, both methodologically and theoretically. Wood et al. (1992; see also DeWitte and Stojanowski 2015; McFadden and Oxenham 2020; Seik 2013; Soltysiak 2015), for example, have suggested that there may be a positive correlation between observed skeletal pathology and good health, given that one must live sufficiently long to register a bony insult rather than dying precipitously, thus providing bioarchaeologists with a seemingly "healthy" skeleton. From an epidemiological perspective, Pinhasi and Turner (2008) criticized the statistical approach taken in constructing the "health index." Cook (2007) expressed concern over the use of stature as a proxy for health, also noting discrepancies between historical accounts and inferences made by using stature data to characterize health.

A further significant issue involves basic differences between the two approaches to studying global health. The Western Hemisphere and European Health projects have emphasized geographic and temporal coverage. The strategy taken by Cohen and colleagues has focused first on defining relatively nuanced, regional patterns. The productive tension between these two contrastive research approaches will doubtless continue, adding to knowledge of health, broadly defined. The European Health project reflects a growing interest of bioarchaeologists and paleopathologists in addressing issues within complex, urban settings (Betsinger and DeWitte 2021).

At present, in both the global and the regional-to-global examples, researchers have focused upon finding universal or nearly universal patterns. In future studies, it may become important to focus upon the explanatory power gained by exploring those cases where expectations fail to be met.

PALEOPATHOLOGY, MUMMY STUDIES, AND MUMMY SCIENCE

Mummies – either human or of other animals – have excited the interest of the lay public and scientists alike since Napoleon invaded Egypt in 1798 (Aufderheide 2003; Buikstra and Nystrom 2021; Cockburn et al. 1998; Lynnerup 2019; Nystrom 2018; Shin and Bianucci

2021). For the paleopathologist, this has meant an opportunity to examine tissues other than bones and teeth with the hope of obtaining information about disease and health beyond that afforded by hard tissues. There are attendant challenges, however, because desiccation alters tissue form such that even very skilled anatomists are challenged to recognize internal organs. Deposition in acid bogs produces tanned corpses or "bog bodies," whose apparent external integrity belies the demineralized osseous tissues within. Artificial mummies inevitably present evidence of tissue destruction during preparation procedures, while the viscera of naturally mummified corpses may be destroyed from within due to bacterial action. Even so, as noted above, there are diseases that have been identified in desiccated soft tissues that are presently unknowable in skeletonized remains. Exemplary is the ongoing interdisciplinary study of Ötzi, "the Tyrolean iceman." As recounted by Zink and Maixner (2019), this desiccated set of remains, ~ 5,300 years old and discovered in Italy's alps in 1991, has been subject to ongoing biomolecular studies that have elucidated pathogen load, diet, ancestry, disease risk, and even eye color. Microbiome and immune system studies are forthcoming.

PALEOPARASITOLOGY

Recovered from mummies (hair, tissues, and alimentary tracks), coprolites, and archaeological deposits such as privies, the remains of parasites, their eggs, nits, and tracks provide key evidence of disease, community health, host diet, and migration history, as well as cultural and climatic change. Disease prevalence may be inferred through studies of egg frequencies in coprolites (Dittmar 2009).

Begun with Ruffer's 1910 recovery of blood fluke eggs in Egypt, methodological advances have increased recovery and identification potential, including recent aDNA applications that have, for example, revealed the presence of parasitic pathogens from 9,000-year-old mummified tissues without other overt evidence. Similarly, coprolites may serve as a source of parasite aDNA. Among the diseases that have been identified by aDNA study are Chagas' Disease, leishmaniasis, and helminthic infections by whipworms, roundworms, and pinworms, along with human fleas and head lice (Dittmar 2009).

Until the 1990s, there was little theory in the study of ancient parasites. Since that time, theoretical developments have led to a proliferation of terms applied to the study, with nuanced differences in emphasis: "Paleoparasitology," typically emphasizes the biological aspect of the study, while "archaeoparasitology" links to the social sciences, especially archaeology and bioarchaeology. "Pathoecology" expressly focuses upon the environmental determinants of disease and symbolized the explicitly interdisciplinary and collaborative nature of the study of ancient parasites (Reinhard and Bryant 2008). Significant advances in knowledge about the evolution and ecology of South American parasites have centered at the Oswaldo Cruz Foundation, Fiocruz, under the direction of Ferreira and Araújo, beginning in 1978, frequently in collaboration with Reinhard at the University of Nebraska (Corrêa Novo and Ferreira 2016).

As emphasized by Dittmar (2013) in her insightful guest editorial to a special issue on paleoparasitology of the *International Journal of Paleopathology*, edited by Le Mort and Mashkour (2013), paleoparasitology offers insights about human mobility, human migrations, animal domestication, hygiene, epidemiology, and climate change. As we develop perspectives from studying the human microbiome and the co-evolution of microbial organisms and our species, a case can also be made for integrating microbial studies with more traditional paleoparasitology as we develop comprehensive evolutionary models.

ANIMAL PALEOPATHOLOGY

The paleopathology envisioned by Schufeldt studied disease of any deceased organism (Cook and Powell 2006). Moodie's (1923a, 1923b) paleopathology was also broad and comparative, while emphasizing animal disease. Although a few scholars, such as Brothwell (Baker and Brothwell 1980), have steadfastly championed animal paleopathology during the twentieth century, the field has become focussed upon human disease. This appears to be changing, however, and the field has moved toward explicitly addressing theoretical and methodological concerns not unfamiliar to those who study human paleopathology: (1) lack of integration with archaeological data and contexts; (2) lack of consistent, standard scoring procedures; and (3) limited understanding of fundamental biomedical processes that underlie pathological lesions (Thomas 2012). Within the past 10 years, animal paleopathology has expanded markedly (e.g., see Bartosiewicz and Gal 2013). Future goals include gaining more methodological sophistication, understanding the nature of diseases for which there are currently no clinical models, developing standardized recording systems, and appreciating greater biological and epidemiological sensitivity to contexts (Thomas 2012, 2019). One great appeal of the approach taken by animal paleopathologists and veterinarians is an emphasis upon broad environmental and cultural contextual concerns in situating diseased animals, similar in form to the ONE Medicine and ONE Health Approaches, associated with the US veterinarian of tropical public health Calvin Schwabe (Dentinger 2018). A collaboration between veterinary pathologist and animal paleopathologist Elizabeth Uhl and human paleopathologist Jane Buikstra (Uhl et al. 2019) has led us to propose an inclusive "ONE Paleopathology" (Buikstra and Uhl 2021).

DISABILITY AND IDENTITY

The study of disability and identity as a form of paleopathology is in a nascent phase. Early attempts to consider compassion and caring for infirm individuals have been effectively critiqued by medical anthropologist Katherine Dettwyler (1991) as being anthropologically naïve and insensitive. In this context, there are two related but distinctive concepts that require definition. For example, Cross (1999) contrasts impairment and disability. The former can readily be estimated directly from studies of diseased bone, but the latter requires consideration of social reactions to an impairment within specific cultural settings. Contemporary definitions of disability are socially mediated and thus vary from culture to culture or even among social classes (Buikstra and Scott 2009; Grauer and Buikstra 2019). In studies of disease or disability in relationship to identity, reactions of *both* the individual and society to a pathological condition are of central significance. More recent studies of impairment and disability have sought further integration of disability theory, interdisciplinarity, and quantitative approaches that step beyond the case study (Byrnes and Muller 2017).

Within the past decade, a rigorous approach for addressing the physical support required for the ill and infirm has developed, initiated and refined by Lorna Tilley (Nystrom and Tilley 2019; Tilley 2015; Tilley and Oxenham 2011; Tilley and Shrenk 2016). The Bioarchaeology of Care method proceeds through a series of stages that include rigorous differential diagnosis, consideration of cultural and environmental contexts, assessment of physical impairment, inference of required care for health maintenance and quality of life. The emotional aspect of "care" or compassion is not the subject of this effort, thus avoiding a portion of Dettwyler's critique. Extending this approach beyond the richly developed case studies to broader contexts, such as institutions, has proved challenging (e.g., Critcher et al. 2016).

INTERPERSONAL VIOLENCE

During the past quarter century, paleopathologists have contributed significantly to issues surrounding violence in the past. While many earlier researchers had accepted prevailing wisdom concerning the lack of violent behaviors among earlier Native Americans, perhaps introduced or at least encouraged by Europeans, recent years have witnessed convincing evidence for warfare and other forms of interpersonal violence well before the fifteenth century (Walker 2001, Milner 1999, 2007). Bioarchaeological evidence has, for example, been used to argue for the presence of anthropophagy, including cannibalism in the American Southwest (Billman et al. 2000; Turner and Turner 1999; White 1992), although archaeologists and bioarchaeologists have proposed alternative interpretations (Darling 1999; Walker 1998). Extreme violence at sites such as Sacred Ridge has also been reported (Osterholtz 2018).

Other studies have focused upon gender-specific violence. Martin and Akins (2001), for example, infer a female underclass for 1000–1300 CE in SW Colorado, while extreme peri-mortem violence has been conjectured as evidence for political intimidation within the same region (Lekson 2002).

STRUCTURAL VIOLENCE

Recently, combining social theory and evidence for ante-mortem and peri-mortem trauma, paleopathologists and bioarchaeologists have focused upon structural violence (Buikstra et al. 2022; de la Cova 2014; Tremblay and Reedy 2020). In such approaches, careful contextualization combined with evidence for disease are used to explore the way institutions create and perpetuate marginalized communities, frequently plagued with poor health and nutrition.

Anchored by Galtung's (1969) definition of structural violence as the institutional, political, and societal limitations upon an individual's ability to achieve their potential, bioarchaeologists and paleopathologists have explored health outcomes associated with marginalization. For example, studies of embodied violence have focused on gendered and racialized structural violence in comparative studies of African Americans and European Americans from late nineteenth and early twentieth century documented skeletal collections (de la Cova 2010, 2011, 2012). A second form of structural violence investigation focusses on postmortem treatment of bodies (Blakely and Harrington 1997; Nystrom 2017). As Watkins and Muller (2015) emphasize, the bodies of the socially marginalized have frequently been dissected to serve educational needs of the white elite. These anonymous, anatomized treatments contrast with the autopsies more frequently directed to upper class individual whose identity and respect are maintained.

In association with raised awareness about societal marginalization and structural violence are concerns raised by descendants and other communities concerned about the exhumation and study of human remains. Laws in Australia, Canada, New Zealand, and the US require consultations and permissions, challenging paleopathologists, bioarchaeologists, and archaeologists to partner with these groups from early stages of research.

Such outreach will doubtless enrich studies of past health and our appreciation of the social outcomes of political actions. The African Burial Ground Project stands as a model for public engagement in partnership with scientific inquiry (Blakey 2010; Blakey and Rankin-Hill 2009).

Studies of aDNA are especially sensitive issues among indigenous communities. Scientists and community members are actively working to establish appropriate procedures for responsible research (Wagner et al. 2020).

Paleopathologists have additional ethical responsibilities, including data access and sharing, along with minimizing destructive sampling procedures. Noninvasive alternatives to standard, destructive autopsy procedures on mummified remains have been advocated (Piombino-Mascali and Gill-Frerking 2019). Researchers specializing in mummy science have raised additional ethical concerns relating to fieldwork and display of the dead (Shin and Biannuci 2021).

PALEOPATHOLOGY AS A PROFESSION: ORGANIZATIONS, CONGRESSES, AND A JOURNAL

The cornerstone, international professional organization for paleopathologists is the Paleopathology Association (PPA), begun in 1973 with an autopsy (PUM II) and symposium attended by medical scientists and anthropologists (Powell 2012). The subject matter and collaborative spirit of the PPA has inspired other developments, including International Congresses on the Epidemiology and Pathology of Infectious Disease. The first of these focused upon syphilis (1993), followed by tuberculosis, leprosy, and plague (Dutour et al. 2012).

Those with special interests in mummified remains and bog bodies have also organized a series of six World Congresses on Mummy Studies, with the inaugural meeting held in 1992. Each Mummy Congress has been well attended by medical and anthropological scientists and practitioners, and a series of Proceedings volumes have been published (Lynnerup et al. 2012).

Beginning in 2011, the Paleopathology Association has supported the publication of the *International Journal of Paleopathology*, whose goal has been to bridge the various disciplines that contribute to the physical study of ancient health and disease (Buikstra 2011). With four issues a year, including Special Topical Issues on specific conditions, such as metabolic diseases, paleoparasitology, violence, oncology, and geographical regions, including the Andes and China, the journal is reaching an international audience and serving well its community of interest.

RECENT ADVANCES AND FUTURE DIRECTIONS

The field of paleopathology has obviously responded effectively to Jarcho's (1966) critique. There are numerous deep syntheses, both as general paleopathology texts and others focussed upon mummy science and specific diseases. The recovery of ancient pathogen DNA fulfills Jarcho's "truly significant" category, including the 1918 influenza virus and the way genomic approaches have truly revolutionized our phylogeographic histories of infectious diseases. International organizations and congresses now regularly promote communication between medical scientists and anthropologists, including mummy studies. The twenty-first century has also witnessed the development of databases grounded in standard terminology for skeletal gross anatomy.

One of the key challenges remaining is to effectively integrate state-of-the-art biomedical technology with the study of ancient disease, both in individual and population perspectives. This is being most effectively accomplished in molecular and histological studies, though in the former, issues of protocols and reporting remain. Non-invasive state-of-the-art imaging technological applications largely remain at the case level, frequently without explicit goals. Another concern is that the proliferating congresses dichotomize the field between the medical sciences, who would naturally attend the mummy congresses, and the anthropologists attending the meetings sponsored by the PPA. A special challenge is integrating genomic studies with archaeological contexts, but the effective integration of these approaches should permit us to truly develop global evolutionary perspectives on ancient diseases as they moved between hosts, whether human or not. What the future holds depends upon continued collaborations between biomedical and anthropological scholars, taking advantage of the new technologies, but always maintaining an evolutionary perspective on disease in cultural and environmental contexts.

NOTE

1 As used here, "Transdisciplinary" refers to studies of disease that explicitly address contemporary issues that threaten wellbeing. Paleopathology is inherently interdisciplinary.

REFERENCES

Agarwal, S. C. "What is Normal Bone Health? A Bioarchaeological Perspective on Meaningful Measures and Interpretations of Bone Strength, Loss, and Aging." *American Journal of Human Biology* 33 (2021): e23647.

Agarwal, S. C., M. Dumitriv, G. A. Tomlinson, et al. "Medieval Trabecular Bone Architecture: The Influence of Age, Sex, and Lifestyle." *American Journal of Physical Anthropology* 124 (2004): 33–44.

Appleby, J., R. Thomas, and J. E. Buikstra. "Increasing Confidence in Paleopathological Diagnosis – Application of the Istanbul Terminological Framework." *International Journal of Paleopathology* 8 (2015): 19–21.

Armelagos, G. J. "Bioarchaeology as Anthropology." *Archaeological Papers of the American Anthropological Association* 13, no. 1 (2003): 27–40.

Armelagos, G. J., and D. P. van Gerven. "A Century of Skeletal Biology and Paleopathology: Contrasts, Contradictions, and Conflicts." *American Anthropologist* 105, no. 1 (2003): 53–64.

Aufderheide, A. C. *The Scientific Study of Mummies.* Cambridge: Cambridge University Press, 2003.

Aufderheide, A. C., and C. Rodríguez-Martín. *The Cambridge Encyclopedia of Human Paleopathology.* Cambridge: Cambridge University Press, 1998.

Baker, J. R., and D. R. Brothwell. *Animal Diseases in Archaeology.* New York: Academic Press, 1980.

Baker, B. J., G. Crane-Kramer, M. Dee, et al. "Advancing the Understanding of Treponemal Disease in the Past and Present." *Yearbook of Physical Anthropology* 71 (2020): 5–41.

Bartosiewicz, L., and E. Gal. *Shuffling Nags, Lame Ducks: The Archaeology of Animal Disease.* Oxford: Oxbow, 2013.

Baten, J., R. Steckel, C. Larsen, et al. "Multidimensional Patterns of European Health, Work, and Violence Over the Past Two Millennia." In *The Backbone of Europe: Health, Diet, Work and Violence over Two Millennia.* Edited by R. Steckel, C. Larsen, C. A. Roberts, et al., 381–396. Cambridge: Cambridge University Press, 2019.

Betsinger, T., and S. DeWitte, eds. *The Bioarchaeology of Urbanization: The Biological, Demographic, and Social Consequences of Living in Cities.* Switzerland: Springer Nature, 2021.

Billman, B. R., P. M. Lambert, and L. L. Banks. "Cannibalism, Warfare, and Drought in the Mesa Verde Region During the Twelfth Century A.D." *American Antiquity* 65, no. 1 (2000): 145–178.

Blakely, R. L., and J. M. Harrington, eds. *Bones in the Basement: Postmortem Racism in Nineteenth-Century Medical Training*. Washington, DC: Smithsonian Institution Press, 1997.

Blakey, M. L. "African Burial Ground Project: Paradigm for Cooperation?" *Museum International* 62, no. 1–2 (2010): 61–68.

Blakey, M. L., and L. M. Rankin-Hill, eds. *The New York African Burial Ground: Unearthing the African Presence in Colonial New York*. Volume 1: *Skeletal Biology of the New York African Burial Ground*. Washington, DC: Howard University in association with the General Services Administration, 2009.

Bos, K. I., K. M. Harkins, A. Herbig, et al. "Pre-Columbian Mycobacterial Genomes Reveal Seals as a Source of New World Human Tuberculosis." *Nature* 514 (2014): 494–497.

Brickley, M. "An Investigation of Historical and Archaeological Evidence for Age-Related Bone Loss and Osteoporosis." *International Journal of Osteoarchaeology* 12 (2002): 364–371.

Brickley, M. B. "*Cribra Orbitalia* and Porotic Hyperostosis: A Biological Approach to Diagnosis." *American Journal of Physical Anthropology* 167, no. 4 (2018): 896–902.

Brickley, M. B., and S. Mays. "Metabolic Disease." In *Ortner's Identification of Pathological Conditions in Human Skeletal Remains*, 3rd edn. Edited by J. E. Buikstra, 531–566. New York: Elsevier, 2019.

Brickley, M. B, and J. L. McKinley, eds. *Guidelines to the Standards for Recording Human Remains*. Reading, UK, 2004.

Brickley, M. B., R. Ives, and S. Mays. *The Bioarchaeology of Metabolic Bone Disease*, 2nd edn. 2020.

Brosch, R., S. V. Gordon, M. Marmiesse, et al. "A New Evolutionary Scenario for the Mycobacterium Tuberculosis Complex." *Proceedings of the National Academy of Sciences, USA* 99 (2002): 3684–3689.

Buikstra, J. E. "A Historical Introduction." In *Bioarchaeology: The Contextual Analysis of Human Remains*. Edited by J. E. Buikstra and L. E. Beck, 7–25. New York: Academic Press, 2006.

Buikstra, J. E. "Welcome to the *International Journal of Paleopathology*." *International Journal of Paleopathology* 1, no. 1 (2011): 1–3.

Buikstra, J. E, ed. "Rigor in Paleopathology: Perspectives from Across the Discipline." *International Journal of Paleopathology* 19 (2017).

Buikstra, J. E., ed. *Ortner's Identification of Pathological Conditions in Human Skeletal Remains*, 3rd edn. New York: Elsevier, 2019.

Buikstra, J. E., and K. Nystrom. "A History of Mummy Studies." In *The Handbook of Mummy Studies*. Edited by D. H. Shin and R. Bianucci, 1–37. Singapore: Springer, 2021.

Buikstra, J. E., and R. E. Scott. "Identity Formation: Communities and Individuals." In *Bioarchaeology and Identity*. Edited by K. Knudson and C. Stojanowski, 24–55. Gainesville: University of Florida Press, 2009.

Buikstra, J. E., and D. Ubelaker, eds. *Standards for Data Collection from Human Skeletal Remains*. Fayetteville: Arkansas Archaeological Survey Press, 1994.

Buikstra, J. E., and E. W. Uhl. "ONE Health: Implications for ONE Paleopathology." *Presentation for 7th Portuguese Conference on Paleopathology*. Portugal: Évora, 2021.

Buikstra, J. E., D. C. Cook, and K. L. Bolhofner. "Scientific Rigor in Paleopathology. *Rigor in Paleopathology: Perspectives from Across the Discipline*." *International Journal of Paleopathology* 19 (2017): 80–87.

Buikstra, J. E., S. N. DeWitte, S. C. Agarwal, et al. "21st Century Bioarchaeology: Taking Stock and Moving Forward." *Yearbook of Biological Anthropology* 178 (2022): 54–114.

Byrnes, J. F., and J. L. Muller, eds. *Bioarchaeology of Impairment and Disability: Theoretical, Ethnohistorical, and Methodological Perspectives*, 201–222. Switzerland: Springer, 2017.

Chhem, R. K. "Paleoradiology: History and New Developments." In *PaleoRadiology: Imaging Mummies and Fossils*. Edited by R. K. Chhem and D. R. Brothwell, 2–14. Berlin, Heidelberg and New York: Springer-Verlag, 2008.

Ciranni, R., F. Garbini, E. Neri, et al. "The 'Braids Lady' of Arezzo: A Case of Rheumatoid Arthritis in a 16th Century Mummy." *Clinical and Experimental Rheumatology* 20 (2002): 745–752.

Cockburn, A., E. Cockburn, and T. A. Reyman, eds. *Mummies, Disease, and Ancient Cultures*, 2nd edn. Cambridge: Cambridge University Press, 1998.

Cohen, M. N., and G. J. Armelagos, eds. *Paleopathology at the Origins of Agriculture*. New York: Academic Press, 1984.

Cohen, M. N., and G. Crane-Kramer. *Ancient Health: Skeletal Indication of Agricultural and Economic Interpretations of the Human Past*. Gainesville: University Press of Florida, 2007.

Cook, D. C. "Maize and Mississippians in the American Midwest: Twenty Years Later." In *Ancient Health: Skeletal Indication of Agricultural and Economic Interpretations of the Human Past*. Edited by M. N. Cohen and G. M. Crane-Cramer, 1–9. Gainesville: University of Florida Press, 2007.

Cook, D. C., and M. L. Powell. "The Evolution of American Paleopathology." In *Bioarchaeology: The Contextual Analysis of Human Remains*. Edited by J. E. Buikstra and L. E. Beck, 281–322. New York: Academic Press, 2006.

Corrêa Novo, S. P., and L. F. Ferreira. "The Paleoparasitology in Brazil and Findings in Human Remains from South America: A Review." *The Korean Journal of Parasitology* 54, no. 5 (2016): 573–583.

Crandall, J. J., and H. D. Klaus, eds. "Advances in the Paleopathology of Scurvy: Papers in Honor of Donald J. Ortner." *International Journal of Paleopathology* 5 (2014): 1–106.

Critcher, L. A. T. "An Exploration of a Modified Bioarchaeology of Care Methodological Approach for Historic Institutionalized Populations." In *New Developments in the Bioarchaeology of Care*. Edited by L. Tilley and A. A. Schrenk, 277–288. Switzerland: Springer International, 2016.

Cross, M. "Accessing the Inaccessible: Disability and Archaeology." *Archaeological Review from Cambridge Archaeology and Disability* 15 (1999): 7–30.

Crowder, C., and S. D. Stout, eds. *Bone Histology: An Anthropological Perspective*. Boca Raton, FL: CRC Press, 2011.

Darling, J. A. "From Hobbes to Rousseau and Back Again." *Science* 285 (1999): 537.

de la Cova, C. "Cultural Patterns of Trauma Among 19th-Century-Born Males in Cadaver Collections." *American Anthropologist* 112, no. 4 (2010): 589–606.

de la Cova, C. "Race, Health, and Disease in 19th Century Born Males." *American Journal of Physical Anthropology* 144, no. 4 (2011): 526–537.

de la Cova, C. "Patterns of Trauma and Violence in 19th-Century-Born African American and Euro-American Females." *International Journal of Paleopathology* 2, no. 2–3 (2012): 61–68.

de la Cova, C. "The Biological Effects of Urbanization and Inmigration on 19th Century-Born African Americans and Euro-Americans of Low Socioeconomic Status: An Anthropological and Historical Approach." *In Modern Environments and Human Health? Revisiting the Second Epidemiological Transition*." Edited by M. K. Zuckermann, 243–264. New York: Wiley Blackwell, 2014. https://doi.org/10.1002/9781118504338.ch13.

Dentinger, R. M. "The Parasitological Pursuit: Crossing Species and Disciplinary Boundaries with Calvin W. Schwabe and the *Echinococcus* Tapeworm, 1956–1975." In *Animals and the Shaping of Modern Medicine: One Health and Its Histories*. Edited by A. Woods, M. Bresalier, A. Cassidy, et al., 161–191. Cham, Switzerland: Springer International Publisher, 2018.

Dettwyler, K. A. "Does Paleopathology Provide Evidence for "Compassion?" *American Journal of Physical Anthropology* 84 (1991): 375–384.

DeWitte, S. N. "Archaeological Evidence of Epidemics Can Inform Future Epidemics." *Annual Review of Anthropology* 45 (2016): 63–77.

DeWitte, S. N. "Misperceptions about the Bioarchaeology of Plague." In *Bioarchaeologists Speak Out*. Edited by J. E. Buikstra, 109–131. Switzerland: Springer Nature, 2019.

DeWitte, S. N., and C. M. Stojanowski. "The Osteological Paradox 20 Years Later: Past Perspectives, Future Directions." *Journal of Archaeological Research* 23 (2015): 397–450.

DeWitte, S. N., and A. Wissler. "Demographic and Evolutionary Consequences of Pandemic Diseases." *Bioarchaeology International* 6 (2022): 15–39.

Dittmar, K. "Old Parasites for A New World: The Future of Paleoparasitological Research. A Review." *Journal of Parasitology* 95 (2009): 365–371.

Dittmar, K. "Guest Editorial." *International Journal of Paleopathology* 3 (2013): 140–141.

Drancourt, M., and D. Raoult. "Palaeomicrobiology: Current Issues and Perspectives." *Nature Reviews: Microbiology* 3 (2005): 23–35.

Dutour, O., G. Pálfi, and C. A. Roberts. "International Congresses on the Evolution and Paleoepidemiology of Infectious Diseases." In *The Global History of Paleopathology: Pioneers and Prospects*. Edited by J. E. Buikstra and C. A. Roberts, 678–683. San Diego: Elsevier, 2012.

Gagneux, S., and P. M. Small. "Global Phylogeography of Mycobacterium Tuberculosis and Implications for Tuberculosis Product Development." *The Lancet Infectious Diseases* 7 (2007): 328–337.

Galtung, J. "Violence, Peace, and Peace Research." *Journal of Peace Research* 6, no. 3 (1969): 167–191.

Giovannetti, G., A. Guerrini, E. Carnieri, et al. "Magnetic Resonance Imaging for the Study of Mummies." *Magnetic Resonance Imaging* 34 (2016): 785–794.

Grauer, A. L., and J. E. Buikstra. "Themes in Paleopathology." In *Ortner's Identification of Pathological Conditions in Human Skeletal Remains*, 3rd edn. Edited by J. E. Buikstra, 21–33. New York: Elsevier, 2019.

Gresky, J., and E. Petiti. "Ancient Rare Diseases: Definition and Concept of 'Rare' in Paleopathology." *International Journal of Paleopathology* (2021).

Grupe, G., and A. Garland, eds. *Histology of Ancient Human Bone: Methods and Diagnosis*. Berlin: Springer-Verlag, 1993.

Jarcho, S. "The Development and Present Condition of Human Palaeopathology in the United States." In *Human Palaeopathology*. Edited by S. Jarcho, 3–30. New Haven: Yale University Press, 1966.

Karlik, S. J., R. Bartha, K. Kennedy, et al. "MRI and Multinuclear MR Spectroscopy of 3,200-year-old Egyptian Mummy Brain." *American Journal of Roentgenology* 189, no. 2 (2007): 105–110.

Kirkpatrick, C. L., R. A. Campbell, K. J. Hunt, et al. "Paleo-oncology: Taking Stock and Moving Forward." *International Journal of Paleopathology* 21 (2018): 3–11.

Klaus, H. "Paleopathological Rigor and Differential Diagnosis: Case Studies Involving Terminology, Description, and Diagnostic Frameworks for Scurvy in Skeletal Remains." In *Rigor in Paleopathology: Perspectives from Across the Discipline*. Edited by J. E. Buikstra. *International Journal of Paleopathology* 19 (2017): 96–110.

Klaus, H., and N. Lynnerup. "Abnormal Bone: Considerations for Documentation, Disease Process Identification, and Differential Diagnosis. 2019." In *Ortner's Identification of Pathological Conditions in Human Skeletal Remains* 3rd edn. Edited by J. E. Buikstra, 59–89. New York: Elsevier, 2019.

Krause-Kyora, B., M. Nutsua, L. Boehme, et al. "Ancient DNA Study Reveals HLA Susceptibility Locus for Leprosy in Medieval Europeans." *Nature Communications* 9 (2018): 1569.

Lagia, A., C. Eliopoulos, and S. Manolis. "Thalassemia: Macroscopic and Radiological Study of a Case." *International Journal of Osteoarchaeology* 17 (2007): 269–285.

Lekson, S. H. "War in the Southwest, War in the World." *American Antiquity* 67, no. 4 (2002): 607–624.

LeMort, F., and M. Mashkour, eds. "Study Cases in Palaeoparasitology from the Palaeolithic to the Modern Times." *International Journal of Paleopathology* 3, no. 3 (2013).

Lynnerup, N. "Mummies and Paleopathology." In *Ortner's Identification of Pathological Conditions in Human Skeletal Remains*, 3rd edn. Edited by J. E. Buikstra, 799–807. New York: Elsevier, 2019.

Lynnerup, N., and H. Klaus. "Fundamentals of Human Bone and Dental Biology: Structure, Function, and\Development." In *Ortner's Identification of Pathological Conditions in Human Skeletal Remains*, 3rd edn. Edited by J. E. Buikstra, 35–58. New York: Elsevier, 2019.

Lynnerup, N., A. Aufderheide, C. Rodríguez-Martín, et al. "The World Congresses on Mummy Studies." In *The Global History of Paleopathology, Pioneers and Prospects*. Edited by J. E. Buikstra and C. A. Roberts, 694–699. Oxford: Oxford University Press, 2012.

Majander, K., S. Pfrengle, A. Kocher, et al. "Ancient Bacterial Genomes Reveal a High Diversity of *Treponema pallidum* Strains in Early Modern Europe." *Current Biology* 30, no. 19 (2020): 3788–3803.

Mancheser, K. "Tuberculosis and Leprosy in Antiquity: An Interpretation." *Medical History* 28 (1984): 162–173.

Marques, C. "Cancer: Lessons to Learn from the Past." In *Bone Cancer*. Edited by D. Heymann, 5–15. San Diego, CA: Academic Press, 2022.

Marques, C., C. Roberts, V. M. J. Matos, et al. "Cancers as Rare Diseases: Terminological, Theoretical, and Methodological Biases." *International Journal of Paleopathology* 32 (2021): 111–122.

Martin, D. L., and N. J. Akins. "Unequal Treatment in Life as in Death: Trauma and Mortuary Behavior at La Plata (A.D. 1000–1300)." In *Ancient Burial Practices in the American Southwest: Archaeology, Physical Anthropology, and Native American Perspectives*. Edited by D. R. Mitchell and J. L. Brunson-Hadley, 223–248. Albuquerque: University of New Mexico Press, 2001.

Mays, S. A. "Human Osteoarchaeology in the UK 2001–2007: A Bibliometric Perspective." *International Journal of Osteoarchaeology* 20, no. 2 (2009): 192–204.

Mays, S. A. "The Palaeopathology of Scurvy in Europe." *International Journal of Paleopathology* 5 (2014): 55–62.

Mays, S. A. "How Should We Diagnose Disease in Paleopathology? Some Epistemological Considerations." *International Journal of Paleopathology* 20 (2018): 12–19.

Mays, S. and M. B. Brickley, eds. "Vitamin D Deficiency in Bioarchaeology and Beyond: The Study of Rickets and Osteomalacia in the Past." *International Journal of Paleopathology* 23 (2018): 1–5. doi: 10.1016/j.ijpp.2018.05.004.

McFadden, C., and M. F. Oxenham. "A Paleoepidemiological Approach to the Osteological Paradox: Investigating Stress, Frailty and Resilience Through Cribra Orbitalia." *American Journal of Physical Anthropology* 173, no. 2 (2020): 205–217.

Moodie, R. L. *Paleopathology: An Introduction to the Study of Ancient Evidence of Disease.* Urbana: University of Illinois Press, 1923a.

Moodie, R. L. *The Antiquity of Disease.* Chicago: University of Chicago Press, 1923b.

Nieves-Colón, M. A., and A. C. Stone. "Ancient DNA Analysis of Archaeological Remains." In *Biological Anthropology of the Human Skeleton*, 3rd edn. Edited by M. A. Katzenberg and A. L. Grauer, 515–544. Hoboken: John Wiley & Sons, 2019.

Milner, G. R. "Warfare in Prehistoric and Early Historic Eastern North America." *Journal of Archaeological Research*, 7 (1999): 105–151. https://doi.org/10.1007/s10814-005-0001-x.

Milner, G. R. "Warfare, Population, and Food Production in Prehistoric Eastern North America." In *North America Indigenous Warfare and Ritual Violence.* Edited by R. J. Chacon and R. G. Mendoza, 182–201. Tucson, AZ: University of Arizona Press, 2007.

Nystrom, K. C., ed. *The Bioarchaeology of Dissection and Autopsy in the United States.* Cham: Springer, 2017.

Nystrom, K. *The Bioarchaeology of Mummies.* London: Routledge, 2018.

Nystrom, K., and L. Tilley, eds. "Mummy Studies and the Bioarchaeology of Care." *International Journal of Paleopathology* 25 (2019): 62–149.

O'Brien, J. J., J. J. Battista, C. Romagnoli, et al. "CT Imaging of Human Mummies: A Critical Review of the Literature (1979–2005)." *International Journal of Osteoarchaeology* 19, no. 1 (2009): 90–98.

Orlando, L., R. Allaby, P. Skoglund, et al. "Ancient DNA Analysis." *Nature Reviews* 1 (2021): 14.

Ortner, D. J. "Foreword." In *The Myth of Syphilis.* Edited by M. L. Powell and D. C. Cook, ix–xx. Gainesville: University Press of Florida, 2005.

Osterholtz, A. "Bioarchaeological Approaches to Southwestern Violence." *Kiva* 84, no. 4 (2018): 399–402.

Pinhasi, R., and K. Turner. "Epidemiological Approaches in Palaeopathology." In *Advances in Human Palaeopathology.* Edited by R. Pinhasi and S. Mays, 177–188. Chichester, UK: Wiley, 2008.

Piombino-Mascali, D., and H. Gill-Frerking. "The Mummy Autopsy: Some Ethical Considerations." In *Ethical Approaches to Human Remains: A Global Challenge in Bioarchaeology and Forensic Anthropology.* Edited by K. A. Squires, D. Errickson, and N. Márquez-Grant, 605–625. Cham: Springer, 2019. https:doi.org/10.1007/978-3-030-32926-6_29.

Powell, M. L. "The History of the Paleopathology Association." In *The Global History of Paleopathology: Pioneers and Prospects.* Edited by J. E. Buikstra and C. A. Roberts, 667–677. San Diego: Elsevier, 2012.

Reid, A. H., T. G. Fanning, J. V. Hultin, et al. "Origin and Evolution of the 1918 'Spanish' Influenza Virus Hemagglutinin Gene." *Proceedings of the National Academy of Sciences* 96 (1999): 1651–1656.

Reinhard, K. J., and V. M. Bryant. "Pathoecology and the Future of Coprolite Studies in Bioarchaeology." In *Reanalysis and Reinterpretation in Southwestern Bioarchaeology.* Edited by A. L. Stodder, 199–216. Arizona State University Anthropological Research Papers No. 59, 2008.

Reinhard, K. J., K. L. Johnson, S. LeRoy-Toren, et al. "Understanding the Pathoecological Relationship Between Ancient Diet and Modern Diabetes Through Coprolite Analysis: A Case Example from Antelope Cave, Mojave County, Arizona." *Papers in Natural Resources* 321 (2012).

Robbins Schug, G., ed. *The Routledge Handbook of the Bioarchaeology of Climate and Environmental Change*. Abingdon: Routledge, 2020.

Roberts, C. A. "Palaeopathology and Archaeology: The Current State of Play". In *The Archaeology of Medicine*. Edited by R. Arnott, 1–20. British Archaeological Reports, International Series 1046. Oxford: Archaeopress, 2002.

Roberts, C. A. *Leprosy Past and Present*. Gainesville: University Press of Florida, 2020.

Roberts, C. A., and J. E. Buikstra. *The Bioarchaeology of Tuberculosis: A Global View on A Reemerging Disease*. Gainesville: University of Florida Press, 2003.

Roberts, C. A., and K. Manchester. *The Archaeology of Disease*, 3rd edn. The Mill, Gloucestershire: The History Press, 2005.

Roberts, C. A., R. Steckel, C. Larsen, et al. "Database Creation, Management, and Analysis." In *The Backbone of Europe: Health, Diet, Work and Violence over Two Millennia*. Edited by R. Steckel, 428–448. Cambridge: Cambridge University Press, 2019.

Rühli, F. J., H. von Waldburg, S. Nielles-Vallespin, et al. "Clinical MR-imaging of Ancient Dry Mummies without Rehydration." *Journal of the American Medical Association* 298 (2007): 2618–2620.

Saab, G., R. K. Chhem, and R. N. Bohay. "Paleoradiographic Techniques." In *PaleoRadiology: Imaging Mummies and Fossils*. Edited by R. K. Chhem and D. R. Brothwell, 15–54. New York: Springer-Verlag, 2008.

Sandison, A. T. "Sir Marc Armand Ruffer (1859–1917) Pioneer of Palaeopathology." *Medical History* 11, no. 2 (1967): 150–156.

Schuenemann, V., C. Avanzi, B. Krause-Kyora, et al. "Ancient Genomes Reveal a High Diversity of *Mycobacterium Leprae* in Medieval Europe." *PLoS Pathogens* 14, no. 5 (2018): e1006997. https://doi.org/10.1371/journal.ppat.1006997.

Schultz, M. "Light Microscopic Analysis of Macerated Pathologically Changed Bones." In *Bone Histology: An Anthropological Perspective*. Edited by C. Crowder and S. D. Stout, 253–296. Boca Raton: CRC Press, 2011.

Shin, D. H., and R. Bianucci, eds. *The Handbook of Mummy Studies*. Singapore: Springer, 2021.

Shin, D. H., I. S. Lee, M. J. Kim, et al. "Magnetic Resonance Imaging Performed on a Hydrated Mummy of Medieval Korea." *Journal of Anatomy* 216, no. 3 (2010): 329–334.

Siek, T. "The Osteological Paradox and Issues of Interpretation in Paleopathology." *Explorations in Anthropology* 13, no. 1 (2013): 92–101.

Soltysiak, A. "The Osteological Paradox, Selective Mortality, and Stress Markers Revisited." *Current Anthropology* 56, no. 4 (2015): 569–570.

Steckel, R., C. S. Larsen, C. A. Roberts, and J. Baten. "Data Collection Codebook." In *The Backbone of Europe: Health, Diet, Work and Violence over Two Millennia*. Edited by R. Steckel et al., 397–427. Cambridge: Cambridge University Press, 2019.

Steckel, R. H., and J. C. Rose, eds. *The Backbone of History: Health and Nutrition in the Western Hemisphere*. Cambridge: Cambridge University Press, 2002.

Stone, A. C., and A. T. Ozga. "Ancient DNA in the Study of Ancient Disease." In *Ortner's Identification of Pathological Conditions in Human Skeletal Remains*, 3rd edn. Edited by J. E. Buikstra, 183–210. New York: Elsevier, 2019.

Stone, A. C., A. Wilbur, J. E. Buikstra, et al. "Mycobacterial Disease in Perspective." *Yearbook of Physical Anthropology* 140 (2009): 66–94.

Stout, S. D., M. E. Cole, and A. M. Agnew. "Histomorphology: Deciphering the Metabolic Record." In *Ortner's Identification of Pathological Conditions in Human Skeletal Remains*, 3rd edn. Edited by J. E. Buikstra, 91–167. New York: Elsevier, 2019.

Thomas, R. "Non-Human Paleopathology." In *The Global History of Paleopathology: Pioneers and Prospects*. Edited by J. E. Buikstra and C. R. Roberts, 652–664. San Diego: Elsevier, 2012.

Thomas, R. "Nonhuman Animal Paleopathology – Are We so Different?" In *Ortner's Identification of Pathological Conditions in Human Skeletal Remains*, 3rd edn. Edited by J. E. Buikstra, 809–822. New York: Elsevier, 2019.

Thompson, R. C., A. H. Allam, G. P. Lombardi, et al. "Atherosclerosis across 4000 Years of Human History: The Horus Study of Four Ancient Populations." *Lancet* 381 (2013): 1211–1222.

Tilley, L. *Theory and Practice in the Bioarchaeology of Care*. Chem, Switzerland: Springer, 2015.

Tilley, L., and M. Oxenham. "Survival Against the Odds: Modeling the Social Implications of Care Provision to Seriously Disabled Individuals." *International Journal of Paleopathology* 1, no. 1 (2011): 35–42.

Tilley, L., and A. A. Shrenk, eds. *New Developments in the Bioarchaeology of Care.* Switzerland: Springer International, 2016.

Tremblay, L. A., and S. C Reedy, eds. *The Bioarchaeology of Structural Violence: A Theoretical Framework for Industrial Era Inequality.* Switzerland: Springer International, 2020.

Turner, C. G. II, and J. A. Turner. *Man Corn: Cannibalism and Violence in the Prehistoric American Southwest.* Salt Lake City: University of Utah Press, 1999.

Uhl, E. W., C. Kelderhouse, J. E. Buikstra, et al. "New World Origin of Canine Distemper: Interdisciplinary Insights." *International Journal of Paleopathology* 24 (2019): 266–278.

Villa, C., B. Frolich, and N. Lynnerup. "The Role of Imaging in Paleopathology." In *Ortner's Identification of Pathological Conditions in Human Skeletal Remains,* 3rd edn. Edited by J. E. Buikstra, 169–182. New York: Elsevier, 2019.

Wagner, J. K., C. Colwell, C. G. Claw, et al. "Fostering Responsible Research on Ancient Disease." *American Journal of Human Genetics* 107, no. 2 (2020): 183–195. https://doi.org/10.1016/j.ajhg.2020.06.017.

Waldron, T. *Palaeoepidemiology.* Walnut Creek, CA: Left Coast Press, 2007.

Walker, W. H. "Where Are the Witches of Prehistory?" *Journal of Archaeological Method and Theory* 5 (1998): 245–308.

Walker, P. L. "A Bioarchaeological Perspective on the History of Violence." *Annual Review of Anthropology,* 30 (2001): 573–596. https://doi.org/10.1146/annurev.anthro.30.1.573.

Watkins, R. J., and J. Muller. "Repositioning the Cobb Human Archive: The Merger of a Skeletal Collection and Its Texts." *American Journal of Human Biology* 27 (2015): 41–50.

White, T. D. *Prehistoric Cannibalism at Mancos 5MTUMR-2346.* Princeton: Princeton University Press, 1992.

White, W. "Databases." In *Advances in Human Palaeopathology.* Edited by R. Pinhasi and S. Mays, 177–188. Chichester, UK: Wiley, 2008.

Wood, J. W., G. R. Milner, H. Harpending, et al. "The Osteological Paradox: Problems of Inferring Prehistoric Health from Skeletal Samples." *Current Anthropology* 33 (1992): 343–370.

Zink, A. R, and F. Maixner. "The Current Situation of the Tyrolean Iceman." *Gerontology* 65, no. 6 (2019): 699–706.

CHAPTER 29 Forensic Anthropology: Current Issues

Douglas H. Ubelaker

With increasing frequency, biological anthropologists apply their knowledge and methodology to issues directed toward their laboratories by the medico-legal community. Collectively, such applications, and the method and theory supporting them, represent the rapidly expanding field of forensic anthropology. Much of this effort is directed toward the identification and interpretation of recovered skeletal remains. More and more frequently, forensic anthropologists also contribute to the evaluation of fleshed remains (especially those in an advanced state of decomposition or other forms of soft tissue alteration) and various issues relating to living persons, such as estimating the age of migrants. Anthropologists have expanded roles at crime scene investigations and those involving mass disasters, human rights, and humanitarian action. Toward these efforts, anthropologists have received substantial support from the American Academy of Forensic Sciences Humanitarian and Human Rights Resource Center and other granting institutions.

The applications of forensic anthropology are largely defined by the circumstances of the cases and the nature of the remains presented. Each case presents unique challenges. To meet these challenges, the forensic anthropologist must consult the supportive published literature, available analytical methodology, and his or her experience to choose the most relevant approaches. Such applications in the last few decades have defined the evolving scientific needs of the field and stimulated considerable research. The result is a vigorous subdiscipline of biological anthropology and forensic science that utilizes the scientific methodology of the parent academic disciplines and includes substantial approaches and databases specific to the field.

Chapter word limits do not allow an exhaustive treatment of the dynamic field of forensic anthropology. Following a brief presentation of the history of the discipline, limited discussion focuses on 10 issues: certification, legal concerns, the laboratory, age estimation, ancestry, population variation, identification, overlap with other disciplines, facial imagery, and emerging technology.

A Companion to Biological Anthropology, Second Edition. Edited by Clark Spencer Larsen.
© 2023 John Wiley & Sons Ltd. Published 2023 by John Wiley & Sons Ltd.

A Brief History

Historical developments in forensic anthropology generally can be traced to European initiatives in comparative anatomy and growth and development. The early history of forensic anthropology is closely linked to the more general field of biological anthropology. Aspects that are particular to forensic anthropology include the early work of Alphonse Bertillon, who attempted to use a detailed system of anthropometry to facilitate medico-legal identification (Spencer 1997).

In the United States, growth of forensic anthropology was initially stimulated by the involvement of physicians and anatomists in local forensic cases. Well-known examples of such involvement include analysis of remains and testimony by Oliver Wendell Holmes (1809–1894) and Jeffries Wyman (1814–1874) in the John W. Webster trial for the murder of Dr. George Parkman at Harvard University, as well as George Dorsey's (1868–1931) contributions to the Adolph Luetgert trial in Chicago (Stewart 1979).

This period also witnessed the beginnings of scholars in biological anthropology extending their research interests into forensic anthropology. Stewart (1979) bestowed the title "the father of forensic anthropology in the United States" upon Thomas Dwight (1843–1911) for his early contributions to the field (Dwight 1878, 1881, 1890a, 1890b, 1894a, 1894b, 1905). Other noteworthy contributors of this early era include Harris Hawthorne Wilder (1864–1928), Paul Stevenson (1890–1971), and T. Wingate Todd (1885–1938), and case involvement by Earnest A. Hooton (1887–1954) and Aleš Hrdlička (1869–1943). Hrdlička initiated casework by the Smithsonian Institution for the FBI Headquarters in Washington D.C. and published on forensic topics (Ubelaker 1999a).

The modern era of forensic anthropology is usually credited to the work of Wilton Krogman (1903–1987), T. D. Stewart (1901–1997), and Mildred Trotter (1899–1991), who among others published key works that provided recognition to the field (e.g., Krogman 1939, 1962; McKern and Stewart 1957; Stewart 1948, 1951, 1970, 1979; Stewart and Trotter 1954, 1955; Trotter and Gleser 1952). Early pioneers also include Alice Brues (1913–2007) and Sheilagh Brooks (1923–2008).

Key historical developments also include organizational advancements. In 1972, 14 founding members created a section of physical anthropology within the American Academy of Forensic Sciences. This new section with its annual meeting provided a forum for research presentation and case discussion focusing specifically on forensic issues and the anthropological application to matters of legal interest. Recently, this section was renamed "anthropology" in recognition of contributions from other academic areas within the field.

With the leadership of Ellis R. Kerley (1924–1998) and others, the American Board of Forensic Anthropology Inc. (ABFA) was formed in 1977. This Board offers certification for forensic anthropologists who qualify by having the necessary degree credentials and passing a written and practical examination.

Another significant development is the 2003 formation of the Forensic Anthropology Society of Europe. This organization, affiliated with the International Academy of Legal Medicine, offers to the European community training and scholarly interaction in forensic anthropology (Baccino 2005).

By 2021, the field of forensic anthropology had grown dramatically to include many educational initiatives, broad research addressing many issues distinct to the field, and active involvement of forensic anthropologists in diverse applications. Noteworthy among these initiatives are contributions to investigations of human rights abuses, natural disasters, and other events leading to mass human fatalities. Employment has expanded beyond university/college teaching and museum research to opportunities in government and non-governmental human rights organizations. Many medical examiner and coroner offices employ or consult with forensic anthropologists as well.

CERTIFICATION

As discussed above, the ABFA represents a key certification body. The ABFA seeks to improve the practice of forensic anthropology and grant certificates to qualified individuals. Diplomate status is limited to those who are permanent residents of the United States, Canada, or their territories (or others by petition for a waiver), possess a PhD with an emphasis in biological anthropology and training (waivers are considered), and have experience in those areas relevant for forensic applications. Candidates must also pass an examination administered by the ABFA. By November 2021, 149 anthropologists had been granted diplomate status.

Diplomate status with the ABFA offers forensic anthropologists a key credential that indicates to the legal system and to others who need forensic anthropological services that the holder is qualified. Ultimately, however, the legal system represents the gatekeeper in determining who is qualified to render opinions on forensic anthropology matters in a court of law (Fulginiti et al. 2019).

For many years, the ABFA represented the only certifying body in forensic anthropology. That is no longer the case. Since 2014, the Forensic Anthropology Society of Europe (FASE) offers two levels of certification. The top level targets the independent practitioner with either an MD or PhD degree. The other level focuses on those with casework experience who hold the equivalent of a master's degree. Both levels also call for knowledge testing (Forensic Anthropology Society of Europe 2020).

The Latin American Forensic Anthropology Association (ALAF) represents another important organizational development within forensic anthropology that also offers certification. Formed in 2003, this organization states among its goals the formation of an "independent accreditation board that will certify qualified practitioners of forensic anthropology" (Argentine Forensic Anthropology Team 2005). Discussion of the standards to be employed in certification emphasizes professional experience, noting the paucity of advanced degree programs in Latin America with a focus on forensic anthropology. The ALAF certification program involves requirements of education and experience as well as testing of applicants (Ubelaker 2018a).

Certification is also available in the United Kingdom sponsored by the Royal Anthropological Institute, the Office of the Forensic Science Regulator, and the British Association of Forensic Anthropology (MacKinnon and Harrison 2016). Like the other certification programs, the British system involves both educational requirements and testing.

Debate continues on certification issues. While certification represents a valuable credential, it is not universally recognized as a prerequisite for casework involvement. Clearly, many anthropologists who are not certified are active in the field and make valuable contributions, including providing court testimony. However, in the absence of the certification credential, decision makers in the medico-legal arena struggle to decide who is qualified.

The value of certification should be emphasized, especially to the legal system. Maintenance of this system requires a great deal of effort for all involved, especially the officers of the relevant organizations. This effort should be rewarded with broader recognition of the importance of certified status.

At the same time, new measures are needed, especially for those residing outside of North America and Europe, to clarify the qualifications of those involved. Mechanisms need to be established to recognize experience, training, formal education, and other forms of preparation. Such recognition coupled with rigorous testing should aid the process of determining who is qualified to participate in forensic anthropological investigations.

LEGAL ACCEPTANCE OF METHODOLOGY

In recent years, issues have emerged regarding the use of forensic science expert testimony in legal procedures. These issues cluster within two general categories: (1) heightened scrutiny and criticism of some aspects of forensic science by the general science community and (2) court decisions that have attempted to define the use of experts and expert methodology in the courtroom.

In 2003, the editor of *Science* wrote an editorial titled "Forensic Science: Oxymoron?" calling attention to growing scientific criticism targeting some areas of forensic science (Kennedy 2003). Reactions have been strong on all sides of the issues raised, but these developments have stimulated review by the National Research Council (2009), as well as both research and discussion within the forensic community. The basic issue questions if some aspects of forensic science are soundly rooted in good science or if they have evolved over the years within the forensic framework in a manner that lacks scientific rigor.

In the legal arena, prior to 1993, most recognized that a 1923 court decision *Frye v. United States* (293 F. 1013 [D.C. Cir. 1923]) offered guidelines regarding expert testimony. If an expert was subject to a "Frye Hearing," then the court examined whether the methodology utilized was generally accepted within the scientific community.

In 1993, a Supreme Court decision in the case of *Daubert v. Merrell Dow Pharmaceuticals, Inc.* (509 US 579 [1993]) produced guidelines that superseded those of the Frye decision. The Daubert decision shifted responsibility to determine acceptance from the scientific community in the Frye ruling to the presiding judge. Acting as the scientific gatekeeper, the judge must evaluate scientific testimony based on five primary criteria. These criteria involve whether the scientific method utilized in a case (1) is testable and has been tested through the scientific method, (2) was subject to peer-review, (3) is based on established standards, (4) has a known error rate, and (5) is widely accepted by the scientific community.

An additional key legal development occurred in 1999 with a Supreme Court decision in the case of *Kumho Tire Co. v. Carmichael* (526 US 137 [1999]). In this decision, the Court concluded that (1) forensic experts can develop theories based on observation and experience and apply those to a case, (2) diverse aspects of forensic testimony should be evaluated with the same degree of rigor, and (3) the Daubert guidelines should be regarded as being flexible and not necessarily applicable universally to scientific testimony.

Although these developments have not targeted forensic anthropology directly, they have stimulated considerable discussion and research within the field (Bohan and Heels 1995; Cheng and Yoon 2005; Faigman et al. 1994; Grivas and Komar 2008; Kaiser 1998; Risinger et al. 2002; Saks 2000; Sanders 2001). The general reactive tendency has been to reexamine techniques to make them more quantifiable and less subjective (Christensen 2004, 2005), as well as to examine accuracy and interobserver and intraobserver error and to recognize and minimize bias. While these developments are positive and have improved the quality of forensic anthropology methodology, many aspects of anthropological analysis remain interpretive. Experience continues to play a dominant role in case interpretation, and most research indicates that holistic approaches produce more accurate results than the use of single techniques. Reducing complex anthropological interpretation to simplified techniques that can easily be tested for error rates risks loss of much of the scholarly punch of a more comprehensive analysis. As supported by the Kumho decision, much of diverse anthropological analysis and interpretation must call upon experience and broad observation to maximize the information retrieved.

The Forensic Anthropology Laboratory

Biological anthropologists who choose to enter the world of forensic anthropology learn quickly (hopefully) that major adjustments need to be made in the quality control of the remains and items examined. Due to the legal context of forensic work, strict controls must be maintained on equipment, evidence, and the environment in which the analysis takes place. It is also critical to document if a breach occurred to any of the protocols employed. Procedures should document the prevention of contamination and the inadvertent loss of evidence that could negatively impact a case interpretation. These concerns call for thoughtful organization and protocols for the forensic anthropology laboratory (Warren et al. 2008).

The bottom line in forensic laboratory management is that procedures need to be in place that secure the evidence and document the chain of custody. Gone are the days when cases could be left unattended on the laboratory table along with other collections of human remains for extended periods of time, fully accessible to students, volunteers, and those involved in unrelated activities. The chain of custody must be maintained to document the location and personnel access to the remains at all times. Security systems need to be capable of not only ensuring safety to the evidence but, if necessary, also to enable documentation of that security (Warren et al. 2008).

To anthropologists accustomed to a more casual approach to the use of materials in their laboratories, the forensic context requires some adjustment. If in the forensic analysis of a complete human skeleton an extra metatarsal from a younger individual is found, does this prove that a second victim is involved or merely that someone used the skeleton for teaching purposes in the laboratory and accidentally mixed in another bone from the teaching collection? If the forensic examiner finds a cut on a bone, then does it suggest a victim of stabbing or merely that a student tried to clean the bone in the laboratory and left the alteration behind? These are the kinds of questions that emerge unless the laboratory has strict controls that clarify the possibilities throughout the analysis process.

Age Estimation

The accurate estimation of age at death represents an important component of forensic anthropological analysis (Rogers 2016). Such estimates can greatly aid the investigation leading to identification of a recovered skeleton. They also can be useful in the exclusion of missing persons mistakenly thought to perhaps be represented by remains. For these reasons, it is essential that estimates advanced in forensic reports are both accurate and realistic, given the nature of the evidence presented. The age range reported must be appropriate to the methods utilized, as well as the skeletal attributes presented by the available evidence.

Research generally has documented that the extent of variation manifest in the skeletal aging process increases with advancing age (Ubelaker 1999b). Thus, whereas it may be possible to estimate reliably the age at death within weeks of fetal remains (Fazekas and Kósa

1978), the age range of older adults may encompass decades. Throughout the aging process, regional variation, lifestyle, diet, and various environmental factors influence the rate and nature of age changes (Stinson et al. 2000). Thus, age estimation is a relatively complex process that is enhanced by the experience of the examiner.

Coupled with the call for quantification, the establishment of error rates and the need for standardization from the legal community, various innovative statistical approaches have been advanced. Notable among these are tests of interobserver error (Bouvier and Ubelaker 1977), testing of different techniques on the same samples (Bouvier and Ubelaker 1977; Galera et al. 1995; Martrille et al. 2007), testing of methods on different samples (Megyesi et al. 2006; Prince and Ubelaker 2002; Ubelaker and Parra 2008), and Bayesian statistics and transition analysis (Boldsen et al. 2002; Getz 2020; Milner et al. 2008). Many of these developments are driven by the fact that individual methods reflect the nature of the samples they are derived from and tested upon. Problems arise when the underlying samples are not representative of the cases the methods are applied to. Fortunately, this concern has stimulated considerable research that has advanced the accuracy of age estimation significantly (Adserias-Garriga 2019; Zapico et al. 2020).

Another key issue involves the selection of which methods to utilize, especially in the estimation of adult age. Should the most accurate single method be employed (Saunders et al. 1992) or are more accurate results obtained by using multiple age indicators (Acsádi and Nemeskéri 1970; Bedford et al. 1993). Selection of aging methodology is complex and should be guided by the nature of the skeletal remains available, as well as judgments regarding method effectiveness. For example, in the analysis of the skeleton of a young child, long bone length and dental eruption provide some useful age information. However, the final estimate should be heavily influenced by the extent of dental formation since research demonstrates that in that age group, dental formation has the highest correlation with chronological age and the least population variation (Scheuer and Black 2000; Ubelaker 1987).

Although research indicates that different adult age indicators are of varying accuracy and are most applicable at different periods in the adult aging process, all offer some useful information. Baccino and Zerilli (1997) suggested a procedure in which pubic symphysis morphology is consulted first. If the initial phases of symphyseal development are found, then they should be extensively relied upon for age determination since research has demonstrated that assessment of pubic symphysis morphology is an effective technique in applications to younger adults. If later phases are found, Baccino and Zerilli (1997) recommend relying more on the Lamendin dental technique (Lamendin et al. 1992), which offers greater reliability in older adults.

In a blind test of four aging methods (pubic symphysis, sternal rib ends, bone histology, and the Lamendin dental technique) on a French autopsy sample of known age at death, two independent observers documented that experience plays a significant role in the accuracy of application, especially with complex histological techniques (Baccino et al. 1999). This research also documented that for each observer, various methods of using multiple techniques all produced more accurate results than any one individual technique.

Research also suggests that some consideration needs to be devoted to population variation in the nature and timing of aging. For example, an application of the Kerley method of histological age determination based on a modern military sample from the United States to a demographically very different sample from the Dominican Republic produced significant variance in estimated ages (Ubelaker 1981). Schaefer and Black (2005) documented that age progression in epiphyseal union in a Bosnian sample differed from that suggested by studies of samples of different populations.

CONCEPTS OF RACE

Most missing persons are described in regard to some sort of racial category. Thus, "race" becomes an issue in forensic anthropological analysis. In attempting to be useful on this issue, anthropologists need to recognize the social dimensions of public perceptions of race and to communicate opinions appropriately. Analysis may reveal a pattern of attributes suggesting that during life the individual represented by the remains was related to a particular group. The pattern may support opinions about the individual's ancestry (Sauer et al. 2016).

Because discussions of "race" stir passions within the scholarly community, word choice is important. It can be argued that the word "race" is no longer a useful term since it seems to mean different things to different people and because of its historical baggage. Nevertheless, forensic anthropologists continue to make significant contributions on this topic, both in casework and in research (Dunn et al. 2020). Recognizing the associated problems, some forensic anthropologists avoid making such assessments. Others have been challenged by these issues and designed research to target the inherent problems. Progress relates to defining the specific groups targeted and developing databases and methods that facilitate their assessment.

The term "Hispanic" is particularly problematic because it can refer to individuals of Spanish heritage regardless of their ancestry, genotype, or phenotype. This and other related issues can be dealt with through adequate description and careful wording in reports. The challenge is to provide useful information that may aid an investigation without offering up categories that are misleading. It is also important not to force an opinion when the data do not permit an assessment. Skeletons (especially the fragmentary ones) of many individuals present such a mixture of traits and measurements that it is not possible to suggest affinity with a particular group.

Although thoughtful analysis of ancestry should utilize both observations and measurements, many forensic anthropologists have utilized the measurement-based software FORDISC 3.1 (Jantz and Ousley 2005). This system offers customized discriminant function equations that utilize whatever measurements can be taken and deliver a classification complete with the relevant statistics needed for interpretation. Although FORDISC represents a valuable tool, it is limited by the nature of the database it draws from. If a skeleton originates from an individual/population not well represented within the database, the quality of the classification is affected (Ubelaker et al. 2002a). Fortunately, the associated statistics can provide hints when such situations occur.

REGIONAL VARIATION AND SECULAR CHANGE

Nearly all areas of forensic anthropology applications are impacted by morphological components of regional variation and secular change. As documented collections and worldwide research in this area increase, the importance of these factors becomes illuminated. Historically, new methods have been developed from well-documented collections showing great promise only to find their utility diminished later when applied to more diverse samples. A major emerging new frontier in forensic anthropology represents the development of such collections and research.

The good news is that this challenge is being met. As interest and activity in forensic anthropology grows worldwide, new collections (of both data and skeletons) are being assembled (Ubelaker 2014a). As existing methods are tested with these new resources, knowledge grows regarding the extent of variation involved. In scholarly areas in which variation is strong (e.g., sexual dimorphism, ancestry assessment, stature calculation) population specific methodology can be developed. Such progress has led the journal *Forensic Science International* to create a section specifically for new emerging datasets within forensic anthropology.

In regard to many of our techniques, decades have passed since their initial formulation. Are these methods and the data they are based upon still relevant to modern applications? To what extent has secular change occurred in the attributes examined? Within the United States, this question can be examined to a limited extent through comparisons of modern samples with the data from the older ones. Of particular value is the modern database contributing to the development of FORDISC, discussed above. This database is constructed using information collected from modern forensic cases that have been identified. Comparison with the samples assembled in decades past reveals aspects of secular change and documents the need to maintain currency in methodology (Jantz and Jantz 1999; Meadows and Jantz 1995).

IDENTIFICATION ISSUES

Much of the effort in forensic anthropological analysis is geared toward identification. Interpretations of age at death, sex, ancestry, living stature, time since death, medical history, and other attributes help narrow the search for the person represented by the recovered remains. A scientific identification results when unique characteristics are found on both recovered remains and the antemortem records of a once living person. Such identifications in forensic anthropology usually originate from radiographic comparisons (Morishita et al. 2021), since images taken of the living person can reveal bony details that can be detected within recovered remains (De Boer et al. 2020; Ubelaker 2018b).

The process of scientific identification involves several stages of interpretation. First, matching attributes must be found in both the antemortem and postmortem materials. Differences must be explained by such factors as quality of the images available, postmortem alterations in the recovered remains, or changes in the living person that occurred between death and the time the antemortem radiographs were taken. Once this process is complete an assessment must be made regarding the uniqueness of the matching features. If the assemblage of matching features is unique, then scientific identification results. If they are judged not to be unique then a determination follows that the remains could be the suggested individual, but the association cannot be proven by the comparison. Thus a "match" does not automatically yield a scientific identification; uniqueness of the attributes being compared must first be established.

In many cases, matching attributes are found but these fall somewhat short of the evidence needed for scientific identification. This problem is especially acute in areas of the world and socioeconomic contexts in which radiographs and other medical/dental records are not available. The antemortem evidence available frequently involves memories of family and friends and results in possible or putative identifications. Material culture also can contribute (Birkby et al. 2008; Komar and Lathrop 2008). Judgments are required to decide at what point the evidence is sufficient to justify identification. Inadequate evidence can lead to errors in identification. While many medical examiner/coroner offices consider a totality of circumstances, misidentification is tragic and can be avoided through science and understanding of the identification process.

INTELLECTUAL BORDERS

Although forensic anthropology has specific methodology and subject matter not shared with other disciplines, it also involves some intellectual overlap with other areas of forensic science. Many anthropologists work with fleshed remains, even those that are subject to conventional autopsy. Although this usually is a cooperative venture with forensic pathologists, it can involve overlapping areas of opinion, especially relating to trauma interpretation (L'Abbe et al. 2019). Forensic pathologists are charged with making the determination of cause and manner and death. However, particularly in skeletal cases, forensic anthropologists may glean the evidence supporting the opinion. Trauma analysis represents a major contribution of forensic anthropologists, supported by extensive experimental research (Dempsey and Blau 2020). Anthropologists are well qualified to differentiate perimortem trauma, sustained at or about the time of death from postmortem alterations and developmental features.

Some intellectual overlap is also apparent in the study of teeth. Forensic odontologists uniquely have the expertise to assess products of dental practice, but forensic anthropologists share their knowledge of dental anatomy and dental age estimation techniques.

Anthropologists frequently work closely with and to some extent overlap expertise with forensic entomologists, forensic botanists, DNA specialists, and tool mark examiners. In analysis, such questions arise as "who is best qualified to interpret and report on tool marks in bone, the forensic anthropologist who has experience in the nature of bone modification or the tool mark examiner who specializes in correlations of tool markings with the tools that produced them?" Answers to such questions vary depending on the experience of those involved.

FACIAL IMAGERY

Facial approximation (estimating what the facial image of a person was from the evidence of a recovered skull) and photographic superimposition (usually comparing an antemortem photograph with a skull) represent two common areas of facial imagery that frequently involve anthropologists. Facial approximation (also termed facial reproduction and facial reconstruction) involves a combination of art and science and is employed only as a last resort to reach out to the public for leads in an investigation. The technique is not used directly, or exclusively, for identification purposes. A variety of approaches are available involving clay modeling, sketches, and computer-generated images (Babacan et al. 2021; Donato et al. 2020). The effort is challenging in that it can involve artists who utilize data produced by anthropologists on the characteristics of the individual, anthropologists who happen to have artist skills or a team approach involving collaboration between the artist and anthropologist. The artist must stay focused on the particular anatomy of the individual skull being examined, rather than ceding to artistic license. This can be challenging.

Interpretations regarding photographic superimposition involve all of the concerns, requirements, and caveats of all identification techniques. In the case of skull/photograph comparisons, the technique is usually used for exclusion or to indicate the possibility that the skull and image may represent the same person. Methodology has improved dramatically with new technology, but the underlying concerns remain the same (Ubelaker et al. 2019).

RECENT ADVANCES AND EMERGING TECHNOLOGY

Major advances in forensic anthropology stem from new databases, new technology, new applications of existing technology, increased conversation among scientists, and sustained experimental research (Zapico et al. 2021). As discussed above, growing collections and databases throughout the world have enabled research and conclusions not possible only a decade ago. The new knowledge on the impact of human variation on methodology greatly augments the field and strengthens interpretation.

A database of analyses of many samples of bone, tooth, and other materials using scanning electron microscopy/energy dispersive spectroscopy allows examiners to differentiate small fragments of bone and tooth from other similarly appearing materials (Ubelaker et al. 2002b). Comparison of the forensic specimen can be made with the spectral database of known materials primarily focusing on the proportions of calcium and phosphorus. This technique will differentiate bone and tooth from most other materials but cannot distinguish human from non-human.

New applications of the technique of protein radio immunoassay (pRIA) allow species identification of small bone and tooth fragments (Ubelaker et al. 2004). This procedure will not only differentiate human from nonhuman fragments but will allow determination of the species of the nonhuman material present. Using small samples (200 mg or less), the technique involves protein extraction followed by a solid-phase double-antibody radioimmunoassay employing controls of antisera produced in rabbits and radioactive-marked antibody of rabbit gamma globulin produced in donkeys.

Studies of cementum formation and racemization in teeth offer great promise for more precise age estimation if taphonomic and other methodological issues can be worked out. Microscopic study of the alternating bands of opaque and translucent dental cementum shows potential in quantifying age at death (Wittwer-Backofen et al. 2004) and clarifying season of death (Wedel 2007). However, reducing interobserver error in the counting of the bands represents a challenge.

Another promising area of research involves racemization methodology assessing changes of L-form amino acids to D-form in human proteins (Ohtani et al. 2005; Ohtani and Yamamoto 2005). The challenge with this approach involves clarifying taphonomic effects when applied to remains recovered from forensic contests of considerable time since death.

Analysis of radiocarbon, especially in regard to the modern bomb curve, enables determinations of time since death more accurately than previously possible (Ubelaker 2001). Atmospheric testing of nuclear weapons in the 1950s and early 1960s produced high levels of artificial radiocarbon that through the food chain were incorporated in humans. Although levels have been steadily reducing since the peak in 1963, they only now approach the pre-1950 values. If radiocarbon analysis of recovered human samples reveals the higher levels, then the investigator knows the tissue formed after 1950. Tissue-specific analysis potentially can produce information regarding both the birth date and the death date (Lynnerup et al. 2008; Spalding et al. 2005; Ubelaker 2014b; Ubelaker and Buchholz 2006; Ubelaker et al. 2006).

New three-dimensional approaches to cranial morphology allow greater precision in assessments of population affinities and ancestry (Ross and Ubelaker 2019; Ross et al. 2002, 2004). Moving beyond caliper-generated measurements, these computer-assisted approaches involve more sophisticated shape analysis offering greater insight into potential population relationships.

Chemical approaches offer great promise in estimating geographical origins of individuals. The value of isotopic analysis has long been recognized in dietary reconstruction (Ambrose and Norr 1993; Katzenberg 1992; Schwarcz and Schoeninger 1991). Recently, researchers have focused attention on isotopic analysis of human materials to assess geographical origins in forensic contexts (Chesson and Berg 2021; Ubelaker and Francescutti 2020). The following two studies represent a case in point.

Beard and Johnson (2000) recognized that the quantities of strontium isotopes vary considerably geologically and geographically. Due to dietary factors, strontium isotopes also vary considerably in human bones and teeth, reflecting the geographical origins of the food and water ingested. Thus, strontium isotope analysis of human tissues yields data providing information regarding geographical origins. The authors note that analysis of bone samples produces average values reflecting materials ingested during the last years of life, since bone remodels and continuously incorporates new dietary strontium during the period of bone formation. In contrast, strontium isotope analysis of dental enamel reveals information about the geographic origins of dietary materials during the childhood of the individual since dental enamel does not remodel.

Ehleringer et al. (2008) address the issue of geographic origins of human remains through the analysis of hydrogen and oxygen isotope ratios in human hair. Like the strontium isotopes discussed above, hydrogen and oxygen isotope concentrations also vary geographically and become incorporated in human hair through the diet, especially drinking local tap water. In a forensic context, hair, specifically keratin, analysis might reveal if the person represented displayed values consistent with a local origin or likely originated elsewhere. Analysis of different aspects of the hair might reflect the geographical history of the individual in the relatively short periods of time before death represented by hair growth patterns.

The future remains particularly bright for forensic anthropology, not only because of these technological developments but also primarily because of the growing student and other scholarly interest in the field. This interest translates into new diverse cohorts of emerging forensic anthropologists who through research and casework will continue to transform the field. The surge of innovative research has led to the development of new regional organizations, as well as new publications such as the *Journal of Forensic Anthropology* sponsored by the University of Florida, Wiley's online WIRE for forensic anthropology, and various podcasts. Experimental research continues to focus on taphonomic and trauma issues. Migrant aging has emerged as an important problem for forensic anthropologists. Although forensic anthropology enjoys a solid scientific foundation and rich history, it continues to evolve in positive ways.

REFERENCES

Acśadi, G., and J. Nemeskéri. *History of Human Life Span and Mortality.* Budapest: Akadémiai Kiadó, 1970.

Adserias-Garriga, J., ed. *Age Estimation: A Multidisciplinary Approach.* London: Elsevier, 2019.

Ambrose, S. H., and L. Norr. "Experimental Evidence for the Relationship of the Carbon Isotope Ratios of Whole Diet and Dietary Protein to Those of Bone Collagen and Carbonate." In *Prehistoric Human Bone: Archaeology at the Molecular Level.* Edited by J. B. Lambert and G. Grupe, 1–38. Berlin: Springer-Verlag, 1993.

Argentine Forensic Anthropology Team. Latin American Forensic Anthropology Association. https://www.eaaf.org/alaf/2005/12/latin_american-html.

Babacan, S., S. Isiklar, I. M. Kafa, et al. "Redesign of Missing Mandible by Determining Age Group and Gender from Morphometric Features of Skull for Facial Reconstruction (Approximation)." *Archaeological and Anthropological Science* 13 (2021): 75.

Baccino, E. "Forensic Anthropology Society of Europe (FASE), a Subsection of the IALM, Is 1 Year Old." *International Journal of Legal Medicine* 119 (2005): N1.

Baccino, E., D. H. Ubelaker, L. C. Hayek, et al. "Evaluation of Seven Methods of Estimating Age at Death from Mature Human Skeletal Remains." *Journal of Forensic Sciences* 44 (1999): 931–936.

Baccino, E., and A. Zerilli. "The Two Step Strategy (TSS) or the Right Way to Combine a Dental (LAMENDIN) and an Anthropological (SUCHEY-BROOKS System) Method for Age Determination (Abstract)." *Proceedings of the American Academy of Forensic Sciences* 3 (1997): 150.

Beard, B. L., and C. M. Johnson. "Strontium Isotope Composition of Skeletal Material Can Determine the Birth Place and Geographic Mobility of Humans and Animals." *Journal of Forensic Sciences* 45 (2000): 1049–1061.

Bedford, M. E., K. F. Russell, C. O. Lovejoy, et al. "Test of the Multifactorial Aging Method Using Skeletons with Known Ages-at-Death from the Grant Collection." *American Journal of Physical Anthropology* 91 (1993): 287–297.

Birkby, W. H., T. W. Fenton, and B. E. Anderson. "Identifying Southwest Hispanics Using Nonmetric Traits and the Cultural Profile." *Journal of Forensic Sciences* 53 (2008): 29–33.

Bohan, T. L., and E. J. Heels. "The Case Against *Daubert*: The New Scientific Evidence 'Standard' and the Standards of the Several States." *Journal of Forensic Sciences* 40 (1995): 1030–1044.

Boldsen, J. L., G. R. Milner, L. W. Konigsberg, et al. "Transition Analysis: A New Method for Estimating Age from Skeletons." In *Paleodemography: Age Distribution from Skeletal Samples.* Edited by R. D. Hoppa and J. W. Vaupel, 73–106. Cambridge: Cambridge University Press, 2002.

Bouvier, M., and D. H. Ubelaker. "A Comparison of Two Methods for the Microscopic Determination of Age at Death." *American Journal of Physical Anthropology* 46 (1977): 391–394.

Cheng, E. K., and A. H. Yoon. "Does *Frye* or *Daubert* Matter? A Study of Scientific Admissibility Standards." *Virginia Law Review* 91 (2005): 471–513.

Chesson, L. A., and G. E. Berg. "The Use of Stable Isotopes in Postconflict Forensic Identification." *Wiley Interdisciplinary Reviews: Forensic Science* 4, issue 2 (2021): e1439.

Christensen, A. M. "The Impact of *Daubert*: Implications for Testimony and Research in Forensic Anthropology (and the Use of Frontal Sinuses in Personal Identification)." *Journal of Forensic Sciences* 49 (2004): 427–430.

Christensen, A. M. "Testing the Reliability of Frontal Sinuses in Positive Identification." *Journal of Forensic Sciences* 50 (2005): 18–22.

De Boer, H. H., Z. Obertová, E. Cunha, et al. "Strengthening the Role of Forensic Anthropology in Personal Identification: Position Statement by the Board of the Forensic Anthropology Society of Europe (FASE)." *Forensic Science International* 315 (2020): 110456.

Dempsey, N., and S. Blau. "Evaluating the Evidentiary Value of the Analysis of Skeletal Trauma in Forensic Research: A Review of Research and Practice." *Forensic Science International* 307 (2020): 110140.

Donato, L., R. Cecchi, M. Goldoni, et al. "Photogrammetry vs. CT Scan: Evaluation of Accuracy of a Low-Cost Three-Dimensional Acquisition Method for Forensic Facial Approximation." *Journal of Forensic Sciences* 4 (2020): 1260–1265. https://doi.org/10.1111/1556-4029.14319.

Dunn, R. R., M, C. Spiros, K. R. Kamnikar, et al. "Ancestry Estimation in Forensic Anthropology: A Review." *Wiley Interdisciplinary Reviews: Forensic Science* 2, no. 4 (2020): e1369.

Dwight, T. *The Identification of the Human Skeleton. A Medico-Legal Study.* Boston: David Clapp & Son, 1878.

Dwight, T. "The Sternum as an Index of Sex and Age." *Journal of Anatomy and Physiology* 15 (1881): 327–330.

Dwight, T. "The Sternum as an Index of Sex, Height and Age." *Journal of Anatomy and Physiology* 24 (1890a): 527–535.

Dwight, T. "The Closure of the Cranial Sutures as a Sign of Age." *Boston Medical and Surgical Journal* 122 (1890b): 389–392.

Dwight, T. "Methods of Estimating the Height from Parts of the Skeleton." *Medical Record* 46 (1894a): 293–296.

Dwight, T. "The Range and Significance of Variations in the Human Skeleton." *Boston Medical and Surgical Journal* 13 (1894b): 361–389.

Dwight, T. "The Size of the Articular Surfaces of the Long Bones as Characteristic of Sex." *An Anthropological Study. American Journal of Anatomy* 4 (1905): 19–32.

Ehleringer, J. R., G. J. Bowen, L. A. Chesson, et al. "Hydrogen and Oxygen Isotope Ratios in Human Hair Are Related to Geography." *Proceedings of the National Academy of Sciences of the United States of America* 105 (2008): 2788–2793.

Faigman, D. L., E. Porter, and M. J. Saks. "Check Your Crystal Ball at the Courthouse Door, Please: Exploring the Past, Understanding the Present, and Worrying about the Future of Scientific Evidence." *Cardozo Law Review* 15 (1994): 1799–1835.

Fazekas, I. G., and F. Kósa. *Forensic Fetal Osteology.* Budapest: Akadémiai Kiadó, 1978.

Forensic Anthropology Society of Europe. http://forensicanthropology.eu. Accessed September 1, 2020.

Fulginiti, L. C., K. Hartnett-McCann, and A. Galloway, eds. *Forensic Anthropology and the United States Judicial System.* Oxford: Wiley, 2019.

Galera, V., D. H. Ubelaker, and L. C. Hayek. "Interobserver Error in Macroscopic Methods of Estimating Age at Death from the Human Skeleton." *International Journal of Anthropology* 10, no. 4 (1995): 229–239.

Getz, S. M. "The Use of Transition Analysis in Skeletal Age Estimation." *Wiley Interdisciplinary Reviews: Forensic Science* 2, no. 6 (2020): e1378.

Grivas, C. R., and D. A. Komar. "*Kumho, Daubert*, and the Nature of Scientific Inquiry: Implications for Forensic Anthropology." *Journal of Forensic Sciences* 53 (2008): 771–776.

Jantz, L. M., and R. L. Jantz. "Secular Change in Long Bone Length and Proportion in the United States, 1800–1970." *American Journal of Physical Anthropology* 110 (1999): 57–67.

Jantz, R. L., and S. D. Ousley. *Fordisc 3.0.* Knoxville: The University of Tennessee, 2005.

Kaiser, J. "Should Engineer Witnesses Meet the Same Standards as Scientists?" *Science* 281 (1998): 1578.

Katzenberg, M. A. "Advances in Stable Isotope Analysis of Prehistoric Bones." In *The Skeletal Biology of Past Peoples: Research Methods.* Edited by S. R. Saunders and M. A. Katzenberg, 105–120. New York: John Wiley and Sons, 1992.

Kennedy, D. "Forensic Science: Oxymoron?" *Science* 302 (2003): 1625.

Komar, D. A., and S. Lathrop. "The Use of Material Culture to Establish the Ethnic Identity of Victims in Genocide Investigations: A Validation Study from the American Southwest." *Journal of Forensic Sciences* 53 (2008): 1035–1039.

Krogman, W. M. "A Guide to the Identification of Human Skeletal Material." *FBI Law Enforcement Bulletin* 8 (1939): 3–31.

Krogman, W. M. *The Human Skeleton in Forensic Medicine.* Springfield, IL: Charles C. Thomas, 1962.

L'Abbe, E. N., S. A. Symes, D. E. Raymond, et al. "The Rorschach Butterfly, Understanding Bone Biomechanics Prior to Using Nomenclature in Bone Trauma Interpretations." *Forensic Science International,* 2019. https://doi.org/10.1016/j.forscint.2019.04.005.

Lamendin, H., E. Baccino, J. F. Humbert, et al. "A Simple Technique for Age Estimation in Adult Corpses: The Two Criteria Dental Method." *Journal of Forensic Sciences* 37 (1992): 1373–1379.

Lynnerup, N., H. Kjeldsen, S. Heegaard, et al. "Radiocarbon Dating of the Human Eye Lens Crystallines Reveal Proteins Without Carbon Turnover Throughout Life." *PLoS One* 3, no. 1 (2008). Electronic document. http://dx.doi.org/10.1371%2Fjournal.pone.0001529.

MacKinnon, G., and K. Harrison. "Forensic Anthropology and Archaeology in the United Kingdom: Are We Nearly There Yet?" In *Handbook of Forensic Anthropology and Archaeology*, 2nd edn. Edited by S. Blau and D. H. Ubelaker, 13–26. London: Routledge, 2016.

Martrille, L., D. H. Ubelaker, C. Cattaneo, et al. "Comparison of Four Skeletal Methods for the Estimation of Age at Death on White and Black Adults." *Journal of Forensic Sciences* 52 (2007): 302–307.

McKern, T. W., and T. D. Stewart. "Skeletal Age Changes in Young American Males." Technical Report EP-45. Natick, MA: Quartermaster Research and Development Center, Environmental Protection Research Division, 1957.

Meadows, L., and R. L. Jantz. "Allometric Secular Change in the Long Bones from the 1800s to the Present." *Journal of Forensic Sciences* 40 (1995): 762–767.

Megyesi, M. S., D. H. Ubelaker, and N. J. Sauer. "Test of the Lamendin Aging Method on Two Historic Skeletal Samples." *American Journal of Physical Anthropology* 131 (2006): 363–367.

Milner, G. R., J. W. Wood, and J. L. Boldsen. "Advances in Paleodemography." In *Biological Anthropology of the Human Skeleton*, 2nd edn. Edited by M. A. Katzenberg and S. R. Saunders, 561–600. Hoboken, NJ: John Wiley and Sons, Inc., 2008.

Morishita, J., N. Ikeda, Y. Ueda, et al. "Personal Identification Using Radiological Technology and Advanced Digital Imaging: Expectations and Challenges." *Journal of Forensic Research* 12, no. 8 (2021): 472.

National Research Council. *Strengthening Forensic Science in the United States: A Path Forward*. Washington DC: The National Academies Press, 2009.

Ohtani, S., and T. Yamamoto. "Strategy for the Estimation of Chronological Age Using the Aspartic Acid Racemization Method with Special Reference to Coefficient of Correlation Between D/L Ratios and Ages." *Journal of Forensic Sciences* 50 (2005): 1020–1027.

Ohtani, S., I. Abe, and T. Yamamoto. "An Application of D- and L-Aspartic Acid Mixtures as Standard Specimens for the Chronological Age Estimation." *Journal of Forensic Sciences* 50 (2005): 1298–1302.

Prince, D. A., and D. H. Ubelaker. "Application of Lamendin's Adult Dental Aging Technique to a Diverse Skeletal Sample." *Journal of Forensic Sciences* 47 (2002): 107–116.

Risinger, D. M., M. J. Saks, W. C. Thompson, et al. "The *Daubert/Kumho* Implications of Observer Effects in Forensic Science: Hidden Problems of Expectation and Suggestion." *California Law Review* 90 (2002): 3–56.

Rogers, T. "Skeletal Age Estimation." In *Handbook of Forensic Anthropology and Archaeology*. Edited by S. Blau and D. H. Ubelaker, 273–292. London: Routledge, 2016.

Ross, A. H., and D. H. Ubelaker. "Complex Nature of Hominin Dispersals: Ecogeographical and Climatic Evidence for Pre-Contact Craniofacial Variation." *Scientific Reports* 9 (2019): 11743. https://doi.org/10.1038/s41598-019-48205-1.

Ross, A. H., D. H. Ubelaker, and A. B. Falsetti. "Craniometric Variation in the Americas." *Human Biology* 74 (2002): 807–818.

Ross, A. H., D. E. Slice, D. H. Ubelaker, et al. "Population Affinities of 19th Century Cuban Crania: Implications for Identification Criteria in South Florida Cuban Americans." *Journal of Forensic Sciences* 49 (2004): 11–16.

Saks, M. J. "The Aftermath of *Daubert*: An Evolving Jurisprudence of Expert Evidence." *Jurimetrics* 40 (2000): 229–241.

Sanders, J. "*Kumho* and How We Know." *Law and Contemporary Problems* 64 (2001): 373–415.

Sauer, N. J., J. C. Wankmiller, and J. T. Hefner. "The Assessment of Ancestry and the Concept of Race." In *Handbook of Forensic Anthropology and Archaeology*, 2nd edn. Edited by S. Blau and D. H. Ubelaker, 243–260. London: Routledge, 2016.

Saunders, S. R., C. Fitzgerald, T. Rogers, et al. "A Test of Several Methods of Skeletal Age Estimation Using a Documented Archaeological Sample." *Canadian Society of Forensic Science Journal* 25 (1992): 97–118.

Schaefer, M. C., and S. M. Black. "Comparison of Ages of Epiphyseal Union in North American and Bosnian Skeletal Material." *Journal of Forensic Sciences* 50 (2005): 777–784.

Scheuer, L., and S. Black. *Developmental Juvenile Osteology*. San Diego: Academic Press, 2000.

Schwarcz, H. P., and M. J. Schoeninger. "Stable Isotope Analyses in Human Nutritional Ecology." *Yearbook of Physical Anthropology* 34 (1991): 283–321.

Spalding, K. L., B. A. Buchholz, L. E. Bergman, et al. "Age Written in Teeth by Nuclear Tests." *Nature* 437, no. 7057 (2005): 333–334.

Spencer, F. "Bertillon, Alphonse (1853–1914)." In *History of Physical Anthropology*, vol. 1. A-L. Edited by F. Spencer, 170–171. New York: Garland Publishing, Inc., 1997.

Stewart, T. D. "Medico-legal Aspects of the Skeleton. I. Sex, Age, Race and Stature." *American Journal of Physical Anthropology* 6 (1948): 315–321.

Stewart, T. D. "What the Bones Tell." *FBI Law Enforcement Bulletin* 20 (1951): 1–5.

Stewart, T. D., ed. *Personal Identification in Mass Disasters*. Washington, D.C.: Smithsonian Institution, 1970.

Stewart, T. D. *Essentials of Forensic Anthropology: Especially as Developed in the United States.* Springfield, IL: Charles C. Thomas, 1979.

Stewart, T. D., and M. Trotter, eds. *Basic Readings on the Identification of Human Skeletons: Estimation of Age.* New York: Wenner-Gren Foundation for Anthropological Research, Inc., 1954.

Stewart, T. D., and M. Trotter. "Role of Physical Anthropology in the Field of Human Identification." *Science* 122 (1955): 883–884.

Stinson, S. et al. "Growth Variation: Biological and Cultural Factors." In *Human Biology: An Evolutionary and Biocultural Perspective.* Edited by S. Stinson, B. Bogin, and R. Huss-Ashmore, 425–464. New York: Wiley-Liss, Inc., 2000.

Trotter, M., and G. C. Gleser. "Estimation of Stature from Long Bones of American Whites and Negroes." *American Journal of Physical Anthropology* 10 (1952): 463–514.

Ubelaker, D. H. "Approaches to Demographic Problems in the Northeast." In *Foundations of Northeast Archaeology.* Edited by D. R. Snow, 175–194. New York: Academic Press, 1981.

Ubelaker, D. H. "Estimating Age at Death from Immature Human Skeletons: An Overview." *Journal of Forensic Sciences* 32 (1987): 1254–1263.

Ubelaker, D. H. "Aleš Hrdlička's Role in the History of Forensic Anthropology." *Journal of Forensic Sciences* 44 (1999a): 724–730.

Ubelaker, D. H. *Human Skeletal Remains, Excavation, Analysis, Interpretation,* 3rd edn. Washington, DC: Taraxacum, 1999b.

Ubelaker, D. H. "Artificial Radiocarbon as an Indicator of Recent Origin of Organic Remains in Forensic Cases." *Journal of Forensic Sciences* 46 (2001): 1285–1287.

Ubelaker, D. H. "Osteology Refence Collections." In *Encyclopedia of Global Archaeology.* Edited by C. Smith, 5632–5641. New York: Springer, 2014a.

Ubelaker, D. H. "Radiocarbon Analysis of Human Remains: A Review of Forensic Applications." *Journal of Forensic Sciences* 59 (2014b): 1466–1472.

Ubelaker, D. H. "A History of Forensic Anthropology." *American Journal of Physical Anthropology* 165 (2018a): 915–923.

Ubelaker, D. H. "Personal Identification in Forensic Anthropology." *The Japanese Journal of Legal Medicine* 72 (2018b): 62–63.

Ubelaker, D. H., and B. A. Buchholz. "Complexities in the Use of Bomb-Curve Radiocarbon to Determine Time Since Death of Human Skeletal Remains." *Forensic Science Communications* 8, no. 1 (2006). Electronic document. https://archives.fbi.gov/archives/about-us/lab/forensic-science-communications/fsc/archives.

Ubelaker, D. H., and C. Franscescutti. "The Role of Stable Isotope Analysis in Forensic Anthropology." In *Forensic Science and Humanitarian Action: Interacting with the Dead and the Living.* Edited by R. C. Parra, S. C. Zapico, and D. H. Ubelaker, 275–280. Hoboken, New Jersey: John Wiley & Sons, Inc, 2020.

Ubelaker, D. H., and R. C. Parra. "Application of Three Dental Methods of Adult Age Estimation from Intact Single Rooted Teeth to a Peruvian Sample." *Journal of Forensic Sciences* 53 (2008): 608–611.

Ubelaker, D. H., A. H. Ross, and S. M. Graver. "Application of Forensic Discriminant Functions to a Spanish Cranial Sample." *Forensic Science Communications* 4, no. 3 (2002a). Electronic document. https://archives.fbi.gov/archives/about-us/lab/forensic-science-communications/fsc/archives.

Ubelaker, D. H., D. C. Ward, V. S. Braz, et al. "The Use of SEM/EDS Analysis to Distinguish Dental and Osseus Tissue from Other Materials." *Journal of Forensic Sciences* 47 (2002b): 940–943.

Ubelaker, D. H., J. M. Lowenstein, and D. G. Hood. "Use of Solid-Phase Double-Antibody Radioimmunoassay to Identify Species from Small Skeletal Fragments." *Journals of Forensic Sciences* 49 (2004): 924–929.

Ubelaker, D. H., B. A. Buchholz, and J. E. B. Stewart. "Analysis of Artificial Radiocarbon in Different Skeletal and Dental Tissue Types to Evaluate Date of Death." *Journal of Forensic Sciences* 51 (2006): 484–488.

Ubelaker, D. H., Y. Wu, and Q. R. Cordero. "Craniofacial Photographic Superimposition: New Developments. Forensic Science International." *Synergy* 1 (2019): 271–274.

Warren, M. W., H. A. Walsh-Haney, and L. E. Freas, eds. *The Forensic Anthropology Laboratory.* Boca Raton: CRC Press, 2008.

Wedel, V. L. "Determination of Season at Death Using Dental Cementum Increment Analysis." *Journal of Forensic Sciences* 52 (2007): 1334–1337.

Wittwer-Backofen, U., J. Gampe, and J. W. Vaupel. "Tooth Cementum Annulation for Age Estimation: Results from a Large Known-Age Validation Study." *American Journal of Physical Anthropology* 123 (2004): 119–129.

Zapico, S. C., D. H. Ubelaker, and J. Adserias-Garriga. "Applications of Physiological Bases of Aging to Forensic Science: New Advances." In *Forensic Science and Humanitarian Action: Interacting with the Dead and the Living*. Edited by R. C. Parra, S. C. Zapico, and D. H. Ubelaker, 183–197. Hoboken, New Jersey: John Wiley & Sons, Inc., 2020.

Zapico, S C., Q. Gauthier, A. Antevska, et al. "Identifying Methylation Patterns in Dental Pulp Aging: Application to Age-at-Death Estimation in Forensic Anthropology." *International Journal of Molecular Sciences* 22, no. 7 (2021): 3717.

30 Diet Reconstruction and Ecology

Margaret J. Schoeninger and Laurie J. Reitsema

BACKGROUND

Stable isotope ratio analysis revolutionized research on present and past diets and ecology, particularly when combined with information from other sources (e.g., see Chapter 32). Physicists discovered that some elements occur in more than one form (i.e., isotopes), expanding their use during World War II. Following the war, chemists and geochemists used them in non-military research, and some of those academics trained anthropologists. In South Africa, geochemist John Vogel worked with archaeologist Nik van der Merwe, and together they published one of the earliest papers on the use of carbon stable isotopes determining the timing of maize introduction into North America (Vogel and van der Merwe 1977). In the USA, geochemist Samuel Epstein trained Michael DeNiro, a zoologist (DeNiro and Epstein 1978, 1981b). DeNiro, in turn, trained a biological anthropologist (Schoeninger and DeNiro 1984; Schoeninger et al. 1983).

The term isotope means "same place" on the periodic table (Hoefs 2009). In carbon, ^{12}C and ^{13}C are stable carbon isotopes, whereas ^{14}C is an unstable, or radioactive, isotope. All three isotopes of carbon have the same number of electrons and protons but differ in the number of neutrons in their nuclei. This chapter deals only with the stable forms. The isotopes of an element share the same chemical properties because chemical reactions are determined largely by electron configurations, but they differ in mass (numbers of neutrons) and so molecules containing different isotopes (e.g., $^{13}CO_2$ versus $^{12}CO_2$) react at different rates and the bond strengths differ between molecules containing different isotopes of the same element. The effects are most apparent among the light elements (H, C, N, O) because the differential between the isotopes is large compared with the average mass of the element. Among the light elements, molecules with the "lighter" isotope (^{12}C) react faster and the bonds break more easily than those molecules containing the "heavier" isotope (^{13}C). In other words, $^{12}C-^{14}N$ bonds form and break more rapidly than do bonds consisting of $^{12}C-^{15}N$, $^{13}C-^{14}N$, or $^{13}C-^{15}N$.

As the isotopes within an element circulate within the biosphere, these reaction rate differences result in products that contain different relative amounts of each stable isotope than those in the starting components (i.e., substrate) of a reaction. For example, bone collagen is a protein made up of individual amino acids, each of which is a product resulting from reactions on starting components from food and the breakdown products from an animal's own tissues. The $^{13}C/^{12}C$ ratio of the carbon in an individual's collagen (product) differs depending on the $^{13}C/^{12}C$ ratio in the combination of consumed amino acids of protein, specific carbohydrates, and lipids (substrate). Bone collagen normally has relatively more ^{13}C than in diet because bonds with ^{12}C break more readily and more ^{12}C is eliminated as waste from the body. Hence, we say that bone collagen is enriched in ^{13}C relative to its substrate (diet), and that excreted materials are depleted in ^{13}C relative to the substrate. Similarly, the $^{18}O/^{16}O$ ratio in bone mineral (product) differs from the $^{18}O/^{16}O$ ratio in the animal's body water, which is the substrate for the oxygen in bone mineral. The difference in isotope ratio between the product and substrate is largely due to fractionation. For collagen synthesis, enzymatic control determines the magnitude of the fractionation; this is a case of kinetic isotope fractionation. For bone mineral synthesis the temperature of the reaction determines the magnitude of fractionation; this is an equilibrium isotope fractionation.

Among heavier elements like strontium (mass of 87.62), the mass difference between the isotopes is trivial compared to the overall mass of the element. Within strontium, metabolic reactions such as photosynthesis, bone mineral synthesis, or amino acid synthesis do not change the $^{87}Sr:^{86}Sr$ ratio of the product (plant tissue or bone mineral) relative to the ratio within the substrate. Instead, the ratio of $^{87}Sr:^{86}Sr$ in biological tissues directly reflects the substrate, which for strontium is a rock or soil, or the water in which soil or rocks have dissolved.

Except for strontium, biological processes result in the transfer of elements from the geosphere to the biosphere as well as between different compartments of each sphere. For example, the transfer of carbon from the ocean to the atmosphere or from plant tissue to animal tissue are associated with predictable, sequential changes from the natural abundance isotope ratios through kinetic and equilibrium isotope fractionation (see Figures 3.1 and 3.2 in Fry 2006). These changes, however, are small so that direct reporting of isotope ratios (e.g., $^{13}C:^{12}C$) is impractical. For this reason, isotope ratios are represented as δ values (e.g., δ ^{13}C), i.e., the difference between the isotope ratio within the sample of interest and that within an internationally recognized standard (e.g., PDB for carbon, AIR for nitrogen, SMOW or PDB for oxygen). These δ values are expressed as per mil (‰) (Hoefs 2009), according to the following equation:

$$\frac{R_{sample} - R_{standard}}{R_{standard}} * 1,000$$

where R_{sample} equals the $^{13}C/^{12}C$ ratio in the material of interest (e.g., bone, hair, plant, etc.) and $R_{standard}$ equals the $^{13}C/^{12}C$ ratio in the standard used in comparison (e.g., for carbon). The stable isotope data on primates, including humans, derive from a variety of tissues including: feces, representing roughly 24 hours or less, hair, representing one year or more, bone mineral (apatite) and organic (collagen), representing years, and tooth dentine and enamel (apatite), representing early life. The applications of the isotope approach are worldwide, and any presentation of short length will necessarily be unable to cover all of them.

CARBON ISOTOPE RATIOS, REPRESENTED AS $\delta^{13}C$

The majority of the world's active cycling carbon is sequestered in the ocean as dissolved carbonate. During the exchange between oceanic carbon with atmospheric carbon dioxide (CO_2), atmospheric CO_2 (product) is depleted in ^{13}C relative to oceanic carbon (substrate) by equilibrium isotope fractionation. Today's atmospheric CO_2 has a $\delta^{13}C$ value around –8‰ while surface ocean CO_2 has a value around 1‰ (Wahlen 1994). Plant $\delta^{13}C$ values are determined by kinetic isotope fractionation during photosynthetic fixation of atmospheric CO_2, which is the source of carbon for all terrestrial plants. The average value for today's plants that follow the dominant terrestrial C_3 pathway (cool season grasses, herbaceous plants, and trees) is around –26 to –28‰, those that utilize the C_4 pathway (warm and dry adapted tropical grasses like maize, amaranths, chenopods, setarias) average around –12‰, and those that utilize the CAM pathway (succulents) commonly have values near those of C_4 plants (Kohn 2010; O'Leary 1988). The large range in C_3 plant values is discussed further below.

The $\delta^{13}C$ value of terrestrial plants and animals dating to more than 100 years ago are approximately 1.5‰ higher than those of today's plants and animals. Large-scale forest burning (i.e., combustion of C_3 plants) and use of fossil fuels (mostly C_3 plants) have dumped huge amounts of ^{13}C-depleted CO_2 (~ –26‰) into our atmosphere, which is termed the Suess effect (Keeling 1961; Keeling et al. 2017). The results are higher atmospheric CO_2 levels than any in the last 5+ million years and atmospheric $\delta^{13}C$ values around –8‰ rather than the –6.5‰ of the nineteenth century (Friedli et al. 1986). More recently, the Suess effect is recognized as lowering dissolved inorganic carbon $\delta^{13}C$ values by up to 0.8‰ in uppermost levels of subtropical regions of relatively shallow oceans currents like the Gulf Stream (Eide et al. 2017). The impact, if any, on marine plants and animals located in nearby regions is not yet known.

In contrast to plants on land, freshwater aquatic plants have multiple potential sources of carbon. Particulate organic matter, from algae and detritus, has values ranging approximately from –18.5 to –22.0‰ (Hoefs 2009). The $\delta^{13}C$ ratios of plants and animals occupying freshwater aquatic niches fall between these values. Variables such as turbulence, depth, and clarity all influence $\delta^{13}C$ values of carbon in waters, even within the same water body (Hecky and Hesslein 1995; Katzenberg and Weber 1999).

Marine plants, most of which follow the C_3 photosynthetic pathway, utilize multiple carbon sources including detritus from local terrestrial plants in nearshore and brackish waters, dissolved CO_2 (–7.0‰), and dissolved carbonic acid (0‰), and have $\delta^{13}C$ values between those of C_3 and C_4 terrestrial plants (Hoefs 2009). Thus, marine animals consuming nearshore marine plants have values closer to C_3 plants whereas higher trophic level marine fish and mammals have $\delta^{13}C$ values that are less negative (Schoeninger and DeNiro 1984; Vika and Theodoropoulou 2012).

In archaeological applications of isotopic diet reconstructions, carbon isotope ratios differ not only with foods consumed, but among different consumer tissue types. For example, collagen and carbonate from the same bone exhibit different, albeit correlated, $\delta^{13}C$ values, owing to differences in how these tissues are formed (see above) (Ambrose and Norr 1993; Tieszen and Fagre 1993). Understanding the relationships between the $\delta^{13}C$ values of different tissue types has provided important complementary information about diet in cases where multiple tissues can be analyzed, and permitted diet reconstructions in cases where only one or another tissue type is available (e.g., where tooth enamel is preserved but bone collagen is not). A meta-analysis (Kellner and Schoeninger 2007) compared experimental data from rats, mice, and pigs (Ambrose and Norr 1993; Howland et al. 2003; Jim et al. 2004). The experimental studies show that $\delta^{13}C_{diet}$ is estimated accurately based on $\delta^{13}C_{apatite}$ as suggested in each individual study. The meta-analysis also showed that $\delta^{13}C_{collagen}$ correlated more tightly with $\delta^{13}C_{diet}$ than with $\delta^{13}C_{diet\ protein}$, i.e., a significant amount of the carbon in bone collagen is coming from the carbohydrate and lipid fraction of diet (i.e., diet energy), and not the diet protein. Fernandes and colleagues (2012) and Froehle and colleagues (2010, 2012) estimate approximately 30–40 percent of the isotopic signature captured in collagen reflects these other dietary fractions rather than diet protein.

In addition, the meta-analysis demonstrated that a plot of $\delta^{13}C_{collagen}$ against $\delta^{13}C_{apatite}$ of all experimental fauna revealed two parallel regression lines with individuals eating only C_3 protein falling about 6‰ to the left (more negative) of those individuals eating only C_4 protein. Those eating only C_3 energy plotted at the lower (more negative) end of the graph while those eating only C_4 energy plotted at the top (less negative) end; those with mixed sources of energy plotted midway along their respective regression lines. Archaeological populations (Harrison and Katzenberg 2003; figure 2) selected for extensive floral and faunal information on human diet largely adhered to the model described by the experimental fauna. Archaeological populations with significant reliance on marine foods did not separate clearly. Subsequent analyses including nitrogen isotope data (Froehle et al. 2009) clarified the situation and is discussed further below.

Collagen and carbonate are the most common materials analyzed in stable isotope studies in archaeology, but there is growing interest in the measurement of isotope ratios of specific compounds, such as individual amino acids. Individual amino acids follow their own metabolic pathways, offering more specific evidence linking consumers to their diets (Hare et al. 1991). For example, research in arid coastal and near-coastal regions of South Africa has disentangled marine protein and C_4 plants as possible sources of high $\delta^{13}C$ values among past humans using $\delta^{13}C$ values of individual amino acids (Corr et al. 2005). Even in cases where $\delta^{13}C_{Collagen}$ values are similar between groups, the $\Delta^{13}C_{Glycine-Phenylalanine}$ values of marine protein consumers are higher than those of C_4 consumers, because phenylalanine is an essential amino acid routed to collagen with little fractionation (~1–2‰), whereas glycine is a non-essential amino acid subject to fractionation between trophic levels when it is synthesized de novo. Marine food webs have more trophic positions than terrestrial food webs (Schoeninger and DeNiro 1984), making enrichment of $^{13}C_{Glycine}$ an indicator of marine resource consumption in an otherwise ambiguous case.

Much of the $\delta^{13}C$ variation within C_3 plants that was mentioned above is associated with the level of canopy cover, which affects both the $\delta^{13}C$ value in the carbon dioxide available to growing plants and the rate of photosynthesis (Kohn 2010). The $\delta^{13}C$ value of CO_2 within semi-evergreen tropical forests (i.e., more closed canopies) is >2‰ below well-mixed atmospheric CO_2. This is partially due to the addition of ^{13}C-depleted CO_2 respired from microbial activity that varies dramatically both temporally and spatially, including vertically (Pataki et al. 2003). Plant tissues integrate this variation (Bowling et al. 2003).

Studies among extant primates demonstrate that $\delta^{13}C$ values in primate tissues track environmental variables including canopy cover, foraging height, and precipitation (Blumenthal et al. 2012; Carlson and Crowley 2016; Schoeninger et al. 1997, 1998, 2016). The increasing frequency with which humans interact with nonhuman primates due to habitat encroachment is impacting the microenvironmental characteristics of primate habitats and has given rise to the field of ethnoprimatology. Stable isotope studies have focused on many key aspects of human–nonhuman primate interactions, including crop raiding (Loudon et al. 2014), provisioning (Schurr et al. 2012), and forest disturbance (Schillaci et al. 2014).

Other research with extant primates focuses on behaviors that are otherwise difficult to observe, such as weaning (Bădescu et al. 2017).

Additional work has used the $\delta^{13}C$ values in various materials to reconstruct general aspects of the ecology of past environments and the diets of our early hominin relatives. Some estimated the presence of C_3 and C_4 plant types and shifting paleoenvironments by analyzing combinations of proxy measures including the $\delta^{13}C$ values in paleosols and carbonate nodules, and bone mineral and tooth enamel of various ungulate species (Kingston 2007; Kingston and Harrison 2007b; Lee-Thorp 2000b). Other studies caution against relying on a single proxy like ungulate tooth enamel because of intrataxon variation in diets (Robinson et al. 2021). Diagenesis (postmortem alteration of the carbonate fraction) can be a significant problem (Koch 2007; Koch et al. 1997). In East Africa, some of the 3.9 million year old tooth enamels were extensively altered mineralogically whereas others, from the same excavation site, were not (Kohn et al. 1999; Schoeninger et al. 2003) and in South Africa, diagenetic alteration of 1–2‰ occurs (Lee-Thorp 2000a).

Still, some fascinating results are now available (summarized by Schoeninger 2014; Sponheimer et al. 2013). One of our earliest relatives, *Ardipithecus*, lived in a wooded environment eating C_3 foods (White et al. 2009). Among East African *Homo habilis* and *Paranthropus boisei* (van der Merwe et al. 2008), and South African *Australopithecus africanus* and *Paranthropus robustus* (Sponheimer et al. 2005) all foraged in open country or drought-type habitats rather than in closed canopy situations. Some individuals (especially *Paranthropus*) apparently ate foods with a C_4 signal although what those foods may have been is still the subject of discussion. Among European Neandertals and early modern humans, the $\delta^{13}C$ values in collagen demonstrate that they foraged in open country habitats (Richards and Trinkaus 2009), even though they may have inhabited forested regions.

Nitrogen Isotope Ratios, Represented as $\delta^{15}N$

The major nitrogen reservoir is the atmosphere and the $\delta^{15}N$ of well-mixed atmosphere is defined at 0.0‰. The transfer of inorganic nitrogen (N_2 gas) into the biological realm depends on specialized organisms such that those found in nodules on the roots of leguminous plants (called nitrogen-fixing plants), which can have values close to zero although the majority of plants take up soil nitrogen and are more positive than atmospheric nitrogen (Virginia and Delwiche 1982). Marine organisms tend to have more positive $\delta^{15}N$ values than do terrestrial organisms except in environments like coral reefs, where nitrogen-fixing blue-green algae comprise the base of the food chain (Schoeninger and DeNiro 1984). The higher marine values result from bacterial activity and from the greater length of trophic chains in the ocean than in terrestrial environments.

The $\delta^{15}N$ values in the tissues of animals are positively correlated with the values in their diets (DeNiro and Epstein 1981b; Schoeninger and DeNiro 1984; Minagawa and Wada 1984; Hare et al. 1991). The source of the nitrogen in bone collagen is largely ingested with a minimal amount recycled from one's own body (Ambrose 2000). There is an increase of approximately 3.5‰ in $\delta^{15}N$ values between trophic levels (Ambrose 2000; Minagawa and Wada 1984; Schoeninger and DeNiro 1984), and human omnivory has been estimated in broad relative terms in some regions (Ambrose et al. 2003) and in more specific terms in other regions where plants are unavailable for much of the year (Richards et al. 2000). Humans eating marine foods often show higher $\delta^{15}N$ than those who do not in similar regions (Sealy and van der Merwe 1986). Exceptions to this general rule occur in specific situations of water or caloric stress (Ambrose and DeNiro 1986; Fuller et al. 2005; Heaton et al. 1986; O'Connell et al. 2001; Sealy et al. 1987), and in warm-water reefs or other areas with shallow coastal margins where blue-green algae directly fix atmospheric nitrogen (Keegan and DeNiro 1988; Wallace et al. 2006).

The $\delta^{15}N$ values and $\delta^{13}C$ values from different tissue types reflect different, complementary aspects of a consumer's diet, and thus can be usefully combined for a more comprehensive picture of overall diet. Mixing models have been developed to account for these multiple lines of evidence (reviewed by Cheung and Szpak 2021; Reitsema and Holder 2018). For example, adding $\delta^{15}N_{collagen}$ values to Kellner and Schoeninger's (2007) comparison of $\delta^{13}C_{collagen}$ and $\delta^{13}C_{apatite}$ values in a multivariate model clarifies specific aspects of the diet of several populations (Froehle et al. 2009). Of C_3-based foragers, those from Ontario had an average $\delta^{15}N_{collagen}$ value of 12.2 ± 1.0‰ compared to 9.5 ± 2.1‰ in those from Georgia, demonstrating the importance of freshwater fish from the Great Lakes in the former (Katzenberg 1989). Among coastal foragers, those from Tierra del Fuego (14.8 ± 3.2‰, range = 10.6–18.8‰) are lower than California islanders (17.8 ± 1.4‰, range = 14.9–20.8‰), and the former show a bi-model distribution that is nonoverlapping (10.6–13.2‰ vs. 15.1–18.8‰) when plotted by region, even though the carbon stable isotope values are virtually similar.

Because they reflect trophic position, $\delta^{15}N$ values of dependent infants (hair; feces) are higher than those of their mothers until the completion of weaning, aiding evaluations of infant care, reproductive strategies, and life history variables (Bădescu et al. 2017; Beaumont et al. 2015; Fuller et al. 2006; Katzenberg et al. 1996; Kendall et al. 2021; Reitsema 2012; Reynard and Tuross 2015; Schurr 1998, 2018; Wright and Schwarcz 1998).

HYDROGEN ISOTOPE RATIOS, REPRESENTED AS δ^2H OR δ

Hydrogen is ubiquitous in the geosphere and the huge relative mass difference between its two stable isotopes (^2H or D and ^1H) means that hydrogen exhibits the largest fractionations among the light stable isotopes. As a result of massive equilibrium isotope fractionations during the transfer of water from the ocean to the atmosphere and in precipitation, δD^2H values in rainwater and surface water, in the plants and animals that rely on them, show patterned differences (White 1989; Ziegler 1989). First suggested over 40 years ago as a tracer in food webs (Estep and Dabrowski 1980), the method was seldom used (Cormie et al. 1994b) because of difficulties in controlling for the exchangeable hydrogen atoms within organic material (Bowen et al. 2005) and the multiple sources of hydrogen in tissues (DeNiro and Epstein 1981a). Recently, however, several laboratories demonstrated the effectiveness of δ^2H values in various tissues for identifying trophic position (Birchall et al. 2005), animal migration patterns (Hobson et al. 2004; Hobson and Wassenaar 1997), paleoclimate (Leyden et al. 2006), human paleodiet (Reynard and Hedges 2008), and forensic cases (Bowen et al. 2009), as well as other applications such as the identification of CAM plants or beans in human diets (Sternberg 1989; Ziegler 1989).

OXYGEN ISOTOPE RATIOS, REPRESENTED AS $\delta^{18}O$

Oxygen has three stable isotopes (^{18}O, ^{17}O, and ^{16}O), but $^{18}O/^{16}O$ is usually measured because it affords the greater relative mass difference. The water cycle of evaporation and condensation produces the general, global patterns of $\delta^{18}O$ in waters (Craig 1961; Gat 1980; Gat and Gonfiantini 1981) and in animal tissues (Longinelli 1984). These studies demonstrate that temperature of precipitation (summer versus winter, altitudinal and latitudinal variation), rainfall amount (e.g., El Niño vs. La Niña), air-circulation patterns, distance from the ocean, and other variables affect the $\delta^{18}O$ in waters must be considered in local situations.

The $\delta^{18}O$ values of phosphate and carbonate in animal bone and tooth enamel show a general correlation with local precipitation (Koch et al. 1989; Kohn 1996; Kohn et al. 1996) although physiological parameters vary across animal species in ways that can differentially affect animal $\delta^{18}O$ values (Bryant and Froelich 1995; Fricke and O'Neil 1996). Animals that obtain the majority of their body water by drinking surface water 'show a strong correlation with the values in surface water' (Huertas et al. 1995). Those that obtain the majority of their body water from their diets show a correlation with local relative humidity (Ayliffe and Chivas 1990; Cormie et al. 1994a). Seasonal variation in rainfall is recorded by intratooth variation in $\delta^{18}O$ values (Balasse et al. 2003; Fricke et al. 1998), proving useful in reconstructing aspects of behavior within pastoral populations (Balasse and Ambrose 2002) or paleoclimatic variables such as temperature, rainfall, and humidity (Bryant et al. 1996, 1994; Fricke et al. 1995; Schoeninger et al. 2000). More recently, the $\delta^{18}O$ values of tooth enamel have been compared with that in bone mineral to determine migration patterns in prehistoric human populations, particularly in Mesoamerica and South America (Knudson and Buikstra 2007; Knudson and Price 2007; White et al. 2004).

Strontium Isotope Ratios: $^{87}Sr/^{86}Sr$

The distribution of ratios of strontium isotopes differs from the discrimination of strontium relative to calcium in biological systems. Because there is no measurable fractionation during transfer between the geosphere and the biosphere, the $^{87}Sr/^{86}Sr$ ratio in animal bones and teeth reflects an averaging of the $^{87}Sr/^{86}Sr$ ratios in an animal's diet and drinking water (Faure 1977). Very old rocks contain significantly more ^{87}Sr than do rocks of recent origin because ^{87}Sr is a long-term decay product of the radioactive isotope ^{87}Rb. This means that in regions where there are distinctive $^{87}Sr/^{86}Sr$ ratios, it can be possible to identify the area of origin. When there is no diagenetic alteration of the original biological level of strontium (Hoppe et al. 2003; Nelson et al. 1986), intra-tooth variation in $^{87}Sr/^{86}Sr$ ratios or the difference between tooth enamel and bone $^{87}Sr/^{86}Sr$ ratios can identify migratory behavior in animals (Hoppe et al. 1999), including humans (Bentley 2006).

The application of $^{87}Sr/^{86}Sr$ ratios for understanding human behavior has been used across many regions. The approach clarified the origin of a highly ranked individual from Tikal in MesoAmerica (Wright 2005), suggested migratory behavior in archaeological and fossil populations in South Africa (Sealy et al. 1991; Sillen et al. 1998), central Europe (Price et al. 1994a), Briton (Montgomery et al. 2003), and the southwestern US (Price et al. 1994b), and revealed possible marriage patterns in South America (Ericson 1985) and warfare involving foreign mercenaries in the ancient Mediterranean region (Reinberger et al. 2021). The most detailed study, however, is in South America, where Knudson and colleagues have addressed patterns of population and individual movements across the Peruvian highlands (Dahlstedt et al. 2021; Knudson and Buikstra 2007; Knudson et al. 2014, 2004).

Sulfur Isotope Ratios, Represented as $\delta^{34}S$

There are three main reservoirs for sulfur on Earth: dissolved sulfate (SO_4) in oceans with $\delta^{34}S$ values of approximately +20‰, sulfate in sediments formed by evaporites, with $\delta^{34}S$ values of approximately +16‰, and sulfide in rocks and soils, with $\delta^{34}S$ values of approximately $-12‰$ (Krouse 1980; Newton and Bottrell 2007). The $\delta^{34}S$ values of plants and animals in a particular region vary according to the varied input of these sources in waters and soils. The mean $\delta^{34}S$ value of sea water is uniquely high, at $+20‰$, and does not vary greatly among regions, due to the sheer massiveness of the oceans as a reservoir. Freshwater organisms have values spanning the range of $\delta^{34}S$ in biological systems ($-22‰$ to $+20‰$), due to the differential inputs of sulfates, weathering sedimentary sulfides, porewater sulfates, and precipitation into waters, as well as the influence of fractionation by anaerobic bacteria (Connolly et al. 2004; Nehlich 2015). Freshwaters tend to have values of between $-5‰$ and $+15‰$ (Nehlich et al. 2012). As in freshwater, the $\delta^{34}S$ values of terrestrial plants and animals are varied but are lower than those of the ocean, with a typical range of $-5‰$ to $+10‰$, clustering around $0‰$ (Nehlich et al. 2012). Terrestrial $\delta^{34}S$ values are the products of weathering of the sulfates and sulfides in rocks, evaporites, and soils, and deposits of oceanic sulfur from sea spray and precipitation (Krouse 1980). This latter factor, termed the "sea spray effect," results in higher terrestrial $\delta^{34}S$ values in coastal regions. Because $\delta^{34}S$ variation is linked both to geography and to diet, the applications of $\delta^{34}S$ values in archaeology tend to follow two paths: reconstructing migration histories (e.g., Bataille et al. 2021), and disambiguating carbon and nitrogen isotope evidence for aquatic foods in human diets (e.g., Nehlich et al. 2010).

CONCLUSIONS

Forty years ago, no one predicted the astounding range of applications that now use stable isotope data within anthropology, and the same difficulty occurs now for predictions into the future. A few areas, however, seem particularly promising. First, the development of new technical methods is truly remarkable. Many of these are published in the *Journal of Archaeological Science* and include residue analyses (Mukherjee et al. 2008), specific amino acid analyses (Corr et al. 2009), and continued development of δ^2H (δD) in climate studies (Kirsanow et al. 2008).

In addition, there are several large overarching projects investigating human biological and social change through time, where stable isotope analysis plays one of several interrelated parts. For example, the Global History of Health Project (co-directed by Clark Larsen, Richard Steckel, and Paul Sciulli) compares estimates of ancient human health with human diet (see Steckel et al. 2002, for a preliminary report) to provide the first rigorous evaluation of the impact of human subsistence strategies on health. In the Andean highland and lowland regions of South America several projects are beginning to clarify how the emergence of two powerful states (Wari and Tiwanaku) combined with environmental change to impact specific local communities. Stable isotope analyses are central to delineating climate change (e.g., Magilligan et al. 2008), identifying migrants (e.g., Buzon et al. 2012; Knudson and Torres-Rouff 2009), and elucidating the variable effect of imperial powers on the subsistence strategies, health, and social structure of peripheral communities (Kellner and Schoeninger 2008). For example, in the Andean region, the interactions between colonial powers and their associated communities clearly differed within the Andean region and across North America (e.g., Garland et al. 2018; Hutchinson 2004; Kellner and Schoeninger 2008; Larsen 2001).

Climate reconstruction both on the archaeological and the paleontological scale is another exciting area given the importance of understanding climate change for today's world. Archaeological samples hold the promise of understanding the specifics of climate change and its impact on actual human populations in the past, which should be useful in our present-day preparations and expectations. Physical and paleo-oceanographers, atmospheric chemists, and geochemists might clarify the variables and processes that cause climate change, but they lack the human scale that bioarcheology and paleoanthropology provide. The Andean projects mentioned above are one example. Another (among many) comprises paleoecology and paleoclimate reconstruction across Africa and Eurasia during the time that the human lineage separated from ape-like ancestors, radiated, and then resulted in the single lineage that we see today. In Africa, the painstaking work of John Kingston and colleagues (Kingston 2007; Kingston et al. 2007; Kingston and Harrison 2007a) includes carbonate nodule and tooth enamel analyses, mapping of modern environmental signatures, and consideration of orbital parameters to provide a background for understanding East African Plio/Pleistocene hominin evolution. Expanding these kinds of study to other geographical regions and placing fossils from multiple time periods in a context was unanticipated prior to the present developments within stable isotope analysis (see Hallin et al. 2012; Hartman 2008; Lee-Thorp and Sponheimer 2006, for examples).

Finally, primate behavioral ecology is also benefiting from stable isotope studies. Combined with observations on diet and behavioral data from long-term field projects, like that of Phillips-Conroy in the Awash National Park in Ethiopia, the dietary and ecological variation recorded by stable isotope data in various samples, including feces (Bădescu et al. 2017; Blumenthal et al. 2012; Codron et al. 2006; Reitsema et al. 2020) and hair (Loudon et al. 2016; Oelze et al. 2016; Schillaci et al. 2019), will establish predictive power that enables isotope analysis of fossils, museum collections, and unhabituated primate populations to expand knowledge of diet and ecology in all these groups.

The list could go on and on, and while this chapter must end, the work will not. Stable isotope data are such powerful proxy measures of multiple variables that it is now impossible to account for the great diversity in applications of relevance to anthropology in a single chapter. Perhaps that is the highest compliment that one can give to the two academics who started us all on this fascinating path with their presentation to the 1976 Annual Meeting of the Society for American Archaeology (Vogel and van der Merwe 1976). We wish they could both find satisfaction in that difficulty.

REFERENCES

Ambrose, S. H. "Controlled Diet and Climate Experiments on Nitrogen Isotope Ratios of Rats." In *Biogeochemical Approaches to Paleodietary Analysis.* Edited by S. H. Ambrose and M. A. Katzenberg, 243–259. New York: Kluwer Academic/Plenum Publishers, 2000.

Ambrose, S. H., and M. J. DeNiro. "The Isotopic Ecology of East African Mammals." *Oecologia* 69 (1986): 395–406.

Ambrose, S, and L. Norr. "Experimental Evidence for the Relationship of the Carbon Stable Isotope Ratios of Whole Diet and Dietary Protein to Those of Bone Collagen and Carbonate." In *Prehistoric Human Bone: Archaeology at the Molecular Level.* Edited by J. B. Lambert and G. Grupe, 1–38. Berlin: Springer-Verlag, 1993.

Ambrose, S. H., J. E. Buikstra, and H. W. Krueger. "Gender and Status Differences in Diet at Mound 72, Cahokia, Revealed by Isotopic Analysis of Bone." *Journal of Anthropological Archaeology* 22, no. 3 (2003): 217–226.

Ayliffe, L. K., and A. R. Chivas. "Oxygen Isotope Composition of the Bone Phosphate of Australian Kangaroos: Potential as a Palaeoenvironmental Recorder." *Geochimica et Cosmochimica Acta* 54 (1990): 2603–2609.

Bădescu, I., M. A. Katzenberg, D. P. Watts, et al. "A Novel Fecal Stable Isotope Approach to Determine the Timing of Age-Related Feeding Transitions in Wild Infant Chimpanzees." *Am. J. Phys. Anthropol.* 162, no. 2 (2017): 285–299.

Balasse, M., and S. Ambrose. "The Seasonal Mobility Model for Prehistoric Herders in the South-Western Cape of South Africa Assessed by Isotopic Analysis of Sheep Tooth Enamel." *Journal of Archaeological Science* 29 (2002): 917–932.

Balasse, M., A. B. Smith, S. H. Ambrose, et al. "Determining Sheep Birth Seasonality by Analysis of Tooth Enamel Oxygen Isotope Ratios: The Late Stone Age Site of Kasteelberg (South Africa)." *Journal of Archaeological Science* 30 (2003): 205–215.

Bataille, C. P., K. Jaoen, S. Milano, et al. "Triple Sulfur-Oxygen-Strontium Isotopes: Probabilistic Geographic Assignment of Archaeological Remains Using a Novel Sulfur Isoscape of Western Europe." *PLoS One* 16, no. 5 (2021): e0250383.

Beaumont, J, J. Montgomery, J. Buckberry, et al. "Infant Mortality and Isotopic Complexity: New Approaches to Stress, Maternal Health and Weaning." *American Journal of Physical Anthropology* 157, no. 3 (2015): 441–457.

Bentley, A. R. "Strontium Isotopes from the Earth to the Archaeological Skeleton: A Review." *Journal of Archaeological Method and Theory* 13, no. 3 (2006): 135–187.

Birchall, J., T. C. O'Connell, T. H. E. Heaton, et al. "Hydrogen Isotope Ratios in Animal Body Protein Reflect Trophic Level." *Journal of Animal Ecology* 74 (2005): 877–881.

Blumenthal, S. A., K. L. Chritz, J. M. Rothman, et al. "Detecting Intraannual Dietary Variability in Wild Mountain Gorillas by Stable Isotope Analysis of Feces." *Proceedings of the National Academy of Sciences* 109, no. 52 (2012): 21277–21282.

Bowen, G. J., L. Chesson, K. Nielson, et al. "Treatment Methods for the Determination of δ^2H and $\delta^{18}O$ of Hair Keratin by Continuous-Flow Isotope-Ratio Mass Spectrometry." *Rapid Communications in Mass Spectrometry* 19 (2005): 2371–2378.

Bowen, G. J., J. R. Ehleringer, L. A. Chesson, et al. "Dietary and Physiological Controls on the Hydrogen and Oxygen Isotope Ratios of Hair from Mid-20th Century Indigenous Populations." *American Journal of Physical Anthropology* 139 (2009): 494–504.

Bowling, D. R., D. E. Pataki, and J. R. Ehleringer. "Ecosystem Isotope Exchange and Whole-Canopy Discrimination in Medicago Sativa." *Agricultural and Forest Meteorology* 116 (2003): 159–179.

Bryant, J. D., and P. N. Froelich. "A Model of Oxygen Isotope Fractionation in Body Water of Large Mammals." *Geochimica et Cosmochimica Acta* 59 (1995): 4523–4537.

Bryant, J. D., B. Luz, and P. N. Froelich. "Oxygen Isotopic Composition of Fossil Horse Tooth Phosphate as a Record of Continental Paleoclimate." *Palaeogeography, Palaeoclimatology, Palaeoecology* 107 (1994): 210–212.

Bryant, J. D., P. N. Froelich, W. J. Showers, et al. "Biologic and Climatic Signals in the Oxygen Isotope Composition of Eocene-Oligocene Equid Enamel Phosphate." *Palaeogeography, Palaeoclimatology, Palaeoecology* 126 (1996): 75–89.

Buzon, M. R., C. A. Conlee, and A. Simonetti. "The Consequences of Wari Contact in the Nazca Region During the Middle Horizon: Archaeological, Skeletal, and Isotopic Evidence." *Journal of Archaeological Science* 39 (2012): 2627–2636.

Carlson, B. A., and B. E. Crowley. "Variation in Carbon Isotope Values Among Chimpanzee Foods at Ngogo Kibale National Park and Bwindi Impenetrable National Park, Uganda." *American Journal of Primatology* 78 (2016): 1031–1040.

Cheung, C., and P. Szpak. "Interpreting Past Human Diets Using Stable Isotope Mixing Models." *Journal of Archaeological Method and Theory* 28, no. 4 (2021): 1106–1142.

Codron, D., J. A. Lee-Thorp, and M. Sponheimer. "Inter- and Intrahabitat Dietary Variability of Chacma Baboons (Papio Ursinus) in South African Savannas Based on Fecal δ13C, δ15N, and %N." *American Journal of Physical Anthropology* 129, no. 2 (2006): 204–214.

Connolly, R. M., M. A. Guest, and A. J. Melville. "Sulfur Stable Isotopes Separate Producers in Marine Food-Web." *Oecologia* 138 (2004): 161–167.

Cormie, A. B., B. Luz, and H. P. Schwarcz. "Relationship Between the Hydrogen and Oxygen Isotopes of Deer Bone and Their Use in the Estimation of Relative Humidity." *Geochimica et Cosmochimica Acta* 58, no. 16 (1994a): 3439–3449.

Cormie, A. B., H. P. Schwarcz, and J. Gray. "Determination of the Hydrogen Isotopic Composition of Bone Collagen and Correction for Hydrogen Exchange." *Geochimica et Cosmochimica Acta* 58, no. 1 (1994b): 365–375.

Corr, L. T., J. C. Sealy, M. C. Hodon, et al. "A Novel Marine Dietary Indicator Utilising Compound-Specific Bone Collagen Amino Acid δ13C Values of Ancient Humans." *Journal of Archaeological Science* 32, no. 3 (2005): 321–339.

Corr, L. T., M. P. Richards, C. Grier, et al. "Probing Dietary Change of the Kwädąy Dän Ts'ìnchį Individual, an Ancient Glacier Body from British Columbia: II. Deconvoluting Whole Skin and Bone Collagen δ13C Values via Carbon Isotope Analysis of Individual Amino Acids." *Journal of Archaeological Science* 36, no. 1 (2009): 12–18.

Craig, H. "Isotopic Variations in Meteoric Waters." *Science* 133 (1961): 1702–1703.

Dahlstedt, A. C., E. E. Schach, S. I. Baitzel, et al. "Stable Oxygen and Radiogenic Strontium Variability in the Osmore Drainage, Peru: Implications for Intra-regional Andean Paleomobility Studies." *Journal of Archaeological Science: Reports* 37 (2021): 102933.

DeNiro, M. J., and S. Epstein. "Influence of Diet on Distribution of Carbon Isotopes in Animals." *Geochimica et Cosmochimica Acta* 42, no. 5 (1978): 495–506.

DeNiro, M. J., and S. Epstein. "Hydrogen Isotope Ratios of Mouse Tissues Are Influenced by a Variety of Factors Other than Diet." *Science* 214 (1981a): 1374–1375.

DeNiro, M. J., and S. Epstein. "Influence of Diet on the Distribution of Nitrogen Isotopes in Animals." *Geochimica et Cosmochimica Acta* 45 (1981b): 341–351.

Eide, M, A. Olsen, U. S. Ninnemann, et al. "A Global Estimate of the Full Oceanic 13C Suess Effect Since the Preindustrial." *Global Biogeochemical Cycles* 31 (2017): 492–514.

Ericson, J. E. "Strontium Isotope Characterization in the Study of Prehistoric Human Ecology." *Journal of Human Evolution* 14 (1985): 503–514.

Estep, M. F., and H. Dabrowski. "Tracing Food Webs with Stable Hydrogen Isotopes." *Science* 209 (1980): 1537–1538.

Faure, G. "Isotope Geology of Strontium." In *Principles of Isotope Geology*, 107–145. New York: John Wiley and Sons, 1977.

Fernandes, R., M.-J. Nadeau, and P. M. Grootes. "Macronutrient-Based Model for Dietary Carbon Routing in Bone Collagen and Bioapatite." *Archaeological and Anthropological Sciences*, 4 (2012): 291–301.

Fricke, H. C., and J. R. O'Neil. "Inter- and Intra-tooth Variation in the Oxygen Isotope Composition of Mammalian Tooth Enamel: Some Implications for Paleoclimatological and Paleobiological Research." *Palaeogeography, Palaeoclimatology, Palaeoecology* 126 (1996): 91–99.

Fricke, H. C., J. R. O'Neil, and N. Lynnerup. "Oxygen Isotope Composition of Human Tooth Enamel from Medieval Greenland: Linking Climate and Society." *Geology* 23, no. 10 (1995): 869–872.

Fricke, H. C., W. C. Clyde, and J. R. O'Neal. "Intra-tooth Variations in δ¹⁸O (PO₄) of Mammalian Tooth Enamel as a Record of Seasonal Variations in Continental Climate Variables." *Geochimica et Cosmochimica Acta* 62, no. 11 (1998): 1839–1850.

Friedli, H., A. Lotscher, H. Oeschger, et al. "Ice Core Record of the 13C/12C Ratio of Atmospheric CO₂ in the Past Two Centuries." *Nature* 324 (1986): 237–238.

Froehle, A. W., C. M. Kellner, and M. J. Schoeninger. "A Three-Variable Analysis of Carbon and Nitrogen Isotope Values Discriminates Between Dietary Energy and Protein Sources in Prehistoric Humans." *American Journal of Physical Anthropology* 138, no. S48 (2009): 130.

Froehle, A. W., C. M. Kellner, and M. J. Schoeninger. "Effect of Diet and Protein Source on Carbon Stable Isotope Ratios in Collagen: Follow up to Warinner and Tuross." *Journal of Archaeological Science* 37 (2010): 2662–2670.

Froehle, A. W., C. M. Kellner, and M. J. Schoeninger. "Multivariate Carbon and Nitrogen Stable Isotope Model for the Reconstruction of Prehistoric Human Diet." *American Journal of Physical Anthropology* 47, no. 3 (2012): 352–369.

Fry, B. *Stable Isotope Ecology*. New York: Springer, 2006.

Fuller, B. T., J. L. Fuller, N. E. Sage, et al. "Nitrogen Balance and δ15N: Why You're Not What You Eat During Nutritional Stress." *Rapid Communications in Mass Spectrometry* 19, no. 2497–2506 (2005).

Fuller, B. T., J. L. Fuller, D. A. Harris, et al. "Breast Feeding and Weaning in Modern Human Infants with Carbon and Nitrogen Stable Isotope Ratios." *American Journal of Physical Anthropology* 129 (2006): 279–293.

Garland, C. J., L. J. Reitsema, C. S. Larsen, et al. "Early Life Stress at Mission Santa Catalina de Guale: An Integrative Analysis of Enamel Defects and Dentin Incremental Isotope Variation in Malnutrition." *Bioarchaeology International* 2, no. 2 (2018): 75–94.

Gat, J. R. "The Isotopes of Hydrogen and Oxygen in Precipitation." In *Handbook of Environmental Isotope Geochemistry*. Edited by P. Fritz and J. Fontes, 21–47. Amsterdam: Elseview, 1980.

Gat, J. R., and R. Gonfiantini, eds. "Stable Isotope Hydrology: Deuterium and Oxygen-18 in the Water Cycle," Volume Series No. 210. International Atomic Energy Agency, Vienna Technical Reports, 1981.

Hallin, K. A., M. J. Schoeninger, and H. P. Schwarcz. "Paleoclimate During Neandertal and Early Modern Human Occupation at Amud and Qafzeh, Israel: The Stable Isotope Data." *Journal of Human Evolution* 62, no. 1 (2012): 59–73.

Hare, P. E., M. Fogel, T. W. Stafford, Jr., et al. "The Isotopic Composition of Carbon and Nitrogen in Individual Amino Acids Isolated from Modern and Fossil Proteins." *Journal of Archaeological Science* 18, no. 3 (1991): 277–292.

Harrison, R. G., and M. A. Katzenberg. "Paleodiet Studies Using Stable Carbon Isotopes from Bone Apatite and Collagen: Examples from Southern Ontario and San Nicolas Island, California." *Journal of Anthropological Archaeology* 22 (2003): 227–244.

Hartman, G. "*The Environmental Origins of Plants and Herbivores in the Southern Levant: An Isotopic Approach.*" Doctoral Thesis, Harvard University, Cambridge, MA, 2008.

Heaton, T. H. E., J. C. Vogel, G. von La Chevallerie, et al. "Climatic Influence on the Isotopic Composition of Bone Nitrogen." *Nature* 322 (1986): 822–823.

Hecky, R. E., and R. H. Hesslein. "Contribution of Benthic Algae to Lake Food Webs as Revealed by Stable Isotope Analysis." *Journal of the North American Benthological Society* 14 (1995): 631–653.

Hobson, K. A., and L. I. Wassenaar. "Linking Breeding and Wintering Grounds of Neotropical Migrant Songbirds Using Stable Hydrogen Isotopic Analysis of Feathers." *Oecologia* 109 (1997): 142–148.

Hobson, K. A., G. J. Bowen, L. I. Wassenaar, et al. "Using Stable Hydrogen and Oxygen Isotope Measurements of Feathers to Infer Geographical Origins of Migrating European Birds." *Oecologia* 141 (2004): 477–488.

Hoefs, Jochen. *Stable Isotope Geochemistry.* New York: Springer-Verlag, 2009.

Hoppe, K. A., P. L. Koch, R. W. Carlson, et al. "Tracking Mammoths and Mastodons: Reconstruction of Migratory Behavior Using Strontium Isotope Ratios." *Geology* 27, no. 5 (1999): 439–442.

Hoppe, K. A., P. L. Koch, and T. T. Furutani. "Assessing the Preservation of Biogenic Strontium in Fossil Bones and Tooth Enamel." *International Journal of Osteoarchaeology* 13 (2003): 20–28.

Howland, M. R., L. T. Corr, S. M. M. Young, et al. "Expression of the Dietary Isotope Signal in the Compound-Specific $\delta^{13}C$ Values of Pig Bone Lipids and Amino Acids." *International Journal of Osteoarchaeology* 13, no. 1–2 (2003): 54–65.

Huertas, A. D., P. Iacumin, B. Stenni, et al. "Oxygen Isotope Variations of Phosphate in Mammalian Bone and Tooth Enamel." *Geochimica et Cosmochimica Acta* 59, no. 20 (1995): 4299–4305.

Hutchinson, D. L. *Bioarchaeology of the Florida Gulf Coast: Adaptation, Conflict, and Change.* Gainesville: University Press of Florida, 2004.

Jim, S., S. Ambrose, and R. P. Evershed. "Stable Carbon Isotopic Evidence for Differences in the Dietary Origin of Bone Cholesterol, Collagen, and Apatite: Implications for Their Use in Paleodietary Reconstruction." *Geochimica et Cosmochimica Acta* 68, no. 1 (2004): 61–72.

Katzenberg, M. A. "Stable Isotope Analysis of Archaeological Faunal Remains from Southern Ontario." *Journal of Archaeological Science* 16 (1989): 319–329.

Katzenberg, M. A., and A. Weber. "Stable Isotope Ecology and Palaeodiet in the Lake Baikal Region of Sibera." *Journal of Archaeological Science* 26, no. 6 (1999).

Katzenberg, M. A., D. A. Herring, and S. R. Saunders. "Weaning and Infant Mortality: Evaluating the Skeletal Evidence." *Yearbook of Physical Anthropology* 39 (1996): 177–199.

Keegan, W. F., and M. J. DeNiro. "Stable Carbon- and Nitrogen-Isotope Ratios of Bone Collagen Used to Study Coral-Reef and Terrestrial Components of Prehistoric Bahamian Diet." *American Antiquity* 53, no. 2 (1988): 320–336.

Keeling, C. D. "A Mechanism for Cyclic Enrichment of Carbon-12 by Terrestrial Plants." *Geochimica et Cosmochimica Acta* 24 (1961): 299–313.

Keeling, R. F., H. D. Graven, L. R. Welp, et al. "Atmospheric Evidence for a Global Secular Increase in Carbon Isotope Discrimination of Land Photosynthesis." *Proceedings of the National Academy of Sciences USA* 114, no. 39 (2017): 10361–10366.

Kellner, C. M., and M. J. Schoeninger. "A Simple Carbon Isotope Model for Reconstructing Human Diet." *American Journal of Physical Anthropology* 133, no. 4 (2007): 1112–1127.

Kellner, C. M., and M. J. Schoeninger. "Wari's Imperial Influence on Local Nasca Diet: The Stable Isotope Evidence." *Journal of Anthropological Archaeology* 27 (2008): 226–243.

Kendall, E., A. Millard, and J. Beaumont. "The 'Weanling's Dilemma' Revisited: Evolving Bodies of Evidence and the Problem of Infant Paleodietary Interpretation." *American Journal of Physical Anthropology* 175, no. S72 (2021): 57–78.

Kingston, J. D. "Shifting Adaptive Landscapes: Progress and Challenges in Reconstructing Early Hominid Enviornments." *Yearbook of Physical Anthropology* 50 (2007): 20–58.

Kingston, J. D., and T. Harrison. "Isotopic Dietary Reconstructions of Pliocene Herbivores at Laetoli: Implications for Early Hominin Evolution." *Palaeogeography, Palaeoclimatology, Palaeoecology* 243 (2007a): 272–306.

Kingston, J. D., and T. Harrison. "Isotopic Dietary Reconstructions of Pliocene Herbivores at Laetoli: Implications for Early Hominin Paleoecology." *Palaeogeography, Palaeoclimatology, Palaeoecology* 243 (2007b): 272–306.

Kingston, J. D., A. L. Deino, R. K. Edgar, et al. "Astronomically Forced Climate Change in the Kenyan Rift Valley 2.7–2.55 Ma: Implications for the Evolution of Early Hominin Ecosystems." *Journal of Human Evolution* 53, no. 5 (2007): 487–503.

Kirsanow, K., C. Makarewicz, and N. Tuross. "Stable Oxygen ($\delta 18O$) and Hydrogen (δD) Isotopes in Ovicaprid Dentinal Collagen Record Seasonal Variation." *Journal of Archaeological Science* 35 (2008): 3159–3167.

Knudson, K. J., and J. Buikstra. "Residential Mobility and Resource Use in the Chiribaya Polity of Southern Peru: Strontium Isotope Analysis of Archaeological Tooth Enamel and Bone." *International Journal of Osteoarchaeology* 17 (2007): 563–580.

Knudson, K. J., and T. D. Price. "Utility of Multiple Chemical Techniques in Archaeological Residential Mobility Studies: Case Studies from Tiwanaku- and Chiribaya-Afficiated Sites in the Andes." *American Journal of Physical Anthropology* 132 (2007): 25–39.

Knudson, K. J., and C. Torres-Rouff. "Investigating Cultural Heterogeneity and Multiethnicity in San Pedro de Atacama, Northern Chile Through Biogeochemistry and Bioarchaeology." *American Journal of Physical Anthropology* 138 (2009): 473–485.

Knudson, K. J., T. D. Price, J. E. Buikstra, et al. "The Use of Strontium Isotope Analysis to Investigate Tiwanaku Migration and Mortuary Ritual in Bolivia and Peru." *Archaeometry* 46 (2004): 5–18.

Knudson, K. J., P. S. Goldstein, A. Dahlstedt, et al. "Paleomobility in the Tiwanaku Diaspora: Biogeochemical Analyses at Rio Muerto, Moquegua, Peru." *Am. J. Phys. Anthropol.* 155, no. 3 (2014): 405–421.

Koch, P. L. "Isotopic Study of the Biology of Modern and Fossil Vertebrates." In *Stable Isotopes in Ecology and Environmental Science*. Edited by R. Mitchener and K. Lajtha, 99–154. Oxford, England: Blackwell Scientific Publications, Ltd., 2007.

Koch, P. L., D. C. Fisher, and D Dettman. "Oxygen Isotope Variation in the Tusks of Extinct Proboscideans: A Measure of Season of Death." *Geology* 17 (1989): 515–519.

Koch, P. L., N. Tuross, and M. L. Fogel. "The Effects of Sample Treatment and Diagenesis on the Isotopic Integrity of Carbonate in Biogenic Hydroxylapatite." *Journal of Archaeological Science* 24 (1997): 417–429.

Kohn, M. J. "A Predictive Model for Animal $\delta^{18}O$: Explaining Old Studies and Designing New Ones." *Geochimica Cosmochimica Acta* 60, no. 23 (1996): 4811–4829.

Kohn, M. J. "Carbon Isotope Compositions of Terrestrial C3 Plants as Indicators of (Paleo)ecology and (Paleo)climate." *Proceedings of the National Academy of Sciences USA* 107, no. 46 (2010): 19691–19695.

Kohn, M. J., M. J. Schoeninger, and J. W. Valley. "Herbivore Tooth Oxygen Isotope Compositions: Effects of Diet and Physiology." *Geochemica et Cosmochemica Acta* 60, no. 20 (1996): 3889–3896.

Kohn, M. J., M. J. Schoeninger, and W. W. Barker. "Altered States: Effects of Diagenesis on Fossil Tooth Chemistry." *Geochimica et Cosmochimica Acta* 63, no. 18 (1999): 2737–2747.

Krouse, H. R. "Sulfur Isotopes in Our Environment." In *Handbook of Environmental Isotope Geochemistry*. Edited by P. Fritz and J. C. Fontes, 435–471. Amsterdam: Elsevier, 1980.

Larsen, C. S., ed. *Bioarchaeology of Spanish Florida: The Impact of Colonialism*. Gainesville: University Press of Florida, 2001.

Lee-Thorp, J. A. "Preservation of Biogenic Carbon Isotopic Signals in Plio-Pleistocene Bone and Tooth Mineral." In *Biogeochemical Approaches to Paleodietary Analysis*, Vol. 5. Edited by S. H. Ambrose and M. A. Katzenberg, 89–115. New York: Kluwer Academic/Plenum Publishers, 2000a.

Lee-Thorp, J. A. "Preservation of Biogenic Carbon Isotopic Signals in Plio-Pleistocene Bone and Tooth Mineral." In *Biogeochemical Approaches to Paleodietary Analysis*. Edited by S. H. Ambrose and M. A. Katzenberg, 89–115. New York: Kluwer Academic/Plenum Publishers, 2000b.

Lee-Thorp, J. A., and M Sponheimer. "Contributions of Biogeochemistry to Understanding Homin Dietary Ecology." *Yearbook of Physical Anthropology* 13, no. S43 (2006): 131–148.

Leyden, J. J., L. I. Wassenaar, K. A. Hobson, et al. "Stable Hydrogen Isotopes of Bison Bone Collagen as a Proxy for Holocene Climate on the Northern Great Plains." *Palaeogeography, Palaeoclimatology, Palaeoecology* 239, no. 1 (2006): 87–89.

Longinelli, A. "Oxygen Isotopes in Mammal Bone Phosphate: A New Tool for Paleohydrological and Paleoclimatological Research?" *Geochimica et Cosmochimica Acta* 48 (1984): 385–390.

Loudon, J. E., J. R. Grobler, M. Sponheimer, et al. "Using the Stable Carbon and Nitrogen Isotope Compositions of Vervet Monkeys (Chlorocebus Pygerythrus) to Examine Questions in Ethnoprimatology." *PLoS One* 9, no. 7 (2014): e100758.

Loudon, J. E., P. A. Sandberg, R. W. Wrangham, et al. "The Stable Isotope Ecology of Pan in Uganda and Beyond." *American Journal of Primatology* 78, no. 10 (2016): 1070–1085.

Magilligan, F. J., P. S. Goldstein, G. B. Fisher, et al. "Late Quaternary Hydroclimatology of a Hyper-arid Andean Watershed: Climate Change, Floods, and Hydrologic Responses to the El Niño-Southern Oscillation in the Atacama Desert." *Geomorphology* 101 (2008): 14–32.

Minagawa, M., and E. Wada. "Stepwise Enrichment of ^{15}N along Food Chains: Further Evidence and the Relation Between δ^{15}N and Animal Age." *Geochimica Cosmochimica Acta* 48, no. 5 (1984): 1135–1140.

Montgomery, J., P. Budd, and T. Neighbour. "Sr Isotope Evidence for Population Movement within the Hebridean Norse Community of NW Scotland." *Journal of the Geological Society* 160 (2003): 649–653.

Mukherjee, A. J., A. M. Gibson, and R. P. Evershed. "Trends in Pig Product Processing at British Neolithic Grooved Ware Sites Traced through Organic Residues in Potsherds." *Journal of Archaeological Science* 35, no. 7 (2008): 2059–2073.

Nehlich, O. "The Application of Sulphur Isotope Analyses in Archaeological Research: A Review." *Earth-Science Reviews* 142 (2015): 1–17.

Nehlich, O., D. Boric, S. Stefanovic, et al. "Sulphur Isotope Evidence for Freshwater Fish Consumption: A Case Study from the Danube Gorges, SE Europe." *Journal of Archaeological Science* 37, no. 5 (2010): 1131–1139.

Nehlich, O., B. T. Fuller, N. Marquez Grant, et al. "Investigation of Diachronic Dietary Patterns on the Islands of Ibiza and Formentera, Spain: Evidence from Sulfur Stable Isotope Ratio Analysis." *American Journal of Biological Anthropology* 143, no. 4 (2012): 512–522.

Nelson, B. K., M. J. DeNiro, M. J. Schoeninger, et al. "Effects of Diagenesis on Strontium, Carbon, Nitrogen, and Oxygen Concentration and Isotopic Composition of Bone." *Geochimica et Cosmochimica Acta* 50 (1986): 1941–1949.

Newton, R., and S. Bottrell. "Stable Isotopes of Carbon and Sulphur as Indicators of Environmental Change: Past and Present." *Journal of the Geological Society* 164 (2007): 691–708.

O'Connell, T. C., R. E. M. Hedges, M. A. Healey, et al. "Isotopic Comparison of Hair, Nail and Bone: Modern Analyses." *Journal of Archaeological Science* 28, no. 11 (2001): 1247–1255.

Oelze, V. M., G. Fahy, G. Hohmann, et al. "Comparative Isotope Ecology of African Great Apes." *J. Hum. Evol.* 101 (2016): 1–16.

O'Leary, M. H. "Carbon Isotopes in Photosynthesis." *BioScience* 38, no. 5 (1988): 328–336.

Pataki, D. E., J. R. Ehleringer, L. B. Flanagan, et al. "The Application and Interpretation of Keeling Plots in Terrestrial Carbon Cycle Research." *Global Biogeochemical Cycles* 17, no. 1 (2003): 1022:1–15.

Price, T. D., G. Grupe, and P. Schröter. "Reconstruction of Migration Patterns in the Bell Beaker Period by Stable Strontium Isotope Analysis." *Applied Geochemistry* 9 (1994a): 413–417.

Price, T. D., C. M. Johnson, J. A. Ezzo, et al. "Residential Mobility in the Prehistoric Southwest United States: A Preliminary Study Using Strontium Isotope Analysis." *Journal of Archaeological Science* 21, no. 3 (1994b): 315–330.

Reinberger, K. L., L. J. Reitsema, B. Kyle, et al. "Isotopic Evidence for Geographic Heterogeneity in Ancient Greek Military Forces." *PLoS One* 16, no. 5 (2021): e0248803.

Reitsema, L. J. "Introducing Fecal Stable Isotope Analysis in Primate Weaning Studies." *American Journal of Physical Anthropology* 74 (2012): 926–939.

Reitsema, L. J., and S. Holder. "Stable Isotope Analysis and the Study of Human Stress, Disease, and Nutrition." *Bioarchaeology International* 2, no. 2 (2018): 63–74.

Reitsema, L. J., C. E. Jones, H. R. Gilbert, et al. "Isotopic and Elemental Corroborates for Wild Bearded Capuchin (Sapajus Libidinosus) Omnivorous Dietary Adaptation at Fazenda Boa Vista, Brazil." *Rapid Commun. Mass Spectrometry* 34, no. 19 (2020): e8856.

Reynard, L. M., and R. E. M. Hedges. "Stable Hydrogen Isotopes of Bone Collagen in Palaeodietary and Palaeoenvironmental Reconstruction." *Journal of Archaeological Science* 35 (2008): 13934–13942.

Reynard, L. M., and N. Tuross. "The Known, the Unknown and the Unknowable: Weaning Times from Archaeological Bones Using Nitrogen Isotope Ratios." *Journal of Archaeological Science* 53 (2015): 618–625.

Richards, M. P., and E. Trinkaus. "Isotopic Evidence for the Diets of European Neanderthals and Early Modern Humans." *Proceedings of the National Academy of Sciences* 106, no. 38 (2009): 16034–16039.

Richards, M. P., P. B. Perritt, E. Trinkaus, et al. "Neanderthal Diet at Vindija and Neanderthal Predation: The Evidence from Stable Isotopes." *Proceedings of the National Academy of Sciences* 97 (2000): 7663–7666.

Robinson, J. R., J. Rowan, W. A Barr, et al. "Intrataxonomic Trends in Herbivore Enamel $\delta^{13}C$ Are Decoupled from Woody Cover." *Nature Ecology and Evolution* 5 (2021): 995–1002.

Schillaci, M. A., J. M. Castillini, C. A. Stricker, et al. "Variation in Hair $\delta^{13}C$ and $\delta^{15}N$ Values in Long-Tailed Macaques (Macaca Fascicularis) from Singapore." *Primates* 55, no. 1 (2014): 25–34.

Schillaci, M. A., J. Lintlop, M. Sunra, et al. "Hair Cortisol and Stable Carbon and Nitrogen Isotope Ratios in Barbary Macaques (Macaca Sylvanus) from Gibraltar." *Rapid Communications in Mass Spectrometry: RCM* 33, no. 9 (2019): 831–838.

Schoeninger, M. J. "Stable Isotope Analyses and the Evolution of Human Diets." *Annual Review of Anthropology* 43, no. 1 (2014): 413–430.

Schoeninger, M. J., and M. J. DeNiro. "Nitrogen and Carbon Isotopic Composition of Bone Collagen from Marine and Terrestrial Animals." *Geochimica et Cosmochimica Acta* 48 (1984): 625–639.

Schoeninger, M. J., M. J. DeNiro, and H. Tauber. "Stable Nitrogen Isotope Ratios of Bone Collagen Reflect Marine and Terrestrial Components of Prehistoric Human Diet." *Science* 220 (1983): 1381–1383.

Schoeninger, M. J., U. T. Iwaniec, and K. E. Glander. "Stable Isotope Ratios Monitor Diet and Habitat Use in New World Monkeys." *American Journal of Physical Anthropology* 103 (1997): 69–83.

Schoeninger, M. J., U. T. Iwaniec, and L. T. Nash. "Ecological Attributes Recorded in Stable Isotope Ratios of Arboreal Prosimian Hair." *Oecologia* 113 (1998): 222–230.

Schoeninger, M. J., M. J. Kohn, and J. W. Valley. "Tooth Oxygen Isotope Ratios as Paleoclimate Monitors in Arid Ecosystems." In *Biogeochemical Approaches to Paleodietary Analysis in Archaeology*, Volume 5: *Advances in Archaeological and Museum Science*. Edited by S. H. Ambrose and M. A. Katzenberg, 117–140. New York: Plenum Press, 2000.

Schoeninger, M. J., H. Reeser, and K. Hallin. "Paleoenvironment of Australopithecus Anamensis at Allia Bay, East Turkana, Kenya: Evidence from Mammalian Herbivore Enamel Stable Isotopes." *Journal of Anthropolgical Archaeology* 22 (2003): 200–207.

Schoeninger, M. J., C. A. Most, J. J. Moore, et al. "Environmental Variables Across *Pan Troglodytes* Sites Correspond with the Carbon, but Not the Nitrogen Stable Isotope Ratios of Chimpanzee Hair." *American Journal of Primatology* (2016). doi:10.1002/ajp.22496.

Schurr, M. R. "Using Stable Nitrogen-Isotopes to Study Weaning Behavior in Past Populations." *World Archaeology* 30, no. 2 (1998): 327–342.

Schurr, M. R. "Exploring Ideas about Isotopic Variation in Breastfeeding and Weaning Within and Between Populations: Case Studies from the American Midcontinent." *International Journal of Osteoarchaeology* 28, no. 5 (2018): 479–491.

Schurr, M. R., A. Fuentes, E. Luecke, et al. "Intergroup Variation in Stable Isotope Ratios Reflects Anthropogenic Impact on the Barbary Macaques (Macaca Sylvanus) of Gibraltar." *Primates* 53, no. 1 (2012): 31–40.

Sealy, J. C., and N. J. van der Merwe. "Isotope Assessment and the Seasonal-Mobility Hypothesis in the Southwestern Cape of South Africa." *Current Anthropology* 27, no. 2 (1986): 135–150.

Sealy, J. C., N. J. van der Merwe, J. A. Lee Thorp, et al. "Nitrogen Isotopic Ecology in Southern Africa: Implications for Environmental and Dietary Tracing." *Geochimica et Cosmochimica Acta* 51 (1987): 2707–2717.

Sealy, J. C., N. J. van der Merwe, A. Sillen, et al. "$^{87}Sr/^{86}Sr$ as a Dietary Indicator in Modern and Archaeological Bone." *Journal of Archaeological Science* 18, no. 3 (1991): 399–416.

Sillen, A., G. Hall, S. Richardson, et al. "87Sr/86Sr Ratios in Modern and Fossil Food-Webs of the Sterkfontein Valley: Implications for Early Hominid Habitat Preference." *Geochimica et Cosmochimica Acta* 62, no. 14 (1998): 2463–2473.

Sponheimer, M., J. L. Thorp, D. de Ruiter, et al. "Hominins, Sedges, and Termites: New Carbon Isotope Data from Sterkfontein Valley and Kruger National Park." *Journal of Human Evolution* 48 (2005): 301–312.

Sponheimer, M., Z. Alemseged, T. Cerling, et al. "Isotopic Evidence of Early Hominin Diets." *Proceedings of the National Academy of Sciences* 110, no. 26 (2013): 10513–10518.

Steckel, R. H., J. C. Rose, C. S. Larsen, et al. "Skeletal Health in the Western Hemisphere from 4000 B.C. to the Present." *Evolutionary Anthropology* 11 (2002): 142–155.

Sternberg, L. S. L. "Oxygen and Hydrogen Isotope Ratios in Plant Cellulose: Mechanisms and Applications." In *Stable Isotopes in Ecological Research*, vol. 68. Edited by P. W. Rundel, J. R. Ehleringer, and K. A. Nagy, 124–141. New York: Springer-Verlag, 1989.

Tieszen, L. L., and T. Fagre. "Effect of Diet Quality and Composition on the Isotopic Composition of Respiratory CO_2, Bone Collagen, Bioapatite, and Soft Tissues." In *Prehistoric Human Bone: Archaeology at the Molecular Level.* Edited by J. B. Lambert and G. Grupe, 121–155. Berlin, Heidelberg: Springer Berlin Heidelberg, 1993.

van der Merwe, N. J., F. Masao, and M. K. Bamford. "Isotopic Evidence for Contrasting Diets of Early Hominins *Homo Habilis* and *Australopithecus Boisei* of Tanzania." *South African Journal of Science* 104 (2008): 153–156.

Vika, E., and T. Theodoropoulou. "Re-examining Fish Consumption in Greek Antiquity: Results from δ13C and δ15N Analysis from Fish Bone Collagen." *Journal of Archaeological Science* 39 (2012): 1618–1627.

Virginia, R. A., and C. C. Delwiche. "Natural 15N Abundance of Presumed N2-Fixing and non-N2-Fixing Plants from Selected Ecosystems." *Oecologia* 54 (1982): 317–325.

Vogel, J. C., and N. J. van der Merwe. "Isotopic Evidence for Early Maize Cultivation in New York State." *Society for American Archaeology National Meetings* 1976 (1976): 11.

Vogel, J. C., and N. J. van der Merwe. "Isotopic Evidence for Early Maize Cultivation in New York State." *American Antiquity* 42 (1977): 238–242.

Wahlen, M. "Carbon Dioxide, Carbon Monoxide and Methane in the Atmosphere: Abundance and Isotopic Composition." In *Stable Isotopes in Ecology and Environmental Science.* Edited by K. Lajtha and R. H. Mitchener, 93–113. Oxford: Blackwell Scientific Publications, 1994.

Wallace, B. P., J. A. Seminoff, S. S. Kilham, et al. "Leatherback Turtles as Oceanographic Indicators: Stable Isotope Analyses Reveal a Trophic Dichotomy Between Ocean Basins." *Marine Biology* 149 (2006): 953–960.

White, J. W. C. "Stable Hydrogen Isotope Ratios in Plants: A Review of Current Theory and Some Potential Applications." In *Stable Isotopes in Ecological Research*, vol. 68. Edited by P. W. Rundel, J. R. Ehleringer, and K. A. Nagy, 142–162. New York: Springer-Verlag, 1989.

White, C. D., R. Storey, F. J. Longstaff, et al. "Immigration, Assimilation, and Status in the Ancient City of Teotihuacan: Stable Isotope Evidence from Tlajinga 33." *Latin American Antiquity* 15 (2004): 176–197.

White, T. D., S. H. Ambose, G. Suwa, et al. "Macrovertebrate Paleontology and the Pliocene Habitat of *Ardipithecus Ramidus*." *Science* 326 (2009): 87–93.

Wright, L. E. "In Search of Yax Nuun Ayiin I: Revisiting the Tikal Project's Burial 10." *Ancient Mesoamerica* 16 (2005): 89–100.

Wright, L. E., and H. P. Schwarcz. "Stable Carbon and Oxygen Isotopes in Human Tooth Enamel: Identifying Breastfeeding and Weaning in Prehistory." *American Journal of Physical Anthropology* 106 (1998): 1–18.

Ziegler, H. "Hydrogen Isotope Fractionation in Plant Tissues." In *Stable Isotopes in Ecological Research*. Edited by P. W. Rundel, J. R. Ehleringer, and K. A. Nagy, 105–123. New York: Springer-Verlag, 1989.

CHAPTER 31 Current Concepts in Bone Biology

Mary E. Cole, James H. Gosman, and Samuel D. Stout

INTRODUCTION

Bone tissue changes substantially in mass and shape during growth. During fetal development, the genome provides positional information for the skeletal outline through diffusible gradients of morphogens. These gradients direct the formation of mesenchymal condensations and cartilage templates throughout the body, which are replaced with bone during skeletal development. During subsequent growth, and throughout the lifespan, mechanical demands on bone tissue alter its distribution, shape, and microstructural composition (Long and Ornitz 2013; Rauch and Schoenau 2001). The cross-sectional size and shape of bone, and the morphometry of bone tissue microstructure, have found broad application in biological anthropology for interpreting mechanical loading history (Ruff and Larsen 2014) and assessing bone tissue quality and strength, particularly in the context of aging and pathological conditions (Stout et al. 2019). To aid these interpretations, this chapter outlines models for bone functional adaptation to mechanical demand, summarizes cellular responses to mechanical loading, and reviews some physiological influences on bone growth and bone loss.

Mechanical strain changes and microscopic tissue damage are sensed by osteocytes embedded in bone tissue, which subsequently trigger modeling or remodeling processes. Bone modeling refers to the uncoupled formative or resorptive actions of bone cells on bone surfaces. Osteoblasts form new bone (formation modeling) under increased mechanical loading, while osteoclasts resorb bone (resorptive modeling) under disuse conditions. Bone remodeling refers to the coupled actions of osteoclastic bone resorption, followed by osteoblastic bone formation, at the same tissue location, carried out by a local group of cells called a "Basic Multicellular Unit" (BMU). Bone remodeling can occur in high strain conditions in response to microdamage (targeted remodeling) and in low strain conditions (disuse-mediated remodeling) (Hughes et al. 2020). Bone cell differentiation, maturation, and coupling within these processes is regulated by the local presence of paracrine factors, produced by nearby cells, and autocrine factors, produced by the cell itself. Levels of local factors are also regulated by endocrine factors produced by distant cells, particularly systemic hormone levels. Physiological conditions thereby modify the sensitivity and functioning of bone cells in response to mechanical demand (Plotkin and Bruzzaniti 2019).

BONE FUNCTIONAL ADAPTATION

Bone functional adaptation is the concept that bone tissue adjusts its shape and structure in response to its mechanical environment during life (Ruff et al. 2006). In the nineteenth century, anatomist Georg Hermann von Meyer and engineer Karl Culmann suggested that trabecular struts were aligned with principal stresses (von Meyer 1867). This work influenced orthopaedic surgeon Julius Wolff (Wolff 1892), who hypothesized that both the internal architecture and external form of bone were the consequence of the direction and pattern of mechanical loads (Bertram and Swartz 1991). "Wolff's Law" has persisted in cultural memory as the basis for bone functional adaptation. However, Wolff assumed that bone adapts to static loads in strict mathematical correspondence, altering bone architecture continually. It was Wilhelm Roux (Roux 1885) who correctly identified bone structure as adaptive to dynamic loads and self-regulating toward a functional stimulus (Lee and Taylor 1999; Roesler 1987).

Frost's Mechanostat Model

Bone functional adaptation characterizes mechanical loading using a dimensionless quantity of strain. When an external load causes bone to deform, or change in size or shape, strain is measured as its relative change in length (Pivonka et al. 2018). Harold M. Frost (1987) proposed the mechanostat model to describe how bone coordinates modeling and remodeling to keep these strains within an equilibrium range. This "Utah Paradigm" initially came together at the University of Utah's Hard Tissue Workshops in the 1960s. The mechanostat works like a thermostat regulates temperature, triggering heating or cooling until the temperature returns to the set range. The underlying concept of the mechanostat is that bone models and remodels to keep its typical strains within a preset range, or "setpoint." If mechanical loading changes enough to deform bone outside of that strain range, bone models or remodels until the new distribution of tissue again deforms at the setpoint strain (Frost 1987). The strain triggers for bone modeling and remodeling are what Frost terms "minimum effective strain" thresholds (MES). Approximate ranges derived from strain gage experiments (Frost 2003) include:

1. **Disuse Window**: Disuse-mode remodeling resorbs more bone than is formed.
2. **Adapted Window**: Conservation mode remodeling produces equal bone resorption and formation above the remodeling threshold (MESr = 50–100 $\mu\varepsilon$).
3. **Mild Overload Window**: Uncoupled bone formation begins at the modeling threshold (MESm = 1,000–1,500 $\mu\varepsilon$) and remodeling is suppressed.
4. **Pathological Overload Window**: Microdamage begins to accumulate faster than it can be remodeled above the microdamage threshold (MESp = ~3,000 $\mu\varepsilon$) until bone failure at ultimate strength (~25,000 $\mu\varepsilon$ in young adults)

Models for Bone Functional Adaptation

Many predictive models have been proposed to explain the frequency and rate of bone modeling and/or remodeling. **Equilibrium models**, following Frost's mechanostat, hypothesize that when a load changes, bone is added or removed until the tissue response returns to a pre-set range. The equilibrium variable that bone seeks to maintain can vary between models, including stress (Kummer 1988), daily tissue level stress (Beaupré et al. 1990), peak strains (Rubin and Lanyon 1984), strain energy density (Huiskes et al. 1987), and a balance of mass, momentum, and energy (Cowin and Hegedus 1976). A challenge for equilibrium models is that both loading environment and tissue response vary substantially between skeletal sites, species, and life stages (Pearson and Lieberman 2004). Consequently, most equilibrium models consider the target range to be inter- and intra-skeletally variable, determined by factors including skeletal location, genetics, hormones, and the breakdown of these physiological influences with senescence and disease (Skerry 2006). Turner (1999) explains intraskeletal variation through cellular accommodation, where cells retain a memory of customary local strain patterns and adapt only to large, abnormal loading deviations. Cell mechanosensivity can be altered through reorganization of the cytoskeleton or extracellular receptors and microenvironment (Robling et al. 2006). Bone curvature may further establish customary local strain, as it induces predictable strain patterns across a range of dynamic load directions and magnitudes (Turner 1998). Carter and Beaupré's (2001) mechanobiology hypothesis accounts for variation with a biological component, including genetic and hormonal regulation of intrinsic growth, and intraskeletal variation in precursor cell populations (Carter and Beaupré 2001). Intra-skeletal variability is more directly addressed by **optimization models**, which hypothesize that bone remodels toward an optimal structure for a given load environment. This often involves maximizing structural stiffness relative to the cost of adding bone mass (Bagge 2000; Pearson and Lieberman 2004; Subbarayan and Bartel 1999). Lieberman and Crompton use this approach to explain limb bone tapering. Distal limbs are more energetically costly to accelerate and favor remodeling to repair strain damage over modeling to add bone mass (Lieberman and Crompton 1998).

Principals of Bone Functional Adaptation

Starting in the 1970s, strain gauge measurements of varied species, skeletal elements, and loading conditions established several important principles of bone functional adaptation:

1. Bone adapts to dynamic strains, not static strains. A continuously applied load will result in bone loss, while intermittent loading will result in bone apposition (Hert et al. 1971).

2. Bone adapts to local strains, not total strains. Lanyon and colleagues (1982) found that when strain is distributed regionally, bone is modeled preferentially on the periosteal surface of the region under higher strain, rather than uniformly around the circumference of the bone (Lanyon et al. 1982). Over 70 percent of longitudinal forces on a bone are not uniform axial compression, but are due to bending, where varying regions of a cross-section are tensed or compressed by the same load (Biewener and Bertram 1993). Bone experiences higher strain ($\times 1.9$) under compression and fails more quickly in tension (Lanyon and Baggott 1976). Bone tissue microstructure often varies morphometrically between cross-sectional regions which typically experience higher-strain compression or lower-strain tension (Stout et al. 2019).

3. Bone adaptation can be stimulated by low strains if they occur at high frequency. Experimental strain stimulus is proportional to strain rate, which is the product of strain magnitude and strain frequency (cycles per second). Strain rate can be increased

either by increasing the frequency of loading or by increasing the magnitude of strain (Turner 1998). Even extremely low-level strains ($< 10\ \mu\varepsilon$) stimulate bone formation at high frequencies (20–50 Hz) (Rubin et al. 2002). While bone experiences relatively few daily high-strain (2,000–3,000 $\mu\varepsilon$), low-frequency (1–3 Hz) loading events, muscle contractions associated with posture create continual low-strain ($<5\ \mu\varepsilon$), high-frequency (10–50 Hz) loads. Sarcopenia (muscle wasting) may contribute to age-associated bone loss through this decline in high-frequency, low-magnitude stimuli (Ozcivici et al. 2010).

4. Bone becomes desensitized to strain, or "saturated," after a fairly short number of loading cycles (Turner 1998). Only four cycles per day are sufficient to prevent disuse-associated bone loss, and minimal gains occur above ~40 cycles per day (Rubin and Lanyon 1984). Numerous loading models have confirmed that inserting rest periods of 10–15 seconds between each loading cycle substantially improves adaptive response (Meakin et al. 2014). Osteocytes sense mechanical loading through strain-induced fluid flow within their lacunar-canalicular network. Repeated load cycles before the fluid has redistributed may be perceived by the osteocyte as a static load, causing saturation of adaptive response (Scheiner et al. 2016).

Accommodating Fatigue Repair in Equilibrium Models

In Frost's original mechanostat model, the remodeling range does not have a high enough setpoint to target and repair fatigue damage (Martin 2003). Human bone tissue releases energy through creating "microcracks," which it subsequently targets for remodeling. This increases the total energy that the bone can withstand before fracturing (Ritchie 2011). Estimates for the frequency of targeted remodeling range from 10 to 30 percent of all remodeling activity (Burr and Martin 1993; Li et al. 2001), although it is theoretically possible that all BMUs are "steering" toward microdamage (Martin 2002). Hughes and colleagues (2020) recently refined the mechanostat model into four adaptive pathways. A reduced strain stimulus can cause peripheral bone loss, preferentially at the endosteum, through uncoupled *resorption modeling*. Bone loss can also occur through coupled *disuse-mediated remodeling*, where bone formation does not equal bone resorption, increasing cortical porosity or trabecular element thinning and loss. An increased strain stimulus can cause peripheral, uncoupled *formation modeling*, preferentially at the periosteum. High strains may also induce the coupled *targeted remodeling* of microdamage within the cortex (Hughes et al. 2020).

Stochastic Remodeling and the Lazy Zone

In some equilibrium models, including the mechanostat and mechanobiology, remodeling within the adapted range or "lazy zone" is stochastic, with minimal net change in bone mass or architecture (Pearson and Lieberman 2004). Animal models have challenged the concept of a strain range where bone is nonresponsive. When limbs are artificially loaded in their natural configuration, bone adaptation tends to occur only when induced strains fall outside the typical range. When limbs are artificially loaded in novel configurations, or with natural loading removed, low to high strains stimulate bone resorption or formation in a linear fashion, without an unresponsive "lazy zone." This suggests that bone becomes nonresponsive to strain stimulus after it has adapted to the associated loading condition, rather than being inherently unstimulated by a given strain range (Meakin et al. 2014; Sugiyama et al. 2012).

Cellular Effectors of Bone Functional Adaptation

A cellular perspective is essential to understanding principles of bone functional adaptation. Strain-induced fluid flow and microdamage-induced osteocyte apoptosis are the key mechanisms of mechanotransduction, whereby osteocytes are mechanically stimulated to trigger bone formation or resorption. These mechanisms explain why adaptation is dynamic, responsive to localized strain or damage, sensitive to strain frequency, and reaches loading cycle saturation. Osteoblast and osteoclast differentiation and function are regulated by osteocyte signaling, by self-regulation from their own cell type, by "cross-talk" from the opposing cell type, and by endocrine factors from the physiological environment (Rauch and Schoenau 2001).

Osteoblast Differentiation and Bone Formation

Osteoblasts deposit the organic matrix of bone, both during initial modeling and during remodeling as replacement for resorbed bone. Their numerous cytoplasmic extensions penetrate the osteoid, or unmineralized bone, as it is newly deposited. To create this osteoid, osteoblasts secrete large amounts of type I collagen. Other chief products include osteocalcin, a non-collagenous protein that controls calcium deposition, and alkaline phosphatase, which blocks pyrophosphates from inhibiting mineralization. These osteoblast-produced factors mediate the accumulation of hydroxyapatite, or calcium phosphate, to mineralize the matrix (Long 2012).

Osteoblasts arise from mesenchymal stem cells (MSCs), which originate in the bone marrow. Mesenchymal stem cells express RUNX2 (also called Cbfa1) as they commit to become osteochondroprogenitors, and RUNX2 and OSX as they mature into osteoprogenitors (Long 2012; Long and Ornitz 2013). Several families of growth factors regulate RUNX2 expression, transcriptional activity, and downstream pathways, including BMPs (bone morphogenetic proteins), TGF-β (transforming growth factor β), FGFs (fibroblast growth factors), and IGFs (insulin-like growth factors). Locally produced parathyroid hormone analog PTHrP (parathyroid hormone-related peptide) promotes expression of RUNX2 and components of these growth factor pathways during early differentiation (Plotkin and Bivi 2014; Plotkin and Bruzzaniti 2019).

RUNX2 is a transcription factor for ligands or receptors that promote osteoblast differentiation, including hedgehog, fibroblast growth factor (FGF), parathyroid hormone-related peptide (PTHrP), Dlx5, and Wnt signaling (Komori 2019). **Canonical** (β-catenin dependent) **Wnt signaling** (Figure 31.1) induces OSX expression, which is necessary for commitment to the osteoblast lineage (Long 2012). Inside the osteoblast progenitor, the protein β-catenin is normally targeted by a multiprotein complex of Axin, APC, CK1α, and GSK-3β. This complex phosphorylates β-catenin, marking it for proteasome-mediated degradation. In canonical Wnt signaling, an extracellular Wnt ligand binds to transmembrane proteins Frizzled and LRP5/6. DVL is recruited intracellularly and phosphorylates GSK-3, rendering the multiprotein complex inactive. Accumulating β-catenin levels in the cytosol stimulate its translocation to the nucleus, where it associates with TCF/LEF and CREB to activate target gene promoters (e.g., RUNX2, OSX, Dlx5) and suppress inducers of other mesenchymal stem cell pathways (PPARγ, C/EBPα) (Houschyar et al. 2019; Maeda et al. 2019). Canonical Wnt signaling can be inhibited by antagonists that bind to LRP5/6 receptors (sclerostin, Dickkopf-1/2, Wise/Sostdc1), accessory transmembrane proteins that facilitate receptor inhibition (LRP4, Kremen), secreted factors that serve as decoy receptors for Wnts (secreted Frizzled-related proteins, Wnt inhibitory factor 1), and secreted Wnt deacylaces that modify Wnts extracellularly (Tiki2, Notum). Wnt signaling also self-downregulates as osteoblastogenesis progresses. The β-catenin gene targets include the LRP5/6 antagonist sclerostin (SOST) and ubiquitin E3 ligases (ZNRF3, RNF43) that degrade the FZD receptor (Brommage et al. 2019; Houschyar et al. 2019; Maeda et al. 2019; Plotkin and Bruzzaniti 2019).

Noncanonical (β-catenin independent) **Wnt signaling** promote cytoskeletal rearrangement, cell polarity, and cell attachment and migration. The two major noncanonical pathways begin with Wnt5a (and perhaps other noncanonical Wnts), binding ROR 1/2 receptors in addition to Frizzled. In the **Wnt/Ca^{2+} pathway**, recruited DVL and G proteins activate the membrane-bound enzyme PLC to cleave PIP_2 into IP_3 and DAG. IP3 activates the release of calcium from the endoplasmic reticulum. Increased intracellular calcium triggers calmodulin, CaMKII, and DAG-activated PKC to cause transcription factors NFAT, NFκB, and CREB to translocate to the nucleus. In the **planar cell polarity pathway** (PCP), intracellular recruitment of DVL signals through Daam1, small GTPases RhoA and Rac, and kinases ROCK and Jnk to promote cytoskeletal reorganization and to activate transcription factors c-Jun and AP1 (Houschyar et al. 2019; Maeda et al. 2019; Pivonka et al. 2018; Plotkin and Bruzzaniti 2019). Wnt binding to FZD can activate additional noncanonical pathways to increase LRP5/6 receptor expression and enhance energy production (Maeda et al. 2019).

Osteoclast Differentiation and Bone Resorption

Osteoclasts are responsible for resorption of bone. They are polykaryons, meaning that they have multiple nuclei resulting from the fusion of multiple progenitors. Osteoclasts attach to the bone using integrins and seal to its surface with a podosome belt made from rings of filamentous actin. Podosome clusters can assemble and disassemble within minutes, promoting rapid osteoclast migration along the bone surface. Within this sealing zone, the osteoclast plasma membrane takes on a "ruffled" appearance due to the fusion of vesicles for secretion of its bone-resorbing products. Protons (H$^+$) are produced from water and carbon dioxide by a carbonic anhydrase II enzyme and enter the sealing zone through a vacuolar H$^+$/ATPase (ATP6I). Extracellular chloride ions (Cl$^-$) are obtained with an HCO$_3^-$/CL$^-$ exchanger and enter the sealing zone through a chloride channel (CIC-7) in complex with transmembrane protein OSTM1. This HCl acidifies the sealing zone, dissolving hydroxyapatite mineral. The exposed type I collagen is digested through enzymes released from lysosomes, including cathepsin K, matrix metalloproteases, and tartrate-resistant acid phosphatase (TRAP). After resorption, osteoclasts detach and undergo apoptosis, or cell death (Bellido et al. 2019; Plotkin and Bruzzaniti 2019; Ross 2013).

Like osteoblasts, osteoclast progenitors are produced in bone marrow, arising from hematopoietic stem cells (HSCs). Cytokines M-CSF and RANKL are essential for osteoclastogenesis (see Figure 31.1). M-CSF binds to the c-Fms receptor and signals through ERK to transcription factor E2F, promoting proliferation of osteoclast precursors. M-CSF induces expression of RANK on osteoclast precursor cell membranes, where it binds its ligand RANKL. Both M-CSF and RANK signal through PI3K to AKT pathways to promote precursor survival and cytoskeletal reorganization, and through ERK to the transcription factor MITF to promote osteoclast differentiation. RANK signaling pathways also activate transcription factors (MITF, AP1, NFATc1, NF-κB) for osteoclast differentiation. These signaling pathways are supported by extracellular matrix (ECM) interactions with integrin αvβ3, and by the activation of TNF-α and IL-1 receptors. Gene targets promote

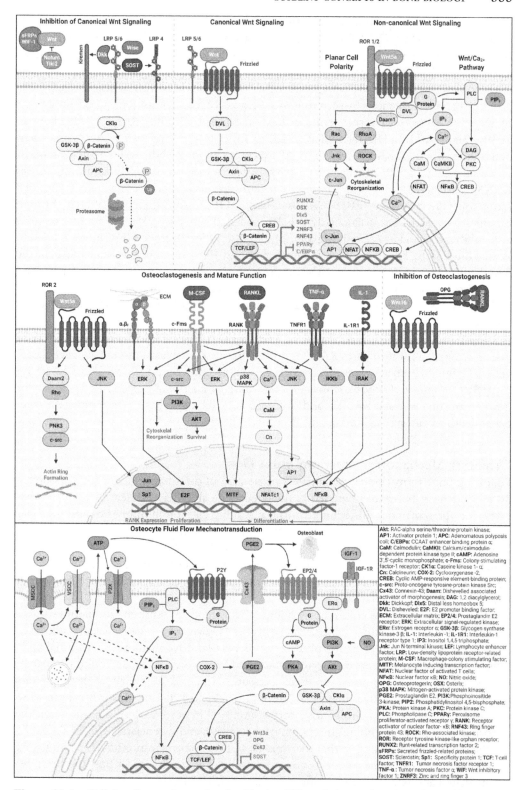

Figure 31.1 Cell signaling pathways involved in the differentiation or function of osteoblasts (top), osteoclasts (middle), and osteocytes (bottom). Figure created with BioRender.com.

osteoclast survival, differentiation, transmembrane proteins for fusion of mononuclear precursors (DC-STAMP, OC-STAMP), and proteins needed for acidifying the sealing zone and resorbing the matrix (e.g., ATP6I, CIC-7, OSTM1, MMP9, TRAP, cathepsin K) (Bellido et al. 2019; Plotkin and Bruzzaniti 2019; Takayanagi 2007).

Osteoblast lineage cells are important regulators of osteoclast differentiation. They can promote osteoclastogenesis by secreting M-CSF and RANKL, or inhibit osteoclastogenesis by secreting OPG (Osteoprotegerin), a decoy receptor that binds RANKL (Maeda et al. 2019) (Figure 31.1). The ratio of RANKL to OPG in the local osteoclast environment determines whether RANKL remains in excess to bind RANK and initiate osteoclast differentiation (Trichilo and Pivonka 2018). In osteocytes, mechanical loading suppresses RANKL and increases OPG, inhibiting osteoclastogenesis and protecting concurrent bone formation (Pivonka et al. 2018). In osteoblasts, OPG expression is increased through canonical Wnt signaling, particularly Wnt16-mediated activation. Wnt16 binding to FZD also inhibits osteoclastogenesis by blocking transcription factors NFATc1 and NF-κB. Wnt5a binding to FZD and ROR 2 signals through JNK, recruiting c-Jun to Sp1 on the RANK promoter to upregulate RANK expression. In mature osteoclasts, Wnt5a binding recruits Rho through the Daam2 adapter protein, causing the Rho effector kinase PKN3 to bind to c-Src, triggering actin ring formation (Kobayashi et al. 2018; Maeda et al. 2019).

Apoptosis of osteoclasts is regulated, in part, by the release of calcium from the resorbed matrix. Low calcium stimulates RANKL production by osteoblasts, increasing osteoclastogenesis. High calcium activates the osteoclast CaSR receptor and downstream pathways for osteoclast apoptosis. Osteoblast lineage cells can also encourage osteoclast apoptosis by down-regulating levels of RANKL and M-CSF and by secreting FasL, which binds the osteoclast death receptor Fas (Plotkin and Bruzzaniti 2019).

Osteocyte Mechanotransduction: Fluid Flow

Following bone formation, approximately 65 percent of osteoblasts die through apoptosis, 10 to 30 percent become embedded in the deposited osteoid and differentiate into osteocytes, and the remainder differentiate into bone-lining cells or chondroid-depositing cells. As osteocytes accumulate through many modeling and remodeling events, they compose approximately 95 percent of all bone cells (Franz-Odendaal et al. 2006). Osteocyte cell bodies are housed in lacunae, which are connected to other lacunae through canaliculi. Osteocytes extend their ~ 50 dendrites into the canaliculi to communicate with other osteocytes (Himeno-Ando et al. 2012).

Cowin, Weinbaum, and colleagues proposed that osteocytes sense the shear stress caused by fluid flow within lacunar–canalicular networks (Cowin et al. 1991; Weinbaum et al. 1994). Mechanical loading creates pressure gradients that drive the flow of interstitial fluid, causing shear stress on the osteocyte surface and drag force in its surrounding matrix. Osteocytes are also responsive to fluid pressure, which is amplified at higher strain frequencies, and which they may sense through the cytoskeleton. However, shear stress appears to be the primary mechanosensory stimulus (Liu et al. 2015). Fluid flow on the endosteal surface also promotes migration of osteoblasts and osteoclasts (Uda et al. 2017). Hughes and colleagues suggest that this fluid flow shear stress is responsible for stimulating formation modeling, while osteocyte apoptosis triggers resorption modeling and both disuse-mediated and targeted remodeling (Hughes et al. 2020).

Osteocytes sense fluid shear stress through focal adhesions and pericellular projections that tether them to the extracellular matrix. Mineralized protrusions from the lacunar–canalicular space form direct focal adhesions with transmembrane integrins ($\alpha V\beta 3$) on the osteocyte cell body and its dendrites. Pericellular transverse fibrils also extend from the osteocyte and bridge the extracellular space. When the osteocyte is deflected against these adhesions by fluid flow, cellular strain is amplified up to 100-fold (Liu et al. 2015; Verbruggen and McNamara 2018).The cell volume stimulated by physiologically active strain (> 3,000 µε) is amplified 10–40 percent by projections of the pericellular matrix and 50–420 percent by focal adhesions of the extracellular matrix. Strain amplification is essential for osteocyte function, as bone experiences mechanical strains of 1,000–2,000 µε, but osteocytes biochemically respond to strains starting around 5,000 µε and generate a substantial response to strains exceeding 10,000 µε (Verbruggen et al. 2012). A strain of 2,000 µε on bone is experienced as over 30,000 µε around osteocyte lacunae (Uda et al. 2017). Bending of the primary cilium of the osteocyte may also play a role in sensing fluid flow, although in a low capacity, as such cilia exist on only ~4% of osteocytes and bone-lining cells (Verbruggen and McNamara 2018).

Membrane stretch and strain causes an intracellular calcium influx through mechanosensitive calcium channels (MSCCs) on the osteocyte plasma membrane (Hughes and Petit 2010) (Figure 31.1). Local depolarization causes further calcium influx through voltage-sensitive calcium channels (VSCCs). ATP is then released extracellularly through vesicular exocytosis or through hemi-channels such as Cx43. ATP binding to the ATP-gated cation channel P2X causes further calcium influx. ATP binding to the G-protein coupled receptor P2Y causes the membrane-bound enzyme PLC to cleave PIP_2 into IP_3, which activates the release of additional calcium from the endoplasmic reticulum. Increased intracellular calcium induces translocation of NF-κB to the nucleus, where it transcribes prostaglandin synthase COX-2. PGE2 is synthesized by COX-2 and released extracellularly through Cx43, where it promotes β-catenin mediated gene transcription in both osteocytes and osteoblasts. PGE2 binding to receptor EP2 or EP4 receptors signal through cAMP/PKA and PI3K/Akt pathways to inhibit GSK-3β, allowing β-catenin to translocate to the nucleus. PI3K/Akt signaling is supported by estrogen (Erα) and nitric oxide. In osteocytes, β-catenin complexed with TCF/LEF and CREB transcribes genes that support osteoblastogenesis (Wnt3a), inhibit osteoclastogenesis (OPG), and promote osteocyte communication (Cx43), while downregulating Wnt signaling antagonist sclerostin (Pivonka et al. 2018; Uda et al. 2017; Verbruggen and McNamara 2018).

Osteocyte Mechanotransduction: Apoptosis

Osteocyte apoptosis (cell death) can occur in response to local microdamage, triggering targeted remodeling, or low strain, triggering resorption modeling or disuse-mediated remodeling. Osteocyte apoptosis occurs as early as 24 hours after microdamage, with resorption following 10 to 14 days later (Hughes et al. 2020). Linear microcracks disrupt pulsatile fluid flow between osteocytes, which may cause osteocyte apoptosis by impairing nutrient transport, destroying Cx43 gaps that facilitate osteocyte communication, and inducing hypoxia followed by oxidative stress (Ru and Wang 2020). Localized osteocyte apoptosis triggers osteocytes in a 100–300 µm "penumbra" radius of the damage site to upregulate RANKL and VEGF and decrease OPG expression, thereby promoting osteoclastogenesis. These peripheral osteocytes protect themselves by expressing the antiapoptotic protein Bcl-2 (Kennedy et al. 2012). Osteocyte apoptosis is required for expression of osteoclastogenic factors in these "bystander" osteocytes (Kennedy et al. 2014). The mechanism may involve the apoptotic release of extracellular ATP through Panx1 channels (McCutcheon et al. 2020). Larger microcracks result in a greater RANKL increase (Mulcahy et al. 2011). Abnormally low strain also triggers osteocyte apoptosis. Diffusion alone is not sufficient for osteocyte nutrient supply. In a state of disuse, the absence of strain-induced fluid flow may cause osteocyte apoptosis through nutrient deficiency and waste accumulation (Hughes and Petit 2010). Disuse-induced osteocyte apoptosis also triggers expression of RANKL and downregulation of OPG (Hughes et al. 2020).

Basic Multicellular Unit Structure and Phases of Remodeling

Remodeling requires osteocytes to coordinate action between osteoblasts and osteoclasts through the formation of a BMU. In cortical bone, the BMU tunnels into the cortex, with osteoclasts resorbing bone in a "cutting cone" and osteoblasts following behind in a "closing cone" to form new bone. In humans, osteons are approximately 250–300 μm in diameter and up to 10 mm long and retain a central Haversian canal for the blood vessel. This structure is called a secondary osteon, in contrast to the primary osteons that form when modeled bone surrounds a blood vessel. In cancellous bone, the BMU sits on the exposed surface of the trabecula. Osteoblasts resorb bone in a hemiosteon, forming a trench 60–70 μm deep, which is then filled with bone by osteoblasts (Robling et al. 2006; Trichilo and Pivonka 2018). The BMU is covered by a canopy of cells of mesenchymal origin, forming the bone remodeling compartment (BRC). In cortical bone, the canopy forms over the osteoblasts of the closing cone, and is penetrated by the central blood vessel. In cancellous bone, the canopy forms through retraction of bone lining cells, and it is penetrated by marrow capillaries (Eriksen 2010).

The remodeling cycle lasts about 120 days in cortical bone and 200 days in cancellous bone, with most of this time (150 days in cancellous bone) occupied by bone formation (Eriksen 2010). The phases of remodeling include (1) **activation** by osteocytes, (2) **resorption** by osteoclasts, (3) **reversal**, where resorption transitions to formation, (4) **formation** by osteoblasts, (5) **mineralization** of the deposited osteoid, and (6) **resting**, or quiescence (Verbruggen and McNamara 2018). The reversal phase, where bone resorption is coupled to bone formation, has been a subject of recent inquiry and discovery. Baron and colleagues (Baron 1977) identified the reversal phase when they observed large mononucleated cells in resorption spaces (Howship's lacunae) between the retreat of osteoclasts and the deposition of osteoid. It remained unknown for more than three decades whether these reversal cells were post-osteoclasts or pre-osteoblasts (Dempster 2017). Immunohistochemistry subsequently determined that reversal cells, which colonize as much as 80 percent of eroded surfaces in bone, belong to the osteoblastic lineage. Reversal cells express Runx2 and alkaline phosphatase, and begin to express the OSX characteristic of mature osteoblasts as they approach the region of osteoid deposition (Andersen et al. 2013; Lassen et al. 2017). Reversal cells clean up demineralized collagen, which is required for subsequent bone formation, through synthesis of matrix metalloproteinases. Reversal cells also deposit the osteopontin and collagen types I and III that compose the secondary osteon's cement line, which marks the extent of resorption before formation begins (Abdelgawad et al. 2016; Andersen et al. 2013). The reversal phase is actually a "reversal–resorption" phase, as osteoclasts are also sparsely distributed amongst reversal cells. "Primary" osteoclasts in the tip of the cutting cone are responsible for canal elongation, while "secondary" osteoclasts on the walls widen the tunnel. Expansion of the canal diameter constitutes the most overall resorption and is halted by osteoid deposition, which prevents further osteoclast activity (Lassen et al. 2017).

Coupling Mechanisms

In order to maintain adult bone mass, the amount of bone resorbed by osteoclasts must be "coupled" with the bone formed by osteoblasts. Sims and Martin (2014) identify four main classes of coupling factors.

1. **Matrix-derived signals:** Stored growth factors are released from the bone matrix by osteoclast resorption. These include TGF- β, BMP-2, IGFs, and platelet-derived growth factor (PDGF-bb), which promote osteoblastic differentiation, as discussed by Sims and Martin (2014).

2. **Osteoclast-secreted factors:** Active and inactive osteoclasts secrete factors that promote osteoblastogenesis and mature osteoblast function, including Wnt10b, CTHRC1 (a Wnt signaling modulator), BMP-6, cardiotrophin-1 (an IL-6 member), sphingosine-1-phosphate (a lipid mediator), and complement factor 3a (Sims and Martin 2014). Nonresorbing osteoclasts also secrete afamin to stimulate pre-osteoblast migration (Kim et al. 2012). TRAP expressed by osteoclasts is taken up by adjacent reversal cells and may promote their osteoblastogenesis (Abdelgawad et al. 2016).

3. **Osteoclast membrane-expressed factors:** Bidirectional signaling can occur through the physical connection of factors expressed on osteoclast and reversal cell membranes. Bone formation is promoted by osteoclast ephrinB2 and osteoblast EphB4 bidirectional signaling, which increases osteoblastogenesis through Runx2 activation and represses osteoclastogenesis through decreasing c-Fos and NFATc1 expression. Osteoclastogenesis can also be inhibited by osteoclast neutrophilin-1 and plexin-A1 binding to osteoblast Semaphorin 3A (Plotkin and Bruzzaniti 2019). Conversely, the transition to bone formation can be delayed by bidirectional signaling that inhibits osteoblastogenesis and promotes osteoclastogenesis. This includes osteoclastic ephrinA2 to osteoblastic EphA2 signaling and osteoclastic semaphorin 4D to osteoblastic plexin-B1 signaling (Abdelgawad et al. 2016; Plotkin and Bruzzaniti 2019).

4. **Topographical changes:** Osteoblast packing may be one mechanism by which osteoblasts sense the size and shape of resorption pits. Osteoid deposition appears to occur only once osteoprogenitors have reached a threshold cell density. This may be associated with acquisition of a cuboidal shape by packed osteoblasts, which is associated with collagen secretion. Slower osteoprogenitor recruitment extends the length of the reversal–resorption phase and expands the osteon's diameter (Lassen et al. 2017).

Physiological Influences on Bone Growth and Bone Loss

Hormones are key regulators of longitudinal growth. Long bones form through endochondral ossification, where a hyaline cartilage template is replaced with bone, starting in primary (diaphyseal) and secondary (epiphyseal) ossification centers. The cartilage growth plates at either end are ossified by osteoblasts adjacent to the primary ossification center, mineralized by hypertrophic chondrocytes intermediately, and lengthened by proliferating chondrocytes most distally (Long and Ornitz 2013; Mackie et al. 2011). **Growth hormone** (somatotropin) induces the liver and growth plate chondrocytes to produce IGF-1, which stimulates chondrocyte proliferation, along with osteoblastogenesis, as discussed. IGF-2 is produced by growth plate chondrocytes directly and is required for embryonic growth (Mackie et al. 2011). Growth hormone also directly stimulates pre-chondrocyte proliferation at the growth plate. **Thyroid hormone** T3 downregulates proliferation and increases hypertrophy of growth plate chondrocytes, while promoting mature osteoblast activity and osteoblast mediation of osteoclastogenesis. **Sex steroids** mediate the effects of the growth hormone/IFG-1 axis on longitudinal bone growth. During puberty, low levels of estrogen in females and testosterone aromatized to estrogen in males triggers growth hormone and IGF-1 production for the growth spurt. In late puberty, rising estrogen levels close the growth plate and stimulate epiphyseal fusion (Bellido and Gallant 2019).

Increasing bone length and body mass during growth increases bending strains on long bones, triggering the radial expansion of their cross-sections (Rauch and Schoenau 2001; Stout et al. 2019). Sex steroids play a key role in radial expansion and maintenance. Testosterone promotes periosteal bone formation, but estrogen stimulates endosteal bone formation while inhibiting periosteal formation. **Estrogens** are secreted by the ovaries in females and aromatized from androgens in males (Bellido and Gallant 2019). Estrogen receptor ERα may increase mechanical adaptation, particularly at the endosteum and in trabecular bone, by activating loading-induced β-catenin signaling, sensitizing PGE2 signaling, and upregulating Cx43 expression for osteocyte communication. ERβ has been suggested to compete with ERα to suppress mechanical adaptation at the periosteal surface. Murine experiments suggest sex differences in estrogen-sensitized responses to loading (Pivonka et al. 2018). When estrogen levels decline in females at menopause, the activation frequency of resorption increases by 33 percent and the endosteum is increasingly resorbed (Han et al. 1997). **Testosterone** is secreted mainly by the testes in males, and by the ovaries, adrenal glands, and through sex steroid conversion in adipose and other peripheral tissues in females (Bellido and Gallant 2019). Males exceed females in cross-sectional bone dimensions during and after menopause, with testosterone-driven expansion of the periosteal radius during aging (Martin 1993). Bone distributed further from the neutral axis is more mechanically effective. Males only need to restore approximately 30 percent of endosteal bone loss through periosteal apposition in order to retain bone bending strength (Martin 1993). However, starting around age 70, males can experience accelerated cortical bone loss in association with declining levels of bioavailable testosterone and the estrogen hormone estradiol (Khosla et al. 2005). Mechanically-induced bone turnover is also modulated over the lifespan by hormones and other factors involved in calcium–phosphate balance (parathyroid hormone, vitamin D), metabolism (insulin, leptin), the immune system (interleukins), and stress (glucocorticoids) (Bellido and Gallant 2019; Takayanagi 2007).

The physiological disregulation of aging also alters the microstructural products of remodeling. Bone resorption is accelerated through declining sex steroids, reduced physical activity, and increased microdamage to brittle tissue. Bone formation is concurrently reduced by osteoblast and osteocyte senescence in sensitivity, function, and survival (Infante and Rodríguez 2018). By decoupling these cellular processes from their mechanical triggers, bone tissue becomes less adapted to its typical loading environment, increasing fragility and fracture risk. We have previously reviewed age-associated changes in the mechanical patterning of cortical bone, including increased cortical porosity and pore system coalescence, decreased osteocyte lacunar density, smaller and more circular secondary osteons, and accumulated microdamage (Stout et al. 2019). Studies of the ontogenetic patterning of human trabecular bone indicate a broad similarity across mechanical sites (humerus, femur, and tibia), with a significant mechanical influence from human bipedal locomotion (Gosman et al. 2018). Trabecular bone loss begins during sex steroid sufficiency, potentially due to declines in serum IGF-I and growth hormone secretion after age 20. Before age 50, lifetime trabecular bone loss reaches 37 percent in females and 42 percent in males, compared to lifetime cortical bone loss of 6 percent in females and 15 percent in males (Riggs et al. 2008). Males preferentially experience trabecular thinning. Females tend to decline in trabecular number, which reduces bone strength more than trabecular thinning. This may contribute to a higher fracture risk in females (Khosla et al. 2005).

Conclusion

In this chapter, we summarized current mechanobiological concepts in skeletal biology. We reviewed principles of bone functional adaptation, cellular effectors of mechanical loading, and some physiological factors that modify mechanical adaptation over the lifespan. Bone tissue can be a useful proxy of physical behavior, health, and aging. It is important to recognize the complex interplay of mechanical, genetic, and physiological influences on its morphometry.

REFERENCES

Abdelgawad, M. E., J.-M. Delaisse, M. Hinge, et al. "Early Reversal Cells in Adult Human Bone Remodeling: Osteoblastic Nature, Catabolic Functions and Interactions with Osteoclasts." *Histochemistry and Cell Biology* 145, no. 6 (2016): 603–615.

Andersen, T. L., M. E. Abdelgawad, H. B. Kristensen, et al. "Understanding Coupling Between Bone Resorption and Formation: Are Reversal Cells the Missing Link?" *The American Journal of Pathology* 183, no. 1 (2013): 235–246.

Bagge, M. "A Model of Bone Adaptation as an Optimization Process." *Journal of Biomechanics* 33, no. 11 (2000): 1349–1357.

Baron, R. "Importance of the Intermediate Phases Between Resorption and Formation in the Measurement and Understanding of the Bone Remodeling Sequence." In *Bone Histomorphometry: Second International Workshop Lyon*. Edited by P. J. Meunier, 179–183. Toulouse: Armour Montagu, 1977.

Beaupré, G. S., T. E. Orr, and D. R. Carter. "An Approach for Time-Dependent Bone Modeling and Remodeling-Application: A Preliminary Remodeling Simulation." *Journal of Orthopaedic Research* 8, no. 5 (1990): 662–670.

Bellido, T. M., and K. M. H. Gallant. "Hormonal Effects on Bone Cells." In *Basic and Applied Bone Biology*, 2nd edn. Edited by D. B. Burr and M. R. Allen, 299–313. London, UK: Academic Press, 2019.

Bellido, T. M., L. I. Plotkin, and A. Bruzzaniti. "Bone Cells." In *Basic and Applied Bone Biology*, 2nd edn. Edited by D. B. Burr and M. R. Allen, 37–55. London, UK: Academic Press, 2019.

Bertram, J. E., and S. M. Swartz. "The "Law of Bone Transformation: A Case of Crying Wolff?" *Biological Reviews of the Cambridge Philosophical Society* 66, no. 3 (1991): 245–273.

Biewener, A. A., and J. E. Bertram. "Mechanical Loading and Bone Growth in Vivo." In *Bone*, vol. VII. Edited by B. K. Hall, 1–36. Boca Raton, FL, 1993.

Brommage, R., J. Liu, P. Vogel, et al. "NOTUM Inhibition Increases Endocortical Bone Formation and Bone Strength." *Bone Research* 7, no. 1 (2019): 1–12.

Burr, D. B., and R. B. Martin. "Calculating the Probability that Microcracks Initiate Resorption Spaces." *Journal of Biomechanics* 26, no. 4–5 (1993): 613–616.

Carter, D., and D. Beaupré. *Skeletal Function and Form: Mechanobiology of Skeletal Development, Aging, and Regeneration.* Cambridge: Cambridge University Press, 2001.

Cowin, S. C., and D. H. Hegedus. "Bone Remodeling I: Theory of Adaptive Elasticity." *Journal of Elasticity* 6, no. 3 (1976): 313–326.

Cowin, S. C., L. Moss-Salentijn, and M. L. Moss. "Candidates for the Mechanosensory System in Bone." *Journal of Biomechanical Engineering* 113, no. 2 (1991): 191–197.

Dempster, D. W. "Tethering Formation to Resorption: Reversal Revisited." *Journal of Bone and Mineral Research* 32, no. 7 (2017): 1389–1390.

Eriksen, E. F. "Cellular Mechanisms of Bone Remodeling." *Reviews in Endocrine & Metabolic Disorders* 11, no. 4 (2010): 219–227.

Franz-Odendaal, T. A., B. K. Hall, and P. E. Witten. "Buried Alive: How Osteoblasts Become Osteocytes." *Developmental Dynamics* 235, no. 1 (2006): 176–190.

Frost, H. M. "The Mechanostat – A Proposed Pathogenic Mechanism of Osteoporoses and the Bone Mass Effects of Mechanical and Nonmechanical Agents." *Bone and Mineral* 2, no. 2 (1987): 73–85.

Frost, H. M. "Bone's Mechanostat: A 2003 Update." *Anatomical Record Part A – Discoveries in Molecular Cellular and Evolutionary Biology* 275a, no. 2 (2003): 1081–1101.

Gosman, J., D. Raichlen, and T. Ryan. "Human Transitions: Current Perspectives on Skeletal Development." In *Children and Childhood in Bioarchaeology*. Edited by P. Beauchesne and S. C. Agarwal, 207–238. Gainesville: University Press of Florida, 2018.

Han, Z.-H., S. Palnitkar, D.S. Rao, et al. "Effects of Ethnicity and Age or Menopause on the Remodeling and Turnover of Iliac Bone: Implications for Mechanisms of Bone Loss." *Journal of Bone and Mineral Research* 12, no. 4 (1997): 498–508.

Hert, J., M. Lisková, and J. Landa. "Reaction of Bone to Mechanical Stimuli. 1. Continuous and Intermittent Loading of Tibia in Rabbit." *Folia Morphologica* 19, no. 3 (1971): 290–300.

Himeno-Ando, A., Y. Izumi, A. Yamaguchi, and T. Iimura. "Structural Differences in the Osteocyte Network Between the Calvaria and Long Bone Revealed by Three-Dimensional Fluorescence Morphometry, Possibly Reflecting Distinct Mechano-Adaptations and Sensitivities." *Biochemical and Biophysical Research Communications* 417, no. 2 (2012): 765–770.

Houschyar, K. S., C. Tapking, M. R. Borrelli, et al. "Wnt Pathway in Bone Repair and Regeneration – What Do We Know so Far." *Frontiers in Cell and Developmental Biology* 6 (2019): 170.

Hughes, J. M., and M. A. Petit. "Biological Underpinnings of Frost's Mechanostat Thresholds: The Important Role of Osteocytes." *Journal of Musculoskeletal & Neuronal Interactions* 10, no. 2 (2010): 128–135.

Hughes, J. M., C. M. Castellani, K. L. Popp, et al. "The Central Role of Osteocytes in the Four Adaptive Pathways of Bone's Mechanostat." *Exercise and Sport Sciences Reviews* 48, no. 3 (2020): 140–148.

Huiskes, R., H. Weinans, H. J. Grootenboer, et al. "Adaptive Bone-Remodeling Theory Applied to Prosthetic-Design Analysis." *Journal of Biomechanics* 20, no. 11–12 (1987): 1135–1150.

Infante, A., and C. I. Rodríguez. "Osteogenesis and Aging: Lessons from Mesenchymal Stem Cells." *Stem Cell Research & Therapy* 9, no. 1 (2018): 244.

Kennedy, O. D., B. C. Herman, D. M. Laudier, et al. "Activation of Resorption in Fatigue-Loaded Bone Involves Both Apoptosis and Active Pro-Osteoclastogenic Signaling by Distinct Osteocyte Populations." *Bone* 50, no. 5 (2012): 1115–1122.

Kennedy, O. D., D. M. Laudier, R. J. Majeska, et al. "Osteocyte Apoptosis Is Required for Production of Osteoclastogenic Signals Following Bone Fatigue in Vivo." *Bone* 64 (2014): 132–137.

Khosla, S., L. J. Melton, R. A. Robb, et al. "Relationship of Volumetric BMD and Structural Parameters at Different Skeletal Sites to Sex Steroid Levels in Men." *Journal of Bone and Mineral Research* 20, no. 5 (2005): 730–740.

Kim, B.-J., Y.-S. Lee, S.-Y. Lee, et al. "Afamin Secreted from Nonresorbing Osteoclasts Acts as a Chemokine for Preosteoblasts via the Akt-Signaling Pathway." *Bone* 51, no. 3 (2012): 431–440.

Kobayashi, Y., S. Uehara, and N. Udagawa. "Roles of Non-Canonical Wnt Signaling Pathways in Bone Resorption." *Journal of Oral Biosciences* 60, no. 2 (2018): 31–35.

Komori, T. "Regulation of Proliferation, Differentiation and Functions of Osteoblasts by Runx2." *International Journal of Molecular Sciences* 20, no. 7 (2019): E1694.

Kummer, B. "Functional Adaption of the Bone to Its Mechanical Stress." In *Fortschritte der Osteologie in Diagnostik Und Therapie*, edited by F. H. W. Heuck and E. Keck, 3–16. Berlin, Heidelberg: Springer, 1988.

Lanyon, L. E., and D. G. Baggott. "Mechanical Function as an Influence on the Structure and Form of Bone." *The Journal of Bone and Joint Surgery* British Volume 58-B, no. 4 (1976): 436–443.

Lanyon, L. E., A. E. Goodship, C. J. Pye, and J. H. MacFie. "Mechanically Adaptive Bone Remodelling." *Journal of Biomechanics* 15, no. 3 (1982): 141–154.

Lassen, N. E., T. L. Andersen, G. G. Pløen, et al. "Coupling of Bone Resorption and Formation in Real Time: New Knowledge Gained from Human Haversian BMUs." *Journal of Bone and Mineral Research* 32, no. 7 (2017): 1395–1405.

Lee, T. C., and D. Taylor. "Bone Remodelling: Should We Cry Wolff?" *Irish Journal of Medical Science* 168, no. 2 (1999): 102–105.

Li, J., T. Mashiba, and D. B. Burr. "Bisphosphonate Treatment Suppresses Not Only Stochastic Remodeling but Also the Targeted Repair of Microdamage." *Calcified Tissue International* 69, no. 5 (2001): 281–286.

Lieberman, D. E., and A. W. Crompton. *Principles of Animal Design.* Cambridge: Cambridge University Press, 1998.

Liu, C., K. Middleton, and L. You. "Bone Cell Mechanobiology Using Micro- and Nano-Techniques." In *Integrative Mechanobiology: Micro- and Nano-Techniques in Cell Mechanobiology.* Edited by C.A. Simmons, D.-H. Kim, and Yu Sun, 245–265. Cambridge: Cambridge University Press, 2015.

Long, F. "Building Strong Bones: Molecular Regulation of the Osteoblast Lineage." *Nature Reviews Molecular Cell Biology* 13, no. 1 (2012): 27–38.

Long, F., and D. M. Ornitz. "Development of the Endochondral Skeleton." *Cold Spring Harbor Perspectives in Biology* 5, no. 1 (2013): a008334.

Mackie, E. J., L. Tatarczuch, and M. Mirams. "The Skeleton: A Multi-functional Complex Organ: The Growth Plate Chondrocyte and Endochondral Ossification." *The Journal of Endocrinology* 211, no. 2 (2011): 109–121.

Maeda, K., Y. Kobayashi, M. Koide, et al. "The Regulation of Bone Metabolism and Disorders by Wnt Signaling." *International Journal of Molecular Sciences* 20, no. 22 (2019): E5525.

Martin, B. "Aging and Strength of Bone as a Structural Material." *Calcified Tissue International* 53, no. Suppl. 1 (1993): S34–S39, discussion S39–S40.

Martin, R. B. "Is All Cortical Bone Remodeling Initiated by Microdamage?" *Bone* 30, no. 1 (2002): 8–13.

Martin, R. B. "Fatigue Microdamage as an Essential Element of Bone Mechanics and Biology." *Calcified Tissue International* 73, no. 2 (2003): 101–107.

McCutcheon, S., R. J. Majeska, D. C. Spray, et al. "Apoptotic Osteocytes Induce RANKL Production in Bystanders via Purinergic Signaling and Activation of Pannexin Channels." *Journal of Bone and Mineral Research* 35, no. 5 (2020): 966–977.

Meakin, L. B., J. S. Price, and L. E. Lanyon. "The Contribution of Experimental in Vivo Models to Understanding the Mechanisms of Adaptation to Mechanical Loading in Bone." *Frontiers in Endocrinology* 5 (2014): 154.

Mulcahy, L. E., D. Taylor, T. C. Lee, and G. P. Duffy. "RANKL and OPG Activity Is Regulated by Injury Size in Networks of Osteocyte-Like Cells." *Bone* 48, no. 2 (2011): 182–188.

Ozcivici, E., Y. K. Luu, B. Adler, et al. "Mechanical Signals as Anabolic Agents in Bone." *Nature Reviews. Rheumatology* 6, no. 1 (2010): 50–59.

Pearson, O. M., and D. E. Lieberman. "The Aging of Wolff's 'Law': Ontogeny and Responses to Mechanical Loading in Cortical Bone." *American Journal of Physical Anthropology* Suppl. 39 (2004): 63–99.

Pivonka, P., A. Park, and M. R. Forwood. "Functional Adaptation of Bone: The Mechanostat and Beyond." In *Multiscale Mechanobiology of Bone Remodeling and Adaptation.* Edited by P. Pivonka, 1–60. CISM International Centre for Mechanical Sciences. Cham: Springer International Publishing, 2018.

Plotkin, L. I., and N. Bivi. "Local Regulation of Bone Cell Function." In *Basic and Applied Bone Biology.* Edited by D. B. Burr and M. R. Allen, 47–73. London, UK: Academic Press, 2014.

Plotkin, L. I., and A. Bruzzaniti. "Molecular Signaling in Bone Cells: Regulation of Cell Differentiation and Survival." *Advances in Protein Chemistry and Structural Biology* 116 (2019): 237–281.

Rauch, F., and E. Schoenau. "The Developing Bone: Slave or Master of Its Cells and Molecules?" *Pediatric Research* 50, no. 3 (2001): 309–314.

Riggs, B. L., L. J. Melton, R. A. Robb, et al. "A Population-Based Assessment of Rates of Bone Loss at Multiple Skeletal Sites: Evidence for Substantial Trabecular Bone Loss in Young Adult Women and Men." *Journal of Bone and Mineral Research* 23, no. 2 (2008): 205–214.

Ritchie, R. O. "The Conflicts Between Strength and Toughness." *Nature Materials* 10, no. 11 (2011): 817–822.

Robling, A. G., A. B. Castillo, and C. H. Turner. "Biomechanical and Molecular Regulation of Bone Remodeling." *Annual Review of Biomedical Engineering* 8 (2006): 455–498.

Roesler, H. "The History of Some Fundamental Concepts in Bone Biomechanics." *Journal of Biomechanics* 20, no. 11 (1987): 1025–1034.

Ross, F. P. "Osteoclast Biology and Bone Resorption." In *Primer on the Metabolic Bone Diseases and Disorders of Mineral Metabolism*, 8th edn. Edited by C. J. Rosen, 25–33. Hoboken, NJ: John Wiley and Sons, Inc., 2013.

Roux, W. "Beitrage Zur Morphologie Der Funktionnellen Anspassung." *Archive of Journal of Anatomy and Physiology* 9 (1885): 120–158.

Ru, J.-Y., and Y.-F. Wang. "Osteocyte Apoptosis: The Roles and Key Molecular Mechanisms in Resorption-Related Bone Diseases." *Cell Death & Disease* 11, no. 10 (2020): 846.

Rubin, C., A. S. Turner, R. Müller, et al. "Quantity and Quality of Trabecular Bone in the Femur are Enhanced by a Strongly Anabolic, Noninvasive Mechanical Intervention." *Journal of Bone and Mineral Research* 17, no. 2 (2002): 349–357.

Rubin, C. T., and L. E. Lanyon. "Regulation of Bone Formation by Applied Dynamic Loads." *The Journal of Bone and Joint Surgery American Volume* 66, no. 3 (1984): 397–402.

Ruff, C. B., and C. S. Larsen. "Long Bone Structural Analyses and the Reconstruction of Past Mobility: A Historical Review." In *Reconstructing Mobility: Environmental, Behavioral, and Morphological Determinants*. Edited by K. J. Carlson and D. Marchi, 13–29. New York, NY: Springer, 2014.

Ruff, C., B. Holt, and E. Trinkaus. "Who's Afraid of the Big Bad Wolff?: 'Wolff's Law' and Bone Functional Adaptation." *American Journal of Physical Anthropology* 129, no. 4 (2006): 484–498.

Scheiner, S., P. Pivonka, and C. Hellmich. "Poromicromechanics Reveals That Physiological Bone Strains Induce Osteocyte-Stimulating Lacunar Pressure." *Biomechanics and Modeling in Mechanobiology* 15, no. 1 (2016): 9–28.

Sims, N. A., and T. J. Martin. "Coupling the Activities of Bone Formation and Resorption: A Multitude of Signals Within the Basic Multicellular Unit." *BoneKEy Reports* 3 (2014).

Skerry, T. M. "One Mechanostat or Many? Modifications of the Site-Specific Response of Bone to Mechanical Loading by Nature and Nurture." *Journal of Musculoskeletal & Neuronal Interactions* 6, no. 2 (2006): 122–127.

Stout, S. D., M. E. Cole, and A. M. Agnew. "Histomorphology: Deciphering the Metabolic Record." In *Ortner's Identification of Pathological Conditions in Human Skeletal Remains, 3rd edn.* Edited by J. E. Buikstra, 91–167. San Diego: Academic Press, 2019.

Subbarayan, G., and D. L. Bartel. "A Reconciliation of Local and Global Models for Bone Remodeling Through Optimization Theory." *Journal of Biomechanical Engineering* 122, no. 1 (1999): 72–76.

Sugiyama, T., L. B. Meakin, W. J. Browne, et al. "Bones' Adaptive Response to Mechanical Loading Is Essentially Linear Between the Low Strains Associated with Disuse and the High Strains Associated with the Lamellar/Woven Bone Transition." *Journal of Bone and Mineral Research* 27, no. 8 (2012): 1784–1793.

Takayanagi, H. "Osteoimmunology: Shared Mechanisms and Crosstalk Between the Immune and Bone Systems." *Nature Reviews Immunology* 7, no. 4 (2007): 292–304.

Trichilo, S., and P. Pivonka. "Application of Disease System Analysis to Osteoporosis: From Temporal to Spatio-Temporal Assessment of Disease Progression and Intervention." In CISM International Centre for Mechanical Sciences, *Multiscale Mechanobiology of Bone Remodeling and Adaptation*. Edited by P. Pivonka, 61–121. Cham: Springer International Publishing, 2018.

Turner, C. H. "Three Rules for Bone Adaptation to Mechanical Stimuli." *Bone* 23, no. 5 (1998): 399–407.

Turner, C. H. "Toward a Mathematical Description of Bone Biology: The Principle of Cellular Accommodation." *Calcified Tissue International* 65, no. 6 (1999): 466–471.

Uda, Y., E. Azab, N. Sun, et al. "Osteocyte Mechanobiology." *Current Osteoporosis Reports* 15, no. 4 (2017): 318–325.

Verbruggen, S. W., and L. M. McNamara. Chapter 6, "Bone Mechanobiology in Health and Disease." In *Mechanobiology in Health and Disease*. Edited by S. W. Verbruggen, 157–214. Academic Press, 2018.

Verbruggen, S. W., T. J. Vaughan, and L. M. McNamara. "Strain Amplification in Bone Mechanobiology: A Computational Investigation of the in Vivo Mechanics of Osteocytes." *Journal of the Royal Society Interface* 9, no. 75 (2012): 2735–2744.

von Meyer, G. H. "Die Architectur Der Spongiosa." *Reichert und du Bois-Reymond's Archiv* 8 (1867): 615–628.

Weinbaum, S., S. C. Cowin, and Y. Zeng. "A Model for the Excitation of Osteocytes by Mechanical Loading-Induced Bone Fluid Shear Stresses." *Journal of Biomechanics* 27, no. 3 (1994): 339–360.

Wolff, J. *Das Gesetz Der Transformation Der Knochen*. Berlin: Verlag von August Hirschwald, 1892.

CHAPTER 32

Deducing Attributes of Dental Growth and Development from Fossil Hominin Teeth

Debbie Guatelli-Steinberg

In 1667, Niels Stensen (also known as "Steno") had an epiphany while dissecting a shark. Its teeth were uncannily similar to commonly found pieces of rock known as *glossopetrae* or "tongue stones," then considered to have magical powers. Steno recognized the true identity of these "tongue stones" as fossilized shark teeth (Maisey 1997). Indeed, much of the vertebrate fossil record consists of teeth, largely because teeth are the hardest elements of the skeleton (Hillson 1996). The same is true of the human fossil record (although fossilized shark teeth are much more common than those of humans, as sharks lose hundreds of teeth during their lives and have been around since the Devonian period).

The hardest component of teeth is enamel, the outer covering of dental crowns, where 96 percent of mature enamel is mineral, composed of hydroxyapatite – a crystalline calcium phosphate (Nanci 2008). No cells are contained in mature enamel, so that, once it is formed, enamel cannot regrow in the way bone can (Nanci 2008)). Incremental growth layers in enamel, somewhat analogous to tree-rings, can therefore be preserved for millennia in fossilized enamel. As enamel in different teeth is formed throughout the span of time between the prenatal period and late childhood (Hillson 1996), the study of enamel growth in human fossil ancestors provides a unique window into growth and development during the early years of life.

Here, I will describe the basic biology of enamel growth and highlight three topics of paleoanthropological inquiry to which the analysis of enamel growth layers yields insights. The first of these is the evolution of human life history. In an evolutionary context, the phrase "life history" most simply refers to "a series of growth and maturational phases ultimately related to the scheduling of reproduction and lifetime reproductive output" (Kelley and Smith 2003). These phases include, or are related to, the gestation period, age at weaning, age at sexual maturity and first breeding, interbirth intervals, and longevity. Among

A Companion to Biological Anthropology, Second Edition. Edited by Clark Spencer Larsen.
© 2023 John Wiley & Sons Ltd. Published 2023 by John Wiley & Sons Ltd.

primates, humans have the most prolonged life histories, with particularly long periods of juvenile growth, commonly referred to as "childhood" (Bogin 1997). Our protracted periods of juvenile growth may be related to the very high energy requirements of growing our large brains. Indeed, during childhood energy saved from reduced somatic growth rates appears to be diverted to brain growth (Kuzawa et al. 2014). The study of enamel growth in fossil hominins has made, and continues to make, major contributions to our understanding of *when* our extended period of childhood growth and development evolved.

While analyzing enamel growth in fossils, researchers have found differences among species (or groups of hominins) in the way in which enamel is formed. Analyzing patterns of enamel growth formation is therefore a second area of inquiry, related to the first, and one that provides insight into differences in growth processes among various species. The third area of research the study of enamel growth addresses is that of physiological stress in fossil hominins. Periods of malnutrition or bouts of disease can disrupt enamel growth, leaving permanent records of these events in fossilized enamel (Hillson 1996). A great deal more has been accomplished in each of these three areas than can be touched upon in this introductory essay. Nevertheless, this essay hits some of the high points involved in the study of hominin enamel growth.

Background: The Incremental Nature of Enamel Growth

From inside out, a tooth crown consists of three major tissues: pulp, dentine, and enamel (Figure 32.1). Pulp is a soft tissue surrounded by dentine, a hard tissue that is 70 percent mineralized. The harder and more brittle enamel covering of the tooth crown gains some protection from fracture through the shock-absorbing quality of the softer dentine, which underlies it (Nanci 2008). The following general account of enamel formation is summarized from descriptions by Nanci (2008) – except where otherwise noted.

Enamel begins to form at the cusp tip of a crown. In response to the first formed dentine, enamel-forming cells called "ameloblasts" secrete an organic matrix of proteins that serves the purpose of "accepting" minerals. Ameloblasts continue to differentiate from epithelial cells sequentially, along the presumptive enamel–dentine junction, in response to the

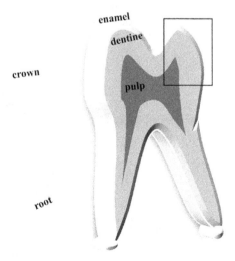

Figure 32.1 Internal structure of a tooth.

sequential formation of dentine along the length of the crown. The rate at which amelo-blast differentiation occurs is known as the "enamel extension rate" (Shellis 1984). As ameloblasts become functional, they migrate away from the enamel–dentine junction and toward what will eventually become the enamel surface, secreting the enamel matrix as they go. During this first step, which is the secretory stage of enamel formation, enamel reaches a state of 30 percent mineralization. After ameloblasts have formed the full thickness of the enamel, they undergo morphological changes associated with the maturation stage of enamel formation, as they cycle between removing water and organic components of the matrix and introducing an additional mineral. Enamel reaches its fully mineralized state at the end of the maturation stage.

The incremental nature of enamel growth is reflected in microstructural details of the enamel formed during the secretory stage. Aside from a small portion of the enamel formed first and last, the enamel formed by each ameloblast has a rod-like structure, and therefore is often referred to as an enamel rod (or alternatively as an enamel prism; Dean 1987). Enamel rods reflect the path of the ameloblasts which formed them (Risnes 1986) (Figure 32.2). In enamel thin sections viewed through a transmitted light microscope, fine lines known as "cross-striations" cross-cut the enamel rods. Over the length of the rod cross-striations appear to form at regular intervals (Dean 1987; see Figure 32.2). Experimental studies from the 1930s first suggested that cross-striations are formed according to a circadian rhythm (that is, a twenty-four-hour rhythm; for a review, see Dean 1987). Bromage (1991) produced experimental confirmation of this rhythm. The exact physiological mechanism(s) underlying this rhythm are not known, but daily variations in the metabolic activity of ameloblasts may underlie the daily rhythm of cross-striations (Boyde 1979; Dean 1987; Fitzgerald 1998).

Cross-striations are sometimes referred to as short-period increments, so as to differentiate them from a second kind of incremental growth, present in enamel, which is represented by long-period increments (Dean 2000). When viewed under a transmitted light microscope, long-period increments in enamel appear as dark lines traversing a series of enamel rods (Figure 32.2 is an idealized diagram). More commonly, long-period increments in the enamel are called "striae of Retzius" (Hillson 1996), after their discoverer Anders Retzius, a Swedish anatomist of the nineteenth century.

Striae of Retzius are actually a series of growth layers in a three-dimensional tooth. These growth layers are formed when all the ameloblasts along the enamel-forming front (Figure 32.2) simultaneously slow their secretion of the enamel matrix (Dean 1987). It has long

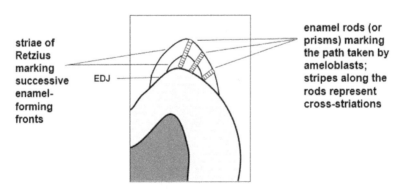

Figure 32.2 Diagram showing how enamel layers form during tooth formation. See the text for further details.

been assumed that the simultaneous slowing of secretory ameloblasts occurs at regular intervals throughout all of the teeth of an individual (Dean 1987; FitzGerald 1998), reflecting a systemic physiological growth rhythm. Recent studies, however, have shown that different tooth types (deciduous vs. permanent; anterior permanent vs. posterior permanent) of the same individual may have slightly different long-period enamel growth rhythms (e.g., Mahoney et al. 2016; McFarlane et al. 2021). Given that whole classes of the dentition appear to retain a common rhythm, these recent studies are not entirely inconsistent with the notion that there is yet a systemic growth rhythm underlying the formation of striae of Retzius. It could be that this fundamental rhythm is altered locally, within tooth types. The source of this rhythm is still a biological mystery, though it has been suggested that it might originate from the suprachiasmic nucleus of the hypothalamus (SCN), an area of the brain that is linked to circadian rhythms (Bromage et al. 2012).

In humans, the average stria of Retzius interval is eight or nine days, ranging from a minimum of six to a maximum of 12 (Reid and Dean 2006). To determine this interval, one counts the number of daily increments or cross-striations that fall between the striae of Retzius. This count, in days, is then referred to as the "periodicity" of the striae.

In a tooth's cuspal or occlusal enamel, the striae of Retzius (layers in three dimensions) cover each other in a series of domes, and so they are not visible from the tooth's surface (Figure 32.3). Thus, in cuspal enamel, the striae of Retzius are sometimes called "hidden" or "buried" increments. However, on the sides of a tooth, in a tooth's lateral enamel, the striae of Retzius form a series of layered planes in three dimensions, which are called "Retzius planes." These "growing planes" actually emerge on to the surface of enamel (Figures 32.3 and 32.4). In the lateral enamel, the growth layers are no longer buried. The surface manifestations of Retzius planes are known as "perikymata" (a plural form of the noun "perikyma"). The name is based on the ancient Greek noun *kyma* (or *kuma*), meaning "wave." This choice was inspired by the wave-like "crests" and "troughs" which perikymata exhibit (Hillson 1996; see Figures 32.3 and 32.4).

With the aid of a microscope, perikymata can be directly observed and counted on fossil enamel surfaces, as long as they have not been worn or eroded away. As perikymata are surface manifestations of the striae of Retzius, they have exactly the same periodicity of the striae in any given tooth. By counting all the perikymata from the cusp of the tooth to its cervix (the "bottom" of the tooth), and by considering a range of possible periodicities, an estimated range can be calculated for the time a fossil tooth's lateral enamel took to form.

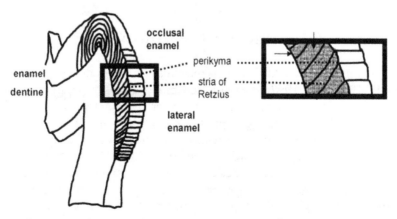

Figure 32.3 Illustration of the relationship between internal and external enamel growth layers in tooth enamel.

Figure 32.4 Scanning electron micrograph of a Neanderthal incisor enamel surface showing the wave-like horizontally oriented structures called perikymata.

Ideally, one would want to have a way of looking inside fossil teeth – through natural fractures, thin-sectioning, or synchrotron techniques (Smith and Tafforeau 2008) – to be able to determine the exact periodicity of the perikymata. The use of X-ray synchrotron microtomography has transformed the study of enamel growth and development in our ancestors (e.g., Smith et al. 2010; Smith and Tafforeau 2008; Xing et al. 2019), making it possible to ascertain multiple aspects of enamel growth. Much of the foundational work on this topic, however, was limited to enamel surfaces, relying on perikymata to obtain estimates of lateral enamel formation time. These earlier studies of fossil teeth focused on counting perikymata on anterior teeth (incisors and canines) rather than on posterior teeth (premolars and molars) – since in the former a much smaller proportion of overall enamel formation time is hidden in the cuspal region (Hillson and Bond 1997).

ENAMEL GROWTH AND THE TEMPO OF FOSSIL HOMININ LIFE HISTORIES

The pace of a primate species' life history is related to its rate of dental development. B. H. Smith (1989, 1991, and 1992) demonstrated this relationship clearly, particularly with respect to the age at which the first permanent molar erupts. Her analyses of 21 species of primates from diverse taxonomic groups showed that the age at which the first molar emerges into the oral cavity is highly correlated with life history variables such as gestation length, weaning age, and age at sexual maturity in females. This relationship exists largely because skeletal growth is slower in species with bigger brains and longer life histories, so that molars cannot emerge into the jaw until the jaw grows big enough to accommodate them (Smith 1992). Larger-brained species with slow life histories tend to have later first molar eruption ages than smaller-brained species with faster life histories. The first molars erupt in humans at around six years of age (Hillson 1996). Hence some refer to these teeth as our "six-year-old" molars. Chimpanzees, humans' closest primate relatives, have brains approximately one-fourth to one-third the size of human brains and an age of first molar eruption that is two to three years earlier than that of humans (Zihlman et al. 2004).

The periodicity of striae of Retzius itself appears to have a relationship to the pace of life history across living primates. Bromage et al. (2009, 2012) found strong positive correlations between primate species' average periodicities and several life history variables. Thus, for example, fast growing ring-tailed lemurs have average periodicities of 2 to 3 days (Hogg et al. 2015) and are weaned much earlier than orangutans, which have average periodicities ranging from 9 to 12 days (McGrath et al. 2019) and are not fully weaned until 7 to 9 years of age (Schuppli et al. 2016).

Armed with this comparative perspective that links aspects of enamel growth to life history, researchers have used, and continue to use, growth increments in fossil hominin tooth enamel to track the evolution of human life histories. Early human ancestors, such as *Australopithecus*, had small brains, not much larger than those of chimpanzees (Smith and Tompkins 1995). Thus, on the basis of the relationship between brain size and first molar eruption, Smith (1991) argued that *Australopithecus* would have had an age of first molar eruption closer to that of chimpanzees than to that of humans. Bromage and Dean (1985) and Beynon and Dean (1988) actually demonstrated that this was true by counting the perikymata on the surfaces of the anterior (incisor and canine) teeth of early hominins. Their analysis of *Australopithecus afarensis* specimen LH2 (from Laetoli, Tanzania, dated to approximately 3.7 mya) illustrates their approach. This ancient hominin died at the point when the lower central incisor crown had just completed its growth and when the first molar had already erupted into the oral cavity. The lower central incisor had 130 perikymata on its lateral surface. Assuming a seven-day periodicity, about average for early hominins (Lacruz et al. 2008), these 130 perikymata represent approximately 2.5 years of growth. Adding an estimate for the age at which the first incisor begins to calcify (approximately 0.5 years after birth in humans) and an estimate for the "buried" Retzius planes in the cuspal enamel (approximately 0.5 years in human teeth), Beynon and Dean (1988) concluded that the LH2 individual was approximately 3.5 years of age at death. Clearly, with a first molar having already erupted at this age, this *Australopithecus afarensis* individual had a rate of dental development far more similar to that of a chimpanzee than to that of a modern human! Other specimens of *Australopithecus* and *Paranthropus* examined by these two researchers were similarly accelerated in their dental development.

More recently, Smith et al. (2015) used X-ray synchrotron microtomography to examine early hominin fossil teeth, finding greater variability in their enamel growth and development than previously realized. The use of synchrotron imaging allowed them to obtain exact periodicities for early hominin fossil teeth, to ascertain periods of growth in the cuspal region of the tooth, and to ultimately produce precise estimates of age at death. (The only unknown component of these authors' estimates was the age of tooth initiation.) Comparing the age at death of these fossil hominins with dental developmental charts of modern humans, Smith et al. (2015) found that although all early hominins had achieved states of dental development that were more advanced than similarly aged modern children, they were not all equally advanced. Nevertheless, the point stands that early hominin dental development was faster than that of modern humans. The median periodicities of early hominins (*Australopithecus*, *Paranthropus*, and early *Homo*) also bear out this conclusion, with those of early hominins having significantly lower periodicities than do people today (Hogg et al. 2020). Because fast growing modern human primates have lower periodicities than slower-growing primates, the lower average periodicities of early human ancestors also suggest they had an overall more rapid pace of growth than we humans do today.

The first glimmerings of growth prolongation in our ancestors occurred with *Homo erectus*, a species with a brain that was larger than that of *Australopithecus* but smaller than our own brain (Smith and Tompkins 1995). Dean and colleagues (2001), using more complex histological methods than can be described here on crown and root sections of the Javanese *Homo erectus* specimen Sangiran S-37, estimated that, in this individual, the first molar emergence would have occurred around 4.4 years of age. These researchers were also able to count perikymata on the anterior teeth of WT-15000, the "Nariokotome boy" (a remarkable, nearly complete skeleton of an African *Homo erectus* individual). Interestingly, for this specimen, estimates of overall crown formation time based on these counts fell well within the estimated range for *Australopithecus*, and below the estimated range for modern humans (Dean et al. 2001). Furthermore, these researchers determined that enamel formation in the Nariokotome boy's lower canine was completed at the age of four years. Dean and colleagues argued that, if the Nariokotome boy was like modern humans in completing enamel formation in his lower canine at the time of M1 emergence, then his first molar would have emerged at approximately four years of age. Hence these data on the enamel formation time and on the estimated first molar emergence in *Homo erectus* suggest only a minimal shift toward the prolongation of growth in this species. Indeed, it is one of the fascinating aspects of the Nariokotome boy that analysis of enamel yields an age at death of eight years, with an approximate height of five feet, three inches. This is, perhaps needless to say, a bit tall for an eight-year-old boy!

So, when did growth periods of the same length as those of modern humans evolve? Bermúdez de Castro and colleagues (1999) reported a modern human pattern of dental development in the 0.8-million-year-old hominins from Atapuerca-TD6 (Spain). The state of *relative* development in pairs of each individual's anterior and posterior teeth was similar to that displayed by modern humans. Similarities in relative dental development can, however, belie differences in the absolute time it takes to form the dentition. For example, the nearly simultaneous eruption of first molars and first incisors in both *Paranthropus* and *Homo sapiens* (Bromage 1990) does not imply that these two taxa shared the same absolute rate of development. Based on the work of Beynon and Dean (1988), we know that they did not, despite this similarity in their relative dental development.

T. Smith and co-workers (Smith et al. 2007) used X-ray synchrotron microtomography to "look inside" the teeth of the approximately 300,000-year-old remains of one of the Jebel Irhoud specimens from Morocco, a site with the oldest known modern humans in the fossil record. In so doing, they found this specimen to have the highest periodicity – ten days – among all hominin fossils yet known. These researchers determined that overall enamel formation times in the teeth of this specimen, which were large by modern human standards, were actually *greater* than those of modern humans. Furthermore, Smith and colleagues determined that this individual died at the age of 7.78 years, when its other teeth (premolars and molars) were at stages of development comparable to those of a modern European child of the same chronological age.

Our research team, led by Song Xing, used synchrotron X-ray microtomography to examine dental growth and development in the more morphologically archaic but also more recent Xujiayao fossil hominin juvenile from China, dated to between 100,000 and 224,000 years before present (Xing et al. 2019). Our analyses revealed an age at death of approximately 6.5 years (Xing et al. 2019) and a stage of dental development comparable to that of some modern human population groups (Xing et al. 2020). Notably, Xujiayao 1, like Jebel Irhoud, had a periodicity of ten days.

If the archaic hominin Xujiayao and early modern humans like Jebel Irhoud had growth periods similar to our own, then were Neandertals also like us in this regard? With brain sizes similar to, or greater than, those of modern humans, Neandertals might be expected to have had prolonged juvenile growth periods. Though much has been published on dental growth and development in Neanderthals – perikymata studies: e.g., Ramirez-Rozzi and Bermudez de Castro (2004); Guatelli-Steinberg et al. (2005); dental development and eruption studies, e.g., Macchiarelli et al. (2006), Smith et al. (2010), Rosas et al. (2017) – the answer to this question has proven surprisingly elusive. For example, Macchiarelli et al. (2006) estimated the age of first molar eruption in the La Chaise Neandertal from France (Macchiarelli et al. 2006) at 6.7 years of age, quite close to the 6.4 years of age which B. H. Smith and Tompkins (1995) had predicted on the basis of the Neandertal brain size. However, T. Smith and colleagues (2010) analyzed dental development in six Neanderthals using X-ray synchrotron microtomography, revealing more accelerated rates of dental development. Finally, Rosas et al. (2017) found the El Sidrón Neanderthal to have comparable rates of dental development to that of modern humans. Are there methodological differences that might explain these apparent contradictions? Or is it perhaps simply that over time and space, Neandertals varied greatly in the amount of time their teeth took to develop, some of them being more like modern humans than others?

Variation in Enamel Growth Patterns

While studying enamel growth in early hominins, Beynon and Dean (1988) noted a difference between *Australopithecus* and *Paranthropus*. In the former, perikymata became much more compact in the final (cervical) third of the crown to form. In the latter, perikymata were more evenly distributed, as well as absolutely more widely spaced over the entire length of the crown. The authors attributed the wider spacing of perikymata in *Paranthropus* to fast enamel extension rates (the rate at which new ameloblasts along the enamel–dentine junction are recruited to form enamel). Beynon and Wood (1987) had previously examined naturally fractured teeth of *Paranthropus*, finding very rapid extension rates in this genus. Consistently faster extension rates in *Paranthropus* may have resulted in more widely spaced, and thus fewer, perikymata on their enamel surfaces. Beynon and Wood (1987) noted that the rapidity with which enamel was formed in *Paranthropus* was especially interesting given the great thickness of this species' enamel. *Paranthropus* was building large teeth with thick enamel in a hurry!

Although the wide spacing of perikymata in *Paranthropus* appears to reflect its rapid rate of enamel extension, one cannot assume as a rule that the spacing of perikymata along the surface reflects the enamel extension rate along the enamel–dentine junction. Other variables such as periodicity, the rate of enamel secretion, enamel thickness, and the course of the striae of Retzius may also affect the absolute spacing of perikymata on the enamel surface (Schwartz and Dean 2001). Further, it is important to note that the absolute spacing of perikymata on the enamel surface (perikymata per mm) is not the same thing as the *distribution pattern* of perikymata over the tooth crown, which can be defined as the percentage of total perikymata present in each tenth (decile) of a tooth's crown height (Dean and Reid 2001). Some species pack their perikymata in the more cervical deciles of the tooth's crown height, while others have perikymata distributed more evenly (Dean and Reid 2001). Figure 32.4 shows a scanning electron micrograph image of a Neanderthal tooth surface that has a more even distribution of perikymata than do modern humans, for whom perikymata become very closely spaced toward the cervix, as depicted in Figure 32.3.

The distribution pattern of perikymata on any tooth reflects changes in the rate of enamel formation as measured along the enamel surface, but again, that variation can be produced by several underlying mechanisms. Despite our uncertainty about what exact growth processes underly the perikymata distribution patterns of different species, what has become clear is that modern humans depart from most recent members of the *Homo* genus (from *Homo erectus* on) in their enamel growth patterns (Guatelli-Steinberg et al. 2007; Modesto-Mata et al. 2020; Ramirez-Rozzi and Bermudez de Castro, 2004). In other words, we modern humans appear to be derived in this regard, as we are in many other aspects of our anatomy, relative to these earlier members of our genus. It has been suggested that this modern human growth pattern in enamel may reflect the longer periods over which modern humans form their crowns (Modesto-Mata et al. 2020).

To complicate matters, our research team found that the recently discovered small-brained hominin *Homo naledi*, a contemporary of Neanderthals and anatomically modern humans, exhibits a unique perikymata distribution pattern (Guatelli-Steinberg et al. 2018), with extremely packed perikymata in the cervical regions of its teeth. In essence, *Homo naledi* appears to be even more derived in its perikymata distribution than are modern humans, with an apparent greater slowing of enamel formation along the enamel surface as the crown grows from cusp to cervix.

What we really need is some work on evaluating what these diverging patterns may mean – do they represent changes in energy allocation during the span of enamel formation that might ultimately tell us something about the evolution of life history? Do similar perikymata distribution patterns reflect similar underlying enamel growth mechanisms? Alternatively, are these patterns simply features of enamel formation unrelated to life history that change over time as species diversify?

Enamel Growth Disruptions

While different species exhibit different enamel growth patterns, another area of inquiry into enamel growth involves the analysis of disruptions during the normal course of enamel growth. Such disruptions can be caused by physiological stress, such as malnutrition, during the period of tooth development. When these stresses disrupt ameloblasts (enamel-producing cells) during the secretory phase of enamel formation (Goodman and Rose 1990; Ten Cate 1994), they can cause enamel hypoplasias – areas of reduced enamel thickness in the form of pits, horizontal grooves, exposed enamel growth planes, and occasionally even missing enamel (Hillson and Bond 1997; Fédération Dentaire Internationale 1982, 1992). Once formed, these defects become permanent features of the crown, unless the defects are worn away by abrasion or attrition. For these reasons, and because teeth are the most abundant of skeletal remains, enamel hypoplasias have become one of the most important sources of information about systemic physiological stress in fossil hominins (e.g., Bombin 1990; Brennan 1991; Brunet et al. 2002; Guatelli-Steinberg 2003, 2004; Guatelli-Steinberg et al. 2004; Hutchinson et al. 1997; Molnar and Molnar 1985; Ogilvie et al. 1989; White 1978).

Linear enamel hypoplasia (LEH) is the most common type of hypoplastic defect; it takes the form of "furrows" on the enamel surface (Hillson and Bond 1997). Among the different types of hypoplastic defects, LEH has the greatest potential to reveal information about the duration of enamel growth disturbances. This potential resides in the crucial facts about enamel formation discussed earlier and in the nature of LEH defects themselves. In a LEH defect, growth disruptions cause ameloblasts to prematurely stop secreting enamel matrix, which results in the exposure of wider than normal portions of the Retzius planes at the enamel surface. Thus, perikymata are clearly associated with LEH defects and can therefore be used to estimate the duration of disruptions in enamel growth (Hillson and Bond 1997).

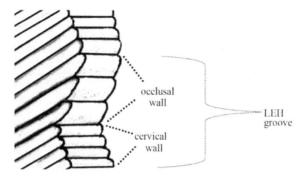

Figure 32.5   The internal anatomy of a linear hypoplastic furrow-form defect (see the text for an explanation).

In my earlier studies, I attempted to use the perikymata in LEH defects for estimating the duration of growth disruptions in fossil hominins (Guatelli-Steinberg 2003, 2004; Guatelli-Steinberg et al. 2004). Through microscopic investigation, Hillson and Bond (1997) determined that perikymata are more widely spaced than normal in the occlusal walls of hypoplastic furrows, and that these "occlusal wall" perikymata therefore reflect the period of disrupted growth. Perikymata in the cervical wall of a defect represent instead a return to normal growth (Hillson and Bond 1997). Figure 32.5 is a diagram showing a linear defect's occlusal and cervical walls and the perikymata they comprise. If perikymata can be seen within a defect on an actual tooth crown, then the duration of disrupted growth can be estimated.

Enamel hypoplasias in Neandertals are of particular interest because researchers have argued that Neandertals lived under conditions of nutritional stress and were inefficient foragers (e.g., Trinkaus 1986; but see Sorensen and Leonard 2001). Several early studies of developmental defects in the enamel of Neandertals indicated that these hominins had relatively high frequencies of enamel hypoplasia (Brennan 1991; Molnar and Molnar 1985; Ogilvie et al. 1989; Skinner 1996). However, Hutchinson and colleagues (1997) found that these high frequencies are matched by similar frequencies in various prehistoric foraging and horticultural populations.

I compared the LEH defects of Neandertals to those of Inupiaq inhabitants of Point Hope, Alaska (Guatelli-Steinberg et al. 2004). Many of the Neandertal specimens included in my study derived from unstable (Hutchinson et al. 1997) or cold environments (Schwartz and Tattersall 2002). The marginal Arctic habitats of the Point Hope Inupiaq would also have imposed harsh living conditions. Stable isotope analyses suggest that Neandertals may have been predominantly, though not exclusively (e.g., Hardy et al. 2012), meat eaters (Bocherens et al. 1999; Richards et al. 2000). The Inupiaq also included a large portion of meat and fish in their diets (Larsen and Rainey 1948). If Neandertals were less efficient foragers than the Point Hope Inupiaq, then they might be expected to have recorded, in their enamel, evidence of having withstood stress episodes of longer duration. The evidence I obtained from counting perikymata within Neandertal defects did not, however, support this view. In fact, based on counting perikymata within defects, the average estimated disruption time for Neandertals was slightly shorter than that for the Inupiaq.

It is obvious that Neandertals must have experienced physiological stress; the presence of LEH makes this clear. The comparison with the Inupiaq, however, tells us that there may be reason to doubt that Neandertals were *more* stressed (through malnutrition or disease) than Inupiaqs. Hutchinson and colleagues (1997) essentially reached the same conclusion in their comparison of LEH frequencies in Neandertals and various modern human for-aging groups: the Neanderthal stress experience may have been high, but is not so unusual.

Most recently, our research team, led by Kate McGrath (2021) analyzed the depth of enamel defects in Neanderthals using 3-D enamel profilometry. Defect depth, in part, may reflect the severity of stress (McGrath et al. 2021). Our study found that compared to many modern human archaeological samples, Neanderthals did not have deeper defects, and that was true even when the defects were scaled to the depth of normal perikymata on their enamel surfaces (McGrath et al. 2021).

I have also examined linear enamel hypoplasias in early *Homo*, *Australopithecus*, and *Paranthropus* (Guatelli-Steinberg 2003, 2004). Unfortunately, comparisons across these genera are complicated by the large differences among them in the duration and manner in which they form enamel. Thus, it is not at all clear exactly what the LEH differences among them might mean in terms of differences in their experience of stress. For example, I found that, of all these early hominins, *Paranthropus* has fewer average LEH defects per tooth. However, I do not think that this result can be clearly interpreted to mean that *Paranthropus* experienced less physiological stress than these other hominin species. In fact, *Paranthropus* would be expected to exhibit fewer defects, simply because its teeth form so quickly, providing a smaller "window of vulnerability" (Vrijenhoek 1985) to disruption than do the longer-forming teeth of *Australopithecus* or early *Homo*. Slow-growing body structures of slow-growing species therefore entail a potentially inherent disadvantage in their prolonged exposure to disruptive influences on their growth.

CONCLUSIONS AND FUTURE DIRECTIONS

The foregoing discussion highlights insights about our ancestors gained from studying incremental growth in fossilized enamel. Analyses of these growth layers have enabled us to trace the evolution of human childhood through the fossil record. It is now clear that a prolonged period of childhood, equal in length to our own, did not evolve until fairly late in human evolutionary history, in early *Homo sapiens* (Smith et al. 2007) and archaic *Homo* (Xing et al. 2019, 2020). Periods of prolonged childhood growth may also have evolved in Neandertals, but additional work is necessary to clarify whether this was so.

In the case of Neandertals, who are so closely related to modern humans, an under-standing of dental growth may not be enough to resolve the question. Part of the problem with resolving questions about Neandertal childhood is that the relationship between overall juvenile growth periods and dental development is stronger at higher levels of the taxonomic hierarchy than it is at lower levels (Dirks and Bowman 2007). For example, it is clear that, compared to monkeys as a whole, lemurs have faster dental development as well as an abbreviated period of juvenile growth (Smith 1989). However, a single monkey species with a more rapid rate of dental development than another closely related monkey species may not have had a shorter juvenile growth period than the latter. There may there-fore be limits to what the study of dental development can tell us about juvenile growth in our fossil ancestors, particularly in species that are most closely related to us.

The study of enamel growth increments in our ancestors has also revealed differences in their patterns of enamel growth. In *Paranthropus* (particularly *P. robustus*), enamel extension tended to occur more quickly and in an apparently more uniform manner down the crown than it did in *Australopithecus* or *Homo*. Neandertals and modern humans differed in their enamel growth patterns, as is reflected by differences in perikymata distribution. Exactly why some hominin species had a more uniform distribution of perikymata than others is not clear. The distribution of perikymata along the length of the crown can be related to changes in extension rates, but it is also potentially related to other variables. Much work needs to be done to discover the mechanisms that result in these different patterns. Our research team made one small step in this direction by comparing perikymata distribution and underlying enamel growth variables in modern humans (Guatelli-Steinberg et al. 2012), but similar studies in fossil hominins are needed.

Finally, the study of enamel growth has yielded insights into physiological stress in our ancestors. Neandertals, for example, appear not to have differed from some modern human foragers in their frequencies of linear enamel hypoplasia (Hutchinson et al. 1997), nor in the duration (Guatelli-Steinberg 2004) or severity (McGrath et al. 2021) of the stress episodes these defects represent. The teeth of *Paranthropus* have fewer defects than those of *Australopithecus* or *Homo* – possibly because, in the former, abbreviated crown formation times prevented the enamel from recording multiple stress episodes (Guatelli-Steinberg 2004). Enamel formation variables, such as the duration of enamel formation, must therefore be considered when one uses linear enamel hypoplasias to try to understand stress in our fossil ancestors.

Although Niels Stensen recognized, in 1667, the fact that teeth fossilized, it is doubtful that he could have anticipated the kinds of information about growth and development that has been gleaned from them. While many intriguing insights have been gained from the study of enamel growth in our ancestors, new technologies promise that there is much more to come.

REFERENCES

Bermúdez de Castro, J. M., A. Rosas, E. Carbonell, et al. "A Modern Pattern of Dental Development in Lower Pleistocene Hominids from Atapuerca-TD6 (Spain)." *Proceedings of the National Academy of Science* 96 (1999): 4210–4213.

Beynon, D., and M. C. Dean. "Distinct Dental Development Patterns in Early Fossil Hominins." *Nature* 335 (1988): 509–514.

Beynon, D., and B. Wood. "Patterns and Rates of Enamel Growth in the Molar Teeth of Early Hominids." *Nature* 326 (1987): 493–496.

Bocherens, H., D. Billiou, A. Mariotti, et al. "Paleoenvironmental and Paleodietary Implications of Isotopic Biogeochemistry of Last Interglacial Neanderthal and Mammal Bones in Scladina Cave (Belgium)." *Journal of Archaeological Science* 26 (1999): 599–607.

Bogin, B. "Evolutionary Hypotheses for Human Childhood." *Yearbook of Physical Anthropology* 40 (1997): 63–89.

Bombin, M. "Transverse Enamel Hypoplasia on Teeth of South African Plio-Pleistocene Hominids." *Naturwissenschaften* 77 (1990): 128–129.

Boyde, A. "Carbonate Concentration, Crystal Centres, Core Dissolution, Caries, Cross Striations, Circadian Rhythms, and Compositional Contrast in the SEM." *Journal of Dental Research* (Special Issue) 58 (1979): 981–983.

Brennan, M. "*Health and Disease in the Middle and Upper Paleolithic of Southwestern France: A Bioarchaeological Study*." PhD Dissertation, New York University, 1991.

Bromage, T. G. "Early Hominid Development and Life History." In *Primate Life History and Evolution*. Edited by C. J. de Rousseau, 105–113. New York: Wiley–Liss, 1990.

Bromage, T. G. "Enamel Incremental Periodicity in the Pig-Tailed Macaque: A Polychrome Fluorescent Labeling Study of Dental Hard Tissues." *American Journal of Physical Anthropology* 86 (1991): 205–214.

Bromage, T. G., and M. C. Dean. "Re-Evaluation of the Age at Death of Immature Fossil Hominids." *Nature* 317 (1985): 525–527.

Bromage, T. G., R. S. Lacruz, R. Hogg, et al. "Lamellar Bone Is an Incremental Tissue Reconciling Enamel Rhythms, Body Size, and Organismal Life History." *Calcified Tissue International* 84, no. 5 (2009): 388–404.

Bromage, T. G., R. T. Hogg, R. S. Lacruz, and C. Hou. "Primate Enamel Evinces Long Period Biological Timing and Regulation of Life History." *Journal of Theoretical Biology* 305 (2012): 131–144.

Brunet, M., P. Fronty, M. Sapanet, et al. "Enamel Hypoplasia in a Pliocene Hominid from Chad." *Connective Tissue Research* 43 (2002): 94–97.

Dean, M. C. "Growth Layers and Incremental Markings in Hard Tissues; A Review of the Literature and Some Preliminary Observations about Enamel Structure in *Paranthropus boisei*." *Journal of Human Evolution* 16 (1987): 157–172.

Dean, M. C. "Incremental Markings in Enamel and Dentine: What They Can Tell Us About the Way Teeth Grow." In *Development, Function, and Evolution of Teeth*. Edited by M. F. Teaford, M. M. Smith, and M. W. J. Ferguson, 119–130. Cambridge: Cambridge University Press, 2000.

Dean, M. C., and D. J. Reid. "Perikymata Spacing and Distribution on Hominid Anterior Teeth." *American Journal of Physical Anthropology* 116 (2001): 209–215.

Dean, C., M. G. Leakey, D. Reid, et al. "Growth Processes in Teeth Distinguish Modern Humans from *Homo erectus* and Earlier Hominins." *Nature* 414 (2001): 628–631.

Dirks, W., and J. Bowman. "Life History Theory and Dental Development in Four Species of Catarrhine Primates." *Journal of Human Evolution* 53 (2007): 309–320.

Fédération Dentaire Internationale. "An Epidemiological Index of Developmental Defects of Dental Enamel (DDE)." *International Dental Journal* 32 (1982): 159–167.

Fédération Dentaire Internationale. "A Review of the Developmental Defects of Enamel Index (DDE Index)." *International Dental Journal* 42 (1992): 411–426.

FitzGerald, C. M. "Do Enamel Microstructures Have Regular Time Dependency? Conclusions from the Literature and a Large-Scale Study." *Journal of Human Evolution* 35 (1998): 371–386.

Goodman, A. H., and J. C. Rose. "Assessment of Systemic Physiological Perturbations from Dental Enamel Hypoplasias and Associated Histological Structures." *Yearbook of Physical Anthropology* 33 (1990): 59–110.

Guatelli-Steinberg, D. "Macroscopic and Microscopic Analyses of Linear Enamel Hypoplasia in Plio-Pleistocene Hominins with Respect to Aspects of Enamel Development and Morphology." *American Journal of Physical Anthropology* 120 (2003): 309–322.

Guatelli-Steinberg, D. "Analysis and Significance of Linear Enamel Hypoplasia in Plio-Pleistocene Hominins." *American Journal of Physical Anthropology* 125 (2004): 199–215.

Guatelli-Steinberg, D., C. S. Larsen, and D. L. Hutchinson. "Prevalence and the Duration of Linear Enamel Hypoplasia: A Comparative Study of Neandertals and Inuit Foragers." *Journal of Human Evolution* 47 (2004): 65–84.

Guatelli-Steinberg, D., D. J. Reid, T. A. Bishop, and C. S. Larsen. "Anterior Tooth Growth Periods in Neandertals Were Comparable to Those of Modern Humans." *Proceedings of the National Academy of Sciences* 102 (2005): 14197–14202.

Guatelli-Steinberg, D., D. J. Reid, and T. A. Bishop. "Did the Lateral Enamel of Neandertals Grow Differently from that of Modern Humans?" *Journal of Human Evolution* 52 (2007): 72–84.

Guatelli-Steinberg, D., B. A. Floyd, M. C. Dean, and D. J. Reid. "Enamel Extension Rate Patterns in Modern Human Teeth: Two Approaches Designed to Establish an Integrated Comparative Context for Fossil Primates." *Journal of Human Evolution* 63, no. 3 (2012): 475–486.

Guatelli-Steinberg, D., M. C. O'Hara, A. Le Cabec, et al. "Patterns of Lateral Enamel Growth in *Homo naledi* as Assessed Through Perikymata Distribution and Number." *Journal of Human Evolution* 121 (2018): 40–54.

Hardy, K., S. Buckley, M. J. Collins, et al. "Neanderthal Medics? Evidence for Food, Cooking, and Medicinal Plants Entrapped in Dental Calculus." *Naturwissenschaften* 99, no. 8 (2012): 617–626.

Hillson, S. *Dental Anthropology*. Cambridge: Cambridge University Press, 1996.

Hillson, S., and S. Bond. "The Relationship of Enamel Hypoplasia to the Pattern of Tooth Crown Growth: A Discussion." *American Journal of Physical Anthropology* 104 (1997): 89–103.

Hogg, R. T., L. R. Godfrey, G T. Schwartz, et al. "Lemur Biorhythms and Life History Evolution." *PLoS One* 10, no. 8 (2015): e0134210.

Hogg, R., R. Lacruz, T. G. Bromage, et al. "A Comprehensive Survey of Retzius Periodicities in Fossil Hominins and Great Apes." *Journal of Human Evolution* 149 (2020): 102896.

Hutchinson, D. L., C. S. Larsen, and I. Choi. "Stressed to the Max? Physiological Perturbation in the Krapina Neandertals." *Current Anthropology* 38 (1997): 904–914.

Kelley, J., and T. M. Smith. "Age at First Molar Emergence in Early Miocene *Afropithecus turkanensis* and Life-History Evolution in the Hominoidea." *Journal of Human Evolution* 44 (2003): 307–329.

Kuzawa, C. W., H. T. Chugani, L. I. Grossman, et al. "Metabolic Costs and Evolutionary Implications of Human Brain Development." *Proceedings of the National Academy of Sciences* 111, no. 36 (2014): 13010–13015.

Lacruz, R, M. C. Dean, F. Ramirez-Rozzi, and T. G. Bromage. "Patterns of Enamel Secretion and Striae Periodicity in Fossil Hominins." *Journal of Anatomy* 213 (2008): 148–158.

Larsen, H., and F. G. Rainey. "Ipiutak and the Arctic Whale Hunting Culture." *Anthrological Papers of the American Museum of Natural History* 42 (1948): 1–276.

Macchiarelli, R., L. Bondioli, A. Debénath, et al. "How Neandertal Molar Teeth Grew." *Nature* 444 (2006): 748–751.

Mahoney, P., J. J. Miszkiewicz, R. Pitfield, et al. "Biorhythms, Deciduous Enamel Thickness, and Primary Bone Growth: A Test of the Havers–Halberg Oscillation Hypothesis." *Journal of Anatomy* 228, no. 6 (2016): 919–928.

Maisey, J. G. *Discovering Fossil Fishes.* New York: Holt, 1997.

McFarlane, G., D. Guatelli-Steinberg, C. Loch, et al. "An Inconstant Biorhythm: The Changing Pace of Retzius Periodicity in Human Permanent Teeth." *American Journal of Physical Anthropology* 175, no. 1 (2021): 172–186.

McGrath, K., L. S. Limmer, A.-L. Lockey, et al. "3D Enamel Profilometry Reveals Faster Growth but Similar Stress Severity in Neanderthal versus *Homo sapiens* Teeth." *Scientific Reports* 11, no. 1 (2021): 1–12.

McGrath, K., D. J. Reid, D. Guatelli-Steinberg, et al. "Faster Growth Corresponds with Shallower Linear Hypoplastic Defects in Great Ape Canines." *Journal of Human Evolution* 137 (2019): 102691.

Modesto-Mata, M., M. C. Dean, R. S. Lacruz, et al. "Short and Long Period Growth Markers of Enamel Formation Distinguish European Pleistocene Hominins." *Scientific Reports* 10, no. 1 (2020): 1–12.

Molnar, S., and I. M. Molnar. "The Prevalence of Enamel Hypoplasia Among the Krapina Neandertals." *American Anthropologist* 87 (1985): 536–549.

Nanci, A. *Ten Cate's Oral Histology: Development, Structure, and Function.* St. Louis: Mosby (Elsevier), 2008.

Ogilvie, M. D., B. K. Curran, and E. Trinkaus. "Prevalence and Patterning of Dental Enamel Hypoplasia Among the Neandertals." *American Journal of Physical Anthropology* 79 (1989): 25–41.

Ramirez-Rozzi, F. V., and J. M. Bermúdez de Castro. "Surprisingly Rapid Growth in Neanderthals." *Nature* 428 (2004): 936–939.

Reid, D. J., and M. C. Dean. "Variation in Modern Human Enamel Formation Times." *Journal of Human Evolution* 50 (2006): 329–346.

Richards, M. P., P. B. Pettitt, E. Trinkaus, et al. "Neanderthal Diet at Vindija and Neanderthal Predation: The Evidence from Stable Isotopes." *Proceedings of the National Academy of Sciences* 97 (2000): 7663–7666.

Risnes, S. "Enamel Apposition Rate and the Prism Periodicity in Human Teeth." *Scandanavian Journal of Dental Research* 94 (1986): 394–404.

Rosas, A., L. Ríos, A. Estalrrich, et al. "The Growth Pattern of Neandertals, Reconstructed from a Juvenile Skeleton from El Sidrón (Spain)." *Science* 357, no. 6357 (2017): 1282–1287.

Schuppli, C., S. I. F. Forss, E. J. M. Meulman, et al. "Development of Foraging Skills in Two Orangutan Populations: Needing to Learn or Needing to Grow?" *Frontiers in Zoology* 13, no. 1 (2016): 1–17.

Schwartz, G. T., and M. C. Dean. "Ontogeny of Canine Dimorphism in Extant Hominoids." *American Journal of Physical Anthropology* 115 (2001): 269–283.

Schwartz, J., and I. Tattersall. *The Human Fossil Record*, Vol. 1. New York: Wiley–Liss, 2002.

Shellis, R. P. "Variation in Growth of the Enamel Crown in Human Teeth and a Possible Relationship Between Growth and Enamel Structure." *Archives of Oral Biology* 29 (1984): 697–705.

Skinner, M. "Developmental Stress in Immature Hominines from Late Pleistocene Eurasia: Evidence from Enamel Hypoplasia." *Journal of Archaeological Science* 23 (1996): 833–852.

Smith, B. H. "Dental Development as a Measure of Life History in Primates." *Evolution* 43 (1989): 683–688.

Smith, B. H. "Dental Development and the Evolution of Life History in Hominidae." *American Journal of Physical Anthropology* 86 (1991): 157–174.

Smith, B. H. "Life History and the Evolution of Human Maturation." *Evolutionary Anthropology* 1 (1992): 134–142.

Smith, B. H., and R. L. Tompkins. "Toward a Life History of the Hominidae." *Annual Review of Anthropology* 24 (1995): 257–279.

Smith, T. M., and P. Tafforeau. "New Visions of Dental Tissue Research: Tooth Development, Chemistry, and Structure." *Evolutionary Anthropology* 17 (2008): 213–226.

Smith, T. M., P. Tafforeau, D. J. Reid, et al. "Earliest Evidence of Modern Human Life History in North African Early *Homo sapiens*." *Proceedings of the National Academy of Science* 104 (2007): 6128–6133.

Smith, T. M., P. Tafforeau, D. J. Reid, et al. "Dental Evidence for Ontogenetic Differences Between Modern Humans and Neanderthals." *Proceedings of the National Academy of Sciences* 107, no. 49 (2010): 20923–20928.

Smith, T. M., P. Tafforeau, A. le Cabec, et al. "Dental Ontogeny in Pliocene and Early Pleistocene Hominins." *PloS One* 10, no. 2 (2015): e0118118.

Sorensen, M. V., and W. R. Leonard. "Neandertal Energetics and Foraging Efficiency." *Journal of Human Evolution* 40, no. 6 (2001): 483–495.

Ten Cate, A. R. *Oral Histology: Development, Structure and Function*. St. Louis, MO: Mosby, 1994.

Trinkaus, E. "The Neandertals and Modern Human Origins." *Annual Review of Anthropology* 15 (1986): 193–218.

Vrijenhoek, R. C. "Animal Population Genetics and Disturbance: The Effect of Local Extinctions and Recolonizations on Heterozygosity and Fitness." In *The Ecology of Natural Disturbances on Patch Dynamics*. Edited by S. T. A. Picket and P. J. White, 266–286. San Diego: Academic Press, 1985.

White, T. D. "Early Hominid Enamel Hypoplasia." *American Journal of Physical Anthropology* 49 (1978): 79–84.

Xing, S., P. Tafforeau, M. O'Hara, et al. "First Systematic Assessment of Dental Growth and Development in an Archaic Hominin (genus, *Homo*) from East Asia." *Science Advances* 5, no. 1 (2019): eaau0930.

Xing, S., P. Tafforeau, M. C. O'Hara, et al. "A Broader Perspective on Estimating Dental Age for the Xujiayao Juvenile, A Late Middle Pleistocene Archaic Hominin from East Asia." *Journal of Human Evolution* 148 (2020): 102850.

Zihlman, A., D. Bolter, and C. Boesch, "Wild Chimpanzee Dentition and Its Implications for Assessing Life History in Immature Hominin Fossils." *Proceedings of the National Academy of Sciences* 101 (2004): 10541–10543.

CHAPTER 33

Skull: Function – New Directions

Qian Wang and Rachel A. Menegaz

The human skull is a highly integrated structure, resulting from an interplay of multifunctional anatomy, structural adaptations, and evolution. In the chapter titled "Understanding skull function from a mechanobiological perspective" in the first edition of this book, Daegling (2010) masterly summarized many research perspectives on skull function and evolution. Since then, significant advances have been made on many fronts, such as bone material properties, the functional roles of joints including craniofacial sutures and the temporomandibular joint, the addition of new genetic data to inform the Masticatory–Functional hypothesis, and the impact of agriculture and contemporary lifestyles on dietary behavior and oral health, and so on. This chapter reviews these new research directions along with recent investigative approaches, and important concepts and findings on skull form and function that capture rapid developments that will broaden and deepen future studies in both theoretical and practical senses.

BONE MATERIAL PROPERTIES – VARIATIONS AND EXTERNAL–INTERNAL INTEGRATION

As a biomaterial building upon mineralized collagen fibers, bone has a particular hierarchical structure with up to seven distinctive levels, and the structure–mechanical relations at each of the hierarchical levels have been recognized. Consequently, changes occurring at lower hierarchical levels affect functionalities of higher hierarchical levels and the whole bone as well (Weiner and Wagner 1998). Thus, the investigation of form and function should be studied at all levels of organization, from molecules, tissue, to whole bone. Bone material strength such as stiffness has been investigated through two approaches, nanoindentation and ultrasonic methods, and both reveal that bone material properties vary according to anatomical regions. Nanoindentation is an engineering technique during

A Companion to Biological Anthropology, Second Edition. Edited by Clark Spencer Larsen.
© 2023 John Wiley & Sons Ltd. Published 2023 by John Wiley & Sons Ltd.

which a hard-tipped material with known material properties and a known force is pressed into the bone surface, usually cortical bone, to assess the stiffness and hardness of the bone (Oyen 2010). Meanwhile, their implications in functional adaptation have been investigated in terms of regional differences associated with different functional demands or loading regimes (Casanova et al. 2017). For example, Daegling et al. (2011) found spatial patterning of surface bone stiffness in facial skeletons of colobus monkeys, in which alveolar bone was found to be less stiff than adjacent basal bone based on nanoindentation data, suggesting a material solution for undertaking occlusal loads through the increase of the compliance of alveolar bone. While density is known to correlate with bone stiffness (Wang and Dechow 2006), density alone does not account for variation in features of cortical bone quality, such as material directionality and anisotropy (Wang and Dechow 2006; Wang et al. 2006a, 2010a). The microstructure of bone reveals that bone is an anisotropic material – the bone stiffness might be different in different directions. The directionality could be linked to the principal orthogonal axes of the bone (longitudinal, transvers, and sagittal).

Ultrasonic investigations of human, rhesus macaque, baboon, chimpanzee, bonobo, and gorilla skulls indicate that cortical density, thickness, elastic and shear moduli, and anisotropy vary throughout the skull in different regions of the craniofacial skeletons (Peterson et al. 2006; Wang and Dechow 2006; Wang et al. 2006a, 2010a; Gharpure et al. 2016). These skeletal properties have been related to the functional adaptations related to feeding (Wang and Dechow 2006; Wang et al. 2010a). For example, there are area-specific patterns of cortical thickness and elastic properties in the human and non-human primate mandibles. The mandibular corpus has the highest elastic and shear stiffness, which might be a material adaption for resisting bending and twisting forces during mastication with compression and shear stress. The symphyseal cortex is thickest yet less stiff and less anisotropic than other regions, which might be adapted to resisting "wishboning," the symphyseal stress patterns produced by lateral transverse bending of the mandible during mastication. The ramus has high density and stiffness but is more anisotropic than that in the non-muscle bearing regions, which suggest interactions between bone and adjacent muscular tissues (Wang et al. 2010a).

Evidence also exists that indicates significant correlations among external morphological and internal material features of the craniofacial skeleton, including: (1) paralleling anatomical axis of the bone or bone parts and the orientation of maximum stiffness; (2) an inverse relationship between cortical thickness and density/elastic stiffness; and (3) bone elastic property changes during ontogeny, aging, and sexual dimorphism (Wang and Dechow 2006; Wang et al. 2006a, 2010a; Dechow et al. 2008, 2010). These findings underline the integration of morphology, material properties, and function of craniofacial skeleton. The negative correlation between cortical density and thickness is also observed at the species level. For example, baboons have thinner yet denser and stiffer cortical bone in the craniofacial skeleton than macaques and humans (Wang et al. 2006a). An inverse relationship between thickness and stiffness may suggest a biomechanical mechanism for functional adaptation adopted to maintain the stability and integrity of the structure in different parts of the skeleton. If loads vary widely in orientation, then a thicker structure may help avoid structural damages, while if the direction of loading varies less, a thinner yet more dense structure may help the bone focus on the principal loading requirements.

The coupling of micro-CT imaging and ultrasonic assessment of 3D elastic properties in human and baboons also reveals the important relationship between tissue elastic anisotropy and the spatial configuration of osteons. The long axes of the osteons, as represented by the Haversian canals, are aligned with the axes of maximum elastic stiffness of the cortical bone. This also aligns with the long axis of the bone or bone parts (Dechow et al. 2008; Wang et al. 2010), demonstrating the structural and material bases of bone mechanical properties at the tissue level. Moreover, comparison of the material properties of craniofacial cortical bone has demonstrated that closely related species, such as rhesus monkeys and baboon, have similar area-specific patterns of variation for density, maximum elastic and shear stiffness, and anisotropy compared to humans (Wang et al. 2006a). This discovery suggests that human and monkey skulls adapt to different masticatory and oral functions through adjustments in cortical bone microstructure and density. The similarity of these two closely related primate species is particularly important for studies of functional morphology, taxonomy, and evolution in extant and extinct human and primate taxa, because mechanical related properties, such as density and stiffness, cannot be measured in extinct species known only from fossils. It is thus hypothesized that the living species could be used as a baseline to study extinct taxa that are phylogenetically closely related (Wang et al. 2006a).

CRANIOFACIAL SUTURES – A NEW FUNCTIONAL CONCEPT

Sutures are fibrous joints in vertebrate craniofacial skeletons that function as growth centers. Sutural disturbances, such as premature closure, result in abnormal skull shape because of adjustments to growth directions (Cohen 2000). Sutures also have potential biomechanical roles. Their mechanical roles have been discussed and investigated using various experimental and computer-aided techniques in both living and fossil species (Behrents et al. 1978; Byron 2009; Byron et al. 2004; Dzialo et al. 2014; Farke 2008; Herring 1972, 2008; Rayfield 2005; Wang et al. 2008, 2010b, 2012; Wang and Dechow 2016). Originally, it was proposed that sutures function as stress dampeners and thus protect the skull (Behrents et al. 1978). This hypothesis would predict that patent sutures remain flexible relative to the surrounding bone and serve as energy sinks in response to applied loads. However, patent sutures fail at relatively modest stress levels (Popowics and Herring 2007). Computer-aided sensitivity analyses of the mechanical effect of sutures in finite element models also demonstrate that the presence of sutures does not profoundly influence global strain patterns in relatively large primate skulls, and their capacity of absorbing the work induced by functional loadings are limited, though local effects are detected (Wang et al. 2010b, 2012).

The new concept of sutures suggests that instead of serving to reduce stress in the skull, the sutures instead are vulnerable structures that should be protected from high stress levels in order to not disrupt normal skull growth timing and direction (Wang et al. 2012). Some stress-reducing cranial structures may serve to shield sutures rather than bone (Dzialo et al. 2014; Wang et al. 2012; Zhang et al. 2019). Adaptations to reducing sutural stress and strain may include increased sutural size, altered sutural morphology (e.g., overlapping squamosal sutures) (Dzialo et al. 2014), or by variation in sutural position (Wang and Dechow 2016). Within primates, the placement of some sutures (e.g., the maxillozygomatic suture) correspond to low stress zones, as seen in a FEA simulation of a cranial model without sutures (Wang and Dechow 2016).

If sutures are biomechanically weak structures that need to be protected, then it is reasonable to predict that sutures should not exist in areas where they would be under constant high stress, or they should be properly protected if found in such an environment. However, the presence of supernumerary sutures dividing the zygoma (divided zygoma – DZ), an area of high stress during biting, directly challenges this hypothesis. A morphological and biomechanical investigation of human and nonhuman primates demonstrated that the DZ condition would alter overall morphology of the midface of the affected side, resulting in facial asymmetry in unilateral DZ skulls (Wang and Dechow 2016). The superior division of the divided zygoma was normally slender along with the adjacent frontal bone parts, while the inferior division of the divided zygoma was normally more robust, along with stronger temporal and maxillary bones. The stresses incurred during normal masticatory activities would be shunted from the upper face to the lower face, especially along the zygomatic arch. These findings revealed that DZ disturbs the pattern of stress distribution during mastication, with compensatory strengthening in the lower midface of the affected side to withstand the increased stress level. Overall, the phenomenon of facial asymmetry in unilateral DZ skulls challenges the protecting roles of sutures yet favors the protected status of sutures (i.e., protected vs. being protected by bones). This knowledge of naturally occurring supernumerary sutures on the facial skeleton brings new insights into the biology sutures and the developmental instability of skulls. The new concept of sutures also opens new insights to the understanding of craniofacial form, adaptation, developmental plasticity, and evolution, and helps to improve therapeutic philosophies in corrective and regenerative medicine of the craniofacial skeleton (Wang and Dechow 2016; Zhang et al. 2019).

MASTICATORY–FUNCTIONAL HYPOTHESIS – A REVISIT

Within recent human evolution, there has been significant somatic change in the human body along with behavioral changes. Since the Neolithic era, there has been a general trend of decreasing body dimensions and cranial size and skull robusticity. The "Masticatory–Functional Hypothesis" proposed by David Carlson pinpoints the decrease of the functional demands placed on the masticatory complex during the transition from hunter–gatherer to agricultural stages to explain the change of human skull form with diminishing skull robusticity (Carlson 1976; Carlson and Van Gerven 1977, 1979). Carlson's analysis of cranial change from the Mesolithic horizon through the Christian horizon in the Nubian region of Northern Africa shows clear patterns of craniofacial change including: (1) a relative increase in height and decrease in length of the cranial vault; (2) a tendency for the midface and lower face to become more inferoposteriorly located relative to the anterior cranial vault; and (3) a decrease in the robusticity of the entire craniofacial complex, especially in those features primarily associated with masticatory function. According to this interpretation, a shift in subsistence adaptation of the Nubian population through time led to a decrease in the functional demands placed on the masticatory complex, which in turn brought about four related alterations of cranial morphology.

While the Masticatory–Functional hypothesis emphasizes the importance of decreasing masticatory stress on the recent evolution of human skulls, there are other competing hypotheses. These include the development of smaller masticatory muscles due to genetic mutation (Stedman et al. 2004) and the decrease of the brain size due to increased roles in collective intelligence with less reliance on the individual in cognition and information management in large-scale societies (DeSilva et al. 2021). Hence, in recent human history, cultural adaption might have become the major selective pressure in human biological evolution (Carlson and Van Gerven 1979), with further roles played by population history, subsistence type, and climate (Larsen 2015; von Cramon-Taubadel 2014; Wang et al. 2019). Moreover, ancient genome analyses charting migrations of early farmers in ancient China reveals that there was movement and admixture of peoples during the Neolithic that gave rise to modern-day populations in East Asia (Yang et al. 2020). This resulted in an influx of agriculturalists to Southeast Asia and the replacement of the local gene pool such that little trace of hunter–gatherer ancestry remains in the genes of people who live in the region today. Similarly, farmers from northern China moved northward into Siberia and supplanted the local gene pool, reducing the presence of the previous local hunter–gatherer ancestry (Yang et al. 2020). This suggests that the transition in morphology in East Asian populations is not primarily due to dietary change as in North Africa, but by gene pool replacement because of the overpowering influx of agriculturalists – which was likely to be the ready-made result of functional masticatory adaptations elsewhere. Ancient DNA studies probably provide more new insights for understanding morphological transition in areas with possible migration and replacement.

EVOLUTIONARY PARADOX AND MISMATCH DISEASES

The application of the Masticatory–Functional Hypothesis to understand changes in dietary behavior has also recently become one of the major fronts in the study of early human evolution due to methodological advances, including microwear analysis and finite element analysis (Grine et al. 2010; Strait et al. 2013, 2009). These studies suggest that the variation in the facial skeletons of australopiths are adaptations to various dietary behaviors including the consumption of hard and/or tough foods. For example, the anterior pillar is a facial strengthening structure for undertaking the stress generated by frequent use of premolars (Strait et al. 2009). However, increasing masticatory force or efficiency is limited by the need to maintain the integrity of the masticatory apparatus. A recent biomechanical analysis revealed that *Australopithecus sediba* could not feed on hard foods on a consistent basis due to increased possibility of failure of the temporomandibular joint (TMJ) (Ledogar et al. 2016b). This finding suggests that TMJ integrity may be a major limiting factor in hominin craniofacial evolution, demonstrating the need for new perspectives on the integrity of the masticatory system in the study of functional morphology in human evolution. At the crux of this debate is how TMJ stability has affected or been affected in recent human evolution, especially during the facial shortening seen in the past several thousand years of modern human history, which reflects the concept of "mismatch diseases," a result of our body inadequately adapted to our environment (Liberman 2013).

In the mammal-feeding apparatus, the overall safety rule is to minimize distractive (tensile) TMJ reaction forces by reducing the activity levels of the chewing muscles on the balancing (nonbiting) side of the skull based on a "constrained lever model" (Greaves 1978). Briefly, as summarized by Ledogar and colleagues (2016a, 2016b), this model predicts that bite force production is constrained by the risk of generating distractive forces at the working (biting) side of the TMJ. During unilateral biting, reaction forces are produced at the bite point, the working side TMJ and the balancing side TMJ. These three points form a "triangle of support," and the line of action of the resultant vector of the jaw elevator muscle forces must intersect this triangle in order to produce a "stable" bite in which compressive reaction forces are generated at all three points. The resultant vector lies in the midsagittal plane when the muscles are recruited with equal force and will pass through the triangle of support during bites. Importantly, molar biting alters the shape of the triangle such that a midline muscle result may lie outside of the triangle of support, generating distractive forces in the working-side TMJ. This force pulls the mandibular condyle from the articular eminence. While the soft tissues of the TMJ are well suited to resist compressive joint reaction forces, they are not configured to resist distractive joint forces as the condyle is pulled away from the cranium (Greaves 1978).

Based on the "constrained lever model," it has been argued that the TMJ has been an "imperfecta", the weakest link prone to failure due to unduly high distractive forces or other conditions, during human evolutionary history, and hence an internal selective pressure. However, the problem may be present in early robust types, gradually becoming

more prominent in recent and contemporary modern humans characterized by the gra-
cilization of skulls. Morphological changes related to subsistence strategies include not only
jaw size and shape, but also the spatial relationship between upper and lower jaws, and
repositioning of masticatory muscles. These changes have led to decreases in bite force production and decreases in the ability to withstand stresses generated by bite forces and
increases in oral disorders such as TMJ dysfunction (TMD) (Liberman 2013; Larsen 2015;
Wang et al. 2019). TMD might be an example of a "mismatch diseases", along with osteoarthritis, lower back pain, flat feet, and hypertensive heart disease; these diseases suggest
that cultural and behavioral factors have altered the modern human environment away from
the evolutionarily context and selective pressures in which most of human evolution
occurred (Liberman 2013). Studies of oral disorders, along with other modern diseases,
could benefit from functional and evolutionary perspectives. For a better understand of the
etymology of TMD, careful research designs are warranted which consider the integrity of
the temporomandibular joint, the recruitment of muscle forces and positioning of biting
points, and overall morphology of the craniofacial skeleton.

Experimental Approaches for Understanding Skull Function

The laboratory has long represented an ideal environment in which to test hypotheses
about feeding biology derived from observations made in the field and in the museum.
Nearly a half century of technological and methodological advances has made it possible to
investigate how changes to dietary composition affect feeding behaviors, which in turn alter
the biomechanical stress applied to the craniofacial complex. The skeletal strain resulting
from these stresses can then be quantified and correlated to observed differential modeling
and remodeling of the hard and soft tissues in wild and laboratory species. Perhaps most
importantly, the theoretical model connecting diet, masticatory strain, and osteogenic
responses can be replicated among multiple primate and nonprimate mammalian species,
thus demonstrating the basic principles of functional morphology within the context of dietary ecology and evolution.

Understanding the relationship between diet and craniofacial form starts with a characterization of dietary variation in terms of elastic (Young's) modulus, or stiffness, toughness,
and hardness (Lucas et al. 2001; Williams et al. 2005). These dietary profiles can then be
recreated in the laboratory, allowing for feeding behaviors to be evaluated under more naturalistic conditions. Feeding behavior can then be quantified through many parameters that
describe the interactions between anatomy and the food item. Aspects of the chewing cycle,
including cycle duration and frequency, have been correlated with both body size and dietary material properties (Ravosa et al. 2010b, 2015; Ross et al. 2009). Recruitment patterns
of jaw adductor musculature and the resultant bite forces can also vary with dietary properties (Hylander 1979b; Hylander et al. 2000; Vinyard et al. 2008), such that more
mechanically resistant food items require more chewing cycles and/or higher peak bite
forces to successfully reduce the food particle sizes for swallowing (Hylander 1979a,
Hylander 1979b; Ravosa et al. 2015). Dynamic imaging techniques, including fluoroscopy
and X-Ray Reconstruction of Moving Morphology (XROMM), can be used to quantify
feeding kinematics and the end results of these interactions among food items, teeth, and
musculoskeletal components (Menegaz et al. 2015; Montuelle et al. 2020; Orsbon et al.
2018; Ross et al. 2010). While many mammals exhibit stereotyped masticatory behaviors,
kinematic studies have demonstrated that some level of flexibility remains such that chewing
cycle dynamics are responsive to changes in food properties (Menegaz et al. 2015; Montuelle

et al. 2020), which both aids in the reduction of food particle size and protects oral structures from excessive bite forces (Williams et al. 2005).

Any changes in feeding behavior – including muscle recruitment, bite force, or jaw kinematics – are predicted to change the distribution and magnitude of bone strain (deformation). *In vivo* studies have documented strain gradients in the mammalian skull, such that strains during feeding are highest at skeletal sites proximal to the oral cavity (Ravosa et al. 1991; Ross and Metzger 2004). Furthermore, the magnitude of strains in regions such as the mandibular corpus vary with food material properties, such that feeding on more resistant food items results in increased bone strain (Hylander 1979b; Hylander et al. 1998). The shear strains observed in mammalian mandibles are similar across a large range in body sizes and, while absolutely less than experienced by the limbs during locomotion, are considered to be osteogenic – or of a sufficient magnitude to elicit a bone formation/remodeling response (Ravosa et al. 2013). The presence of osteogenic strain levels is supported by observations of increased bone mass in predicted high strain regions, e.g., the mandibular corpus, condylar neck, and zygomatic arch (Daegling and Hotzman 2003; Hylander 1979b).

The collection of *in vivo* strain data is, by its very nature, an invasive procedure, requiring the surgical implantation of strain gauges directly on to bone. For this reason, it is not always practical or desirable to obtain in *vivo* strain data for all primate species. *In silico*, FEA combines digital models of skull architecture, often obtained from computed tomography, with anatomical-based estimates of muscle and bite forces to generate predicted stress and strain patterns. When validated by in *vivo* and *in vitro* strain data, FEA can be a useful tool for testing hypotheses regarding the functional morphology of feeding (Smith et al. 2021; Strait et al. 2009). Model validity can be strengthened by incorporating tissue heterogeneity data (e.g., material property differences within and among cortical bone, and trabecular bone) (Strait et al. 2005; Wroe et al. 2007). Recent intraspecific applications of FEA provide support for the idea that osteogenic responses to increased dietary loading result in decreased craniofacial strain (Mitchell et al. 2021).

The laboratory setting provides yet another option for testing functional morphology hypotheses through *in vivo* modification of dietary composition. These dietary manipulation studies rely on the mechanism of phenotypic plasticity, or the ontogenetic modulation of a phenotype across an environmental gradient (West-Eberhard 2005). Phenotypic plasticity can function as a mechanism for the fine-tuning of form–function relationships across an individual's lifespan. In skeletal tissues, phenotypic plasticity is accomplished through functional adaptation, or the dynamic processes by which bone tissue is modeled and remodeled in order to maintain a skeletal element's structural integrity in a given loading environment (Biewener 1993; Frost 1987; Lanyon and Rubin 1985). Thus, it is possible to test the biomechanical role of specific structures within the skull by modifying dietary material properties of a single laboratory species and quantifying the resultant changes in musculoskeletal morphology, all while controlling for other factors such as genetic variation, age, reproductive status, environment, nutrition, etc. While some early plasticity studies used primate species (Bouvier and Hylander 1981, 1982, 1996b), for practical and ethical reasons most modern plasticity research uses non-primate mammals (e.g., suids, lagomorphs, rodents, and carnivorans). Such studies have contributed to our understanding of the common responses of mammalian bone to loading and unloading, thus providing a basis by which the functional significance of craniofacial morphologies can be understood in wild and fossil primate taxa.

Experimental studies have shown that an increase in masticatory loading influences craniomandibular size and shape, including but not limited to: temporomandibular joint morphology (Bouvier and Hylander 1981, 1984; Nicholson et al. 2006; Ravosa and Kane 2017; Ravosa et al. 2008a); mandibular corpus dimensions and cortical bone distribution (Bouvier and Hylander 1984; Franks et al. 2016; Kiliaridis et al. 1996); mandibular symphysis morphology (Ciochon et al. 1997; Ravosa et al. 2007, 2008a); dental occlusion, tooth row length, and placement of the bite point relative to the joint (Ciochon et al. 1997; Menegaz et al. 2010; Organ et al. 2006); the size, shape, and cortical bone thickness at attachment sites for jaw adductor musculature, including the sagittal crest, temporal fossa, coronoid process, zygomatic arch, angular process, and pterygoid plates (Bouvier and Hylander 1996a; Kiliaridis et al. 1996; Nicholson et al. 2006; Menegaz et al. 2010; Menegaz and Ravosa 2017); and hard palate dimensions and cross-sectional morphology (Franks et al. 2016; Menegaz et al. 2009).

In addition to shedding light on the functional significance of craniofacial skeletal morphology at a macroscopic level, plasticity studies also provide the opportunity to collect data that can be difficult to obtain from wild species or museum specimens. This includes bone microstructure and material properties data, and morphological data for soft tissues such as bone and cartilage. Modern experimental approaches highlight the various hierarchical levels at which functional adaptation to diet and biomechanical loading may occur (Wang and Dechow 2006; Wang et al. 2006a; Dechow et al. 2010). Changes in external morphology, cross-sectional geometry (e.g., cortical bone thickness, trabecular density), biomineralization, and bone material properties all represent potential functional adaptations to increased loading. However, all of these parameters may not be seen simultaneously within a single craniofacial region or structure (Franks et al. 2016). Thus, absence of macroscopic changes in morphology (e.g., size/shape) does not necessarily indicate the absence of dietary adaptations at the microscopic level. This poses additional questions related to the utilization of skeletal morphology to interpreting dietary behaviors and evolutionary relationships: Are some craniofacial regions more canalized, or less plastic, with regards to masticatory loading (Collard and Lycett 2008; Franks et al. 2016; Wood and Lieberman 2001)? Is the mechanostat "set point," or the level of strain above which bone demonstrates an osteogenic response (Frost 1987), consistent across all regions of the craniofacial skeleton? Potential insight into this latter question may come from the cranial vault, which despite exhibiting low strain values relative to the facial skeleton during loading (Hylander and Johnson 1992) has also been found to have elevated strains at sutural interfaces (Wang et al. 2008, 2010, 2012), and plastic responses to loading through increased cortical bone thickness in cranial vault bones (Menegaz et al. 2010; Pearson and Lieberman 2004) and increased sutural complexity (Byron et al. 2004). Additionally, soft tissues such as muscle and cartilage may respond differentially to variation in masticatory loading. The consumption of mechanically resistant diets is associated with increased masticatory muscle size, physiological cross-sectional area (a proxy for muscle force), and altered fiber type distributions (Ciochon et al. 1997; Ravosa et al. 2010a; Taylor et al. 2006). Cartilages such as the articular cartilage at the temporomandibular joint also show plastic responses to loading in terms of layer thickness, chondrocyte apoptosis rates, and altered protein expression in the extracellular matrix (Bouvier and Hylander 1982; Ravosa and Kane 2017; Ravosa et al. 2008a).

Finally, an individual's ability to respond to changing loading conditions via musculoskeletal adaptations is strongly influenced by ontogeny. As aging progresses, morphological plasticity may decrease as growth rates and bone modeling rates decrease (Bertram and Swartz 1991; Pearson and Lieberman 2004; Ravosa et al. 2008b). Feeding behaviors also change across ontogeny, suggesting that the growth and plasticity of structures involved in different behaviors such as suckling and chewing may change as well (Menegaz and Ravosa 2017). Experimental studies provide support for decreasing plasticity during aging, with different mechanisms of skeletal adaptation seen in immature versus mature animals. Young individuals may demonstrate more pronounced bone modeling, appositional growth, and changes in bone geometry in response to increased loading. Adults or aged individuals may primarily respond to changes in loading via remodeling, the redistribution of bone mass, or changes in bone microstructure (Menegaz and Ravosa 2017; Mitchell et al. 2021; Pearson and Lieberman 2004; Ruff et al. 1994; but see Scott et al. 2014). Due to the highly modular nature of the craniofacial skeleton (Zelditch et al. 2008), experimental approaches such as plasticity studies represent an opportunity to better understand the nature of aging and functional adaptation within distinct regions of the primate skull.

Conclusions

There has been a rapid development in the study of skull form and function in terms of theory, approaches, and concepts. Investigations have extended to a wider range of vertebrate animals including humans and nonhuman primates. Studies have been conducted at various material and theoretical perspectives, from tissue to individual bones and from bone *per se* to joints and regional skeletons, from genetics to dietary behavior, and from hunter-gatherers to modern agricultural populations. With new hypotheses and new research techniques, the quest for functional mechanisms continues to broaden and deepen our knowledge of the skull, especially in the context of genetic, developmental, behavioral, cultural, and environmental diversity, conditions, and limitations.

REFERENCES

Behrents, R. G., D. S. Carlson, and T. Abdelnour. "*In Vivo* Analysis of Bone Strain about the Sagittal Suture in Macaca Mulatta During Masticatory Movements." *Journal of Dental Research* 57 (1978): 904–908.

Bertram, J. E. A., and S. M. Swartz. "The 'Law of Bone Transformation'. *A Case of Crying Wolff?*" *Biological Reviews of the Cambridge Philosophical Society* 66 (1991): 245–273.

Biewener, A. A. "Safety Factors in Bone Strength." *Calcified Tissue International* 53 (1993): 568–574.

Bouvier, M., and W. L. Hylander. "Effect of Bone Strain on Cortical Bone Structure in Macaques Macaca Mulatta." *Journal of Morphology* 167 (1981): 1–12.

Bouvier, M., and W. L. Hylander. "The Effect of Dietary Consistency on Morphology of the Mandibular Condylar Cartilage in Young Macaques Macaca Mulatta." In *Factors and Mechanisms Influencing Bone Growth*. Edited by A. D. Dixon and B. G. Sarnat, 569–579. New York: AR Liss, 1982.

Bouvier, M., and W. L. Hylander. "The Effect of Dietary Consistency on Gross and Histologic Morphology in the Craniofacial Region of Young Rats." *American Journal of Anatomy* 170 (1984): 117–126.

Bouvier, M., and W. L. Hylander. "The Mechanical or Metabolic Function of Secondary Osteonal Bone in the Monkey Macaca Fascicularis." *Archives of Oral Biology* 41 (1996a): 941–950.

Bouvier, M., and W. L. Hylander. "Strain Gradients, Age, and Levels of Modeling and Remodeling in the Facial Bones of Macaca Fascicularis." In *The Biological Mechanisms of Tooth Movement and Craniofacial Adaptation*. Edited by Z. Davidovitch and L. A. Norton, 407–412. Boston: Harvard Society for the Advancement of Orthodontics, 1996b.

Byron, C. D. "Cranial Suture Morphology and Its Relationship to Diet and Encephalization in Cebus." *Journal of Human Evolution* 57 (2009): 649–655.

Byron, C. D., J. Borke, J. Yu, et al. "Effects of Increased Muscle Mass on Mouse Sagittal Suture Morphology and Mechanics." *Anatomical Record* 279A (2004): 676–684.

Carlson, D. S. "Temporal Variation in Prehistoric Nubian Crania." *American Journal of Physical Anthropology* 45 (1976): 467–484.

Carlson, D. S., and D. P. Van Gerven. "Masticatory Function and Post-Pleistocene Evolution in Nubia." *American Journal of Physical Anthropology* 46 (1977): 495–506.

Carlson, D. S., and D. P. Van Gerven. "Diffusion, Biological Determinism, and Biocultural Adaptation in the Nubian Corridor." *American Anthropologist* 81 (1979): 561–580.

Casanova, M., A. Balmelli, D. Carnelli, et al. "Nanoindentation Analysis of the Micromechanical Anisotropy in Mouse Cortical Bone." *Royal Society Open Science* 4, no. 2 (2017): 160971.

Ciochon, R. L., R. A. Nisbett, and R. S. Corruccini. "Dietary Consistency and Craniofacial Development Related to Masticatory Function in Minipigs." *Journal of Craniofacial Genetics and Developmental Biology* 17, no. 2 (1997): 96–102.

Cohen, M. M. "Sutural Biology." In *Craniosynostosis*. Edited by M. M. Cohen and R. E. Mclean, 11–23. Oxford, UK: University Press, 2000.

Collard, M., and S. J. Lycett. "Does Phenotypic Plasticity Confound Attempts to Identify Hominin Fossil Species?" *Folia Primatologica* 79 (2008): 111–122.

Daegling, D. J. "Understanding Skull Function from a Mechanobiological Perspective." In *A Companion to Biological Anthropology*. Edited by C. S. Larsen, 501–515. Hoboken, NJ: Wiley-Blackwell, 2010.

Daegling, D. J., and J. L. Hotzman. "Functional Significance of Cortical Bone Distribution in Anthropoid Mandibles: An in Vitro Assessment of Bone Strain under Combined Loads." *American Journal of Physical Anthropology* 122, no. 1 (2003): 38–50.

Daegling, D. J., M. C. Granatosky, W. S. McGraw, et al. "Spatial Patterning of Bone Stiffness Variation in the Colobine Alveolar Process." *Archives of Oral Biology* 56, no. 3 (2011): 220–230.

Dechow, P. C., D. H. Chung, and M. Bolouri. "Relationship Between Three-Dimensional Microstructure and Elastic Properties of Cortical Bone in the Human Mandible and Femur." In *Primate Craniofacial Function and Biology, Developments in Primatology Series*. Edited by C. J. Vinyard, M. J. Ravosa, and C. E. Wall, 265–292. New York: Springer, 2008.

Dechow, P. C., Q. Wang, and J. Peterson. "Edentulation Alters Material Properties of Cortical Bone in the Human Craniofacial Skeleton: Functional Implications for Craniofacial Structure in Primate Evolution." *Anatomical Record* 293, no. 4 (2010): 618–629.

DeSilva, J. M., J. F. A. Traniello, A. G. Claxton, et al. "When and Why Did Human Brains Decrease in Size? A New Change-Point Analysis and Insights from Brain Evolution in Ants." *Frontiers in Ecology and Evolution* 9 (2021): Article 742639.

Dzialo, C., S. A. Wood, M. Berthaume, et al. "Functional Implications of Squamosal Suture Size in *Paranthropus Boisei*." *American Journal of Physical Anthropology* 153 (2014): 260–268.

Farke, A. A. "Frontal Sinuses and Head-Butting in Goats: A Finite Element Analysis." *Journal of Experimental Biology* 211 (2008): 3085–3094.

Franks, E. M., N. E. Holton, J. E. Scott, et al. "Betwixt and Between: Intracranial Perspective on Zygomatic Arch Plasticity and Function in Mammals." *Anatomical Record* 299, no. 12 (2016): 1646–1660.

Frost, H. M. "Bone "Mass" and the "Mechanostat": A Proposal." *Anatomical Record* 219 (1987): 1–9.

Gharpure, P., E. D. Kontogiorgos, L. A. Opperman, et al. "Elastic Properties of Chimpanzee Craniofacial Cortical Bone." *Anatomical Record* 299 (2016): 1718–1733.

Greaves, W. S. "The Jaw Lever System in Ungulates: A New Model." *Journal of Zoology* 184 (1978): 271–285.

Grine, F. E., F. Judex, D. J. Daegling, et al. "Craniofacial Biomechanics and Functional and Dietary Inferences in Hominin Paleontology." *Journal of Human Evolution* 58 (2010): 293–308.

Herring, S. W. "Sutures: A Tool in Functional Cranial Analysis." *Acta Anatomica (Basel)* 83 (1972): 222–247.

Herring, S. W. "Mechanical Influences on Suture Development and Patency." *Frontiers of Oral Biology* 12 (2008): 41–56.

Hylander, W. L. "The Functional Significance of Primate Mandibular Form." *Journal of Morphology* 160 (1979a): 223–240.

Hylander, W. L. "Mandibular Function in *Galago Crassicaudatus* and *Macaca Fascicularis*: An *in Vivo* Approach to Stress Analysis of the Mandible." *Journal of Morphology* 159, no. 2 (1979b): 253–296.

Hylander, W. L., and K. R. Johnson. "Strain Gradients in the Craniofacial Region of Primates." In *The Biological Mechanisms of Tooth Movement and Craniofacial Adaptation*. Edited by Z. Davidovitch, 559–569. Columbus: The Ohio State University Press, 1992.

Hylander, W. L., M. J. Ravosa, C. F. Ross, et al. "Mandibular Corpus Strain in Primates: Further Evidence for a Functional Link Between Symphyseal Fusion and Jaw-Adductor Muscle Force." *American Journal of Physical Anthropology* 107, no. 3 (1998): 257–271.

Hylander, W. L., M. J. Ravosa, C. F. Ross, et al. "Symphyseal Fusion and Jaw-Adductor Muscle Force: An EMG Study." *American Journal of Physical Anthropology* 112 (2000): 469–492.

Kiliaridis, S., A. Bresin, J. Holm, et al. "Effects of Masticatory Muscle Function on Bone Mass in the Mandible of the Growing Rat." *Acta Anatomica* 155 (1996): 200–205.

Lanyon, L., and C. T. Rubin. "Functional Adaptation in Skeletal Structures." In *Functional Vertebrate Morphology*. Edited by M. Hildebrand, D. M. Bramble, K. F. Liem, and D. B. Wake, 1–25. Cambridge: Harvard University Press, 1985.

Larsen, C. S. 2015. *Bioarchaeology: Interpreting Behavior from the Human Skeleton*, 2nd edn. Cambridge, UK: Cambridge University Press.

Ledogar, J. A., P. C. Dechow, Q. Wang, et al. "Human Feeding Biomechanics: Performance, Variation, and Functional Constraints." *PeerJ*. (2016a). https://doi.org/10.7717/peerj.2242.

Ledogar, J. A., A. L. Smith, S. Benazzi, et al. "Mechanical Evidence that *Australopithecus Sediba* Was Limited in Its Ability to Eat Hard Foods." *Nature Communications* 7 (2016b): 10596.

Liberman, D. *The Story of the Human Body: Evolution, Health, and Disease*. New York, NY: Knopf Doubleday, 2013.

Lucas, P. W., T. Beta, B. W. Darvell, et al. "Field Kit to Characterize Physical, Chemical and Spatial Aspect of Potential Primate Foods." *Folia Primatologica* 72 (2001): 11–25.

Menegaz, R. A., D. B. Baier, K. A. Metzger, et al. "XROMM Analysis of Tooth Occlusion and Temporomandibular Joint Kinematics During Feeding in Juvenile Miniature Pigs." *Journal of Experimental Biology* 218, no. 16 (2015): 2573–2584.

Menegaz, R. A., and M. J. Ravosa. "Ontogenetic and Functional Modularity in the Rodent Mandible." *Zoology* 124 (2017): 61–72.

Menegaz, R. A., S. V. Sublett, S. D. Figueroa, et al. "Phenotypic Plasticity and Function of the Hard Palate in Growing Rabbits." *Anatomical Record* 292A (2009): 277–284.

Menegaz, R. A., S. V. Sublett, S. D. Figueroa, et al. "Evidence for the Influence of Diet on Cranial Form and Robusticity." *Anatomical Record* 293A (2010): 630–641.

Mitchell, D. R., S. Wroe, M. J. Ravosa, et al. "More Challenging Diets Sustain Feeding Performance: Applications Toward the Captive Rearing of Wildlife." *Integrative Organismal Biology* 3, no. 1 (2021): 10.1093/iob/obab030.

Montuelle, S. J., R. A. Olson, H. Curtis, et al. "Effects of Food Properties on Chewing in Pigs: Flexibility and Stereotypy of Jaw Movements in a Mammalian Omnivore." *PLoS One* 15, no. 2 (2020): e0228619.

Nicholson, E. K., S. R. Stock, M. W. Hamrick, et al. "Biomineralization and Adaptive Plasticity of the Temporomandibular Joint in Myostatin Knockout Mice." *Archives of Oral Biology* 51 (2006): 37–49.

Organ, J. M., C. B. Ruff, M. F. Teaford, et al. "Do Mandibular Cross-Sectional Properties and Dental Microwear Give Similar Dietary Signals?" *American Journal of Physical Anthropology* 130, no. 4 (2006): 501–507.

Orsbon, C. P., N. J. Gidmark, and C. F. Ross. "Dynamic Musculoskeletal Functional Morphology: Integrating diceCT and XROMM." *Anatomical Record* 301 (2018): 378–406.

Oyen, M. L. *Handbook of Nanoindentation: With Biological Applications*. Boca Raton, FL: Jenny Stanford Publishing, 2010.

Pearson, O. M., and D. E. Lieberman. "The Aging of Wolff's 'Law': Ontogeny and Responses to Mechanical Loading in Cortical Bone." *American Journal of Physical Anthropology* 125, no. S39 (2004): 63–99.

Peterson, J., Q. Wang, and P. C. Dechow. "Material Properties of the Dentate Maxilla." *Anatomical Record* 288A (2006): 962–972.

Popowics, T. E., and S. W. Herring. "Load Transmission in the Nasofrontal Suture of the Pig, Sus Scrofa." *Journal of Biomechanics* 40 (2007): 837–844.

Ravosa, M. J., and R. J. Kane. "Dietary Variation and Mechanical Properties of Articular Cartilage in the Temporomandibular Joint: Implications for the Role of Plasticity in Mechanobiology and Pathobiology." *Zoology* 124 (2017): 42–50.

Ravosa, M. J., K. R. Johnson, and W. L. Hylander. "Strain in the Galago Facial Skull." *Journal of Zoology (London)* 207 (1991): 125–136.

Ravosa, M. J., R. Kunwar, S. R. Stock, et al. "Pushing the Limit: Masticatory Stress and Adaptive Plasticity in Mammalian Craniomandibular Joints." *Journal of Experimental Biology* 210 (2007): 628–641.

Ravosa, M. J., E. K. López, R. A. Menegaz, et al. "Adaptive Plasticity in the Mammalian Masticatory Complex: You are What, and How, You Eat." In *Primate Craniofacial Biology and Function*. Edited by C. J. Vinyard, M. J. Ravosa, and C. E. Wall, 293–328. New York: Springer Academic Publishers, 2008a.

Ravosa, M. J., E. K. López, R. A. Menegaz, et al. "Using 'Mighty Mouse' to Understand Masticatory Plasticity: Myostatin-Deficient Mice and Musculoskeletal Function." *Integrative and Comparative Biology* 48 (2008b): 345–359.

Ravosa, M. J., J. Ning, D. B. Costley, et al. "Masticatory Biomechanics and Masseter Fiber-Type Plasticity." *Journal of Musculoskeletal & Neuronal Interactions* 10 (2010a): 46–55.

Ravosa, M. J., C. F. Ross, S. H. Williams, et al. "Allometry of Masticatory Loading Parameters in Mammals." *Anatomical Record* 293, no. 4 (2010b): 557–571.

Ravosa, M. J., K. A. Congdon, and R. A. Menegaz. "Experimental Approaches to Musculoskeletal Function in Primates." In *A Companion to Paleoanthropology*, 55–74. Hoboken, New Jersey: Wiley-Blackwell, 2013.

Ravosa, M. J., J. E. Scott, K. R. McAbee, et al. "Chewed Out: An Experimental Link Between Food Material Properties and Repetitive Loading of the Masticatory Apparatus in Mammals." *Peer J.* 3 (2015): e1345.

Rayfield, E. J. "Using Finite-Element Analysis to Investigate Suture Morphology: A Case Study Using Large Carnivorous Dinosaurs." *Anatomical Record* 283 (2005): 349–365.

Ross, C. F., and K. A. Metzger. "Bone Strain Gradients and Optimization in Vertebrate Skulls." *Annals of Anatomy – Anatomischer Anzeiger* 186, no. 5 (2004): 387–396.

Ross, C. F., D. A. Reed, R. L. Washington, et al. "Scaling of Chew Cycle Duration in Primates." *American Journal of Physical Anthropology* 138, no. 1 (2009): 30–44.

Ross, C. F., A. L. Baden, J. Georgi, et al. "Chewing Variation in Lepidosaurs and Primates." *Journal of Experimental Biology* 213, no. 4 (2010): 572–584.

Ruff, C. B., A. Walker, and E. Trinkaus. "Postcranial Robusticity in Homo. III: Ontogeny." *American Journal of Physical Anthropology* 93, no. 1 (1994): 35–54.

Scott, J. E., K. R. McAbee, M. M. Eastman, et al. "Teaching an Old Jaw New Tricks: Diet-Induced Plasticity in a Model Organism, from Weaning to Adulthood." *Journal of Experimental Biology* 217 (2014): 4099.

Smith, A. L., C. Robinson, A. B. Taylor, et al. "Comparative Biomechanics of the Pan and Macaca Mandibles During Mastication: Finite Element Modelling of Loading, Deformation and Strain Regimes." *Interface Focus* 11, no. 5 (2021): 20210031.

Stedman, H., B. Kozyak, A. Nelson, et al. "Myosin Gene Mutation Correlates with Anatomical Changes in the Human Lineage". *Nature* 428 (2004): 415–418.

Strait, D. S., Q. Wang, P. C. Dechow, et al. "Modeling Elastic Properties in Finite-Element Analysis: How Much Precision Is Needed to Produce an Accurate Model?" *Anatomical Record* 283 (2005): 275–287.

Strait, D. S., G. W. Weber, S. Neubauer, et al. The Feeding Biomechanics and Dietary Ecology of *Australopithecus Africanus*. *Proceedings of the National Academy of Sciences*, 106(7) (2009): 2124–2129.

Strait, D. S., P. Constantino, P. W. Lucas, et al. "Diet and Dietary Adaptations in Early Hominins: The Hard Food Perspective." *American Journal of Physical Anthropology* 151 (2013): 339–355.

Taylor, A. B., K. E. Jones, R. Kunwar, et al. "Dietary Consistency and Plasticity of Masseter Fiber Architecture in Postweaning Rabbits." *Anatomical Record* 288A (2006): 1105–1111.

Vinyard, C. J., C. E. Wall, S. H. Williams, and W. L. Hylander. "Patterns of Variation Across Primates in Jaw-Muscle Electromyography During Mastication." *Integrative and Comparative Biology* 48, no. 2 (2008): 294–311.

von Cramon-Taubadel, N. "Evolutionary Insights into Global Patterns of Human Cranial Diversity: Population History, Climatic and Dietary Effects." *Journal of Anthropological Sciences* 92 (2014): 43–77.

Wang, Q., and P. C. Dechow. "Elastic Properties of External Cortical Bone in the Craniofacial Skeleton of the Rhesus Monkey." *American Journal of Physical Anthropology* 131, no. 3 (2006): 402–415.

Wang, Q., and P. C. Dechow. "Divided Zygomatic Bone in Primates with Implications of Skull Morphology and Biomechanics." *Anatomical Record* 299 (2016): 1801–1829.

Wang, Q., D. S. Strait, and P. C. Dechow. "A Comparison of Cortical Elastic Properties in the Craniofacial Skeletons of Three Primate Species and Its Relevance to the Study of Human Evolution." *Journal of Human Evolution* 51, no. 4 (2006a): 375–382.

Wang, Q., D. S. Strait, and P. C. Dechow. "Fusion Patterns of Craniofacial Sutures in Rhesus Monkey Skulls of Known Age and Sex from Cayo Santiago." *American Journal of Physical Anthropology* 131 (2006b): 469–485.

Wang, Q., P. C. Dechow, B. W. Wright, et al. "Surface Strain on Bone and Sutures in a Monkey Facial Skeleton: An in Vitro Approach and Its Relevance to Finite Element Analysis." In *Primate Craniofacial Function and Biology. Developments in Primatology: Progress and Prospects.* Edited by C. J. Vinyard, M. J. Ravosa, and C. E. Wall, 149–172. Boston, MA: Springer, 2008.

Wang, Q., D. W. Ashley, and P. C. Dechow. "Regional, Ontogenetic, and Sex-Related Variations in Elastic Properties of Cortical Bone in Baboon Mandibles." *American Journal of Physical Anthropology* 141 (2010a): 526–549.

Wang, Q., A. L. Smith, D. S. Strait, et al. "The Global Impact of Sutures Assessed in a Finite Element Model of a Macaque Cranium." *Anatomical Record* 293 (2010b): 1477–1491.

Wang, Q., S. Wood, I. Grosse, et al. "The Role of the Sutures in Biomechanical Dynamic Simulation of a Macaque Cranial Finite Element Model: Implications for the Evolution of Craniofacial Form." *Anatomical Record* 295 (2012): 278–288.

Wang, Q., Q. Zhang, T. Han, et al. "Masticatory Properties in Pre-modern Holocene Populations from Northern China." *HOMO Journal of Comparative Human Biology* 70, no. 1 (2019): 15–30.

Weiner, S., and H. D. Wagner. "The Material Bone: Structure-Mechanical Function Relations." *Annual Review of Materials Science* 28 (1998): 271–298.

West-Eberhard, M. J. "Developmental Plasticity and the Origin of Species Differences." *Proceedings of the National Academy of Sciences of the United States of America*, 102 (2005): 6543–6549.

Williams, S. H., B. W. Wright, V. D. Truong, et al. "Mechanical Properties of Foods Used in Experimental Studies of Primate Masticatory Function." *American Journal of Primatology* 67, no. 3 (2005): 329–346.

Wood, B., and D. E. Lieberman. "Craniodental Variation in Paranthropus Boisci: A Developmental and Functional Perspective." *American Journal of Physical Anthropology* 116, no. 1 (2001): 13–25.

Wroe, S., K. Moreno, P. Clausen, et al. "High-Resolution Three-Dimensional Computer Simulation of Hominid Cranial Mechanics." *Anatomical Record* 290 (2007): 1248–1255.

Yang, M. A., X. Fan, B. Sun, et al. "Ancient DNA Indicates Human Population Shifts and Admixture in Northern and Southern China." *Science* 369, no. 6501 (2020): 282–288.

Zelditch, M. L., A. R. Wood, R. M. Bonett, et al. "Modularity of the Rodent Mandible: Integrating Bone, Muscles, and Teeth." *Evolution & Development* 10 (2008): 756–768.

Zhang, Q., Q. Zhang, S. Yang, et al. "Divided Zygoma in Holocene Human Populations from Northern China." *American Journal of Human Biology* 31, no. 6 (2019): e23314. 10.1002/ajhb.23314.

CHAPTER 34

Dental Microwear Analysis: *Wear* We Are Going, *Wear* We Have Been

Christopher W. Schmidt and Peter S. Ungar

There is probably no more important element of craniofacial function than the role of the dentition in mastication of food. The dentition provides the elements of tooth use as they pertain to oral reduction of food into digestible elements. In our view, the record of dental microwear provides a fundamental window on to dietary adaptation and masticatory function in general and the role of dentition in reducing food in particular. In this regard, there is a large and growing body of research that highlights the role of teeth as tribiological structures, namely structures that include mechanical elements involving wear, friction, and lubrication as it pertains to tooth use.

DENTAL BIOTRIBOLOGY AND MICROWEAR FORMATION

Dental microwear research rests at the boundary between biology and engineering. More specifically, it combines basic principles of ecology with tribology, "the science and technology of interacting surfaces in relative motion and the practices related thereto" (Jost 1966; see Zhou et al. 2013). Microwear forms during chewing as a result of interactions between opposing surfaces and abrasives in or on foods between those surfaces. Aristotle wrote around 350 BC, "teeth have one invariable office, namely the reduction of food." When we think about how teeth reduce foods, we need to consider that foods break in different ways depending on their fracture properties (Lucas 2004). Some foods are hard and must be crushed with force to initiate cracks. Such foods are often brittle, resulting in cracks easily spreading easily once started. Other foods are tough, and while they might be soft, they require work to generate tension through shearing or slicing to spread cracks. In this sense, chewing is a problem of relative motion between opposing, interacting surfaces. Indeed, as Simpson (1933) noted long ago, vertical movement of cusps into basins results in crushing (he called it *opposition*), whereas vertical movement with steep crests running parallel to the plane of motion results in shearing. Horizontal movements of opposing crests or cusps across basins result in grinding.

The basic theory behind microwear interpretation begins with the notion that the relative motions of food particles and opposing teeth vary with the fracture properties of the items eaten. For example, abrasives in or on foods should cause pits when hard objects are crushed between opposing enamel surfaces; scratches form when tough items are sheared between enamel surfaces as they slide past one another (Gordon 1982). Consider the actions of cutting paper with a pair of scissors and crushing a horseshoe between hammer and anvil. Thus, a hard object diet (e.g., nuts or bone) should result in heavily pitted microwear surfaces whereas a tough food diet (e.g., leaves or meat) should leave long parallel striations on tooth wear facets.

The idea of using microwear as an indicator of tooth–tooth movements is not new. Simpson (1926) proposed nearly a century ago that the direction of scratches on molar facets might be used to determine how past mammals chewed. This became a popular go-to approach for inferring masticatory behaviors of fossil mammals in the 1950s and 1960s (e.g., Butler 1952; Mills 1955 et seq.). The idea that feature shapes evince masticatory movements (e.g., crushing causes pits, shearing or grinding causes scratches) came later (e.g., Grine 1977) and paved the way to connecting microwear directly with food preferences. However, working out the details – "seeing" how tooth surfaces interact with each other and the abrasives in or on foods with different properties – is a formidable task. Wear facets can be less than a millimeter across and movements between them, precise to microns, are masked by cheek or adjacent teeth. Wear facets are generally angled on the inside slopes of cusps, making it even more difficult to work out occlusal dynamics and the relationships of jaw movements and relative motions of contact surfaces. Then there is the challenge of establishing and confirming relationships between microwear pattern and diet. There are three approaches: (1) comparative analyses of teeth from individuals living under natural conditions – typically specimens archived in museums or other research collections, (2) *in vitro* studies simulating chewing with machines, and (3) *in vivo* experiments with live animals fed different foods.

COMPARATIVE STUDIES

The earliest studies to document relationships between microwear pattern and diet were comparative in nature. The idea was to determine whether species with known food preferences had distinctive and predictable microwear signatures. Teaford and Walker (1984), for example, used wild-shot primates from museum collections representing species reported to be hard-object feeders, folivores, and frugivores. The ratios of pits to scratches on their molar wear facets were high, low, and intermediate, respectively, as predicted. Studies of other mammals followed, from antelope to zebra, bat to mole, pig to sheep, marsupials, cats, and hyenas, etc. (e.g., Hayek et al. 1991; Mainland 1998; Rivals and Semprebon 2006; Robson and Young 1986; Silcox and Teaford 2002; Solounias and Hayek 1993; Strait 1993; van Valkenbugh et al. 1990; Ward and Mainland 1999). The general patterns were clear – among closely related mammalian species, those reported to consume tougher foods tended to have more scratches on their molars, whereas those that ate harder ones tended to have more pits. More recent work examining surface textures using metrological techniques has confirmed that, among a broad spectrum of mammals, those reported to consume softer, tougher foods tend to have higher wear surface anisotropy, and those that crush hard, brittle foods tend to have higher texture complexity (e.g., Arman et al. 2019; DeSantis et al. 2020; Donoghue et al. 2013; Haupt et al. 2013; Kubo and Fujita 2021; Kubo et al. 2017; Purnell et al. 2013; Prideaux et al. 2009; Schubert et al. 2010; Scott 2012; Scott et al. 2012; Tanis et al. 2018; Ungar et al. 2007, 2010).

That said, many such studies have been based on museum specimens collected in the early twentieth century, with little information on where they were trapped and no detail on food preferences of individuals included in analyses. Diet-pattern associations were by necessity general and broad given food preferences and availabilities to individuals over time and space. The whole point of microwear analysis, and other "foodprints" (Ungar 2017) – remnant traces of actual feeding activity – is to understand what individuals eat on a daily basis, not just to document general trends for populations or species. This has led some to focus on samples collected at specific locations to determine the limits of microwear for diet reconstruction (e.g., Stuhlträger et al. 2019; Teaford and Robinson 1989; Teaford and Runestad 1992). Some researchers even began ambitious catch-and-release microwear programs on wild primates to look for similarities and differences between groups and individuals within them (Nystrom et al.; 2004; Teaford and Glander 1996). Others have attempted to connect microwear to stomach contents (Merceron et al. 2010; Purnell et al. 2012) or fat reserves (Ungar et al. 2021) of wild-caught individuals. Such studies have produced varying results, but by and large have confirmed that microwear can provide insights into diet, oftentimes with details related to variation by season, ecological zone, or individual preference.

In Vitro Studies

While comparative studies are the cornerstone of microwear research – they provide the baseline for inferring diet in fossil and bioarchaeological samples – there has also been a push to understand the etiology of dental microwear by experimental means. How do tooth–tooth movement, abrasive type and concentration, and food substrate properties combine to form specific microwear patterns? Studies have involved a variety of approaches, from scraping enamel surfaces with abrasives by hand to a myriad of mechanical masticators or chewing simulators (e.g., Gügel et al. 2001; Hua et al. 2015, 2020; Karme et al. 2016; Maas 1994; Peters 1982; Ryan 1979). These machines have varied in design, from those producing single-stroke movements in a fixed plane (e.g., Karme et al. 2016; Ryan 1979) to reciprocally rotating antagonistic wheels (Gügel et al. 2001) to a three-dimensional contraption wherein the angle of approach between opposing enamel samples can be varied (Hua et al. 2015, 2020). In some cases, abrasives and food items are put into slurries and in others foods are placed between opposing enamel surfaces (Figure 34.1).

While "real-world" oral environments are more complex with many variables difficult to simulate in vitro, chewing machines do allow for control over conditions and easy testing of effects of abrasive type and load, food material properties, etc. A variety of other instruments, such as the atomic force microscope, microtribometer, and material testing system have also been used to simulate wear with precise forces and to assess results (e.g., Daegling et al. 2016; Lucas et al. 2013; Van Casteren et al. 2020; Xia et al. 2017, 2015). Results of these studies have varied with methods employed and are sometimes contradictory, but a few things are clear. First, it seems that different sorts of microscopic abrasives under different loads can produce different and sometimes unexpected microwear patterns. That said,

Figure 34.1 A = Bitemaster II chewing simulator with a sample of meat. B = microwear generated with force perpendicular to the surface (crushing), C = microwear generated with force 45 degrees to the surface, D = microwear formed with force near parallel to the surface (shearing). Note that there are more small pits on B than on D. The top image of each surface is the baseline/pre-experiment (see Hua et al. 2015 for details).

the angle of approach between opposing surfaces clearly drives feature shape: pits are caused by compression and scratches by drag (e.g., Gügel et al. 2001; Hua et al. 2015). Other key findings have been the observation that similar microwear patterns can occur with markedly different levels of gross wear (Karme et al. 2016) and that microwear formation depends both on mechanical properties of food and abrasives (Hua et al. 2020).

In Vivo Studies

Another increasingly popular approach to working out relationships between microwear and diet involves feeding laboratory animals different foods with varying types and amounts of abrasive under controlled conditions. While this approach does not replicate the complexity of "real-world" natural settings either, it is a step closer than possible using a chewing machine. Kay and Covert's (1983) early study of opossums fed cat food supplemented with plants and insect chitin was pivotal in establishing protocols for quantitative microwear analysis. Teaford and Oyen's (1989a) benchmark work on vervet monkeys fed wet and dry monkey chow was the first to demonstrate variation in microwear among laboratory primates fed foods with different properties. It also demonstrated the fleeting lifespans of individual features, which is on the order of days (e.g., Teaford and Oyen 1989b). The rapid rate of microwear turnover was confirmed recently by Teaford et al. (2017, 2020, 2021) in studies of lemurs and capuchin monkeys. Human volunteers have also been used to assess impacts of diet and rates of microwear turnover (Romero et al. 2012; Teaford and Lytle 1996; Teaford and Tylenda 1991).

Indeed, the number of in vivo studies has increased in recent years and have expanded to many other species, from fishes to rodents, rabbits, and sheep (Ackermans 2020; Baines et al. 2014; Calandra et al. 2016; Gallego-Valle et al. 2020; Hoffman et al. 2015; Kropacheva et al. 2019; Merceron et al. 2017, 2016; Mihlbachler et al. 2019; Muller et al., 2014; Ramdarshan et al. 2017; Schulz et al. 2013; Winkler et al. 2019). As with in vitro studies, results have varied depending on the questions asked, animals considered, and analytical protocols used. Some have considered abrasive size, composition, and concentration as confounding factors that can throw a wrench into the works and confuse microwear interpretation, whereas others have focused on how we can amplify the diet signal. Results indicate that external abrasives added to the diet can affect microwear pattern in different ways depending on concentration, size, and type. On the other hand, these differences need not swamp the diet signal – animals fed different types of food tend to have distinctive microwear patterns. Sheep fed clover differ from those fed grass, whether these foods are covered in dust or not (Merceron et al. 2016). In vivo studies in aggregate speak to the potential of microwear as a diet proxy, but caution that its formation is complex, and this should be considered when using microwear to infer diets of bioarchaeological and paleontological samples.

PHYTOLITHS, GRIT, AND INSIDE BASEBALL

A major question debated recently in the literature is, "do phytoliths scratch teeth?" This has been a surprisingly difficult question to answer. Some in vitro experiments have suggested that phytoliths are too soft to scratch enamel (e.g., Atkins and Liu 2007; Lucas et al. 2013, 2014; Sanson et al. 2007). Other research focusing on relationships between tooth wear and enamel thickness (Rabenold and Pearson 2011, 2014), grass components of the diet (Kubo and Yamada 2014), the ability of other soft materials to scratch enamel (Xia et al. 2016, 2018), and in vitro experiments (Schulz-Kornas et al. 2020; Winkler et al. 2019) suggest that phytoliths can wear teeth. Indeed, Rodriguez-Rojas and colleagues (2020) recently confirmed that phytoliths and silica grit suspended in artificial saliva can scratch teeth to a similar extent.

Another question involves the impact of large exogenous particles (e.g., sand) on the microwear feature shape. Such particles have been implicated in the formation of microwear pits in the absence of a hard food diet (e.g., Daegling and Grine 1999; Hoffman et al. 2015; Ackermans 2020). Other properties of food, such as water content (Winkler et al. 2019) and pliability and porosity (Hua et al. 2020) also play a role in feature formation; but the arcane and esoteric details of microwear etiology are, for this review at least, "inside baseball" (*sensu* Safire 1988), largely unintelligible and of little interest to nonexperts. What is important here is that while microwear formation is complex, the noise generally does not overwhelm the diet signal (e.g., Burgman et al. 2016; Hedberg and Desantis 2017; Merceron et al. 2016).

Interpretations of DMTA

The sources cited in this summary represent a fraction of the hundreds of papers published in just the past few decades exploring microwear in extant and extinct primates, and modern and ancient humans. The variety of animals studied with DMTA alone is quite impressive and, to date, includes antelope, armadillos, bats, bears, cows, deer, dire wolves, dogs, elephants, fishes, fossil mammals (including cave bears, diprotodons, flat-headed peccary, mastodons, Paraceratherians, saber-toothed cats, Xenarthrans), horses, hyenas, marsupials, panthers, pigs, rabbits, reptiles, rodents, shrews, and sloths (e.g., DeSantis 2016; DeSantis et al. 2012; Donohue et al. 2013; El Zaatari 2008; El Zaatari and Hublin 2014; Haupt et al. 2013; Louys et al. 2021; Merceron et al. 2010; Percher et al. 2017; Prideaux et al. 2009; Purnell et al. 2013; Purnell and Darras 2016; Schmidt 2008; Schmidt et al. 2019; Schubert et al. 2010; Schulz et al. 2013; Scott et al. 2009, 2012, 2005, 2006; Stynder et al. 2012; Ungar et al. 2012, 2007, 2010; White et al. 2021). Although not exhaustive, the list above exemplifies the scope of microwear application. Despite the concerns and limitations described in this chapter, it is clear that microwear textures are useful indicators of the foods that animals eat (e.g., Adams et al. 2020; Percher et al. 2018).

Of course, dietary information comes from many sources; for example, the animals listed above have quite distinct dental morphologies, ranging from sharp carnassials to flat cheek teeth. It is important to note, however, that gross dental shapes do not always reflect the foods most often consumed by a particular species at a particular time (e.g., Ungar 2009, Ungar et al. 2016). Dental microwear indicates that cusp morphology and enamel thickness do not invariably reflect the preferred foods of extant primates (e.g., Teaford and Oyen 1989a; Teaford and Robinson 1989; Teaford and Ungar 2014; Teaford et al. 2017). Thus, morphology is an initial condition regarding what any fossil creature, or ancient human, could eat or is adapted to eat, but it is dental wear that indicates what an individual did eat, which may or may not agree with morphology (see Ungar 2009). Disagreements between dental form and function are valued findings and invoke a variety of considerations, including the dietary contributions of fallback foods, individual nuances in food preference, and, at least among humans and their ancestors, food preparation.

Interpretations in Humans and Human Ancestors

The teeth of human ancestors provide one such place where DMTA contradicted expectations. Ungar et al. (2008) found that the megadont hominin *Paranthropus boisei*, long thought to be a hard food consumer, probably preferred softer foods. *P. boisei* had large flat molars and muscular jaws capable of crushing hard seeds and nuts. By 1.5 to 2 million years ago, *P. boisei* focused more on foods that generated fewer pits and more scratches. In the end, it was the microwear texture analysis that changed the dietary paradigm for *P. boisei* and opened the door for new interpretations of its way of life.

Sireen El Zaatari and colleagues have been instrumental in exposing the importance of plant foods in Neandertal diets using microwear. Isotopic studies indicated Neandertals were top predators, comparable to canids in their meat consumption, yet the texture data indicated that Neandertal jaw movements were consistent with consuming tough, fibrous plant foods that varied by the region in which they lived (e.g., Richards et al. 2000; El Zaatari et al. 2011, 2016). Interpretations of Neandertal textures by Almudena Estalrrich, Jessica Droke, and Whitney Karriger are similar in that they see regionally dependent patterns of plant consumption (Droke et al. 2020; Estalrrich et al. 2017; Karriger et al. 2016; Williams et al. 2018, 2019, 2021); interestingly the DMTA results are congruent with reports of DNA and plant remains in Neandertal calculus (e.g., Weyrich et al. 2017; Power et al. 2018).

Less surprisingly, Upper Paleolithic humans had DMTA evidence of plant consumption (e.g., El Zaatari and Hublin 2014). Subsistence nuances of Upper Paleolithic peoples of the Levant include a notable reliance on cereal grains prior to their domestication. Such a situation occurred at the 19,000 year-old site of Ohalo II, which produced a sizable quantity of wild barley and edible grasses, as well as processed starch grains, despite there being no evidence of domestication (Kislev et al. 1992; Piperno et al. 2004). A young adult from the site bore a microwear signature more typical of people consuming highly processed domesticates (Mahoney 2006). A similar situation occurred among Natufian people, who immediately preceded the origins of agriculture. Natufian microwear texture is nearly indistinguishable from that of later Neolithic farmers, but dissimilar to pre-agricultural groups around the globe (Mahoney 2006; Schmidt et al. 2019).

Interpreting meat in the diet remains difficult when using DMTA. Meat itself is not hard enough to generate microwear features (Hua et al. 2015). Moreover, it is so pliant that abrasives in or on it may sink into the tissue during mastication, preventing them from scoring enamel in many cases. Currently, efforts are nevertheless underway in the field and lab to better coax meat consumption signatures from DMTA data. El Zaatari (2008, 2010) studied recent coastal and arctic foragers thought to have consumed a diet rich in meat. Those foragers had high complexity and high anisotropy values, indicative of jaw movements in consistent directions. This makes sense if meat consumption results in repeated vertical and lateral excursion of the mandible to shear it. Schmidt et al. (2016) found a similarly high anisotropy among Iron Age pastoralists, who also were thought to have consumed meat and dairy products, but their complexities were quite low. Paleoindian foraging groups, thought to have consumed large amounts of meat based on their stable isotope values, had high complexities and low anisotropies. For these foragers, the high complexity is probably due to eating hard, wild foods like seeds and nuts, while the low anisotropy is probably due to eating a diverse diet that leads to jaw movements in many directions (e.g., Da Gloria and Schmidt 2020). Thus, high meat diets do not necessarily generate consistent DMTA signatures and, in fact, they can be swamped by signatures of other foods, particularly hard, abrasive ones (see Schmidt 2010, 2021; Schmidt et al. 2019). In order to refine our understanding of microwear's relationship to the foods that cause it, researchers are looking to new experimental approaches (e.g., Krueger et al. 2021; see above) as well as expanding the micro-topographic variables studied. In recent years, analysts have added to DMTA a battery of surface metrology parameters that calculate areal distributions of height values in the z-plane (e.g., ISO 25178; see Leach 2013; Purnell et al. 2013; Schulz et al. 2010).

Interpretations of human microwear texture are additionally obscured by the advent of agriculture, because for millennia farmers have processed their foods in ways that significantly alter the crop's original physical properties (Figure 34.2). Foragers also processed foods, via cooking and stone grinding (Shoemaker et al. 2017). However, in general, farmers process foods far more than do their foraging counterparts; they tend to mill their

(a)   (b)

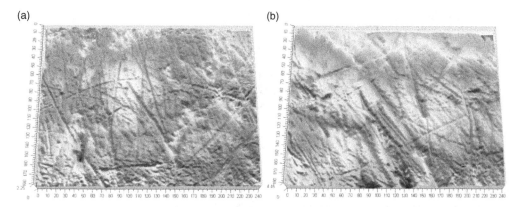

Figure 34.2 Microwear texture of food producers. The difference in dietary hardness may relate to differences in food preference and/or processing. A = few pit features, B = more pit features. Scales are in microns.

cereal grains to meals or flours and cook foods extensively in well-constructed ceramic vessels (e.g., Briggs 2016; Feathers 2006). Early farming diets had some abrasive components, particularly early on when stone grinding implements would contaminate ground grains with grit particles, but over time, this kind of contamination diminished, particularly as wooden implements became more common (e.g., Greenlee 2006). From the Early Bronze age to the Iron Age of England, texture signatures decreased in complexity as milling technology improved (Schmidt et al. 2019). Diets also became softer in precontact North America with the adoption of maize as the primary late precontact staple. However, some very late precontact peoples of the Ohio River valley had diets creating microwear textures that were far more complex than preceding groups. In fact, their microwear signatures looked like they consumed primarily wild foods (i.e., see Holmes 2021; Schmidt 2021), although their stable isotope values indicate maize consumption (Cook and Schurr 2009). A possible explanation for this microwear signature is that the late precontact peoples supplemented their domesticate-based diet with wild nuts (Emerson et al. 2005). Another possibility is that they consumed dried maize kernals in the form of a coarsely ground hominy. Although hominy was often prepared as a pudding-like dish or bread, it is plausible that some preparations could have retained hard kernel fragments (Mihesuah 2015). If it is determined that the cause of the elevated complexity values relates to nut consumption, then we have another discrepancy between indicators of diet. In this case it would not be between form and function, but rather between chemical and textural signatures. The benefit of such discrepancies is that they serve as fertile ground for gaining greater insights into questions of ancient diets.

Conclusion

Dental microwear analysis stems from an understanding of the manners by which dental surfaces change as they contact other teeth, food, and anything else introduced into the oral environment. In all, DMTA provides unique dietary insights that may or may not agree with dental morphology, the archaeological record of foods consumed, or geochemistry of oral or skeletal remains. In the end, however, it may be that DMTA provides a data source providing an essential record of diet and tooth use that may contradict earlier expectations.

REFERENCES

Ackermans, N. L. "The History of Mesowear: A Review." *Peer J* 8 (2020): e8519.

Adams, N. F., T. Gray, and M. A. Purnell. "Dietary Signals in Dental Microwear of Predatory Small Mammals Appear Unaffected by Extremes in Environmental Abrasive Load." *Palaeogeography, Palaeoclimatology, Palaeoecology* 15 (2020):109929.

Arman, S. D., T. A. A. Prowse, A. M. C. Couzens, et al. "Incorporating Intraspecific Variation into Dental Microwear Texture Analysis." *Journal of the Royal Society Interface* 16 (2019): 20180957.

Atkins, A. G., and J. H. Liu. "Toughness and the Transition Between Cutting and Rubbing in Abrasive Contacts." *Wear* 262 (2007): 146–159.

Baines, D. C., M. A. Purnell, and P. J. B. Hart. "Tooth Microwear Formation Rate in *Gasterosteus Aculeatus.*" *Journal of Fish Biology* 84 (2014): 1582–1589.

Briggs, R. V. "The Civil Cooking Pot: Hominy and the Mississippian Standard Jar in the Black Warrior Valley, Alabama." *American Antiquity* 81 (2016): 316–332.

Burgman, J. H. E., J. Leichliter, N. L. Avenant, et al. "Dental Microwear of Sympatric Rodent Species Sampled Across Habitats in Southern Africa: Implications for Environmental Influence." *Integrative Zoology* 11 (2016): 111–127.

Butler, P. M.. The Milk-Molars of Perissodactyla, with Remarks on Molar Occlusion. *Proceedings of the Zoological Society of London* 121 (1952): 777–817.

Calandra, I., and G. Merceron. "Dental Microwear Texture Analysis in Mammalian Ecology." *Mammal Review* 46 (2016): 215–228.

Calandra, I., G. Labonne, E. Schulz-Kornas, et al. "Tooth Wear as a Means to Quantify Intra-Specific Variations in Diet and Chewing Movements." *Scientific Reports* 6 (2016): 34037.

Casserly, A., R. Van Sessen, and C. Schmidt. "Determining Onset of Significant Facial Pathology Using Dental Wear and Microwear Texture Analysis: A Case Study from the Middle Archaic (~ 5,500 BP) of Indiana." *Dental Anthropology* 27 (2014): 5–7.

Cook, R. A., and M. R. Schurr. "Eating Between the Lines: Mississippian Migration and Stable Carbon Isotope Variation in Fort Ancient Populations." *American Anthropologist* 111 (2009): 344–359.

Daegling, D. J., and F. E. Grine. "Terrestrial Foraging and Dental Microwear in *Papio Ursinus.*" *Primates* 40 (1999): 559–572.

Daegling, D. J., L. C. Hua, and P. S. Ungar. "The Role of Food Stiffness in Dental Microwear Feature Formation." *Archives of Oral Biology* 71 (2016): 16–23.

Da Gloria, P., and C. W. Schmidt. "Dental Microwear Texture Analyses of the Paleoamericans of Lagoa Santa, Central-Eastern Brazil." In *Dental Wear in Evolutionary and Biocultural Contexts*. Edited by C. W. Schmidt and J. T. Watson, 243–262. Academic Press, 2020.

Delezene, L. K., M. F. Teaford, and P. S. Ungar. "Canine and Incisor Microwear in Pitheciids and Ateles Reflects Documented Patterns of Tooth Use." *American Journal of Physical Anthropology* 161 (2016): 6–25.

DeSantis, L. R. G. "Dental Microwear Textures: Reconstructing Diets of Fossil Mammals." *Surface Topography: Metrology and Properties* 4 (2016): 1–12.

DeSantis, L. R. G., B. W. Schubert, J. R. Scott, et al. "Implications of Diet for the Extinction of Saber-Toothed Cats and American Lions." *PLoS One* 7 (2012): 1–9.

DeSantis, L. R. G., A. C. Sharp, B. W. Schubert, et al. "Clarifying Relationships Between Cranial Form and Function in Tapirs, with Implications for the Dietary Ecology of Early Hominins." *Scientific Reports* 10 (2020): 1–11.

Donohue, S. L., L. R. G. DeSantis, B. W. Schubert, et al. "Was the Giant Short-Faced Bear a Hyper-Scavenger? A New Approach to the Dietary Study of Ursids Using Dental Microwear Textures." *PLoS One* 8 (2013): 1–7.

Droke, J., C. W. Schmidt, F. L. Williams, et al. "Regional Variability in Diet Between Northern European and Mediterranean Neandertals: Evidence from Dental Microwear Texture Analysis." In *Dental Wear in Evolutionary and Biocultural Contexts*. Edited by C. Schmidt and J. T. Watson, 225–241. Academic Press, 2020.

El Zaatari, S. "Occlusal Molar Microwear and the Diets of the Ipiutak and Tigara Populations (Point Hope) with Comparisons to the Aleut and Arikara." *Journal of Archaeological Science* 35 (2008): 2517–2522.

El Zaatari, S. "Occlusal Microwear Texture Analysis and the Diets of Historical/Prehistoric Hunter-Gatherers." *International Journal of Osteoarchaeology* 20 (2010): 67–87.

El Zaatari, S., and J.-J. Hublin. "Diet of Upper Paleolithic Modern Humans: Evidence from Microwear Texture Analysis." *American Journal of Physical Anthropology* 153 (2014): 570–581.

El Zaatari, S., F. E. Grine, P. S. Ungar, et al. "Ecogeographic Variation in Neandertal Dietary Habits: Evidence from Occlusal Molar Microwear Texture Analysis." *Journal of Human Evolution* 61 (2011): 411–424.

El Zaatari, S., F. E. Grine, P. S. Ungar, and J.-J. Hublin. "Neandertal Versus Modern Human Dietary Responses to Climatic Fluctuations." *PloS One* 11 (2016): e0153277.

Emerson, T. E., K. M. Hedman, and M. L. Simon. "Marginal Horticulturalists or Maize Agriculturalists? Archaeobotanical, Paleopathological, and Isotopic Evidence Relating to Langford Tradition Maize Consumption." *Midcontinental Journal of Archaeology* 30 (2005): 67–118.

Estalrrich, A., S. El Zaatari, and A. Rosas. "Dietary Reconstruction of the El Sidrón Neandertal Familial Group (Spain) in the Context of Other Neandertal and Modern Hunter-Gatherer Groups. A Molar Microwear Texture Analysis." *Journal of Human Evolution* 104 (2017): 13–22.

Feathers, J. K. "Explaining Shell-Tempered Pottery in Prehistoric Eastern North America." *Journal of Archaeological Method and Theory* 13 (2006): 89–133.

Gallego-Valle, A., L. Colominas, A. Burguet-Coca, et al. "What Is on the Menu Today? Creating a Microwear Reference Collection Through a Controlled-Food Trial to Study Feeding Management Systems of Ancient Agropastoral Societies." *Quaternary International* 557 (2020): 3–11.

Gordon, K. D. "A Study of Microwear on Chimpanzee Molars: Implications for Dental Microwear Analysis." *American Journal of Physical Anthropology* 59 (1982): 195–215.

Greenlee, D. "Dietary Variation and Prehistoric Maize Farming in the Middle Ohio Valley." In *Histories of Maize, Multidisciplinary Approaches to the Prehistory, Biogeography, Domestication, and Evolution of Maize.* Edited by J. Staller, R. H. Tykot, and B. Benz, 215–233. New York: Academic Press, 2006.

Grine, F. E. Analysis of Early Hominid Deciduous Molar Wear by Scanning Electron Microscopy: A Preliminary Report. *Proceedings of the Electron Microscopy, Society of South Africa* 7 (1977): 157–158.

Gügel, I. L., G. Grupe, and K. H. Kunzelmann. "Simulation of Dental Microwear: Characteristic Traces by Opal Phytoliths Give Clues to Ancient Human Dietary Behavior." *American Journal of Physical Anthropology* 114 (2001): 124–138.

Haupt, R. J., L. R. G. DeSantis, J. L. Green, et al. "Dental Microwear Texture as a Proxy for Diet in Xenarthrans." *Journal of Mammalogy* 94 (2013): 856–866.

Hayek, L.-A. C., R. L. Bernor, N. Solounias, et al. "Preliminary Studies of Hipparionine Horse Diet as Measured by Tooth Microwear." *Annales Zoologici Fennici* 28 (1991): 187–200.

Hedberg, C., and L. R. G. DeSantis. "Dental Microwear Texture Analysis of Extant Koalas: Clarifying Causal Agents of Microwear." *Journal of Zoology* 301 (2017): 206–214.

Henry, A. G., A. S. Brooks, and D. R. Piperno, "Microfossils in Calculus Demonstrate Consumption of Plants and Cooked Foods in Neanderthal Diets (Shanidar III, Iraq; Spy I and II, Belgium)." *Proceedings of the National Academy of Sciences* 108 (2011): 486–491.

Hoffman, J. M., D. Fraser, and M. T. Clementz. "Controlled Feeding Trials with Ungulates: A New Application of in Vivo Dental Molding to Assess the Abrasive Factors of Microwear." *Journal of Experimental Biology* 218 (2015): 1538–1547.

Holmes, G. "Dental Microwear Texture Analysis of Caborn-Welborn People in Comparison to Late Precontact and Early/Middle Woodland People." MS Thesis, Indianapolis, IN: University of Indianapolis, 2021.

Hua, L. C., E. T. Brandt, J.-F. Meullenet, et al. "Technical Note: An in Vitro Study of Dental Microwear Formation Using the BITE Master II Chewing Machine." *American Journal of Physical Anthropology* 158 (2015): 769–775.

Hua, L., J. Chen, and P. S. Ungar. "Diet Reduces the Effect of Exogenous Grit on Tooth Microwear." *Biosurface and Biotribology* 6 (2020): 48–52.

Jost, P. "Lubrication (Tribology) – A Report on the Present Position and Industry's Needs." *Department of Education and Science*, London, UK: HM Stationary Office, 1966.

Karme, A., J. Rannikko, A. Kallonen, et al. "Mechanical Modelling of Tooth Wear." *Journal of the Royal Society Interface* 13, no. 120 (2016): 1–9.

Karriger, W. M., C. W. Schmidt, and F. H. Smith. "Dental Microwear Texture Analysis of Croatian Neandertal Molars." *Paleoanthropology* (2016): 172–184. 10.4207/PA.2016.ART102.

Kay, R. F., and H. H. Covert. "True Grit: A Microwear Experiment." *American Journal of Physical Anthropology* 61 (1983): 33–38.

Kislev, M. E., D. Nadel, and I. Carmi. "Epipalaeolithic (19,000 BP) Cereal and Fruit Diet at Ohalo II, Sea of Galilee, Israel." *Review of Palaeobotany and Palynology* 73 (1992): 161–166.

Kropacheva, Y. E., S. V. Zykov, N. G. Smirnov, et al. "Dental Microwear and Mesowear of Microtus Voles Before and After Experimental Feeding of Owls." *Доклады Академии Наук* 486 (2019): 638–642.

Krueger, K. L., E. Chwa, A. S. Peterson, et al. "Technical Note: Artificial Resynthesis Technology for the Experimental Formation of Dental Microwear Textures." *American Journal of Physical Anthropology* 176 (2021): 703–712. https://doi.org/10.1002/ajpa.24395.

Kubo, M. O., and M. Fujita. "Diets of Pleistocene Insular Dwarf Deer Revealed by Dental Microwear Texture Analysis." *Palaeogeography, Palaeoclimatology, Palaeoecology* 562 (2021): 110098.

Kubo, M. O., and E. Yamada. "The Inter-Relationship between Dietary and Environmental Properties and Tooth Wear: Comparisons of Mesowear, Molar Wear Rate, and Hypsodonty Index of Extant Sika Deer Populations." *PLoS One* 9, no. 3 (2014): e90745.

Kubo, M. O., E. Yamada, T. Kubo, et al. "Dental Microwear Texture Analysis of Extant Sika Deer with Considerations on Inter-Microscope Variability and Surface Preparation Protocols." *Biosurface and Biotribology* 3 (2017): 155–165.

Leach, R. "Introduction to Surface Topography." In *Characterisation of Areal Surface Texture* Edited by R. Leach, 1–13. Berlin, Heidelberg: Springer, 2013.

Louys, J., Y. Zaim, Y. Rizal, et al. "Sumatran Orangutan Diets in the Late Pleistocene as Inferred from Dental Microwear Texture Analysis." *Quaternary International* 603 (2021): 74–81.

Lucas, P. W. *Dental Functional Morphology: How Teeth Work.* Cambridge: Cambridge University Press, 2004.

Lucas, P. W., R. Omar, K. Al-Fadhalah, et al. "Mechanisms and Causes of Wear in Tooth Enamel: Implications for Hominin Diets." *Journal of the Royal Society Interface* 10 (2013): 1–9.

Lucas, P. W., A. van Casteren, K. Al-Fadhalah, et al. "The Role of Dust, Grit and Phytoliths in Tooth Wear." *Annales Zoologici Fennici* 51 (2014): 143–152.

Maas, M. C. "A Scanning Electron-Microscopic Study of in Vitro Abrasion of Mammalian Tooth Enamel under Compressive Loads." *Archives of Oral Biology* 39 (1994): 1–11.

Mahoney, P. "Dental Microwear from Natufian Hunter-Gatherers and Early Neolithic Farmers: Comparisons Within and Between Samples." *American Journal of Physical Anthropology* 130 (2006): 308–319.

Mainland, I. L. "Dental Microwear and Diet in Domestic Sheep (*Ovis Aries*) and Goats (*Capra Hircus*): Distinguishing Grazing and Fodder-Fed Ovicaprids Using a Quantitative Analytical Approach." *Journal of Archaeological Science* 25 (1998): 1259–1271.

Merceron, G., C. Blondel, N. Brunetiere, et al. "Dental Microwear and Controlled Food Testing on Sheep: The TRIDENT Project." *Biosurface and Biotribology* 3 (2017): 174–183.

Merceron, G., G. Escarguel, J.-M. Angibault, et al. "Can Dental Microwear Textures Record Inter-Individual Dietary Variations?" *PLoS One* 5 (2010): 1–9.

Merceron, G., A. Ramdarshan, C. Blondel, et al. "Untangling the Environmental from the Dietary: Dust Does Not Matter." *Proceedings of the Royal Society B: Biological Sciences,* 283 (2016): 20161032.

Mihesuah, D. A. "Sustenance and Health Among the Five Tribes in Indian Territory, Post Removal to Statehood." *Ethnohistory* 62 (2015): 263–284.

Mihlbachler, M. C., M. Foy, and B. L. Beatty. "Surface Replication, Fidelity and Data Loss in Traditional Dental Microwear and Dental Microwear Texture Analysis." *Scientific Reports* 9 (2019): 1–13.

Mills, J. R. E. "Ideal Dental Occlusion in the Primates." *Dental Practitioner* 6 (1955): 47–61.

Müller, J., M. Clauss, D. Codron, et al. "Growth and Wear of Incisor and Cheek Teeth in Domestic Rabbits (*Oryctolagus Cuniculus*) Fed Diets of Different Abrasiveness." *Journal of Experimental Zoology. Part A, Ecological Genetics and Physiology* 321 (2014): 283–298.

Nystrom, P., J. E. Phillips-Conroy, and C. J. Jolly. "Dental Microwear in Anubis and Hybrid Baboons (*Papio Hamadryas*, Sensu Lato) Living in Awash National Park, Ethiopia." *American Journal of Physical Anthropology* 125 (2004): 279–291.

Percher, A. M., A. Romero, J. Galbany, et al. "Buccal Dental-Microwear and Dietary Ecology in a Free-Ranging Population of Mandrills (*Mandrillus Sphinx*) from Southern Gabon." *PLoS One* 12 (2017): e0186870.

Percher, A. M., G. Merceron, G. N. Akoue, et al. "Dental Microwear Textural Analysis as an Analytical Tool to Depict Individual Traits and Reconstruct the Diet of a Primate." *American Journal of Physical Anthropology* 165 (2018): 123–138.

Peters, C. R. "Electron-Optical Microscopic Study of Incipient Dental Microdamage from Experimental Seed and Bone Crushing." *American Journal of Physical Anthropology* 57 (1982): 283–301.

Piperno, D. R., E. Weiss, I. Holst, et al. "Processing of Wild Cereal Grains in the Upper Palaeolithic Revealed by Starch Grain Analysis." *Nature* 430 (2004): 670–673.

Prideaux, G. J., L. K. Ayliffe, L. R. G. DeSantis, et al. "Extinction Implications of a Chenopod Browse Diet for a Giant Pleistocene Kangaroo." *Proceedings of the National Academy of Sciences* 106 (2009): 11646–11650.

Power, R. C., D. C. Salazar-García, M. Rubini, et al. "Dental Calculus Indicates Widespread Plant Use Within the Stable Neanderthal Dietary Niche." *Journal of Human Evolution* 119 (2018): 27–41.

Purnell, M. A., and L. P. G. Darras. "3D Tooth Microwear Texture Analysis in Fishes as a Test of Dietary Hypotheses of Durophagy." *Surface Topography: Metrology and Properties* 4 (2016): 1–11.

Purnell, M. A., O. Seehausen, and F. Galis. "Quantitative Three-Dimensional Microtextural Analyses of Tooth Wear as a Tool for Dietary Discrimination in Fishes." *Journal of the Royal Society Interface* 9, no. 74 (2012): 2225–2233.

Purnell, M. A., N. Crumpton, P. G. Gill, et al. "Within-Guild Dietary Discrimination from 3-D Textural Analysis of Tooth Microwear in Insectivorous Mammals." *Journal of Zoology* 291 (2013): 249–257.

Rabenold, D., and O. M. Pearson. "Abrasive, Silica Phytoliths and the Evolution of Thick Molar Enamel in Primates, with Implications for the Diet of Paranthropus Boisei." *PLoS One* 6 (2011): 1–11.

Rabenold, D., and O. M. Pearson. "Scratching the Surface: A Critique of Lucas et al. (2013)'s Conclusion That Phytoliths Do Not Abrade Enamel." *Journal of Human Evolution* 74 (2014): 130–133.

Ramdarshan, A., C. Blondel, D. Gautier, et al. "Overcoming Sampling Issues in Dental Tribology: Insights from an Experimentation on Sheep." *Palaeontologia Electronica* 20 (2017): 1–19.

Richards, M. P., P. B. Pettitt, E. Trinkaus, et al. "Neanderthal diet at Vindija and Neanderthal predation: The evidence from stable isotopes." *Proceedings of the National Academy of Sciences.* 97 (2000):7663-6.

Rivals, F., and G. M. Semprebon. "A Comparison of the Dietary Habits of a Large Sample of the Pleistocene Pronghorn *Stockoceros Onusrosagris* from the Papago Springs Cave in Arizona to the Modern *Antilocapra Americana*." *Journal of Vertebrate Paleontology* 26 (2006): 495–500.

Robson, S. K., and W. G. Young. "Tooth Microwear of *Thylacinus-Cynocephalus* and *Sarcophilus-harrisii*." *Journal of Dental Research* 65 (1986): 483–483.

Rodriguez-Rojas, F., O. Borrero-Lopez, P. J. Constantino, et al. "Phytoliths Can Cause Tooth Wear." *Journal of the Royal Society Interface* 17 (2020): 20200613.

Romero, A., J. Galbany, J. De Juan, et al. "Brief Communication: Short- and Long-Term in Vivo Human Buccal–Dental Microwear Turnover." *American Journal of Physical Anthropology* 148 (2012): 467–472.

Ryan, A. S. "Wear Striation Direction on Primate Teeth: A Scanning Electron Microscope Examination." *American Journal of Physical Anthropology* 50 (1979): 155–167.

Safire, W. "On Language: Inside Baseball." *New York Times Magazine*, June 19, 1988.

Sanson, G. D., S. A. Kerr, and K. A. Gross. "Do Silica Phytoliths Really Wear Mammalian Teeth?" *Journal of Archaeological Science* 34 (2007): 526–531.

Schmidt, C. W. "Dental Microwear Analysis of Extinct Flat-Headed Peccary (*Platygonus Compressus*) from Southern Indiana." *Proceedings of the Indiana Academy of Science* 117 (2008): 95–106.

Schmidt, C. W. "On the Relationship of Dental Microwear to Dental Macrowear." *American Journal of Physical Anthropology* 142 (2010): 67–73.

Schmidt, C. W. *Long "On" the Tooth: Dental Evidence of Diet.* London: Academic Press, 2021.

Schmidt, C. W., J. J. Beach, J. I. McKinley, and J. T. Eng. "Distinguishing Dietary Indicators of Pastoralists and Agriculturists via Dental Microwear Texture Analysis." *Surface Topography: Metrology and Properties* 4 (2016): 014008.

Schmidt, C. W., A. Remy, R. V. Sessen, et al. "Dental Microwear Texture Analysis of *Homo sapiens*: Foragers, Farmers, and Pastoralists." *American Journal of Physical Anthropology* 169 (2019): 207–226.

Schmidt, C. W., S. El Zaatari, and R. Van Sessen. "Dental Microwear Texture Analysis in Bioarchaeology." In *Dental Wear in Evolutionary and Biocultural Contexts.* Edited by C. W. Schmidt and J. T. Watson, 143–168. London: Academic Press, 2020.

Schubert, B. W., P. S. Ungar, and L. R. G. DeSantis. "Carnassial Microwear and Dietary Behaviour in Large Carnivorans." *Journal of Zoology* 280 (2010): 257–263.

Schulz, E., I. Calandra, and T. M. Kaiser, "Applying Tribology to Teeth of Hoofed Mammals." *Scanning* 32 (2010): 162–182. doi: 10.1002/sca.20181.

Schulz, E., I. Calandra, and T. M. Kaiser. "Feeding Ecology and Chewing Mechanics in Hoofed Mammals: 3D Tribology of Enamel Wear." *Wear* 300 (2013): 169–179.

Schulz-Kornas, E., D. E. Winkler, M. Clauss, et al. "Everything Matters: Molar Microwear Texture in Goats (*Capra Aegagrus Hircus*) Fed Diets of Different Abrasiveness." *Palaeogeography, Palaeoclimatology, Palaeoecology* 552 (2020): 109783.

Scott, J. R. "Dental Microwear Texture Analysis of Extant African Bovidae." *Mammalia* 76 (2012): 157–174.

Scott, J. R., L. R. Godfrey, W. L. Jungers, et al. "Dental Microwear Texture Analysis of Two Families of Subfossil Lemurs from Madagascar." *Journal of Human Evolution* 56 (2009): 405–416.

Scott, R. S., P. S. Ungar, T. S. Bergstrom, et al. "Dental Microwear Texture Analysis Shows Within-Species Diet Variability in Fossil Hominins." *Nature* 436 (2005): 693–695.

Scott, R. S., P. S. Ungar, T. S. Bergstrom, et al. "Dental Microwear Texture Analysis: Technical Considerations." *Journal of Human Evolution* 51 (2006): 339–349.

Scott, R. S., M. F. Teaford, and P. S. Ungar. "Dental Microwear Texture and Anthropoid Diets." *American Journal of Physical Anthropology* 147 (2012): 551–579.

Shoemaker, A. C., M. I. J. Davies, and H. L. Moore. "Back to the Grindstone? The Archaeological Potential of Grinding-Stone Studies in Africa with Reference to Contemporary Grinding Practices in Marakwet, Northwest Kenya." *African Archaeological Review* 34 (2017): 415–435.

Silcox, M. T., and M. F. Teaford. "The Diet of Worms: An Analysis of Mole Dental Microwear." *Journal of Mammalogy* 83 (2002): 804–814.

Simpson, G. G. "Are *Dromatherium* and *Microconodon* Mammals?" *Science* 63 (1926): 548–549.

Simpson, G. G. "Critique of a New Theory of Mammalian Dental Evolution." *Journal of Dental Research* 13 (1933): 261–272.

Solounias, N., and L.-A. Hayek. "New Methods of Tooth Microwear Analysis and Application to Dietary Determination of Two Extinct Antelopes." *Journal of Zoology* 229 (1993): 421–445.

Strait, S. G. "Molar Microwear in Extant Small-Bodied Faunivorous Mammals: An Analysis of Feature Density and Pit Frequency." *American Journal of Physical Anthropology* 92 (1993): 63–79.

Stuhlträger, J., E. Schulz-Kornas, R. M. Wittig, et al. "Ontogenetic Dietary Shifts and Microscopic Tooth Wear in Western Chimpanzees." *Frontiers in Ecology and Evolution* 7 (2019): 298.

Stynder, D. D., P. S. Ungar, J. R. Scott, et al. "A Dental Microwear Texture Analysis of the Mio-Pliocene Hyaenids from Langebaanweg, South Africa." *Acta Palaeontologica Polonica* 57 (2012): 485–496.

Tanis, B. P., L. R. G. DeSantis, and R. C. Terry. "Dental Microwear Textures across Cheek Teeth in Canids: Implications for Dietary Studies of Extant and Extinct Canids." *Palaeogeography, Palaeoclimatology, Palaeoecology* 508 (2018): 129–138.

Teaford, M. F., and K. E. Glander. "Dental Microwear and Diet in a Wild Population of Mantled Howling Monkeys (*Alouatta Palliata*)." In *Adaptive Radiations of Neotropical Primates.* Edited by M. A. Norconk, A. L. Rosenberger, and P. A. Garber, 433–449. New York: Plenum Press, 1996.

Teaford, M. F., and J. D. Lytle. "Brief Communication: Diet-Induced Changes in Rates of Human Tooth Microwear: A Case Study Involving Stone-Ground Maize." *American Journal of Physical Anthropology* 100 (1996): 143–147.

Teaford, M. F., and O. J. Oyen. "In Vivo and in Vitro Turnover in Dental Microwear." *American Journal of Physical Anthropology* 80 (1989a): 447–460.

Teaford, M. F., and O. J. Oyen. "Differences in the Rate of Molar Wear Between Monkeys Raised on Different Diets." *Journal of Dental Research* 68 (1989b): 1513–1518.

Teaford, M. F., and J. G. Robinson. "Seasonal or Ecological Differences in Diet and Molar Microwear in *Cebus Nigrovittatus*." *American Journal of Physical Anthropology* 80 (1989): 391–401.

Teaford, M. F., and J. A. Runestad. "Dental Microwear and Diet in Venezuelan Primates." *American Journal of Physical Anthropology* 88 (1992): 347–364.

Teaford, M. F., and C. A. Tylenda. "A New Approach to the Study of Tooth Wear." *Journal of Dental Research* 70 (1991): 204–207.

Teaford, M. F., and P. S. Ungar. "Dental Adaptations of African Apes." In *Handbook of Paleoanthropology*, 2nd edn. Edited by W. Henke and I. Tattersall, 1465–1493. Berlin, Heidelberg: Springer, 2014.

Teaford, M. F., and A. Walker. "Quantitative Differences in Dental Microwear Between Primate Species with Different Diets and a Comment on the Presumed Diet of *Sivapithecus*." *American Journal of Physical Anthropology* 64 (1984): 191–200.

Teaford, M. F., P. S. Ungar, A. B. Taylor, et al. "In Vivo Rates of Dental Microwear Formation in Laboratory Primates Fed Different Food Items." *Biosurface and Biotribology* 3, no. 4 (2017): 166–173.

Teaford, M. F., P. S. Ungar, A. B. Taylor, et al. "The Dental Microwear of Hard-Object Feeding in Laboratory *Sapajus Apella* and Its Implications for Dental Microwear Formation." *American Journal of Physical Anthropology* 171 (2020): 439–455.

Teaford, M. F., C. F. Ross, P. S. Ungar, et al. "Grit Your Teeth and Chew Your Food: Implications of Food Material Properties and Abrasives for Rates of Dental Microwear Formation in Laboratory *Sapajus Apella* (Primates)." *Palaeogeography, Palaeoclimatology, Palaeoecology* 583 (2021): 110644.

Ungar, P. S. "Tooth Form and Function: Insights into Adaptation Through the Analysis of Dental Microwear." In *Frontiers of Oral Biology*. Edited by T. Koppe, G. Meyer, and K. W. Alt. 38–43. Basel: KARGER, 2009.

Ungar, P. S. *Evolution's Bite: A Story of Teeth, Diet, and Human Origins*, 110–139. Princeton: Princeton University Press, 2017.

Ungar, P. S., G. Merceron, and R. S. Scott. "Dental Microwear Texture Analysis of Varswater Bovids and Early Pliocene Paleoenvironments of Langebaanweg, Western Cape Province, South Africa." *Journal of Mammalian Evolution* 14 (2007): 163–181.

Ungar, P. S., P. S. Scott, J. R. Scott, et al. "Dental Microwear Analysis: Historical Perspectives and New Approaches." In *Technique and Application in Dental Anthropology*. Edited by J. D. Irish and G. C. Nelson, 389–425. Cambridge: Cambridge University Press, 2008.

Ungar, P. S., J. R. Scott, B. W. Schubert, et al. "Carnivoran Dental Microwear Textures: Comparability of Carnassial Facets and Functional Differentiation of Postcanine Teeth." *Mammalia* 74 (2010): 219–224.

Ungar, P. S., K. L. Krueger, R. J. Blumenschine, et al. "Dental Microwear Texture Analysis of Hominins Recovered by the Olduvai Landscape Paleoanthropology Project, 1995–2007." *Journal of Human Evolution* 63 (2012): 429–437.

Ungar, P. S., J. R. Scott, and C. M. Steininger. "Dental Microwear Differences Between Eastern and Southern African Fossil Bovids and Hominins." *South African Journal of Science* 112 (2016): 1–5.

Ungar, P. S., N. A. Sokolova, J. Purifoy, et al. "Assessing Molar Wear in Narrow-Headed Voles as a Proxy for Diet and Habitat in a Changing Arctic." *Mammalian Biology* 101 (2021): 137–151.

van Casteren, A., D. S. Strait, M. V. Swain, et al. "Hard Plant Tissues Do Not Contribute Meaningfully to Dental Microwear: Evolutionary Implications." *Scientific Reports* 10 (2020): 1–9.

Van Valkenburgh, B., M. F. Teaford, and A. Walker. "Molar Microwear and Diet in Large Carnivores: Inferences Concerning Diet in the Sabretooth Cat, Smilodon Fatalis." *Journal of Zoology* 222 (1990): 319–340.

Ward, J., and I. L. Mainland. "Microwear in Modern Rooting and Stall-Fed Pigs: The Potential of Dental Microwear Analysis for Exploring Pig Diet and Management in the Past." *Environmental Archaeology* 4 (1999): 25–32.

Weyrich, L. S., S. Duchene, J. Soubrier, et al. "Neanderthal Behaviour, Diet, and Disease Inferred from Ancient DNA in Dental Calculus." *Nature* 544 (2017): 357–361.

White, J. M., L. R. G. DeSantis, A. R. Evans, et al. "A Panda-like Diprotodontid? Assessing the Diet of *Hulitherium Tomasettii* Using Dental Complexity (Orientation Patch Count Rotated) and Dental Microwear Texture Analysis." *Palaeogeography, Palaeoclimatology, Palaeoecology* 583 (2021): 110675.

Williams, F. L., J. L. Droke, C. W. Schmidt, et al. "Dental Microwear Texture Analysis of Neandertals from Hortus Cave, France." *Comptes Rendus Palevol* 17 (2018): 545–556.

Williams, F. L., C. W. Schmidt, J. L. Droke, et al. "Dietary Reconstruction of Spy I Using Dental Microwear Texture Analysis." *Comptes Rendus Palevol* 18 (2019): 1083–1094.

Williams, F. L., C. W. Schmidt, J. L. Droke, et al. "Reconstructing the Diet of Kůlna 1 from the Moravian Karst (Czech Republic)." *Journal of Paleolithic Archaeology* 4 (2021): 1–23.

Winkler, D. E., E. Schulz-Kornas, T. M. Kaiser, et al. "Dental Microwear Texture Reflects Dietary Tendencies in Extant Lepidosauria Despite Their Limited Use of Oral Food Processing." *Proceedings of the Royal Society B: Biological Sciences* 286 (2019): 20190544.

Xia, J., J. Zheng, D. Huang, et al. "New Model to Explain Tooth Wear with Implications for Microwear Formation and Diet Reconstruction." *Proceedings of the National Academy of Sciences* 112 (2015): 10669–10672.

Xia, Y., A. Ren, and M. K. Pugach. "Truncated Amelogenin and LRAP Transgenes Improve Amelx Null Mouse Enamel." *Matrix Biology* 52–54 (2016): 198–206.

Xia, J., Z. R. Tian, L. Hua, et al. "Enamel Crystallite Strength and Wear: Nanoscale Responses of Teeth to Chewing Loads." *Journal of the Royal Society Interface* 14 (2017): 1–8.

Xia, J., Z. Zhou, L. Qian, et al. "Comment on van Casteren et al. (2018): Cofter Metallic Spheres Do Abrade Harder Enamel." *Royal Society Open Science* 5 (2018): 181376.

Zhou, Z.-R., H.-Y. Yu, J. Zheng, et al. *Dental Biotribology*. New York: Springer, 2013.

35 Primate Locomotion: A Comparative and Developmental Perspective

Michael C. Granatosky and Jesse W. Young

INTRODUCTION

The Primates have a long evolutionary history associated with the arboreal milieu (Cartmill 1985, 1992; Szalay 1968). While such a statement is almost cliché, the importance cannot be understated. Most aspects of primate postcranial anatomy and locomotion are either a direct response to the challenges of arboreality or phylogenetic holdovers from an arboreal ancestor (Cartmill 1992; Chester et al. 2017). Arboreal environments can be generalized as unpredictable. To effectively move through this environment (i.e., *not fall*) primates must navigate across substrates of varying diameter, compliance, orientation, and gap-distance (Preuschoft 2002). Accordingly, primates have evolved several anatomical and neuromuscular adaptations to mitigate these challenges (Gebo 2010). Here, we review these adaptations and discuss current knowledge of primate locomotor biomechanics and behavior. This chapter is not meant to be exhaustive; our goal rather is to excite a new generation of biological anthropologists to the joys of primate locomotion.

PRIMATE LOCOMOTOR ONTOGENY

Field and laboratory investigations of primate locomotion have traditionally been limited to observations of adult animals. To some degree, this focus on adults makes sense. Only adults can reproduce and pass genetic material on to the next generation (i.e., maintain evolutionary fitness). Additionally, limiting research to individuals of a single age class reduces sample variability, thus increasing the likelihood of observing broad-scale

A Companion to Biological Anthropology, Second Edition. Edited by Clark Spencer Larsen.
© 2023 John Wiley & Sons Ltd. Published 2023 by John Wiley & Sons Ltd.

differences among species. However, recent reviews have highlighted primate locomotor development as an important locus of investigation unto itself (Bezanson 2017; Young and Shapiro 2018). Studies of primate locomotor development can contribute to our understanding of primate evolution and adaptation in two ways. First, locomotor development is a critical component of primate life history variation. The pace at which a primate moves from a being dependent, nonmobile infant to an ecologically independent juvenile influences how quickly it can forage for itself (i.e., wean), escape predation unaided, and participate in larger group social interactions (Smith et al. 2020; Young and Shapiro 2018). In fact, because (by definition) infants and juveniles have yet to reach reproductive age, immaturity could be viewed as something of an evolutionary bottleneck; an immature primate that falls to its death or is captured by a predator before reaching puberty will never pass on genetic material. Any functional aspect of ontogeny that serves to increase juvenile survivability – including locomotor behaviors – should therefore experience strong selective pressures for improved performance. Moreover, because nonmobile primate infants must depend on their mothers or other caregivers for transport, the pace of locomotor development also has important ramifications for the energy budgets and fitness of adult members of the group (Altmann and Samuels 1992; Gursky 2015).

Second, the infant/juvenile period is a time of rapid morphological change that takes place alongside equally pronounced changes in locomotor behaviors. Anyone who has ever watched a human toddler struggle to run on relatively short limbs, or watched older children effortlessly glide across playground equipment that adults would hesitate to even climb, knows how much the biomechanical properties of changing bodies can influence locomotor development. As such, careful study growth and locomotor ontogeny offers a "natural laboratory" in which to investigate how targeted changes in anatomy (i.e., relative limb length, center of mass position, or overall body mass) dictate which locomotor behaviors are optimal, or even possible (Doran 1992; Shapiro and Raichlen 2006; Shapiro et al. 2014; Young and Shapiro 2018). In the sections below, we discuss several examples of how studies of primate locomotor ontogeny have contributed to our understanding of primate biology and adaptation.

MAJOR LOCOMOTOR MODES

It is often asserted that primates display the highest locomotor diversity compared to any other mammalian group (Vilensky and Larson 1989). However, quantitative analyses of locomotor diversity reveal that primates display no greater locomotor diversity than other arboreal lineages (Granatosky 2018). Of the 42 total locomotor modes that have been reported across primates, quadrupedalism, climbing, suspension, leaping, and bipedalism account for ~90 percent of the locomotor behaviors utilized (Granatosky 2018; Figure 35.1). With these considerations in mind, and for purposes of expediency, we will limit our discussion to these five most common locomotor modes.

Quadrupedalism

Quadrupedal walking in primates is unusual compared to most other mammals, due to a trio of gait characteristics (Granatosky 2020). Perhaps most noticeable are the extended forelimbs at touchdown (Figure 35.2). Such a posture increases stride length, in turn reducing the number of strides needed to travel a given distance and reducing branch movement (Demes et al. 1990). Second, primates walk using a diagonal sequence gait (Cartmill et al. 2002; Hildebrand 1967; Wimberly et al. 2021) where hindlimb footfalls are

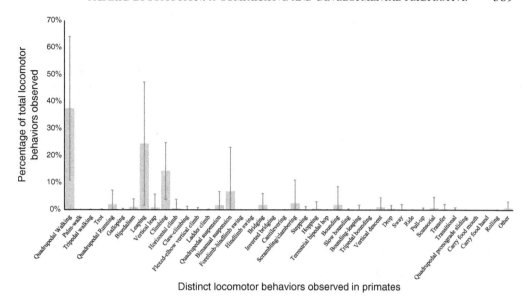

Figure 35.1 Bar plots (mean ± standard deviation) of percentages of various locomotor behaviors (42 distinct locomotor modes reported) observed across Primates (157 published studies; 94 species) (Granatosky 2018). Quadrupedalism (walking and running), leaping, climbing, suspensory (below branch quadrupedalism and bimanual suspension), and bipedalism account for ~ 90 percent of the locomotor behaviors utilized by species across the order.

Figure 35.2 Quadrupedal locomotion, (A) arboreal or (B) terrestrial, represents the most common locomotor mode observed in Primates. Gorillas and chimpanzees use a specialized form of quadrupedal locomotion referred to as (C) knuckle-walking. Images were made available by: (A and B) William Warby, CC BY 2.0, https://creativecommons.org/licenses/by/2.0, via Wikimedia Commons; and (C) Soham Banerjee, CC BY 2.0, https://creativecommons.org/licenses/by/2.0, via Wikimedia Commons.

followed by forelimb footfalls on the opposite side of the body (such that contacts proceed "diagonally" beneath the body). In contrast, most other mammals use lateral sequence gaits where hindlimb footfalls are followed by forelimb footfalls on the same side of the body (such that contacts proceed laterally beneath the body). Cartmill et al. (2002) showed that diagonal sequence gaits improve stability when moving on narrow, precarious arboreal supports. Third, unlike most other mammals, primates demonstrate hindlimb-biased weight support, carrying the majority of body weight on their hindlimbs during locomotion (Demes et al. 1994). Hindlimb dominance can be achieved in several ways, including an active process of using hindlimb muscles to "lift" the anterior body (Reynolds 1985a) or changes in the position of the limbs relative to the center of mass (Raichlen et al. 2009;

Young 2012). Shifting body weight on to the hindlimbs allows primates to reduce loads on their highly mobile, but unstable, forelimb joints and "test" the stability of supports prior to committing the entirety of their mass (Cartmill et al. 2002). Such a weight shift has been hypothesized as an evolutionary precursor to bipedalism (Reynolds 1985a, 1985b).

Quadrupedal primates have a generalized anatomy with grasping hands and feet, fore-limbs and hindlimbs of generally of equal lengths (i.e., intermembral index ~ 100 percent, where the intermembral index is equal to the forelimb length expressed as a percentage of hindlimb length), and a narrow, cylindrical thorax (Fleagle 2013). Compared to arboreal species, terrestrial quadrupedal primates have relatively longer limbs, shorter, more robust digits, cranially curved ulnae with large olecranon processes, restricted joint mobility, and reduced tail lengths (Fleagle 2013; Milne and Granatosky 2021).

The African apes demonstrate a specialized form of quadrupedal locomotion referred to as knuckle-walking (Tuttle 1967). During knuckle-walking, the proximal phalanges and palms are elevated above the substrate, and weight is borne by the intermediate phalanges and proximal phalangeal heads. The metacarpo-phalangeal joints are maintained in a near-neutral position (i.e., ~180°) to a slightly hyper-extended position (Tuttle 1967). A dorsal ridge on the distal radius is thought to reduce muscular stabilization of the wrist during the stance phase (Richmond et al. 2001; Susman 1979). Knuckle-walking is believed to have evolved as a consequence of subjecting an animal adapted to climbing/suspensory locomotion to the heightened forces of terrestrial movement (Tuttle 1967).

The quadrupedal gait kinematics of immature primates are quite variable compared to adults. In some ways, infant primate gait kinematics more closely resemble those of nonprimate mammals, rather than following the modal patterns of adult primates. For instance, young primates frequently use lateral sequence gaits and are initially forelimb dominant in weight support (Rollinson and Martin 1981; Young 2012; Young and Shapiro 2018). In both cases, this ephemeral use of "aberrant" gait kinematics appears to be associated with allometric changes in relative limb length, whole-body center of mass position, and joint postures – illustrating how primate locomotor development can serve as a "natural experiment" through which to investigate the proximate determinants of kinematic variation.

High-Speed Quadrupedalism in Primates: The Neglected Gaits

Recent work has also highlighted some unusual aspects of primate high-speed quadrupedalism. Quadrupedal primates generally walk at the slowest speeds and use gallops or bounds at the highest speeds. However, in the "transitional" zone between walks and gallops/bounds, primates avoid the use of running trots that are characteristic of most other mammals (Hildebrand 1967). Running trots tend to be high-impact "bouncy" gaits, potentially upsetting arboreal stability and causing musculoskeletal injury (O'Neill and Schmitt 2012). To avoid such loads, primates instead use ambles or canters, gaits that avoid the whole-body aerial phases characteristic of running trots, thereby mitigating loading forces (Schmitt et al. 2006).

Leaping

Whereas larger primates span gaps between supports by bridging or suspensory locomotion, smaller primates tend to cross such gaps by leaping (Figure 35.3). Leaping is a ballistic activity: once an animal departs the launching support, how far it travels is solely dependent on the animal's velocity at launching (Napier and Walker 1967). Simply put, to leap high

(A)   (B)

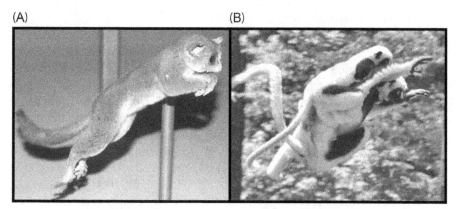

Figure 35.3 Musculoskeletal traits associated with leaping serve to maximize force production or take-off distance prior to launching, thus maximizing take-off velocity. Both (A) small-bodied and (B) large-bodied leapers have elongated hindlimbs and hypertrophied hindlimb extensor muscula-ture. The smallest, most derived leaping species (e.g., galagids: A) further increase hindlimb length by dramatically elongating the proximal tarsal bones of the foot. Images were made available by: (A) David J. Stang, CC BY-SA 4.0, https://creativecommons.org/licenses/by-sa/4.0, via Wikime-dia Commons; and (B) David Haring, Duke Lemur Center, permission for use granted to MCG.

or far an animal must maximally accelerate its center of mass prior to launch, either by exert-ing high forces or undergoing large center of mass excursions during the take-off period. Anatomical adaptations to leaping to primates can thus be understood as biomechanical means of increasing take-off force or take-off distance (Napier and Walker 1967).

Musculoskeletal traits associated with high-force production in leaping primates include hypertrophied extensor muscles (particularly at the knee and ankle; Demes et al. 1998), with a high percentage of Type II "fast" muscle fibers, facilitating powerful high-speed con-tractions to extend the hindlimb joints (Sickles and Pinkstaff 1981a, 1981b). Additionally, primate leapers often have anteroposteriorly deep femoral condyles, increasing the mechanical advantage (i.e., leverage) of the powerful quadriceps muscle. Chief among the leaping traits associated with increased center of mass displacement are long hindlimbs (Connour et al. 2000). The smallest, most derived leaping species further increase hindlimb length by dramatically elongating the proximal tarsal bones of the foot. Second, unlike at the knee joint, the hip and ankle joints of leaping primates typically provide low mechanical advantage for extensor muscles (Anemone 1993). Though this may seem counter-intuitive, low joint mechanical advantage is akin to a high gear in a wheeled vehicle, maximizing linear displacement but requiring a relatively high input force to generate the torque required to move the joint. Finally, the hindlimb joint surfaces of leaping primates are often relatively large and highly curved (Dagosto 1988; Yapuncich and Boyer 2014). These expanded joint surfaces serve two purposes. First, they increase the angular excursion at the joint, further increasing displacement for a given muscle contraction. Second, expanded joint surfaces relieve the articular stresses during the launching and landing phases of the leap.

Because leaping requires both high force production and high precision (particularly dur-ing landing), leaping behaviors tend to develop relatively late during primate ontogeny. For instance, sifakas, galagos, and tarsiers – all of whom are committed, highly specialized vertical clingers and leapers as adults – are primarily quadrupedal walkers and climbers dur-ing the first several months of life, and arboreal leaping is frequently the last locomotor skill to be mastered (Smith et al. 2020).

Suspensory Locomotion

Suspensory locomotion is any form of forward progression in which the animal's center of mass is positioned below the substrate (Cartmill 1985; Fujiwara et al. 2011; Granatosky et al. 2016; see Figure 35.4). These behaviors are often discussed with specific references to the hominoids, atelines, and to some extent the Asian colobines (Byron et al. 2017; Fleagle 1974; Granatosky 2020). However, it should be noted that all primates can, and do, engage in suspensory locomotion, although some lineages emphasize these behaviors more effectively, or for longer periods of time (Mittermeier and Fleagle 1976; Stern 1975). For most, suspensory locomotion brings to mind images of arm-swinging (i.e., brachiation), where the animal hanging below a branch and the forelimbs provide the entirety of weight support and propulsion (Bertram 2004; Byron et al. 2017; Chang et al. 2000; see Figure 35.4B). Arm-swinging may involve the use of the tail in the atelines (Schmitt et al. 2005). The morphology of arm-swinging primates has been studied extensively, and are often cited as a functional suite of characteristics to improve efficient pendular locomotion (Byron et al. 2017; Larson 1998). Arm-swinging primates have long, curved digits, mobile wrist, shoulder, hip, and ankle joints, a short olecranon process, relatively longer forelimbs than hindlimbs (i.e., intermembral index > 100 percent), a broad, barrel-shaped thorax with a dorsally positioned scapula, and a short, stable lumbar region (Byron et al. 2017; Erikson 1963; Fleagle 2013; Gebo 2014; Larson 1998; Milne and Granatosky 2021).

The fluid, swinging motion observed when brachiators move below branches naturally recalls the oscillations of a pendulum and the repeated interchange of potential and kinetic energy (Byron et al. 2017; Fleagle 1974; Schmitt et al. 2005). As such, it is tempting to assert that arm-swinging primates use natural pendular movement to reduce energetic expenditure necessary to travel (Bertram 2004; Chang et al. 2000; Fleagle 1974). Whereas

(A)   (B)   (C)

Figure 35.4 Suspensory locomotion in primates includes both (A) below-branch quadrupedalism and (B) arm-swinging (i.e., brachiation). Primates are the only animal order that move using arm-swinging. Several studies of catarrhine primates have repeatedly shown that infants and juveniles more frequently engage in suspensory locomotion than adults (C). This ontogenetic shift is especially prevalent in the African apes. Images were made available by: (A) David Haring, Duke Lemur Center, permission for use granted to MCG; (B) Bernard DuPont, CC BY-SA 2.0, https://creativecommons.org/licenses/by-sa/2.0, via Wikimedia Commons; and (C) Charles J. Sharp, CC BY-SA 4.0, https://creativecommons.org/licenses/by-sa/4.0, via Wikimedia Commons.

some studies have demonstrated that arm-swinging primates can match the expectations of a simple pendulum, this is only true during very slow speeds and continuous-contact locomotion (Byron et al. 2017; Chang et al. 2000). Simple pendular locomotion is restrictive and to optimize the energetic expenditure animals must limit themselves to a narrow range of stride frequency and length. Arboreal environments are discontinuous and characterized by supports of uneven distances. As such, brachiators often sacrifice energetic efficiency for flexibility when locomoting (Byron et al. 2017; Chang et al. 2000). The highly acrobatic gibbons take such deviations from pendular movement to an extreme by adopting a ricochetal brachiation in which a full-body aerial phase is observed (Bertram 2004; Chang et al. 2000).

In addition to specialized arm-swinging locomotion, many primates – including lorises, orangutans, platyrrhine monkeys, and extinct sloth lemurs – utilize a form of suspensory movement called below-branch quadrupedalism, in which the torso is maintained in a pronograde position and the fore- and hindlimbs are loaded in tension (Granatosky and Schmitt 2019; see Figure 35.4A). Compared to arm-swinging, no specific anatomical modifications are required to adopt below-branch quadrupedalism beyond the ability to flex the digits into a functional hook (Fujiwara et al. 2011). Specialized below-branch quadrupeds also have increased forelimb flexor mass (Fujiwara et al. 2011), commensurate with the use of the forelimb as the primary weight bearing and propulsive limb (Granatosky and Schmitt 2019). Such a finding has led some to suggest that below-branch quadrupedalism served as a locomotor precursor prior to the evolution of more specialized bimanual suspensory behaviors (Byron et al. 2017; Granatosky and Schmitt 2019).

Several studies of catarrhine primates have repeatedly shown that infants and juveniles more frequently engage in suspensory locomotion than adults. The transition away from predominantly forelimb-dominated suspensory locomotion toward arboreal and terrestrial quadrupedalism is particularly dramatic in the African apes (Doran 1992, 1997; Sarringhaus et al. 2014). For instance, in a fine-grained analysis of the ontogeny of locomotion in common chimpanzees (*Pan troglodytes*) in Uganda, Sarringhaus et al. (2014) found that the incidence of suspensory locomotion declined 10-fold between infants and juveniles, alongside a four-fold increase in the incidence of quadrupedalism. Similar ontogenetic trajectories have been observed in bonobos (Doran 1992) and mountain gorillas (Doran 1997). Though less dramatic, developmental decreases in suspensory locomotion have also been observed in cercopithecoid monkeys (Druelle et al. 2018; Workman and Covert 2005; Zhu et al. 2015). The increased incidence of suspensory locomotion among young primates is probably due to a combination of smaller body size and relatively longer forelimbs early in life (i.e., in most primates, the intermembral index decreases during development; see Smith et al. 2020).

Climbing and Descent

As moving in a three-dimensional environment involves the vertical use of space, the ability to climb, and accordingly descend, is essential (Fleagle 1976; Fleagle et al. 1981; Preuschoft 2002). Climbing is ubiquitous in primates and even terrestrially specialized species will often climb rocky outcrops or trees to increase foraging potential and avoid terrestrial predators (Granatosky 2018; Preuschoft 2002). Whereas the importance of climbing to primates is well recognized, there are numerous and often conflicting opinions about what truly constitutes the biomechanical necessities of ascending arboreal substrates. Preuschoft (2002) provided a comprehensive perspective on the issue, specifically aiming to describe the biomechanical necessities of climbing and moving on thin arboreal supports.

First, because climbing engenders force components parallel to the substrate, primates must use their prehensile hands and feet to create the high grasping forces required to increase friction and maintain adhesion (Cartmill 1985; Preuschoft 2002). Similarly, many species also apply medially directed limb forces that further aid the ability to grasp the support between limbs (Granatosky and Schmitt 2017). The South American callitrichids and some strepsirrhines have "re-evolved" functional claws to increase adhesion on arboreal supports (Preuschoft 2002). Second, climbing creates a gravitational torque that could pitch the animal away from the support (Cartmill 1985; Fleagle 1976; Fleagle et al. 1981). To prevent falling, climbing animals must have at least one limb positioned cranial to the center of mass that pulls the body toward the support and another limb caudal to the center of mass that pushes. To gain height, both fore- and hindlimbs produce a net propulsive function, whereas the hindlimb serves as the primary weight support (Hanna et al. 2017).

Generally, primates utilize two distinct forms of climbing. The first involves the primate wrapping its forelimbs around the support while the hindlimbs are flexed and the foot is held in a dorsiflexed position. This is most commonly observed among the callitrichids, tarsiers, or in situations where the diameter of the support is larger than the diameter of the body (Figure 35.5A). Progression is achieved by an asymmetrical bounding-like gait in which as the hindlimbs are extending the forelimbs are quickly swung upwards synchronously. Once the forelimbs are firmly anchored, the hindlimbs swing upwards (Nyakatura

(A)   (B)

Figure 35.5 Climbing is ubiquitous across primates. In (A) small-bodied species, or when the diameter of substrate is larger than the size of the animal, the forelimbs and hindlimbs are wrapped around the support, and progression is achieved by an asymmetrical bounding-like gait. The second form of climbing (B) is a symmetrical gait common on small-diameter substrates and in the hominoids. While most species use their grasping hands and feet in inverted positions to maintain appropriate grip (A), many climbing catarrhines, including humans, use extreme dorsiflexed angle positions to walk with the sole of the foot contacting the support (B). Images were made available by: (A) Kok Leng Yeo, CC BY 2.0, https://creativecommons.org/licenses/by/2.0, via Wikimedia Commons, and (B) Abhishek Singh, CC BY-SA 2.0, https://creativecommons.org/licenses/by-sa/2.0, via Wikimedia Commons.

et al. 2008). The second form of climbing is a symmetrical gait most commonly observed on small-diameter substrates and in the hominoids. However, compared to quadrupedal locomotion (see above) lateral sequence diagonal couplet gaits are most common (Granatosky et al. 2019). While most species use their grasping hands and feet in inverted positions to maintain an appropriate grip, many climbing catarrhines, including humans, use extreme dorsiflexed angle positions to walk with the sole of the foot contacting the support (Isler 2005; Venkataraman et al. 2013).

Studies of primate locomotion often ignore that "what goes up must come down" (Perchalski 2021). Descent in primates is likely to be as common as climbing behaviors, but stark disparity in reported percentages of ascent versus descent probably indicates that such movement is dismissed in studies of positional behavior (Granatosky 2018; see Figure 35.1). Perchalski (2021) demonstrated that strategies for descending substrates vary considerably across species, with small-bodied species typically using head-first descent in all cases, whereas species > 1 kg vary substantially in the type of descending behavior they employ. Perchalski's (2021) study was limited to strepsirrhines, and further work is needed to identify broad descent strategies across primates.

Bipedalism

Movement using only the hindlimbs for support and progression has been observed in many non-human primates. However, some species are more adept than others (Granatosky 2018, 2020). When moving terrestrially, sifakas adopt a bipedal gallop in which the hindlimbs produce a sideways hopping movement and the forelimbs are held up for balance (Figure 35.6A), a gait observed in no other mammal (Wunderlich et al. 2014). Bipedalism in other nonhuman primates is more facultative in nature, especially during load-carrying (Hanna et al. 2015). Facultative bipedalism has been extensively studied in chimpanzees, in the hope of unravelling the evolution of striding bipedalism in humans (Demes et al. 2015). Both bipedal capuchin monkeys and bipedal chimpanzees use a compliant bent-hip, bent-knee gait during bipedal locomotion characterized by short steps and high stride frequencies (Demes 2011; Pontzer et al. 2014a). In both species, mediolateral forces are quite high, likely to prevent lateral falling when moving on one limb during a single-limb stance phase (Hanna et al. 2015; Pontzer et al. 2014a). Considering their crouched gait and high stride frequencies, it is not surprising that the bipedal walking in chimpanzees is costly, requiring 41 percent more energy than expected for a mammal of similar body mass (Pontzer et al. 2014a). However, knuckle-walking in chimpanzees is equally inefficient, and bipedal and quadrupedal locomotion require similar metabolic energy expenditure in chimpanzees. This finding led Sockol et al. (2007) to suggest that small anatomical changes (see below) to improve the efficiency of bipedal locomotion would have had large adaptive benefits.

Humans are the only obligate striding bipeds of the primate order (Figure 35.6D). As reviewed above, bipedal locomotion in nonhuman primates is either facultative (e.g., capuchin monkeys, chimpanzees) or nonstriding (i.e., the bipedal galloping of sifakas). This distinctive form of bipedalism is well suited to one particular function: efficient travel over long distances. Sockol et al. (2007) showed that bipedal humans use less metabolic energy to move a kilogram of body mass than either bipedal or quadrupedal chimpanzees. The energetic efficiency of modern humans is predicated on unique aspects of our gait mechanics and distinct features of our post-cranial anatomy.

First, bipedal humans keep their lower limbs erect and adducted during bipedal stance and locomotion – particularly in comparison to other bipedal primates (O'Neill et al. 2015).

(A)   (B)   (C)   (D)

Figure 35.6   Bipedal locomotion has been extensively studied in primates and varies considerably across species. Because of their specialized leaping anatomy, (A) sifakas use a bipedal galloping gait when moving terrestrially. Many primates adopt facultative bipedalism when carrying objects (B) with their forelimbs. This is especially prevalent in (B) capuchins and (C) hominoids. Humans (D) are the only extant obligate striding biped. Images were made available by: (A) Moongateclimber, CC BY-SA 3.0, http://creativecommons.org/licenses/by-sa/3.0, via Wikimedia Commons; (B) Rennett Stowe, CC BY 2.0, https://creativecommons.org/licenses/by/2.0, via flickr; (C) Eric Kilby, CC BY-SA 2.0, https://creativecommons.org/licenses/by-sa/2.0, via Wikimedia Commons; (D) Lukáš Rychvalský, CC0 1.0 Universal (CC0 1.0), https://creativecommons.org/publicdomain/zero/1.0, via shutterstock.

This limits the muscular effort required to maintain posture, saving metabolic energy with every step (Biewener et al. 2004). Second, lower limb muscle contractions are isometric or eccentric during bipedal walking, rather than concentric (Rose and Gamble 1994). Isometric and eccentric contractions are metabolically cheaper, creating another energy-saving mechanism (McMahon 1984). Third, the rolling motion of the human foot effectively reduces the mechanical (and metabolic) power required to redirect body mass during a walking step (Adamczyk and Kuo 2013).

Humans also show morphological adaptations associated with improving energetic efficiency during bipedalism. Perhaps the most obvious is limb length. Whereas all other apes have intermembral indices of > 100 percent, modern humans have an intermembral index of only 88 percent (Aiello and Dean 1990). Pontzer (2005) showed that long limbs, and the longer strides they permit, reduce the metabolic cost of locomotion by allowing humans to get more "bang for their buck" (i.e., any mechanism that carries the body further with each step will naturally reduce the energy required to travel a given distance). Additionally, human lower limb muscle fibers are typically much shorter than those of the other great apes, reducing the overall volume of limb muscle that must be activated to effect locomotion and thus decreasing overall energetic costs (Pontzer et al. 2009).

Additional distinctive features of the human skeleton are better explained as solutions to the potential balance problems and increased musculoskeletal stresses of bipedalism (Aiello et al. 1990). For instance, the spine is marked by posteriorly concave curvatures in the cervical and lumbar regions (i.e., lordoses) and anteriorly concave curvatures in the thoracic and sacral regions (i.e., kyphoses). The zig-zag pattern of curvatures balances the center of mass over the hindlimb joints, ensuring that little metabolic energy is required to maintain stance. The short, sagittally oriented iliac blades of modern humans redirect the pull of the lesser gluteal muscles, making it easier for a human to balance the trunk during periods of single limb stance (Stern and Susman 1981). Similarly, a medially directed (i.e., valgus) femoral shaft places the foot directly under the center of gravity during a single-limb stance, further securing balance. Finally, lower limb joints are relatively large compared to those of apes and monkeys, decreasing joint stress and the potential for injury (Jungers 1988).

It should also be noted that some features of the modern human musculoskeletal system may be better associated with adaptation for bipedal running than walking *per se*. In their review of endurance running in human evolution, Bramble and Lieberman (2004) listed 26 different features of the musculoskeletal system that could serve as adaptations to variably stabilize the head, stabilize the trunk, reduce joint stresses, prevent overheating, and minimize energetic cost during endurance running. For instance, the spring-like Achilles tendon at the back of the ankle stores and releases energy during a running stride (Foster et al. 2021), but would be of little use during walking.

FUTURE DIRECTIONS

Though the study of primate locomotion has a long history (e.g., Muybridge 1957), there remains much work to be done. Most quantitative research on primate locomotion has focused on captive animals in laboratory environments. Though there is a long, distinguished history of studying primate locomotion in the field as well (Garber 2007), most of this research has been observational and only broadly quantitative. The appeal of the research laboratory is twofold. First, working in the laboratory more easily facilitates experimental control, allowing the researcher to isolate specific factors thought to influence the locomotor behavior in question (e.g., support diameter, compliance, orientation, or distribution in space). Second, many of the standard techniques used to quantitively study primate locomotion have traditionally been feasible to use only in the laboratory (e.g., high-speed cameras, force plates, electromyography). However, primates did not evolve to move on standardized poles in a laboratory environment. Only in the field is it feasible to sample the rich environmental variability that primates face daily (Vereecke and D'Août 2011). Moreover, financial and ethical concerns continue to make *in vivo* research on captive primates increasingly difficult. Some species, due to remoteness, lack of biomedical interest, or conservation status, might never be studied in the laboratory. Locomotor research in the field could thus expand the taxonomic breadth of our knowledge.

How then should primate locomotor researchers interested in field work address the lack of experimental control and measurement precision that would seem to be uniquely the purview of laboratory environments? First, an alternative approach to experimental control is statistical control. Through robust, quantitative sampling of the locomotor behaviors of interest and the ecological and phylogenetic factors hypothesized to influence the behavior, researchers can gain a mechanistic understanding of a biological system despite the lack of experimental control. Second, modern recording technologies have advanced to the point where collecting high-fidelity quantitative data collection is possible in natural environments. High-speed video, laser scanning, and other photogrammetric methods can be used to remotely sample primate locomotor kinematics, morphometrics, and environmental variation (Dunham et al. 2018). Tags and collars with integrated accelerometers and GPS units can be used to get precise biomechanical data on animal movement during fitness-critical activities in natural environments (Wunderlich et al. 2014). Even direct physiological measurements of primate musculoskeletal function are possible in natural environments, as shown by the work of Williams and colleagues (2008) on masticatory electromyography in free-ranging howler monkeys. Vanguard technologies such as these will continue to advance our understanding of primate locomotor evolution and adaptation for years to come.

One especially promising area of inquiry using these emerging technologies is primate locomotor energetics. Locomotion is essential for survival, yet the energy that an animal expends while moving can significantly decrease the amount that it has available for growth and reproduction, or, more proximately, the reserve energy left for seeking a mate and avoiding a predator (Halsey 2016). Therefore, it is likely that natural selection favors animals that move at speeds and select travel paths that allows them to traverse across the landscape at the lowest energy cost possible. However, in the wild, where various interests can compete, an animal may select a movement speed that does not optimize energy economy, sacrificing this currency for an alternative (e.g., stability). Primates are ideal model systems to understand the interplay between locomotor energetic economy and alternative selective pressures. While studies of primate locomotor energetics are limited, data suggest that primate locomotor strategies may not be particularly efficient (Sockol et al. 2007). Further, arboreal environments are complex in nature, and the continuous substrates necessary to maximize an animal's locomotor efficiency are simply not present. However, measurements of daily energy expenditure indicate that primates, including humans, expend only half of the calories expected for mammals of a similar body size (Pontzer et al. 2014b). Such a paradox suggests that primates are actively making decisions about travel paths and/or movement patterns to keep total energy expenditure low. Indirect measures of energy consumption, such as doubly labelled water (Speakman et al. 2019), urinary C-peptide (Sacco et al. 2021), and accelerometers (Bryce et al. 2017), are becoming more accurate and affordable, leading to the possibility of measuring locomotor energetics outside the laboratory. Considerations of primate locomotor energetics in the field will surely spark new and exciting investigations of how primates mitigate the challenges of their complex arboreal environment.

REFERENCES

Adamczyk, P. G., and A. D. Kuo. "Mechanical and Energetic Consequences of Rolling Foot Shape in Human Walking." *Journal of Experimental Biology* 216, no. 14 (2013): 2722–2731.

Aiello, L., and C. Dean. *An Introduction to Human Evolutionary Anatomy*. London, UK: Academic Press, 1990.

Altmann, J., and A. Samuels. "Costs of Maternal Care: Infant-Carrying in Baboons." *Behavioral Ecology and Sociobiology* 29 (1992): 391–398.

Anemone, R. L. "The Functional Anatomy of the Hip and Thigh in Primates." In *Postcranial Adaptation in Nonhuman Primates*. Edited by D. L. Gebo, 150–174. DeKalb, Illinois: Northern Illinois University Press, 1993.

Bertram, J. E. "New Perspectives on Brachiation Mechanics." *American Journal of Physical Anthropology* 39 (2004): 100–117.

Bezanson, M. "Primate Positional Behavior Development and Evolution." *Annual Review of Anthropology* 46 (2017): 279–298.

Biewener, A. A., C. T. Farley, T. J. Roberts, and M. Temaner. "Muscle Mechanical Advantage of Human Walking and Running: Implications for Energy Cost." *Journal of Applied Physiology* 97, no. 6 (2004): 2266–2274.

Bramble, D. M., and D. E. Lieberman. "Endurance Running and the Evolution of Homo." *Nature* 432, no. 7015 (2004): 345–352.

Bryce, C. M., C. C. Wilmers, and T. M. Williams. "Energetics and Evasion Dynamics of Large Predators and Prey: Pumas vs. Hounds." *Peer J.* 5 (2017): e3701.

Byron, C. D., M. C. Granatosky, and H. H. Covert. "An Anatomical and Mechanical Analysis of the Douc Monkey (Genus Pygathrix), and Its Role in Understanding the Evolution of Brachiation." *American Journal of Physical Anthropology* 164, no. 4 (2017): 801–820.

Cartmill, M. "Climbing." In *Functional Vertebrate Morphology*. Edited by M. Hildebrand, D. M. Bramble, K. F. Liem, and D. B. Wake, 73–88. Cambridge, MA: Belknap, 1985.

Cartmill, M. "New Views on Primate Origins." *Evolutionary Anthropology: Issues, News, and Reviews* 1, no. 3 (1992): 105–111.

Cartmill, M., P. Lemelin, and D. Schmitt. "Support Polygons and Symmetrical Gaits in Mammals." *Zoological Journal of the Linnean Society* 136, no. 3 (2002): 401–420.

Chang, Y. H., J. E. A. Bertram, and D. V. Lee. "External Forces and Torques Generated by the Brachiating White-Handed Gibbon (*Hylobates Lar*)." *American Journal of Physical Anthropology* 113 (2000): 201–216.

Chester, S. G. B., T. E. Williamson, J. I. Bloch, et al. "Oldest Skeleton of a Plesiadapiform Provides Additional Evidence for an Exclusively Arboreal Radiation of Stem Primates in the Palaeocene." *Royal Society Open Science* 4, no. 5 (2017): 170329.

Connour, J. R., K. Glander, and F. Vincent. "Postcranial Adaptations for Leaping in Primates." *Journal of Zoology* 251, no. 1 (2000): 79–103.

Dagosto, M. "Implications of Postcranial Evidence for the Origin of Euprimates." *Journal of Human Evolution* 17 (1988): 35–56.

Demes, B. "Three-Dimensional Kinematics of Capuchin Monkey Bipedalism." *American Journal of Physical Anthropology* 145, no. 1 (2011): 147–155.

Demes, B., W. L. Jungers, and U. Nieschalk. "Size-and Speed-Related Aspects of Quadrupedal Walking in Slender and Slow Lorises." In *Gravity, Posture and Locomotion in Primates*. Edited by F. K. Jouffroy, M. H. Stack, and C. Niemetz, 175–197. Florence: Il Sedicesimo, 1990.

Demes, B., S. G. Larson, J. T. Stern, et al. "The Kinetics of Primate Quadrupedalism: 'Hindlimb Drive' Reconsidered." *Journal of Human Evolution* 26 (1994): 353–374.

Demes, B., J. G. Fleagle, and P. Lemelin. "Myological Correlates of Prosimian Leaping." *Journal of Human Evolution* 34, no. 4 (1998): 385–399.

Demes, B., N. E. Thompson, M. C. O'Neill, and B. R. Umberger. "Center of Mass Mechanics of Chimpanzee Bipedal Walking." *American Journal of Physical Anthropology* 156 (2015): 422–433.

Doran, D. M. "The Ontogeny of Chimpanzee and Pygmy Chimpanzee Locomotor Behavior: A Case Study of Paedomorphism and Its Behavioral Correlates." *Journal of Human Evolution* 23 (1992): 139–157.

Doran, D. M. "Ontogeny of Locomotion in Mountain Gorillas and Chimpanzees." *Journal of Human Evolution* 32 (1997): 323–344.

Druelle, F., J. Young, and G. Berillon. "Behavioral Implications of Ontogenetic Changes in Intrinsic Hand and Foot Proportions in Olive Baboons (*Papio Anubis*)." *American Journal of Physical Anthropology* 165 (2018): 65–76.

Dunham, N. T., A. McNamara, L. Shapiro, et al. "A User's Guide for the Quantitative Analysis of Substrate Characteristics and Locomotor Kinematics in Free-Ranging Primates." *American Journal of Physical Anthropology* 167, no. 3 (2018): 569–584.

Erikson, G. E. "Brachiation in New World Monkeys and in Anthropoid Apes." *Symposia of the Zoological Society of London* 10 (1963): 135–164.

Fleagle, J. G. "Dynamics of a Brachiating Siamang [*Hylobates* (*Symphalangus*) *Syndactylus*]." *Nature* 248, no. 5445 (1974): 259–260.

Fleagle, J. G. "Locomotion, Posture, and Comparative Anatomy of Malaysian Forest Primates." 1976. Dissertation, Harvard University.

Fleagle, J. G. *Primate Adaptation and Evolution*, 3rd edn. San Diego: Academic Press, 2013.

Fleagle, J. G., J. T. Stern, W. L. Jungers, et al. "Climbing: A Biomechanical Link with Brachiation and with Bipedalism." *Symposia of the Zoological Society of London* 48 (1981): 359–375.

Foster, A. D., B. Block, F. Capobianco, et al. "Shorter Heels Are Linked with Greater Elastic Energy Storage in the Achilles Tendon." *Scientific Reports* 11, no. 1 (2021): 9360.

Fujiwara, S., H. Endo, and J. R Hutchinson. "Topsy-Turvy Locomotion: Biomechanical Specializations of the Elbow in Suspended Quadrupeds Reflect Inverted Gravitational Constraints." *Journal of Anatomy* 219, no. 2 (2011): 176–191.

Garber, P. A. "Primate Locomotor Behavior and Ecology." In *Primates in Perspective*. Edited by C. J. Campbell, A. Fuentes, K. C. MacKinnon, et al., 543–560. Oxford: Oxford University Press, 2007.

Gebo, D. L. "Locomotor Function Across Primates (Including Humans)." In *A Companion to Biological Anthropology*. Edited by C. S. Larsen, 530–544. Hoboken, New Jersey: Wiley-Blackwell, 2010.

Gebo, D. L. *Primate Comparative Anatomy*. Baltimore: Johns Hopkins University Press, 2014.

Granatosky, M. C. "A Review of Locomotor Diversity in Mammals with Analyses Exploring the Influence of Substrate-Use, Body Mass, and Intermembral Index in Primates." *Journal of Zoology* 306, no. 4 (2018): 207–216.

Granatosky, M. C. "Primate Locomotion." In *Encyclopedia of Animal Cognition and Behavior*. Edited by J. Vonk and T. Shackelford, 1–7. Cham: Springer International Publishing, 2020.

Granatosky, M. C., and D. Schmitt. "Forelimb and Hind Limb Loading Patterns During Below Branch Quadrupedal Locomotion in the Two-Toed Sloth." *Journal of Zoology* 302, no. 4 (2017): 271–278.

Granatosky, M. C., and D. Schmitt. "The Mechanical Origins of Arm-Swinging." *Journal of Human Evolution* 130 (2019): 61–71.

Granatosky, M. C., C. H. Tripp, and D. Schmitt. "Gait Kinetics of Above and Below Branch Quadrupedal Locomotion in Lemurid Primates." *Journal of Experimental Biology* 219 (2016): 53–63.

Granatosky, M. C., D. Schmitt, and J. Hanna. "Comparison of Spatiotemporal Gait Characteristics Between Vertical Climbing and Horizontal Walking in Primates." *Journal of Experimental Biology* 222, no. 2 (2019): jeb185702.

Gursky, S. L. *The Spectral Tarsier*. Abingdon-on-Thames, UK: Routledge, 2015.

Halsey, L. G. "Terrestrial Movement Energetics: Current Knowledge and Its Application to the Optimising Animal." *Journal of Experimental Biology* 219, no. 10 (2016): 1424–1431.

Hanna, J. B., D. Schmitt, K. Wright, et al. "Kinetics of Bipedal Locomotion During Load Carrying in Capuchin Monkeys." *Journal of Human Evolution* 85 (2015): 149–156.

Hanna, J. B., M. C. Granatosky, P. Rana, and D. Schmitt. "The Evolution of Vertical Climbing in Primates: Evidence from Reaction Forces." *Journal of Experimental Biology* 220 (2017): 3039–3052.

Hildebrand, M. "Symmetrical Gaits of Primates." *American Journal of Physical Anthropology* 26, no. 2 (1967): 119–130.

Isler, K. "3D-Kinematics of Vertical Climbing in Hominoids." *American Journal of Physical Anthropology* 126, no. 1 (2005): 66–81.

Jungers, W. L. "Relative Joint Size and Hominoid Locomotor Adaptations with Implications for the Evolution of Hominid Bipedalism." *Journal of Human Evolution* 17, no. 1 (1988): 247–265.

Larson, S. G. "Parallel Evolution in the Hominoid Trunk and Forelimb." *Evolutionary Anthropology: Issues, News, and Reviews* 6 (1998): 87–99.

McMahon, T. A. *Muscles, Reflexes, and Locomotion. Muscles, Reflexes, and Locomotion*. Princeton, NJ: Princeton University Press, 1984.

Milne, N., and M. C. Granatosky. "Ulna Curvature in Arboreal and Terrestrial Primates." *Journal of Mammalian Evolution* 28, no. 3 (2021): 897–909.

Mittermeier, R. A., and J. G. Fleagle. "The Locomotor and Postural Repertoires of *Ateles Geoffroyi* and *Colobus Guereza*, and a Reevaluation of the Locomotor Category Semibrachiation." *American Journal of Physical Anthropology* 45 (1976): 235–255.

Muybridge, E. *Animals in Motion*. New York, NY: Dover Publications, 1957.

Napier, J. R., and A. C. Walker. "Vertical Clinging and Leaping – A Newly Recognized Category of Locomotor Behaviour of Primates." *Folia Primatologica* 6 (1967): 204–219.

Nyakatura, J. A., M. S. Fischer, and M. Schmidt. "Gait Parameter Adjustments of Cotton-Top Tamarins (*Saguinus Oedipus*, Callitrichidae) to Locomotion on Inclined Arboreal Substrates." *American Journal of Physical Anthropology* 135 (2008): 13–26.

O'Neill, M. C., and D. Schmitt. "The Gaits of Primates: Center of Mass Mechanics in Walking, Cantering and Galloping Ring-Tailed Lemurs, Lemur Catta." *The Journal of Experimental Biology* 215 (2012): 1728–1739.

O'Neill, M. C., L. Lee, B. Demes, et al. "Three-Dimensional Kinematics of the Pelvis and Hind Limbs in Chimpanzee (Pan Troglodytes) and Human Bipedal Walking." *Journal of Human Evolution* 86 (2015): 32–42.

Perchalski, B. "Headfirst Descent Behaviors in a Comparative Sample of Strepsirrhine Primates." *American Journal of Primatology* 83, no. 6 (2021): e23259.

Pontzer, H. "A New Model Predicting Locomotor Cost from Limb Length via Force Production." *Journal of Experimental Biology* 208, no. 8 (2005): 1513–1524.

Pontzer, H., D. A. Raichlen, and M. D. Sockol. "The Metabolic Cost of Walking in Humans, Chimpanzees, and Early Hominins." *Journal of Human Evolution* 56, no. 1 (2009): 43–54.

Pontzer, H., D. A. Raichlen, and P. S. Rodman. "Bipedal and Quadrupedal Locomotion in Chimpanzees." *Journal of Human Evolution* 66 (2014a): 64–82.

Pontzer, H., D. A. Raichlen, A. D. Gordon, et al. "Primate Energy Expenditure and Life History." *Proceedings of the National Academy of Sciences* 111, no. 4 (2014b): 1433–1437.

Preuschoft, H. "What Does 'Arboreal Locomotion' Mean Exactly and What Are the Relationships Between Climbing, Environment and Morphology?" *Zeitschrift Für Morphologie Und Anthropologie* (2002): 171–188.

Raichlen, D. A., H. Pontzer, L. J. Shapiro, and M. D. Sockol. "Understanding Hind Limb Weight Support in Chimpanzees with Implications for the Evolution of Primate Locomotion." *American Journal of Physical Anthropology* 138, no. 4 (2009): 395–402.

Reynolds, T. R. "Mechanics of Increased Support Weight by the Hindlimbs in Primates." *American Journal of Physical Anthropology* 67 (1985a): 335–349.

Reynolds, T. R. "Stresses on the Limbs of Quadrupedal Primates." *American Journal of Physical Anthropology* 67, no. 4 (1985b): 351–362.

Richmond, B. G., D. R. Begun, and D. S. Strait. "Origin of Human Bipedalism: The Knuckle-Walking Hypothesis Revisited." *American Journal of Physical Anthropology: The Official Publication of the American Association of Physical Anthropologists* 116, no. S33 (2001): 70–105.

Rollinson, J., and R. D. Martin. "Comparative Aspects of Primate Locomotion, with Special Reference to Arboreal Cercopithecines." *Symposia of the Zoological Society of London* 48 (1981): 377–427.

Rose, J., and J. G. Gamble. *Human Walking*, vol. 3. Philadelphia, PA: Williams & Wilkins, 1994.

Sacco, A. J., M. C. Granatosky, M. F. Laird, and K. M. Milich. "Validation of a Method for Quantifying Urinary C-Peptide in Platyrrhine Monkeys." *General and Comparative Endocrinology* 300 (2021): 113644.

Sarringhaus, L. A., L. M. Maclatchy, and J. C. Mitani. "Locomotor and Postural Development of Wild Chimpanzees." *Journal of Human Evolution* 66 (2014): 29–38.

Schmitt, D., M. D. Rose, J. E. Turnquist, and P. Lemelin. "Role of the Prehensile Tail During Ateline Locomotion: Experimental and Osteological Evidence." *American Journal of Physical Anthropology* 126, no. 4 (2005): 435–446.

Schmitt, D., M. Cartmill, T. M. Griffin, et al. "Adaptive Value of Ambling Gaits in Primates and Other Mammals." *Journal of Experimental Biology* 209, no. 11 (2006): 2042–2049.

Shapiro, L. J., and D. A. Raichlen. "Limb Proportions and the Ontogeny of Quadrupedal Walking in Infant Baboons (*Papio Cynocephalus*)." *Journal of Zoology* 269 (2006): 191–203.

Shapiro, L. J., J. W. Young, and J. L. VandeBerg. "Body Size and the Small Branch Niche: Using Marsupial Ontogeny to Model Primate Locomotor Evolution." *Journal of Human Evolution* 68 (2014): 14–31.

Sickles, D. W., and C. A. Pinkstaff. "Comparative Histochemical Study of Prosimian Primate Hindlimb Muscles. I. Muscle Fiber Types." *American Journal of Anatomy* 160, no. 2 (1981a): 175–186.

Sickles, D. W., and C. A. Pinkstaff. "Comparative Histochemical Study of Prosimian Primate Hindlimb Muscles. II. Populations of Fiber Types." *American Journal of Anatomy* 160, no. 2 (1981b): 187–194.

Smith, T. D., V. B. DeLeon, J. W. Young, and C. Vinyard. *Skeletal Anatomy of the Newborn Primate.* Cambridge, UK: Cambridge University Press, 2020.

Sockol, M. D., D. A. Raichlen, and H. Pontzer. "Chimpanzee Locomotor Energetics and the Origin of Human Bipedalism." *Proceedings of the National Academy of Sciences* 104, no. 30 (2007): 12265–12269.

Speakman, J. R., H. Pontzer, J. Rood, et al. "The International Atomic Energy Agency International Doubly Labelled Water Database: Aims, Scope and Procedures." *Annals of Nutrition and Metabolism* 75, no. 2 (2019): 114–118.

Stern, J. "Before Bipedality." *Yearbook of Physical Anthropology* 19 (1975): 59–68.

Stern, J. T., and R. L. Susman. "Electromyography of the Gluteal Muscles in *Hylobates, Pongo*, and *Pan*: Implications for the Evolution of Hominid Bipedality." *American Journal of Physical Anthropology* 55 (1981): 153–166.

Susman, R. L. "Comparative and Functional Morphology of Hominoid Fingers." *American Journal of Physical Anthropology* 50 (1979): 215–236.

Szalay, F. S. "The Beginnings of Primates." *Evolution* 22, no. 1 (1968): 19–36.

Tuttle, R. H. "Knuckle-Walking and the Evolution of Hominoid Hands." *American Journal of Physical Anthropology* 26, no. 2 (1967): 171–206.

Venkataraman, V. V., T. S. Kraft, and N. J. Dominy. "Tree Climbing and Human Evolution." *Proceedings of the National Academy of Sciences* 110, no. 4 (2013): 1237–1242.

Vereecke, E. E., and K. D'Août. "Introduction. Primate Locomotion: Toward a Synergy of Laboratory and Field Research". In *Primate Locomotion: Linking Field and Laboratory Research, Developments in Primatology: Progress and Prospects*. Edited by K. D'Août and E. E. Vereecke, 1–6. New York, NY: Springer, 2011.

Vilensky, J. A., and S. G. Larson. "Primate Locomotion: Utilization and Control of Symmetrical Gaits." *Annual Review of Anthropology* 18 (1989): 17–35.

Williams, S. H., C. J. Vinyard, K. E. Glander, et al. "Telemetry System for Assessing Jaw-Muscle Function in Free-Ranging Primates." *International Journal of Primatology* 29, no. 6 (2008): 1441.

Wimberly, A. N., G. J. Slater, and M. C. Granatosky. "Evolutionary History of Quadrupedal Walking Gaits Shows Mammalian Release from Locomotor Constraint." *Proceedings of the Royal Society B: Biological Sciences* 288, no. 1957 (2021): 20210937.

Workman, C., and H. H. Covert. "Learning the Ropes: The Ontogeny of Locomotion in Red-Shanked Douc (*Pygathrix Nemaeus*), Delacour's (*Trachypithecus Delacouri*), and Hatinh Langurs (*Trachypithecus Hatinhensis*). I. Positional Behavior." *American Journal of Physical Anthropology* 128 (2005): 371–380.

Wunderlich, R. E., A. Tongen, J. Gardiner, et al. "Dynamics of Locomotor Transitions from Arboreal to Terrestrial Substrates in Verreaux's Sifaka (*Propithecus Verreauxi*)." *Integrative and Comparative Biology* 54 (2014): 1148–1158.

Yapuncich, G. S., and D. M. Boyer. "Interspecific Scaling Patterns of Talar Articular Surfaces Within Primates and Their Closest Living Relatives." *Journal of Anatomy* 224, no. 2 (2014): 150–172.

Young, J. W. "Ontogeny of Limb Force Distribution in Squirrel Monkeys (*Saimiri Boliviensis*): Insights into the Mechanical Bases of Primate Hind Limb Dominance." *Journal of Human Evolution* 62, no. 4 (2012): 473–485.

Young, J. W., and L. J. Shapiro. "Developments in Development: What Have We Learned from Primate Locomotor Ontogeny?" *American Journal of Physical Anthropology* 165 (2018): 37–71.

Zhu, W.-W., P. A. Garber, M. Bezanson, et al. "Age- and Sex-Based Patterns of Positional Behavior and Substrate Utilization in the Golden Snub-Nosed Monkey (*Rhinopithecus Roxellana*)." *American Journal of Primatology* 77 (2015): 98–108.

CHAPTER 36

Teaching Biological Anthropology: Pedagogy of Human Evolution and Human Variation

Briana Pobiner

INTRODUCTION

While biological anthropology intersects with science education via numerous topics, and many practicing biological anthropologists are college or university faculty members, studies of biological anthropology pedagogical best practices at the undergraduate level are scarce. The purpose of this chapter is to (1) outline obstacles and opportunities in teaching two content areas in biological anthropology perceived as "controversial": human evolution and human variation (sometimes understood as "race") and (2) present evidence-based recommendations for pedagogical best practices and approaches that US college and university faculty members can use when teaching these topics in undergraduate classrooms.

LOW ACCEPTANCE OF HUMAN EVOLUTION IN THE US

In 1982, Gallup began the longest running periodic poll of Americans on their acceptance of (or attitudes toward) human evolution.[1] The poll uses the following question and three statements as choices for an answer: "Which of the following statements comes closest to your views on the origin and development of human beings?" (1) "Human beings have developed over millions of years from less advanced forms of life, but God guided this process;" (2) "Human beings have developed over millions of years from less advanced forms of life, but God had no part in this process;" and (3) "God created human beings pretty much in their present form at one time within the last 10,000 years or so." The proportion of respondents who choose each of these statements has remained remarkably consistent in

A Companion to Biological Anthropology, Second Edition. Edited by Clark Spencer Larsen.
© 2023 John Wiley & Sons Ltd. Published 2023 by John Wiley & Sons Ltd.

the total of 14 polls since that time, including the most recent poll in June 2019. Between 31 and 40 percent of respondents have agreed with the first statement; between 9 and 22 percent of respondents have agreed with the second statement, with an overall increase, especially in the last decade or so; and between 38 and 47 percent have agreed with the third statement. The only real change in the most recent poll is an increase – more than doubling, in fact, since 1982 – of those who agree with the second statement. Those having "no opinion" have fluctuated between 4 and 9 percent.

In addition to the increase in people agreeing with Gallup's second statement, there is more recent evidence regarding the acceptance of human evolution acceptance by the American public, which Jon Miller and colleagues (Miller et al. 2021) analyzed via a series of national surveys collected between 1985 and 2020 in which US adults were asked to agree or disagree with the following statement: "Human beings, as we know them today, developed from earlier species of animals." They found that the level of public acceptance of evolution in the US increased in the last decade, from 40 to 54 percent; and, in 2016, for the first time, a majority of US adults agreed with this statement. They attributed this change to increasing enrollment in baccalaureate-level programs, increased exposure to college-level science courses, a declining level of religious fundamentalism, and a rising level of civic scientific literacy (Miller et al. 2021).

The low acceptance of evolution in the US is unusual among Western countries and most of the Global North. In 2006, Jon Miller and colleagues (Miller et al. 2006) published what is still the most extensive comparative international study of human evolution acceptance, including the United States, Japan, and 32 European countries. They found that only Turkish adults were less likely to accept human evolution than American adults. Importantly, though, relevant Pew Research Center data indicate that how a question about human evolution acceptance is phrased can have a strong influence on how it is answered by people from highly religious groups.[2] Specifically, a two-question "branched choice format," in which survey respondents were first asked if they believe humans evolved over time and then those who said "yes" were asked a second question about their views about the processes behind evolution, including the role of God in those processes, led to 66 percent of white evangelical Protestants and 59 percent of Black Protestants taking a "creationist" stance, saying that "humans have always existed in their present form since the beginning of time." In contrast, when survey respondents were asked a single question about their views on whether or not human evolution has occurred, the processes behind evolution, and the role of God in those processes, the majority of white evangelical (62 percent) and Black (71 percent) Protestants agreed with the position that humans evolved over time. This indicates that highly religious people may feel uncomfortable agreeing with the idea that humans evolved over time unless they can express their views about the role of God in these natural processes.

Why is acceptance of evolution in the US so low relative to other Global North countries? Miller and colleagues (Miller et al. 2006) concluded that it is a combination of factors, namely a low level of genetic literacy, the politicization of science, a tendency to see humans as exceptions from the rest of the animal kingdom, and religious influence. Ranney (2012) proposed Reinforced Theistic Manifest Destiny (RTMD) as an explanation. This concept focuses on spiritually linked feedback regarding the US's military and industrial prowess and associations observed among beliefs regarding afterlife, theism, nationalism, global warming, and the origins of species. Other studies have identified myriad factors in the low acceptance of evolution among Americans, including religiosity, religious denomination, openness to experience, educational attainment and focus, and evolutionary content knowledge, along with demographic factors such as gender, age, and political affiliation.[3]

Especially pronounced, however, is the lack of understanding of the nature of science (e.g., Dunk et al. 2017; Heddy and Nadelson 2013). In addition to influences from specific religious or other culturally influenced worldviews, there are three common cognitive barriers to understanding evolution. These are *essentialism*, which is a belief in immutable categories or kinds, sometimes causing people to overlook the significance of individual differences within a species (variation) and randomly occurring differences between parents and offspring (inheritance); *teleology*, meaning that explanations for the form of something assume that its function or design are need-based or invoke an ultimate purpose; and *intentionality*, which assumes that events are purposeful, progressive, or goal-directed, and may be caused by an intentional agent (Gregory 2009; Pobiner 2016 and references therein). For a broader and more extensive review of the challenges to understanding and accepting evolution, including human evolution, see Pobiner (2016); for more international perspectives on evolution education, see Harms and Reiss (2019).

Religious factors are central to public views on only a few science topics. Human evolution usually tops the list. However, are science and religion actually in conflict for Americans? A 2014 Pew Research Center poll found that most Americans (59 percent) think science and religion often conflict, but only 30 percent of Americans say their personal religious beliefs conflict with science.[4] Paradoxically, this "conflict view" is particularly common among Americans who are not very religious (73 percent) or who have no religious affiliation (76 percent), while only 50 percent of the most religious Americans – those who attend services on a weekly basis – hold the conflict view. The proportion of Americans who perceive a conflict between science and their own religious beliefs declined somewhat from 36 percent in 2009 to 30 percent in 2014.[4]

Data from different polls suggest that Americans accept evolution in plants and animals at higher levels than evolution in humans, although this assumption has not been directly tested in a comparative study. Yet, teaching about evolution in humans can paradoxically be an opportunity for biological anthropologists to engage students in science. In this regard, growing research demonstrates that a pedagogical focus on human examples along with evolution of other organisms in high school and college biology classrooms can be an effective and engaging way to teach core concepts of evolution (e.g., Ashmore 2005; Pobiner 2012, 2016; Pobiner et al. 2018, 2019). However, a recent study found that student acceptance of evolution and prior scientific content knowledge can affect student outcomes (perceived content relevance, learning gains, students' engagement, and level of discomfort) when teaching evolution using human versus nonhuman mammal examples in an introductory college biology course (Grunspan et al. 2021).

HUMAN VARIATION AND "RACE"

Human populations differ in their distribution and frequency of traits they display, which are the result of both genetic and nongenetic forces, such as epigenetic and environmental factors (Chakravarti 2015). The relationship between this variation and the concept of "race" is complex; the concept of "race" has different meanings and practices depending on the social, historical, and political context. One definition of "race" is that it refers to "groupings of people according to common origin or background and associated with perceived biological markers."[5] In racist physical anthropology scholarly work, human groups were explicitly classified through biology and culture and then arranged hierarchically in socioevolutionary terms, in an attempt to understand human variation in explicitly racial terms (Benn Torres 2019; Van Arsdale 2019). Skin color is the primary physical criterion by which people have been classified into racial groups because it is visible – yet skin color is generally not associated with other traits that have been used to characterize and classify human races (Jablonski 2021). The current scientific understanding of the pattern and amount of human variation is inconsistent with popular notions of race, because most human traits vary on a continuous basis rather than separating people into discrete racial groups and genetic diversity is greater within populations or geographic groups than between them (Benn Torres 2019; Goodman et al. 2012; Graves 2015; Rivera 2019). Race is a recent human invention and is largely a cultural construct; yet race and racism are embedded in institutions and everyday life in the US and racial thinking is deeply entrenched in the science of human biological variation and the subjective classification systems used for human phenotypes (Benn Torres 2019; Fuentes 2021; Goodman et al. 2012; Graves 2015; Lasisi 2021; Van Arsdale 2019). The American Association of Biological Anthropologists (formerly the American Association of Physical Anthropologists) 2019 statement on race and racism[6] makes it clear that "race does not provide an accurate representation of human biological variation" but is "a social reality that structures societies and how we experience the world." Both biological anthropology and human genetics as fields of study are grappling with how to reconcile their legacies of scientific racism and continue to struggle with conceptualizing and describing geographic and population-based genetic variation, as racial categories are not products of human evolutionary history (e.g., Byeon et al. 2021; Fuentes 2021; Graves 2015; Lasisi 2021).

Biological essentialism of race is "the belief the races are natural 'biological kinds' that differ in humanly important ways (e.g., in complex psychological traits and abilities) because each race possesses a different genetic or biological essence" (Donovan 2015: 1096). Similarly, genetic essentialism is "the belief that a 'race' is a genetically homogenous grouping of people, and that races differ physically, cognitively, and behaviorally primarily because they differ in a discrete manner at the genetic level" (Donovan 2022: 1). Consequently, genetic essentialists believe that complex traits are only minimally influenced by the social environment (Dar-Nimrod and Heine 2011). Biological and genetic essentialism are not supported by scientific research; human groups do not possess a genetic essence that makes members of one group highly uniform and different from other groups, as people of the same group are different in their variable DNA, and racial groups are not discrete (Donovan 2015; Donovan et al. 2019; Fuentes 2021; Rosenberg 2011). The same pattern holds for all other studies of human variation that is not under selection pressure in disparate populations – including skull shape, facial structure, and blood types (Relethford 2002). Additionally, scientific data falsify racialized assertations about the causal role of genes in complex human social outcomes and refute assertions of continental groupings as either biologically meaningful or evolutionarily derived distributions of human genetic variation (Fuentes 2021; Van Arsdale 2019). Yet biological essentialism of race causes people to perceive more variation between racial groups and less variation within racial groups and facilitates social stratification based on race because it causes people to categorically differentiate humans into nonoverlapping races (Chao et al. 2013). This essentialism has been used to rationalize prejudice and justify the social acceptability of racial inequality (and inequity) for a century (Donovan et al. 2019). Recent estimates suggest that 20 percent of non-Black US citizens believe in genetic essentialism of race (Morning et al. 2019).

Human genetics education is not socially neutral because genetic arguments for the existence of racial inequality have been used to oppose social policies that promote racial equality for over a century, and students actively construct explanations for racial difference in middle and high school (Donovan et al. 2019). This extends to undergraduate contexts including business, sociology, nursing, health sciences, and pre-med curricula (Hubbard

2017b; McChesney 2015). Some current teaching material and approaches seem to sustain racial inequality (Donovan 2017) and many teachers avoid the topic entirely – yet "the sensitive topics we avoid in the classroom become the significant problems we avoid in our communities" (Hubbard 2017b: 542). Intuitive thinking, teachers, textbooks, and the media affect secondary students' development of erroneous or outdated ideas related to genetics (Stern and Kampourakis 2017). There is over a century-long history of discussing race in American biology textbooks at the secondary and undergraduate levels (Donovan 2015, 2017). While social Darwinist and eugenicist framings of human racial difference became less prevalent between 1940 and 1960, as recently as the 1960s the biology curriculum continued to communicate a biological essentialist conception of race by explaining the evolutionary origin and adaptive differences between races (Donovan 2015; Skoog 2005). Many high school biology textbooks published between 1993 and 2002 include definitions and characterizations of different races and descriptions of how races originated, and 90 percent of high school biology textbooks in use at the turn of the twenty-first century included references to race (Morning 2008).

Unfortunately, it is possible to tacitly communicate biological essentialism of race in the classroom even while attempting to challenge it (Donovan 2015). Experimental evidence with 8th and 9th grade students indicates that simply reading about the association between genetic disease and racial groups in biology textbooks activated students' belief in biological essentialism, and that students transfer this essentialist thinking to understand racial difference in nondisease contexts such as differences in academic ability (Donovan 2014, 2015, 2016; Donovan et al. 2019). Donovan (2017) found that biology students in 7th to 9th grades who learned about human variation using repeated racial terminology (e.g., "race," "African Americans," "Caucasians," "Ashkenazi Jews") inferred from their curriculum that if races differ in genetic disease prevalence or skeletal structure, then genetic difference would probably cause them to differ cognitively and behaviorally too – even though this was not implied by the curriculum. This was not the case with students who learned with an identical curriculum, but without racial terminology (the aforementioned terms were replaced with "American(s)" and "healthy people"). These 7th to 9th graders perceived 43 percent of genetic and phenotypic differences between racial groups and 57 percent within racial groups, while the scientific estimate of genetic variation across continents commonly associated with US census races is 4.5 percent (Donovan 2017). These findings are consistent with nationally representative experimental findings demonstrating that beliefs in racial essentialism in the American public are increased with subtle references to race in journalistic reports about the genetic basis of disease (Condit et al. 2004; Phelan et al. 2013). Other studies confirm that simply reading news articles about behavioral genetics can activate genetic essentialism beliefs in adults (Morin-Chassé 2014, 2020). When reading science texts that include "gene for" language, adults increase in genetic essentialist beliefs (Lynch et al. 2008).

As noted above, students perceive far too little genetic variation within races and far too much genetic variation across races (Donovan et al. 2019). Many middle and high school student misconceptions about genetics exhibited in essays have their roots in deterministic thinking and an overly simplified view of inheritance patterns, and at least 25 percent of secondary science students exhibit gene-deterministic reasoning about the relationship between genes and complex human traits (Mills Shaw et al. 2008; Stern and Kampourakis 2017). In the context of human genetics education, *basic genomics literacy*, which refers to Mendelian and molecular genetics, tells a mechanistic story about the relatively rare human traits that are influenced by a single gene with two alleles, is focused on inheritance patterns within individuals or families, and is the easiest form of genomics literacy to use for essentialist arguments because the gene is conceptualized as the only cause of a trait (Donovan 2022; Donovan et al. 2020; Fuentes 2021). Studies indicate that when students learn genetic concepts in a curriculum oriented toward basic genetic literacy and Mendelian inheritance, there is a greater probability that their genetic essentialist beliefs will increase rather than decrease because they begin to view human variation as discrete rather than continuous, which reinforces the idea that there are "genes for" traits (Donovan 2014, 2016, 2017; Donovan et al. 2020; Stern and Kampourakis 2017).

Standard genomics literacy focuses on the complex relationship between genetic and phenotypic variation within populations and is grounded in the concepts of population thinking, which emphasizes that human populations are aggregates of genetically varying individuals rather than genetic types, and multifactorial genetics, which contends that most human traits are polygenic and influenced by tens or even thousands of alleles. It also includes the understanding that physical, social, and ecological (environmental) factors strongly influence complex traits and can moderate gene expression (Donovan 2022; Donovan et al. 2020). This form of genomics literacy is more difficult to use for essentialist arguments, and a study with 9th to 12th graders indicated that students with higher (versus lower) genomics literacy exhibited greater reductions in the perception of racial differences and belief in genetic essentialism after learning how patterns of human genetic variation refute genetic essentialism via multifactorial genetics and population thinking (Donovan et al. 2021). *Humane genomics literacy* differs from standard genomics literacy in purpose, not content. It focuses on how population thinking and multifactorial genetics refute genetic essentialist beliefs about race, is derived from anti-racist educational approaches, and makes humane genomics literacy impossible to use for essentialist arguments (Donovan 2022; Donovan et al. 2021). An education that helps students develop both standard and humane genomic literacy could reduce the prevalence of genetic essentialism (Donovan et al. 2021).

The Undergraduate Student Audience

Students do not walk into college classrooms as blank slates. They may have stronger or weaker science content knowledge or understanding of the broader nature of science. They may also have had K-12 teachers reluctant to teach evolution or who taught evolution and creationism as "both sides" of a (inappropriate) debate about the cause of the diversity of life on Earth, whether they attended school in the US or elsewhere. They may have received anti-evolution messaging from other parts of their lives including their family, religious institutions, their peers, their K-12 teachers, books they have read, and the media (Bertka et al. 2019; Glaze and Goldston 2015; Long 2011; Scott 1987; Tolman et al. 2021; Winslow et al. 2011; Woods and Scharmann 2001). If they did not learn about evolution until late in high school, or not at all, then they may experience significant cognitive dissonance when presented with information that strongly contradicts what they have been taught to accept in other aspects of their lives. They may also feel threatened by the mere idea of studying evolution (Reed 2017; Schrein 2017). They may be taking a biological anthropology class in order to avoid another class in a "hard" science. Yet, while they bring their religious worldviews and understandings to their science classes (Borgerding 2020), a student's understanding or acceptance of evolution cannot necessarily be predicted just from knowing their educational background, their religion or religiosity, or their major.

What level of understanding and acceptance of evolution might be expected among undergraduate students in biological anthropology classes? US college students' religiosity has been shown to be negatively correlated with their understanding of evolution (Hawley et al. 2011) and predicts their understanding of evolution even more strongly than the evolution content of their high school biology course (Moore et al. 2011; Rissler et al. 2014). Yet the relationship between understanding evolution and accepting evolution is not straightforward (Dunk et al. 2017). Some studies have found a positive correlation between the two (e.g., Shtulman and Calabi 2012) and some have not (e.g., Sinatra et al. 2003). It is possible for someone to understand evolution and not accept that it is true (e.g., Hermann 2012). It is also possible for someone to accept that evolution is true without actually understanding it (e.g., Lord and Marino 1993). In sum, while there is likely to be a positive relationship between understanding and accepting evolution, this relationship is complex and rife with mitigating factors (e.g., Allmon 2011; Glaze and Goldston 2015; Nelson 2012; Pobiner 2016; Smith and Siegel 2004, and additional references therein). While there is some variation, many teachers and evolution education researchers focus on the goal of helping students understand evolution through classroom teaching, rather than focusing on evolution acceptance (e.g., Barnes and Brownell 2016, 2017; Bertka et al. 2019; Meadows 2009; Reiss 2009; Scharmann 2005).

Research in high school and college biology classrooms has shown that when students' worldviews include religious or other cultural concerns about engaging with evolution content in the classroom, leaving these concerns unaddressed can be detrimental to student learning because it can leave them feeling excluded and uncomfortable (Barnes and Brownell 2017; Hermann 2012; Southerland and Scharmann 2013). More recent approaches explicitly work toward reducing perceived conflicts undergraduate students might feel between evolution and their religious faith (e.g., Barnes and Brownell 2017; Manwaring et al. 2015; Truong et al. 2018). A recent study of students in 26 biology courses across 11 states found that student perceived conflict between evolution and their religion was the strongest predictor of evolution acceptance among all variables measured (including religiosity, religious affiliation, understanding of evolution, and demographics), and even mediated the impact of religiosity on evolution acceptance (Barnes et al. 2021b).

Recent research exploring the experience of Christian undergraduate and graduate students in biology determined that many Christian students think the biology community holds strong negative stereotypes against Christians and sometimes conceal their Christian identities to avoid them (Barnes et al. 2021a). Collectively, Christians are an under-represented religious group in science within the US (compared with Jewish, Buddhist, or Muslim communities) (Ecklund and Scheitle 2007), and college students perceive a bias against Christians in science that may reflect a real bias, at least in academic biology (Barnes et al. 2020). Undergraduate biology students also reported adverse experiences when instructors had negative dispositions toward religion and when they were rigid in their instructional practices when teaching evolution (Barnes et al. 2017). While similar research has not been undertaken among biological anthropology students, it should serve as a signal that even "subtle and infrequent" negative interactions, such as highlighting the conflict between religion and evolution, making fun of religious people who do not accept evolution, making a joke at the expense of a religious individual, making anti-religious comments, or trying to force students' acceptance of evolution could have a significant negative impact on Christian students in college classrooms. Even just the lack of acknowledging religious students or their beliefs during relevant instruction can make students feel invisible or excluded (Barnes et al. 2017). Instead, acknowledging religious students or their beliefs and presenting evolution and religion as compatible can lead to positive experiences for students (Barnes et al. 2017).

There have only been two studies that explore an understanding of the nature of science and misconceptions about evolution among undergraduate biological anthropology students. Cunningham and Wescott (2009) created a survey that they gave to 547 undergraduate students enrolled in an Introduction to Biological Anthropology class. The authors characterized the students enrolled in the course as "generally averse to science and intimidated by the other 'hard' science courses" (Cunningham and Wescott 2009: 513). Barely over half (51 percent) of these students had been taught evolutionary principles in high school without creationism, although most (77 percent) were exposed to evolutionary theory in high school. A slim majority (55 percent) agreed that the theory of evolution correctly explains the development of life. The misconception that a scientific theory is a best guess was fairly common (40 percent), the idea of "need"-driven evolution was widely accepted (66 percent), as was the idea that the environment determines which new traits will appear in a population (78 percent), and that "survival of the fittest" means "only the strong survive" (64 percent). The authors concluded from the survey data that students seem to be able to recognize the scientifically accurate answer when a statement is phrased correctly, yet when a statement included a common misconception, students tended to agree with the misconception. Still, these students did not exhibit other common misconceptions about the importance of population size and variation on species evolution, Lamarckian explanations for skin color, and the importance of "wanting" to evolve. The majority (59 percent) of students realized that evolution does not always result in an improvement. In agreement with other studies, these students' confidence in science was unrelated to their competency (Cunningham and Wescott 2009).

Beggrow and Sbeglia (2019) explored whether the disciplinary context for learning about evolution – anthropology (human evolution) versus biology – had an effect on understanding of and reasoning patterns related to evolution. They had 268 students in classes in these two disciplines complete two widely used evolution knowledge instruments, the CINS (Concept Inventory of Natural Selection) and ACORNS (Assessment of Contextual Reasoning about Natural Selection). While scores on these measures of evolution understanding were generally poor for both groups of students, the anthropology students had lower CINS scores, understood fewer key concepts, had more naive ideas, and displayed lower frequencies of accurate reasoning models. Key concept scores were comparable when background and demographic factors were controlled, but anthropology students continued to display lower measures for the other variables. Additionally, anthropology students had more trouble transferring concepts from a human/primate context to other contexts, making them more novice-like in their evolutionary knowledge and reasoning patterns. However, the anthropology and biology students had significantly different academic and demographic backgrounds, making direct comparisons between the two student groups complex (Beggrow and Sbeglia 2019).

As outlined in the previous section, many students are likely to enter college with biological or genetic essentialist misconceptions about race. These misconceptions may then be inadvertently reinforced in college biology courses that focus only on basic genomics literacy, because focusing on rare, single-gene traits in genetics instruction leads to student misconceptions that this fully describes inheritance and "is clearly not compatible with modern understandings of genetics" (Dougherty 2009: 10). A study of genetics instructors of undergraduate nonmajor biology courses found that they spent the greatest amount of genetics lecture time on genetics transmission (meiosis and Mendel) and the least amount of lecture time on "gene regulation," the broad category that included multifactorial traits and the underlying genetics (Hott et al. 2002). An estimated 75 percent of college students taking introductory biology and genetics courses do not know that there is proportionally more genetic variation within groups that between them (Bowling et al. 2008). Similarly, the study described below found that 29 percent of biological anthropology students believed that there is proportionally more biological difference between two races than between individuals within a single race (Hubbard 2017b).

Hubbard conducted the only study to date on teaching about race in a biological anthropology course (Hubbard 2017b). She explored data collected from 296 undergraduate students in a large-enrolment, general education, natural science course surveying the field of biological anthropology to assess how student understanding of four common misconceptions about the nature of human biological and genetic variation in relation to "human racial variation"[7] changed between teaching interventions, and which concepts were most pervasive. The misconceptions were: (1) individual traits (like skin color or hair color) can be used to reliably distinguish people by race; (2) combinations of traits (like skin color and hair color) can be used to reliably distinguish people by race; (3) there are more biological/genetic differences between people of different races than between people of the same race; and (4) racial differences are best explained by biology, not culture or society. Before exposure to the course content, students generally believed that multiple biological traits can be used to divide people into distinct racial groups, with slightly better understanding that single traits cannot be used to define races; that there is more biological variation among members of the same race; and that races are culturally variable categories. After watching the first 50 minutes of Episode 1 of "Race: The Power of an Illusion,"[8] correct student understanding increased by 16–32 percent (depending on the question). On the same day, the students then attended a two-hour lab where they were shown a series of photos and asked to assign a "race" and to describe specific physical features used to categorize each individual. Through sharing of data among members of their lab group, students were challenged to "prove" that there are individual traits or trait combinations that can be used to reliably assign individuals to racial groups. A final reflective assignment asked students to use these results to explain to a friend why racial differences have no basis in biology. The next day the students attended a 50-minute lecture debunking the core myths of the biological race concept. Student understanding did not change more than 6 percent after the lab and lecture. While students appear to have understood all concepts equally well after a single exposure to the course materials, the idea that we cannot use suites of biological traits to reliably assign individuals to racial groupings (misconception 2) was a sticking point. Only 74–78 percent of students could recognize the fallacy presented in misconception 2, as opposed to the 84–90 percent of students who recognized the fallacies presented with the other three misconceptions. Still, these results suggest that a single exposure to accurate pedagogical content about race might lead to a significant change in student understanding.

TEACHING HUMAN EVOLUTION AND VARIATION IN US BIOLOGICAL ANTHROPOLOGY UNDERGRADUATE COURSES IN ACCURATE, EFFECTIVE, AND INCLUSIVE WAYS

Barnes and Brownell (2017) recently introduced a framework called Religious Cultural Competence in Evolution Education (ReCCEE), particularly for secular college instructors when teaching evolution to religious college biology students. They describe cultural competence as "the ability of individuals from one culture (in this case, primarily secular instructors who are teaching evolution) to bridge cultural differences and effectively communicate with individuals from a different culture (in this case, primarily religious undergraduate biology students)" (Barnes and Brownell 2017: 1). This framework is particularly relevant for academic scientists, who are much less religious than the general US public. In this regard, 52 percent of academic scientists in the Religion Among Academic Scientists study

(RAAS) see themselves as having no religious affiliation, compared with 14 percent of the adult US population (Ecklund and Scheitle 2007). University faculty members are highly accepting of evolution, and knowledge of and acceptance of evolution are positively correlated for university faculty, regardless of level of science education (Rice et al. 2015).

These culturally competent practices can help instructors reduce students' perceived conflict between evolution and religion, increase students' acceptance of evolution, and create more inclusive undergraduate biology classrooms (Barnes and Brownell 2017). These approaches can, and should, be extended to students in biological anthropology classes. They are outlined in Table 36.1, which has been adapted from Table 36.2 in Barnes and Brownell (2017) and extended to include useful resources. Although it was developed for Advanced Placement high school biology classrooms, another similar approach that could be used to reduce perceived conflict between evolution and religion in biological anthropology classrooms is the Cultural and Religious Sensitivity (CRS) Teaching Strategies Resource described by Bertka et al. (2019). This freely downloadable resource focuses on creating a classroom environment where individual worldviews are respected while encouraging a sound scientific understanding of evolution and includes in-class activities.[9]

It is possible to reduce belief in genetic essentialism among biology students if instructors teach genetics in a manner that helps students understand the flaws in such arguments by orienting biology education toward humane genomics literacy instead of basic genomics literacy. Humane genomics literacy is the story of how population thinking and multifactorial genetics refute genetic essentialist beliefs about race. Similar to the framework outlined above for teaching evolution, humane genomics literacy can be considered a cultural relevant pedagogy for teaching "when teaching genetics concepts that, if

Table 36.1 Culturally competent practices for teaching evolution and related resources available for classroom use

Culturally Competent Practice	Description	Resources
Acknowledge	Acknowledge that students may see a conflict between evolution and their religious beliefs.	CRS Resource[5]
Explore	Discuss and encourage the exploration of students' personal views on evolution and religion.	Borgerding (2020)
Teach the nature of science	Explain to students the bounded nature of science and different ways of knowing.	Understanding Science website,[10] Borgerding (2020)
Outline the spectrum of viewpoints	Explain that there are diverse viewpoints on the relationship between evolution and religion, and that viewpoints are not restricted to atheistic evolution and special creationism.	CRS Resource[5]
Provide role models	Highlight biological anthropologists and other scientists who are religious.	AAAS DoSER Profiles in Science Engagement with Faith Communities,[11] National Academies Science and Religion Resources[12]
Highlight potential compatibility	Explicitly discuss the potential compatibility between evolution and religion.	CRS Resource[5], National Academies Science and Religion Resources,[8] Sager (2008), Martin (2010)

Table 36.2 Effective themes to emphasize and approaches to use when teaching about human variation (especially as related to concepts of "race")

Theme/Approach	Description	Reference
Theme		
There are no biological human "races."	The idea of biologically distinct races is not supported by research on genetic or physical (biological) differences among humans.	Hubbard (2017a)
"Race" is real in society and culture.	However, social and cultural constructions of race and its use as an identifier are real.	Hubbard (2017a)
Racism impacts our biology.	Race is not biologically determined, but racism has impacts on our biology.	Hubbard (2017a)
Racial inequality (and inequity) is not the inevitable product of genes.	It is incorrect to infer that races differ socially or behaviorally for genetic reasons (on the basis that they differ medically for genetic reasons).	Donovan (2017)
Genetic essentialism is flawed.	Genetic essentialism is ontologically flawed from a population genetics point of view. Biologists and anthropologists discredited essentialism in the mid-twentieth century by challenging the epistemology of racialist science.	Donovan (2022)
Racial groups are not discrete.	Only 0.1 percent of human DNA varies between individuals. Most (95.7 percent) of this human genetic variation occurs between individuals within continental populations commonly associated with US census racial groups. Although some (7.53 percent) gene variants are unique to a single group, on average none of these variants are possessed by > 1.65 percent of any population. Most variants within the human genome are found in two or more continental groups of humans.	Donovan et al. (2019)
The causes of within-group variation in a trait can be different from the causes of between-group variation in that same trait.	Even when trait differences between individuals within a population are entirely inherited, differences between populations can still be caused entirely by environmental factors.	Donovan et al. (2019)
Approach		
Use refutational texts or curriculum materials to challenge biological essentialism of race.	Refutational texts explicitly challenge scientific misconceptions *and* explain the consensus scientific understanding of a concept by triggering a misconception, labelling it as incorrect, refuting it with evidence, and providing an alternative way of understanding the phenomenon originally explained by the misconception.	Donovan (2015); Donovan et al. (2019)

(Continued)

Table 36.2 *(Continued)*

Theme/Approach	Description	Reference
Use only appropriate and accurate language and metaphors.	Do not use gene-deterministic concepts and language when describing genes, such as "gene" for language or DNA as a "blueprint" rather than a "recipe" metaphor.	Hubbard (2017a); Donovan (2022)
Teach about the complexities of human genetics.	Provide information that helps students understand the genetic flaws in specificity, proximity, stability, immutability, determination, uniformity, and/or discreteness beliefs.	Donovan (2022); Donovan et al. (2019, 2020)
Teach a humane genetics education.	A humane genetics education reduces racial bias by changing the way that students perceive human genetic variation and helps them understand that claims about race and genetics are not socially neutral.	Donovan et al. (2019)

misunderstood, have damaging sociopolitical consequences" (Sparks et al. 2020). Donovan et al. (2019) reported the results of a study in which 8th and 9th grade students learned scientifically accurate information about genetic variation within and between the US census races. This helped students to construct an accurate understanding of genetic variation within and between groups, which changed how students perceived between group variation, which in turn reduced racial bias – causing a significant decrease in their scores on instruments assessing cognitive forms of prejudice. They replicated these results with adults and high school (9th–12th grade) biology students and assert that teaching about human variation in the domain of genetics has potentially powerful effects on social cognition during adolescence.

Given the success of humane genomics instruction in decreasing belief in genetic essentialism in middle and high school students and adults (Donovan et al. 2019, 2020), there is ample reason and opportunity in undergraduate biological anthropology classrooms to take this approach to learning about variation. An accurate understanding of genetic variation undermines the apparent validity of prejudiced beliefs because it refutes scientifically flawed assumptions, including (1) people of the same race are genetically uniform; (2) people of disparate races are categorically different (races are discrete, nonoverlapping categories); (3) biologically influenced abilities are immutable; and (4) genes are the single best explanation for racial disparities (Donovan et al. 2019, 2021; Jackson and Depew 2017). Recommendations for effective themes to emphasize and approaches to take when teaching about race using a humane genomics literacy framework are outlined in Table 36.2. Additionally, similar to the approach outlined previously for teaching human evolution, when teaching about race "simply stating what students are feeling allows space for them to relax in such contexts" (Hubbard 2017a: 517).

It is important to choose words and phrases carefully in the classroom so as to not reinforce misconceptions. Regarding evolution, this is particularly relevant for words that have multiple meanings such as "select," "adapt," "pressure," "need," and "must" (Nehm et al. 2010; Pobiner 2016; Rector et al. 2013). Instructors also may need to provide a more clear, concise, and accurate definition of evolution than what is presented in their anthropology textbook. In this regard, a study concluded that anthropology textbooks often do not provide a single, accurate definition of evolution and that none of the definitions of evolution provided in the textbooks studied mentioned both common ancestry and descent with modification (White et al. 2009). These issues extend to representations of evolution in K-12 textbooks and the media (Padian 2013). Rather than removing racial terminology from the biology curriculum altogether (an approach not advocated by Donovan 2017), Hubbard (2017a) advises to explicitly and correctly define terms often used when teaching about race, including race/racial group, ethnicity/ethnic group, and genetic ancestry. Wade (2021) also advises scientists communicating about race and genetics for the general public not to avoid addressing race. Her advice is to explain what race is and what it is not, and explain why you cannot tell what race someone is by looking at their genome, rather than saying race is not real. She also suggests using humanizing language regarding scientific "samples" to describe people, including the voices of people from the groups who were studied, especially if they are racially marginalized, not playing into racist tropes, and acknowledging that continental categories often used in modern ideas about race are not consistent or eternal (Wade 2021). Fuentes (2021) admonishes that we cannot speak of race without also speaking of racism; doing so reinforces racism and confuses public discourse.

OPPORTUNITIES BEYOND THE COLLEGE CLASSROOM

While the proportion of US adults obtaining bachelor's degrees has been steadily increasing over the past 15 + years,[13] high school biology is often the best and last formal evolution education for many Americans (Long 2012). Additionally, most science learning for most Americans happens outside of formal classroom settings (Falk and Dierking 2010). To reach a broader audience beyond undergraduate students, and actively engage misrepresentation and oversimplification of human evolution and genomics, biological anthropologists will need to engage in concerted outreach efforts outside the academy (Fuentes 2021). This might include signing up for the Skype a Scientist[14] program that connects scientists with classrooms across the globe through virtual classroom visits; writing an article for a freely available online website aimed at a younger student audience, such as Frontiers for Young Minds[15] or Science News for Students[16]; offering a lecture or similar program at a local library; volunteering for a local school, after-school, summer camp, or other organization's STEM program; engaging with the American Association for the Advancement of Science's Dialogue on Science, Ethics, and Religion Program (AAAS DoSER), especially if you are a scientist of faith[17]; volunteering as a scientific consultant for the Clergy Letter Project[18]; becoming familiar with the National Center for Science Education (NCSE)'s work and activities supporting K-12 teachers helping students learn about evolution, climate change, and the nature of science[19]; or getting involved with the American Association of Biological Anthropologists Education Committee[20].

CONCLUSIONS

While biological anthropology college classrooms offer myriad opportunities to engage students who do not see themselves as science oriented via relevant human-focused content, some biological anthropology topics – including human evolution and variation – can be challenging to teach accurately, effectively, and in sensitive ways that appeal to rather than alienate students. This chapter draws on broader pedagogical scholarship to outline these challenges. It also describes culturally competent, inclusive approaches to teaching human evolution and variation based on current evidence and best practices that instead create opportunities for college faculty members to help students overcome misconceptions and learn correct information.

ACKNOWLEDGMENTS

I have drawn on the unpublished 2021 Smithsonian's Human Origins Program's Education and Outreach Strategy document for parts of this chapter, and acknowledge the strong collaboration I had with Rick Potts in writing this document, which we recently updated from the original 2009 version. I did not have the space in this chapter to do justice to the scholarly writing of biological anthropologists on studies of human variation and communication about race, and I apologize for any unintended omissions of key literature in this area. I also thank Rob O'Malley and an additional anonymous reviewer for their suggested edits and comments, which greatly improved this chapter.

NOTES

1 https://news.gallup.com/poll/21814/evolution-creationism-intelligent-design.aspx.
2 https://www.pewresearch.org/fact-tank/2019/02/06/how-highly-religious-americans-view-evolution-depends-on-how-theyre-asked-about-it.
3 https://www.pewforum.org/2013/12/30/publics-views-on-human-evolution.
4 http://www.pewinternet.org/2015/10/22/science-and-religion.
5 https://understandingrace.org/Glossary#r.
6 https://physanth.org/about/position-statements/aapa-statement-race-and-racism-2019.
7 Human racial variation is defined in this study as "the notion that phenotypic variation mirrors underlying genetic variation, making the biological variants we see as racially specific produced by underlying genetic differences between racial groups" (Hubbard 2017b).
8 https://www.racepowerofanillusion.org.
9 https://humanorigins.si.edu/education/teaching-evolution-through-human-examples.
10 https://undsci.berkeley.edu.
11 https://sciencereligiondialogue.org/resources/profiles-listing.
12 https://www.nationalacademies.org/evolution/science-and-religion.
13 https://www.census.gov/library/publications/2021/acs/acsbr-009.html.
14 https://www.skypeascientist.com.
15 https://kids.frontiersin.org.
16 https://www.sciencenewsforstudents.org.
17 https://sciencereligiondialogue.org.
18 https://www.theclergyletterproject.org.
19 https://ncse.ngo.
20 https://physanth.org/about/committees/education-committee-page.

REFERENCES

Allmon, W. D. "Why Don't People Think Evolution Is True? Implications for Teaching, In and Out of the Classroom." *Evolution: Education and Outreach* 4, no. 4 (2011): 648–665.
Ashmore, P. C. "Role of Physical Anthropology in Intermediate and Secondary Education." *American Journal of Physical Anthropology* 128, no. S41 (2005): 154–162.

Barnes, M. E., and S. E. Brownell. "Practices and Perspectives of College Instructors on Addressing Religious Beliefs When Teaching Evolution." *CBE – Life Sciences Education* 15, no. 2 (2016): ar18.

Banes, M. E., and S. E. Brownell. "A Call to Use Cultural Competence When Teaching Evolution to Religious College Students: Introducing Religious Cultural Competence in Evolution Education (Reccee)." *CBE – Life Sciences Education* 16, no. 4 (2017): es4.

Barnes, M. E., J. Elser, and S. Brownell. "Impact of a Short Evolution Module on Students' Perceived Conflict Between Religion and Evolution." *The American Biology Teacher* 79, no. February (2017): 104–111.

Barnes, M. E., K. Supriya, H. M. Dunlop, et al. "Relationships Between the Religious Backgrounds and Evolution Acceptance of Black and Hispanic Biology Students." *CBE – Life Sciences Education* 19, no. 4 (2020): ar59.

Barnes, M. E., S. A. Maas, J. A. Roberts, et al. "Christianity as a Concealable Stigmatized Identity (CSI) Among Biology Graduate Students." *CBE – Life Sciences Education* 20, no. 1 (2021a): ar9.

Barnes, M. E., K. Supriya, Y. Zheng, et al. "A New Measure of Students' Perceived Conflict Between Evolution and Religion (Pcore) Is a Stronger Predictor of Evolution Acceptance than Understanding or Religiosity." *CBE – Life Sciences Education* 20, no. 3 (2021b): ar42.

Beggrow, E. P., and G. C. Sbeglia. "Do Disciplinary Contexts Impact the Learning of Evolution? Assessing Knowledge and Misconceptions in Anthropology and Biology Students." *Evolution: Education and Outreach* 12, no. 1 (2019): 1.

Benn Torres, J. "Anthropological Perspectives on Genomic Data, Genetic Ancestry, and Race." *Yearbook of Physical Anthropology* 171, no. S70 (2019): 74–86.

Bertka, C. M., B. Pobiner, P. Beardsley, et al. "Acknowledging Students' Concerns About Evolution: A Proactive Teaching Strategy." *Evolution: Education and Outreach* 12, no. 1 (2019): 3.

Borgerding, L. "Science and Religion in Higher Education." In *Making Sense of Science and Religion: Strategies for the Classroom and Beyond*. Edited by J. W. Shane, L. Meadows, R. S. Hermann, and I. C. Binns, 91–102. Arlington, VA: NSTA Press, 2020.

Bowling, B. V., E. E. Acra, L. Wang, et al. "Development and Evaluation of a Genetics Literacy Assessment Instrument for Undergraduates." *Genetics* 178, no. 1 (2008): 15–22.

Byeon, Y. J. J., R. Islamaj, L. Yeganova, et al. "Evolving Use of Ancestry, Ethnicity, and Race in Genetics Research – A Survey Spanning Seven Decades." *The American Journal of Human Genetics* 108 (2021): 2215–2223.

Chakravarti, A. "Perspectives on Human Variation Through the Lens of Diversity and Race." *Cold Spring Harbor Perspectives on Biology* 7, no. 9 (2015): a023358.

Chao, M. M., Y. Hong, and C. Chiu. "Essentializing Race: Its Implications on Racial Categorization." *Journal of Personality and Social Psychology* 104, no. 4 (2013): 619–634.

Condit, C. M., R. L. Parrott, B. R. Bates, et al. "Exploration of the Impact of Messages About Genes and Race on Lay Attitudes." *Clinical Genetics* 66 (2004): 402–408.

Cunningham, D. L., and D. J. Wescott. "Still More 'Fancy' and 'Myth' than 'Fact' in Students' Conceptions of Evolution." *Evolution: Education and Outreach* 2, no. 3 (2009): 505–517.

Dar-Nimrod, I., and S. J. Heine. "Genetic Essentialism: On the Deceptive Determinism of DNA." *Psychological Bulletin* 137, no. 5 (2011): 800–818.

Donovan, B. M. "Playing with Fire? The Impact of the Hidden Curriculum in School Genetics on Essentialist Conceptions of Race." *Journal of Research in Science Teaching* 51, no. 4 (2014): 462–496.

Donovan, B. M. "Reclaiming Race as a Topic of the U.S. Biology Textbook Curriculum." *Science Education* 99, no. 6 (2015): 1092–1117.

Donovan, B. M. "Framing the Genetics Curriculum for Social Justice: An Experimental Exploration of How the Biology Curriculum Influences Beliefs About Racial Difference." *Science Education* 100, no. 3 (2016): 586–616.

Donovan, B. M. "Learned Inequality: Racial Labels in the Biology Curriculum Can Affect the Development of Racial Prejudice." *Journal of Research in Science Teaching* 54, no. 3 (2017): 379–411.

Donovan, B. M. "Ending Genetic Essentialism Through Genetics Education." *Human Genetics and Genomics Advances* September (2022): 100058.

Donovan, B. M., R. Semmens, P. Keck, et al. "Toward a More Humane Genetics Education: Learning About the Social and Quantitative Complexities of Human Genetic Variation Research Could Reduce Racial Bias in Adolescent and Adult Populations." *Science Education* 103, no. 3 (2019): 529–560.

Donovan, B. M., M. Weindling, and D. M. Lee. "From Basic to Humane Genomics Literacy." *Science & Education* 29 (2020): 1479–1511.

Donovan, B. M., M. Weindling, B. Salazar, et al. "Genomics Literacy Matters: Supporting the Development of Genomics Literacy Through Genetics Education Could Reduce the Prevalence of Genetic Essentialism." *Journal of Research in Science Teaching* 58 (2021): 520–550.

Dougherty, M. J. "Closing the Gap: Inverting the Genetics Curriculum to Ensure an Informed Public." *The American Journal of Human Genetics* 85 (2009): 6–12.

Dunk, R. D. P., A. J. Petto, J. R. Wiles, et al. "A Multifactorial Analysis of Acceptance of Evolution." *Evolution: Education and Outreach* 10, no. 1 (2017): 4.

Ecklund, E., and C. Scheitle. "Religion Among Academic Scientists: Distinctions, Disciplines, and Demographics." *Social Problems – SOC PROBL* 54, no. May (2007): 289–307.

Falk, J., and L. Dierking. "The 95 Percent Solution: School Is Not Where Most Americans Learn Most of Their Science." *American Scientist* 98 (2010): 486–493.

Fuentes, A. "Biological Anthropology's Critical Engagement with Genomics, Evolution, Race/Racism, and Ourselves: Opportunities and Challenges to Making a Difference in the Academy and the World." *American Journal of Physical Anthropology* 175, no. 2 (2021): 326–338.

Glaze, A., and M. Goldston. "U.S. Science Teaching and Learning of Evolution: A Critical Review of the Literature 2000–2014." *Science Education* 99, no. 3, May (2015): 500–518.

Goodman, A. H., Y. T. Moses, and J. L. Jones. *Race: Are We So Different?* London: Wiley-Blackwell, 2012.

Graves, J. L., Jr. "Why the Nonexistence of Biological Races Does Not Mean the Nonexistence of Racism." *American Behavioral Scientist* 59, no. 11 (2015): 1474–1495.

Gregory, T. R. "Understanding Natural Selection: Essential Concepts and Common Misconceptions." *Evolution: Education and Outreach* 2 (2009): 159–175.

Grunspan, D. Z., R. D. P. Dunk, M. E. Barnes, et al. "A Comparison Study of Human Examples vs. Non-Human Examples in an Evolution Lesson Leads to Differential Impacts on Student Learning Experiences in an Introductory Biology Course." *Evolution: Education and Outreach* 14, no. 1 (2021): 9.

Hawley, H., S. D. Short, L. A. McCune, et al. "What's the Matter with Kansas?: The Development and Confirmation of the Evolutionary Attitudes and Literacy Survey (EALS)." *Evolution: Education and Outreach* 4, no. 1 (2011): 117–132.

Harms, U., and M. J. Reiss, eds. *Evolution Education Reconsidered: Understanding What Works*, 1st edn. Switzerland: Springer Nature, 2019.

Heddy, B. C., and L. S. Nadelson. "The Variables Related to Public Acceptance of Evolution in the United States." *Evolution: Education and Outreach* 6, no. 1 (2013): 3.

Hermann, R. S. "Cognitive Apartheid: On the Manner in Which High School Students Understand Evolution Without Believing in Evolution." *Evolution: Education and Outreach* 5, no. 4 (2012): 619–628.

Hott, A. M., C. A. Huether, J. D. McInerney, et al. "Genetics Content in Introductory Biology Courses for Non-Science Majors: Theory and Practice." *Bioscience* 52, no. 11 (2002): 1024–1035.

Hubbard, A. R. "Teaching Race (Bioculturally) Matters: A Visual Approach for College Biology Courses." *The American Biology Teacher* 79, no. 7 (2017a): 516–524.

Hubbard, A, R. "Testing Common Misconceptions About the Nature of Human Racial Variation." *The American Biology Teacher* 79, no. 7 (2017b): 538–543.

Jablonski, N. G. "Skin Color and Race." *American Journal of Physical Anthropology* 175, no. 2 (2021): 437–447.

Jackson, J. P., Jr., and D. J. Depew. *Darwinism, Democracy, and Race: American Anthropology and Evolutionary Biology in the Twentieth Century.* New York, NY: Routledge, 2017.

Lasisi, T. "The Constraints of Racialization: How Classification and Valuation Hinder Scientific Research on Human Variation." *American Journal of Physical Anthropology* 175, no. 2 (2021): 376–386.

Long, D. E. *Evolution and Religion in American Education: An Ethnography*. Volume 4: *Cultural Studies of Science Education*. Dordrecht, The Netherlands: Springers, 2011. https://doi.org/10.1007/978-94-007-1808-1.

Long, D. E. "The Politics of Teaching Evolution, Science Education Standards, and Being a Creationist." *Journal of Research in Science Teaching* 49, no. 1 (2012): 122–139.

Lord, T., and S. Marino. "How University Students View the Theory of Evolution." *Journal of College Science Teaching* 22, no. 6 (1993): 353–357.

Lynch, J., J. Bevan, P. Achter, et al. "A Preliminary Study of How Multiple Exposures to Messages About Genetics Impact on Lay Attitudes Towards Racial and Genetic Discrimination." *New Genetics and Society* 27, no. 1 (2008): 43–56.

Manwaring, K. F., J. L. Jensen, R. A. Gill, et al. "Influencing Highly Religious Undergraduate Perceptions of Evolution: Mormons as a Case Study." *Evolution: Education and Outreach* 8, no. 1 (2015): 23.

Martin, J. W. "Compatibility of Major U.S. Christian Denominations with Evolution." *Evolution: Education and Outreach* 3 (2010): 420–431.

McChesney, K. Y. "Teaching Diversity: The Science You Need to Know to Explain Why Race Is Not Biological." *SAGE Open* 5, no. 4 (2015): 2158244015611712. https://doi.org/10.1177/2158244015611712.

Meadows, L. *The Missing Link: An Inquiry Approach for Teaching All Students about Evolution*, Illustrated edn. Portsmouth, NH: Heinemann, 2009.

Miller, J. D., E. C. Scott, and S. Okamoto. "Public Acceptance of Evolution." *Science* 313, no. 5788 (2006): 765–766.

Miller, J. D., E. C. Scott, M. S. Ackerman, et al. "Public Acceptance of Evolution in the United States, 1985–2020." *Public Understanding of Science* August (2021): 09636625211035919.

Mills Shaw, K. R., K. Van Horne, H. Zhang, et al. "Essay Contest Reveals Misconceptions of High School Students in Genetics Content." *Genetics* 178, no. 3 (2008): 1157–1168.

Moore, R., D. Brooks, and S. Cotner. "The Relation of High School Biology Courses & Students' Religious Beliefs to College Students' Knowledge of Evolution." *The American Biology Teacher* 73, no. March (2011): 222–226.

Morin-Chassé, A. "Public (Mis)understanding of News about Behavioral Genetics Research." *BioScience* 64, no. 12 (2014): 1170–1177.

Morin-Chassé, A. "Behavioral Genetics, Population Genetics, and Genetic Essentialism: A Survey Experiment." *Science & Education* 29, no. 6 (2020): 1595–1619.

Morning, A. "Reconstructing Race in Science and Society: Biology Textbooks, 1952–2002." *American Journal of Sociology* 114 (2008): 106–137.

Morning, A., H. Brückner, and A. Nelson. "Socially Desirable Reporting and the Expression of Biological Concepts of Race." *Du Bois Review: Social Science Research on Race* 16, no. 2 (2019): 439–455.

Nehm, R. H., M. A. Rector, and M. Ha. ""Force-Talk" in Evolutionary Explanation: Metaphors and Misconceptions." *Evolution: Education and Outreach* 3, no. 4 (2010): 605–613.

Nelson, C. E. "Why Don't Undergraduates Really 'Get' Evolution? What Can Faculty Do?" In Evolution Challenges, Integrating Research and Practice in Teaching and Learning About Evolution. Edited by K. S. Rosengren, S. K. Brem, E. M. Evans, and G. M. Sinatra, 311–347. Oxford: Oxford University Press, 2012.

Padian, K. "Correcting Some Common Misrepresentations of Evolution in Textbooks and the Media." *Evolution: Education and Outreach* 6 (2013): 11.

Phelan, J. C., B. G. Link, and N. M. Feldman. "The Genomic Revolution and Beliefs About Essential Racial Differences: A Backdoor to Eugenics?" *American Sociological Review* 78, no. 2 (2013): 167–191.

Pobiner, B. L. "Use Human Examples to Teach Evolution." *The American Biology Teacher* 74, no. 2 (2012): 71–72.

Pobiner, B. "Accepting, Understanding, Teaching, and Learning (Human) Evolution: Obstacles and Opportunities." *American Journal of Physical Anthropology* 159, no. S61 (2016): 232–274.

Pobiner, B., P. Beardsley, C. Bertka, et al. "Using Human Case Studies to Teach Evolution in High School A.P. Biology Classrooms." *Evolution: Education and Outreach* 11 (2018): 3.

Pobiner, B., W. A. Watson, P. M. Beardsley, et al. "Using Human Examples to Teach Evolution to High School Students: Increasing Understanding and Decreasing Cognitive Biases and Misconceptions." In *Evolution Education Re-Considered*. Edited by U. Harms and M. J. Reiss, 185–205. Switzerland: Springer Nature, 2019.

Ranney, M. A. "Why Don't Americans Accept Evolution as Much as People in Peer Nations Do? A Theory (Reinforced Theistic Manifest Destiny) and Some Pertinent Evidence." In *Evolution Challenges: Integrating Research and Practice in Teaching and Learning About Evolution*. Edited by K. S. Rosengren, S. K. Brem, E. M. Evans, and G. M. Sinatra, 233–269. Oxford: Oxford University Press, 2012.

Rector, M. A., R. H. Nehm, and D. Pearl. "Learning the Language of Evolution: Lexical Ambiguity and Word Meaning in Student Explanations." *Research in Science Education* 43, no. 3 (2013): 1107–1133.

Reed, L. K. "Resources for Teaching Biological Evolution in the Deep South." In *Evolution Education in the American South: Culture, Politics, and Resources In and Around Alabama*. Edited by C. D. Lynn, A. L. Glaze, W. A. Evans, and L. K. Reed, 163–178. New York, NY: Palgrave Macmillan US, 2017.

Reiss, M. J. "The Relationship Between Evolutionary Biology and Religion." *Evolution* 63, no. 7 (2009): 1934–1941.

Relethford, J. H. "Apportionment of Global Human Genetic Diversity Based on Craniometrics and Skin Color." *American Journal of Physical Anthropology* 118, no. 4 (2002): 393–398.

Rice, J. W., M. P. Clough, J. K. Olson, et al. "University Faculty and Their Knowledge & Acceptance of Biological Evolution." *Evolution: Education and Outreach* 8, no. 1 (2015): 8.

Rissler, L. J., S. I. Duncan, and N. M. Caruso. "The Relative Importance of Religion and Education on University Students' Views of Evolution in the Deep South and State Science Standards Across the United States." *Evolution: Education and Outreach* 7, no. 1 (2014): 24.

Rivera, M. B. C. "Race and Human Variation." In *Explorations: An Open Invitation to Biological Anthropology*. Edited by B. Shook, K. Nelson, K. Aguilera, and L. Braff, 489–515. Arlington, VA: American Anthropological Association, 2019. https://pressbooks-dev.oer.hawaii.edu/explorationsbioanth/chapter/__unknown__-12.

Rosenberg, N. A. "A Population-Genetic Perspective on the Similarities and Differences Among Worldwide Human Populations." *Human Biology* 83, no. 6 (2011): 659–684.

Sager, C. *Voices for Evolution*. National Center for Science Education, 2008.

Scharmann, L. C. "A Proactive Strategy for Teaching Evolution." *The American Biology Teacher* 67, no. 1 (2005): 12–16.

Schrein, C. "Evolution Acceptance Among Undergraduates in the South." In *Evolution Education in the American South: Culture, Politics, and Resources in and around Alabama*. Edited by C. D. Lynn, A. L. Glaze, W. A. Evans, and L. K. Reed, 121–133. New York, NY: Palgrave Macmillan US, 2017.

Scott, E. C. "Antievolutionism, Scientific Creationism, and Physical Anthropology." *American Journal of Physical Anthropology* 30, no. S8 (1987): 21–39.

Shtulman, A., and P. Calabi. Cognitive Constraints on the Understanding and Acceptance of Evolution. In *Evolution Challenges: Integrating Research and Practice in Teaching and Learning about Evolution*. Edited by K. S. Rosengren, S. K. Brem, E. M Evans, and G. M. Sinatra, 47–65. Oxford: Oxford University Press, 2012.

Sinatra, G. M., S. A. Southerland, F. McConaughy, et al. "Intentions and Beliefs in Students' Understanding and Acceptance of Biological Evolution." *Journal of Research in Science Teaching* 40, no. 5 (2003): 510–528.

Skoog, G. "The Coverage of Human Evolution in High School Biology Textbooks in the 20th Century and in Current State Science Standards." *Science & Education* 14 (2005): 395–422.

Smith, M. U., and H. Siegel. "Knowing, Believing, and Understanding: What Goals for Science Education?" *Science & Education* 13, no. 6 (2004): 553–582.

Southerland, S. A., and L. C. Scharmann. "Acknowledging the Religious Beliefs Students Bring into the Science Classroom: Using the Bounded Nature of Science." *Theory into Practice* 52, no. 1 (2013): 59–65.

Sparks, R. A., K. E. Baldwin, and R. Darner. "Using Culturally Relevant Pedagogy to Reconsider the Genetics Canon." *Journal of Microbiology & Biology Education* 21, no. 1 (2020): 1–6.

Stern, F., and K. Kampourakis. "Teaching for Genetics Literacy in the Post-Genomic Era." *Studies in Science Education* 53, no. 2 (2017): 193–225.

Tolman, E.R., S. G. Ferguson, G. Hubble, et al. "To Teaching Evolution in Higher Education." *Evolution: Education and Outreach* 14, no. 12 (2021): 16 pages.

Truong, J., E. M. Barnes, and S. Brownell. "Can Six Minutes of Culturally Competent Evolution Education Reduce Students' Level of Perceived Conflict Between Evolution and Religion?" *The American Biology Teacher* 80, February (2018): 106–115.

Van Arsdale, A. P. "Population Demography, Ancestry, and the Biological Concept of Race." *Annual Review of Anthropology* 48 (2019): 227–241.

Wade, L. "Tips for Scientists Writing about Race and Genetics for the General Public." *American Journal of Physical Anthropology* 175, no. 2 (2021): 505–506.

White, J., C. D. Tollini, W. A. Collie, et al. "Evolution and University-Level Anthropology Textbooks: The 'Missing Link'?" *Evolution: Education and Outreach* 2, no. 4 (2009): 722–737.

Winslow, M., J. Staver, and L. Scharmann. "Evolution and Personal Religious Belief: Christian University Biology-Related Majors' Search for Reconciliation." *Journal of Research in Science Teaching* 48, no. November (2011): 1026–1049.

Woods, C., and L. Scharmann. "High School Students' Perceptions of Evolutionary Theory." *Electronic Journal of Science Education* 6, no. 2 (2001): 1–30.

Index